LOURDES COLLEGE
DUNS SCOTUS LIBRARY
REFERENCE DEPARTMENT

LOURDES COLLEGE LIBRARY

3 0379 1003 9411 5

P9-BVM-844

m 27
v. 3

Revised Second Edition

Masterplots

1,801 Plot Stories and Critical Evaluations
of the World's Finest Literature

Revised Second Edition

Volume 3
Con – Dul
1239 – 1868

Edited by
FRANK N. MAGILL

Story Editor, Revised Edition
DAYTON KOHLER

Consulting Editor, Revised Second Edition
LAURENCE W. MAZZENO

SALEM PRESS
Pasadena, California   Englewood Cliffs, New Jersey

96-276

Editor in Chief: Dawn P. Dawson

Consulting Editor: Laurence W. Mazzeno   *Managing Editor:* Christina J. Moose
Project Editors: Eric Howard   *Research Supervisor:* Jeffry Jensen
Juliane Brand   *Research:* Irene McDermott
Acquisitions Editor: Mark Rehn   *Proofreading Supervisor:* Yasmine A. Cordoba
Production Editor: Cynthia Breslin Beres   *Layout:* William Zimmerman

Copyright © 1949, 1952, 1953, 1954, 1960, 1968, 1976, 1996, by Salem Press, Inc. All rights in this book are reserved. No part of this work may be used or reproduced in any manner whatsoever or transmitted in any form or by any means, electronic or mechanical, including photocopy, recording, or any information storage and retrieval system, without written permission from the copyright owner except in the case of brief quotations embodied in critical articles and reviews. For more information address the publisher, Salem Press, Inc., P. O. Box 50062, Pasadena, California, 91115.

∞ The paper used in these volumes conforms to the American National Standard for Permanence of Paper for Printed Library Materials, Z39.48-1984.

Library of Congress Cataloging-in-Publication Data
Masterplots / edited by Frank N. Magill; consulting editor, Laurence W. Mazzeno. — Rev. 2nd ed.
    p.   cm.
Expanded and updated version of the 1976 rev. ed.
Includes bibliographical references and indexes.
1. Literature—Stories, plots, etc. 2. Literature—History and criticism. I. Magill, Frank Northen, 1907-   . II. Mazzeno, Laurence W.
PN44.M33   1996
809—dc20   96-23382
ISBN 0-89356-084-7 (set)   CIP
ISBN 0-89356-087-1 (volume 3)

Revised Second Edition
First Printing

PRINTED IN THE UNITED STATES OF AMERICA

LIST OF TITLES IN VOLUME 3

MASTERPLOTS

Revised Second Edition

CONFESSIONS

Type of work: Autobiography
Author: Saint Augustine (Aurelius Augustinus, 354-430)
First transcribed: Confessiones, 397-401 (English translation, 1620)

> *Principal personages:*
> SAINT AUGUSTINE
> MONICA, his mother
> ADEODATUS, his natural son
> FAUSTUS, the bishop of the Manichaean sect
> AMBROSE, the bishop of Milan
> ALYPIUS, a friend from Tagaste

The *Confessions* was a new form in literature. Others, like Marcus Aurelius, had set down meditations, but this was different. Others had written biographies and autobiographies, but Saint Augustine did not follow that model exactly. True, he does tell about his life, but his method is a departure from a narrative of dates and events. He was more interested in his thievery of pears than in more important actions, and he makes the fruit as meaningful in his life as the Old Testament symbolism of the apples in the garden of Eden. Other episodes are selected because of their revelation of the grace and provision of God: "I pass over many things, hastening on to those which more strongly compel me to confess to thee."

"My *Confessions*, in thirteen books," wrote Saint Augustine, looking back from the age of sixty-three at his various writings, "praise the righteous and good God as they speak either of my evil or good, and they are meant to excite men's minds and affections toward him. . . . The first through the tenth books were written about myself, the other three about the Holy Scripture." In the year before his death, writing to Darius, he declared: "Take the books of my *Confessions* and use them as a good man should. Here see me as I am and do not praise me for more than I am." One may argue that it took the invention of the Christian faith to lead to the creation of the confession as a genre of literature.

In fact, Augustine's life story might be looked on as a parallel to the parable of the prodigal son, with his heart "restless till it finds its rest in God"; he brings his account to an end, after his struggles to free himself from pride and sensuality, with his return to his home at Tagaste. Half his life still lay ahead of him. Although his friends, his teachers, and his mother appear in the *Confessions*, they lack any physical details by which one may visualize them. Two lines cover the death of his father. Neither name nor description is given to his mistress and the mother of his child, nor of the friend whose death drove him from his native city. Detail was of less importance to Saint Augustine than theological meditation and interpretation.

Taking his text from the psalmist who would "confess my transgressions unto the Lord," this work is one long prayer beginning, "Great art thou, O Lord, and greatly to be praised," and ending with the hope that "thus shall thy door be opened."

From the very first, the consolation of God's mercy sustained Saint Augustine. His memories of infancy made him wonder what preceded that period, as later he theorized about what had been before the creation. His pictures of himself crying and flinging his arms about because he could not make his wants known were symbols to him of the Christian life, even as the acquisition of facts about this early period from his mother impressed on him the need for help from others to gain self-knowledge.

Though his mother Monica was a devout Christian and her son had been brought up in that faith, young Aurelius Augustinus was more interested in the hero Aeneas than in God. Once, at the point of death from a stomach ailment, he begged to be baptized, but his mother refused to have him frightened into becoming a Christian. So he went on, reading Latin and disliking Greek and taking delight in the theater. A frank but modest description of his many abilities, the gift of his God to one not yet dedicated to God, ends the first book of this revealing work.

Book 2 concentrates on the sixteenth year of lazy, lustful, and mischievous Aurelius. He and his companions robbed a pear tree, not because they wanted the fruit, since they threw it to the swine, but because it was forbidden. His confession that he loved doing wrong made him ponder his reasons for wandering from the path of good and becoming a "wasteland." When he traveled to Carthage to study, at the age of nineteen, his chief delights were his mistress and the theater. In the course of his prescribed studies he read an essay by Cicero, *Hortensius*, now lost, urging the study of philosophy. Remembering his mother's hopes that he would become a Christian, he tried to read the Scriptures; he found them inferior in style to Cicero. He did, however, become involved with a pseudo-Christian sect, founded by the Persian religious teacher Mani (c. 216-277), because he approved of their logical approach to the problems of evil and good, represented by the dualistic concept of the universe. During the nine years that he was a Manichaean, his mother, encouraged by a dream that he would eventually see his error, kept loyally by him.

Back in Tagaste, he wrote plays, taught rhetoric, and lived with a mistress. He had no patience with a bishop, sent by his mother, to instruct him in Christianity. He was equally scornful of a magician who offered to cast spells to insure his success in a drama competition. He thought he was sufficient to himself, and by his own efforts he won a rhetoric contest. His temporary interest in astrology ended when he was unable to prove that successful divinations were more than chance. The death of a dear friend, who during his last illness became a Christian and denounced the life Aurelius was leading, so profoundly affected him that he returned to Carthage. There, still following the Manichaean beliefs, he wrote several essays, now lost. He was soon to be disillusioned. Faustus, reputed to be the most learned of Manichaean bishops, came to Carthage, and Aurelius Augustinus went to him to clear his religious doubts. Augustinus found Faustus more eloquent than logical. Hoping to improve himself, Augustinus then went to Rome to teach rhetoric; students there were reported to be less rowdy than those in his classes in Carthage. In Rome, malaria, the teaching of the skeptics who upset his confidence in the certainty of knowledge, and above all, the lack of classroom discipline induced him to accept the invitation of officials to resume his teaching career in Milan.

In Milan he enjoyed the companionship of two friends from Tagaste, Alypius and Nebridius. His mother, coming to live with him, persuaded Bishop Ambrose to try to convert her son. About the same time efforts to get him married and to regularize his life caused a break with his mistress, who on her departure left him with his young son Adeodatus. The group around the young rhetorician often discussed philosophy, and in Neoplatonism he found an answer to his greatest perplexity: If there is a God, what is the nature of his material existence? Finally, he was ready to study Christianity, especially the writings of Saint Paul. In book 7, which describes this period of his life, appears one of Saint Augustine's two ecstatic visions, a momentary glimpse of the One.

Book 8 recounts his conversion. Anxious to imitate those who had gained what he himself sought, he listened to an account of the conversion of the orator Marius Victorinus. While returning home, still upset and uncertain, he heard a child chanting: "Pick it up and read it." Taking these words as God's command, he opened the Bible at random and found himself reading Romans 13:13: "Put on the Lord Jesus Christ." Convinced, he called Alypius, and they found Monica and reported to her their newly acquired convictions.

Giving up his teaching, Saint Augustine prepared for baptism, along with his friend and Adeodatus. He was baptized by Bishop Ambrose during Easter Week, 387. Then the party set out to return to Tagaste. During their journey, and following another moment of Christian ecstasy, Monica died at Ostia on the Tiber. Her son's *Confessions* contains touching chapters of affection and admiration for her; sure of his faith at the time of her death, however, he fell into no period of abject mourning such as that which had followed the death of his friend at an earlier time.

With book 10, Saint Augustine turned from episodes of his life to self-analysis, detailing the three steps of the soul's approach to God, passing from an appreciation of the beauties of the outside world to an introspective study of itself, and ending with an inexplicable anticipation of the blessedness of the knowledge of God, the "truth-given Joy," that crowns the soul's pilgrimage.

Book 11 represents one of Saint Augustine's great contributions to Christian thought, the analysis of time. Pondering the mysteries of creation in an "eternal world," he saw it not as measured by "the motion of sun, moon, and stars," but as determined by the soul, the past being its remembrance; the present, its attention; and the future, its anticipation. He wrote: "The past increases by the diminution of the future, until by the consumption of all the future, all is past."

The last two books present speculation on the methods of creation and on the truth of the Scriptures, with most of the chapters devoted to interpretation of the opening verses of Genesis. The Old Testament account is open to many interpretations, and the final book of the *Confessions* deals with the material and allegorical possibilities of the story of the Creation. At the end, Saint Augustine acknowledges the goodness of creation, and meditates on verses describing the rest on the seventh day. He begs that God will bestow the rest and blessedness of that Sabbath in the life eternal that is to come.

Bibliography:

Brown, Peter. *Augustine of Hippo.* Berkeley: University of California Press, 1967. Generally considered the most reliable and complete biography of Augustine. Contains an excellent bibliography and a thorough description of Saint Augustine's intellectual and spiritual development.

Gilson, Étienne. *The Christian Philosophy of Saint Augustine.* Translated by L. E. M. Lynch. New York: Random House, 1960. Describes Saint Augustine's central importance in the development of early Christian thought. Describes *Confessions* as a truly original work of literature.

O'Donnell, James J. *Augustine.* Boston: Twayne, 1985. Contains a thoughtful and clear introduction to the rich diversity of Saint Augustine's writings on grace, free will, and scripture. Annotated bibliography. Chapter 5 analyzes the theological aspects of *Confessions*.

Portalié, Eugène. *A Guide to the Thought of Saint Augustine.* Translated by Ralph Bastian. Chicago: Regenery, 1960. Originally published in French in 1923, this work still remains the clearest general survey of Saint Augustine's life, works, and influence. Examines Saint Augustine's contributions to Christian theology.

Starnes, Colin. *Augustine's Conversion: A Guide to the Argument of Confessions I-IX.* Waterloo, Ontario: Wilfred Laurier University Press, 1990. Presents a clear exposition of the levels of meaning in the first nine books of *Confessions*. Describes the theological and the philosophical dimensions of the work.

CONFESSIONS

Type of work: Autobiography
Author: Jean-Jacques Rousseau (1712-1778)
First published: Les Confessions de J.-J. Rousseau, 1782, 1789 (English translation, 1783-1790)

Jean-Jacques Rousseau undoubtedly succeeded in his effort to write an autobiography of such character that he could present himself before "the sovereign Judge with this book in my hand, and loudly proclaim, Thus have I acted; these were my thoughts; such was I. With equal freedom and veracity have I related what was laudable or wicked, I have concealed no crimes, added no virtues." Rousseau's revolutionary view of the human psyche led to the flowering of the autobiography as a form of expression. There are few examples before his. Rousseau's *Confessions* (full title: *The Confessions of J.-J. Rousseau*) has been praised as perhaps the first instance of a writer's being candid and honest with the world about the writer. The book became a model for what, paradoxically, is indeed an art form: being honest, telling all.

Only a person attempting to tell all would have revealed so frankly the sensual satisfaction he received from the spankings administered by Mlle Lambercier, the sister of the pastor at Bossey, who was his tutor. Only a writer finding satisfaction either in truth or self-abasement would have gone on to tell that his passion for being overpowered by women continued throughout his adult life: "To fall at the feet of an imperious mistress, obey her mandates, or implore pardon, were for me the most exquisite enjoyments; and the more my blood was inflamed by the efforts of a lively imagination, the more I acquired the appearance of a whining lover." Having made this confession, Rousseau probably found it easier to tell of his extended affair with Madame de Warens at Annecy and of his experiences with his mistress and common-law wife, Thérèse Levasseur.

Rousseau records that he was born at Geneva in 1712, the son of Isaac Rousseau, a watchmaker, and Suzanne Bernard. His mother died at his birth, "the first of my misfortunes." According to the son's account of his father's grief, Isaac Rousseau had mixed feelings toward his son, seeing in him an image of Suzanne and, at the same time, the cause of her death. Rousseau writes: "[N]or did he ever embrace me, but his sighs, the convulsive pressure of his arms, witnessed that a bitter regret mingled itself with his caresses. When he said to me, 'Jean Jacques, let us talk of your mother,' my usual reply was, 'Yes, father, but then you know we shall cry,' and immediately the tears started from his eyes."

Rousseau describes his first experiences with reading. He turned to the romances that his mother had loved, and he and his father sometimes spent the entire night reading aloud alternately. His response to these books was almost entirely emotional, but he finally discovered other books in his grandfather's library, works which demanded something from the intellect: Plutarch, Ovid, Molière, and others.

He describes with great affection how his Aunt Suzanne, his father's sister, moved him with her singing; and he attributes his interest in music to her influence. After his stay at Bossey with Pastor Lambercier, Rousseau was apprenticed to an engraver, Abel Ducommun, in the hope that he would succeed better in the engraver's workshop than he had with City Registrar Masseron, who had fired him after a brief trial. Ducommun is described as "a young man of a very violent and boorish character," who was something of a tyrant, punishing Rousseau if he failed to return to the city before the gates were closed. Rousseau was by this time, according to his account, a liar and a petty thief, and without reluctance he stole his master's tools in order to misplace them.

Returning from a Sunday walk with some companions, Rousseau found the city gates closing an hour before time. He ran to reach the bridge, but he was too late. Reluctant to be punished by the engraver, he suddenly decided to give up his apprenticeship.

Having left Geneva, Rousseau wandered aimlessly in the environs of the city, finally arriving at Confignon. There he was welcomed by the village curate, M. de Pontverre, who gave him a good meal and sent him on to Madame Louise de Warens at Annecy. Rousseau expected to find "a devout, forbidding old woman"; instead, he discovered "a face beaming with charms, fine blue eyes full of sweetness, a complexion whose whiteness dazzled the sight, the form of an enchanting neck." He was sixteen, she was twenty-eight. She became something of a mother to him (he called her "Maman") and something of a goddess, but within five years he was her lover, at her instigation. Her motive was to protect him and to initiate him into the mysteries of love. She explained what she intended and gave him eight days to think it over; her proposal was intellectually cool and morally motivated. Since Rousseau had long imagined the delights of making love to her, he spent the eight days enjoying thoughts more lively than ever; but when he finally found himself in her arms, he was miserable: "Was I happy? No: I felt I know not what invincible sadness which empoisoned my happiness: it seemed that I had committed an incest, and two or three times, pressing her eagerly in my arms, I deluged her bosom with my tears."

Madame de Warens was at the same time involved with Claude Anet, a young peasant with a knowledge of herbs who had become one of her domestics. Before becoming intimate with Rousseau she had confessed to him that Anet was her lover, having been upset by Anet's attempt to poison himself after a quarrel with her. Despite her generosity to the two young men, she was no wanton; her behavior was more a sign of friendship than of passion, and she was busy being an intelligent and gracious woman of the world.

Through her efforts Rousseau had secured a position registering land for the king in the office at Chambery. His interest in music, however, led him to give more and more time to arranging concerts and giving music lessons; he gave up his job in the survey office. This was the turning point of his life, the decision which threw him into the society of his times and made possible his growing familiarity with the world of music and letters. His alliance with Madame de Warens continued, but the alliance was no longer of an intimate sort, for he had been supplanted by Winzenreid de Courtilles during their stay at Les Charmettes. Winzenreid came on the scene after the first idyllic summer, a period in his life which Rousseau describes as "the short happiness of my life." He tells of rising with the sun, walking through the woods, over the hills, and along the valley; his delight in nature is evident, and his theories concerning natural man become comprehensible. On his arrival Winzenreid took over physical chores and was forever walking about with a hatchet or a pickax; for all practical purposes Rousseau's close relationship with Madame de Warens was finished, even if a kind of filial affection on his part survived. He describes other adventures in love, and although some of them gave him extreme pleasure, he never found another "Maman."

Rousseau, having invented a new musical notation, went to Paris hoping to convince others of its value. The system was dismissed as unoriginal and too difficult, but Rousseau had by that time been introduced to Parisian society and was known as a young philosopher as well as a writer of poetry and operas. He received an appointment as secretary to the French ambassador at Venice, but he and M. de Montaigu irritated each other and he left his post about a year later.

Returning to Paris, Rousseau became involved with the illustrious circle containing the encyclopedist Diderot, Friedrich Melchior Grimm, and Mme Louise d'Epinay. He later became involved in a bitter quarrel with all three, stemming from a remark in a play by Diderot, but

Rousseau was reconciled with Diderot and continued the novel he was writing at the time, *The New Héloïse* (1761). The account of the quarrel and the letters that marked its progress are one of the liveliest parts of the *Confessions.*

As important an event as any in Rousseau's life was his meeting with Thérèse Levasseur, a tailor between twenty-two and twenty-three years of age, with a "lively yet charming look." Rousseau reports that "At first, amusement was my only object," but in making love to her he found that he was happy and that she was a suitable successor to "Maman." Despite the difficulties put in his way by her mother, and despite the fact that his attempts to improve her mind were useless, he was satisfied with her as his companion. She bore him five children who were sent to the foundling hospital against Thérèse's will and to Rousseau's subsequent regret.

Rousseau describes the moment on the road to Vincennes when the question proposed by the Academy of Dijon—"Has the progress of sciences and arts contributed to corrupt or purify morals?"—so struck him that he "seemed to behold another world." The discourse that resulted from his inspired moment won him the prize and brought him fame. Yet it may be that here, as elsewhere in the *Confessions,* the actual circumstances have been considerably altered by a romantic and forgetful author.

The *Confessions* carries the account of Rousseau's life to the point when, having been asked to leave Bern by the ecclesiastical authorities as a result of the uproar over *Emilius and Sophia: Or, A New System of Education* (1762), he set off for England, where David Hume had offered him asylum.

Rousseau's *Confessions* offers a personal account of the experiences of a great writer. The events which history notes are mentioned—his literary triumphs, his early conversion, his reconversion, his romance with Madame d'Houdetot, his quarrels with Voltaire, Diderot, and churchmen, his musical successes—but they are all transformed by the passionate perspective from which Rousseau, writing years after most of the events he describes, imagines his own past. The *Confessions* leaves the reader with the intimate knowledge of a human being, full of faults and passions, but driven by ambition and ability to a significant position in the history of literature. The *Confessions* has, since its publication, been a model for the artistic endeavor of the confession.

Bibliography:
Babbitt, Irving. *Rousseau and Romanticism.* New York: Meridian, 1955. Originally published in 1919; useful study, despite the author's dislike for his subject matter. Analyses of Romantic genius, imagination, morality, love (including love of nature), irony, and melancholy provide a good checklist of topics to look for in Rousseau.
De Mijolla, Elizabeth. *Autobiographical Quests: Augustine, Montaigne, Rousseau, and Wordsworth.* Charlottesville: University Press of Virginia, 1994. Stimulating study, especially for readers familiar with some of the other authors discussed.
Ellis, Madeleine M. *Rousseau's Venetian Story: An Essay upon Art and Truth in "Les Confessions."* Baltimore: The Johns Hopkins University Press, 1966. Reinforces the fact that what Rousseau has said about himself often is seriously inaccurate.
Gay, Peter. *The Enlightenment: An Interpretation.* 2 vols. New York: W. W. Norton, 1977. Both volumes include numerous references to Rousseau. A source on his historical and intellectual contexts.
Kelly, Christopher. *Rousseau's Exemplary Life: The "Confessions" as Political Philosophy.* Ithaca, N.Y.: Cornell University Press, 1987. Asserts that regarding the *Confessions* as primarily a political statement negates criticism of its inaccuracies.

CONFESSIONS OF AN ENGLISH OPIUM EATER

Type of work: Essays
Author: Thomas De Quincey (1785-1859)
Type of plot: Fantasy
Time of plot: Early nineteenth century
Locale: England and Wales
First published: 1821

Principal personages:
THOMAS DE QUINCEY, the narrator
ANN, a prostitute

The Story:

Intense stomach pains drove Thomas De Quincey, at age twenty-eight, to take opium daily for relief. He had begun taking opium almost ten years before. These stomach pains were a legacy from hardships that he endured as an adolescent. De Quincey's father had died when the boy was seven. Thomas, the responsibility of four guardians, was sent to school, where he became an excellent Greek scholar. Later, at the Manchester Grammar School, he was so superior to his teachers in Greek that he soon felt a desire to leave the school. His guardians being against this plan, however, he asked an old friend for money, received it, and planned to make his escape from a school that he felt had nothing to offer him intellectually.

The day of his escape came. When the groom of his hall was carrying his book-laden trunk down a narrow stairway, the man slipped and fell, the trunk clattering noisily to the floor below. Young De Quincey was sure he would be caught. The noise, miraculously, did not arouse the curiosity of the resident master, and the youth was able to get away.

Seventeen-year-old De Quincey headed westward, walking through Wales, where, in Bangor, he took a room. His landlady was the former servant of a bishop's family. On one of her regular visits to the bishop's house, she disclosed that she was taking in lodgers. When she reported her disclosure to De Quincey, he took exception to the tenor of her remarks concerning him, moved out of her house at once, and found lodging in inns. That type of lodging being relatively expensive, the young man soon found himself reduced to eating only once a day, and this a meal of only coffee or tea. The mountain air of Wales and the walking made him abnormally hungry, so that his having to subsist off berries and charitable handouts hurt him physically. As time went by, he managed to earn a meager living by writing letters for the illiterate and by doing odd jobs. The damage to his health, however, had been done.

His travels then took him from Wales to London, where, utterly destitute and afraid to reveal himself to any friends of his family, he lived for several months on little more than a small ration of bread. Also, at that time, he slept out of doors. At last, in cold weather, an acquaintance gave him shelter in a large, almost empty house, where De Quincey's companion was a ten-year-old girl. Pains in his stomach prevented his ever getting a proper night's sleep; consequently, he slept by fits and snatches both day and night. The master of the house was a legal representative of moneylenders, but despite the man's apparent lack of principles De Quincey found him generous in his way. The little girl appeared to be a servant in the large house, which was situated near Soho Square.

De Quincey walked the streets and often sat all day in parks, until Ann, a sixteen-year-old streetwalker, befriended him. One night, when he had a violent attack of his stomach complaint,

Ann spent part of her scant savings on wine and spices for him. Soon afterward he met an old family acquaintance who gave him money, thus ending De Quincey's period of extreme poverty. Previously, he had been afraid to appeal to family friends for help for fear that his guardians would send him back to the grammar school. That he might have taken on literary work of some kind never occurred to him. Now, solvent for the moment, he made arrangements to get an advance on his patrimony, which would not be legally his until his twenty-first birthday.

After saying good-bye to Ann, he took a coach to Eton to get a signature that was required for an advance on his patrimony. At Eton he called upon an acquaintance, young Lord Desart, who invited him to breakfast. Finding that he could not keep down the food, he took wine to his great comfort. Lord Desart, who was only eighteen, was reluctant to sign for security, but he finally consented. De Quincey returned to London, where he found that Lord Desart's signature did not impress the moneylenders with whom he was negotiating for the advance. Again he was threatened with hardship; again, however, he was saved, for his reconciled relatives sent him to Oxford University. Meanwhile, before he left London, he searched unsuccessfully for Ann. She was nowhere to be found, and he never saw her again.

De Quincey, nineteen, made frequent weekend trips to London from Oxford. One Sunday, while in the metropolis, he suffered greatly from neuralgic pains in the head, and a fellow student whom he encountered recommended opium for relief. He thereupon bought a small amount of laudanum, the tincture of opium, from an apothecary. He returned to his room and took the prescribed amount. The result seemed phenomenal to him; all his pain ceased, and he knew boundless pleasure. There was no intoxication, as from wine or spirits; there was only a protracted sense of being utterly at peace with the world and with himself. The opium uplifted the intellect rather than the animal spirits, and when its effect wore off there was no period of depression such as spirits induced.

As a college student, De Quincey's two great pleasures were to hear Grassini, an Italian soprano who often sang in London, or to take opium and afterward join the Saturday night crowds in the London markets. Even greater than these pleasures, however, was that of withdrawing himself at the time when the opium had reached its maximum effect on his mind, so that he could get the most complete enjoyment from his opium-induced dreams and visions.

De Quincey left Oxford. In 1812 he took a cottage, where he studied German metaphysics and continued to take opium once a week. His health was apparently never better. Even after eight years of taking opium, he was able to say that he had not become a slave to the drug; he was still able to control the amount taken and the intervals between doses.

A recurrence, in 1813, of his old stomach disorder led him to take the drug every day. That he was already partially addicted was a secondary reason for his increased use of opium. For two years he took three hundred and twenty grains of opium daily, but at last he was able to reduce the amount to forty grains. Staying on that allowance, he experienced the happiest year of his life.

About that time a Malay, traveling afoot, stopped for a night at the cottage. De Quincey was impressed by the aspect and garb of the traveler. Before the man left the next morning, De Quincey gave him enough opium, divided into three parts, to kill a man if taken all at once. The Malay clapped all three pieces into his mouth and departed. De Quincey felt concern for several days, but to his relief he never heard or read of the untimely death of a Malay in his part of Great Britain.

In his little cottage in the mountains of northern England, De Quincey, in the winter of 1816-1817, knew complete happiness in his experience with opium. Deep snows, heavy rains, a snug cottage, a roaring fire, a large collection of good books, plenty of tea, and daily consumption of laudanum brought him idyllic happiness.

Matters changed. Having become addicted to the daily taking of opium, it became impossible for him to reduce his daily allowance without bringing on abnormal perspiration and excruciating abdominal pains. He soon lost interest in reading and the study of mathematics and philosophy. A friend sent him David Ricardo's *Principles of Political Economy and Taxation* (1817). The book aroused him from his lethargy long enough to write for publication on that popular subject. Then, unable to write a preface for his work, he shelved the project. He neglected household responsibilities. At night he lay awake in his bed, processions of visions passing through his mind. These visions consisted largely of scenes from the English Civil War and from ancient Rome. Soon he found it difficult to distinguish between the real and the unreal. Furthermore, other dreams and visions took him into frightful abysses. Constantly depressed, he lost all normal sense of space and time, and he often had the sensation of having lived through a millennium. Also, he found himself able to recall insignificant events of his childhood, details which he had never been conscious of remembering.

The opium dreams were periodic: There were nights during which he dreamed historical scenes; then there was a period of architectural dreams—vast piles of buildings and enormous cities; these were followed by dreams of water—lakes, lagoons, vast oceans; and next a period of dreams in which countless human faces presented themselves in peculiar situations to his mind's eye.

In May, 1818, his dream visions took on an Oriental theme. At times he was in Egypt, then in China, or in India. Where in previous dream sequences he had known only spiritual horrors, in these Oriental ones he sensed physical horror from reptiles and frightful birds. In the summer of 1819, De Quincey, still addicted to opium, dreamed of a graveyard in his own little valley. In the dream he arose and walked out of his cottage yard to enjoy the air. He thought he saw an Oriental city and, beneath a palm tree, Ann, the streetwalker friend of his youth. She did not speak; the dream faded and he found himself walking with her in the streets of London. In 1820 one vision was so terrifying in its profundity and breadth that he awoke and declared that he would never sleep again.

Finally, he reasoned that he would surely die if he continued to take opium and that he might die in the attempt to break the habit. With so little choice, he decided to try, at least, to free himself from opium. He reduced his ration gradually and finally broke free, thus proving to himself that an addict may end a habit of seventeen years' duration.

Critical Evaluation:

A book that many have heard of but few have read, De Quincey's *Confessions of an English Opium Eater* remains the most arresting and touchingly human account in English literature of the widespread phenomenon of opium addiction in the early nineteenth century. Laudanam, or tincture of opium, was readily available at pharmacies in De Quincey's time, and was considered an effective cure for extreme headaches and depression. Coleridge also took laudanam for his neuralgic pains, and most readers of Romantic literature are familiar with the exotic fragment "Kubla Khan," which is purported to be the result of an interrupted attempt to capture the elusive memories of an opium dream.

In his *Confessions of an English Opium Eater*, De Quincey refrains from trying to construct art, even in fragments, from his opium reveries. Instead he is a kind of impressionistic reporter, a writer who shares, in a descriptive and evenhanded way, his visions and their sources in the experiences of his life. The result is a curious taming of the marvelous, a domestication of the horrific. De Quincey's quite accomplished writing style has kept this book, despite its title, from being much read in the times since its publication. Deliberate displays of erudition, sentimentality, long sentences emulating Latin, and wordy digressions do not appeal to many readers.

Although to many readers the book may seem prolix, it is compellingly constructed. When readers first encounter the gentle and simple Ann, a child prostitute, De Quincey knows that readers will recognize her at the end of his book in the terrifying dream of "female forms" crying "everlasting farewells." This dream, one of the "Pains of Opium," recalls the agonizing inability of De Quincey to find Ann again after their separation in London. The opium dream becomes a final farewell to this pathetic adolescent experience. As terrifying as it is, the dream is also cathartic and humanizing. In a sense, the dream finally "finds" Ann.

Opium dreams may revivify haunting memories; they may also immortalize trivial moments. The chance visit of the Malay sailor at De Quincey's cottage in the Lakes becomes the source of a series of opium dreams on Oriental themes. These dreams become increasingly terrifying and fantastic; they reveal De Quincey's deep fears of the unknown and his subconscious racial prejudices. It is in this sense that De Quincey's work belongs to the confessional tradition. Implicit in the autobiography and in the visions are the writer's traits, good and bad, as a human being.

Bibliography:
Hayter, Alethea. "De Quincey (I)" and "De Quincey (II)." In *Opium and the Romantic Imagination*. Berkeley: University of California Press, 1968. Discusses De Quincey's conviction that creativity was rooted in one's dreams, and that he felt opium enhanced those dreams.
Rzepka, Charles J. "The Body, the Book, and 'The True Hero of the Tale': De Quincey's 1821 Confessions and Romantic Autobiography as Cultural Artifact." In *Studies in Autobiography*, edited by James Olney. New York: Oxford University Press, 1988. Argues that the person who is supposedly De Quincey in *Confessions of an English Opium Eater* is a fabrication, and this fabrication is created anew in the mind of each reader.
Whale, John C. "De Quincey's Anarchic Moments." *Essays in Criticism: A Quarterly Journal of Literary Criticism* 33, no. 4 (October, 1983): 273-293. Discusses that although many critics compare De Quincey's book to William Wordsworth's *The Prelude* (1850), often critics do not point out that whereas Wordsworth celebrates as fruitful the link between past, present, and future, De Quincey finds the link menacing. Argues that De Quincey concentrates his attention on powers of individual consciousness, which can be capricious.
Wordsworth, Jonathan. "The Dark Interpreters: Wordsworth and De Quincey." *The Wordsworth Circle* 17, no. 2 (Spring, 1986): 40-50. Argues that the reader's chief problem is to discern how De Quincey's perception of suffering reconciles with the perception of darkness as horror and of darkness as wisdom. Points out that in De Quincey's understanding, suffering earns hope for the future.
Young, Michael Cochise. " 'The True Hero of the Tale': De Quincey's *Confessions* and Affective Autobiographical Theory." In *Thomas De Quincey: Bicentenary Studies*, edited by Robert Lance Snyder. Norman: University of Oklahoma Press, 1985. Argues that De Quincey's preoccupation with time pushes the book in opposite directions. The book attempts closure within time and transcendence of chronological limits.

CONFESSIONS OF FELIX KRULL, CONFIDENCE MAN
The Early Years

Type of work: Novel
Author: Thomas Mann (1875-1955)
Type of plot: Picaresque
Time of plot: Early twentieth century
Locale: Germany, Paris, and Lisbon
First published: Bekenntnisse des Hochstaplers Felix Krull: Der Memoiren erster Teil, 1954
(English translation, 1955)

Principal characters:
> FELIX KRULL, alias Armand, a hotel employee
> ENGELBERT KRULL, his father
> FRAU KRULL, his mother
> OLYMPIA, his sister
> HERR SCHIMMELPREESTER, his godfather
> MÜLLER ROSE, an actor and a friend of Engelbert Krull
> MADAME HOUPFLÉ, a sentimental novelist
> DOM ANTONIO JOSÉ KUCKUCK, a Portuguese museum director
> DONA MARIA PIA KUCKUCK, his wife
> SUSANNA (ZOUZOU) KUCKUCK, their daughter
> MARQUIS DE VENOSTA, a wealthy young nobleman
> ZAZA, the marquis' mistress

The Story:

Felix Krull was born in the Rhine Valley, the son of a champagne maker named Engelbert Krull. Townspeople considered the Krull family upper class but frowned on the easygoing way of life in the Krull household; Engelbert Krull, for one thing, showed too much interest in one of his female employees. The Krulls frequently invited friends, among them Felix's godfather, Herr Schimmelpreester, for merry parties, in which Felix and his sister Olympia were allowed to take part.

The greatest experience of Felix's youth was a dramatic performance by a famous actor, Müller Rose. Since the actor was a friend of his father, Felix was allowed to visit backstage. When he saw the actor removing his makeup, he was completely disillusioned, but he marveled at the impressions an actor could create. Before long, Felix himself became an actor. He started extending school vacations by falsifying his father's signature on absentee notes, but he found even more satisfaction from feigning sickness so convincingly as to leave the family doctor completely at sea.

The champagne business unfortunately did not prosper. Krull's champagne was bottled exquisitely, but the wine was of such poor quality that even Herr Schimmelpreester spoke of it only with disdain. The loss of his business and, soon thereafter, his friends was too much for Engelbert Krull, who shot himself. Herr Schimmelpreester recommended that Frau Krull open a rooming house in Frankfurt. He arranged for Olympia to be employed in a light opera company and Felix to be apprenticed in a Paris hotel. When the prospect of military conscription prevented Felix's departure, he was free to explore city life in Frankfurt, although lack of financial means restricted his role to that of an outside observer. He studied the behavior of society at theaters and learned from window displays what was recommended for gentlemen. With equal interest, he studied the lives of prostitutes. Until now he had had only one experience with one of his father's female employees. He met Rosza and, while her procurer was in jail, became her lover.

If Felix wanted to follow Herr Schimmelpreester's advice to seek employment in Paris, he had two alternatives: to serve his military term or to be excused entirely from service. After careful preparation, he went to the army medical examination center. While declaring his fervent desire to serve the fatherland, he managed to convey the most unfavorable information about his background, and he crowned his performance with a pretended epileptic fit. Pretending to be heartbroken because of his military rejection, he left for Paris. During the confusion at customs inspection, he inadvertently, as he assured himself, slipped the jewel case of a woman traveler into his suitcase.

In Paris he found himself the lowest member of the hotel hierarchy. With the help of a roommate, he sold some of the stolen jewels. As an elevator operator in a luxury hotel, he made every effort to please his customers, especially the women. The hotel director gave him the name Armand. One of the guests in his elevator turned out to be the original owner of the jewel case, Madame Houpflé, the wife of a rich Strasbourg merchant. When Armand realized that the woman did not suspect him of the theft, he was very considerate toward her and was rewarded with an invitation to visit her during off-duty hours.

Armand became her lover. Madame Houpflé especially enjoyed the humiliating aspect of the affair and talked about her need to be humiliated. Armand considered the moment appropriate for confessing the theft of the jewel case. Madame Houpflé enjoyed the confession because it increased her abasement, and she suggested that he should rob her of all her valuables. He gladly obliged.

After he had sold the valuables, he rented a room in town. A dual life began: During the day, he was Armand the hotel employee; during the night, he was Felix Krull, man about town. Thanks to his excellent manners, he was soon promoted to the post of waiter. Difficulties, however, arose when the sixteen-year-old daughter of a wealthy family fell hopelessly in love with him, and when the Scottish Lord Strathbogie was determined to have Armand as his valet. Armand said no to all offers; freedom to do as he pleased seemed to him the most valuable goal in life.

His favorite customer was the young Marquis de Venosta, who enjoyed the witty remarks of the waiter Armand. The nobleman's mistress, a Parisian dancing girl named Zaza, also approved of him because he did not fail to call her Madame la Marquise. It was de Venosta who finally discovered Armand's double life when he came across Felix dining in a famous restaurant.

A great dilemma had developed for de Venosta. His parents did not approve of his relationship with Zaza and planned to send him on a trip around the world. Because he found the thought of parting from Zaza unbearable, the marquis was happy to find in Felix a sympathetic listener. Felix explained that the only way for him to stay with Zaza would be to let someone else assume his identity and travel under his name. Delighted with the idea, de Venosta decided that Felix was the best candidate.

After elaborate preparations and much coaching, Felix received a letter of credit and took the train to Lisbon. On the way, he met Dom Antonio José Kuckuck, director of the Museum of Natural History in Lisbon. Impressed by the high social standing of his fellow traveler, the professor explained the outline of his philosophy. Felix found in the professor's theories an explanation of his own being; all developments of natural history seemed to him only steps toward himself. The professor's opinion that all phases of development were still with us and around us gave Felix a clue to the stagelike appearance of the world. He gladly accepted an invitation to visit Kuckuck in Lisbon.

When he met Dona Maria Pia Kuckuck and her daughter Susanna, who was called Zouzou, Felix was struck by the beauty of the two women, who were in turn equally impressed with the handsome "marquis." Determined to kiss Zouzou before his departure but finding his time in Lisbon running short, Felix wrote a letter to "his parents," presenting his stay in Lisbon in such a favorable light that they agreed to the postponement of the scheduled trip to South America. Under the pretext of wanting to show some of his drawings to Zouzou, Felix met her secretly in Kuckuck's garden. The incident resulted in a kiss, which was suddenly interrupted by Dona Maria, who sternly asked "the marquis" to come into the house and reprimanded him for abusing her hospitality. Outspoken Dona Maria wanted to know why Felix could not appreciate maturity instead of asking satisfaction from childishness. Dona Maria threw herself into his arms, and he realized that his attempted seduction of the daughter had ended with the unforeseen conquest of the mother.

Critical Evaluation:

Confessions of Felix Krull, Confidence Man, the last work by Thomas Mann and the only one that can be categorized as humorous, is a twentieth century version of the classic picaresque novel. The picaresque approach, in which social criticism is made more palatable by a liberal application of humor, reveals the discrepancy between what people are and what they think they are. Yet because the picaresque approach aims at vice, not at the person who has it, the protagonist or picaro becomes a hero—or, to be more precise, an antihero. Appropriately, picaresque fiction is often categorized as black humor; the picaro is earth-bound and filled with angst and an existential, if comically portrayed, anguish. He is the perpetual outsider gazing into the light but forever condemned to the dark side of reality; he epitomizes the individual who is a member of society but is alienated from and isolated by it. The picaro is forced to survive by whatever means he finds available, most commonly chicanery and illusion. Thus, he projects a respectable illusion onto a receptive world, already enmeshed in delusion. Readers of picaresque fiction must be constantly aware that the presentation is subjective, the perception superficial and the point of view (generally first person) dominated by illusion, disguise, and literal and figurative masks.

Pretense, role-playing, mask-wearing and disguise are thus traditional elements in the picaresque novel; however, in *Confessions of Felix Krull, Confidence Man*, Mann takes the pretense one step further, for in this work the mask eventually replaces the man. Felix Krull is a chameleon, constantly altering his color to fit his environment. He hides behind multiple personae until "the real I, could not be identified because it actually did not exist." Felix Krull personifies the twentieth century picaro—a hero one step beyond rebellion with no viable religion or creed, a lost soul who is floating on an island of his own imagination. It is ironic that, for perhaps the first time in the picaresque genre, the reader is allowed to penetrate the inner dimensions of a rounded character only to find that too is a disguise. Felix sculpts himself and those around him to support his role-playing. From his childhood dress-up and pretend games to feigning epilepsy at his military induction examination, Felix is so adept an actor that he is lost in the impersonations, separated not only from society but from himself.

Although he is more sophisticated than his fellow picaros and his criminal behavior is the by-product of chance and not contrivance, Felix Krull demonstrates that survival with style still takes precedence over morality. He moves through initiation fully aware that the person who loves the world shapes himself to please it and that, in turn, he who loves himself shapes the world to suit himself. Despite his dealings in illusion and verbal magic, the character is a realist, knowing well the darkness beyond, of which he is a product. He is also aware that regardless of how thoroughly he may succeed in deceiving his fellows, the darkness still waits, ready to topple him from his temporary pedestal of success and suck him back into obscurity. Felix Krull subsists in a dual struggle with the illusion he creates to survive and the reality that it is an illusion.

Felix, alias Armand, alias the marquis, proposes a theory of interchangeability according to which the sole difference between people is monetary; with a change of clothes, the servant can become the master. This theory becomes the controlling factor in the work and in the protagonist himself who becomes so adept at it that the real Felix, if there ever was one, disappears and the character becomes no more than a sponge, soaking up each new identity in turn and altering his shape at will.

Through his association with the professor of natural history, Professor Kuckuck, Felix grasps that all humanity is created from raw material much as he has created himself. Mann dedicates long passages of the work to anthropological discussions of the rationalization that if evolution created humans from primeval slime, humans should be able to re-create themselves from whatever material is available. The professor explains evolutionary theory as stages of three spontaneous generations, and it is not inconceivable to relate this hierarchy to the three stages of Felix Krull's life, which culminate in his rebirth as a marquis.

Given his century's overpopulation and zealous mass media, the twentieth century picaro, in contrast to the picaro of previous ages, is forced inward into the chaotic world of the unconscious. Mann does not use the character Felix Krull to castigate the potential disintegration of society, for he sees it as already complete. Rather, it becomes Felix Krull's chore to symbolize the disintegration of the individual.

Confessions of Felix Krull, Confidence Man, Thomas Mann's last work, remained uncompleted at his death. Although readers of picaresque fiction are accustomed to episodic wanderings and the unresolved cessation of action, this novel cries out for additional details to dispel the impression of the unfinished. All the easier, however, is it for the reader able to agree with Mann that "life is an episode, on the scale of aeons, a very fleeting one."

"Critical Evaluation" by Joyce Duncan

Bibliography:

Alter, Robert. *Rogue's Progress: Studies in the Picaresque Novel.* Cambridge, Mass.: Harvard University Press, 1964. One of the better-known works on the picaresque novel, the book discusses changes in the genre as it moved across generations and national borders. The book treats several novels considered picaresque, including *Confessions of Felix Krull, Confidence Man.*

Hatfield, Henry. *From the Magic Mountain: Mann's Later Masterpieces.* Ithaca, N.Y.: Cornell University Press, 1979. A critical look at the novels of Thomas Mann based, in part, on Mann's correspondence. The work addresses Mann's increasing political awareness, his use of myth and comedy, and how he was viewed by his contemporaries.

Lewis, R. W. B. *The Picaresque Saint.* Philadelphia: J. B. Lippincott, 1959. A critical survey of the picaresque genre with a primary concentration on other novelists but many references to Mann; *Confessions of Felix Krull, Confidence Man* is judged to be one of his masterpieces and the "logical hero" of the age.

Mann, Erika. *The Last Year of Thomas Mann.* Freeport, N.Y.: Books for Libraries Press, 1958.

A firsthand account by Mann's daughter of the inception and construction of *Confessions of Felix Krull, Confidence Man*. Written in memoir form, the work gives an intimate portrait of the author.

Torrance, Robert M. *The Comic Hero.* Cambridge, Mass.: Harvard University Press, 1978. Traces the origin of the comic hero from his mythological antecedents through the modern novel. Contains an extended discussion of *Confessions of Felix Krull, Confidence Man* as representative of the picaresque.

THE CONFESSIONS OF NAT TURNER

Type of work: Novel
Author: William Styron (1925-   )
Type of plot: Psychological realism
Time of plot: c. 1810-1831
Locale: Southeastern Virginia
First published: 1967

> *Principal characters:*
> NAT TURNER, slave leader of an insurrection
> SAMUEL TURNER, one of Nat's owners
> MARGARET WHITEHEAD, white woman acquaintance of Nat
> HARK, a slave
> THOMAS GRAY, a lawyer
> JEREMIAH COBB, a judge
> WILL, a runaway slave

The Story:

Nat Turner was imprisoned and awaiting his death as a result of leading a slave insurrection. A self-proclaimed preacher, Turner was unable to pray and felt abandoned by his God. Thomas Gray arrived to obtain a confession. Gray's concept of his job was to prove that Nat Turner was not a typical slave but a fanatic whose revolt was an isolated event and therefore no threat to the institution of slavery. He tried to convince Turner that the major reason for his defeat was that most of the slaves defended their owners. While Gray talked about the rebellion, Turner thought back to his various owners, from Benjamin and Samuel Turner to Joseph Travis. The memory that dominated from the Travis years concerned Jeremiah Cobb, the man who eventually sentenced Nat Turner to death. Cobb had been impressed with the slave's intelligence while listening to him explain that Hark, a fellow slave, was disoriented because of the sale of his wife and children. After the conversation with Cobb, Turner had decided that Cobb would "be among the few spared the sword." Turner's memory shifted to Cobb's voice in the courtroom that had warned him to stay awake. Thomas Gray, although he represented Turner, had agreed with the prosecution's call for "swift retribution." Gray had stated that a slave rebellion was not likely to happen again because of "the basic weakness and inferiority, the moral deficiency of the Negro character." It was a rationalization of slavery that the public wanted to hear. During the trial, Turner had been thinking of Margaret Whitehead. Although she was the only person he had killed, she had also been one of the whites he had been close to. He recalled the day she had read her poem to him and had told him that he was the only person at home that she could confide in.

His reverie had been interrupted by Cobb's voice sentencing him to death by hanging. Back in jail after the trial, Thomas Gray arrived and attacked Christianity, saying that it had accomplished nothing but "misery and suffering for untold generations." Pondering Gray's words, Turner had doubts about being called by God for his "divine mission."

The condemned man recalled that he had tried to escape from his dilemma by thinking about his youth at Turner's Mill. Nat had learned to read by smuggling a book out of the Turner library. When Samuel Turner discovered his slave's ability, he was delighted. It validated his belief that "slaves were capable of intellectual enlightenment." While Samuel had argued with his brother Benjamin over the potential of slaves, Nat Turner became aware as never before that he was indeed a slave himself, a piece of property. The conservative Benjamin soon died. Nat became a pet of the family and was encouraged to read and to learn. Samuel Turner apprenticed him as a carpenter and eventually promoted Nat to a position of authority on the plantation. This led to the promise of emancipation at the age of twenty-five, a promise that was not kept when the plantation began to decline. Four slaves were sold. Although Nat Turner had sexual fantasies of golden-haired white girls, his only shared sexual experience had been a homosexual encounter with another slave named Willis.

Samuel Turner eventually lost the plantation, and Nat became the property of Reverend Alexander Eppes who, after unsuccessfully trying to rape Nat, relegated him to hard labor as the only slave in the village of Shiloh. Nat's loneliness and frustration continued when he was sold to Thomas Moore. The latter's response to Nat's ability to read was to whip him.

The prisoner next contemplated his developing hatred, the obsession he had to kill all whites in Southampton County. During his almost ten-year tenure with Thomas Moore, Nat nursed his hatred and planned his insurrection. He became a preacher and the subjects of his sermons were black pride and the necessity of rebellion. He created objectives and recruited members of his army. The plan included the destruction of local farms and plantations, the killing of all whites, the conquest of the village of Jerusalem for the purpose of possessing its armory, and the establishment of headquarters in the Dismal Swamp.

When Thomas Moore died, Nat Turner was transferred to Joseph Travis. Despite the better life for Nat, he was determined to fulfill his mission. He convinced himself that he had heard the mandate from God. Independence Day of 1831 was chosen as the beginning of the rebellion, but the plan was cancelled when Will, a slave on a nearby plantation, assaulted his master and ran away, producing an atmosphere of suspicion. Nat Turner interrupted his reflection on the insurrection to recall an episode with Margaret Whitehead. She had sympathized with Will for attacking his cruel master. She had wondered "why darkies stay the way they do." Margaret had asked Nat about a biblical passage that he identified as: "There is no fear in love; but perfect love casteth out fear." Nat remembered his lust for her, but at the time, he had converted it into hatred for the "godless white bitch" who was attempting to distract him from his mission of vengeance. Nat turned his thoughts to the Sunday night the rebellion was launched with an attack on the Joseph Travis farm. When Nat was unable to kill Travis with the first blow, Will, the runaway who had joined the rebel group, killed Travis and his wife. He taunted Nat for being a weak leader.

Thomas Gray intruded into the prisoner's reveries by arriving at his cell and asking if Nat felt any remorse. When Nat admitted to none, Gray gave his analysis of the defeat of the insurrection, stressing the role played by the faithful retainers, the slaves who had defended their masters. After Gray's visit, Nat "was affected by fear and uneasiness." Except for the slaying of Margaret, however, he knew that he had done what was necessary.

Nat's memory returned to the conflict with Will during the beginning of the rebellion. In order to regain control, Nat killed Margaret Whitehead. After the act, he circled the body aimlessly and envisioned Margaret rising from the blazing field. After recovering from the killing, Nat Turner returned to the battle. At the Harris farm, Nat saw a girl escape, but he made no attempt to stop her. Once the alarm was sounded, the insurrection was doomed. He had let himself be doomed. Nat awoke in his cell on the morning of his execution. He talked to Hark in the neighboring cell, but he could find no consolation for his despair, no sign of redemption. Thomas Gray appeared and gave him a Bible, but Nat did not open it. He observed the morning star and thought of Margaret. He remembered their discussion about "the perfect Christian love of God, and of one another." He felt redeemed. As the executioner arrived, he heard a voice say, "Come, My son," and he surrendered to the morning star.

Critical Evaluation:

Based on an actual slave insurrection and employing historical characters, the novel received critical acclaim when it was published in 1967. In 1968, it was awarded the Pulitzer Prize in fiction. Nine months after the publication, a book of vehement disapproval appeared. *William Styron's Nat Turner: Ten Black Writers Respond* attacked the novel for distorting the image of a black hero. The book pointed out the dangers inherent in the attempt of a white writer to portray a black historical figure, especially when the novel is told from the viewpoint of the black protagonist. The major critical question concerned Nat Turner's sexual preferences, particularly his fascination with white womanhood. *The Confessions of Nat Turner* has been a controversial novel, but the effect has been to increase its readership. It is, however, a book that can stand on its artistic merits. In order to create a round character, Styron had to expand upon the limited material of the slave's life that is presented in the actual confession. The result is a fictional character of credibility. The negative side of Styron's approach is that it left him vulnerable to the charges of racism and historical falsification.

Nat Turner is revealed as a sensitive person who is driven to desperation by the evil in the institutions that surround him: slavery and Christianity. As a slave, he sees his predicament as similar to that of Moses and the Israelites. The chance for freedom offered by Samuel Turner is destroyed by economics, and the tribulations suffered while in the hands of Eppes and Moore turn him into a religious fanatic who dreams of leading the slaves out of bondage. Learning to read from the Bible and John Bunyan's *The Life and Death of Mr. Badman*, books cherished by the owner of the slaves, Nat Turner, ironically, evolves into a rebel who plots to kill those slave owners. The novel depicts the development, then, of a monster. He is the natural product of a society that enslaved him and nourished, in part, his intellectual curiosity. Unable to pray while in jail, in a confused state bordered by Christian love and Old Testament violence, Margaret Whitehead's image provides Turner an answer. Nat Turner feels redeemed when he recognizes her message of love, which he equates with the morning star. He is able to face death with confidence.

In working out Nat Turner's destiny, Styron captures the essence of a major moral issue in nineteenth century America. Nat lives with the fears and tensions of surviving in a delicately balanced society. He is daily faced with the problems of pleasing a master and of role-playing for protection and for personal advancement. The various social aspects of slavery are set against a crumbling economic system that threatens to make slavery obsolete. Told from a slave's view, in a series of flashbacks that examine the making of a fictional, if not the historical, Nat Turner, the novel has won its place as at least a minor classic.

Noel Schraufnagel

Bibliography:

Betts, Richard A. "'The Confessions of Nat Turner' and the Uses of Tragedy." *College Language Association Journal* 27, no. 4 (June, 1984): 419-435. Discusses the novel as having the conventions of classical tragedy, including Nat Turner as tragic hero.

Casciato, Arthur D., and James L. W. West. "William Styron and the Southampton Insurrection." *American Literature: A Journal of Literary History, Criticism, and Bibliography* 52, no. 4 (1981): 564-577. Argues that the novel was carefully researched but that the author took a risk in inventing detail.

Clarke, John Henrik, ed. *William Styron's Nat Turner: Ten Black Writers Respond.* Boston: Beacon Press, 1968. An attack on Styron for distorting historical facts about a black hero. Some valid criticism, some merely racist.

Lang, John. "The Alpha and the Omega: Styron's *The Confessions of Nat Turner.*" *American Literature* 53, no. 3 (1981): 499-503. Explains Nat Turner's religious views, particularly the redeeming role of Margaret Whitehead.

Mallard, James M. "The Unquiet Dust: The Problem of History in Styron's *The Confessions of Nat Turner.*" *Mississippi Quarterly: The Journal of Southern Culture* 36, no. 4 (1983): 525-543. Claims that Nat Turner's personal quest for salvation tends to subvert his slave rebellion.

THE CONFIDENCE MAN
His Masquerade

Type of work: Novel
Author: Herman Melville (1819-1891)
Type of plot: Satire
Time of plot: Nineteenth century, before the Civil War
Locale: Mississippi River
First published: 1857

Principal characters:
THE CONFIDENCE MAN, referred to as such only in the title
THE MAN IN CREAM COLORS, a deaf-mute, a guise of the Confidence Man
DER BLACK GUINEA, a lame beggar, a guise of the Cofidence Man
JOHN RINGMAN, an unfortunate gentleman, a guise of the Confidence Man
THE MAN IN THE GRAY COAT AND WHITE TIE, a collector for charities,
   a guise of the Confidence Man
JOHN TRUMAN, the president and transfer agent of the Black Rapids Coal
   Company, a guise of the Confidence Man
THE HERB-DOCTOR, a dealer in herbal medicine, a guise of the
   Confidence Man
A REPRESENTATIVE OF THE PHILOSOPHICAL INTELLIGENCE OFFICE, a
   guise of the Confidence Man
FRANCIS GOODMAN, a cosmopolitan, a guise of the Confidence Man
ROBERTS, a country merchant
THE COLLEGE SOPHOMORE
THE MISER, a wealthy but sickly old man
PITCH, a Missourian
CHARLIE NOBLE, an amiable passenger
MARK WINSOME, a mystic
EGBERT, his practical disciple
WILLIAM CREAM, the ship's barber

The Story:
   On an April morning in St. Louis, a deaf-mute boarded the steamer *Fidèle* ("faith"). Many passengers gathered around a placard advertising a reward for the capture of a mysterious impostor, and some took this opportunity to purchase money belts or biographies of famous criminals. The deaf-mute approached the placard, wrote platitudes about charity on a slate, and displayed them to the crowd. Meanwhile, a barber opened his shop and hung a sign that read "No Trust." Rebuffed, the mute walked to the forecastle and fell asleep at the foot of a ladder.
   After the ship left dock, a group of passengers amused themselves by tossing pennies (or, more cruelly, buttons) to a lame black who caught them in his mouth. He identified himself as Der Black Guinea, but was confronted by a man with a wooden leg who accused him of being a sham. An Episcopalian minister interceded, and when the beggar described several people on the ship who would vouch for him, went to find them. The wooden-legged man renewed his attack, but a Methodist minister rebuked him until he withdrew. Although the Methodist had apparently triumphed, he immediately demonstrated similar suspicion. Further complications

were averted when a kind merchant offered the beggar alms, in the process accidentally dropping a business card, which the beggar surreptitiously covered with his stump.

Roberts, the merchant, was soon accosted by a man with a weed in his hat who identified himself as John Ringman and claimed to be an old acquaintance. When Roberts protested he had no recollection of their meeting, Ringman pressed him to admit he had had a fever at about that time which might have erased his memory. Ringman related a story of profound personal misfortune, until the merchant offered him a bank note, and then a larger one. In return, Ringman told Roberts that the president of the Black Rapids Coal Company, which represented a rare investment opportunity, was on board.

Ringman next encountered a college sophomore reading Tacitus. In impassioned rhetoric, he urged the student to toss the volume overboard before he lost confidence in his fellows. Nonplused, the young man departed.

The Episcopalian minister's search for someone who knew Der Black Guinea concluded when he encountered a man in a gray coat and white tie, exactly as the beggar had described. The unnamed man bore witness to Guinea's authenticity. The wooden-legged man reappeared, and amusedly ridiculed human credulity. Wanting to distance himself from this cynicism, the minister gave the stranger money for the beggar. The stranger then extracted an additional contribution for the Seminole Widow and Orphan Asylum.

This unnamed man managed to compel a donation for this charity from another gentleman, then a further contribution to support an ambitious plan to unite all of the world's charities under one organization. The man concluded his operations by obtaining a donation for the asylum from a woman reading the Bible. Quoting the New Testament, he then departed.

The sophomore was approached by John Truman, the president and transfer agent of the Black Rapids Coal Company. Truman claimed to be searching for Ringman in order to give him money, and to have just spoken with the man in the gray coat. The sophomore invested an undisclosed amount in the company. The hapless Roberts followed suit, and in the process informed Truman of the existence of an old miser onboard. The miser, sickly and confused, invested one hundred dollars. He immediately regretted his decision, but was too weak to pursue Truman.

Not all of the financial transactions aboard the *Fidèle* involved large sums. After Truman's departure, an herb-doctor moved about the ship selling his wares, alternately called Omni-Balsamic Reinvigorator and Samaritan Pain Dissuader. Several passengers, including the miser, made purchases for two or three dollars. Only a Missourian, professing universal distrust of people and nature, resisted.

Pitch, the Missourian, told of a succession of untrustworthy boys he had employed on his farm. Shortly after the herb-doctor's departure, however, a representative of the Philosophical Intelligence Office, an employment agency, persuaded him to try another, sight unseen. Pitch gave the stranger a small fee and passage money. He later had second thoughts, but was interrupted by a man describing himself as a cosmopolitan who argued against a solitary life. Despite the cosmopolitan's protests, Pitch welcomed him as a fellow misanthrope, which compelled him to leave.

Francis Goodman, the cosmopolitan, next met a talkative passenger calling himself Charlie Noble. Noble related a long tale about an Indian-hater named Colonel John Moredock. Finding that they shared a low opinion of misanthropy, Noble and Goodman struck up an immediate friendship over wine, though Noble seemed determined to drink less than his companion. All went well until Goodman claimed to need money and asserted that Noble would lend him fifty dollars. Noble erupted, and Goodman insisted he had been joking. Goodman told a story about a young merchant, Charlemont, who without warning had turned away from his friends. Noble claimed fatigue and left.

Mark Winsome, a mystic philosopher who had overheard the previous conversation, introduced himself to Goodman. Using obscure references to ancient Egypt and Greece, Winsome warned that Noble was out to cheat him. Goodman thanked the mystic, but insisted that he saw no reason to lack confidence in Noble's nature. Winsome introduced Goodman to his disciple, Egbert, and departed.

Egbert proved to be as practical as his mentor had been abstruse. Apparently interested in understanding Winsome's philosophy, Goodman asked Egbert to act out a scenario involving a man in need who begs a loan of a friend. The two men did so at great length, with Goodman requesting the loan and Egbert justifying his refusal. To support his argument, Egbert told of China Aster, who came to ruin and death through a friendly loan. Defeated, the cosmopolitan withdrew.

Goodman went to the ship's barbershop with its "No Trust" sign displayed. After great effort, he convinced the barber to give him a shave on credit and continue the policy for the rest of the voyage for other passengers. He signed an agreement to compensate the barber for any losses. After Goodman left, however, the barber rehung his sign and tore up the agreement.

Goodman retired to the cabin, where he encountered a well-to-do old man reading the Bible by lamplight. The two men agreed on the importance of having confidence in one's fellow. Afterward, the old man bought a traveler's lock and money belt from a young peddler. Goodman refused to purchase anything. Extinguishing the light, he led the man, holding his money belt and a life preserver, into the darkness.

"The Story" updated by Richard Alan Nanian

Critical Evaluation:

Herman Melville's work was largely forgotten during his own lifetime, and it was only in the 1920's that this author began to receive his due, for the first time, as one of the most important writers the United States has ever produced. *The Confidence Man: His Masquerade* was still not appreciated, however, until some thirty years later. As *Moby Dick* (1851) appealed to modernists in the 1920's because of its symbolic investigations of human evil and its experimental form, so *The Confidence Man*, the last of Melville's novels published in his lifetime (*Billy Budd, Foretopman* was published posthumously in 1924), found its audience in post-World War II readership's cynicism, sense of the absurd, and interest in language play. Its dense structure, paradoxes, and puns remind the reader less of Melville's contemporaries than of such postmodern authors as Vladimir Nabokov and Jorge Luis Borges.

Yet *The Confidence Man* is a work deeply rooted in its own time. Gertrude Stein once wrote that no writer is ahead of his or her time, but a unique writer's understanding of his or her own time may not be understood by others also living in that moment: The writer may be living in the present while all others are still living in the past. This is certainly true of Melville in *The Confidence Man*. For while the United States remained obsessed with its own promises of freedom and democracy, Melville was interested in showing how the manipulation of the language of freedom and democracy could become the true discourse of the nation. Incidental historical references make clear to the reader the historical correlative of ruse, swindle, and appearance that Melville is interested in exposing. The hoaxes of circus showman P. T. Barnum and the financial panics and wildcat banking of the nineteenth century manipulated public trust for profit. In *The Confidence Man*, hucksters and con artists try to sell one another bogus stock, swindle one another out of services, and rob one another of whatever property they might have. The masquerade in the title suggests that the novel is not interested in describing a single individual but rather a type. The American confidence man dons any number of masks, but one thing always remains the same: He is trying to sell something, and to do so he must gain the trust of his potential victim. As one character says: "Confidence is the indispensable basis of all sorts of business transactions. Without it, commerce between man and man, between country and country, would, like a watch, run down and stop." No character can steer clear of potential swindles, for to do so would mean distrust of an entire system: capitalism and the American project. Nearly every character in the novel is practicing his own type of shell game, so mutual wariness abounds. The implicit criticism of business and capitalism is clear.

The idea of the masquerade also leads to a very unconventional novel. There is no plot per se. Rather, the novel relies on an intricate plan to structure its narrative. It is forty-five chapters in length: Twenty-two of these occur before twilight, and twenty-two after, in the darkness of night. The characters' actions, as well, grow gradually darker, ending with the planned robbery and murder of an old man whose lantern (symbolizing the light of God) has been extinguished moments before, after midnight. The action takes place aboard a steamship traveling down the Mississippi River, during the period of tension between the North and South prior to the Civil War. In chapter twenty-three, the book's middle chapter, the boat sits still in Cairo, at the southern tip of Illinois. From there on, the characters enter slave territory, which Melville suggests is a state of moral darkness. Thereafter, too, the various guises of the confidence man coalesce into one figure, the cosmopolitan.

In the first half of the novel, transactions have taken place in the light of day. People have been swindled, but the stakes have been low and the consequences not altogether severe. Things take a decidedly more serious turn in the second half of the novel, after the pivotal twenty-third chapter. A chapter concerning "the metaphysics of Indian hating" makes clear that biases against Native Americans have not been based so much upon reality as on the stories that have been built up over the years characterizing Indians as deceitful, treacherous, and bloodthirsty. It is not the truth of a situation upon which people act, but its appearance. As any student of American history knows, massacres resulted on the basis of such fictions. The masks that truth wears are thus of great concern to all if people intend to have anything resembling justice in the world.

The difficulty of ascertaining what is true in a world of appearances makes for a hazardous existence. At the beginning of the novel, a mute man with a chalkboard inscribes various messages, about the virtue of charity, from Corinthians. In a world where what purports to be charity may be villainy in disguise, however, it is not easy to recognize charity when it appears. This is the dark world that Melville describes, a world in which the light of God fades and is replaced by the confusions of evil. The virtues of trust in one's fellow human being, including geniality, philanthropy, fidelity, and consistency, are all, at various times in the novel, manipulated for personal gain. Behind all cons, moreover, is the threat of violence. When, at the end of the novel, the cosmopolitan "kindly" leads the old man to his stateroom, the reader has no doubt that murder and robbery await the old man. The old man, suspicious of the world, having bought a lock for his room and a money belt in which to hide his valuables, is nevertheless trusting of the cosmopolitan, who has spent time with him discussing the Bible. The true (or at least the more successful) criminals of the world, Melville suggests, are those who seem to be benefactors and who know how to use a language that will make themselves attractive.

"Critical Evaluation" by Ted Pelton

Bibliography:
Leyda, Jay. *The Melville Log.* 2 vols. New York: Harcourt Brace Jovanovich, 1951. A collection
of documents important to the life and career of Melville, including excerpts from letters,
reviews of his work, and passages from Melville's novels that allude to biographical data.
Lindberg, Gary. *The Confidence-Man in American Literature.* New York: Oxford University
Press, 1982. A discussion of Melville's novel frames this investigation of the confidence man
in American literature and history. Includes discussions of Huckleberry Finn, P. T. Barnum,
Walt Whitman, and Thomas Jefferson among others.
Melville, Herman. *The Confidence-Man: His Masquerade.* Edited by Bruce Franklin. India-
napolis: Bobbs-Merrill, 1967. Franklin's edition of this novel contains substantial footnotes
to the main text, giving the reader reliable critical elucidations of the text's complex symbolic
structure and historical and mythic allusions.
_____. *Journals.* Edited by Howard C. Horsford and Lynn Horth. Evanston, Ill.:
Northwestern University Press, 1989. Includes entries and passages written soon after
Melville finished *The Confidence Man.*
Rogin, Michael Paul. *Subversive Genealogy: The Politics and Art of Herman Melville.* Berke-
ley: University of California Press, 1979. Incisive psychological and Marxist reading of
Melville's life and work, arguing that Melville was one of the leading thinkers of his age.
The reading of Melville's family's place in the historical context of the 1840's is unparal-
leled. Includes an excellent discussion of *The Confidence Man.*

THE CONFIDENTIAL CLERK

Type of work: Drama
Author: T. S. Eliot (1888-1965)
Type of plot: Comedy of manners
Time of plot: Mid-twentieth century
Locale: London
First performed: 1953; first published, 1954

Principal characters:
SIR CLAUDE MULHAMMER, a successful financier
EGGERSON, his former confidential clerk
COLBY SIMPKINS, his new confidential clerk
B. KAGHAN, a businessman and Lucasta's fiancé
LUCASTA ANGEL, Sir Claude's illegitimate daughter
LADY ELIZABETH MULHAMMER, Sir Claude's wife
MRS. GUZZARD, Colby's aunt

The Story:

Sir Claude Mulhammer, a successful middle-aged financier, had invited his retired confidential clerk, Eggerson, down to London from his home in the suburbs. He had asked Eggerson for the specific purpose of meeting Lady Elizabeth's plane on her return from a trip to Switzerland and telling her that he had been replaced in his position by a young man named Colby Simpkins. Sir Claude and Eggerson were apprehensive that Lady Elizabeth would be suspicious and disapproving, and Sir Claude wanted to keep from her the fact that Colby was his illegitimate son until after she accepted him in the household and had come to like him. Sir Claude and Eggerson hoped that Lady Elizabeth might even decide that she liked him enough to want to adopt him, to take the place of a son she gave up in her youth.

Before Eggerson could leave for the airport, Lady Elizabeth returned unexpectedly and had to be introduced to Colby without any preparation. Lady Elizabeth, however, preoccupied by her spiritual life and convinced that she was the one who had recommended Colby to begin with, eagerly took him under her wing. Colby made a favorable impression on all the members of the household, including Sir Claude's daughter Lucasta and her fiancé B. Kaghan.

An unsuccessful musician, Colby agreed to introduce Lucasta to the pleasures of music. During a long introspective conversation in Colby's new flat, which Sir Claude had acquired for him and Lady Elizabeth enthusiastically offered to decorate, Colby and Lucasta discovered a mutual liking. Lucasta, who began to question her feelings for Kaghan, confided to Colby that she was Sir Claude's daughter. Colby was shocked to learn that she was his half sister, a fact he was, however, unable to reveal to her. Lucasta was disappointed in Colby's reaction, which she misunderstood, and reclaimed Kaghan as her fiancé when he arrived to see Colby's new flat.

Lady Elizabeth appeared soon after, and once she had nudged Lucasta and Kaghan on their way, she began to question Colby closely about his background. Upon discovering that he had been raised by an aunt, Mrs. Guzzard, in Teddington, just outside London, she became convinced that he was the son she had had as a very young woman. She had relinquished the baby to his father and knew that the child had been adopted by a couple with an unusual name from a place she now recalled was Teddington. Because she did not tell Colby what she suspected, he could not understand her interest in his background and tried to turn the conversation. When they were joined by Sir Claude, Lady Elizabeth announced her belief that Colby was her lost son.

Sir Claude decided she must be told the truth about Colby's relationship with him, but Lady Elizabeth remained convinced that he was mistaken. Colby was frustrated to have both a mother and a father claiming him as their own, and he demanded that his real identity be determined. All agreed that Mrs. Guzzard must be summoned and questioned.

Sir Claude arranged a meeting in his business room. While waiting for the arrival of Eggerson, who was to chair the meeting, Sir Claude and Lady Elizabeth spoke honestly and gained a deeper understanding of each other. When Eggerson arrived, he was accompanied by an uninvited guest, Lucasta, who was looking for Colby. When Sir Claude informed her that Colby was her half brother, Lucasta understood the reason for Colby's shock at her earlier disclosure and she thereupon formally announced her marriage to Kaghan.

Mrs. Guzzard was shown in by Kaghan, and when Eggerson began to question her, she revealed that Kaghan was the son Lady Elizabeth had given up; the child had remained with the Guzzards for a while before being adopted by the Kaghans, formerly of Teddington. Mrs. Guzzard also revealed that her sister, who had been expecting Sir Claude's baby, had died before giving birth and that Colby was actually her own son. She had been recently widowed when Sir Claude sought them out and had played along with his belief that Colby was his illegitimate son so that she would receive some financial help for his upbringing. When Colby learned that he was the son of Herbert Guzzard, a disappointed musician, he resolved on music as a career, even if he lacked great talent. Colby refused Sir Claude's offer that he continue to think of him as at least a father figure and to stay at the Mulhammer home. Instead, he decided to apply for the post of organist at the parish church in Eggerson's neighborhood. Sir Claude, inclined to doubt Mrs. Guzzard's revelation about Colby's lineage, dolefully accepted it when he saw that Eggerson, whom he trusted explicitly, believed her. Bereft, the Mulhammers turned for consolation to Sir Claude's daughter Lucasta and Lady Elizabeth's son Kaghan, who promised that their relationship would help stabilize the newly established family.

Critical Evaluation:

T. S. Eliot, best known as one of the greatest English poets of the modern age, also produced several poetic dramas, of which *The Confidential Clerk*, first staged in Edinburgh in 1953, is perhaps the least known and appreciated. Eliot is reported to have said at a press conference after the play's first stage production that "if one wanted to say something serious nowadays it was easier to say it in comedy"; this play can be considered both a serious tale conveyed comically and a high farce dramatized in serious tones. Certainly Eliot was inspired by Greek tragicomedies. The plot of *The Confidential Clerk* is based on Euripides' *Ion* (fifth century B.C.E.). With its lost children, searching parents, and mistaken identities, Eliot's play also resembles the kind of comedy of manners made famous by Oscar Wilde. Despite the appearance of frivolity, however, a serious undertone is integrated into the pattern of events, and behind the farcical interchange of parents and children lies the spiritual revelation that all earthly relationships are swallowed up in one's relation to God.

T. S. Eliot explored the worlds of spirituality and religion widely and deeply in all his writing. In this play, the central concept is Colby's search for a way to integrate the outer world of action with the world of spiritual being, the two aspects of reality. He discovers, in the course of the play, that the path lies through the fulfillment of his true relationships to others, especially to his dead father (the failed musician Herbert Guzzard) and to God, and it is hinted that he may finally find his true vocation in the church. The other characters in the play find their spiritual peace in their own way. Eggerson, for example, finds physical and spiritual solace in retiring regularly to his "secret garden," where he tends vegetables to bring back to his wife.

The play exists simultaneously at two levels: There is the comic, farcical world, in which long-lost relatives, parents, and children are revealed and reunited, and there is the world of spiritual discovery, in which self-knowledge is the goal. The play's ultimate revelation is that the only way to unite the outer (public) and inner (private) worlds is through love and communion with another human being and/or with God. As in much of Eliot's other work, especially the plays *The Family Reunion* (1939) and *The Cocktail Party* (1949), a choice is made between normal family life and a dedicated life that leads away from family, probably to God. Lucasta wisely discovers that though she feels an attraction to Colby, he does not really need another human being and that her family-oriented future lies with Kaghan and the Mulhammers. Sir Claude, who craves human closeness and desires Colby for a son, has to learn the hard lesson that he must let Colby go. Eliot emphasizes the need for people to try to understand each other's needs and motivations. Even Lady Elizabeth, who despite her idiosyncratic nature is wiser at the end of the play, expresses the hope that she and Sir Claude may try to understand each other better "and perhaps that will help us to understand other people."

Colby's brief presence among them inspires these new attempts at understanding; his departure does not split the family but reinforces their newfound solidarity. This allows Eliot to end the play on a note of hope. Although Colby's departure saddens the Mulhammers, it makes clear to them the need for self-knowledge and mutual understanding, which are the two prominent themes of *The Confidential Clerk*.

The play is structured in three acts: Act I introduces and explains, Act II develops, and Act III provides revelations and closure. A preliminary dialogue between Sir Claude and Eggerson clarifies the situation for the reader/audience, after which the rest of the characters are introduced slowly. Eliot carefully leads up to Lady Elizabeth's entrance and then gives the actual moment dramatic flair: Sir Claude, Eggerson, and Lucasta have all talked about her and raised suspense about how she will react to Colby; her unexpected arrival quickly becomes a comic anticlimax when she declares that it was she who had interviewed and recommended Colby.

Act II begins with another exploratory dialogue, which, however, approaches the level of intensity associated with poetry. The poetry is not sustained in this play but appears in passages in which Eliot highlights religious and spiritual experience. At other moments, the tone is conversational, with only a touch of poetic language giving it elegance or depth at moments when the characters are expressing their innermost thoughts and feelings.

Act III unravels the mysteries and provides closure. In the course of the play, a sense of unity is established between the characters, each of whom seems equally important and involved in the play's development. A weakness in the play may be that there is no compelling, central episode, no passage of heightened poetic beauty. Instead, Eliot's message is in the design of the entire plot and in the relationships of all the characters to one another. Eliot is considered a writer of poetic drama, but *The Confidential Clerk* exists at the borders of prose where the dramatist, instead of confining the focus to a single revelation, has concentrated on overall plot development and the experiences of an entire group.

Brinda Bose

Bibliography:
Browne, Elliot Martin. *The Making of T. S. Eliot's Plays*. London: Cambridge University Press, 1969. The classic testament to the writing and production of Eliot's plays from the man who

collaborated in their staging and provided invaluable help and criticism to the dramatist at every stage.

Jones, David Edwards. *The Plays of T. S. Eliot*. London: Routledge & Kegan Paul, 1960. Provides a useful chapter-length analysis of *The Confidential Clerk* as well as an introductory discussion of the genre of poetic drama.

Smith, Carol H. *T. S. Eliot's Dramatic Theory and Practice*. Princeton, N.J.: Princeton University Press, 1963. A good basic account of Eliot's ideas of dramatic theory and practice, which gives the reader a sense of what Eliot intended to achieve in his work.

Smith, Grover. *T. S. Eliot's Poetry and Plays: A Study in Sources and Meanings*. 2d ed. Chicago: University of Chicago Press, 1974. An essential reference guide for any interested reader of Eliot's work, which provides details of his sources and inspirations as well as a comprehensive analysis of the explicit and implicit meanings.

Ward, David. *T. S. Eliot Between Two Worlds: A Reading of T. S. Eliot's Poetry and Plays*. London: Routledge & Kegan Paul, 1973. Provides a useful reading of the conflicts and complexities in Eliot's thinking, a discussion that is relevant to an understanding of the play.

CONINGSBY
Or, The New Generation

Type of work: Novel
Author: Benjamin Disraeli (1804-1881)
Type of plot: Bildungsroman
Time of plot: 1832-1840
Locale: England and Paris
First published: 1844

Principal characters:
HARRY CONINGSBY, a young nobleman
MARQUIS OF MONMOUTH, his grandfather
SIDONIA, a wealthy young Jew and Coningsby's friend
EDITH MILLBANK, Coningsby's sweetheart
OSWALD MILLBANK, Edith's father
MR. RIGBY, a member of Parliament
LUCRETIA, a young Italian noblewoman and later Lord Monmouth's wife
FLORA, a member of a troop of actors

The Story:

Harry Coningsby was fourteen years old when he met his grandfather, the Marquis of Monmouth, for the first time. He had been placed in his grandfather's charge when he was still very young with the understanding that his widowed mother, a commoner, was never to see him again. He had been turned over, sight unseen, to the care of Mr. Rigby, a member of Parliament who sat for one of Lord Monmouth's ten boroughs.

Lord Monmouth, who preferred to live abroad, had returned to his native land in 1832 in order to help fight the Reform Bill. Hearing favorable reports of his grandson, he had ordered Mr. Rigby to bring the boy from Eton to Monmouth House. Unfortunately, young Coningsby was unable to put out of his mind thoughts of his mother, who had died when he was nine years old, and he burst into tears at the sight of his grandfather. Lord Monmouth, disgusted by this sign of weakness, ordered him to be led away. He thought to himself that the sentimental boy's future probably lay with the church. Fortunately, the boy became friendly with the marquis' guests, Princess Colonna and her stepdaughter, Lucretia. The princess passed on such glowing descriptions of Coningsby to his grandfather that they were on excellent terms by the time he returned to school.

At Eton, one of Coningsby's close friends was Oswald Millbank, a manufacturer's son. When Coningsby left Eton in 1835, he went to explore Manchester's factories before going to Coningsby Castle to join his grandfather. During his journey, he visited the Millbank mills. Oswald was abroad, but he was hospitably greeted by his friend's father. At the Millbank mansion, Coningsby met beautiful but shy young Edith Millbank and learned from her Whig father that he favored the rise of a new force in government—a natural aristocracy of able men, not one composed of hereditary peers.

Before departing for Coningsby Castle, young Coningsby was tempted to inquire about the striking portrait of a woman which graced the diningroom wall. His host, much upset by his question, made a brusque, evasive answer.

Lord Monmouth, backing Mr. Rigby for re-election to Parliament, had returned to his borough and scheduled an elaborate program of dances, receptions, and plays to gain a following for his Conservative candidate. Princess Colonna and Lucretia were again his grandfather's guests. Coningsby had no need, however, to confine his attentions to them; as Lord Monmouth's kinsman and possible heir, he found himself much sought after by society. He also found time to encourage Flora, a member of the troop of actors entertaining the marquis' guests. The girl was shy and suffered from stage fright.

Here Coningsby met Sidonia, a fabulously wealthy young Jew. Coningsby found his new friend impartial in his political judgments, not only because his fortune allowed him to be just but also because his religion disqualified him as a voter. During their lengthy discussions, Sidonia taught him to look to the national character for England's salvation. He believed that the country's weakness lay in developing class conflicts.

Lucretia made a brief effort to attract Coningsby when she observed the favor in which his grandfather held him, but, before long, she found Sidonia, a polished man of the world, more intriguing. Sidonia, however, was not to be captured. He was attracted by others' intellects, and Lucretia could not meet him on his own level.

After his holiday, Coningsby went to Cambridge for his last years of study. During his first year there, King William IV died, and the Conservative cause fell in defeat. Mr. Rigby was, as he had been for many years, the candidate from his borough, and with the marquis to back him, his victory seemed certain until Mr. Millbank entered the field. The manufacturer and the marquis had been enemies for many years, and their feud reached a climax when Millbank not only bought Hellingsley, an adjoining estate which Lord Monmouth had long coveted, but also defeated Monmouth's candidate.

Prepared for the worst, the defeated Mr. Rigby went to Monmouth House, where the marquis was in residence. He was pleasantly disappointed, however, for his employer's thoughts were not on him. Lord Monmouth was preparing to marry Lucretia, who was determined at least to obtain power and riches through marriage even if she could not have the man she desired. A year after the wedding, Coningsby was invited to join his grandfather and his bride in Paris for Christmas. Stopping at his banker's on his way through London, he was given a package of his mother's correspondence. In the packet was a locket with an exact copy of the portrait he had seen at Millbank. It was a picture of his mother.

While visiting an art gallery in Paris with Sidonia, Coningsby again met Edith Millbank, who was traveling with her relatives, Lord and Lady Wallinger. Coningsby, who fell in love with her immediately, was distressed to hear reports that Sidonia intended to marry her. Finding the couple conversing on familiar terms one evening, he regretfully decided to withdraw from the scene. He returned to England. Disappointed in love, Coningsby devoted himself to his studies for the remainder of his stay at Cambridge. Then, learning that Edith had not married and that Sidonia was no more than an old family friend, he went to Coningsby Castle in order to be near the Millbanks.

Coningsby spent every possible moment with Edith and her family during the next few weeks. When her father discovered the lovers' feelings, he asked Coningsby to leave. He would not, he explained, submit his daughter to the same fate the young man's mother had suffered at Lord Monmouth's hands. In this manner, Coningsby learned that his mother had once been Mr. Millbank's fiancée. Leaving Hellingsley, Coningsby went on a sea voyage from which he was called home by the marquis. Parliament faced another crisis, and Lord Monmouth had decided that Coningsby should stand as his candidate. Coningsby refused, for he was of the opinion that men should cut across party lines to establish recognition of the bond between property and labor. The same day that Lord Monmouth faced his rebellious grandson, he separated from Lucretia, who had proved unfaithful.

The marquis died at Christmas of that year. He left most of his fortune to Flora, who turned out to be his natural daughter. Coningsby was cut off with the interest on ten thousand pounds. Deeply disappointed in his expectations, Coningsby gave up his clubs and most of his friends and began to study law. He had resigned himself to the prospect of years of drudgery when Mr. Millbank repented his decision. The manufacturer withdrew his candidacy in the 1840 election to back Coningsby as the Tory candidate. Rigby was his rival candidate, but he was easily defeated. A few months later, Edith became Coningsby's bride and went with him to live at Hellingsley, their wedding present from Mr. Millbank. As a final blessing, though not an unmixed one, Flora, who had always been weak, died, leaving the fortune she had inherited to the man who had befriended her many years before at Coningsby Castle.

Critical Evaluation:

Benjamin Disraeli had dual careers as a statesman and a novelist. He published several novels before entering Parliament, continued writing during his political career, and published one novel after completing his service as prime minister in 1880. *Coningsby* represents both the political and artistic interests of Disraeli. Politically, the novel is important because it documents the rise of the Young England group, a small group of young members of Parliament with which Disraeli was associated after the 1841 Tory victory. The novel provides a fictionalized account of the political climate the decade after the passage of the 1832 Reform Bill, which provided for somewhat wider voting privileges and for greater representation of the large manufacturing centers. Artistically, the novel is written as a traditional *Bildungsroman*, a study of the maturation of the novel's hero. Harry Coningsby develops from a fourteen-year-old who, overcome by emotion, cries in an early scene, to a twenty-three-year-old newly elected member of Parliament. Disraeli intertwines his political and personal themes by having his protagonist involved with the politics of his day. An adolescent when the Reform Bill passes, Coningsby grows from an unquestioned acceptance of the conservative politics of his grandfather Lord Monmouth to a state of independence in which he accepts neither the Whig nor Tory Party politics. Instead, becoming the leader of the Young England group, he searches for principles that he feels should be the basis of life in England. *Coningsby* and two later novels, *Sybil* (1845) and *Tancred* (1847), function as a trilogy documenting the political, social, and religious views of the Young England group. The Young England trilogy is often considered the best of Disraeli's fiction.

Claiming to present impartially the various prevailing political views of the day, the narrator of *Coningsby* is intrusive. Through the narrator's characterizations and political wit, the Young England group is most often favored, while the established politicians, both Whig and Tory, are satirized. The political events and some of the characters in the novel so closely follow history that keys have been devised equating characters with their historic counterparts. So when the narrator openly judges the quality of the characters, he indirectly comments on some historical figures. Sidonia, an important influence on Coningsby and therefore on the Young England Group, is valorized. "Sidonia, indeed, was exactly the character who would be welcomed in our circles." On the other hand, the narrator satirizes characters representing the established politicians. Rigby, a member of Parliament, the narrator tells us, "was not treacherous, [on a specific evening] only base, which he always was." Sometimes the wit is more general. "We live in an age of prudence. The leaders of the people, now, generally follow." In this way, the novel favors the upcoming generation of political leaders who accept neither the Whig nor the Tory Party lines.

A major theme of the novel is introduced in its subtitle: *The New Generation*. In promoting the cause of Young England, the novel argues for the virtues of youth, genius, and heroism. Along with these romantic virtues comes the belief in the importance of the individual. All these characteristics are inherent in the Young England group, but they have already reached fulfillment in the idealized character of Sidonia. His wealth, intelligence, international reputation, high connections, and virtue indicate the possibilities of life if only the proper course is followed. Outside formal government because he is Jewish, Sidonia nevertheless embodies the ideals that the Young England group professes. (In Sidonia, Disraeli champions his own Jewish background.)

The movement of the novel suggests Disraeli's view of history—more a spiral than a circle or a horizontal line. Tradition and the past were important in Disraeli's politics, yet he was aware that a static policy would not be successful in a changing world. The spiral figure suggests a constant move back to what has been proven good, while at the same time presenting an understanding that there must be a movement forward to keep up with the changing world. Coningsby, in his politics, reached back to a belief in the responsibilities of the property owners, but he was ready to accept that the manufacturing cities in England were to play an important role. His marriage to Millbank's daughter Edith merges the aristocratic with the manufacturing segments of society. He does not proceed in a straight line, having the manufacturers overtake the aristocrats, or in a circle, coming back to the aristocracy without including the manufacturers. Coningsby, like Disraeli, wanted to reinvigorate, not eradicate, the conservative perspective.

As Coningsby grows politically, he also matures socially and personally. Although much of the novel deals with political views and intrigues, other passages describe the social life of the aristocracy. At first awkward in social situations and unable to tell the difference between genuine affection and idle flattery, Coningsby learns to judge character. He chooses his role models wisely. He is influenced by both Sidonia and Eustace Lyle, men who act with sensitivity and concern for others. Coningsby is never taken in, even at a young age, by Rigby's hypocrisy or self-interest. Although respectful of his grandfather, as a young man Coningsby refuses to act for Lord Monmouth's self-interest, acting instead according to his own principles, even when his inheritance is at stake. He falls in love with a manufacturer's daughter, someone of whom his wealthy grandfather and patron would certainly disapprove, but, by remaining steadfast in his choice and being willing to relinquish any inheritance and work in order to establish a living and a reputation, Coningsby manages to get everything—wealth, a seat in Parliament, and love. The rapid change in Coningsby's fortune from isolation and despair when he loses his inheritance to his final success marks the conclusion of the novel as improbable. Yet Coningsby's ultimate success is based on reward for his character. The ending fits an ideal if not a real world.

"Critical Evaluation" by Marion Boyle Petrillo

Bibliography:
Bivona, Daniel. "Disraeli's Political Trilogy and the Antinomic Structure of Imperial Desire." *Novel: A Forum on Fiction* 22, no. 3 (Spring, 1989): 305-325. Sees *Coningsby* as addressing the problem of how to join aristocrats and bourgeoisie so as to renew England while maintaining a stable hierarchy. Views the answer provided in the novel—Coningsby's marriage to Edith—as a form of imperialism.
Cazamian, Louis. "Disraeli: Social Toryism." In *The Social Novel in England, 1830-1850.* Boston: Routledge & Kegan Paul, 1973. Places Disraeli's political trilogy—*Coningsby*,

Sybil, and *Tancred*—in the context of his political position of social Toryism. Refers to *Coningsby* as a "hybrid," part political tract, part "fashionable novel."

Edelman, Maurice. "A Political Novel: Disraeli Sets a Lively Pace." *Times Literary Supplement*, August 7, 1959, 10-11. Presents *Coningsby* as a political novel still read more than one hundred years after its publication. Explores the novel's strong characters, some of whom are shown to reflect Disraeli's own situations and concerns.

Masefield, Muriel. *Peacocks and Primroses: A Survey of Disraeli's Novels*. London: Geoffrey Bles, 1953. Contains two chapters on *Coningsby* written for an audience not familiar with Disraeli's works. Provides plot, lengthy quotations from the novel, background historical information, and identifications of characters with historical figures.

O'Kell, Robert. "Disraeli's *Coningsby*: Political Manifesto or Psychological Romance?" *Victorian Studies* 23, no. 1 (Autumn, 1979): 57-78. Believes *Coningsby* is much more similar to Disraeli's earlier romance novels than is often accepted. Presents political portions of the novel as secondary to the theme of personal identity.

THE CONJURE WOMAN

Type of work: Short fiction
Author: Charles Waddell Chesnutt (1858-1932)
Type of plot: Regional
Time of plot: Post-Civil War
Locale: North Carolina
First published: 1899

Principal characters:
THE NARRATOR
ANNIE, his wife
UNCLE JULIUS, his black coachman
AUNT PEGGY, the conjure woman

The Story:

When the Narrator's wife began to suffer ill effects from the severe Great Lakes climate, he began to look for a suitable place to take her. He had been engaged in grape culture in Ohio, and when he learned of a small North Carolina town that seemed to offer what he needed in climate and suitable land, he decided to buy an old, dilapidated plantation and settle there. An untended vineyard was already on the property; with a little care and expense, the vines would flourish once more. On the day that he took his wife, Annie, to look at the plantation, they happened upon an ancient African American who called himself Uncle Julius. He advised them not to buy the plantation because it was goophered. Realizing they did not know that anything goophered was bewitched (conjured), the old man asked permission to tell them the story of the vineyard.

Many years before the war, when Uncle Julius was still a slave, the plantation owner had made many thousands of dollars from the grapes. Because the master could never keep the slaves from eating the rich grapes and stealing the wine made from them, he conceived the idea of having Aunt Peggy, a conjure woman living nearby, put a goopher on the vines. She made one that said that any black person eating the grapes would die within a year. Most of the slaves stayed away from the grapes, but a few tried them in spite of the conjure, and they all died. When a new slave came to the plantation, no one remembered to tell him about the conjure, and he ate some of the grapes. So that he would not die, Aunt Peggy made him a counter-goopher. Then a strange thing happened. Every year, as the grapes ripened, this slave became so young and sprightly that he could do the work of several men, but in the fall, when the vines died, he withered and faded. This strange action went on for several years, until the master hit upon the idea of selling the slave every spring when he was strong and buying him back cheaply in the fall. By this transaction, he made money each year.

One year, the master hired an expert to prune his vines, but the expert cut them out too deeply and the vines were ruined. Soon afterward, the slave who had bloomed and withered with the vines also died. Some said he died of old age, but Uncle Julius knew that it was the goopher that finally overcame him. Uncle Julius advised strongly against buying the land because the conjure was still on.

The Narrator bought the plantation, however, and it prospered. Later, he learned that Uncle Julius had been living in a cabin on the place and sold the grapes. He always suspected that the story was told to prevent ruination of the old man's business. He gave Uncle Julius employment as a coachman, and so the former slave was well cared for.

When Annie wanted a new kitchen, her husband decided to tear down an old schoolhouse on the place and use the lumber from it for the new building. Uncle Julius advised him against the plan. Strangely enough, that schoolhouse was goophered, too. Uncle Julius' story was that a slave called Sandy was borrowed by others so often that his woman was afraid they would be separated forever. She was a conjure woman, so she turned him into a tree. Each night, she would turn him back into a man, and they would slip into her cabin until morning, when she would again change him into a tree. One day, the woman was sent away from the plantation before she could change Sandy back into a man. While she was away, the master had the tree that was Sandy cut down to build a new kitchen. The slaves had a hard time felling the tree, which twisted and turned and tried to break loose from the chains. At last, they got it to the sawmill. Later the house was built, but it was never much used. The slaves refused to work there because at night they could hear moaning and groaning, as if someone were in great pain. Only Sandy's woman, when she returned, would stay in the building, and she, poor girl, went out of her mind.

Uncle Julius advised against using goophered lumber for the new kitchen. It seemed that Uncle Julius needed the old schoolhouse for his church meetings. The goopher would not bother the worshipers; in fact, the preaching helped Sandy's roaming spirit. Because no one would want to use goophered wood, there was nothing for the wife and her husband to do but buy new lumber for her kitchen.

When the Narrator was about to buy a mule to use in cultivating some land, Uncle Julius warned him against mules because most of them were conjured. Uncle Julius did, however, know of a horse for sale. After his employer bought the horse, which died within three months, Uncle Julius appeared in a new suit he had been admiring for some time.

One day, when Annie felt depressed and listless, Uncle Julius told her and her husband about Becky, a slave who had been traded for a horse. Taken away from her child, she grieved terribly. Aunt Peggy, the conjure woman, turned the baby into a hummingbird so that he could fly down to his mother and be near her and soothe her. Later the conjure woman arranged to have Becky and her baby reunited. Uncle Julius knew that she would never have had all that trouble if she had owned the hindfoot of a rabbit to protect her from harm. The story seemed to cheer Annie, and her husband was not surprised later to find Uncle Julius' rabbit's foot among her things.

When the Narrator prepared to clear a piece of land, Uncle Julius warned him that the land was goophered and told him a harrowing tale about a slave turned into a gray wolf and tricked into killing his own wife, who had thereupon been changed into a cat. Although the gray wolf was said to haunt the patch of land, it did not seem to bother a bee tree from which Uncle Julius gathered wild honey.

One day, Annie's sister Mabel and her fiancé quarreled bitterly. Uncle Julius had another story for them about Chloe, a slave who ruined her life because she was jealous. Chloe listened to a no-account rival and believed his story that her lover was meeting another woman. When she learned that she had lost her lover because she allowed her jealousy to trick her, she sorrowed and died. Even the conjure woman could not help her. Mabel listened to the story and then ran to her fiancé, who just happened to be close to the spot where Julius had stopped their carriage. Later on, the young man seemed to develop a special fondness for Uncle Julius. After the wedding, he tried to persuade the old man to enter his service, but Uncle Julius remained faithful to his employers. He thought they needed his advice and help.

1273

Critical Evaluation:

The Conjure Woman is Charles W. Chesnutt's first collection of short fiction. It includes seven short stories that are loosely connected but unified by parallel format, characters, and thematic similarities. Each story is presented against the unifying background of post bellum Southern life. The apparent model is the Joel Chandler Harris collection of Uncle Remus tales. Chesnutt's method differs from that of Harris by presenting an outside story providing the framework for the inside narrative, which is an original tale. Harris, on the other hand, based his inside material on existing folk tales. An African American, Chesnutt places a distinctive black perspective on his folk material, which is liberally sprinkled with dialect. *The Conjure Woman* preserves a relatively inaccessible and easily overlooked portion of American social and literary history.

The outside narrative usually consists of some type of journey that offers an opportunity to relate the inside narrative in dialect by Uncle Julius. Each inside narrative, which usually involves a major change in a newly introduced character, can stand alone. Chesnutt uses the frame-within-a-frame technique to mute the racial implications of the inside narrative.

Chesnutt also contrasts *The Conjure Woman*'s outside and inside narratives. The outside narrative is solidly based in the real world, one that treats the weak harshly and rewards the wealthy and powerful. The inside narrative is more imaginative and entertaining than didactic. This complex method masks much of the intent to educate the reader about the plight of the African American without becoming offensive or maudlin.

Uncle Julius relates to his white employers in a manner that parallels that with which the artist relates to his audience. Using this paradigm, Chesnutt educates his white audience by correcting the flawed vision of the outside narrative. In a very real sense, Charles Chesnutt conjures his readers by employing this complex methodology.

Some of these stories, in the author's words, "are quaintly humorous; others wildly extravagant, revealing the Oriental cast of the negro's imagination; while others . . . disclose many a tragic incident of the darker side of slavery." These tales are less amusing and more complex than the Uncle Remus stories: Both sets of tales recall the treasury of African American folklore, replete with birds and animals, witches and spells, spirits and haunts, horrors, wonders, protests, and fright.

The Conjure Woman presents several unique problems, one of which is the question of unity in the diversity of these seven stories. That unity is derived from Uncle Julius and consistently similar personas, plot development, and narrative thread, which concerns the trickster overcoming the deceptions of a hostile environment.

The exterior story is narrated in standard English by whites, and the interior story is narrated in dialect by Uncle Julius. The interior stories begin to develop after a catalyst such as an interrupted journey or task. The supernatural elements thereupon take over, with a full-blown story-within-a-story. The entire tale ends when the strands of all the outside plots are gathered up and brought to a satisfactory conclusion.

At the core of each of these seven stories is a desire to promote a better understanding of race relations in the antebellum South with which Chesnutt was so familiar. It also appears that Chesnutt was writing for the white audience a series of stories that appeal for more humane treatment of minorities in the United States.

All of the stories in *The Conjure Woman* are deftly and competently developed, but three are outstanding: "The Conjurer's Revenge," "The Goophered Grapevine," and "The Gray Wolf's Ha'nt." "The Goophered Grapevine" is the first story in the collection, deliberately placed to entice the reader to read the entire volume. It remains the most widely known and frequently anthologized of Chesnutt's short stories. At a seminal level, "The Goophered Grapevine" is about the economics of slavery; although Chesnutt masks his message, the story remains a powerful indictment.

"The Conjurer's Revenge" is properly placed as the fourth story in the collection. It is the centerpiece for unifying character and plot line and is the most complex of the seven stories. It concerns appearance versus reality, illustrated in many ways like Zora Neale Hurston's "The Gilded Six Bits."

"The Gray Wolf's Ha'nt," the sixth story in the collection, is a genuine sojourn in the world of the supernatural. Dan is evil personified; although he starts out with apparently good intentions, he develops a dangerous jealous streak and is transformed into a wolf and a multiple killer. It is a dark, brooding tale of act and revenge.

When *The Conjure Woman* was published in March, 1899, reviews were almost universally favorable. Chesnutt was given credit as the equal of Paul Laurence Dunbar, a new African American literary talent, and a master of short story. All of these tributes inspired Chesnutt to continue writing short stories, many of which were collected in *The Wife of His Youth and Other Stories of the Color Line* (1899).

"Critical Evaluation" by Joe Benson

Bibliography:
Andrews, William L. *The Literary Career of Charles W. Chesnutt.* Baton Rouge: Louisiana State University Press, 1980. Traces Chesnutt's career from his early success with the dialect stories contained in *The Conjure Woman* to the writings of his final years. Gives a full reading of *The Conjure Woman* in terms of the local color tradition, race relationships, and folklore.
Heermance, J. Noel. *Charles W. Chesnutt: America's First Great Black Novelist.* Hamden, Conn.: Archon Books, 1974. A fine overview of Chesnutt's life and a discussion of how his fiction emerged from his literary interests and social concerns. One chapter focuses on *The Conjure Woman* stories.
Keller, Frances Richardson. *An American Crusade: The Life of Charles Waddell Chesnutt.* Provo, Utah: Brigham Young University Press, 1978. A biography of Chesnutt that includes discussion of the events surrounding the publication of *The Conjure Woman.* Photographs of Chesnutt and his family.
Pickens, Ernestine Williams. *Charles W. Chesnutt and the Progressive Movement.* New York: Pace University Press, 1994. A biography focusing on Chesnutt's commitment to social equality for his fellow African Americans. Contains a useful discussion of his using fiction as a vehicle for African Americans to gain national recognition.
Render, Sylvia Lyons. *Charles W. Chesnutt.* Boston: Twayne, 1980. Perhaps the most complete discussion available of Chesnutt's literary career. Traces his development as a writer of fiction and shows that his social and political milieu were central to the meaning of his stories. Includes a biographical chronology, as well as primary and secondary bibliographies.

A CONNECTICUT YANKEE IN KING ARTHUR'S COURT

Type of work: Novel
Author: Mark Twain (Samuel Langhorne Clemens, 1835-1910)
Type of plot: Social satire
Time of plot: Late nineteenth and early sixth centuries
Locale: England
First published: 1889

Principal characters:
HANK MORGAN, the Connecticut Yankee, known as the Boss
CLARENCE, his right-hand man, originally a young court page
KING ARTHUR
SANDY (ALISANDE), a young maiden, later Hank's wife
SIR SAGRAMOUR LE DESIROUS, a short-tempered knight
MERLIN, the court magician

The Story:

Struck on the head during a quarrel in a New England arms factory, a skilled Yankee mechanic (later identified as Hank Morgan) awoke to find himself being prodded by the lance of an armored knight on horseback. The knight was Sir Kay Seneschal of King Arthur's Round Table and the time was June, 528 C.E., in England. So a foppish young page named Clarence informed the incredulous Hank as the knight took him to white-towered Camelot. Remembering that there had been a total eclipse of the sun on June 21, 528, Hank decided that should the eclipse take place, he would know that he was indeed a lost traveler in time turned backward to the days of chivalry.

At Camelot, Hank listened to King Arthur's knights as they bragged of their mighty exploits. The magician, Merlin, repeated his story of Arthur's coming. Finally, Sir Kay told of his encounter with Hank, and Merlin advised that the prisoner be thrown into a dungeon to await burning at the stake on June 21.

In prison, Hank thought about the coming eclipse. Merlin, he told Clarence, was a humbug, and he sent the boy to the court with a message that on the day of his death, the sun would darken and the kingdom would be destroyed. Just as Hank was about to be burned, the sky began to dim. Awed, the king ordered the prisoner released. The people shouted that he was a greater magician than Merlin and the king made him his prime minister. Soon, however, the populace demanded another display of his powers. With the help of Clarence, Hank mined Merlin's tower with some crude explosives he made and then told everyone he would cause the tower to crumble and fall. When the explosion occurred, Hank was assured of his place as the new court magician. Merlin was thrown into prison temporarily.

The lack of mechanical devices in King Arthur's castle bothered the ingenious New Englander, and the illiteracy of the people hurt his American pride in education. He decided to raise the commoners above mere slaves to the nobility. After several years passed, he had a title of his own, for the people called him "The Boss." As the Boss, he intended to modernize the kingdom.

His first act was to set up schools in small communities throughout the country. He had to work in secret because he feared the interference of the Church. He trained workmen in mechanical arts. Believing that a nation needed a free press, he instructed Clarence in journalism. He had telephone wires stretched between hamlets, haphazardly, as it turned out, because there were no maps by which to be guided.

After Sir Sagramour challenged Hank to a duel, the king decided that Hank should go on some knightly quest to prepare himself for the encounter. His mission was to help a young woman named Alisande, whose precise story he was unable to get straight. With many misgivings, he put on a burdensome suit of armor and on his heavy charger started off with Alisande, whom he called Sandy. Sandy told endless tall tales as they traveled through the land. Along the way, Hank marveled at the pitiable state of the people under the feudal system. Whenever he found a man of unusual spirit, he sent him back to Clarence in Camelot, to be taught reading, writing, and a useful trade. He visited the dungeons of a castle at which he stayed and released prisoners unjustly held by the king's cruel sister, Morgan le Fay.

In the Valley of Holiness, he found another opportunity to prove his magic skill. There a sacred well had gone dry because, according to legend, a sin had been committed. When he arrived, Merlin, now released from prison, was attempting magic to make the spring flow. Hank repaired a leak in the masonry at the bottom of the well; then, with much pomp, he restarted the water flow. As the well filled, Merlin went home in shame.

By chance, Hank came on one of his telephone installations in a cave nearby. He talked to Clarence, who told him that King Arthur was on his way to the Valley of Holiness to see the flowing spring. He returned to the spring to find a fake magician assuring the gaping pilgrims that he could tell what anyone was doing at that moment. Hank asked him about King Arthur. The magician said that he was asleep in his bed at Camelot. Hank grandly predicted that the king was on his way to the Valley of Holiness. When the king did arrive, the people were again awed by Hank's magic.

Anxious to learn about the condition of the people, Hank proposed to disguise himself as a commoner and travel through the country. The king insisted on joining him. Hank knew that Arthur was not to blame for his own social doctrines; he was a victim of his place in society. On their journey, the king proved to be courageous and kind. Misfortune overtook them, however, when they were seized by an earl and sold as slaves because they were unable to prove themselves free men. As slaves they were taken to London, where Hank picked the lock that held him, killed the slave driver, and escaped. After his escape, the rest of the slaves were ordered to be hanged, but Hank located a telephone and called Clarence in Camelot, ordering him to send help. The next day, Sir Launcelot and five hundred knights mounted on bicycles arrived in time to save Hank and the king.

Hank returned to Camelot in glory, but he still had to fight a duel with Sir Sagramour— a fight which in reality would be a battle between him and Merlin. Merlin professed to cover Sir Sagramour with an invisible shield, but the credulous knight was invisible to no one but himself. Wearing no armor and riding a small pony, Hank met the heavily armored Sir Sagramour on the tournament field, where he dodged the charging knight until the latter grew tired. Hank then lassoed Sagramour and pulled him from his horse. After Hank bested other knights in this manner, Sagramour returned to the field; this time, Merlin stole Hank's lasso. Seeing no alternative, Hank shot Sir Sagramour with a revolver, after which he challenged all the knights of the land. He had only eleven rounds left in two revolvers, but after he had killed nine charging knights, the line wavered and gave up.

Three years passed. By this time, Hank had married Sandy, and they had a little girl. He and Clarence were planning to declare a republic after the death of Arthur, for the sixth century kingdom was now a nineteenth century land with schools, trains, factories, newspapers, the telephone, and the telegraph. Although the code of chivalry had been abolished, the knights still insisted on wearing their armor. When little Hello-Central, Hank's daughter, became ill, he and Sandy took the child to France to recuperate. During a return visit to England, Hank found Camelot in shambles. Clarence, his only follower who remained loyal, explained what had happened. King Arthur and Sir Launcelot had fought over Queen Guenever. Now the king was dead, and the Church had destroyed Hank's new civilization by interdict.

Hank and Clarence fortified a cave, surrounding it with electrically charged barriers. In a battle with the massed chivalry of England, Hank was stabbed. When an old woman came to the fortress from the enemy lines and offered to nurse him, no one recognized her as Merlin in disguise. The magician cast a spell on Hank and declared that he would sleep for thirteen hundred years. Hank awoke to find himself once more in the nineteenth century.

Critical Evaluation:

A Connecticut Yankee in King Arthur's Court should have offered Mark Twain one of his best opportunities to attack the repressive and antidemocratic forces that he saw in post-Civil War America as well as in sixth century England. That the attack becomes in large part an exposé of the very system he sought to vindicate reveals as much the deep division in the author's own nature as any problem inherent in the material itself. Ironically, much of the interest the work continues to hold for readers is based on the complications resulting from Mark Twain's inability to set up a neat conflict between the forces of progress and those of repression. Hank Morgan's visit to King Arthur's court not only unveils the greed and super-stition associated with the aristocracy and the established Church but also reveals some of the weaknesses in humans that enable oppressive parasitical institutions to exist. The industrial utopia Hank tries to establish in sixth century England is no more than a hopeless dream.

As a character, Hank is, in many respects, a worthy successor to Huckleberry Finn. Like Huck, Hank is representative of the common people and, at his best, he asserts the ideal qualities Mark Twain associates with those who escape the corruption of hereditary wealth and power and the conditioning of tradition. Unlike Huck, however, who was largely an observer power-less to change the system, Hank is given the opportunity to make his values the basis of a utopian society. While Huck sees being "civilized" as an infringement on his individuality and freedom, Hank is, in his own way, fully civilized according to the standards of the world he represents. The pragmatic wit that enables Huck Finn to survive against all odds becomes for Hank the basis of his rise in the industrial system to a position of authority and success. He fully accepts the nineteenth century doctrines of laissez-faire capitalism, progress, and technology as the best social and human principles. Hank represents Mark Twain's vision of technological humankind as a social ideal, the greatest product of the greatest society.

Mark Twain's choice of Arthur's court as the testing ground for Hank's ideas was not accidental. Most immediately, the author was offended by Matthew Arnold's attacks on the American glorification of the common man and the view of America as a cultural desert. In attacking the golden age of chivalry, Mark Twain simultaneously sought to expose English history, culture, and traditions of aristocratic privilege. At the same time, he associates the age of Arthur with the sorts of romantic attitudes he exposes in *Huckleberry Finn* (1884) as the ruin of the American South. Making his spokesman, Hank, a product of the society Arnold had deplored, Mark Twain mounts a two-pronged attack against Europeanism and sophistication and, in his own view, the dangerously reactionary attitudes that asserted the superiority of the "romantic" past over the present.

What begins for Hank, with his prediction of the moment of the eclipse, as a simple expedient for survival, quickly becomes open war between Merlin (and the Church) and the Machine Age represented by Hank. Hank sees himself as a Promethean bringer of new knowledge and new order to the oppressed masses. Hank's humanitarian values are pitted against the selfishness and greed of the aristocracy and the Church, and his reason challenges their superstition. Based on Mark Twain's view of technological human beings as the apex of human development, Hank naturally assumes that he is the rightful ruler of the world. Hank seems to assume that because he takes up the cause of the oppressed people against their oppressors, he necessarily has a moral superiority to those against whom he fights. Neither Hank nor Mark Twain seems to give consideration to the question of ends and means.

It is particularly ironic that Hank, ostensibly the bringer of light to this benighted people, should rely no less than his archenemy Merlin on the power of superstition to gain ascendancy over the masses. From the moment he discovers the profound effect that his prediction of the eclipse has on the audience, Hank begins to challenge Merlin to ever greater miracles. Such episodes as the destruction of Merlin's tower or the restoring of the Holy Well represent Hank's use of technology to create the fear and awe that Merlin previously commanded. Recognizing that humans are essentially base and weak, Hank, like Merlin, maintains his power through exploitation of ignorance and gullibility.

It is humanity, not technology, that ultimately fails Hank. With the exception of the fifty-two young men who have never been exposed to the teachings of the Church, the society that Hank constructs through his technology reverts to its former state the minute his back is turned. Humans, as Hank perceives them, are no more than conditioned animals, and none of his modern miracles can change that fact. In the end, Hank's technology too fails him and his companions and his dream of progress becomes a nightmare, a sacrifice to the very ignorance it would replace. Promethean Hank Morgan, the bringer of light and knowledge, finally vindicates only Mark Twain's pessimistic view of human nature.

The ending of *A Connecticut Yankee in King Arthur's Court* is as bleak as anything the author ever wrote. The scenes of Hank's utopia destroyed by perverse human nature, the destruction unleashed by the power of technology, and, finally, the prospect of Hank's forces being overcome by the pollution of the bodies piled in their trenches are frightening to contemplate. Mark Twain, having apparently set out to affirm the nineteenth century doctrine of progress, finally comes full circle to suggest that something permanent within human nature makes such dreams hopeless. Clearly, there is here an anticipation of the author who, having lost hope in the human potential of his Huck Finn, would become a misanthropic voice crying out against the "damned human race."

"Critical Evaluation" by William E. Grant

Bibliography:
Foner, Philip S. *Mark Twain, Social Critic*. New York: International Publishers, 1958. Explains the novel's vindication of democracy as a response to such foreign critics as the British historian Matthew Arnold, and analyzes Mark Twain's fear of American sympathies toward monarchy, aristocracy, and established churches. Includes a bibliography.
Hill, Hamlin. Introduction to *A Connecticut Yankee in King Arthur's Court*. San Francisco: Chandler, 1963. Hill's introduction to this fully illustrated facsimile reprint of the first edition explains the caricatures of illustrator Dan Beard, and Mark Twain's attitude toward them.
Rasmussen, R. Kent. *Mark Twain A to Z: The Essential Reference to His Life and Writings*. New York: Facts On File, 1995. Contains a detailed synopsis of *A Connecticut Yankee in King Arthur's Court*, cross-referenced to analytical entries on both real and fictional names,

places, and events. With additional entries on Mark Twain's illustrators and publishers, this volume is an excellent resource for placing the novel within the broad context of Mark Twain's work.

Sloane, David E. E. *Mark Twain as a Literary Comedian.* Baton Rouge: Louisiana State University Press, 1979. Defines, with many examples, the traditions of American humor, seeing *A Connecticut Yankee in King Arthur's Court* as their literary culmination. Identifies the novel's allusions to persons, events, and conditions of Mark Twain's time. Discusses the book's diction, combining humorous caricature with corrective satire. Includes a bibliography.

Smith, Henry Nash. *Mark Twain's Fable of Progress: Political and Economic Ideas in "A Connecticut Yankee."* New Brunswick, N.J.: Rutgers University Press, 1964. Compares Mark Twain's novel to works by Charles Dudley Warner, William Dean Howells, and Henry Adams, contemporary authors who treated problems of changing American values during post-Civil War industrialization. Discusses Mark Twain's ambivalence as a critic of political corruption in America and a defender of entrepreneurship over feudalism.

Twain, Mark. *A Connecticut Yankee in King Arthur's Court.* Edited by Bernard Stein. Berkeley: University of California Press, 1979. The definitive, revised edition of the novel, prepared by the Mark Twain Project in Berkeley. Contains all of Dan Beard's original illustrations, as well as extensive annotations and an elaborate editorial apparatus.

THE CONSCIENCE OF THE RICH

Type of work: Novel
Author: C. P. Snow (1905-1980)
Type of plot: Psychological realism
Time of plot: Early twentieth century
Locale: England
First published: 1958

Principal characters:

LEWIS ELIOT, a young lawyer
CHARLES MARCH, a friend of Lewis
LEONARD MARCH, Charles's father
SIR PHILIP MARCH, Leonard's older brother
KATHERINE MARCH, Charles's sister
ANN SIMON, a young activist
HERBERT GETLIFFE, the lawyer with whom Lewis studies
FRANCIS GETLIFFE, Herbert's brother, a scientist

The Story:

After they finished writing their final examinations for the British Bar, Lewis Eliot and Charles March went out together to celebrate. A month later, both of the young men learned that they had passed the test, and they began a year of apprenticeship in London. They saw each other often and soon became the closest of friends. Although Lewis often spoke about personal matters, as well as his problems with Herbert Getliffe, with whom he was studying, Charles remained secretive for a long time. One day, he invited Lewis to dinner at his father's London house and mentioned that his family was Jewish.

Lewis was dazzled by the March establishment and charmed by both Charles's vivacious sister, Katherine, and his father, Leonard, a wonderful storyteller. When Katherine balked at attending one of the dances where wealthy Jewish young people were supposed to meet their future mates, Leonard became extremely angry. When Charles took his sister's side, Leonard turned on him as well.

Charles later told Lewis that he intended to leave the law, so that he would no longer be trapped in the small society of which his family was a part. Both Leonard and his brother, Sir Philip March, found it hard to believe that this was not just a passing fancy. Leonard threatened action if Charles persisted in his plan.

During the summer, Herbert Getliffe's brother Francis, a likable, sensible young scientist, was a frequent guest at the March country house, even though, like Lewis, he was a Gentile and therefore presumably not a marital possibility. When Ann Simon, an attractive Jewish girl, came to visit, she argued with Charles about Herbert. Her antipathy was based on what she had been told by Ronald Porson, an unsuccessful lawyer. At dinner, Leonard was shocked to discover that Ann was a political radical, but when he found that she had good family connections, he was somewhat reassured.

Now desperately in love, Ann and Charles began meeting secretly in Lewis' room. Ann urged Charles to become a doctor, like her father, and Charles became convinced that it was a good idea. Leonard thought it was ridiculous, and informed Charles that he had changed his mind about making him financially independent. He would continue paying an allowance, but otherwise, Charles could fend for himself.

Ironically, Katherine, not Charles, was in love with someone outside of the faith. When she announced her engagement to Francis, Leonard put up only a token struggle and then proceeded with wedding plans. His brother was marrying into the March family, so Herbert Getliffe felt he should warn them, through Lewis, that Ronald Porson was agitating for a government inquiry into Herbert's financial affairs. Porson alleged that Herbert had used insider information, obtained in dealings with the government, for his own advantage. Katherine and Francis were married, and Charles and Ann began to make their own wedding plans. With Charles's permission, Katherine approached their father, hoping he would now change his mind and make Charles independent, but Leonard remained adamant.

Five years later, the family celebrated Leonard's seventieth birthday. Katherine and Francis had two children and were expecting a third. Charles and Ann had none, but Charles had completed his medical studies and had a good practice.

Porson was still hoping for revenge, not only on Herbert, but on the family of the man who had taken Ann away from him. This time the rumors about government leaks involved several officials, including Philip, a parliamentary secretary with hopes of a ministry. Lewis discovered that Ann had been working for the Communist newspaper that was leading this new attack, and that she had gathered the information they intended to print. He begged Ann to get the story stopped, if only out of consideration for Charles. Ann tried, but won only a postponement.

At Charles's insistence, Ann accepted Leonard's invitation to dinner, although she did not feel well. During the evening, she became much worse, and her illness was diagnosed as pneumonia. She had to remain at the March home. When she realized that she might die, Ann told Charles where she had secreted some documents that, if published, would result in the newspaper's being suppressed. Charles, she said, could decide whether or not to use them.

During Ann's long illness, Leonard had to face the fact that he wanted her to die; however, she survived. Shortly before Ann was finally well enough to leave the March home, Francis and Katherine confronted Charles and asked him what he intended to do. If he asked her, they pointed out, Ann would stop the newspaper. Charles said that he would never ask that of his wife, not even to spare his father and the family reputation. In that case, Katherine and Francis said, they never wanted to see Ann again, and Charles regretfully replied that also meant a complete break with him.

When the final article in the series appeared, Philip was dismissed from his government post. His career was finished. Leonard called Charles to his home in order to inform him that from now on, there would be no monthly allowance. Lewis continued to attend Leonard's parties. One evening after he had left the March house, Lewis happened to look back. Before long, he thought, the lights would go out and Leonard would be left alone.

Critical Evaluation:

C. P. Snow was one of the most important intellectuals of his time. As a physicist, he was involved in the important molecular research that was being conducted at Cambridge University during the 1930's. As a wartime government official, he so distinguished himself that he was made Commander of the Order of the British Empire. Snow is best remembered, however, for his third career, that of a writer. "Strangers and Brothers," a series of eleven novels published over a period of thirty years, brilliantly illuminates the crucial issues of the modern era.

As Snow points out in his introduction to *The Conscience of the Rich*, the publication dates of his novels do not indicate their actual order in the series. In fact, he says, although a number of the novels appeared before *The Conscience of the Rich*, it should be the second in the "Strangers and Brothers" sequence. It can also be considered singly, as a work complete in itself.

Although Lewis Eliot appears in every book of the "Strangers and Brothers" series, either as protagonist or as an observer, in *The Conscience of the Rich* he serves a special purpose. Lewis is no more a part of elite Anglo-Jewish society than the author himself; by telling his story from Lewis' point of view, instead of writing as an insider, Snow makes sure that it will ring true.

The primary conflict in the novel is a familiar one, the struggle between those who wish to preserve a highly traditional society and those who work for change, or at least welcome it. As head of the extended family, Sir Philip feels it is his duty to direct the younger members in the right path, and Leonard feels a similar obligation toward his own offspring. Two of the most important decisions that a young person makes are the choice of a career, which in the early years of the twentieth century applied only to men, and the choice of a mate. In offering guidance to Katherine and Charles, their elders believe that they are not only being helpful, but perhaps even averting tragedy.

On Lewis' first visit to the March household, however, he sees that Katherine and Charles do not have the reverence for tradition that their elders do. The dance that Leonard expects Katherine to attend is not just a casual social function; it is one of the periodic gatherings at which the members of the Jewish elite can meet suitable marriage partners. Katherine does not wish to be so circumscribed, and Charles voices his own understanding of her attitude. As it turns out, Katherine and Charles both marry people whom their elders consider unsuitable. Francis is a Gentile, and Ann, although Jewish, is a Communist, dedicated to overturning the social order and, as events prove, quite willing to destroy Charles's own family in the process.

On one level, *The Conscience of the Rich* describes a conflict between two philosophies; however, the characters' actions and reactions are motivated as much by emotion as by rationality. Leonard is likable, kind, and generous, but he is also domineering. He is not interested merely in the welfare of his children; he is also bent on demonstrating his power over them. One can understand his disappointment when Charles leaves the law and merely loafs; clearly this is the waste of a good mind and an embarrassment to the family. Charles's decision to become a doctor, however, cannot injure the family; Leonard is furious simply because the career choice was Ann's idea, not his.

Leonard hates Ann because he sees her as his enemy in a battle for control over Charles. What he never realizes is that in Lewis' terms, Ann is really not Charles's master, but his slave. If Charles tries to please her, it is only because he recognizes her total devotion to him. Leonard loses his son because he does not understand either himself or anyone else. In contrast, Charles achieves happiness because he recognizes the truth. His problem is not his Jewish blood, but his sense of guilt, which arises from the realization that his wealth is not being used to benefit society (hence the title of the book) and from his recognition of a defect in his character, a tendency to be heartless and cruel. In his new career, Charles suppresses his evil propensities and dedicates himself to the service of others. Ironically, Leonard contributes to his son's happiness by disinheriting him.

Although Snow himself was of the party of change, not that of tradition, it is a measure of his genius that none of the characters in his story is totally unsympathetic. What is tragic about *The Conscience of the Rich* is that it shows how basically good people, operating from principle and motivated by honest concern, can do so much harm to those they love.

Rosemary M. Canfield Reisman

Bibliography:
De la Mothe, John. *C. P. Snow and the Struggle of Modernity.* Austin: University of Texas Press, 1992. Asserts the writer's primary concern is the need for "mediation between the private and the public spheres." A demanding study in intellectual history, but worth the effort. Photographs and bibliography.

Halperin, John. *C. P. Snow: An Oral Biography.* New York: St. Martin's Press, 1983. A series of interviews conducted during the last two years of Snow's life. Not indexed, but contains frequent references to *The Conscience of the Rich* and related matters. A brief conversation with Lady Snow (Pamela Hansford Johnson) is recorded in an appendix. Some photographs.

Karl, Frederick F. *C. P. Snow: The Politics of Conscience.* Carbondale: Southern Illinois University Press, 1963. The chapter on *The Conscience of the Rich* concentrates primarily on three characters. Charles and Lewis are discussed as "Snow's alternatives to the typical existential hero," and Leonard as a reactionary who, although charming, is essentially a fool. Interesting but oversimplified. Includes a fictional chronology based on the first eight books of the "Strangers and Brothers" series.

Ramanathan, Suguna. *The Novels of C. P. Snow: A Critical Introduction.* London: Macmillan, 1978. Short but insightful. Although references to *The Conscience of the Rich* are scattered, provides a good overview of Snow's novels and useful comments about his originality. Bibliography.

Shusterman, David. *C. P. Snow.* Rev. ed. Boston: Twayne, 1991. A good starting point for the study of Snow. Three chapters are devoted to the "Strangers and Brothers" series. Biographical information, including a chronology, extensive notes and references, and a select bibliography. Secondary sources are annotated.

THE CONSCIOUS LOVERS

Type of work: Drama
Author: Sir Richard Steele (1672-1729)
Type of plot: Sentimental
Time of plot: Early eighteenth century
Locale: London
First performed: 1722; first published, 1723

> *Principal characters:*
> YOUNG BEVIL, a young gentleman of fortune
> SIR JOHN BEVIL, young Bevil's father
> INDIANA DANVERS, a young woman befriended by young Bevil
> LUCINDA SEALAND, engaged to young Bevil
> MR. SEALAND, Lucinda's father
> MR. MYRTLE, young Bevil's friend, in love with Lucinda Sealand
> MR. CIMBERTON, a suitor for Lucinda Sealand's hand

The Story:

Young Bevil, a gentleman of some fortune, was engaged to marry the daughter of Mr. Sealand. Although he was not in love with the woman, he had agreed to marry her at his father's request. On the day of the marriage, however, there was some doubt that the marriage would take place, for the bride's father had discovered that Bevil was paying the bills of a young woman he had brought back from France. Fearing that the young woman, called Indiana, was Bevil's mistress, Mr. Sealand did not want to see his daughter married to a man who kept another woman.

The fathers did not know that Bevil had sent a letter to Lucinda Sealand which gave her his permission to break off the marriage at that late date. Bevil had done so because he knew that Lucinda was really in love with his friend, Mr. Myrtle, and because he himself wanted to marry Indiana. After the letter had been sent, Sir John's valet told young Bevil that the marriage would probably be broken by Mr. Sealand. Bevil then confided in the servant that Indiana was the daughter of the British merchant named Danvers, who had disappeared in the Indies soon after the ship in which Indiana, her mother, and her aunt had been traveling to join him had been captured by French privateers.

Myrtle then arrived at Bevil's apartment and told his friend that a third marriage arrangement was in the wind that day. Mrs. Sealand was trying to wed her daughter to Mr. Cimberton, a queer fellow with peculiar ideas about wives and a great deal of money; Mrs. Sealand was willing to overlook strange notions in favor of the fortune her daughter might marry. The only thing that prevented the marriage contract from being settled that day was the nonappearance of Cimberton's wealthy uncle. Bevil suggested to Myrtle that he and Bevil's servant Tom, an artful rascal, disguise themselves as lawyers and go to the Sealand house in an attempt to prevent the marriage or, at least, to find out what could be done to keep the contract from being signed.

Meanwhile Indiana's aunt was cautioning her against the attentions of Bevil. The aunt could not believe, despite Indiana's reports of Bevil's behavior, that the young man was helping Indiana and paying her bills without intending to make her his mistress. As they continued to argue, Bevil appeared. Indiana tried to learn in private conversation what his intentions were, for she loved him very much. He would only reply that he did everything for her because he found pleasure in doing good. Wanting him to love her, she felt rather hurt. Secretly, Bevil had promised himself that he would never tell her of his affection as long as his father had not given permission for a marriage to her.

At the Sealand house, in the meantime, Lucinda was subjected to the humiliation of an inspection by Mr. Cimberton, who in company with Mrs. Sealand looked at Lucinda as he might look at a prize mare he was buying for his stable. While they were talking over her good and bad points, Myrtle and Bevil's servant, disguised as lawyers, put in their appearance. They learned very little, except that Mrs. Sealand was determined to wed her daughter to Cimberton as soon as possible. Upon leaving the house, Bevil's servant received a letter from Lucinda for his master. Myrtle, who suspected duplicity on Bevil's part, sent him a challenge to a duel.

Myrtle appeared at Bevil's apartment a few minutes after his challenge. Bevil refused at first to be a party to a duel, but when Myrtle heaped many insults upon Bevil and Indiana, calling the latter Bevil's whore, his language so enraged Bevil that he said he would fight. A moment later Bevil regained control of himself. Realizing how foolish a duel would be, he showed Myrtle the letter from Lucinda, which only thanked Bevil for giving her permission to break off the wedding.

Sir John and Mr. Sealand met. Mr. Sealand refused to go on with the marriage that day until he had satisfied himself as to the relationship between Indiana and Bevil. Sir John agreed to wait until the investigation had been made.

Bevil and Myrtle decided to make one more attempt to terminate the possible marital arrangements of Mrs. Sealand for her daughter. Myrtle disguised himself as Cimberton's uncle and went to the Sealand house. There Lucinda discovered his identity, but she kept it from her mother and the unwelcome suitor.

At the same time Mr. Sealand had gone to Indiana's home. As soon as he entered the house Indiana's aunt recognized him as someone she had known before, but she decided not to reveal herself to him. Questioned, Indiana said that she had been befriended by Bevil but that he had made no effort to seduce her. Her deportment and her narrative assured Mr. Sealand that there was no illicit relationship between the two. When she had finished her story, telling of her lost father and the capture of herself, her mother, and her aunt by French privateers, he asked her father's name. She told him it was Danvers. Mr. Sealand then announced that Indiana was his long-lost daughter, and he identified some trinkets she had as those belonging to his first wife and their child. When Indiana's aunt appeared, identifying herself as Mr. Sealand's sister, he recognized her at once. He told them that he had changed his name after undergoing certain difficulties in the Indies.

Mr. Sealand readily agreed to a marriage between his new found daughter and Bevil. At that moment Sir John, young Bevil, and a group from the Sealand house arrived. Sir John, hearing the news, was pleased at the prospect of a marriage between Indiana and his son. Bevil, anxious to aid his friend Myrtle, then requested that a marriage be arranged between his friend and Lucinda Sealand. Cimberton tried to intercede on his own behalf until Mr. Sealand informed him that only half his fortune would now go to Lucinda. Cimberton, who was more anxious for the money than for the woman, departed in a huff, whereupon Myrtle, who was still disguised as Cimberton's uncle, threw off the disguise and claimed Lucinda for his bride.

Critical Evaluation:

The opening night on November 7, 1722, at Drury Lane of *The Conscious Lovers* proved to be an important event in the development of English drama. The play may be marked as the end of Restoration comedy and the beginning of sentimental comedy. The play was a success as indicated by what was then considered a long initial run—eighteen nights.

Sir Richard Steele is probably most widely acclaimed for his journalism in *The Tatler*, *The Spectator*, *The Guardian*, and *The Theatre* and for his contribution to the periodical essay. His appointment to the governorship of Drury Lane by George I enabled him, however, to maintain a close contact with theatrical affairs. When Steele in this controlling position came under attack for failing to support new plays, he undertook *The Theatre*, which appeared twice weekly from January 2, 1720, to April 5, 1720. This periodical was to be closely allied to *The Conscious Lovers*, which was at that time called *Sir John Edgar*.

For his spokesman in *The Theatre*, Steele chose Sir John Edgar, the title character of the unfinished play on which he had been working for approximately ten years. Sir John Edgar's son Harry, who appears in the periodical, is taken from his counterpart in the drama. Like the dramatic character, Harry has an overwhelming filial devotion and a reckless friend named Myrtle. In No. 3 of *The Theatre*, Steele again borrows from the play when he proposes a board of theatrical visitors that parallels in description several of the dramatic characters of the play—Mr. Sealand and his daughter Lucinda, Charles Myrtle, and Humphrey. *Sir John Edgar* was titled *The Conscious Lovers* shortly before it was produced, and Sir John Edgar and his son were renamed Sir John Bevil and Bevil Junior.

The Conscious Lovers has a threefold purpose. The first purpose, probably the least significant, is to attack the practice of dueling. That this was a subject of concern for Steele is apparent by its frequency as a topic in his periodical essays. Steele wished to promote the idea that a man who refused to duel was not a coward or a knave. A scene in Act IV between Bevil and Myrtle is designed to exemplify this theory.

Steele's second purpose is to justify the merchant as worthy of a high position in social circles. The merchant had been much abused by Restoration dramatists. Steele was not the earliest author to make this point in dramatic form. *The Beaux Merchant*, a play "by a Clothier" identified as John Blanch, published in 1714, crusades for just recognition for merchants and precedes the production of *The Conscious Lovers*. In *The Conscious Lovers*, Steele's mouthpiece for this issue is apparently Mr. Sealand, who says in Act IV: "We Merchants are a Species of Gentry, that have grown into the World this last Century, and are as honourable, and almost as useful, as you landed Folks, that have thought yourselves so much above us." Indeed, the two most despicable characters of the play, Cimberton and Mrs. Sealand, suffer from the flaw Mr. Sealand points out—assumption of superiority by right of gentle birth.

The third purpose for writing *The Conscious Lovers* was, as Steele states in the prologue, "To chasten wit, and moralize the stage." In this endeavor Steele was taking up the cry for dramatic reform that had been precipitated by the bawdiness and cynicism of Restoration comedy. Jeremy Collier's attack on the theater in 1698, titled *A Short View of the Immorality and Profaneness of the English Stage*, was widely read. Steele, however, held that the stage could serve a beneficial, educational purpose. On April 16, 1709, he wrote in *The Tatler* (No. 3), "I cannot be of the same opinion with my friends and fellow laborers, the Reformers of Manners, in their severity towards plays; but must allow, that a good play, acted before a well-bred audience, must raise very proper incitements to good behaviour, and be the most quick and most prevailing method of giving young people a turn of sense and breeding." Steele put his theory in motion with the production of *The Conscious Lovers*. That it was thought to achieve its purpose can be seen among other things in King George I's gift to Steele of five hundred guineas for the play's contribution to the reform of the stage.

The reform of the stage that Steele achieved came by replacing Restoration comedy with another type—sentimental comedy. The first attempt at this variety of comedy was made in 1696 with Colley Cibber's *Love's Last Shift*. The play, however, was tainted by bawdy Restoration dialogue and hypocrisy. Although Steele wrote other plays in this vein, it was not until *The Conscious Lovers* that a decisive turning point occurred and the sentimental drama seemed to find its place in the history of English drama. Sentimental drama is marked by a number of elements. One is the idea of the innate goodness of people rather than the idea of the depravity of the self that marks Restoration comedy. Second, sentimental comedy makes appeal to the emotions that surpasses the appeal to the intellect, again in direct opposition to Restoration comedy. Third, in sentimental comedy there is an obvious moral. Fourth, sentimental comedy makes an attempt to place the ideal in a realistic setting, which leads to a certain amount of improbability and exaggeration. Fifth, there is a stress upon pity and the evocation of tears. Sixth, there is a tendency to serious discussion of ethical questions. Seventh, there is an element of mystery, such as the lost child recovered, and eighth, there are romantic love scenes.

Steele is also credited with establishing several character types that regularly appear in sentimental comedy: a man and maiden whose concepts of marriage are untainted by cynicism or contempt for the institution; the loyal friend; the debauchee redeemed in time for the fifth-act curtain; the rejected mistress who is reunited with her lover in marriage; and the loyal wife who, though tempted, remains virtuous. *The Conscious Lovers* has hints, if not fully formed representations, of both the characteristics and characters of the sentimental comedy.

Steele's model for the new dramatic hero is Bevil Junior, who exudes innate goodness by his filial devotion, romantic love, gentlemanly behavior, and lack of narcissistic tendencies. He provides quite a contrast to the Restoration comedy hero. The comedy of the play is provided by Tom and Phillis, whom Steele worked into a farcical subplot at the suggestion of Colley Cibber. Tom and Phillis imitate their social betters and thus provide a satirical look at the manners and customs of the time. More humor is provided by Cimberton, a character who recalls Restoration comedy. He boldly exhibits a self-love that blinds him to the true virtues of Lucinda and enables him only to see her as a means to his self-improvement. Steele's new play does not release itself completely from previous models, for Cimberton is the epitome of a Restoration character.

The influence of Steele's *The Conscious Lovers* went beyond England. When the first professional company of actors in America decided to move to New York from Williamsburg, they confronted considerable difficulty in obtaining a license to perform because of the Puritan influence in the area. Once they obtained the license, they chose a play from their repertory that they felt would satisfy the moral ethics of the Puritan community. Steele's *The Conscious Lovers*, billed as "a moral comedy," opened on September 17, 1753, was a success, and thus contributed to the beginning of theater in New York City. *The Conscious Lovers* was also significant to American theater in another way. The first play written by an American on a native subject and produced by professional actors was Royall Tyler's *The Contrast*, produced at the John Street Theatre on April 16, 1787, by the American Company. For the context of the play, Tyler borrowed heavily from *The Conscious Lovers*. Thus, *The Conscious Lovers* became not only noteworthy in the history of English theater but was also instrumental in beginning the history of American theater.

"Critical Evaluation" by Phyllis E. Allran

Bibliography:
Aitken, G. A. Introduction to *Richard Steele*, edited by G. A. Aitken. Westport, Conn.: Greenwood Press, 1968. An introduction to a collection of Richard Steele's plays. Section 9 focuses on *The Conscious Lovers*, providing a production history and accounts of early

performances, and a discussion of the eighteenth century philosophical debates about the play.

Bernbaum, Ernest. *The Drama of Sensibility*. Gloucester, Mass.: Peter Smith, 1958. Traces eighteenth century English drama from the rakish Restoration comedy to the sentimental comedy exemplified by Richard Steele's plays. Discusses *The Conscious Lovers* as a cultural artifact and provides interesting information about the play's debt to Terence.

Loftis, John. *Comedy and Society From Congreve to Fielding*. Stanford, Calif.: Stanford University Press, 1959. Discusses the changes in English comedy resulting from social upheavals in eighteenth century England. Places *The Conscious Lovers* in the middle of social change. Treats the play as a comedy of ideas with a definite Whiggish bias and suggests that political ideas interfere with the dramatic development of the play.

_____. *Steele at Drury Lane*. Westport, Conn.: Greenwood Press, 1973. Detailed discussion of *The Conscious Lovers*. Discusses the play as the culmination of Steele's efforts to reform the English stage. Examines the play's origins and production history, analyzes the controversy over the play, and defines sentimental comedy as a genre best exemplified by *The Conscious Lovers*.

Steele, Richard. *The Conscious Lovers*. Edited and with an introduction by Shirley Strum Kenny. Lincoln: University of Nebraska Press, 1968. The introduction places the play in its cultural, historical, philosophical, and theatrical contexts. Describes the play as a moral comedy that features good-natured characters and shows the influence of Richard Steele's work on the plays of Oliver Goldsmith and Richard Sheridan.

THE CONSOLATION OF PHILOSOPHY

Type of work: Philosophy
Author: Boethius (c. 480-524)
First transcribed: De consolatione philosophiae, 523 (English translation, late ninth century)

The Consolation of Philosophy by Anicius Manlius Severinus Boethius is the most significant and final work to come from the thinker known as "the last of the Romans, the first of the Scholastics." It is the author's most significant work because it draws on a lifetime of studying the writings of Plato, Aristotle, Porphyry, Proclus, Plotinus, and other classical figures; it is a piece, therefore, that proved to be critical to medieval philosophers of Christianity throughout Europe, as well as to such literary figures as Dante Alighieri and Geoffrey Chaucer. For, while *The Consolation of Philosophy* contains elements of Aristotelianism, Stoicism, and Neoplatonism, it is also ruled by the concept of a personal God to whom one can pray and from whom one might seek salvation.

It is Boethius' final work, written during his imprisonment in Pavia as he awaited execution under the authority of the Ostrogothic king Theodoric for the crime of treason against Pope John I. *The Consolation of Philosophy,* then, belongs to the ancient genre of Greek and Roman philosophy known as the *consolatio,* which is designed to provide the soul with a kind of moral and spiritual medication in times of distress. This aspect of the work had an influence on a number of literary masterworks of the Middle Ages, including Dante's *Divine Comedy* (c. 1320) and the fourteenth century Middle English *Piers Plowman.* Boethius' distress of the soul was extreme, since he had fallen from a position of favor in the Roman court to a position of disgrace after being unjustly accused of treason. This context of the work's authorship lends it an aspect of urgency and seriousness that many philosophical and literary texts do not have.

Divided into five books, with thirty-nine poems interspersed throughout the discourse, *The Consolation of Philosophy* is written in the form of a dialogue between Boethius and the feminine spirit of Philosophy, who visits him in his cell. The poems serve a purpose similar to that of the chorus in Greek tragedy: They summarize and at times advance the discussion between Boethius and the figure of Philosophy. In his commentaries on Porphyry, Boethius had maintained that philosophy, being the love of wisdom, brings to the mind the "reward of its own divinity" and thereby returns it to its own nature. This is the role of Philosophy in *The Consolation of Philosophy* as well, where Philosophy opens up to the author the path to God that belongs to the soul of the rational being. Philosophy conceives God to be the rational Being of all beings, belonging to the invisible and infinite realm of reason that transcends the finite realm of the material world. The soul that ascends to the realm of reason frees itself from the confines of matter—including the confines of prison walls—and therefore from suffering to enjoy the true freedom of the good that inheres in God alone.

Philosophy allows the soul to ascend through a process not only of education but also of remembering. This feature of the work reflects the influence on Boethius of Plato's doctrine of *anamnesis,* or recollection. Other important influences seen in the work include the idea of fate, as developed by Proclus, and the notion of God as the center of all things, which was expounded by Plotinus. This combination of Proclus and Plotinus proves to be especially important in Boethius' discussion of the distinction between fate and providence. Both of the earlier thinkers maintained that essential to the soul's approach to God is its divorce from material things: The movement toward is a movement inward, which philosophy reveals to be a movement upward.

Book 1 of *The Consolation of Philosophy* opens with a poem about the despair into which Boethius had fallen after fate robbed him of worldly power and position and cast him at death's door. The poem no sooner ends, however, than the awe-inspiring figure of Philosophy appears and casts out the muses of poetry. Boethius describes Philosophy as a "physician" who comes to heal him of the sickness in his soul by showing him who he truly is. He tries to justify himself before Philosophy by pointing out his good intentions and by complaining about the prosperity of the wicked. Philosophy answers him with an argument that true freedom and well-being come with the submission to God's will. Therefore, she says, the source of Boethius' illness lies not in having been abandoned by God but in having forgotten his own true, rational nature, which is not subject to the winds of fortune.

In book 2, Philosophy follows up her remarks with a discussion of the evils of turning to fortune as a basis for our understanding of ourselves and the world. It is not bad fortune that is at the root of his suffering, she explains to Boethius, but misguided belief (a principle held by the Stoic thinker Marcus Aurelius). If he would be happy, then he must alter his belief, for example, that the good amounts to good fortune. In order to do that, he must determine that happiness is to be found only within, not outside, himself. For Boethius, this "within oneself" means within one's rational nature as it comes from God. It is impossible to be happy without being who one is, a rational being created in the image of God. Since fortune pertains to what is external to one and external to one's nature, it is a false source of happiness.

The question of what characterizes genuine happiness is pursued further in book 3. Here, Philosophy affirms that the good and only the good distinguishes true happiness, since the good alone is inherently valuable. Neither money nor power, neither fame nor security, falls into the category of the good, because all of these derive their value from their relation to something else in the world; they are a means to something else, while the good is an end unto itself. As for the value of the good, it is determined by the God who alone is good and who alone is the source of all that is good. If the perfect good is true happiness, then, says Philosophy, true happiness is to be found only in God, who is the perfect good: God is the essence of happiness. From this claim it follows that happiness is possessed through the possession of divinity; where the divine image is manifest in the human being, happiness also is manifest. Therefore "the good itself and happiness are identical," and anyone who is happy is in possession of the divine image.

While Boethius is receptive to these arguments of Philosophy, in book 4 he is still unsettled by the fact that evil often goes unpunished. Philosophy assures him, however, that evil never goes unpunished or virtue unrewarded, suggesting that the world that has come from God's hand is the best of all possible worlds. She demonstrates her claim by arguing that all human activity derives from a combination of will and power and that all people will the good, since all people desire happiness. Those who fail to obtain the good do so because they lack a certain power; people who succumb to the lures of pleasure and vice, for example, do so because they are too weak to exercise self-control. Since to be good is to be who one is, those who are too weak to be good are too weak to be: To lose one's goodness is to lose one's being. Hence those who are so weak that they sink to doing evil are punished with non-being; similarly, those who have the power to do good are rewarded, for to be good is to be happy, and happiness is the greatest of all rewards. Philosophy thus responds to Boethius not by appealing to an external system of behavior modification but by positing a universal, internal, and necessary condition in which the soul suffers what it inflicts.

Having determined that reward and punishment are part of the inescapable condition of rational beings, Philosophy goes on to show that a good power rules the world, since, with the inevitable punishment of evil and rewarding of good, everything happens in a just and good manner. This design according to which all things transpire she calls providence, which is "divine reason itself." Providence, she explains, is the plan that derives from God's understanding, whereas fate is the unfolding of that plan through the order of things in the world. Human beings, according to this conception, may escape the rule of fate by divorcing themselves from the things of the world and using their own reason to draw near to divine reason. Those who cling to providence are free from ill fortune, since their happiness depends not on the twists and turns of fate but on the tranquility and truth of reason.

In book 5, Boethius concludes *The Consolation of Philosophy* with a discussion of free will that arises from Philosophy's earlier remarks on fate and providence. Boethius begins by suggesting that there is a contradiction between God's foreknowledge and freedom of the will. Worse than a contradiction, he maintains, there is an injustice at work here, since it is unjust to punish people for doing evil when they cannot do otherwise. In addition, argues Boethius, such a condition renders prayer useless and hope pointless, since there is no hope of changing what is preordained. Philosophy replies by pointing out that foreknowledge does not result in predestination; to know what will happen is not to make it happen. Because God is eternal, she adds, all things and events from all times are simultaneously present; since God is above the realm of cause and effect, which is the realm of time, he does not cause anything to happen. What God knows, he knows necessarily, but the necessity of his knowing about the course of events does not imply the necessity of their happening.

Boethius ends his work by declaring that the key to understanding everything that Philosophy sets forth is the cultivation of virtue. For the cultivation of virtue takes people beyond the material world and into the realm of reason and divinity, where they become who they are by becoming good. The one necessity that God imposes upon humanity is the necessity to be good. In this, Boethius tells himself, lies the essence of humanity's being.

David Patterson

Bibliography:
Barrett, Helen M. *Boethius: Some Aspects of His Times and Work.* New York: Russell & Russell, 1965. Provides an informative discussion of the relation between Boethius and Theodoric the Ostrogoth, as well as thorough background information on Western Europe in the fifth century. Two chapters examine *The Consolation of Philosophy.*

Gibson, Margaret, ed. *Boethius: His Life, Thought, and Influence.* Oxford, England: Basil Blackwell, 1981. Contains fourteen essays on Boethius, five of which are devoted to *The Consolation of Philosophy* and deal with the work's literary design and its influence on medieval literature.

Lerer, Seth. *Boethius and Dialogue: Literary Method in "The Consolation of Philosophy."* Princeton, N.J.: Princeton University Press, 1985. Discusses the tradition of dialogue in the works of Cicero, Augustine, and Fulgentius and relates that tradition to *The Consolation of Philosophy.* Examines the function of the poems in that work and the use of dialogue as a means of arriving at truth.

Means, Michael H. *The Consolatio Genre in Medieval English Literature.* Gainesville: University of Florida Press, 1972. Explores the significance of Boethius' *The Consolation of Philosophy* as a prototype for the consolatio genre in medieval English literature. Also examines the influence of the work on Dante's *Divine Comedy, Piers Plowman,* and other works.

Patch, Howard Rollin. *The Tradition of Boethius: A Study of His Importance in Medieval Culture*. New York: Oxford University Press, 1935. Contains fascinating legends and traditions surrounding the life of Boethius, as well as discussions of the importance of Boethius to medieval thought. Includes a useful examination of medieval translations of *The Consolation of Philosophy*.

CONSUELO

Type of work: Novel
Author: George Sand (Amandine-Aurore-Lucile Dupin, Baronne Dudevant, 1804-1876)
Type of plot: Historical
Time of plot: Eighteenth century
Locale: Venice, Bohemia, and Vienna
First published: 1842-1843 (English translation, 1846)

> *Principal characters:*
> CONSUELO, a singer
> ANZOLETO, her betrothed
> PORPORA, her music master and godfather
> COUNT RUDOLSTADT, a Bohemian nobleman
> ALBERT, his son
> CORILLA, Consuelo's rival
> JOSEPH HAYDN, a composer

The Story:

At the church of the Mendicanti in Venice, Consuelo was the most gifted of all the pupils of the famous teacher, Porpora. Consuelo was a poor orphan child, and Porpora had made her his goddaughter. Before the death of her mother, Consuelo had promised that she would one day become betrothed to Anzoleto, another poor musician of Venice.

Through the efforts of Anzoleto, Consuelo was engaged as the prima donna at the theater of Count Zustiniani, replacing Corilla, who had also been Porpora's student. Consuelo was a great success, but Anzoleto, who had also been engaged in the theater at the insistence of Consuelo, was not much of a musician and was not well received. Anzoleto, afraid that he would be discharged, pretended to be in love with Corilla, thinking that he would be safe if both singers were in love with him. Porpora had never liked Anzoleto, and at last he contrived to have Consuelo visit Corilla's home. When they found Anzoleto there, Consuelo was so hurt that she left Venice at once, vowing that she would never set foot on the stage again and renouncing the false Anzoleto forever.

From Venice, Consuelo went to Bohemia, where she was engaged by Count Rudolstadt as a companion for his niece, Amelia. This young noblewoman had been betrothed to young Count Albert Rudolstadt, but she feared him because he seemed to be insane. Albert often had visions in which he saw scenes of the past and often imagined himself to be the reincarnated body of some person long dead. When Albert first heard Consuelo sing, he called her by her name, even though she had taken another name to hide her unhappy life in Venice. Albert told Consuelo and the whole family that she was his salvation—that she had been sent to remove the curse from him. Consuelo was bewildered.

Albert often disappeared for many days at a time; no one knew where he went. Consuelo followed him but could never find his hiding place until the night she descended into a deep well and found steps leading to a grotto where Albert and an idiot called Zdenko spent many days together. Zdenko loved Albert more than his own life; when he saw Consuelo coming into the well, he thought she wanted to harm Albert, and he almost killed her. Consuelo escaped from Zdenko and found Albert. After she spoke soothingly to him, he ceased his mad talk and seemed to regain normal behavior. She persuaded him to return to his family and not to go back to the grotto without her. Albert told Consuelo that he loved her and needed her, but, although she no longer loved Anzoleto, she could not forget how she had once loved him, and she asked Albert to wait a while for her answer.

Albert's father and the rest of the family were grateful to Consuelo for helping restore Albert to his senses. The father, Count Rudolstadt, even told Consuelo that he would give his consent to a marriage between his son and her, for the old gentleman believed that only Consuelo could keep his son sane. While Consuelo was debating whether she loved Albert and could accept the honor, Anzoleto, having deserted Corilla, came to the castle in search of her. Consuelo slipped away from the castle, leaving a note for Albert. She went to Vienna to rejoin Porpora.

Without funds, Consuelo had great difficulty in reaching Vienna and had to walk most of the way. In her travels, she met Joseph Haydn, a young composer who had been on his way to the castle to find her; he had hoped he could persuade her to take him to Porpora, under whom he wished to study. Dressed as a peasant boy, Consuelo accompanied Haydn to Vienna. One night they took refuge in the home of a canon of the church. While they were there, Corilla came to the door, seeking a safe place to give birth to her child. Consuelo had pity on her former enemy and took Corilla to an inn, where she helped to deliver the child. From a maid, Consuelo learned that Anzoleto was the father. Corilla did not recognize Consuelo, who continued to wear the disguise of a boy.

When Joseph and Consuelo finally reached Vienna, the girl found Porpora overjoyed to see her again. Haydn became Porpora's pupil, and Consuelo sang for the Empress. Then Corilla, who had also come to Vienna and learned that it was Consuelo who befriended her during the birth of her child, arranged for Consuelo to sing in the theater there. Corilla hoped to seal the lips of Consuelo, who knew of the illegitimate child and knew also that Corilla had abandoned the baby in the home of the canon who had given Consuelo and Joseph shelter. Anzoleto was never heard from again.

Consuelo wrote to Albert, telling him that she was almost ready to return to him, but Porpora intercepted the letter and destroyed it. Consuelo waited in vain for a reply from Albert. At last, Porpora told her that he had received a letter from the count, saying that he did not wish his son to marry an actress and that Albert had concurred in the decision. Consuelo so trusted her godfather that she believed him, not realizing how ambitious Porpora was for her musical career.

Porpora went with Consuelo to accept a theater engagement in Berlin. On the way, they met the brother of Count Rudolstadt. Albert had asked his father to have someone at a certain place on the road on a specific day and at a specific hour, saying that the messenger was to bring the travelers he would meet there to the castle at once. Albert was very ill, and Consuelo persuaded Porpora to allow her to go to Albert. When she arrived at the castle, she learned that his father had received a letter from Porpora saying that he would never consent to a marriage between Consuelo and Albert and that Consuelo herself had renounced Albert. It had been the deathblow. Albert grew very weak and begged Consuelo to marry him before he died so that his soul could find peace; he still believed that only through Consuelo could he find salvation. The marriage vows were repeated, and Albert, crying that he was now saved, died in Consuelo's arms.

Consuelo stayed with her husband all night, leaving him only when he was carried to his bier. She then bade Albert's family good-bye, refusing to accept any of the fortune which was now hers. Then she left the castle and went to join Porpora in Berlin, where Frederick the Great himself worshiped both her beauty and her art.

Critical Evaluation:

George Sand is important in literary history for being a pioneer in the development of the category of fiction known as the romantic novel. Some modern classics are Daphne du

Maurier's *Rebecca* (1938) and Margaret Mitchell's famous Civil War novel *Gone with the Wind* (1936). Earlier classics in the genre include Emily Brontë's *Wuthering Heights* (1847) and Charlotte Brontë's *Jane Eyre* (1847). It is interesting to note that *Consuelo* contains some of the elements that have come to be practically indispensable to such novels. Two of the most popular elements are the "Cinderella" theme and the theme of a woman torn between love for two different men. George Sand uses both in *Consuelo*, the story of a poor girl who marries a handsome aristocrat and becomes a wealthy countess. The heroine is torn between love for the passionate but fickle Anzoleto and the noble but neurotic Albert.

The element of the vagabond in *Consuelo* undoubtedly appealed to female readers of her time, many of whom lived housebound, dependent lives and could identify with a heroine who had the courage to live under the open sky, travel wherever she pleased, and obtain the necessities of life through her own wit and talent. The book is a powerful statement about the rights of the individual—male or female. It attacks corruption and hypocrisy and explores the difficulties that face an independent woman. Sand knew the pain of independence, and she steered her heroine through the traps waiting for any woman who tried to achieve success in her own right. Consuelo saves herself much suffering by avoiding financial or psychological dependence on men, subjugating her personality to no one. Her character explores the experience of a woman searching for personal integrity.

Her novels are often neglected because they have old-fashioned characteristics which annoy impatient readers. The modern reader may find *Consuelo* too long, too rambling, too digressive, too full of melodramatic events and inflated dialogue expressing impossibly noble sentiments. Some of the characters that were original creations in Sand's time have become stereotypes from too much copying by inferior writers. Consuelo herself is a slightly implausible character. She was raised on the streets of Venice but remains a chaste, high-minded girl throughout her harrowing adventures, which include attempts to seduce and rape her. Without any formal education, she has a huge vocabulary and impeccable grammar; she speaks Spanish, Italian, and German. She has the ability to pick up new languages practically overnight. Her voice captivates everyone who hears her. Men fall madly in love with her at first sight.

What saved Sand's best novels from oblivion was the keen mind of their author. Noteworthy in *Consuelo* are Sand's mini-essays contained in her many interesting digressions from the main thread of her tale. Chapter 56 contains an essay on folk art which displays Sand's intelligence, learning, and socialistic ideology. Chapter 74 contains a poetic essay on loneliness. Chapter 97 contains a moving description of the silence and mystery of an empty theater. Chapter 101 contains a profound discussion of the function of art. *Consuelo* is also remarkable for its demonstration of Sand's musical knowledge, part of which she acquired during her famous love affair with the great Polish pianist and composer Frederic Chopin. Perceptive readers are willing to overlook *Consuelo*'s faults in favor of its wealth of information about history, famous personalities of the eighteenth century, music, architecture, fashions, furnishings, social conditions, and human nature. The novel's portrait of the young Franz Joseph Haydn, "father of the symphony" and teacher of the great Wolfgang Amadeus Mozart, is another of its interesting features.

Sand is regarded by contemporary feminists as an early heroine of the women's liberation movement who outraged society by dressing in men's clothes, smoking cigars, and living a life of sexual freedom normally permitted only to men. This recognition of Sand as a dynamic personality has brought about a renewed interest in her fiction. *Consuelo* can be read as a protest against the suppressed condition of women. Sand's revolutionary concerns went beyond that, however; she wanted nothing less than a complete reconstruction of society based on evangelical love. She was appalled by the glaring contrast between the wealthy minority and the impoverished, overworked majority. *Consuelo* belongs to what has been called Sand's "Middle Period." In later years, she withdrew from active life and wrote a number of pastoral romances which celebrate the virtues of a life of contemplation. Her life mirrored the turbulent period of history she lived through, which included the French Revolution of 1848 and its reactionary aftermath. *Consuelo*, like most of Sand's novels, is intensely autobiographical and reveals the real-life courage as well as the lofty ideals and powerful emotions of a remarkable woman.

"Critical Evaluation" by Bill Delaney

Bibliography:
Datlof, Natalie, Jeanne Fuchs, and David A. Powell, eds. *The World of George Sand.* New York: Greenwood Press, 1991. This collection of essays dealing with Sand's life, work, political views, and literary influence includes essays on *Consuelo*, along with much valuable reference material.

Maurois, André. *Lelia: The Life of George Sand.* Translated by Gerard Hopkins. New York: Harper and Bros., 1954. One of the best of many biographies of Sand. Maurois, a distinguished French author and historian, treats his subject with remarkable intelligence, sensitivity, and feeling.

Naginski, Isabelle Hoog. *George Sand: Writing for Her Life.* New Brunswick, N.J.: Rutgers University Press, 1991. This biographical work emphasizes Sand's influence as a feminist. It discusses Sand's great success as a professional writer, which enabled her to lead a life of adventure and independence at a time when female authors were considered second-rate.

Powell, David A. *George Sand.* Boston: Twayne, 1990. This biography of Sand by an authority on her life and works provides a great deal of criticism and interpretation. Powell devotes many pages to discussions of both *Consuelo* and its sequel *The Countess of Rudolstadt* (1843). The compact, functional volume contains considerable bibliographical material.

Sand, George. *The Story of My Life: The Autobiography of George Sand.* Albany: State University of New York Press, 1991. This is an English language edition of Sand's *Histoire de ma vie* (1854-1855), a work which is regarded as a classic of French literature because of its eloquent prose and sensitive self-revelations of a free-spirited woman making her way in a "man's world."

CONVERSATION IN THE CATHEDRAL

Type of work: Novel
Author: Mario Vargas Llosa (1936-   )
Type of plot: Social realism
Time of plot: 1960's
Locale: Lima, Peru
First published: Conversación en la catedral, 1969 (English translation, 1975)

Principal characters:
SANTIAGO ZAVALA, a journalist
AMBROSIO PARDO, a dogcatcher and former chauffeur

The Story:

Santiago Zavala was the son of the late Peruvian industrialist Fermín Zavala. Lima was suffering an epidemic of rabies, and Zavala was writing editorials for the tabloid *La Crónica* attacking the city administration's handling of the stray dog problem. Zavala set out in search of his wife's dog, which had been caught by dogcatchers eager to earn a commission, which, ironically, was part of the city's response to the crisis and to Zavala's editorials. While on his search, he encountered Ambrosio, a dogcatcher who once had been Zavala's father's chauffeur as well as the chauffeur and bodyguard of the notorious Cayo Bermudez, minister of security under the regime of the dictator Manuel Odría during Santiago's university days. The meeting of Santiago and Ambrosio initiated a four-hour conversation in The Cathedral, the bar-restaurant-brothel where Santiago and Ambrosio went to drink and reminisce.

The conversation drifted to the eight years of Odría's presidency, the time when Santiago and Ambrosio were young men on the verge of independence from their families. Both had fathers who were closely connected to the corrupt regime. Santiago's father was deeply involved in deals with Cayo Bermudez. Ambrosio's father worked as a member of the secret police. Ambrosio and Santiago attempted to separate themselves from their fathers' paths; both ultimately recognized that they had failed.

Framed by the conversation between the two men in The Cathedral bar, the narration of *Conversation in the Cathedral* includes more than one hundred characters. Almost twenty separate subplots, in the form of separate conversations, occur within the main conversation between Santiago and Ambrosio. During their conversation, Santiago asked Ambrosio several questions about the past. Santiago wanted to discover the identity and motivation of a notorious prostitute's killer. On another level, however, Santiago sought to unravel the puzzle of when and how his life and his country began to disintegrate.

Santiago's inquiry led him to retrace his steps as a wealthy young man caught in an identity crisis that, metaphorically, was a historical crisis for his class. The favorite son of a wealthy upper-class family, Santiago was expected to enter a profession and have a lifestyle that continued to uphold the values and privileges of his predecessors. His older brother, Chispas, managed his father's pharmaceutical factories and continued his father's traditions. Neither Fermín nor Chispas ever appeared as cruel, arrogant, or oppressive men. Their mother, Zoila, however, adhered to strict class distinctions and had a fear and anxiety of "race mixtures." As far as she was concerned, Santiago adhered to the wrong values in his concern for the nation's, rather than his class's, destiny, and associated with the wrong people. Santiago rejected his family's wealth, ideology, and privileged position in Peruvian society. His mother's worst fears

1298

materialized when Santiago married his nurse, a simple, lower-class nonwhite woman. Santiago defied his father's desire and mother's advice and chose to enter San Marcos University. There he became acquainted with an activist communist group whose members believed that only a Marxist revolution would enable Peruvians to set the nation on a road of de- velopment and justice. Santiago was unaware that the dictator's regime suspected his father of having joined a new alliance of rich men against General Odría. Santiago and his father were placed under surveillance, and the Zavala phone was tapped. Santiago's group was arrested, but Santiago's father used his connections, especially with Cayo Bermudez, to obtain Santiago's release.

Although he did not attempt to help any of the group members, Santiago viewed his father's actions as a final affront and broke with his parents. He went to live with a renegade bohemian uncle, who eventually found him a job with *La Crónica*. Santiago's writing skills were quickly recognized, and he was assigned to reporting crime. As part of his duties, he performed an investigation into the murder of Lima's most famous prostitute, La Musa. In the course of the investigation Santiago discovered that his father was the famed homosexual, Bola de Oro. Santiago knew that Ambrosio, as chauffeur to two powerful and corrupt men, shuffled between the sites of their domestic and public activities. Ambrosio witnessed the Zavala family's tensions as well as the political crisis that Fermín and Cayo Bermudez had to face and surmount. Santiago assumed that Ambrosio held the answer to the riddle of the Zavala family. Ambrosio, indifferent to Santiago's anxieties and obsessions, and unreflective himself, told his story in his own way and in his own time.

Santiago learned from Ambrosio that Cayo Bermudez had been groomed for advancement by Fermín a senator in the dictator's mock parliament. Bermudez invited several of his old friends to his home, where La Musa and her lover, the mulatta Queta, played the roles of hostesses and prostitutes to the group. Bermudez, observing that Fermín was a homosexual, procured for Fermín his somewhat reluctant chauffeur, Ambrosio. Ambrosio killed La Musa in order to protect Fermín (Ambrosio's much-admired employer) from scandal and blackmail at her hands. Santiago learned the truth, but this truth culminated in more riddles and no answers and no prospects for a brighter future. Santiago's quest ended with the despair and alienation with which it had begun.

Critical Evaluation:

Mario Vargas Llosa's major contribution to Latin American literature has been in his passionate, articulate literary denunciation of his society's ills. Vargas Llosa uses narrative structures and techniques that enable him to portray the multifaceted experiences of urban Peru. The life depicted in the Peru of his fiction is the life of a society in a furious process of urbanization. In this society, many of the existing social structures enter into a process of disintegration. The decay of the old order and the violence resulting from social alienation, class disparity, and racism stamp Vargas Llosa's fictional world with a terrifying sense of pain. Vargas Llosa's narrative structures encapsulate not only nostalgia for a beautiful and departing rural order but also the velocity of change in the everyday life of common individuals. Vargas Llosa captures a nation's movement from an unacceptable old order into the terrifying and relentless life of the city.

The length, complexity of plot, and subtlety of character motivation of *Conversation in the Cathedral* place great demands on the reader's memory and attention. Just as Santiago finds incredible the idea of his father's being the legendary Bola de Oro, the reader has difficulty making this same identification because information comes in bits and pieces, glimpses of scenes, and tails of gossipy conversations. Although the entire narrative is constituted out of the conversation between Santiago and Ambrosio, it has other conversations superimposed on it. One dialogue contains another dialogue that contains another dialogue, and so on. Each dialogue involves different characters speaking at different times and different spaces.

In the midst of Ambrosio or Santiago's recollections, other voices intervene to tell their versions or contribute their information. Vargas Llosa presents a view that sensory perception is experienced in terms of memory and language. Sensory perception becomes the screen onto which all consciousness is projected in *Conversation in the Cathedral*.

By means of conversation, Vargas Llosa not only narrates the action in a series of crisscrossing retrospective scenes but also delves into complexity of character. In the novel, the author portrays the myriad complexities of Peru's social and racial class system, catching it in the middle of its process of decomposition. The dramatic, even melodramatic, experiences of the characters announce a farewell to Zoila's world. In the dictatorship there were no heroes or martyrs; it produced only failures.

In *Conversation in the Cathedral*, young university students have passed tests, their rites of initiation. They consider themselves autonomous, mature individuals responsible for themselves and for the future of their country. No longer isolated within the confines of their neighborhoods, they plunge into university life, defined by one of the characters as a microcosm of Peruvian political life. The novel takes university life as the point of departure for the story, but the total narrative breadth of *Conversation in the Cathedral* extends into other sectors and periods of Peru's social fabric. The plot chronicles the years of the Odría dictatorship (1948-1956) and the disastrous effects that this oppressive and corrupt regime had on Peruvian society as a whole. Directly (the planning of a student-labor uprising) and indirectly (the conversations of politicians, maids, prostitutes, and journalists), the novel's discourse is centered on the question of power. *Conversation in the Cathedral* is a quintessential political novel.

In *Conversation in the Cathedral*, the multiplicity of stories creates an overwhelming sense of circularity. At the end of each story there seems to be a connection with the beginning of another story of a previous time. The novel has four sections of roughly equal length. Each part is focused on a major event in the plot and theme of the story: the awakening of Santiago's social and moral consciousness, La Musa's settling in as Bermudez's lover and hostess, La Musa's murder, the defeat of Santiago's investigative consciousness.

At the end of the novel the reader, like Santiago, is persuaded that it is necessary to learn more about the nature of evil. The reader may even be tempted to try to find an answer to Santiago's initial question: "When did Peru get all screwed up?" It is the need to find an answer to this question that sustains the reader's interest as Santiago plunges through various sordid histories. The novel is an exhaustive inquiry into the nature and dynamics of evil in relation to the corrupting influence of power. It is considered by many critics to be Vargas Llosa's most pessimistic text.

Genevieve Slomski

Bibliography:
Castro-Klaren, Sara. *Understanding Mario Vargas Llosa.* Columbia: University of South Carolina Press, 1990. Provides an introduction to the life and writings of Vargas Llosa and explicates his most important works. Bibliography.
Gerdes, Dick. *Mario Vargas Llosa.* Boston: Twayne, 1985. Good overview of Vargas Llosa's fiction in a historical and social context. Bibliography.

McMurray, George R. "The Novels of Mario Vargas Llosa." *Modern Language Quarterly* 29, no. 3 (September, 1968): 329-340. Discusses structural and thematic concerns in *Conversation in the Cathedral*.

Rossman, Charles, and Alan Warren Friedman, eds. *Mario Vargas Llosa*. Austin: University of Texas Press, 1978. Examines individual novels as well as major themes and concerns of Vargas Llosa's work.

Williams, Raymond L. *Mario Vargas Llosa*. New York: Frederick Ungar, 1986. Introduction to Vargas Llosa's works. Bibliography.

COPLAS ON THE DEATH OF HIS FATHER

Type of work: Poetry
Author: Jorge Manrique (c. 1440-1479)
First published: Coplas por la muerte de su padre, 1492 (English translation, 1833)

Jorge Manrique, regarded as having been among the most accomplished of late medieval Spanish poets, belonged to an aristocratic Castilian family, one that left its mark upon the cultural as well as the political history of the fifteenth century. His father, Rodrigo, Count of Paredes, rose to be Master of Santiago and Constable of Castile. Jorge's uncle, Gómez Manrique, was one of the finest poets of the reign of King Enrique IV (1454-1474). Among more distant kinsmen, Jorge could claim as a great-uncle the celebrated writer Iñigo Lopez de Mendoza, Marquis of Santillana. Thus, Jorge Manrique was part of a brilliant vein of literary culture that marked at least certain individuals and families among the fifteenth century warrior aristocracy of Castile. Characteristic of his time, he was torn between the claims of a soldier's, a courtier's, and a poet's life, eventually dying in battle in 1479 fighting on behalf of Queen Isabel.

The *Coplas on the Death of His Father* has been called the greatest poem in the Spanish language, but even without it, Manrique's approximately fifty *canciones* (lyric poems) and *decires* (narrative, panegyric, or satirical poems) would have established him among the leading poets of his time. As it was, *Coplas on the Death of His Father* so touched the imagination of subsequent generations that for more than two hundred years, criticism was written that sought to discover new and esoteric meanings in Manrique's masterpiece. Lope de Vega Carpio esteemed it so highly that he declared that it should have been written in letters of gold. Manrique's most eloquent English translator, Henry Wadsworth Longfellow, thought it to be the most beautiful "moral" poem in the Spanish language, and Pedro Salinas wrote that the poem represents the culmination of the elegiac lyric in Spanish. Manrique's critics concur that in this work he excels all other poets of the fifteenth century in Spain.

The poem, which consists of approximately five hundred lines, divided into forty-two *coplas* (or stanzas), is a memorial to Manrique's father, Rodrigo, who died in 1476 at the height of his fame. An intensely emotional poem, it integrates the poet's personal loss, the medieval world-view, concern for the passing of time, the vagaries of fortune, the inevitability of death, and the hope of salvation. Its uniqueness lies in Manrique's ability to employ familiar and rather well-worn themes in such a way as to extend their aesthetic potential. A mark of Manrique's greatness is his ability to render the grief of one individual in such a way that it became a grief universally shared by his readers.

The poem uses the form known as the *copla de pie quebrado*, familiar in Spanish poetry from the time of Juan Ruiz, the Archpriest of Hita, in the fourteenth century. In the *pie quebrado*, the tetrasyllabic (four-syllable) line is used with the octosyllabic (eight-syllable) line, thus reducing some lines to half the metrical length of the others, in mixed trochaic meter. These half-lines, when handled by a master, create an effect of suspense or hesitation. Manrique's use of the *pie quebrado* form became so famous that thereafter the term *copla manriqueña* (after Manrique), or simply the *copla de Jorge Manrique*, became as distinctive as the Shakespearean sonnet became in English letters.

The dominant motifs in the *Coplas on the Death of His Father* reflect characteristic medieval themes: the *ubi sunt qui ante nos in mundo fuere?* ("what has become of those who have gone before us?"); the *memento mori* ("in the midst of life we are in death"); and the *contemptus mundi* (or contempt for the things of this world); death personified; death as the great equalizer; the fleeting nature of fame and honor in this world; and the eternal promise of Christian salvation. Manrique, in presenting these well-known themes, achieves a rare intensity with his simple and direct vernacular Castilian. This was peculiarly significant for his time, because, in an age of classical translations, Castilian poets were increasingly abandoning vernacular forms of expression in favor of imitations of classical themes and forms. The poem, in exploiting every possibility of the vernacular language, demonstrates the fullest potentiality of Spanish versification. Furthermore, Manrique exemplifies the mood of his age, a period of profound pessimism and self-doubt. Such a mood is characteristic of an age of economic and demographic decay, as well as of plague and pestilence.

The poem can be divided into three sections. The first is a discussion of the theme of human mutability, the second pursues that of *ubi sunt*, while the third is an elegy for the late don Rodrigo. It begins by expressing a mood that is general and universal, meditating upon the transitory nature of this world, and then, following a series of examples taken from recent and ancient history, turns to the core of the poem, the reputation of the dead man himself.

In the first section, the poet contemplates the passage of time and the significance of memory. He explores the theme of life as a journey, which eventually merges with death, and thus returns to the source of all life: "Our lives are like rivers," he writes, gliding to the "boundless sea" which is the grave, in which "all earthly pomp and boast" are swallowed up. This section then develops the stock medieval theme of *contemptus mundi* as a prescription for attaining salvation: Things such as beauty and wealth, which are admired and esteemed in this temporal world, must perish, while those things that partake of the eternal, such as the human soul, endure. What men and women desire and pursue in this world are mere fleeting things that have no meaning and that offer no sustenance to the soul. At this point, death is introduced as the equalizer, for all are united in death. It is better, then, to regard this world as a journey until, in encountering death, one attains a better life beyond the grave. This present world is subject to mutability, chance, disaster, and decay, from which not even those in the highest places can escape. Manrique uses a favorite late medieval metaphor, the goddess Fortuna, ever inconstant, raising up men and women with the ascent of her wheel, only to cast them down again in despair.

Manrique turns to a second medieval theme, *ubi sunt*, posing a series of questions which ask, what has happened to the men and women of the past? The answer is that they have all passed away because they were a part of this transitory and impermanent world, a theme that recalls the earlier theme of *contemptus mundi*. While the reiteration of the *ubi sunt* theme is ubiquitous in medieval literature, it is indicative of Manrique's inventiveness that in his use of it he is superior to all his contemporaries. He invokes those names associated with the life of his father, don Rodrigo, beginning with his king Juan II (1406-1454), the Infantes of Aragon, and don Alvaro de Luna, the notorious favorite of the king. He evokes the chivalric trappings of the royal court, the festivities and the tournaments, but in describing all this, he underscores the transitory nature of worldly splendor and of a life "false and full of guile," observing that "our happiest hour is when, at last,/ the soul is freed."

In the final section, the poet introduces don Rodrigo as "Spain's champion," implying for his readers a comparison with another Rodrigo, El Cid. He declares that there is no need for a eulogy because "ye saw his deeds!" His father's name "dwells on every tongue." There then follows an elaborate passage of comparisons with the Roman heroes of old—Caesar and Octavian, Titus, Trajan, and Hadrian, Antoninus Pius and Constantine—Manrique claims for his father "Scipio's virtue" and "the indomitable will/ of Hannibal."

In the last part of the poem, Death appears in person and courteously addresses don Rodrigo. Here, Death is not the typical macabre figure familiar to contemporaries from the dance of death but is a mediator assisting don Rodrigo in transcending the mortal state and attaining fame and immortality: "Let virtue nerve thy heart again," says Death, proclaiming the ideal of the "brave knight whose arm endures/ Fierce battle, and against the Moors/ His standard rears." Rodrigo replies: "O Death, no more, no more delay!/ My spirit longs to flee away/ And be at rest."

In its perfect use of medieval topics, the poem represents a high point, and thus a change, in medieval consciousness. In contrast with a work such as *The Poem of the Cid* (twelfth or early thirteenth century), which glorifies action, *Coplas on the Death of His Father* embodies the contemplative spirit. This treatment of examining the meaning of life and the nature of reality makes the poem distinctive. Although the poem is a traditional elegy, the genius of the poet transforms the experience of personal loss into a universal statement of the transitory nature of earthly happiness and an affirmation of the Christian ideal of salvation.

Donna Berliner

Bibliography:
Bell, Alan S. "Tradition and Pedro Salinas's Original Approach to Jorge Manrique." *South Atlantic Bulletin* 39, no. 4 (November, 1974): 38-42. A critique of Salinas' widely read essay on Manrique.
Brenan, Gerald. *The Literature of the Spanish People from Roman Times to the Present Day.* New York: Cambridge University Press, 1970. The definitive study in English of Spanish literature.
Danker, Frederick E. "The *Coplas* of Jorge Manrique." *The Boston Public Library Quarterly* 10 (July, 1958): 164-167. An introduction, including the poem's early printing history.
Deyermond, A. D. *A Literary History of Spain: The Middle Ages.* London: Ernest Benn, 1971. The best introduction to medieval Spanish literature.
Dunn, Peter N. "Themes and Images in the *Coplas* . . . of Jorge Manrique." *Medium Aevum* 33 (1964): 169-183. A close reading of the poem, more concerned with aesthetic integrity than with literary history.
Krause, Anna. *Jorge Manrique and the Cult of Death in the Cuatrocientos.* Berkeley: University of California Press, 1937. Emphasizes late medieval attitudes toward mortality and death.
Longfellow, Henry Wadsworth, trans. "Ode on the Death of His Father," by Jorge Manrique. In *Ten Centuries of Spanish Poetry: An Anthology of English Verse with Original Texts from the Eleventh Century to the Generation of 1898*, edited by Eleanor L. Turnbull. Baltimore: The Johns Hopkins University Press, 1955. Longfellow's translation remains highly readable. See also Pedro Salinas' introduction in this book.
Post, C. R. *Medieval Spanish Allegory.* Cambridge, Mass.: Harvard University Press, 1915. An old but splendid study of the literary milieu of medieval Spanish writers.
Vinci, Joseph. "The Petrarchan Source of Jorge Manrique's *Las coplas.*" *Italica* 45 (1968): 314-328. Vinci makes a good case for Petrarch being a major influence on Manrique. Contains textual comparisons.

CORIOLANUS

Type of work: Drama
Author: William Shakespeare (1564-1616)
Type of plot: Tragedy
Time of plot: Third century
Locale: Rome, Corioli, and Antium
First performed: c. 1607-1608; first published, 1623

Principal characters:
CAIUS MARCIUS CORIOLANUS, a noble Roman
TITUS LARTIUS and
COMINIUS, generals against the Volscians
MENENIUS AGRIPPA, a friend of Coriolanus
TULLUS AUFIDIUS, a general of the Volscians
SICINIUS VELUTUS and
JUNIUS BRUTUS, tribunes of the people
VOLUMNIA, the mother of Coriolanus
VIRGILIA, the wife of Coriolanus

The Story:

Caius Marcius, a brilliant soldier, was attempting to subdue a mob in Rome when he was summoned to lead his troops against the Volscians from Corioli. The Volscians were headed by Tullus Aufidius, also a great soldier and perennial foe of Marcius. The hatred the two leaders had for each other fired their military ambitions. Marcius' daring as a warrior, known by all since he was sixteen, led him to pursue the enemy inside the very gates of Corioli. Locked inside the city, he and his troops fought so valiantly that they overcame the Volscians. Twice wounded, the victorious general was garlanded and hailed as Caius Marcius Coriolanus.

On his return to Rome, Coriolanus was further proclaimed by patricians, consuls, and senators, and he was recommended for the office of consul, an appointment wholeheartedly approved by the nobles. Because the citizens too had to vote on his appointment, Coriolanus, accompanied by Menenius Agrippa, went to Sicinius and Brutus, the plebeian tribunes, to seek their approval.

The people had long held only contempt for Coriolanus because of his arrogance and inhumane attitude toward all commoners. Although coached and prompted by Menenius to make his appeal as a wound-scarred soldier of many wars, Coriolanus could not bring himself to solicit the citizens' support but instead demanded it. He was successful in this with individuals he approached at random on the streets, but Brutus and Sicinius, who represented the common people, were not willing to endorse the elevation of Coriolanus to office. They voiced the opinions of many citizens when they accused Coriolanus of insolence and of abuses such as denying the people food from the public storehouses. Urging those citizens who had voted for him to rescind their votes, Brutus and Sicinius pointed out that his military prowess was not to be denied but that this very attribute would result in further suppression and misery for the people. Coriolanus' ambitions, they predicted, would lead to his complete domination of the government and to the destruction of their democracy.

Menenius, Cominius, and the senators repeatedly pleaded with Coriolanus to approach the tribunes civilly, and Volumnia admonished him that if he wanted to realize his political ambitions he must follow their advice. Appealing to his responsibility as a Roman, Volumnia pointed out that service to one's country was not shown on the battlefield alone and that Coriolanus must use certain strategies and tactics for victory in peace as well as in war.

Coriolanus misconstrued his mother's suggestions. She had taught him arrogance, nurtured his desires in military matters, and boasted of his strength and of her part in developing his dominating personality. Coriolanus now inferred that his mother in her older years was asking for submissiveness and compliance. Although he promised Volumnia that he would deal kindly with the people, it was impossible for him to relent, even when his wife, Virgilia, who had never condoned his soldiership, lent her pleas to those of the group and appealed to his vanity as a capable political leader and to his responsibility as a father and husband.

Coriolanus' persistence in deriding and mocking the citizens led to an uprising against him. Drawing his sword, he would have stood alone against the mob, but Menenius and Cominius, fearing that the demonstration might result in an overthrow of the government, prevailed upon him to withdraw to his house before the crowd assembled. Coriolanus misinterpreted the requests of his friends and family that he yield to the common people, and he displayed such arrogance that he was banished from Rome. Tullus Aufidius, learning of these events, prepared his armies to take advantage of the civil unrest in Rome.

Coriolanus, in disguise to protect himself against those who wanted to avenge the deaths of the many he had killed, went to Antium to offer his services to Aufidius against Rome. When Coriolanus removed his disguise, Aufidius, who knew the Roman's ability as a military leader, willingly accepted his offer to aid in the Volscian campaign. Aufidius divided his army in order that he and Coriolanus each could lead a unit, thereby broadening the scope of his efforts against the Romans. In this plan, Aufidius saw the possibility of avenging Coriolanus' earlier victories over him; once they had taken Rome, Aufidius thought, the Romans' hatred for Coriolanus would make possible his dominance over the arrogant patrician.

The Romans heard with dismay of Coriolanus' affiliation with Aufidius; their only hope, some thought, was to appeal to Coriolanus to spare the city. Although Menenius and Cominius blamed the tribunes for Coriolanus' banishment, they went as messengers to the great general in his camp outside the gates of Rome. They were unsuccessful, and Cominius returned to inform the citizens that in spite of old friendships, Coriolanus would not be swayed in his intentions to annihilate the city. Cominius reported that Coriolanus refused to take the time to find the few grains who were his friends among the chaff he intended to burn.

Menenius, sent to appeal again to Coriolanus, met with the same failure. Coriolanus maintained that his ears were stronger against the pleas than the city gates were against his might. Calling the attention of Aufidius to his firm stand against the Romans, he asked him to report his conduct to the Volscian lords. Aufidius promised to do so and praised the general for his stalwartness. While Coriolanus vowed not to hear the pleas of any other Romans, he was interrupted by women's voices calling his name. The petitioners were Volumnia, Virgilia, and young Marcius, his son. Telling them that he would not be moved, he again urged Aufidius to observe his unyielding spirit. Then Volumnia spoke, saying that their requests for leniency and mercy were in vain, since he had already proclaimed against kindliness, and that they would therefore not appeal to him. He had also made it impossible for them to appeal to the gods: They could not pray for victory for Rome because such supplication would be against him, and they could not pray for his success in the campaign because that would be to betray their country. Volumnia proclaimed that she did not seek advantage for either the Romans or the Volscians but asked only for reconciliation. She predicted that Coriolanus would be a hero to both sides if he could arrange an honorable peace between them.

Finally moved by his mother's reasoning, Coriolanus announced to Aufidius that he would frame a peace agreeable to the two forces. Aufidius declared that he too had been moved by Volumnia's solemn pleas and wise words. Volumnia, Virgilia, and young Marcius returned to Rome, there to be welcomed for the success of their intercession with Coriolanus. Aufidius withdrew to Antium to await the return of Coriolanus and their meeting with the Roman ambassadors, but as he reviewed the situation, he realized that peace would nullify his plan for revenge against Coriolanus. Moreover, knowing of the favorable regard the Volscians had for Coriolanus, he felt he had to remove the man who had been his conqueror in war and who might become his subduer in peace. At a meeting of the Volscian lords, Aufidius announced that Coriolanus had betrayed the Volscians by depriving them of victory. In the ensuing confusion, he stabbed Coriolanus to death. Regretting his deed, he then eulogized Coriolanus and said that he would live forever in men's memories. One of the Volscian lords pronounced Coriolanus the most noble corpse that was ever followed to the grave.

Critical Evaluation:

Coriolanus, which first appeared in 1607 or 1608, marked a vision quite distinct from and unlike the earlier great tragedies *Hamlet* (1600-1601), *King Lear* (1605-1606), and *Macbeth* (1606), which retain their appeal as much for their differences as for their likenesses to later ages. *Coriolanus*, on the other hand, remains modern in a number of significant ways. For one thing, there are no noble kings in the quasi-democratic society being portrayed, no amusing comic interludes with clowns and jesters that epitomize the jolly side of English sensibility, no fundamentally decent great men marred only by one tragic flaw, no declamatory soliloquies, no uplifting philosophical or poetic musings, no reassurances of a better future after the tragic hero's downfall. Instead, the landscape not only reflects the pessimism of Jacobean London but also distressingly resembles that of the twentieth century. The play presents a proudly democratic and secular society marred by the corrosive effects of established wealth in tandem with rigid social class divisions, a populace easily distracted by concerns of the moment and appeals to narrow self-interest (which allow rabble-rousers and charlatans to use their false rhetoric to great effect), a guns-or-butter debate that pits military preparedness against social welfare, and a fundamental question about the role of the exceptional individual in a supposedly egalitarian society. These remained the concerns of later ages as well, and they give *Coriolanus* a political and social resonance with twentieth century audiences that is not the case in those great Shakespearean tragedies that focus more exclusively on questions of individual morality.

Three related themes have particular resonance. In a society that at least tips its hat toward egalitarian ideals, the character of Coriolanus is a Shakespearean version of the Nietzschean *Übermensch* or superman. This was a figure the Renaissance regarded with fear and fascination both in literature—as in Christopher Marlowe's characters Doctor Faustus and Tamburlaine and in John Milton's Satan—and in real life, as in such figures as Sir Francis Drake and Sir Walter Ralegh. These Renaissance overreachers took advantage of the new freedoms of their liberated age to accomplish wonders but in doing so shook the foundations of their society, which, though initially valuing what they represented, usually ended by destroying them. A Macbeth, Lear, or Richard III might temporarily threaten the state as a result of personal ambition, foolishness, or corruption, but these figures were not, like Coriolanus, a barely contained force whom those around him tolerated for his usefulness but never ceased to regard nervously. (Othello comes closest to this description, but he is a basically good man led astray by personal weakness.) The dilemma William Shakespeare develops in *Coriolanus* anticipates the historical situations of individuals with a will to dominate, generals who accomplish what society wanted and who then turn on their own people with ferocity. Such strong personalities are needed in crisis but dangerous any other time, and from Napoleon to Adolf Hitler, Joseph Stalin to Mao Tse-tung, society has been terrorized by such figures. Whether we agree with those critics who regard *Coriolanus* as a play about politics or see it, as Algernon Charles Swinburne did, as a "drama of individuality" focused on an outsize hero, the problem is timeless.

As perhaps nowhere else in his works, Shakespeare in *Coriolanus* ties the character of his hero to his upbringing. This is in contrast to the way he explores the forces that shape Prince Hal in the *Henry IV* (1597-1598) and *Henry V* (1598-1599) series, where it is shown how little power they had over the prince. Here, Shakespeare looks at Coriolanus' nature as peculiarly male rather than as simply natural for a great warrior, and in the scenes with his mother, Volumnia, and his wife, Virgilia, he suggests the power of upbringing. Volumnia, a stalwart Roman matron, is fiercely "masculine" in her martial virtues and has proudly raised Coriolanus in this model of manhood. Virgilia, more conventionally feminine, deplores her husband's violent ways and their influence on their son. Few other Shakespearean heroes have their natures so linked to environment, and nowhere else, saving in the frothy problems of the comedies, is the gender difference confronted so directly. As with the superman type, the male ego in its purest untamed form has practical uses for guarding the city, but Shakespeare asks what is to be done with it during peacetime. The easy answer, and the one the Romans first choose, is exile, but this backfires when Coriolanus thereupon embraces the worst enemy of those who had rejected him. Critic John Holloway called Coriolanus a typical "scapegoat figure," a disturbing influence in the society to be symbolically driven out to restore peace. Yet such figures cannot easily be pushed into the desert permanently as were biblical scapegoats. Those like Coriolanus must be accepted as part of society itself, to be endured or dealt with.

Another concern in the play that had surfaced during Shakespeare's Renaissance and continues to be relevant is that of mob psychology. It would be several generations before the English Civil War and almost two hundred years before the terrors of the French Revolution, but fear of mob rule was endemic in Britain since the earliest days of Elizabeth I's rule, during Shakespeare's childhood. This fear runs through *Coriolanus*, balancing the equally abhorrent specter of rule by an undisciplined general teetering on the edge of manic fury. The play offers no solution to this Hobson's choice between governance by the whim of the "many-headed multitude" and that by aristocratic contempt for the concerns of the commonality, but it establishes the problem. The world of *Coriolanus* exemplifies the dilemma between distrust of the failed values of a self-serving aristocracy and distrust in the alternative, the passions of a "democratic" mob, and it explores that problem in connection with ambition, social stratification, and gender roles. Shakespeare's entire tragic canon illuminates human nature as no other dramatist's has done, but in *Coriolanus* he also provides insight into the problems of an age that was just beginning.

"Critical Evaluation" by Gina and Andrew Macdonald

Bibliography:
Barton, Anne. "*Julius Caesar* and *Coriolanus*: Shakespeare's Roman War of Words." In *Shakespeare's Craft: Eight Lectures*, edited by Philip H. Highfill, Jr. Carbondale: Southern Illinois University Press, 1982. Barton points out that in a world dependent on verbal rhetorical persuasion, Coriolanus' distrust of language alienates and isolates him, as does his personal use of language without regard to audience response.
Crowley, Richard C. "*Coriolanus* and the Epic Genre." In *Shakespeare's Late Plays: Essays in*

Honor of Charles Crow, edited by Richard Tobias and Paul Zolbrod. Athens: Ohio University Press, 1974. Argues that *Coriolanus* merges tragedy and epic and has at its heart the conflict between mercy and honor.

McAlindon, T. "*Coriolanus:* An Essentialist Tragedy." *Review of English Studies* 44 (November, 1993): 502-520. Rather than as a metaphor for England's problems, McAlindon regards *Coriolanus* as a political tragedy of class conflict and manipulation of power in a realistic, historically specific society .

McKenzie, Stanley D. " 'Unshout the Noise That Banish'd Marcius': Structural Paradox and Dissembling in *Coriolanus.*" *Shakespeare Studies: An Annual Gathering of Research, Criticism, and Reviews* 18 (1986): 189-204. Argues that in a world of chaotic reversals, betrayals, and paradoxes where only the adaptable survive, Coriolanus' unchanging consistency dooms him.

Miller, Shannon. "Topicality and Subversion in William Shakespeare's *Coriolanus.*" *Studies in English Literature, 1500-1900* 32, no. 2 (Spring, 1992): 287-310. Discusses *Coriolanus'* intricate structure of topical references and draws parallels with the career of James I, early seventeenth century issues of authority and monarchy, and other conflicts and contradictions of Shakespeare's age.

Rackin, Phyllis. "*Coriolanus:* Shakespeare's Anatomy of 'Virtus.'" *Modern Language Studies* 13, no. 2 (Spring, 1983): 68-79. Interprets *Coriolanus* as a cautionary illustration of the narrow, exclusive inadequacy of the Roman ideal. The hero's Roman virtues ironically are the vices that doom him.

THE CORNERSTONE

Type of work: Novel
Author: Zoé Oldenbourg (1916-   )
Type of plot: Historical
Time of plot: Early thirteenth century
Locale: France and the Holy Land
First published: La Pierre Angulaire, 1953 (English translation, 1955)

Principal characters:
ANSIAU, the old lord of Linnières and a pilgrim to the Holy Land
LADY ALIS, his wife
HERBERT LE GROS, Ansiau's son and heir
DAME AELIS, his wife
HAGUENIER OF LINNIÈRES, Herbert's oldest son
EGLANTINE, Herbert's half sister and lover
ERNAUT, Herbert's bastard son
LADY MARIE DE MONGENOST, the object of Haguenier's chivalric love
AUBERI, Ansiau's young squire
RIQUET, a renegade monk and Ansiau's traveling companion
GAUCELM OF CASTANS, called Bertrand, another traveling companion

The Story:

Ansiau, an old crusader, had left his fief in Champagne and his family to make a pilgrimage to the Holy Land. The half-blind lord hoped that at the grave of his eldest son and in the holy city of Jerusalem, he would find release from his grief. He was given a twelve-year-old boy, Auberi, as his squire.

The new lord of Linnières was another son, the licentious and unscrupulous Herbert le Gros. Herbert's mother, the Lady Alis, so disapproved of his behavior that she refused to live with him. She moved to a farmhouse, along with her husband's illegitimate daughter Eglantine, who was having a clandestine affair with her half brother.

Herbert sent to Normandy for his son Haguenier, who for years had been training to be a knight. On his way home, Haguenier met the beautiful, bored Lady Marie of Mongenost and swore allegiance to her, hoping that devotion would propel her into his arms.

After ten years of absence, Haguenier felt like a stranger in his own home. However, he soon found friends, including his brother Ernaut, who had been refused the hand of a cousin's daughter because of his illegitimate birth. Ernaut was threatening to kill himself. Herbert decided to send Ernaut for a papal document which might help his case. Meanwhile, Herbert proceeded with his other plans. Haguenier and his two illegitimate brothers were knighted, and Haguenier was married to a wealthy, older widow. After Haguenier made a poor showing in a tournament, Herbert sent him to prove himself in the crusade against the Albigensians.

On the road to Marseilles, Ansiau was joined by a lighthearted runaway monk, Riquet, and by Bertrand, or Gaucelm of Castans, who, because of his wife's Albigensian enthusiasm, had been blinded as punishment for heresy. Riquet left the party to remain with a village girl, and the other three proceeded through the war-ravaged countryside. At Pamiers, Bertrand was reunited with his son but found him determined to die for his new faith. In despair, Bertrand departed.

Fearful of his mother and, to a lesser degree, of damnation, Herbert broke off his affair with his half sister. Eglantine aborted their child and, bent on destroying Herbert, haunted the forest, experimenting with witchcraft.

After distinguishing himself in battle, Haguenier became ill and had to abandon the crusade. His wife produced a beautiful little girl. Haguenier was captivated, but because the child was not a male to carry on the line, Herbert was furious. Despite Haguenier's objections, Herbert had the marriage annulled. However, Haguenier said that unless Marie became available, he would not marry again. Marie continued to test her lover, pushing him into a battle with a rival, which Haguenier lost, then insisting that he fight in a tournament using only a mirror for a shield. Amazingly, he survived and triumphed over four knights. By now, Haguenier was the complete chivalric lover. To show his devotion to Marie, he had even forsworn physical love.

One disaster after another came upon Herbert and those associated with him. Ernaut was heartbroken when, despite the papal document, he was once again rejected and the girl he loved was betrothed to another man. Haguenier tried desperately to get his half brother through this crisis, but, when the marriage took place, Ernaut hanged himself, just as he had threatened to do.

Discovering his affair with Eglantine, the Lady Alis disowned Herbert and placed a curse upon him. Then came a bitter drought. When rain fell everywhere except on Herbert's lands, the peasants blamed Eglantine's witchcraft. A mob swept down upon Lady Alis' farmhouse, injured her, and killed Eglantine. Convinced that his mother's curse was working, Herbert confessed his many sins to a priest and was given a number of penances. Herbert did make a fairly short pilgrimage. However, he hired someone else to go to the Holy Land in his place.

In Marseilles, Ansiau and his two friends were delighted to have Riquet rejoin them. The monk promptly began making money to pay their way to the Holy Land and turning it over to Ansiau for safekeeping. When Ansiau was robbed, Riquet had to begin all over again. In desperation, he went into a church to pray. While he was there, a woman left a necklace of precious stones at the shrine of Saint Mary Magdalene. Assuming that his prayer had been answered, Riquet took the necklace, sold it, and procured passages to the Holy Land for his friends and himself.

In Acre at last, Ansiau searched for his son's grave without success. He decided to continue on his way to Jerusalem. Unfortunately, Bertrand was now too ill to walk but fearful of remaining behind alone. Ansiau and Riquet decided to take turns carrying him. The four left Acre with a large convoy, accompanied by armed men. However, a band of Muslim warriors swept down from the hills, killed the guards, and took the rest captive. Young, strong men like Riquet were sent to be sold as slaves. Those who were not of much use, such as Bertrand, were marched until they died of exhaustion. In fact, Bertrand chose to die; he left the line of prisoners and was decapitated. Seeing that Ansiau, though blind, still had considerable physical power, the Muslims set him to work turning a mill. Because they believed that Auberi was Ansiau's son, they permitted the boy to remain with the old man.

While Herbert was away, his wife Aelis was so indiscreet that Haguenier was forced into a duel with her lover. On his return, when Herbert learned about the scandal, he began beating his wife. Chivalrously, Haguenier went to her defense. In the ensuing scuffle, Herbert's back was broken. During the days that followed, Herbert forgave his son, and the Lady Alis, regretting her curse upon him, forgave Herbert. On his deathbed, Herbert asked Haguenier to marry off his one-year-old daughter and turn over the family estates to her husband. Haguenier, he said, should enter a monastery. Haguenier obeyed his father's wishes and became Brother Ernaut. When his wife died, Haguenier had his daughter sent to Marie to be reared.

In the Holy Land, Ansiau persuaded the faithful Auberi to make his escape, and, eventually, the boy found his way to a group of Christian pilgrims. Among the Muslims, Ansiau gained the reputation of being a holy man and a healer. He died on a hill above Jerusalem.

"The Story" by Rosemary M. Canfield Reisman

Critical Evaluation:
The Cornerstone is not so much a historical novel as a work of fiction in which medieval men and women live. This distinction is important. What now passes for the historical novel is little more than an adventure story filled with bombast or a record of bedroom escapades in fancy dress. Zoé Oldenbourg's book is the exception that justifies a literary form debased by most of her contemporaries. Her novel has all the qualities readers expect of a story enclosing long perspectives of time and change and the mysteries of life and death.

No small part of Oldenbourg's effectiveness is the result of her insight into the mind and heart of medieval people. Her characters come together, talk, or go about their intimate affairs, and, in so doing, they reveal themselves and their private concerns, loyalties, superstitions, hopes of heaven, and fears of hell. Nothing seems contrived or forced; situations arise as casually as they do in Geoffrey Chaucer's *The Canterbury Tales* (1380-1390) or the stories of Giovanni Boccaccio, but everything adds up to the stir and spirit of an age. Life is harsh, disappointing, and sad. Men seize at excitement or happiness in the pageantry of a tournament, the rituals of a court of love, an illicit passion, or the violence of war. Always, above everything else, Christian faith gives meaning and purpose to experience and guides humanity's quest for spiritual salvation. Through these matters, Oldenbourg brings to life and motion the gentry and the whole of medieval society—knights and their ladies, crusaders, troubadours, wandering scholars, holy pilgrims, serfs, priests, merchants, clerks, and beggars—in the days when Philip Augustus reigned in Paris and Pope Innocent III had summoned the chivalry of France to a new crusade against the Albigensian heretics of Provence and Toulouse.

In a novel so solid in construction, so varied in detail, certain comparisons are inevitable. There is something massive here, like the soaring bulk of a Gothic cathedral built in an age when people lived in daily intimacy with God and churches became powerful upsurges of buttressed masonry. In this connection, the title of Oldenbourg's book is symbolic, for Christian faith was the cornerstone on which rested the whole structure of the feudal period. Again, reading this novel is like inspecting at close hand a medieval tapestry in which every figure, leafy tree, and symbolic beast has been worked lovingly and with care, or like turning the pages of a beautifully limned Book of Hours, the figures of its decorative groupings a little stiff and archaic in their poses but believable and very human, with every face and gesture clear-cut and revealing.

Father, son, and grandson stand in the foreground of this landscape with figures. In his old age, Ansiau de Linnières, part of whose story was told in an earlier novel, *The World Is Not Enough* (1946), turns over his fiefs in Champagne to his heir and sets out on a pilgrimage to the Holy Land in order to win forgiveness for the sins of his rough life. A veteran of the Third Crusade, he hopes to see Jerusalem once more before he dies and to visit the grave of his oldest son, buried at Acre. His sight failing, he goes blind on the way and wanders through a countryside ravaged by the Albigensian wars in the company of a young squire, a blinded heretic, and a renegade monk. In Palestine, he is captured and forced into slave labor. His capacity for faith, however, allows him to overcome all agonies of the body and spirit, and, in his last hour, dying alone on a hillside near Jerusalem, he trustingly calls on God to be his priest.

His son Herbert, aptly nicknamed the Gross, is a man of brutal nature and prodigious physical appetites. Greedy, lecherous, cruel, disliked by his neighbors and alienated from his children, he has murdered, fornicated, and blasphemed his way into middle age. When he commits incest with his half sister Eglantine and is cursed by his mother, the Lady Alis, the pilgrimage he makes in expiation of his sins is little more than an impious fraud. On his return, he is fatally injured by his son, Haguenier, while he is trying to beat his wife to death.

Haguenier, the young knight of Linnières, represents the more tender and idealistic side of the medieval temperament. He might have become an even worthier son of an unworthy father if he had not been afflicted by physical weakness or come under the spell of Lady Marie de Mongenost, whom he served faithfully but hopelessly, according to the rules of chivalric love. In repentance, after his sin of patricide, he left the older woman to whom he was married and his baby daughter and entered a religious order.

It is plain that the three Linnières of the novel illustrate three different facets of medieval life and belief. Bluff old Ansiau and Herbert le Gros stand at opposite poles of that age of contradictions and extremes. Haguenier, too sensitive for the rough life to which he has been trained, confusing his adoration of the Virgin with his love for an earthly woman, dreamy, but manly in his capacity for fidelity and suffering, points to the more humanistic age which was soon to follow.

Oldenbourg has expressed a belief that in the contemporary novel there is too little concern with what is great and eternal in man. In this somber, richly imagined, and starkly imaged story of thirteenth century France, she has held up a mirror of human conduct and faith which illumines the past to reflect the hopes and fears of the present.

Bibliography:
Ames, Alfred C. "Mounting Power in Rare Novel." *Chicago Sunday Tribune*, January 9, 1955, p. 3. Praises the author for her "proud lack of compromise" in treating a complicated subject. Despite the fact that their way of life and their modes of thought are foreign to twentieth century readers, all of Oldenbourg's characters come to life and become objects of concern.
Janeway, Elizabeth. "Courage and Faith in a Distracted Age." *The New York Times Book Review*, January 9, 1955, 4. States that Oldenbourg's theme is the triumph of "courage and faith" in a period of conflict, violence, and rapid change. Although she reveals the worst side of Christianity, as well as the best, the author sees religion as the only sound basis for existence.
"Medieval Tapestry." *Time* 65 (January 10, 1955): 88. States that the novel is "artfully written." The accounts of vicious behavior and brutality are justified by Oldenbourg's intention to present a "huge and intricate tapestry" which shows clearly what life was like in the thirteenth century.
Pick, Robert. "Eros in a Wimple." *Saturday Review* 38 (January 8, 1955): 10. *The Cornerstone* is the first modern novel to re-create the world of chivalric love in all its subtlety and its innocent blasphemy. Additionally, the characters symbolize historical change. Herbert is a man of the Middle Ages, and the son who kills him is a Renaissance humanist. Interesting comments.
Raymond, John. Review of *The Cornerstone*. *New Statesman and Nation* 48 (December 4, 1954): 762. Blending historical events with her characters' very human reactions to them, the author has produced a "great historical novel." The three major figures—crusader, son, and grandson—are seen not merely as individuals but also as representatives of an era.

THE CORSICAN BROTHERS

Type of work: Novel
Author: Alexandre Dumas, *père* (1802-1870)
Type of plot: Adventure
Time of plot: 1841
Locale: Corsica and Paris
First published: Les Frères corses, 1844 (English translation, 1880)

Principal characters:
ALEXANDRE DUMAS, the narrator of the story and a traveler in Corsica
LUCIEN DE FRANCHI, a Corsican
LOUIS DE FRANCHI, Lucien's brother and a law student in Paris
EMELIE, a married woman with whom Louis is in love
MONSIEUR DE CHATEAU-RENAUD, Louis' rival for Emelie's affections

The Story:

In March, 1841, Alexandre Dumas was traveling, with his horse and guide, on the island of Corsica. One day, he arrived at the top of a hill overlooking the towns of Olmeto and Sullacaro; and in accordance with the custom followed by travelers on that island, he surveyed the scene before him in order to decide at whose house he would spend the night. Hospitality was an ancient art on Corsica, where it was considered an honor to entertain a guest without recompense. From his vantage point, Dumas decided upon a house which his guide informed him was the Sullacaro property of Madame Savilia de Franchi.

The weary traveler was cordially welcomed by Madame de Franchi and shown to the room of her absent son, Louis. She promised that her other son would soon be home and would pay his respects on his arrival. A few minutes later, young Lucien de Franchi knocked at the guest's door.

Dumas gathered from the youth's conversation that there was little likeness between the twin de Franchi brothers in appearance or tastes. Lucien, browned and robust, was dressed in riding clothes. He could not, he said, be forced to leave his native mountains. Louis, he declared, was a student who had spent most of his time indoors with his books. In spite of variance in interests, Lucien continued, they were devoted to each other.

Since they wished to continue their conversation while he dressed, Lucien invited the guest to his room, a chamber in contrast with that of the absent Louis. The student's room was furnished in the modern French manner and filled with books. Lucien's furniture was all of the fifteenth and sixteenth centuries, and the walls were hung with weapons of every type. Lucien exhibited two pistols, each bearing a similar date and inscription on its butt, which had belonged to his father and mother.

When the two men rejoined Madame de Franchi, she anxiously asked Lucien if he had anything to tell her about Louis. He replied that he had not. Lucien explained to the guest that the brothers, born attached and cut apart, experienced like impressions at the same time. He had felt melancholy for the past few days, so he knew his brother must be in trouble. He knew Louis was not dead, however, for if he had been, he would have seen his twin in a vision.

At dinner Lucien explained that he had to go out later, as he had been chosen mediator to resolve an ancient vendetta between the Orlandi and Colonna families. That evening Lucien was to meet with the Orlandi clan leader at a ruin about a league from town so that a reconciliation might take place the following day. He invited Dumas to accompany him.

In the moonlight, they climbed a hill on which stood the ruins of an old house which had belonged to an ancestress of the de Franchis, a woman who some four hundred years before had become involved in a feud with the de Guidice family. The pistols in Lucien's room celebrated the end of the vendetta, concluded when his parents had simultaneously killed two brothers, the last of their hereditary enemies.

After some urging, the head of the Orlandi clan agreed to bring his family to Sullacaro the following morning so that a peace treaty with the Colonna clan might be signed. After Lucien had shot a pheasant, he and his guest began their descent to the town.

The following morning, Dumas was on hand to witness the conciliation of the Orlandi and Colonna families as they marched from either end of the town to stand before the church. After a pact had been signed before the village notary, the clan leaders attended mass together.

That afternoon Dumas was forced to leave for Paris. After exchanging his hunting belt for one of Lucien's daggers, he started for the coast. Lucien had given Dumas a letter for his brother, and Madame de Franchi had begged that he himself should deliver it. The author sought out the young man immediately on his arrival in Paris. Louis was not at home. In answer to a note left by Dumas, he came to call the next day. Dumas was surprised at the resemblance between Louis and his brother. In response to inquiries, Louis admitted that he had been suffering from a bitter private grief. Unfortunately, he was in a hurry and could not stay long that day. It was agreed that he and Dumas would meet the following night at an opera ball.

When he kept his appointment with his new friend, Louis appeared distraught and at first did not want to accompany Dumas to a supper party to be given after the ball by D——, a friend of the writer. When he understood, however, that a Monsieur de Chateau-Renaud would be present and that this gentleman had a bet with his host that he would bring a certain unidentified personage with him, the Corsican declared he would go.

At the party, Dumas and Louis discovered that de Chateau-Renaud had gambled on bringing a young married woman with him and on being able to present her before four o'clock. The couple arrived only a few minutes before the hour, the man forcing rather than escorting his companion. When she realized, from the few words which de Chateau-Renaud let slip to their host, that she had been the object of a bet, she insisted on leaving immediately and asked Louis to take her home. When the young man consented, he was challenged by de Chateau-Renaud. Although he had never handled a weapon, Louis accepted the challenge.

Later that day, Dumas called on his young friend and agreed to serve as a second in the duel. Louis explained that Emelie, the young woman whose cause he had championed, had been entrusted to his care by her husband, a sea captain. Deeply in love with her, he had made every effort to conceal his passion. When, to his dismay, he realized she was carrying on an affair with de Chateau-Renaud, he had attempted to reprove her but had been accused of jealousy for his pains. Then, by chance, he had been invited to D——'s party, where Emelie had appeared as the result of de Chateau-Renaud's wager.

The pistol duel was to take place next morning at nine. Dumas arrived at Louis' rooms at seven-thirty and found him writing a letter in which he informed his mother and brother that he was writing in a lucid interval but that he would soon be dead of brain fever. He explained to Dumas that he had been visited by his father the previous night and been told that he would die. Not wishing his family to know the true circumstances of his death, he asked his friend to send the letter so that Lucien would not come to Paris seeking vengeance and so, perhaps, be killed.

The young Corsican died, as he had predicted. A bullet entered below his sixth rib and came out just above his hip on the other side of his body. Dumas mailed the letter as he had promised.

Five days later he was surprised by a visit from Lucien, who could not yet have learned of his brother's fate. The Corsican declared he had been out riding the day his brother was killed; at the moment of Louis' death, he had felt as though a bullet had also pierced him. To Dumas' astonishment, he showed an inflamed mark below the sixth rib on his own body. The following morning, he had set out for Paris, with his mother's blessing.

Two days later, Lucien stood facing de Chateau-Renaud on the spot where his brother had fallen. An instant later, de Chateau-Renaud lay dead, a bullet through his head, and Lucien shed his first tears since Louis' death.

Critical Evaluation:

The Corsican Brothers belongs to that most productive period in the career of Alexandre Dumas, *père*, the 1840's. This period, which followed the years of play writing, saw the publication of Dumas' best-known works, including *The Three Musketeers* (1844), *The Count of Monte-Cristo* (1844-1845), and *Twenty Years After* (1845). Although he was much given to producing stage versions of his fiction, Dumas recognized the relatively small merit of *The Corsican Brothers* and never adapted it to play form. In London, however, the story about the incredible bond between twin brothers, who were born physically attached and had to be cut apart, created a sensation; so many English melodramas based on Dumas' plot sprang up that the story soon gave rise to a rash of burlesques.

That Dumas was a playwright before he was a novelist is evident throughout his fiction; the action is always bold and dramatic, unfolding in a series of varied and vivid scenes, with scenery and costumes more than adequately re-created through the narrative description. This is especially true in *The Corsican Brothers*, where the setting is based on Dumas' observations during his travels in Corsica in 1841. The element in Dumas' fiction which continues to attract a reading audience, however, is the author's success as a historical novelist; he so skillfully blends actual history with events spawned in his own fertile imagination that often only a very trained eye can separate the two. Thus in *The Corsican Brothers*, the carefully reproduced landscape and faithfully rendered pictures of the island inhabitants are merged with a plot full of the supernatural element, to create a final product that—despite the novel's many flaws—seems a vivid and realistic account of true events. Dumas' characters aid this impression of verisimilitude; they are very alive and have colorful, distinctive personalities. At the same time, they are not drawn with any psychological depth—in the sense that their subtler emotions and motivations are not delineated—and they do not grow or change appreciably throughout the story; they are clearly subordinate in importance to the plot. Nevertheless, Dumas' characters have a certain irresistible energy that captures the reader's sympathy; like their creator, they have a boundless zest for living and joy in adventure that make them perfect vehicles for romantic escapism in the audience.

Thus, *The Corsican Brothers* illustrates Dumas' usual weaknesses—his tendency to string together random and often inaccurate bits of history and geography, his unpolished style, and his shallow characterizations—as well as his distinctive strengths: a fast-moving story full of suspense and surprises and characters lovable for their passion and exuberance.

Bibliography:

Dumas, Alexandre, *père*. *The Road to Monte Cristo: A Condensation from "The Memoirs of Alexandre Dumas."* Translated by Jules Eckert Goodman. New York: Charles Scribner's Sons, 1956. An abridged translation of Dumas' memoirs that relate to his source material for his novels, including *The Corsican Brothers*.

Galan, F. W. "Bakhtiniada II, *The Corsican Brothers* in the Prague School: Or, The Reciprocity of Reception." *Poetics Today* 8, nos. 3/4 (1987): 565-577. Approaches Dumas' *The Corsican Brothers* using the critical apparatus of Bakhtin. While the reading is sometimes difficult, this is the only paper published in English on *The Corsican Brothers*.

Maurois, André. *The Titans, a Three-Generation Biography of the Dumas*. Translated by Gerard Hopkins. New York: Harper & Row, 1957. Considered the authoritative biography of Dumas *père*, his father, and his son. Includes an excellent bibliography. Discusses *The Corsican Brothers* in a cursory fashion.

Schopp, Claude. *Alexandre Dumas: Genius of Life*. Translated by A. J. Koch. New York: Franklin Watts, 1988. A biographical and critical approach to the life and works of Alexandre Dumas, *père*. The volume contains a discussion on Dumas' adaptation of *The Corsican Brothers* into a drama in order to pay his bills.

Stowe, Richard S. *Alexandre Dumas (père)*. Boston: Twayne, 1976. An excellent starting place for an analysis of the life and works of Alexandre Dumas *père*, probably the best source in English. *The Corsican Brothers* is addressed in part 2 of chapter 10.

THE COSSACKS

Type of work: Novel
Author: Leo Tolstoy (1828-1910)
Type of plot: Psychological realism
Time of plot: Nineteenth century
Locale: The Caucasus
First published: Kazaki, 1863 (English translation, 1873)

Principal characters:
OLYENIN, a Russian aristocrat
MARYANKA, a Cossack woman
LUKASHKA, a young Cossack, betrothed to Maryanka
UNCLE YEROSHKA, an old Cossack retired from service

The Story:

Olyenin, a young Russian aristocrat, decided to leave the society of Moscow and enter the army as a junior officer for service in the Caucasus. There were a number of reasons for his decision. He had squandered a large part of his estate, he was bored with what he considered an empty life, and he was in some embarrassment because of a love affair in which he could not reciprocate the woman's love.

Olyenin left the city after a farewell party one cold, wintry night. He and his servant, Vanyusha, traveled steadily southward toward the Caucasus, land of the Cossacks. The farther Olyenin went on his journey the better he felt about the new life he was about to begin. In a year's service, he saw the opportunity to save money, to rearrange his philosophy, and to escape from a mental state which did not permit him to love. He was sure that in a new environment he could become less egocentric and could learn to love others as he loved himself.

Shortly after he joined his unit, he was one of a force sent out along the Terek River to guard against depredations by the tribes who lived in the mountains and on the steppes south of the river. The troops were to reinforce the Cossacks who lived in the narrow strip of verdant land which bordered the river. Olyenin's unit was stationed in the village of Novomlin, a small settlement of houses and farms with a population of less than two thousand people, mainly Cossacks.

The Cossack men spent their time in hunting and standing guard at posts along the Terek River, while the women tended the homes and farms. When Olyenin's unit moved into the village, he, as an aristocrat, was not assigned duties with the troops, and so his time was largely his own. The Cossacks did not like the Russian troops, for the tensions of differing cultures and the years of enmity between them had not been assuaged. Olyenin was quartered in the house of a Cossack ensign and soon learned that he was not welcome. They were accepting him and his servant only because the household had to take them.

In the house lived an ensign, his wife, and their daughter Maryanka. Maryanka had been spoken for in marriage by a young Cossack, Lukashka, a hero in his village because he had saved a boy from death by drowning and had killed a mountain tribesman who had attempted to swim across the river during a raid. Olyenin quickly became infatuated with Maryanka. He did not know how to act in her presence, however, because he was bewildered by the possibility of a love affair between himself and the young, uncultured Cossack.

Olyenin made friends with Lukashka, whom he met at an outpost while hunting, and Uncle

Yeroshka, an old Cossack whose days of service were over. In Yeroshka's company, Olyenin went hunting almost every day. He disliked drinking bouts, gambling at cards with the other officers, and the pleasure they found in pursuing the women of the village whose husbands and sweethearts were away on duty. Olyenin was happier alone or hunting with Yeroshka in the woods along the Terek, where he could try to work out his emotional problems.

At last, Olyenin began to feel that he could be happy through generosity to others. He discovered that he enjoyed giving a horse to Lukashka and presenting old Yeroshka with small gifts that meant little to Olyenin but a great deal to the old man. In addition, Olyenin won the respect of the Cossacks by his ability to shoot pheasants on the wing, a new feat to the Cossacks, who had never seen it done.

As time passed, Olyenin became more and more aware of Maryanka's presence. When her parents announced that she was formally engaged to young Lukashka, the announcement made Olyenin decide that he, too, was really in love with her. He turned over in his mind the possibilities that such a love would entail. He could not imagine taking her back to Moscow, into the society to which he had expected to return after his tour of duty, nor could he imagine settling down for life in the Cossack village. Although his stay there meant a great deal to him, he knew that he could never be happy following the primitive life he saw there, for he had too many ties, both social and material, in the world he had temporarily left.

While Olyenin helped Maryanka pick grapes in the vineyards, he had an opportunity to declare his love. Maryanka neither became angry nor repulsed him, although she gave him little encouragement. Later Olyenin, able to press his suit at various times, promised to marry the Cossack woman. She, on her part, refused to say that she would marry him, for she too realized the difficulties of such a marriage. Unlike most of the Cossack women, she was not free with her favors and refused to let either Olyenin or Lukashka share her bed. Lukashka was well aware of what was happening but was not worried; he felt that the situation would right itself because he was the better man of the two.

One day a small band of marauders from across the Terek appeared a short distance from the village. When the Cossacks, accompanied by Olyenin, made a sortie against them, the outlaws tied themselves together so that they could not run away while they made a stand against the Cossacks. After the battle, Lukashka, wounded by a gunshot, was carried back to the village, where it was discovered that he could not recover from his wound. Faced with the death of the man her parents had chosen to be her husband, Maryanka realized that her life and people were widely separated from Olyenin and the culture for which he stood. Deciding that she could never have any lasting affection for the Russian, she told Olyenin bluntly of her decision. Olyenin requested a change of duty to another unit. After permission for the transfer was granted, he and his servant left the village and the kind of life he never could learn to accept.

Critical Evaluation:

The character of Olyenin, the hero of *The Cossacks*, is largely autobiographical in origin. Like his young hero, Leo Tolstoy left Moscow in 1852 and joined an army regiment stationed in the Caucasus, the land of the Cossacks. Throughout his four years of service—during which he fought in expeditions in the Caucasus, the Danube, and the Crimea—Tolstoy kept very careful, detailed diaries, which years later were to provide invaluable material for his fiction. In the Caucasus diaries, he recorded all aspects of his life as a soldier, including not only the fighting but also the hunting and drinking, the time spent reading and writing, and the periods of idleness and boredom; it is to this minute observation and recording of firsthand experience that *The Cossacks* owes much of its verisimilitude of plot and setting, its vividness of atmosphere and impression. In addition to using his army experiences in molding the character of Olyenin, Tolstoy provided his hero with a background nearly identical to his own; both Olyenin and his creator were young noblemen who left Moscow as a result of large debts and an unsuccessful love affair, and both are concerned with discovering new values amid a different way of life from that to which they had been accustomed.

This escape from life in a teeming city, with its juxtaposition of culture and decadence, attractiveness and corruption, creativeness and stagnation, is at the thematic center of *The Cossacks*. The novel revolves around the concern for humanity's return to a more natural state from the debilitating influences of urban civilization. This idea is embodied in Olyenin's flight from the whirl of Moscow society to the Caucasus. The important question to be answered, however, is what Tolstoy does with the nature-versus-civilization hypothesis. Certainly, in the first chapters, it would appear that the hero is headed toward an environment that will heal and renew him. However, the extent to which the remaining course of the narrative proves the Caucasus to be the natural life that Olyenin is seeking remains in question.

Tolstoy is able to see both strengths and shortcomings in each way of life and condemns neither one. One illustration of his objectivity is seen in his characterization of old Yeroshka, who, if this novel were a polemic against civilization, would be the obvious candidate to represent Cossack wisdom and the superiority of their way of life. Instead, he is portrayed as a brave hunter and fighter but a fault-ridden and quite human individual; he is a lovable, if slightly lecherous old reprobate. Rather than dispensing profound insight and ancient wisdom to young Olyenin, Yeroshka simply rides, hunts, drinks, and encourages the youth to enjoy sensual pleasures without worrying about the future. Likewise, the other main Cossack figure, Lukashka, combines strength and virtue, weakness and pettiness. Yeroshka, Lukashka, and their people are admirable in their bravery, their energy, and their closeness to the land; yet at the same time they murder, steal, and lose themselves in drunkenness and debauchery.

In the same way, Tolstoy attacks all the evils of his own and his hero's class: their idleness, selfishness, shortsightedness, hypocrisy, temper, and irresponsibility. Although he sees these vices in the nobility and includes many of them in Olyenin's personality, he does not lose sight of redeeming qualities in the aristocracy. Olyenin's merit lies in his basic morality, which will not allow him to be complacent about his weaknesses; he is dissatisfied with his faults and his former way of life and seeks, although in an imperfect fashion, to find remedies and to grow as a person.

Olyenin vacillates throughout the story in his opinion of what comprises happiness. In chapter twenty, he exclaims to himself, "Happiness consists in living for others," while, in chapter thirty-three, he is convinced that "Self-renunciation is all stuff and nonsense . . . in my heart there is nothing but love for myself and the desire to love her and live her life with her." Olyenin never finds the key to happiness throughout the novel, although he enjoys a brief period of unreflecting enjoyment with the Cossacks, but he does discover that the urban, aristocratic way of life and the Cossack culture are incompatible. He learns this lesson on the personal level when his attempt to form a relationship with Maryanka fails, and on a more general level in his inability ever to feel truly a part of Cossack culture.

In addition to the cohesiveness which Olyenin's search for happiness gives *The Cossacks*, the novel is also strongly unified through its richly evocative descriptive passages. In a powerful style marked by its clarity and simplicity, Tolstoy paints an unforgettable picture of Cossack life and of the people who cultivate the land. In this early work, all the author's love of nature, farming, and country life emerges in scenes of riding, hunting, and harvesting to create a vividness of effect that foreshadows the genius of his later novels.

Leo Tolstoy conceived the idea of writing *The Cossacks* in 1852, although it took him ten years of intermittent work to complete the novel. The basic idea for the work was inspired by the author's long talks with an old Cossack friend, Epishka. Tolstoy's projected plan, first jotted down in a brief diary entry, was for a story "(a) about hunting, (b) about the old way of life of the Cossacks, and (c) about his expeditions in the mountains." Tolstoy's original intention was to write a long and complex novel that would include a substantial background of Cossack history, faithful renditions of the folk customs of the Caucasus, and all the tales of the area told to him by Epishka. As it transpired, however, Tolstoy was forced, for financial reasons, to finish the novel hastily for a publication deadline in 1863; the final length was approximately two hundred pages, since much of the original plan for the work had either been altered over the years or sacrificed in the hurry to complete it. *The Cossacks* is therefore a work of many peculiarities of structure and style; nevertheless, it marks an important step in Tolstoy's development, being his first work to be translated into another language and to capture an enthusiastic audience abroad. Above all, it remains an unsurpassed description of Cossack life and an excellent psychological study of a young man casting about for values which will fill the moral void he fears has entered his life.

"Critical Evaluation" by Nancy G. Ballard

Bibliography:
Bayley, John. *Tolstoy and the Novel*. Chicago: University of Chicago Press, 1988. For the nonspecialist, this book is the most readable survey of Tolstoy's long fiction in the English language. Compares *The Cossacks* with other examples of Tolstoy's fiction set in the Caucasus and finds it wanting.
Kornblatt, Judith Deutsch. *The Cossack Hero in Russian Literature: A Study in Cultural Mythology*. Madison: University of Wisconsin Press, 1992. Kornblatt places Tolstoy's *The Cossacks* in a Russian tradition that runs from early nineteenth century writer Alexander Pushkin through twentieth century novelist Mikhail Sholokhov.
Turner, C. J. G. "Tolstoy's *The Cossacks*: The Question of Genre." *Modern Language Review* 73, no. 3 (July, 1978): 563-572. A detailed examination of Tolstoy's conflicting intentions in *The Cossacks*, which he declares "a hybrid" of such genres as sketch, tale, novel, idyll, and autobiography. Elucidates this position by recounting the decade-long process of the novel's composition.
Wasiolek, Edward. *Tolstoy's Major Fiction*. Chicago: University of Chicago Press, 1978. Notes that *The Cossacks* "has some clear deficiencies," particularly in terms of the point of view it presents, but differs with Bayley as to the nature and extent of the problem. Argues that Tolstoy needed to establish two points of view, subjective and objective, but did not handle their juxtaposition skillfully.
Wilson, A. N. *Tolstoy*. New York: W. W. Norton, 1988. A lengthy biography in which Wilson calls *The Cossacks* Tolstoy's "first masterpiece" and an example of his ability to make new, fresh use of clichéd material.

THE COUNT OF MONTE-CRISTO

Type of work: Novel
Author: Alexandre Dumas, *père* (1802-1870)
Type of plot: Historical
Time of plot: Nineteenth century
Locale: France
First published: 1844-1845 (English translation, 1846)

> *Principal characters:*
> EDMOND DANTÈS, a young sailor
> MERCÉDÈS, his sweetheart
> FERDINAND MONDEGO, a rival
> M. DANGLARS, an ambitious shipmate
> M. VILLEFORT, a deputy
> VALENTINE, his daughter
> ABBÉ FARIA, a prisoner at Chateu D'If
> CADEROUSSE, an innkeeper
> M. MORREL, a shipping master
> MAXIMILIAN, his son
> ALBERT, Mondego's son
> HAIDEE, an Albanian

The Story:

When Edmond Dantès sailed into Marseilles harbor in 1815, he was surrounded by enemies. One of his shipmates, Danglars, coveted his appointment as captain of the *Pharaon*, and another, Ferdinand Mondego, wished to wed Mercédès, who was betrothed to Edmond.

Danglars and Ferdinand wrote a note accusing Edmond of carrying a letter from Elba to the Bonapartist committee in Paris. Caderousse, a neighbor, learned of the plot but kept silent. On his wedding day Edmond was arrested and taken before a deputy named Villefort, a political turncoat, who, to protect himself, had Edmond secretly imprisoned in the dungeons of the Château D'If. There Dantès' incarceration was secured by the plotting of his enemies outside the prison, notably Villefort, who wished to cover up his own father's connections with the Bonapartists.

Napoleon came from Elba, but Edmond lay forgotten in his cell. The cannonading at Waterloo died away. Years passed. Then one night Edmond heard the sound of digging from an adjoining cell. Four days later, a section of the flooring fell in, and Edmond saw an old man in the narrow tunnel below. He was the Abbé Faria, whose attempt to dig his way to freedom had led him only to Edmond's cell. Thereafter the two met daily, and the old man taught Edmond history, mathematics, and languages. In Edmond's fourteenth year of imprisonment Faria, mortally ill, told Edmond where to find a tremendous fortune should he escape after the old man's death. When death did come, the abbé's body was placed in a sack, and Edmond conceived the idea of changing places with the dead man, whom he dragged through the tunnel into his own bed. Jailers threw the sack into the sea. Edmond ripped the cloth and swam through the darkness to an islet in the bay.

At daybreak he was picked up by a gang of smugglers with whom he worked until a stroke of luck brought him to the island of Monte-Cristo, where Faria's fortune lay. He landed on the island with the crew of the ship, and, feigning injury in a fall, persuaded the crew to leave him behind until they could return for him. Thus he was able to explore the island and to find his treasure hidden in an underground cavern. He returned to the mainland and there sold some small jewels to provide himself with money enough to carry out his plans to bring his treasure from Monte-Cristo. He learned that his father had died and that Mercédès, despairing of Edmond's return, had married Ferdinand.

Disguised as an abbé, he visited M. Caderousse to seek information about those who had caused his imprisonment. M. Villefort had gained fortune and station in life. Danglars was a rich banker. Ferdinand had won wealth and a title in the Greek war. For this information Edmond gave Caderousse a diamond worth fifty thousand francs.

He learned also that his old shipping master, M. Morrel, was on the verge of bankruptcy. In gratitude, because Morrel had given the older Dantès money to keep him from starvation, Edmond saved Morrel's shipping business.

Edmond took the name of his treasure island. As the Count of Monte-Cristo he dazzled all Paris with his fabulous wealth and his social graces. He and his mysterious protégée, a beautiful girl named Haidée whom he had bought during his travels in Greece, became the talk of the boulevards.

Meanwhile he was slowly plotting the ruin of the four men who had caused him to be sent to the Château D'If. Caderousse was the first to be destroyed. Monte-Cristo had awakened his greed with the gift of a diamond. Later, urged by his wife, Caderousse committed robbery and murder. After being released from prison, he attempted to rob Monte-Cristo but was mortally wounded by an escaping accomplice. As the man lay dying, Monte-Cristo revealed that his true name was Edmond Dantès.

In Paris, Monte-Cristo succeeded in ingratiating himself with the banker Danglars and was secretly ruining him. The next victim on his list was Ferdinand, who had gained his wealth by betraying Pasha Ali in the Greek revolution of 1823. Monte-Cristo persuaded Danglars to send to Greece for confirmation of Ferdinand's operations there. Ferdinand was exposed and Haidée, daughter of the Pasha Ali, appeared to confront him with the story of her father's betrayal. Albert, the son of Mercédès and Ferdinand, challenged Monte-Cristo to a duel to avenge his father's disgrace. Monte-Cristo intended to make his revenge complete by killing the young man, but Mercédès came to him and begged for her son's life. Aware of Monte-Cristo's true identity, she interceded with her son as well, and at the scene of the duel the young man publicly declared that his father's ruin had been justified. Mercédès and her son left Paris, and Ferdinand shot himself.

Monte-Cristo had also become intimate with Madame Villefort and encouraged her desire to possess the wealth of her stepdaughter, Valentine. The count had slyly directed Madame Villefort in the use of poisons, and the depraved woman murdered three people. When Valentine, too, was poisoned, Maximilian Morrel, son of the shipping master, went to Monte-Cristo for help, who then learned that his friend Maximilian loved Valentine. Monte-Cristo vowed to save the young girl, but she had apparently died. Monte-Cristo promised future happiness to Maximilian.

Danglars' daughter, Eugénie, ran off to seek her fortune, and Danglars found himself bankrupt. He deserted his wife and fled the country. When Villefort discovered his wife's treachery and crimes, he threatened her with exposure. She then poisoned herself and her son Edward, for whose sake she had poisoned the others. Monte-Cristo revealed his true name to Villefort, who subsequently went mad.

But Monte-Cristo had not deceived Maximilian. He had rescued Valentine while she lay in a drugged coma in the tomb. Now he reunited the two lovers on his island of Monte-Cristo. They were given the count's wealth, and Monte-Cristo sailed away with Haidée never to be seen again.

Critical Evaluation:

The Count of Monte-Cristo, Alexandre Dumas' best-known novel after *The Three Musketeers* (1844), is, improbable as it might seem, based on a true story. Dumas, who has become almost legendary for his prolific literary output of nearly three hundred volumes, employed collaborators to search through published memoirs for suitably exciting plots. Through this process a volume entitled *Mémoires tirés des archives de la Police de Paris* by Jacques Peuchet, the Keeper of the Archives at the Prefecture of Police, came to Dumas' attention.

In Peuchet's memoirs, which contained a treasure of potential plots for novels, was a record of a case of wrongful imprisonment and vengeance that strongly appealed to the French author. In 1807, a young shoemaker in Paris, François Picaud, was engaged to marry Marguerite Vigoroux, a beautiful orphan with a fortune of one hundred thousand gold francs. When four of Picaud's friends, jealous of his good fortune, accused him of being an English agent, Picaud was spirited away in the night by the police, who at the time were worried about certain insurrectionary movements. The unfortunate man's parents and his betrothed made inquiries but, failing to obtain any satisfaction, resigned themselves to the inevitable. In 1814, with the fall of the empire, Picaud was released from the castle of Fenestrelle where he had all that time been imprisoned. While in captivity, he had, with great devotion, looked after an Italian prelate who had been imprisoned on a political charge and had not long to live. The dying man bequeathed to Picaud a treasure hidden in Milan. After his release, the shoemaker recovered the treasure and returned under an assumed name to the district in which he had been living. He made inquiries and soon discovered the plot against him by his jealous friends. He then spent ten years of his life engaged in an elaborate plot against the perpetrators of his suffering, which resulted in the eventual destruction of his former friends.

Dumas delighted in the idea of creating a character possessed of a fabulous fortune who was an avenger in some great cause. This impulse was natural, for Dumas, in spite of his exuberant exterior, harbored many grievances against society at large and against individual enemies in particular. His father had been persecuted; he himself was harassed by creditors and slandered. He shared with other unjustly treated writers that longing for vengeance that has engendered so many masterpieces. The experiences of Picaud gave him the story for which he had been longing, but it was a stroke of genius by which he came up with the name, Count of Monte-Cristo, which has come to be embedded in the memories of countless readers. The mysterious creative forces that lead to the birth of great works came into play one day when Dumas went boating among the islands around Elba and his guide pointed out a beautiful island named Monte-Cristo.

The Count of Monte-Cristo had a greater success than any of Dumas' books prior to *The Three Musketeers*. Like most of Dumas' major novels, it was first serialized in the daily newspaper, and he kept his public in suspense from one day to the next by means of romantic love affairs, intrigues, imprisonments, hairbreadth escapes, and innumerable duels. Dumas had great gifts of narrative and dialogue and a creative imagination, but only a limited critical sense and an even smaller concern for historical accuracy. He had, however, a knack for seizing situations and characters to render a satisfactory historical atmosphere. He believed sincerely that action and love were the two essential things in life and thus in fiction. His writing was never complicated by analysis or psychological insights, and his best works, such as *The Count of Monte-Cristo* and *The Three Musketeers*, can be read with effortless enjoyment.

Critics rightly point to the excessive melodrama of Dumas' work, and to his lack of psychological perception and his careless style. The characters are one-dimensional, stranded in the conventional molds the author has set for them. There is no change, no sudden insight, and no growth in the players upon Dumas' stage. Yet despite many defects, this novel remains a breathtaking narrative and a dramatic tale filled with mystery and intrigue. For thousands of years the unhappy human race has found release in cathartic tales such as this one. The most popular characters have been the magician and the dispenser of justice. The injured and weak live with the hope, which no ill-success can weaken, of the arrival of the hero who will redress all wrongs, cast down the wicked, and give the deserving their desserts.

At the time Dumas was writing, the magician had been confused with the rich man whose wealth permits him to indulge his every whim and to use his treasure to provide justice for the innocent man and to punish the guilty. Dumas dreamed of becoming just such a distributor of earthly happiness, and *The Count of Monte-Cristo* gave him the framework for which he was looking. The author's hero is not a savage murderer but an implacable avenger who obtains justice and disappears. *The Count of Monte-Cristo* finds its audience among people of all ages and of all times who like a romantic adventure tale with a larger-than-life hero.

"Critical Evaluation" by Patricia Ann King

Bibliography:
Bell, A. Craig. *Alexandre Dumas: A Biography and Study.* London: Cassell, 1950. Discusses the origins and the genesis of *The Count of Monte-Cristo*, including notes from Dumas to his collaborator Auguste Maquet. Provides clear analysis of character, settings, and theme.
Hemmings, F. W. J. *Alexandre Dumas: The King of Romance.* New York: Charles Scribner's Sons, 1979. Good introductory source describing the origins of the plot of *The Count of Monte-Cristo* in an earlier story, "Georges," and in the imprisonment of François Picaud. Argues that the work is the greatest revenger's tragedy in the history of the novel and that it employs the hero as an instrument of divine providence. Clear analysis of theme and character.
Ross, Michael. *Alexandre Dumas.* Newton Abbot, Devon, England: David and Charles, 1981. Explores the relationship between Dumas and his collaborator Auguste Maquet, discussing the role each played in the plot development of *The Count of Monte-Cristo*. Compares the real and fictionalized versions of the story of François Picaud.
Schopp, Claude. *Alexandre Dumas: Genius of Life.* Translated by A. J. Koch. New York: Franklin Watts, 1988. Detailed biography that provides a good introduction to Dumas' life and work, including the events surrounding the creation of *The Count of Monte-Cristo* and an account of public response. Provides insights into Dumas' working methods.
Stowe, Richard. *Alexandre Dumas (pere).* Boston: Twayne, 1976. Provides a clear plot summary of *The Count of Monte-Cristo* and detailed analysis of character, setting, and atmosphere. Compares Dantès with other Dumas heroes and traces the novel's development, focusing on its interesting blending of reality and fantasy.

THE COUNTERFEITERS

Type of work: Novel
Author: André Gide (1869-1951)
Type of plot: Psychological realism
Time of plot: Early 1920's
Locale: Paris
First published: Les Faux-monnayeurs, 1925 (English translation, 1927)

Principal characters:
ÉDOUARD, a writer
OLIVIER MOLINIER, his nephew
GEORGE MOLINIER, Olivier's younger brother
VINCENT MOLINIER, Olivier's older brother
BERNARD PROFITENDIEU, Olivier's friend and Édouard's secretary
LAURA DOUVIERS, Édouard's friend
COMTE ROBERT DE PASSAVANT, a libertine
ARMAND VEDEL, Laura's brother and Olivier's friend

The Story:

When seventeen-year-old Bernard Profitendieu discovered an old love letter of his mother's and realized that he was an illegitimate son, he left a scathing letter for the man whom he had considered his real father and ran away from home. He spent that night with his friend, Olivier Molinier. Olivier told him of his Uncle Édouard, a writer, who would be arriving from England the following day, and also of a woman with whom his older brother Vincent was involved.

The next morning, Bernard left before Olivier had awakened. For a time he wondered what to do. He idly decided to go to the station and watch Olivier meet his uncle. That same morning Vincent visited his friend, the notorious homosexual, Comte Robert de Passavant. Vincent was disturbed over his affair with Laura Douviers, a married woman whom he had met while both were patients in a sanatorium. Upon her release, she had followed Vincent to Paris.

Édouard was returning to Paris because of a promise to Laura. He had known her before her marriage and had told her to call upon him whenever necessary. He was also looking forward to seeing his nephew Olivier, of whom he was very fond. He was so excited, in fact, that, after checking his bag, he threw away his checkroom ticket. The meeting with his nephew, however, proved unsatisfactory. Although unobserved, Bernard had watched the meeting between the two. He picked up the checkroom ticket Édouard had dropped and claimed the bag. In it he discovered a large sum of money, which he quickly pocketed, Édouard's journal, which he read without scruple, and Laura's supplicating letter.

With no definite plan in mind, Bernard called on Laura. Laura was disturbed by the young man who knew so much about her affairs, but his actions became understandable when Édouard arrived and Bernard admitted the theft of the bag. He said that he had stolen it as a means of getting in touch with Édouard. Édouard was impressed with the young man's impudent charm. When Bernard suggested that he might fill the role of a secretary, Édouard agreed. A few days later, with Bernard as his secretary, Édouard took Laura to Switzerland. Bernard wrote to Olivier in glowing terms about his new position. Olivier was jealous of Bernard, who, he felt, had taken his place in Édouard's affections. He decided to take an editorial assignment offered to him by de Passavant.

1326

In the meantime, Bernard fell in love with Laura. When he confessed his love, Laura showed him a letter from her husband, begging her to come back to him with her child and Vincent's. She had decided to return to him. Bernard and Édouard returned to Paris. A letter then arrived from Olivier to Bernard. He was in Italy with de Passavant, and he wrote complacently about the wonderful journal they intended to publish. Bernard showed the letter to Édouard, who failed to realize that the letter disguised the boy's real feelings of jealousy and hurt.

Although still serving as Édouard's secretary, Bernard had enrolled in the Vedel School and was living in the Vedel household. The Vedels were Laura's parents and Édouard's close friends. Édouard was particularly fond of Rachel, Laura's older sister, and it distressed him to see that she was devoting all of her time and energy to managing the school. Bernard told Édouard about some children, including George Molinier, Olivier's younger brother, who were engaged in some underhanded activities. The boys, as Bernard was soon to learn, were passing counterfeit coins.

Olivier returned to Paris to get in touch with Bernard. The meeting between the two was strained. As they parted, Olivier invited Édouard and Bernard to a party which de Passavant was giving that evening. Olivier then went to visit another old friend, Armand Vedel, Laura's younger brother. Armand refused the invitation to the party but suggested that Olivier ask his sister Sarah to go in his place. Bernard, who was living at the school, was to serve as her escort.

The party was an orgy. Olivier became drunk and quarrelsome. Édouard led him from the room, and Olivier, ashamed, begged his uncle to take him away. Bernard escorted Sarah home. Her room was beyond Armand's, and her brother handed Bernard the candle to light the way. As soon as Bernard had gone into her bedroom, Armand bolted the door. Bernard spent the night with Sarah.

The next morning, Bernard found Édouard attempting to revive Olivier. After spending the night with his uncle, the boy had risen early in the morning on the pretext that he wanted to rest on the sofa. Getting up later, Édouard had discovered his nephew lying on the bathroom floor unconscious, the gas jets turned on. Édouard nursed Olivier until the boy recovered. When Olivier's mother went to see her son, she expressed to Édouard her concern for George and his wayward habits. Édouard promised to speak to George. He also learned that Vincent had gone away with Lady Griffith, a friend of de Passavant.

A few days later, Édouard received a call from M. Profitendieu, the man Bernard had thought was his father. Ostensibly he had called in his office as magistrate to ask Édouard to speak to his nephew George, who was suspected of passing counterfeit coins. It soon became evident, however, that the real object of his visit was to inquire about Bernard. Since the boy had left home, Profitendieu had worried about him. He wanted very much to have him home once more.

Meanwhile, Bernard's affair with Sarah had attracted Rachel's attention, and she asked him to leave the school. Bernard went to Édouard, who told him of the interview with Profitendieu. For some time Bernard had regretted the harsh letter he had written, and the hatred he had felt for his foster father had changed to sympathy and fondness. It was evident that Bernard was no longer needed as Édouard's secretary. He therefore decided to return home.

Armand had succeeded Olivier as editor of de Passavant's journal. He went to see Olivier and showed him a letter from an older brother in Egypt. The writer told of a man with whom he was living who was almost out of his mind. From what he could gather from the fellow's ravings, the man had been responsible for his female companion's death. Neither Armand nor Olivier guessed that the man was Olivier's brother Vincent.

George and his friends caused a tragedy at their school. Boris, the young grandson of an old friend of Édouard, had been invited to join a secret society if he would perform the act of initiation—standing up before the class and shooting himself through the temple. It was understood that the cartridge would be a blank. Only one person knew there was a live cartridge in the gun; he told no one. When Boris, pale but resolute, walked to the front of the class and shot himself, the joke became a tragedy. The experience was terrible enough to bring George to his senses. Meanwhile, after Olivier had completely recovered from his suicide attempt, Édouard settled down again to writing his book, with a great sense of peace and happiness.

Critical Evaluation:

One year after André Gide published *Corydon* (1924), which provoked a literary furor, he completed *The Counterfeiters* together with its complementary *Le Journal des faux-monnayeurs* (1926; *Journal of the Counterfeiters*, 1931). Both books had taken six years to write. The idea for the novel, however, came to the author at least as early as 1906, when he cut out from the September 16 issue of the newspaper *Le Figaro* an article concerning a case of counterfeiting in which several children from respectable families had been involved. He also had on file a report of the suicide of Neny, a young student at the Lycée Blaise-Pascal. Furthermore, in 1907, news of a gang of anarchist counterfeiters was widely publicized. By 1919, Gide began a tentative draft of the novel, which he continued intermittently while he was writing his critical study *Dostoïevsky* (1923) and completing his sexual research. *The Counterfeiters*, a culmination of such long and careful thought, is generally regarded as Gide's masterpiece, although he preferred the more scandalous *Corydon*.

In a sense, *The Counterfeiters* summarizes the major ideas that Gide had presented up to that point in his career. Later, he would publish other major books—*Si le grain ne meurt* (1926; *If I Die . . .* , 1935), *L'École des femmes* (1929; *The School for Wives*, 1929), for example—but they would not break new ground. With *The Counterfeiters*, Gide's high place in European literature was assured. While its roots are in the tradition of the nineteenth century social novel and novel of ideas—for example, Gustave Flaubert's *A Sentimental Education* (1869) and Fyodor Dostoevski's *The Possessed* (1871-1872)—its influence, both in matters of style and in philosophy, is unmistakable in such important twentieth century novels as Aldous Huxley's *Point Counter Point* (1928) and Lawrence Durrell's *The Alexandria Quartet* (1957-1960). Like these books, *The Counterfeiters* is at once a novel of ideas, of artistic development, and of psychological realism.

Gide's title, which is partly ironic, was the projected title of a yet unfinished—and, according to *The Journal of the Counterfeiters*, never-to-be-completed—novel by Édouard. Throughout the book, Édouard talks about his novel, describes its theme, and, at one point, allows George Molinier to read a selection from it; George not only fails to understand the meaning of the passage but also scorns the name of the protagonist. On reflection, Édouard agrees with his critic. Édouard is never satisfied with the direction that his writing takes. At first, he insists that his book has no subject, that it is a mere slice of life. Later, he catches sight of its "deep-lying subject," which is "the rivalry between the real world and the representation of it which we make to ourselves." That subject is expressed in the symbolism of a counterfeit coin. In the important chapter "Édouard Explains His Theory of the Novel," he shows Bernard Profitendieu a counterfeit ten-franc piece. If Bernard were to understand that the coin is not genuine, he would naturally despise it; if he were deluded into thinking that it is real, he would value it beyond its worth. Value, therefore, depends upon perception, but perception has nothing to do with reality. Later, the reader learns that the coin is more than a symbol of counterfeit values. George is suspected of passing counterfeit money.

Gide's trick upon the reader is characteristic of his artistic method, which is one of ironic contrast, of allowing his protagonists to play games that prove finally to be serious, or to turn their serious problems into farcical games. *The Counterfeiters* presents a wide diversity of ideas, exposes their absurdities, yet sometimes salvages their values. On one level, the book explores the risks along with the liberating energies of criminality. Bernard, who comes upon Édouard's checkroom ticket, takes the writer's bag, which contains money, a literary journal, and a letter from Laura Douviers. He keeps the money, at least for a while, excusing himself with the rationalization that he is not a thief, reads the confidential journal, and uses the letter as a pretext to involve himself in Laura's life as her protector. Thus, he commits a "gratuitous act," outrageous in its casual, motiveless interference in the lives of others. Yet the consequences, both for Bernard and for those concerned, are not as crass as the reader might expect. By exercising his total capacity for freedom, he has broken into life, enjoyed a more exciting and richer life-experience than he might otherwise have known. To be sure, the ultimate consequences of his act are dangerous, and he learns that one's boldness may often cause other people unhappiness, but the lesson is not entirely cautionary. By the end of the book, more liberated than at the outset, Bernard makes his peace with his stepfather and returns to his family as a more responsible young man.

Bernard, though perhaps the most extraordinary example of this, is not the only character in the novel who asserts his philosophies by living them. Just as Bernard's fortunes are on the rise because of his impetuosity, Vincent Molinier's decline. The seducer of Laura, whom he callously abandons, Vincent himself is destroyed by Lady Griffith. Her sensuality is greater and more destructive than his. Still other characters temporize, frozen in will, and allow the world to come to them. Gide's method is to provide brief scenes presenting encounters between characters, usually two characters at a time. The personalities express their ideas, sometimes debate, and at other times agree. Yet matched with a different partner, a different encounter, the characters change their minds, often subtly and without understanding the results of their actions. Thus, the sense of reality shifts, just as the circumstances appear to turn one direction or another. Reality is not absolute. The author, who is himself a voice in the novel, is not above suspicion of error. Surely Gide's major spokesman, the writer Édouard, is at times wise, at times foolish.

More than a complex novel of ideas that explores the limitations of perceiving reality, *The Counterfeiters* is an aesthetic novel that treats the development of the artist. To be sure, there are two novelists in the book. Édouard, the more important figure, is a discreet homosexual, stoic, troubled by problems of moral ambiguity, but generous, open-natured, and, like Gide, insistent that sincerity is his chief resource as an artist. His rival is Comte Robert de Passavant, also a homosexual, more successful as a writer but more devious as a human being. The comte is also Édouard's rival for the affections of Olivier Molinier. As Édouard develops—through constantly changing and refining—his aesthetic, it becomes clear that his rivalry with Passavant is never far from the springs of his invention. Édouard explains his theory of art both in dialogues—or encounters—with other characters or, more fully, to himself in his journals. Like Gide's famous literary journals, Édouard's notebooks examine the philosophy and strategies of composition, relate anecdotes, puzzle over problems of structure, and attempt to analyze the writer's own motives. As an exploration both of art and of himself, the journals are filled with undigested, often contradictory, but urgent material for further investigation. It is a measure of Gide's excellence as an artist that he never exhausts but generally augments the subject he treats.

His understanding of the craft of fiction carries over to an interest in the artist's psychology. Perhaps this concern of Gide's novel is less satisfactory for most readers, because the writer's homosexual bias allows for only a partial, inadequate view of the subject. One theme of *The Counterfeiters* is the psychosexual development of the two university friends, Bernard and

Olivier. At the beginning of the novel, both prepare for their *bachot*, the baccalaureate examinations at the Sorbonne. By the end, both pass. Similarly, they undergo a sensual education that results in a certain homosexual orientation for Olivier and a very nearly certain one for Bernard. Olivier is clearly disposed to homosexuality when he first encounters Bernard (and they share a bed), but he discovers, first through the comte de Passavant and later through Édouard, that the relationship he prefers involves the companionship of an older patron. As for Édouard, a genteel and delicate pederast, the arrangement is ideal. Having achieved the satisfaction he has always craved from the love of Olivier, he is prepared to resume work on his novel.

Bernard's sexuality is more ambiguous, but without doubt it is mainly homoerotic. His sexual encounter with Sarah Vedel is almost farcical. Sarah, the aggressor throughout, is—incredible to say—assisted by her brother Armand, who bolts the bedroom door to make sure that the couple perform the act of love. As soon as Bernard wakes up, he runs from Sarah's chamber, never wishing to see her again. Bernard is capable only of veneration for women, as he idolizes Laura and admires Rachel, her sister, but feels for them nothing akin to desire. He is more finely attracted to Olivier. Yet, following Gide's homosexual fantasy, he bows out of the picture so that Édouard has the youth to himself. To complete the fantasy, Gide allows Olivier's mother, Pauline, in a ludicrous scene, to bestow her blessings on the union. Curious though the scene is from the standpoint of heterosexual psychology, it is perfectly satisfactory from the context of the author's purpose in the novel. The description of the meeting, after all, is part of Édouard's journal. How much of it is imagined and how much real? Indeed, to what extent are the actions of the characters real or pretended? Gide, master of disguises, makes his characters speak their parts, cleverly or stupidly as may be, but withholds his own moral judgments.

"Critical Evaluation" by Leslie B. Mittleman

Bibliography:
Brée, Germaine. *Gide*. New Brunswick, N.J.: Rutgers University Press, 1963. One of the best introductions to Gide and his work available in English. Brée's analysis of *The Counterfeiters* and *The Journal of "The Counterfeiters"* emphasizes sociological aspects, connections to Gide's life, and the importance of the readers' own participation in the novel's meaning.
Cordle, Thomas. *André Gide*. Updated ed. New York: Twayne, 1993. Contains a good analysis of *The Counterfeiters*, which Cordle considers Gide's greatest work. The social critique of early twentieth century petty bourgeoisie comes out as an important theme of the novel. Selected bibliography.
Gide, André. *Journal of "The Counterfeiters."* Translated by Justin O' Brien. In *The Counterfeiters* by André Gide. Translated by Dorothy Bussy. New York: Knopf, 1951. Gide's own account of his novel's genesis is a fascinating document in its own right and provides many insights into its meaning.
Guerard, Albert J. *André Gide*. Cambridge: Harvard University Press, 1951. Still an important introduction to Gide's work. Places *The Counterfeiters* in the tradition of the modern novel of the turn of the century, and makes some interesting parallels with the work of Russian novelist Fyodor Dostoevski, who was an important influence on Gide.
Walker, David H. *André Gide*. New York: St. Martin's Press, 1990. Contrasts *The Counterfeiters* with Gide's earlier work. Analyzes the psychological aspects of the novel and the problem of causality.

THE COUNTESS CATHLEEN

Type of work: Drama
Author: William Butler Yeats (1865-1939)
Type of plot: Allegory
Time of plot: Indeterminate
Locale: Ireland
First published: 1892; first performed, 1899

> *Principal characters:*
> COUNTESS CATHLEEN, an Irish noblewoman
> OONA, her childhood nurse and present companion
> ALEEL, a visionary poet in love with Cathleen
> SHEMUS RUA, a peasant
> MARY, his wife
> TEIGUE, their son
> TWO DEMONS, disguised as merchants

The Story:

During a famine, an Irish peasant family was talking about strange creatures that had appeared, portents that evil supernatural forces were abroad in the land. The Countess Cathleen and her companions arrived, searching for the way to her castle. The peasants bitterly complained to her of their state, and she gave them what she had left in her purse after previous charity to other starving folk. She invited the family to her castle the next day to receive more.

After her departure, Shemus and Teigue complained at the meagerness of her charity, while Mary scolded them for ingratitude. Irked by his wife's words, Shemus asserted his independence by rashly calling three times on the supernatural creatures of the woods to enter his house. Two traveling merchants appeared, ostentatiously displaying their wealth. They offered money for souls and sent Shemus and Teigue to broadcast their offer to the countryside. Cathleen arrived at her castle, where Aleel tried to distract her with a story about Queen Maeve of the fairies, who wept for a mortal who died of love for her—not because she loved him too, but because she had forgotten his name. Oona recalled her to the concerns of the day, earning a curse from Aleel for having prevented him from relieving Cathleen of distress for ten minutes. The castle steward told Cathleen that men had broken into the castle to steal food; to Oona's consternation, Cathleen declared the theft to be no sin, since the men must have been starving. Shemus and Teigue then arrived with their tale of merchants buying souls; Cathleen, appalled, offered to buy their souls back. Father and son declined the offer, having concluded that God had turned his back on Ireland. Cathleen then instructed the steward to sell all her property, save only the house, and use the money to buy food for the starving, stating that she intended from that time forward to dedicate herself to others.

Aleel tried to get Cathleen to flee by telling her a dream he had had of an angel who urged her to flee. She refused, asserting that it had been a pagan god, not an angel. She tenderly dismissed Aleel from her company to find the peace she could not have herself, and went in to pray and sleep.

While she slept, the merchants entered and robbed her treasury, then woke Cathleen to tell her lies—that her relief efforts had come to nothing—and to pass on rumors about their own appearance in the land. They explained men's willingness to sell their souls as a kind of joy in despair, and told her her own soul would be worth half a million crowns. She began to suspect their true identities, and they departed as their pursuers closed in on them.

Cathleen bade peasants fleeing the evil times welcome to a place where they would be safe, but at that moment, Oona discovered the empty treasury. Although close to personal despair, Cathleen urged all with her to pray for the souls of the famine victims. Meanwhile, other peasants passed the castle, talking about the power and beauty of gold as the merchants followed in silence. They moved on, and a forlorn Aleel passed by, singing in a vain attempt to soothe his love-stricken heart.

The merchants set up shop in the house of Shemus Rua and began dealing for souls, with Shemus and Teigue as their lieutenants. Mary Rua had refused food bought with the devil's money and lay dead on her bed. Two peasants exchanged their souls for money, finding themselves to be worth less than anticipated since the merchants had records of their darkest, most hidden secrets. Aleel, too, offered his soul—for free, since he had no need of it if it could not help Cathleen. He was refused, since his soul already belonged to the countess. An old, nearly sinless woman sold her soul for a thousand crowns and wished God's blessing on the merchants, whereupon she screamed as a burning pain passed through her. This frightened the other peasants, who began to shrink from the merchants.

Cathleen came to the cottage, offering her soul for the half million crowns on the condition that the other bartered souls be returned to their owners. After the sale, the merchants followed her out, vowing to watch over her until her impending death from a broken heart allowed them to take her soul.

Aleel had a vision of the old gods and heroes returning, and Oona arrived at the hut to be told that her mistress had already sold her soul. As they both knelt, in prayer or despair, Cathleen was carried in to die. Outside, a ferocious storm brewed, terrifying the peasants, whose fear was increased by Aleel's response to the storm: a curse on fate for leaving no hope. Aleel then described a vision of angels and devils battling in the middle of the storm. He seized one of the angels to demand word of Cathleen's fate. The angel described her arrival in heaven, redeemed by her sacrifice despite the sin of having sold her soul. Aleel knelt before this revelation, while Oona begged for her own death, bemoaning her separation from Cathleen.

Critical Evaluation:

William Butler Yeats first published a version of the story of the Countess Kathleen O'Shea in his collection *Fairy and Folk Tales of the Irish Peasantry* (1888), and appears to have conceived of a play based on the story at around the same time. Although he later dismissed the play, his first and longest major dramatic work, as merely "a piece of tapestry," Yeats was unable to dismiss the idea from his imagination. For over thirty years, he repeatedly revised *The Countess Cathleen* to bring it into line with his evolving vision of poetry and the theater.

Unable to fit the play into the formalized symbolism of Yeats's later drama, many writers have examined *The Countess Cathleen* only in terms of its role in the development of the Irish theater. Yeats published an early version in 1892. The play was not performed, however, until 1899, after at least one major revision, when it was half of the playlist of the inaugural season of the Irish National Theater.

The Dublin premiere was politically controversial; protestors objected to the play's unorthodox theology and allegedly slanderous depiction of Irish peasants—even before the play was staged. Religious authorities objected to Yeats's conclusion that, "The Light of Lights/ Looks always on the motive, not the deed"; while nationalists insisted no Irishman would ever sell his soul. These sorts of objections were prophetic of later conflicts between Irish playwrights and the public. Organized hecklers tried to disrupt the first performance, disgusting the young James

Joyce, who was present. Despite these protests, however, the first performance was enthusiastically received by much of the audience.

The play's role in theater history has distracted attention from the play itself, which critics of Yeats's drama seldom treat favorably. The frequent revisions, none of which brought out the "personal thought and feeling" that Yeats claimed where his real goal in writing it, make it easy to see *The Countess Cathleen* as a failure. The more intense poetry and more accomplished drama of his later plays also contributed to a critical focus on the play's flaws, as did Yeats's own judgment.

Such dismissals obscure the play's thematic strengths: the patterned exposition of conflicts between private and public roles, between responsibility to the real world and fulfillment of the dream, between the motive and the deed. Yeats sought to portray this metaphysical conflict in the person of Cathleen and conceded that, insofar as she undergoes no dramatic transformation, the play does not succeed. The internal conflict is over almost before it begins. Cathleen vows in the second scene to place others' joys and sorrows before her own, and never thereafter appears seriously tempted to renege on the vow.

Even the play's detractors grant that its strength is lyric rather than dramatic. Linguistic expression, not plot and characterization, is what is most impressive and original about the play. In some versions, the play was subtitled "A Mystery Play," suggesting another way to read it. Placing its story of sacrifice and redemption in the context of medieval religious mysteries shifts the emphasis from drama of character to the contrasts between the allegorical figures of the play. Each major figure occupies a different position in the debate between the demands of public and private life, highlighting different aspects of Cathleen's choices. Aleel, the poet, urges Cathleen to embrace his dream of love, and thus to transfer (but not abandon) her public responsibility to the peasantry to others. He fails to tempt Cathleen with his songs of fairyland, but his poetic vision enables him to see her final assumption into heaven, confirming her choice and his visionary perspective. Mary Rua, the peasant's wife, holds to orthodox theology; she will have no dealings with devils, and so saves her soul even as her body dies. A countess, unlike a peasant, has a public as well as a private responsibility, so Cathleen's choice must be to compromise with evil in the interests of a greater good. Her compromise represents the triumph of public responsibility over personal satisfaction. It is a subtle reading of the relationship between good and evil.

Yeats's play can be seen as an allegory cataloging the forms of response to worldly concerns. Cathleen's willingness to sacrifice herself in the interest of her peasants contrasts to the selfish desperation of the peasants who sell their souls, to the distant refusal of Aleel to abandon hopeless love, and to the stern refusal to compromise of Mary Rua, none of which prove useful in relieving suffering. Despite the objections of dogmatists, the play presents a fairly orthodox response to the problem of evil, a response from which Yeats would move away as his artistic vision developed.

A. Waller Hastings

Bibliography:
Lucas, F. L. *The Drama of Chekhov, Synge, Yeats, and Pirandello.* London: Cassell, 1963. Places *The Countess Cathleen* in the context of European drama. Finds the play wanting.
Nathan, Leonard E. *The Tragic Drama of William Butler Yeats: Figures in a Dance.* New York: Columbia University Press, 1965. Examines Yeats's failure to realize completely his goal of a metaphysical drama about the conflict between the natural and supernatural worlds.

O'Connor, Ulick. *All the Olympians: A Biographical Portrait of the Irish Literary Renaissance.* New York: Atheneum, 1984. The chapter on *The Countess Cathleen* provides unusual detail about the play's first Dublin production in 1899 and its hostile reception by some segments of the Irish public.

Rajan, Balachandra. *W. B. Yeats: A Critical Introduction.* London: Hutchinson University Library, 1965. Includes a good, brief account of the play's failure to achieve Yeats's vision and places the work in the context of his later successes, arguing that these successes unfairly color critical vision of *The Countess Cathleen.*

Ure, Peter. "The Evolution of Yeats's *The Countess Cathleen.*" *Modern Language Review* 57, no. 1 (January, 1962): 12-24. Traces Yeats's development of the conflict between dreams and responsibility through several stages of revision.

A COUNTRY DOCTOR

Type of work: Novel
Author: Sarah Orne Jewett (1849-1909)
Type of plot: Bildungsroman
Time of plot: Mid-nineteenth century
Locale: Oldfields, Maine
First published: 1884

> *Principal characters:*
> NAN PRINCE, a student of medicine
> MRS. THACHER, her grandmother
> DR. LESLIE, her guardian
> MISS NANCY PRINCE, her aunt

The Story:

One cold winter night while Mrs. Thacher and two of her neighbors were sitting around the stove and gossiping about neighborhood activities, they were interrupted by a noise at the door. Adeline Thacher Prince had fallen on the doorstep. In her arms she held her infant daughter, Nan. Dr. Leslie was sent for at once, but by the next day, Adeline was dead. According to her wishes, Dr. Leslie became the little child's guardian, though she lived with her maternal grandmother.

Nan's mother had left home to go to work in a textile mill in Lowell. There she had fallen in love with a young man from Dunport, Maine, and after a short courtship, she had married him. The marriage had been far from happy. Adeline had inherited a wild, rebellious tendency, and it was whispered in Dunport that she had eventually started to drink. Furthermore, Adeline resented the strong opposition of her husband's family to the marriage, and, in particular, the views of her husband's sister, Miss Nancy Prince. After Adeline's husband died, she tried for a time to support both herself and the child. When she could do so no longer, she trudged back to Oldfields to die in her mother's home.

Nan seemed to exhibit some of her mother's traits, for she was mischievous and inclined to pleasure. Her grandmother often thought her a trial, but to Dr. Leslie she was something quite different. One day, Nan retrieved a fallen bird with a fractured leg and applied a splint, as she had seen Dr. Leslie do to his patients. The doctor began to wonder if Nan had not inherited some tendency toward medicine from her father. He did not insist that she go to school. He thought that the training she received in the woods and the fields was far more beneficial than any she would obtain in the schoolroom.

When Mrs. Thacher died, Nan went to live with Dr. Leslie. There was a great feeling of affection between the two. Nan, who continued to go out on calls with the doctor, exhibited much interest in his work. The time came at last for her to be sent to boarding school. At first, she was shy and rather backward in her studies, but after a while, she made admirable progress. She would have been completely satisfied with her life if she had not wondered, from time to time, about the mysterious aunt of whom she had heard only rumors. Mrs. Thacher had never explained anything of the girl's family background to her, and Nan had conjured up the figure of a wealthy aristocratic relative who would one day send for her. Miss Prince, who had inherited a large estate, regularly sent money to Dr. Leslie to help provide for Nan's upkeep.

The doctor never touched a penny of it. When Adeline had died, Miss Prince had asked for custody of the child, but Mrs. Thacher and Dr. Leslie had refused her request.

When Nan grew older, she told Dr. Leslie of her desire to study medicine. Although the doctor was aware of the difficulties she would face, he approved heartily of her interest. Yet, the town of Oldfields did not, and many were shocked at the idea of a woman doctor. Nan continued her studies using the doctor's books, however, and acted as his nurse. She was to continue training at a medical school in a nearby city.

When the time came for her to leave Oldfields, Nan wrote a brief note to her aunt, Miss Prince, and asked if she might visit her father's sister. Miss Prince, although she feared that Nan might be like her mother, consented to receive her niece. On Nan's arrival in Dunport, Miss Prince, genuinely pleased with her, helped Nan to make friends and openly acknowledged her young relative. Yet, when Nan expressed her wish to study medicine, everyone was shocked, even Miss Prince, who in a large measure blamed Dr. Leslie for Nan's unladylike desire for a professional career. Nan, although made unhappy by her aunt's objections, remained adamant.

Her aunt and her friends, however, sought to lead her astray from her work. Miss Prince had a favorite friend, young George Gerry, to whom she intended leaving her money. When Nan grew fond of George, everyone hoped that they would marry. One day, during an outing, Nan and George stopped at a farmhouse, and Nan treated a farmer who had thrown his arm out of joint. Sometime later, George asked Nan to marry him. She refused, both because she wanted to become a doctor and because she was afraid that her inherited characteristics might cause her to be a bad wife.

At last, she told her aunt that she would have to return to Oldfields. On her arrival, the doctor, who had been apprehensive that Nan might have been influenced by Miss Prince and her money, was pleasantly surprised. She was the same Nan she had been before, and all the more ambitious for a successful medical career.

Nan went away to study. When she returned, Dr. Leslie was older and needed more help in his practice. Nan settled down in Oldfields and slowly the community accepted her. Before many years passed, she had succeeded Dr. Leslie in the affections of the men and women of the village.

Critical Evaluation:

Sarah Orne Jewett uses the conventional novel pattern of the development of a young person to explore why a nineteenth century woman may choose not to follow a traditional path. The book further argues that a woman should be encouraged in an alternative path if her inclinations and talents lead her toward a career rather than a home life. Jewett subsumes a courtship plot into the novel of development and portrays the heroine's rejection of marriage as an important step in her growing up. In *A Country Doctor*, an independent career rather than a dependent marriage is the final goal.

The primary plot of the novel is Nan Prince's development, and Jewett intertwines exposition with event to demonstrate how a woman might grow into a vocation instead of into marriage. Nan's guardian and mentor Dr. Leslie makes her a test case with which to try out his theory that a child, like a plant, should be allowed to grow naturally rather than to be clipped, tied, and trained according to predetermined notions. Nan discovers her vocation rather than having Dr. Leslie or society choose it for her. The novel suggests that some combination of inheritance, environment, and the will of God makes people what they are. From her father, Nan inherits a talent for medicine and a determination to pursue goals. From her mother she inherits a wild streak that, the novel suggests, is better channeled into a career than into domestic life. Nan has no inclination toward domestic pursuits nor romantic love, and so comes to believe that she should fulfill what she believes to be her God-given life purpose of practicing medicine.

After she decides to become a doctor, Nan confronts a series of hurdles that threaten to deter her, and when she has successfully cleared each one, she has proven she deserves the glorious future she thanks God for in the novel's final lines. Nan is first discouraged by people who persistently trivialize her goals. Many refuse to take her aspiration seriously, assuming that she will grow out of her fancy for working or that she will fall in love and give it up. She successfully maintains her own conviction, however, that her vocation is medicine and not marriage. When she goes to Dunport for an extended visit with her wealthy Aunt Nancy, whom she has never seen before, she faces additional hurdles. She could become her aunt's heiress if she stayed in Dunport, and not be obliged to work for a living at all. Mrs. Fraley, a friend of her aunt and a force to be reckoned with in Dunport society, invites Nan to tea in order to denounce her desire to be a doctor. Rather than buckle under the pressure, Nan politely but assertively defends her choices. The toughest obstacle of all, however, comes from within Nan. She surprises herself by falling in love with George Gerry, Aunt Nancy's young protégé. The courtship scenes are subsumed into the novel's overall purpose of tracing Nan's growth toward a career. Her knowledge of herself is strong and she knows she could not give herself entirely to George and to marriage. She knows her marriage would eventually prove to be unhappy, and she knows she would regret turning aside from her life's purpose, so she rejects George's marriage offer and her aunt's insistence that she make Dunport her home. Having successfully overcome these challenges and proven herself true to her convictions, Nan returns to her childhood home, Oldfields, to take up her study of medicine and to begin to establish a practice.

Jewett attempts to present Nan's rebellion against conventional roles for women as nonthreatening. The novel stresses several times that many women can and should find fulfillment in marriage and homemaking, and that a married woman should devote herself to her husband and home. Nan professes to regard marriage highly; that is one reason she rejects it for herself. Jewett never hints that Nan might both marry and practice medicine. The heroine must choose between those paths. Jewett's handling of the courtship between Nan and George unsettles the cultural dictate in favor of marriage nevertheless. In the key scene in which Nan, out on a pleasure trip with George, confidently and successfully adjusts a separated shoulder for a suffering farmer, Jewett shows that a woman can have power to command men. The farmer and George obey Nan's directions because she offers them with such confidence, and while the farmer is astonished and grateful at the outcome, George is disturbed. He cannot conceive of a relationship with a woman in which she has superior command, and he begins to conceive of his courtship of Nan as a battle in which he is endeavoring to master her, to persuade her to give up her silly idea of becoming a woman doctor. When he has been defeated, he is forced to recognize his inferiority to Nan, a self-awareness that Jewett suggests will inspire him to work harder toward his own goals. The novel claims on one hand to hold marriage sacred; it also reveals on the other that a woman might prove herself independent of romantic love, stronger than men, and fully satisfied with a career.

Jewett is frequently praised for her precise rendition of New England scenes, characters, and language, but the relevance of her work to American literature and culture goes beyond its successful representation of isolated rural communities. *A Country Doctor* argues that human nature is the same everywhere, and that life may be observed and lived to its fullest in a small New England town as well as anywhere else. When Jewett presents this study of how one young woman found her vocation and proved herself worthy of it, she implies that the lessons learned by Nan are relevant beyond the confines of nineteenth century New England. She shows how an individual may be influenced by her environment and biological heritage and yet exert her free will to choose her own path in life.

"Critical Evaluation" by Karen Tracey

Bibliography:
Blanchard, Paula. *Sarah Orne Jewett: Her World and Her Work.* Reading, Mass.: Addison-Wesley, 1994. Discusses *A Country Doctor* as an autobiographical novel. Dr. Leslie resembles Jewett's physician father, and Nan's decision to pursue vocation over marriage is drawn from Jewett's personal experience.
Donovan, Josephine. *Sarah Orne Jewett.* New York: Frederick Ungar, 1980. Analyzes her fictional themes of city versus country and isolation versus community.
Nagel, Gwen L., ed. *Critical Essays on Sarah Orne Jewett.* Boston: G. K. Hall, 1984. Reprints early reviews and contains original critical essays on her works, several of which discuss *A Country Doctor*'s relation to Jewett's other fiction.
Roman, Margaret. *Sarah Orne Jewett: Reconstructing Gender.* Tuscaloosa: University of Alabama Press, 1992. Argues that Jewett creates male and female characters who do not conform to conventions in order to challenge accepted notions about the sexes and to project a world in which any person may live and grow freely.
Westbrook, Perry D. *Acres of Flint: Sarah Orne Jewett and Her Contemporaries.* Rev. ed. Metuchen, N.J.: The Scarecrow Press, 1981. Shows how Jewett's work relates to the local-color literary tradition developed by New England women writers after the Civil War.

THE COUNTRY OF THE POINTED FIRS

Type of work: Novella
Author: Sarah Orne Jewett (1849-1909)
Type of plot: Social realism
Time of plot: Late nineteenth century
Locale: Maine seacoast
First published: 1896

Principal characters:
THE NARRATOR, a woman writer who is no longer young
ALMIRA TODD, an herbalist
MRS. BLACKETT, her mother
WILLIAM BLACKETT, Almira's younger brother, a fisherman and farmer

The Story:

The narrator, a woman writer, came to Dunnet Landing one summer to escape a too busy life in Boston. In this Maine coastal town, which had impressed her on an earlier visit, she hoped to find a quiet haven in which to complete a long-delayed, important piece of writing. She stayed with Mrs. Almira Todd, a widowed herbalist who turned out to be a central person in the village. Almira was a kind of partner both to the doctor and the minister in dealing with physical and emotional ills, especially of the women and children of Dunnet Landing. Almost without realizing it, the narrator found herself drawn into helping Almira with her work. While Almira gathered herbs in the countryside, the narrator sold remedies and spruce beer at Almira's house on the edge of the village.

When she realized she was getting little writing done, the narrator resigned her informal sales position and rented the schoolhouse just outside the village as a hermitage for writing during the day. Instead of causing a break between the narrator and Almira, this change brought them closer together. During the early summer evenings, Almira gradually told the narrator the story of her life, including the fact that she and the man she loved most had been prevented by his family from marrying.

In the course of the summer, and with help from Almira, the writer gradually came to know and treasure the people of Dunnet Landing and to appreciate the richness of lives and characters that had at first seemed isolated, insular, and reticent. The aged recluse Captain Littlepage came to her at the schoolhouse, eager to confide in someone seemingly like himself. He told her the story of his shipwreck in the northern polar regions and of an account he had come to believe of a mysterious island near the North Pole, the waiting place for dead souls before they move on to the next world. The narrator proved adept at persuading him to converse comfortably, even though she was skeptical of his story and a little impatient at the interruption.

The narrator grew increasingly interested in the people of the region and came to look forward to meeting and befriending more of them. She met Almira's brother, William Blackett, and their mother, Mrs. Blackett, when Almira took her to Green Island for a visit.

William was a fisherman and farmer who sold bait and raised sheep. Almira was critical of him, thinking that he had made too little of his opportunities. He seemed shy and reserved, but the narrator met him while he was digging potatoes for their dinner, and they quickly became friends. Soon after they met, he showed her his favorite view of the island. In the afternoon, Almira took the narrator to her favorite place, where the best pennyroyal grew, and confided more about her relationship with her husband, Nathan, and his early death. She thought him the best of husbands and was sorry to lose him so soon but was consoled that he had died before discovering that she loved another more than him.

Before leaving the island, the narrator learned that Mrs. Blackett had a golden gift for making friends that few people possess, "so that they make a part of one's own life that can never be forgotten." In one brief visit, the narrator formed a deep and lasting friendship with Mrs. Blackett. They communicated intimately and silently when Mrs. Blackett showed the narrator her favorite place, the view from her rocking chair.

Soon after the visit to Green Island, Susan Fosdick, a childhood friend who lived to circulate news, came to stay with Almira. It became clear that the two guests would get along well, and the conversation became intimate, finally turning to the story of Joanna Todd, Almira's cousin by marriage. "Poor Joanna" came to believe that God would never forgive her for having blamed him when her fiancé deserted her. She isolated herself from the community on Shell-heap Island, a place that was difficult to reach, but the community continued to watch over her. The narrator saw an image of herself in Joanna's chosen isolation. Not long after hearing the story, the narrator visited Joanna's grave on the island.

The high point of the summer was the reunion of the Bowden family, of which Mrs. Blackett was the matriarch. Almira, the narrator, and Mrs. Blackett drove a wagon to the reunion, making short visits at several houses along the way. The reunion brought together many members of the family who saw one another no more than once a year, allowing them a short time to express their affection and concern for one another. The reunion included a grand march of the families across a field and into a grove, where they enjoyed a great outdoor feast and a few ceremonies. The narrator had succeeded so well during the summer in becoming a part of the community that she was made an honorary Bowden by Almira and Mrs. Blackett. The narrator felt not only that she had become a member of a new family, but that this family represented all of history's families. As the summer drew to a close, the narrator got to know another of the reticent old sea captains, Elijah Tilley. Having learned how to relate to these people, the narrator was more at ease with him than with Captain Littlepage as she drew out the story of his persisting grief for his long-dead wife.

When it was time for the narrator to return to the city, Almira's feelings were so strong that she could not bear to prolong her farewell. She left the narrator parting gifts to show those feelings. Among the gifts was the coral pin that Almira's husband had brought home for his cousin Joanna, who had refused to accept it. Steaming away from Dunnet Landing, the narrator reflected on the rich life of the village as she looked back with love.

Critical Evaluation:

When *The Country of the Pointed Firs* was published, Sarah Orne Jewett's friend Rudyard Kipling said, "I maintain (and will maintain with outcries if necessary) that that is the reallest New England book ever given us." Willa Cather wrote in 1925 that this book, along with Nathaniel Hawthorne's *The Scarlet Letter* (1850) and Mark Twain's *Adventures of Huckleberry Finn* (1884), would stand up to the tests of time.

Jewett wrote four short sequels to this novella: "The Queen's Twin" (1899); "A Dunnet Shepherdess" (1899), in which she introduces William's fiancée, Esther Hight; "The Foreigner" (1900); and "William's Wedding" (1910). In all of these stories, as in the novella, one of Jewett's main themes is the centrality of friendship to a meaningful life. The narrator goes to Dunnet Landing to isolate herself in order to write. She finds that isolation is not really what she needs, although she does need to escape what she characterizes in "William's Wedding" as "the hurry of life in a large town, the constant putting aside of preference to yield to a most unsatisfactory activity." The narrator discovers that what she really needs is to cultivate friendships, to be let into the confidence of the people of Dunnet Landing, and to learn to know them. She is somewhat reluctant at first and a little impatient to get on with her work, but as she gets to know the often eccentric but delightful people such as Captain Littlepage, the Blacketts, and Susan Fosdick, she comes to value the treasures in this rich, if sparsely populated, mine of life. Each new acquaintance challenges her in some way to extend and perfect her skills of conversation. By the end of the summer, she has new friends, a new family, and a new home. Her skills of friendship have been honed to a fine edge, so that she can listen with sympathy and warmth to the somewhat ridiculous but touching devotion of Captain Tilley for his dead wife. She has learned to open herself to the epiphany of a sudden revelation of spiritual beauty in another and to the communion of sharing such revelations.

Jewett adopted an unusual form for her novella, which gives it the appearance of a collection of superficially related sketches. The narrator's discovery of the richness of the community, her cultivation of friendships, and her development of the skills of conversation give strong thematic unity to these sketches. There is also strong structural unity provided by the gradual integration of the narrator into the community, as well as by the narrator's growth in understanding and appreciation: Chapter 1 brings her to Dunnet Landing; chapters 2-6 show her somewhat reluctantly drawn into intimacy with Almira and earning her trust; chapters 7-11 show her integration into Almira's immediate family; chapters 12-15 develop the contrasting example of Joanna, who left community behind permanently; chapters 15-19 reveal the unity of Almira's immediate family with the larger Bowden family, and that of the Bowden family with all families throughout human history; chapter 20 provides balance and contrast for the narrator's encounter with Captain Littlepage (this time she eagerly and easily pursues the intimacy Captain Tilley offers); and the final chapter takes her away from Dunnet Landing. This organization results in a subtle plot that may seem static to some readers but that inspired later writers to similar experiments. Several major works of twentieth century fiction—among them William Faulkner's *Go Down, Moses* (1942) and Eudora Welty's *The Golden Apples* (1949)— are structurally indebted to Jewett's novella. In the century following its publication, Cather's prophecy proved true. Recognition of the stature of *The Country of the Pointed Firs* increased and the work received more sophisticated attention in scholarship, literary criticism, and literature classrooms.

"Critical Evaluation" by Terry Heller

Bibliography:
Blanchard, Paula. *Sarah Orne Jewett: Her World and Her Work*. Reading, Mass.: Addison-Wesley, 1994. In this literary biography, Blanchard devotes one chapter to discussing the novella in the context of Jewett's life and other works. Also provides photographs, relevant background and biographical information, and a bibliography.
Donovan, Josephine. *Sarah Orne Jewett*. New York: Frederick Ungar, 1980. Includes a biographical sketch followed by a discussion of Jewett's artistic principles and main themes. One chapter discusses the novella as a realization of Jewett's themes and purposes. Also includes bibliography.
Nagel, Gwen L., ed. *Critical Essays on Sarah Orne Jewett*. Boston: G. K. Hall, 1984. The introduction to this collection summarizes critical response to all of Jewett's works. Contains contemporary reviews and several more recent critical essays on the novella and the other Dunnet Landing stories.

Roman, Margaret. *Sarah Orne Jewett: Reconstructing Gender*. Tuscaloosa: University of Alabama Press, 1992. Examines the attitudes toward gender in Jewett's fiction. One chapter shows how the novella reflects Jewett's mature ideas about gender identity. Includes bibliography.

Sherman, Sarah Way. *Sarah Orne Jewett: An American Persephone*. Hanover, N.H.: University Press of New England, 1989. Explores the extensive development and use of the myth of Persephone by Jewett and her contemporary writers. Much of the second half of the book shows how Jewett uses the myth in the novella. Includes bibliography.

THE COUNTRY WIFE

Type of work: Drama
Author: William Wycherley (1641?-1715)
Type of plot: Comedy
Time of plot: Seventeenth century
Locale: London
First performed: 1675; first published, 1675

> *Principal characters:*
> MR. HORNER, a gallant alleged to be impotent
> MR. PINCHWIFE, a jealous husband
> MRS. PINCHWIFE, his dissatisfied wife
> ALITHEA, Mr. Pinchwife's sister, a society woman
> HARCOURT, a gallant in love with Alithea

The Story:

Mr. Horner, a gallant with a bad reputation for seduction, pretended that he had been made impotent through disease and caused word of his misfortune to be spread throughout the town by his quack doctor. Immediately, men who had been afraid to let him meet their wives for fear of seduction hastened to assure him that he could come to their homes and escort their women anywhere. Horner's old companions among the town gallants teased him unmercifully and at first the women would have nothing to do with him. Among his friends was Jack Pinchwife, who was vastly afraid of being made a cuckold. He had not even let it be known that he was married. His wife was a woman from the country; she, he thought, did not know enough about fashionable city life to think of taking a lover.

Pinchwife made the mistake, however, of escorting his wife to a play, where she was seen by Horner and some of his friends. When Pinchwife returned to his lodgings, his wife, tired of being kept locked in the house, asked her husband to let her go walking. A relative, a woman from the town, spoke for her as well. Pinchwife became angry with both: at his wife for wanting to go out and at his relative who had, he claimed, been corrupting her morals. Pinchwife foolishly told his wife what she was missing in town life—plays, dinners, parties, and dances— and so aroused her interest in all that he was attempting to keep from her for the sake of his honor.

When a party of women came to take his wife to the latest play, Pinchwife refused to let her go or even to see the visitors. He gave out the excuse that she had smallpox. The excuse failed. At the same time Horner and some other gallants came to call.

The women were urged by their husbands to let Horner take them to the theater, but they, in disgust, refused, until Horner himself whispered to one of them that the rumor spread about his impotency was untrue. Mrs. Pinchwife was forgotten and left behind.

After some time Mrs. Pinchwife became melancholy because she wished to enjoy the gaiety her husband told her about but refused to let her see. At last Pinchwife agreed to take her to a play if she would dress as a man. On the way to the play, accompanied by Pinchwife's sister Alithea, they met the sister's fiancé, a simpleton who let his friend, Harcourt, pay court to Alithea. She, realizing that her fiancé was a fool, tried to treat Harcourt coolly, even though her fiancé was angry with her for doing so.

Before they arrived at the theater they met Horner. Pinchwife, in spite of all he had heard about Horner's impotence, was worried lest Horner discover Mrs. Pinchwife's disguise. Horner, recognizing Mrs. Pinchwife, teased the jealous husband by kissing the young "gentleman" and telling "him" the kiss was for his sister, Mrs. Pinchwife. Horner, in addition, told the "young man" that he was in love with Mrs. Pinchwife.

The following morning Alithea was dressed to marry her fiancé. The bridegroom came with a parson, actually Harcourt in disguise. Harcourt was still determined to take Alithea for his own, if he could. After some discussion, the marriage was put off for a day.

Meanwhile, Pinchwife tried to force his wife to send a letter calculated to discourage Horner's attentions, but she substituted a love letter for the one her husband had dictated. After taking the letter, Pinchwife locked her in her room and told her to stay away from the window.

In his own rooms, Horner held a discussion with his quack doctor and told him how well his scheme to fool husbands was working. In proof, a well-bred woman came to his rooms, but the opportunity was lost when her husband followed her. A few moments later two other women arrived, much chagrined when they found Horner entertaining other visitors. Pinchwife, knowing nothing of the substitution, delivered the letter. Upon his return home he found his wife writing another love letter to Horner. Angered, he drew his sword, but he was interrupted by the entrance of Alithea's fiancé.

Mrs. Pinchwife lied her way out of the situation by saying she was writing the letter for Alithea, who, she said, was in love with Horner. Pinchwife, knowing that Horner was of as good family and as wealthy as his sister's fiancé, thought that by marrying Alithea to Horner he could keep his wife away from the rake. When he agreed to take Alithea to Horner, his wife disguised herself in Alithea's clothing and presented herself as Alithea to be taken to Horner's lodgings.

Pinchwife unsuspectingly took his wife to Horner and left to get a clergyman to marry the couple. On the way he met his sister's fiancé, who was puzzled by Pinchwife's tale. When they met the real Alithea, all were confused. Shortly after Pinchwife had gone, three women appeared at Horner's lodgings. During the visit all three discovered that Horner had enjoyed their favors, while they each thought he was hers alone. After they left, Horner got rid of Mrs. Pinchwife after some trouble; she wanted to leave her husband and live with Horner.

Pinchwife, Alithea, Harcourt, and the fiancé all arrived to clear up the mystery of the disguised Alithea. The men accused Horner of double-dealing, and Pinchwife threatened the gallant with his sword. Mrs. Pinchwife, who had been loitering nearby, entered the room. To save the honor of all concerned, Alithea's maidservant took the blame for lying. The doctor came in unexpectedly and testified again to the impotency of Horner. His report put all husbands at their ease again. Only Mrs. Pinchwife, who had been unable to leave her husband or to have Horner's favors, was out of sorts.

Critical Evaluation:
This play is the epitome of the spirit of the reign of Charles II. The plot is presented with Restoration boldness, depending as it does on the supposition of Horner's impotence and his amorous adventures with various wives who have been gulled into believing that he is incapable of feelings for the opposite sex. While the main device of the play is frankly indecent, the handling of the theme, particularly in the dialogue, is brilliant. Clever dialogue and the whimsicality of Mrs. Pinchwife's naïveté save the drama from approaching pornography and raise the play to the realm of art. As a result of the play's deftness, readers usually find themselves laughing, along with the characters, at the duplicity of the women and their lover.

William Wycherley's comedies were his contribution to English dramatic literature and in one of them, *The Country Wife*, the Restoration comedy reached its height. Wycherley's first play, *Love in a Wood*, was performed in the spring of 1671 and occasioned the start of a relationship between Wycherley and the Duchess of Cleveland, who was mistress to the king. Wycherley was, as a result, brought into the court circle and into the favor of the king. *The Gentleman Dancing Master*, his second play, apparently opened at Dorset Garden in the fall of 1672. It was not well received by the Restoration audience, perhaps because of its simplicity and lack of vulgarity. *The Plain-Dealer*, first produced in December, 1676, has the distinction of being Wycherley's last play, his most morally ambiguous, and thus the most discussed of the Restoration comedies, with the exception perhaps of William Congreve's *The Way of the World* (1700). It is from a character in this play that Wycherley received his nickname of "Manly" from John Dryden.

Wycherley's third play, *The Country Wife*, is considered by most critics to be the best of the Restoration comedies. *The Country Wife* was apparently first produced by the King's Company at the Theatre Royal in Drury Lane on January 12, 1675, and was obviously well received by the audiences of the time, for it immediately became a part of the repertory at the Theatre Royal. Its popularity is still apparent in the fact that it is one of the most often revived of the comedies from its period.

The ethos of the Restoration period presumably had its effect on *The Country Wife*. The theater was being promoted by a libertine, Charles II, who surrounded himself with an equally profligate court. Many aristocrats of the period viewed humanity as depraved and affected a contempt for morality, especially in the form of Puritanism or Republicanism. The bawdiness of *The Country Wife* seems suited to the temper of its times.

The licentious nature of the play, however, brought it criticism during the Restoration, though perhaps it was that some people did not like their mirrored image. As Richard Steele wrote of Horner in *The Tatler* of April 16, 1709, after seeing a production on April 14: He "is a good representation of the age in which that comedy was written; at which time, love and wenching were the business of life, and the gallant manner of pursuing women was the best recommendation at court." Steele also criticized Pinchwife, but again as a representative of the age, "one of those debauchees who run through the vices of the town and believe when they think fit, they can marry and settle at their ease." Steele in his criticism was contributing to the general criticism of the theater that occurred from about 1695 to 1745 and had reached a high point in 1698 with Jeremy Collier's *A Short View of the Immorality and Profaneness of the English Stage*. Collier, unlike Steele, was not generous to Wycherley or his characters, calling Horner "horridly Smutty" and accusing Mrs. Pinchwife, Horner, and Lady Fidget of a "Rankness and Indecency of their Language." Criticism of the play continued into the Victorian period, when perhaps it met its strongest criticism under the pen of Thomas Babington Macaulay in an 1841 essay "The Comic Dramatists of the Restoration." He said of Wycherley's comedies: "In truth Wycherley's indecency is protected against the critic as a skunk is protected against the hunters. It is safe because it is too filthy to handle and too noisome to approach." Despite the adverse criticism of the play, it was following, perhaps more strongly than some, the satiric method employed by Restoration comedy, which was to present on the stage characterizations that were true to life—some of them to be emulated and some of them to be avoided. The use of laughter in *The Country Wife* closely follows Thomas Hobbes's observation that people laugh because they suddenly recognize their superiority to others. As Hobbes says, "Sudden glory is the passion which maketh those grimaces called laughter; and is caused either by some sudden act of their own that pleaseth them, or by the apprehension of some deformed thing in another, by comparison whereof they suddenly applaud themselves." The fact that Wycherley chose to follow these examples is reinforced by his epigraph to *The Gentleman Dancing Master*, in which he acknowledges that a great comedy does not merely make the audience laugh; it should say something.

What Wycherley has to say in *The Country Wife* concerns the lack of deep feeling and selfish motives that permeated the sexual morality of his time. Women are not sought after as wives, or even concubines, but rather as mere strumpets. Once the man's sexual desires have been gratified, he will go out looking for another encounter. To make his play instructive as well as illustrative, Wycherley conceived three intrigues in his plot—involving Pinchwife, Horner, and Harcourt—that allow the reader to make a value judgment about how well a character is able to drop his pretense and channel his natural desires into constructive results. Thus, Pinchwife exhibits the least desirably imitative character; despite his selfishly motivated, zealous guarding of his wife, Margery, he is cuckolded. Horner, though admirable in wit and clear in an understanding of himself and others, never drops the role of eunuch and its fringe benefits and thus remains a slave to lust and what he terms the "greatest Monster" in nature—affectation. Harcourt becomes the most admirable as a "rake converted" who is able to translate his desires into true love and respect for the woman Alithea and, at play's end, intends to be a husband to her.

In his concern with the three intrigues of *The Country Wife*, Wycherley introduces a wide variety of Restoration comedy types. There is the jealous man whose jealousy is reproved, the hypocritical ladies of refinement who wish to protect their honor yet are proved lustful wenches, the trusting man whose trust is proved foolish, the rakes whose sole desire is satiating themselves in pleasure, and the fashionable narcissistic Restoration fop. Within this gallery, Horner is perhaps the central character despite the fact that he does not, as previously mentioned, face a totally happy end. In Horner's character Wycherley presents aspects to be applauded and condemned. His name suggests what he is—a cuckold maker who gains great satisfaction by awarding horns to betrayed husbands. Wycherley's idea for Horner's trick came from *Eunuchus* by the Roman playwright Terence. In the play, a young man pretends to be a eunuch so that he can be admitted freely into the company of a young girl. However, unlike Terence's character, Horner does not rape; he uses his disguise only to gain access to willing partners. In this pursuit he is a villain of sorts. Yet in his villainy—cuckolding of husbands and bedding of mistresses—he is to be commended, for he proves that the selfish nature of the foolish men is deplorable, and that the honor of the virtuous ladies is hypocritical. He is also to be pitied, however, because he never rises above base desire. As Horner expresses it, "Ceremony in love is as ridiculous as in fighting; falling on briskly is all should be done on such occasions."

In *The Country Wife* the women characters and their social behavior also meet with varying degrees of censure and praise. With Lady Fidget, Margery Pinchwife, and Alithea, Wycherley presents the differing levels of feminine conduct as he saw them in the Restoration period. These levels ranged from those lustful women who were equal to the men in their desires, to those women of true virtue who sought a love based on more than sexual gratification. Although there are other women of "honor" in the play—Mrs. Dainty Fidget and Mrs. Squeamish—Lady Fidget is the most verbal and active and thus more self-incriminating. In her lustful behavior she is little different from a strumpet except for her hypocrisy, which perhaps makes her more damnable. For instance, at the moment she is about to give herself to Horner her train of thought runs thus: "You must have a great care of your conduct; for my acquaintances are so censorious . . . and detracting, that perhaps they'll talk to the prejudice of my Honour, though you should not let them know the dear secret." So that his dislike of such hypocrisy is made absolutely clear, by the end of the play Wycherley has had Horner partaking of pleasure with all the ladies of virtue. Contrasting Lady Fidget is Margery Pinchwife, lustful but honest about her lust. As Horner says about the love letter she writes him, " 'Tis the first love letter that ever was without flames, darts, fates, destinies, lying and dissembling in it." She is perhaps more admirable for her honesty, yet at the end of the play she is taught to lie by the "virtuous" set. The final female character of note, Alithea, is virtuous in all aspects and is heading for a commendable marriage based on a true love and would seem to be, as the opposite of Lady Fidget, the character for emulation.

One of the comic devices used adeptly by Wycherley in *The Country Wife* is the double entendre. This was the apparatus to which Collier took such offense, writing that "when the Sentence has two Handles, the worst is generally turn'd to the Audience. The matter is so contrived that the Smut and Scum of the Thought now rises uppermost; And, like a Picture drawn to *Sight*, looks always upon the Company." Indeed, Wycherley's double entendres are as powerful as Collier describes them (although one may not react to them in the same manner that Collier did), and in Act IV, scene iii—the "china scene"—Wycherley is at his best.

The importance of *The Country Wife* lies in the fact that it signals the height, and therefore the beginning of the fall, of Restoration comedy. With its adept social satire, telling visions of selfishness and hypocrisy, and the seldom surpassed farcical china scene, *The Country Wife* stands at the pinnacle of Restoration comedy. However, within the representation of the apparently romantic love of Alithea and Harcourt was the seed of what was to grow within the comedy of that period until it destroyed it. This representation of the ideal in a realistic setting was the chief characteristic of the comedy to come—sentimental or "weeping comedy."

"Critical Evaluation" by Phyllis E. Allran

Bibliography:
Harwood, John T. *Critics, Values, and Restoration Comedy.* Carbondale: Southern Illinois University Press, 1982. Provides a lucid account of the play in its context of the history and conventions of Restoration drama.
Holland, Norman N. *The First Modern Comedies: The Significance of Etherege, Wycherley and Congreve.* Cambridge, Mass.: Harvard University Press, 1959. Perhaps the most influential account of the play. Takes the Harcourt-Alithea relationship as the moral standard by which the actions of the others are measured.
Marshall, W. Gerald. *A Great Stage of Fools: Theatricality and Madness in the Plays of William Wycherley.* New York: AMS Press, 1993. The chapter on *The Country Wife* is contentious and not entirely convincing, but deserves consideration for its impressive scholarship and insight, especially into the relationship of Margery and Pinchwife.
Milhous, Judith, and Robert D. Hume. *Producible Interpretation: Eight English Plays, 1675-1707.* Carbondale: Southern Illinois University Press, 1985. Highly recommended for anyone interested in Restoration drama. The chapter on *The Country Wife* provides what is probably the best available introduction to the play and includes a valuable overview of modern critical approaches. A commendatory blend of wit, exemplary scholarship, and common sense.
Zimbardo, Rose. *Wycherley's Drama: A Link in the Development of English Satire.* New Haven, Conn.: Yale University Press, 1965. Argues that *The Country Wife* is foremost a satire, one against "lust that disguises itself." Persuasive.

THE COURTESAN

Type of work: Drama
Author: Pietro Aretino (1492-1556)
Type of plot: Satire
Time of plot: Early sixteenth century
Locale: Rome
First published: La cortigiana, 1534 (English translation, 1926); first performed, 1537

Principal characters:
MESSER MACO, a would-be courtier
MAESTRO ANDREA, a clever charlatan
SIGNOR PARABOLANO, a nobleman
VALERIO, Parabolano's chamberlain
ROSSO, Parabolano's groom, a rogue
ALVIGIA, a procuress
ARCOLANO, a baker
TOGNA, his young wife

The Story:
Messer Maco, a wealthy Sienese fop and a fool, came to Rome with the intention of becoming a cardinal. Upon his arrival he met Maestro Andrea, who informed him that he would first have to become a courtier. Maco thereupon announced his desire to become a courtier, and Andrea obligingly promised to transform him into one.

Signor Parabolano, learning that Maco was in town, ordered his groom, Rosso, to have all the lampreys he could find sent to Maco as a gift of welcome. When Parabolano left, Rosso made fun of his master's love affairs to the other servants. Valerio, Parabolano's faithful chamberlain, overheard him and ran him off. Rosso swindled a fisherman out of his lampreys by posing as a servant of the pope. When discovered, he convinced the authorities that the fisherman was mad.

Maco received his first lesson in being a courtier. He was instructed in being, among other things, a blasphemer, a gambler, an adulator, a slanderer, an ingrate, a whore-chaser, an ass, and a nymph.

Next, Rosso visited Alvigia, a procuress. Rosso, having overheard Parabolano talking in his sleep, had learned that his master was in love with the matron Livia. If, he told Alvigia, he could successfully pander to his master's lust, he would secure his position and could also be revenged on Valerio, Parabolano's chamberlain. Alvigia agreed to help the groom.

Meanwhile, Maco had fallen in love with Camilla, a courtesan who was being kept by a Spanish lord. Andrea feared that this new interest would interrupt his fleecing of Maco, but Maco was now all the more determined to become a courtier. He was impatient about Camilla, however, and disguised himself as a groom to gain access to her house. To hinder him, Andrea and Maco's own groom cried out that the sheriff was after him for illegal entry into Rome. Afraid to appear in his own clothes, Maco ran off, still in his disguise as a servant.

Rosso and Alvigia were having their problems, too. Although Parabolano had agreed to allow Rosso to secure the services of the procuress for him, Livia proved unapproachable. The two then devised the following plan: Rosso was to tell Parabolano that Livia was willing to meet him, but that, being proper and shy, she would do so only in the profoundest dark; he must promise not to embarrass her with any light whatsoever. Once assured that Parabolano would not be able to see his mistress, Alvigia would substitute the baker's young wife, Togna, for the virtuous Livia. Parabolano, his lust now almost consuming him, was willing to agree to any stipulations. He was willing, even, to believe the calumnies of his groom, and he put his chamberlain, Valerio, in disgrace.

Maco, hiding in Parabolano's house from the supposed sheriff, finally mustered enough courage to emerge for the final courtier-making process. He was placed in a vat that, according to Andrea, was a courtier-mold. There he was thoroughly steamed. Once recovered, he headed for Camilla's house as a full-fledged courtier. Andrea and Maco's groom pretended to be Spaniards storming the house. Maco leaped from the window, terrified, and fled in his underwear.

His embarrassment was followed by that of Parabolano. Togna had planned to go to her assignation in her husband's clothes. Suspicious of her design, the old baker feigned drunken sleep while he watched her put on his garments and steal away. He then dressed in her clothes and followed her to the house of the procuress.

Parabolano discovered the ruse once he was alone with Togna. At first he was enraged, but Valerio, embittered and determined to leave Rome and the fickleness of courtiers, arrived in time to calm him down. Admitting that, blinded by lust, he had allowed himself to be led around like a fool, Parabolano restored Valerio to favor and begged his forgiveness. Valerio advised him to admit the whole escapade openly and to treat it as a joke so that, by owning up to his own folly, he would be safe from having his enemies use it against him.

As Parabolano was beginning to see the humor in the situation, the baker Arcolano appeared, dressed in his wife's clothes. He too was enraged, but Parabolano convinced him that he had no designs on his wife. The two, Togna and Arcolano, were forced to kiss and make up. Then, in keeping with the comic ending that Parabolano insisted upon, everyone was forgiven—even the conniving Rosso, once he had returned a diamond that Parabolano had given him to help seduce Livia. He was a Greek, Parabolano observed, and was only acting according to his nature. Finally Maco appeared, seeking help from the "Spaniards." When their true identity was revealed, Maco was shown what a fool he really was. He, in turn, was forced to forgive Andrea.

Critical Evaluation:

By the time of Pietro Aretino, the Italian Renaissance had become overripe. It would be another half-century or more before England's attitudes and culture reached a similar stage of decadence, but the Italians were already experiencing a decline.

With the new concentration upon the world of mortal life, casting aside considerations for the afterlife, it was inevitable that pleasure should come to be regarded as the major purpose of life. Power was important, of course, as Nicolò Machiavelli attested, but, as always, the product of power was pleasure, even if it was only the pleasure of exerting control over one's contemporaries.

Aretino, though he ridicules lechery in this play, was known for his own indulgence in excesses of sensuality. Perhaps that is why he does not excoriate sexual liberties nearly so sharply as he does the inhumanities of court politics. Those who are clever but lacking in wisdom and compassion have always enjoyed clambering over their fellows in their attempts to gain tactical advantage. Aretino seems to have recognized this at an early stage in his life, while discovering also the efficacy of his vituperative pen. The son of a prostitute, he could not rely on kindness or justice from such a world to make his life bearable. It would be difficult to believe that anyone, finding himself living the life of a servant as described by Rosso in Act V, would not seize any available means of moving to a position offering more pleasure and power (as Aretino's writings moved him). Aretino's poison pen is often amusing, sometimes distasteful, occasionally boring, but, given the circumstances, it is always understandable.

Rome, the setting of the play, is as much the butt of Aretino's jokes as is courtly politics. Indeed, Rome and the life at court seem inextricably bound together in the author's mind, perhaps because he was himself nearly murdered once as a result of court intrigues surrounding the papacy. He appears to have adopted Venice instead as his home, lavishing his praise upon that city in Act III, and, at tiresome length, upon some of its citizens. The names of those receiving his encomiums did not simply pop into Aretino's head unbidden; aside from those few, like Titian, who seem to have been his friends, he carefully praises those who can be of use to him. He is often quite forthright about this, at one point even going so far as to cause a character to mention his name and his hopes. The fact that such tactics were immensely successful reminds us that whereas Aretino's life may have had an offensive odor about it, so did his age.

Although he was neither a great dramatist nor a great poet, Aretino displays great ability to mingle several dialects, assigning different ones to different characters and relishing especially those vigorous speech patterns associated with the illiterate and the poor. At times, the delight his characters show in the scatological can be entertaining.

He seems uninterested in, or incapable of, weaving circumstances of credibility into his characters' entrances and exits or into their shifts in conversational subjects. Often characters simply announce that the subject will change. In many instances the author flings personages on stage and then plucks them off again with no rationale other than the exigencies of his plot.

Only once in the play does he reach the heights of bitter wisdom scaled regularly by the Jacobeans, and that is when Maco catechizes Andrea on life:

> MACO: Tell me, how does one come into the world, Maestro?
> ANDREA: Through a cave.
>
> . . . .
>
> Maco: But what happens when a man is through living?
> ANDREA: He dies in a hole as spiders do.

These lines, with their gothic imagery and cynical accuracy, might easily have excited the envy of John Webster.

One recognizes in *The Courtesan* the topsy-turvy world picture painted so often by other Renaissance dramatists and moralists. Servants here, as elsewhere, are insolent and presumptuous with their masters, and their masters are lustful, foolish, and purblind. When Rosso dupes Parabolano, his deceit being exposed only in the last scene, this bears a similarity to the comedies of Ben Jonson, especially to his *Volpone* (1605). Mosca is a much more fully drawn character, wittier and more alive, but there are definite debts owed by Jonson to just such Italian comedies as this one. If there were nothing else in Aretino to attract Jonson's attention, the Italian's acidic wit would most probably have impressed the Englishman as emanating from a kindred spirit.

Rosso's arguement that the way to advancement is through pandering to the lusts of the powerful, has echoes in Cyril Tourneur's *The Revenger's Tragedy* (1606-1607) and in Webster's *The Duchess of Malfi* (1614). Perhaps a more revealing, if less definite, parallel lies in Andrea's tutoring of Maco in the art of being a courtier. The tutor-pupil relationship has great dramatic potential for satire on the subject taught, and Aretino makes use of this potential, as does William Shakespeare in *As You Like It* (c. 1599-1600) when Rosalind, in disguise, instructs

Orlando on the many aspects of love. Admittedly, Rosalind is much less harsh in her criticism of lovers and ladies than is Andrea on courtiers and fops, but Andrea's subject is more deserving of acrimony. In addition, Rosalind is the future beneficiary of her precepts; she is dressing a husband, while Andrea is simply plucking a chicken.

Aretino is noted for his realism, sometimes described as "unpleasant." *The Courtesan* contains many examples of realism, among which are the hawking of "histories" in Act I, the selling of lampreys, and the description of meal-taking in the servants' quarters. It is the last that exemplifies the sort of realism that earned the adjective "unpleasant," but it is worth remembering that few realists have escaped the adjective. Aretino, though inconsistent, is in the main a true realist.

"Critical Evaluation" by John J. Brugaletta

Bibliography:
Chubb, Thomas C. *Aretino: Scourge of Princes*. New York: Reynal & Hitchcock, 1940. Comprehensive, scholarly life study of the courtier and author. Discusses the composition of Aretino's writings, including *The Courtesan*. Stresses the libertine character of Aretino's life and works.
Cleugh, James. *The Divine Aretino*. New York: Stein and Day, 1966. Highly readable biography of the statesman and writer. Comments on Aretino's prose style in *The Courtesan* and other writings, explaining how he used his experience to vivify his creative works.
Hutton, Edward. *Pietro Aretino: The Scourge of Princes*. London: Constable & Co., 1922. Biographical study of the writer, examining the myths surrounding his licentious lifestyle. A separate chapter discusses his writings, citing examples from *The Courtesan* to highlight Aretino's ability to recreate the life he saw around him.
Roeder, Ralph. *The Man of the Renaissance: Four Lawgivers*. New York: Viking, 1933. Excellent summary of the life and accomplishments of this key figure of the late Renaissance. Highlights the popularity of his writings and examines biographical influences.
Symonds, J. A. *Renaissance in Italy*. Vol. 2. New York: Modern Libraries, 1935. A chapter on Aretino sketches his influence on Italian politics and letters and offers detailed commentary on his contemporaries. Especially helpful for gaining an appreciation of the author's style.

THE COURTSHIP OF MILES STANDISH

Type of work: Poetry
Author: Henry Wadsworth Longfellow (1807-1882)
Type of plot: Sentimental
Time of plot: 1621
Locale: Massachusetts
First published: 1858

Principal characters:
MILES STANDISH, a soldier
JOHN ALDEN, Miles Standish's friend
PRISCILLA, a young woman loved by Standish and Alden

The Story:
Miles Standish was a gruff captain of the soldiers, whose wife had died after the landing of the *Mayflower* the previous fall. In the Pilgrim colony, he shared a cabin with John Alden, a young scholar. One night, Standish dropped his copy of *Caesar's Commentaries* and turned to John, who was writing a letter in which he praised Priscilla, one of the young women of the colony. Standish spoke of the loneliness and weariness of his life, and of the fact that Priscilla, too, was living alone, her parents having died during the winter. Because he himself was no scholar but only a blunt soldier, he asked John to convey his proposal of marriage to Priscilla. Taken aback by the request, John stammered that it would be wiser for Standish to plead his own case. When the captain asked the favor in the name of friendship, the young man could no longer refuse.

Priscilla was singing the Hundredth Psalm, and when John opened the door of her cabin, he saw her industriously spinning. Filled with woe at what he must do, he nevertheless stepped resolutely inside. Seizing what seemed an opportune moment, he blurted out the captain's proposal. Priscilla flatly refused, for she believed that Standish himself should have come if she were worth the wooing. She further confused the young man by asking him why he did not speak for himself. Caught between his own love for Priscilla and his respect for Standish, John decided to go back to England when the *Mayflower* sailed the next day.

Miles Standish was enraged when he heard the outcome of John's wooing, but the captain's tirade was interrupted by news of Indians on the warpath. He strode into the colony's council room and there saw a snakeskin full of arrows, the challenge to battle. Pulling out the arrows, he filled the skin with bullets and powder, and defiantly handed it back to the Indian. The savage quickly disappeared into the forest. Captain Standish, his eight men, and their Indian guide left the village the next morning before anyone else was awake.

Alden did not sail that day. Among the people on the beach, he saw Priscilla, who looked so dejected and appealing that he decided to stay and protect her. They walked back to the village together, and John described Miles Standish's reaction to Priscilla's question. He also confided that he had planned to leave the colony but was remaining to look after her.

Miles Standish, marching northward along the coast, brooded over his defeat in love but finally concluded that he should confine himself to soldiering and forget wooing. When he returned to the village from his attack on the Indian camp, he brought with him the head of one of the savages and hung it on the roof of the fort. Priscilla was glad then that she had not accepted Miles Standish.

That autumn, the village was at peace with the Indians. Captain Standish was out scouring the countryside. John Alden had built his own house and often walked through the forest to see Priscilla. One afternoon, he sat holding a skein of thread as she wound it. As they sat talking, a messenger burst in with the news that Miles Standish had been killed by a poisoned arrow and that his men were cut off in ambush.

At last, John felt free to make his own declaration. He and Priscilla were married in the village church, before all the congregation. The magistrate had read the service and the elder had finished the blessing when an unexpected guest appeared at the door. It was Miles Standish—recovered from his wound—and he came striding in like a ghost from the grave. Before everyone, the gruff soldier and the bridegroom made up their difference. Then, Standish tenderly wished John and Priscilla joy, and the wedding procession set off merrily through the forest to Priscilla's new home.

Critical Evaluation:

The Courtship of Miles Standish is one of the lasting results of Henry Wadsworth Longfellow's interest in and examination of New England history and literature. The poem is basically a Puritan love story, which has its factual roots in Longfellow's own distant maternal ancestor John Alden. The obvious pastoral qualities are borne out in the pleasant remoteness of the scene, the physical descriptions of the land, and the simplicity of the people about whom the story is told. The central theme of innocence and youthful love ties this pastoral romance together.

The landscape of the poem is definitely Puritan in its dimensions. Everything is seen through the eyes of the Pilgrims, who looked realistically and often harshly at the Indians and the life around them. The action of the poem takes place from the early spring to the fall, yet the tone of the poem takes on a wintry feeling that is very much in keeping with the austerity of the Puritan outlook. The ocean is, for example, pictured as "sailless, sombre and cold with the comfortless breath of the east wind."

The scriptural imagery and language is evident, further emphasizing the poem's pastoral character. There are references to the spirit of the Old Testament in event and name. Longfellow describes John Alden and Priscilla on their wedding day as "Fresh with the youth of the world, recalling Rebecca and Isaac." Despite the placid tone, there are glimpses of freshness and light, as this is a poem about youth and love and new beginnings. The magnificence of the sun on the wedding day is testimony to the poet's romantic ideals for his young bride and groom.

Longfellow's use of hexameter is an appropriate means of establishing the mood of the poem. The hexameters are looser and more flexible than those used in *Evangeline* (1847). The effect is more relaxed and far less stately, and free use of trochees provides a freshness not found in *Evangeline*.

Longfellow found it sufficient to acquaint himself very generally with the history and spirit of the times and the people about whom he was writing. A careful and scrupulous examination of the poem will find some deviations from chronology and fact, though certainly not anything that would take away from the broad appeal of this work.

Bibliography:
Arvin, Newton. *Longfellow: His Life and Work.* Boston: Little, Brown, 1963. Sees *The Courtship of Miles Standish* as an unpretentious domestic comedy, presented with simple truthfulness, appropriate Puritan coloration, and biblical imagery.
Ferguson, Robert A. "Longfellow's Political Fears: Civic Authority and the Role of the Artist in *Hiawatha* and *Miles Standish*." *American Literature* 50 (May, 1978): 187-215. Interprets

John Alden as representing both the helpless, authority-fearing artist and the personally conflicted Longfellow himself. Interprets Miles Standish's admiration for Julius Caesar as intended to be an unpleasant characteristic.

Wagenknecht, Edward. *Henry Wadsworth Longfellow: His Poetry and Prose*. New York: Ungar, 1986. Praises *The Courtship of Miles Standish* for its faultless narrative flow, skillfully evoked atmosphere, unfaltering plot elements, and detailed, realistically presented, and developed characters. Asserts that the work neatly balances comedy and serious drama.

Williams, Alicia Crane. "John and Priscilla, We Hardly Knew Ye." *American History Illustrated* 23 (December, 1988): 40-47. Explains that, although John Alden and Priscilla Mullins were elevated by Longfellow to legendary status, biographical information concerning the real pair is sketchy. John, a cooper who became a civil officer, and Priscilla, who inherited considerable money, married about 1623 and by 1650 had eleven children.

Williams, Cecil B. *Henry Wadsworth Longfellow*. New York: Twayne, 1964. Provides a detailed plot summary of *The Courtship of Miles Standish* that includes carefully chosen quotations. Extols the work as part of America's cultural heritage and refers to Longfellow's journals for details about the work's composition.

COUSIN BETTE

Type of work: Novel
Author: Honoré de Balzac (1799-1850)
Type of plot: Social realism
Time of plot: Early nineteenth century
Locale: Paris
First published: La Cousine Bette, 1846 (English translation, 1888)

Principal characters:
BARON HULOT
ADELINE, his wife
HORTENSE, their daughter
VICTORIN, their son
LISBETH, Adeline's Cousin Bette
MONSIEUR CREVEL, Baron Hulot's enemy
CÉLESTINE, Victorin's wife and the daughter of Monsieur Crevel
COLONEL HULOT, the baron's older brother
MADAME VALÉRIE MARNEFFE, Baron Hulot's mistress
MONSIEUR MARNEFFE, Madame Marneffe's husband
COUNT STEINBOCK, Hortense's husband
BARON MONTÈS, Madame Marneffe's lover

The Story:
One day in the summer of 1838, M. Crevel called on Adeline, the Baroness Hulot, to offer to make her his mistress, but she refused him. M. Crevel had sworn to be revenged on Baron Hulot, who had stolen his former mistress. The baron had, however, spent his fortune in the process and was now unable to give his daughter Hortense a satisfactory dowry. Hortense was able to forget her sorrow over her own marriage prospects by teasing Adeline's cousin Lisbeth, or Cousin Bette, about her lover. Cousin Bette was the old maid of the family, and her lover was a sculptor and Polish refugee named Count Steinbock. The attachment between them was that of mother and son, but Cousin Bette was wildly jealous of his other friends.

That evening, the baron's older brother, Colonel Hulot, and his son and daughter-in-law, Victorin and Célestine, came for dinner. Célestine, the daughter of M. Crevel, did not share her father's dislike of Baron Hulot. After dinner, the baron escorted Cousin Bette home and then went to see his mistress. He found that she had deserted him for a rich duke.

The next morning, Baron Hulot laid plans to seduce Madame Marneffe, the wife of a clerk who worked for him. In the meantime, Hortense had managed to speak to Count Steinbock by buying one of his pieces of sculpture. He called shortly afterward. The Hulots felt that the penniless young nobleman might be a good match for Hortense, but the plan was kept secret from Cousin Bette.

Baron Hulot arranged to meet Madame Marneffe in Cousin Bette's rooms. Later, he moved the Marneffes into a more lavish establishment in the Rue Varennes, and Cousin Bette went there to live. Through her new friend, Cousin Bette learned of the coming marriage between Hortense and Count Steinbock, for Baron Hulot had no secrets from Madame Marneffe. Cousin Bette had always been treated in the family as the eccentric old maid and the ugly duckling;

their stealing her lover was the final humiliation. She swore vengeance on the whole Hulot family, and Madame Marneffe agreed to help her.

As a first step, Cousin Bette introduced M. Crevel to Madame Marneffe. Then she had Count Steinbock imprisoned for debt, and she told Hortense that he had returned to Poland. No one suspected that Cousin Bette had put him in prison. Once he had obtained his release through friends, the wedding plans went ahead. Baron Hulot managed to raise a dowry for Hortense and planned to keep himself solvent by sending Adeline's uncle to Algiers. There, Baron Hulot hoped to steal money from the government through dealings with the army commissary; the uncle was to be the innocent dupe.

As soon as Hortense was married, Baron Hulot moved Adeline to a more modest house so that he could spend more money on Madame Marneffe. She and the baron conducted their affair quietly and attracted little notice. At the same time, she was also intimate with M. Crevel. M. Marneffe gave little trouble to either of these gentlemen as long as they kept him supplied with money and a good position at the war office.

When Baron Montès, an old lover of Madame Marneffe, appeared one evening, Baron Hulot and M. Crevel became worried. That same night, Madame Marneffe refused to let Baron Hulot enter her apartment. M. Crevel told Baron Hulot that he too had been Madame Marneffe's lover. The two old rivals were reconciled and went to see Madame Marneffe the next day. She agreed to consider M. Crevel's offer to marry her after her husband died, but she told Baron Hulot that he need not hope to be her lover again. After the two old men had left, she asked Cousin Bette to try to get Count Steinbock to come to her. She had always wanted to make a conquest of him, and his downfall would also be Cousin Bette's revenge on Hortense.

Count Steinbock was in need of money, and Cousin Bette slyly suggested borrowing from Madame Marneffe. After the count secretly went to see her, Madame Marneffe made a complete conquest of him.

When Madame Marneffe found herself to be pregnant, she told each lover separately that he was the father. Hortense believed that Count Steinbock was the father and deserted him to return to her mother. Baron Hulot found it necessary to visit Adeline to see Hortense and ask her to return to her husband. Hortense refused and made a violent scene. Cousin Bette arrived to take Hortense's side. She said that she could no longer stay with Madame Marneffe; she would keep house for old Colonel Hulot. It was her plan to marry the old man and gain control of the only money left in the family.

The baron's affairs were growing desperate. Adeline's uncle in Algiers wrote that the plot to steal from the government had been discovered and that money was needed to stop an investigation. Madame Marneffe was insisting on money for her child and a better position for her husband. One night, Madame Marneffe led Baron Hulot into a trap; when M. Marneffe brought the police to the lovers' room, saying he would prosecute unless he were promoted at the war office, the baron agreed.

At last, the Algerian scandal broke, and the uncle killed himself. Colonel Hulot was crushed by this blow to the family honor. He paid the necessary money from his own savings and died only a few days later from wounded pride. Cousin Bette had her revenge. Baron Hulot was a ruined man. In his disgrace, he sought shelter with the mistress who had deserted him for the duke. She provided him with some capital and a pretty seamstress to keep him company, and he lived in the slums under an assumed name. Through the efforts of Victorin, now a successful lawyer, the family slowly regained its wealth. Madame Marneffe's child was stillborn, and her husband died. Victorin was determined to keep his father-in-law from throwing himself away on the woman. He hired an underworld character to inform Baron Montès that Madame Marneffe was having an affair with Count Steinbock and was to marry M. Crevel. Baron Montès took his revenge on Madame Marneffe and M. Crevel by infecting them with a fatal tropical disease; they both died soon after their marriage.

Adeline began to do charity work in the slums. On one of her visits, she discovered her husband and brought him back to live with his family. Meanwhile, Cousin Bette had retired to her bed with consumption; she died soon after Baron Hulot's return, who had become a model husband. Soon after his wife hired a new cook, however, Adeline discovered her husband in the servants' quarters with the peasant girl. Adeline died three days later. Baron Hulot left Paris, and as soon as he could, he married the peasant girl, Agathe. This impropriety caused Victorin to remark that parents can hinder the marriages of their children; but children can do nothing about the actions of their parents in their second childhood.

Critical Evaluation:

Cousin Bette, Honoré de Balzac's last masterpiece, is one of the last novels of his huge, unfinished project, *La Comédie humaine* (*The Human Comedy*), and, together with *Cousin Pons* (1847), belongs to the *Scenes from Parisian Life* segment. The book presents some of Balzac's most somber visions of human depravity but also emphasizes loyalty and devotion. Balzac wrote *Cousin Bette* during the winter of 1846 under the greatest possible pressure from his indebtedness and emotional strain; the strain, coming on top of many years of arduous work, may finally have broken the novelist's strength. It is one of Balzac's longest novels and one of the most perfectly organized and most densely constructed. There are none of the digressions or padding that he sometimes used to lengthen stories. All the different characters in the tale—the black "angel" Bette, the debauched Hulot, the ambitious Valérie Marneffe, and her scheming husband—interact like the pieces of a vast machine grinding toward the inevitable, ironic conclusion.

Balzac saw society as a unit, a great drama with endless links and relationships. This theme is everywhere evident in *Cousin Bette*. All social levels are portrayed and are shown to be interwoven beneath the surface by the threads of human emotions. Hatred ties Bette to the Hulots, passion ties Baron Hulot to Madame Marneffe, ambition connects Marneffe to the baron, love ties Hortense to Steinbock, and debt ties Steinbock to Bette. The tangle is at once extremely complicated and entirely plausible. Amazingly enough, Balzac was able to keep not only the threads of this novel in his head but also the threads for the entire series of novels, which included nearly three thousand named characters.

Balzac believed that individuals' antecedents, environment, and upbringing shape their destiny. In this, he anticipated the realist school and such naturalists as Émile Zola. Balzac saw that apparently trivial changes or new conditions had the capacity to bring out latent possibilities in people and to alter the entire course of someone's life. In his novels and stories, Balzac emphasized the importance of his characters' physical surroundings, the towns and streets and houses in which they lived, the rooms that seemed to trap them, the clothes and gestures that gave them away, and all the other minutiae of life. In *Cousin Bette*, the descriptions of Paris range from the run-down neighborhood near the Louvre, in which Bette lives, to the shabby elegance of the Hulots' establishment. Everything is vividly detailed, explained, and placed in context. Nothing exists in isolation.

The place of women in society is reflected on many levels in *Cousin Bette*. Bette herself earns her own way with her needlework and always has. Valérie uses her beauty to further her unscrupulous husband's career and ends up being kept by rich men. Hortense, Bette's cousin, was bred to be a wife and must find a husband or be a burden to her family; she knows this, but she also knows that her father must provide her with a dowry and that she herself is not sufficient to acquire a man's name and place in society. Hortense's mother, Adeline, suffers her husband's indiscretions in silence because there is no socially acceptable recourse. The women must all resort to intrigue and deceit to accomplish anything in the society dominated and controlled by males. Bette is the most independent of the women and the most ruthless, but her efforts—whatever their motivation—are all clandestine. Whatever success she has is possible only because nobody is aware of it. People do not suspect her because she is a woman, no longer young, and plain, characteristics that render her almost invisible.

In *Cousin Bette*, as in so many of Balzac's novels, the contrast between the provinces and Paris is an ever-present theme, for it is Bette's peasant shrewdness, her lack of sophistication that gives the novel its momentum. Bette is a provincial fighting to make her way in the jungle of Paris. The reader cannot help but feel that Balzac admired her ruthless, astute maneuvering. Balzac was always fascinated by the theme of the individual in conflict with society, and with the rebel or criminal personality. His villains often were more vigorous and interesting than his virtuous people, and Cousin Bette is no exception. She is one of Balzac's most intriguing and complex characters, totally unlikable yet hypnotic in her power. Her individuality is symbolized by the way in which she stubbornly reduces her hand-me-down garments from their urban fashion to countrified, colorless rags; she makes the clothes conform to her self-image. Shy and wild, vicious and hard, only her highly developed will keeps Bette from physically attacking her beautiful and resented cousin, Adeline. From the beginning, the reader knows that Bette is capable of anything. Resentment had grown within her until it possessed her and changed her into a monster. The countrywoman's pride will not stop short of complete revenge. Yet, strangely enough, she is content with a secret revenge. It does not matter to her if the Hulots never know that she was the instrument of their ruin. The silent satisfaction is enough for this peasant spinster.

After a long and detailed preparation and exposition in which Balzac establishes the characters and their setting, the pace of the novel increases and the tension mounts to a climax that is as inevitable as that of a classic tragedy. The Hulots and Valérie, Marneffe and Steinbock, all pay the consequences of their sins; all of them have let an obsession rule their life. Only Bette emerges triumphant, for she is victorious even after death.

"Critical Evaluation" by Bruce D. Reeves

Bibliography:
Hemmings, F. W. J. *Balzac: An Interpretation of "La Comédie Humaine."* New York: Random House, 1967. Chapter 4, "The Cancer," presents a comparative analysis of *Cousin Bette*, *Eugénie Grandet*, and *Père Goriot* as a trilogy of related studies centering on a father whose private obsession jeopardizes his family.
Levin, Harry. *The Gates of Horn: A Study of Five French Realists.* New York: Oxford University Press, 1963. A study of literary realism in France. Chapter 4, an influential overview of Balzac's work, includes several specific references to *Cousin Bette.*
Maurois, André. *Prometheus: The Life of Balzac.* Translated by Norman Denny. Harmondsworth, England: Penguin, 1971. The definitive biography by France's premier literary biographer. A thorough, generally objective, and highly readable account of Balzac's life. Provides detailed context for and some commentary on all of the major works.
Prendergast, Christopher. *Balzac: Fiction and Melodrama.* New York: Holmes & Meier, 1978. Argues for the importance of the conventions and devices of melodrama for the interpreta-

tion of Balzac's analyses of French society. Contains a detailed analysis of *Cousin Bette* as well as an overview of previous critical work on the novel.

Stowe, William W. *Balzac, James, and the Realistic Novel.* Princeton, N.J.: Princeton University Press, 1983. Discusses the solutions Balzac and Henry James adopted in solving various problems of realistic fictional representation. Includes a comparative study of the dramatic elements in *Cousin Bette* and James's *The Wings of the Dove.*

COUSIN PONS

Type of work: Novel
Author: Honoré de Balzac (1799-1850)
Type of plot: Naturalism
Time of plot: 1840's
Locale: Paris
First published: Le Cousin Pons, 1847 (English translation, 1880)

Principal characters:
SYLVAIN PONS, an elderly musician and amateur art collector
SCHMUCKE, Pons's friend and fellow musician
MADAME CIBOT, a portress at Pons's residence
MONSIEUR DE MARVILLE, Pons's cousin
MADAME DE MARVILLE, Monsieur de Marville's wife and an enemy of
  Pons
FRAISIER, a rascally attorney
REMONENCQ, a friend and accomplice of Madame Cibot

The Story:

Sylvain Pons was an ugly man who had no family except one cousin, Monsieur de Marville, a rich and influential government official. As a result of his connection, Cousin Pons, as the de Marvilles called him, was able to dine out at a rich man's home at least once a week. These opportunities satisfied one of Pons's two pleasures in life, a delight in good food well served. Pons's job as conductor of the orchestra at a ballet theater and his series of private music pupils gave him the money to live and to satisfy his other delight in life, collecting works of art.

By the time he was in his sixties, Pons had built up a collection worth more than one million francs, though neither he nor anyone else realized that it was so valuable. Pons's only friend was a musician in his orchestra, an old German named Schmucke. The two men lived together in an apartment filled with Pons's art treasures. Their lives were extremely simple; the portress at the house, Madame Cibot, cooked for them and cleaned the apartment, and their work kept them busy most of the time. The only flaw in their existence, as Schmucke saw it, was the fact that Pons went out to dinner once a week and sometimes twice.

Even that flaw was remedied when Madame de Marville, the wife of Pons's cousin, grew tired of having the old man in her home and made her attitude obvious to him. He then began eating all of his meals at home with Schmucke. Pons, however, was too fond of dining out on rich food to be happy with the arrangement, and he missed the company that he had enjoyed for more than forty years. With Schmucke's help, Pons determined to try to make peace with Madame de Marville by securing a rich husband for Cécile, the de Marvilles' daughter. The attempt was a dismal failure and as a result the de Marvilles' house and those of all their friends became closed to Pons.

The shock of finding that his cousin and all of his cousin's connections regarded him as vicious and hateful and would no longer speak to him was too much for Pons. He fell ill, and nothing the doctor could do helped. His friend Schmucke tried to keep their small establishment going with the aid of Madame Cibot, who acted as a nurse while Schmucke worked at the theater or gave music lessons.

It was unfortunate for the two old men that Madame Cibot learned that the art treasures lying about the apartment were extremely valuable. At first she thought only of having Pons set up

1360

an annuity for her at his death, in return for her nursing care, but her avarice eventually led her to conceive the idea of getting the entire fortune into her own hands. She took into her confidence a small dealer in bric-a-brac named Remonencq, who in turn enlisted the aid of Elie Magus, a Jew with a passion for art. The Jew, with the help of the other two, gained admittance to Pons's apartment and made an estimate of the collection's value. At the same time, he made an agreement to pay Madame Cibot more than forty thousand francs if she would get Schmucke, who knew nothing of art, to sell four of his friend's pictures for money to pay Pons's doctor bills.

Poor Schmucke, who thought only of saving his friend's life, readily agreed to sell four masterpieces, whose value he did not know, for a fraction of their true value. After they had been sold, thinking that Pons would never notice, he simply hung four other pictures in their places. Delighted at her success in fleecing the old men, Madame Cibot decided to try to get all the collection and enlisted the aid of the doctor, who was a poor man, and a rascally attorney named Fraisier. Fraisier knew of Pons's influential relatives and pointed out to Madame Cibot that the relatives would fight any attempt by the portress to get the old man's estate. He also convinced her that they were powerful enough to send her to the guillotine if they could prove her guilt. Feeling that her only chance of success lay with him, Madame Cibot agreed to follow the attorney's advice.

The attorney went to Madame de Marville, who was also avaricious, and told her of Pons's wealth and his determination to leave it to Schmucke. Madame de Marville immediately agreed to do anything she could to gain the fortune for herself, for all the family's wealth had gone into her daughter's dowry. She promised to have her husband get good appointments for Fraisier and the doctor, and she consented to set up an annuity for Madame Cibot. When she told her husband, he agreed.

Fraisier and Madame Cibot then began to lay plans to find a way into Pons's confidence. Unfortunately, Pons became suspicious of Madame Cibot. His suspicions were confirmed when he awoke one afternoon to find Elie Magus, his rival collector, examining the art objects on the walls and tables. Summoning his remaining strength, Pons left his sickbed, staggered to the other rooms, and discovered that his paintings were gone. He realized immediately that someone had been attempting to fleece him at poor Schmucke's expense. That night, after Schmucke had confessed to selling the paintings, he and Schmucke discussed what they could do. Pons forgave Schmucke, for he knew that the German had no idea of the cash values of the paintings or the more personal value they had for Pons himself.

Pons drew up a will naming Madame Cibot as one of his heirs, in an attempt to deceive her as to his real intentions. He even left the will where she would see it. The portress was pleased, although the will did not provide for as much as she wanted. Fraisier also saw the document and was pleased because it was a will that could easily be broken in court for the benefit of the de Marville family. Pons had hoped that they would react in that way, and the following day he secretly made a new will which left his fortune to the crown, with the stipulation that in return the government should give Schmucke a lifetime annuity.

When Pons died shortly afterward, his death left poor Schmucke in a dreadful state. The German musician knew little of the world, and Pons's death left him without judgment or willpower. All he cared about was dying quickly in order to meet his friend in heaven. Because of his state of mind, the plotters believed it would be easy to take the estate away from him.

The de Marvilles, bringing a suit to break the will, hoped that Schmucke, to avoid trouble, would accept a small annuity and let them have the bulk of the estate. They were right in their belief, but just as the papers were about to be signed, a messenger brought Schmucke a copy of the charges made in court against the old man, charges that he had influenced his friend in an attempt to get the estate. The shock to Schmucke was so great that he died within a few days, allowing the estate to go unchallenged to the de Marvilles, who had denied their cousin and despised him during his last years.

Many people gained by the deaths of Pons and Schmucke. The de Marvilles recouped their fortune; Fraisier, the rascally attorney, received an office of trust for his part in the affair; the doctor who had tended Pons received a sinecure; Elie Magus, the Jew, had his coveted pictures; and Madame Cibot had her annuity. She also had a new husband, for Remonencq, her fellow conspirator, poisoned her husband and then married her. Everyone, except Schmucke, the man Pons had wanted most to help, had benefited from Pons's fortune.

Critical Evaluation:

Honoré de Balzac stood at the dividing line between Romanticism and realism. He was inclined toward the fantastic and supernatural and to the exaggeration of normal human types, but his desire to reproduce concrete fact and to visualize the scene or object made him a superb painter of French society in the first half of the nineteenth century. Both of these aspects of his writing are easily observed in *Cousin Pons*, part of the *Scenes from Parisian Life* segment of Balzac's *La Comédie humaine* (*The Human Comedy*).

Balzac's own interest in the supernatural and hereafter is seen in the discussion of fortune-telling and astrology when Madame Cibot calls on the witchlike Madame Fontaine in her den. Balzac devotes several pages to an analysis of the plausibility of the seer's art and the reality of certain types of divination. Human beings do not understand everything that exists in the universe, he says, and should not close their eyes to some possibilities simply because they cannot be explained. This idea leads to a belief that is fundamental in Balzac's philosophy and that played an important part in his writing and in the structure of *The Human Comedy*: predestination. Balzac believed that the fates conspired to lead human beings to their ultimate destinies. Given the circumstances of people's backgrounds and the makeup of their characters and factors of their lives, they have no way of avoiding a particular fate. Balzac considered his job to be that of a recorder setting down the causes and effects of the lives and destinies of his characters, and he believed that his method was scientific and objective.

In *Cousin Pons*, readers see the characters of the old collector Pons and his beloved friend, Schmucke, and how their good and trusting natures are taken advantage of by the avaricious people around them. Given the nature of human beings, it is not surprising that the story works its way to a pathetic and painful conclusion. It would be incorrect to say that Balzac created men and women more horrible than any who lived; Balzac knew very well that people who have been taught that material values are the only important ones will stop at nothing until they have acquired everything they can see within their grasp. The morality or lack of morality in Madame Cibot, Fraisier, Remonencq, and the other characters is the result of many factors, which Balzac draws with his usual skill. None of these people stands outside of society; they all are influenced by it and in turn influence it. This is one of the fundamental themes in *The Human Comedy*.

The friendship between Pons and Schmucke is portrayed with a touching humor and sensitivity. The devotion between the two old men provides a counterpoint to the grasping, almost savage, natures of Madame Cibot and the others. Seldom did Balzac portray such a low level of society, but he shows both sides of the coin, the love and generosity possible between human beings as well as the cruelty and hypocrisy. If the negative powers ultimately are victorious, that is merely—Balzac implies—the fates at work. That does not mean, however, that he believes that the negative always wins.

Cousin Pons was intended as a companion volume to *Cousin Bette* (1846). In *Cousin Pons* there is the poor male relation, cruelly treated, but gentle of heart, and in *Cousin Bette* there is the poor female relation, also cruelly treated, but revenging herself. The symmetry pleased Balzac, and, read together, the two novels form a powerful structure and a devastating picture of human nature and its possibilities for good and evil.

The collection of old Pons is one that Balzac, himself an avid collector, would have wanted to own. Pons's passion for antiques was shared by Balzac, as was the old man's terror of other people gazing upon or possibly stealing them. Balzac was always at his best when describing a mania—as in connection with Père Goriot, Eugénie Grandet, and César Birotteau—whether the subject was greed, a passion for collecting, or obsessive parental affection. Balzac did more than sympathize with Pons's mania: He felt with Pons as the old man put together and tried to guard his rooms. The passion for the collection, also shared by the old Jew, Magus, is portrayed with so much intensity that the reader comes to feel some of it as well.

Pons and Schmucke are two of the great characters in Balzac's vast gallery and in all of European literature. They both are extremely funny and very touching. They are "odd" yet never absurd, and they are portrayed with a truth of observation and a subtlety of touch that render them sympathetic despite their quirks of personality. Their strange habits and costumes, their odd passions for collecting, for good food, for company, are not applied by the writer from the outside but emerge from within their living, breathing beings. That is why their ultimate fates are so devastating to the reader; their gentle, unworldly natures soon become objects of concern, and their lives present moral pictures of the most painful kind.

Despite its grim, brutal aspects, *Cousin Pons* is actually a very gentle book. The greater part of the story is devoted to the friendship and the devotion of Schmucke and old Pons. Pons's loyalty for his old friend and his effort to care for Schmucke even after his own death are touchingly shown. When the grasping natures of Madame Cibot and her allies are held up before this picture of unselfish love, they appear doubly horrible. A tone of quiet melancholy pervades the book, a sadness on the part of Balzac that such a fate should await two such good men. As the chronicler of human nature in all of its forms, however, he cannot flinch. He draws the de Marville household in all of its pettiness and Madame Cibot, a woman who rivals even Cousin Bette when it comes to merciless scheming. Before Balzac, few authors had attempted such an uncompromising look at the varieties of human nature. So honest was his gaze that, even today, readers find themselves flinching at the picture he painted.

"Critical Evaluation" by Bruce D. Reeves

Bibliography:
Bertault, Philippe. *Balzac and "The Human Comedy."* Translated by Richard Monges. New York: New York University Press, 1963. A general survey of Balzac's novels that offers little in-depth analysis of individual works but usefully locates them in relation to Balzac's major themes and interests. Includes a brief biographical sketch.
Hemmings, F. W. J. *Balzac: An Interpretation of "La Comédie Humaine."* New York: Random House, 1967. Hemmings' chapter 8, "The Dialectic," presents an analysis of *Cousin Pons*, finding the late novel to be one of Balzac's most pessimistic but also one of his most profound works.
Levin, Harry. *The Gates of Horn: A Study of Five French Realists.* New York: Oxford University Press, 1963. A study of literary realism in France. Levin's chapter 4, an influential overview of Balzac's work, includes several specific references to *Cousin Pons*.

Maurois, André. *Prometheus: The Life of Balzac*. Translated by Norman Denny. Harmonds-worth, England: Penguin, 1971. The definitive biography by France's premier literary biographer. A thorough, generally objective, and highly readable account of Balzac's life. Provides detailed context for and some commentary on all of the major works, including *Cousin Pons*.

Wilkinson, Lynn R. "*Le Cousin Pons* and the Invention of Ideology." *PMLA* 107, no. 2 (March, 1992): 274-289. Analyzes the complex relationships between ideology and representation in Balzac's novel from a Marxist perspective. Includes a discussion of the influence of mechanical technology, especially the then-new science of photography, on literature.

CRANFORD

Type of work: Novel
Author: Elizabeth Gaskell (1810-1865)
Type of plot: Domestic realism
Time of plot: Early nineteenth century
Locale: England
First published: 1851-1853

Principal characters:
MARY SMITH, the narrator
MISS DEBORAH JENKYNS, a genteel spinster
MISS MATILDA JENKYNS (MATTY), her sister
PETER JENKYNS, their long-lost brother
MRS. JAMIESON, a leader of society
LADY GLENMIRE, Mrs. Jamieson's sister-in-law
MARTHA, Miss Matilda's faithful servant

The Story:

Cranford was a small English village inhabited mostly by ladies. Few gentlemen took up residence there, and most of those who did seemed to disappear on various and mysterious errands. The doctor, the shopkeepers, and a few male servants were the only representatives of their sex who crossed the ladies' vision with any regularity.

Most of the ladies lived in "elegant economy." The spending of money was considered vulgar and showy, and one did not mention being poor unless in private to one's dearest friend. When semiretired Captain Brown moved to Cranford and talked openly about being poor, it was quite an affront to the ladies. The captain was, however, so kind and considerate to everyone, whether they were more or less fortunate than he, that the ladies could not long resent his vulgar behavior and talk. He had two daughters. The elder, dying of an incurable illness, had a tongue sharpened by pain, but the kind women of Cranford joined the younger daughter in trying to make the dying girl's last days pleasant and comfortable.

The women experienced great sorrow when the kind captain was killed while rescuing a small child from an oncoming train. When his elder daughter died soon after, all of the ladies were hard-pressed to make suitable arrangements for the younger daughter. One day, a former suitor appeared and took her for his wife. The village ladies rested happily in the knowledge that Captain Brown would be pleased with his daughter's security.

Until her death, Miss Deborah Jenkyns was one of the more dominant spinsters in the town. She made all decisions for her younger sister, Miss Matilda, who was fifty-five years old. Miss Matilda, affectionately called Miss Matty by all but her sister, knew that Deborah had the better mind and did not resent her sister's dominance. After Miss Deborah's death, Miss Matty almost had to learn how to live again. Her particular friends were Miss Pole, Mrs. Forrester, and Mrs. Jamieson, who became the social leader of Cranford after Miss Deborah's death. Miss Mary Smith also often visited Miss Matty and brought her the good advice of her father, who was Miss Matty's financial adviser. Mary was surprised to learn that Miss Matty had long ago had a suitor whom she rejected in order to stay with her mother. Not long after Miss Deborah's death, that gentleman returned to Cranford for a visit. Mary was disappointed that he did not renew his courtship of Miss Matty. Miss Matty grieved too, but only in secret, for she would never have admitted to such vulgar sentiments openly. Mary also learned that Miss Deborah and Miss Matty had a brother who had disappeared many years before, after being severely punished by their father for playing a practical joke on Miss Deborah. Peter Jenkyns was believed dead, although Miss Matty had heard rumors that he was living in India.

The genteel ladies were thrown into a flurry of excitement when they heard that Mrs. Jamieson's sister-in-law, Lady Glenmire, was to settle in Cranford. Since she was the first noblewoman they had encountered, they spent long hours discussing how they should address her. Their worries were for naught, however, for Mrs. Jamieson subtly but firmly informed them that they would not be included in her guest list. At first, the ladies were greatly hurt. Later, Mrs. Jamieson was forced to relent and invite them to call, for most of the county gentility were away or otherwise occupied. Miss Matty, Miss Pole, and Mrs. Forrester first thought they would be engaged elsewhere for the fateful night, but their innate kindness, as well, perhaps, as their curiosity, prevailed, and they accepted the invitation. They found Lady Glenmire delightful and no more refined or genteel than they themselves.

Mrs. Jamieson departed from Cranford for a time, leaving Lady Glenmire in charge of her home. Soon after, Lady Glenmire became engaged to the doctor of the town, a man whose presence the ladies did not even acknowledge except when his services were needed for bleeding. He was no higher socially than a shopkeeper, but it was exciting that the ladies at last knew someone who was to be married. They awaited Mrs. Jamieson's return with fear and anticipation, and they were not disappointed, for Mrs. Jamieson, deciding to cut Lady Glenmire, stated that she had always known her to be of low taste.

The engaged couple were married before Mrs. Jamieson returned. By that time, a great tragedy had befallen Miss Matty. The bank in which her estate was deposited had to close its doors, and she was left with only thirteen pounds a year. She made no complaint; her biggest worry was whether Mrs. Jamieson would allow the ladies to continue their friendship with her. Mary Smith sent for her father to see what he could plan for Miss Matty. Careful that she should not know of their gift, Miss Pole, Mrs. Forrester, and another friend gave up some of their own small incomes so that they could help their friend. Mary and Mr. Smith persuaded Miss Matty to sell tea, but it took a good deal of convincing to assure her that this would be a genteel way for a lady to supplement her income. Miss Matty's faithful maid, Martha, forced her young man to marry her sooner than he had anticipated so that they could rent Miss Matty's house and have her for a lodger. In this way, Martha could continue to look after her old mistress without injuring Miss Matty's pride. Everyone was happy when Mrs. Jamieson returned and said that the ladies could continue to call on Miss Matty because her father had been a rector and his daughter, who had never married, was entitled to the position he had left her.

More good fortune followed. Mary Smith wrote to Miss Matty's brother in India. When he received the letter, Peter Jenkyns sold his property and returned to Cranford to keep his sister in comfort and in some prosperity. Peter also brought about a reconciliation between Mrs. Jamieson and Lady Glenmire, who now called herself Mrs. instead of Lady. Once more, there was peace in Cranford.

Critical Evaluation:

Elizabeth Gaskell began writing *Cranford* in 1851 when Charles Dickens invited her to send tales for his new weekly journal, *Household Words*. Dickens and Gaskell were so pleased with the first two *Cranford* stories, which depicted a community of genteel single women in a retired country village, that Gaskell went on to write fourteen more, and what she had initially intended as a lighthearted sketch developed into one of her most subtle fictional creations.

Gaskell's first two novels, *Mary Barton* (1848) and *Ruth* (1853), which she had begun before starting *Cranford*, were both greeted by controversy, *Mary Barton* for what some Victorian readers perceived as an alarming siding with the working class against the employing class, and *Ruth* for its sympathetic treatment of an unwed mother. *Cranford* seemed safer, more distant from such troubling nineteenth century issues. It became particularly popular after Gaskell's death, its biggest sales coming at the turn of the century, and it was praised with such words as "charming," "delightful," "delicate." Well into the twentieth century it continued to be read as a nostalgic portrait of a quaint, old-fashioned, feminine world.

The quaintness and charm are there, and so is some nostalgia, for *Cranford*'s narrator, Mary Smith, writes with a constant awareness that the life she describes is already anachronistic and likely soon to disappear altogether in a rapidly modernizing society. However, the novel is also marked by a clear-sighted probing into the conditions of its female characters' lives in a society that expected the genders to occupy separate spheres.

The opening sentence—"In the first place, Cranford is in possession of the Amazons"— implies that separate spheres might mean immense power for women. Cranford's circle of widows and single ladies pride themselves on their self-sufficiency; they rule their world, and it is one in which men are superfluous.

If, however, the image of Amazons leads readers to expect warrior-women who challenge Victorian orthodoxies about pursuits appropriate for females, Gaskell quickly sets them right in her descriptions of the most conventional of ladies. They may own their own houses—a right denied married Englishwomen until the Married Women's Property Acts passed after 1870— but their economic power is severely curtailed. They glory in their "elegant economy," but such economy is required of them because they live on very small inherited incomes and because they devote themselves to preserving the social rules with which they maintain the class status determined for them by their relation to fathers or husbands. They visit one another and play cards, they fantasize about threats from thieves who turn out not to exist, they read little and are vastly ignorant about the wider world, and in real crises, they need help from men.

Gaskell develops the pathos and grotesqueries of the Cranford ladies' lives by focusing on the Jenkyns sisters. The older sister, Deborah, had devoted herself to her authoritarian clergy-man father; she never married and was always available to read to him and help him with correspondence. Gaskell portrays her as something of a social tyrant devoted to preserving the cultural status quo, whether this be a matter of literary style (she scorns any deviation from the formal eighteenth century sentences of Samuel Johnson, her father's favorite author) or social status (she has prevented her younger sister, Miss Matty, from marrying the farmer Mr. Holbrook, a free spirit who cared nothing about social advancement). After Deborah's death, Miss Matty, who has been allowed no independent will or intellectual development, seems nearly helpless.

The narrative nevertheless leads readers to feel admiration and considerable sympathy for the Cranford ladies. Gaskell's narrator, Mary Smith, contrasts significantly with the women whose lives she describes, for she lives not in Cranford but in Drumble, an industrial city. She is a young woman still residing with her father yet in possession of independent opinions. She responds enthusiastically to modern culture—standing up for Dickens, for example, against Miss Jenkyns' advocacy of Dr. Johnson, and cheering when the visiting Lady Glenmire outrages her status-conscious sister-in-law Mrs. Jamieson by marrying a mere surgeon with the plebeian name of Hoggins. Mary Smith easily sees through the Cranford ladies' snobberies and subterfuges. Yet she also loves them. The Jenkyns sisters are her particular friends; she visits them often, and for her the limited lives of the Cranford ladies are full of human interest.

Moreover, she sees not only the limitations but the largely good-humored strength with which Cranford's women make the best of these limitations. Above all, she recognizes Miss Matty's sweetness, kindness, and integrity, and she is a perceptive reader of the hidden pain in Miss Matty's life. The novel's climax comes when the women rally around Miss Matty after her livelihood is threatened by the failure of the bank in which Deborah had invested their inheritance. At such points, the narration emphasizes the importance of the kind of mutual support the Cranford ladies, despite their frequent competitiveness, can give one another. The novel's great achievement is the blending of tones with which Mary Smith tells her stories: ironic, satiric, amused, sad, and deeply loving.

That Mary Smith is both an outside observer and an engaged participant also gives her an important role in the novel's action. When Miss Matty loses most of her income, Mary Smith is able to persuade Miss Matty and the other Cranford ladies that she would not lose social status by setting up a shop and earning money. Furthermore, as someone willingly belonging to the wider world, she manages to get a letter to Miss Matty's long-lost brother Peter, who returns from India and, evading suggestions of marriage, establishes a household with his sister. Peter has a particularly interesting relation to the novel's concern with Victorian separations between men and women. He had left Cranford in a spirit of rebellion against his father's sternness and his sister Deborah's sexual prudery; he returns as a man comfortably able to express the "feminine" qualities of kindness and loyalty that are Cranford's great strength. In this, he is like male characters who appeared earlier in the novel: Mr. Brown, the proponent of Dickens in the first two chapters; the surgeon Hoggins; and Miss Matty's lost love, Holbrook. If *Cranford* gives something of the impression of a utopian fiction, this is the product not only of its nostalgic love for an older world but also of its proposal that the best human society will cease to insist that men and women construct themselves as different kinds of beings.

"Critical Evaluation" by Anne Howells

Bibliography:
Auerbach, Nina. *Communities of Women: An Idea in Fiction.* Cambridge, Mass.: Harvard University Press, 1978. Stresses the virtues of Cranford as a cooperative female community and speculates that the novel may have been influenced by Gaskell's friendship with Charlotte Brontë.
Keating, Peter, ed. Introduction to *"Cranford" and "Cousin Phillis,"* by Elizabeth Gaskell. Harmondsworth, Middlesex, England: Penguin, 1976. An informative introduction that stresses *Cranford's* representations of social change.
Schor, Hilary M. *Scheherezade in the Marketplace: Elizabeth Gaskell and the Victorian Novel.* New York: Oxford University Press, 1992. Explores *Cranford's* experimentation with narrative, which is especially interesting for its references to other literary works and for its narrator's attentiveness to Miss Matty's hidden "woman's story."
Stoneman, Patsy. *Elizabeth Gaskell.* Bloomington: Indiana University Press, 1987. A survey of Gaskell's works that stresses *Cranford's* depiction of women as limited and marginalized by society. Includes a useful bibliography on Gaskell, Victorian women and women writers, and feminist theory and literary criticism.
Uglow, Jennifer. *Elizabeth Gaskell: A Habit of Stories.* New York: Farrar, Straus, Giroux, 1993. An excellent biography that describes Gaskell's writing of *Cranford* and discusses perceptively the novel's themes, characters, and structure. Sees the novel as "an appeal against separate spheres" for men and women.

THE CREAM OF THE JEST

Type of work: Novel
Author: James Branch Cabell (1879-1958)
Type of plot: Satire
Time of plot: Twentieth century
Locale: Virginia
First published: 1917

> *Principal characters:*
> FELIX KENNASTON, an author
> KATHLEEN KENNASTON, his wife
> RICHARD HARROWBY, his neighbor
> ETTARRE, a woman in his novel and his dreams

The Story:

Felix Kennaston told his neighbor, Richard Harrowby, about his dreams. In writing his novels, Kennaston had created a world much different from the ordinary world of the Virginia countryside, and his dreams contained similar elements of the romantic and the marvelous. To Harrowby, the whole thing seemed indecent, for Harrowby was a conventional, unimaginative gentleman farmer who had made his money in soaps and beauty aids.

Kennaston was writing a novel called *The Audit at Storisende*, and in his dreams he identified himself with a character named Horvendile, who was looking for that elusive and highly improbable creature, the ideal woman. In Ettarre, his heroine, Kennaston felt he had found her. Much of his plot centered on a broken round medallion bearing mysterious symbols, a medallion he called the sigil of Scoteia.

One afternoon, Kennaston, walking in his garden, stooped to pick up a little piece of shining metal, apparently a broken half of a small disc, and casually dropped it into his pocket. Later, while looking over some books in his library, he thought of the little piece of metal in his pocket. He brought it out and laid it where the light of the lamp fell upon it. At once, he seemed to be talking with Ettarre, who explained that he had picked up half the broken sigil of Scoteia and that it had brought him back to her imagined world of romance and dream. As he reached out to touch her, she disappeared, and Kennaston found himself sitting again in his library.

Kennaston's novel was published as *The Men Who Loved Allison*, a title that his publisher assured him would bring better sales. When several readers, shocked by what they called indecency in the novel, wrote indignant letters to the newspapers, the book became a best-seller. Mrs. Kennaston, who made it a point never to read her husband's books, enjoyed his success. She treated Kennaston with polite boredom.

Strange things happened to Kennaston. One day at a luncheon, a famous man took him aside and asked him whether he bred white pigeons. This question puzzled Kennaston, as did the little mirror the man held in his hand. Another time, he saw an ugly old woman who told him that there was no price of admission to her world, but that one paid upon leaving. Several times he talked to Ettarre in his dreams.

One day, Kennaston received an invitation to call on a prelate who had come to Lichfield to attend the bishop's funeral. The prelate praised Kennaston's book. He spoke of pigeons, too, and mentioned how useful he found his little mirror. Kennaston was frankly puzzled. He returned to his dreamland, where, as Horvendile, he experienced almost every passion and emotion known; and always, as he reached out to touch Ettarre, the dream would come to an end.

Kennaston read widely in philosophy and the classics, and he began to question the reason for his own existence. He came to the conclusion that the present moment was all that was real—that the past and future had no part in the reality of today. As a man of letters, he became interested in the artistry of creation and decided that God must have been happy over his creation of the character of Christ. Probably because of his interest in God as an artist, Kennaston was confirmed in the country church nearby. This act on his part increased his stature among the people of the neighborhood. They even elected him to the vestry.

One day, Kennaston went to the station to meet his wife's train. While he was waiting, a woman with whom he had once been in love came up to him and started to talk. She was about to go back to her home in St. Louis. They recalled the past, and as she left him to get on her train, he had a moment in which he identified her with Ettarre. His remark to his wife about her, however, was that she was not keeping her good looks as she grew older. What haunted him, however, was that the woman had drawn from her purse a medallion resembling the sigil of Scoteia.

Kennaston—as Horvendile—dreamed of being in many parts of the world in many eras; and one of the mysteries was that he was always a young man approximately twenty-five years of age. He was at Queen Elizabeth's court; he was at Whitehall with Cromwell; he was at the French court of Louis XIV; he was among the aristocrats about to be beheaded during the French Revolution; and always beside him was Ettarre, whose contact would bring his dreams to an end.

One afternoon he found, quite by accident, the missing piece of the sigil of Scoteia in his wife's bathroom. After securing the other piece, he put them together on his wife's dressing table and began speculating about the relation of his wife to Ettarre. He hoped that the discovery of the entire sigil would express to her what he had never been able to convey. She paid no attention to it, and their life continued its banal rounds. Eleven months later, Mrs. Kennaston died in her sleep without ever having discussed the sigil or its significance with her husband. After her death, he showed Harrowby the two halves of the sigil, by which he had almost made his dreams come true. Far from being a magic emblem, the pieces proved to be merely the broken top of a cold cream jar. It was the final disillusionment for Kennaston, who was at last compelled to give up romantic, youthful dreaming for the realities of middle age.

Critical Evaluation:

The Cream of the Jest: A Comedy of Evasions was a pivotal novel in James Branch Cabell's career, marking the change of direction that allowed him to find and perfect a unique literary voice. His earlier novels had made little or no use of the supernatural in their scrupulous investigation of the nature of love and the problems involved in finding and maintaining sexual relationships. His first-published novel, *The Eagle's Shadow: A Comedy of Purse Strings* (1904)—the book that first introduced the character of Felix Kennaston and Kennaston's best-selling novel *The Men Who Loved Allison*—and his first-written book, *The Line of Love* (1905), were contemporary fictions of a fairly light nature. The collections *Gallantry* (1907) and *Chivalry* (1909), and the novel *The Soul of Melicent* (1913; revised as *Domnei: A Comedy of Woman Worship,* 1920), were romances in a more traditional sense, reexamining the literary roots of the mythology of romantic love. In both types of work, Cabell maintained the strict discipline of decency that was required by the prudish publishers of the day, but he became acutely aware of the ironic folly of attempting to purge the idea of romance of its erotic essence. *The Cream of the Jest* began a merciless satirization of the evasions inherent in prudery. Cabell continued the satirization in an increasingly gaudy and flamboyant fashion, by means of a series of baroque fantasies in which the lofty but anemic ideals of *Gallantry* and *Chivalry* were infused with a dramatic and glorious—but poignantly futile—virility.

In a narrow sense, Felix Kennaston's situation is a fictionalization of Cabell's own; in a broader sense, it embodies and dramatizes a fundamental aspect of the human condition. Every human being has a public and a private self, the former bound and controlled by social rules and conventions, while the latter retains the precious freedom of dreams and daydreams. Everyone, therefore, is acutely aware of the evasions that the public self is forced by politeness to practice. Such evasions are the everyday acts of censorship by which the "indecency" of private desires and fantasies must be carefully hidden. Everyone admits that the wilder impulses of the private self need to be kept in check if civilized social life is to be preserved, but everyone feels that there is something very precious in the emotion-laden dreams whose total suppression would be a terrible tragedy. Everyone, male or female, has a shadowy alter ego like Felix Kennaston's Horvendile and could, if pressed, envision a secret ideal such as Kennaston's Ettarre.

The final movement of the novel's plot is one of deflation, in which it follows the precedent set by all actual erotic adventures. The precious sigil of Scoteia, to whose reunion Kennaston's beloved but excessively dutiful wife remained oblivious, turns out to be nothing more than the broken lid of a jar of cosmetic cream. What the body of the text reminds readers, however, is that people do not live only in reality; people also live in the inner world of the imagination, where the sigil of Scoteia is indeed a sigil, a powerful magical talisman, a symbol of the true heart of human aspiration and human achievement. Richard Harrowby cannot see this, any more than Mrs. Kennaston could, but readers can. Readers can also see the irony in Harrowby's failure; although he is a farmer whose heritage is based in the fecundity of the land and a businessman whose wealth comes from products whose main purpose is to enhance sexual attractiveness, he maintains the conventional pretense that any public reference to sexual matters, however carefully veiled, is indecent.

The Cream of the Jest proved, ironically, to be prophetic. Felix Kennaston's carefully retitled account of *The Audit at Storisende* is charged with indecency, and the resultant publicity makes it a best-seller. James Branch Cabell's next novel—his first full-blown fantasy, heavily spiced with teasing innuendo—was *Jurgen: A Comedy of Justice* (1919), which fell afoul of the courts as well as public opinion, and was made famous by the resultant publicity. In the same way that the Volstead Act, passed in the year of *Jurgen's* publication, gave birth to speakeasies, so the application of the spirit of Prohibition to U.S. literature gave birth to an opposition. The boldest spokespeople of this opposition were writers who used fantasy, fabulation, and allegory to make fierce fun of their enemies; John Erskine and Thorne Smith played leading roles, but Cabell was the leader, and *The Cream of the Jest* provided the materials for all his later broadsides.

Just as Felix Kennaston followed up *The Men Who Loved Allison* with *The Tinctured Veil* ("that amazing performance which he subsequently gave to a bewildered world"), so Cabell went on to produce further adventures of an uncompromisingly amazing—and, to the reading public, somewhat bewildering—nature. Horvendile and Ettarre were to return time and time again, in slightly different guises, throughout the multistranded complex of works that ultimately came to be known as *The Biography of the Life of Manuel* (1927-1930).

In the eighteen-volume edition of this sprawling masterpiece, *The Cream of the Jest* is the concluding volume, the key to all that has gone before. It is described in the author's afterword as the most potent of all his books. In painstakingly mapped genealogies, Felix Kennaston— Cabell's alter ego within the eighteen-volume series—becomes the ultimate descendant and modern inheritor of the adventurous tradition that descends from Manuel, the legendary hero of *Figures of Earth: A Comedy of Appearances* (1921), whose quest is continued by his followers in *The Silver Stallion: A Comedy of Redemption* (1926). The erotic subtext of *The Cream of the Jest* is elaborated and somewhat revised in the last-written novel of the series, *Something About Eve: A Comedy of Fig-Leaves* (1927), but the jest remained the same throughout, and the sequence deserves to be considered the cream of twentieth century fantasy writing in the United States.

"Critical Evaluation" by Brian Stableford

Bibliography:
Davis, Joe Lee. *James Branch Cabell.* New York: Twayne, 1962. Considers all of Cabell's works as confessional pieces and intensely personal romantic flights of fancy. Allots a central role to *The Cream of the Jest.*
Inge, Thomas M., and Edgar E. MacDonald, eds. *James Branch Cabell: Centennial Essays.* Baton Rouge: Louisiana State University Press, 1983. A compilation of essays that were presented at Virginia Commonwealth University, 1979, in commemoration of the centennial of Cabell's birth. Valuable biographical information and criticism.
McDonald, Edgar. "James Branch Cabell." In *Supernatural Fiction Writers: Fantasy and Horror,* edited by Everett F. Bleiler. New York: Charles Scribner's Sons, 1985. A compact commentary on the author's excursions into fantasy.
Tarrant, Desmond. *James Branch Cabell: The Dream and the Reality.* Norman: University of Oklahoma Press, 1967. A Jungian analysis that considers Horvendile and Ettarre as archetypal images.
Wells, Arvin. *Jesting Moses: A Study in Cabellian Comedy.* Gainesville: University of Florida Press, 1962. Relates Cabell's work to the tradition of French satirical fabulation that descends from François Rabelais to Anatole France.

CRIME AND PUNISHMENT

Type of work: Novel
Author: Fyodor Dostoevski (1821-1881)
Type of plot: Psychological realism
Time of plot: Mid-nineteenth century
Locale: Russia
First published: Prestupleniye i Nakazaniye, 1866 (English translation, 1886)

> Principal characters:
> RASKOLNIKOV, a Russian student
> DOUNIA, his sister
> SONIA, a prostitute
> PORFIRY, the inspector of police
> RAZUMIHIN, Raskolnikov's friend

The Story:

Rodion Raskolnikov, an impoverished student in St. Petersburg, dreamed of committing the perfect crime. He murdered an old widowed pawnbroker and her stepsister with an ax and stole some jewelry from their flat. Back in his room, Raskolnikov received a summons from the police. Weak from hunger and illness, he prepared to make a full confession. The police, however, had called merely to ask him to pay a debt his landlady had reported to them. When he discovered what they wanted, he collapsed from relief. Upon being revived, he was questioned; his answers provoked suspicion.

Raskolnikov hid the jewelry under a rock in a courtyard. He returned to his room, where he remained for four days in a high fever. When he recovered, he learned that the authorities had visited him while he was delirious and that he had said things during his fever that tended to cast further suspicion on him.

Luzhin, betrothed to Raskolnikov's sister Dounia, came to St. Petersburg from the provinces to prepare for the wedding. Raskolnikov resented Luzhin because he knew his sister was marrying to provide money for Raskolnikov. Luzhin visited the convalescent and left in a rage when the young man made no attempt to hide his dislike for him.

A sudden calm came upon the young murderer; he went out and read the accounts of the murders in the papers. While he was reading, a detective joined him. The student, in a high pitch of excitement caused by his crime and by his sickness, talked too much, revealing to the detective that he might well be the murderer. No evidence, however, could be found that could throw direct suspicion on him.

Later, witnessing a suicide attempt in the slums of St. Petersburg, Raskolnikov decided to turn himself over to the police; but he was deterred when his friend, a former clerk named Marmeladov, was struck by a carriage and killed. Raskolnikov gave the widow a small amount of money he had received from his mother. Later, he attended a party given by some of his friends and discovered that they, too, suspected him of complicity in the murder of the two women.

Back in his room, Raskolnikov found his mother and his sister, who were awaiting his return. Unnerved at their appearance and not wanting them to be near him, he placed them in the care of his friend, Razumihin, who, upon meeting Dounia, was immediately attracted to her.

1373

In an interview with Porfiry, the chief of the murder investigation, Raskolnikov was mentally tortured by questions and ironic statements until he was ready to believe that he had been all but apprehended for the double crime. Partly in his own defense, he expounded his theory that any means justified the ends of a man of genius and that sometimes he believed himself a man of genius. Raskolnikov proved to his mother and Dounia that Luzhin was a pompous fool, and the angry suitor was dismissed. Razumihin had by that time replaced Luzhin in the girl's affections.

Meanwhile Svidrigailov, who had caused Dounia great suffering while she had been employed as his governess, arrived in St. Petersburg. His wife had died, and he had followed Dounia, as he explained, to atone for his sins against her by settling upon her a large amount of money.

Razumihin received money from a rich uncle and went into the publishing business with Dounia. They asked Raskolnikov to join them in the venture, but the student, whose mind and heart were full of turmoil, declined; he said good-bye to his friend and to his mother and sister and asked them not to try to see him again.

He went to Sonia, the prostitute daughter of the dead Marmeladov. They read Sonia's Bible together. Raskolnikov was deeply impressed by the wretched girl's faith. He felt a great sympathy for Sonia and promised to tell her who had committed the murders of the old pawnbroker and stepsister. Svidrigailov, who rented the room next to Sonia's, overheard the conversation; he anticipated Raskolnikov's disclosure with interest. Tortured in his own mind, Raskolnikov went to the police station, where Porfiry played another game of cat-and-mouse with him. Raskolnikov's conscience and his paranoia had resulted in immense suffering and torment of mind for him.

At a banquet given by Marmeladov's widow for the friends of her late husband, Luzhin accused Sonia of stealing money from his room. He had observed Raskolnikov's interest in Sonia, and he wished to hurt the student for having spoken against him to Dounia. The girl was saved by the report of a neighbor who had seen Luzhin slipping money into Sonia's pocket. Later, in Sonia's room, Raskolnikov confessed his crime and admitted that in killing the two women he had actually destroyed himself.

Svidrigailov had overheard the confession and disclosed his knowledge to Raskolnikov. Believing that Porfiry suspected him of the murder and realizing that Svidrigailov knew the truth, Raskolnikov found life unbearable. Then Porfiry told Raskolnikov outright that he was the murderer, at the same time promising Raskolnikov that a plea of temporary insanity would be placed in his behalf and his sentence would be mitigated if he confessed. Raskolnikov delayed his confession.

Svidrigailov had informed Dounia of the truth concerning her brother, and he now offered to save the student if Dounia would consent to be his wife. He made this offer to her in his room, which he had locked after tricking her into the meeting. He released her when she attempted unsuccessfully to shoot him with a pistol she had brought with her. Convinced at last that Dounia intended to reject him, Svidrigailov gave her a large sum of money and ended his life with the pistol.

Raskolnikov, after being reassured by his mother and his sister of their love for him, and by Sonia of her undying devotion, turned himself over to the police. He was tried and sentenced to serve eight years in Siberia. Dounia and Razumihin, now successful publishers, were married. Sonia followed Raskolnikov to Siberia, where she stayed in a village near the prison camp. In her goodness to Raskolnikov and to the other prisoners, she came to be known as Little Mother Sonia. With her inspiring example, Raskolnikov began his regeneration.

Critical Evaluation:

Crime and Punishment was Fyodor Mikhailovich Dostoevski's first popularly successful novel after his nine-year imprisonment and exile for alleged political crimes (the charges were of doubtful validity) against the czar. After his release from penal servitude, Dostoevski published novels, short stories, novellas, and journalistic pieces, but none of these brought him the critical and popular acclaim which in 1866 greeted *Crime and Punishment*—possibly his most popular novel. This book is no simple precursor of the detective novel, no simplistic mystery story to challenge the minds of Russian counterparts to Sherlock Holmes's fans. It is a complex story of a man's turbulent inner life and his relationship to others and to society at large. The book must be considered within the context of Dostoevski's convictions at the time he wrote the novel, because Dostoevski's experience with czarist power made a lasting impression on his thinking. Indeed, Dostoevski himself made such an evaluation possible by keeping detailed notebooks on the development of his novels and on his problems with fleshing out plots and characters.

Chastened by his imprisonment and exile, Dostoevski shifted his position from the youthful liberalism (certainly not radicalism) which seemed to have precipitated his incarceration to a mature conservatism which embraced many, perhaps most, of the traditional views of his time. Thus, Dostoevski came to believe that legal punishment was not a deterrent to crime because he was convinced that criminals demanded to be punished; that is, they had a spiritual need to be punished. Today, that compulsion might be called masochistic; but Dostoevski, in his time, related the tendency to mystical concepts of the Eastern Orthodox church. With a skeptical hostility toward Western religion and culture, born of several years of living abroad, Dostoevski became convinced that the Western soul was bankrupt and that salvation—one of his major preoccupations—was possible only under the influence of the church and an ineffable love for Mother Russia, a devotion to homeland and to the native soil which would brook neither logic nor common sense: a dedication beyond reason or analysis. Thus, expiation for sins was attained through atonement, a rite of purification.

The required expiation, however, is complicated in *Crime and Punishment* by the split personality—a typically Dostoevskian ploy—of the protagonist. The schizophrenia of Raskolnikov is best illustrated by his ambivalent motives for murdering the pawnbroker. At first, Raskolnikov views his heinous crime as an altruistic act that puts the pawnbroker and her sister out of their misery while providing him the necessary financial support to further his education and mitigate his family's poverty, thus relieving unbearable pressures on him. He does intend to atone for his misdeed by subsequently living an upright life dedicated to humanitarian enterprises. Raskolnikov, however, shortly becomes convinced of his own superiority. Indeed, he divides the human race into "losers" and "winners": the former, meek and submissive; the latter, Nietzschean supermen who can violate any law or principle to attain their legitimately innovative and presumably beneficial ends. Raskolnikov allies himself with the "superman" faction. He intends to prove his superiority by committing murder and justifying it on the basis of his own superiority. This psychological configuration is common enough, but, unlike most paranoid schizophrenics, Raskolnikov carries his design through—a signal tribute to the depth of his convictions.

The results are predictably confusing. The reader is as puzzled about Raskolnikov's motives as he is. Is it justifiable to commit an atrocity in the name of improvement of the human condition? This essential question remains unanswered in *Crime and Punishment*; Raskolnikov, ego-centrically impelled by pride, cannot decide whether or not he is superior, one of those supermen entitled to violate any law or any principle to serve the cause of ultimate justice, however justice might be construed. Likewise, in his notebooks, Dostoevski implied that he, too, was ambivalent about Raskolnikov's motives. Yet he added that he was not a psychologist but a novelist. He was thus more concerned with consequences than with causality. This carefully planned novel therefore expands upon a philosophical problem embodied in the protagonist.

The philosophical problem in *Crime and Punishment* constitutes the central theme of the novel: the lesson Raskolnikov has to learn, the precept he has to master in order to redeem himself. The protagonist finally has to concede that free will is limited. He has to discover and admit that he cannot control and direct his life solely with his reason and intellect, as he tried to do, for such a plan leads only to emptiness and to sinful intellectual pride. Abstract reason takes the place of a fully lived life and precludes the happiness of a fully lived life; happiness must be earned, and it can be earned only through suffering. Thus, Raskolnikov has to learn that happiness is achieved through suffering—another typically Dostoevskian mystical concept. The climactic moment in the novel, therefore, comes when Raskolnikov confesses his guilt at the police station, for Raskolnikov's confession is tantamount to a request for punishment for the crime and acceptance of his need to suffer. In this way, Raskolnikov demonstrates the basic message of *Crime and Punishment*: that reason does not bring happiness; happiness is earned through suffering.

The epilogue—summarizing the fates of other characters; Raskolnikov's trial, his sentencing, and his prison term; and Sonia's devotion to Raskolnikov during his imprisonment—confirms the novel's central theme. Artistically, however, the epilogue is somewhat less than satisfactory. First, Dostoevski's notes indicate that he had considered and rejected an alternate ending in which Raskolnikov committed suicide. Such a conclusion would have been psychologically sound. The very logicality of Raskolnikov's suicide, however, would have suggested a triumph of reason over the soul. That idea was not consonant with Dostoevski's convictions; thus, he dropped the plan. Second, the ending that Dostoevski finally wrote in the epilogue implies that the meek and submissive side of Raskolnikov's personality emerged completely victorious over the superman. Such an ending contradicts Raskolnikov's persistent duality throughout the novel. Raskolnikov's dramatic conversion thus strains credulity, for it seems too pat a resolution of the plot. For the sophisticated reader, however, it does not greatly detract from the powerful psychological impact of the novel proper or diminish the quality of a genuinely serious attempt to confront simultaneously a crucial social problem and a deeply profound individual, human one.

"Critical Evaluation" by Joanne G. Kashdan

Bibliography:
Jackson, Robert Louis, ed. *Twentieth Century Interpretations of "Crime and Punishment."* Englewood Cliffs, N.J.: Prentice-Hall, 1974. Includes an essay by Dostoevski on *Crime and Punishment*. Offers many theories on Raskolnikov's personality. Considers the metaphysical point of view in *Crime and Punishment*.
Johnson, Leslie A. *The Experience of Time in "Crime and Punishment."* Columbus, Ohio: Slavica Publishers, 1984. Explains the use of time in the novel as a means for building anxiety and suffering in the characters. Shows how time is manipulated in *Crime and Punishment* and how the treatment of time in other works by Dostoevski is different.
Jones, Malcolm V. *Dostoyevsky: The Novel of Discord.* London: Elek Books Limited, 1976. Gives an overview of the complexity and chaos that are to be expected in Dostoevski. Extended selection on *Crime and Punishment*.

Leatherbarrow, William J. *Fedor Dostoevsky*. Boston: Twayne, 1981. Includes a biographical sketch of Dostoevski. Commentary on his works, including *Crime and Punishment*. Bibliography, index.

Miller, Robin Feuer. *Critical Essays on Dostoevsky*. Boston: G. K. Hall, 1986. Contains an essay by Leo Tolstoy and criticism and commentary on Dostoevski. Indicates how perceptions of Dostoevski have changed over time.

CRIMES OF THE HEART

Type of work: Drama
Author: Beth Henley (1952-   )
Type of plot: Comedy
Time of plot: 1974
Locale: Hazlehurst, Mississippi
First performed: 1979; first published, 1981

> *Principal characters:*
> LENNY,
> MEG, and
> BABE, sisters
> CHICK, their cousin
> DOC, Meg's old boyfriend
> BARNETTE LLOYD, Babe's lawyer

The Story:

Lenny lit a candle in a cookie to celebrate her thirtieth birthday. Chick, Lenny's cousin, came over before going to bail Lenny's sister, Babe, out of jail. Lenny also wired her sister Meg to come home. After Doc Porter, Meg's old boyfriend, came over to tell Lenny that her horse, Billy Boy, had been struck by lightning, Meg came home to find out that Zackery had been shot by his wife, Babe, because she did not like his looks. Meg also found out that Old Granddaddy had been in the hospital for three months with strokes. Old Granddaddy had been proud of Babe's marriage to Zackery, the most influential man in Hazlehurst. Old Granddaddy also had had high hopes for Meg's singing career, but Meg had stopped singing and was working for a dog food company. Meg was further surprised to find out that Doc Porter was married to a Yankee and had two children by her.

Babe returned home with Chick, who had to leave when told that her two children had eaten paint. Babe realized that Chick had hated the three sisters ever since their father had left them and their mother had come to live with Old Granddaddy. Chick had been embarrassed by mother Magrath's suicide and now by Babe's shooting of Zackery. Babe wondered why Mama had hanged herself. After her husband had left, Mama had been depressed, spending her days on the porch smoking and killing bugs while she sat next to the old yellow cat that she eventually had hanged along with herself.

Babe would not tell why she shot Zackery because she was protecting someone, but she did admit that she shot to kill. Lenny came back to tell Meg and Babe that Chick's children were all right and not to make a mess. Lenny was becoming as fussy as Old Grandma. She did not do anything but work in the brickyard and take care of Old Granddaddy. She only made love to one man, Charlie, a boyfriend she met through a lonely heart's club. According to Lenny, the romance had broken off because Charlie had found out that Lenny had a shrunken ovary and could not have children. Meg suspected that Old Granddaddy had recommended that Lenny break off the relationship. Meg noticed Chick's birthday present to Lenny, and Meg and Babe decided to order a huge cake to celebrate Lenny's birthday.

When Barnette, Babe's lawyer, came over, Babe refused to see him. Barnette was a young but qualified lawyer who had a personal vendetta against Zackery and wanted to prove that Zackery beat Babe and drove her to shoot him. Babe's medical record showed numerous injuries, and Barnette wanted Babe to corroborate that she had been abused. Barnette also assured Meg that he would not betray Babe just to get even with Zackery because he was fond of Babe. When Barnette left, Babe not only confirmed the abuse but also told Meg why she shot Zackery. Lonely and isolated, Babe had engaged in a sexual relationship with Willy Jay, a fifteen-year-old black boy. One day Zackery had seen Willy Jay at his house and had hit him. After contemplating shooting herself, Babe realized she really wanted to kill Zackery, so she shot him. After Meg convinced Babe to speak to Barnette, Babe confessed to Barnette that after she had shot Zackery she had made a pitcher of lemonade before calling the police. Zackery had damaging evidence that Barnette went to find. Barnette, whose father had been ruined by Zackery, was eager to win the case and get even.

Lenny came home angry at Meg for lying to Old Granddaddy about her career. Meg came home disgusted at herself for being obliged to lie. The sisters looked at family pictures and decided to play a game of cards when Doc called and Meg invited him over. When Doc came over Meg blamed herself for leaving Doc after he hurt his leg. Meg had stopped singing when she had had a nervous breakdown. Meg and Doc went out to enjoy the moonlight.

Barnette showed Babe photographs that Zackery had of Babe and Willy Jay making love. That night Old Granddaddy had another stroke and went into a coma. The next morning, Meg came home able to sing because she could care for Doc (although nothing had happened between them), and he had gone back to his wife. Barnette, who had evidence of Zackery's political corruption, would make a deal with him to save Babe. Zackery called Babe to tell her he was having her committed to a mental institution. After chasing Chick up a tree for insulting Meg, Lenny called Charlie and invited him over. After a failed attempt to hang herself, Babe stuck her head in the oven with the gas on. Meg rescued Babe, and Meg and Babe surprised Lenny with an enormous birthday cake. The three sisters laughed and ate huge pieces of cake.

Critical Evaluation:

Crimes of the Heart is Beth Henley's first full-length play, and it launched her career as a playwright. The play was originally produced in Louisville in 1979. In 1981, it opened Off-Broadway at the Manhattan Theatre Club, becoming the first play to win the Pulitzer Prize before opening on Broadway. In 1981, the play also won the coveted New York City Drama Critics Circle Award for best new American play. Later, the play opened to good reviews at the Golden Theatre on Broadway, where it became a box-office hit and was nominated for a Tony Award for the best play for the 1981-1982 Broadway season. Eventually, the play became a staple in regional repertory theater and was made into a film, starring Sissy Spacek and Jessica Lange, in 1987.

The drama is tightly structured, taking place in little more than a day. Suspense builds around Babe's shooting of her husband and her possible jail sentence. The play is also structured around Lenny's thirtieth birthday. The play opens with Lenny lighting one candle on a cookie and ends with the three sisters celebrating Lenny's birthday by eating huge pieces of cake. The other unifying structure is the offstage dying of Old Granddaddy in hospital. Early in the play, Lenny announces that Old Granddaddy has gotten worse in the hospital. Later, Meg and Lenny come back from visiting him. Act II ends on the jolting announcement that Old Granddaddy has had a stroke. Act III begins with the announcement that he is in a coma. Old Granddaddy and his dying absorb a considerable portion of the play's time. His dying focuses the play on two themes: the world of death, decay, and disease that absorbs the characters and the false values that Old Granddaddy has tried to instill in his granddaughters.

Reflecting Old Granddaddy's dying, the world is filled with death, disease, and decay. From Lenny's hair falling out and Meg's slicing pains in her chest to Mrs. Porter's tumor in her bladder, illness is pervasive. Meg reads Old Granddaddy's book on diseases of the skin and Babe keeps news clippings of her mother's suicide in her scrapbook. Old Granddaddy is not alone among the ailing men in the play. Zackery is in the hospital with a bullet in his stomach. Doc Porter has a crippled leg. Willy Jay is beaten. Other signs of disease, decay, and death include Mama's cat's being hung and Billy Boy's being struck by lightning. The audience may wonder if, in some symbolic sense, all the death and destruction has something to do with the baleful and unseen influence of Old Granddaddy.

Old Granddaddy has also influenced the lives of his three granddaughters. They have tried to live out his dreams for them. He has filled them with illusions that have led them to self-destructive behavior. Old Granddaddy wanted Babe to marry the influential Zackery so she could rise up in society. Babe is not suited to be among Zackery's social set and winds up unhappily married to a brutish man. Old Granddaddy pumped Meg up with ideas about becoming a Hollywood celebrity. He told her that with her singing talent, all she needed was exposure and she could make her own breaks. Her attempt to live the life Old Granddaddy set for her brought her to the brink of madness. She makes up stories about her fame and then feels guilty afterward. Whether she tries to fulfill Old Granddaddy's dream or acts to spite him, she is still controlled by him. Lenny is also acting out Old Granddaddy's image of what she should be. Old Granddaddy has made her feel self-conscious about her shrunken ovary. She has become Old Granddaddy's nursemaid. She does not know what she will do with her life after Old Granddaddy dies. He advised her to give up the one man with whom she had a relationship.

On the day of their mother's funeral, Old Granddaddy filled them so full of banana splits for breakfast that they got sick. His attempts to fill them with the rich desserts of life has left them physically and mentally ill. Babe shoots her husband then swills down three glasses of her favorite lemonade until she is bloated. Meg tries to harden herself against life by looking at pictures of crippled children, then using money she might have donated to the March of Dimes to buy a double-scoop ice cream cone. When Lenny is filled with Old Granddaddy's advice, she feels like vomiting.

Critics have debated whether the play has a clear resolution. Some critics believe that the final celebration signifies a change in the lives of the three sisters. The resolution, however, is uncertain because the ending is clearly linked to the sisters' reactions to Old Granddaddy. The final scene of the three sisters laughing replicates the previous scene of laughing over Old Granddaddy's coma. Their laughter comes more out of hysteria than joy. The scene in which the sisters stuff themselves with huge pieces of cake for breakfast reenacts Old Granddaddy's stuffing them full of banana splits for breakfast. Although they have made discoveries about themselves, their gorging themselves with birthday cake repeats the pattern of what Old Granddaddy has instilled in them. They still seek solace in empty pleasures.

Crimes of the Heart is a well-crafted drama that blends a fine mixture of comedy and tragedy in the Southern gothic style. It blends the grotesque with the touching, the eccentric with the realistic, and the laughter of hysteria with the laughter of celebration.

Paul Rosefeldt

Bibliography:
Adler, Thomas P. *Mirror on the Stage: The Pulitzer Prize Plays as an Approach to American Drama.* West Lafayette, Ind.: Purdue University Press, 1987. A brief discussion of *Crimes of the Heart* as a play of female solidarity.

Gagen, Jean. "Most Resembling Unlikeness and Most Unlikely Resemblance: Beth Henley's *Crimes of the Heart* and Chekhov's *Three Sisters.*" *Studies in American Drama: 1945-Present* 4 (1989): 119-128. A comparison that finds *Crimes of the Heart* lacking in the subtlety of the *Three Sisters*.

Guerra, Jonnie. "Beth Henley: Female Quest and the Family Play Tradition." In *Making a Spectacle: Feminist Essays on Contemporary Women's Theatre*. Ann Arbor: University of Michigan Press, 1989. A feminist study of Henley's plays that focuses on women's breaking away from the patriarchy in *Crimes of the Heart*.

Hargrove, Nancy D. "The Tragicomic Vision of Beth Henley's Drama." *Southern Quarterly* 22 (Summer, 1984), pp. 54-70. An exploration of the mixture of tragedy and comedy in Henley's plays.

Karpinski, Joanne B. "The Ghosts of Chekhov's *Three Sisters* Haunt Beth Henley's *Crimes of the Heart*." In *Modern American Drama: The Female Canon*, edited by June Schlueter. Madison, N.J.: Fairleigh Dickinson University Press, 1990. A comparison that finds *Crimes of the Heart* more accessible to modern audiences than *Three Sisters*.

THE CRISIS

Type of work: Novel
Author: Winston Churchill (1871-1947)
Type of plot: Historical
Time of plot: 1860's
Locale: Missouri and Virginia
First published: 1901

> *Principal characters:*
> STEPHEN BRICE, a young lawyer from Boston
> VIRGINIA CARVEL, his sweetheart
> CLARENCE COLFAX, Brice's rival for Virginia Carvel
> JUDGE WHIPPLE, Brice's employer and friend
> COLONEL CARVEL, Virginia's father
> ABRAHAM LINCOLN

The Story:

In 1858, Stephen Brice moved from Boston to St. Louis with his widowed mother. He went to accept the offer of Judge Whipple, his father's friend, who had promised Stephen an opportunity to enter his law firm. A personable young man, Stephen Brice found favor among the people of St. Louis, including Colonel Carvel, and the colonel's daughter, Virginia. Stephen promptly fell in love with Virginia Carvel. He was not encouraged by the young woman at first because he was a New Englander.

One day, Judge Whipple sent Stephen to Springfield, Illinois, with a message for the man who was running for senator against Stephen A. Douglas. When Stephen Brice finally found his man, Abraham Lincoln, he was in time to hear the famous Freeport debate between Lincoln and Douglas. Lincoln made a deep impression on Stephen, who went back to St. Louis a confirmed Republican, as Judge Whipple had hoped. Feeling that Stephen would some day be a great politician, the judge had sent him to Lincoln to catch some of Lincoln's idealism and practical politics.

Convinced by Lincoln that no country could exist half-slave and half-free, Stephen Brice became active in Missouri politics on behalf of the Republicans, a dangerous course to take in St. Louis because of the many Southerners living in the city. His antislavery views soon alienated Stephen from the woman he wanted to marry, who then promised to marry Stephen's rival, her cousin and fellow Southerner, Clarence Colfax.

Lincoln lost the election for the Senate, but in doing so won for himself the presidency of the United States in 1860. During both campaigns, Stephen Brice worked for the Republican party. An able orator, he became known as a rising young lawyer of exceptional abilities.

The guns at Fort Sumter reverberated loudly in St. Louis in 1861. The city was divided into two factions, proslavery Southerners and antislavery Northerners. Friends of long standing no longer spoke to one another, and members of the same family found themselves at odds over the question of which side Missouri should favor, the Union or the Confederacy. It was a trying time for Stephen Brice. Having a widowed mother and his political activities to look after, he was unable to join the army. Judge Whipple convinced him that, for the time being, he could do more for his country as a civilian. It was hard for the young man to believe the judge when all of Stephen's friends and acquaintances were going about the city in uniform.

When war was declared, Missouri had a little campaign of its own, for the state militia, under the direction of the governor, tried to seize the state. This attempt was defeated by the prompt action of Federal forces in capturing the militia training camp without firing a shot. A spectator at that minor engagement, Stephen made the acquaintance of a former army officer named William T. Sherman and of another shambling man who claimed he should be given a regiment. The young officers laughed at him; his name was Ulysses S. Grant.

Among those captured when Federal troops overcame the Missouri militia was Clarence Colfax, Stephen's rival. Clarence refused to give his oath and go on parole, and he soon escaped from prison and disappeared into the South. Virginia Carvel thought him more of a hero than ever.

Communications with the South and the Southwest had been cut by the Union armies, and as a result Colonel Carvel went bankrupt. He and his daughter aided Southern sympathizers attempting to join the Confederate Army. At last, the colonel felt that it was his duty to leave St. Louis and take an active part in the hostilities.

The war continued, putting the lie to those optimists who had prophesied that hostilities would end in a few months. By the time of the battle at Vicksburg, Stephen had become a lieutenant in the Union Army. He distinguished himself in that battle and came once more to the attention of Sherman. When the city fell, Stephen found Clarence Colfax, now a lieutenant-colonel in the Confederate Army. The Southerner had received a severe wound. To save Clarence's life, Stephen arranged for him to be sent to St. Louis on a hospital ship. Stephen knew that he was probably sending his rival back to marry Virginia Carvel. Young Colfax realized what Stephen had done and told Virginia as much while he was convalescing in St. Louis. The girl vowed that she would never marry a Yankee, even if Colfax were killed.

Judge Whipple had fallen ill, and he was nursed by Virginia and by Stephen's mother. While the judge was sinking fast, Colonel Carvel appeared. At the risk of his life, he had come through the lines in civilian clothes to see his daughter and his old friend. There was a strange meeting at Judge Whipple's deathbed. Clarence Colfax, Colonel Carvel, and Stephen Brice were all there. They had all risked their lives, for the Confederates could have been arrested as spies, and Stephen, because he was with them, could have been convicted of treason. That night, Virginia realized that she was in love with Stephen.

After the judge's death, Stephen returned to the army. Ordered to General Sherman's staff, he accompanied the general on the march through Georgia. At the battle of Bentonville, Stephen again met Clarence Colfax, who had been captured by Union soldiers while in civilian clothes and brought to Sherman's headquarters as a spy. Once again, Stephen interceded with Sherman and saved the Southerner's life. Soon afterward, Stephen, promoted to the rank of major, was sent by Sherman with some dispatches to General Grant at City Point, Virginia. Stephen recognized Grant as the man he had seen at the engagement of the militia camp back in St. Louis.

During the conference with the general, an officer appeared to summon Stephen to meet another old acquaintance, Abraham Lincoln. The president, like Grant, wished to hear Stephen's firsthand account of the march through Georgia to the sea. When Stephen asked for a pardon for Clarence Colfax, Lincoln said he would consider the matter. Stephen went with Lincoln to Richmond for an inspection of that city after it had fallen to Grant's armies.

Virginia Carvel, not knowing of Stephen's intercession on behalf of Clarence Colfax, traveled to Washington to ask Lincoln for a pardon. She gained an audience with the president, during which she met Stephen once again. Lincoln granted them the pardon, saying that with the war soon to end, the time to show clemency had come. He left Virginia and Stephen alone when he hurried to keep another appointment. The young people had realized during their talk with Lincoln that there was much to be forgiven and forgotten by both sides in the struggle that was drawing to a close. The emotion of the moment overcame their reticence at last, and they declared their love for each other. They were married the following day.

After the wedding, they went to visit Virginia's ancestral home in Annapolis. A few days later, word came to them that Lincoln had died from an assassin's bullet.

Critical Evaluation:

America's Winston Churchill—not to be confused with Great Britain's Winston Churchill— was one of the most popular novelists in the early twentieth century. Descended from one of the earliest families of New England, Churchill was born in St. Louis, Missouri, in 1871 and raised there. He received an appointment to the U.S. Naval Academy; although he did well at Annapolis, and in spite of his lack of personal wealth, he chose a literary career. His first novel, *The Celebrity*, was published in 1897, but it was his second, *Richard Carvel* (1899), a historical novel set during the American Revolution, that made Churchill a household name and brought him both popular and critical praise.

The Crisis is something of a sequel to *Richard Carvel*, with Richard's descendants, Virginia Carvel and her father, among the major characters. Churchill initially envisioned *The Crisis* (originally titled *The Third Generation*) as a saga covering the period from the Civil War to the time of its writing, but then restricted the time to the Civil War era alone. The story is set largely in St. Louis, a simple choice since it was Churchill's home until he moved to New Hampshire in 1900. It also gave the author certain advantages in structuring the novel. Missouri was both a slave state and a border state, and Churchill's St. Louis was populated not only by Southerners but also by emigrants from New England who were unsympathetic to the Southern way of life, to its aristocratic values, and to slavery. Churchill explicitly postulates in *The Crisis* that the Civil War was, in many ways, a direct continuation of the struggle between the aristocratic Cavaliers who supported King Charles II during the English Civil War of the 1640's and their opponents, the Parliamentary Puritans. The Puritans migrated to New England, the Cavaliers to Southern states, and in the mid-nineteenth century their descendants met, uneasily, in St. Louis.

Churchill's historical interpretation is not accurate. The Southern aristocracy—and most Southerners were not aristocrats—was a U.S. development with no direct connection to England's Cavaliers, but his reading of the past gives *The Crisis* a dramatic structural conflict of opposites. A more historically accurate choice is Churchill's including as a third community in St. Louis the recent emigrants from Germany, whom he made symbolic representatives of the values of liberty and union.

What made *The Crisis* vastly popular was its Civil War setting. The greatest U.S. tragedy was the stuff of drama. In the early twentieth century, the war's memories, real and imagined, were still fresh and relevant to Churchill's readers. North and South were only recently reconciled, in part because of the recent Spanish-American War of 1898. Feelings were still strong, but enough time had passed that both sides could better understand the position of their opponents.

It is apparent that Churchill agrees with history's verdict: The North's cause was the better cause and deserved to be victorious. Early in the novel, Stephen Brice, a recently arrived upper-class New Englander, views a slave auction and buys a young woman to save her from a worse fate. The South was destined to lose because of its defense of slavery and for its attempt to destroy the Union. Churchill was a man of his times, for whom freedom and liberty for the slaves was necessary and inevitable. Also reflecting his times, Churchill depicts African Americans as free, but not necessarily equal to white Europeans. African Americans in *The Crisis*, as in the later and even more popular novel, Margaret Mitchell's *Gone with the Wind* (1936), were generally presented as being inferior. The recent German emigrants from northern Europe, on the other hand, could play an important role in the preservation of the Union. In the early twentieth century, slavery might belong to the past but racism was still deeply entrenched in American society.

The Civil War setting gives *The Crisis* its continuing popularity; it is the only one of Churchill's novels that remained in print after his death in 1947. Fast-paced, full of dramatic incidents and confrontations, and driven by profound moral and philosophical issues that have continued to affect Americans, *The Crisis* seems destined to maintain a broad and lasting readership.

For all of its virtues, *The Crisis* cannot compare with the best American novels of its generation. Churchill's novels were popular among American readers—Theodore Roosevelt wrote words of praise to the author from the White House—but Churchill did not receive the lasting critical recognition accorded to his contemporaries, such as Stephen Crane, Theodore Dreiser, or Frank Norris. Churchill's greatest failure as a novelist is that his major characters are types rather than individuals: Their actions and responses are largely predictable. Stephen Brice and his mother represent the staunch and upright traditional New England Puritans. Virginia Carvel and her father, the Colonel, exemplify the Southern aristocracy at its best, while Virginia's admirer and Brice's rival, Clarence Colfax, epitomizes the Southerner as the cavalier warrior. Eliphalet Hopper is also from New England, but symbolizes the corrupted Puritan: materialistic, opportunistic, and amoral. Judge Whipple is the uncompromising abolitionist who is willing to sunder even old friendships for the cause. Churchill's characters never transcended their two-dimensional construction.

Paradoxically, the best-realized character in *The Crisis* is not one of Churchill's fictional creations but Abraham Lincoln. Churchill took his historical responsibility seriously and did considerable research before writing *The Crisis*, and he successfully captures many of Lincoln's qualities. He is equally successful in his portrayal of William T. Sherman and, to a lesser degree, Ulysses S. Grant, both prominent Civil War generals. The portrayal of Virginia Carvel, Stephen Brice, and the other fictional figures, and their resulting predictable actions, however, limit and date *The Crisis*. Still, Churchill tells an exciting and fast-moving story, with the Civil War as the stage, that became and has remained popular.

"Critical Evaluation" by Eugene Larson

Bibliography:
Knight, Grant C. *The Strenuous Age in American Literature*. Chapel Hill: University of North Carolina Press, 1954. Classic study of American literature covering the period 1900 to 1910, largely coinciding with the presidency of Theodore Roosevelt. Successfully integrates the authors, including Churchill, and their works with the times.
Pattee, Fred Lewis. *The New American Literature, 1890-1930*. New York: Century, 1930. Although dated, the work has valuable comments on Churchill's *The Crisis* as being in the Romantic tradition of the Waverley novels of Sir Walter Scott.
Schneider, Robert W. *Five Novelists of the Progressive Era*. New York: Columbia University Press, 1965. Compares Churchill with the other major authors of the period: William Dean Howells, Stephen Crane, Frank Norris, and Theodore Dreiser. Concludes with the argument that Churchill's liberalism was fundamentally affected by the events of World War I.

_____. *Novelist to a Generation: The Life and Thought of Winston Churchill.* Bowling Green, Ohio: Bowling Green University Popular Press, 1976. This biographical study by an eminent scholar is the most satisfactory work about Winston Churchill. Combines a discussion of his life with an analysis of his novels.

Titus, Warren Irving. *Winston Churchill.* New York: Twayne, 1963. Combines biography and literary analysis. Was the major study of Churchill until the appearance of Schneider's analytical biography.

THE CRITIC
Or, A Tragedy Rehearsed

Type of work: Drama
Author: Richard Brinsley Sheridan (1751-1816)
Type of plot: Satire
Time of plot: Late eighteenth century
Locale: London
First performed: 1779; first published, 1781

> *Principal characters:*
> MR. DANGLE, a Londoner with a passion for theatrical affairs
> MRS. DANGLE, his wife
> MR. SNEER, Mr. Dangle's friend and resident sneer
> MR. PUFF, a puff writer and dramatist
> SIR FRETFUL PLAGIARY, a dramatist

The Story:

Mr. Dangle, a well-to-do gentleman of London, sat one morning with his wife at breakfast. While he read the newspapers, Mrs. Dangle complained that her husband's hobby, the theater, was making her house unlivable, with disappointed authors, would-be actors, musicians, and critics making it their meeting place. Dangle protested vigorously, but as he did so a stream of callers arrived to prove her point.

The first caller was Mr. Sneer. He and Mrs. Dangle got into a discussion on the morality of the stage and the proper material for comedies. Then Sir Fretful Plagiary, a dramatist, was announced. Before he entered, Dangle reported that Plagiary was a close friend but that he could not accept criticism of his work. Sir Fretful told how his new play had been sent to the Covent Garden theater, rather than to Drury Lane, because of the envy he had uncovered there.

Sneer, Dangle, and Sir Fretful Plagiary began to discuss the latter's new play. In the discussion all criticism of his drama was brushed aside in one way or another by the author, who ended up with a diatribe against all who would say anything against his work, including the newspapers. At the end of their talk, a group of musicians entered looking for Dangle's assistance in securing work with the theaters. They were led by an Italian who knew no English and a Frenchman who knew little English, but was to act as interpreter.

The Frenchman and the Italian tried to make Dangle understand what they wanted, but with little success. After a trilingual conversation, in which not one of the participants could understand the others, Mrs. Dangle took the musicians into another room for refreshment and so relieved her husband of their troublesome presence. As the musicians left Dangle and Sneer alone in the room, Mr. Puff, another dramatist who had a play in rehearsal at the theater, entered. Puff was introduced to Sneer by Dangle as a puffing writer for the newspapers, whose job it was to praise anyone or anything for a price; he was, in short, an eighteenth century press agent. He explained for the benefit of Mr. Sneer the various kinds of "puffs" he wrote: the direct, the preliminary, the collateral, the collusive, and the oblique. At the end of the conversation, the three agreed to meet at the theater to watch a rehearsal of Puff's new play.

Later the three met, and Puff informed his two friends, Dangle and Sneer, that the time of his play was the days following defeat of the Spanish Armada during the reign of Elizabeth. The under-prompter, appearing to notify the author that the rehearsal was ready to begin, said that the play had been somewhat shortened. The actors, informed that anything they found unnecessary in the tragedy could be cut, had taken full liberties with Mr. Puff's script.

When the curtain rose, two watchmen were found asleep at four in the morning. Sir Christopher Hatton and Sir Walter Raleigh appeared on the stage and began the exposition of the plot. They were interrupted at intervals by protestations and explanations by the author, who spoke to the actors on the stage and to his two friends observing the rehearsal.

In the second act of the play a love story between the daughter of the fort commander and a captured Spanish prince was introduced, again with continued interruptions by the dramatist, who was enraged at the liberties taken by the actors in cutting his lines and parts of scenes. He and his friends, Sneer and Dangle, continued to discuss dramatic art as the rehearsal continued and found various aspects of the play to point up their discussion. Puff was particularly proud of the second sight credited to the heroine, a device by which he was able to describe the defeat of the Spanish Armada without showing the sea fight on the stage.

He was also quite proud of a verbal fencing match between the heroine and the Spanish prince. When Sneer and Dangle found the repartee ambiguous, Puff explained that he had written the dialogue completely in fencing terms, an explanation which his friends found scarcely more intelligible. Puff irritated the actors by directing them as the rehearsal progressed, and they, in turn, continued to irritate him by cutting out more lines. At their protestations that they could not act because of his interruptions, he replied heatedly that he had feelings, too, and did not like to see his play shredded by the players.

At the end of the love scene in the play, Puff began an argument with the under-prompter, who informed him that it was impossible to rehearse the park scene because the carpenters had not built the scenery. Puff angrily announced that they could cut his play as they would; he intended to print it in its entirety.

The next scene in the rehearsal of Puff's play was a sentimental discovery scene not connected with the main story. In reply to his friends' comments, Puff explained that there was no need to have a logical connection between the main plot and the subplot. Then came what Puff called the most perfect scene in the play. An actor entered, sat down, shook his head, arose, and went off the stage. The shaking of the head, according to Puff, said more than all the words he could have written.

In the last scene of the play the Spanish prince was killed in a duel, and his English sweetheart went mad. After her exit from the stage, a masque procession of all the British rivers and their tributaries passed over the stage, while an orchestra played Handel's *Water Music*. Following the procession, Puff announced to his friends that the rehearsal was good, but that the actors were not yet perfect. To the actors he announced that another rehearsal would be held the next day.

Critical Evaluation:

In Richard Brinsley Sheridan's time *The Critic: Or, A Tragedy Rehearsed* was probably best known for its bitingly satirical portrait of Sheridan's fellow dramatist, Richard Cumberland, who was the model for Sir Fretful Plagiary. Today the play is most important for the light it sheds on what Sheridan thought of the drama prevalent in his own time. By showing the reader the insipidity of the tragedy rehearsed within the play, the laughable defense of trite dramatic devices by its author, and the comments by the actors, Sheridan lets the reader see what he thought of the state of drama during his age.

The principal theme of *The Critic* is the dynamic interplay of illusion and reality. The central focus is on the role language plays in that interplay. Dangle, Sneer, and Puff—the names prepare one for the spirit of the comedy—form the play's comic center, where each character either ridicules or is ridiculed, sometimes both. The play's themes derive from the portrayal of characters who pretend to be better than they are.

Act I begins the play's attacks on fakery and moral blindness. Sneer characterizes the age as "luxurious and dissipated," saying it is nevertheless hypocritical enough to produce a drama that ignores "the follies and foibles of society" in favor of dramatizing "the greater vices and blacker crimes of humanity." With the arrival of Sir Fretful Plagiary, the play's attention shifts to a type of individual author. On the pretext of repeating what newspaper reviewers have said, Sneer and Dangle attack Sir Fretful's plagiarism, coarse language, and dullness. The play's main target, however, is Puff and his production of *The Spanish Armada*, a tragedy that illustrates, in comic reversal, the play's plea for elevated standards in the theater and for literary and personal honesty.

The second and third acts present a world within a world and a tragedy within a comedy. Puff's play is a burlesque of the tragic spirit. One of the ways that Sheridan effects his burlesque is to mix the comic outer drama with the highly stylized language and actions of the actors in rehearsal. Puff's understanding of the elevated world of tragedy is satirized by his play's ridiculous actions and by the stilted, hackneyed dialogue of its characters, who bear such names as Whiskerandos and Tilburnia.

Act I has alerted the audience to the significance of language in the way people create their own reality and to the potential of language as an instrument of comic ridicule. When introducing Sneer to Mrs. Dangle, for example, Mr. Dangle draws attention to the comic resources of language: "My dear, here's Mr. Sneer." Sir Fretful's crime is not only that he steals ideas from others but that he coarsens and dulls what he takes—and is unaware of the fact. Puff boasts an ability to "insinuate obsequious rivulets into visionary groves" and to live off charitable donations by exaggerating his misfortunes.

Such portrayals illustrate the inability of people in general to escape the linguistic prison they erect around themselves, or that is erected around them by others. When Sneer ironically proposes that a statue of Mercury be erected in honor of Puff, a god "of fiction," he offers an apt symbol of Puff, whose nature is expressed in his devotion to artifice, to making a lie seem real. Making illusion seem real, the essence of drama, is one of the play's themes, and Sheridan seems to be saying that the artifice is morally acceptable as long as the writer keeps clear the line separating truth from fiction. Sir Fretful and Puff are morally reprehensible because they do not keep the line clear, and the irony is that they cannot understand their failure to do so. This failure makes them fools despite their expertise in fakery.

The play argues that people tend to see only what they wish to see—or see only what their natures allow them to see. During the rehearsal of his tragedy, Puff, blinded by vanity, is unable to see how absurd the performance of his tragedy is. When Sneer points out that "the clown seems to talk in as high a style as the first hero," Puff declares he does not make "slavish distinctions." He is incapable of distinguishing good language from bad language, tragedy from farce, or truth from fiction. His failure to achieve this kind of intellectual keenness is the chief lesson of the final two acts. Puff represents a tendency toward vanity and self-delusion in everyone; the play constitutes a moral indictment of human nature.

In Act I, the duty of drama to inculcate morals is made an issue. Sheridan's play, by implication, offers an example of the principle working as it should, helping the audience to see, through satire and comedy, that people make fools of themselves, and create bad art in the process, when they cannot distinguish fiction from reality. When Sneer says that the theater "in proper hands, might certainly be made the school of morality," Sheridan seems to be inviting the audience to view his play as an exercise in distinguishing right from wrong.

Part of the play's aim is to define good tragedy by showing bad tragedy. In a comic twist, Puff is the guide. Puff's final announcement—"we'll rehearse this piece again to-morrow"—is followed by the stage direction, "Curtain drops/finis." By ending both plays together, Sheridan is suggesting that the worlds of the two plays are interconnected. Puff's tragedy will recycle, and so will the world outside the play. By ridiculing the vanity and blindness of Puff, and by suggesting that Puff's world coincides with that of the audience, *The Critic* serves as a warning.

"Critical Evaluation" by Bernard E. Morris

Bibliography:
Auburn, Mark S. *Sheridan's Comedies*. Lincoln: University of Nebraska Press, 1977. The first chapter characterizes the nature of comedy between 1748 and 1780, emphasizing Sheridan's role in its development. A separate chapter is devoted to *The Critic*.

Ayling, Stanley. *A Portrait of Sheridan*. London: Constable, 1985. Places *The Critic* in its social and political context. Describes Sheridan's involvement with the theater.

Danziger, Marlies K. *Oliver Goldsmith and Richard Brinsley Sheridan*. New York: Frederick Ungar, 1978. The initial chapter places Sheridan's plays in their social and literary context. Another chapter analyzes *The Critic* as a complex study of the relationship of art and life.

Durant, Jack D. *Richard Brinsley Sheridan: A Reference Guide*. Boston: G. K. Hall, 1981. Lists the major editions of Sheridan's work and offers nearly 300 pages of critical studies dating from 1816 to 1979. Extensive annotations.

Loftis, John. *Sheridan and the Drama of Georgian England*. Oxford: Basil Blackwell, 1976. Contains a chronology of Sheridan's life and a bibliography that includes critical studies of Sheridan's plays, background studies, and biographies. Connects *The Critic* to the political climate that influenced the play's satire and to the burlesque tradition.

CRITIQUE OF PURE REASON

Type of work: Philosophy
Author: Immanuel Kant (1724-1804)
First published: Kritik der reinen Vernunft, 1781 (English translation, 1838)

Immanuel Kant's *Critique of Pure Reason* is a masterpiece in metaphysics designed to explore the possibility of synthetic a priori judgments. A synthetic judgment is one whose predicate is not contained in the subject; an a priori judgment is one whose truth can be known independently of experience. Kant therefore in effect questioned how it is that statements in which the idea of the subject does not involve the idea of the predicate can nevertheless be true and can also be known to be true without recourse to experience.

To make the question clearer, Kant offered examples of analytic and synthetic judgments. The statement that "All bodies are extended" is offered as an analytic judgment because it would be impossible to think of a body, that is, a physical object, that was not spread out in space; the statement "All bodies are heavy" is offered as a synthetic judgment, because Kant believed that it is possible to conceive of a body without supposing that it has weight.

The judgment that "All red apples are apples" is analytic because it would be impossible to conceive that something that was red and an apple could possibly not be an apple; the predicate is, in this case, included in the subject. The judgment "All apples are red," however, is synthetic, because it is possible to think of an apple without supposing it to be red; in fact, some apples are green. Synthetic judgments can be false, but analytic judgments are never false.

A priori knowledge is knowledge "absolutely independent of all experience," whereas a posteriori knowledge is empirical knowledge, that is, knowledge possible only through experience. Human beings can know a priori that all red apples are apples (and that they are red), but to know that a particular apple has a worm in it is something that can be known only a posteriori.

The question whether synthetic a priori judgments are possible concerns judgments that must be true—because they are a priori and can be known to be true without reference to experience—even though, being synthetic, their predicates are not conceived in thinking of their subjects. As an example of a synthetic a priori judgment Kant offers the statement: "Everything that happens has its cause." He argues that he can think of something happening without considering whether it has a cause; the judgment is, therefore, not analytic. Yet he supposes that it is necessarily the case that everything that happens has a cause, even though his experience is not sufficient to support that claim. The judgment must be a priori. How are such synthetic a priori judgments possible?

One difficulty arises at this point. Critics of Kant have argued that Kant's examples are not satisfactory. The judgment that everything that happens has a cause is regarded either as being an analytic rather than a synthetic a priori judgment (every event being a cause relative to an immediately subsequent event, and an effect relative to an immediately preceding event) or as being a synthetic a posteriori rather than an a priori judgment (which leaves open the possibility that some events may be uncaused). A great many critics have maintained that Kant's examples are bound to be unsatisfactory for the obvious reason that no synthetic a priori judgments are possible. The argument is that unless the predicate is involved in the subject, the truth of the judgment is a matter of fact, to be determined only by reference to experience.

Kant's answer to the problem concerning the possibility of synthetic a priori judgments was that pure reason—that is, the faculty of arriving at a priori knowledge—is possible because the human way of knowing determines, to a considerable extent, the character of what is known.

Whenever human beings perceive physical objects, they perceive them in time and space; time and space are what Kant calls "modes of intuition," that is, ways of apprehending the objects of sensation. Because human beings must perceive objects in time and space, the judgment that an object is in time must be a priori but, provided the element of time is no part of the conception of the object, the judgment is also synthetic. It is somewhat as if a world were being considered in which all human beings are compelled to wear green glasses. The judgment that everything seen is somewhat green would be a priori (since nothing could be seen except by means of the green glasses), but it would also be synthetic (since being green is no part of the conception of object).

In Kant's terminology, a transcendental philosophy is one concerned not so much with objects as with the mode of a priori knowledge, and a critique of pure reason is the science of the sources and the limits of what contains the principles by which human beings know a priori. Space and time are the forms of pure intuition, that is, modes of sensing objects. The science of all principles of a priori sensibility, that is, of those principles that make a priori intuitions (sensations) possible, Kant calls the transcendental aesthetic.

Human beings do more than merely sense or perceive objects; they also think about them. The study of the existence of a priori concepts, as distinguished from intuitions, is called transcendental logic. This study is divided into transcendental analytic, dealing with the principles of the understanding without which no object can be thought, and transcendental dialectic, showing the error of applying the principles of pure thought to objects considered in themselves.

Using Aristotle's term, Kant calls the pure concepts of the understanding categories. The categories are of quantity (unity, plurality, totality), quality (reality, negation, limitation), relation (substance and accident, cause and effect, reciprocity between agent and patient), and modality (possibility-impossibility, existence-nonexistence, necessity-contingency). According to Kant, everything that is thought is considered according to these categories. It is not a truth about things in themselves that they are one or many, positive or negative, but that all things fall into these categories because the understanding is so constituted that it can think in no other way.

Kant maintained that there are three subjective sources of the knowledge of objects: sense, imagination, and apperception. By its categories, the mind imposes a unity on the manifold of intuition; what would be a mere sequence of appearances, were the mind not involved, makes sense as the appearance of objects.

The principles of pure understanding fall into four classes: axioms of intuition, anticipations of perception, analogies of experience, and postulates of empirical thought in general. The principle of the axioms of intuition is that "All intuitions are extensive magnitudes," proved by reference to the claim that all intuitions are conditioned by the spatial and temporal mode of intuition.

The principle by which all perception is anticipated is that "the real that is an object of sensation has intensive magnitude, that is, a degree." It would not be possible for an object to influence the senses to no degree, hence various objects have different degrees of influence on the senses. The principle of the analogies of experience is that "Experience is possible only through the representation of a necessary connection of perceptions." Human experience would be meaningless were it not ordered by the supposition that perceptions are of causally related substances which are mutually interacting.

Kant's postulates of empirical thought in general relate the possibility of things to their satisfying the formal conditions of intuition and of concepts, the actuality of things to their satisfying the material conditions of sensation, and the necessity of things to their being determined "in accordance with universal conditions of experience" in their connection with the actual.

A distinction that is central in Kant's philosophy is the distinction between the phenomenal and the noumenal. The phenomenal world is the world of appearances, the manifold of sensation as formed spatially and temporally and understood by use of the categories. The noumenal world is the world beyond appearance, the unknown and unknowable, the world of "things-in-themselves."

In the attempt to unify experience, reason constructs certain ideas—of a soul, of the world, of God. These ideas are, however, transcendental in that they are illegitimately derived from a consideration of the conditions of reason. To rely on them leads to difficulties that Kant's "Transcendental Dialectic" was designed to expose. The "Paralogisms of Pure Reason" are fallacious syllogisms for which the reason has transcendental grounds; that is, the reason makes sense out of its operations by supposing what, on logical grounds, cannot be admitted. The "Antinomies of Pure Reason" are pairs of contradictory propositions, all capable of proof provided the arguments involve illegitimate applications of the forms and concepts of experience to matters beyond experience.

Kant concludes the *Critique of Pure Reason* with the suggestion that the ideas of God, freedom, and immortality arise in the attempt to make moral obligation intelligible. This point was developed at greater length in his *Metaphysics of Morals* (1785) and his *Critique of Practical Reason* (1788).

Bibliography:
Cassirer, H. W. *Kant's First "Critique."* New York: Humanities Press, 1954. Highlights several of the weaknesses in Kant's "critical philosophy"; balanced by an assessment of Kant's strengths. Recommended for the more advanced student.
Ewing, A. C. *A Short Commentary on Kant's "Critique of Pure Reason."* 1938. Chicago, Ill.: University of Chicago Press, 1987. Presents an objective exegesis of Kant's work, suitable for the beginner. Careful, perceptive discussion of many of Kant's terms and therefore also useful for the more advanced student. Points out the contributions made by both Paton and Smith, despite their opposed critical views. Highly recommended.
Paton, H. J. *Kant's Metaphysic of Experience.* 1936. New York: Macmillan, 1951. Covers first half of *Critique of Pure Reason.* Disagrees sharply with N. K. Smith on its composition. Argues for the organic coherence of Kant's "critical philosophy." A standard and well-received commentary.
Smith, Norman Kemp. *A Commentary to Kant's "Critique of Pure Reason."* 1918. Rev. ed. London: Macmillan, 1930. An important source, though some of its arguments are controversial. Employs Hans Vaihinger's "patchwork" theory of the composition of *Critique of Pure Reason.* Recommended to be read alongside Paton's commentary for a fuller range of critical views.
Weldon, T. D. *Introduction to Kant's "Critique of Pure Reason."* Oxford, England: The Clarendon Press, 1945. A useful work for all levels. Discusses *Critique of Pure Reason* thoroughly; also covers Kant's earlier works, his philosophical influences and context, and his place in the philosophy of science.

THE CROCK OF GOLD

Type of work: Novel
Author: James Stephens (1882-1950)
Type of plot: Fantasy
Time of plot: Indeterminate
Locale: Irish countryside
First published: 1912

Principal characters:
THE PHILOSOPHER
THE THIN WOMAN, his wife
SEUMAS and
BRIGID, two children
ANGUS OG, an early Irish god
CAITILIN, his mortal wife

The Story:

In the center of a very dark pinewood lived the two old Philosophers and their wives, the Grey Woman of Dun Gortin and the Thin Woman of Inis Magrath. One couple had a little boy named Seumas, the other a little girl named Brigid. Both were born on the same day. When the children were ten years old, one of the old Philosophers decided that he had now learned all that he was capable of learning. This conclusion depressed him so much that he decided to die. It was unfortunate, as he pointed out, that at the time he was in the best of health; however, if the time had come for him to die, then die he must. He took off his shoes and spun around in the center of the room for fifteen minutes until he fell over dead. So grieved was the Grey Woman that she, too, killed herself, but since she was much tougher than her husband, she spun for forty-five minutes before she died. The Thin Woman calmly buried the two bodies under the hearthstone.

The people who lived on the edge of the pinewood often came to see the Thin Woman's husband when they needed advice. One day, Meehawl MacMurrachu came to the Philosopher to learn who had stolen his wife's scrubbing board. The Philosopher, after much questioning, finally decided that the fairies had taken it. He advised Meehawl to go to a certain spot and steal the Crock of Gold that the Leprechauns of Gort na Gloca Mora had buried there. For years, the Leprechauns had been filling their Crock of Gold by clipping the edges of gold coins that they found in people's houses at night. They needed the gold to ransom any of the little people caught by human beings.

Losing their gold to Meehawl made the Leprechauns angry, and they tried to make Meehawl bring it back by giving him and his wife all kinds of aches and pains. Next, they came stealthily and lured Brigid and Seumas down into a little house in the roots of a tree; but fear of the Thin Woman was on them, and they set the children free. Then the Great God Pan, the god of the beast that is in every human, lured away Caitilin, Meehawl's daughter, with the music of his pipes. When Meehawl came with his tale of sorrow, the Philosopher sent Brigid and Seumas to tell Pan to release the girl. Pan, however, refused to answer their questions. When they told the Philosopher, he became so angry that he ordered his wife to bake him some cakes to eat on the way, and he started off by himself to visit Pan. None of the Philosopher's arguments, however, could persuade Pan to free Caitilin, and the Philosopher went off to get the help of Angus Og of the old gods.

Angus Og went to see Pan and the girl in their cave and forced the girl to choose between them. Caitilin, who had learned the true meaning of hunger and desire with Pan, did not know how to choose. Angus Og explained to her that he was Divine Inspiration, and that if she would come and live with him and be his wife, he would show her peace and happiness. He proved by several signs that he was the favorite of the gods of the earth and had more power than Pan. Caitilin sensed that true happiness would be found with Angus Og and that only hunger could be found with Pan; so she chose to leave Pan and go with Angus Og and was saved from the beast in humanity.

The Philosopher, on his way back home, delivered several messages from the god. He gave one message to a young boy, a promise from Angus Og that in time the old gods would return and that before they did, the boy would write a beautiful poem in their praise. Cheered by the news that the gods would soon come back, the Philosopher finally arrived home and greeted his wife with such affection that she decided always to be kind to him and never again to say a cross word. Unknown to them, the Leprechauns had informed the police in the village that there were two bodies buried under the hearthstone in the Philosopher's house. One day, the police broke into the house, found the bodies, and accused the Philosopher of murder. Meanwhile, Brigid and Seumas were playing in the woods, and, quite by chance, they happened to dig a hole and find the Crock of Gold where Meehawl had buried it. They gave it back to the Leprechauns, but the return of the gold was not enough to set matters right. The police kept the Philosopher in jail. Then the Thin Woman baked some cakes and set out to find Angus Og, dragging the children behind her and saying the worst curses there were against the police. The first gods she met were the Three Absolutes, the Most Beautiful Man, the Strongest Man, and the Ugliest Man. By her wisdom, the Thin Woman was able to answer their questions and save herself and the children from their frightful powers. When they had passed these gods, they found the house of Angus Og. He was waiting for someone to come and ask him to aid the Philosopher, for it is impossible for the gods to help anyone unasked.

Calling all the old gods together, Angus Og and his wife led a great dance across the fields, and then they went down into the town with all the gods following. In the town, their merry laughter brought happiness to all who saw them except the most evil of men. The charges against the Philosopher were forgotten, and he was free to go back to his house in the pine woods and dispense wisdom once more. Then the gods returned singing to their own country to await the birth of Caitilin and Angus Og's child and the day when the old Irish gods could again leave their hidden caves and hollows and rule over the land with laughter and song.

Critical Evaluation:

On its publication in 1912, *The Crock of Gold* placed James Stephens in the vanguard of writers guiding the Irish Literary Revival of that period. This movement, led by the poet William Butler Yeats among others, sought to revitalize Irish culture with inspiration derived from ancient Irish myths and legends. The movement placed a strong emphasis on the Irish language and had a mystic reverence for the customs and folklore of poor people, particularly those living off the land. Yeats saw *The Crock of Gold* as an indication that Dublin, the capital of Ireland, was living a deeper spiritual life because the city had nurtured its author, James Stephens.

The extravagant praise heaped on *The Crock of Gold* on its publication was matched by its popularity with the reading public. It became a best-seller immediately and remains James

Stephens' most popular work. As a novel, it is impossible to categorize. Part fairy tale, part philosophy, part mythology, part social history with a conscience, it is very comic, tremendously imaginative, and always extravagant in its celebration of language and life.

Stephens' influences in writing the book are marked and in many cases easily traceable. The huge upsurge in writing with native themes and pastoral settings in Ireland in the 1890's and early 1900's gave Stephens the inspiration for much of the plot. Stephens' mentor and one of the leaders of the Irish Literary Revival, Æ (George Russell), believed literally in the existence of spirits, fairies, and gods, and prophesied their materialization in the Irish countryside and cities. The verbose Philosopher in the novel seems to be at least partly based on Æ, who had a comic tendency to pontificate. On a deeper level Stephens owes a huge and acknowledged debt to the English poet William Blake. Blake saw life as warring extremes—good and evil, intellect and emotion, spirit and matter—that spark the fires of progress. Blake often vilified authority, organized religion, materialism, and the horrors of industrialized society. Stephens touches on all these themes in *The Crock of Gold*, if sometimes in a muted form.

Chief among the protagonists are the Philosopher and Caitilin, the former representing intellectual nature, the latter emotional nature. At the beginning readers see the Philosopher as a rather pedantic, joyless creature with a huge store of information but little knowledge of life's essentials and no capacity for love. His journey to meet the ancient Irish god, Angus Og, transforms him. First the Philosopher meets Pan, representing animal nature, and, despite the Philosopher's anger, he notices that he feels more alive than he has for years after his contact with a pure physicality. Traveling on, he perceives the sadness of some people he meets and their unsureness of how to conduct their affairs. His rendezvous with Angus Og brings him to ecstasy, marrying his intellect with his spirit and awakening a dormant love for his fellow human beings.

Caitilin, whose name suggests she represents the personification of Ireland (Caitilín Ní Houlaháin), also has encounters with these two gods. Meeting Pan entices her sensual nature to blossom and, in imitation of him, she discards her clothes to better express this side of herself. The Philosopher, in this scene representing the repressed domesticated member of civilization, is horrified by this and rails against her and Pan to no avail. Subsequently, Angus Og comes to seek her out and, in a crucial scene of the plot, gets her to leave Pan and come with him. This episode may be interpreted in many ways but can probably best be seen as a prophecy by Stephens that Ireland should gravitate toward what is her own (Pan is a Greek god) and, in Caitilin's terms, as a union with her spiritual roots which will bear offspring to revitalize Ireland.

Intertwined with these and other journeys (such as the one undertaken by the Thin Woman of Magrath), Stephens places his philosophical discourses, some of them pages long. Though he seems serious, his manner of dealing with them smacks of whimsicality if not irreverence. Everything is turned upside down in this novel, the momentous and the commonplace exchange places and importance on most every page.

Stephens' theme is straightforward: imagination, love, joy, and dance need their proper place in modern life. In Ireland, these things should spring from Ireland's own culture. Modern society has placed too much reliance on reason and the intellect. The result is loneliness and lack of fulfillment. The philosopher's experience in prison, held by uncomprehending policemen obeying the mindless dictates of law, shows Stephens at his most serious. Two fellow prisoners tell wretched stories of society's lack of charity to the old and the sick. At the end, when the Thin Woman asks Angus Og to free her husband, all the gods and spirits of old join him in setting the people free from their bondage, literal and mental.

The Crock of Gold has survived as literature because it is funny, profound, elusive, and charming. One could argue that the parts are greater than the whole. Some of the philosophizing, for instance seems half-digested, as if Stephens had read ideas elsewhere and not quite made them his own. What works best are the less deliberate moments: insects talking to cows, children playing with Leprechauns, offhand humor, encounters with peasants. With the beautiful and poetic language, they make it a story that has become a classic of fantasy writing.

"Critical Evaluation" by Philip Magnier

Bibliography:
Bramsback, Birgit. *James Stephens: A Literary and Biographical Study.* Cambridge, Mass.: Harvard University Press, 1959. Has a good chapter on Stephens that may be useful as a short overview of his life and work.
Finneran, Richard J. *The Olympian and the Leprechaun: W. B. Yeats and James Stephens.* Dublin, Ireland: Dolmen Press, 1978. Has many quotes and insights from Yeats on Stephens and his place in Irish literature.
McFate, Patricia. *The Writings of James Stephens: Variations on a Theme of Love.* New York: St. Martin's Press, 1979. Good at placing Stephens in historical and literary context.
Martin, Augustine. *James Stephens: A Critical Study.* Totowa, N.J.: Rowman & Littlefield, 1977. Strong in critical analysis and debating themes.
Pyle, Hilary. *James Stephens: His Work and an Account of His Life.* New York: Barnes & Noble Books, 1965. Groundbreaking work in separating fact from fiction in Stephens' life. A sympathetic account traces his origins, motivations, and influence.

CROME YELLOW

Type of work: Novel
Author: Aldous Huxley (1894-1963)
Type of plot: Social satire
Time of plot: 1920's
Locale: England
First published: 1921

> *Principal characters:*
> HENRY WIMBUSH, the owner of Crome
> ANNE WIMBUSH, his niece
> DENIS STONE, a young poet
> MR. SCROGAN, a man of reason
> GOMBAULD, an artist
> MARY BRACEGIRDLE, a victim of repressions
> JENNY MULLION, a deaf but keen-eyed observer

The Story:

Denis Stone, a shy young poet, went to a house party at Crome, the country home of Henry Wimbush and his wife. He went because he was in love with Wimbush's niece, Anne. Anne looked down on Denis because he was four years younger than she, and she treated him with scorn when he attempted to speak of love. Mr. Wimbush was interested in little except Crome and the histories of the people who had lived in the old house. Mrs. Wimbush was a woman with red hair, probably false, and an interest in astrology, especially since she had recently won a bet on a horse with her star-given information. Other guests at the party included Gombauld, an artist who had been invited to paint Anne's picture; the diabolically reasonable Mr. Scrogan; deaf Jenny Mullion; and Mary Bracegirdle, who was worried about her Freudian dreams. Denis and Anne quarreled, this time over their philosophies of life. Denis tried to carry all the cares of the world on his back, but Anne thought that things should be taken for granted as they came. The quarrel cost Denis his first opportunity to tell Anne that he loved her.

Mary Bracegirdle discussed her dreams and repressions with Anne. Having decided to secure either Gombauld or Denis for a husband, she chose the wrong times to talk with both men. Gombauld was busy painting when Mary came up to him. Denis was smarting with jealousy over the time Anne and Gombauld spent together.

Ivor Lombard arrived for the party. Ivor, a painter of ghosts and spirits, turned his attentions toward repressed Mary and secretly visited her one night in the tower. He went away without seeing her again.

At various times, Mr. Wimbush called the party together while he read stories of the early history of Crome. These stories were from a history at which Mr. Wimbush had worked for thirty years. Denis often wondered if he would ever get a chance to tell Anne that he loved her. Walking in the garden after a talk with Mr. Scrogan, whose cold-blooded ideas about a rationalized world annoyed him, he found a red notebook in which Jenny had been writing for the past week. The notebook contained a collection of sharply satirical cartoons of all the people at the house party. Jenny had drawn him in seven attitudes that illustrated his absurd jealousy, incompetence, and shyness. The cartoons deeply wounded his vanity and shattered his self-conception.

He was further discouraged by the fact that there was nothing for him to do at a charity fair held in the park outside Crome a few days later. Mr. Scrogan made a terrifying and successful fortune-teller; Jenny played the drums; Mr. Wimbush ran the various races; and Denis was left to walk aimlessly through the fair as an official with nothing to do. Gombauld made sketches of the people in the crowd, and Anne stayed by his side.

The night after the fair, Denis overheard part of a conversation between Gombauld and Anne. Denis was unaware that Anne had repulsed Gombauld, for she had made up her mind to accept Denis if he ever got around to asking her; consequently, he spent hours of torture thinking of the uselessness of his life. At last, he decided to commit suicide by jumping from the tower. There he found Mary grieving, because she had received only a brisk postcard from Ivor. She convinced Denis that both their lives were ruined and advised him to flee from Anne. Convinced, Denis arranged a fake telegram calling him back to London on urgent business. When it arrived, Denis realized with dismay that Anne was miserable to see him go. The telegram was the one decisive action of his life. Ironically, it separated him from Anne.

Critical Evaluation:

Aldous Huxley published this, his first novel, when he was twenty-seven years old. Themes announced in this satirical, loosely knit work were to characterize his future production also: How can people of the modern world find the solutions required by the present to the age-old problems of humanity? What constitutes value? To what extent can historical imperatives be avoided, or, if they still mean something, to what extent can they continue to be implemented? In his justly famous novel of 1932, *Brave New World*, Huxley poses these problems in a way far more integral to the plot. In *Crome Yellow*, such questions—and putative solutions—are put in the mouths of various characters. Since none of these (even Denis Stone, the protagonist and point-of-view) is clearly sympathetic, it is not possible to discern in which direction Huxley himself throws his weight. It is more a case of "a plague on all your houses"—nobody escapes Huxley's satirical deconstruction. Romanticism is especially attacked, and such attacks are repeated and developed throughout what might be considered the trilogy formed by his first three novels—*Crome Yellow, Antic Hay* (1923), and *Those Barren Leaves* (1925)—and even through the seven-novel series, including *Point Counter Point* (1928), *Brave New World*, *Eyeless in Gaza* (1936), and *After Many a Summer Dies the Swan* (1939), that constitutes Huxley's novelistic output up to 1939. Yet there are many Romantic elements in his writing.

Huxley's work is rife with such contradictions. It well illustrates the poet William Butler Yeats's aphorism that, if rhetoric is what results from one's arguments with others, poetry is the outcome of one's argument with oneself. For example, Huxley knew enough history to deplore the historicism of contemporary thinkers, yet was unable himself to avoid sweeping statements concerning historical tendencies. In *Brave New World*, the vision of the lockstep future is a nightmare, but the few nonconforming characters are not impressive either. *Crome Yellow* might be a better book had Huxley found an organizing idea—Carl Jung's theory of psychological types comes to mind—to impart a positive spin to the relativism of his people; as it stands, they tend to cancel each other out rather than complement and augment one another.

Huxley's popularity began with the publication of *Crome Yellow* and grew with each successive novel, especially with the people of his own generation, which indicates that Huxley spoke for his peers, that his unresolved contradictions were theirs as well, and that they welcomed such a mirroring—which was, after all, a focusing of their confusions and despair.

Crome Yellow also is an entertaining work, in part because of its setting, an ancient and splendid English country house standing amid sumptuous gardens in a beautiful countryside, at the end of a train ride that passes through stations with such names as Spavin Delawarr, Knipswich for Timpany, and Camlet-on-the-Water. In the grand house itself, there are secret doors, winding staircases, parapets, and towers. As they dine in style or stroll the garden paths, Huxley's characters may articulate radical notions concerning the end of civilization as they know it, and the feeling resulting from the massive destruction and loss of life during World War I may color their behavior, but much proceeds according to traditions that have succeeded through many generations, and a sense of coziness and safety mitigates the dire predictions that are voiced in much of *Crome Yellow*.

The characters are certainly entertaining—or the caricatures, one might almost call them, for Huxley is a gifted cartoonist in prose. The red sketchbook that Jenny Mullion keeps, and at which Denis steals a look, is an emblem of the novel, which is itself a kind of sketchbook filled with uncomfortably accurate lampoons. Like cartoon people, the cast of *Crome Yellow* is composed of static people, of types; no one is changed by his or her experiences in the course of these 150 or so pages. Huxley is interested in human diversity, but not much given to representing its development.

Huxley capably demonstrates throughout *Crome Yellow* his own diverse talents, as satirist, parodist, purveyor of little-known details from history; as poet, versifier, memorizer of—or inventor of—fascinating conversation; as theorist, philosopher, psychologist. At times, these demonstrations amount to nothing more than a half-baked genius strutting his stuff, as certain critics allege; so it must appear to readers, then and now, who are unable to identify with a pert wit fresh out of Eton and Oxford. To many of his contemporaries, who included a number of the brightest intellects as well as the "bright young things," Aldous Huxley, in *Crome Yellow*, was the first to announce the coming of a new sensibility, one that would spurn traditional Great Britain and Europe, and that would not let its own lack of constructive thought deter it from remarking on the wholesale flaws in the thought it was meant to inherit.

As one reviewer at the time wrote, many of Huxley's contemporaries found him "amusing," a word that meant a lot more than "funny." It was their highest term of praise. In an era when the values that had persisted throughout the lengthy Victorian period were now perceived as having failed and led directly to the holocaust of World War I by the more prescient members of the British public, it seemed enough to say so in an engaging and provocative way: Without sounder grounds of value, "amusing" had to suffice. As the grandson of Thomas Henry Huxley, who had championed Darwin, and the relative of Matthew Arnold, who in his famous poem "Dover Beach" (1867) had announced the withdrawal of faith in Christendom, Aldous Huxley inherited a considerable burden of family responsibility for the condition of the present. He was to spend his life seeking for solutions, and *Crome Yellow* makes a start by clearing the air of the outdated and the stultifying.

"Critical Evaluation" by David Bromige

Bibliography:
Baker, Robert S. *The Dark Historic Page: Social Satire and Historicism in the Novels of Aldous Huxley, 1921-1939.* Madison: University of Wisconsin Press, 1982. Invaluable work, especially the chapter entitled *"Crome Yellow* and the Problem of History."
Bedford, Sybille. *Aldous Huxley: A Biography.* 1st ed. New York: Alfred A. Knopf, 1974. First-rate, extensive biography.
Birnbaum, Milton. *Aldous Huxley's Quest for Values.* 1st ed. Knoxville: University of Tennessee Press, 1971. Deals with Huxley's novels by theme rather than by chronology, but the

index references to *Crome Yellow* are worth looking up. Birnbaum, a college student in the 1920's, writes in his preface, "In debunking the traditional sources of value he was, in a sense, acting as our surrogate."

Bowering, Peter. *Aldous Huxley: A Study of the Major Novels*. New York: Oxford University Press, 1969. Notes the counterpull, beneath the benign skepticism of its surface, of an underlying gravity in *Crome Yellow*.

Firchow, Peter. *Aldous Huxley: Satirist and Novelist*. Minneapolis: University of Minnesota Press, 1972. Sound insights into Huxley's procedure in *Crome Yellow*.

Watt, Donald, ed. *Aldous Huxley: The Critical Heritage*. London: Routledge & Kegan Paul, 1975. Fascinating compendium of reviews, articles, and letters, arranged chronologically. F. Scott Fitzgerald, at that time the author of one published novel, said in his review of *Crome Yellow*, "Huxley . . . is said to know more about French, German, Latin, and medieval Italian literature than any man alive. I refuse to make the fatuous remark that he should know less about books and more about people." Watt's introduction provides further insights into *Crome Yellow*.

CROTCHET CASTLE

Type of work: Novel
Author: Thomas Love Peacock (1785-1866)
Type of plot: Fiction of manners
Time of plot: Nineteenth century
Locale: England
First published: 1831

Principal characters:
EBENEZER MAC CROTCHET, a country squire
YOUNG CROTCHET, his son
LEMMA CROTCHET, his daughter
SUSANNAH TOUCHANDGO, the beloved of young Crotchet
MR. CHAINMAIL, an antiquarian
CAPTAIN FITZCHROME, a young army officer
LADY CLARINDA BOSSNOWL, the beloved of Fitzchrome

The Story:

The squire of Crotchet Castle was descended from Scottish and Jewish ancestors, but he tried to assume the demeanor of a traditional English country squire. He had great ability in making money, and he used his wealth to buy a manor and a coat of arms. With his wife dead and his son in London, the squire lived alone with his daughter. Young Crotchet, who had inherited his father's love for money, had taken his father's gift of a large sum and turned it into enormous profits. His business dealings were shady, however, and many people thought his day of reckoning would come. For the present, however, his luck held. He had been engaged to Miss Susannah Touchandgo, the daughter of a great banker, but when that gentleman had absconded with the bank's funds, leaving his daughter almost penniless, young Crotchet had deserted his love without a backward glance. Susannah had gone to Wales, where she made her living in simple surroundings, teaching a farmer's children.

Squire Crotchet's daughter Lemma bore some resemblance to her ancestors, a fact that was compensated in the eyes of local swains by the size of her father's fortune. A suitor had not yet been selected for her, but there were many who sought her hand and her purse.

Crotchet Castle was a gathering place for philosophers and dilettantes picked at random by Squire Crotchet. These would-be intellectuals engaged in long and tiresome disputes on all branches of philosophy and science. One of them, Mr. Chainmail, longed for a return to the customs and morals of the Middle Ages, believing that the present was decidedly inferior to the past. He was violently opposed by other members of the group who worshiped mammon. None of the philosophers ever changed his views, and each found much pleasure in expounding his own pet theory.

While strolling through the grounds one day, some of the gentlemen came upon a young army officer, Captain Fitzchrome. Invited to join the group, the captain accepted readily, for he was in love with Lady Clarinda Bossnowl, one of the guests. Lady Clarinda obviously loved the captain, but she had been promised to young Crotchet in a match that was purely a business arrangement: his money for her title. The captain pleaded with her at every opportunity, but she silenced him and her own heart by ridiculing his lack of funds. Lemma Crotchet, in the meantime, became pledged to Lady Clarinda's brother. The four young people spent many hours together, much to Captain Fitzchrome's sorrow.

One day, the squire took his guests on a river voyage down the Thames. They visited places of learning and culture but saw little of either except the buildings supposed to house those attributes. During the trip, the captain finally gave up his hopes of winning Lady Clarinda, and he left the party without notifying anyone. He settled in a village inn, where he was later joined by Chainmail, the antiquarian, who had left the party to study a ruined castle in the neighborhood. Since the captain knew the way to the castle, he offered to guide Chainmail, but he was called back to London on business before they could undertake their expedition. Chainmail went on alone.

During his researches, Chainmail caught a glimpse of a nymphlike creature who fascinated him so much that he could not rest until he had made her acquaintance. When he finally met her, he learned that she was Susannah Touchandgo. Chainmail found her perfect in every way but one. He knew she would share the simple, old-fashioned life he loved, but he had determined to marry a lady of gentle birth. Susannah, ashamed of her father's theft, would tell him nothing of her family background. In spite of her reluctance in this respect, Chainmail loved her and spent many happy hours at the farmhouse in which she lived.

When Captain Fitzchrome returned and learned of his friend's plight, he encouraged Chainmail to ask for the lady's hand. The antiquarian was, however, unable to change his views. The situation was brought to a climax when they saw in the paper an announcement of the approaching marriage of Lady Clarinda and young Crotchet. Susannah was temporarily overcome by the news, and in trying to comfort her, Chainmail inadvertently proposed. Then Susannah told him of her father's crime. Chainmail, however, could overlook that fact in his joy over the discovery that Susannah was of gentle blood. In a few days, the two were married.

The following Christmas, most of the friends gathered again at Crotchet Castle. Lemma Crotchet had married Lord Bossnowl, but Lady Clarinda Bossnowl had not yet married young Crotchet. The young man was a little dismayed at seeing Susannah married to Chainmail, for he still held her in affection. Lady Clarinda cast longing glances at the captain, even to the point of singing a song that was obviously intended for him. She was not sorry, therefore, when young Crotchet disappeared. His firm had failed, and he was penniless. It was assumed that he had crossed the Atlantic to join forces with Susannah's father, who had set up business there. Lady Clarinda refused to be put up for sale again. She gladly accepted Captain Fitzchrome and his smaller but stabler fortune.

Critical Evaluation:

Crotchet Castle is something of a historical novel, not because it attempts to re-create the past but because it reflects so clearly the life and times of its author. Published in 1831, the work was written during the preceding year or two. The setting of the novel extends from the valley of the Thames to Oxford, through a canal to the Severn, and from there to northern Wales. These areas were well known to Thomas Love Peacock, who had undertaken a walking journey upriver from the Thames valley in 1809 and then written a long poem about it, *The Genius of the Thames* (1810). In 1815, accompanied by the poet Percy Bysshe Shelley and some other friends, Peacock made a boat trip up the Thames from Windsor that included visits to Oxford and Lechlade. The same itinerary appears in chapters 9 and 10 of *Crotchet Castle*, except that in the novel the group is able to afford passage through the canal, an economic hurdle that in 1815 forced Shelley and Peacock to change their plans.

Peacock's first trip to northern Wales was in the winter of 1808-1809. During that visit he went on long walks to enjoy the mountain scenery, and he met Jane Gryffydh, the well-educated daughter of a Welsh clergyman, with whom he discussed books. Peacock himself was a prodigious reader, as is apparent in his works, and it is surprising to learn that he only attended school from the age of six to thirteen. Yet he read not only English literature but Greek, Latin, French, and Italian, all in the original languages. Predictably, he was scornful of the university education he never had, an attitude that appears in several of his novels but never more prominently so than in the Oxford portion, chapter 9, of *Crotchet Castle*.

Peacock lacked not only formal education (for which he more than compensated) but also significant vocational experience. Only in 1819 did he apply for and attain a position in the Examiner's Department of the East India Company. Now financially secure and at age thirty-four in want of a wife, he proposed by mail to Jane Gryffydh (whom he had not seen for years) and was accepted. Though the marriage was not entirely a success, Jane's knowledge of Wales and of its language and literature influenced several of Peacock's novels. She was almost certainly the original of Susannah Touchandgo, the nymph of Merionethshire. Peacock writes meaningfully in chapter 14 that her favorite author was Jean-Jacques Rousseau, the radical eighteenth century Swiss philosopher and novelist who taught his readers to appreciate the society of children, the beauty of nature, and the pleasure of mountain solitude. Peacock himself shared these tastes.

Like several of Peacock's other novels, *Crotchet Castle* has a full cast of ideologically committed characters, some of whom reflect actual persons known to the author. These include friends of Shelley, a poet of unconventional ideas whom Peacock had known since the autumn of 1812. (Shelley left England in 1818, but corresponded regularly with Peacock until his death four years later in Italy.) It was largely through his association with Shelley that the more conservative Peacock came to learn of, and sometimes to mock, the various utopian schemes for worldwide reformation. These appear throughout his novels in dialogue, most prominently in chapter 6 ("Theories") of *Crotchet Castle*. As the author declares there, all such reforms are doomed to failure, among other reasons for want of money.

At the time Peacock was writing *Crotchet Castle*, money and reform were issues that aroused extreme public agitation. Though spared the revolutions that swept through Europe in 1848 (and had already rocked the French monarchy in 1830), England was wracked in 1831 by riots and incendiary vandalism. Masses of unenfranchised laborers, whose traditional occupations had been destroyed by technological advances (weavers put out of work by power looms, for example), had no other means of expressing their discontent than through violence, mob action, and burnings.

Peacock describes such a group in chapter 18 as they attempt to storm Chainmail Hall under their mythical leader, Captain Swing. A preliminary reform bill finally achieved passage through Parliament in 1832. It was followed by other legislation that alleviated the working conditions of women and children in particular, extended the franchise, and eventually established public schools. Peacock, who had not written of such issues in any of his previous novels, deals only briefly with the workers' discontent in *Crotchet Castle*.

Although Peacock may well be charged with being cold or impercipient toward the social and intellectual changes of his own century—a criticism that is largely valid—in this regard *Crotchet Castle* does not entirely conform to the author's other works. The novel reflects Peacock's awareness of the importance of earned money in achieving and maintaining position not only in British society but in British thought as well. Political and economic power was shifting from the aristocracy to the middle class, which explains the shift to the more concrete taste of mercantilists that dominated the Victorian period.

Yet as the establishment realigned itself to some extent, the position of women within society and within the power structure as a whole remained controversial. Like Shelley, Peacock favored a greater degree of female intellectual freedom than was commonly vouchsafed to women in his time. He expressed his belief in women's intelligence and potential by creating a series of unusually perceptive heroines, of whom Lady Clarinda in *Crotchet Castle* is the most outstanding example. Even so, however, the specter of marriage as a primarily commercial transaction haunts the novel throughout and is not altogether resolved at the end.

The dominant theme of *Crotchet Castle* is money and the fact that all aspects of society and thought ultimately depend upon it. Peacock's awareness of the pound's importance no doubt made him a valuable employee of the East India Company, even as his kind of literary education based on classical and foreign languages slipped into obscurity.

"Critical Evaluation" by Dennis R. Dean

Bibliography:
Burns, Bryan. *The Novels of Thomas Love Peacock.* Totowa, N.J.: Barnes & Noble Books, 1985. Sound criticism, with unsurprising insights. Includes a good discussion of *Crotchet Castle.*

Butler, Marilyn. *Peacock Displayed: A Satirist in His Context.* London: Routledge & Kegan Paul, 1979. The most influential book on Peacock of its time, with acute critical discussions of all seven novels, especially *Crotchet Castle.*

Dawson, Carl. *His Fine Wit: A Study of Thomas Love Peacock.* Berkeley: University of California Press, 1970. A comprehensive survey of Peacock's poetry, nonfictional prose, and novels. Good discussions of the Peacockian novel in general and of the individual novels, including *Crotchet Castle.*

Kjellin, Hakan. *Talkative Banquets: A Study in the Peacockian Novels of Talk.* Stockholm: Almqvist & Wiksell, 1974. An interesting study of Peacock's relations with the dialogue and dramatic traditions. Discusses five of his seven novels, including *Crotchet Castle.*

McKay, Margaret. *Peacock's Progress: Aspects of Artistic Development in the Novels of Thomas Love Peacock.* Stockholm: Almqvist & Wiksell, 1992. Traces Peacock's growth as a novelist through his seven novels.

Peacock, Thomas Love. *Novels.* Edited by David Garnett. 2 vols. London: Rupert Hart-Davis, 1963. Discusses *Crotchet Castle* in volume 2. This edition is recommended for its annotations, which are by Peacock himself and by Garnett.

Priestley, J. B. *Thomas Love Peacock.* London: Macmillan, 1927. A classic essay, still worth consulting.

CROW
From the Life and Songs of the Crow

Type of work: Poetry
Author: Ted Hughes (1930-   )
First published: 1970

A reader coming upon Ted Hughes's *Crow* for the first time will realize immediately its forceful, almost savage turning-away from English poetic tradition. In its harsh treatment of human relations, religious and moral assumptions, and the function of consciousness in the natural world, *Crow* offers page after page of profoundly raucous poetic rebellion.

Hughes's protagonist is Crow—omnivorous, homely, solitary, and ubiquitous. Borrowing from Celtic mythology, the Old Testament, and various aboriginal legends, the poet creates a rich, potent mythology of his own for this figure. "Two Legends" introduces the book's central concerns. It is a litany of enigmatic statements focusing on muscle and organ, on force as the origin of life: "Black was the without eye/ Black the within tongue/ Black was the heart/ Black the liver, black the lungs." This incantation of the body's tissues ultimately leads to the soul, black also, the sum here of the struggle to overcome or contain the Genesis-like void from which everything springs. Thus in the second legend of the poem, an "egg of blackness" hatches a crow, the figure who will for the rest of the collection symbolize alternately the life force and the primal element of chaos. He will speak for both intuition and deception, preserver as much as destroyer. An ambiguous semideity whose hoarse cry celebrates the cyclic processes of birth and death, the crow is "a black rainbow/ Bent in emptiness/ over emptiness/ But flying"—that is (in Hughes's final, unpunctuated line of the poem), immutable and free of social, religious, or scientific attempts to organize or define elemental realities.

These rational or spiritual attempts are alluded to in many of the poems in *Crow* as Hughes turns Crow's baleful stare upon one conventional system of thought after another. Following the biblical "begat" sequence in "Lineage," Hughes offers a trio of poems describing Crow's birth and his paradoxical reliance upon death. "Examination at the Womb-Door" offers a bleak catechism in which the answer to all but two questions is "Death." The interrogator, never identified, reduces Crow—and by implication all creatures, human beings included—to mere anatomical features possessed ultimately by death: "Who owns these scrawny little feet?. . . this bristly scorched-looking face?. . . these unspeakable guts?. . . these questionable brains?" Yet even thus dissected, Crow is only "held pending trial" by this negating power of death. Although death "owns all of space" and is "stronger" than hope, love, and life, Crow is allowed to pass after realizing that he, embodiment of the life force, can paradoxically overcome or outlast death itself. The stark refrain of "death" throughout the poem in fact makes Crow's final response all the more forceful: "But who is stronger than death?/ Me, evidently."

Here, as elsewhere in *Crow*, the tone is equivocal, tentative. Crow is at one level the spirit of inventiveness, of making do. In both "A Kill" and "Crow and Mama" Crow's experiences resemble nothing so much as crash landings after which he must improvise for survival. He smashes into the "rubbish" of the ground in the former poem and crashes on the moon in the latter, only to crawl out and take up the struggle that Hughes sees as the essential reality.

Crow proves resourceful. In "A Childish Prank" he already thrives on malicious humor, as the poem revises the origins of human sexuality into a quintessentially Hughesian myth of pain and misunderstanding. Pondering the problem of how to invest Adam and Eve with souls, God falls asleep, thereby allowing Crow to invest the parents of humanity with the two writhing halves of a bitten worm, which have been dragging man and woman toward each other ever since. The same supplanting of the spiritual or Godly with the physical and naturalistic takes place in "Crow's First Lesson," in which God tries to teach Crow to say—if not to feel or to understand—"love." Every attempt to speak the word results in the creation of something dangerous or grotesque. A final try produces only the sexual grappling of man and woman. God cannot part them, and Crow flies "guiltily off."

The next several poems in the volume involve Crow's sojourns, following his various adventures throughout a blasted world, where civilizations have risen and fallen against the background of an essentially predatory, immutable natural order. "Crow Alights" brings him to mountains, sea, and stars before he comes upon an old shoe, a rusted garbage can, and other refuse of the twentieth century. Though he scrutinizes the evidence, Crow cannot piece it together nor explain the motionlessness of the human face and hand he perceives through a window. The last five lines of the poem—separate, end-stopped one-line stanzas of clipped or fragmented sentences—effectively communicate the sense of wreckage out of which Crow must somehow derive his existence. "That Moment" describes a similar situation. The human race may have just extinguished itself, but the event is merely another opportunity for Crow, who starts searching for his next meal.

On the other hand, when "Crow Hears Fate Knock on the Door" it is a prophecy he feels inside him, more troubling for his being its source, a feeling "like a steel spring/ Slowly rending the vital fibres." It is because of this unease, perhaps, that Crow begins to question his own conduct in the very next poem, "Crow Tyrannosaurus." Like the prehistoric Rex, Crow is bound by the most elemental of laws—"the horrible connection," as one critic puts it, "between creature and creature: kill to live." Observing bird and beast and human around him, Crow wonders at all the deaths "gulped" in order to survive. No sooner does he consider the morality of such a natural order than he is compelled by it to kill again. He may wish to change, to refine himself out of the blood and guts of creation, but he cannot escape his design and function. Kill-and-eat mechanism that he is, Crow finds himself stabbing at grubs even as he questions the action. He survives the dinosaur and may outlast humanity, but not through any transcending of his given role.

Nevertheless, Crow does seem to develop something like a conscience. "Conscience" cannot be understood in its religious sense but instead as Crow's coming to terms with the consequences of his actions, both for himself and for others. Even in a poem such as "Crow's Theology" Hughes does not allow the presumably benign realization of God's love to go uncontested. Just as he cannot keep himself from stabbing the grub earlier, Crow must meditate fiercely upon this God and his relationship with the rest of Creation. If God "speaks" Crow's language and Crow's mere existence is somehow a form of divine revelation, as the poem has it, then "what/ Loved the stones and spoke stone?" What, indeed, speaks and loves the silences of creation, including the silence of death? Crow's answer, arrived at through the only philosophy he can know, is that there are two Gods, one much bigger than the other, loving his enemies, and having "all the weapons."

As if to test this hypothesis, Crow mounts a challenge in "Crow's Fall," Hughes's rendering of Lucifer's ill-fated aspiring. Here, Crow is described as having once been white, an angelic figure who decided that "the sun was too white" and so tried to attack and defeat it. Crow summons all his powers, but the sun only brightens at this futile assault, leaving Crow so charred that even his voice is left scorched. Like Lucifer, Crow is not killed; also like Lucifer, he manages out of his pride to fashion his own version of events: "Up there . . . Where white is black and black is white, I won." Also like Lucifer, Crow is a "light bringer"; his lessons in endurance, in the rapaciousness of existence, are bitter epiphanies.

After his fall, Crow embarks on a series of experiments with language, testing his powers of perception and creation against the memory of his disastrous try at "love." He discovers in "Crow Goes Hunting" that words bound away like hares, fly off like starlings. He concocts other words to shoot at those escaping him, but none stays within his control. Crow gazes after them "speechless with admiration," beginning to intuit the vexed relation of words to the things they name.

The fablelike "Crow's Elephant Totem Song" dramatizes a similar disquiet. The elephant, originally "delicate and small," is set upon by hyenas maddened with envy and torn into pieces which they carry away into their respective "hells." At the Resurrection—in this tale, not Christ's Second Coming—the elephant reassembles himself: "Deadfall feet," "toothproof body," "bulldozing bones," and "aged eyes, that were wicked and wise." Like Crow's fall from an arrogant purity (whiteness), the elephant's death-and-rebirth into a "wicked and wise" homeliness provides a morality play for Hughes, one based on the law of the jungle or veldt rather than Judaic or Christian tradition.

From "Crow's Playmates" on, the book rushes to its conclusion, as scene after scene has Crow creating and miscreating. All Crow can do is watch his "works" take on lives of their own and then try to survive the destruction they cause. After he creates gods to keep him company, each tears from him some part of his power until he is but a "remnant, his own leftover, the spat-out scrag." A parallel event occurs in "Crow Blacker Than Ever." Here God and Adam, disgusted with each other, turn toward their respective paradises—heaven and Eve—when Crow mischievously nails together the two realms. The agony this produces, God and humanity unwillingly connected, is what Crow deems his "Creation," victoriously flying "the black flag of himself." The apocalyptic "Crow's Last Stand" begins with a "burning" that Hughes breaks across several lines until reaching what the sun could not burn any further. The sun "rages and chars" against this last obstacle, obviously an emblem of survival and resilience in the midst of catastrophe: "Crow's eye-pupil, in the tower of its scorched fort." This eye, as pure perception, may be the final, irreducible image of consciousness in Hughes's mythology.

Ted Hughes has said his idea in *Crow* was to reduce his style "to the simplest clear cell—then regrow a wholeness and richness organically from that point." The collection's mythic power, brutal diction, and sardonic bleakness of vision make it one of the truly landmark works in post-World War II English poetry. Whether attracted to or repulsed by these qualities, no poet or reader of poetry can claim not to hear the dark echoes of Hughes's *Crow* in the literature of other writers since this collection's appearance.

James Scruton

Bibliography:

Gifford, Terry, and Neil Roberts. *Ted Hughes: A Critical Study.* Winchester, Mass.: Faber & Faber, 1981. A thematic approach to the poet's works, with special attention to the relation of humanity to nature in Hughes's "animal" poems.

Hamilton, Ian. *A Poetry Chronicle: Essays and Reviews.* Winchester, Mass.: Faber & Faber, 1973. An example of how widely divergent the critical responses to *Crow* have been. Hamilton points out the "excesses" of the book, such as its "bludgeoning" diction.

Sagar, Keith. *The Art of Ted Hughes.* 2d ed. New York: Cambridge University Press, 1978. The chapter on *Crow* is perhaps the best general introduction to the volume. Clear explanations of various mythic sources and helpful extracts from Hughes's essays and interviews.

Scigaj, Leonard M. *The Poetry of Ted Hughes.* Iowa City: University of Iowa Press, 1986. Examines the aesthetic and philosophical purposes behind Hughes's most-criticized elements in *Crow* and in other Hughes volumes, from violent subject matter to awkward structure.

Thwaite, Anthony. *Twentieth-Century English Poetry.* London: Heinemann, 1978. A brief but balanced assessment of *Crow* in terms of its impact on contemporary poetry and its position in the Hughes canon. Thwaite cites the specific shortcomings of several negative critical reactions to the themes and forms of *Crow*.

THE CRUCIBLE

Type of work: Drama
Author: Arthur Miller (1915-   )
Type of plot: Historical
Time of plot: 1692
Locale: Salem, Massachusetts
First performed: 1953; first published, 1953

Principal characters:

THE REVEREND SAMUEL PARRIS, Salem's minister
BETTY PARRIS, his daughter
TITUBA, Parris family's household slave
JOHN PROCTOR, respected farmer
ELIZABETH PROCTOR, his wife
MARY WARREN, their servant
ABIGAIL WILLIAMS, Parris' niece and former servant to the Proctor family
DEPUTY GOVERNOR DANFORTH, chief magistrate
JUDGE HATHORNE, his assistant
THE REVEREND JOHN HALE, scholar of the supernatural
FRANCIS NURSE, farmer
REBECCA NURSE, his wife and a beloved matriarch
GILES COREY, an old but vigorous farmer

The Story:

The Reverend Samuel Parris prayed over his daughter, who lay stricken with a nameless malady. As he prayed, he was angered by the interruption of his Negro slave, Tituba, whom he had brought with him from the island of Barbados. Parris was frightened and furious, for he had discovered his daughter Betty, Tituba, and some of the village girls dancing in the woods. Now two of the girls, Betty and Ruth Putnam, lay ill and witchcraft was rumored about the village. His daughter Betty and his ward and niece, Abigail Williams, had been participants in a secret and sinful act. Parris felt his position as minister to the community of Salem was threatened. Moreover, he suspected that more than dancing had taken place.

The frightened Parris sent for the Reverend John Hale, a reputed scholar familiar with the manifestations of witchcraft. While waiting for Hale to arrive, the parishioners revealed the petty grievances and jealousies hidden beneath the veneer of piety of the Puritan community. Parris felt that the community had failed to meet its financial obligations to him. He suspected John Proctor, a respected farmer, of undermining his authority. Proctor resented Parris for preaching of nothing but hellfire and the money owed to the parish. Thomas Putnam, a grasping landholder, disputed the boundaries of his neighbors' farms. Ann Putnam had lost seven babies at childbirth, and she suspected witchcraft of mothers with large families, most especially Rebecca Nurse, who had had eleven healthy children.

Amid this discontent, the learned Reverend Hale arrived with his books of weighty wisdom. Under Hale's close questioning concerning the girls' illicit activities in the woods, Abigail Williams turned the blame away from herself by accusing Tituba of witchcraft. Terrified by the threat of hanging, Tituba confessed to conjuring up the Devil. Thomas Putnam asked Tituba if she had seen the old beggar Sarah Good or Goodwife Osborne with the Devil. Sensing her survival at stake, Tituba named both women as companions of the Devil. Abigail Williams picked up the accusations and added the names of other villagers. Soon the rest of the girls began hysterically chanting out the names of village men and women seen in company with the Devil.

At the Proctor farm, Proctor told Elizabeth that Abigail Williams had revealed that the dancing in the woods was only "sport." When Proctor hesitated to go to the authorities with this information, Elizabeth Proctor quietly reminded her husband of his past infidelities with Abigail Williams. Their argument was interrupted by the arrival of the Reverend Hale, who had come to inquire into the sanctity of the Proctor home. Elizabeth Proctor suspected that Abigail Williams meant to destroy her so that she might become Proctor's wife. Mary Warren, another of the afflicted girls and the Proctors' servant, returned from court where she had been giving testimony. She gave Elizabeth a rag doll that she had made in court.

At this point, officers of the court arrived at the Proctor farm with an arrest warrant for Elizabeth Proctor on the charge of witchcraft. They searched the house for poppets (dolls) and found the one Mary Warren had given to Elizabeth. They discovered a pin in its stomach and took it for proof that Abigail Williams' stomach pains were the result of Elizabeth Proctor's witchcraft. Elizabeth was taken away in chains. Proctor confronted Mary Warren, demanding that she tell the court the truth. At the court of Deputy Governor Danforth, Giles Corey, Francis Nurse, and John Proctor presented evidence to save their wives from the charge of witchcraft. Danforth confiscated the list of names brought by Francis Nurse testifying to Rebecca Nurse's good character and marked the petitioners for arrest. Giles Corey refused to name the people who backed him, so the deputy governor had Corey arrested. When Proctor brought Mary Warren to court to recant, Abigail pretended to be possessed by the evil spirits brought by Mary Warren. Proctor accused the girls of lying and confessed to having committed adultery with Abigail Williams. Danforth refused to believe that Abigail could be guilty of so great a sin, but Proctor swore that Abigail was dismissed as the Proctors' servant by Elizabeth because she knew of the affair. Danforth brought Elizabeth to the court and questioned her regarding Proctor's adultery with Abigail. Elizabeth lied to Danforth to save Proctor's name, and ironically condemned him as a perjurer.

In the Salem jail, the Reverend Parris and the Reverend Hale begged Rebecca Nurse and John Proctor to confess to witchcraft in order to save their lives. Hale and Parris realized too late that the accused had been victims of the girls' hysteria and the townspeople's private grievances. Rebecca Nurse remained firm in her convictions, refusing to confess, but John Proctor wavered. Proctor thought that in lying to the court, he would only be adding a lie to the sin of adultery. Full of self-contempt, Proctor confessed to witchcraft. Having confessed, he refused to let the court keep his signed confession. He recanted his confession and went to the gallows to save his name.

Critical Evaluation:

Arthur Miller's *The Crucible* was first presented at the Martin Beck Theatre in New York on January 22, 1953, when Senator Joseph McCarthy's House Committee on Un-American Activities was casting a pall over the arts in America. Writers, especially those associated with the theater and the film industry, came under the particular scrutiny of the committee. Those who were blacklisted as communists were banned from employment. Guilt was a matter of accusation, of being named. The parallels between these two periods of social and political persecution in American history were obvious to playgoers in the 1950's. In both the witch trials and the committee hearings, people were summoned before an unchallengeable authority, interrogated, intimidated, and frequently coerced into the betrayal of others in order to escape being persecuted themselves. Miller's work may also be examined for its intrinsic merit rather than for its status as a political tract. With the passage of time, it becomes clear that *The Crucible* is more than a polemic. It transcends its topical boundaries and speaks of universals common to the human condition. In *The Crucible*, Miller balances the social tragedy of the Salem community against the personal tragedy of John Proctor, whose triumph over self restores a sense of moral order in a community torn apart by ignorance, hysteria, and malice. The superstitious ignorance of the Salem villagers transforms a youthful escapade into a diabolic act. Despite Ann Putnam's staunch religious beliefs, she admits to having sent her daughter Ruth to Tituba to conjure up the souls of her dead babies so that Ruth, her one remaining daughter, may discover the cause of their seemingly unnatural deaths. Abigail Williams' motives are darker yet. She seeks Tituba's aid to put a curse on Elizabeth Proctor's life so that she can replace her in John Proctor's affections. The villagers' religious beliefs are so suffused with superstition that they readily accept the notion that the girls are bewitched. No one questions the assumption that the girls are under the spell of supernatural forces except John Proctor, whose challenge takes the form of oblique dissent, and Rebecca Nurse, who asserts that teenage girls often go through "silly seasons."

When the Reverend Parris discovers the girls cavorting in the forest, it is not surprising that they feign illness as a means of hiding from the accusations of their superstitious elders, for they have broken terrible taboos. When Abigail Williams seizes upon the device of accusing others to deflect blame away from herself, she sets in motion the forces of envy, greed, and malice. As the hysteria spreads, the townspeople turn on one another, profiting from their neighbors' misfortunes, wreaking vengeance for real or imagined grievances, substituting spite and fear for love and trust.

The court, an extension of the governing theocracy, was meant to ensure stability and social order. It is tragically ironic that as the court grows in power, the community disintegrates. Crops rot in the fields, cows bellow for want of milking, and abandoned children beg in the streets. Having fled England to escape intolerance and persecution, the Puritans establish a community so narrow and closed that deviation from the norm is regarded as sinful and dissent as diabolic. As *The Crucible* so forcefully dramatizes, such a community must implode. Narrow minds cannot be allowed to prevail over the Proctors and Nurses of this world, who are condemned for their generosity of spirit.

John Proctor is a reluctant hero. He knows that the court has been deceived by Abigail's seeming virtue. He hesitates to expose the fraudulent proceedings, however; to do so means he must reveal his adulterous affair. When he finally bares his heart to the court, his confession is in vain. Unable to believe that he has been deceived, Deputy Governor Danforth sends for Elizabeth Proctor to discover if she supports Proctor's charge. She knows that Proctor is a proud man who values his good name, so she denies her knowledge of the affair, unaware that in telling her first lie she will condemn Proctor as a perjurer. It is at this point that John Proctor breaks with the community, damning the court's proceedings and all the hypocrites associated with it, not unaware that he is including himself within the compass of his curse.

Faced with hanging, Proctor protests to Elizabeth that for him to "mount the gibbet like a saint" is a pretense. Sainthood is for the likes of Rebecca Nurse, not John Proctor. Yet Proctor refuses to let the court keep his signed confession, for it is hard evidence of a lie. Like his predecessors, Oedipus and Hamlet, Proctor insists on the truth even if it means his destruction. Rather than sanctify his name on the altar of duplicity, he becomes a martyr for truth, and in doing so preserves the sanctity of individual freedom.

In *All My Sons* (1947) and *Death of a Salesman* (1949), Arthur Miller explored the erosion of family structure in the wake of materialism, and audiences were moved to compassion. In *The Crucible*, his exploration of the destruction of freedom by an ignorant and despotic society moved many viewers to anger. The themes were too close to home, and for Miller, ironically prophetic. In 1956, summoned before the House Committee on Un-American Activities, Arthur Miller was cited for contempt of Congress for refusing to name names.

David Sundstrand

Bibliography:
Bonnet, Jean-Marie. "Society Versus the Individual in Arthur Miller's *The Crucible.*" *English Studies* 63, no. 1 (February, 1982): 32-36. Solid analysis of the central themes. Contends that *The Crucible* explores the balance between social responsibility and individual freedom.
Martin, Robert A. "Arthur Miller's *The Crucible*: Background and Sources." *Modern Drama* 20, no. 3 (September, 1977): 279-292. Contends that the play transcends the topical parallel of the House Committee on Un-American Activities and stands on its own merits.
Miller, Arthur. *Conversations with Arthur Miller.* Edited by Matthew C. Roudane. Jackson: University Press of Mississippi, 1987. Miller discusses his work with various interviewers. Two useful discussions of *The Crucible.*
Warshow, Robert. "The Liberal Conscience in the Crucible." In *The Immediate Experience: Movies, Comics, Theatre and Other Aspects of Popular Culture.* New York: Doubleday, 1962. Warshow considers the work a wooden political polemic, historically inaccurate, without a central point.

CRY, THE BELOVED COUNTRY

Type of work: Novel
Author: Alan Paton (1903-1988)
Type of plot: Social realism
Time of plot: Mid-twentieth century
Locale: South Africa
First published: 1948

Principal characters:
THE REVEREND STEPHEN KUMALO, a Zulu clergyman
GERTRUDE, his sister
ABSALOM, his son
MSIMANGU, his friend
MR. JARVIS, his white benefactor

The Story:

The letter brought fear to the hearts of the Reverend Stephen Kumalo and his wife. To a Zulu, letters were rare and frightening. Once opened, they could never be closed again, their contents forgotten. Kumalo waited until he could control his fear before he opened the letter from Johannesburg telling him that his sister was sick and needed his help. The trip would be costly for a poor Zulu clergyman, but he had to go. Perhaps there he could also find their son Absalom, who had never been heard from since he had left the village. Stephen and his wife knew in their hearts that, in Johannesburg, Absalom had succumbed to the evil resulting from the white man's breaking up the tribes and compelling black men to work in the mines.

Taking their small savings, Kumalo journeyed to the city. He went first to the mission and met Msimangu, who had written the letter. Msimangu was also a clergyman, working for his people in the city as Kumalo worked in the country. He sorrowfully told Kumalo that his sister Gertrude was a prostitute and a dealer in illegal liquor. She and her child were impoverished, even though she had once made much money from her trade. Kumalo located Gertrude, with the help of Msimangu, and found her willing to go with him to the temporary rooms he had found with a good woman. When his business was finished, she and the child would go with him to his home, away from temptation.

Before looking for his son, Kumalo visited his brother John, a successful merchant and a politician who was under surveillance by the police for his ability to stir up the blacks. John was discreet; he took no chance of being arrested and losing his business. Many of the black leaders sacrificed everything to help their people, but not John. Expediency was his only thought. He had left the church and turned a deaf ear to his brother's pleas that he return to a holier life.

Kumalo began his search for Absalom. With Msimangu, he searched everywhere. Each place they visited added to his fear, for it became clear from their investigation that Absalom had been engaged in stealing, drinking, and worse. Often they walked for miles, for the black leaders were urging their people to boycott the buses in order to get the fares reduced. Kumalo learned that Absalom had been in the company of John's son, and both of them had been in and out of trouble. The trail led to a reformatory, but Absalom had been dismissed shortly before because of his good behavior. The white teacher of the reformatory joined Kumalo in his search, because the boy's behavior reflected on his training. Next, Kumalo found a girl who, soon to bear Absalom's child, waited to marry him. The old man knew at once that if Absalom were not found, the girl must return to the hills with him and make her home there.

At last, he found Absalom in prison. Absalom, John's son, and another boy had robbed and killed Arthur Jarvis, a white man who had befriended the blacks. Brokenhearted, the old man talked with his son. He could tell that Absalom did not truly repent but only said the right things out of fear. His one ray of goodness was his desire to marry the young woman in order to give his unborn child a name. Kumalo wept for his son, but he wept also for the wife and children, the father and mother of the slain man.

At the trial, Absalom was defended by a lawyer found by Kumalo's friends. The plea was that the murder was not planned and that the boy had shot in fear. The judge, a good man, weighed all the evidence and pronounced a verdict of guilty; the punishment, death by hanging. John's son and the other boy were acquitted for lack of evidence. The verdict was a gross miscarriage of justice, but John was more powerful than Kumalo.

Before Kumalo left Johannesburg, he arranged for the marriage between his son and the girl. Then he started home, taking the girl and Gertrude's child with him. Gertrude had disappeared the night before they were to leave, but no one knew where she had gone. She had talked of becoming a nun, but Kumalo feared that she had gone back to her old life; Gertrude liked laughter and fun.

At home, the people welcomed their minister, showering love and blessings upon him. The crops were poor that season, and people were starving. Kumalo prayed for his people and worked for them. He knew that they must learn to use the land wisely but was helpless to guide them. He went to their chief to ask for cooperation, but the chief was concerned only for himself and his family.

Hope came to the people in the form of a child. He was the grandchild of Mr. Jarvis, the father of the man Absalom had murdered. Mr. Jarvis had always helped the black people, and, after his son's death, he gave all of his time to the work started by his murdered son. He sent milk for the children and brought in an agricultural demonstrator who would help the people restore fertility to the soil. Mr. Jarvis built a dam and sent for good seed. His grandchild became Kumalo's friend; through him, the white man learned of the needs of the people. Kumalo, whose son had killed his benefactor's son, was at first ashamed to face Mr. Jarvis. When they met, few words were exchanged, but each read the heart of the other and understood the sorrow and grief there.

The bishop came and told Kumalo that it would be best for him to leave the hills and the valley, to go where his son's crime was unknown. Kumalo grieved and stood silent. Before the bishop left, a letter came from Mr. Jarvis, thanking Kumalo for his friendship and offering to build his people a new church. The bishop felt ashamed.

When the day came for Absalom's execution, Kumalo went into the mountains. He had gone there before when struggling with fear. Mr. Jarvis, knowing the torment that was in his soul, bade him to go in peace. When the dawn came, Kumalo cried out for his son. He cried too for his land and his people. When would dawn come for them?

Critical Evaluation:

Cry, the Beloved Country is a novel of social protest—a protest against apartheid, the policy of racial segregation that existed in South Africa. When the Reverend Stephen Kumalo travels from his home in Ndotsheni to the capital city of Johannesburg to find his missing family members, he encounters a disintegration of tribal customs and family life. The Reverend Kumalo learns quickly that the whites, through the policy of apartheid, have disrupted African values and social order. He notes that city life leads to a demoralized lifestyle of poverty and crime for the natives. Even the Reverend Theophilus Msimangu, a priest who offers his assistance to the

Reverend Kumalo, believes that this disintegration of social values cannot be mended. The Reverend Msimangu does, however, envision hope for "when white men and black men . . . desiring only the good of their country, come together to work for it." The land, in this case, South Africa, is the center of this novel. As the land becomes divided and eroded, so, too, do the people who live on it. Because James Jarvis and the Reverend Stephen Kumalo reach a shared responsibility for their actions and thoughts as they attempt to understand the loss of their sons, Alan Paton believes that the country of South Africa has hope for restoration of its values and order in its new generation, especially in the sons of Arthur Jarvis and Absalom Kumalo.

Cry, the Beloved Country is structured into three sections. To depict the land as the central focus of this novel, Paton opens chapter 1 with a poetic reverence for "the fairest valleys of Africa." Here the connection between land and people becomes evident. Book 1 points to the erosion of the land as the people leave their native soil. This section focuses on the native soil of the blacks, the Reverend Stephen Kumalo in particular. It is difficult to maintain the beauty and fertility of the land when the tribal natives head for the promises of the city. The land, then, stands desolate. This deterioration is further illustrated in the shantytowns dishearteningly discovered by the Reverend Kumalo as he enters Johannesburg.

The opening lines are repeated in chapter 18, which begins book 2. The melodic description of the land is now in reference to the whites' partition of South Africa, namely, James Jarvis. The land is not depleted, but well tended. The openness and vitality of the land offer a sheer contrast to the depiction contained in book 1. James Jarvis' farm, the finest one of the countryside, "stands high above Ndotsheni." Paton thus symbolically portrays the destructiveness and divisiveness of apartheid in the ownership of land.

The third section holds a twofold purpose. Chapter 30 brings to light the drought that covers the land of Ndotsheni. Saddened by the land's deterioration, the Reverend Kumalo knows he must find a way to restore its beauty and fertility. Subsequently, this is assisted by a brewing rainstorm and, most notably, by the generosity of James Jarvis, who hires an agricultural demonstrator to ready plans for tillage. Symbolically, Paton realizes the Reverend Msimangu's words of hope that only love "has power completely." The reconstruction of the land becomes a joint venture between Kumalo and Jarvis, between black and white. Taking responsibility for one's actions has brought a new understanding and renewed principles for the good of all humanity.

Stylistically, Paton parallels character to character and action to action to dramatize the social ills of South Africa and its native people, while contrasting these vivid portraits to the lives of the white South Africans. As noted previously, the novel's three sections structurally suggest the two different worlds of Africans and Europeans, then offer a prospective solution and hope in the third book in the coming together of the two fathers. The safe, calm village life of Kumalo and the farm life of Jarvis is paralleled to the city life in Johannesburg, a city of evil, corruption, and moral inequities for both blacks and whites. The need for truth and justice is paralleled by Kumalo's search for his son Absalom, whom he finds in prison, with Jarvis' news of his son's death. Each father must come to terms with a loss. Although paralleled, it is Jarvis who claims an affinity, "for there is something between" them. Ironically, it is Kumalo's son who shot and killed Arthur Jarvis. Paton allows this parallel to function in two ways: first, to reflect the suffering of each father; second, to reveal that both Absalom and Arthur fell victim to apartheid. Paralleling, then, is more than just a structural device, but rather a focus on the issue of race relations in South Africa.

Alan Paton uses unique literary techniques to enhance the poignancy of his themes. Paton employs intercalary chapters to dramatize the historical setting of the novel. These intercalary chapters serve as Paton's social criticism of the divisive political and social order in South Africa. Paton also uses dashes to indicate dialogue, allowing not only for the realistic portrayal of conversation, but also for the rapid dramatic actions among characters. This simple literary technique generates the movement of plot and points directly to the language. Diction remains simple, yet eloquent in its delivery by the various characters. The Reverend Kumalo speaks in a mildly solemn language emphasizing his ecclesiastic background; the Reverend Msimangu often speaks in an oratory fashion to proclaim his views. John Kumalo, the brother of the Reverend Kumalo, uses the language of violence to demonstrate his anger over apartheid and his love for power as a black leader in Johannesburg. The tribal language brings the novel credence and revelation of a people rooted in tradition and honor.

In 1946, Alan Paton began writing *Cry, the Beloved Country*. Less than four months later, he finished it. Born in South Africa, Paton knew firsthand the tragedy that marks his homeland. He notes that although the story is not true, it is a social record of the truth. *Cry, the Beloved Country* is a classic work of world literature, not only for bringing to light a destructive political system, but also for depicting the humanity among people that can be lost in the struggle for justice and power. *Cry, the Beloved Country* is a cry for one's land, a cry for justice, a cry for understanding, and certainly, a cry for hope. Indeed, this novel speaks for all lost generations who seek direction in a dark world.

"Critical Evaluation" by Carmen Carrillo

Bibliography:
Alexander, Peter F. *Alan Paton: A Biography*. New York: Oxford University Press, 1994. A particularly engaging, well-documented, enormous biography. Provides important background information on the genesis of the novel in chapters 12 and 13.
Brutus, Dennis. "Protest Against Apartheid." In *Protest and Conflict in African Literature*, edited by Cosmo Pieterse and Donald Munro. New York: Africana, 1969. A notable and substantive critique of *Cry, the Beloved Country* from a black South African perspective. Argues that the novel's simple, direct protest against apartheid is not forceful enough against the monstrosity of racism.
Callan, Edward. *Alan Paton*. Rev. ed. Boston: Twayne, 1982. Contains ten chapters based on Paton's own 1981 volume of autobiography, *Towards the Mountain*. Provides significant general background on Paton's life and times, and a critical evaluation of his fiction, drama, biography, and poetry, including a full chapter on *Cry, the Beloved Country*.
_____. *"Cry, the Beloved Country": A Novel of South Africa*. Boston: Twayne, 1991. A supplement to the 1982 study, focused on the historical and literary context. Includes an eight-chapter critical reading and interpretation of the novel.
Paton, Jonathan. "Comfort in Desolation." In *International Literature in English: Essays on the Major Writers*, edited by Robert L. Ross. New York: Garland, 1991. A general discussion of Alan Paton's work, written by the younger of his two sons. Identifies a Christian ethic that calls for comfort in desolation as the single, most significant element of *Cry, the Beloved Country*.

CULTURE AND ANARCHY

Type of work: Social criticism
Author: Matthew Arnold (1822-1888)
First published: 1869

In *Culture and Anarchy*, Matthew Arnold sought a center of authority by which the anarchy caused by the troubled passage of the Reform Bill of 1867 might be regulated. At its best his style is clear, flexible, and convincing. He wrote in such a complicated mood of indignation, impatience, and fear, however, that his style and his argumentative method are frequently repetitious and unsystematic. The book is nevertheless a masterpiece of polished prose, in which urbane irony and shifts of ridicule are used to persuade the Victorian middle class that it must reform itself before it could begin to reform the entire nation.

Writing as a so-called Christian humanist, Arnold primarily directed his criticism against the utilitarianism of the followers of Jeremy Bentham and John Stuart Mill and against the various movements of liberal reform. Disturbed by the social and political confusion, by Fenianism and the Hyde Park Riots of 1866, and by the inability of either the church or the government to cope with the growing unrest both in England and on the Continent, Arnold attempted to describe an objective center of authority that all, regardless of religious or social bias, could follow.

This center of authority is culture, which he defined on the level of the individual as "a pursuit of our total perfection by means of getting to know, on all matters which most concern us, the best which has been thought and said in the world." Because this authority is internal, it is a study of perfection within the individual, a study that should elevate the "best self" through a fresh and free search for beauty and intelligence. By following "right reason," the disinterested intellectual pursuits of the "best self," Arnold foresaw a way to overcome the social and political confusion of the 1860's and to prepare for a future in which all could be happy and free. With this basically romantic view of human beings as a means and human perfectibility as the end, Arnold turned to social criticism, carefully showing that no other center of authority was tenable. The ideal of nonconformity, the disestablishment of the church, led to confusion or anarchy because it represented the sacrifice of all other sides of human personality to the religious. The ideal of the liberal reformers, on the other hand, led to anarchy because it regarded the reforms as ends rather than means toward a harmonious totality of human existence.

Arnold clarifies his definition of culture by tracing its origin to curiosity or "scientific passion" (the desire to see things as they really are) and to morality or "social passion" (the desire to do good). Christianity, as he saw it, was like culture in that it also sought to learn the will of God (human perfection) and make it prevail. Culture went beyond religion, however, as interpreted by the Nonconformists in that it was a harmonious expansion of all human powers. In even sharper terms, culture was opposed to utilitarianism, which Arnold considered "mechanical" because it worshiped means rather than ends. In fact, anything—materialism, economic greatness, individual wealth, bodily health, Puritanism—that was treated as an end except that of human perfectibility was to Arnold mere "machinery" that led to anarchy. Only culture, the harmonious union of poetry (the ideal of beauty) and religion (the ideal of morality), saw itself as a means that preserved the totality of the individual. Culture looked beyond machinery; it had only one passion—the passion for "sweetness" (beauty) and "light" (intelligence) and the passion to make them prevail. With such a passion it sought to do away with social classes and religious bias to make the best that has been thought and known in the world ("right reason") the core of human endeavor and institutions.

After establishing his definition of culture in terms of the individual, Arnold turned toward the problem of society. He saw the characteristic view of English people toward happiness as the individual freedom, but he also saw that each class had its own opinion as to what it considered freedom to be. In other words, there was a strong belief in freedom but a weak belief in "right reason," which should view freedom disinterestedly. This misplacing of belief was to Arnold one of the chief causes of anarchy; it was the mistake of acting before thinking. Ideally, "right reason" should precede action, and the state should be the disinterested union of all classes, a collective "best self." In reality, the state was being led toward anarchy by class interests because the aristocracy, or "Barbarians," was inaccessible to new, fresh ideas; the middle class, or "Philistines," had zeal but not knowledge; and the working class, or "Populace," was raw and untrained. Because culture alone could join the two sides of the individual, culture alone could overcome the narrow views of the three classes. Members of the different classes possessed the same human nature and saw happiness as freedom; also, the "best self" was common to all classes. Therefore, since authority could be found neither in religion nor in politics, it could be found only in individuals who, by following "right reason" rather than class bias, could assert their "best selves" in a harmonious union that sought the best for everyone. The major impediments to such a state were what Arnold called "Atheism," the outright denial of such a thing as "right reason," and "Quietism," the utilitarian belief that reason was the result of habit. These impediments Arnold rejected on the basis of intuition and faith. Ethics can be known intuitively, and by building faith on the individual's intuition the spirit of culture could overcome the present anarchy.

The enlargement of his terms from the individual to the state naturally led Arnold to consider the historical development of the social and political confusion that he confronted. In the famous chapter titled "Hebraism and Hellenism," Arnold accounted for the very ground and cause out of which actual behavior arises, by distinguishing between the energy in human affairs that drives at practice, the obligation of duty, self-control, and work (Hebraism) and the energy that drives at those ideas that are the basis of right practice (Hellenism). Like the "scientific passion," Hellenism's chief function is to see things as they really are, and like the "social passion," Hebraism seeks proper conduct and obedience. In other words, what Arnold earlier analyzed as the opposing drives in the individual, he now enlarges to a historical context, all human endeavor in the Western world being associated with either the one or the other drive. Both drives aim at human perfection or salvation, but their means and ideals are sharply different. Hebraism, or "strictness of conscience," inculcates a sense of sin, but Hellenism, the "spontaneity of consciousness," teaches what Arnold has called culture.

The rise of Christianity marked the great triumph of Hebraism over Hellenism, but the Renaissance marked the resurgence of Hellenism. The anarchy of the 1860's Arnold saw as the result of Puritanism's reaffirmation of Hebraism in the seventeenth century, a reaffirmation that was against the currents of history. The problem was intensified by the Puritan belief that duty was an end in itself, whereas in reality both great drives are no more than contributions to human development. Thus, in England there was too much Hebraism, so much, in fact, that religion and politics had become mechanical. As a solution, Arnold suggested that Hellenism be imported. In Hellenism, which ultimately is a synonym for culture, the ideals of internal harmony, or the unity of the total human being, and of harmony with things overcome the one-sidedness of Hebraism. The other drive, however, should not be excluded, for Hellenism alone leads to moral relaxation. There should be a harmony of both sides, a union from which would come the awakening of a healthier and less mechanical activity.

After analyzing culture in terms of the individual, the state, and history, Arnold turned to the particular issues before Parliament at the time he wrote. He directed his wit and some of his most vivacious ridicule against the four political reforms that were at the heart of liberalism—the disestablishment of the Irish church, the Real Estate Intestacy Bill, the Deceased Sister's Wife Bill, and free trade—and showed that the liberal reformers lacked disinterestedness, displayed a remarkable absence of reason, and were unconsciously leading to anarchy. By leaving the issues that were uppermost in his mind to the last, he dramatically illustrated that only culture could lead to perfection. For him the four bills were examples of the lack of belief in "right reason" and the philistine endeavor to act without thought. He warned that without "right reason" there could be no society and without society there could be no perfection. Only "right reason," the disinterested search for the best that has been thought or done regardless of class interests, could defeat anarchy by establishing the way to happiness through harmony.

Culture and Anarchy is one of those works that transcend their generic limitations. Ostensibly an analysis of the contemporary political situation in England and specifically a critique of the growing attitude of liberalism promoted in works such as John Stuart Mill's *On Liberty* (1859), the essays Matthew Arnold published originally in the *Cornhill Magazine* under the series title "Anarchy and Authority" have become regarded as the *locus classicus* of a certain conservative viewpoint that has generated strong reactions for more than one hundred years. The basic premise for Arnold's judgment of contemporary society is that there is an inherent urge toward perfection that resides in every individual. Arnold believed every person capable of being governed by "culture." For him, this meant living by the dictates of reason, in such a way that people realize they are not always the touchstone for judgments about either art or conduct; in the estimation of Lionel Trilling, one of his most distinguished critics, the attainment of culture was by Arnold's definition "the conscious effort of each man to come to the realization of his complete humanity." In Arnold's view, self-interest is the major enemy of both individual and social perfection; only when individuals are able to act disinterestedly, putting aside individual and class distinctions to work in harmony for the common good, would they become capable of realizing their "best selves."

Although Arnold is eloquent and penetrating in his social criticism, he lacks epistemological sophistication. The question he never addresses is how to determine what is best for individuals and society. He was attacked by contemporaries and criticized by succeeding generations for what many have seen as imperious dogmatism. Arnold claims that right reason—or, as he expresses it in *Culture and Anarchy* and elsewhere, "imaginative reason"—can serve as a guide for determining what a person or a society ought to do. He hopes that all will one day be educated to see what is best but argues that until then it is the business of government to restrain individual freedoms when they allow behavior inconsistent with what is good for society. It is understandable that this view leads to charges that Arnold is actually advocating state control and opting for a kind of approach giving those in authority permission to restrict conduct, perhaps even thought.

In the twentieth century, when all writing has come to be considered a political act and all conservative writing subjected to close scrutiny, Arnold became a principal target for literary theorists; their emphasis on the significance of political subtexts negatively affected the reputation of a writer who had considered himself a strong promoter of liberalism and a believer in people's ability to improve their individual and common lots in life.

Updated by Laurence W. Mazzeno

Bibliography:
Anderson, Warren D. *Matthew Arnold and the Classical Tradition*. Ann Arbor: University of Michigan Press, 1965. Examines Arnold's lifelong interest in classical literature and civilization. In writing *Culture and Anarchy*, Arnold drew heavily on Greek thought, and he was especially influenced by Plato.
Cockshut, A. O. J. "Matthew Arnold: Conservative Revolutionary." In *Matthew Arnold: A Collection of Critical Views*, edited by David J. DeLaura. Englewood Cliffs, N.J.: Prentice-Hall, 1973. Looks at *Culture and Anarchy* and four of Arnold's overtly religious works to trace the basic assumptions of his religious position. Arnold's combination of conservatism and skepticism made him seek established religion, but he also sought to change it.
Jump, J. D. *Matthew Arnold*. London: Longmans, 1965. Reassesses the achievement of Arnold the man, the poet, and the critic. Provides an excellent and accessible introduction to *Culture and Anarchy*, tracing the history of composition, political and social contexts, major arguments, and the author's intentions.
McCarthy, Patrick J. *Matthew Arnold and the Three Classes*. New York: Columbia University Press, 1964. A full-length study of *Culture and Anarchy*. Examines Arnold's own relationships with the three classes delineated in his work. Extensive notes, index, and bibliography.
Neiman, Fraser. "Anarchy and Authority." In *Matthew Arnold*. New York: Twayne, 1968. A brief but clear presentation of the major points in *Culture and Anarchy*, with an emphasis on explaining Arnold's terminology. Also includes a chronology, bibliography, and thorough index.

CUPID AND PSYCHE

Type of work: Fable
Author: Unknown
Type of plot: Mythic
Time of plot: Antiquity
Locale: Greece
First transcribed: Unknown (first English translation, probably 1566)

Principal characters:
    PSYCHE, the daughter of a Greek king
    CUPID, the god of love
    VENUS, the goddess of love and beauty

The Story:

Psyche, daughter of a Greek king, was as beautiful as Venus and sought after by many princes. Her father, seeking to know what fate the gods might have in store for her, sent some of his men to Apollo's oracle to learn the answer. To the king's horror, the oracle replied that Psyche was to become the mate of a hideous monster, and the king was ordered to leave his daughter to her fate upon a mountaintop, to prevent the destruction of his people. Clad in bridal dress, Psyche was led to a rocky summit and left there alone. The sad and weary young woman soon fell into a swoon.

Venus, jealous of Psyche's beauty, called her son Cupid and ordered him to use his arrows (whoever was struck with one of his arrows fell in love with whomever they were looking at) to turn Psyche's heart toward a creature so hideous that mortals would be filled with loathing at the sight of Psyche's mate. As Cupid saw his victim, however, as he was preparing to shoot his arrow, he was transfixed by her beauty. He dropped his arrow and it struck him in the leg. He fell in love with her and decided that Psyche should be his forever. While Psyche slept, Zephyrus came at Cupid's bidding and carried her to the valley in which Love's house stood. There she awoke in a grove of trees in which stood a magnificent golden palace. She entered the building and wandered through the sumptuously furnished rooms.

At noon, Psyche found a table lavishly spread. A voice invited her to eat, assured her that the house was hers, and told her that the being who was to be her lover would come that night.

As she lay in bed that night a voice close beside her told her not to be afraid. The voice spoke so tenderly that Psyche welcomed her unseen suitor and held out her arms to him. When Psyche awoke the next morning, her lover had gone, but he had left behind a gold ring and had placed a circlet on her head.

For a time Psyche lived happily in the golden palace, visited each night by the lover whose face she had not seen. At last, however, she became homesick for her two sisters and her father. One night, she asked her lover to permit her sisters to visit her the next day. He gave his consent, but he warned that she was not to tell them about him.

Zephyrus carried the sisters to the valley. Overjoyed to see them, Psyche showed them the beauties of the palace and loaded them with gifts. Jealous of her good fortune, they tried to make her suspicious of her unseen lover. They suggested that her lover was a serpent who changed into the form of a youth at night, a monster who would at last devour her. To save herself, they advised her to hide a lamp and a knife by her bed so that she might see him and slay him as he slept.

Psyche did as they had suggested. That night, as her love lay asleep, she lit the lamp and brought it close so that she might look at him. When she saw the perfectly handsome young man by her side, she was powerless to use her knife. As she turned, sobbing, to extinguish the flame, a drop of burning oil fell on Cupid's shoulder. Awaking with a cry, he looked at her reproachfully. With the warning that love cannot live with suspicion, he left the palace. Psyche tried to follow but fell in a swoon at the threshold.

When she awoke, the palace had vanished. Determined to seek her lover, she wandered alone across the countryside and through cities hunting the god. Meanwhile, Cupid took his vengeance on her sisters. To each he sent a dream that she would become his bride if she were to throw herself from the mountaintop. Both sisters, obeying the summons, found only the arms of Death to welcome them.

No god would give the wandering Psyche shelter or comfort or protect her from the wrath of Venus. At the temples of Ceres and Juno, she was turned away. At last, she came to the court of Venus herself. Warned by her heart to flee, she was nevertheless drawn before the throne of the goddess. Venus decided that Psyche should be kept as a slave. She was to be given a new task to do each day and was to live until she once more began to hope.

Psyche's first task was to sort a huge pile of mixed seeds and grain into separate heaps, with the warning that if there were so much as one seed in the wrong pile she would be punished, but by dusk, she had separated only small heaps of grain. Cupid so pitied her that he commanded myriad ants to complete the task for her.

The next day, Psyche was ordered to gather the golden fleece of Venus' sheep. Obeying the advice of a reed at the edge of the river, she waited until the animals had lain down to sleep and then collected the wool which had been left clinging to the bushes.

Psyche's third task was to fill a jug with the black water that flowed down a steep mountain into the rivers Styx and Cocytus. She was able to complete this task with the aid of a bird who carried the jug to the stream, collected the water, and brought it back to her.

On the fourth day, Psyche was given her most difficult task; she was to go to the land of the dead and there collect some of the beauty of the goddess Proserpine in a golden box. If she succeeded, Venus promised, she would treat Psyche kindly thereafter. To visit Proserpine—in the land of the dead—and to return, however, was an impossible achievement. In despair, Psyche determined to cast herself from a tower, but as she was about to kill herself a voice called to her and told her how she might fulfill her mission.

Following instructions, Psyche traveled to Proserpine's realm. There she might have stayed on forever if she had not thought suddenly of her love. On her way back, she had almost reached the daylight when envy seized her. She opened the box, thinking she would have whatever it contained for herself, but no sooner had she lifted the lid than she fell into a deep sleep filled with nightmares. She might have lain that way forever if Cupid, going in search of her, had not found her. He awoke her with one of his arrows and sent her on to his mother with the box.

Then he flew off and presented himself before Jove with his petition that Psyche be made immortal. Jove, after hearing his pleas, sent Mercury to conduct Psyche into the presence of the gods. There she drank from the golden cup of ambrosia that Jove handed her and became immortal. She and Cupid were at last united for all time.

Critical Evaluation:

Although the story of Cupid's love for Psyche (or at least a maid) was known by Hellenistic times, the one known literary source for this complete tale is the *Metamorphoses* (c. 180-190) of Lucius Apuleius. Better known as *The Golden Ass*, this Latin book deals with the transformation of Lucius into an ass, his year-long journey and checkered adventures, his ultimate restoration to human shape, and his devotion to the Egyptian goddess Isis. At the center of this eleven-book work is couched the story of Cupid and Psyche, as told by an old crone to a beautiful young woman. This "pleasant tale and old wives' story," as the old woman put it, belongs to the genre of the folktale, and throughout the world variations on this story are known. Apuleius' readers would have immediately recognized the character Psyche as typical of the heroines of Greek "novels" or "romances": She is lovely and in love, but she is also timid, pious, naïve, and curious. This last characteristic, her most serious fault, Apuleius uses to relate Psyche to Lucius, the central figure of the novel. As a result of curiosity, both are violently thrown into a life of suffering and despair; both overcome their trials and achieve true happiness by devotion to a deity.

Through the years, *Cupid and Psyche* has been recognized for its allegorical possibilities. Cupid ("desire," Eros in Greek) is one of the oldest allegorical divinities. Psyche, in turn, means "soul." That Apuleius intended symbolic reflection of the larger work is hardly debatable, but that he saw the story as a vehicle of teaching Christian virtue is unfounded. Nevertheless, the universal charm of the story prompted Fulgentius Planciades (sixth century) to allegorize thus: The city is the world, Psyche's father is God, her mother is matter, her sisters represent flesh and the will, Venus is lust, and Cupid is "cupidity"; Fulgentius' allegory, however, does not have satisfactory consistency. Pedro Calderón de la Barca (seventeenth century) saw the three daughters as paganism, Judaism, and the Church, the last of whom was wedded to Christ. The Platonists, who no doubt recognized echoes from Plato's *Phaedrus* (fourth century B.C.E.), saw the sisters as the tripartite soul: Desire and spirit are overcome by sure reason, and the ultimate acceptance of the rational soul among the gods symbolized freedom from the Orphic cycle of death and rebirth. Jungians see Psyche as the psychic development of the feminine; Venus symbolizes fertility, and the marriage to Cupid is sexual bondage.

In this story, Cupid is considerably more mature than the familiar Hellenistic winged archer-cherub, and his beauty is emphasized; nevertheless, he is still mischievous and his mother's minion. Venus, however, is an outright burlesque; she seems to have grown more vain with age and motherhood, and her jealousy of the beautiful young virgin Psyche is decidedly un-Christian. Still, such a characterization is necessary if Venus is to be given the role of the folktale witch who sets the apparently impossible tasks, which are also appropriate to Venus' role as mother-in-law, since the wool, grain, water, and beauty are Psyche's symbolic dowry, representing wifely abilities and virtues.

Tasks and journeys are traditional themes in heroic tales, especially when they are punishments for some sacrilege. Psyche's crime, despite her original guilelessness, is twofold: She has offended Venus, and she has violated her husband's trust. It is interesting to observe how in Apuleius' version Psyche, who is so simple that she cannot even lie to her sisters about her husband, even after being told not to mention him, loses her innocence as soon as she is persuaded by them to kill the "monster." Thereafter she has a part in the trouble that follows. Psyche, therefore, loses innocence, but she gains knowledge and a chance to regain happiness— eternally. This is the theme of the larger work, the *Metamorphoses*, in which Lucius is initiated into the Isiac mysteries and becomes the priest of Isis, forsaking the evils of a world of asses in human flesh.

Another addition to the synopsis above must be included. Apuleius has Cupid warn Psyche that if she keeps secret the strange nature of their marriage, the child she is bearing will remain divine. Apuleius ends his story with the birth of a child who is fittingly called Voluptas, or "Joy." Thus, the eternal union of love and the soul does result in the soul's divine, that is, immortal, joy.

As a product of the classical age, *Cupid and Psyche* is full of familiar classical literary and mythological illusions. The "labors" motif includes the traditional journey to the underworld (such as with Herakles, Orpheus, Odysseus, and Aeneas). The deserted Psyche recalls the despair of Ariadne, Andromeda, and Dido. The theme of the opened container recalls Pandora. Psyche's apotheosis, or deification, finds precedent especially in the myth of Herakles. As for the gods, their portraits become near parodies of Homeric models, in that they act with stereotypical predictability. Later versions of *Cupid and Psyche* are found in Giovanni Boccaccio's *Genealogies of the Gentile Gods* (1350-1375) and in Walter Pater's *Marius the Epicurean* (1885). In addition Calderón, Molière, Pierre Corneille, Thomas Heywood, and Joseph Beaumont have told their versions of the Cupid and Psyche fable.

"Critical Evaluation" by E. N. Genovese

Bibliography:
Franz, Marie-Louise von. *The Golden Ass of Apuleius.* Boston: Shambhala, 1992. Psychological interpretation of the Cupid and Psyche myth. An excellent resource for the study and analysis of this myth.

Haight, Elizabeth Hazelton. *Apuleius and His Influence.* New York: Longmans, Green, 1927. Although much research has followed in subsequent years, this remains a significant source for comparative studies. Traces the tradition of Cupid and Psyche from classical to modern literature. Cites various interpretations of the myth in different historical periods.

Labouvie-Vief, Gisela. *Psyche and Eros.* New York: Cambridge University Press, 1994. Illustrates theories of the mind and gender using this myth as foundation. Interprets myth as a psychological development to overcome dualistic thinking in terms of gender. Comprehensive examination of the psychological components of mythmaking.

Neumann, Erich. *Amor and Psyche.* New York: Harper & Row, 1962. Provides detailed commentary that includes classical sources, art illustrations, and occurrences in other literature. Argues that Psyche represents the development of the feminine psyche.

Schlam, Carl C. *The Metamorphoses of Apuleius.* Chapel Hill: University of North Carolina Press, 1992. Detailed commentary on sources of the myth of Cupid and Psyche and an extensive bibliography. Includes theories of a number of other critics to explain the myth's origin.

Tatum, James. *Apuleius and "The Golden Ass."* Ithaca, N.Y.: Cornell University Press, 1979. Identifies and compares a number of sources and interpretations of the Cupid and Psyche myth. Characterizes and analyzes individual parts of the story.

CUSTER DIED FOR YOUR SINS
An Indian Manifesto

Type of work: Social criticism
Author: Vine Deloria, Jr. (1933-   )
First published: 1969

Vine Deloria, Jr., one of the most important Native American intellectuals, first achieved prominence with the publication of *Custer Died for Your Sins: An Indian Manifesto*, a collection of eleven essays and an "afterword" on a variety of topics related to American Indian social, legal, and political issues of the 1960's. Coming at the end of a decade in which the fundamental values of American culture were being rigorously questioned, when American history was being rewritten, and when the younger generation was eagerly searching for alternative lifestyles, Deloria's book quickly became a best-seller praised for the wit, humor, and energy of its style as well as for its articulate and witty presentation of the Native American point of view and its penetrating critique of mainstream American culture.

Earlier in the 1960's, interest in American Indians had been generated by the reissue, in 1962, of *Black Elk Speaks* (1932), the life story of an Oglala Sioux holy man which had become a cult classic on college campuses. Then, in 1968, the Pulitzer Prize in fiction was awarded to N. Scott Momaday, the American Indian author of *House Made of Dawn* (1968), the first novel written by a Native American to be so honored. Next came *Custer Died for Your Sins* in 1969, quickly followed by Dee Brown's revisionist presentation of the history of the Indian wars in *Bury My Heart at Wounded Knee* (1970), which also became a national best-seller. In their different ways, these four books urged the rejection of the old stereotypes of American Indians and gave a more realistic and much more sympathetic view of them than had previously been available in literature that was written almost exclusively from the perspective of white Americans.

Thus, in his opening essay, "Indians Today: The Real and the Unreal," Deloria comments that he intends to discuss the Indian people's feeling of unreality that "has been welling up inside us and threatens to make this decade [the 1970's] the most decisive in history for Indian people." Among the "unreal and ahistorical" beliefs and attitudes that Deloria goes on to enumerate is the claim by many white people to have an Indian ancestor, usually an Indian princess grandmother, and Deloria humorously comments that he "once did a projection backward and discovered that evidently most tribes were entirely female for the first three hundred years of white occupation." Indians, Deloria comments, suffer from misconceptions and stereotyping because white people believe that they are so easy to understand: "Anyone and everyone who knows an Indian or who is *interested*, immediately and thoroughly understands them." Among these "understandings," Deloria lists many myths about Indians, beginning with Christopher Columbus' mistaken belief that the native peoples he met were the inhabitants of India, the later view that they were the ten lost tribes of Israel, and the yet later view that they were little better than wild animals to be "hunted and skinned. Bounties were set and an Indian scalp became more valuable than beaver, otter, marten, and other animal pelts."

However, Deloria argues, not all the harm was done by the Indians' enemies; much of it was done by their "friends," the white do-gooders, missionaries, promoters, scholars, "and every conceivable type of person who believed he could help. White society failed to understand the situation because this conglomerate of assistance blurred the real issues beyond recognition." The essay ends with an enumeration of tribal governments and political organizations as they existed in the 1960's, an analysis of their accomplishments and prospects for the future, and a plea for "fewer and fewer 'experts' on Indians. What we need is a cultural leave-us-alone agreement in spirit and in fact."

The essays which follow take up individually the concerns that are outlined in "Indians Today: The Real and the Unreal." The second essay, titled "Laws and Treaties," begins by pointing out a tragic irony in the history of the United States government's treatment of the Native Americans. President Lyndon Johnson stressed the importance of the United States keeping its commitments in Southeast Asia, and President Richard Nixon pictured the Soviet Union as a menace to world peace because it did not honor its treaties. However, Deloria comments, "Indian people laugh themselves sick when they hear these statements. America has yet to keep one Indian treaty or agreement despite the fact that the United States government signed over four hundred such treaties and agreements with Indian tribes. . . . It is doubtful that any nation will ever exceed the record of the United States for perfidy." Deloria argues, however, that this perfidy is not merely a fact of America's past; more damage is being done to Indian people in the 1960's than was done in the entire nineteenth century. Adding to the Indian people's resentment of their treatment at the hands of a government which daily tramples on Indian treaty rights while insisting on maintaining its commitments in Vietnam is their outrage at the complicity of the Christian churches in the mistreatment of Native Americans. Why, Deloria asks, if the churches actually want justice, do they not speak out about the mistreatment of the Indians?

The essay concludes that America "has always been a militantly imperialistic world power eagerly grasping for economic control over weaker nations," including the Indian nations which were conquered one after another in the United States' march across the North American continent. The war in Vietnam is seen in the essay as only the most recent symptom of the basic lack of integrity of the American government, "a side issue in comparison with the great domestic issues which must be faced—and justly faced—before this society destroys itself."

The next four essays, "The Disastrous Policy of Termination," "Anthropologists and Other Friends," "Missionaries and the Religious Vacuum," and "Government Agencies," discuss the ways in which those white people who were sympathetic to the Indians have inadvertently caused them more harm than good. Termination was a policy, initiated in the 1950's, intended to end the federally recognized status of Indian tribes, thereby solving the "Indian problem" by assimilating the Indian people into the general population. According to Deloria, however, it was used as another excuse by the government to get its hands on Indian lands.

Anthropologists, no matter how well intentioned, treat Indian people "as objects for observation . . . for experimentation, for manipulation, and for eventual extinction. The anthropologist thus furnishes the justification for treating Indian people like so many chessmen available for anyone to play with." Deloria urges Indian people to reject the anthropologists' "compilation of useless knowledge" and argues that Indians should not cooperate with those who raise no hand to help them. "During the crucial days of 1954, when the Senate was pushing for termination of all Indian rights, not one single scholar, anthropologist, sociologist, historian, or economist came forward to support the tribes against the detrimental policy." According to Deloria, these scholars were not really interested in helping Indian people but merely in exploiting them to further their own academic careers.

Deloria attacks Christian do-gooders and especially Christian denominations which are determined to keep Indian congregations in a mission status and refuse to admit Indians to the ministry for fear that the "purity" of the doctrine would suffer. Thus, Indian people are offended and the "impotence and irrelevancy" of the churches has meant a return to traditional religion and the rapid expansion of the Native American Church. Deloria believes that Indian religion, not Christianity, will be the salvation of Indian people, primarily, he says, because Indian religions, regardless of the tribe, view death as a natural occurrence and not a punishment from God. If the Christian missions were really interested in serving the Indians' best interests, they would assist in the creation of a national Indian Christian Church incorporating all existing missions and programs into one all-encompassing organization to be put wholly in the hands of the Indian people themselves.

In "Government Agencies," Deloria explains the structure and history of the Bureau of Indian Affairs (BIA), points out its inefficiencies and failures, and offers proposals for changes that need to be made if Indians are to be able to make progress comparable to that of the rest of society. Programming should be based on the size of the tribe, with special consideration for funding given to the thirty-five or so tribes with sufficient population, land, and resources to make large programs feasible. Area BIA offices should be given the bulk of the budgets in discretionary funds in order to maximize flexibility to meet local needs. People employed directly by the tribes should be given civil service status so that they can leave the BIA and work directly for tribal governments without losing time in grade and retirement benefits. The BIA itself should be transferred from the Department of the Interior to the Department of Commerce, where it could be merged with the Economic Development Administration, an agency better able to match tribal projects to available government and private sector programs.

The best-known and most often quoted essay in the collection is the one entitled "Indian Humor." It is based on the premise that one of the best ways to understand a culture is to know what it finds humorous. For too long, Deloria thinks, the stereotype of the humorless, "granite-faced grunting redskin has been perpetuated by American mythology." In contrast, Deloria points out that humor was an integral part of traditional Indian cultures. Teasing was used as a method of social control for centuries before the white invasion; it made it possible to correct and mold social behavior while preserving egos and minimizing disputes of a personal nature—an alternative to direct confrontation and public denunciation that preserved the dignity of the accused. In the politically charged atmosphere of the 1960's, humor served as a method of bringing Indian people from various tribes together by focusing on commonalities and creating goodwill, and thus it was an important political tool in the struggle to gain "red power." Satire can circumscribe problems so that possible solutions are suggested, and people are often awakened and "brought to a militant edge" because of jokes.

Among the most politically useful targets of Indian humor are the BIA, where Deloria often counsels Indians to run in case of earthquake because nothing can shake the BIA, and General Custer, who was well dressed for the occasion of his last stand, his body having been found afterward dressed in an Arrow shirt. Humor, according to Deloria, is the cement which holds the Indian movement together: "When a people can laugh at themselves and laugh at others and hold all aspects of life together without letting anybody drive them to extremes, then it seems to me that that people can survive."

The remaining essays are more dated, focusing on what Indian people can do to help themselves in the 1960's. Deloria concludes by reminding Indian people of the great war chief Crazy Horse, who "never drafted anyone to follow him" but was followed because people recognized that what he did was for the people. When he was dying, bayoneted in the back, Crazy Horse said to his father, "Tell the people it is no use to depend on me any more now." Deloria writes, "Until we can once again produce people like Crazy Horse all the money and help in the world will not save us."

Dennis Hoilman

Bibliography:
Carriker, Robert C. "The American Indian from the Civil War to the Present." In *Historians and the American West*, edited by Michael P. Malone. Lincoln: University of Nebraska Press, 1983. Criticizes Deloria for being more political than historical.

Champagne, Duane, ed. *The Native North American Almanac: A Reference Work on Native North Americans in the United States and Canada*. Detroit: Gale Research, 1994. Comments on Deloria's impact on the views of Native American religious movements.

Ruoff, A. Lavonne. *American Indian Literatures: An Introduction, Bibliographic Review, and Selected Bibliography*. New York: Modern Language Association, 1990. Comments on Deloria's "keen wit, sharp satire, and political insight."

Steiner, Stan. *The New Indians*. New York: Dell, 1968. Contains scattered comments on Deloria and his place in the red power movement, providing a context for the issues raised in *Custer Died for Your Sins*.

Wiget, Andrew. *Native American Literature*. Boston: Twayne, 1985. Describes Deloria's "witty, acerbic style."

THE CUSTOM OF THE COUNTRY

Type of work: Novel
Author: Edith Wharton (1862-1937)
Type of plot: Social realism
Time of plot: Late nineteenth century
Locale: New York and Paris
First published: 1913

Principal characters:
UNDINE SPRAGG, a predatory woman
ABNER E. SPRAGG, her father
ELMER MOFFATT, her first husband
RALPH MARVELL, her second husband
PAUL, Undine and Ralph Marvell's son
RAYMOND DE CHELLES, her third husband
PETER VAN DEGEN, her lover

The Story:

Undine Spragg, who came to New York from Apex City with her parents, had been in the city for two years without being accepted in society. Her opportunity came at last when she was invited to a dinner given by Laura Fairford, whose brother, Ralph Marvell, had taken an interest in her. Although his family was socially prominent, Ralph had little money. He was an independent thinker who disliked the superficiality of such important people as Peter Van Degen, the wealthy husband of Ralph's cousin, Clare Dagonet, with whom Ralph had once been in love.

About two months after their meeting, Undine and Ralph became engaged. One night, they went to see a play, where Undine was shocked to find herself sitting next to Elmer Moffatt, someone who knew about her past. She promised to meet him privately in Central Park the next day. When they met, Moffatt, a blunt, vulgar man, told Undine that she must help him in his business deals after she married Ralph. Moffatt also went to see Undine's father and, threatening to reveal Undine's past if Mr. Spragg refused, asked him to join in a business deal.

Mr. Spragg was fortunate in his business deal with Moffatt and was able to give Undine a big wedding. After Ralph and Undine were married, Ralph gradually realized that Undine cared less for him than for the social world. He also became aware of Undine's ruthless desire for money. Her unhappiness and resentment increased when she learned that she was pregnant.

During the next several years, Moffatt became a significant financial figure in New York. Ralph, in an attempt to support Undine's extravagance, went to work in a business to which he was ill-suited. Undine, meanwhile, kept up a busy schedule of social engagements. She also accepted some expensive gifts from Peter Van Degen, who was interested in her, before Peter left to spend the season in Europe. One day, Undine saw Moffatt, who had come to propose a disreputable business deal to Ralph; the deal succeeded and Undine went to Paris to meet Peter, where soon she had spent all the money. She met the Comte Raymond de Chelles, a French aristocrat, whom she thought of marrying until Peter told her that if she stayed with him, he would give her everything she wanted. At this point, Undine received a telegram announcing that Ralph was critically ill with pneumonia and asking her to return to New York immediately. Undine decided to stay in Paris.

Ralph recovered. After her uncontested divorce from Ralph, Undine lived with Peter Van Degen for two months. When he learned that Undine had not gone to Ralph while he was ill, Peter was disillusioned and left her without getting the promised divorce from his wife Clare. Ralph, meanwhile, had returned to the Dagonet household with his son, Paul, for whose sake he began to work hard at the office. He also resumed work on a novel. Then he learned that Undine was engaged to Comte Raymond de Chelles and badly needed money to have her marriage to Ralph annulled by the Church. Undine agreed to waive her rights to her son if Ralph would send her one hundred thousand dollars to pay for her annulment. Ralph borrowed half of the needed sum and went to Moffatt to make another business deal. As Undine's deadline approached, with the deal not yet concluded, Ralph went to see Moffatt, who told him that the matter was going more slowly than expected and that it would take a year to materialize. Moffatt told Ralph that he himself was once married to Undine, back in Apex City, but that Undine's parents had forced the young couple to get a divorce. After hearing this story, Ralph went home and committed suicide.

Undine, now in possession of her son, married Raymond de Chelles. She was very happy in Paris, even though Raymond was strict about her social life. After three months, they moved to the family estate at Saint Desert to live quietly and modestly. When Raymond began to ignore her, Undine became bored and resentful of her husband's family for not making allowances for her extravagance, which continued unabated.

One day, she invited a dealer from Paris to appraise some of the priceless Chelles tapestries. When the dealer arrived, the prospective American buyer with him turned out to be Moffatt, now one of the richest men in New York. Over the next several weeks, Undine saw a great deal of her first husband. When the time came for Moffatt to return to New York, Undine invited him to have an affair with her. Moffatt told her that he wanted marriage or nothing.

Undine went to Reno, Nevada, where she divorced Raymond and married Moffatt that same day. Moffatt gave Undine everything she wanted, but she realized that in many personal ways he compared unfavorably with her other husbands. The Moffatts settled in a mansion in Paris to satisfy Undine's social ambitions and her husband's taste for worldly display. When Undine learned that an old society acquaintance, Jim Driscoll, had been appointed ambassador to England, she decided that she would like to be the wife of an ambassador. Moffatt told her bluntly that that was the one thing she could never have because she was a divorced woman. Still dissatisfied, Undine was certain that the one thing she was destined to be was an ambassador's wife.

Critical Evaluation:

The Custom of the Country, one of Edith Wharton's major achievements, was published midway through her productive period between 1905 and 1920, which culminated in a Pulitzer Prize in fiction. As in *The House of Mirth* (1905), Wharton examines the old New York in which she grew up with an anthropologist's eye. As in her masterpiece, *The Age of Innocence* (1920), she shrewdly examines the conventions of society and the men and women who try to break out of them. *The Custom of the Country* reflects not only her concern with American cultural inadequacies and her contempt for the values of the newly moneyed and growing middle class (in this concern she resembles her contemporary, Henry James) but also her interest in the issue of the role of women in society.

Wharton's portrait of Undine is remarkable; nothing quite like it had been attempted in American literature, except perhaps in Theodore Dreiser's *Sister Carrie* (1900). Like Dreiser, Wharton shatters the conventions of the age, which sentimentalized women and consigned them to passive roles in melodramas or staid drawing room comedies and romances. The novel ends with Undine still unsatisfied. Her marriage to Moffatt, financially by far her most successful, is marred by her insatiable desire for more, particularly for anything that might enhance her position in society. From the time she leaves Apex and comes to New York to cut a figure in society, she thrives only when she is noticed and treasured and when her extravagance is indulged. She grows more sophisticated but her character does not change. It is unlikely that she would ever be content, which is why Wharton ends the novel with Undine's longing to be an ambassador's wife.

It would be simplistic merely to see Undine as a villainess—indeed, Wharton does not treat her as such. Rather, Undine represents her times, late nineteenth and early twentieth century America, when the number of business speculators such as Moffatt rose sharply and the old New York of Edith Wharton's childhood gave way to a new class of entrepreneurs. Undine is a kind of robber baron, boosting her stock and conniving at investments in her human capital. She is every bit as ruthless as Moffatt, but since she is a woman she has far less latitude than he does and must depend on pleasing men and on insinuating herself in good society.

Undine is as much a victim as she is a villainess. Neither her father nor the other men in her life tell her the slightest thing about business. Her father has spoiled her with gifts even as he complains that her demands tax his resources. Because she always gets what she wants she thinks that her father exaggerates his worries about money. To her, money is something men get to please their women, and the men do not disabuse her of that idea. Even Ralph's sad, desperate effort to pay her off with one hundred thousand dollars merely confirms her judgment that men will get her what she wants. It is not surprising that she sees society as rapacious. In this competitive context, she is hardly alone in indulging her appetites.

What does set Undine apart from other self-serving, cold-blooded, and unsympathetic fictional women is her almost complete lack of feeling for her son. Moffatt is quite tender with the boy and behaves sensitively as a stepfather, but Undine ignores her son even after she has remarried Moffatt. As Moffatt says, Undine simply cannot help herself. She is so self-obsessed that even her own family will always be ancillary to her.

If Undine remains attractive to Moffatt and to some readers even after the worst is known about her, it is because of her incredible energy. As a woman she has so little room to maneuver or ability to decide on the kind of life she wants. Her life involves constant transitions, yet she never despairs. She is at her finest when she rebels against Raymond de Chelles, her third husband. It is true that she is horribly blind to what home and family mean to him—she proposes to sell the family heirlooms so that she could continue her brilliant seasons in Paris—but she also protests against the stifling double standard that allows Raymond to travel and live his life while she is supposed to sacrifice her wants. Undine refuses to be passive.

Wharton portrays her heroine without so much as a veneer of sentimentality. This has prompted some critics to suggest that she despises Undine, but this view seems untenable given the novel's carefully controlled narrative voice. Undine is not blamed but viewed, rather, in anthropological terms as a product of her times—as are the other characters. Ralph, for example, elicits much sympathy for his efforts to please Undine and for his acceptance of Undine's behavior. He even tolerates her neglect of their son. Yet Ralph is weak; he does not fight for what he loves, and his suicide is a wasteful, pathetic ending to a life that had some promise. Having begun as a critic of old New York society, he eventually capitulates to its dictates. That he should be so undone demonstrates how ill-prepared he was to contend with life.

Narrow and unimaginative as Undine's parents are, they at least instilled in their daughter a will not merely to live but to prevail. What she wants may be vulgar and worthless, yet without energy like hers, social change would be impossible. Without her kind of irreverence, women would be at the mercy of either the Ralphs or the Raymonds. In the context of the dynamic, rapidly changing early twentieth century society, Undine is an appropriate and brilliantly realized creation.

"Critical Evaluation" by Carl Rollyson

Bibliography:

Lewis, R. W. B. *Edith Wharton: A Biography.* New York: Harper & Row, 1975. This standard biography provides important background information on the novel and a sensitive critical discussion placing it in the context of Wharton's other work.

McDowell, Margaret B. *Edith Wharton.* Boston: Twayne, 1976. An introductory study that includes a separate chapter on *The Custom of the Country*, which discusses its critical reception, compares it to other Wharton works, and analyzes its structure, Wharton's use of satire, and her deft treatment of minor characters.

Nevius, Blake. *Edith Wharton: A Study of Her Fiction.* Berkeley: University of California Press, 1953. An early but still valuable study that compares Wharton's Undine to the creation of the "new woman" in other early twentieth century novels, calling her a "symbolic victim" of the forces shaping modern America.

Raphael, Lev. *Edith Wharton's Prisoners of Shame: A New Perspective on Her Neglected Fiction.* New York: St. Martin's Press, 1991. Compares *The Custom of the Country* with *The House of Mirth* and provides a close analysis of the novel's structure.

Wolff, Cynthia Griffin. *A Feast of Words: The Triumph of Edith Wharton.* New York: Oxford University Press, 1977. A critical study with significant biographical material that helps illuminate the author's readings of the novels. Includes a thorough interpretation of *The Custom of the Country*, emphasizing Wharton's anthropological view of her characters.

CUTTLEFISH BONES

Type of work: Poetry
Author: Eugenio Montale (1896-1981)
First published: Ossi di seppia, 1925 (English translation, 1992)

Along with Giuseppe Ungaretti and Salvatore Quasimodo, writers of the Hermetic school, Eugenio Montale is one of the most influential poets to shape Italian letters in the twentieth century. Although Montale also wrote literary criticism and about fifteen hundred newspaper and periodical articles, it was his first volume of poetry, *Cuttlefish Bones,* marked by its precision, concision, and concreteness, that gained him public recognition. In its prosody, the collection breaks from traditional Italian poetry in many ways. Most significantly, it marks a final shift from the style of Gabriele D'Annunzio. Montale abandons the linear and rhetorically flourished narrative line and works instead in a highly associative style, in an Italian really spoken, with images as the loci of meaning and abstractions arising from the images. The tone becomes direct and sometimes conversational, and fixed stanzaic patterns modulate to a mix of free verse with varied meters. Montale declared his aesthetic intent: "to rid myself of all waste" in the interest of precision.

Montalean images derive in large part from the world of nature. The imagery of *Cuttlefish Bones* is extremely influenced by the environs of the Cinque Terre area of the Ligurian coast, with its "enchanting arc of rocks and sky," where he went during summers until he was thirty years old. The title refers to fragments of remains of the octopus washed ashore. Indeed, throughout the collection, the sea tosses its "bones" onto the shore and hurls the "sea-wrack starfish cork" "onto the beaches": All of this flotsam is heaved up, "hurled aside by the torrent of life." The section within *Cuttlefish Bones* with the same title abounds in recurring Ligurian images of the seacoast, the bright sun and the evocation of heat ("that land of searing sun where the air/ goes hazy with mosquitos"), the rocky shoreline, and the cuttlebones. The desolate images of rocks, of "stonebound suffering," are every now and then juxtaposed with messages of inspiration like those of the epiphany of light in the lemon trees, of the re-creation of the winter wonderland of childhood, and of the sunflower, "crazed with light," which can be found where "life evaporates as essence." In contrast, "The Mediterranean" evokes the expansiveness of the sea. Montale apostrophizes: "O immensity, it was you, redeeming/ even the stones in their suffering."

Cuttlefish Bones presages the rest of Montale's work both aesthetically and thematically. The symbol system of the collection is established in "In limine," wherein images of walls, which are representative of boundaries and stasis as well as of the preestablished, are contrasted by the fluidity of the water and the unconfined movement of the wind, which are shown to be emblematic of change, movement, and transformation.

Montale described himself in "The Mediterranean" as "a man intent/ on observing, in himself, and others, the furor/ of fleeting life." He treats this theme and others typical of his times: alienation and anguish in living; isolation and enclosure emblematized by recurrent images of walls and the transgressing of those walls into boundlessness; exile from place, from childhood, from nature; the mixed virtues of being unencumbered by relationships; and the search for the authentic self.

The collection was originally received as a metaphysical statement. The face of a passerby on a crowded street, for instance, shows for a moment "an invisible suffering," but no one notices. Facing the abyss of "nothingness at my back,/ emptiness behind me," the speaker says:

"I will feel the terror of the drunken man." After that flash of metaphysical anguish, things of commonplace reality return. Having seen life as void of meaning once, he calls those everyday objects, the "trees, houses and hills," "the usual deception"; he states quietly that he will continue on, "silently," "bearing my secret among the men who do not look back." The "real" world becomes unreal—a motif in his early poetry.

In "The Mediterranean," he describes the sense of futility of a poet trying to say something in the presence of the sea with its "vast language," which contrasts his "moldy dictionary words" and his "clichés/ which student rabble might tomorrow steal in real poetry." Overwhelmed and overawed by the elemental power of the Mediterranean, his consciousness is razed: "My thoughts fail, they leave me." His senses leave him as well, but this has its beneficent side also, in that having no thoughts, and no senses, he is no longer conscious and therefore no longer bound. He has, as he says, "No limit."

Montale's work is not void of the kind of inspiration that can often mount to a statement of faith in the human spirit's drive to endure. In "The Lemon Trees," he describes and defines his poetic, separating it from its predecessors, whom he shows as "the laureled poets" of tradition who walk among "shrubs/ with learned names." He eschews them, the lushness of tradition, and their poetics in favor of those streets that "end in grassy/ ditches" in which boys catch "a few famished eels from drying puddles"—an image which exemplifies Montale's aesthetic decision to create in a language of sparseness, bringing thoughts to meaning through evocative images. In contrast to the images of dryness, paths of water wend their way "into the orchards, among the lemon trees." The smell of the earth "rains its restless sweetness in the heart," and the "smell of the lemon trees" becomes one of the "riches of the world" in which even "we the poor share." These riches, the lemon trees, have the power to melt the "heart's ice," as they transform into "trumpets of gold" which "pour forth/ epiphanies of Light!"

"Don't ask me for words" provided for many the basis on which to term *Cuttlefish Bones* a volume exemplifying Montale's skepticism. The poem confronts with negations. The poet establishes an anti-idealistic situation by telling readers that he cannot give words that will tell about the soul, and he ends by telling he cannot use language to "open worlds"; all he can tell is a negation, he says: "what we are *not*, what we do *not* want." He cannot, he says, cast what he cannot tell in "letters of fire," emblazoning and illuminating as if it were at once a shining harbinger of hope against a background of emptiness and decay, "lost crocus in a dusty field," and also an emblem of the difficulty of speaking to his generation immediately after the First World War. Humanity, he says, confident and "striding," connected with others, is unaware that its impress, its "shadow"—perhaps its soul—might become emblazoned on "a crumbling wall." People are unaware that even their soul, in becoming part of or associated with this crumbling wall, this thing of substance that fades and fails, will not be eternal. Montale the poet speaks directly to the reader, going against Romanticism in saying the poet has only "gnarled syllables," which are "branch-dry," through which he can tell of nothing eternal: not of the soul, and truly not of "formulas" that will help people to see.

"To laze at noon, pale and thoughtful," known to most readers of Italian poetry, almost suspends itself in its lack of action verbs and the repetition of infinitives: "to laze," "to listen," "to gaze," "to peer." The image of the blaze is repeated from the first poem in the series in the image of "a blazing garden wall." In the last sequence of this poem, the action finally moves, and "walking out, dazed with light," the realization dawns on the speaker that life is "trudging along a wall," and that the wall is "spiked/ with jagged shards of broken bottles"—an image typical in rural northern Italy.

"Don't take shelter in the shade" repeats images from "To laze at noon, pale and thoughtful":

the shade, the waves, the cliffs, the action of "lazing," and, again, dazzling light, stated to be the "one certainty." The poem "To laze at noon" is transformed: The "lazing" is done by the waves in a time of "distress," and the very material images of earthiness transform into the evanescent; a windhover is like summer lightning, life "powders away," and our passing is done "in a shimmer of dust," the cliffs "fray/ in a webbing of haze," and even the light becomes a "flare of ash." The ash, however, in the last stanza, is illusion burning (or purifying) and vanishing into the certainty of "light"; the movement counters the previous movement in the admonition to another, "let's not throw our strayed lives/ to a bottomless abyss."

Montale acknowledges that one is always part of one's tradition, even when seeming to write against it. In his allusions to such writers as Dante Alighieri and Giacomo Leopardi, he situates himself distinctly in the history of Italian letters as he diverges into new directions. One of the most significant literary artists of the twentieth century, Montale focuses in his poetry upon fragments of objects in order to attempt to transform fragmented vision into a vision of wholeness.

Donna Berliner

Bibliography:
Almansi, Guido, and Bruce Merry. *Eugenio Montale: The Private Language of Poetry.* Edinburgh: Edinburgh University Press, 1977. Provides close reading and examination of sources.
Arrowsmith, William, ed. and trans. *Cuttlefish Bones: 1920-1927,* by Eugenio Montale. New York: W. W. Norton, 1992. Arrowsmith's extensive notes and commentary provide invaluable insight into the collection.
Becker, Jared. *Eugenio Montale.* Boston: Twayne, 1986. Biographical background of Montale. Chapter on *Cuttlefish Bones* examines themes, images, and characters.
Cambon, Glauco. *Eugenio Montale's Poetry: A Dream in Reason's Presence.* Princeton, N.J.: Princeton University Press, 1982. Cambon's section on *Cuttlefish Bones* treats not only the themes of the book, but also the prosody and influences.
Huffman, Claire de C. L. *Montale and the Occasions of Poetry.* Princeton, N.J.: Princeton University Press, 1983. Challenging and rewarding, this book discusses Montale and Eliot in terms of the poetry of objects, then traces the development of Montale's poetics.
Pipa, Arshi. *Montale and Dante.* Minneapolis: University of Minnesota Press, 1968. First full study in English. Explores Dante's tremendous and formative influence on Montale.
Singh, Ghan Shyam. *Eugenio Montale: A Critical Study of His Poetry, Prose, and Criticism.* New Haven, Conn.: Yale University Press, 1973. An excellent discussion by a translator who received personal commentary from Montale. The introduction effectively places Montale within his tradition.
West, Rebecca J. *Eugenio Montale: Poet on the Edge.* Cambridge, Mass.: Harvard University Press, 1981. An invaluable and detailed study of Montale's themes, style, and poetics.

CYCLOPS

Type of work: Drama
Author: Euripides (c. 485-406 B.C.E.)
Type of plot: Satyr play
Time of plot: Antiquity
Locale: Mt. Aetna in Sicily
First performed: Kyklōps, c. 421 B.C.E. (English translation, 1782)

> *Principal characters:*
> ODYSSEUS, king of Ithaca
> THE CYCLOPS
> SILENUS, aged captive of the Cyclops
> CHORUS OF SATYRS
> COMPANIONS OF ODYSSEUS

The Story:

As he raked the ground before the cave of his master, the Cyclops, old Silenus lamented the day he was shipwrecked on the rock of Aetna and taken into captivity by the monstrous, one-eyed offspring of Poseidon, god of the sea. About Silenus gamboled his children, the Chorus of Satyrs, who prayed with their father to Bacchus for deliverance. Suddenly, Silenus spied a ship and the approach of a group of sailors who were clearly seeking supplies. Odysseus and his companions approached, introduced themselves as the conquerors of Troy, driven from their homeward journey by tempestuous winds and desperately in need of food and water. Silenus warned them of the cannibalistic Cyclops' impending return, urged them to make haste, and then began to bargain with them over the supplies. Spying a skin of wine, the precious liquid of Bacchus which he had not tasted for years, Silenus begged for a drink. After one sip he felt his feet urging him to dance. He offered them all the lambs and cheese they needed in exchange for one skin of wine.

As the exchange was taking place, the giant Cyclops suddenly returned, ravenously hungry. The wretched Silenus made himself appear to have been terribly beaten and accused Odysseus and his men of plundering the Cyclops' property. Odysseus denied the false charge, but although he was supported by the leader of the Chorus of Satyrs, the Cyclops seized two of the sailors, took them into his cave, and made a meal of them. Horrified, Odysseus was then urged by the satyrs to employ his famed cleverness, so effective at Troy, in finding some means of escape.

After some discussion, Odysseus hit upon a subtle plan: First they would make the Cyclops drunk with wine; then, while he lay in a stupor, they would cut down an olive tree, sharpen it, set it afire, and plunge it into the Cyclops' eye. After that escape would be easy. When the Cyclops emerged from his cave, Odysseus offered him the wine, and the giant and Silenus proceeded to get hilariously drunk. So pleased was the monster with the effects of the Bacchic fluid that Silenus without much trouble persuaded him not to share it but to drink it all up by himself. The grateful Cyclops asked Odysseus his name (to which the clever warrior replied "No man") and promised that he would be the last to be eaten. Soon the Cyclops found the earth and sky whirling together and his lusts mounting. He seized the unhappy Silenus and dragged him into the cave to have his pleasure with him.

As the Cyclops lay in a stupor, Odysseus urged the satyrs to help him fulfill the plan they had agreed upon, but the cowardly satyrs refused and Odysseus was forced to use his own men for the task. Soon the agonized Cyclops, shouting that "no man" had blinded him, came bellowing out of the cave. The chorus mocked and jeered him for this ridiculous charge and gave him false directions for capturing the escaping Greeks. The berserk giant thrashed about and cracked his skull against the rocks. When the escaping Odysseus taunted him with his true name, the Cyclops groaned that an oracle had predicted that Odysseus would blind him on his way home from Troy, but he told also that the clever one would pay for his deed by tossing about on Poseidon's seas for many years. The satyrs hastened to join the escape so that they could once more become the proper servants of Bacchus in a land where grapes grew.

Critical Evaluation:

By purely aesthetic standards, *Cyclops* cannot be considered a valuable or important play, but it otherwise has a twofold interest as the only complete satyr play preserved from ancient Greece and as a dramatization of an episode from Homer's *Odyssey* (c. 800 B.C.E.). Euripides has kept the main line of Homer's tale, but for the sake of enhanced humor has added the character of old Silenus and the Chorus of Satyrs. Furthermore, the exigencies of stage presentation made it necessary for him to change Homer's ingenious escape device to slipping through the rocks past the blind Cyclops. The light tone of the play must have been a welcome relief to the Greek audience, for the play followed three tragedies presented in succession.

The satyr play was traditionally presented at a Greek dramatic festival after three tragedies had been staged. It made fun of tragic characters and themes, deflating tragedy's conceits and devices. As such, it is usually thought to have been designed to provide some comic relief from the prevailing gloom and tension of the three preceding plays. An ancient critic called Demetrius of Phalerum called it "tragedy on holiday," which indicates both its parodic character and its connections with the bawdy celebration of the Dionysian festival. The satyr play may on occasion have had a close connection with the tragedies that preceded it—the satyr play that followed the Oedipus trilogy, for instance, was called *The Sphinx*—but in other cases the link seems more tenuous.

Various opinions have been expressed on the purpose of the satyr play. The notion that it provided light relief after the tragedies is widely held. Others have suggested that it was designed to accompany heavy wine-drinking at the end of the day's celebration of Dionysus. Alternatively, the plays may reflect the incorporation of older, animalistic, agricultural rites involving satyrs into the urban festival of Dionysus in which the dramas were performed. It is known that people dressed up as satyrs, mythical creatures that are humanlike but with elements of horses and goats. Satyrs are described in ancient sources as mischievous, playful, lusty, and hedonistic. They have pointed ears and snub noses and a horse's tail. They represent the unleashed forces of physical desire that normally have to be kept under control. This is why they are closely connected with Dionysus, the god of wine, dancing, and release of pent-up emotions.

Evidence from *Cyclops* and other fragmentary satyr plays suggests some common elements of the genre: the captivity and liberation of the Chorus of Satyrs, the presence of a miraculous invention or substance (wine, fire, the flute), the theme of rebirth or escape from the underworld, and a lively interest in sexual activity. In spite of the similarities with Greek comedy, the satyr play retained its close links with tragedy in meter and language, and in its use of mythological, as opposed to topical, subject matter.

Cyclops is the only complete satyr play that survives. Its moments of slapstick humor—such as the Cyclops' entrance on stage to the strains of a wedding song, the scene of Silenus drinking behind the Cyclops' back, and the final episode with the blinded creature stumbling around the stage—make it an effective burlesque of a well-known Homeric story. Euripides changed Homer's Cyclops from a man-eating savage into a more human personage: He has an intellect, the ability to argue his position, and a sophisticated ideology. He owns cattle as well as sheep and keeps a retinue of slaves. He is even something of a gourmet cook. At the same time, the Cyclops retains his penchant for eating humans. It is this combination of the old and the new, of the barbaric and the civilized, in the Cyclops that makes him such a bizarre character.

The play presents an Odysseus who is a clever and unscrupulous trickster, rather than the noble hero of traditional mythology. Odysseus is the little man fighting against the giant and gets the audience's sympathy as a result. The bullying Cyclops gets the punishment he deserves. The audience nevertheless may feel some sympathy for the Cyclops, who suffers a terrible punishment. The Cyclops in the *Odyssey* is a complex figure, and Polyphemus in this satyr play is more than just a buffoon. The emphasis on the painful effects of the blinding of the Cyclops serves to engage the audience's sympathy. The downfall of the Cyclops, in fact, acquires some tragic coloring.

Cyclops is also the dramatization of the initiation of an individual into the rites of the worship of Dionysus. Polyphemus, for all his knowledge and sophistication, is unfamiliar with wine. He is presented as akin to such figures as Lycurgus or Pentheus, who also have to be converted to Dionysian ways. The liberation of the imprisoned satyrs at the end of the play represents the triumph of the god Bacchus over all obstacles and enemies. Euripides has successfully brought Dionysus into an old Homeric story: Building on the detail of the Cyclops' unfamiliarity with wine, a sign of his savagery and lack of humanity, the playwright has produced a representation of the power of Dionysus.

Cyclops thus offers a fitting end to the tragic trilogy that preceded it. In tragedy, the power of the gods is demonstrated, as well as the inevitability of human fate. The satyr play offers the same basic lesson: Polyphemus takes the place of the tragic hero who is brought low by the god or his agent (in this case, Odysseus is the agent of Dionysus). There may also have been a provocative contemporary reference: The Sicilian setting of the action might well have recalled to the Athenian audience their city's disastrous naval expedition to Sicily a few years before. Such an allusion might point to the fact that the Athenians, like Odysseus and the satyrs, were lucky to get away with their lives; on the other hand, it might suggest that the Athenian populace had acted like a Polyphemus, drunk with ambition and blind to the dangers of arrogance and greed.

"Critical Evaluation" by David H. J. Larmour

Bibliography:
Arnott, Peter D., trans. *Three Greek Plays for the Theatre: Euripides, "Medea," "Cyclops"; Aristophanes, "The Frogs."* Bloomington: Indiana University Press, 1961. A fine translation of the play, with an introduction. *Cyclops* is described as a tragedy and a comedy.
Green, Roger L. *Two Satyr Plays: Euripides' "Cyclops" and Sophocles' "Ichneutai."* New York: Penguin Books, 1957. A good translation, with an introduction. Sophocles' *The Searching Satyrs*, an incomplete satyr play, offers a useful opportunity for comparison.
Seaford, Richard. Introduction to *Cyclops*, by Euripides. Oxford, England: Clarendon Press, 1984. Offers a 60-page survey of the features of satyric drama in general and of *Cyclops* in particular. The connections of satyr drama with the cult of Dionysus in Athens are emphasized.

Sutton, Dana F. *The Greek Satyr Play*. Meisenheim an Glan, Germany: Hain, 1980. A comprehensive survey of the genre. Traces the history of the satyr play, offers a critical appraisal and provides a useful bibliography.

Webster, T. B. L. *Monuments Illustrating Tragedy and Satyr Play*. London: Institute of Classical Studies, University of London, 1967. Presents visual evidence from archaeological sources of satyrs and their role in drama. Explores the links between tragedy and the satyr play.

CYMBELINE

Type of work: Drama
Author: William Shakespeare (1564-1616)
Type of plot: Tragicomedy
Time of plot: First century B.C.E.
Locale: Britain, Italy, and Wales
First performed: c. 1609-1610; first published, 1623

> *Principal characters:*
> CYMBELINE, the king of Britain
> THE QUEEN, Cymbeline's wife
> CLOTEN, the queen's son by a former husband
> IMOGEN, Cymbeline's daughter by a former marriage
> POSTHUMUS LEONATUS, Imogen's husband
> PISANIO, a servant of Posthumus
> IACHIMO, an Italian braggart
> BELARIUS, a banished lord
> GUIDERIUS and
> ARVIRAGUS, Cymbeline's sons, reared by Belarius
> CAIUS LUCIUS, a Roman ambassador

The Story:

Gullible Cymbeline and his conniving queen intended that his daughter Imogen should marry his stepson Cloten. Instead, Imogen chose the gentle Posthumus and secretly married him. In a fit of anger, the king banished Posthumus, who fled to Italy after promising to remain loyal and faithful to his bride. As a token of their vows, Imogen gave Posthumus a diamond ring that had belonged to her mother; in turn, Posthumus placed a bracelet of rare design on Imogen's arm.

In Rome, Posthumus met Iachimo, a vain braggart who tried to tempt Posthumus by appealing to his sensuality. Posthumus, not to be tempted into adultery, told Iachimo of his pact with Imogen and of the ring and bracelet they had exchanged. Iachimo scoffingly wagered ten thousand ducats against Posthumus' ring that he could seduce Imogen.

Iachimo went to Britain with letters to which he had forged Posthumus' name, which persuaded Imogen to receive him. Using ambiguous implications and innuendo, Iachimo played on her curiosity about her husband's faithfulness. When that failed to win her favor, he gained access to her bedroom in a trunk which, he had told her, contained a valuable gift he had bought in France that was intended for the Roman emperor; he had asked that the trunk be placed in her chamber for safekeeping. While Imogen slept, he noted the details of the furnishings in the room, took the bracelet from her arm, and observed a mole on her left breast.

Back in Italy, Iachimo described Imogen's room to Posthumus and produced the bracelet, which he said Imogen had given him. Incredulous, Posthumus asked Iachimo to describe some aspect of Imogen's body as better proof of his successful seduction. Iachimo's claim that he had kissed the mole on Imogen's breast enraged Posthumus. He sent a letter to Pisanio, commanding that the servant kill Imogen, and a letter to Imogen asking her to meet him in Milford Haven. Pisanio was to kill Imogen as they traveled through the Welsh hills.

On the journey Pisanio divulged the real purpose of their trip when he showed Imogen the letter ordering her death. Unable to harm his master's wife, Pisanio instructed her to dress as a boy and join the party of Caius Lucius, who was in Britain to collect tribute to the Emperor Augustus and who was soon to return to Rome. Then Imogen would be near Posthumus and could try to disprove Iachimo's accusations against her. Pisanio also gave Imogen a box containing a restorative, which the queen had entrusted to him ostensibly in case Imogen became ill during her trip. The queen actually thought the box contained a slow-acting poison, which she had procured from her physician; he, suspecting chicanery, had reduced the drug content so that the substance would do no more than induce a long sleep. Pisanio took leave of his mistress and returned home.

Dressed in boy's clothing, hungry, and weary, Imogen came to the mountain cave of Belarius, who had been banished from Cymbeline's court twenty years earlier and had kidnapped Guiderius and Arviragus, Cymbeline's infant sons. In Wales, the two boys had been brought up to look upon Belarius as their father. Calling herself Fidele, Imogen won the affection of the three men when she asked shelter of them. Left alone when the men went out to hunt food, Imogen, worn out and ill, swallowed some of the medicine that Pisanio had given her.

Cymbeline, meanwhile, had refused to pay the tribute demanded by Rome, and the two nations prepared for war. Cloten, who had been infuriated by Imogen's coldness to him, tried to learn her whereabouts. Pisanio hoped to trick her pursuer and showed him the letter in which Posthumus asked Imogen to meet him at Milford Haven. Disguised as Posthumus, Cloten set out to avenge his injured vanity.

In Wales, he came upon Belarius, Arviragus, and Guiderius while they were hunting. Recognizing him as the queen's son, Belarius assumed that Cloten had come to arrest them as outlaws. He and Arviragus went in search of Cloten's retinue while Guiderius fought with and killed Cloten. Guiderius then cut off Cloten's head and threw it into the river. Returning to the cave, the three men found Imogen, as they thought, dead, and they prepared her for burial. Benevolent Belarius, remembering that Cloten was of royal birth, brought his headless body for burial and laid it near Imogen.

When Imogen awoke from her drugged sleep, she was grief-stricken when she saw lying nearby a body dressed in Posthumus' clothing. Sorrowing, she joined the forces of Caius Lucius as the Roman army marched by on their way to engage the soldiers of Cymbeline.

Posthumus, who was a recruit in the Roman army, now regretted his order for Imogen's death. Throwing away his uniform, he dressed himself as a British peasant. Although he could not restore Imogen to life, he did not want to take any more British lives. In a battle between the Romans and Britons, Posthumus vanquished and disarmed Iachimo. Cymbeline was taken prisoner and rescued by Belarius and his two foster sons. These three had built a fort and, aided by Posthumus, had so spurred the morale of the fleeing British soldiers that Cymbeline's army was victorious.

Since he had not died in battle, Posthumus identified himself as a Roman after Lucius was taken, and he was sent to prison by Cymbeline. In prison, he had a vision in which Jove assured him that he would yet be the lord of the Lady Imogen. Jove ordered a tablet placed on Posthumus' chest. When Posthumus awoke and found the tablet, he read that a lion's whelp would be embraced by a piece of tender air and that branches lopped from a stately cedar would revive. Shortly before the time set for his execution, he was summoned to appear before Cymbeline.

In Cymbeline's tent, the king conferred honors upon Belarius, Guiderius, and Arviragus and bemoaned the fact that the fourth valiant soldier, so poorly dressed, was not present to receive his reward. Cornelius, the physician, told Cymbeline that the queen had died after her villainies. Lucius pleaded for the life of Imogen, still dressed as a boy, because of the page's youth. Pardoned, Imogen asked Iachimo to explain his possession of the ring he wore. As Iachimo confessed having lied to win the ring from Posthumus, Posthumus entered and identified himself as the murderer of Imogen. When Imogen protested against his confession, Posthumus struck her. Pisanio then identified Imogen to keep Posthumus from striking her again. The truth disclosed, Belarius understood his foster sons' affinity for Imogen. Posthumus and Imogen, reunited, professed to remain devoted to each other for the rest of their lives.

After Guiderius confessed to the murder of Cloten, Cymbeline ordered him bound, but he stayed the sentence when Belarius identified himself and the two young men. Cymbeline then blessed his three children who stood before him. A soothsayer interpreted Jove's message on the tablet left on Posthumus' chest. The lion's whelp was Posthumus, the son of Leonatus, and the piece of tender air was Imogen. The lopped branches from the stately cedar were Arviragus and Guiderius, long thought dead, now restored in the king's love. Overjoyed, Cymbeline made peace with Rome.

Critical Evaluation:

Cymbeline, together with *The Winter's Tale* (1610-1611) and *The Tempest* (1611), belongs to William Shakespeare's final period of writing. These last three plays are marked by their mood of calmness, maturity, and benevolent cheerfulness; a kind of autumnal spirit prevails. This is not to say that *Cymbeline* lacks villains, traumatic events, or scenes of violence—the play contains all these elements—but that the tone is serene in spite of them. *Cymbeline* may be classified as a tragicomedy to distinguish it from such more dazzling predecessors among Shakespeare's comedies as *Love's Labour's Lost* (1594-1595) and *Twelfth Night: Or, What You Will* (1600-1602), which have roguish heroes and heroines, dialogues filled with witty and sparkling repartee, and plots abounding in mischievous scheming and complications. The main characters in *Cymbeline*, by contrast, are remarkable for their virtue rather than their cleverness, wit, or capacity for mischief; Posthumus is a model of earnestness and fidelity, and Imogen is the picture of purity and wifely devotion. The text is memorable not for the brilliance and sparkle of its dialogue, but for its moving poetry. Much of the plot consists of the trials and sufferings of the good characters, brought on by the scheming of the bad ones. However, the play ends as comedy must, with the virtuous rewarded and the wicked punished.

In the plot of *Cymbeline*, Shakespeare combined two lines of action: the political-historical story line of the British king preparing for war with Rome, and the love story of Imogen and Posthumus. For the historical background, Shakespeare once again used Holinshed's *The Chronicles of England* (1577). Finding, however, that Cymbeline, a descendant of King Lear, was too dull to provide for interesting drama, he took the liberty of assigning to that king the refusal to pay the Roman tribute, which action Holinshed had attributed to Cymbeline's son Guiderius. In this way, he enlivened the plot with a war, which was resolved in a peace treaty at the end. Imogen's story, however, provides the primary interest in *Cymbeline*, a love story centering on a wager between a cunning villain and a devoted husband regarding the faithfulness of the absent wife; for this story Shakespeare was indebted to one of the tales in Boccaccio's *Decameron* (1349-1351). In addition to the two main story lines, the plot of *Cymbeline* contains many characters traveling in disguise and cases of mistaken identity. In a subplot of Shakespeare's invention, the story is further complicated with the consequences of Belarius having abducted and subsequently reared the king's infant sons in Wales. Such elements lend a certain extravagance to the plot of *Cymbeline*.

Cymbeline bears many resemblances to previous plays of Shakespeare. The figure of the gullible king influenced by his wicked queen reminds one of *Macbeth*, as does the scene of supernatural intervention, the ghosts of Posthumus' family, and the tablet bearing a prophecy. Iachimo does not approach Iago in malignancy, but nevertheless calls to mind Othello's tormentor through his cunning strategies and his manipulation of Posthumus' capacity for jealousy. Likewise, the scenes of Imogen's travels disguised as a boy and her eventual reunion with her lost brothers are reminiscent of Viola's similar adventures in *Twelfth Night: Or, What You Will*. Perhaps most important, however, is the relation it bears to that final masterpiece, *The Tempest.*

Bibliography:
Bergeron, David M. "*Cymbeline*: Shakespeare's Last Roman Play." *Shakespeare Quarterly* 31, no. 1 (Spring, 1980): 31-41. Traces the historical and political factors at work in the play.
Frye, Northrop. *A Natural Perspective: The Development of Shakespearean Comedy and Romance.* New York: Columbia University Press, 1965. Frye puts the play in the context of other late romances. The most interesting commentary available on the role of Imogen and on the visions experienced by Posthumus toward the end of the play.
Hieatt, A. Kent. "*Cymbeline* and the Intrusion of Lyric." In *Unfolded Tales: Essays on Renaissance Romance*, edited by George M. Logan and Gordon Teskey. Ithaca, N.Y.: Cornell University Press, 1989. Hieatt displays *Cymbeline*'s relationship to Edmund Spenser's sonnet sequence "The Ruins of Rome" and other treatments of the theme of historical inheritance in the frame of lyricism. A major reinterpretation of the play and a valuable commentary.
Miola, Robert S. *Shakespeare's Rome.* Cambridge, England: Cambridge University Press, 1983. Places *Cymbeline* in the context of Shakespeare's Roman plays. Emphasizes how Shakespeare's portrait of Britain has an ambiguous relationship to the Roman imperial legacy.
Parker, Patricia. "Romance and Empire: Anachronistic *Cymbeline*." In *Unfolded Tales: Essays on Renaissance Romance*, edited by George M. Logan and Gordon Teskey. Ithaca, N.Y.: Cornell University Press, 1989. Speculates on what has always been one of the most vexing issues surrounding *Cymbeline*, the fact that half of it seems set in ancient Roman times and the other half in the Italian Renaissance of Shakespeare's lifetime. Parker also traces the influence on the play of Vergil's *Aeneid* (29-19 B.C.E.), particularly as regards the roles of oracles, prophecy, and kingship.

THE CYPRESSES BELIEVE IN GOD

Type of work: Novel
Author: José María Gironella (1917-   )
Type of plot: Historical realism
Time of plot: 1931-1936
Locale: Gerona, Catalonia, northeastern Spain
First published: Los cipreses creen en Dios, 1953 (English translation, 1955)

Principal characters:
MATÍAS ALVEAR, a telegraph operator
CARMEN ELGAZU, his wife
IGNACIO,
CÉSAR, and
PILAR, their children
MOSÉN ALBERTO, a priest
DAVID and
OLGA POL, teachers

The Story:

Matías Alvear was transferred by his government employer from Málaga, where his children were born, to Gerona. Though Matías was indifferent to religion, his wife Carmen was very devout and gave her children a strong religious upbringing. Ignacio entered the seminary when he was ten but after a few years decided that he did not want to be a priest. He went to work in a bank while going to high school at night. In the meantime, César entered another seminary when he was old enough. During this period, Spain became a republic in 1931.

After being reproached by Ignacio for being indifferent to the poor, César learned how to be a barber, shaving and cutting the hair of invalids and the poor. He taught the slum children reading and arithmetic, but was forbidden by the railroad workers to teach them the catechism. Ignacio began studying with David Pol and his wife Olga, a very modern couple. His anarchist cousin José visited from Madrid and got involved in heckling at conservative political meetings. José and Ignacio were involved in a riot disrupting a dance called to distract attention from a strike.

Ignacio was upset after visiting the insane asylum and finding that the inmates were fed spoiled food. He was expelled from an anarchists' meeting when he objected to destroying the printing press, housed in the local orphanage, on which the conservative paper was printed and which provided the orphanage with much of its income. Doña Amparo, wife of the policeman Julio García, seduced Ignacio.

The anarchists destroyed the orphanage's print shop and were arrested but released since no one could prove their guilt. Ignacio passed his examinations and while vacationing at the seashore with his family, met Ana María. She was of a higher social class (her father a businessman) but tired of the *señoritos* (little gentlemen) and found Ignacio refreshing. After the summer visit, Ignacio did not answer her letters but instead had an affair with the prostitute Candela, from whom he contracted a venereal disease. After his recovery he reformed, made a good confession, and was forgiven by his family.

Catalonia declared autonomy from the Spanish central government. A general strike in

1445

Gerona called to support this autonomy was countered with martial law. Soldiers stormed a meeting of autonomy supporters, and the major was shot by the deputy Santeló. Those at the meeting were imprisoned, among them David, Olga, and Julio García. Mosén Alberto ministered to those imprisoned but most rejected his efforts. While the Costa brothers were in jail, their sister Laura instituted reforms in their industries such as a clinic and a child-care center, under the guidance of Mosén Francisco. Major Martínez de Soria tried those imprisoned and told Julio that he would be shot if the real culprit was not disclosed. Information from Barcelona implicated Santeló, who was executed. The other prisoners were released, but Julio lost his post as police chief.

Mateo Santos organized a cell of the Fascist Falange, while Cosme Vila quit his job at the bank to open Communist Party headquarters. Ignacio fell in love with Marta Martínez de Soria, whose brother joined the Falange and was killed in Valladolid. The Popular Front, a merger of all leftist parties, won a violence-plagued election. Julio returned as chief of police, while David and Olga became commissioners of education and forbade the clergy and nuns to teach while wearing religious habits. The anarchists called a general strike; when it was broken, they set off bombs. To discredit them, the Communists bombed the Diocesan Museum, killing one of Mosén Alberto's maids. At a meeting in the Albéniz theater, the Communists stated their demands, including a Workers' Militia and Julio's being replaced. The Socialists and liberals demurred. After Julio rejected most of the Communist demands, the Communists proclaimed a general strike, burned a Christian Brothers church and school, and lynched the sexton. Mateo and his Falangist comrades beat up Dr. Relken, a German archaeologist whom they suspected of being a spy, and went into hiding.

The general strike spread. The Communists got food for the strikers from the tenant farmers, who withheld the share due their landlords, but gave the food only to Party members. The Workers' Militia began to drill, but was sent home by the police (headed by Julio). Cosme Vila was arrested but rescued by the truckers bringing food for the strikers. Gerona became polarized between Left and Right. The assassination of the Rightist leader José Calvo Sotelo triggered a civil war in Spain that began with a military insurrection in Africa. Major Martínez de Soria and the Falange occupied Gerona and released the landowners who had been imprisoned for owning firearms. When the military in Barcelona was defeated and surrendered, those in Gerona followed orders and yielded. Julio and the loyalist officers arrested Major Martínez while the Communists and Anarchists stormed the barracks and got arms. Since Julio would not let them murder the officers who surrendered, the militia burned churches, commandeered cars and garages, and arrested suspects.

A revolutionary committee organized a series of executions. The Alvear family was guarded by a militiaman to whom Ignacio once gave blood, but they were unable to save César, who returned from Collell and was arrested while trying to protect communion wafers from desecration. He and several others were executed; his last view was that of Mosén Francisco, who had disguised himself as a militiaman and gave those executed the last rites.

Critical Evaluation:

The Cypresses Believe in God was José María Gironella's third novel and the first to attain widespread success, being translated into several other languages. It is the first part of a trilogy about the Spanish Civil War, the other volumes being *One Million Dead* (1961) and *Peace After War* (1966). A subsequent volume, *Men Cry Alone* (1968), was not as successful. Critics agree that *The Cypresses Believe in God* is the best book in the four-volume chronicle of the Alvear family.

The author set himself a threefold task in his study, set in the years preceding the outbreak of the Spanish Civil War and ending with the first incidents of the military insurrection that was eventually victorious under General Francisco Franco. His first concern was a chronicle of the Alvear family with the coming to maturity of the three children the central feature. His next concern was the portrayal of the small city of Gerona with its population of 25,000 as represented by the characters with whom members of the Alvear family interact: Ignacio's fellow workers at the bank, César's career as a seminarian, Pilar's maturing and falling in love with Mateo Santos, fellow law student with Ignacio, son of the tobacconist with whom Matías plays dominoes, and organizer of the Falange in Gerona. Finally, as a backdrop there are the incidents of the coming of the civil war, at first distant and then coming increasingly closer.

Several influences have been found on Gironella's novel: The family chronicles of Benito Galdós and John Galsworthy are most frequently mentioned, but also the historical novels of Honoré de Balzac and Charles Dickens. Gironella had read Leo Tolstoy's monumental *War and Peace* (1865-1869) shortly before beginning work on *The Cypresses Believe in God*. A negative influence were the general developments in the early twentieth century novel, which many Spanish critics thought were overly intellectualized. Gironella returned to the techniques of realism and couched his work in a narrative prose style that some critics have considered crude and others factual and direct. His narration contrasts with the linguistic virtuosity, psychologizing, and stream-of-consciousness writing of Gironella's immediate predecessors. The novel is rather slow-moving, since the author is seeking to depict the rhythms of a small Spanish city, organized around the seasons and the main religious holidays. Yet it is also a novel of action that increases in tempo as the civil war approaches.

There is such a multiplicity of characters in the novel that in the English translation the author placed, at the end, a list of the fictional characters, a list of actual historical figures whose names appear in the novel, and identification of the main political movements in Spain at that time. The reader needs this guidance. The portrayal of the characters is for the most part sympathetic; though the novel is written from the point of view of the insurgents, its protagonists are not saints, and except at the end, the opponents are not demons. Gironella has various characters state in everyday language the political philosophies that they espouse, thus providing the reader an idea of the complexity of Spanish politics at that time. The destructive aspect of the civil war is revealed in the development of the characters: Mateo Santos, though a good friend of Ignacio and Pilar's sweetheart, organizes and leads the beating of Dr. Relken, whereas Cosme Vila, Ignacio's colleague at the bank, first appears as a character that Charles Dickens might have portrayed and ends as the organizer of executions, including César's. One criticism lodged against the novel is that the coup by the insurgents is portrayed as bloodless, with Dr. Relken's beating their only atrocity, whereas the counter-coup by the anarchists and Communists is characterized by the machine-gunning of praying nuns.

The title of the book comes from the cypress trees that adorn most Spanish cemeteries. As a young seminarian, César had to be forbidden by his spiritual advisers from spending as much time as he did in visiting cemeteries, and at the end of the novel it is in a cemetery that he is executed. Ignacio's character development parallels that of the author himself. Both were born at approximately the same time, had initial aspirations toward the priesthood, then worked in a bank. Gironella went on to serve in the insurgent army, and at the time of writing *The Cypresses Believe in God* was working in a bookstore in Gerona. His novel was enthusiastically received in the United States at the time of its appearance, was a selection of the Catholic Digest Book Club, and was extensively reviewed. It should be read as a counterbalance to novels of the

Spanish Civil War that take the Loyalist side, such as Ernest Hemingway's *For Whom the Bell Tolls* (1940) and André Malraux's *Days of Hope* (1937).

R. M. Longyear

Bibliography:
Ilie, Paul. "Fictive History in Gironella." *Journal of Spanish Studies: Twentieth Century* 2 (1974): 77-94. Shows that Gironella points out relationships between the novel and historical events of the time. Citations from the novels are all in the original Spanish.

Preston, Paul. *Revolution and War in Spain, 1931-1939*. New York: Methuen, 1984. This set of twelve essays shows that the Spanish Civil War was not one but many wars. Most pertinent to the background of *The Cypresses Believe in God* are the essay by Frances Lannon on the responsibilities of the anticlericals and the Catholic church in polarizing Spanish society in the 1930's and the chapter by Juan Pablo Pusi on the conflicts between the micronationalism of Catalonia and the Second Republic.

Schwartz, Ronald. *José María Gironella*. Boston: Twayne, 1972. Covers the author's career to 1968. The chapter on *The Cypresses Believe in God* contains several errors, such as identification of David, Olga, and El Responsable as Communists, and thus should be used with caution.

Thomas, Gareth. *The Novel of the Spanish Civil War*. New York: Cambridge University Press, 1990. Gironella's trilogy receives a chapter, and the introductory chapters are valuable in providing a context. The citations from Gironella and his critics are all in the original Spanish or French.

CYRANO DE BERGERAC

Type of work: Drama
Author: Edmond Rostand (1868-1918)
Type of plot: Tragicomedy
Time of plot: Seventeenth century
Locale: France
First performed: 1897; first published, 1898 (English translation, 1898)

> *Principal characters:*
> CYRANO DE BERGERAC, poet and soldier
> ROXANE, with whom Cyrano is in love
> CHRISTIAN DE NEUVILLETTE, a clumsy young soldier

The Story:

In the theater hall of the Hôtel de Burgundy, a young soldier named Christian de Neuvillette anxiously waited for the beautiful Roxane to appear in her box. Christian had fallen passionately in love with this woman whom he had never met. While he was waiting for her arrival, Christian became increasingly upset because he feared that he would never be able to summon sufficient courage to address her, for he believed she was as brilliant and as graceful as he was doltish and clumsy.

Also in the audience, waiting for the curtain to go up, was one Ragueneau, a romantic tavern-keeper and tosspot poet, whose friends praised his verses to his face while behind his back they helped themselves to the pastries that he made. Ragueneau inquired of another poet concerning the whereabouts of Cyrano de Bergerac. The actor Montfleury, Cyrano's enemy and one of Roxane's suitors, was to star in the play, and Cyrano had threatened him with bodily injury if he appeared for the performance. Cyrano, however, had not yet arrived.

At last Roxane appeared. The play began, and Montfleury came out on the stage to recite his lines. Suddenly a powerful voice ordered him to leave the stage. After the voice came the man, Cyrano de Bergerac, one of the best swordsmen in France. The performance was halted abruptly.

Another of Roxane's suitors tried to provoke a fight with Cyrano by ridiculing de Bergerac's uncommonly big nose. Cyrano, sensitive about his disfiguring nose, became the insulter instead of the insulted. Words led to a duel. To show his contempt for his adversary, Cyrano composed a poem while he was sparring with his opponent, and when he had finished the last word of the last line, Cyrano staggered his man. Le Bret, Cyrano's close friend, cautioned the gallant swordsman against making too many enemies by his insults.

Cyrano confessed that he was exceptionally moody lately because he was in love with his lovely cousin Roxane, despite the fact he could never hope to win her because of his ugliness. While Le Bret tried to give Cyrano confidence in himself, Roxane's chaperone appeared to give Cyrano a note from his cousin, who wanted to see him. Cyrano was overcome with joy. The place selected for the meeting between Cyrano and Roxane was Ragueneau's tavern. Cyrano arrived early, and, while he waited for his beautiful cousin, he composed a love letter, which he left unsigned because he intended to deliver it in person. When Roxane appeared, she confessed to Cyrano that she was in love. Cyrano thought for a moment that she was in love with him, but he soon realized that the lucky fellow was not Cyrano himself, but Christian. Roxane asked Cyrano to take the young soldier under his wing, to protect him in battle. Cyrano sadly consented to do her bidding.

Later, when Christian dared jest with Cyrano concerning the latter's nose, Cyrano restrained himself for Roxane's sake. When he learned that Cyrano was Roxane's cousin, Christian confessed his love for Roxane and begged Cyrano's help in winning her. Christian was a warrior, not a lover; he needed Cyrano's ability to compose pretty speeches and to write tender, graceful messages. Although his heart was broken, Cyrano gave the young man the letter he had written in Ragueneau's tavern.

Cyrano visited Roxane to inquire about her love affair with Christian. Roxane, who had recently received a letter from Christian, was delighted by his wit. Cyrano did not tell her that he was the writer of the letter.

Shortly afterward Christian told Cyrano that he now wanted to speak for himself in his wooing of Roxane. Under her balcony one evening Christian did try to speak for himself, but he became so tongue-tied that he had to ask the aid of Cyrano, who was lurking in the shadows. Cyrano, hidden, told Christian what to say, and Roxane was so delighted by these dictated protestations that she bestowed a kiss on Christian.

A friar appeared with a letter from the Count de Guiche, commander of Cyrano's regiment, to Roxane. The count wrote that he was coming to see her that night, even though by so doing he was deserting his post. Roxane deliberately misread the letter, which, she said, ordered the friar to marry her to Christian. Roxane asked Cyrano to delay de Guiche until after the ceremony, a request which de Bergerac effectively carried out by making the count think that Cyrano was mad. After learning that Roxane and Christian were already married, the duped de Guiche ordered Christian to report immediately to his regiment.

In a battle which followed, Cyrano and the other cadets were engaged against the Spanish. During the conflict Cyrano risked his life to send letters to Roxane through the enemy's lines, and Roxane never suspected that the author of these messages was not Christian. Later Roxane joined her husband, and to him she confessed that his masterful letters had brought her to his side.

Realizing that Roxane was really in love with the nobility and tenderness of Cyrano's letters, Christian begged Cyrano to tell Roxane the truth. Christian, however, was killed in battle shortly afterward, and Cyrano swore never to reveal Christian's secret. Rallying the cadets, Cyrano charged bravely into the fight, and under his leadership the Spanish were defeated.

Fifteen years passed. Roxane, grieving for Christian, had retired to a convent. Each week Cyrano was accustomed to visit Roxane. One day, however, he came late. When he arrived, he concealed under his hat a mortal wound which one of his enemies had inflicted by dropping an object from a building on Cyrano's head. While talking about her dead husband, Roxane recited to Cyrano Christian's last letter, which she kept next to her heart. With Roxane's permission, Cyrano read the letter which he himself had written, even though it had grown so dark that neither he nor Roxane could see the words.

Suddenly Roxane realized that Cyrano knew the contents of the letter by heart, that he must have written it. With this realization came her conviction that for fifteen years she had unknowingly loved the soul of Cyrano, not Christian. Roxane confessed her love for Cyrano, who died knowing that at last Roxane was aware of his love and that she shared it with him.

Critical Evaluation:

Edmond Rostand's family was wealthy, and he never seemed to need to be commercial. He worked at a slow and sure pace and chose his themes as they came to him. His canon includes one volume of poetry, *Les Musardises* (1890), and the dramas *Les Romanesques* (1894), *La Princess lointaine* (1895), *La Samaritaine* (1897), *Cyrano de Bergerac* (1897), *L'Aiglon* (1900), and *Chantecler* (1910).

Dramatic invention, the use of splendid and spectacular settings, the presence of an eloquent, witty, and adventuresome hero, the conflict of love versus honor, the recklessness and self-sacrifices of the characters, and the point of honor upon which the whole play turns—all are elements of the romance tradition and are present in *Cyrano de Bergerac*. *Cyrano de Bergerac* is a perennial favorite with theater audiences. Cyrano is more than a hot-tempered swordsman who gets into trouble because he resents people who make fun of his nose. Cyrano de Bergerac symbolizes magnanimity, unselfishness, and beauty of soul. Motion picture and television adaptations as well as several successful stage revivals of *Cyrano de Bergerac* over the years demonstrate that Rostand's popular turn-of-the-century verse play is a classic. Written shortly before the beginning of the twentieth century, *Cyrano de Bergerac* reflects the themes and symbols of late nineteenth century romanticism, with its emphasis on the heroic individual who feels he has failed. In its story of ill-fated lovers and wasted lives, and its symbolic moon as mother-and-home of the hero, and in its historical context, *Cyrano de Bergerac* is the culmination of a romantic revival in French literature.

In tone the play charts a drastically different course from the "decadent" products that filled the theaters during the same period. In creating Cyrano, Rostand reached into the seventeenth century for his character. The real Cyrano was a little-known writer who lived in France from 1619 until his death in 1655. The bearer of an unusually large nose, he wrote about it in his books—books that may be described as the early ancestors of the science fiction genre.

It is tempting to speculate that Rostand also found his proper tone in the seventeenth century, for *Cyrano de Bergerac* is a play based on certain Renaissance-like assumptions, such as the reality of honor and the drama it can create when confronted with a passion like love. The theme of the play—"the making of a style out of despair"—also has affinities with seventeenth century values. People in Europe during the Renaissance were still experiencing the example as well as the ideal of the heroic individual: the exhilarating belief that one can, with courage, strength, and intellectual ability, will into being—create—the world as one chooses. It remained for Rostand's age to turn the coin from "man is everything" to "man is nothing." An underlying assumption of *Cyrano de Bergerac* is the presence of despair, but Rostand handles it lightly, and it is the style which one can create within this framework of despair that interests him. Rostand's word for style becomes "panache"—literally "white plume" but a word with broad symbolic connotations in the play. The word signifies something of a swashbuckling quality. It conveys a sense of superiority, courage, pride. A man with "panache" would swagger, and, like Cyrano, he is almost bound to have enemies.

In spite of its evident stage popularity, *Cyrano de Bergerac* has taken its share of critical abuse from reviewers, who have panned it as insincere, mere shallow, bustling physical activity, and a study in useless sacrifice. The extravagance of the play, in terms of setting, language, and action, and its improbabilities also clash with the expectation of critics more accustomed to realism. Cyrano, however, is a poet, like his author; Rostand uses this play, as he does all of his works, as a vehicle for his own lyric voice.

This important point brings up a related problem the play offers to those who cannot read it in the original French. Those unfamiliar with French must depend upon translations, and although there are several English ones from which to choose, all suffer to some extent because of linguistic and cultural differences which accompany language barriers. Rostand uses the Alexandrine couplet, which gives the language of the play a weighty balance of rhyme and rhythm. Rhyming couplets in French are simply easier on the ear than they are in English. French has more rhyming endings and more acceptable combinations of its rhyming words than have proved possible in English. Out of five readily accessible English translations, three attempt to retain the poetic tone by using blank verse or rhymed verse. The other two avoid the restrictive nature of Rostand's preferred rhyme scheme. One is unrhymed, but a close literal translation; the other uses various rhyme schemes freely and attempts to find English or American parallels for Rostand's witty references to French life and history, providing a lengthy introduction to explain why the changes were made. Regardless of what translation is used, the high lyrical style of the play is evident. One translation focuses on the concept of "panache" by using the French term in different contexts throughout the play. It helps define this last word of Cyrano's which serves as a key to the play's meaning. For example, early in the play at the Pont Nesle battle, Cyrano declares that he came alone except for his triple-waving plume, this "proud panache." Later, in the debate with de Guiche over whether it was honorable for the latter to throw off his white scarf to escape, Cyrano argues that the white plume is a man's panache, a manifestation of his very soul, not to be bartered or squandered but to be preserved as a sign of contempt for his enemies.

Finally, at the end of the play and the end of his life, Cyrano describes the leaves as falling with a certain panache: They float down like trailing plumes of fading beauty, masking their fear of returning to the inevitable ashes and dust of biblical prophecy; they fall gracefully, with style, as though they were flying. Truly, *Cyrano de Bergerac* is about style created out of despair.

"Critical Evaluation" by Jean G. Marlowe

Bibliography:
Chandler, Frank Wadleigh. *The Contemporary Drama of France*. Boston: Little, Brown, 1920. Rostand is depicted as "an idealist endowed with a sense of humor." Ranks *Chantecler*, however, at a slightly higher level than *Cyrano de Bergerac*, for "the scintillating wit, the brilliant extemporization, the profusion of words and images that make us dizzy." Good for comparing the tone of *Cyrano de Bergerac* with the rest of the canon.
Clark, Barrett Harper. *Contemporary French Dramatists*. Cincinnati: Stewart & Kidd, 1915. A short but informative essay on Edmond Rostand, his work habits, and his thin but excellent canon. Helps put *Cyrano de Bergerac* in perspective, and explains why subsequent dramas did not measure up to the masterpiece. Discusses the "nose" monologue in some detail.
Matthews, Brander. *French Dramatists of the Nineteenth Century*. 3d ed. New York: Charles Scribner's Sons, 1901. Unusual in criticizing *Cyrano de Bergerac* for lacking passions, real action, and realism. Questions *Cyrano de Bergerac* as a lasting piece of stagework—"at bottom too slight a thing to serve as the corner-stone of a new school."
Rostand, Edmond. *Cyrano de Bergerac: A Heroic Comedy in Five Acts*. Translated and edited by Louis Untermeyer. New York: Heritage Press, 1954. This deluxe edition, with color illustrations by Pierre Brissard, features a foreword introducing the person on whom the stage figure is based. Brief biographical notes and a performance history to 1947.
Smith, Hugh Allison. *Main Currents of Modern French Drama*. New York: Henry Holt, 1925. Acknowledges *Cyrano de Bergerac* as definitive in evaluating the qualities and worth of Rostand's poetic drama. Summarizes articles that appeared after the first production. Finds the play's "freshness and salubrity" the main source of its popularity. Cyrano was not the beginning of a new school but rather an indication of "the survival and culmination of Romanticism."

CYROPAEDIA

Type of work: History
Author: Xenophon (c. 431-c. 354 B.C.E.)
First transcribed: Kyrou paideia, after 371 B.C.E.? (English translation, 1560-1567)

Among the surviving authors of ancient Greek literature, Xenophon has the distinction of being the first who wrote in a variety of prose genres, forms that in turn deal with an even greater variety of subject matter. Most of the early prose writers of Greece devoted themselves with notable single-mindedness to either history, the philosophic or scientific treatise of a given sort, dialogue, or rhetoric. Xenophon, however, wrote in nearly all of these forms. What is more, one of his latest works is a composition which even now is essentially *sui generis*. The *Cyropaedia*, or *Education of Cyrus*, has been called a historical romance. The name may be convenient, but there is in fact no adequate classification for the work. "Didactic-romantic-political-fictional-biography" might come closer.

Xenophon has incorporated into the *Cyropaedia* some treatment of nearly all the topics that he developed separately in his more restricted works. Of his historical interests, despite the title and ostensible subject, there is only a slight trace: The historical and geographical reliability of Xenophon's tale is minimal. The *Hellenica*, covering Greek history from the point where Thucydides left off in 411 B.C.E. to the death of Epaminondas in 362 B.C.E., and the *Anabasis* remain his only strictly historical creations. The latter, a famous account of the author's participation as a young man in a Greek mercenary army expedition deep into the Persian Empire, is probably his best work. The *Cyropaedia* resumes some of the *Anabasis*' telling of expert generalship in exotic terrain. The extensive discussions of Cyrus' wise arrangements in military, political, social, and economic order recall the concerns reflected in Xenophon's *Constitution of Sparta, Agesilaus* (on the Spartan king, here treated as a model leader), *Hiero*, and *Oeconomicus*, all written in the fourth century B.C.E. The account of Cyrus' education and the portrait of his personal virtues and world-wisdom, which culminates in his deathbed discourse to his sons on the soul, continue in their way, the philosophical writings of Xenophon that are centered on Socrates, chiefly in the *Memorabilia*. The attentions devoted to horseman-ship, hunting, and conviviality ("Cyrus at Banquet," as it were) are vestiges of still other works of his. As a final seasoning for the whole, Xenophon includes the first love romance in Western literature, the story of Pantheia and Abradatas.

This topical cross section presents a complex of matters from which a writer of genius might well have woven an absorbing tapestry comprising an intellectual and cultural summary of the age, an encyclopedic *Bildungsroman*, such as Johann Wolfgang von Goethe's *Wilhelm Meister's Apprenticeship* (1795-1796) or Thomas Mann's *The Magic Mountain* (1924). Xenophon failed to do so. The quality of the product can be assessed after the following summary.

In book 1, Cyrus the Great is born of Cambyses, king of Persia, and Mandane, the daughter of Astyages, king of Media. Reared until his twelfth year in Persian simplicity and discipline, he then visits Media for five years. There, he learns to ride a horse and hunt, and he wins the friendship and admiration of the Medes by his virtues. He returns home and completes his training under his father's guidance. When Media is threatened by an Assyrian invasion, Cyaxares, the son of the now-deceased Astyages, asks aid of the Persians. Cyrus is sent in command of the Persian forces.

Book 2 begins in Media, where Cyrus reorganizes his army and prepares it physically and psychologically for combat. The king of Armenia, a vassal to Cyaxares, revolts.

In book 3, Cyrus reconquers the king of Armenia by brilliant strategy and recovers his allegiance to Cyaxares by equally brilliant diplomacy. He executes a similar feat with the Chaldeans, the neighbors of the Armenians. Cyaxares and Cyrus then advance together to meet the Assyrians, and, thanks largely to Cyrus' generalship, the Assyrians are defeated in a first engagement at the border.

In book 4, Cyaxares becomes jealous of Cyrus' reputation and decides to stay behind with his own army, allowing Cyrus to move ahead as he pleases. Cyrus, however, persuades most of the Median army to accompany him as well. He wins over to his side the Hyrcanians, a subject people of the Assyrians. After a second defeat of the Assyrians, he provides the Persians with a cavalry force of their own. In growing vexation, Cyaxares orders that the Median "volunteers" with Cyrus be sent home. Cyrus sends a message in justification of his noncompliance. Gobryas, a vassal of the Assyrian king, defects to Cyrus.

Cyrus advances to the walls of Babylon in book 5, but postpones an assault on the city. Three more subject peoples accede to the Persians. Cyrus returns to the border of Media and there confronts the spleen and chagrin of Cyaxares with such dexterity that his uncle is publicly reconciled to him. Book 6 covers the further military preparations being carried on in winter quarters. Pantheia, the wife of a noble subject of the Assyrian king, had been captured earlier and given into the keeping of Araspas, a Median officer in Cyrus' entourage. Araspas now attempts to seduce her. She appeals to Cyrus and is protected. In consequence, her husband, Abradatas, is won over to Cyrus.

In book 7, a massive army of Assyrians and allies under the command of Croesus, king of Lydia, is defeated. Before the battle, Pantheia takes pathetic leave of Abradatas, who dies a hero's death in the fighting. Pantheia kills herself over his body. Croesus, captured after the siege of Sardis, is generously treated by Cyrus. After several other campaigns, Babylon is taken by stratagem and victory is complete.

In book 8, Cyrus organizes his empire, marries the daughter of Cyaxares, and after a long reign holds a final edifying discourse on his deathbed. A surprising postscript sarcastically details the degeneration of the Persians since the time of Cyrus.

On the very face of it the arrangement is unpromising. The action advances without complication except for such essentially irrelevant episodes as those involving Pantheia. In no other fashion is there sufficient human richness to sustain the objective material. Xenophon's political and moral concerns, to be sure, are worked in by a superabundant series of dialogues and speeches, devices that Thucydides had employed with brilliant effect. (Mann's *The Magic Mountain* again provides some parallels.) For Thucydides, however, the issues and personalities of the Peloponnesian War were problematic and many-sided to an overwhelming degree. Xenophon's Cyrus, by contrast, is so mercilessly idealized that no counterforce can be set up to provide enough tension to launch issues or personalities. The nearest thing to such a confrontation lies in the theme of the growing jealousy of Cyaxares. Thucydides would have been capable of presenting in Cyaxares a potent distillate of everything vital in Spartan and Athenian culture that opposed the composite of Athenian-Spartan ideals read by Xenophon into the figure of Cyrus. Xenophon's Cyaxares, however, is no such foil; he is a pathetic also-ran who is graciously manipulated by his hero-gentleman nephew.

The didactic material is not simply embedded in the framework of successive events, without human complication; a degree of lapidary attention to context could still have made the segments memorable. For the most part, however, when Xenophon settles into a discourse or dialogue, he produces a run of facile, repetitious, platitudinous elegance. Skill in specious conversation was clearly part of the Greek ideal of the gentleman. In this fashion, he managed to pad out his stick-figure design to some four hundred pages.

One moral to be drawn, then, is that the *Cyropaedia* should never be read straight through except in Greek, since it is only the grace of its style that gives some spice to many a dull page. It should also, in justice, be admitted that a wisely condensed English version is worth its reading time. Anecdotes possessed of point and humor, moments with some vividness of situation and character, do occur. For example, some country bumpkin rookies in training are told that they must march behind their lieutenant. When the lieutenant is by chance sent on a postal errand, the entire platoon obediently runs off behind him. At times, the practical wisdom has its interest. Cambyses Cyrus tells how to manage his men: When encouraging them by hopes which are not certain to be fulfilled, one should not personally suggest these doubtful hopes; get someone else to act as mouthpiece.

More important, however, some rapid acquaintance with the text of the *Cyropaedia* will always be worthwhile because of the position this book occupies in the development of the ancient political imagination. Both Xenophon and another Socratic enthusiast gave their minds to the problem of the inadequacy of existing Greek political systems. In its artistry and profundity, Plato's *Republic* (388-366 B.C.E.) transcends Xenophon beyond all compare. Plato, however, never conceived of a satisfactory political order larger than the city-state, and the times were leaving him behind.

Bibliography:

Due, Bodil. *The "Cyropaedia": Xenophon's Aims and Methods*. Aarhus, Denmark: Aarhus University Press, 1989. Provides a concise and general summary of the characters, themes, and structures of the work. Recommended for those with some knowledge of ancient Greek.

Gera, Deborah Levine. *Xenophon's "Cyropaedia."* Oxford, England: Clarendon Press, 1993. A rigorously argued close reading that also gives attention to questions of the work's sources in the Greek and Persian traditions.

Hirsch, Steven. *The Friendship of the Barbarians*. Hanover, N.H.: University Press of New England, 1985. Uses Xenophon's work to explore the Greeks' views of other peoples. Argues that far from being ethnocentric, the Greeks admired many aspects of their Persian adversaries' culture. Addresses anthropological and historical as well as literary concerns.

Tatum, James, ed. *The Search for the Ancient Novel*. Baltimore: The Johns Hopkins University Press, 1994. Indispensable reference for the study on the narrative form of the Hellenistic romance, of which *Cyropaedia* is the earliest available example.

_____. *Xenophon's Imperial Fiction: On "The Education of Cyrus."* Princeton, N.J.: Princeton University Press, 1989. The best treatment of the *Cyropaedia* available for the general reader. Illuminates rhetoric, political leadership, literary history, and the canon of ancient classics.

DAISY MILLER
A Study

Type of work: Novella
Author: Henry James (1843-1916)
Type of plot: Psychological realism
Time of plot: Mid-nineteenth century
Locale: Vevey, Switzerland, and Rome
First published: 1878

Principal characters:
DAISY MILLER, an American tourist
WINTERBOURNE, an American expatriate
GIOVANELLI, Daisy's Italian suitor

The Story:
Winterbourne was a young American who had lived in Europe for quite a while. He spent a great deal of time at Vevey, which was a favorite spot of his aunt, Mrs. Costello. One day, while he was loitering outside the hotel, he was attracted by a young woman who appeared to be related to Randolph Miller, a young American boy with whom he had been talking. After a while, the young woman exchanged a few words with him. Her name was Daisy Miller. The boy was her brother, and they were in Vevey with their mother. They came from Schenectady, Winterbourne learned, and they intended to go next to Italy. Randolph insisted that he wanted to go home. Winterbourne learned that Daisy hoped to visit the Castle of Chillon. He promised to take her there, for he was quite familiar with the old castle.

Winterbourne asked his aunt, Mrs. Costello, to meet Daisy. Mrs. Costello, however, would not agree because she thought the Millers were common. That evening, Daisy and Winterbourne planned to go out on the lake, much to the horror of Eugenio, the Millers' traveling companion, who was more like a member of the family than a courier. At the last moment, Daisy changed her mind about the night excursion. A few days later, Winterbourne and Daisy visited the Castle of Chillon. The outing confirmed Mrs. Costello's opinion that Daisy was uncultured and unsophisticated.

Winterbourne made plans to go to Italy. When he arrived, he went directly to the home of Mrs. Walker, an American whom he had met in Geneva. There he met Daisy and Randolph. Daisy reproved him for not having called to see her. Winterbourne replied that she was unkind, as he had just arrived on the train. Daisy asked Mrs. Walker's permission to bring an Italian friend, Mr. Giovanelli, to a party that Mrs. Walker was about to give. Mrs. Walker agreed. Then Daisy said that she and the Italian were going for a walk. Mrs. Walker was shocked, as young unmarried women did not walk the streets of Rome with Italians. Daisy suggested that there would be no objection if Winterbourne would go with her to the spot where she was to meet the Italian and then walk with them.

Winterbourne and Daisy set out and eventually found Giovanelli. They walked together for a while. Then Mrs. Walker's carriage drew alongside the strollers. She beckoned to Winterbourne and implored him to persuade Daisy to enter her carriage. She told him that Daisy had been ruining her reputation by such behavior; she had become familiar with Italians and was quite heedless of the scandal she was causing. Mrs. Walker said she would never speak to

Winterbourne again if he did not ask Daisy to get into the carriage at once. Daisy, refusing the requests of Mrs. Walker and Winterbourne, continued her walk with the Italian.

Mrs. Walker was determined to snub Daisy at the party. When Winterbourne arrived, Daisy had not made her appearance. Mrs. Miller arrived more than an hour before Daisy appeared with Giovanelli. Mrs. Walker had a moment of weakness and greeted them politely; but, as Daisy came to say goodnight, Mrs. Walker turned her back upon her. From that time on, Daisy and Giovanelli found all doors shut to them. Winterbourne saw her occasionally, but she was always with the Italian. Everyone thought they were having an affair. When Winterbourne asked her if she were engaged, Daisy said that she was not.

One night, despite the danger from malarial fever, Giovanelli took Daisy to the Colosseum. Winterbourne, encountering them in the ancient arena, reproached the Italian for his thoughtlessness. Giovanelli said that Daisy had insisted upon viewing the ruins by moonlight. Within a few days, Daisy was dangerously ill. During her illness, she sent word to Winterbourne that she had never been engaged to Giovanelli. A week later, she was dead.

As they stood beside Daisy's grave in the Protestant cemetery in Rome, Giovanelli told Winterbourne that Daisy would never have married her Italian suitor, even if she had lived. Then Winterbourne realized that he himself had loved Daisy without knowing his own feelings and that he could have married her had he acted differently. He reasoned, too late, that he had lived in Europe too long and that he had forgotten the freedom of American manners and the complexity of the American character.

Critical Evaluation:

Henry James's *Daisy Miller*, which explores the social expectations placed upon Americans traveling in Europe, reveals the hypocrisy inherent in judging other people. Throughout the novella, the reader is provided with numerous clues that the Miller family is not particularly sophisticated, although clearly wealthy. Winterbourne, for example, observes that Daisy has beautiful clothing, but that her appearance suffers from "a want of finish." Daisy's mother, Mrs. Miller, who makes little attempt to control her children, has a habit of saying the wrong thing at the wrong time and is unaware that her daughter's behavior is unacceptable. Eugenio, the Millers' courier, acts shocked and disapproving when Daisy displays her inappropriate social conduct. He simply expects the Millers to know better.

Daisy Miller, a young woman who knows her mind in a time in which women were considered incapable of complex thought, confounds characters such as Mrs. Walker, who represents European standards of social conduct. Daisy, through her innocent, logical assessment of the social restrictions to which she is expected to adhere, reveals the hypocrisy of these expectations. When Winterbourne tells her, for example, that flirting is considered inappropriate behavior for young, unmarried women, Daisy retorts that flirting would seem more proper in unmarried women than in married women. Her logic is irrefutable; ironically, as Winterbourne discloses, there are married women with whom flirting might take a serious turn. Daisy flirts fearlessly, in public, but she is the most exemplary among her peers. She is the most honest.

In contrast, Winterbourne is reputed to have spent a great deal of time in Geneva in the company of an older woman whom no other character in the novel has seen. Moreover, the text implies that this woman may be married. In light of this possibility, Winterbourne's hypocrisy is clear. Daisy, too, spends a great deal of time with an attractive, unmarried Italian who dotes on her, but her relationship with him is chaste. The sexist double standard that ruled Victorian morality made Winterbourne's behavior acceptable and Daisy's not.

Daisy's behavior, in fact, is a refreshing deviation from the standard presentation of women of her time in art and literature as weak, fragile creatures. Winterbourne's aunt, Mrs. Costello, suffers from numerous headaches and hence spends a lot of time resting, for example. Even Mrs. Miller, who adheres to so few social rules, manages to be ill most of the time; she rarely sees the beautiful artifacts of the countries she visits and is virtually unable even to go for short walks. When Winterbourne arrives in Italy, he hopes to find a Daisy Miller who fits his own image of ideal femininity, one who gazes out the window of an antediluvian Roman dwelling, longing for his arrival. Winterbourne finds no such creature. Daisy Miller is vivacious, strong-minded, and refreshingly assertive. She asserts to Winterbourne, for example, that she has "never allowed a gentleman to interfere with anything" that she does. In a time when women were the property of men, this sentiment is refreshing, even to Winterbourne.

Winterbourne, for all of his supposed sophistication, cannot shake his attraction to Daisy Miller. He continually attempts to make her behavior conform to his dualistic expectations for women. As far as Winterbourne is concerned, Daisy Miller is either good or bad. She cannot simply be who she is. Ironically, when Winterbourne finds, upon his arrival in Italy, that Daisy is spending a great deal of time with Mr. Giovanelli, he believes that she should have instinctively known that Giovanelli was inappropriate company. The irony lies in his own inability to recognize that perhaps he is inappropriate company for Miss Miller, or she for him. The hypocrisy of his thinking is thus continually revealed.

Throughout the novella, Miss Miller confounds other Americans who are traveling abroad, as was the custom of well-to-do Americans of the late nineteenth century. Yet, sadly, as the novella reaches its conclusion, Daisy Miller, who catches a fever after recklessly going out late in the evening, loses her life. Her death is not dramatized in an overt attempt to impart a moralistic message about prudence to the reader. Rather, her death provides her with a level of social acceptance that she never attained in life. She is buried in a small Protestant cemetery; the burial in consecrated ground professes her innocence and morality. Her funeral is well attended, another clear indication of her virtue. As if these indications are not enough, Giovanelli tells Winterbourne outright that Daisy Miller was innocent. Another subtle irony emerges in that although Winterbourne may think himself socially superior to Giovanelli, he is clearly Giovanelli's inferior, as Winterbourne is uncouth enough to insult Giovanelli at Daisy's funeral. Furthermore, Giovanelli never questions Daisy's innocence, while Winterbourne continually wavers in his judgment of Daisy's character, even telling her at one point that she should not flirt with anyone except him.

One of the greatest tragedies of the novella is not that Daisy is continually misjudged by her hypocritical peers for her nonconformist behavior, but that she eventually conforms. The beautiful virgin dies in the prime of her life. In so doing, she conforms to another common portrayal of ideal femininity in art and literature. Winterbourne learns the gravity of his misjudgment of Miss Miller not only through Giovanelli but through Mrs. Miller, who informs Winterbourne that Miss Miller spoke of him on her deathbed. Daisy's greatest concern was that Winterbourne know that she was not engaged to Giovanelli. The novella then makes clear that Daisy might very well have been in love with Winterbourne, although she refused to adhere to the social standards of what was considered appropriate behavior toward him or toward Giovanelli. The novella ends with a reference to Winterbourne's possible relations with a foreign woman in whom he is much interested, implying that his own adherence to the hypocritical double standard continues. Daisy Miller, after all, was also much interested in a foreign man, yet her behavior cost her her life.

"Critical Evaluation" by Dana Reece Baylard

Bibliography:

Graham, George Kenneth. *Henry James: The Drama of Fulfilment.* Oxford, England: Clarendon Press, 1975. Concentrates on the tragicomedy of Winterbourne's attempt to understand Daisy. Examines the interplay between the social and the personal, and the rational and the emotional.

Hoffmann, Charles G. *The Short Novels of Henry James.* New York: Bookman Associates, 1957. Examines how *Daisy Miller* presents European social codes as constraints on evil—and Daisy's defiance as foolish American innocence of evil. Looks at the theme of appearance (Daisy's corruption) versus reality (Daisy's innocence).

Samuels, Charles Thomas. *The Ambiguity of Henry James.* Champaign: University of Illinois Press, 1971. Shows how *Daisy Miller* fits into James's view of the guilt of innocence. Daisy is culpable, as are her persecutors—especially the fastidious Winterbourne, yearning for American purity in a fallen world.

Tintner, Adeline R. *The Museum World of Henry James.* Ann Arbor: University of Michigan Press, 1986. Concentrates on James's use of the portrait of Pope Innocent X as analogy and contrast to Daisy's innocence in the work. Points out the ironic ending: that Winterbourne will be subject to the gossip he sought to avoid.

Wagenknecht, Edward. *Eve and Henry James: Portraits of Women and Girls in His Fiction.* Norman: University of Oklahoma Press, 1978. Looks at the origins of the work, the controversy it aroused, and its literary counterparts. Considers Daisy's character, her refusal to conform, and her ignorance of corruption.

DAME CARE

Type of work: Novel
Author: Hermann Sudermann (1857-1928)
Type of plot: Domestic realism
Time of plot: Nineteenth century
Locale: Germany
First published: Frau Sorge, 1887 (English translation, 1891)

Principal characters:
PAUL MEYERHOFER, a simple farmer
MAX MEYERHOFER, his father
ELSBETH MEYERHOFER, his mother
ELSBETH DOUGLAS, a neighbor girl

The Story:

About the time their third son, Paul, was born, the Meyerhofers lost their country estate, Helenenthal, through forced sale. Meyerhofer tried to keep his wife, Elsbeth, in ignorance of what was going on, but she was so uneasy that at last he told her that a family named Douglas had bought his property.

Meyerhofer was a violent man, given to grandiose schemes to gain wealth and endowed with a martyr complex. It suited him to move his family to a humble farm, within sight of Helenenthal, where they would be constantly reminded of their lost prosperity. Elsbeth, who was a docile woman, shuddered at the prospect.

Mrs. Douglas, a kindhearted woman, came to see the mother and her baby. She assured Elsbeth Meyerhofer that she could stay on at Helenenthal as long as the family wished. The two women became good friends. Mrs. Douglas acted as godmother for Paul, and Mrs. Meyerhofer was godmother for Elsbeth, a daughter born to the Douglases a short time later. In spite of their friendship, however, Meyerhofer took offense at a fancied slight and moved his family in bleak November to a farm on the moor.

In those poor surroundings, Paul had a secluded childhood. His mother, sensing his retiring disposition, was kind to him, but his father was brutal. He continually ridiculed his son by comparing him unfavorably with his two lively older brothers. He often beat Paul, and after the beatings his mother comforted him. She often told him stories; the one he remembered best was a frightening tale about Dame Care, a gray woman who laid great burdens on poor people. Some years after they moved, Elsbeth Meyerhofer had twin daughters, Katie and Greta.

About the time Paul was learning to whistle, bad times came to the farm. The mortgage was due, and there was no money to pay it. Day after day, Meyerhofer drove into town and came back very late, usually drunk. Despite her fear of her husband, Elsbeth Meyerhofer determined to seek help. She took Paul with her to Helenenthal on a memorable visit. There she explained her husband's dislike for the Douglas family and asked for their help. The amiable Mr. Douglas gave her the money to pay the mortgage. Paul played with Elsbeth while the grown-ups visited.

Paul did not succeed easily at school. He had to study a long time to get his work done, and he had to memorize all the answers to problems. His handwriting, however, was very good. The Erdmann brothers, wild-eyed and saucy, made his life miserable for years. They often beat him, stole his lunch, and threw his clothes into the river.

The Meyerhofer property was surrounded by a peat bog. Always too busy to pay attention to his farm, Meyerhofer bought a used steam engine to harvest peat. He gave half his harvest as down payment to Levy, a sharp trader, and hired an engineer whom Levy had recommended. The old engine, however, would never run, and Meyerhofer learned that the supposed engineer was only a tramp hired by Levy for a few days' imposture. That winter, when Levy came to collect the other half of the harvest, the duped Meyerhofer drove him off with a whip. Levy, a shrewd man of business, went to a lawyer. Meyerhofer was compelled to give up his harvest and, in addition, pay a heavy fine.

After the older brothers had been sent away to school, there was no money to educate Paul, who was sent to confirmation classes. He saw Elsbeth there, and he even sat near her. She was kind to the boy and went out of her way to speak to him. The Erdmann brothers teased them about the friendship and said that Paul was sweethearting. Hating ridicule, Paul seldom spoke to Elsbeth after that.

Paul toiled on the farm for five years and got little help from his father. Once, when he was out seeding a distant field, Paul saw Elsbeth. Delighted to see him again, she gave him a book of Heinrich Heine's poetry; she was impressed with his ability to whistle whole symphonies. Once after she had been abroad for a long time, a party was given on her return, to which Paul and his family were invited. The rest of the Meyerhofers went early in the day, but Paul went after dark so that no one would see his shabby clothes. He watched his two sisters having a merry time, and he saw his father talking grandly with Mr. Douglas.

Out of sympathy for Paul, Mr. Douglas agreed to go in with Meyerhofer on one of his schemes. On the strength of Douglas' endorsement, Meyerhofer borrowed money recklessly. When he heard what was going on, Mr. Douglas came to the farm and told Meyerhofer to stop. Meyerhofer set the dog on him, but Mr. Douglas, though bitten, choked the savage beast. While Paul was apologizing to his neighbor, Meyerhofer attacked a servant, Michel, who had watched the scene. Michel picked up an ax. Paul took it away from him and threw it down a well. Then he carried his struggling father into the house. From that day on, Paul was master in the household.

While Paul was wandering late one night near Helenenthal, he saw brilliant flames shooting from his farm buildings. Michel had fired the barn. Paul was able to save the house, the livestock, and the old steam engine, but everything else was lost.

Beaten in spirit, Elsbeth Meyerhofer died a lingering death. At the funeral, Paul saw Elsbeth again. Since her own mother was incurably ill, she felt a strong bond of sympathy for Paul. Later Paul, with the aid of books on mechanics sent by his remote brothers, began to rebuild the steam engine that had been his father's folly. He worked so hard that he had little time to look after his sisters. One night he overheard them in the meadow with the Erdmann boys and learned that his sisters' honor had been smirched by his old enemies. Waiting in a deserted road for them at night, he forced them at pistol point to swear they would marry Katie and Greta.

Paul finally got the old steam engine operating, and he began to cut and market peat. As his trade increased, he became a man of substance and traveled about Germany. He heard of Elsbeth from time to time and knew that she planned to marry her cousin.

One night, eight years after their barn burned, Paul suspected that his father was planning to burn the Douglas barn. To divert him from his mad deed, he set fire to his own house and barn and was seriously burned in the flames.

Paul was taken to Helenenthal. The searchers had found Meyerhofer dead of a stroke near the Douglas barn, a broken pot of petroleum by his side. Although it was Elsbeth's wedding day, she insisted on staying by Paul's bed. The vicar was sent away, and her cousin left. For many weary days, Elsbeth watched over Paul.

After his recovery, Paul was tried for the deliberate burning of his own house. Admitting his guilt, he blamed himself for always having been so timid and withdrawn. Now that he had lost everything, he felt free at last. Dame Care, who had been his nemesis all of his life, had been routed. Paul was sentenced to two years in prison. On his release, Elsbeth and Mr. Douglas met him to take him home. Both Helenenthal and Elsbeth would be his.

Critical Evaluation:

Dame Care is an outstanding example of German Romanticism, a style colored by a kind of world-sadness, completely rural settings, and a sentimental tone. *Dame Care* covers a wide span of years in its action, but it is gracefully concise without being abrupt. Hermann Sudermann exhibits a paternal sympathy for his characters; perhaps his greatest gift is his understanding of all classes of people.

The novel is an extraordinary study of a human being who becomes trapped by circumstances into sacrificing his life to his family. With great subtlety and psychological penetration, Sudermann portrays the gradual development of Paul's conviction that his life must be the way it is. Paul longs to be selfish but can never bear to shirk responsibility. He knows that people take advantage of him, but he cannot deny help to those who need him. Sudermann poignantly describes the plight of this conscientious young man, carefully avoiding sentimentality or falseness of tone. He captures the right sympathetic note as he writes about Paul, and the novel's style is even and restrained throughout, allowing the events to produce the emotional reaction.

Fairy tales form a background for the story of Paul's growing up and subsequent bondage. They are the only frame of reference young Paul has, as he tries to comprehend the dark and mysterious world. It is natural that he should think of Elsbeth in the white house as a fairy princess far above him. The subtle, tender, slowly maturing relationship between Paul and Elsbeth is related by the author with a mastery of nuance and suggestion; the mutual pain that the two young people experience is never made melodramatic or false, although their situation might seem to be that of a romantic melodrama.

The power of selfishness is hauntingly dramatized in the book, as Paul's family convinces him that he must live apart from the joys of ordinary mortals. All he can do, he tells Elsbeth, is watch over the happiness of others and make them as happy as possible. After the final catastrophe, however, he realizes that nobody has appreciated his sacrifices, nobody has noticed that he has given away his own happiness. People who take do so without concerning themselves about those who must do the giving.

Sudermann shows as much skill with scenes of action as he does with psychological analysis. The dramatic moment when Paul saves his father's life and establishes himself as master of the farm is brilliantly rendered; the two fires that destroy the farm are described with vivid, vigorous prose. The countryside around the farms and village is pictured clearly, with concise, yet poetic, descriptions. Sudermann is as successful at bringing to life the minor characters as he is the major ones; Paul's selfish and self-centered brothers and sisters and guilt-tormented, half-mad father are particularly well done. Elsbeth Meyerhofer, Paul's mother, might have become a cliché figure, the long-suffering wife, but she is portrayed with a sensitive and subtle understanding that makes her a genuine human being; her suffering is completely understandable and therefore pitiable. Many of the characters are unlikable, and often the story is painful to read, but it is, thanks to the author's great skill, completely engrossing from beginning to end. *Dame Care* presents a stark but realistic view of human nature, alleviated only by the decency of a few rare individuals.

Bibliography:
Bithell, Jethro. *Modern German Literature, 1880-1950.* London: Methuen, 1959. Brief sketch of Sudermann's career that concentrates on the dramas. Illustrates linkages between *Dame Care* and the writer's later works. Concludes that the novel is a *Bildungsroman* that praises the value of hard work.

Dukes, Ashley. *Modern Dramatists.* 1912. Reprint. Freeport, N.Y.: Books for Libraries Press, 1967. Brief sketch of Sudermann's accomplishments as a dramatist. Useful for understanding the author's concerns about social conditions, which influenced both his dramas and his fiction, including *Dame Care.*

Hale, Edward Everett. *Dramatists of Today.* New York: Henry Holt, 1905. Examines Sudermann's career in the context of other popular playwrights. Much of the discussion centers on his dramas, for which Sudermann is chiefly noted. Also examines his motives and interests and the styles that influenced him and led to his writing *Dame Care.*

Mainland, W. F. "Hermann Sudermann." In *German Men of Letters,* edited by Alex Natan. Vol. 2. London: Oswald Wolff, 1963. Surveys Sudermann's accomplishments and notes how his popularity as a dramatist led to a revival of interest in his novels, which were written during the early years of his career. Briefly comments on the themes in *Dame Care.*

Phelps, William Lyon. *Essays on Modern Novelists.* New York: Macmillan, 1918. Includes a chapter on Sudermann's novels. Uses his works as examples for highlighting strengths and weaknesses of late nineteenth century German fiction. Praises *Dame Care* for its structural unity and its qualities of realism, calling it "an anatomy of melancholy."

THE DAMNATION OF THERON WARE

Type of work: Novel
Author: Harold Frederic (1856-1898)
Type of plot: Social realism
Time of plot: 1890's
Locale: New York State
First published: 1896

Principal characters:

THERON WARE, a young Methodist minister
ALICE WARE, his wife
FATHER FORBES, a Catholic priest
CELIA MADDEN, a rich young Irish-Catholic woman
DR. LEDSMAR, Father Forbes's friend
MR. GORRINGE, a trustee of Theron's church

The Story:

Theron Ware had gone to the annual statewide meeting of the Methodist Episcopal Church with great expectation of being appointed to the large church in Tecumseh. He was greatly disappointed, therefore, when he was sent to Octavius, a small rural community. To the minister and his wife, the town and its citizens did not appear formidable at first, but a hint of what was to come occurred the first morning after their arrival. A boy who delivered milk to Mrs. Ware informed her that he could not deliver milk on Sunday because the trustees of the church would object. Shortly afterward, the trustees told the new minister that his sermons were too dignified and that Mrs. Ware's Sunday bonnet was far too elaborate for a minister's wife. Theron and his wife were depressed. Unhappy in his new charge, Theron decided to write a book about Abraham.

One day, Theron assisted an injured Irish-Catholic workman and went home with him to see what help he might give. At the man's deathbed, Theron observed the parish priest and a pretty young redhead, Celia Madden, who assisted him. Upon their acquaintance, the minister was surprised to find that his earlier hostility to Catholics and the Irish was foolish. These people were more cultured than he, as he learned a few evenings later when he went to the priest for some advice in connection with his proposed book.

At the priest's home, he met Dr. Ledsmar, a retired physician interested in biblical research. The priest and the doctor knew a great deal about the actual culture of Abraham and his people. They tried to be tactful, but the young minister quickly saw how wrong he had been to think himself ready to write a religious book on any topic; all he knew was the little he had been taught at his Methodist seminary.

Upon leaving Father Forbes and the doctor, Theron walked past the Catholic church. Hearing music within, he entered to find Celia Madden at the organ. Later, he walked home with her and discovered that she was interested in literature and art as well as music. Once again that evening, Theron was made to realize how little he actually knew. He went home with the feeling that his own small world was not a very cultured one.

Three months later, there was a revival at Theron's church. Mr. and Mrs. Soulsby, two professional exhorters, arrived to lead a week of meetings which were designed to pay off the church debt and put fervor into its members. The Wares, who entertained the Soulsbys, were surprised to find that the revival leaders were very much like insurance salespeople, employing similar tactics. During the revival week, Theron was nonplussed to discover what he thought were the beginnings of an affair between his wife and one of the trustees of his church, Mr. Gorringe.

In a long talk with Mrs. Soulsby, Theron told her that he had almost decided to give up the Methodist ministry because of the shallowness he had discovered in his people and in his church. Mrs. Soulsby pointed out to him that Methodists were no worse than anyone else in the way of hypocrisy and that all they lacked was an external discipline. She also reminded him that he was incapable of making a living because he lacked any worldly training.

Theron's life was further complicated when he realized that he was beginning to fall in love with Celia Madden. As a result of her interest in music, he had asked her advice in buying a piano for his home, and she had, unknown to him, paid part of the bill for the instrument. He also found time to call on Dr. Ledsmar, whose peculiar views on the early church interested him. He disgusted the old doctor, however, with his insinuations of an affair between Father Forbes and Celia.

In September, the Methodists of Octavius had a camp meeting. Its fervor did not appeal to Theron, after his more intellectual religious reading and his discussions with Celia and Father Forbes, and he went off quietly by himself. In the woods, he came upon a picnic given by Father Forbes's church. At the picnic, he met Celia and had a long talk with her, kissed her, and told her of his unhappiness in his double bondage to church and wife.

Soon afterward, he alienated Celia by telling her that he was afraid of scandal if he were seen talking with her. He also offended Father Forbes by reports that Dr. Ledsmar had spoken slightingly of Celia. The priest told his housekeeper that he was no longer at home to Theron Ware.

One day, Theron openly confronted his wife with his suspicions about her and Mr. Gorringe. She denied the charges, but her very denial seemed to speak against her in her husband's mind. In his unhappiness, he went to see Celia. She was not at home, but her brother, who was dying slowly of tuberculosis, saw him. With the license of the dying, he said that when Theron arrived in Octavius he had the face of an angel, full of innocence, but that in the eight months the minister had spent in the little town, his face had taken on a look of deceit and cunning. Celia's brother continued by warning the minister that he should stay among his own people, that it was bad for him to tear himself from the support which Methodism had given him.

Leaving the Madden home, Theron learned that Celia was going to New York City. It occurred to him that Father Forbes was also going to the city that evening and perhaps they were traveling together. He went home and told his wife that urgent business called him to Albany; then he went to the station and boarded the train unseen. In New York, he saw the priest and Celia meet, and he followed them to a hotel. After the priest had left the hotel, he went upstairs and knocked at Celia's door. She told him that she was busy and did not wish to see him, adding that she had noticed him following her earlier in the journey. While he pleaded with her, Father Forbes came in with some other gentlemen and informed Theron that they had come to New York to get another brother of Celia out of a bad scrape.

Dismissed, Theron stumbled down the stairs. A few days later, he arrived at the Soulsby house at dawn. He told an incoherent story of having tried to commit suicide, of stealing money from the church at Octavius, and of wandering alone about the city for hours while he tried to drink himself to death.

The Soulsbys took him in and sent for his wife. He was ill for months. After his recovery, both he and his wife realized that he was never meant for the ministry. Through the Soulsbys, Theron was finally able to make a new start in a real estate office in Seattle. Theron knew he would make a successful real estate agent; or, if that failed, he could try politics. There was still time enough for him to be in Congress before he was forty.

Critical Evaluation:

The often controversial and always turbulent course of Harold Frederic's life centered on his struggle to be recognized as a novelist. Born the son of a freight conductor in Utica, New York, in 1856, Frederic rose from relatively humble beginnings. His father died before Frederic was two, and lacking substantial resources, Frederic got little education beyond high school. Like so many of the noted American writers of his time, Frederic began writing as a journalist. His strong political views almost immediately led him into a series of controversies, and he changed papers frequently, eventually landing at *The New York Times*, where he received acclaim for his work as London correspondent. Life was never smooth, however, for Frederic. Late in life, he endured constant criticism for his extramarital affair with a woman who bore him three children. Even his death inspired scandal. Bedridden in 1898 with a stroke, Frederic requested a doctor, but his Christian Scientist mistress summoned a faith healer who proved ineffective in preventing Frederic's death. The mistress and faith healer were acquitted of manslaughter, but not before their highly publicized trial received international notoriety.

Throughout his life, Frederic sought artistic recognition. Although he published several novels, few received any acclaim. *The Damnation of Theron Ware* nevertheless enjoyed commercial success and earned critical recognition during the author's lifetime. Its stature continued growing after his death, and by the middle of the twentieth century, the novel had come to be seen as a literary masterpiece. A fine example of literary realism with strong elements of naturalism, *The Damnation of Theron Ware* creates a biting portrait of life in post-Civil War America, as drawn from the author's varied experiences and acquaintances. Read superficially, *The Damnation of Theron Ware* offers an excellent story, but this often delightful surface rests on a complicated web of elements that supports multiple interpretations. For example, the novel can be read as a representation of the intellectual and theological turmoil of the late nineteenth century and as a sophisticated psychological study of a flawed individual.

The characters of the novel can symbolize conflicting social and ideological forces in post-Civil War America. For example, Theron's congregation at Octavius, and the Methodist establishment in general, represent a middle America which, in Frederic's view, has stubbornly maintained the traditional forms of Protestantism but has lost touch with its moral and spiritual underpinnings. Consequently, Theron's society plods unreflectingly on as an intellectually narrow, prudish, and blatantly hypocritical mob easily susceptible to emotional appeals. On the other hand, Dr. Ledsmar, an atheist researcher who performs medical experiments on unwitting subjects, reflects new scientific thought. Ledsmar's Darwinian view of humanity and its institutions, along with his callous indifference to individual rights and dignity, depicts the amoral objectivity of science carried to an extreme. At the same time, the Catholic Father Forbes, who should exemplify spiritual devotion, follows a philosophical trend similarly lacking in moral integrity. Father Forbes sees different religions as simply various results of humanity's need for ritual and security; for the priest, Christianity is simply another useful myth. Ledsmar sees people as objects for study, whereas Forbes sees them as childlike savages who alternately interrupt his hedonistic pleasures or serve as subjects for his intellectual amusements. Father Forbes views his priestly functions as a necessary service for the benefit of the ignorant masses.

The two women who act as catalysts for Theron, Celia Madden and Sister Soulsby, also represent particular ideologies. Celia may be seen as the true Emersonian romantic, the artistic individualist who creates her own rules. As an Irish Catholic, Celia may be interpreted as a stereotype of her unusual background; however, her differences seem more likely designed to distinguish her from the Protestant mainstream. Celia differs from Father Forbes in that she appears to have a strong sense of morality; nevertheless, her high moral tone does not prevent her from amusing herself with Theron's discomfort. Celia's professed Hellenism and her disdain of propriety blatantly announce her nonconformity; Sister Soulsby readily conforms with any ideology that is useful. She represents a pragmatism inherent in American culture since the Puritans. Her pragmatism, however, lacks moral purpose. Although Sister Soulsby works for the Methodists, she has just as readily plied her talents for less savory causes. Soulsby differs from the Methodist establishment in having no illusions about her hypocritical actions. As she indicates to Theron, she assumes that the ends justify the means and believes, as does Father Forbes, that values are relative.

Theron seems to represent the struggle to find some moral center among the turbulent social and intellectual landscape of his time, but his flawed character dooms this quest. Seen from a psychological perspective, much of Theron's plight seems his own fault. Theron suffers from great pride and ambition. He sees his assignment to the provincial Octavius as a slight by people incapable of appreciating him, so he is predisposed to scorn the members of his new parish as backward and unworthy. However, the naïve and inexperienced minister greatly overestimates his knowledge and intellect, thereby opening himself to disaster when he ventures outside the familiar environment of Methodism. By emphasizing Theron's perspective of events, Frederic highlights Theron's many self-serving misperceptions. Dazzled by Celia's attention and by her risqué behavior, Theron mistakenly assumes that she finds him romantically desirable. Impressed by Father Forbes's casual derision of religion, Theron foolishly tries to emulate the priest's intellectual approach and incorrectly assumes that Father Forbes will appreciate derogatory remarks about Methodists. When Theron must finally confront his misplaced optimism and inflated self-image (the British version of the novel was titled *Illumination*), he tries to kill himself. Theron's illumination does not last long. He ends the novel engrossed in new delusions of his own greatness.

Frederic ensures that his readers share Theron's dilemma. By undermining all the sources of moral and intellectual value in the novel, the author leaves blind stupidity as the only path by which Theron can avoid being disillusioned, at best. As a result, Frederic masterfully captures the anxiety and confusion brought about by the rapid changes of the late nineteenth century. Not surprisingly, despite all of his weaknesses, Theron is typically seen as one of the more sympathetic characters of American fiction.

"Critical Evaluation" by Tom E. Hockersmith

Bibliography:
Briggs, Austin, Jr. *The Novels of Harold Frederic*. Ithaca, N.Y.: Cornell University Press, 1969. A starting point for any discussion of the novel. While considering Frederic's work as a whole, it considers sources for, influences on, and critical reactions to the novel.
MacFarlane, Lisa Watt. "Resurrecting Man: Desire and *The Damnation of Theron Ware*." *Studies in American Fiction* 20, no. 2 (Fall, 1992): 127-143. Focuses on "the convergence of gender and religion" in the novel and argues that Frederic uses Theron as a transitional or mediating figure for the evolving roles of women in society.

Michelson, Bruce. "Theron Ware in the Wilderness of Ideas." *American Literary Realism, 1870-1910* 25, no. 1 (Fall, 1992): 54-73. Focuses on the place and especially the time in which the action takes place. Argues that the novel uses Theron's character to express the particular difficulties of maintaining identity in the turmoil of the age.

O'Donnell, Thomas F., and Hoyt C. Franchere. "The Damnation of Theron Ware." In *Harold Frederic*. New York: Twayne, 1961. A chapter in a standard biography of Frederic, this study places the novel in the context of the author's life and offers a general critical analysis.

Oehlschlaeger, Fritz. "Passion, Authority, and Faith in *The Damnation of Theron Ware*." *American Literature* 58, no. 2 (May, 1986): 238-255. While emphasizing the sociological and gender themes of the novel, Oehlschlaeger argues that the novel focuses on the breakdown of traditional authorities in the late nineteenth century.

THE DANCE OF DEATH

Type of work: Drama
Author: August Strindberg (1849-1912)
Type of plot: Psychological realism
Time of plot: Late nineteenth century
Locale: Sweden
First performed: 1905; first published, 1901 as *Dödsdansen, första delen* and *Dödsdansen, andra delen* (English translation, 1912 as *The Dance of Death I* and *The Dance of Death II*)

Principal characters:
EDGAR, a captain in the Swedish coast artillery
ALICE, his wife
JUDITH, their daughter
CURT, Alice's cousin
ALLAN, Curt's son, in love with Judith

The Story:

For twenty-five years Edgar, a captain in the Swedish coast artillery, and his wife Alice had lived an unhappy existence. Their unhappiness was caused by Edgar's contempt for everyone else in the world; he thought of himself as a better being than others, even his wife, and he had made their marriage a tyranny. They lived on an island off the coast, where Edgar was the commanding officer of the artillery detachment. Living in an old prison, they avoided the other people of the island as well as officers of the post and their wives. Indeed, Alice was virtually a prisoner in her home. The only means of communication she had with the mainland was through a telegraph key, which she had taught herself to operate. She kept her skill with the telegraph a secret, for her husband did not want her to have any means of communication with the outside world.

Alice's only hope of release from her husband's tyranny lay in the fact that he was ill and might die at any time. On their silver wedding anniversary Curt, Alice's cousin, arrived on the island to officiate as the quarantine officer. On his first visit to Edgar and Alice he learned about the life which they led, when Edgar suffered an attack and Alice gloated over her husband's illness. Curt, who had been divorced by his wife, also learned that Edgar had caused the divorce and persuaded the court to award the custody of the children to Curt's wife.

During the two days that Edgar lay ill, grave changes took place in the three people. Alice turned gray-haired. Feeling that the time had come when she should admit her age, she had stopped tinting her hair. She also became an object of distrust to Curt, for she tried to make love to her cousin while her husband lay ill. Curt, unable to understand her actions, could not fully realize how much she hated her husband and how much she had suffered during the past twenty-five years. Edgar himself resembled a corpse after his illness; but he immediately tried, upon his recovery, to dominate the others.

On the third day after his attack the captain told his wife he was going to divorce her. In retaliation, she tried to have him convicted of the embezzlement of government funds, of which he was innocent. She also embraced her cousin Curt in her husband's presence, at which time Edgar tried to kill her with his saber. After that incident, both husband and wife calmed, admitting they had tortured each other enough. They both said they hoped that they could get along with each other peaceably, if not happily.

A few months later Curt's son Allan, a cadet stationed with Edgar's artillery company, fell in love with Judith, the daughter of Alice and Edgar. The parents, failing to realize the youngsters were serious in their affair, thought that Judith was making game of Allan at her father's request, for Edgar hated Allan because he was Curt's son. At the time Edgar was trying to arrange a marriage for Judith with a major in the regiment, a man older than Edgar. The lovers' quarrels of the two young people only served to heighten the illusion under which the three grownups labored.

Edgar, meanwhile, was also busy undermining Curt's position as quarantine officer. After gleaning information from Curt, he then published articles about quarantine management in periodicals and thus gained a reputation for himself in a field in which he was actually ignorant. After his retirement, the result of his illness, he planned to run for the national legislature, in opposition to Curt, who had expected to try for an office. Edgar completely discredited Curt with the voters by taking up a subscription for his rival, who, acting on Edgar's advice, had lost a great deal of money in an unwise investment. With deliberate malice, Edgar did everything he could to discredit Curt in the eyes of the world and to reduce him to abject poverty and dependence.

After Curt had lost his money, Edgar bought his house and its furnishings and then left the house exactly as it was, in order to make the loss more poignant to Curt. Then Edgar was made an inspector of quarantine stations, an appointment which made him Curt's superior in employment. Curt, accepting his reverses calmly and stoically, refused to lose his head, although Alice tried to make him seek revenge. Alice still hoped that her ailing husband might die quickly, before he could completely ruin the lives of Curt, his son Allan, Judith, and Alice herself.

In the meantime the captain continued his plan to marry Judith to a man who could help to fulfill Edgar's ambitions. Instead of marrying her to the major, he arranged a marriage to the colonel of his old regiment, notwithstanding the fact that the colonel was more than forty years older than Judith. So far as anyone could suppose, the marriage was to take place; Judith herself seemed to be agreeable to the match. Alice made one last attempt to spoil the plan, but a letter she had written was intercepted by Edgar and returned by him to his wife.

Judith herself ruined Edgar's scheme by revealing her true love to Allan. To prevent the marriage, she called the colonel on the telephone, insulted him, and broke off the engagement. Then, with her mother's aid, she arranged to go to Allan at the military post to which Edgar had sent him. The failure of his plan was too much for Edgar. He suffered an apoplectic stroke, much to the delight of his wife, who saw revenge at last for all that she and the other members of the family had suffered at the sick man's hands. Unable to control her delight at Edgar's approaching death, she taunted him on his deathbed with the fact that he was hated and that his evil plans were finally going awry. His only answer, since he had lost the power of speech, was to spit in her face.

After Edgar's death, which occurred within a few hours, both his wife and her cousin admitted that death had changed their attitudes toward the dead man. Alice said she must have loved him as well as hated him, and she hoped that peace would rest with his soul.

Critical Evaluation:

This particular play was written in two parts, in a way that is comparable to the two parts of William Shakespeare's *Henry IV* (c. 1597-1598) in that *Henry IV* is two plays for the most part because it is too long to be one. The first part of *The Dance of Death* deals with the parents and the second with their children.

August Strindberg's specialty in his plays was the stripping bare of "that yawning abyss which is called the human heart," as one of his characters calls it. Perhaps only Fyodor Dostoevski in modern literature has penetrated equally to the depths of psychological torment. His characters say things that most people feel at times, but which they restrain themselves from expressing or even admitting to themselves. Strindberg was obsessed with the dual nature of the human brain, with the contrast between inner feelings and their outer expression. The power and horror of *The Dance of Death* comes from this expression of the normally suppressed thoughts of the characters. This startling honesty seems to shatter moral and social conventions and to leave both characters and audience vulnerable and exposed. "It's horrible," says one of the characters in one of Strindberg's later plays, "don't you find life horrible?" The reply is, "Yes, horrible beyond all description." The endurance of the characters in the face of madness and violence suggests that they see, in spite of everything, that there is no acceptable alternative.

From the first lines of *The Dance of Death*, one is struck by the intensity of the speeches. Alice and Edgar are caught in the midst of a duel, or, rather, in the last and brutally final stages of a duel. When the play opens, the conflict is only verbal, but it soon becomes more passionate and more violent. At times, the dialogue seems to be on the verge of becoming no more than an insane ranting, and yet there are moments when Strindberg rises above his fury and sums up the tragedy of life in a few sentences.

It is vital to understand the intimate relationship between Strindberg's life and work to comprehend fully his dramas, particularly *The Dance of Death*. Essentially pessimistic, August Strindberg lived a tortured existence, from a childhood of poverty and insecurity to years as a minister and then a medical student to a period as a journalist. His first major play, a historical drama, was rejected by the Swedish Royal Theatre. He became famous with the publication of his first novel, *The Red Room* (1879), but he continued writing plays. The conflict between the sexes inspired some of his most intense dramas, including *The Father* (1887) and *Miss Julie* (1888), and, ultimately, *The Dance of Death*. Although Strindberg was married three times, the central relationship of his life was his violent and tormented first marriage. Like D. H. Lawrence, Strindberg was obsessed with the idea of the lower-class male, himself, marrying the aristocratic lady and then bringing her down to his own level. This obsession is reflected in *Miss Julie* and in the relationship between Alice and Edgar in *The Dance of Death*. The disaster of his marriage and the loss of his four children drove him into alcoholism, and, despite his growing fame as a writer, he became a lonely and unhappy man, unable to find steady employment.

In his later plays, Strindberg combined the techniques of naturalism with his unique vision of psychology. These bold dramas, with realistic dialogue, highly wrought symbols (such as the wedding ring, the fortress, the wreaths, and the piano in *The Dance of Death*), and stark settings, brought about a revolution in European drama. One of his last and greatest plays, *The Dance of Death* reflects his first marriage and the collapse of his life afterward. All of his work possesses extraordinary vitality, but in *The Dance of Death*, Strindberg transforms essentially autobiographical material into a drama of exceptional power. His work influenced later playwrights such as Elmer Rice, Eugene O'Neill, Luigi Pirandello, and Edward Albee.

Strindberg has been accused of hating his female characters, and no character has prompted this statement more than Alice in *The Dance of Death*. Were Strindberg's greatest plays the product of a dangerous and intense misogyny? Is this what gives his brilliant psychological dramas their peculiarly perverse power? No doubt he did suffer from paranoia, brought on by his many personal problems, and his writing suggests, in places, paranoiac tendencies. The women in the plays, such as Julie and Alice, tend to be strong and vengeful creatures, who deliberately try to lead men to destruction. The power of *The Dance of Death* and other dramas of this late period must be due, also, to a deep introspective analysis of his sufferings, for, between his bouts of madness, Strindberg was able to examine his mental disturbance and to make use of the knowledge he gained from such examinations. From a reckless, Bohemian existence, he emerged, in his last years, into a guilt-ridden form of Christianity, Swedenborgian mysticism, and a Schopenhauerian pessimism according to which the real world exists outside human understanding. His third marriage, to the young actress Harriet Bosse, dissolved after less than three years, and he discovered that he had inoperable cancer. Then, suddenly, the Swedish people recognized his greatness and began speaking of a Nobel Prize for him. "The anti-Nobel Prize is the only one I would accept," he retorted. When his first wife died in 1912, he collapsed, although he had not seen her for twenty years. Three weeks later, he was dead.

Some critics have said that both Edgar and Alice are monsters battling to the death, like a pair of dinosaurs clashing in some ancient swamp, but the fact is that they are not monsters any more than are the characters of *The Father* or *Miss Julie* or any other of his plays. They are two trapped individuals struggling desperately to survive, but not knowing what to do; every frantic gesture that they make only wounds them more. They are, perhaps, two of the most pitiful characters in modern literature. The scenes in which Alice plays the Hungarian dance on the piano and Edgar performs the violent jig with his jangling spurs and in which Alice hurls her wedding ring at Edgar are excruciatingly painful, cutting beneath the layers usually left by more conventional playwrights. Alice and Edgar are bound together by a love-hate relationship that neither can escape, except into death. As Strindberg knew, distance and time cannot release a man or woman from certain types of bondage. At the end of the first part of the play, Edgar realizes how hopelessly he and his wife are bound, and laughs that they might as well celebrate their silver wedding anniversary. "Let us pass on," he cries. Somehow, they endure, and that, perhaps, is the message of the play. Alice, when Edgar dies at the end of the second part, finally understands that she loved Edgar, as well as hated him, and she prays for peace for him. By implication, she also prays for herself.

"Critical Evaluation" by Bruce D. Reeves

Bibliography:
Brady, Philip. "The Dance of Death." *Times Literary Supplement*, February 10, 1995, 18. Brief review affirms the relevance of the play in the twentieth century. Argues that the drama moves beyond the warring of the sexes to the inefficacy of life.
Hildeman, Karl-Ivan. "Strindberg, *The Dance of Death*, and Revenge." *Scandinavian Studies* 35, no. 4 (November, 1963): 267-294. Asserts that character sketches and events in *The Dance of Death* are based on Strindberg's sister and brother-in-law. Concludes that Strindberg created these characters as punishment or revenge for real or imagined injury.
Johnson, Walter. "Strindberg and the *Danse Macabre*." In *Strindberg: A Collection of Critical Essays*, edited by Otto Reinert. Englewood Cliffs, N.J.: Prentice-Hall, 1971. Discusses Strindberg's use of the medieval image of Death characterized by the *danse macabre* (the dance of death) as a symbol in parts 1 and 2. Contends that the dance symbolizes life as an evil dream while death becomes a release from the horrors of hell/life. Includes a detailed bibliography.
Meyer, Michael. *Strindberg: A Biography*. New York: Random House, 1985. Includes relevant biographical information on many of Strindberg's major plays, including *The Dance of Death*. Meyer has translated eighteen of Strindberg's plays to English and is knowledgeable

about the playwright. His biography is concerned primarily with Strindberg's influence on modern theater. Includes subject index.

Valency, Maurice. *The Flower and the Castle: An Introduction to Modern Drama*. New York: Macmillan, 1963. Comprehensive discussion of all of Strindberg's major plays and his contribution to modern theater. Includes subject index and selected bibliography.

A DANCE TO THE MUSIC OF TIME

Type of work: Novel
Author: Anthony Powell (1905-   )
Type of plot: Social realism
Time of plot: 1914-1971
Locale: London, various other locales in Great Britain, and Venice, Italy
First published: 1976: *A Question of Upbringing,* 1951; *A Buyer's Market,* 1952; *The Acceptance World,* 1955; *At Lady Molly's,* 1957; *Casanova's Chinese Restaurant,* 1960; *The Kindly Ones,* 1962; *The Valley of Bones,* 1964; *The Soldier's Art,* 1966; *The Military Philosophers,* 1968; *Books Do Furnish a Room,* 1971; *Temporary Kings,* 1973; *Hearing Secret Harmonies,* 1975

Principal characters:

NICHOLAS JENKINS, the narrator and a novelist
KENNETH WIDMERPOOL, a school acquaintance of Jenkins; the only character besides the narrator to figure in all twelve volumes of the cycle
PETER TEMPLER, a school friend of Jenkins
JEAN TEMPLER, Peter's younger sister and Jenkins' lover before his marriage
CHARLES STRINGHAM, another school friend
SILLERY, a manipulative don
J. G. QUIGGIN, a fellow student at the university with Jenkins who later attains celebrity as a left-wing critic
MARK MEMBERS, a fellow student who achieves recognition as a poet
CAPTAIN GILES JENKINS, Jenkins' raffish uncle
SIR MAGNUS DONNERS, an industrialist
EDGAR DEACON, a bad painter
RALPH BARNBY, another painter, superior to Deacon
MRS. MILLY ANDRIADIS, a socialite
MONA, Peter Templer's first wife and a former model
BOB DUPORT, Jean Templer's first husband and an entrepreneur
ST. JOHN CLARKE, an Edwardian novelist despised by Jenkins
MRS. MYRA ERDLEIGH, a friend of Uncle Giles and a clairvoyant
CHIPS LOVELL, a friend of Jenkins and fellow scriptwriter
LADY MOLLY JEAVONS, Chip Lovell's aunt by a former marriage
TED JEAVONS, her husband
LADY PRISCILLA TOLLAND, a debutante who is pursued and later married by Chips Lovell
LADY ISOBEL TOLLAND, Priscilla's older sister, who becomes Jenkins' wife
ERRIDGE, Priscilla and Isobel's eldest brother, later Lord Warminster
GENERAL AYLMER CONYERS, an old family friend of the Jenkinses
HUGH MORELAND, a composer and one of Jenkins' closest friends
MATILDA WILSON, an actress whose second marriage is to Moreland
MACLINTICK, a music critic and admirer of Moreland

DR. TRELAWNEY, a cult leader and magus

CAPTAIN ROWLAND GWATKIN, Jenkins' company commander in the Welsh regiment in which he is commissioned at the outset of World War II

PAMELA FLITTON, Stringham's niece who becomes Widmerpool's wife

LINDSAY "BOOKS-DO-FURNISH-A-ROOM" BAGSHAW, a disreputable journalist

X. TRAPNEL, a novelist and short-story writer of the immediate postwar period

RUSSELL GWINNETT, an American professor who writes a biography of Trapnel

SCORPIO MURTLOCK, a cult leader in the late 1960's who claims to be a reincarnation of Dr. Trelawney

FIONA CUTTS, a niece of the Jenkinses and one of Murtlock's disciples

The Story:

Nicholas Jenkins was in school at Eton along with three other young men, Charles Stringham, Peter Templer, and Kenneth Widmerpool. Jenkins used his friendship with the other boys to cement his acquaintance with various areas of life: Widmerpool's ambition, Stringham's aristocratic connections, and Templer's social ease and familiarity with sex. A visit from Jenkins' scapegrace Uncle Giles forecast unstable elements in the adult world. On a visit to Templer's family, Jenkins met Templer's sister Jean, for whom he developed a crush. He then went to France to practice the language in a French home, only to encounter Widmerpool, who was the object of jest and abuse on the part of the French people who knew him. Jenkins also fell in love with the daughter of his host. Returning to England, Jenkins entered Oxford, where he became initiated into literary circles, meeting two young writers, Mark Members and J. G. Quiggin, who seemed to have an odd love-hate relationship with each other.

Jenkins moved to London and worked for a publisher of art books. He encountered a bizarre array of people ranging from the artist Edgar Deacon to the industrialist Sir Magnus Donners. He attended a whirl of parties and initiated several unsuccessful love affairs, encountering Widmerpool several times along the way. He spent a weekend at Peter Templer's country house, where he once again met Jean, and began a serious relationship with her. Jenkins decided on a career as a writer of fiction, even as Members and Quiggin vied for the patronage of a prominent novelist. Stringham, meanwhile, began his descent into drunkenness and depression. Jean abruptly left Jenkins and returned to her husband, accompanying him to South America.

Jenkins began encountering various members of the large, aristocratic, and quite eccentric Tolland family. Through the offices of Quiggin, he met the family's head, the left-wing gadfly Lord Erridge, and, eventually, Erridge's sister Isobel. Jenkins knew as soon as he saw Isobel that he would marry her, and indeed the two did marry some months later. Widmerpool also got engaged, to an older widow, but the outcome was disastrous, and Widmerpool emerged humiliated and chastened, causing amused comment on the part of Jenkins' family friend, the octogenarian General Aylmer Conyers.

The composer Hugh Moreland was probably Jenkins' best friend. Moreland's wife Matilda was the former mistress of Donners, and helped Moreland secure patronage in the aristocracy. Stringham's mother, Amy Foxe, held a party for Moreland, at which Stringham momentarily showed some of his old vigor. The darker side of the Bohemian world, however, was revealed when Moreland's friend, the music critic Maclintick, committed suicide.

It was the late 1930's, and war clouds were gathering. Jenkins thought back to the beginning of World War I in 1914, when a disturbance in the domestic staff of his parents' household had mystically heralded the instigation of the war, announced dramatically by Uncle Giles. Another element of the 1914 tableau, the mystical cult leader Dr. Trelawney, reappeared mysteriously at the seaside in 1939, months after Jenkins had sensed the coming of the war in a masque of the Seven Deadly Sins held at Donners' castle in Stourwater. Widmerpool assisted Jenkins in obtaining a commission in the Army, and Moreland was shocked to find Matilda had gone back to Donners.

Jenkins was appointed a major in a Welsh regiment stationed in Northern Ireland. He developed a close bond with the regiment's melancholy captain, Rowland Gwatkin, and generally adapted well, if unevenly, to army life. Isobel gave birth to a son, whom Jenkins was able to see on a leave home. Gwatkin compromised his army career by silliness over a woman, and Jenkins was transferred to Divisional Headquarters, where, to his tremendous surprise, he found his immediate superior was Widmerpool.

Another surprise was in store for Jenkins, as he discovered Stringham was a waiter in the division's mess unit. Although his circumstances were reduced, Stringham had conquered his alcoholism and had regained his integrity. Jenkins went back to London only to experience the height of the Blitz, in which several of his relatives and old friends were killed. On the same trip, Jenkins attempted to transfer into a liaison unit that worked with various allied countries; this effort eventually proved successful.

Jenkins met Pamela Flitton, Stringham's hostile and sexually aggressive niece. Pamela began to cut a wide swath through Jenkins' network of friends and acquaintances, having an affair with Templer, among others. Jenkins found out that Stringham, eager to go to the front lines, had been sent to Singapore, where he was tortured and killed during the Japanese occupation. Templer died while attempting to aid the Yugoslav resistance. Moreland lingered on, but was never the same and died some years after the end of the war. The war ended, and Jenkins attended the victory celebration at Westminster Cathedral. After the service, he met Jean Templer, now the wife of a Latin American diplomatic aide. Widmerpool, who had risen rapidly through the ranks during the war, amazed everyone by marrying Pamela Flitton.

The war changed Jenkins' social landscape forever. Most of his close friends were dead. His literary career, however, continued, and he became involved with editing the periodical *Fission*. Through this post he encountered Quiggin and Members again, as well as meeting the prominent cultural opinion-maker Lindsay "Books-do-furnish-a-room" Bagshaw. Jenkins became friendly with the younger novelist X. Trapnel. Trapnel was a tragic figure whose artistic talents were never matched by stability in life. He fell in love with Pamela Widmerpool, whose husband had been named a Life Peer. Pamela left Widmerpool for Trapnel, but then spurned Trapnel as well, leading him to suicide.

Widmerpool was found to have intrigued with a Communist puppet government in Eastern Europe and was disgraced. Pamela became involved with the American academic Russell Gwinnett, who was writing a biography of Trapnel; she killed herself in the course of pursuing a relationship with Gwinnett. Gwinnett's biography of Trapnel was eventually awarded the Sir Magnus Donners Prize (the financier had died some years previously). At the prize banquet, Jenkins encountered Widmerpool, who had become an enthusiast for the 1960's youth counter-culture. Widmerpool eventually joined a cult led by the insidious and charismatic Scorpio Murtlock, a spiritual disciple of Trelawney. Murtlock abused Widmerpool and finally caused his death. One of Murtlock's disciples, however, escaped from the cult and rescued a painting by Stringham that had come to Widmerpool through his marriage to Pamela. As this painting was exhibited at an art gallery, Jenkins encountered Jean and had a final meeting with his first love. Jenkins contemplated the course of his life, and meditated on the nature of the seasons and the patterns that govern "the music of time."

"The Story" by Margaret Boe Birns

Critical Evaluation:

Anthony Powell's *A Dance to the Music of Time* is a *roman-fleuve*, a long sequence of novels that together make up a single unified work. Other examples of the *roman-fleuve* in English fiction include C. P. Snow's *Strangers and Brothers* (1972), comprising eleven individual novels, and Henry Williamson's *A Chronicle of Ancient Sunlight* (1951-1969), comprising fifteen novels. In French, examples of the *roman-fleuve* include Romain Rolland's *Jean Christophe* (1904-1912, ten volumes), Jules Romains' *Men of Good Will* (1932-1946, twenty-seven volumes), Roger Martin du Gard's *Les Thibaults* (1922-1940, eight volumes), and Marcel Proust's *Remembrance of Things Past* (1913-1927, seven volumes).

The length of the *roman-fleuve* allows the novelist to develop characters over a long span of time, to convey something of the density and complexity of life itself. Powell memorably achieves these effects; at the same time, he is virtually unique among practitioners of the *roman-fleuve* in that his viewpoint is essentially comic.

A Dance to the Music of Time draws its title from a painting by Nicolas Poussin. At the beginning of the novel, Jenkins watches some workmen gathered around a fire and is reminded of Poussin's painting, the one

in which the Seasons, hand in hand and facing outward, tread in rhythm to the notes of the lyre that the winged and naked greybeard plays. The image of Time brought thoughts of mortality: of human beings, facing outward like the Seasons, moving hand in hand in intricate measure: stepping slowly, methodically, sometimes a trifle awkwardly, in evolutions that take recognisable shape.

This image of "the music of time," to the tune of which "partners disappear only to reappear again, once more giving pattern to the spectacle," governs the entire sequence.

The twelve novels of the cycle are grouped in four subsections, or movements. The first movement, which includes *A Question of Upbringing*, *A Buyer's Market*, and *The Acceptance World*, traces the progress of narrator Nicholas Jenkins from youth to experience. Powell's treatment of this passage is highly unsentimental; for Jenkins, youth is something to be endured and gotten over with, and the prevailing mood of the opening novels is one of waiting for life to begin in earnest. This mood is not Jenkins' alone; indeed, throughout the cycle, Jenkins himself is rarely the focus of attention. He is, rather, a participant-observer through whose experience the reader comes to know an extraordinary diversity of characters.

A Question of Upbringing begins in December, 1921. (Although Powell does not always supply exact dates for the action, they can usually be reconstructed with reasonable accuracy following the internal chronology of the cycle, and with reference to historical events mentioned throughout.) The location is an exclusive English public school; among Jenkins' schoolmates are three characters destined to play an important role in the cycle. Of these, the most important is Kenneth Widmerpool. Widmerpool is the only character other than the narrator to figure in all twelve volumes of the sequence. A disagreeable youth and, ultimately, a despicable man, Widmerpool appears at intervals throughout Jenkins' life; their relationship embodies the metaphor of the dance, according to which one is bound to one's "partners" by an inscrutable design. More sympathetic characters are Jenkins' friends Charles Stringham and Peter Templer. Stringham is appealing yet self-destructive; Templer is smooth, confident, and mature beyond his years.

The first section of *A Question of Upbringing* introduces these characters in the school setting. In the summer following his graduation, Jenkins visits the Templers and meets Peter's younger sister, Jean, then about sixteen or seventeen, to whom he is greatly attracted. In the fall of 1923, following a farcical interlude in France, Jenkins enters the university (unnamed, but presumably Oxford). A long comic scene set several months later in the rooms of a power-hungry don, Sillery, introduces two of Jenkins' fellow students who become recurring characters in the cycle: J. G. Quiggin, later to attain celebrity as a Marxist critic and all-around man of letters, although he leaves the university without a degree, and Mark Members, who makes his reputation as a poet and then, like Quiggin, branches out into the role of man of letters.

A Buyer's Market, the second novel in the sequence, opens in the summer of 1928 or 1929, four or five years after *A Question of Upbringing*, and concludes in October of the same year. Jenkins, having been graduated from the university, has found employment in London, where he works for a publisher that specializes in art books but issues other sorts of books as well. Stringham and Widmerpool, in a coincidence typical of the entire sequence, both find themselves working for Sir Magnus Donners, a prominent industrialist. In structure, this volume follows the pattern established in the first volume. It consists of four chapters, each of which centers on a comic episode or set piece. With some variation, this is the method that Powell follows throughout.

A Buyer's Market introduces the first of many artists and artists *manqué* that populate the cycle: Edgar Deacon, a seedy, egotistical, untalented painter with a taste for young men (he dies in the course of the novel after a drunken fall), and Ralph Barnby, a far better painter than Deacon but one whose art is very much tied to the *Zeitgeist* of the 1920's; he is also a notorious womanizer. The central scene of the novel is a party at the home of Mrs. Milly Andriadis, a socialite in her mid-thirties who has a brief affair with Stringham before his marriage, which takes place near the end of the volume. This party continues Jenkins' initiation into the world of experience: "I was . . . more than half aware," he reflects, "that such latitudes are entered by a door through which there is, in a sense, no return."

A second set piece features Sir Magnus Donners giving a tour of the dungeons at Stourwater Castle, his home, which occasions comment on his voyeuristic and otherwise perverse sexual proclivities. Among the party is the former Jean Templer, now Jean Duport; her loutish husband, Bob Duport, several years older than Jenkins and his contemporaries, is an aggressive entrepreneur who makes and loses great sums of money.

The Acceptance World (the title is British financial jargon for what is known in the United States as "trading in futures") completes Jenkins' initiation. In the course of this volume, which spans the period from autumn 1931 to summer 1933, Jenkins publishes his first novel and carries on an intense affair with Jean Duport, still going as the book ends but showing signs of running down. Later, Jenkins learns that while their affair was still going, Jean had already taken up with the man for whom she eventually leaves him, Jimmy Brent, an odious character whose appeal to Jean is incomprehensible to Jenkins.

An important figure in this volume is the novelist St. John Clarke, introduced briefly in *A Buyer's Market*. Clarke, an Edwardian writer who in his time attains both popular and critical success, becomes a kind of litmus test: Referred to in various ways by various characters throughout the sequence, he represents for Jenkins all that is artistically cheap and meretricious.

Also introduced here is the clairvoyant Mrs. Myra Erdleigh, whom Jenkins meets in the hotel rooms of his Uncle Giles. This scene, the opening scene of *The Acceptance World*, is one of the most important in the entire twelve volumes. Throughout the sequence there are many references to occult phenomena, in addition to the often uncanny coincidences that are the very texture of the action. Powell's attitude toward such phenomena is neither credulous nor debunking. He clearly believes that some experiences of occult phenomena—second sight, telepathy (at least of a low-grade variety), and so on—are valid. Their recurring presence in the cycle (along with instances of obvious charlatanry) has a larger import as well, for they point to the mystery of human existence—a mystery not confined to realms designated "occult."

When Mrs. Erdleigh reads the cards and tells Jenkins his future, he is immediately startled by her perspicacity, but he quickly discounts that effect, observing that "such trivial comment, mixed with a few home truths of a personal nature, provide, I had already learnt, the commonplaces of fortune-telling." Yet Mrs. Erdleigh's insights into Jenkins' character are genuinely perspicacious, and, as the reader gradually appreciates, her specific predictions concerning his future are all, in time, fulfilled—genuinely fulfilled, not merely finding the loose "confirmation" of a fortune-cookie oracle.

The first movement of the cycle, then, concludes with Jenkins and his contemporaries firmly established in

the Acceptance World . . . the world in which the essential element—happiness, for example—is drawn, as it were, from an engagement to meet a bill. Sometimes the goods are delivered, even a small profit made; sometimes the goods are not delivered, and disaster follows; sometimes the goods are delivered, but the value of the currency is changed.

The second movement includes *At Lady Molly's*, *Casanova's Chinese Restaurant*, and *The Kindly Ones*. It is 1934 as *At Lady Molly's* begins, and Jenkins has moved from his publishing job to work as a scriptwriter for a British studio, having meanwhile published his second novel. A fellow scriptwriter, Chips Lovell, about five years younger than Jenkins (who is by this time twenty-eight or twenty-nine), is nephew by marriage to the Lady Molly of the title, Molly Jeavons, and early in the novel, he takes Jenkins to a party at the Jeavonses, where he hopes to meet Priscilla Tolland, a young woman whom he is pursuing. Later, at the country cottage of J. G. Quiggin (currently domiciled with Peter Templer's former wife, Mona, a former model), Jenkins meets Priscilla's older sister Isobel. They are but two of the ten children of Lord Warminster; the eldest, Erridge, is Quiggin's landlord and patron, sharing his Marxist views. In his understated way, Jenkins reports that he knew at first sight that Isobel would be his wife. The novel begins by introducing, via Jenkins' reminiscences of long family friendship, the character of General Aylmer Conyers, one of the most delightful and most warmly portrayed figures in the entire sequence. Retired, nearing the age of eighty, General Conyers is still formidable: He trains dogs, plays the cello, and discusses the works of Carl Gustav Jung, which he has recently discovered and absorbed with great interest. This volume also follows the fates of Widmerpool, whose fiancée breaks their engagement when he cannot perform as a lover, and Stringham, whose alcoholism and alienation are severe.

Casanova's Chinese Restaurant begins with a flashback to 1928-1929 that introduces Hugh Moreland, a composer who is one of Jenkins' closest friends and who becomes an important recurring character. The first section of this novel, discounting the flashback, is set in 1933 and 1934 and overlaps in time some of the action of *At Lady Molly's*. By this stage, the fifth novel in the sequence, the special effects of the *roman-fleuve* begin to come into play. The texture is denser; much can be accomplished simply by mentioning the name of a familiar character in a new (and often surprising) context.

Much of *Casanova's Chinese Restaurant* is concerned with marriage and marriages. Jenkins marries Isobel; Moreland marries the actress Matilda Wilson (to whom Jenkins is introduced by Moreland after a performance in John Webster's *The Duchess of Malfi*, 1614), a former mistress of Sir Magnus Donners. There is also the bitterly—indeed, pathologically—unhappy marriage of the Maclinticks; Maclintick, a music critic who worships Moreland, in his own words, "with the proper respect of the poor interpretive hack for the true creative artist," ends by committing suicide after his wife Audrey leaves him. His suicide dissuades Moreland from pursuing his affair (as yet unconsummated) with Priscilla Tolland; a week later, her engagement to Chips Lovell is announced. The movement concludes with *The Kindly Ones*, which begins with a long flashback to 1914. Jenkins recalls his governess' lesson, that the Greeks so greatly feared the Furies that they renamed them the Eumenides—the Kindly Ones—hoping thus to placate them. The flashback evokes the mood of imminent disaster, the sense that the Furies are about to strike again, yet it does so in an oblique fashion, for much of the action is broad comedy involving the Jenkinses' servants. Introduced in this section is the cult leader and magus Dr. Trelawney. After another brief flashback, to 1928 or 1929, and sections set in 1938 and 1939, the novel concludes in the fall of 1939, several weeks after the outbreak of World War II, with the brother of Ted Jeavons (Lady Molly's husband) promising Jenkins to expedite his call-up by the army.

The third movement, which includes *The Valley of Bones*, *The Soldier's Art*, and *The Military Philosophers*, spans the war years. As *The Valley of Bones* opens early in 1940, Jenkins has been commissioned as a second-lieutenant in a Welsh regiment, soon to be stationed at a school for chemical warfare quartered on a decaying estate in Northern Ireland. Much of the action of this volume centers on the tragicomic fate of Jenkins' immediate superior, Captain Rowland Gwatkin (in civilian life an employee of a small bank), whose romanticism proves his downfall. When, at the end of the volume, Jenkins is transferred and then told to report to the DAAG (Deputy-Assistant-Adjutant-General) at Divisional Headquarters in Northern Ireland, it is no surprise that the officer to whom he reports turns out to be Widmerpool.

Widmerpool's machinations and running battles with fellow officers figure prominently in the next volume, *The Soldier's Art*. Stringham makes an unexpected reappearance as a waiter in the mess where Jenkins regularly eats; Widmerpool not only rejects Jenkins' suggestion that they help Stringham in some way but also arranges for his transfer to a Mobile Laundry Unit due to be sent to the Far East—an eventuality concerning which Stringham maintains indifference ("Awfully chic to be killed"). On leave in London, Jenkins meets Chips Lovell, currently estranged from Priscilla (who is carrying on an affair) but hopeful of getting her back. Later, after Chips has left the restaurant where he and Jenkins met, Jenkins sees Priscilla and her lover, Odo Stevens. That night, both Chips and Priscilla (and Lady Molly, at whose house Priscilla is staying) are killed in air raids at different locations.

In the final volume of the third movement, *The Military Philosophers*, Jenkins has a new posting, working in the War Office in Whitehall in Allied Liaison, with special responsibility for Polish forces. Widmerpool, who has been promoted, is also working in Whitehall, with access to policy makers at the highest levels. Early in the volume, Jenkins meets Peter Templer and is struck by his air of detachment and fatalism. Templer has recently had an affair with Stringham's niece, Pamela Flitton, a beautiful but malicious femme fatale who inexplicably turns her attention to Widmerpool, to whom she is soon engaged. Later in the volume, when Templer is sent to the Balkans on a secret mission and killed by Communist partisans, Pamela accuses Widmerpool of complicity in Templer's death. There is also word, confirmed by Widmerpool, that Stringham was captured by the Japanese at the fall of Singapore and died in a prisoner-of-war camp. Finally, this volume features the reappearance of Jean Duport, at first unrecognizable to Jenkins as the wife of a Latin American attaché, Colonel Flores, some years her junior.

The deaths of Templer and Stringham are symbolic of the end of a period and, indeed, a way of life. The postwar world presents a strange new landscape. Such is the mood of the final movement, comprising *Books Do Furnish a Room*, *Temporary Kings*, and *Hearing Secret Harmonies*. In *Books Do Furnish a Room*, which begins in the winter of 1945-1946 and concludes in the fall of 1947, Jenkins, who was unable to write during the war and finds that he is still not ready to attempt a novel, undertakes a study of Robert Burton, entitled *Borage and Hellebore*. Much of this volume is concerned with the postwar literary scene, especially with the antics of J. G. Quiggin and the crowd associated with his magazine *Fission*, edited by the disreputable journalist Lindsay "Books-do-furnish-a-room" Bagshaw ("Books" for short). Also introduced in this context is one of the most interesting characters in the cycle, X. Trapnel (based on Powell's acquaintance with the writer Julian Maclaren-Ross). Trapnel is a novelist and short-story writer of enormous gifts and idiosyncratic manner whose immediate postwar success is not followed up; his decline to a premature death is hastened by an affair with Pamela Widmerpool.

Between the time of *Books Do Furnish a Room* and that of *Temporary Kings*, there is an interval of more than ten years—the first such substantial gap in the sequence. *Temporary Kings* begins in the summer of 1958 at an international writers' conference in Venice. The arrival of an American professor, Russell Gwinnett, who is at work on a biography of X. Trapnel, prompts memories of Trapnel's death. After a leisurely and blackly comic account of the conference and its attendant intrigues, the scene shifts back to England, where Widmerpool is about to be charged with espionage on behalf of the Soviets. (Later, the case is dropped, presumably in exchange for information from Widmerpool.) Pamela pursues Gwinnett and dies in bed with him in a hotel, having taken an overdose of drugs; there are rumors of necrophilia, consistent with Gwinnett's past. Hugh Moreland, long in ill health and living in reduced circumstances with Maclintick's widow, Audrey, dies at the end of this volume.

There is another ten-year interval between the conclusion of *Temporary Kings* and the opening of the final volume of the sequence, *Hearing Secret Harmonies*, in the spring of 1968. Several new characters are introduced in this volume, including the cult leader Scorpio Murtlock (who claims to be a reincarnation of Dr. Trelawney) and the Jenkinses' niece, Fiona Cutts, who is one of Murtlock's disciples. (The time of the action is the same as that of the Manson family and similar phenomena of the 1960's.) Familiar figures appear as well: Widmerpool, after a stint in California, has returned to England in a new guise, as a champion of the counterculture, while Gwinnett's book on X. Trapnel, *Death's-Head Swordsman*, thought to have been abandoned, not only is published but also wins the Sir Magnus Donners Prize. New and old characters come together when Widmerpool joins Murtlock's cult (which he tries to take over) and Gwinnett, in England to receive the Donners Prize and pursue research for his new book, *The Gothic Symbolism of Mortality in the Texture of Jacobean Stagecraft*, attends the cult's rites and witnesses Murtlock's assertion of supremacy over Widmerpool. A year or so later, Widmerpool dies on a dawn run with fellow cultists; meanwhile, Gwinnett has married Fiona.

The final volume concludes with Jenkins lighting an autumn bonfire, the smoke of which reminds him of the workmen's fire that he contemplated at the beginning of the first volume.

In turn, the memory brings to mind a long passage from Robert Burton's *The Anatomy of Melancholy*, asserting with a kind of biblical eloquence the cyclical order of human life ("one purchaseth, another breaketh; he thrives, his neighbor turns bankrupt; now plenty, then again dearth and famine.").

A Dance to the Music of Time is a remarkable achievement for many reasons, but above all it is distinguished by its richly varied cast of characters. It is a mistake to claim, as some critics have, that Powell has documented the British experience in the middle decades of the twentieth century. Certainly, his novels give the flavor of the period as it was experienced by a certain class, but his interest is always in his characters as individuals, not as types.

Indeed, insofar as it is possible to summarize the message of a twelve-volume sequence of novels, that message may be found in Powell's approach to his characters. Powell himself has observed that if one writes about people as they are, one will inevitably write comedy. His characters are unpredictable, frequently contradictory in their twists and turns, yet for that reason they are extremely lifelike. *A Dance to the Music of Time* suggests that at the heart of human experience, as of every individual life, there is an irreducible mystery.

Bibliography:
Birns, Margaret Boe. "Anthony Powell's Secret Harmonies: Music in a Jungian Key." *The Literary Review* 27 (Fall, 1981): 80-92. Analyzes the psychological and discursive elements in Powell's novel from the perspective of Carl Gustav Jung's archetypal theories, focusing especially on the Jenkins-Widmerpool relationship.
Harrington, Henry R. "Anthony Powell, Nicolas Poussin, and the Structure of Time." *Contemporary Literature* 24, no. 4 (1983): 431-448. This learned and eloquent piece is essential to any serious reading and study of the novel. Illuminates the grandeur and totality of Powell's novelistic design.
Joyau, Isabelle. *Understanding Powell's "A Dance to the Music of Time."* New York: St. Martin's Press, 1994. Wide-ranging and full of provocative observations. Especially good on the minor characters, whose significance is often missed. Convincingly establishes Powell as a major modern novelist.
Russel, John. *Anthony Powell: A Quintet, Sextet, and War.* Bloomington: Indiana State University Press, 1970. This pioneering study of Powell remains surprisingly relevant despite the fact that it was written when the novel was only three-fourths complete. Good on the psychology of Jenkins and the moral significance of Stringham.
Selig, Robert L. *Time and Anthony Powell.* Madison, N.J.: Fairleigh Dickinson University Press, 1991. Definitely the most skillful and comprehensive work on Powell to date. Selig artfully explores the novel's relevance to contemporary narrative theory.

DANCING AT LUGHNASA

Type of work: Drama
Author: Brian Friel (1929-   )
Type of plot: Psychological realism
Time of plot: Summer, 1936
Locale: County Donegal, Ireland
First performed: 1990; first published, 1990

Principal characters:

MICHAEL MUNDY, the narrator, a young man, looking back on the
summer when he was seven years old
KATE, Michael's schoolteacher aunt
MAGGIE, Michael's aunt, who keeps house for the family
AGNES, Michael's aunt, who works at home as a knitter
ROSE, Michael's aunt, also a knitter
CHRIS, Michael's unmarried mother
GERRY EVANS, Michael's father
JACK, Michael's uncle, a missionary priest just returned from Uganda

The Story:

The adult Michael reflected aloud on the summer of 1936, when he was seven years old and lived in rural County Donegal. His mother Chris, his father Gerry, his uncle Father Jack, and his four aunts formed a silent, motionless tableau as the backdrop for his monologue. That was the summer they got their first radio and their first contact with Dublin music. It was also the summer in which Father Jack, sick, came home to die after twenty-five years of missionary work in Uganda, uninterrupted except for a brief stint as a chaplain in the British army, which explained the ornate officer's uniform he wore.

The adult Michael, Kate, Gerry, and Father Jack then left the stage. It was a warm summer afternoon. The domestic routines of a loving family in the kitchen of a remote, rural cottage proceeded. Maggie was preparing food for the hens; Agnes was knitting gloves to meet her assigned quota of two dozen per week; Rose was replenishing the supply of turf (peat) for the fire; Chris was ironing; the sisters made amiable small talk. Rose, unexpectedly, broke into a bawdy music-hall song and dance; Maggie joined her. The simple Rose, the others were chagrined to learn, had a date planned with a local married man, Danny Bradley.

The young Michael (invisible to the spectator, his lines spoken by the adult Michael) worked on his two kites in the garden. While his did this, his aunt Maggie asked him the first of five riddles she had for him. The child recounted his and their disappointment over the recent return of the missionary priest, Jack, broken in health and mind.

Kate, the grade-school teacher, returned from Ballybeg, where she had been shopping for all of them, quinine for Father Jack included. Rose teased her about her crush on old Austin Morgan. All the talk in Ballybeg, Kate reported, was of the upcoming harvest festival; the sisters agreed in a verbal rush of enthusiasm to go to it. Rose spontaneously threw herself into a mad dance, following which Kate vetoed the whole scheme as inappropriate.

Out in the yard, Maggie, miming a bird, paid back young Michael for having frightened her earlier by pretending to see a rat. She came inside and received her cigarettes, sharing the gossip

1483

from Kate's shopping expedition. When they learned of a village boy badly burned at the pagan Lughnasa Festival in the hills, it was Rose who supplied the details. Maggie learned of a former girlfriend of hers visiting from London with her children and remembered a dance they had attended in a foursome years ago. While the women talked, Father Jack wandered in and out, his memory disturbed. In the background, the radio played Irish dance music. Maggie launched into a wild solo dance, joined soon by the others; only Kate danced alone. They all continued, rapt, even after the very unreliable radio stopped working.

The sisters were squabbling about their division of domestic labor when they were disturbed by the approach of Gerry, the Welsh father of Michael, Chris's child. Kate relented sufficiently to allow Chris to invite Gerry inside; she had not seen him in more than a year. At the front door, Chris learned that he had been teaching dancing in Dublin but was now selling gramophones door-to-door. She told him young Michael was now in school. It was his intention, he told her, to fight with the International Brigade in Spain. When the radio spontaneously started inside the house, the couple responded to "Dancing in the Dark" by dancing down the lane, while Kate watched from inside the house. Even though Gerry promised to be back in two weeks before he left for Spain, Chris would not agree to marry him.

The lives of the other family members were also not going well. Kate felt her world was collapsing; the local parish priest was threatening her with the loss of her job. Father Jack's mind was disturbed. Befuddled by his African experiences and having trouble with the English language, he wandered into the kitchen. He had seen a white bird on his windowsill that morning. When Agnes told him that it was Rose's pet rooster, it caused him to reminisce about the African rituals and native dances he had known.

The narrator, the adult Michael, concluded Act I with an omniscient, informative monologue. Father Jack had indeed been sent home in disgrace after giving up his faith and joining the native culture. Kate was fired from her teaching position. Rose was romantically involved with a married man, and both she and her mentor Agnes' knitting contracts were canceled. Michael saw his mother and father dancing again, in harmony despite the lack of music, but there was to be no marriage. The family community was rapidly disintegrating.

The final act opened three weeks later. Maggie sang a romantic song and talked to young Michael, who was expecting a bicycle from his father, a bicycle that would never arrive. She posed riddles to him, only the last of which—Why is a gramophone like a parrot?—was not answered. It was becoming increasingly clear that Father Jack's religious context was no longer Christian. After he seemed to be getting healthier, he died suddenly, within a year of his coming home. Rose disappeared, returning later to confess that she had been with Danny Bradley up in the hills where the Lughnasa Festival had been held. She and Agnes secretly left for England, where, the narrator reported, they eventually died miserable deaths: Agnes of exposure on the Thames Embankment, Rose in a hospice.

Michael's parents carried on with their separate lives. Gerry, who also had danced with Agnes and Maggie before he left, was injured in Spain in a fall from his motorcycle. Eventually, he married another woman and started a new family in Wales. Chris went to work in the new knitting factory for the rest of her life. Michael finally closed the Lughnasa time in his memory; he saw dancing everywhere as the stage lights, wordlessly, were brought down.

Critical Evaluation:

Brian Friel is one of Ireland's most prolific and successful contemporary dramatists. *Dancing at Lughnasa* won both London's Olivier Award and New York's Tony Award for Best Play. Though successful in New York with *Philadelphia Here I Come* (1964), Friel is better known in Dublin and London for dramatic triumphs such as *Faith Healer* (1979), the more political *Translations* (1980), and *Molly Sweeney* (1994).

Friel was educated for the priesthood at Maynooth Seminary, Ireland, but, instead of taking Holy Orders, he became a teacher like his father. Following the success of his very elegant short stories, available in two collected editions, *The Saucer Full of Larks* (1962) and *The Gold in the Sea* (1966), he gave up teaching and devoted himself to the theater, working in 1963 at the Guthrie Theater in Minneapolis.

Dancing at Lughnasa (pronounced LOO-na-sah) represents Friel's utilization in his writing of the regional life he knows so well. Young artists are often advised to write about what they know, and Friel demonstrates just how satisfying this course can be for a much wider audience than simply the people of his home, the northern counties of Ireland, the locale in which he situates *Dancing at Lughnasa* and much of his writing. This geographic area and this family life become metaphors for a wider audience by far. Friel's concern here is to show the fragility of any community and his keen awareness of the slippery quality of language as a means of communication.

The dominant metaphor in this play is the dance, a claim which becomes much clearer in a theatrical production than in a simple reading of the text. Ironically, for a wordsmith as skilled, careful, and responsible as Friel, it is the dancing in the play, as opposed to the frozen immobility of the tableaux that open and close the drama, which most makes his point about the necessity of honest communication, or connection, between and among people in any context.

Behind the action, never appearing on stage, is the pagan dancing of the Lughnasa Festival in the hills. Lugh (pronounced "Loo") is an ancient pre-Christian, Celtic god of fertility and harvest, still honored by some of the "Christians" in Ballybeg (Gaelic for "small town"). Father Jack's beating of rhythms with young Michael's kite sticks supplies yet another pre-Christian art form to the mix. The radio the sisters enjoy so much is their intermittent link to the traditional Irish folk music and dance; it is also their link to the popular dance music of the time in which the play is set. Chris and Gerry dance together beautifully, though marriage is out of the question because of Gerry's lack of reliability as a provider.

This play suggests that communities, including family communities, are under a severe threat. Many writers have extolled the virtues of local communities in the late twentieth century, while failing to offer a clearer solution to prevent their erosion. Here, Friel shows us the doomed cottage industry of knitting; the corrosive religious prejudice from religious orthodoxy that leads to Kate's dismissal from her teaching post because of her link to the lapsed Catholic, Father Jack. Political engagement, a thorny issue for Irish writers like Friel, is evidently not Friel's answer to these problems. Gerry's involvement in the Spanish Civil War is bathetic and ridiculous; he gets his war wound from falling off of his motorcycle.

For Friel, communication is evidently an important key to community at all levels. Words have come dangerously close to failing in the late twentieth century Irish politics that includes a litany of broken treaties. What might work better, Friel suggests in this play, is the necessary trust and harmony needed to dance. Everyone in this family does dance, with the exception of Michael. As the lights are brought down finally on the stage, the tableau moves ever so slightly to the music, the mysterious source of which is not the radio: "Dancing . . . because words were no longer necessary."

Archibald E. Irwin

Bibliography:

Dantanus, Ulf. *Brian Friel: The Growth of an Irish Dramatist*. London: Faber, 1987. A thorough appraisal of Friel's work and themes through 1986.

Foster, Roy. "Pleasing the Local Gods: *Dancing at Lughnasa*." *Times Literary Supplement*, October 26, 1990, 1152. A very favorable review of the London production, in which it is claimed that the play is about "ceremonies of innocence against a background of encroaching despair." For Foster, the essentials are not dancing but "mental retardation, illegitimacy, priestly social control, economic decline, and, eventually, emigration and destitution."

Lahr, John. "Brian Friel's Blind Faith." *The New Yorker* 70 (October 17, 1994): 107-110. With a full-page photograph of Friel, explores his work up to 1994 and sympathetically fits *Dancing at Lughnasa* into its context: Dancing becomes "a means of approaching the non-sectarian religions."

MacNeil, Maire. *The Festival of Lughnasa*. Dublin: University College, 1982. Situates the pagan harvest festival in its European context, surviving as it did in Ireland at least until 1962.

Peacock, Alan, ed. *The Achievement of Brian Friel*. Gerrard's Cross, England: Colin Smythe, 1994. A broad collection of sixteen essays from scholars and theater professionals on Friel's breadth and sympathy of interest and on his dramaturgical creations, including *Dancing at Lughnasa*.

Rich, Frank. "A Drama of Language [*Dancing*]." *The New York Times*, October 25, 1991, C1. A very favorable review of the New York production in which Rich concludes, "let us dance and dream just before night must fall."

DANGEROUS ACQUAINTANCES

Type of work: Novel
Author: Pierre Choderlos de Laclos (1741-1803)
Type of plot: Psychological realism
Time of plot: Mid-eighteenth century
Locale: Paris and environs
First published: Les Liaisons dangereuses, 1782 (English translation, 1784)

> *Principal characters:*
> CÉCILE DE VOLANGES, a young girl of good family
> MADAME DE VOLANGES, her mother
> THE COMTE DE GERCOURT, Cécile's fiancé
> THE CHEVALIER DANCENY, Cécile's admirer
> THE MARQUISE DE MERTEUIL, a fashionable matron and Gercourt's
> former mistress
> THE VICOMTE DE VALMONT, a libertine
> MADAME DE TOURVEL, the wife of a judge
> SOPHIE CARNAY, Cécile's confidante
> MADAME DE ROSEMONDE, Valmont's aunt

The Story:

When Cécile de Volanges was fifteen years old, her mother removed her from a convent in preparation for the girl's marriage to the Comte de Gercourt. The match had been arranged by Madame de Volanges without her daughter's knowledge. Shortly after her departure from the convent, Cécile began an exchange of letters with Sophie Carnay, her close friend. Cécile had few contacts with her fashionable mother except for trips they made together to shops to purchase an elaborate wardrobe. The little she knew about the plans for her future she learned from her maid.

The unscrupulous Marquise de Merteuil saw in the proposed marriage an opportunity to be revenged on Gercourt, who some time before had deserted her for a woman of greater virtue. In her wounded vanity, she schemed to have the Vicomte de Valmont, a libertine as unscrupulous as herself, effect a liaison between Cécile and the Chevalier Danceny. Such an affair, circulated by gossip after Cécile and Gercourt were married, would make the husband a laughingstock of the fashionable world. To complete her plan for revenge, the marquise also wanted Valmont to seduce Madame de Tourvel, the woman for whom Gercourt had abandoned her. Madame de Tourvel was the wife of a judge. As a reward for carrying out these malicious schemes, the Marquise de Merteuil promised to reinstate Valmont as her own lover.

Valmont was able to arrange a meeting between Cécile and Danceny. Although she was attracted to the young man, Cécile hesitated at first to reply to his letters. She concealed her eventual consent to write to him, even to speak of love, from her mother. Valmont had meanwhile turned his attention to Madame de Tourvel, who was a virtuous woman and, aware of the vicomte's sinister reputation, tried to reject his suit. Nevertheless, she found herself attracted to him, and in time she agreed to write to him but not to see him. She also stipulated that Valmont was not to mention the subject of love or to suggest intimacy. Eventually Valmont and Madame de Tourvel became friends. Aware of her indiscretion even in friendship, she finally told Valmont that he must go away, and he accepted her decision.

In the meantime, although she wrote him letters in which she passionately declared her love, Cécile was steadfast in her refusal to see Danceny. Cécile had grown more mature. She still wrote to Sophie Carnay, but not as frankly as before. Instead, she turned for advice to the Marquise de Merteuil, whom she saw as a more experienced woman. The marquise, impatient with the slow progress of the affair between Cécile and Danceny, informed Madame de Volanges of the matter, with the result that the mother, in an angry interview with her daughter, demanded that Cécile forfeit Danceny's letters. The marquise's plan produced the effect she had anticipated; Cécile and Danceny declared themselves more in love than ever.

Hoping to end her daughter's attachment to Danceny, Madame de Volanges took Cécile to the country to visit Madame de Rosemonde, Valmont's ailing aunt. Valmont soon followed, on the Marquise de Merteuil's instructions, to keep the affair alive between Cécile and the young chevalier and to arrange for Danceny's secret arrival. Valmont, bored with rustic life, decided to take Cécile for himself. Under the pretext of making it safer for him to deliver Danceny's letters, he persuaded her to give him the key to her room. At the first opportunity, Valmont seduced her. At first the girl was angered and shocked; before long, however, she was surrendering herself to him willingly. Valmont was at the same time continuing his attentions to Madame de Tourvel. Deciding that persistence accomplished nothing, he tried ignoring her, whereupon Madame de Tourvel wrote to offer her friendship.

Cécile, deeply involved with Valmont, wrote the Marquise de Merteuil, asking for her advice on how to treat Danceny. Madame de Volanges, who was unaware of the situation, also wrote the marquise, telling her that she was considering breaking off the match with Gercourt; her daughter's happiness, she declared, was perhaps worth more than an advantageous marriage. In reply, the marquise earnestly cautioned Madame de Volanges on a mother's duty to guide a daughter and to provide for her future.

When Madame de Tourvel also became a guest of Valmont's aunt, she gave that gallant the opportunity to seduce her. He was tempted, but took greater pleasure in seeing her virtue humbled. After his rejection and her own moral scruples had forced Madame de Tourvel to flee in shame, she wrote Madame de Rosemonde a letter in which she apologized for her abrupt departure and explained her emotional straits. Madame de Rosemonde's reply was filled with noble sentiments and encouragement.

Valmont was surprised to find himself deflated by Madame de Tourvel's departure. His ego suffered another blow when Cécile locked him out of her room. The marquise was more impatient than ever with Valmont's slow progress, and she decided to work her revenge through Danceny. Her first step was to captivate the young chevalier. He succumbed to her, but nevertheless continued to write impassioned letters to Cécile.

Valmont decided to possess Madame de Tourvel. Afterward, he described her initial hesitation, surrender, and complete abandon in a triumphant letter to the Marquise de Merteuil, closing his account with the announcement that he was coming at once to claim the promised reward. The marquise managed to put off his claim, however, by reproving him for his handling of his affair with Madame de Tourvel. The difference between this and his other affairs, she said, was that he had become emotionally involved; his previous conquests had been smoothly and successfully accomplished because he had regarded them only as arrangements of convenience, not relationships of feeling. The irony underlying her attitude was that she was still in love with Valmont and had not counted on losing him, even for a short time. She had lost control of the strings by which she had dangled Valmont to satisfy her desire for vengeance.

Valmont tried to free himself of his emotional involvement with Cécile and Danceny. Cécile had miscarried his child; Danceny's devotion no longer amused him. Although Valmont made every effort to win the favor of the marquise, she held him off and, after a quarrel, capriciously turned from him to Danceny and made that young man a slave to her charms and will.

Both Valmont and the marquise were eventually defeated in this duel of egotistic and sexual rivalry. Danceny, having learned of Valmont's dealings with Cécile, challenged the vicomte to a duel and mortally wounded him. As he was dying, Valmont gave the chevalier his entire correspondence with the marquise. Once her malice was exposed, she was ruined socially. When an attack of smallpox left her disfigured for life, she fled to Holland. Madame de Tourvel, already distressed because of the treatment she had received from Valmont, died of grief at his death. Cécile entered a convent. Danceny gave the incriminating letters to Madame de Rosemonde and, vowing celibacy, entered the order of the Knights of Malta. Madame de Rosemonde sealed the letters that had brought disaster or death to everyone who had been involved with so dangerous an acquaintance as the Marquise de Merteuil.

Critical Evaluation:

Dangerous Acquaintances, the only novel by the French artillery officer Pierre Choderlos de Laclos, is a slow-paced but fascinating story, in which Laclos proved himself a master of the epistolary form popularized by Samuel Richardson and other novelists of the eighteenth century. The letters are so skillfully arranged, and the characterizations so scrupulously presented, that the reader willingly accepts the letters as real and the characters as people rather than as devices for telling a story. The illusion is furthered by Laclos' use of frequent footnotes to explain details in the letters.

Frequently in the history of Western literature, certain works that were initially castigated as indecent, immoral, or blasphemous later came to be acknowledged not only as artistic triumphs but as powerful moral statements. Such is the case with Laclos' *Dangerous Acquaintances*. Enormously popular, yet roundly condemned, the novel was seen as outright scandalous. The real hostility toward the book, however, may have stemmed not from its immoral themes but from Laclos' ruthless honesty in portraying the social, intellectual, and erotic climate of mid-eighteenth century French society, unmitigated by stylistic indirection or sentimental distortion. Moreover, it seems curious to call a book corrupt in which the transgressors are so thoroughly punished for their machinations. Indeed, to later readers, the ending seems too easy and perhaps melodramatic. Valmont's deathbed conversion is almost sentimental, and Madame de Merteuil's smallpox seems gratuitous.

There is in the work a chilling quality in the manner in which Valmont and Madame de Merteuil manipulate and destroy the lives of others as players would move pieces around a chessboard. Although called an erotic novel, there is, in fact, little sexual passion and no emotional involvement in these intrigues. Love is an almost entirely intellectual activity, and this is Laclos' primary moral point. Valmont and Madame de Merteuil represent the final product of eighteenth century rationalism; they have reasoned their feelings out of existence.

A closer look at the "game" suggests yet deeper and more complex motivations than the simple pleasures of manipulation and petty spite. Although Valmont and Madame de Merteuil for the most part maintain a tone of light, elegant bantering between themselves, comparing notes as friendly rivals, their competition is in deadly earnest, yet their ultimate opponents are not their various victims but they themselves. Cécile de Volanges, Chevalier Danceny, and Madame de Tourvel are merely surrogates that Valmont and Madame de Merteuil use to get at each other. *Dangerous Acquaintances* is truly one of the most brilliant, elegant, and brutal "battle-of-the-sexes" works ever written.

Valmont and Madame de Merteuil are at once products and victims of their society. They have absorbed and accepted its rationalistic basis. They have subjugated their emotional impulses to it, and they are both suppressed by its social norms and rituals. Valmont is a soldier without a war. Predisposed by training to military command, Valmont is bored and restless in the stagnant, aimless, ritualized society in which he finds himself. He uses amatory combat as a weak substitute for the real thing.

Madame de Merteuil's situation and psychology are somewhat more complicated. As an aristocratic woman, her freedom of action is severely circumscribed. She has the potential to be passionate but is forced into an arranged marriage with a dull old man. She is brilliant and resourceful but faces a lifetime of meaningless social activity that will eventually stultify her capacities. She is free-spirited and experimental but bound by behavioral norms and a rigid double standard that threatens to ostracize her for the slightest dereliction. Madame de Merteuil has refused to accept these limitations for herself; she has, in fact, determined to use them to her own advantage. "Ought you not to have concluded," she writes Valmont, "that, since I was born to avenge my sex and to dominate yours, I must have created methods unknown to anybody but myself?" Thus, although Madame de Merteuil impresses readers as a "moral monster," Laclos does raise the question as to how she came to be that way. In many ways, she seems to be an earlier version of Henrik Ibsen's Hedda Gabler, whose frustrated passions and abilities also turned to viciousness and eventually to self-destruction.

Madame de Merteuil destroys herself, because both her suppressed passion for Valmont and her need to dominate him are too strong to remain in equilibrium. For his part, Valmont, too, feels the need to dominate, as is clear when he presents his ultimatum to Madame de Merteuil—"from this day on I shall be either your lover or your enemy." To that, she responds "Very well—War!" and rationalistic erotic intrigue becomes mutual self-destruction. Because the emotions cannot remain suppressed, rational self-control gives way to vindictive impulse, and love is replaced by self-defeating hate.

Bibliography:

Conroy, Peter V. *Intimate, Intrusive and Triumphant: Readers in the "Liaisons dangereuses."* Amsterdam: Benjamins, 1987. Concludes that the fictional reader is the most powerful character "in" the book, more powerful than the narrator. Discusses form and technique from the perception of the reader.

Free, Lloyd R., ed. *Laclos: Critical Approaches to "Les Liaisons dangereuses."* Madrid: Studia Humanitas, 1978. Eleven essays by critics discussing evil, characterization, suspense structures, language, and contemporary consciousness.

Meltzer, Françoise. "Laclos' Purloined Letters." *Critical Inquiry* 8, no. 3 (Spring, 1982): 515-529. Points out that in the epistolary novel, it is the fictional reader who most clearly creates the text. Discussion, which is informed by the work of Jacques Derrida and Jacques Lacan, argues ironically that a purloined letter always arrives at its destination.

Miller, Nancy K. "Rereading as a Woman: The Body in Practice." *Poetics Today* 6, nos. 1/2 (1985): 291-299. Examines the scene in which the Vicomte de Valmont writes a letter to Madame de Tourval literally on Emilie's body and gives a feminist reading of male production of reading and its "rules."

Roussel, Roy. "The Project of Seduction and the Equality of the Sexes in *Les Liaisons dangereuses." Modern Language Notes* 96, no. 4 (May, 1981): 725-745. Presents an argument that seduction almost wishes not to succeed, since the process itself is enjoyable. Seducers seek to define themselves against traditional codes that demonstrate their arbitrary nature.

DANIEL DERONDA

Type of work: Novel
Author: George Eliot (Mary Ann Evans, 1819-1880)
Type of plot: Social realism
Time of plot: Mid-nineteenth century
Locale: Rural England, London, and the Continent
First published: 1876

Principal characters:
DANIEL DERONDA
MIRAH LAPIDOTH, a girl he saves from drowning
SIR HUGO MALLINGER, Daniel's guardian
LADY MALLINGER, his wife
GWENDOLEN HARLETH, a beautiful young lady
MRS. DAVILOW, her mother
MRS. GASCOIGNE, Mrs. Davilow's sister
MR. GASCOIGNE, her husband
REX, their son
ANNA, their daughter
MALLINGER GRANDCOURT, Gwendolen's husband and Sir Hugo's heir
LUSH, his follower
HERR KLESMER, a musician
CATHERINE ARROWPOINT, his wife and an heiress
HANS MEYRICK, one of Deronda's friends
MRS. MEYRICK, his mother
EZRA COHEN, a shopkeeper in the East End
MORDECAI, a boarder with the Cohens and Mirah's brother
MRS. LYDIA GLASHER, Grandcourt's former mistress

The Story:

Gwendolen Harleth, a strikingly beautiful young woman, was gambling at Leubronn. Playing with a cold, emotionless style, she had been winning consistently. Her attention was suddenly caught by the stare of a dark, handsome gentleman whom she did not know and who seemed to be reproving her. When her luck changed and she lost all her money, she returned to her room to find a letter from her mother requesting her immediate return to England. Before she left, Gwendolen decided that she would have one more fling at the gaming tables. She sold her turquoise necklace for the money to play roulette, but before she could get to the tables, the necklace was repurchased and returned to her with an anonymous note. Certain that the unknown man was her benefactor, she felt that she could not very well return to the roulette table. She went back to England as soon as she could. Her mother had recalled her because the family had lost all their money through unwise business speculations.

A high-spirited, willful, accomplished, and intelligent young woman, Gwendolen was Mrs. Davilow's only child by her first marriage and her favorite of all her children. By her second marriage to Mr. Davilow, who was now dead, she had had four colorless, spiritless daughters. About one year earlier, she had moved to Offendene to be near her sister and brother-in-law, the prosperous, socially acceptable Gascoignes and because she wished to arrange a profitable marriage for her oldest daughter. Gwendolen's beauty and manner had impressed all the surrounding gentry. Her first victim had been her affable cousin Rex Gascoigne, who had been willing to give up his career at Oxford for Gwendolen. His family refused to sanction this unwise move, however, and Rex, broken in spirit, was sent away for the time being. Gwendolen remained unmoved by the whole affair.

Soon afterward, the county became excited over the visit of Mallinger Grandcourt, the somewhat aloof, unmarried heir to Diplow and several other large properties owned by Sir Hugo Mallinger. All the young ladies were eager to get Grandcourt to notice them, but it was Gwendolen, apparently indifferent and coy in her conversation, whom the well-mannered but monosyllabic Grandcourt courted for several weeks. Gwendolen's mother, uncle, and aunt urged her to try to secure Grandcourt, and just when it seemed that Grandcourt would propose and Gwendolen accept, Mrs. Lydia Glasher appeared. Grandcourt's scheming companion, Lush, had brought Mrs. Glasher to tell Gwendolen that she had left her husband to live with Grandcourt and was now the mother of four of his illegitimate children. She begged Gwendolen not to accept Grandcourt so that she might have the chance to secure him as the rightful father of her children. Gwendolen, promising not to stand in Mrs. Glasher's way, had gone immediately to join friends at Leubronn.

Before he came to Leubronn, Daniel Deronda, the man whom Gwendolen had encountered in the gambling casino, had been Sir Hugo Mallinger's ward. He did not know his parents, but Sir Hugo had always treated him well. Sir Hugo, who had married late in life, had only daughters. Although he lavished a great deal of expense and affection on Deronda, his property was to go to his nephew, Mallinger Grandcourt. At Cambridge, Deronda had been extremely popular. There, he had earned the undying gratitude of a poor student named Hans Meyrick, whom Deronda helped to win a scholarship at the expense of his own studies. One day after leaving Cambridge while in a boat on the river, Deronda saved a pale and frightened young woman, Mirah Lapidoth, from committing suicide. She told him that she was a Jewess who had returned after years of wandering with a brutal and blasphemous father to look for her lost and fondly remembered mother and brother in London. Deronda took her to Mrs. Meyrick's home, where Mrs. Meyrick and her daughters nursed the penniless Mirah back to health.

When Gwendolen returned to Offendene, she learned that her family would be forced to move to a small cottage and that she would have to become a governess. The idea oppressed her so strongly that when she saw Grandcourt, who had been pursuing her on the Continent, she agreed at once to marry him in spite of her promise to Mrs. Glasher. Her mother, aunt, and uncle knew nothing of Mrs. Glasher; Grandcourt knew only that she had spoken to Gwendolen, knowledge that he kept to himself.

After their marriage, Grandcourt was revealed to be a mean, domineering, and demanding man. He set out to break Gwendolen's spirit. In the meantime, at several house parties, Gwendolen met Daniel Deronda and found herself much attracted to him. At a New Year's party at Sir Hugo Mallinger's, Gwendolen, despite her husband's disapproval and biting reprisals, spoke to Deronda frequently. When she told him her whole story and confessed having broken her promise to Mrs. Glasher, Deronda suggested that she show her repentance by living a less selfish life and begin to care for and help those less fortunate than she. Gwendolen, realizing the folly of her marriage to Grandcourt and wishing to find some measure of happiness and peace, decided to follow the course Deronda had proposed.

Meanwhile, Deronda was attempting to secure Mirah's future and, if possible, to find her family. Mirah had been an actress and had some talent for singing. Deronda arranged an interview for her with Herr Klesmer, a German-Jewish musician with many connections, who could get Mirah started on a career. Herr Klesmer was very much impressed with Mirah's singing. He had known Gwendolen at Offendene and had refused to help her when she had asked for singing engagements because he had thought her without sufficient talent; that had been the first blow to Gwendolen's ego. Herr Klesmer had married Miss Arrowpoint, next to Gwendolen the most talented and attractive girl in Offendene.

Still trying to find Mirah's family, Deronda wandered in the London East End. There he became friendly with the family of Ezra Cohen, a crafty but generous shopkeeper. On the basis of some slight evidence, Deronda for a time believed that the man might be Mirah's brother. Through Ezra's family, he also met Mordecai, a feeble and learned man, with whom he immediately felt a great kinship. Mordecai took Deronda to a meeting of his club, a group of men who discussed scholarly, political, and theological topics.

Deronda was delighted when he learned that Mordecai was really Mirah's brother. This discovery helped Deronda to acknowledge and accept his own spiritual and literal kinship with the Jews. The boy of unknown origin, able to move successfully in the high society of England, had found his real home in London's East End.

Critical Evaluation:

George Eliot published her last novel, *Daniel Deronda*, in 1876, shortly after the highly successful *Middlemarch* (1872). The novel chronicles the growth in consciousness of a self-conscious and self-seeking young man, Daniel Deronda, whose moral perception broadens as he becomes aware of his own identity and his mission as a Jew. His growth is encouraged by Mordecai, who is the incarnation of what unifies the Jews and who reflects George Eliot's sympathetic understanding.

Deronda's growth in consciousness and sympathetic understanding are mirrored in and facilitated by Gwendolen Harleth's parallel growth from utter selfishness to a broader and deeper sense of herself and her fellows. Deronda's growing ability to communicate with her and to experience mutual understanding prepares him for the deeper affinity that he comes to feel for Mordecai and his dreams of Jewish nationalism.

As of the very first reviews, many critics saw the novel as being divided into two parts: the Daniel Deronda or Jewish part, which includes Mirah and Mordecai, and the Gwendolen Harleth or English part, which includes Grandcourt. Almost everyone found fault with the character and mission of Deronda and described him as being effeminate, wooden, lifeless, helpless, pedantic, clumsy, unsatisfying, analytical, vague, and tentative; he was described as lacking vitality and as being too theorizing, melodramatic, and dull. At the same time the English part was highly praised, and Gwendolen was judged to be one of the most successful heroines Eliot had created. Critics found Gwendolen Harleth to be charming, interesting, and psychologically realistic. Indeed, among George Eliot's women, Gwendolen is the most rebellious against patriarchal traditions, and her struggle to overcome her egoism and learn submission is totally believable.

Even the style and philosophy of the two parts of the novel have been compared for their differences. The Deronda part is idealistic and deals in allegorical and epic terms with the history and the heritage of the Jewish people; the Gwendolen part is realistic in every sense.

Deronda's Jewish heritage is effectively used to symbolize the principles of solidarity that underline George Eliot's moral message. Many readers have responded positively and with appreciation to Eliot's extensive knowledge of Jewish culture, the depth of her Talmudic studies, and her sympathetic treatment of the plight of the Jews in Britain (the character Daniel Deronda was thought to be patterned after Benjamin Disraeli and Deronda's mother after Disraeli's mother).

The unifying element for both plots is found in the use of imagery and other artistic devices that incorporate both plots into the major theme and demonstrate the growth in sympathetic understanding that Deronda and Gwendolen exhibit. Both characters are in the crisis of alienation and acquisition of self until they gradually learn to recognize their own identities and intended purposes; in the course of that, each learns submission. Their heritage is revealed in relation to their mothers and in their growing sexual awareness. Patterns of imagery involving vision, light, eyesight, and reflecting pools and glasses define and chronicle their growing self-perception and insight into the hearts of others.

As the characters experience the inner conflict between sympathy and selfishness, references to and experiences with theater and music help enlarge their sympathies. River imagery is used in many ways. At first the characters are merely drifting with a lack of purpose, but as they mature, they begin to row energetically. Bridges of understanding develop in meetings that take place on actual bridges. Other significant patterns of images that delineate the growth of sympathy involve specific reactions to gems and precious stones and the interpretation of writing, texts, and language. Dreams chronicle crises in spiritual growth, and sensuous relationships provide opportunities to analyze morality within complex social networks.

Daniel Deronda grows as he becomes Gwendolen's moral leader and helps her to outgrow her narrow egoism; being directed by his nobler nature and seeing him assume his cosmic role shocks her into an awareness of self. She learns to accept her own limitations, to fulfill her obligations to her mother and others, to outgrow her dependence on Deronda, and to stand alone. She is released from the bondage of her marriage to the sinister Grandcourt. Deronda's involvement with Gwendolen serves as a catalyst to bring him to admit that Mirah is the woman he loves and to usher him into his public role. Both Deronda and Gwendolen learn that to lose one's life is to find it.

As a young man, Deronda believed he was the illegitimate child of Sir Hugo Mallinger, who has raised him as his son. By the time Deronda goes to Genoa to learn the truth about his birth, he has been prepared in every possible way to receive the knowledge that his mother, Madame Alcharisi, imparts to him. Even though she has neglected her duty to her race and to her family, her son is mature enough to be glad that he is a Jew. He is ready to learn more of her personal and national heritage from the manuscripts and family records in the trunk that her grandfather had preserved for him, and he allows Mordecai to interpret the documents to him and instruct him in the meaning of her inheritance.

George Eliot's last novel is a powerful and in some ways inspired work, as fascinating for its defects as for its successes, since both reflect not only the author's established strengths as a novelist but also her inventiveness and willingness to explore new areas and strive for greater depth and breadth in her fiction. *Daniel Deronda* shares with its predecessors a penetrating insight into human relationships, a sensitive portrayal of individual moral and emotional growth, an astute and critical analysis of Victorian values, and a unifying moral vision of life.

"Critical Evaluation" by Constance M. Fulmer

Bibliography:
Caron, James. "The Rhetoric of Magic in *Daniel Deronda*." *Studies in the Novel* 15, no. 1 (Spring, 1983): 1-9. Reprinted in *The Critical Response to George Eliot*, edited by Karen L. Pangallo. Westport, Conn.: Greenwood Press, 1994. Argues that Eliot's techniques and rhetoric support her theme of characters moving toward ideal humanity, and that she uses such elements from romance as evil, witches, sorcery, and divination to fuse ideas and actions.

Pell, Nancy. "The Fathers' Daughters in *Daniel Deronda.*" *Nineteenth Century Fiction* 36, no. 4 (March, 1982): 424-451. Pell reviews the theme of inheritance and family relations, as well as women's difficulties in establishing cultural and social legitimacy within a patriarchal society.

Swann, Brian. "Eyes in the Mirror: Imagery and Symbolism in *Daniel Deronda.*" *Nineteenth Century Fiction* 23 (1969): 434-445. Swann interprets the novel as a drama of damnation and salvation and of the acquisition of selfhood and the establishment of standards and values.

Weisser, Susan Ostrov. "Gwendolen's Hidden Wound: Sexual Possibilities and Impossibilities in *Daniel Deronda.*" *Modern Language Studies* 20, no. 3 (Summer, 1990): 3-13. Weisser examines the treatment of restraint and self-interest in relation to sexuality.

Zimmerman, Bonnie. "Gwendolen Harleth and 'The Girl of the Period.'" In *George Eliot: Centenary Essays and an Unpublished Fragment*, edited by Anne Smith. Totowa, N.J.: Barnes & Noble, 1980. This analysis of Gwendolen's role describes her as the culmination of Eliot's theory on women; she is Eliot's most rebellious and egoistic heroine and receives the most dreadful punishment.

DANTON'S DEATH

Type of work: Drama
Author: Georg Büchner (1813-1837)
Type of plot: Tragedy
Time of plot: Spring, 1794
Locale: Paris
First published: Dantons Tod, 1835 (English translation, 1927); first performed, 1902

> *Principal characters:*
> GEORGES DANTON and
> CAMILLE DESMOULINS, deputies of the National Convention
> ROBESPIERRE and
> SAINT-JUST, members of the Committee of Public Safety
> JULIE, Danton's wife
> LUCILLE, Desmoulins' wife
> MARION, a prostitute

The Story:

The action occurred between March 24 and April 5, 1794, during the French Revolution's Reign of Terror. Georges Danton, who had raised armies that had saved the Republic, had become indifferent to politics, yet he retained sufficient popularity to pose a threat to the extremist Revolutionary leader Robespierre, who gained and kept power by executing leaders of his opposition.

Danton, several friends, and their ladies exchanged witticisms as they played cards through most of a night. At the same time, Camille Desmoulins tried to bring Danton back into the political arena to lead the attack against Robespierre's totalitarian faction. Meanwhile Robespierre invited citizens to follow him to the Jacobin Club, where he dominated the Committee of Public Safety. At the club, Robespierre proclaimed in a long tirade that he was an incorruptible leader and that his government was forced to proceed despotically against the villainy of Royalists, foreigners, and other enemies. To punish such oppressors of humankind was mercy, he insisted; to forgive them would be stupid and even barbaric. He maintained that the French Republic needed to deploy weapons of terror to save its ideals, and he asked his listeners to trust his policies.

Instead of opposing Robespierre, Danton preferred to flirt with the prostitute Marion, who rhapsodized the joys of the body in a monologue in which she compared herself to a sea that swallowed all men. Danton's moderate friends, who had heard Robespierre's impassioned oratory, warned him of the latter's enmity, but Danton only shrugged off their advice, certain that Robespierre's people would not dare arrest him. When the two leaders met in debate, Danton urged Robespierre to stop his massive slaughter of alleged conspirators, while the latter countered that a Revolution that was only half-finished was digging its own grave. After Danton left the room, Robespierre, in an extended soliloquy, convinced himself that even though some people might accuse him of acting out of personal jealousy, Danton was a threat to the Republic and had to be eliminated.

The Committee of Public Safety ordered the arrests of the Dantonists. Instead of fleeing or fighting, Danton remained passive and introspective, brooding remorsefully about the bloodshed of the September, 1793, massacres of Royalists, for which he took responsibility. His wife, Julie, reminded him that he had thereby saved the nation, but he remained unconvinced that those massive executions had been necessary. At the National Convention, Robespierre sought to justify his decision to move against Danton's group. He compared himself to Moses leading his people into the desert on their way to the promised land.

Danton and a number of his associates were now imprisoned, joining friends and acquaintances who had previously been arrested. Formally arraigned by Robespierre's subordinates, Danton demanded that his accusers appear before him. The session of the Revolutionary Tribunal adjourned without granting his demand. Robespierre's leading deputy, Saint-Just, then "discovered" a plot by the Dantonists to blow up the National Convention. The Dantonists were thereupon condemned to the guillotine, even though Danton publicly accused Robespierre's Committee of Public Safety of high treason.

Awaiting execution, Danton meditated extensively on death and bade farewell to his beloved body, about to become a "broken fiddle." He prophesied that Robespierre's violent death would follow his within six months, a historically accurate forecast. As the Dantonists were taken by cart to the execution square, they bantered among themselves and forgave one another's sins. After the guillotine had done its grisly work, Desmoulins' wife, Lucille, deliberately shouted, "Long live the King!" She was immediately arrested as a Royalist, sure to share her husband's fatal fate.

Critical Evaluation:

Georg Büchner's life was brief but intense, and his extraordinary talents merit no less than the word genius. Before he died of typhoid fever at the age of twenty-three, he had obtained a doctorate in philosophy, taught comparative anatomy at the University of Zurich, been formidably active as a political revolutionary, composed scientific papers, translated two dramas by Victor Hugo into his native German, and outlined a course of lectures on the history of German philosophy. Above all, he had written three plays and one story that mark him as one of Germany's, indeed Europe's, most brilliant authors.

Büchner's impact was felt, directly or indirectly, by virtually every important playwright after him. He can be studied as a forerunner of naturalism, social realism, psychological irrationalism, expressionism, existentialism, and the theater of the absurd. In the search for the taproot of twentieth century drama, one need dig no further than his texts.

Danton's Death may well be the best first play ever written. It is profound, relentless, passionate, eloquent, complex, and tragic. Above all, it is remarkably original, even though Büchner was influenced by earlier German dramatists and by William Shakespeare. Like Johann Wolfgang Von Goethe's *Götz von Berlichingen* (1773), *Danton's Death* presents a vast historical panorama composed of short, episodic, loosely connected scenes, and with broad strokes it achieves a fullness and earthiness of detail and creates a multitude of characters. Goethe's *Götz*, however, is an idealized robber baron, and his play demonstrates the possibility of heroic action; Büchner's Danton is an antihero and this work shows extreme skepticism about the feasibility of heroism.

The playwright who most clearly commanded Büchner's admiration is Shakespeare. Danton's self-communing soliloquies go straight back to Hamlet's. Like Hamlet, Danton is passive, introspective, melancholy, bored, witty, morbid, and prone to subject the assumptions of others to ironic analysis. Büchner's Lucille, when she gives way to hysteria, recapitulates Ophelia's mad scene. And Büchner casts the French Revolution in the Roman world of such Shakespearean texts as *Julius Caesar* (1599), *Antony and Cleopatra* (1607), and *Coriolanus* (1608); each of these features, as *Danton's Death* does, a recklessly blind protagonist and coarse, obscene, easily swayed mobs.

Büchner is faithful to respected scholarly sources for the struggle between Danton and Robespierre that occurred in France during the early 1790's. His primary historic debt is to F. A. Mignet's *Histoire de la Révolution française* (1826) and L. A. Thiers' *Histoire de la Révolution française* (1825-1827). He derived many of the external events in *Danton's Death* from these sources and sometimes reproduces verbatim whole speeches by the historic Danton. His portrait is historically accurate in featuring Danton's joviality, generosity, passionate temperament, hedonism, and carelessness in courting danger. His stress on Danton's laziness, fatalism, sensuality, and disillusionment has aspects that are both traditional and contemporary.

Büchner is highly original, however, in presenting Danton as an unheroic hero who, even when capable of stirring action, chooses not to engage in it. Because of his disillusionment with politics and human nature, his only desire is for death. Unlike such classic, developing heroes as Oedipus or Lear, the static Danton fails to experience any moments of insight or recognition, and he does not begin in an initial state of innocence or ignorance from which, as a result of the dramatic action, he enters the world of experience and increased knowledge. Without choosing to wrestle with his fate, Danton indicates repeatedly that he has come to regard all human behavior as ultimately futile, doomed to destruction, without hope or reason. Each man, he declares, is isolated in his impenetrable shell, unable to come to know his fellow, adrift on a sea of anguish and desolation.

The play's first scene illustrates this pessimism and Büchner's adroit juggling of dramatic styles. The initial conversation, ostensibly about love, is loaded with wit and bawdry. Julie, Danton's devoted wife, is concerned about his cynicism. "Don't you believe in me?" she asks him. He replies:

> How should I know! We know little enough about one another. We're thick-skinned creatures who reach out our hands toward one another, but it means nothing—leather rubbing against leather—we're very lonely.

The apprehensive Julie tries to obtain emotional reassurance from her husband, but he refuses to comfort her, instead asserting that for people to know one another, it would be necessary to crack open their skills and draw forth their thoughts one by one from their brain fissures. Danton will restate the same idea several times in the play.

Büchner's plot is anti-Aristotelian, in that the central emotional crisis of the drama is not released through the contrivances of plot structure. Instead of being clearly organized with a beginning, middle, and end, the text begins at the end of the middle and continues as one extended end. Robespierre organizes the accusations against the Dantonists, followed by their arrest, trial, and execution. Danton, by contrast, refuses to offer any resistance and thereby resigns himself to his fate. What the play amounts to is a slow dance of death, with Danton invoking life's nullity in richly metaphoric imagery as he prepares himself for extinction.

The pervasive dramatic confrontation is in the opposed temperaments of Robespierre and Danton. Büchner shows the former as a damaged psychopath who projects his vengeful, aggressive impulses on others and sees himself as a divinely appointed instrument of justice who can do no wrong. His language anticipates the twentieth century rhetoric of totalitarianism: It is loaded with absolute assertions and dogmatic clichés, devoid of humor, and dominated by abstractions such as "virtue," "immorality," and "the healthy strength of the people." While Robespierre is prepared to sacrifice any number of people to what he is convinced is his absolutely necessary program, Danton refuses to set in motion any further acts of political violence, resigned instead to the futility of politics and history.

Although he is the passive antihero, Danton is mentally and morally superior to his opponent. He jibes at Robespierre's pomposity, jokes with the mob, eschews self-pity, and contrives an endless succession of striking metaphors to express his stoic resignation. He uses wit as an alternative to anger and dilutes his despair in affectionate teasing of his friends. In the conflict between these leaders, Büchner achieves a timeless, universal polarity between the impatient zealot filled with self-righteous fervor and the weary humanist who can no longer believe in a better life to come.

Gerhard Brand

Bibliography:
Hamburger, Michael. "Georg Büchner." In *Contraries: Studies in German Literature.* New York: Dutton, 1970. Hamburger is a distinguished critic and translator of German literature. His essay focuses on the profound boredom that saps the willpower of Büchner's heroes.
Hilton, Julian. *Georg Büchner.* New York: Grove Press, 1982. Hilton pays special attention to the scenic structure of *Danton's Death* and to Büchner's influence on such contemporary playwrights as Bertolt Brecht, John Arden, and David Storey.
Knight, A. H. F. *Georg Büchner.* Oxford, England: Basil Blackwell, 1951. This is the first full-length study of Büchner in English. It examines all of Büchner's writings thoroughly, including his letters. In the discussion of *Danton's Death*, Knight examines at length Büchner's use of historic sources.
Lindenberger, Herbert. *Georg Büchner.* Carbondale: Southern Illinois University Press, 1964. Lindenberger writes gracefully and perceptively, with particular sensitivity to Büchner's uses of rhetoric and dramatic form. His chapter on Büchner's forebears and descendants is illuminating.
Schwartz, Alfred. *From Büchner to Beckett: Dramatic Theory and the Modes of Tragic Drama.* Athens: Ohio University Press, 1978. Schwartz distinguishes and traces various patterns of tragedy. He examines Büchner's kaleidoscopic art of composition, in which each scene expresses the violent assaults of history on people's lives.

DAPHNIS AND CHLOË

Type of work: Fiction
Author: Longus (fl. third century C.E.)
Type of plot: Pastoral
Time of plot: Indeterminate
Locale: Island of Lesbos
First transcribed: Poimenika ta kata Daphnin kai Chloen, third century C.E. (English translation, 1587)

Principal characters:
DAPHNIS, a young shepherd
CHLOË, a shepherdess

The Story:

On the Greek island of Lesbos, a goatherd named Lamo one day found a richly dressed infant boy being suckled by one of his goats. Lamo and his wife, Myrtale, hid the purple cloak and ivory dagger the boy had worn and pretended he was their own son. They named him Daphnis. Two years later, a shepherd named Dryas discovered an infant girl being nursed by one of his sheep in a cave of the nymphs. This child also was richly dressed. Dryas and his wife, Nape, kept the girl as their own, giving her the name Chloë.

When the two children were fifteen and thirteen years old respectively, they were given flocks to tend. Daphnis and Chloë played happily together, amusing themselves in many ways. One day, while chasing a goat, Daphnis fell into a wolf pit, from which he was rescued unharmed by Chloë and a herdsman she had summoned to help her. Daphnis began to experience delightful but disturbing feelings about Chloë. Dorco, a herdsman, asked permission to marry Chloë but was refused by Dryas. Disguising himself in a wolf skin, Dorco shortly afterward attempted to seize Chloë. Attacked by the flock dogs, he was rescued by Daphnis and Chloë, who innocently thought he had merely been playing a prank. Love, little understood by either, grew between Daphnis and Chloë.

In the autumn some Tyrian pirates wounded Dorco, stole some of his oxen and cows, and took Daphnis away with them. Chloë, who heard Daphnis calling to her from the pirate ship, ran to aid the mortally wounded Dorco. Dorco gave her his herdsman's pipe, telling her to blow upon it. When she blew, the cattle jumped into the sea and overturned the ship. The pirates drowned, but Daphnis, catching on to the horns of two swimming cows, came safely to shore.

After the celebration of the autumn vintage, Daphnis and Chloë returned to their flocks. They attempted in their innocence to practice the art of love, but they were not successful. Some young men of Methymne came to the fields of Mitylene to hunt. When a withe used as a cable to hold their small ship was gnawed in two by a goat, the Methymneans blamed Daphnis and set upon him. In a trial over the affair, Daphnis was judged innocent. The angry Methymneans later carried away Chloë. The god Pan warned the Methymnean captain in a dream that he should bring back Chloë, and she was returned. Daphnis and Chloë joyfully celebrated holidays in honor of Pan.

The two lovers were sad at being parted by winter weather, which kept the flocks in their folds. In the spring the lovers happily drove their flocks again to the fields. When a woman named Lycaenium became enamored of the boy, Daphnis finally learned how to ease the pains he had felt for Chloë; but Lycaenium warned him that Chloë would be hurt the first time she experienced the ecstasy of love. Through fear of doing physical harm to his sweetheart, the tender Daphnis would not deflower his Chloë. Meanwhile, many suitors, Lampis among them, asked for the hand of Chloë, and Dryas almost consented. Daphnis bewailed his inability to compete successfully with the suitors because of his poverty. With the aid of the nymphs he then found a purse of silver, which he gave Dryas in order to become contracted to Chloë. In return, Dryas asked Lamo to consent to the marriage of his son, but Lamo answered that first he must consult his master, Dionysophanes.

Lamo, Daphnis, and Chloë prepared to entertain Dionysophanes; but Lampis ravaged the garden they had prepared because he had been denied Chloë's hand. Fearing the wrath of his master, Lamo lamented his ill fortune. Eudromus, a page, helped to explain the trouble to Lamo's young master Astylus, who promised to intercede with his father and blame the wanton destruction on some horses in the neighborhood. Astylus' parasite, Gnatho, fell in love with Daphnis but was repulsed. Finally, the depraved Gnatho received Astylus' permission to take Daphnis with him to the city. Just in time, Lamo revealed the story of the finding of Daphnis, who was discovered to be Dionysophanes' son. Meanwhile, Lampis stole Chloë, who was later rescued by Gnatho. After Dryas told how Chloë had been found as a child, it was learned that she was the daughter of Megacles of Mitylene. Thus the supposed son and daughter of Lamo and Dryas were revealed as the children of wealthy parents who were happy to consent to their marriage. The wedding was celebrated amid the rural scenes dear to both bride and groom. Daphnis became Philopoemen, and Chloë was named Agele. On her wedding night Chloë at last learned from Daphnis how the delights of love might be obtained.

Critical Evaluation:

Daphnis and Chloë (the work has also been translated as *The Pastoral Loves of Daphnis and Chloë*, 1924, and as *The Story of Daphnis and Chloë*, 1908) first appeared in English in a version by Richard Waldegrave in 1587, but the translation made by George Thornley in 1657 is more familiar. More recent translations by George Moore and Jack Lindsay are considerably more readable but have not enjoyed wide circulation. *Daphnis and Chloë* was an influential work throughout Renaissance Europe, its subject matter and style being respectfully recapitulated in pastoral romances produced in the vernacular throughout Europe. Like many late classical works, however—the most notorious examples are credited to Petronius and Lucian—*Daphnis and Chloë* came to be considered an indecent work because of its relative frankness about sex. For this reason the English text retired for a while in the nineteenth and early twentieth centuries into the shady realm of privately printed editions. Unlike the satires of Petronius and Lucian, however, *Daphnis and Chloë* contains nothing deliberately coarse or obscene; its allegory of the growth and maturation of sexual love is handled with scrupulous delicacy that seems intended to avoid giving offense.

Although the labored and archaic style of the Thornley translation obscures the fact, *Daphnis and Chloë* is in several ways a strikingly modern work. It has better claims to be considered the first protonovel than any other work of classical literature. Its plot—which comprises an event-crowded obstacle course that continually parts the two lovers but finally delivers them to a marriage blessed with unexpected wealth and status—foreshadows the formula that has by far been the most successful in the popular fiction of more than a century. It is also one of the earliest works to take it for granted that the life of rural folk needs to be tactfully explained and sentimentally glorified for the benefit of a thoroughly "civilized" (in its literal sense of city-bred) audience. The nostalgic reverence for the pastoral in *Daphnis and Chloë* is identical in spirit to that which infects a great deal of nineteenth and twentieth century fiction; even its disapproval of Gnatho's homosexuality is far more reminiscent of modern attitudes than of what are usually thought of as the attitudes of ancient Greece.

What remains classical about *Daphnis and Chloë* is its careful use of allegory, particularly in its use of the Greek pantheon. Its invocation of Pan is, however, self-consciously metaphorical and artificial. Unlike the dramas of several centuries earlier, in which the gods are treated with reverent awe as overlords of human destiny, the attitude of *Daphnis and Chloë* is conspicuously casual. This offhandedness is a natural partner of the somewhat anecdotal style of early prose fiction, but it is as much a cause as an effect. The author can refer to the gods without excessive stylization because he is fully conscious of the fact that they are, for him, symbolic. His account of the myth of Echo and the tale of Pan and Syrinx assumes that the audience knows them as fables or amusing stories. When Pan afflicts the Methymneans with the panic named after him, he acts as a friend doing a favor, not as a loftily offended god wreaking havoc upon human playthings.

It is not merely Pan's name that is carefully diminished by the author of the romance; the names "Daphnis" and "Chloë" have their own significance. One attribute of the name "Chloë" is "Blooming," and it has been used as a surname of the goddess Demeter, protectress of the green fields. The original Daphnis was the alleged son of Hermes and a nymph, who was brought up by the nymphs and taught by Pan to play the flute; he became a shepherd and the inventor of bucolic poetry. Pan symbolizes nature; the names allotted to the hero and heroine of the story symbolize agriculture and animal husbandry. As the plot finally emphasizes, these are essentially technologies, but they are products of civilization which must work within the framework of nature. Necessity rules that they must be harmonized, at least to some extent, with nature's wildness and seasonally patterned fecundity. The nostalgic manner of the tale is a gentle reminder to a civilized audience that all their triumphs of artifice and manners remain rooted in the soil and the pastures.

There remains in all this a certain honest reverence, but it is a buoyant politeness rather than the somber and fatalistic reverence of Greek tragedy. The name that Daphnis takes after his marriage, Philopoemen, would also have been well known to the original hearers of the tale, being that of the last great military leader Greece produced before losing its political independence. Having come into his proper heritage, Daphnis is transformed from herdsman to hero. This indicates nostalgia for an era when Greece was the fountainhead of civilization rather than a mere handmaiden of Rome.

Few people today would read *Daphnis and Chloë* for pleasure; the text is too cluttered and too discursive, the prose irredeemably primitive even in more sensitive and less florid translations than Thornley's. Those who read the tale for instructive purposes, however, cannot help but notice that in almost everything that is currently read for pleasure some echo of *Daphnis and Chloë* sounds. The message that it puts across is still being broadcast. To say that it stands as the remote ancestor of all modern romance stories is not to insult it but rather to confirm that it contains the seeds of a vast and flourishing literary growth, and is—in its assiduously modest fashion—a great work.

"Critical Evaluation" by Brian Stableford

Bibliography:
Barber, Giles. *Daphnis and Chloë: The Markets and Metamorphoses of an Unknown Bestseller.* London: The British Library, 1989. The text of the 1988 Panizzi Lectures. A fascinating study of the bibliographic history of the work and its reception by various audiences.

Longus. *Daphnis and Chloë.* Translated by Jack Lindsay. London: Daimon Press, 1948. Lindsay discusses in an essay the mythological background of the story, comparing Greek nature myths to Babylonian and Celtic ones, and analyzing the significance of the names contained in the narrative.

_____. *Daphnis and Chloë.* Translated by George Thornley and with an introduction by J. M. Edwards. New York: Putnam, 1924. The Thornley translation is revised and augmented by J. M. Edwards, whose introduction details the various manuscript sources. There is a useful appendix on the origins of the work.

_____. *The Pastoral Loves of Daphnis and Chloë.* Translated and with an introduction by George Moore. London: Heinemann, 1924. Moore's introduction is cast as a dialogue between himself and Thomas Whittaker, in which the merits of the text and the need for a new translation are considered at length.

_____. *The Story of Daphnis and Chloë.* Translated, annotated, and edited by W. D. Lowe. Cambridge, England: Deighton Bell, 1908. Perhaps the most useful edition for academic purposes, by courtesy of the elaborate annotations.

THE DARK JOURNEY

Type of work: Novel
Author: Julien Green (1900-   )
Type of plot: Psychological realism
Time of plot: Early twentieth century
Locale: France
First published: Leviathan, 1929 (English translation, 1929)

Principal characters:
    PAUL GUÉRET, a neurotic tutor
    ANGÈLE, a young laundress
    MADAME LONDE, a restaurant proprietress
    MONSIEUR GROSGEORGE, Guéret's employer
    MADAME GROSGEORGE, his wife
    FERNANDE, a young girl

The Story:

Paul Guéret was an incompetent, prematurely aged tutor hired to instruct the sickly, unintelligent son of a prosperous provincial family named Grosgeorge. Knowing himself to be a failure and tired of his wife, whom he no longer loved, he had hoped that life would be better in Chanteilles; within a month, however, he was just as wretched there as he had been in Paris, where his feelings of self-pity and frustration had often driven him into sordid love affairs. In Chanteilles, bored by his dreary surroundings, he soon found himself infatuated with Angèle, a young woman who worked in a laundry. Hoping to become her lover, he began to write letters asking her to meet him. Sometimes he followed her at a distance when she delivered the washing to her customers.

One night he accosted her at a footbridge on the outskirts of the town. Hating himself for his shabby clothes and stammering speech, he offered her a cheap ring stolen from his wife. Although she accepted the ring, the laundress did not encourage his attentions. His abrupt yet furtive ardor both attracted and repelled her.

That same night, Guéret went by chance to the Restaurant Londe in nearby Lorges. There Madame Londe, the proprietress, presided majestically behind her cashier's desk. A sly woman whose days were given over to spying and gossip, she delighted in alternately cajoling and bullying her patrons, who seemed to hold her resentfully in awe. When Guéret entered, she was disturbed because he was a stranger and she knew nothing about him. She refused to let him pay for his dinner and had him write his name in her account book. Her desire was to add him to her regular clientele.

Madame Londe's hold over her patrons was a sinister one, maintained through her niece, Angèle. Because the girl was indebted to her for food and a room, she forced Angèle to sell her favors to the regular customers of the restaurant. With knowledge thus gained of the guilt and secret vices of her patrons, Madame Londe was able to dictate to them as she pleased. Her own position as a procuress gave her no worry; her only concern was her lust for power over others.

Upset by his desire for Angèle, Guéret paid little attention to his duties as a tutor. André Grosgeorge was a poor student, but his mother shrewdly blamed Guéret for her son's slow progress. Madame Grosgeorge was a woman in whom the starved passions of her girlhood had turned to a tortured kind of love which found its outlet in cruelty and treachery. Because the husband whom she despised ignored her nagging tirades, she took special pleasure in beating her son and in humiliating Guéret.

Monsieur Grosgeorge felt sorry for the browbeaten tutor. Having guessed that Guéret was unhappily married, Grosgeorge bluntly advised him to find a mistress before he wasted his years in moping dullness. Grosgeorge admitted that that was the course he himself had followed. One day, he boastingly produced a note in which the writer asked Grosgeorge to meet her the next night. Guéret, staring at the letter, shook with suppressed rage. He recognized the scrawl as Angèle's handwriting.

After several meetings with Guéret, Angèle became more independent in her attitude toward Madame Londe. Because his conduct was quite different from that of other men who sought her favors, she no longer wished to sell herself in order to act as her aunt's informant. During a quarrel Angèle, who refused to keep an assignation the old woman had arranged, threatened to leave. Madame Londe was worried. Afraid that she would lose her hold over her patrons, she began to train Fernande, a twelve-year-old girl, to take Angèle's place.

Guéret returned to the Restaurant Londe. During the meal, he learned from the talk of the other diners that Angèle was Madame Londe's niece and that she had given herself to most of the men there. That night, driven to desperation by his knowledge, he broke into her bedroom. It was empty. When Madame Londe, aroused by his entry, screamed for help, he ran away and hid in a wood. On his way back to Chanteilles, he met Angèle. In a sudden, brutal fury, he picked up a branch and struck her until blood covered her face and head.

All that day he skulked beside the river. While he was sneaking back into town after dark, he met a feeble old man. Fearing capture, he seized the old man's stick and beat him to death. Filled with blind terror, he fled across the yards of unknown houses and through back streets of the town.

The neighborhood was shocked by the brutality of Guéret's crime, and for weeks the townspeople refused to venture into the streets at night. Angèle, disfigured for life, refused to give the name of her assailant and remained shut up in her room above the restaurant. Only Madame Grosgeorge scoffed at those who bolted their doors at dusk. Indeed, she seemed to relish the fact that the shabby, blundering tutor had scarred the face of her husband's mistress and violently disrupted the monotony of her own existence.

At last, the hue and cry diminished. Unable to stay away from Angèle, Guéret returned to the district. Madame Grosgeorge saw him near the footbridge and called after him that she would meet him there the next evening. Guéret did not appear, although she waited impatiently for more than an hour. Later, he came to her villa, and she, unknown to her husband, hid the fugitive in her private sitting room. She promised that she would give him money and some of her husband's clothing before she sent him away in the morning.

His presence in the house, however, gave her such strange satisfaction that she refused to let him go as she had promised. The next morning, she went to her sitting room and tried to talk to him about his crimes. When his answers showed only that he was still in love with Angèle, Madame Grosgeorge felt cheated. She had admired him for his violence, but she now despised him for his foolish passion. Again, she locked him in the room while she tried to decide what to do. Little Fernande came to deliver some laundry. On impulse, Madame Grosgeorge wrote a note telling Angèle that Guéret was in her house and asking that the police be called.

Madame Londe, always on the alert, intercepted the message and hurried to give the alarm. Angèle, learning what had happened, sent Fernande to warn the fugitive that he must escape at once. Meanwhile, Madame Grosgeorge had returned to Guéret. When he insisted that she let him go, she locked the door and threw the key out of the window. Then she told him that Angèle knew his whereabouts and that, if he were betrayed, the laundress would be to blame. She took a revolver from her desk, put it in her belt, and calmly prepared to write a letter. Fernande ran into the garden. Guéret, leaning out of the window, asked her to pick up the key and unlock the door. He then heard the sound of a shot behind him. Madame Grosgeorge had shot herself.

Critical Evaluation:

Writing always somewhat outside the mainstream of French (and American) fiction, Julien Green managed literally to survive most of his contemporaries, remaining active as a writer and granting frequent interviews well into his nineties. In Green's case, the happy accidents of longevity and sustained productivity assured a continued interest in his work, including those novels published near the start of his career. *The Dark Journey* was the third of Green's novels to be published while the author was still in his twenties. His early novels were marked by a sureness of touch rare for his age, especially in the creation and delineation of his characters. Green's characters imposed themselves upon the reader, drawing him or her deeply into a threatening reality that lurked just beneath the surface of everyday life. Thus do Guéret's yearnings, harmless enough at the start, pass quickly into obsession, violence, and murder.

Using shifting viewpoints, although always narrating in the third person, Green shows society as a potential danger zone of conflicting preoccupations and obsessions. Like some of the most memorable characters in Honoré de Balzac's multivolume *Comédie humaine* (1843-1846), written a century earlier, many of Green's personages tend to be monomaniacs, motivated by a single overriding passion. Unlike Balzac, however, Green presents his characters in inevitable conflict rather than in isolation, showing the society portrayed to be more menacing than entertaining. As Glenn Burne points out in his major survey of Green's work, of all the characters' preoccupations, Guéret's obsession with sex and love is, in a sense, the most normal. Like many of Green's featured characters, however, he proves hopelessly inarticulate, unable to communicate with Angèle or anyone else, perhaps because his lack of attractiveness, even if only self-perceived, has hampered his social development. In the hands of another writer, a character such as Guéret might prove comic or even sympathetic; for Green, however, he becomes and remains a danger both to himself and to others. Likewise, Madame Londe, whose peculiar lust for power might emerge as laughable in another context, poses dangers of which she herself might well be unaware. As Burne observes, the traditional concept of fate looms large in *The Dark Journey*, often invoked or blamed by the characters themselves as they proceed to their doom. No doubt, the characters' extreme self-centeredness has much to do with their fate; were any of them less self-absorbed, they might well find time to understand one another.

Although it precedes by at least a decade the more religious and mystical phases of Green's career as a novelist, *The Dark Journey* in many ways invites comparison with certain novels of François Mauriac, a frankly religious and Roman Catholic novelist in whose dark narratives God was most often revealed by his absence; in other words, the misadventures of Mauriac's characters, in the author's view, might well prepare them for the revelation or discovery of God. For the haunted, driven characters of *The Dark Journey*, however, no such revelation seems possible or even imaginable. The unrelieved bleakness of the moral and emotional landscape invites the reader to consider other options.

"Critical Evaluation" by David B. Parsell

Bibliography:

Burne, Glenn S. *Julian Green*. New York: Twayne, 1972. Provides a comprehensive overview of the first forty-five years of Green's career, culminating in his induction into the Académie Française in 1971. Provides a good interpretation of *The Dark Journey*.

Dunaway, John M. *The Metamorphosis of the Self: The Mystic, the Sensualist, and the Artist in the Works of Julien Green*. Lexington: University Press of Kentucky, 1978. Revised from a doctoral dissertation, Dunaway's study traces the sources and evolution of Green's narrative art. It deals only in passing with *The Dark Journey*, relating it to the prevalence of violence in Green's early fiction.

Peyre, Henri. *French Novelists of Today*. New York: Oxford University Press, 1967. Provides a good overview of Green's career, presenting him as standing outside both the French and the American traditions from which his work derives. Includes useful readings of Green's early and midcareer fiction.

Stokes, Samuel. *Julian Green and the Thorn of Puritanism*. New York: King's Crown Press, 1955. Stokes's volume, like Dunaway's, is a revised doctoral dissertation and the first full-length study of Green in English. It is still useful for the analysis of Green's religious evolution as reflected in his novels.

DARK LAUGHTER

Type of work: Novel
Author: Sherwood Anderson (1876-1941)
Type of plot: Psychological realism
Time of plot: 1920's
Locale: Old Harbor, Indiana
First published: 1925

Principal characters:
BRUCE DUDLEY, formerly John Stockton, a Chicago reporter
SPONGE MARTIN, a workman close to the grass roots
FRED GREY, owner of an automobile wheel factory
ALINE, his wife

The Story:

Bruce Dudley's name was not actually Bruce Dudley but John Stockton. He had grown tired of being John Stockton, reporter on a Chicago paper and married to Bernice. His wife, who worked on the same paper and wrote magazine stories on the side, thought him flighty, and he admitted it. He wanted adventure, and he wanted to go back to Old Harbor, the river town in Indiana where he had spent his childhood. With less than three hundred dollars, he left Chicago, Bernice, and his job on the paper. He picked up the name Bruce Dudley from two store signs in an Illinois town. After a trip down the Mississippi River to New Orleans, he went to Old Harbor and got a job varnishing automobile wheels in the Grey Wheel Company, which was owned by Fred Grey.

Working in the same room with Bruce was Sponge Martin, a wiry old fellow with a black mustache who lived a simple, elemental life. That was the reason, perhaps, why Bruce liked him so much. Sometimes when the nights were fair and the fish were biting, Sponge and his wife packed up sandwiches and moonshine whiskey and went down to the river. They would fish for a while and get drunk, and then Sponge's wife would make him feel like a young man again. Bruce wished he could be as happy and carefree as Sponge.

When Bruce had been making his way down the Mississippi, he had stayed for five months in an old house in New Orleans, where he watched African Americans and listened to their songs and laughter. It seemed to him, listening to them laughing their dark laughter, that they lived as simply as children and were happy.

Aline, the wife of Fred Grey, saw Bruce Dudley walking out the factory door one evening as she sat in her car waiting for Fred. She did not know who he was, but she remembered another man to whom she had felt attracted in the same way. In Paris, after the war, she had seen a man at Rose Frank's apartment whom she had wanted. Then she had married Fred, who was recovering from the shock of the war, even though he was not the man for whom she wished.

One evening, Bruce Dudley passed by the Grey home as Aline stood in the yard. He stopped and looked first at the house and then at Aline. Neither spoke, but something passed between them. They had found each other.

Aline, who had advertised for a gardener, hired Bruce after turning down several other applicants. Bruce had quit his job at the factory shortly before seeing her advertisement. When he first began to work for Aline, they both maintained some reserve, but each of them carried on many imaginary conversations with the other. Fred seemed to resent Bruce's presence on the grounds, but he said nothing to the man, and when he questioned his wife, he learned that she knew nothing of Bruce except that he was a good worker.

Aline watched her husband leave for the factory each morning and wondered how much he knew or guessed. She thought a great deal about her own life and about life in general. Her husband was no lover. Few women nowadays had true lovers. Modern civilization told people what they could not have, and people belittled what they could not possess. Because people did not have love, they made fun of it, were skeptical of it, and besmirched it. The play between Aline and the two men continued silently. Two black women who worked in Aline's house watched the proceedings. From time to time, they were heard laughing, and their dark laughter sounded mocking. White folks were queer, making life so complicated, whereas black people took what they wanted simply, openly, happily.

One day in June, after Fred had gone to march in a veterans' parade and the servants had gone to watch the parade, Aline and Bruce remained on the property alone. She sat and watched him work in the garden. Finally, when he looked at her, he followed her into the house through a door she purposely left open. Bruce had left the house before Fred returned, and he disappeared from Old Harbor.

Two months later, Aline told Fred she was expecting a child.

When Fred came home one evening in the early fall, he saw his wife and Bruce together in the garden. Aline calmly called to him and announced that the child she was expecting was not his. She and Bruce had waited, she went on, to let him know they were leaving. Fred pleaded with her to stay, knowing she was hurting herself, but they walked away; Bruce carried her two heavy bags.

Fred stood with his revolver in his hand a few minutes later, telling himself that he could not dispassionately let another man walk away with his wife. His mind was filled with confused anger, and for a moment he thought of killing himself. Then he followed the pair along the river road. He was determined to kill Bruce, but he lost sight of the two in the darkness. In a blind fury, he shot at the river. On the way back to his house, he stopped to sit on a log. The revolver fell to the ground, and for a long time he sat crying like a child.

After Fred had returned to his home and gone to bed, he tried to laugh at what had happened, but he could not. Outside in the road, he heard a sudden burst of laughter. It was the younger of the two black servants who worked in the Grey home. She cried out loudly that she had known it all the time, and again there came a burst of dark laughter.

Critical Evaluation:

Sherwood Anderson's *Dark Laughter* is a serious novel that emerged from the aftermath of World War I and reflects the literary and stylistic devices pioneered in that era. For writers, artists, and thinkers, World War I represented the end of intellectual, scientific, political, moral, and psychological certainties. Before the war, intellectuals considered Western culture to be the finest flowering and the highest expression of human civilization. In its barbarism and in the duration and intensity of its savagery, unprecedented in human history, the war shattered that belief. Scientific discoveries shook hitherto unquestioned assumptions about the Newtonian universe. Marx's theories and the Russian Revolution undermined confidence in social classes and political systems. Freud, by elaborating a theory of an active unconscious and an unconscious life, destroyed the idea that human beings were a given, known quantity.

All of these developments form the context for the movement in literature in which accepted patterns of characterization, sequence, and symbols were radically altered. It is in this context that Anderson's *Dark Laughter* can be understood best. In the novel. Anderson tries both to formulate a criticism of the old values made disreputable by the war and to set forth new values by which people could live.

Anderson establishes two dramatic poles in the novel: One embodies a natural, honest, sincere relationship to life; the other (embodying the old, prewar values) represents an artificial, mechanical, and dishonest approach. Fred Grey and Bernice Stockton are characters who lead superficial and distant lives. Grey imagines himself to be sensitive, cultured, and generous, but he is actually morally coarse, suspicious, and tightfisted. Above all, he is separated from the realities of life by his economic position and inner sterility.

Bernice Stockton, the wife from whom Bruce Dudley fled, is a variation of the same type. Her specialty is literature, but from hints of the story she is writing—a precious, unreal thing—it becomes clear that her characters and plot reflect her own superficial romanticism rather than the actual conditions of life. She is a member of an "in group" of writers and intellectuals, and Anderson indicates that this membership is more important to her than infusing her art with truth.

In contrast to these characters are Bruce Dudley, Sponge Martin, and, to some extent, Aline Grey. Anderson casts these people as representatives of the new, hopeful values that have come to life after the trauma of war. Sponge Martin and his wife, for example, have a genuine connection to real life. Their sexual life is natural and unaffected, they have few pretensions; and they are generous and simple. Dudley himself, the central character in the novel, is a writer more interested in the truth than in "word slinging." Leaving Bernice was a rejection of her literary pretensions. In falling in love with Aline, and fathering her child, he was answering the deeper, underlying currents in life.

For Aline, who vacillates between these poles, the marriage to Grey had represented a confused surrender to the conventional life. Running away with Dudley meant coming to terms with life as it is, not as it exists in the decadent literary circles of postwar France, in the romantic fantasies of her adolescence, or in the expected routines of upper-middle-class life in the United States.

It is clear that, just as Anderson is criticizing an outworn and mechanical value system, he is also criticizing an earlier literary tradition, which did not come to terms with the natural, primitive side of life or seek out and explore the unconscious. If literary tradition discusses only the superficial and agreeable aspects of life, then Anderson heartily disapproved of it. He hoped that *Dark Laughter* would support and represent a new literary tradition to correspond to the new postwar values.

Anderson himself admitted that *Dark Laughter* was influenced by James Joyce, for he used such modernist techniques as breaking sections of narrative into fragments, scattering parts of poems throughout the text, using subjective, semi-stream-of-consciousness narration, and switching points of view. As a matter of fact, the techniques employed in *Dark Laughter* probably reflect more generally the literary climate of the 1920's rather than a specifically Joycean influence.

Dark Laughter also displays certain negative features of the American literary climate of the 1920's, perhaps most visible among them a racist component in many passages. With his title *Dark Laughter*, Anderson refers to the natural, honest pole of human behavior that he espouses. Yet associated with this naturalness are "primitive," "uncivilized," and "amoral" qualities that Anderson links to black people. In fact, *Dark Laughter* refers to the laughter of black maids in the Grey household when they learn of Aline's adultery. Such prejudices, commonplace in the era in which *Dark Laughter* was written, need not overshadow the major intent of the book. *Dark Laughter* expresses an important opposition of ideas in mid-twentieth century literary terms: The reader is asked to choose between real life and superficial life; and, in that sense, Anderson has presented the reader with a profound moral choice.

"Critical Evaluation" by Howard Lee Hertz

Bibliography:
Anderson, David D. "Anderson and Myth (1976)." In *Critical Essays on Sherwood Anderson*, edited by David D. Anderson. Boston: G. K. Hall, 1981. Connects content to the writer's effort to define the myth underlying his own life. Concludes that in *Dark Laughter* Anderson is pleading for individualism in a materialistic America and that the novel is the rejection of rejection.

Burbank, Rex. *Sherwood Anderson*. New York: Twayne, 1964. An accessible text with a chapter-long consideration of *Dark Laughter* that gives historical context for the novel. Provides an effective interpretive plot summary and critical analysis of the work. Includes a preface and chronology, minimal notes and references, a selected bibliography, and an adequate index.

Flanagan, John T. "The Permanence of Sherwood Anderson." In *Critical Essays on Sherwood Anderson*, edited by David D. Anderson. Boston: G. K. Hall, 1981. Emphasizes the autobiographical nature of Anderson's fiction, connects his lifestyle to that of characters like Bruce Dudley, and addresses his writing style. Flanagan presents *Dark Laughter* in a positive light.

Townsend, Kim. *Sherwood Anderson*. Boston: Houghton Mifflin, 1987. An excellent literary view of the novel, including the influence of various writers. Sees Anderson as seeking complete identification with the "niggers" of his novel. Townsend evaluates the work as a failure, despite the fact that it captures the rhythms of life in the 1920's.

White, Ray Lewis. *Sherwood Anderson's Memoirs: A Critical Edition*. Chapel Hill: University of North Carolina Press, 1969. Collection offers a good selection of the writer's reflections on *Dark Laughter*. Includes an account of how the family maid, Kate, inspired the novel. Also includes a selected bibliography and index.

DARKNESS AT NOON

Type of work: Novel
Author: Arthur Koestler (1905-1983)
Type of plot: Social realism
Time of plot: 1930's
Locale: Russia
First published: 1940

> *Principal characters:*
> NICHOLAS RUBASHOV, a political prisoner
> IVANOV, a prison official
> GLETKIN, another official
> MICHAEL BOGROV, another prisoner
> KIEFFER (HARE-LIP), an informer
> NUMBER 1, the supreme leader of the party

The Story:

Nicholas Rubashov, former Commissar of the People and once a power in the party, was in prison. Arrested at his lodgings in the middle of the night, he had been taken secretly to cell 404, which bore his name on a card just above the spy hole. His cell was located in an isolation block for political suspects.

At seven o'clock in the morning, Rubashov was awakened by a bugle, but he did not get up. Soon he heard sounds in the corridor. He imagined that someone was to be tortured, and he dreaded hearing the first screams of pain. When the footsteps reached his own section, he saw through the eye hole that guards were serving breakfast. Rubashov did not receive any breakfast because he had reported himself ill. He began to pace up and down the cell, six and a half steps to the window, six and a half steps back.

Soon he heard a quiet knocking from the wall of the adjoining cell, 402. In communicating with one another, prisoners used the "quadratic alphabet," a square of twenty-five letters, five horizontal rows of five letters each. The first series of taps represented the number of the row; the second series the number of the letter in the row. Thus, words could be spelled. From the communications Rubashov had had with his neighbor, Rubashov had come to picture him as a military man, one not in sympathy with the methods of the great leader or with the views of Rubashov himself. From his window he saw prisoners walking in the courtyard for exercise. One of these, a man with a harelip, looked repeatedly up at Rubashov's window. From his neighbor in cell 402, Rubashov learned that Hare-Lip was a political prisoner who had been tortured in a steam bath the day before. A little later Hare-Lip, in cell 400, sent Rubashov his greetings, via the inmate of 402, but he would not give his name.

Three days later, Rubashov was brought up for his first examination. The examiner was Ivanov, Rubashov's old college friend and former battalion commander. During the interview the prisoner learned that he was accused of belonging to the opposition to the party and that he was suspected of an attempt on the party leader's life. Ivanov promised a twenty-year prison term instead of the death penalty if Rubashov confessed. The prisoner was given a fortnight to arrive at a decision.

After the hearing Rubashov was given paper and pencil. He used them to formulate his ideas on the party, society, and his own predicament. As he did so, he remembered a German called

Richard whom he had expelled from the party, thereby ensuring Richard's certain death at the hands of the Gestapo. Three weeks later, Rubashov himself had been arrested by the German police but had resisted giving any information despite hideous torture. Pacing his cell, he also cast his mind back on Little Loewy, a tireless advocate for the party in the Belgian ports. Rubashov had expelled him, too, for deviating from the party line, and Loewy had hanged himself. In a somber mood, Rubashov finally remembered Arlova, his secretary and mistress, whose cries for Rubashov's help he had totally ignored.

The night before the time set by Ivanov had expired, Rubashov felt a tenseness in the atmosphere. His friend in 402 communicated to him that one of the prisoners was to be shot. This prisoner was Michael Bogrov, who had always been Rubashov's close friend. As the condemned man was brought through the corridors, the prisoners tapped his progress from one cell to another and drummed on the doors of their cells as he passed. The beaten, whimpering figure of Bogrov came by Rubashov's cell. Rubashov heard his friend shout to him as his friend was dragged down the stairs.

Rubashov's second hearing took place late at night. Ivanov came to Rubashov's cell with a bottle of brandy and persuaded him that to keep faith with the living was better than betrayal of the dead. Accordingly, Rubashov wrote a letter to the Public Prosecutor renouncing his own oppositional attitude and acknowledging his errors. The third night after delivering the letter to the warder, Rubashov was awakened and taken to the office of Gletkin, another official of the prison. Under blinding lights in Gletkin's office, he was questioned day and night for an interminable period of time. He learned that Ivanov had been liquidated for conducting Rubashov's case negligently. Gletkin called in Hare-Lip as a witness against Rubashov. It was only with great difficulty that Rubashov recognized in that broken, cringing man the son of his former friend and associate, Kieffer. The bright spotlight, the lack of sleep, the constant questionings—these factors combined to make Rubashov sign a trumped-up charge that he had plotted to take the life of the party leader.

Rubashov had committed none of these crimes. He was merely the victim of Number 1's megalomania. One night he heard the sound of drumming along the corridor. The guards were taking Hare-Lip to be executed. When the drumming started again, Rubashov knew that his time had come. He was led into the cellar. Another party incident was closed.

Critical Evaluation:

When Arthur Koestler began writing *Darkness at Noon* in 1938, much of Europe squirmed under the heel of totalitarian forces. The threat of fascism was very apparent to many intellectuals, but that of communism not nearly so much. Many naïve and prominent figures looked to the Soviet Union for leadership in the long march to a distant utopia. Koestler, a Communist Party activist for most of the 1930's, knew the reality at first hand. He had seen countless numbers of friends censored and executed by the Communist Party. He had traveled extensively in the Soviet Union and seen its economic backwardness and widespread famine. Against this historical background, *Darkness at Noon* may be viewed first of all as a factually accurate account that uses the techniques of fiction. Koestler writes in a spare, straightforward fashion without stylistic flights. The understatement of the horrors and madness of the prison conveys its sordidness without adornment. The characters are not the anguished superhumans of Greek tragedy but small gray figures in a bureaucratic nightmare. They ride along in a train of destiny over which they not only have no control but also have no understanding.

Koestler focuses on the show trials as the particular manifestation of the Communist suppression. These trials took place throughout the 1930's and represented the bloodthirsty, paranoid effort of Joseph Stalin (who is represented as Number 1 in the novel) to consolidate his position as dictator by liquidating all opposition, including his own former comrades in the Russian Revolution. The protagonist of the novel, Rubashov, is fictional, but he represents many Communist Party leaders who did exist and met their deaths through trumped-up charges brought against them by the Soviet police. Much of the narrative takes place inside the mind of Rubashov and presents a brilliant psychology study. Rubashov is a man trying to reconcile his present dilemma with the beliefs and actions of his earlier years. More specifically, Koestler addresses an issue that puzzled political analysts of his day: Why did those accused in the show trials plead guilty in open court to crimes that they did not commit? In answering this question, Koestler leads the reader through many dark labyrinths of Rubashov's logical mind. The book on one hand sheds light on Rubashov's conviction in the ultimate rightness of all the Communist Party's actions and on the other shows his cynicism about the economic and political realities of the time. Koestler describes Rubashov's sad mistreatment in the prison and then demonstrates with flashbacks that the high-ranking Communist is no innocent. Previously he has thrown people to the wolves for political reasons and once merely to save himself. Ultimately Koestler seems to suggest that Rubashov confesses because of exhaustion and his reasoned conviction that in doing so he will render the Party one last service. Rubashov had previously resisted torture successfully in a fascist prison. While in the service of the Communist Party, he had shown great moral and physical courage.

Koestler's theme is means and ends. To Rubashov, the push to an honorable and humanitarian goal justifies unsavory actions to achieve that goal. In this case the goal is a utopian Communist society in which no one wants economically, in which the upper class withers away, and in which people rule themselves spontaneously and fairly. The means to this end are best determined by the utterly ruthless "militant philosophers"—the leaders of the Communist Party. Koestler also wrote on this theme in his first novel, *The Gladiators* (1939), concerning a revolution by slaves against the Roman Empire. The hero, Spartacus, has great success at first, but his unwillingness to quell disorder among his own troops and followers causes his downfall. Spartacus' revolution failed whereas the Russian Revolution succeeded. Koestler implies that the difference was that the Communist leaders stopped at nothing to achieve their ends. In so doing they negated their highest aspirations and, in a sense, therefore also failed in their revolution to bring a classless perfect world. All through the book Rubashov wrestles with this problem of means and ends. Rubashov hopes, faintly, that the Communist Party will be proven right by history. He abases himself publicly to this end, gambling his only remaining card, his logic, that the Party will ultimately be proven to be on the true path.

Except for remembered incidents, the novel takes place almost entirely inside a prison. It could be argued that Koestler loses some breadth of vision with this setting. Some critics have pointed out that the novel has no middle ground, no ordinary lives lived by Russians who were not in prison and who were not members of the Communist Party. This observation misses the point of Koestler's writing the book, which was to examine and expose the Communist Party's mentality. The suffocating prison, with its dark corridors, closed off from the outside world and operating under its own logic, is a concretization of the Communist dystopia and a metaphor for the Communist rationale. *Darkness at Noon* has a place as one of the great political novels of the twentieth century and puts Arthur Koestler in the forefront of political writers such as George Orwell and Aleksandr Solzhenitsyn. On its publication in France after World War II, *Darkness at Noon* influenced public opinion against the Communist Party and possibly prevented it from gaining power. With the end of the Cold War in the 1980's, the historical events it depicts became less relevant but, as an allegory of the fallacy of using pure logic as a guide to human affairs and of the dangers of justifying immoral behavior with political expediency, it remains as potent as ever.

"Critical Evaluation" by Philip Magnier

Bibliography:
Koestler, Arthur. *The Invisible Writing: The Second Volume of an Autobiography, 1932-1940.* London: Hutchinson, 1969. Koestler discusses his activism in the Communist Party, his travels to the Soviet Union, his imprisonment in fascist Spain, and his denunciation of communism in *Darkness at Noon.*

Levene, Mark. *Arthur Koestler.* New York: Frederick Ungar, 1984. Overview of Koestler's political writing, including a chapter on *Darkness at Noon.*

Pearson, Sidney A. *Arthur Koestler.* Boston: Twayne, 1978. Includes a chapter on *Darkness at Noon.*

Rothkopf, Carol Z. *"Darkness at Noon": A Critical Commentary.* New York: American R.D.M., 1963. Scholarly, complete, and well-written discussion.

Sperber, Murray A. ed. *Arthur Koestler: A Collection of Critical Essays.* Englewood Cliffs, N.J.: Prentice-Hall, 1977. Includes essays by George Orwell and Saul Bellow. With an intellectually tortuous attack on *Darkness at Noon* by a French Marxist.

DAVID COPPERFIELD

Type of work: Novel
Author: Charles Dickens (1812-1870)
Type of plot: Bildungsroman
Time of plot: Early nineteenth century
Locale: England
First published: 1849-1850

Principal characters:
DAVID COPPERFIELD, the narrator
CLARA, his mother
MISS BETSEY TROTWOOD, David's grandaunt
CLARA PEGGOTTY, a nurse
MR. DANIEL PEGGOTTY, her brother
EMILY, his orphan niece
HAM, his orphan nephew
MR. MURDSTONE, David's stepfather
MISS JANE MURDSTONE, his sister
MR. CREAKLE, the master of Salem House
JAMES STEERFORTH, David's schoolmate
TOMMY TRADDLES, a student at Salem House
MR. WILKINS MICAWBER, a man of pecuniary difficulties
MR. WICKFIELD, Miss Trotwood's solicitor
AGNES WICKFIELD, his daughter
URIAH HEEP, a clerk
MR. SPENLOW, the man under whom David studied law
DORA SPENLOW, his daughter and later David's wife
MR. DICK, Miss Betsey's protegé

The Story:
David Copperfield was born at Blunderstone, in Suffolk, six months after his father's death. Miss Betsey Trotwood, an eccentric grandaunt, was present on the night of his birth, but she left the house abruptly and indignantly when she learned that the child was a boy, since only a girl could have been named after her. David spent his early years with his pretty young mother and a devoted servant named Peggotty.

The youthful widow was soon courted by Mr. Murdstone. Soon after his mother married him, he proved to be stingy and cruel. David was packed off with Peggotty to visit her relatives at Yarmouth. Her brother had converted an old boat into a home by the sea, where he lived with his niece, who was called Little Em'ly, and his sturdy young nephew, Ham. Little Em'ly and Ham were David's first real playmates, and his visit to Yarmouth remained one of the few happy memories of his lonely childhood. After Mr. Murdstone's sister, Jane, arrived to take charge of her brother's household, David and his mother never again felt free from the dark atmosphere of suspicion and gloom the Murdstones created about them.

One day, in a fit of childish terror, David bit his stepfather on the hand. He was immediately sent off to Salem House, a wretched school near London, where his life was more miserable than ever under a brutal headmaster named Creakle. In spite of Mr. Creakle's harsh treatment and bullying, however, David's life was endurable because of his friendship with two boys, the lovable Tommy Traddles and the handsome, lordly James Steerforth.

David's school days ended suddenly with the death of his mother and her newborn infant. When he returned home, he discovered that Mr. Murdstone had dismissed Peggotty. Barkis, the stage driver, whose courtship had been meager but earnest, had taken Peggotty away to become Mrs. Barkis, and David found himself friendless in his former home. Soon he was put to work in an export warehouse in London, in which Murdstone had an interest. As a ten-year-old worker in the dilapidated establishment of the wine merchants Murdstone and Grinby, David was overworked and half-starved, and he loathed his job and the people with whom he had to associate. He did meet the Micawber family, however, in whose house David lodged. The impecunious Mr. Micawber was sent to debtor's prison shortly afterward and decided, on his release, to move with his family to Plymouth. After he lost these good friends, David decided to run away.

The only relative he knew of was his father's aunt, Miss Betsey Trotwood, of whom he knew only that she lived in Dover and had been indignant at his birth. He nevertheless set out, full of hope; on the way he was robbed of the few things he possessed and consequently arrived at Miss Betsey's home in a wretched state. At first, his reception was not encouraging, but Miss Betsey took the advice of Mr. Dick, a feebleminded distant kinsman who lived with her, and let David into the house. While she deliberated about what to do with her bedraggled nephew, she wrote to inform Mr. Murdstone, who thereupon came with his sister to Dover. Miss Betsey, disliking both Murdstones intensely at first sight, again took Mr. Dick's advice and kept David.

Much to the boy's joy, Miss Betsey almost immediately sent him to a school in Canterbury run by a Mr. Strong, a headmaster quite unlike Mr. Creakle. During his stay at school, David lodged with Miss Betsey's lawyer, Mr. Wickfield and his daughter Agnes, with whom he was very happy. He also met Uriah Heep, Mr. Wickfield's cringing, hypocritical clerk with the clammy handclasp.

When David finished school at the age of seventeen, Miss Betsey suggested that he take some time before deciding on a profession. On his way to visit his old nurse Peggotty, David met James Steerforth again and went home with his former schoolmate. There he met Steerforth's mother and Rosa Dartle, a young woman who was passionately in love with Steerforth. Years before, the quick-tempered Steerforth had struck Rosa, who still carried the scar.

David persuaded Steerforth to come with him to see Peggotty and her family. At Yarmouth, Steerforth met Little Em'ly, who was by that time engaged to Ham. She and Steerforth were immediately attracted to each other.

David finally decided that he wished to study law. Accordingly, he was articled to the law firm of Spenlow and Jorkins in London. When he said good-bye to Agnes, she told him she distrusted Steerforth's influence over him; she also expressed uneasiness about Uriah Heep, who was on the point of entering into partnership with her father, who was showing signs of feebleness. As he left the house, David encountered Uriah himself, who told him that he wanted to marry Agnes, which outraged David.

After his new life began in London, David was invited to the home of his employer, where he met and instantly fell in love with Mr. Spenlow's pretty daughter, Dora. Soon they became secretly engaged. About the same time, however, David heard the distressing news that Little Em'ly had run away with Steerforth. Shortly after he became engaged to Dora, Betsey Trotwood came to London to tell David that she had lost all of her money. After failing in his attempt to recover some of the money for his articles with Spenlow and Jorkins, David took a part-time job as secretary to Mr. Strong, his former headmaster. Because that job paid very little, David also began to study to be a reporter of parliamentary debates.

Mr. Spenlow's sudden death dissolved the partnership of Spenlow and Jorkins, and David learned to his dismay that his former employer had died almost penniless. After studying hard, David became a reporter, and at the age of twenty-one, he married Dora. While these events were happening, David had kept in touch with Mr. Micawber, who now became Uriah Heep's confidential secretary. Though something had finally turned up for Mr. Micawber, his relations with David and even with his own family became somewhat mysterious, but Mr. Micawber's conscience soon got the better of him and at a meeting he arranged at Mr. Wickfield's home, he revealed Uriah Heep's criminal perfidy. Uriah Heep had for years robbed and cheated Mr. Wickfield, and Miss Betsey discovered that it was he who had been responsible for her own financial losses.

Mr. Micawber, having cleared his conscience, decided to take his family to Australia, where he was sure something would turn up. By that time Emily, whom Steerforth had deserted, had returned to her uncle Peggotty and they, too, went to Australia. As David watched their ship put out to sea, it seemed to him that the sunset was a bright promise for their new life.

The great cloud in David's life now became his wife's delicate health. Day after day she failed, and in spite of his tenderest care, he was forced to see her grow more feeble and wan. Agnes Wickfield, like the true friend she had always been, was with him on the night of Dora's death. As in his earlier troubles, he turned to Agnes in the days that followed and found comfort in her sympathy and understanding. Upon her advice, he decided to go abroad for a while. First, however, he went to Yarmouth to put a last letter from Emily into Ham's hands. While he was there, a storm caused a ship to founder off the coast. Ham died in a courageous attempt to rescue a survivor clinging to a broken mast. Later that day, the waves washed his body ashore and that of the false Steerforth.

David lived in Europe for three years. One day, soon after his return, Miss Betsey slyly suggested that Agnes might soon be married. Heavyhearted, David went off to offer her his good wishes. When she burst into tears, he realized that what he had hoped was true—her heart was his. To the great delight of matchmaking Miss Betsey, Agnes and David were married, and David settled down to begin his career as a successful novelist.

Critical Evaluation:

"But, like many fond parents, I have in my heart of hearts a favorite child. And his name is David Copperfield." This is Charles Dickens' final, affectionate judgment of the work that stands exactly in the middle of his novelistic career, with seven novels preceding and seven following it (excluding the unfinished *The Mystery of Edwin Drood*, 1870). When he began the novel, he was in his mid-thirties, secure in the continuing success that had begun with *Sketches by Boz* (1836) and *Pickwick Papers* (1836-1837). It was a good time to take stock of his life and to make use of the autobiographical manuscript he had put by earlier; he did not try to conceal the personal element from his public, who eagerly awaited each of the nineteen numbers of the serialized first publication of *David Copperfield* between May, 1849, and November, 1850. Charles Dickens is readily identified with David Copperfield, and as Dickens phrased it, he viewed his life through the "long Copperfieldian perspective."

Although much in the life of the first-person narrator corresponds to Dickens' own life, the author altered a number of details. Unlike David, Dickens was not a genteel orphan but the eldest son of living and improvident parents; his own father served as the model for Micawber. Dickens' childhood stint in a shoeblacking factory seems to have been somewhat shorter than

David's drudgery in the warehouse of the wine distributors Murdstone and Grinby, but the shame and suffering he felt were identical. Whereas young Dickens failed in his romance with a pretty young girl, David is permitted to win his first love, Dora, but Dickens then imparts to Dora's character the faults of his own wife, Kate.

However fascinating the autobiographical details, *David Copperfield* stands primarily on its merits as a novel endowed with the bustling life of Dickens' earlier works but controlled by his maturing sense of design. In addition to the compelling characterization of the protagonist, the novel abounds with memorable portrayals. The square face and black beard of Mr. Murdstone, always viewed in conjunction with that "metallic lady," Miss Murdstone, evoke the horror of dehumanized humanity. Uriah Heep's writhing body, clammy skin, and peculiarly lidless eyes suggest a subhuman form more terrifying than the revolting nature of his "'umbleness." Above all the figures that crowd the lonely world of the orphan rises the bald head of Mr. Micawber, flourishing his command of the English language and his quizzing glass with equal impressiveness.

These vivid characters notwithstanding, David Copperfield is very definitely the hero of his own story. This is a novel of initiation, organized around the two major segments of the hero's development, childhood and early manhood. The plot focuses steadily on the testing he receives that is to qualify him for full manhood. He makes his own choices, but each important stage of his moral progress is marked by the intervention and aid of his aunt.

Initially, David is weak simply because he is a child, the hapless victim of adult exploitation; but he is also heir to the moral weakness of his childish mother and his dead father, who was an inept, impractical man. Portentously, David's birth is the occasion of a conflict between his mother's Copperfieldian softness and Aunt Betsey's firmness, displayed in her rigidity of figure and countenance. From a state of childish freedom, David falls into the Murdstone world. The clanking chains of Miss Murdstone's steel purse symbolize the metaphorical prison that replaces his innocently happy home. Indeed, for David, the world becomes a prison. After his five days of solitary confinement at Blunderstone, he enters the jail-like Salem House School, and after his mother's death, he is placed in the warehouse, apparently for life. His involvement with the Micawbers offers no escape, either, for he is burdened with their problems in addition to his own.

Although David repudiates the tyrannical firmness of which he is for a time a victim, he does not actively rebel except once, when he bites Mr. Murdstone. Instead, like his mother, he submits—fearfully to the Murdstones and Creakle, and worshipfully to the arrogant Steerforth. He also escapes into the freedom of fantasy through books and stories and through the lives of others, which he invests with an enchantment that conceals from him whatever is potentially tragic or sordid.

David's pliant nature, nevertheless, shares something of the resolute spirit of Aunt Betsey. Looking back on his wretched boyhood, David recalls that he kept his own counsel and did his work. From having suffered in secret, he moves to the decision to escape by his own act. The heroic flight is rewarded when Aunt Betsey relents and takes him in. In accordance with her character, she trusses up the small boy in adult clothes and announces her goal of making him a "fine fellow, with a will of your own," with a "strength of character that is not to be influenced, except on good reason, by anybody, or by anything." The first cycle of testing is complete.

The conventionally happy years in Dover and Canterbury mark an interlude before the second major cycle of the novel, which commences with David's reentry into the world as a young man. Significantly, he at first resumes the docile patterns of childhood. Reunited with Steerforth, he once again takes pride in his friend's overbearing attitude, and he allows himself to be bullied by various people, above all servants. He evades the obligation to choose his own career by entering into a profession that affects him like an opiate. In Dora's childlike charms, he recaptures the girlish image of his mother. At this point, however, the firm Aunt Betsey, having cut short his childhood trials, deliberately sets in motion his adult testing with her apparent bankruptcy.

Responding to his new challenges, David falls back upon his childhood resources. At first, in unconscious imitation of Murdstone, he tries to mold Dora, but then consciously rejects tyranny and chooses instead resignation and understanding for the fact that she can be no more than his "child-wife." He responds with full sympathy to the tragedy of Emily's affair with Steerforth, but he needed that proof to be finally disenchanted with the willfulness that had captivated his boyish heart. Most important, he recovers the saving virtue of his childhood, his ability to suffer in secrecy, to keep his own counsel, and to do his work. As his trials pile up—poverty, overwork, disappointment in marriage, his wife's death, and the tribulations of the friends to whom his tender heart is wholly committed—he learns to conquer his own undisciplined heart.

The mature David who emerges from his trials has profited from his experiences and heritage. His capacity for secret suffering is, for him as for Aunt Betsey, a source of strength, but his, unlike hers, is joined to the tenderheartedness inherited from his parents. Her distrust of humans has made her an eccentric. His trusting disposition, on the other hand, though rendering him vulnerable, binds him to humankind.

Although Aunt Betsey sets a goal of maturity before David, Agnes Wickfield is the symbol of the hard-won self-discipline that he finally achieves. She is from the beginning his "better angel." Like him, she is tenderhearted and compliant, yet far from being submissive; she is in control of herself in even the most difficult human relationships. Since it is never distorted by distrust of humankind, her firmness of character is the only influence David should accept in his pursuit of the moral goal Aunt Betsey has set before him.

By the time David has recognized his love for Agnes, he has also attained a strength of character similar to hers. The appropriate conclusion to his quest for maturity is his union with Agnes—who is from the beginning a model of the self-disciplined person in whom gentleness and strength are perfectly balanced. Furthermore, the home he builds with her is the proper journey's end for the orphaned child who has grasped at many versions of father, mother, family, and home: "Long miles of road then opened out before my mind, and toiling on, I saw a ragged way-worn boy forsaken and neglected, who should come to call even the heart now beating against him, his own." He has outgrown the child-mother, the child-wife, the childhood idols, even the childhood terrors, and he is a mature man ready to accept love "founded on a rock." In the context of a successful completed quest, the novel ends with a glimpse of the complete man, who writes far into the night to erase the shadows of his past but whose control of the realities is sufficient in the presence of the woman who is always symbolically "near me, pointing upward!"

"Critical Evaluation" by Catherine E. Moore

Bibliography:
Bloom, Harold, ed. *Charles Dickens' "David Copperfield."* New York: Chelsea House, 1987. Bloom's introduction considers the novel as the original portrait of the artist as young man. Eight other essays, all written after 1969, include examinations of the novel's moral unity and mirror imagery.

Collins, Philip. *Charles Dickens: "David Copperfield."* London: Edward Arnold, 1977. Brief study that focuses on the work itself rather than on Dickens or his methods. Discusses the novel's specific strengths and weaknesses and examines how the novel's serial publication affected its structure. Most useful for the student who has read some of Dickens' contemporaries.

Dunn, Richard J., ed. *Approaches to Teaching Dickens' "David Copperfield."* New York: Modern Language Association of America, 1984. Intended for teachers but fascinating and helpful for students. Includes descriptions of other books and materials useful for understanding the novel and for determining discussion topics and approaches for classroom use.

Storey, Graham. *"David Copperfield": Interweaving Truth and Fiction.* Boston: Twayne, 1991. A very accessible study. After three chapters that discuss the novel's autobiographical elements and critical reception, Storey presents an extended reading focusing on children and childhood. Includes a bibliography and chronology.

Vogel, Jane. *Allegory in Dickens.* Tuscaloosa: University of Alabama Press, 1977. In the chapters about *David Copperfield*, which make up a great deal of the book, the author proposes that the novel can be read—and was written—as a Christian allegory of the spiritual journey from Creation to Heaven. Thought-provoking, though not always convincing.

THE DAY OF THE LOCUST

Type of work: Novel
Author: Nathanael West (Nathan Weinstein, 1903-1940)
Type of plot: Social realism
Time of plot: 1930's
Locale: Hollywood
First published: 1939

Principal characters:
TOD HACKETT, novice costume and set designer
CLAUDE ESTEE, a successful screenwriter
FAYE GREENER, a would-be actress
HARRY GREENER, a has-been vaudeville clown
HOMER SIMPSON, a retired bookkeeper

The Story:

Tod Hackett, a set and costume designer, arrived in Hollywood, still idealistic from Yale. He worked on his painting, *The Burning of Los Angeles,* to fulfill his dream of becoming a successful artist. As he watched people from his movie studio window, he saw soldiers moving like a mob, with a fat man cursing at them through a megaphone. Tod observed how people masqueraded by dressing in roles and how houses reflected odd mixtures of architectural styles. He recalled the day when Abe Kusich showed him his seedy hotel, and Tod immediately had become obsessed with Faye Greener.

At Claude Estee's party, Tod was initiated into Hollywood's perverse pleasures. To amuse guests, Estee decorated his pool with a life-size rubber reproduction of a grotesque dead horse, its stiff legs straight up, distended belly enormous, and black tongue hanging out. Joining the partygoers at Audrey Jenning's brothel, Tod watched part of a pornographic film; then seeing Faye's best friend, Mary Dove, he tried to engage Faye's services.

Failing to do so, he ingratiated himself, keeping Faye and her sickly father, Harry, company. One day, after Homer Simpson appeared with flowers and wine to court Faye, Tod learned that while selling homemade polish, Harry had collapsed at Homer Simpson's house. Then Tod met another rival for Faye's attention, Earle Shoop. The three went to the hillside camp of Miguel, a Mexican who raised fighting gamecocks. After they had eaten, they drank tequila. Unable to stand Faye's seductive dancing with Miguel, Earle cracked him in the head. Tod, caught up in the frenzy, grabbed at Faye as she ran past him. Until his passion and anger were exhausted, Tod envisioned his artistic depiction of violence: Los Angeles burning amid a gala holiday crowd.

Although Faye had abandoned him, the following evening (while Faye went to the movies with Homer), Tod got trapped into hearing her sick father reminisce about his vaudeville career. The next day Harry died. To pay for funeral expenses, Faye worked at Mrs. Jenning's brothel. Harry's funeral resembled a theatrical performance, with arguments about the cheap casket, dramatic hymns pleading for Christ's coming, and curious onlookers being urged to view the corpse. Tod convinced Faye that venereal disease from prostitution would destroy her beauty.

Instead of relying on Tod for support, Faye moved in with Homer Simpson, who paid her expenses (a business arrangement: She would become a star and would pay him back with interest) and did the housework. Their daily routine consisted of shopping, dinner out, movies, and ice cream sodas. Homer's neighbor was Maybelle Loomis, a stage mother desperately trying to make a child star of Adore, her eight-year-old, who was dressed like a man, with plucked and shaped eyebrows. He performed upon command a sexually suggestive song, complete with erotic gestures. Adore and Faye deserved to be in pictures, agreed Tod and Homer.

No longer wanting to be sexually aroused but rejected by Faye, Tod avoided her for several months. He went to bizarre Hollywood churches and sketched worshipers. In one church he observed people whipped into religious fervor by a man preaching messianic rage with threats of the Tiger of Wrath and the Jackal of Lust.

Against his better judgment late one night, Tod joined Homer and Faye at a nightclub featuring female impersonators. While Faye danced with a stranger, Homer admitted that to please Faye, he let Earle and Miguel live in his garage, despite Miguel's disgusting game chickens. When Tod and Claude attended a cockfight there, they witnessed this brutal sport that ended with the losing cock's death. Homer invited them in for drinks, and the erotic Faye, whom Tod called a whore, took center stage. She drunkenly danced with Miguel and Earle. A scuffle broke out. Later, after Homer and Earle found Faye in bed with Miguel, she moved out, leaving Homer distraught.

Tod returned to Homer's the next morning to comfort Homer. Faye would survive because of her sexual opportunism, Tod realized. Although he imagined raping her, he could not complete his violent sexual fantasy. Leaving a restaurant, he saw Kahn's Persian Palace Theatre had attracted thousands for a world movie premiere. A radio announcer described the frenzied crowd, like a revival preacher whipping an audience to hysteria. Tod fought his way through the surging crowd, getting kicked and swept away. Then he spotted Homer walking dazed, in a catatonic stupor, with his suitcases and with his pants over his night clothes. He said he was going back to Iowa. While sitting on a bench to wait for a taxi, Homer was hit in the face with a stone thrown by Adore. Homer went berserk, stomping Adore despite Tod's attempts to pull him off. Suddenly, the crazed mob tore Tod away from Homer and engulfed the child-attacker. Another part of the wild mob surged, and Tod felt his ribs cracking and his leg throbbing. People in the mob enjoyed the riotous free-for-all that had started with a sighting of Gary Cooper. Desperately clinging to a fence, Tod envisioned his painting, with Faye, Harry, Homer, Claude, and himself fleeing a mob. After a policeman rescued him, Tod asked to be taken to Claude's. In his hysteria, he imitated the police car siren in a loud scream.

Critical Evaluation:

Nathanael West (born Nathan Weinstein) worked in Hollywood in 1933 on the script for his novel *Miss Lonelyhearts* (1933) but was disillusioned when his suggestions were ignored, and his book twisted beyond recognition, retitled in its script form as *Advice to the Lovelorn*. In 1935, he returned to Hollywood to gather material for his fourth and last novel, *The Day of the Locust*. He lived in poverty for many months, supported by his brother-in-law, humorist S. J. Perelman, until he found work as a scriptwriter. His first produced film was, ironically enough, *Ticket to Paradise* (1936). For most of the next five years, he worked for several major studios until his death in 1940 in a car accident. He was fascinated by and cynical about Hollywood, knowing that screenwriters had their writing revised or rejected. They could not write anything really good, but they could make good money if they were lucky. West preferred mechanical work on lesser quality, formulaic pictures so he could save his creative energies for his own fiction. Writing movie scripts came easily, and West was considered a competent craftsman at his trade. West's screenwriter friends F. Scott Fitzgerald and William Faulkner also considered screenwriting to be mere hack work for Hollywood's dream factory. Fitzgerald (who, coincidentally, died the day before West was killed in a car accident in 1940) left unfinished a Hollywood novel, *The Last Tycoon* (1941). Along with Fitzgerald's novel, West's *The Day of the Locust* is considered among the finest in the Hollywood novel genre.

Structured into twenty-seven chapters like movie scenes, the book presents an insider's perspective of Hollywood's dream factory and underworld society. West achieves a sense of reality with his richly detailed, accurate settings of the Hollywood landscape—movie lots, hotels, churches, restaurants, bars, brothels, streets, and canyons. In fact, this realistic detail merges with grotesquely exaggerated images to create a sense of surrealism. Comedy is juxtaposed with tragedy, and as a result the plot's pace seems somewhat uneven. The disjointed feeling conveys exactly the dual nature of Hollywood's reality and fantasy. Being familiar with his father's construction business, West uses architectural images—of houses, theaters, and churches—to depict Hollywood as home of the grotesque, the gaudy, the materialistic. Tod comments on the comic artificiality of the houses: "It is hard to laugh at the need for beauty and romance, no matter how tasteless, even horrible. . . . Few things are sadder than the truly monstrous." This third-person limited omniscient viewpoint (through Tod's consciousness) often reflects West's views. Tod fears that in selling out to Hollywood, he is prostituting his talents to a lesser art. The fascination-repulsion is at the emotional heart of the novel, which West began in 1935 while he lived in Hollywood, a seedy section of Los Angeles. Earlier in the thirties he managed two New York City hotels catering to low-life clientele; he was well acquainted with writers, artists, prostitutes, vaudeville comics, and dwarfs, so he knew from experience how the desperate, the unemployed, and the poverty-stricken stood on breadlines during the Great Depression. They obsessively attended movies and read magazines to get their vicarious thrills of glamour and wealth.

The studio lot's dream-dump becomes a central metaphor for Hollywood's chaos and shoddiness. Movies promised paradise, the South Sea dream of escape. They became instead a dream-dump, like the studio's pile of discarded props and sets. Tod's seedy hotel is a microcosm of the world of dreamers. The movie lot is a microcosm of dream makers. The collapse of the Waterloo set is only one of many images of total chaos and destruction in this surrealistic world of grotesquerie.

The portrayal of Hollywood's artificiality directly relates to the dream-become-nightmare theme. Claude's home, a reproduction of a Southern antebellum mansion, well exemplifies the grotesquely comic impulse to startle and amuse. Images of phony structures in "Caliphonia" parallel the phony people. Not only in their various costumes that represent their make-believe roles, but also in their physical descriptions, West's characters are degenerate—for example, Homer's weird hands, Harry's mechanical laugh, Earle's two-dimensional face like a mechanical drawing. Moreover, a sense of unreality exists in the decadence of Faye, Earle, Abe, and Miguel. No healthy sexual relationships are depicted—only violent erotic fantasies, prostitution, sadism and masochism, female impersonators, impotence, and promiscuity. By satiric reduction, love becomes a vending machine. For many who come to the land of sunshine and oranges, Hollywood's artificiality is a cheat. Tod captures people's despair in his series called *The Dancers*; he draws people (based on his friends) as they "spin crazily and leap into the air with twisted backs like hooked trout." Betrayed and cheated after years of slaving away for nothing, people become victims or they resort to violence.

The fury of the living dead, with their anarchic power, epitomizes both Tod's vision in *The Burning of Los Angeles* and West's prophecy in *The Day of the Locust*. West had seen at movie premieres how people worshipped glamorous stars with such insane jealousy, almost like hatred, that they could have shredded the stars' flesh as much as their clothes. Through violence, the cheated and betrayed ultimately take revenge. West's vision of the apocalypse, when locusts ravage the land, turns the American dream into the Hollywood nightmare.

Laura M. Zaidman

Bibliography:
Comerchero, Victor. *Nathanael West: The Ironic Prophet.* Syracuse: Syracuse University Press, 1964. Argues that the novel should be read as a satire of a declining Western culture. Perceptive analysis of West's apocalyptic vision.

Madden, David, ed. *Nathanael West: The Cheaters and the Cheated.* De Land, Fla.: Everett/ Edwards, 1973. Contains five assessments of the novel, and several general essays on West's work.

Malin, Irving. *Nathanael West's Novels.* Carbondale: Southern Illinois University Press, 1972. Offers a close textual analysis of West's images, metaphors, and symbols as clues to the novel's themes and characterization.

Martin, Jay. *Nathanael West: The Art of His Life.* New York: Farrar, Straus & Giroux, 1970. The first full-length biography and critical study. Analyzes the novels in the context of West's Hollywood years; also includes twenty pages of pictures and a detailed listing of his film writing.

_____, ed. *Nathanael West: A Collection of Critical Essays.* Englewood Cliffs, N.J.: Prentice-Hall, 1971. Includes short essays by West's contemporaries William Carlos Williams and W. H. Auden.

DE PROFUNDIS

Type of work: Letter
Author: Oscar Wilde (1854-1900)
First published: 1905

The eighty-page manuscript of this letter rests in the British Museum. It was written in Reading Gaol on prison paper during the last months, from January to March, of Oscar Wilde's two-year sentence for "unnatural practices." It was addressed to Lord Alfred Douglas, but when Wilde was not allowed to send it from prison he handed it to his friend Robert Ross the day after he was released on May 19, 1897, with instructions to type a copy and send the original to Lord Alfred, who always claimed he never received it. Part of the work was first published under Ross's title, *De Profundis*, in 1905, and again in 1908. A typescript was given by Ross to Vyvyn Holland, Wilde's younger son, who published it in 1949. Rupert Hart-Davis has shown that this first complete edition contained hundreds of errors, and he has now published the manuscript after it was released by the British Museum from the fifty-year restriction Ross placed on it when he deposited the manuscript in 1909. As a letter, it becomes the center of the definitive edition of Wilde's letters; in the shorter form edited by Ross it is both an apologia and a literary essay. Nevertheless, in its entirety it has a unity and a unique value as Wilde's testament to his life as an artist which should encourage its publication for the first time as an independent work of art under the title which is customarily given it.

Since it is cast in the form of an epistle, the work needs some contextual reference to Wilde's life and works before and after his imprisonment and the composition of the letter. The prison sentence marked the end of his marriage, his income, and his life in England; thereafter he lived in exile as Sebastian Melmoth. One link with the past, however, was not broken, the association with Lord Alfred Douglas. Wilde's return to the young man, the cause of his imprisonment, divorce, and bankruptcy, and to the kind of associates whose evidence had convicted him, seems to invalidate the promise to lead a new life with which *De Profundis* closes. Wilde claimed, however, that while, on the one hand, the conditions of exile, disgrace, and penury drove him to those acquaintances, on the other, they were the creations of his art and not the conditions of his life. Wilde's one conviction was that he was an artist, and he doggedly transposed the terms of life and art. His term for the new life was *La vita nuova* (c. 1292) of Dante. Similarly, *The Picture of Dorian Gray* (1891) was to be the parable of his life; it was more true to his life because of its artistry than was his biography. The strain of maintaining this paradox ended his life three years after his release and finished his writing career shortly after the composition of *De Profundis*. The resolution of the paradox is the intention of the long letter.

This epistle is therefore connected both with Wilde's biography (in which sense it is autobiography) and with his literary canon. In the letter, he suggests that his sentence and fate are "prefigured" in works like *The Picture of Dorian Gray*. The immediate artistic fruits of the "new life" are the two letters to the *Morning Chronicle* and *The Ballad of Reading Gaol* (1898), his only writing after *De Profundis*; parts of the last amount to a prose poem falling somewhere between the prose of the two letters and poetry of the ballad, Wilde's longest and most effective poem. The two letters are included in Ross's 1908 edition and show plainly the real conditions under which *De Profundis* was written. Wilde sums them up as constant hunger, diarrhea from the rotten food, and insomnia from the diarrhea and the plank bed in his cell. His description of prison life is vivid and awful; out of his experience, immediately after his release, he showed courage in writing letters to defend a discharged warder and to plead for decent treatment of child prisoners. Perhaps he could have played a prominent role in prison reform had not exile intervened; yet it is difficult to see Wilde in that role unless he really meant what he said in *De Profundis*. As it was, events showed that this epistle belonged to the realm of art and not to life.

Wilde's request to have the letter copied by Ross showed that he thought of it as art, his "letter to the world." The covering letter to Ross described his three intentions. He would explain, not defend, his past, describe his spiritual and mental crisis in prison, and outline his future plans. The aptness of Ross's title from Psalm 130 is obvious, but the work is not so much the salvation of a lost soul as it is Wilde's artistic equivalent of this, the groping toward an artistic resolution of the paradox that the pursuit of beauty leads to the ugliness of Reading Gaol. The past is covered mostly in the longer first half of the letter, in reproaches to Lord Alfred Douglas, which were at least somewhat merited but relevant only if Wilde recognized Lord Alfred as the alter ego of that past and not of the future. This failure to interpret his past life as a work of art indicates the failure of the remaining portion of the letter, printed in Ross's edition of 1908.

This general section of *De Profundis* is in two related parts. The first states Wilde's reliance on the paradox that art is life, life art; his problem is to see the art in his present situation, which he sums up in the word "sorrow." If he really feels sorrow, then sorrow must be artistic or of artistic value; he decides that his art (that is, life) lacked the dimension of shadow (that is, sorrow), and his present sorrow must have been intended for the purpose of improving his art. If Wilde can transpose his prison sentence into an aspect of art, then his paradox holds good. We have evidence in the letters of his friends that he did just this soon after his release, when he wittily described Reading Gaol as an enchanted castle, complete with ogres, dungeons, and devices of torture.

The second part of this section then plays with an artistic creation or symbol of sorrow: the Man of Sorrows, by which Wilde indicated himself, Christ, and all people to the limited extent that he could be interested in anyone but himself. He pursues the Christian analogy daringly to argue not that he is Christ but that Christ (like Wilde) was the supreme artist of life. He had the imagination to feel the sufferings of a leper without being that leper, while at the same time Christ preserved his individuality. Similarly, his sympathetic imagination and artistry compelled him to turn himself into an artistic symbol of the truth about life: the Man of Sorrows. Wilde is thus not serving a prison sentence; as an artist, he is creating an artistic (that is, symbolic) statement about life. In this way he is able to absorb the most "sorrowful" experience of his life, the half-hour he stood on the center platform at Clapham Junction on his way to Reading Gaol and endured the mockery of the populace.

Having accomplished this artistic stroke (and advised Lord Alfred as a fellow poet to do likewise), Wilde proposes the two subjects on which he would like now to write. The first, the presentation of Christ as the forerunner of the Romantic movement in life, was largely covered in his previous outrageous analogy; its extension here leads him to the proposition that the sinner is as near a perfect human as humans can know because, in repenting, he can actually alter his past; thus he is the artist of the present and of the past.

The second subject, the life of art considered in relation to conduct of life, is much more the nub of Wilde's attitude to his past and his future. As he admits, everybody will simply point to Reading Gaol as the logical conclusion of the artistic life as Wilde practiced it. He dodges the logic by three lofty assertions. He is now so much the repentant sinner that he can even pity those who mocked him at Clapham Junction; that it was reliance on the Philistines (that is, the original legal action he instituted against Queensbury) that brought him to Reading Gaol; that the supreme concern of the artist is what he says of himself, not what others say. His own statements, Wilde asserted, must be the truth because what he says will be an artistic creation.

Thus Wilde's perverse reading of the obvious analogies in the Christian story made him miss its whole point of sacrifice (though he considers he was sacrificed for Lord Alfred) and confirms his original paradox, absolves him from all blame, and nullifies the whole meaning of Reading Gaol. The artist had triumphed over his real situation but only at the cost of life itself.

Bibliography:
Ellman, Richard, ed. *The Artist as Critic: Critical Writings of Oscar Wilde*. Chicago: University of Chicago Press, 1968. Explores Wilde's theory that suffering could be important for an artist; Wilde believed in "the realization of man through suffering." Examines Wilde's mentality when writing *De Profundis*.

_____. *Oscar Wilde: A Collection of Critical Essays*. Englewood Cliffs, N.J.: Prentice-Hall, 1969. Discusses Lord Alfred Douglas' obligation to answer Wilde's letter to him, also known as *De Profundis*. Looks at Wilde's attitude toward Christ as the supreme artist and forgiver.

Gide, André. *Oscar Wilde: "In Memoriam," "De Profundis."* Translated by Bernard Frechtman. New York: Philosophical Library, 1949. Examines M. Davray's translation of *De Profundis* in French and compares the translated version containing four letters by Wilde from prison to the English edition which does not include the other letters. Presents his personal reaction to Wilde's life.

Nassaar, Christopher S. *Into the Demon Universe: A Literary Exploration of Oscar Wilde*. New Haven, Conn.: Yale University Press, 1974. Deeply analyzes *De Profundis*. Compares it to the "demon universe" since Wilde had warned that a balance must be maintained in the "demon universe of life." In *De Profundis*, Wilde loses this perspective. Claims Wilde creates a personal myth in which he views his own life and in which Christ becomes an important symbol.

Pearson, Hesketh. *Oscar Wilde: His Life and Wit*. New York: Harper & Brothers, 1946. Covers Wilde's biography, but utilizes *De Profundis* to describe Wilde's later state of mind. Presents this letter as revealing the feeble aspects of Wilde, although the letter is unconvincing and too dramatic.

DEAD SOULS

Type of work: Novel
Author: Nikolai Gogol (1809-1852)
Type of plot: Social satire
Time of plot: Early nineteenth century
Locale: Russia
First published: Myortvye Dushi, part 1, 1842; part 2, 1855 (English translation, 1887)

Principal characters:
PAVEL IVANOVITCH TCHITCHIKOFF, an adventurer
MANILOFF, the man from whom he bought souls
TENTETNIKOFF, the bachelor whom he tried to marry off
PLATONOFF, Tchitchikoff's later traveling companion
KLOBUEFF, a spendthrift whose estate he bought
KONSTANTIN SKUDRONZHOGLO, a wealthy landholder who lent him
    money
ALEXEI IVANOVITCH LYENITZEN, the official who threw him into jail

The Story:
Pavel Ivanovitch Tchitchikoff had arrived in the town accompanied by his coachman, Selifan, and his valet, Petrushka. He had been entertained gloriously and had met numerous interesting people, many of whom insisted on his visiting them in their own homes. Nothing could have suited Tchitchikoff better. After several days of celebration in the town, he took Selifan and began a round of visits to the various estates in the surrounding country.

His first host was Maniloff, a genial man who wined and dined him in a manner fit for a prince. When the time was ripe, Tchitchikoff began to question his host about his estate. To his satisfaction, he learned that many of Maniloff's souls, as the serfs were called, had died since the last census and that Maniloff was still paying taxes on them and would continue to do so until the next census. Tchitchikoff offered to buy these dead souls from Maniloff and so relieve him of his extra tax burden. The contract was signed, and Tchitchikoff set out for the next estate.

Selifan got lost and in the middle of the night drew up to a house which belonged to Madame Korobotchkina, from whom Tchitchikoff also bought dead souls. When he left his hostess, he found his way to an inn in the neighborhood. There he met Nozdreff, a notorious gambler and liar. Nozdreff had recently lost a great deal of money at gambling, and Tchitchikoff thought he would be a likely seller of dead souls. When he broached the subject, Nozdreff asked him the reason for his interest in dead souls. For every reason Tchitchikoff gave, Nozdreff called him a liar. Then Nozdreff wanted to play at cards for the souls, but Tchitchikoff refused. They were arguing when a police captain came in and arrested Nozdreff for assault on a man while drunk. Tchitchikoff thought himself well rid of the annoying Nozdreff.

His next host was Sobakevitch, who at first demanded the unreasonable sum of one hundred rubles for each name of a dead soul. Tchitchikoff finally persuaded him to accept two and a half rubles apiece, a higher price than he had planned to pay.

Pliushkin, with whom he negotiated next, was a miser. He bought one hundred twenty dead souls and seventy-eight fugitives after considerable haggling. Pliushkin gave him a letter to Ivan Grigorievitch, the town president.

Back in town, Tchitchikoff persuaded the town president to make his recent purchases legal. Since the law required that souls, when purchased, be transferred to another estate, Tchitchikoff told the officials that he had land in the Kherson province. He had no trouble in making himself sound plausible. Some bribes to minor officials helped.

Tchitchikoff proved to be such a delightful guest that the people of the town insisted that he stay on and on. He was the center of attraction at many social functions, including a ball at which he was especially interested in the governor's daughter. Soon, however, rumors spread that Tchitchikoff was using the dead souls as a screen, that he was really planning to elope with the governor's daughter. The men, in consultation at the police master's house, speculated variously. Some said he was a forger; others thought he might be an officer in the governor-general's office; one man put forth the fantastic suggestion that he was really the legendary Captain Kopeykin in disguise. They questioned Nozdreff, who had been the first to report the story of the purchase of dead souls. At their interrogation, Nozdreff confirmed their opinions that Tchitchikoff was a spy and a forger who was trying to elope with the governor's daughter.

Meanwhile, Tchitchikoff had caught a cold and was confined to his bed. When at last he had recovered sufficiently to go out, he found himself no longer welcome at the houses of his former friends. He was, in fact, turned away by servants at the door. Tchitchikoff realized it would be best for him to leave town.

The truth of the matter was that Tchitchikoff had begun his career as a humble clerk. His father had died leaving no legacy for his son, who served in various capacities, passing from customs officer to smuggler to pauper to legal agent. When he learned that the Trustee Committee would mortgage souls, he hit upon the scheme of acquiring funds by mortgaging dead souls that were still on the census lists. It was this purpose which had sent him on his current tour.

He turned up next on the estate of Andrei Ivanovitch Tentetnikoff, a thirty-three-year-old bachelor who had retired from public life to vegetate in the country. Learning that Tentetnikoff was in love with the daughter of his neighbor, General Betrishtcheff, Tchitchikoff went to see the general and won his consent to Tentetnikoff's suit. He brought the conversation around to a point where he could offer to buy dead souls from the general. He gave as his reason the story that his old uncle would not leave him an estate unless he himself already owned some property. The scheme so delighted the general that he gladly made the transaction.

Tchitchikoff's next stop was with Pyetukh, a generous glutton whose table he enjoyed. There he met a young man named Platonoff, whom Tchitchikoff persuaded to travel with him and see Russia. The two stopped to see Platonoff's sister and brother-in-law, Konstantin Skudronzho-glo, a prosperous landholder. Tchitchikoff so impressed his host that Skudronzhoglo agreed to lend him ten thousand rubles to buy the estate of a neighboring spendthrift named Klobueff. Klobueff said he had a rich old aunt who would give great gifts to churches and monasteries but would not help her destitute relatives. Tchitchikoff proceeded to the town where the old woman resided and forged a will to his own advantage, but he forgot to insert a clause canceling all previous wills. On her death, he went to interview His Excellency, Alexei Ivanovitch Lyenitzen, who told him that two wills had been discovered, each contradicting the other. Tchitchikoff was accused of forging the second will and was thrown into prison. In the interpretation of this mix-up, Tchitchikoff learned a valuable lesson in deception from the crafty lawyer he consulted. The lawyer managed to confuse the affair with every public and private scandal in the province, so that the officials were soon willing to drop the whole matter if Tchitchikoff would leave town immediately. The ruined adventurer was only too glad to comply.

Critical Evaluation:
 When Gogol began work on *Dead Souls* in the 1830's, he developed a picaresque anecdote, initially suggested by poet Alexander Pushkin, that was crudely satiric. Eventually the concept grew into a "poema," or an epic, signaling its broad scope, patriotic flavor, and symbolic content. Although the censors forced him to alter the "Tale of Captain Kopeykin" in the tenth chapter of the novel and to change the title "Dead Souls," with its blasphemous and politically charged implications, to "The Adventures of Tchitchikoff," the work drew universal admiration. By the time the work was published in 1842, Gogol anticipated two more volumes describing the moral rebirth of Tchitchikoff and the ideal state of the Russian nation. Gogol's consistent dissatisfaction with the draft prevented him from publishing the continuation. The five chapters of volume 2 did not appear until three years after his death, in 1852.

 Gogol's contemporaries emphasized the accuracy of his portraits of Russian life, his realism. Some critics viewed Gogol's Russia as a faithful copy or justified the negative portrayals as necessary for a balanced depiction of Russia, while others objected to his cruel depiction of Russian life. The novel was interpreted variously from purely satiric to morally uplifting. Although Gogol's work was frequently discussed as a commentary on the unjust institution of serfdom, *Dead Souls* instead emphasizes the imperfections of government bureaucracy and satirizes officials working within that system. Gogol focuses his attention primarily on the middle class, rather than the high nobility, noble landowners, urban bureaucrats, or the peasantry. The provincial setting allows, however, for ample presentation of varied social groups. *Dead Souls* develops generalizations about Russian manners, speech, characters, and spirit within episodes of comic and lyric digression.

 The first six chapters of the novel establish Tchitchikoff's mirrorlike amiability as he visits a series of Russian landowners: the vapid and obliging Maniloff, the suspicious Madame Korobotchkina, the misanthropic Sobakevitch, the hyperbolic Nozdreff, and the miserly Pliushkin. In order to buy the legal titles to recently deceased serfs, he mimics the dominant obsession of each. Gogol manages to sustain the enigma of Tchitchikoff through these shifts of behavior. Only near the end of the novel does Gogol flesh out his hero by supplying his biography and preparing him for the next stage on the road. The late inclusion of the biography makes it apparent that the Tchitchikoff mirroring has been mutual. Maniloff now appears as a parody of Tchitchikoff decorum; Korobotchkina's bargaining emerges as a variant of his cunning; Nozdreff represents his prevarication; Sobakevitch manifests his calculating maneuvers; Pliushkin figures as his acquisitional passion.

 In the first half of the novel, Gogol delineates a gallery of portraits by outlining each landowner's physical appearance, home, family, hospitality, and reaction to Tchitchikoff's proposal. Gogol's methods of characterization exhibit a tension between the general and the particular, between typical traits and idiosyncratic detail. Although all the main characters belong to the same social class, they represent distinct personality types: Maniloff's sentimental inertia, Nozdreff's wild prevaricating, Sobakevitch's bearlike bluster, Pliushkin's disfiguring thrift acquire significance as typifying generalities. Even when drawing the abundant minor figures, Gogol emphasizes the generalized nature of certain looks or behavior, and yet gives them unique and comic names. At the same time, the traits of Gogol's characters, particularly Tchitchikoff's acquisitiveness, are features of the times.

 The metaphysical implications of the title, denying of the soul's immortality, drew controversy. The title actually seems to describe the characters though, all of whom represent varying degrees of spiritual or intellectual deadness. Throughout the text, categories of living and dead commingle. The deceased serfs are sometimes treated as if they were alive, while minor figures appear in great detail only to disappear without further mention. The fragmentary second part of the novel begins to trace the spiritual rebirth of Russia as well as that of Tchitchikoff.

The road embodies the dominant structural principle of the work. The novel begins with Tchitchikoff's arrival and ends with the continuation of his journey. The celebrated closing paragraph likening Russia to a speeding troika establishes the connection between Russia and Tchitchikoff, whose destinies are both unresolved. As the instrument of Tchitchikoff's quest, the road represents experience, movement, and change. The dynamic of the road balances the inertia of the landowners. Finally, the road describes the narrative itself. Since the concept of a journey loosely structures the novel, digressions, random events, and episodic characters seem natural. In his lyric asides, the narrator compares his enterprise to a journey where unexpected turns create significant developments. Gogol takes his cue from the picaresque novel, with its wandering heroes, outlandish adventures, and digressive narrators.

The first volume is characteristic in its lack of plot or resolution. From the opening paragraph, essentials are blurred and irrelevancies are sharply etched. Gogol is particularly fond of suspending the action while he develops a simile at such length that it functions as a tale in its own right. While the epic simile generates beauty out of mundane details or broadens the significance of events, Gogol's extended similes often become comic digressions. Similes emerge mocking conventions of epic narration and making fun of the characters and events of Gogol's own tale. Gogol combines comedy of situation and slapstick physical humor with verbal humor, including witty puns, absurd neologisms, purposefully vague dialogue, and exaggerated formulaic expressions. The plot is consistently overwhelmed by comic details and lyric digressions.

Dead Souls is largely a book written about how it is written. The authorial interruptions are confessions, admonishments, pleas for sympathy, and complaints about probable misunderstandings. Throughout the text, the narrator anticipates objections to his "low" language, his use of a scoundrel as a hero, the lack of love intrigue, and other differences from conventional novels. The interpolated "Tale of Captain Kopeykin" in the tenth chapter is a masterpiece of *skaz*, or mannered narration in which the speaker unwittingly vies with his story for attention using a vivid manner that overshadows the content of the story. Ultimately, the entire narrative exists as a performance, a colloquial stylization replete with outlandish words and irrelevancies balanced by a desire for lofty lyricism and moral uplift. *Dead Souls* finally emerges as an enigmatic work that continues to fluctuate between the comic and the tragic, the epic and the picaresque.

"Critical Evaluation" by Pamela Pavliscak

Bibliography:
Fanger, Donald. *The Creation of Nikolai Gogol.* Cambridge, Mass.: Harvard University Press, 1979. An interesting consideration of the relationship between Gogol and his readers. Evaluates Gogol's commentary on literature within his texts and explores the road as the dominant metaphor of *Dead Souls.*
Gippius, V. V. *Gogol.* Edited and translated by Robert Maguire. Ann Arbor, Mich.: Ardis, 1981. This classic treatment of Gogol's life and works is enhanced by glosses on contemporary figures. The book treats Gogol's literary influences in detail. The chapter on *Dead Souls* considers the structure of the novel as a gallery of caricatures and explores Gogol's reformulation of the picaresque novel.
Griffiths, Frederick, and Stanley Rabinowitz. *Gogol, Dostoevsky, and National Narrative.*

Evanston, Ill.: Northwestern University Press, 1990. Places Gogol's work within the frame-work of the epic tradition. Evaluates stylistic aspects of the text, such as Homeric similes and hyperbole, that create the mock-heroic mood of *Dead Souls*.

Maguire, Robert, ed. and trans. *Gogol from the Twentieth Century*. Princeton, N.J.: Princeton University Press, 1974. A collection of well-known Russian essays. These varied approaches to Gogol's work include a consideration of Gogol as a realist depicting provincial life, a psychoanalytic evaluation of his prose, and a stylistic analysis of his wordplay. The intro-duction provides a thorough overview of the criticism.

Nabokov, Vladimir. *Nikolai Gogol*. Norfolk, Conn.: New Directions, 1944. The clever tone of Nabokov's book mirrors that of Gogol's prose. While the stylistic analysis is eclectic and brilliant, the primary focus is on banality. Gogol's genius is his attention to the absurd in everyday life.

DEATH AND THE KING'S HORSEMAN

Type of work: Drama
Author: Wole Soyinka (1934-   )
Type of plot: Tragedy
Time of plot: 1944
Locale: Oyo, Nigeria
First published: 1975

> *Principal characters:*
> ELESIN OBA, the king's horseman
> PRAISE-SINGER, leader of Elesin's retinue
> IYALOJA, a senior woman of the Oyo market
> SIMON PILKINGS, a colonial district officer
> JANE PILKINGS, his wife
> SERGEANT AMUSA, a colonial police officer
> JOSEPH, the Pilkingses' houseboy
> BRIDE, a young woman
> OLUNDE, Elesin's oldest son

The Story:

The alafin (king) had died. It was time for his chief lieutenant, Elesin Oba, to will his own death, so that he might accompany the alafin on his passage to the next life. As Elesin entered the market, the Praise-Singer pleaded with him to tarry a while, to enjoy the last fruits of life in this world. Elesin, a man of enormous courage, rejected this plea and boasted of his readiness to meet death without fear. He talked of the Not-I bird that sounded at the approach of death, echoed by people from all levels of society who sought to flee death—all but he, the king's horseman, who had been born and lived for this moment.

The women of the marketplace, led by Iyaloja, also asked whether he was truly ready to face death, praising him all the while for his strength of will. On this night, nothing could be denied him: rich clothing, fine food, beautiful women, all were at his pleasure. A beautiful young woman, the Bride, caught his eye. He determined that he would have her, even though she was already promised as a bride to Iyaloja's son. Tactfully, Iyaloja suggested that he should not claim the Bride, just as an honorable man will leave food at a feast for the children. The insistence of the king's horseman at this moment could not be denied, however, and Elesin and the woman retired to the bridal chamber.

At the district officer's house, the Pilkingses prepared to attend a costume ball in honor of the visiting British prince. They were modeling their disguises, ritual masks of the Yoruba dead cult, when Sergeant Amusa arrived to report a disturbance in the marketplace caused by Elesin's preparations for death. A Muslim, Amusa was flustered by the Pilkingses' blasphemous use of the death masks in a nonreligious context and could not express himself clearly. The Pilkingses' servant, Joseph, a convert to Christianity, explained what was happening, whereupon Mr. Pilkings decided to halt the ritual suicide, upholding Western ideals of the sanctity of life. Pilkings ordered Amusa to make the arrest while he and his wife went to meet the Prince.

Back in the marketplace, Amusa's attempt to enter the bridal chamber and arrest Elesin was blocked by Iyaloja and the young women, who mocked the policeman as a eunuch neutered by the white colonial authorities. Defeated by the women, Amusa retreated to seek reinforcement.

Then Elesin emerged from the bridal chamber bearing bloodstained bedclothes, evidence of the Bride's virginity and his success in impregnating her, creating a union of life and the passage to death. Filled with vitality and sexual satisfaction, he momentarily lost his will to die, but recovered and fell gradually into a trance. As his spirit moved away from this world, his body began a heavy dance accompanied by the Praise-Singer's ritual pronouncements.

Amusa arrived at the ball in tattered clothing to report his failure to arrest Elesin. Mr. Pilkings, admonished by his supervisor to maintain control, took matters into his own hands, going off to arrest Elesin. While he was gone, Elesin's son Olunde, whom the Pilkingses had befriended and sent to England to study medicine, arrived, expecting to bury his father after hearing in England of the alafin's death. As Jane and Olunde spoke of England, Olunde showed that he did not accept British values, despite his Western education.

Seeking a topic on which they might agree, Olunde and Jane discussed the progress of the war. Jane told him of an English naval captain who had died while destroying his ship, thereby saving the city. She found his self-sacrifice difficult to understand, convinced there must have been another way. Olunde found the self-sacrifice life-affirming, being death in the cause of life. Jane then informed him that her husband was en route to prevent Elesin's suicide. Olunde explained that Pilkings' success would be catastrophic because of the ritual importance of the horseman's death. Pilkings returned and became nervous and distracted on hearing Olunde's words. The mood was explained when a heavily chained Elesin arrived on the scene; Pilkings had succeeded. Olunde first ignored his father's presence and then rejected him, calling him, like Amusa, an eater of leftovers.

In his prison cell beneath the resident's palace, Elesin first blamed Pilkings for arresting him. The moment at which Elesin should have joined the alafin on his journey to heaven had passed with the arrest, and it was too late to restore the cosmic order. Elesin claimed to have regained his sense of purpose after experiencing the contempt of his son, but Elesin was no longer able to carry out his own death. When Pilkings was called away, Elesin shifted blame to the Bride for tempting him away from his destiny. In truth, the white man had only provided an excuse for him to succumb to his desire to remain in the world, enjoying its pleasures.

The Pilkingses returned to the cell to announce a visitor, Iyaloja, who castigated Elesin for his loss of will and the betrayal of his people. She also announced that a volunteer had been found to carry Elesin's last message: that he would not come to the waiting alafin. When the body of this messenger was carried into the prison area, Pilkings and Elesin were both horrified to recognize Olunde, who had taken his father's place. In a final affront to Elesin's lost honor, Pilkings refused to allow Elesin to whisper the ritual message in his son's ear, thus—from the Yoruba perspective—completing the destruction of the cosmic order. Left with nothing to salvage, Elesin strangled himself with his own chains before the colonial authorities could react. His death, however, came too late to fulfill his hereditary function. What hopes remained lay with the unborn child the Bride carried, the only fruit of the night's events.

Critical Evaluation:

When Wole Soyinka became the first African to win the Nobel Prize in Literature in 1986, his work was cited for its strongly mythic blending of African—specifically Yoruban—ritual with Western dramatic forms, a blending that is particularly evident in *Death and the King's Horseman*. The play is based on an actual event in Nigerian colonial history. In 1946, British officials intervened to prevent a ritual suicide such as Elesin Oba attempts in the play. In the traditional Yoruba cosmology, which by the 1940's was already eroded by the introduction of Christianity, the dead king must be joined by his courier, who acts as a mediator between the living and the dead. Insofar as the continuity of living and dead is central to Yoruba concepts of community, Elesin's failure to carry out his suicide threatens the social order.

The play begins with an evocation of African ritual. The scene in the marketplace appears completely out of time: There are no white people, no mention whatever of the colonial circumstances, and the ritual suicide being undertaken is one that has occurred repeatedly in Yoruba history. It is into this world that the first intimations of Elesin's lack of will are introduced. The audience witnesses his desire for the young woman, who represents life. Despite Elesin's protestations, his fear of death is evident. Only after this theme has been established does the play shift, in Act II, to a more familiar Western pattern of realistic drama, when it moves to the topic of the colonial powers.

The British colonial officer and his wife demonstrate their inability to comprehend spiritual values not only by their profaning of profoundly religious symbols for use as costumes at a masked ball but also by Simon Pilkings' blasphemous references to Christianity before his devout servant Joseph. It is their obliviousness to the sacred that enables them to bring about Elesin's failure. His understanding of his spiritual role makes his failure tragic. The role of the colonial district officer, Pilkings, in stopping the suicide, tempts the audience to see the play as enacting the cultural conflict between African traditions and the usurping colonial power. Soyinka warned against such a reductive reading and in fact altered events to make the colonial intervention less significant than it was in the historical antecedent. Further, by moving events from the postwar period to 1944, he creates parallels between sacrifices undertaken by the British and the sacrifice that Elesin fails to make.

Soyinka complicates matters by presenting two models of sacrifice among the British: the naval captain who destroyed his damaged munitions ship to preserve the city and the prince who risks his life to bolster morale among the colonists. Matters are further complicated by Olunde's decision to substitute for his father, despite his manifest lack of belief in the tradition that calls for this sacrifice. At the beginning of the play, the Western-educated Olunde expects, after the burial of his father, to resume his medical studies rather than to inherit his father's ritual role.

Instead of a limited political tract on the colonial suppression of Yoruba customs, then, Soyinka presents a more complex metaphysical conflict within the soul of his protagonist. Much of the play's first act is given to Elesin's song about the "Not-I bird," the desire to deny death that, he claims, afflicts all human beings but himself. At the moment of truth, however, Elesin proves as vulnerable to fear as the rest of humanity; called upon to die for the sake of his community, he chooses to live for himself.

The play's merging of Western and traditional motifs and its tendency to complicate apparently clear lines of division reflects Soyinka's conviction that there is no pure literature, that all art reflects the combination and complication of various traditions. The inability to cast the play into a simple cultural category marks its continuity with other great works of modernist art. In *Death and the King's Horseman*, Soyinka appropriates Western forms to speak for Africans.

A. Waller Hastings

Bibliography:
Katrak, Ketu H. *Wole Soyinka and Modern Tragedy: A Study of Dramatic Theory and Practice.* Westport, Conn.: Greenwood Press, 1986. Extended study of the roots of Soyinka's art in Yoruba ritual and Western dramatic traditions. Argues that the play dramatizes the common

fear of death that can be allayed only with ritual suicide, while criticizing the tradition itself and seeking a mythic revision suitable for the modern world.

Ogundele, Wole. *"Death and the King's Horseman:* A Poet's Quarrel with His Culture." *Research in African Literatures* 25, no. 1 (Spring, 1994): 47-60. Treats the play from a social and political perspective, focusing on the social conditions influencing Elesin's moral position.

Ralph-Bowman, Mark. "'Leaders and Left-Overs': A Reading of Soyinka's *Death and the King's Horseman." Research in African Literatures* 14, no. 1 (February, 1983): 81-97. Emphasizes the spiritual aspects of the play, portraying Elesin as a failed Christ figure whose actions constitute blasphemy and Olunde as a redemptive figure, upholding his culture despite exposure to the West.

Whitaker, Thomas R. "Wole Soyinka." In *Post-Colonial English Drama*, edited by Bruce King. New York: St. Martin's Press, 1992. Describes the play as a revision of Yoruba folk opera, under the influence of Western tragedy and Ibsen-like realism. Argues that all moral positions in the play are made problematic by the mingling of Western and African traditions.

Williams, Adebayo. "Ritual and the Political Unconscious: The Case of *Death and the King's Horseman." Research in African Literatures* 24, no. 1 (Spring, 1993): 67-79. Applies to the play the concept that ritual acts carry out political functions through a kind of collective unconscious. Argues that Elesin's suicide acts to reinforce the ruling class.

DEATH COMES FOR THE ARCHBISHOP

Type of work: Novel
Author: Willa Cather (1873-1947)
Type of plot: Historical realism
Time of plot: Last half of the nineteenth century
Locale: New Mexico and Arizona
First published: 1927

Principal characters:
BISHOP JEAN MARIE LATOUR, Vicar Apostolic of New Mexico
FATHER JOSEPH VAILLANT, his friend and a missionary priest
KIT CARSON, a frontier scout
JACINTO, an Indian guide

The Story:

In 1851, Father Jean Marie Latour reached Santa Fé, where he was to become Vicar Apostolic of New Mexico. His journey from the shores of Lake Ontario had been long and arduous. He had lost his belongings in a shipwreck at Galveston and had suffered painful injury in a wagon accident at San Antonio. When he arrived, accompanied by his good friend Father Joseph Vaillant, the Mexican priests refused to recognize his authority. He had no choice but to ride three thousand miles into Mexico to secure the necessary papers from the bishop of Durango.

On the road, he lost his way in an arid landscape of red hills and gaunt junipers. His thirst became a vertigo of mind and senses, and he could blot out his own agony only by repeating the cry of the Savior on the Cross. As he was about to give up all hope, he saw a tree growing in the shape of a cross. A short time later, he arrived in a Mexican settlement called Agua Secreta (hidden water). Stopping at the home of Benito, Father Latour first performed marriage ceremonies and then baptized all the children.

At Durango, he received the necessary documents and started the long trip back to Santa Fé. Father Vaillant had in the meantime won over the inhabitants of Santa Fé and had set up the episcopal residence in an old adobe house. On the first morning after his return, Father Latour, now officially bishop, heard the unexpected sound of a bell ringing the Angelus. Father Vaillant told him that he had found the bell, bearing the date 1356, in the basement of old San Miguel Church.

On a missionary journey to Albuquerque in March, Father Vaillant acquired a handsome cream-colored mule as a gift and another just like it for Bishop Latour. These mules, Contento and Angelica, faithfully served the men for many years. On another trip, as the two priests were riding together on their mules, they were caught in a sleet storm and stopped at the rude shack of the American Buck Scales. His Mexican wife warned the travelers by gestures that their lives were in danger, so they rode on to Mora without spending the night. The next morning, the Mexican woman appeared in town and told them that her husband had murdered and robbed four travelers and that he had killed her three babies. As a result, Scales was brought to justice and his wife, Magdalena, was sent to the home of Kit Carson, the famous frontier scout. From that time on, Kit Carson was a valuable friend of the two priests. Magdalena later became the housekeeper and manager for the kitchens of the Sisters of Loretto.

During his first year at Santa Fé, Bishop Latour was called to a meeting of the Plenary Council in Baltimore. On the return journey, he brought back with him five nuns sent to establish the school of Our Lady of Light. Attended by Jacinto, an American Indian who served as his guide, Latour spent some time visiting his own vicariate. Padre Gallegos, whom he visited at Albuquerque, acted more like a professional gambler than a priest, but because he was very popular with the natives, Latour did not remove him at that time. At last, he arrived at the end of his long journey, the top of the mesa at Acoma. On that trip, he heard the legend of Fray Baltazar, killed during an uprising of the Acoma Indians.

A month after his visit, he suspended Padre Gallegos and put Father Vaillant in charge of the parish at Albuquerque. On a trip to the Pecos Mountains, Vaillant fell ill with an attack of the black measles. Bishop Latour, hearing of his illness, set out to nurse his friend. Jacinto again served as guide on the cold, snowy trip. When Latour reached his friend's bedside, he found that Kit Carson had arrived before him. As soon as the sick man could sit in the saddle, his friends took him back to Santa Fé.

Bishop Latour decided to investigate the parish of Taos, where the powerful old priest Antonio José Martinez was the ruler of both spiritual and temporal matters. The following year, the bishop was called to Rome. When he returned, he brought with him four young priests from the Seminary of Montferrand and a Spanish priest to replace Padre Martinez at Taos.

Bishop Latour had one great ambition, to build a cathedral in Santa Fé. He was assisted by the rich Mexican rancheros, but above all by his good friend Don Antonio Olivares. When Don Antonio died, it was found that he had left his estate to his wife and daughter during their lives, after which it was to go to the church. Don Antonio's brothers contested the will on the grounds that the daughter, Señorita Inez, was too old to be Doña Isabella's daughter. The bishop and his vicar had to persuade the vain, coquettish widow to swear to her true age of fifty-three, rather than the forty-two years she claimed. Thus the estate eventually went to the church.

Father Vaillant was sent to Tucson, but after several years, Bishop Latour decided to recall him to Santa Fé. When he arrived, the bishop showed him the stone for building the cathedral. About that time, Bishop Latour received a letter from the bishop of Leavenworth. Because of the discovery of gold near Pike's Peak, he asked to have a priest sent there from Bishop Latour's diocese. Father Vaillant, the obvious choice, spent the rest of his life in Colorado, though he returned to Santa Fé with the papal emissary when Bishop Latour was made an archbishop. Father Vaillant later became the first bishop of Colorado, and he died there after years of service. Archbishop Latour attended his impressive funeral services.

After the death of his friend, Father Latour retired to a modest country estate near Santa Fé. He had dreamed during all his missionary years of the time when he could retire to his own fertile green Auvergne in France, but in the end he decided that he could not leave the land of his labors. He spent his last years with memories of the journeys he and Father Vaillant had made over thousands of miles of desert country. Bernard Ducrot, a young seminarian from France, became like a son to him during those last years.

When Father Latour knew that his time had come to die, he asked to be taken into town to spend his last days near the cathedral. On the last day of his life, the church was filled with people who came to pray for him, as word that he was dying spread through the town. He died in the still twilight, and the cathedral bell, tolling in the early darkness, carried the news to the waiting countryside that death had come for Father Latour.

Critical Evaluation:

When writing of her great predecessor and teacher, Sarah Orne Jewett, Willa Cather expressed her belief that the quality that gives a work of literature greatness is the "voice" of the author, the sincere, unadorned, and unique vision of a writer coming to grips with the material chosen. If any one characteristic can be said to dominate the writings of Cather, it is that of a true and moving sincerity. She never tried to twist her subject matter to suit a preconceived purpose, and she resisted the temptation to dress up homely material. She gave herself absolutely to her chosen material, and the result was a series of books both truthful and rich with intimations of the destiny of the American continent. By digging into the roots of her material, she exposed deeper meanings, which she expressed with a deceptive simplicity. Her vision and craftsmanship were seldom more successful than in *Death Comes for the Archbishop*. So completely did Cather merge her voice with her material that some critics have felt that the book is almost too polished and lacks the sense of struggle necessary in a truly great novel. This, in fact, indicates the magnitude of the author's achievement and the brilliance of her technical skill. *Death Comes for the Archbishop* resonates with the unspoken beliefs of the author and the resolved conflicts that went into its construction. On the surface, it is cleanly wrought and simple, but it is a more complicated and profound book than it appears at first reading. Cather learned well from Sarah Orne Jewett the secrets of artless art and of sophisticated craftsmanship that disarms by its simplicity.

Death Comes for the Archbishop is a novel that reaffirms part of the American past, the history of the Catholic Southwest beautifully told through the re-creation of the lives of Bishop Lamy and Father Macheboeuf, two devout and noble missionary priests in the Vicariate of New Mexico during the second half of the nineteenth century. The novel combines the narrative with bright glimpses into the past in stories that cut backward into time. Tales and legends that extend beyond the period of American occupation into three centuries of Spanish colonial history and back to the primitive tribal life of the Hopi, the Navajo, and the vanished cliff-dwellers break the chronicle at many points, giving it density and variety and allowing the work to recapture completely the spirit and movement of the pioneer West. It is true that this novel is an epic and a regional history, but much more than either, it is a tale of personal isolation, of one man's life reduced to the painful weariness of his own sensitivities. Father Latour is a hero in the most profound sense of the word, displaying virtues of courage and determination, but he is also a very human protagonist, with doubts and inner conflicts. His personality is held up in startling contrast to that of his friend, Father Vaillant, a simpler, though no less good, individual. Cather's austere style perfectly captures the scholarly, urbane, religious devotion that characterizes Father Latour, and the reader is always aware of a sense of the dignity of human life, as exemplified in the person of one individual. Cather was not afraid to draw a good man, a man who could stand above others because of his deeds and innate quality.

Although based on a true sequence of events, the book focuses less on plot than on character and, perhaps more specifically, the interplay of environment and character. Throughout the book, the reader is aware of the human reaction to the land, and that of one man to the land he has chosen. Subtly and deeply, the author suggests that the soul of the man is profoundly altered by the soul of the land. Cather never doubts that the land, too, possesses a soul and that this soul can transform a human being in complex and important ways. She was fascinated by the way the landscape of the Southwest, when reduced to its essences, seemed to reduce human beings to their essences. Cather abandoned traditional realism in this book and turned toward the directness of symbolism. With stark pictures and vivid styles, she created an imaginary world rooted in but transcending realism. The rigid economy with which the book is written gives it unusual power in the reader's mind long after the reading. The greatest symbol is provided by the personality of Bishop Latour, who stands like a windswept crag in the vast New Mexico landscape and represents the nobility of the human spirit despite the inner conflicts against which all must struggle.

The descriptions of place set the emotional tone of the novel. The quality of life is intimately related to the landscape, and the accounts of the journeys and the efforts to survive in the barren land help to create an odd warmth and almost surreal passion in the narrative. Bishop Latour and Father Vaillant establish a definite emotional relationship with the country; if the other characters in the book are less vividly realized as individuals, it is perhaps because they do not seem to have the same relationship with the land. Certainly none of them is involved in the intense love-hate relationship with the land with which the two main characters struggle for so many years.

Although the narrative encompasses many years, the novel is essentially static and built of a series of rich images and thoughtful movements highlighted and captured as by a camera. This quality of the narrative is a characteristic of Cather's style: The frozen moments of contemplation and glimpses into Father Latour's inner world and spiritual loneliness are the moments that give the book its greatness. Despite the presence of Kit Carson, the novel is not an adventure story any more than it is merely the account of a pair of churchmen attempting to establish their church in a difficult new terrain. The cathedral becomes the most important symbol in the final part of the book, representing the earthly successes of a man dedicated to unworldly ambitions. This conflict between the earthly and the spiritual is at the heart of Bishop Latour's personality and at the heart of the book. The reader understands, at the end, when the bell tolls for Father Latour, that the man's victory was greater than he ever knew.

"Critical Evaluation" by Bruce D. Reeves

Bibliography:
Fryer, Judith. *Felicitous Space: The Imaginative Structures of Edith Wharton and Willa Cather.* Chapel Hill: University of North Carolina Press, 1986. An important inquiry into the meaning of actual and imagined spaces in the works of the two writers. Explores Cather's unfurnished rooms and landscapes and gives particular attention to her use of color and light in *Death Comes for the Archbishop.*

Gerber, Philip. *Willa Cather.* Boston: Twayne, 1975. A brief but solid introduction to Cather's life and literary career. *Death Comes for the Archbishop* is seen as a retreat into the past and as an implicit comparison to an inferior present, which accounts for its elegiac tone. Contains a select annotated bibliography of criticism.

March, John. *A Reader's Companion to the Fiction of Willa Cather.* Westport, Conn.: Greenwood Press, 1993. An excellent source for any reader of Cather. Contains, alphabetically listed, often lengthy explanations of place names, proper names, and other objects of importance in Cather's fiction.

Murphy, John J. "Willa Cather's Archbishop: A Western and Classical Perspective." *Western American Literature* 13 (Summer, 1978): 141-150. Argues that the novel reflects Cather's cyclical view of history and her belief that American experience repeats the European. In this reading, Latour becomes a variation of the Western hero.

Skaggs, Merrill Maguire. *After the World Broke in Two: The Later Novels of Willa Cather.* Charlottesville: University Press of Virginia, 1990. Provides an intellectual history that focuses on the works of Cather's artistic maturity. Sees *Death Comes for the Archbishop* as Cather's greatest achievement because of its ability to ask and provide answers to questions of faith, art, and the continuity of life.

DEATH IN THE AFTERNOON

Type of work: Autobiography
Author: Ernest Hemingway (1899-1961)
First published: 1932

Ernest Hemingway's *Death in the Afternoon* is a personal examination of bullfighting in Spain during the 1920's and 1930's. Hemingway began visiting Spain in the summer of 1923 and quickly became involved in the world of bullfighting. He stayed in the same hotels, ate in the same restaurants, and drank in the same bars as the matadors. He followed them as they performed in different cities. Eventually, he began making annual trips to Pamplona, where bullfights were held in connection with the religious festival of San Fermín. Pamplona became the setting for the climactic scenes of *The Sun Also Rises* (1926).

Drawing on this background, Hemingway attempts in *Death in the Afternoon* to celebrate "the modern Spanish bullfight" and to explain it "both emotionally and practically" for an audience of Americans. Hemingway assumes that his readers may be disgusted by the idea of bullfighting, but wishes them to give him the opportunity to show them what it is all about before they arrive at a judgment.

Death in the Afternoon is more than a book about bullfighting, however. The book is as much a book about Ernest Hemingway as it is a book about bullfighting. It is filled with his perceptions, his experiences, and his way of looking at life. So much of the information given in the book is autobiographical that it must be read in order to understand the life of Hemingway.

Chapter 1 begins with a narration of Hemingway's own early experience with bullfighting. He reports that he first went to the bullfights because of the influence of Gertrude Stein. Before going, Hemingway says that he expected to be horrified by the killing of the horses in the ring during the bullfight. He went, however, because it served a goal of his writing. He was trying to learn how to "put down what really happened in action; what the actual things were which produced the emotion you experienced."

With this goal in mind, Hemingway went to Spain to study the bullfights, but once there he found them to be so complicated and so compelling to him that he began to study bullfighting for its own sake.

The rest of chapter 1 is an interesting mixture of essay and personal observation. Hemingway deals with the question of the morality of bullfighting by writing on the difference between people who identify psychologically with animals (and thus who think the bullfights are barbaric because bulls and frequently horses are killed) and people who identify with humans (and become upset only when the matador performs poorly or is injured). He deals with the question of the aesthetics of bullfighting by writing about how the enjoyment of the art of bullfighting increases in the same way that a person develops an ear for music or a sensitive palate for wine. The basic thread of the narrative is always bullfighting, but Hemingway cannot keep himself from engaging in asides, telling anecdotes, and making lengthy commentaries on other subjects. In this book on bullfighting, Hemingway is creating a persona that developed over the years into the voice of "Papa" Hemingway. In letters that Hemingway writes before *Death in the Afternoon* he often apologizes for the advice that he gives to family and friends, calling himself a Dutch uncle. At the time of the writing of *Death in the Afternoon*, he is beginning to stop apologizing. His tone throughout the book is one of a kindly, knowledgeable guide who knows what is best for the reader.

Hemingway was not an old man when he wrote *Death in the Afternoon*. He was relatively young. The arrogance that cost Hemingway many friends over the years is, in this book, beginning to show. There are passages in the book in which Hemingway sounds more like a bully than a kindly guide, and the overall impression that he gives of himself is that of a much older and much more experienced man. This arrogance is seen in an extreme degree in his attacks on other authors, which are sprinkled throughout the book. Hemingway suggests that some writers write the way they do because they are sexually frustrated; if they would take care of this problem, their writing would improve greatly. The book contains vicious asides about fellow writers such as William Faulkner, Aldous Huxley, André Gide, and Jean Cocteau. The book was widely condemned by critics for this meanness when it first appeared.

Hemingway also shows his fascination with technical trivia in *Death in the Afternoon*. Hemingway loved any type of activity that involves the complicated use of equipment. With bullfighting Hemingway was able to indulge this fascination to an extreme degree. His discussion of the various pieces of equipment and the techniques used in bullfighting takes up four chapters. Hemingway also demonstrates an almost encyclopedic knowledge of the bulls that are specifically bred for bullfights. He devotes another four chapters to a discussion of the size, weight, power, and mating habits of the bulls.

Another example of Hemingway's love for technical trivia is the book's series of appendices. One appendix contains sixty-four pages of black and white photos of bulls, bullfighters, fight techniques, and even of a horn wound on a matador's leg as it is being operated on. Hemingway includes detailed captions that explain the significance of each photo. Another appendix defines the meaning of hundreds of Spanish bullfighting terms, but also has whimsical entries on pickpockets, sodomites, and "tarts about town."

When *Death in the Afternoon* was first published, some critics accused Hemingway of padding the book with appendices that were of little use to the reader. Certainly, many of the appendices are very useful to the student of bullfighting, but some of them probably are padding. One appendix, for example, is nothing more than a series of notebook entries from Hemingway's Paris years about the reactions of his friends and family members (whom he does not identify by name) to their first bullfight.

In addition to Hemingway's evolving persona and his obsession with details, *Death in the Afternoon* also demonstrates the author's recurrent fascination with death. One of the book's major themes is the decadence of modern bullfighting, as opposed to the purity of bullfighting's earlier years. Decadence in bullfighting involves the matador's using tricks to appear to be a lot closer to the bull (and thus to danger and death) than he really is. The decadent matador causes the crowd of onlookers to feel an emotion that is false because he is really in no great danger.

True bullfighting, according to Hemingway, is something else. Bullfighting is not really a sport, since it is not an equal contest between man and bull. The drawing power of the fight is tragedy. The odds of the matador being killed are small. However, the competent matador can "increase the amount of danger of death that he runs" to the precise degree that he wishes. It is to the matador's credit if he deliberately attempts something that is extremely dangerous. It is to his dishonor if he does something dangerous through ignorance or torpidity. To Hemingway, that a man hazards death, while working at the limits of his skill to avoid it, makes a bullfight worth seeing.

Hemingway evaluates a number of bullfighters against the standard of their genuineness in hazarding death. He discusses great matadors of the past, such as Joselito and Belmonte, and bullfighters of his time, such as Sidney Franklin, the "pride of Brooklyn," an American who was trying to earn a living in Spain as a matador in the 1930's.

There are passages in the book in which Hemingway also seems intent on shocking his readers. He graphically describes the goring of bullfighters in the ring and the subsequent operations in hospitals. He includes one of his short stories, "A Natural History of the Dead," at the end of chapter 12.

The reader of *Death in the Afternoon* can learn a great deal of technical information about bullfighting. The greater appeal of this book is not what it teaches about bullfighting but rather what it teaches about a man who loved bulls, bullfights, matadors, and Spain: Ernest Hemingway.

In *Death in the Afternoon* Ernest Hemingway is encountered as a human being, without the veil of fiction. He is a writer at the height of his creative powers and at the height of his own arrogance. Hemingway shows his readers a clear picture of who he is by describing the things he loves and the things he hates. This picture is not always a flattering one. It contains his greatness, his pettiness, and his cruelty. The picture is, however, an extraordinarily accurate one. *Death in the Afternoon* must be read by anyone who wants to understand Ernest Hemingway.

Howard Cox

Bibliography:
Castillo Puche, José. *Hemingway in Spain.* Translated by Helen R. Lane. Garden City, N.Y.: Doubleday, 1974. Enlightening account of the time that Hemingway spent in Spain during the last years of his life.

Eastman, Max. "Bull in the Afternoon." In *Art and the Life of Action.* New York: Alfred A. Knopf, 1934. Scathing review of *Death in the Afternoon* that describes Hemingway's literary style as one of "wearing false hair on his chest." Hemingway and Eastman came to blows over this review.

Griffin, Peter. *Along with Youth.* New York: Oxford University Press, 1985. Chapter 1 discusses early influences on Hemingway's writing and argues that *Death in the Afternoon* is Hemingway's version of Mark Twain's *Life on the Mississippi.*

Hemingway, Ernest. *The Dangerous Summer.* New York: Charles Scribner's Sons, 1960. In many ways a rewriting of *Death in the Afternoon.* It concerns the 1959 bullfighting season and parallels the earlier book almost exactly in form and structure. Hemingway reexamines some of the ideas about bullfighting that he discussed in his earlier book.

Hotchner, A. E. *Hemingway and His World.* New York: Vendome Press, 1989. Recounts all of the events in Hemingway's life that went into the making of *Death in the Afternoon* and gives a sampling of the critical reaction to the book. Lavishly illustrated with photographs of the places in Spain that Hemingway visited and of Hemingway as a young man.

A DEATH IN THE FAMILY

Type of work: Novel
Author: James Agee (1909-1955)
Type of plot: Domestic realism
Time of plot: Summer, 1915; May 15-20, 1916
Locale: Knoxville, Tennessee
First published: 1957

> *Principal characters:*
> RUFUS FOLLET, a six-year-old boy
> JAY, Rufus' father
> MARY, Jay's wife and Rufus' mother
> CATHERINE, Rufus' younger sister
> FRANK and
> RALPH, Jay's brothers
> ANDREW, Mary's brother
> HANNAH LYNCH, Jay and Mary's friend and helper

The Story:

The novel's nostalgic evocation of an earlier, quiet time is set by "Knoxville: Summer 1915," a poetic reminiscence Agee had written in 1936. It was selected by an editor to be a preface to the novel, which was not quite complete when James Agee died. The preface re-creates childhood memories of the peaceful summer evenings of Agee's middle-class Knoxville home as the women finished their kitchen work and the men, collars open and in shirtsleeves, watched by their children and older relatives, turned out to water their lawns. Such evenings were filled with shapes formed by spraying hoses, the sounds of nozzles being adjusted, and the recollections of the family, its work set aside momentarily, sitting outside on a quilt making small talk, watching the sky, waiting for the night to come. The preface closes with a life-affirming benediction: "May God bless my people, my uncle, my aunt, my mother, my good father, oh, remember them kindly in their time of trouble; and in the hour of their taking away."

Part 1 of the novel's three parts opens with Rufus—Agee's real, and detested, nickname— being taken, joyously, by Jay, his father, to see a slapstick Charlie Chaplin movie, one that was all the funnier for being slightly risqué. Afterward, deciding to "hoist a couple," Jay took Rufus into a bar where Jay bragged about his boy's reading ability, which Rufus, somewhat dismayed, realized was his father's way of not embarrassing him about his inability to fight off other boys. Balance was soon restored, the bonding tightened, and the contract between them reaffirmed, as Rufus was offered a Life Saver—man-to-man—as Jay used another to cloak his breath and Rufus grasped that when his father set out on a slow, contented pace homeward it was because Jay genuinely savored time spent with his son. That gentle night, as Rufus drifted into sleep, he heard his father telling his mother that he would return before the kids were awake and then the grinding sounds of the family Ford being cranked. In the morning, Mary explained why Jay was not at breakfast.

His parents had been wakened by a phone call from Jay's younger brother, Ralph. Ralph and Jay's ill father lived on a farm miles out of Knoxville, and the message was that their father was dying. Jay had decided, chancing that his brother was right, to make the trip. Mary prepared Jay for his journey while Rufus and his younger sister, Catherine, slept.

Rufus imagined his father's thoughts as he drove to the farm: Jay's thoughts of home, encounters at the ferry, and the pleasant feel of Jay moving into his home country. Rufus imagined Mary too, strict and religious, lying in bed, reviewing her marriage: its flaws, her dislike of Jay's rural background, his lack of religion, her unconcern for his father, her resentment that others forgave Jay his weaknesses because of his generous ways, and her deep anger over the burdens he imposed upon her. She thought of the gulf that widened between them, but she grimly saw her duty to put the future in the children and to raise them Catholic.

Rufus meanwhile dreamed of his father exorcising his childish fears during a nightmare by joking and singing to him, and of his mother's different comforting and songs. He recalled both parents' discussing the imminent birth of his sister, Catherine. Together, these were Rufus' filtered remembrances of the varieties of love he received and of the loves he perceived between others.

Part 2 deals with the accidental death that would shatter the sense that Rufus and his family had made of their world: the phone call conveying the ominous news of the accident, the family's trying to cushion Mary's shock with confirmation of Jay's instantaneous death, Mary's efforts to shield the children, and the full realization of the tragic event rippling through the family. Rufus, meanwhile, reflected on visits with relatives that bared to him the network of familial relationships. His family life he contrasted with the torture and tensions he suffered at the hands of other boys.

Mary, in part 3, explained Jay's death to Rufus and Catherine, answering their questions as best she could, but not quite clarifying the meaning of death. A priest was called. Relatives and friends arrived in preparation for the funeral. Finally Mary allowed her children a last view of their father before his interment, Rufus all the while trying to comfort a bewildered Catherine. Afterward, placed in others' charge, Rufus glimpsed his father's coffin and was proud Jay was so heavy and that it took several men to handle it. When the graveyard ceremony concluded, Uncle Andrew confided a miracle to Rufus: Andrew had seen a beautiful butterfly land on Jay's coffin, a sign of Jay's ascent to Heaven. Andrew then bitterly denounced the priest, the funeral's religious claptrap, and those who prayed, leaving Rufus baffled and full of unasked questions before he was taken home.

Critical Evaluation:

Cast as a novel, *A Death in the Family* is James Agee's long-planned autobiographical memorial to his father. The event that inspired the memorial was a simple one, though its consequences were not. Hugh James (Jay) Agee died in an automobile accident outside of Knoxville, Tennessee, on May 18, 1916. Jay had been responding to an emergency call from a brother that their father was dying. The brother had been drinking and, ironically, there was no emergency, a situation made more poignant by the reader's foreknowledge of what was to happen. Six-year-old Rufus, Jay's son, whose childhood memories, dreams, and reconstructions informed the story, had idolized his father (rather than his mother, Mary) as the nurturing parent, the model around whom he sensed his place in the world and the beginning of his own identity. His father's death shattered the delicate balance and tranquillity of Rufus' childhood, and, in fact, marked James Agee for the remainder of his own rather brief life.

A 1958 Pulitzer Prize winner, Agee's *A Death in the Family* is a touching and lyrical novel of domestic love. Combining strains that are romantic and modernist, it works at different levels around a number of important themes. Agee's—Rufus'—childhood love of his father, delicate and balanced but prone to damage by a wrong word or look on the part of those who composed Rufus' world, provides the novel's main theme. Agee's story, however, goes beyond this theme.

Agee was a Southern writer who could be associated with a particular southern locale and era. Within that framework he was also in many ways a Southern traditionalist, although the novel's abundant detail includes the depiction of sentiments and situations that are universal. Agee carefully documented the erosion of rural values among people like his father by Knoxville's growing industrialization during the years of his childhood. The harsh noises of passing streetcars that made his little sister Catherine cry, and the grinding, whirring metallic sounds of Jay cranking his Ford, a disturbance to family and neighborhood alike, are only two of many examples of this erosion that Agee sought to evoke.

The clash of rural and urban values was likewise played out within his parents' mutual love. Jay remained countrified at heart while Mary, quite consciously, was an urban Catholic. Socially, Mary and her relatives looked down on Jay. To be sure, Jay dominated his household, but he was oblivious to the price Mary paid in chagrin at his ways. Gentle enough, patient in his way, generous, hardworking, practical, devoted, and deeply attached to his country roots, he nonetheless was sometimes an embarrassment. While he acceded to Mary's wish to raise the children as Catholics, he was personally unreligious and unbaptized, a sore point with Mary's priest as well as occasion for her brother Andrew's outrage at the funeral. Jay's humor, in addition, ran to the vulgar, or so it seemed in his day; he swore, spat, enjoyed bending the elbow, and lapsed into rural idioms and songs. His death by a prime symbol of modernization, the Ford, and his father's wasting away, are metaphors for the decline of the old rural South.

In addition to the evocations of tensions between Rufus' parents and within the extended family (some of them healthy tensions that stitched together the framework of family loves), Agee laced the novel with concerns about the forces that were pulling those networks asunder. Those forces manifested themselves in physical separations and in those fragmentations that attended urban living. In this light, Jay was "a victim of progress," but so too were Rufus, Mary, and Catherine; no one could say how the family might have developed differently had Jay lived.

A Death in the Family is like a photograph, sharp in its details of a family in a moment in time, during an age in passage, never to be experienced again, and all the more precious in recognition of the photograph's ephemeral qualities. Enduring qualities remained, evoked by the photograph: Jay and Mary singing their son through his nightmares, Rufus feeling his father's hands stroking his head, Rufus smelling Jay's leather and tobacco, kids on their bellies reading comics, parental admonitions to Rufus about respecting differences (those of black people, relatives, and old folks): all archetypal memories, recognizable to everyone and timeless.

Clifton K. Yearley

Bibliography:
Bergreen, Laurence. *James Agee: A Life.* New York: E. P. Dutton, 1984. A fascinating biography that discusses *A Death in the Family.* Many fine photos.
Doty, Mark A. *Tell Me Who I Am: James Agee's Search for Selfhood.* Baton Rouge: Louisiana State University Press, 1981. An interesting study of Agee's search for selfhood, in which the remembrances in *A Death in the Family* play a major role.
Kramer, Victor A. *James Agee.* Boston: Twayne, 1975. A lifelong Agee scholar, Kramer has invaluable insights on the novel.
Lofaro, Michael A., ed. *James Agee: Reconsiderations.* Knoxville: University of Tennessee Press, 1992. Thirteen essays detail the full range of Agee's writings.
Madden, David, ed. *Remembering James Agee.* Baton Rouge: Louisiana State University Press,

1974. Includes essays and recollections by Agee's friends, which provide human dimensions to the novel.

Moreau, Geneviève. *The Restless Journey of James Agee*. Translated by Miriam Kleiger. New York: William Morrow, 1977. A sensitive portrayal of Agee and his work.

DEATH IN VENICE

Type of work: Novella
Author: Thomas Mann (1875-1955)
Type of plot: Symbolic realism
Time of plot: Early twentieth century
Locale: Italy
First published: Der Tod in Venedig, 1912 (English translation, 1925)

> *Principal characters:*
> GUSTAV VON ASCHENBACH, a middle-aged German writer
> TADZIO, a young Polish boy

The Story:

Gustav von Aschenbach was a distinguished German writer whose work had brought him world fame and a patent of nobility from a grateful government. His career had been honorable and dignified. A man of ambitious nature, unmarried, he had lived a life of personal discipline and dedication to his art. In portraying heroes who combined the forcefulness of a Frederick the Great with the selfless striving of a Saint Sebastian, he believed that he had spoken for his race as well as for the deathless human spirit. Yet his devotion to the ideals of duty and achievement had brought him close to physical collapse.

One day, after a morning spent at his desk, he left his house in Munich and went for a walk. His stroll took him as far as a cemetery on the outskirts of the city. While he waited for a streetcar to take him back to town, he suddenly became aware of a man who stood watching him from the doorway of the mortuary chapel. The stranger, who had a rucksack on his back and a walking staff in his hand, was evidently a traveler. Although no word passed between watcher and watched, Aschenbach felt a sudden desire to take a trip, to leave the cold, wet German spring for the warmer climate of the Mediterranean lands. His impulse was strengthened by the fact that he had encountered a problem of technique that he was unable to solve in his writing. He decided to take a holiday and leave his work for a time, hoping to find relaxation for mind and body in Italy.

He went first to an island resort in the Adriatic but became bored with his surroundings before too long and booked passage for Venice. On the ship, he encountered a party of lively young clerks from Pola. With them was an old man whose dyed hair and rouged cheeks made him a ridiculous but sinister caricature of youth. In his disgust, Aschenbach failed to notice that the raddled old man bore a vague resemblance to the traveler he had seen at the cemetery in Munich.

Aschenbach's destination was the Lido. At the dock in Venice, he transferred to a gondola that took him by the water route to his Lido hotel. The gondolier spoke and acted so strangely that Aschenbach became disturbed. Because of his agitation, he never noticed that the man looked something like the drunk old scarecrow on the ship and the silent stranger at the cemetery. After taking his passenger to the landing stage, the gondolier, without waiting for his money, hastily rowed away. Other boatmen suggested that he might have been afraid of the law because he had no license.

Aschenbach stayed at the Hotel des Bains. That night, shortly before dinner, his attention was drawn to a Polish family, which consisted of a beautiful mother, three daughters, and a handsome boy of about fourteen. Aschenbach was unaccountably attracted to the youngster, so much so that he continued to watch the family throughout his meal. The next morning, he saw the boy playing with some companions on the beach. His name, as Aschenbach learned while watching their games, was Tadzio.

Disturbed by the appeal the boy had for him, the writer decided to return home. On his arrival at the railroad station in Venice, however, he discovered that his trunks had been misdirected to Como. There was nothing for him to do but wait for his missing luggage to turn up, so he went back to the hotel. Although he despised himself for his vacillation, he realized that his true desire was to be near Tadzio. For Aschenbach there began a period of happiness in watching the boy and anguish in knowing they must remain strangers. One day, he almost summoned up enough courage to speak to the boy. A moment later, he became panic-stricken for fear that Tadzio might be alarmed by an older man's interest. The time Aschenbach had set for his holiday passed, but the writer had almost forgotten his home and his work. One evening, Tadzio smiled at him as they passed each other. Aschenbach trembled with pleasure.

Guests began to leave the hotel; there were rumors that a plague had broken out in nearby cities. While loitering one day on the Piazza, Aschenbach detected the sweetish odor of disinfectant in the air, for the authorities were beginning to take precautions against an outbreak of the plague in Venice. Aschenbach stubbornly decided to stay on despite the dangers of infection.

A band of entertainers came to the hotel to serenade the guests. In the troupe was an impudent, disreputable-looking street singer whose antics and ballads were insulting and obscene. As he passed among the guests to collect money for the performance, Aschenbach detected on his clothing the almost overpowering smell of disinfectant, an odor suggesting the sweetly corruptive taints of lust and death. The ribald comedian also bore a strange similarity to the gondolier, the rouged old rake, and the silent traveler whose disturbing presence had given Aschenbach the idea for his holiday. Aschenbach was torn between fear and desire. The next day, he went to a tourist agency where a young clerk told him that people were dying of the plague in Venice. Even that confirmation of his fears failed to speed Aschenbach's departure from the city. That night, he dreamed that in a fetid jungle, surrounded by naked orgiasts, he was taking part in horrible, Priapean rites.

By that time his deterioration was almost complete. Even though he allowed a barber to dye his hair and tint his cheeks, he still refused to see the likeness between himself and the raddled old fop whose appearance had disgusted him on shipboard. His behavior became more reckless. One afternoon, he followed the Polish family into Venice and trailed them through the city streets. Hungry and thirsty after his exercise, he bought some overripe strawberries at an open stall and ate them. The odor of disinfectant was strong on the sultry breeze.

Several days later, Aschenbach went down to the beach where Tadzio was playing with three or four other boys. They began to fight, and one of the boys threw Tadzio to the ground and pressed his face into the sand. As Aschenbach was about to interfere, the other boy released his victim. Humiliated and hurt, Tadzio walked down to the water. He stood facing seaward for a time, as remote and isolated as a young Saint Sebastian, then he turned and looked with a somber, secret gaze at Aschenbach, who was watching from his beach chair. To the writer, it seemed as though the boy were summoning him. He started to rise but became so giddy that he fell back into his chair. Attendants carried him to his room. That night, the world learned that the great Gustav von Aschenbach had died suddenly of the plague in Venice.

Critical Evaluation:

Together with James Joyce and Marcel Proust, Thomas Mann is often considered one of the great writers of the early twentieth century. Mann, who was awarded the Nobel Prize in Literature in 1919, was born into an upper-middle-class German family and left his country in 1933 because of his opposition to Adolf Hitler and the Nazi regime. He later came to the United States, where he taught and lectured. A scholar as well as an artist, Mann shows in his works the influence of such diverse thinkers as Friedrich Nietzsche, Arthur Schopenhauer, Richard Wagner, and Sigmund Freud. The problem of the artist's role in a decadent, industrialized society is a recurring theme in many of his works, including *Buddenbrooks* (1901), *Tonio Kröger* (1903), *Death in Venice* (1912), and *The Magic Mountain* (1924).

   Death in Venice, Mann's best-known novella, is a complex, beautifully wrought tale dealing with the eternal conflict between the forces of death and decay and the human attempts to achieve permanence through art. Mann portrays the final triumph of death and decay, but not before the hero, Aschenbach, has experienced an escape into the eternal beauty created by the imagination of the artist. The escape of the famous writer is accomplished, however, not by his own writings but by the art of his creator, Thomas Mann. Form and order do finally impose themselves on the chaos of his life; corruption and death are transformed into the purity of artistic beauty.

   The characterization of a literary hero of his age is subtle and complex. Author of prose epics, philosophical novels, novels of moral resolution, and aesthetics, Aschenbach has created the hero for his generation. He is aware that his success and talent rely on a basis of physical stamina as well as moral and mental discipline, and his work is a product of strain, endurance, intellectual tenacity, and spasms of will. He recognizes, however, that his writing has been to some degree a "pursuit of fame" at the expense of turning his back on a full search for truth. As the novella opens, Aschenbach is exhausted and no longer finding joy in his craft; he has become aware of approaching old age and death, and is faced with the fear of not having time to finish everything he desired to write. Restlessly walking in the beauty of the English Garden of Munich, Aschenbach is inspired to leave his relatively rootless life on a pilgrimage for artistic renewal in Venice, the perfect symbol of human art imposed on nature's chaos. This journey motif begins with his glimpse of a stranger in a cemetery, a foreigner with a skull-like face and a certain animal ruthlessness.

   Arriving at the port of Venice, he discovers that his gondolier is taking him out to sea rather than into the city; the gondolier's physical description ominously echoes that of the stranger of the cemetery. The gondola itself is specifically compared to a black coffin. The trip becomes the archetypal journey of life to death and of a man into the depths of himself. Aschenbach discovers Venice, the symbol of perfect art in his memory, to be dirty, infected, corrupt, and permeated by the odor of the human disease and pollution spread in the natural swamp on which the artifice is built. Aschenbach's own transformation to a "foreigner," one who belongs in Venice, is accomplished at an increasingly mad tempo after the moment when, turning his back on the possibility of escaping Venice by train, he collapses at a fountain in the heart of the city. His death becomes almost self-willed; he dies not because of the plague, not because of his love of Tadzio, but because of his will to live and to create atrophy.

   The exterior events of the story, which are minimal, can be properly explained only in terms of the inner conflict of the artist. To produce art, Aschenbach believes he must practice absolute self-denial, affirming the dignity and moral capacity of the individual in the face of a world of self-indulgence that leads to personal abasement. Yet he is also a man and, as such, has drives connecting him to the chaos of the formless elements of nature. This inner conflict is objectified in the boy Tadzio, who embodies all that Aschenbach has rejected in fifty long years of dedication to Apollonian art. As his desire for Tadzio becomes obsessive and drives him to neglect his body and dignity, disintegration sets in and death becomes irrevocable. Subconsciously, Aschenbach is choosing to pursue the basic sensual, Dionysian side of himself that he has always denied.

Mann uses dream visions to underline and clarify Aschenbach's subconscious conflicts. His first hallucination of the crouching beast in the jungle is evoked by the glimpse of the stranger at the Byzantine chapel in Munich. This vision literally foreshadows the trip to Venice and metaphorically foreshadows the inner journey during which Aschenbach discovers the jungle and beast within himself. The second vision on the beach in Venice, in the form of a Platonic dialogue, explores the interrelatedness of art, love, and beauty with human bestiality. In a third major dream hallucination, Aschenbach is initiated into the worship of the Dionysian rite and finally glimpses "the stranger god" of sensual experience, formless chaotic joy, and excesses of emotion. The most striking vision occurs at the end of the novella, when Aschenbach, viewing the amoral beauty of perfection of form in Tadzio silhouetted against the amoral, formless beauty of the sea, accepts the promise inherent in the sea's chaos as the equivalent of the beauty produced by order and moral discipline. Readers assume the vision to be objective reality until brought sharply and suddenly into the present reality of Aschenbach's dead body. Ernest Hemingway used this same technique later in his own novella-length study of death and art, "The Snows of Kilimanjaro" (1961).

Mann's use of natural, geographical symbols also underlines the central conflicts of the novella. Aschenbach identifies the discipline of his art with Munich, a city of northern Europe, and with the snowy mountains. These places are associated with health, energy, reason, will, and Apollonian creative power. Against them, Mann juxtaposes the tropical marshes, the jungle animal and plant life, the Indian plague, the sun and the sea, which are associated with Dionysian excesses of emotion and ecstasy in art. The beast, the jungle, the plague, chaos lie within the nature of humanity and art just as clearly as do mountains, self-denial, will, and reason, qualities that enable human beings to construct artifice upon the chaos of nature. Great art, Nietzsche says in *The Birth of Tragedy Out of the Spirit of Music* (1909), is a product of the fusion rather than the separation of the calm, ordered, contemplative spirit of Apollo and the savage, sensual ecstasy of Dionysus. This is what both Aschenbach and the reader discover in Mann's *Death in Venice*.

"Critical Evaluation" by Ann E. Reynolds

Bibliography:
Berlin, Jeffrey B., ed. *Approaches to Teaching Mann's "Death in Venice" and Other Short Fiction.* New York: Modern Language Association of America, 1992. Designed for teachers, this book contains several useful shorter essays, especially that by Naomi Ritter on the story in the context of European decadence. Includes a useful bibliographical essay.
Cohn, Dorrit. "The Second Author in *Der Tod in Venedig.*" In *Critical Essays on Thomas Mann*, compiled by Inta M. Ezergailis. Boston: G. K. Hall, 1988. An examination of the highly ironic relationship between the narrator of the story and his protagonist, Gustav von Aschenbach. An excellent example of close textual analysis of one specific aspect of the novella.
Heller, Erich. "The Embarrassed Muse." In *Thomas Mann: The Ironic German.* 1958. Reprint. South Bend, Ind.: Regnery/Gateway, 1979. Places the novella in the context of Mann's other works before embarking on a detailed discussion of the irony Mann employs in the narrative. Heller pays special attention to the story's focus on art and the artist.

Reed, T. J. *"Death in Venice": Making and Unmaking a Master.* New York: Twayne, 1994. The best general overview of the story with sections on literary and historical context, good close readings, and a look at the story's genesis and its relationship to Mann and German history. Also includes an annotated bibliography.

Weiner, Marc A. "Music and Repression: *Death in Venice.*" In *Undertones of Insurrection: Music, Politics, and the Social Sphere in the Modern German Narrative.* Lincoln: University of Nebraska Press, 1993. A brief but thorough analysis of musical tropes and meanings in the novella. Focuses on interpretation and provides an excellent discussion of the musical aspects of *Death in Venice.*

DEATH OF A HERO

Type of work: Novel
Author: Richard Aldington (1892-1962)
Type of plot: Political
Time of plot: World War I
Locale: England
First published: 1929

> *Principal characters:*
> GEORGE WINTERBOURNE, the protagonist
> MR. GEORGE WINTERBOURNE, his father
> MRS. GEORGE WINTERBOURNE, his mother
> ELIZABETH, his wife
> FANNY WELFORD, his mistress

The Story:

When word came that George Winterbourne had been killed in the war, his friend tried to reconstruct the life of the dead man to see what forces had caused his death. The friend had served with George at various times during the war, and it was his belief that George had deliberately exposed himself to German fire because he no longer wanted to live.

George Winterbourne's father was a sentimental fool and his mother a depraved wanton. The elder Winterbourne had married primarily to spite his dominating mother, and his bride had married him under the mistaken notion that he was rich. They resigned themselves to mutual hatred, and the mother showered her thwarted love on young George. She imagined herself young and desirable and was proud of her twenty-two lovers. Her husband went to a hotel when she was entertaining, but he prayed for her soul. They were the most depressing parents to whom a child could be exposed, and they caused young George to hate them both. Soon after receiving word of their son's death, the elder Winterbourne was killed in an accident. After thoroughly enjoying her role as a bereft mother and widow, Mrs. Winterbourne married her twenty-second lover and moved to Australia.

By the time he reached young manhood, George had mingled with all sorts of unusual people. He had dabbled in writing and painting, and sexual freedom was his goal, even though he experienced little of it. At the home of some pseudointellectual friends, he first met Elizabeth. They were immediately compatible: Both hated their parents, and both sought freedom. At first, Elizabeth was shocked by George's attacks on Christianity, morals, the class system, and all other established institutions, but she soon decided that he was a truly "free" man. In fact, it was not long before she adopted his ideas; soon free love was the only thing she would talk or think about.

George and Elizabeth considered themselves extremely sensible. They did not talk of love, only sex, and they saw no reason why they should marry to experience sex as long as they were careful not to have a baby. They decided that there would be no sordidness to cloud their affair, and that they were both free to take all the other lovers they pleased. That was freedom in an intelligent way. Elizabeth was even more insistent of that than George.

When, however, Elizabeth mistakenly thought that she was pregnant, her progressive ideas disappeared and she insisted that George must marry her at once for the sake of her honor and reputation. They were married, much to the horror of their families. When Elizabeth learned that she was not pregnant—in fact, the doctor told her that she could not possibly have a child without an operation—her old ideas returned. She became an evangelist for sex, even though she detested the word. Marriage made no difference in George's and Elizabeth's lives. They continued to live separately and to meet as lovers.

When Elizabeth made a trip home, George became the lover of her best friend, Fanny Welford, another enlightened woman. He was sure that Elizabeth would not mind, for she had become the mistress of Fanny's lover, but to his surprise Elizabeth created a scene over Fanny. On the surface, the young women remained friends, each unwilling to admit a bourgeois dislike of the situation.

When war broke out, George was drafted and immediately sent to France. The war and the killing horrified George, and obsessively he began to think about his own death. He was brave, but not from any desire to be a hero; rather, the monotony of his existence seemed to demand that he keep going even though he was ready to drop from fatigue. The knowledge of the ill-concealed dislike between Fanny and Elizabeth began to prey on his mind. There seemed to be only two solutions: To drift along and accept whatever happened or to get himself killed in the war. It seemed to make little difference to him or anyone else which course he chose. His letters to his two women depressed each of them. He could have spared himself his anxiety, for each had taken other lovers and gave little thought to George.

George's depression increased. He felt that he was degenerating mentally as well as physically and that he was wasting what should have been his best years. He knew that he would be terribly handicapped if he did live through the war, that those not serving would have passed him by.

George was made an officer and sent back to England for training. There he lived again with Elizabeth, but she left him frequently to go out with other men. Fanny, too, seemed to care little whether she saw him or not. Talk of the war and his experiences obviously bored them, and they made only a small pretense of interest. He spent his last night in England with Fanny while Elizabeth was off with someone else. Fanny did not bother to get up with him the morning he left. She awoke lazily and went back to sleep again before he had even left the flat.

Back at the front, George found that he was ill-suited to command a company. Although he did his best, he was constantly censured by his colonel, who blamed George for all the faults of his untrained and cowardly troops. George could think of little but death. During a particularly heavy German shelling, he simply stood up and let the bullets smash into his chest.

Critical Evaluation:

Although two-thirds of *Death of a Hero* is concerned with the life of George Winterbourne before World War I, the novel presents the prewar era as a prelude to the great catastrophe that followed. Richard Aldington leaves no doubt about the ultimate target of his satire, vociferously denouncing the hypocritical Victorian platitudes that held killing to be chivalrous and erotic love to be shameful: "It was the regime of Cant before the War which made the Cant during the War so damnably possible and easy." Although Aldington blames the war on the older generation, he finds the younger generation, including the supposedly enlightened intelligentsia, almost equally guilty. Not only was the conduct of the war itself dishonest, he claims, but it was also the expression of a pervasive dishonesty in English society.

Death of a Hero is more than simply a war novel, for it treats the experience of the whole generation of men who fought in the war and makes an urgent appeal for a less repressive society. The events of the book are closely based on Aldington's personal experiences both as a member of the avant-garde in prewar England and as a runner and officer during the war, yet the novel presents George Winterbourne's experience as representative. His death is ambiguous: Although his final act is clearly suicidal, the implication is that he has been driven to it by the tragic fate of the young men of his time whom society had denied such basic necessities as love and truth.

George's death takes place on the same day as that of Wilfred Owen (1893-1918), the preeminent poet of "the pity of war," on November 4, 1918, just one week before the armistice. Owen's poems, like *Death of a Hero*, gave expression to the camaraderie between fighting men and the great psychological abyss that the war experience opened between soldiers and civilians.

In his section headings Aldington suggests that his novel is constructed like a symphony, with four movements (a prologue and three parts) in progressively slower tempos: allegretto, vivace, andante cantabile, and adagio. In the prefatory letter to Halcott Glover, however, Aldington also describes it as a jazz novel, constructed on principles such as those he had used for his long poem *A Fool i' the Forest* (1924). Although certain musical motifs are brilliantly used in the descriptions of bombardment in part 3, it is difficult to see how the musical analogy functions continuously to give the novel its form, and the tempo indications seem superfluous to the reading experience.

In part 1, it is clear that Aldington wants to make his characters, especially George's contemptible parents, stand for all of society. To have drawn them three-dimensionally might have detracted from that purpose, but his presenting them as caricatures makes it difficult for the reader to find them interesting or significant, especially as the war episode (which gives point to Aldington's satire) is yet to come. The reader feels that these "grotesques," as Aldington describes them, are made of straw—targets too trivial to warrant such lurid invective.

Part 2 further shows how George is betrayed by those who profess to care about him. Although George's love interests, Elizabeth and Fanny, at first appear to be more sympathetic and human than his parents, they too eventually betray George and come to stand in contrast to the comparatively guileless, trusting protagonist. Several of Aldington's famous literary friends appear in this section as amusing, absurdly self-absorbed, and pretentious characters in George's London bohemian set—the poet Ezra Pound as the sculptor Upjohn, the novelist D. H. Lawrence as Comrade Bobbe, and the poet T. S. Eliot as Waldo Tubbe.

Only when George enters the army does he find companions whose simple courage is admirable and inspiring. His commanding officer, Evans, is honest and hardworking, yet he would certainly have been an object of scorn had he appeared in parts 1 or 2. Here, however, he is a sympathetic character, suggesting that the war somehow humanizes men and enables them to transcend cant. The war section, which includes vivid descriptions of the horror of the trenches, has generally been considered to be the most effective and praiseworthy of the novel's three parts. Aldington's skill as a poet, even as an imagist poet devoted to precise description and fresh cadences, has been perceived in his magnificent accounts of bombardment and combat.

Aldington was well known in literary circles as a poet, but his first novel made him famous on both sides of the Atlantic, for although it received mixed reviews in the press, it was an immediate best-seller. (An unexpurgated edition was published in France in 1930 though most of the phrases that the original publishers had censored were far from offensive.) *Death of a Hero* was in the vanguard of a great wave of literature about World War I that began to appear in 1929, after a decade in which there had been little interest in war writing. The work remains one of the more distinguished contributions to this body of work, although it has received only modest critical attention. In retrospect, it is clear that it gave early expression to the major themes of World War I prose and shows unusual insight into such frequently neglected questions as the relationship between the war and changing attitudes toward women and sexuality. Some writers were, however, able to find more satisfactory solutions to the problem of expressing protest against the war than the fierce invective that often interrupts the narrative in *Death of a Hero*.

Most commentary on Aldington's work tends to concentrate either on his notorious biographical works or on his role in the Imagist movement. Both the novel's admirers and its detractors tend to react to the same quality: its relentless ferocity. The narrator at times almost browbeats the reader, and Bernard Bergonzi compares the novel unfavorably with more patient denunciations of the war such as Robert Graves's *Goodbye to All That* (1929) and Edmund Blunden's *Undertones of War* (1928). For its admirers, however, it is precisely as a novel whose flaws are owing to its overwhelming bitterness that it gives a voice to the "lost generation."

"Critical Evaluation" by Matthew Parfitt

Bibliography:
Bergonzi, Bernard. *Heroes' Twilight: A Study of the Literature of the Great War.* New York: Coward, McCann, 1966. Bergonzi devotes several pages of this readable and wide-ranging study to *Death of a Hero*, arguing that the novel suffers from the author's lack of detachment from his subject.
Doyle, Charles. "Port-Cros and After, 1928-1929." In *Richard Aldington: A Biography.* Carbondale: Southern Illinois University Press, 1989. Includes a substantial, balanced discussion of *Death of a Hero*, with critical commentary on its principal themes and literary merits. Acknowledges the stylistic flaws but argues that the novel was essential work to the "imaginative reconstruction" of the war.
McGreevy, Thomas. *Richard Aldington: An Englishman.* London: Chatto & Windus, 1931. McGreevy, a personal friend of Aldington, includes an extensive, if rather subjective, study of *Death of a Hero*. Focuses on the novel's formal characteristics.
Morris, John. "Richard Aldington and *Death of a Hero*—or Life of an Anti-Hero?" In *The First World War in Fiction: A Collection of Critical Essays,* edited by Holger Klein. New York: Barnes & Noble Books, 1977. Judicious and attentive critique of the novel, with a particular focus on the problems of satiric tone.
Smith, Richard Eugene. *Richard Aldington.* Boston: Twayne, 1977. An accessible introduction to Aldington's life and works. Includes a chapter on *Death of a Hero* and a useful bibliography of criticism to 1976.

DEATH OF A SALESMAN

Type of work: Drama
Author: Arthur Miller (1915-   )
Type of plot: Tragedy
Time of plot: 1940's
Locale: New York and Boston
First performed: 1949; first published, 1949

> *Principal characters:*
> WILLY LOMAN, a traveling salesman
> LINDA, his wife
> BIFF, their oldest son
> HAPPY, their younger son
> CHARLEY, their neighbor
> BERNARD, Charley's son
> UNCLE BEN, Willy's successful brother
> HOWARD WAGNER, Willy's boss

The Story:

Very late one night, having that morning set out on what was to have been a sales trip to Portland, Maine, Willy Loman returned to his Brooklyn home because he had repeatedly driven his car off the side of the road. Now sixty-three years old, Willy had worked as a traveling salesman for the Wagner Company for more than thirty years. Of late, his sales had declined because his old customers had died or retired, and the company had taken away his salary and made him work on straight commission. His wife, Linda, comforted Willy when he returned and encouraged him to ask Howard Wagner for a position in the New York office, where he would not have to travel and could once again earn a guaranteed salary.

Upstairs in their old bedroom, Willy's sons, Biff and Happy, reminisced about their happier times as adolescents and talked about how disappointing their lives had become. At thirty-four years of age, Biff had held many different kinds of jobs since leaving high school and he felt that he was not progressing toward anything. He had been a high school football star but had failed to win a college scholarship because he had failed a mathematics course and had refused to make up the credits to graduate at summer school. Biff had just returned home from working on a farm in Texas, and that morning Willy had already begun criticizing him about his failure to make money and find a prestigious profession. Biff's younger brother Happy had remained in New York City, working in a low-level sales position and spending most of his time seducing women. As they talked, Biff and Happy decided they could be successful and much happier if they went into business together.

While Biff and Happy talked upstairs, Willy sat in the kitchen and talked loudly to himself, reliving moments from his past such as Biff preparing for an important football game, Biff and Happy cleaning the family car, Willy's own joy in working with his hands on projects around the house, and his afternoons in a hotel room with a woman on one of his sales trips to Boston. Eventually, Willy's neighbor, Charley, came over from next door. As Charley and Willy talked and played cards, Willy imagined that he was talking to his older brother Ben, who had once invited Willy to join him in Alaska to make his fortune. After Charley returned home, Willy moved outside, still caught up in his imagined conversation. Linda came back downstairs and told Biff and Happy of her fear that Willy had been planning to kill himself; she had discovered a piece of rubber hose connected to a gas pipe in the basement. When Willy came back into the house, the conversation turned to the dreams Willy had had of Biff becoming a successful salesman and entrepreneur. At Willy's urging, the family agreed that the next morning Biff should see Bill Oliver, one of his former bosses, and ask for a loan to start a sporting goods business.

The next morning, Willy went to his own boss, Howard Wagner, to ask for a position in the New York office. Instead of getting a new position, however, he was fired from his job. Willy left Wagner's office and went to Charlie's office to ask for a loan to pay his bills. There he encountered Charlie's son, Bernard, a boyhood friend of Biff and Happy and now a successful lawyer arguing cases in front of the Supreme Court. Willy asked how Bernard had managed to succeed when Biff and Happy had failed, but Bernard asked why Biff, after flunking mathematics, had never gone to summer school so as to graduate from high school.

Happy had gone to a local restaurant to arrange a dinner to celebrate Biff's successful meeting with Mr. Oliver, but when Biff arrived he reported that Oliver had not remembered him and that, in his anger, Biff had impulsively stolen Oliver's fountain pen. When, however, he heard his father's news that he had been fired, Biff lied about his meeting with Oliver and, to console his father, described it as a success. Happy had arranged for two women to join them at the restaurant. When Willy went to the washroom, Biff and Happy left the restaurant with the two women and abandoned their father. In the washroom, Willy had a flashback and remembered the time, right after Biff had flunked his mathematics course, when Biff came to Boston on a surprise visit and caught Willy with another woman in his hotel room. It was this discovery that had kept Biff from going to summer school and from graduating from high school.

After leaving the restaurant, Willy decided on the way home that the best way he could provide for his wife and sons was to commit suicide, so that the life insurance settlement of $20,000 would come to them after his death. Happy and Biff returned home from their dates with the two women and were greeted by Linda's reprimand that they had abandoned Willy at the restaurant. Biff responded angrily, accusing Willy and Happy of not facing the reality of their ordinary lives. He claimed that he finally understood himself and would go back to farming and working with his hands, outdoors, where he was genuinely happy. This emotional confrontation ended with Biff crying on his father's shoulder. Moved by his son's display of affection, Willy left the house and drove the car to his death. In the play's last scene, in the cemetery after Willy's funeral, Linda talked to Willy over his grave and reflected on the irony that he had killed himself just as they had finished paying for their house.

Critical Evaluation:

Following in the tradition of the classic Norwegian playwright Henrik Ibsen, Arthur Miller is concerned above all with the relationship between the individual and society. His investigations range from his portrait of the industrialist Joe Keller in *All My Sons* (1947), who sacrifices the safety of World War II fighter pilots and ruins his business partner to satisfy his desire for financial success, to examining the connection between the dysfunctional marriage of Sylvia and Phillip Gellburg and the rise of Nazism in *Broken Glass* (1994). In *Death of a Salesman,* Miller focuses on the relationship between society and the individual's concept of self. As a consequence of living in a capitalistic society that emphasizes materialistic values, Willy Loman has a defective sense of self. He is obsessed not only with financial success but more specifically with appearances and impressions, with being considered important and "well-liked" by others, and he has passed these superficial values on to his two sons, Biff and Happy.

In the course of the play, Biff becomes more aware of his real needs and feelings and frees himself from this destructive concept of self. Only then is Biff able to care more deeply for his father, and he breaks down and cries in his arms. Willy is moved by his son's love but his understanding is incomplete, as becomes clear when he commits suicide under the impression that this is the only way to give Biff financial prosperity. At the play's end it is clear that Biff will heal himself and go back out West to find work that suits his genuine concept of self, while Happy will probably repeat the misdirected life of his father.

Miller's plays often mix his characteristically realistic style with expressionistic techniques. In *Death of a Salesman,* he enhances the theme of self-awareness by using techniques to distort time and space and to represent the working of Willy's mind. While playing cards with his neighbor Charlie, for example, Willy imagines that he sees his brother Ben, who appears on the stage as if he were a real person. By allowing the past and the present to intermingle freely, Miller represents the confusion and distress in Willy's mind. In fact, Miller's working title for the play was "The Inside of His Head" and his original concept for the stage set was a model of an enormous face, inside of which the action was to take place. In having the action follow and portray Willy's meandering mind, Miller creates a psychological quality that reflects Willy's confusion about identity. As Willy's mind wanders in his past, talking to his brother Ben or remembering building projects around the house, Willy's true self is revealed. He is a man who loves to work outdoors with his hands, the kind of man that Biff finally comes to accept as his true self. As Biff says over Willy's grave, "there's more of him in that front stoop than in all the sales he ever made."

Death of a Salesman is of crucial importance to twentieth century literature because it once again posed raised the question whether tragedy is possible with a common hero. The Aristotelian concept of tragedy, which dominated dramatic literature until the nineteenth century, insisted that only characters of noble birth or soul could be tragic heroes. In the eighteenth and nineteenth centuries, however, an increasing number of plays with tragic endings were written about common people. In 1949, concurrent with his play's appearance on Broadway, Miller published a defense of the play as a genuine tragedy in the essay "Tragedy and the Common Man," in which he argued that all that was required for tragic stature was a hero willing to "lay down his life" to secure "his 'rightful' position in his society."

Miller won a Pulitzer Prize in drama in 1949 for *Death of a Salesman,* and for many years thereafter he was considered, alongside Eugene O'Neill and Tennessee Williams, one of America's greatest playwrights. Of his many subsequent plays, perhaps only *The Crucible* (1953) and *After the Fall* (1964), had a comparable popular and critical impact. Undoubtedly his masterpiece, *Death of a Salesman* remains Miller's most enduring work.

Terry Nienhuis

Bibliography:
Bloom, Harold, ed. *Willy Loman.* New York: Chelsea House, 1991. A collection of sixteen focused extracts from books and articles, with ten complete essays providing an excellent selection of criticism focusing on Willy as a literary character. Includes a provocative introduction by Bloom in which he discusses Willy as a tragic hero.
Dukore, Bernard F. *"Death of a Salesman" and "The Crucible."* Atlantic Highlands, N.J.: Humanities Press International, 1989. An excellent introduction for beginning students. Analyzes the text from both literary and theatrical points of view and examines selected productions of the play to demonstrate the rich embodiment of literary ideas.

Koon, Helene Wickham, ed. *Twentieth Century Interpretations of "Death of a Salesman."* Englewood Cliffs, N.J.: Prentice-Hall, 1983. An anthology of ten essays that provide a wide variety of critical approaches to the play. A standard source.

Miller, Arthur. *"Salesman" in Beijing.* New York: Viking Press, 1984. Miller's fascinating and highly readable diary account of the famous production he directed of *Death of a Salesman* in Beijing, China, in 1983, where the universality of the play became most evident. Includes photographs by his wife, Inge Morath.

Roudané, Matthew C., ed. *Conversations with Arthur Miller.* Jackson: University Press of Mississippi, 1987. Transcriptions of thirty-nine interviews with Miller between 1947 and 1986. Notable for personal insights into Miller and the productions of his plays. The interviews persistently return to questions concerning *Death of a Salesman* and Miller's theories on tragedy.

THE DEATH OF ARTEMIO CRUZ

Type of work: Novel
Author: Carlos Fuentes (1928-   )
Type of plot: Social realism
Time of plot: 1889-1959
Locale: Mexico
First published: La muerte de Artemio Cruz, 1962 (English translation, 1964)

Principal characters:
ARTEMIO CRUZ, a dying tycoon
CATALINA, his wife
LORENZO, his son, who was killed in the Spanish Civil War
TERESA, his daughter
GLORIA, his granddaughter
GERARDO, his son-in-law
DON GAMALIEL BERNAL, his father-in-law
GONZALO BERNAL, a young lawyer executed by Villistas
FATHER PAEZ, a priest
REGINA, a dead woman Artemio had loved
LILIA and
LAURA, Artemio's mistresses
PADILLA, Artemio's secretary
LUNERO, a mulatto peon

The Story:

Artemio Cruz was on his deathbed after having been stricken by a gastric attack upon his return from a business trip to Hermosillo on April 9, 1959. As he lay in his mansion in a fashionable section of Mexico City, the stench in his nostrils was as much from the moral corruption of his life as from the processes of decay already at work in his body. Disregarding Cruz' protests, who had abandoned the church years before, an officious priest tried to administer the last sacrament. Doctors subjected him to indignities with their instruments as they examined his body. In the background stood his estranged wife and the daughter who despised him. Although they pretended concern for the dying man, their greatest anxiety concerned his will, and he refused to tell them where he had put it. His only hold on reality was a tape recording with an account of business deals and proposed transactions, which his secretary, Padilla, played for him. While the people jostled about in his room, Artemio Cruz drifted between past and present in a series of flashbacks tracing the events that had brought him to his present state.

In 1919, he was an ambitious young veteran of the revolution arriving at the home of the Bernal family in Perales. Ostensibly he was there to bring to a bereaved father and sister an account of Gonzalo Bernal's death before a Villista firing squad. In reality, he meant to insinuate himself into the confidence of the old *hacendado,* marry his daughter, Catalina, and get possession of the Bernal estates. After he married Catalina, however, his wife never realized that Artemio had really fallen in love with her; influenced by Father Paez, the family priest, she believed that she paid with her soul for her father's security, and she hated herself for the passion to which Artemio could move her at night. Husband and wife ended up despising each other, and she blamed him when their son, whom he removed from her control, was killed while fighting in the Spanish Civil War. Before Catalina, Cruz had loved Regina, a camp follower who was taken hostage by Villa's troops and hanged. After her death, there had been other women, including Lilia, the young mistress he took on a holiday in Acapulco and who betrayed him there, and Laura, who later married someone else.

In addition to his adventures with women, Artemio recalled ruining his neighbors at Perales and getting possession of their lands, using bribery and blackmail to buy his first election as a deputy, giving lavish parties, negotiating business deals, ruining competitors, and all the while preparing himself for the loneliness and desolation he would feel when his time came to die.

Two episodes throw light on the later years of Artemio's career. One is the story of his capture by a Villista troop. Sentenced to death, he decided to give information to the enemy. Although he later killed the officer to whom he had promised betrayal, he was guilty by intent. Some justification for his deed came from Gonzalo Bernal, the disillusioned idealist who nevertheless went bravely to his death, who declared that once a revolution has been corrupted by those who act only to live well and to rise in the world, battles may still be fought and won but the uncompromising revolution has been lost.

In the last episode, Artemio Cruz returned to his beginnings. He had been born on the petate, the mat symbolic of the peon's condition, son of a decayed landowner and a half-caste girl. His only friend during his early years had been Lunero, a mulatto who served the needs of Artemio's half-crazed old grandmother and his lazy, drunken uncle. After the boy accidentally shot his uncle, he ran away to Veracruz. There, a schoolmaster tutored Artemio and prepared him for the part he would play in the revolution before he lost his ideals and chose betrayal and the rejection that ultimately led him to the corrupting use of power over other men's lives and the spiritual ruin of his own.

Critical Evaluation:

To many Mexicans, the Revolution of 1910 is the great and inescapable fact in their country's destiny and their own personal identity. A second conquest of the land and the past, it was the climax of four centuries of turbulent history and the adumbration of all that had happened since. The revolution did more than topple the paternal dictatorship of Porfirio Diaz: It tore a nation apart with fratricidal strife and put it together again in a strange new way that continued to disturb and puzzle its citizens. The war swept away lingering remnants of colonialism, brought a long-lived oligarchy into being, created a new middle class, moved Mexico into the twentieth century, and helped to shape a literature both ancestral and prophetic in its depictions of a sad and violent land.

In some ways, the situation can be compared to the aftermath of the Civil War in the United States, where for decades Americans tried to see their fraternal conflict in perspectives of cause and consequence. Among American Southerners, especially, there remained a sense of the uniqueness of the experience, a sense of national tragedy. A somewhat similar spirit prevails in some aspects of Mexican life, but on a greater scale and complicated by a growing belief that the revolution failed and the real revolution was still to come. In fact, Mexican intellectuals in the late twentieth century were often self-conscious in much the same manner that William Faulkner and writers of his generation were self-conscious, obsessed with feeling for place, burdened by the past, uneasy in the new society and with what had been lost in the process of change, and seeking to reclaim old values in their stories and poems. Feeling that history had isolated them in their own particular moment in time—the parochialism of the revolution— Mexican writers often turned inward to create a literature veering between fury and outrage and the poetry of nocturnal silence. They lived, to borrow a phrase from the poet Octavio Paz, in a "labyrinth of solitude." It was Jose Luis Cuevas, the avant-garde painter, who first used the term "Cactus Curtain" in protest against the isolation of the Mexican artist. In an earlier novel, *Where the Air Is Clear* (1958), Carlos Fuentes said that it is impossible to explain Mexico but only to believe in it with anger, a feeling of outrage, passion, and a sense of alienation.

This statement makes clear that the author rejects Mexican life of his time but at the same time uses it in his novels to test his sensuous powers and dramatic vigor. The country he writes about is not the land that tourists see or a land of tradition; it is the country of art, a place and people transformed by compelling imagination into something rich, strange, and meaningful. This is one explanation for his restless technical experiments with broken narrative structures, shifting points of view, solemn hymns to landscapes and time, and the interior monologues by which he tries to probe the conscience and consciousness of his people. If he has not yet assimilated in his own writing the influences he has absorbed from such varied figures as Marcel Proust, James Joyce, Faulkner, John Dos Passos, and Thomas Wolfe, he has nevertheless put his borrowings to brilliant use in catching the tempo of Mexican life in its present stage of uncertainty and indirection.

Although his methods may vary in his discontinuity of form and the labyrinthine turnings of his style, his theme remains constant. His novels are studies in the responsibility that power, knowingly or unknowingly, brings and the corruption that almost necessarily accompanies power. He began with *Where the Air Is Clear*, a novel set against the background of Mexico City, where the extremes of poverty and wealth allowed a study in breadth of what had happened on all levels of society after the revolution failed to fulfill its promises. Central to Fuentes' theme is Federico Robles, once an ardent revolutionary but now a driving power in the country's political and financial life. His rise in the world through treachery, bribery, ruthless exploitation and his corruption of better men have made him many enemies. The novel presents the story of more than one man's ruin, however. Underlying the events of the story are the long shadows the failed revolution has thrown into the present, the realization of wasted effort, of lives lost to no purpose, of high aims given over to meaningless deeds of sensuality, folly, and outrage. As can be seen at the end, Robles is what he is because others in their selfishness and pride have assisted in his rise. Now they hate him because they see in him an enlarged image of themselves. *Where the Air Is Clear* is saved from becoming an ideological polemic by the underlying consideration of much that is flawed and gross in the human condition.

Fuentes tells a similar story in *The Good Conscience* (1959), although in that novel his concern is with a family, grandfather, father, and son rather than with a single individual. The setting is Guanajuato, where the oldest of the Ceballos, a dry-goods merchant, laid the foundation of a family fortune. Representative of the new middle class, the materialistic, ambitious Ceballos men marry for position, play cynical political games for security, and carry on shady business deals for gain. Society accepts them, the state protects them, and the Church sustains them. The writer's picture of chicanery and corruption is magnificent, but the book breaks abruptly in the middle to present in Jaime Ceballo, the youngest of the family, a story of adolescent confusion and rebellion. Torn between the self-seeking practices of his family and the teachings of the Church, he attempts to follow the example of Christ, fails, and falls back on radicalism as the only alternative to the greed, lust for power, and hypocrisy of his class. The ending, unconvincing after the ironical, somber overtones orchestrated through the earlier sections of the novel, suggests that it was dictated more by the writer's Marxist beliefs than the logic of character and experience.

The Death of Artemio Cruz is more limited in its presentation of this theme than Fuentes' previous work. The book is somewhat flawed by a bewildering cross-chronology, in which the points of view constantly shift and intermingle, and by the varied stylistic effects. In the end, however, the novel rises above its faults in its compelling picture of one man's life and the relation of that life to the years of disorder and change that had conditioned the course of twentieth century Mexican history. The central figure is again a force in the land, a millionaire who has climbed to his position of wealth and power by violence, blackmail, bribery, and brutal exploitation of the workers. Like Federico Robles, he is a former revolutionist who stands for the Mexican past and its present. (The robber bands who represented the extreme of the revolutionary effort, Fuentes seems to say, have now been replaced by the robber barons of modern finance and politics.) On the wall of his office, a map shows the extent of his holdings: a newspaper, mines, timber, hotels, and foreign stocks and bonds; not shown are sums of money on deposit in English, Swiss, and United States banks.

Fuentes handles the character of Artemio Cruz with considerable subtlety and skill. He does not gloss over his character's cynicism, opportunism, or brutal ruthlessness, but he saves him from being presented as a monster of calculation by showing his relationships with the three people who mean most in his life: Lunero, the devoted mulatto for whose sake he committed a murder; Regina, the girl killed by Villistas; and his son, Lorenzo. Through the novel, like a refrain, runs a reference to the time just before Lorenzo went off to fight in the Spanish war when father and son took a morning ride toward the sea. By the end of the novel, Artemio's story fulfills all that it promised to a young boy, one man's journey with no real beginning or end in time, marked by love, solitude, violence, power, friendship, disillusionment, corruption, forgetfulness, innocence, and delight. There is also in this story the depiction of how a man's death is joined to his beginning.

Fuentes employs three voices in the narrative. The first is the third person, used to present in dramatic form the events of Artemio's life as they are pieced together in past time. The second is the "I" of the present, as the old man lies dying, shrinking from the decay of his body, and taking fitful account of what is going on around him. The third is a vatic presence never identified that addresses Artemio as "you." This, perhaps, is the unrealized Artemio, the man he might have been. He is a lover of the land that the real Artemio Cruz robbed and raped, the product of history, or the re-created moral conscience of the revolution. He speaks in metaphors, poetry, and prophecy about history and time, and places and people, because they belong to the beautiful but sad and tragic land of his birth.

The Death of Artemio Cruz is a divided book, terse, chaotic, passionate, and ironic. Too much has been made, undoubtedly, of Carlos Fuentes as one of Mexico's angry young men. In spite of his Marxist beliefs, he is essentially a romantic, and he possesses an exuberant, powerful talent. Aside from the surface effects of undisciplined but compelling style, Fuentes' writing is strikingly clear and unhackneyed, even in translation.

Bibliography:
Faris, Wendy B. *Carlos Fuentes*. New York: Frederick Ungar, 1983. Fine overview of Fuentes' works with considerable detailed analysis. Includes a twenty-two-page chapter that focuses solely on *The Death of Artemio Cruz*, discussing the novel's plot, theme, and presentation.
Guzmán, Daniel de. *Carlos Fuentes*. New York: Twayne, 1972. Excellent overview of Fuentes' life and career through the 1960's. Discusses initial critical reception of *The Death of Artemio Cruz*, presents a description of the narrative and a plot summary, and considers the significance of the novel in Fuentes' evolution as a writer.
Harss, Luis, and Barbara Dohmann. *Into the Mainstream: Conversations with Latin American Writers*. New York: Harper & Row, 1967. Includes a chapter entitled "Carlos Fuentes, or the

New Heresy," which provides an interview-based discussion of Fuentes and his works and includes considerable background on post-revolutionary Mexican society and literature.

Sommers, Joseph. *After the Storm: Landmarks of the Modern Mexican Novel.* Albuquerque: University of New Mexico Press, 1968. A twelve-page discussion of *The Death of Artemio Cruz* treats the novel's tone, structure, point of view, and treatment of time, followed by more detailed consideration of the work's theme and its literary quality. Includes some comparison to Fuentes' earlier novel *Where the Air Is Clear.*

Vázquez Amaral, José. *The Contemporary Latin American Narrative.* New York: Las Américas, 1970. A brief chapter on *The Death of Artemio Cruz,* part overview and part review, compares Fuentes' novel and Mariano Azuela's *The Underdogs* (1915) as novels of the Mexican Revolution.

THE DEATH OF EMPEDOCLES

Type of work: Drama
Author: Friedrich Hölderlin (1770-1843)
Type of plot: Tragedy
Time of plot: Fifth century B.C.E.
Locale: Agrigentum and Mount Etna
First published: Der Tod des Empedocles, 1826 (English translation, 1966)

> Principal characters:
> EMPEDOCLES, a prophet and healer
> KRITIAS or MECADES, the ruler of Agrigentum
> MANES, Empedocles' former teacher
> MECADES,
> HEMOCRATES,
> PAUSANIAS,
> PANTHEA, and
> DELIA, observers and commentators

The Death of Empedocles is a verse drama of Friedrich Hölderlin's middle period (1793-1799), when his worldview of idealistic pantheism—that the human being is part of a cosmos in which all things express the nature of divinity—was called into question by issues raised in his intense study of the philosophical works of Johann Gottlieb Fichte. Fichte asserts in his philosophy that it is the individual consciousness alone that gives meaning to the world. Such a view challenges the holistic aspect of pantheism. While in many respects *The Death of Empedocles* has been seen as Hölderlin's dramatization of his inner conflict, it is also a representative work of the movement of many Romantics away from an interest in classical themes toward their struggle to express innovative perceptions of the relationship between humanity and nature and between humanity and divinity. *The Death of Empedocles* is one of the works that marks this transformation.

Like his contemporaries and immediate predecessors, Hölderlin considered the problem of what is proper to humankind and what is not: some abilities and some knowledge are not appropriate for the mortal state because, being primarily of the flesh and not solely of the spirit, people do not have the powers of perception to understand. Ironically, humanity desires to understand those very things that it cannot. Empedocles attempts to expose the secrets of the soul and of the workings of the universe to a humanity that cannot have the capacity to understand them.

The Death of Empedocles, which takes place at Agrigentum and at the foot of Mount Etna, is a version of the legend of the Greek philosopher, poet, and statesman, Empedocles. Empedocles, who lived c. 490 to 430 B.C.E., threw himself, according to legend, into the crater of Mount Etna to prove that he was a god. Empedocles was reputed to know many of the secrets of the gods and of the universe and of life and death. In the play, Empedocles' problem is that he has aspired to be more than a man but will always be less than the gods. Critics have noted the similarity between Hölderlin's Empedocles and Christ in many respects, the most significant being that they are both figures of matter and spirit, both of whom overcame their states through death and transformation to another state—deification for Christ, reunion with elemental nature for Empedocles. Empedocles' tragedy is that he becomes one with the divine spirit of the universe, and thereby alienates the ruling powers of Agrigentum. He chooses to share his visions with the people, undermining the authority of the religious establishment. According to Hölderlin's plan for his final version, Empedocles is a redeemer figure who must die in order for his civilization to flourish. Hölderlin's vision of the universe is Romantic and cyclical; for him, death and life become part of the same process, harmony is broken and reestablished, and things form, decay, and reassemble themselves—even civilization is subject to decay and restoration.

The drama remains in three fragments, none of which Hölderlin finished. Versions 1 and 2 show Empedocles as a prophet with the tragic flaw of pride. Half tragic hero and half Christ figure, Empedocles has the powers of the magician to heal and to move the elements, but his desire to be reunited with the gods causes him to disregard the pleas of his followers that he return to them from his exile. In the second version, before the action of the play begins, Empedocles, "That tender soul . . . run to waste," wishes to share his understanding with his people, but in this version, he is insolent and despotic. This tragic hero of the second version is a Romantic who not only falls but who also bemoans his own fall. His first speech shows him imploring the gods and the forces of nature to consider him in his solitariness. His vision of the universe contributes to his fall; ultimately, he understands that his own powers of perception and his ability to control the elemental forces condemn him to solitude. By the third version, Hölderlin transcends his own self-imposed strictures of classical tragedy to create, in fragmentary form, a work in which Empedocles' personal motive for suicide, that of reuniting with the gods, takes on the universal significance of the redemption of civilization.

In the first version, Kritias, the archon or ruler in Agrigentum, who represents government, remarks that Empedocles' teachings have so affected the people that they, in their belief that he has ascended into heaven, are disaffected against the laws of the state. Hermocrates, who represents religion, counsels that Empedocles has been abandoned by the gods, who formerly so favored him, because he came to be on such familiar terms with them that he actually forgot that he could never be one of them, and "forgot the difference" between them. It is Hermocrates who will curse him, and who plans to show the people that Empedocles, rather than having risen, was actually in his garden in a state of abject depression.

The second version omits this scene, and opens instead with the interchange between the priest and the archon, Kritias, who is renamed in this version Mecades. As in the first version, in discussing the stature of Empedocles among the citizenry of Agrigentum, Mecades and Hermocrates say that Empedocles has overreached his own boundaries: Because of his familiarity with the gods, the people adulate him excessively, honoring him for stealing the "fire of life" from Heaven, and have ceased honoring their laws and customs. Hermocrates describes the downfall of the noble-minded Empedocles, how he became like the "superstitious rabble with no soul," which caused the loss of his power.

Empedocles' meditative soliloquy, which in version 1 is the third scene, opens version 2. Empedocles reflects on his fallen state, on his previous state as a powerful seer to whom people had applied for renovation of their spirits, and on the necessity of his being punished for his pride in presuming to be too much of the world of the gods. He calls out to the divinities of the earth and sky.

In dialogue with Pausanias, he reveals his pantheism: He recalls having heard the melodies of the powers of nature and her "ancient harmony," and he regrets that nature's powers have deserted him, claiming that the greater one's good fortune, the worse one's downfall. Pausanias then asks of Empedocles one of the key questions of the drama: Can one control one's own feelings, or can the forces of darkness reach even into the human heart? Another way to phrase the question: Do we have free will, or are we ruled by fate? He implores Empedocles to remember that Empedocles has been and still is a person. Empedocles counters with the Romantic statement, "You do not know me, nor yourself, nor life, nor death." In his bitterness, he says that the world is a "dead stringed instrument" without him to animate it with "a language and a soul"; nature has become his serving girl, and the gods live for the people only insofar as he proclaims them. He informs Pausanias that the things for which Pausanias admires him are those things that destroy him: the vast extent of his powers of understanding the universe, and his abilities to control the elements, often for the good of humanity. This scene breaks off as Empedocles begins a disquisition on the transformative power of the word.

In versions 1 and 2, Empedocles explains to Pausanias that his fall from grace is due to being too blessed by the gods, that ultimately he has become too insolent in his pride. In the fragmentary conclusions to Act II of the second version, there follows an interchange between Panthea and Delia. In the second version, in contrast to the first, the question of the morality of Empedocles' contemplated suicide is emphasized through the discussion of Panthea, Delia, and Pausanias. Panthea is supportive of Empedocles, and Pausanias rather glorifies him in his decision, but Delia objects.

Panthea expresses the dichotomy between the gods and nature, proclaiming that it was nature rather than the gods who gave Empedocles his lofty soul. Delia comments on the death of Empedocles in lines that bemoan the transitory nature of existence. Panthea remarks upon the fact that living things fade, that "the best,/ Even they seek out their destroyers," which are the "gods of death." In anguish, she implores, "O Nature, why do you/ Make it so easy?/ For your hero to die?" With his death, Panthea moans, the hearts of humanity draw away from nature and from "the holy All": She closes with the comment, "For we who are blind?/ Needed a miracle once." The real problem is not merely that Empedocles has suffered a tragic fall through pride but also that in so doing, he has created a state of disharmony with nature, having lost sight of the holiness of all living things. In Hölderlin's Romantic philosophy, the drawing of human hearts away from "the holy All" constitutes communal spiritual cataclysm. It is in his third version that he tries dramatically to redeem this act through Empedocles.

Version 1 continues with the visit to Empedocles in his garden by several people, including Kritias and Hermocrates, the latter of whom curses Empedocles in his wish to commit suicide, and who spurs the crowd on to drive Empedocles into exile. The action builds to a turning point when, on Mount Etna, Empedocles and Pausanias see the crowd coming up the mountainside. Hermocrates claims to the people that Empedocles is forgiven, but Pausanias tells them that Empedocles intends to commit suicide. The people threaten to kill Hermocrates and proclaim their desire to make Empedocles their king. Empedocles, however, remarks that the era of democracy has arrived, and that although he will not go home with them, he will give them a message, that message being the holiest thing he has to give. He then speaks to them of death and life, and of the transformative nature of civilization. He implores them to defy the old ways and to engage in a worship of nature, for only then will humanity attain true peace, the "life of the world."

Critics have noted Christological allusions. Empedocles becomes aware that the time of his own purification and transformation is at hand; he has been as one lent to life for a short time; he has fulfilled his purpose to the people. Having become too aware of the divine in the world, he knows he must pass on, and he bids Pausanias arrange things, including a last supper. Version 2 concludes as, invoking Jupiter, Empedocles passes out of this state in an overwhelming cognizance of the divinity of the universe.

Although the third version consists of only three finished scenes, Hölderlin's notes for its completion give a fairly good notion of the direction in which he intended to take the work. He intended to expand the first act and to include four more acts, in which the bewildered crowd would come to understand the implications of the death of Empedocles. While in versions 1 and 2, Empedocles' fall from grace is a central issue, in version 3, the thematic focus shifts to the moral questions, including those that attend the contemplation of suicide by a leader who is a poet, prophet, magician, and healer.

Version 3 opens with Empedocles in exile, awakening, describing his position between "Father Etna and his close relative, the Thunderer." High up in a place where he sings "natural songs" with the eagles, he is in harmony with nature as well as in proximity to the gods. Dramatic tension in this version has been significantly heightened with the introduction of a new character, Strato, as king of Agrigentum, and brother of Empedocles. In soliloquy, Empedocles tells that his brother has exiled him, but that he has nevertheless made a new life for himself; he knows he himself sinned against humanity by serving them blindly as the elements like "fire or water" serve, but not as a human being with a human heart would serve. He therefore deserved to have been driven out by his people, and it is this forced exile which has in fact recreated the bond between him and nature. He pronounces that "death is what I seek. It is my right," and that his need for the human heart has ended.

In the third scene of the third version, Hölderlin departs in a radically different direction, one that lifts this work out of the realm of an imitative tragic classicism and into that of innovative Romanticism. In it, Manes, Empedocles' former teacher, admonishes Empedocles for his decision to commit suicide and causes him to come to terms with this decision. Manes admits to Empedocles, however, that there is one very specific situation in which suicide may be allowed, and that concerns a very specific individual in a very specific situation. While remaining doubtful throughout, he describes Empedocles as this kind of individual: one who partakes of both the human and divine realms in a time of transformative social and political upheaval. This would be a person who could so absorb the conflicts in the world into himself that he would serve as an example to humanity of what is possible: of the strength of the peace that is within their power to create. He must die, then, because he would himself be worshipped, and people would forget that their objective in his example is not for them to worship him, but to do as he has done. Cosmically, his death is to herald a new order, a new civilization. Had Hölderlin completed the third version, he would have used this presentation; Hölderlin's notes make this clear. In the projected conclusion, Manes believes that Empedocles is actually the "historical redeemer," "the chosen one who kills and gives life, in and through whom a world is at once dissolved and renewed." Manes is to give to the people the great secret of Empedocles, his last will, as the basis for the new civilization.

The historical Empedocles presumably attracted Hölderlin: Fundamentally a pantheist, Empedocles was adept at manipulating the forces of nature; essentially an idealist, he believed in political democracy. It may have been Empedocles' theory of the cyclic nature of the universe that attracted Hölderlin as well. Ultimately, however, *The Death of Empedocles* represents the influences of the German Romantics who preceded Hölderlin. Hölderlin was acutely aware that people are of the world of matter, not only of the world of spirit, and, being so, people cannot really ever become part of the realm of pure spirit. In other words, people may strive and strive for perfection, but human perfection is paradoxically very imperfect: It can be only a shadow of true spiritual perfection. Not to recognize the vast difference between the ideal state and the real state is cosmically disastrous. Empedocles' pride postpones his recognition of this difference.

It is most unfortunate that Hölderlin never finished this play. Even as it stands, it is a major document in the history of European Romanticism. There is the curious circumstance of three versions, which, read together (and with Hölderlin's notes) as one work, provide a substantial view of the progress of a poet's mind in a time of artistic as well as social and political transformation.

Donna Berliner

Bibliography:
George, Emery E., ed. *Friedrich Hölderlin: An Early Modern.* Ann Arbor: University of Michigan Press, 1972. Shows how Hölderlin's work presages treatments and techniques that developed later in the nineteenth century.

Hamburger, Michael. "Hölderlin." In *Contraries: Studies in German Literature.* New York: E. P. Dutton, 1970. Contains a significant discussion of Hölderlin's interpretation of the notion of the poet as seer and the place of *The Death of Empedocles* in this tradition.

Hölderlin, Friedrich. "The Ground for Empedocles." In *Friedrich Hölderlin: Essays and Letters on Theory.* Translated and edited by Thomas Pfau. Albany: State University of New York Press, 1988. Discusses *The Death of Empedocles* and the nature of drama, as well as the opposing principles of the rational consciousness and the irrational forces of nature.

Pike, Burton. "The Idealist Element in Hölderlin's *Empedokles.*" *Germanic Review* 32, no. 1 (February, 1957): 178-185. Shows Empedocles as a figure who embodies the most idealistic aspects of Hölderlin's worldview.

Stahl, E. L. "The Dramatic Structure of Hölderlin's *Empedokles.*" *Modern Language Review* 62, no. 1 (January, 1967): 92-97. Discussion of the dramatic structure and the projected execution of the fragments.

_____. "Hölderlin's Idea of Poetry." In *The Era of Goethe: Essays Presented to James Boyd.* Oxford: Basil Blackwell, 1959. Discusses Hölderlin's aesthetic notions in the context of those of his contemporaries.

Unger, Richard. *Friedrich Hölderlin.* Boston: Twayne, 1984. Accessible chapter on *The Death of Empedocles* examines the changes from version to version.

_____. *Hölderlin's Major Poetry: The Dialectics of Unity.* Bloomington: Indiana University Press, 1975. Places Hölderlin's work in the framework of his notion of the oneness of the universe.

THE DEATH OF IVAN ILYICH

Type of work: Novella
Author: Leo Tolstoy (1828-1910)
Type of plot: Psychological realism
Time of plot: 1880's
Locale: St. Petersburg and nearby provinces
First published: Smert Ivana Ilicha, 1886 (English translation, 1887)

> *Principal characters:*
> IVAN ILYICH GOLOVIN, a prominent Russian judge
> PRASKOVYA FEDOROVNA GOLOVINA, his wife
> PETER IVANOVITCH, his colleague
> GERASIM, his servant boy

The Story:

During a break in a hearing, a group of lawyers gathered informally. One, Peter Ivanovitch, interrupted the good-natured arguing of the others with the news that Ivan Ilyich, a colleague they greatly respected, was dead. Unwittingly, each thought first of what this death meant to his own chances of promotion, and each could not help feeling relief that it was Ivan Ilyich and not himself who had died.

That afternoon, Peter Ivanovitch visited the dead man's home, where the funeral was to be held. Although he met a playful colleague, Schwartz, he attempted to behave as correctly as possible under such sorrowful circumstances, as if by observing the proper protocol he could persuade himself into the proper feelings. He looked respectfully at the corpse and talked with Ivan's widow, Praskovya Fedorovna, but he was continually distracted during his talk by an unruly spring in the hassock on which he sat. While he struggled to keep his decorum, Praskovya spoke only of her own exhaustion and suffering. Peter, suddenly terrified by their mutual hypocrisy, longed to leave; once the widow had pumped him for information about her pension, she, too, was glad to end the conversation. At the funeral, Peter saw Ivan's daughter and her fiancé, who were angrily glum, and Ivan's little son, who was tearstained but naughty. Only the servant boy, Gerasim, spoke cheerfully, for he was the only one who could accept death as natural. Peter left and hurried to his nightly card game.

Ivan Ilyich had been the second and most successful of the three sons of a superfluous bureaucrat. An intelligent and popular boy, he seemed able to mold his life into a perfect pattern. As secretary to a provincial governor after completing law school, and later as an examining magistrate, he was the very model of conscientiousness mingled with good humor. He managed the decorum of his official position as well as the ease of his social one. Only marriage, although socially correct, did not conform to his ideas of decorum; his wife, not content to fulfill the role he had chosen for her, became demanding and quarrelsome. As a result, he increasingly shut himself off from his family (which had grown with two children) and found the order and peace he needed in his judiciary affairs.

In 1880, however, he was shattered by the loss of two promotions. In desperation, he went to St. Petersburg, where a chance meeting led to his obtaining a miraculously good appointment. In the city, he found precisely the house he had always wanted, and he worked to furnish it to his taste. Even a fall and a resulting bruise on his side had not dampened his enthusiasm. He and his wife were delighted with their new home, which they thought was aristocratic, although it looked like the homes of all those who wished to appear well-bred. To Ivan, life was at last as it should be: smooth, pleasant, and ordered according to an unwavering routine. His life was properly divided into the official and the personal, and he kept the two halves dexterously apart.

Ivan began to notice an increasing discomfort in his left side. He finally consulted a specialist, but the examination left him frightened and helpless, for although he understood the doctor's objective attitude as akin to his own official one, he felt that it had given his pain a terrible significance. For a time, he felt that he was recovering by following prescriptions and learning all he could about his illness, but renewed attacks terrified him. Gradually Ivan found his whole life to be colored by the pain. Card games became trivial; friends seemed to do nothing but speculate on how long he would live. When Ivan's brother-in-law came for a visit, his shocked look told Ivan how much illness had changed him, and he suddenly realized that he faced not illness but even death. Through deepening terror and despair Ivan shrank from this truth. Other men died, not he. Desperately, he erected screens against the pain and the knowledge of death it brought, but it lurked behind court duties and quarrels with his family. The knowledge that it had begun with the bruise on his side only made his condition harder to bear.

As Ivan grew steadily worse, drugs failed to help him, but the clean strength and honesty of the peasant boy, Gerasim, nourished him, for Ivan felt that his family were hypocrites who chose to pretend that he was not dying. Death to them was not part of that same decorum he, too, had once revered and was therefore hidden as unpleasant and shameful. Only Gerasim could understand his pain because only he admitted that death was real and natural.

Ivan retreated increasingly into his private anguish. He hated his knowing doctors, his plump, chiding wife, his daughter and her new fiancé. Lamenting, he longed to have his old, happy life again, but only memories of childhood revealed true happiness. Unwillingly he returned again and again to this knowledge as he continued questioning the reasons for his torment. If he had always lived correctly, why was this happening to him? What if he had been wrong? Suddenly, he knew that the faint urges he had consciously stilled in order to do as people thought proper had been the true urges. Since he had not known the truth about life, he also had not known the truth about death. His anguish increased as he thought of the irrevocable choice he had made.

His wife brought the priest, whose sacrament eased him until her presence reminded him of his deceptive life. He screamed to her to leave him, and he continued screaming as he struggled against death, unable to relinquish the illusion that his life had been good. Then the struggle ceased, and he knew that although his life had not been right, it no longer mattered. Opening his eyes, he saw his wife and son weeping by his bedside. Aware of them for the first time, he felt sorry for them. As he tried to ask their forgiveness, everything became clear to him. He must not hurt them; he must set them free and free himself from his sufferings. The pain and fear of death were no longer there. Instead, there was only light and joy.

Critical Evaluation:

The Death of Ivan Ilyich is quite short, but it is one of the greatest pieces of fiction in any language. In it, Leo Tolstoy examines the hollowness of bourgeois existence. Ivan Ilyich is a successful member of the state bureaucracy. Throughout his life he has carefully adjusted his conduct so as to please his superiors and to arrange a life that runs smoothly and without complication. He is the perfect example of the conforming, "other-directed" man. Only shortly before his death does he discover the horror that lies behind his seemingly successful life.

The story opens in an unusual but significant way. Rather than tell the reader of Ivan's early years, Tolstoy presents the dead Ivan stretched out at home, attended by his wife and closest friend, Peter Ivanovitch. The behavior of the mourners indicates more about Ivan's life than any chronicle could. Rather than grieve over his death, they are worried about their own affairs. His wife asks Peter Ivanovitch about her pension, hoping to persuade him to help her arrange for an increase, while he frets about missing the bridge game he had planned. They both pretend to feelings of grief they do not feel. The work proceeds to answer the question what was it about Ivan's life that could have resulted in so little concern for him after his death. This portion of the novella dramatizes the statement that opens the second section: "Ivan Ilyich's life had been most simple and most ordinary and therefore most terrible."

Ivan's progress from law school to the position of examining magistrate is marked by careful obedience to authority both in legal matters and in matters of taste and style of life. His early pangs of conscience at youthful actions are overcome when he sees people of good position doing the same thing without qualms. Still, he never becomes a rake or hell-raiser; he is, rather, anxiously correct and proper. He makes a proper marriage—one that serves to advance him—and then gradually proceeds to alienate his wife and children by avoiding domestic complications in the name of his job. In this separation between his private life, with its potential for affection, and his public duties, he furthers the process of fragmentation within himself. He becomes punctilious at home as well as at work. All of his life takes on an official and artificial character, from which only the natural process of dying can release him as it educates him. In the opening scene, readers are told that "his face was handsomer and above all more dignified than when he was alive." His death is a form of rescue.

His job is a game that he had played with great seriousness—like the bridge games he hurries to after work. He never abuses his power as a magistrate but always conducts himself "by the book." Most of all, he is careful never to become personally involved in the carrying out of justice. He is a perfect arm of the state, a perfect product of its bureaucratic machinery. Naturally, he never questions the system of justice he is paid to administer. It is significant that he rises no higher than the middle rank of officialdom. Those above him have perceived that he is essentially mediocre.

Nevertheless, his life seems to flow along easily, pleasantly, and correctly. He decorates his new home, supervising much of the work closely. He imagines that the result is very special, but Tolstoy states that Ivan's home, characteristically, looks exactly like the homes of other people of his class and station. Underneath the smooth surface of this life something is wrong, and it refuses to stay concealed. Instead, it manifests itself in the form of an illness, probably cancer, which gradually consumes Ivan's vitality. When he goes to the doctor he feels guilty and desperately uncertain. For the first time, he learns what it is like to be the recipient of the games those in authority play—like a criminal dragged to the bar. The doctor cannot or will not tell him what is wrong (he probably does not know). Gradually, Ivan declines until he is bedridden. His disintegrating flesh begins to give off a strange and unpleasant odor. He becomes hateful to himself and to his wife, who up to now has pursued a life of idle and superficial pleasure. Even more than physical pain, Ivan suffers from spiritual torment. His prior habits of life have given him no resources with which to face death. Moreover, he is perpetually troubled by the question of why he is suffering when he took such pains to lead a correct life. What if he has been wrong all along? In the grip of despair, he searches for hope at any hand, but no hope presents itself until he finds it possible to accept the kind attentions of his servant Gerasim.

Gerasim is the opposite of Ivan. A healthy, simple peasant, he has never known the artificial life of a bureaucrat and social climber. He does not fear death and, thus, does not mind being in the presence of the dying Ivan. He is in tune with the natural. Ivan is able to accept him because he feels that there is no deception in Gerasim's attitude toward him, whereas he sees nothing but deception in the kind and cheerful attitudes of his wife and friends (a reaction, in part, to the falseness of his former life). When Gerasim sits for hours with his master's legs propped up on his shoulders, Ivan feels unaccountable relief. Still, Gerasim's presence only partially modifies Ivan's agony. Essentially, he must go through the process of dying by himself. Perhaps Gerasim's naturalness does bring Ivan to the conviction of the worthlessness of his former life, but death is Ivan's best educator. It gradually and painfully strips away the artificial and the vain. It reduces Ivan to the elemental position of an organism dependent on the natural processes of life. Interestingly, Ivan thinks most of all of his early youth at this time. He recalls when he was still an innocent, uncorrupted by the false system he slavishly aspired to enter. In a sense, he is yearning to recapture the natural instincts represented by Gerasim. Death offers him the chance. In the final hours of his interminable decline, Ivan grows still. He has a vision of light and freedom. Death becomes for him a door to a larger and purer existence.

"Critical Evaluation" by Benjamin Nyce

Bibliography:
Christian, R. F. *Tolstoy: A Critical Introduction.* London: Cambridge University Press, 1969. Discusses *The Death of Ivan Ilyich* and compares the novella with Franz Kafka's *The Trial* (1925). Also relates the plot and structure of *The Death of Ivan Ilyich* to the works of later writers whom it may have influenced.
Courcel, Martine de. *Tolstoy: The Ultimate Reconciliation.* Translated by Peter Levi. New York: Charles Scribner's Sons, 1988. A thorough discussion of Tolstoy. Explains the social and political atmosphere at the time of *The Death of Ivan Ilyich*. Finds many parallels between it and Tolstoy's life.
Jahn, Gary R. *"The Death of Ivan Ilich": An Interpretation.* New York: Twayne, 1993. Includes an extensive chronology of Tolstoy and the literary and historical context of the work. Presents critical reception, social, psychological and philosophical issues, as well as a section on structure and style. Also gives an extensive reading of the plot.
Noyes, George Rapall. *Tolstoy.* New York: Dover, 1968. Discusses the interconnection of Tolstoy's many works and refers to biographical information pertinent to the understanding of his writings. Finds *The Death of Ivan Ilyich* to be more intense and focused than other works by the author.
Rowe, William W. *Leo Tolstoy.* Boston: Twayne, 1986. Contains a chronology of Tolstoy's life, bibliography, and index. Chapters include biographical information and treatments of several novels and stories. An excellent companion for the Tolstoy reader. Discusses the structure and main character of *The Death of Ivan Ilyich*.

THE DEATH OF THE HEART

Type of work: Novel
Author: Elizabeth Bowen (1899-1973)
Type of plot: Psychological realism
Time of plot: After World War I
Locale: London and Seale, England
First published: 1938

Principal characters:
THOMAS QUAYNE, the owner of Quayne and Merrett, an advertising
agency
ANNA QUAYNE, his wife
PORTIA QUAYNE, his sixteen-year-old half sister
ST. QUENTIN MILLER, an author and a friend of the Quaynes
EDDIE, an employee of Quayne and Merrett
MAJOR BRUTT, a retired officer
MRS. HECCOMB, Anna's former governess

The Story:

Anna Quayne's pique demanded an outlet—she could no longer contain it all within herself; therefore, while St. Quentin Miller shivered with cold, she marched him around the frozen park, delivering herself of her discontent. The trouble, of course, had started with Portia, for the Quayne household had not been the same since the arrival of Tom's sixteen-year-old half sister. Not that Portia was all to blame; the business had begun with a deathbed wish. Who could expect dying old Mr. Quayne to ask Tom to take a half sister he hardly knew, keep her for at least a year, and give her a graceful start in life? As she explained to St. Quentin, Anna herself hardly knew how to cope with the arrangement, although she had tried to accept it with outward tranquillity. Now she had stumbled across the girl's diary, glimpsed her own name, and had been tempted to read. It was obvious that Portia was less than happy and that she was scanning the atmosphere of her brother's house with an unflattering eye.

While Anna was thus unburdening herself, the subject of her discussion returned home quietly from Miss Paullie's lessons. She was vaguely disturbed to learn from Matchett, the housekeeper, that Anna had commented upon the clutter in Portia's bedroom. Later, she shared tea with Anna and St. Quentin when they came in, tingling with cold; but the atmosphere seemed a bit stiff, and Portia readily agreed with Anna's suggestion that she join her brother in his study. Portia felt more at ease with Tom, even though he clearly found conversation with her awkward.

By now, Portia knew that there was no one in whom she could readily confide. At 2 Windsor Terrace, Matchett offered a certain possessive friendship; at school, only the inquisitive Lilian took notice of her. Major Brutt was better than either of these; in her presence, his eyes showed a fatherly gleam, and she liked the picture puzzle he had sent. Anna tolerated the Major—he was her only link with an old friend, Pidgeon—but Major Brutt seldom ventured to call, and Portia saw him mostly in the company of others.

Another of Anna's friends whom Portia sometimes saw was Eddie. Eddie, however, was seemingly beyond the range of Portia's clumsy probing for companionship. He was twenty-three years of age and brightly self-assured as well. Anna found it amusing to have him around, although she often rebuked his conceit and presumption; she went so far as to find him a job with Quayne and Merrett. One day, Portia handed Eddie his hat as he took leave of Anna; the next day he wrote to her. Before long, they were meeting regularly and secretly.

Having no wish to alienate Anna, Eddie cautioned Portia not to mention him in her diary, but he reveled in Portia's uncritical adoration. They went to the zoo, to tea, and ultimately to his apartment. Matchett, who found Eddie's letter under Portia's pillow, soon became coldly jealous of his influence. Even Anna and Tom became slightly restive as they began to realize the situation. Meanwhile, Portia was falling deeper and deeper in love. When Eddie lightly declared that it was a pity they were too young to marry, Portia innocently took his remarks as a tentative proposal. Although he carefully refrained from real lovemaking, Portia felt sure he returned her love.

With the approach of spring, Anna and Tom revealed their intention of spending a few weeks in Capri. Since Matchett would houseclean while they were gone, they decided to send Portia to Mrs. Heccomb, Anna's former governess, who lived in a seaside house at Seale. Portia, dismayed by the prospect of separation from Eddie, was only partially consoled by his promise to write.

Eddie did write promptly; so did Major Brutt, with the promise of another picture puzzle; and Seale, happily, turned out better than Portia had expected. Having none of Anna's remoteness, Mrs. Heccomb deluged her guest with carefree chatter. Her two grown-up stepchildren reacted somewhat more cautiously, because they were prepared to find Portia a highbrow. When they realized she was only shy, they quickly relaxed; the radio blared while they vigorously shouted over it about roller skating, hockey games, and Saturday night parties. Portia gradually withdrew from her shell of loneliness. Within a few days, she felt enough at home to ask Daphne Heccomb if Eddie might spend a weekend at Seale. Daphne consented to relay the request to her mother, and Mrs. Heccomb affably approved.

Eddie's visit was not a success. His efforts to be the life of the party soon had Mrs. Heccomb wondering about the wisdom of her invitation. At the cinema, his good fellowship extended to holding hands enthusiastically with Daphne. When a distressed Portia uttered mild reproaches, he intimated that she was a naïve child. Walking together in the woods on their final afternoon, Portia learned that Eddie had no use for her love unless it could remain uncritical and undemanding. Her vision of an idyllic reunion shattered as she began to see his instability. Two weeks later, her stay at Seale ended. Back in London, Matchett triumphantly informed her that Eddie had left word that he would be out of town a few days.

Walking home from school not long afterward, Portia encountered St. Quentin, who inadvertently revealed Anna's perusal of the diary. Upset, she sought comfort from Eddie once more. No longer gratified by her devotion, he made her feel even more unwanted; and the sight of a letter from Anna, lying on Eddie's table, convinced Portia that they were allied against her. As she left his apartment, it seemed unthinkable that she could ever return to Windsor Terrace; her only possible refuge now was Major Brutt. She went, therefore, to the Karachi Hotel, surprising the worthy major as he finished his dinner. Surprise changed to alarm as she pleaded her case: Would he take her away, would he marry her? She could relieve his loneliness, she could care for him, she could polish his shoes. With as much serenity as he could muster, the major affirmed that polishing shoes was a job with which women had little success; with a little time and patience, her position would soon appear less desperate. He wished very much to call the Quaynes, for it was getting late and they would be worried. Portia believed that she had been defeated, but she could still choose ground on which to make a final stand. Very well, she finally agreed, he might call them, but he was not to tell them she was coming. That would depend, she finished enigmatically but firmly, on whether they chose to do the right thing.

The major had been right; the Quaynes were worried. After the telephone rang, their momentary relief was succeeded by real confusion. What, after all, would Portia consider the right thing for them to do? It would have to be simple. With help from St. Quentin, they finally decided, and Matchett was sent in a taxi to fetch her.

Critical Evaluation:

Elizabeth Bowen is most often at her best as a writer when she is writing from the perspective of the marginalized—in *Eva Trout* (1969), Bowen writes from the margins of madness. In *The House in Paris* (1935) and *The Death of the Heart*, the marginalized experience is depicted through the eyes of a commonly peripheral period of experience, through the perspective of the child and the adolescent. Portia Quayne is the observing consciousness through which the adult world is revealed for the hypocrisy and shallowness that marks the relationship between Thomas and Anna Quayne.

Portia, the half sister of Thomas, is brought to live in the Quayne household after being orphaned. Her presence in the house brings to a head the many tensions that were brewing there before her arrival. Bowen's use of the child's consciousness gives perspective to the adult world. This emphasis on the "fallenness" of adult perspective is reinforced in the titles of the three sections of the novel, "The World," "The Flesh," and "The Devil." These three section titles both relate to the baptismal rites of the Anglican Book of Common Prayer, and, more generally, signify the three obvious sources of spiritual temptation that mark the Quaynes' dispirited lifestyle and Portia's own falling into the world of the adult.

The title of the story has a double resonance: It relates to the condition of the Quaynes in their marriage, and, perhaps more important, it serves as a caveat for Portia, whose heart, or center of feeling, is being systematically worn down throughout the novel.

Bowen's writing often captures the fading era of the stout British character and the passing of the world of manners that attends the era's demise. The novel's title thus also relates in a general way to the fatal end of an entire empire's place in the world. The death of the heart of British character is at stake throughout the novel, as it is seen to reside at last in the type of people that the Quaynes represent. The world of British manners about which Bowen wrote so clearly had suffered a double blow as a result of the two world wars. In *The Death of the Heart*, all the characters suffer under a cultural malaise that not even the introduction of the young can surmount. Bowen shows the British upper middle class as being too self-involved to give any clear direction to the young, especially young women.

Bowen's decision to make her central character an orphan serves various dramatic purposes. First, Portia's status as an orphan works to exonerate her from the situation into which she is forced. She does not do anything to create the tensions between Anna and Thomas, and, as a parentless child, she is placed in the position of observing the adult world, while only being indirectly related to what takes place within it. Second, Portia's status as an orphan gives her the privilege of serving as a somewhat distanced narrative consciousness. Her interactions with Anna are not fraught with the same tensions that one could expect from a typical parent-child relationship. Portia, being parentless, can double as Anna's own not yet fully developed self. Portia learns from the Quaynes that emergence into the adult world, at the threshold of which she stands, brings with it a certain "death" or loss of innocence. Portia's surrogate position with regard to Anna's own maternal sense, however, teaches Anna that, contrary to the way she is living, the heart does not have to die completely to develop to its greatest extent.

Bowen's narrative style combines the use of the third-person narrator with interpolations from Portia's diary, thus giving the reader a firsthand look at what Portia is thinking and how events are registering with her. Significantly, Portia's diary excerpts are found in the section "The Flesh," underscoring that even processes of reflection must take place through the senses. In this way, Bowen plays with the notion that the flesh, or the world of bodily sensation and gratification, is also humankind's foundation for building a more intuitive and spiritual understanding of the world around it.

Bowen manipulates her narrative technique according to the section headings; through indirection, the primary means in the novel by which the characters understand one another; and by showing Portia's growth over a period of time. Bowen aims for a psychological realism throughout the story by limited use of the techniques of the *Bildungsroman*, or novel of personal development. Portia is a personality in the making. Because the central character is a young woman at a formative stage in her life, the reader can interpret the story as a coming-of-age novel, in which both the adults and the child reach a point of perception about themselves and one another.

Finally, the novel must be understood within the context of the novel of manners. Bowen excels at writing about the manners and mores of the British upper middle class. *The Death of the Heart* is generally considered one of her finest achievements in the genre. Although it explores the darker side of human relations, it is not without humor and the ability to entertain.

"Critical Evaluation" by Susan M. Rochette-Crawley

Bibliography:
Austin, Allan E. *Elizabeth Bowen*. Rev. ed. Boston: Twayne, 1989. Good introduction discusses Bowen's style, syntax, use of narrator, and evocative settings. Analyzes careful blending of the two themes—loss of innocence and the revival of a stagnant relationship—praising narrative voice for awareness, perception, humor, compassion. Annotated bibliography.
Coles, Robert. *Irony in the Mind's Life*. Charlottesville: University Press of Virginia, 1974. Clear, insightful analysis of setting, theme, and character, especially the adolescent Portia's innocent capacity for malevolence as she struggles with the seven deadly sins. Discusses the importance of Lilian and Eddie.
Glendinning, Victoria. *Elizabeth Bowen: Portrait of a Writer*. London: Weidenfeld & Nicolson, 1977. Presents Bowen as the last of the Anglo-Irish writers, discussing incidents and individuals in Bowen's life that are reflected in *The Death of the Heart*. Evaluates innovative authorial voice over technique.
Heath, William. *Elizabeth Bowen: An Introduction to Her Novels*. Madison: University of Wisconsin Press, 1961. Discusses the novel's structure, including transitions between its three sections. Analyzes character and theme, finding Matchett the moral authority of the novel. Compares Bowen with Henry James, Jane Austin, and T. S. Eliot. Extremely helpful introduction and annotated bibliography.
Kenney, Edwin, Jr. *Elizabeth Bowen*. Cranbury, N.J.: Bucknell University Press, 1975. Presents *The Death of the Heart* as a culmination of Bowen's themes of youthful innocence confronting a world of unsympathetic fallen adults. Describes Bowen's contrasting the child with the adult, innocence with experience, and the past with the present, including detailed analysis of the relationship between Portia and Anna.

THE DEATH OF VIRGIL

Type of work: Novel
Author: Hermann Broch (1886-1951)
Type of plot: Philosophical
Time of plot: 19 B.C.E.
Locale: Brundisium (Brindisi, Italy)
First published: Der Tod des Vergil, 1945 (English translation, 1945)

> *Principal characters:*
> PUBLIUS VIRGILIUS MARO, the chief poet of Rome
> AUGUSTUS CAESAR, the emperor of Rome
> PLOTIA HIERIA, a woman Virgil had once loved
> LYSANIAS, a young boy
> A SLAVE

The Story:

The imperial fleet returned from Greece to Brundisium, bearing with it the Emperor Augustus and his poet, Virgil, who lay dying. Augustus had sought Virgil and brought him back from the peace and calm in Athens to the shouting Roman throngs—to the mob with its frightening latent capacity for brutality, its fickle adoration of its leaders. Yet these were the Romans whom Virgil had glorified; the nobles he had seen on shipboard greedily eating and gaming were their leaders. Dapper, sham-majestic Augustus was their emperor.

Fever-ridden, the poet heard a boy's song as the ship entered the harbor. Later, as he was carried from the ship, a beautiful boy appeared from nowhere to lead his litter away from the tumult surrounding the emperor, through narrow streets crowded with garbage ripening into decay, streets full of the miseries of the flesh where women jeered at him for being rich and weak. The women's insults made him aware of his own sham-divinity and of the futility of his life. Dying, he at last saw clearly what hypocrisy his life had been, like the shining, hollow emperor whom he served.

At the palace, he was taken to his chambers. The boy, Lysanias, remained with him as night fell. In the depths of a violent seizure, Virgil recognized his own lack of love. As he lay, conscious of his dying body and the infested night, he knew that, like the Augustus-worshiping masses, he had followed the wrong gods; that in his devotion to poetry he had from the beginning given up the service of life for that of death; that it was too late for him to be fulfilled, for even his *Aeneid* lay unperfected. Some recurrence of vigor drove him to the window. Looking into the night, he knew that not only his poem remained to be fulfilled; some knowledge still lay ahead for him to achieve. For the necessity of the soul is to discover itself, since through self-discovery it finds the universe: The landscape of the soul is that of all creation. Human beings must learn, not through the stars but through other human beings.

Two men and a woman interrupted his thoughts when they came through the streets quarreling and shouting good-natured obscenities, guffawing their bawdiness with that male laughter whose matter-of-factness annihilates rather than derides. This laughter in the beautiful night revealed something of the nature of beauty itself. Beauty is the opponent of knowledge; because it is remote, infinite, and therefore seemingly eternal, it is pursued wrongly for its own sake. The same nonhuman laughter is hidden in it. The artist who pursues beauty plunges into loneliness and self-idolatry; because he chooses beauty rather than life, his work becomes adornment rather than revelation. This path Virgil had chosen: Beauty's cold egotism instead of love's warm life, which is true creativity. Thus he had died long before, even before his renunciation of the lovely Plotia, whom he now remembered.

The need for contrition because of his refusal of love, a refusal of the pledge given to all, overwhelmed him. The fever rose within him, bringing strangely prophetic visions of Rome in ruins with wolves howling, of giant birds droning. As reality returned, he knew that for his own salvation he had to burn the *Aeneid*.

Lysanias read to him as he drifted into a calm dream, shining with a knowledge of all past earthly happenings and a vision of something to come. Not yet, but soon, would come one in whom creation, love, and immortality would be united; one who would bear salvation like a single star, whose voice he seemed to hear bidding him open his eyes to love, for he was called to enter the creation. As the fever left him and dawn broke, he momentarily doubted the voice. Then came the vision of an angel and, at last, undisturbed sleep.

Virgil awoke to find two old friends who had come to cheer him. Their bluff reassurances changed to incredulity when they heard that he planned to burn the *Aeneid*. Their arguments against his own conviction that his book lacked reality because he himself lacked love were blurred by his fevered perception. Lysanias, whose existence seemed questionable to his friends, appeared with a Near Eastern slave to reaffirm that Virgil was the guide, although not the savior. Plotia came and called him to an exchange of mutual love and the destruction of his work, the renunciation of beauty for love. Suddenly he and Plotia were exposed, and power thundered around him.

Augustus had come to ask Virgil not to burn the *Aeneid*. In the ensuing interview, Virgil's rising delirium made him not only supernaturally aware of truth but also confused as to reality: The invisible Plotia guarded the manuscript; the invisible Lysanias lurked nearby; the room sometimes became a landscape. Augustus insisted that the poem was the property of the Romans, for whom it had been written. Virgil tried to explain that poetry is the knowledge of death, for only through death can one understand life; that unlike Aeschylus, whose knowledge had forced him to poetry, he, Virgil, had sought knowledge through writing poetry and had therefore found nothing.

Augustus and the slave seemed to be talking, and Augustus was the symbol of the state he had created, which was order and sobriety and humanity's supreme eternal reality. The slave, awaiting the birth of the supreme ancestor's son, was steadfastness and the freedom of community. The truth of the state must be united to the metaphysical by an individual act of truth, must be made human to realize perfection. Such a savior will come, whose sacrificial death will be the supreme symbol of humility and charity. Virgil still insisted that he must sacrifice his work because he had not sacrificed his life, that destroying a thing that lacked perception would redeem both himself and the Romans.

Augustus, growing angry, accused Virgil of envy. In a moment of love, Virgil gave him the poem, agreeing not to destroy it. He asked, however, that his slaves might go free after his death. As he talked of his will to his friends, renewed attacks of fever brought him ever stranger hallucinations. He called for help and found he could at last say the word for his own salvation.

After he had finished dictating his will, it seemed to him that he was once more on a boat, one smaller than the one that had brought him into the harbor the day before, rowed by his friend Plotius and guided by Lysanias. About him were many people he knew. Gradually, all disappeared as he floated into the night; the boy became first a seraph whose ring glowed like a star, then Plotia, who led him into the day again. Reaching shore, they entered a garden where, somehow, he knew that she had become the boy and the slave and that he had become all of them; then he was also the animals and plants, then the mountains, and finally the universe, contained in a small white core of unity—and nothing. He was commanded to turn around, and the nothing became everything again, created by the word in the circle of time. Finally, he was received into the word itself.

Critical Evaluation:

In 1938, Hermann Broch had to flee his native Austria because he was Jewish. It was only through the intervention of sympathetic friends and acquaintances, among them James Joyce, that Broch succeeded in leaving Europe. Once in America, he set to work finishing the novel *The Death of Virgil.*

At the heart of this novel lies the queston whether or not to destroy Virgil's last great creation, the epic poem the *Aeneid* (29-19 B.C.E.). A dying artist contemplates the value of his art and confronts the hard reality of politics, trying to come to grips with the fact that his work, the *Aeneid,* celebrates the Roman state and its new ruler, Augustus Caesar (first Roman emperor, also called Octavian when younger, 27 B.C.E.-14 C.E.).

During approximately the first half of the book, Virgil contemplates the imperfection of the world and the resulting fallibility of art. He concludes that art, even his own art, is incapable of rectifying the state of imperfection and that the artist is doomed to failure. Thus the *Aeneid* becomes the ultimate symbol of all that is wrong with the world and of art's inability to impose perfection.

Beauty has come to frighten Virgil. In a fever, he makes his way to the window to witness a vulgar, disgusting scene on the street between two men and a woman. As they teeter off, however, they blend into the night and become part of a greater beauty. He, the poet, who has dedicated his life to beauty, must face beauty's indifferent incorporation of the vile. He wonders what his own responsibility is to the world around him, thus reflecting Broch's thoughts at a time when most of Europe had succumbed to Fascism.

Virgil arrives at his decision to burn his work through an inner monologue, in isolation. Once he discloses his intent to burn the *Aeneid,* those around him raise their voices in protest. It is, however, not until Augustus enters the room that the protests begin to carry weight for Virgil. In the long debate between the two, which consumes about one-fifth of the novel, Virgil manages to parry Augustus' many attempts at persuasion. It is not Virgil's debt to himself, to art, nor to the Roman people that sways Virgil from his resolve to burn his epic poem. It is a flash of Augustus' anger, which penetrates Virgil's protective façade. When Augustus questions Virgil's fidelity toward him, his longtime patron and now leader of the Roman world, Virgil realizes that the ultimate sacrifice would be not to destroy his work but to give it to Augustus. Virgil's act, one of love, proclaims a new, Christian era.

In Broch's novel, an essential element of Virgil's dissatisfaction with the *Aeneid* is that it glorifies a worldly age that he senses is passing. Although he had been raised in the Jewish faith, Broch, like so many of his generation, had converted to Christianity as an adult. The "Christian Virgil" is an essential element of Broch's image of Virgil. In the novel, the Roman poet has a vision adumbrating the coming of Christ. Indeed, for Broch, Virgil was the ideal figure symbolizing the passing of one age to another.

In the early part of the twentieth century, it was commonly thought that many parallels existed between those times and the Roman age. Thinkers such as the German historian Oswald Spengler and the British historian Arnold Toynbee used Rome—particularly Rome's disintegration—as a model with which to analyze contemporary twentieth century culture. This attitude generally prevailed when the Virgil bimillennial celebration took place in 1930, and it was reflected in Theodor Haecker's 1931 book *Virgil, Father of the West.* Broch read the book and especially liked Haecker's interpretation of Virgil as proto-Christian. In 1936, Broch wrote a first, much shorter version of his Virgil story for a radio broadcast in March, 1937. Eventually, there were five versions, each successively building into the final, grand, lyrical narrative.

Broch had no formal training in classics, and he gleaned almost everything he knew about Virgil's life from Haecker's book. In the first versions of Broch's novel, he focused on the death of the poet and his crisis of art. Only later did he introduce what became the central theme of the book: the destruction of the *Aeneid*. He learned about the legend through a friend's translation of the preface to an old edition of Virgil. From early versions of his novel, it is clear that Broch knew Virgil's *Eclogues* (43-37 B.C.E.), but reference to the *Aeneid* is curiously absent. Since the *Eclogues* provide the main focus of Christian attention to the Roman poet, this is another indication that Broch's interest in the Roman poet was driven by the image of the Christian Virgil.

Although *The Death of Virgil* is usually referred to as a novel, Broch tried to avoid any particular genre. He himself referred to the work as a poem extending over more than five hundred pages. The German language lends itself to long, convoluted constructions, but Broch pushed even German conventions to the limit, with some sentences going on for page after page. The book is separated into four sections—Water, the Arrival; Fire, the Descent; Earth, the Expectation; and Ether, the Homecoming—which Broch conceived of in musical terms. (The American conductor Leonard Bernstein once made plans to write a symphony based on Broch's novel, envisioning four movements to correspond to the four sections, and the French composer Jean Barraqué actually did base parts of a symphony on the work.) Much of the novel is cast in a stream-of-consciousness style, which represents Virgil's inner universe. This gives way in part three to the external world of conversation. Here, the utterances, as in the dialogue between Virgil and Augustus, resemble the brief thrusts and parries of a fencing duel.

"Critical Evaluation" by Scott G. Williams

Bibliography:
Dowden, Stephen D., ed. *Hermann Broch: Literature, Philosophy, Politics (The Yale Broch Symposium 1986)*. Columbia, S.C.: Camden House, 1988. Includes articles by Luciano Zagari (" 'Poetry is Anticipation': Broch and Virgil") and Vasily Rudich ("Mythical and Mystical in *The Death of Vergil*: A Response to Luciano Zagari"), which deal directly with *The Death of Virgil*, as well as other essays from the 1986 Yale Broch Symposium, which offer insights into the entire corpus of Broch's work.

Lützeler, Paul Michael. *Hermann Broch: A Biography*. Translated by Janice Furness. London: Quartet Books, 1987. A thorough and interesting study, which helps to illuminate the circumstances surrounding the creation of *The Death of Virgil*.

Untermeyer, Jean Starr. "Midwife to a Masterpiece." In *Private Collection*. New York: Alfred A. Knopf, 1965. The personal account of the translator of *The Death of Virgil*, who worked closely with Broch on the translation during his time at Princeton.

Wiegand, Hermann J. "Broch's *Death of Vergil*: Program Notes." PMLA 62 (1947): 525-554. Offers a solid discussion of the novel. Includes a letter from Broch to Wiegand which is historically interesting, though later scholarship shows that Broch's memory of events leading to the writing of the novel is not always completely reliable.

Ziolkowski, Theodore. *Virgil and the Moderns*. Princeton, N.J.: Princeton University Press, 1993. Particularly valuable for its discussion of Broch's use of Virgil in relation to other twentieth century writers.

THE DEATH SHIP

Type of work: Novel
Author: B. Traven (Berick Traven Torsvan, 1890?-1969)
Type of plot: Social realism
Time of plot: 1920's
Locale: Belgium, Holland, France, Spain, and the Mediterranean Sea
First published: Das Totenschiff, 1926 (English translation, 1934)

> *Principal characters:*
> GERARD "PIPPIP" GALES, a young American sailor
> STANISLAV, a Polish sailor and Gerard's friend

The Story:

Gerard Gales was stranded in Antwerp when his ship returned to New Orleans without him. The passport had displaced the sun as the center of the universe. Unable to prove his citizenship (American), he was a man without a country, and his physical presence was no proof of his birth to officialdom. Immigration officials solved the problem of his presence by smuggling him from Belgium into Holland, then back into Belgium, then into France, where he was jailed for riding a train without a ticket and later sentenced to be shot as a suspected spy. He sensed the universal animosity toward Americans and pretended to be a German. When he did, he was treated well. He made his escape. In Spain, he was left entirely alone. Ostensibly politically oppressed, the Spanish seemed freer than other Europeans, and Gerard loved them. The Spanish peasants were in fact so good to him that he felt useless and hated himself. He realized the error of the Communist state, in which the individual is denied the privilege of taking his or her own risks. Wanting to return to sailing and to his woman, Gerard signed aboard *The Yorikke.*

Aboard *The Yorikke,* he descended into a sailor's hell. He was a drag man in a stokehold. The filthiest job on the ship was that of the drag man, who performed the most loathsome chores. Its name obscured on the bow, *The Yorikke,* too, appeared to lack a proper birth certificate. It seemed ashamed of its name. Gerard exhibited a kind of nationalism when he withheld his true name and country and signed on as an Egyptian. No American would sail on such a ship, and he realized that, despite his country's many faults, he loved it and was wretchedly homesick. *The Yorikke* resembled no ship he had ever seen. It had no life jackets. It was, in sailor slang, a death ship, so called because its owners had decided to put it to sea, in its dilapidated, unseaworthy condition, in the hope that it would sink, so that they could collect the insurance. The crew, desperate men called "deads," already at the end of their tether when they came aboard, did not know when the ship would go down. The sea, Gerard imagined, would probably burp or spit the diseased ship out for fear of infection. No supplies—spoons, coffee cups, blankets—were provided; the men repeatedly stole a single bar of soap from one another until it had been through every filthy hand. Conditions were worse than those in a concentration camp. The only thing in ample supply was work. Any man who tried to collect overtime on that ship pathologically committed to profits, could find himself in a black hold with rats that would, individually, terrify a cat. Gerard had a vivid sense of the ship personified, as a she; he thought the ship was insane. Gerard thought of *The Yorikke* in female terms.

Gerard admired his mysterious captain, whose intelligence set him apart from the old-style pirate. He supported his men, and they would rather have sunk with the ship than inform the authorities that it was carrying contraband. *The Yorikke* crew was the filthiest Gerard had ever seen. The men wore bizarre rags. Some appeared to have been shanghaied off the gallows to work on the ship. In the towns, other sailors shunned them; men, women, and children feared them; and the police, afraid they would leave the town in ashes, followed them. Gerard, despite his misery, learned to live and laugh on the ship. He sensed, nevertheless, *The Yorikke*'s imminent doom.

Gerard and his friend Stanislav were shanghaied from *The Yorikke* to serve on the new but disastrously slow *Empress of Madagascar*, which was to be scuttled in a few days. The *Empress*, however, in Gerard's personifying view, managed to kill her plotting captain. She stood like a tower between the rocks before she sank. Stanislav got to eat as a shipowner would before he drowned. He and Gerard were safely tied to a piece of wreckage, but Stanislav had a hallucination in which he saw *The Yorikke* leaving the dock. Wanting to go with the ship, he detached himself from the wreckage and slipped into the sea. Gerard offered his respects to his comrade while waiting to be rescued.

Critical Evaluation:

Based on the author's experiences and written when he was about twenty-four, *The Death Ship* is in some ways unlike any other novel. The book may be classified as a proletarian novel, written in the style of tough-guy fiction. Its thesis, however, is not as doctrinaire as that of a typical proletarian novel. *The Death Ship* also bears resemblances to other types of novels. For example, as does Franz Kafka's K., Gerard moves through a labyrinth of bureaucracy. Gerard confronts the modern inquisition of officials empowered to dispense passports, certificates, sailor's books, receipts, affidavits, seals, and licenses. Gerard also experiences different locales in Europe, which recalls, with irony, a novel of the lost generation. The novel also is frank about money in a manner that recalls naturalism. No plot or story line as such holds the novel together; one mishap simply follows another in Gerard's life. In this respect the novel resembles a picaresque novel. Gerard is a storyteller who never tires of retelling a tale. The consulate scenes are repetitious; readers get variations on the same routine. Stanislav tells Gerard a story about himself that closely resembles Gerard's earlier experiences. Gerard tells his general story the way a sailor would, commenting with joking metaphors and reflecting constantly on the meaning of events. The reader is visualized as a captive audience for a man who has at last found a way to speak his mind without interruption on social, political, and economic topics. The novel has some poignant moments, too: As is typical of a tough-guy novel, sentimentality occasionally intrudes.

Work is at the center of this novel—the struggle to get it and, under extreme conditions, the horror and ultimate beauty of it. Traven gives all the details of various work routines. One of the most horrific passages in literature is Traven's description of putting back fallen grate bars while the boiler is white hot. After a first bout at what becomes a daily task, Gerard declares that he is free, unbound, above the gods; he can do what he wishes and curse the gods, because no hell could be greater torture.

Gerard resurrects the literary theme of male bravery. Bravery on the battlefield is nothing compared to the bravery of men who do the work that keeps civilization afloat. No flag drapes the bodies of casualties; they go, like garbage, over the fantail. On a death ship, no laws keep a crew member in line; each worker is crucially necessary, and work is a common bond. With no sense of heroics, Gerard helps save two men and is himself saved. His true countrymen, he discovers, are those workers who are scalded and scorched by the same furnace. He does not desert because his friend Stanislav would then have to work alone. Traven appears to show how men grow accustomed to misery and filth, but he insists that nobody really gets used to them.

Few fictive descriptions of the life, the hopes, the illusions, and the attitudes of the doomed sailor—his qualities of ingenuity, improvisation, and audacity—are as complete as Traven's.

The style of the story—rough, garrulous, and full of profanity—sounds translated, but it is consistent with Gerard's semiliterate immigrant background. The style becomes wearisome in three hundred pages, but the sheer energy of the telling achieves a special eloquence. Traven is overly fascinated by figurative rhetoric; many of the book's wisecracks seem forced and writerly. The book's humor, wit, and comedy are, however, interwoven artfully with its grim and dark plot. Traven is also fond of ridiculing popular fiction and film versions of the seafaring life, and his narration of Gerard's brush with bureaucracy verges on the satiric.

Traven's book seems not to carry the calculated uplift of a proletarian novel with a political message. *The Death Ship* carries a significant cargo of fatalism. Gerard and Stanislav are more victims of the nature of things than of conditions that can be reformed. Gerard may gripe with every breath he takes, but he does not whine. He proudly insists that he can do work any man can do, anywhere. He contemptuously refuses to bow to circumstance. He refuses to blame the shipowners; having failed to take his fate in his own hands by jumping ship, he has no right to refuse to be a slave. He can only hope that he will be resurrected from the "deads" by his own will and fortitude. He knows that for the courageous man who survives the ordeal of *The Yorikke*, anything is possible. Gerard preaches the gospel of hard work, not because work is good for the soul, but because it is good for the flesh. Unlike most proletarian writers, Traven achieves a kind of mystique about work.

Bibliography:

Baumann, Michael L. *B. Traven: An Introduction.* Albuquerque: University of New Mexico Press, 1976. Discusses Traven as a proletarian writer, focusing on his attitudes toward nationalism and capitalism. Compares language and subject matter in the 1926 German version of *The Death Ship* with the 1934 English one.

Chankin, Donald O. *Anonymity and Death: The Fiction of B. Traven.* University Park: Pennsylvania State University Press, 1975. Clear, insightful psychoanalytic analysis of character and theme in *The Death Ship.* Provides historical and geopolitical background. Discusses literary parallels in the works of Joseph Conrad, Herman Melville, and others.

Mezo, Richard E. *A Study of B. Traven's Fiction: The Journey to Solipaz.* San Francisco: Mellon Research University Press, 1993. A comprehensive critical analysis of theme, character, style and structure in Traven's fiction. Discusses the development of Gales's persona in *The Death Ship* and later works. Extensive bibliography. A very good introduction to Traven and his fiction.

Raskin, Jonah. *My Search for B. Traven.* New York: Methuen, 1980. An interesting account of the many mysteries surrounding B. Traven's multiple identities. Compares manuscript, typescript, and various print editions of *The Death Ship*, tracing the development of Gales, the introduction of Stanislaw, the growing symbolic importance of the ship.

Stone, Judy. *The Mystery of B. Traven.* Los Altos, Calif.: William Kaufmann, 1977. Includes excerpts from the only extended series of interviews with B. Traven, including a discussion of the theme of *The Death Ship* and revealing his complex social philosophy. An important source for analyzing Traven's fiction.

THE DECAMERON

Type of work: Fiction
Author: Giovanni Boccaccio (1313-1375)
Type of plot: Stories-within-a-story
Time of plot: Antiquity and the Middle Ages
Locale: Italy
First transcribed: 1349-1351 (English translation, 1620)

Principal characters:
THE THREE TEDALDO SONS, three gentlemen of Florence
ALESSANDRO, their nephew
THE DAUGHTER OF THE KING OF ENGLAND
TANCRED, Prince of Salerno
GHISMONDA, his daughter
GUISCARDO, her lover
ISABETTA, a young woman of Messina
LORENZO, her lover
GALESO, a stupid young man of Cyprus, known as Cimone
EFIGENIA, his love
LISIMACO, a young man of Rhodes
FEDERIGO DEGLI ALBERIGHI, a young man of Florence
MONNA GIOVANNA, his love
PERONELLA, a wool comber of Naples
PERONELLA'S HUSBAND
STRIGNARIO, her lover
NATHAN, a rich man of Cathay
MITRIDANES, a rich man envious of Nathan
SALADIN, Sultan of Babylon
MESSER TORELLO, a wealthy countryman of Pavia
GUALTIERI, the son of the Marquess of Saluzzo
GRISELDA, his wife

The Story:
A terrible plague was ravaging Florence, Italy. To flee from it, a group of seven young women and three young men, who had met by chance in a church, decided to go to a villa out of town. There they set up a working arrangement whereby each would be king or queen for a day. During the ten days they stayed in the country, each told a story, following certain stipulations laid down by the daily ruler. The stories ranged from romance to farce, from comedy to tragedy.

Pampinea's Tale About the Three Tedaldo Young Men. When Messer Tedaldo died, he left all of his goods and chattels to his three sons. With no thought for the future, they lived so extravagantly that they soon had little left. The oldest son suggested that they sell what they could, leave Florence, and go to London, where they were unknown.

In London, they lent money at a high rate of interest, and in a few years, they had a small fortune. Then they returned to Florence. There they married and began to live extravagantly again, while depending on the monies still coming to them from England.

A nephew named Alessandro took care of their business in England. At that time, there were such differences between the king and a son that Alessandro's business was ruined. He stayed in England, however, in the hope that peace would come and his business would recover. Finally, he returned to Italy with a group of monks who were taking their young abbot to the pope to get a dispensation for him and a confirmation of the youthful cleric's election.

On the way, Alessandro discovered that the abbot was a woman, and he married her in the sight of God. In Rome, the woman had an audience with the pope. Her father, the King of England, wished the pope's blessing on her marriage to the old King of Scotland, but she asked the pope's blessing on her marriage to Alessandro instead.

After the wedding, Alessandro and his bride went to Florence, where she paid his uncles' debts. Two knights preceded the couple to England and urged the king to forgive his daughter. After the king had knighted Alessandro, the new knight reconciled the king and his rebellious son.

Fiammetta's Tale of Tancred and the Golden Cup. Tancred, Prince of Salerno, loved his daughter Ghismonda so much that, when she was widowed soon after her marriage, he did not think to provide her with a second husband, and she was too modest to ask him to do so. Being a lively woman, however, she decided to have as her lover the most valiant man in her father's court. His name was Guiscardo. His only fault was that he was of humble birth.

Ghismonda noticed that Guiscardo returned her interest, and they met secretly in a cave, one entrance to which was through a door in the young widow's bedroom. Soon she was taking her lover into her bedroom, where they enjoyed each other frequently.

Tancred was in the habit of visiting his daughter's room at odd times. One day, when he went to visit, she was not there. He sat down to wait in a place where he was, by accident, hidden by the bed curtains from his daughter and her lover, who soon came in to use the bed.

Tancred remained hidden, but that night he had Guiscardo arrested. When he berated his daughter for picking so humble a lover, she scolded him for letting so brave a man remain poor in his court. She begged nothing from Tancred except that he kill her and her lover with the same stroke.

The prince did not believe Ghismonda would be as resolute as she sounded. When her lover was killed, Tancred had his heart cut from his body and sent to her in a golden cup. Ghismonda thanked her father for his noble gift. After repeatedly kissing the heart, she poured poison into the cup and drank it. Then she lay down upon her bed with Guiscardo's heart upon her own. Tancred's own heart was touched when he saw her cold in death, and he obeyed her last request that she and Guiscardo be buried together.

Filomena's Tale of the Pot of Basil. Isabetta lived in Messina with her three merchant brothers and a young man named Lorenzo, who attended to their business affairs. Isabetta and Lorenzo fell in love. One night, as she went to Lorenzo's room, her oldest brother saw her. He said nothing until the next morning, when the three brothers conferred to see how they could settle the matter so that no shame should fall upon them or upon Isabetta.

Not long afterward, the three brothers set out with Lorenzo, claiming that they were going part way with him on a journey. Secretly, however, they killed and buried the young man.

After their return home, the brothers answered none of Isabetta's questions about Lorenzo. She wept and refused to be consoled in her grief. One night Lorenzo came to her in a dream and told her what had happened and where he was buried. Without telling her brothers, she went to the spot indicated in her dream and found her lover's body there. She cut off his head and wrapped it in a cloth to take home. She buried the head in dirt in a large flowerpot and planted basil over it. The basil flourished, watered by her tears.

She wept so much over the plant that her brothers took away the pot of basil and hid it. She asked about it often, so the brothers grew curious. At last they investigated and found Lorenzo's head. Abashed, they left the city. Isabetta died of a broken heart.

Pamfilo's Tale of Cimone, Who Became Civilized Through Love. Galeso was the tallest and handsomest of Aristippo's children, but he was so stupid that the people of Cyprus called him Cimone, which meant "Brute." Cimone's stupidity so embarrassed his father that the old man sent the boy to the country to live. There Cimone was contented, until one day he came upon Efigenia, whose beauty completely changed him.

He told his father that he intended to live in town. The news worried his father for a while, but Cimone bought fine clothes and associated only with worthy young men. In four years, he was the most accomplished and virtuous young man on the island.

Although he knew she was promised to Pasimunda of Rhodes, Cimone asked Efigenia's father for her hand in marriage. He was refused. When Pasimunda sent for his bride, Cimone and his friends pursued the ship and took Efigenia off the vessel, after which they let the ship's crew go free to return to Rhodes. In the night, a storm arose and blew Cimone's ship to the very harbor in Rhodes where Efigenia was supposed to go. Cimone and his men were arrested.

Pasimunda had a brother who had been promised a wife, but this woman was loved by Lisimaco, a youth of Rhodes, as Efigenia was loved by Cimone. The brothers planned a double wedding.

Lisimaco made plans with Cimone. At the double wedding feast, Lisimaco, Cimone, and many of their friends snatched the brides away from their prospective husbands. The young men carried their beloved ones to Crete, where they lived happily in exile for a time, until their fathers interceded for them. Then Cimone took Efigenia home to Cyprus, and Lisimaco took his wife back to Rhodes.

Fiammetta's Tale of Federigo and His Falcon. Federigo degli Alberighi was famed in Florence for his courtesy and his prowess in arms. He fell in love with Monna Giovanna, a woman who cared nothing for him, though he spent his fortune trying to please her. Finally he was so poor that he went to the country to live on his farm. There he entertained himself only by flying his falcon, which was considered the best in the world.

Monna's husband died, leaving her to enjoy his vast estates with one young son. The son struck up an acquaintance with Federigo and particularly admired the falcon. When the boy became sick, he thought he might get well if he could own Federigo's bird.

Monna, as a last resort, swallowed her pride and called upon Federigo. She told him she would stay for supper, but Federigo, desperately poor as he was, had nothing to serve his love except the falcon, which he promptly killed and roasted for her.

After the meal, with many apologies, Monna told her host that her son, thinking he would get well if he had the falcon, desired Federigo's bird. Federigo wept to think that Monna had asked for the one thing he could not give her.

The boy died soon after, and Monna was bereft. When her brothers urged her to remarry, she finally agreed to do so, but she would marry no one but the generous Federigo, who had killed his pet falcon to do her honor. So Federigo married into great riches.

Filostrato's Tale of Peronella, Who Hid Her Lover in a Butt. Peronella was a Neapolitan wool comber married to a poor bricklayer. Together they made enough to live comfortably. Peronella had a lover named Strignario, who came to the house each day after the husband went to work.

One day, when the husband returned unexpectedly, Peronella hid Strignario in a butt (large keg or barrel). Her husband had brought home a man to buy the butt for five florins. Thinking quickly, Peronella told her husband that she already had a buyer who had offered seven florins for the butt and that he was at that moment inside the butt inspecting it.

Strignario came out, complaining that the butt was dirty. The husband offered to clean it. While the husband was inside scraping, Strignario cuckolded him again, paid for the butt, and went away.

Filostrato's Tale of Nathan's Generosity. Once, in Cathay, lived a very rich and generous old man named Nathan. He had a splendid palace and many servants, and he entertained lavishly anyone who came his way.

In a country nearby lived Mitridanes, who was not nearly so old as Nathan but just as rich. Since he was jealous of Nathan's fame, he built a palace and entertained handsomely everyone who visited. One day, a woman came thirteen times asking alms. Furious when Mitridanes called her to task, she told him that she had once asked alms of Nathan forty-two times in one day without reproof. Mitridanes decided that he would have to kill Nathan before his own fame would grow.

Riding near Nathan's palace, Mitridanes discovered Nathan walking alone. When he asked to be directed secretly to Nathan's palace, Nathan cheerfully took him there and established him in a fine apartment. Still not realizing Nathan's identity, Mitridanes revealed his plan to kill his rival. Nathan arranged matters so that Mitridanes came upon him alone in the woods.

Mitridanes, curious to see Nathan, caught hold of him before piercing him with a sword. When he discovered that Nathan was the old man who had first directed him to the palace, made him comfortable, and then arranged the meeting in the woods, Mitridanes realized that he could never match Nathan's generosity, and he was greatly ashamed.

Nathan offered to go to Mitridanes' home and become known as Mitridanes, while Mitridanes would remain to be known as Nathan. By that time, however, Mitridanes thought his own actions would tarnish Nathan's fame, and he went home humbled.

Pamfilo's Tale of Saladin and Messer Torello. In the time of Emperor Frederick the First, all christendom united in a crusade for the recovery of the Holy Land. To see how the Christians were preparing themselves and to learn to protect himself against them, Saladin, the Sultan of Babylon, took two of his best knights and made a tour through Italy to Paris. The travelers were disguised as merchants.

Outside the little town of Pavia, they came upon Messer Torello, who was on his way to his country estate. When they asked him how far they were from Pavia, he told them quickly that the town was too far to be reached that night and sent his servants with them to an inn. Messer Torello sensed that the three men were foreign gentlemen and wanted to honor them; he had the servants take them by a roundabout way to his own estate. Meanwhile, he rode directly home. The travelers were surprised when they saw him in his own place, but, realizing that he meant only to honor them, they graciously consented to spend the night.

The next day, Messer Torello sent word to his wife in town to prepare a banquet. The preparations were made, and both Torellos honored the merchants that day. Before they left, the wife gave them handsome suits of clothes like those her husband wore.

When Messer Torello became one of the crusaders, he asked his wife to wait a year and a month before remarrying if she heard nothing from him. She gave him a ring with which to remember her. Soon afterward, a great plague broke out among the Christians at Acre and killed many men. Most of the survivors were imprisoned by the sultan. Messer Torello was taken to Alexandria, where he trained hawks for Saladin and was called Saladin's Christian. Neither man recognized the other for a long time, until at last Saladin recognized a facial gesture in Torello and made himself known as one of the traveling merchants. Torello was freed and lived happily as Saladin's guest. He expected daily to hear from his wife, to whom he had sent word of his adventures. His messenger had been shipwrecked, however, and the day approached when his wife would be free to remarry.

At last Torello told Saladin of the arrangement he and his wife had made. The sultan took pity on him and had Torello put to sleep on a couch heaped with jewels and gold. Then the couch, whisked off to Italy by magic, was set down in the church of which his uncle was abbot. Torello and the abbot went to the marriage feast prepared for Torello's wife and her new husband. No one recognized Torello because of his strange beard and oriental clothing, until he displayed the ring his wife had given him. Then with great rejoicing they were reunited, a reward for their earlier generosity.

Dioneo's Tale of the Patient Griselda. Gualtieri, eldest son of the Marquess of Saluzzo, was a bachelor whose subjects begged him to marry. Although he was not anxious to take a wife, he decided to wed poor Griselda, who lived in a nearby hamlet. When he went with his friends to bring Griselda home, he asked her if she would always be obedient and try to please him and never be angry. Upon her word that she would do so, Gualtieri had her stripped of her poor gown and dressed in finery becoming her new station.

With her new clothes, Griselda changed so much in appearance that she seemed to be a true noblewoman, and Gualtieri's subjects were pleased. She bore him a daughter and a son, both of whom Gualtieri took from her. In order to test her devotion, he pretended to have the children put to death, but Griselda sent them off cheerfully since that was her husband's wish.

When their daughter was in her early teens, Gualtieri sent Griselda home, clad only in a shift, after telling her that he intended to take a new wife. His subjects were sad, but Griselda remained composed. A short time later, he called Griselda back to his house and ordered her to prepare it for his wedding, saying that no one else knew so well how to arrange it. In her ragged dress, she prepared everything for the wedding feast. Welcoming the guests, she was particularly thoughtful of the new bride.

By that time Gualtieri thought he had tested Griselda in every possible way. He introduced the supposed bride as her daughter and the little boy who had accompanied the girl as her son. Then he had Griselda dressed in her best clothes, and everyone rejoiced.

Critical Evaluation:

Giovanni Boccaccio, Dante Alighieri, and Francesco Petrarch were the leading lights in a century that is considered the beginning of the Italian Renaissance. Dante died while Boccaccio was a child, but Petrarch was a friend during his middle and later life. Dante's work was essentially of the spirit; Petrarch's was that of the literary man; Boccaccio's broke free of all tradition and created a living literature about ordinary people. *The Decameron* is his most famous work. Since its composition, readers and critics have made much of its hundred entertaining and worldly tales, comic and tragic, bawdy and courteous, satiric and serious, that compose this work. Unfortunately, much early criticism was moralistic, and Boccaccio was faulted for devoting his mature artistic skill to a collection of "immoral" stories.

The Decameron has fared better in the twentieth century, with more solid critical inquiries into the work's literary significance and style. Boccaccio's collection has been considered representative of the Middle Ages; it has also been viewed as a product of the Renaissance. The work is both. *The Decameron* not only encompasses literary legacies of the medieval world, but also goes far beyond Boccaccio's own time, transcending, in tone and style, artistic works of both previous and later periods.

The structure, with its frame characters, has many analogues in medieval literature; the frame story—a group of tales within an enclosing narrative—was a device known previously, in

Europe and in the Orient. The material for many of Boccaccio's stories was gleaned from Indian, Arabic, Byzantine, French, Hebrew, and Spanish tales.

Although *The Decameron* is not escapist literature, the idea and nature of the framework have much in common with medieval romance. There is the idealistic, pastoral quality of withdrawal into the pleasant place or garden, away from the ugly, harsh reality of the surrounding world. The ten young people who leave Florence—a dying, corrupt city that Boccaccio describes plainly in all of its horrors—find only momentary respite from the charnel house of reality; but their existence for ten days is that of the enchanted medieval dreamworld: a paradise of flowers, ever-flowing fountains, shade trees, soft breezes, where all luxuries of food and drink abound. Virtue and decorum reign. There is no cynicism or lust in the various garden settings, where the pastimes are strolling, weaving garlands, or playing chess. Even Dioneo, who tells the most salacious stories, is as chaste in his conduct as Pampinea, Filomena, Filostrato, and the others. One critic has even seen in these frame characters a progression of virtues, and described their stories as groups of exempla praising such qualities as wisdom, prudence, or generosity.

Against this refined and idealized medieval framework are the stories themselves, the majority marked by realism. The locale of each story is usually an actual place; the Italian cities of Pisa, Siena, and especially Florence figure largely as settings. The entire Mediterranean is represented, with its islands of Sicily, Corfu, Rhodes, Cyprus, and Ischia. France, England, and Spain also serve as backgrounds. In one story, the seventh tale on the second day, beautiful Altiel, the Sultan of Babylon's daughter, after being kidnapped, travels in the space of four years over most of the Mediterranean, the islands, Greece, Turkey, and Alexandria. Boccaccio is also concerned with restricted spatial reality, and he sketches, in close detail, internal settings of abbeys, bedrooms, churches, marketplaces, castles, and inns. Different social classes have their own language and clothing. Many characters—such as Ciappelletto, living in profanation of the world; Rinaldo abandoned in nakedness and cold by his fellowmen; Peronella, the deceitful Neapolitan wool comber cuckolding her husband; the whole convent of nuns eagerly lying with the youth Masetto—these Boccaccio describes in believable, human situations.

Although he draws upon the entire arsenal of medieval rhetoric, the author of these one hundred stories goes beyond figures of speech and linguistic tools in his modern paradoxical style and cynical tone. Although his satire often bites deeply, his comic mood generally embraces evil and holiness alike with sympathy and tolerance. His treatment of themes, situation, and character is never didactic. Like Geoffrey Chaucer, Boccaccio is indulgent, exposing moral and social corruption but leaving guilty characters to condemn themselves.

A novella such as the comic tale of Chichibio, told on the sixth day, is pure comic farce, moving rapidly by question and answer, playfully rollicking to a surprise ending brought about by this impulsive, foolish cook. The story of Rossiglione and Guardastagno, ninth tale of the fourth day, has a tragic plot, but the narrators draw no moral in either case. The interaction of character, scene, and plot brings into relief forces that motivate the world of humanity and allow the readers to judge if they must. Again and again, characters in the tales are relieved from moral responsibility by the control of fortune.

Throughout *The Decameron*, Boccaccio concerns himself primarily with presenting a human world as he observed and understood it. In this presentation, there is no pedantry or reticence; he paints men and women in all of their rascality, faithlessness, nobility, and suffering, changing his Italian prose to suit the exigency of purpose, whether that results in a serious or comic, refined or coarse, descriptive or analytical style. Boccaccio has command of many styles and changes easily from one to another.

In utilizing fables and anecdotes from many medieval sources, in employing figurative and rhythmical devices from books on medieval rhetoric, and in structuring his framework according to the chivalric world of valor and courtesy, among other things, Boccaccio's work is a product of the Middle Ages. In its frank, open-minded treatment of worldly pleasures, in its use of paradox and cynicism, and in its realistic handling of character, however, *The Decameron* transcends the medieval period and establishes a literary pattern for the Renaissance and after.

"Critical Evaluation" by Muriel B. Ingham

Bibliography:
Branca, Vittore. *Boccaccio: The Man and His Work.* Edited by Dennis J. McAuliffe, translated by Richard Monges and Dennis J. McAuliffe. New York: New York University Press, 1976. Offers critical biography and critical analysis of *The Decameron.* Details of Boccaccio's life and culture are chronologically correlated to his body of work; analysis emphasizes literary traditions.
Deligiorgis, Stavros. *Narrative Intellection in "The Decameron."* Iowa City: University of Iowa Press, 1975. Organized by day, treating each successive story in its turn. Provides a comprehensive view of the work's themes and its narrative framework.
De Sanctis, Francesco. "Boccaccio's Human Comedy." In *Critical Perspectives on "The Decameron,"* edited by Robert S. Dombroski. 1972. Reprint. New York: Barnes & Noble Books, 1976. Analyzes the purpose, tone, and focus of *The Decameron.* Includes an incidental comparison of Boccaccio's style and emphasis in *The Decameron* to Dante's.
Lee, A. C. *"The Decameron": Its Sources and Analogues.* New York: Haskell House, 1966. An annotated list of possible and probable sources for the individual tales told by the characters in *The Decameron*, plus parallels where the same stories are told by different writers of other ages and cultures. Careful collation and synthesis; a helpful index.
Mazotta, Giuseppe. *"The Decameron*: The Marginality of Literature." In *Critical Perspectives on "The Decameron,"* edited by Robert S. Dombroski. 1972. Reprint. New York: Barnes & Noble Books, 1976. Discusses *The Decameron* as a vehicle for interpreting history, as well as for using secular literature as a means of coping with mutability and death.

DECLINE AND FALL
An Illustrated Novelette

Type of work: Novel
Author: Evelyn Waugh (1903-1966)
Type of plot: Social satire
Time of plot: Twentieth century
Locale: England and Wales
First published: 1928

Principal characters:

PAUL PENNYFEATHER, a serious-minded young Oxonian
SIR ALASTAIR DIGBY-VAINE-TRUMPINGTON, a young aristocrat
ARTHUR POTTS, a noble-minded young man
DR. AUGUSTUS FAGAN, the head of Llanabba Castle School
FLOSSIE and
DIANA, his daughters
MR. PRENDERGAST, a former clergyman
CAPTAIN GRIMES, a public-school man
PETER BESTE-CHETWYNDE, one of Paul's pupils
MARGOT BESTE-CHETWYNDE, his mother
SOLOMON PHILBRICK, a confidence man
SIR HUMPHREY MALTRAVERS, later Lord Metroland, a British politician

The Story:

At Scone College in Oxford, the annual dinner of the Bollinger Club ended with the breaking of glass. Reeling out of Sir Alastair Digby-Vaine-Trumpington's rooms, the drunken aristocrats ran to earth the inoffensive divinity student Paul Pennyfeather and forcibly left him trouserless before they went roaring off into the night. Bollinger members could be fined, but the college authorities felt that Paul deserved more severe punishment for running across the quadrangle in his shorts. As a result, he was sent down for indecent behavior. After informing him that under his father's will his legacy could be withheld for unsatisfactory behavior, his unsympathetic guardian virtuously announced his intention to cut off Paul's allowance.

Through a shoddy firm of scholastic agents, Paul became a junior assistant master at Llanabba Castle, Wales. Llanabba was not a good school. Its head was Dr. Augustus Fagan, whose lectures on service were intended to cover up the inadequacies of his institution. He had two daughters: Flossie, a vulgar young woman with matrimonial ambitions, and Diana, who economized on sugar and soap. One of the masters was Mr. Prendergast, a former clergyman who suffered from doubts. The other was Captain Grimes, who wore a false leg and was, as he frankly admitted, periodically in the soup. A bounder and a scoundrel, he put his faith in the public-school system, which may kick a man out but never lets him down. Grimes thought he had been put on his feet more often than any public-school man alive. His reluctant engagement to Flossie was his protection against the next time he found himself in trouble.

Paul was in charge of the fifth form. When he met his class for the first time, most of the boys claimed that their name was Tangent. An uproar arose between the would-be Tangents and a few non-Tangents, but Paul put an end to the situation by announcing that the writer of the longest essay would receive half a crown. After that, he had no more trouble. Mr. Prendergast, whose own students behaved outrageously and made fun of his wig, wondered why Paul's classes were always so quiet. Paul considered young Peter Beste-Chetwynde the most interesting of his pupils.

Arthur Potts was one of the few men Paul had known at Scone; he wrote that Alastair Trumpington had regretted Paul's dismissal and wanted to send him twenty pounds. Hearing of the offer, Grimes wired for the money in Paul's name.

When several parents expressed their intention to visit Llanabba Castle, Dr. Fagan decided to honor their visit with the annual field sports meet. Philbrick, the butler, objected to his extra duties. He confided to Paul that he was a crook who had taken the post in order to kidnap little Lord Tangent, but that he had reformed after falling in love with Diana. He told Mr. Prendergast that he was really Sir Solomon Philbrick, a millionaire shipowner, and he left Grimes under the impression that he was a novelist collecting material for a book.

The sports meet was not a success. Lady Circumference, Lord Tangent's mother, was rude to everyone when she distributed the prizes. The Llanabba Silver Band played. Margot Beste-Chetwynde created a social flurry when she arrived with a black man. In carrying out his function as the starter, Mr. Prendergast accidentally shot Lord Tangent in the heel and later became drunk and abusive. Paul fell in love at first sight with Peter Beste-Chetwynde's beautiful widowed mother.

The term dragged to a close. Lord Tangent's foot became infected, and he died. Grimes, landing in the soup once more, announced his engagement to Flossie, but the marriage turned out as badly as he had expected. When detectives arrived to arrest Philbrick on charges of false pretense, he had already flown. A few days later, Grimes's clothing and a suicide note were discovered on the beach.

Engaged to tutor Peter during the vacation, Paul went to his home, King's Thursday. At the time Margot Beste-Chetwynde bought the place from her impoverished bachelor brother-in-law, Lord Pastmaster, it had been the finest example of Tudor domestic architecture in England. Bored with it, however, she had commissioned Otto Silenus, an eccentric designer, to build a modernistic house in its place. Silenus built a structure of concrete, glass, and aluminum. It was a house for dynamos, not people, but people came there anyway for an endless round of house parties.

When Paul finally found enough courage to propose to Margot, she accepted him because Peter thought the young Oxonian would make a better stepfather than Margot's rival suitor, Sir Humphrey Maltravers, the minister of transport. During preparations for the wedding, Paul learned that Margot still carried on her father's business, a syndicate vaguely connected with amusement enterprises in South America. Grimes turned up mysteriously in her employ. Potts, now working for the League of Nations, also took an unexplained interest in Margot's business affairs.

A few days before the wedding, Margot asked Paul to fly to Marseilles and arrange for the passage of several cabaret entertainers to Rio de Janeiro. He did so without realizing that he was bribing the officials he interviewed. On his wedding morning, Paul was having a final drink with Alastair Trumpington when a Scotland Yard inspector appeared and arrested him on charges of engaging in international white-slave trafficking.

Margot fled to her villa at Corfu and did not appear at the trial. Potts, a special investigator for the League of Nations, was the chief witness for the prosecution. Convicted of Margot's crimes, Paul was sentenced to seven years' penal servitude. He served the first part of his sentence at Blackstone Gaol, where he found Philbrick a trustee and Mr. Prendergast the chaplain. Shortly after, Prendergast was killed by a crazed inmate, and Paul was removed to Egdon Health Penal Settlement. Grimes was briefly one of his fellow prisoners, but one day, while serving on a work gang, he walked off into the fog. Everyone but Paul assumed that he perished in a swamp. Grimes, whose roguery was timeless, could never die. Margot came to visit Paul. She announced her intention to marry Maltravers, now Lord Metroland and the Home Secretary.

Paul's escape from Egdon Heath was carefully contrived. On orders from the Home Secretary, he was removed for an appendicitis operation in a nursing home owned by Dr. Fagan, who had forsaken education for medicine. After a drunken doctor had signed a death certificate stating that Paul had died under the anesthetic, Alastair Trumpington, who had become Margot's young man, put him on a yacht that carried him to Margot's villa at Corfu. Officially dead, Paul enjoyed the rest he thought he deserved. Wearing a heavy mustache, he returned to Scone some months later to continue his reading for the church. When the chaplain mentioned another Pennyfeather, a wild undergraduate sent down for misconduct, Paul said that the young man was a distant cousin.

At Scone, the annual dinner of the Bollinger Club ended with the breaking of glass. Paul was reading in his room when Peter Beste-Chetwynde, Lord Pastmaster since his uncle's death, came in; he was very drunk. Paul's great mistake, Peter said, was that he had become involved with people like Margot and himself. After his departure, Paul settled down to read another chapter in a book on early church heresies.

Critical Evaluation:

Decline and Fall mingles farce with grim tragedy. Episodic in form, with many of its scenes no more than a page or so in length, it is a penetrating yet hilarious study of disordered English society in the period between the wars. Evelyn Waugh insisted that his books were not intended as satires, since the satirical spirit presupposes a stable and homogeneous society against which to project its critical exposure of folly and vice. For all that, the writer demonstrates in this novel a tremendous talent for comic satire. Paul Pennyfeather's misadventures reflect one phase of the contemporary mood of disillusionment. The character of Grimes, on the other hand, who is a bounder and a cad, is timeless—a figure who would have been as much at home in the days of the Caesars as he was in the reign of King George V. Waugh's distortions and exaggerations have also the quality of fantasy, for in his pages the impossible and the believable exist simultaneously on the same plane.

Decline and Fall is the first and possibly the best work of Waugh, a luminary of the English satirists. The novel is notable for its economy of time and space. The action extends over one year, and the protagonist's circumstances at the beginning and end are virtually identical, which neatly rounds off the story. Waugh's prose is sparse, his epigrams unlabored, as in, for example, Paul Pennyfeather's quip that the English public school is a perfect conditioner for life in prison. Waugh lays low individuals and whole classes of society with a flick of a proper name: Digby-Vaine-Trumpington for a vain, trumpeting young aristocrat; Maltravers for a secretary of transportation; Prendergast for a clergyman aghast at his apprehension of divine indifference; Grimes for an earthy rascal; Pennyfeather for an impecunious, half-fledged scholar.

The tone is persistently cheerful. No amazement is expressed, even by the innocent and beleaguered protagonist, at anything that befalls him. Tragedies occur offstage. The death of Prendergast, for example, is revealed in a hymn. Lord Tangent's demise is recorded as follows: In chapter 8, he is shown crying because he has been wounded in the foot by a bullet from the starter's pistol; in chapter 12, Beste-Chetwynde reports in an aside that Tangent's foot is gangrenous; in chapter 13, the news comes that the foot is being amputated; finally in chapter 19, it is reported in an offhand way that he has died.

The list of groups and institutions that excite the author's scorn is extensive; his opprobrium falls on the aristocracy, the newly rich, the universities, the public schools, old-school penology, newfangled penology, the House of Lords, the House of Commons, the Church of England, historical landmarks, modern architecture, and the League of Nations, to name a few. Although the novel manages to be hilarious at the expense of practically everybody, it has a serious side, or rather a serious center, namely, the schoolboy virtue of Pennyfeather contrasted with the cheery rascality of Grimes.

It is evident from the start that Paul Pennyfeather is a right thinker and a square shooter. He owes his educational opportunities as much to his own industry, intelligence, and moderation as to the legacy left by his parents. He is earnest, diffident, and idealistic; in short, he is the very model of a middle-class English divinity student. The incredible things that happen to him seem at first reading to represent repeated assaults of a corrupt society on a genuinely decent character. Captain Grimes, on the other hand, shows up as a bounder of the very worst kind, a poseur who relies on public-school connections to rescue him from his frequent immersions in "the soup." He milks the fellowship of honor and duty for all it is worth and does not hesitate to abandon ship at the first sign of bad weather—women, children, and gentlemanly behavior notwithstanding.

For all his roguery, however, Grimes is not a villain. He is instead the most sympathetic character in the novel. The chief element of his personality is common sense; it is he, and not Pennyfeather, who is the author's persona, who embodies the impulses of sanity as opposed to the precepts of class and culture. During the war, for example, when faced with court-martial or honorable suicide, he relies on drink and old school ties to see him through alive, and they do. Trapped into marriage, he simply bolts, once into the public schools, once into the sea. Imprisoned, he makes his escape by sinking into a quicksand from which, Paul and the reader are confident, he will rise to drink his pint in new guise but with the old elemental verve. He is self-indulgent, brave, resourceful, and not to be humbugged.

Although self-disciplined, Paul is meek, credulous, and fundamentally passive by contrast. Everything that happens to him, good or bad, simply happens. His rather mild passion for Margot Beste-Chetwynde strikes him like lightning; his actual proposal of marriage is all Margot's doing. He acquiesces alike to expulsion from college and rescue from prison with the same spongy plasticity cloaked beneath the ethical pose of being a good sport. In fact, it may be argued that believers in this schoolboy code of ethics suffer from a profound moral laziness and invite the outrages perpetrated on them in its name by those who do not believe in it. Paul's explanation of why he does not outface Potts and take money from Trumpington is illustrative. He defines a gentleman as someone who declines to accept benefits that are not his by right or to profit from windfall advantage. Implicit in this stance is a kind of flabby ethical neutrality disguised as self-respect, a certain pride in taking no action. Grimes's judgment is sounder and more vigorous, for he recognizes Potts as a stinker in prosecuting Paul for a crime he committed inadvertently.

The author remarks at one stage that Paul does not have the makings of a hero. No more has he the makings of a villain, for villainy requires the kind of enterprise exemplified by Margot. It is not Paul's decline and fall that are recorded here but the degeneration of a society in which custom and privilege combine to nurture all manner of waste and wickedness. Paul is merely part of the problem. Grimes, the voice of blackguardism and good sense, is part of the solution. Paul toasts the stability of ideals, Grimes the passing moment.

Despite Grimes, however, *Decline and Fall* ends on a rather grim note, with Peter Beste-Chetwynde a wastrel and Paul embracing a pinched orthodoxy. The underlying sense is of honorable old forms giving way to a new and nastier regime, a theme that Waugh also pursued in later works. Indeed, he espoused it in his own life to the extent of rejecting the new order altogether. As a result, he was virtually a hermit at the time of his death.

"Critical Evaluation" by Jan Kennedy Foster

Bibliography:
Beaty, Frederick L. *The Ironic World of Evelyn Waugh: A Study of Eight Novels.* DeKalb: Northern Illinois University Press, 1992. Argues that Waugh is more an ironist than a satirist and examines his various uses of irony. Chapter 2 is a study of *Decline and Fall.*
Carens, James F. *The Satiric Art of Evelyn Waugh.* Seattle: University of Washington Press, 1966. Published in the year of Waugh's death, this study of all his major works concentrates on specific satiric effects and the way in which the author achieved them. *Decline and Fall* is discussed in chapters 1 through 7.
Cowley, Malcolm. *"Decline and Fall."* In *Critical Essays on Evelyn Waugh,* edited by James F. Carens. Boston: G. K. Hall, 1987. This essay, first published only three years after the appearance of *Decline and Fall,* compares that novel with *Vile Bodies* and concludes that the first is greatly superior. An interesting early evaluation of Waugh.
Crabbe, Katharyn W. *Evelyn Waugh.* New York: Continuum, 1988. Following a brief biography in chapter 1, the author devotes the six remaining chapters to the novels; *Decline and Fall* is analyzed in chapter 2.
Stopp, Frederick J. *Evelyn Waugh: Portrait of an Artist.* Boston: Little, Brown, 1958. A standard work, which suffers only from having been published before Waugh completed his World War II trilogy. All the other novels, including *Decline and Fall,* are discussed in detail.

THE DEERSLAYER
Or, The First War-Path, a Tale

Type of work: Novel
Author: James Fenimore Cooper (1789-1851)
Type of plot: Historical
Time of plot: 1740
Locale: Northern New York State
First published: 1841

Principal characters:
NATTY BUMPPO, a woodsman called Deerslayer by the Delawares
HURRY HARRY, a frontier scout
CHINGACHGOOK, Deerslayer's Delaware friend
THOMAS HUTTER, owner of the lake
JUDITH HUTTER, a young woman Thomas Hutter claims as his daughter
HETTY HUTTER, Judith's sister
WAH-TA!-WAH, Chingachgook's beloved

The Story:

Natty Bumppo, a young woodsman known as Deerslayer, and Hurry Harry traveled to the shores of Lake Glimmerglass together. It was a dangerous journey, for the French and their Iroquois allies were on the warpath. Deerslayer was planning to meet his friend Chingachgook, the young Delaware chief, so that they might go against the Iroquois. Hurry Harry was on his way to the lake to warn Thomas Hutter and his daughters that hostile Indians were raiding along the frontier. Harry was accustomed to hunt and trap with Hutter during the summer, and he was an admirer of Hutter's elder daughter, the spirited Judith.

Hutter and his daughters lived in a cabin built on piles in the middle of the lake. Hutter had also built a great, scowlike vessel, known among frontiersmen as the ark, on which he traveled from one shore of the lake to the other on his hunting and trapping expeditions. On their arrival at the lake, the two found a hidden canoe. Having paddled out to the cabin and found it deserted, they proceeded down the lake and came upon the ark anchored in a secluded outlet. Hutter had already learned of the Indian raiders. The party decided to take refuge in the cabin, where they could be attacked only over the water. The men managed to maneuver the ark out of the narrow outlet and sail it to the cabin. They had one narrow escape, for as the ark was clearing the outlet, six Indians tried to board the boat by dropping from the overhanging limbs of a tree. Each missed and fell into the water.

Under cover of darkness, Hutter, Deerslayer, and Hurry Harry took the canoe and paddled to shore to get Hutter's two remaining canoes hidden there. They found the canoes and, on their way back to the ark, sighted a party of Indians camped under some trees. While Deerslayer waited in a canoe offshore, the other two men attacked the Iroquois camp in an attempt to obtain scalps, for which they could receive bounties. They were captured. Deerslayer, knowing that he was powerless to help them, lay down to sleep in the canoe until morning.

When Deerslayer awoke, he saw that one of the canoes had drifted close to shore. To rescue it, he was forced to shoot an Indian, the first man he had ever killed. Returning to the fort with his prizes, Deerslayer told the girls of their father's fate. It was agreed that they should delay any attempt at rescue until the arrival of Chingachgook, whom Deerslayer was to meet that night.

Under cover of darkness, the party went in the ark and met Chingachgook at the spot where the river joined the lake. Back in the cabin, Deerslayer explained that the Delaware had come to the lake to rescue his sweetheart, Wah-ta!-Wah, who had been stolen by the Iroquois. Suddenly, they discovered that Hetty Hutter had disappeared. The girl, who was somewhat feebleminded, had cast off in one of the canoes with the intention of going to the Indian camp to rescue her father and Hurry Harry.

The next morning, Wah-ta!-Wah came upon Hetty wandering in the forest. She took the white girl to the Iroquois camp. Because the Indians believed deranged persons were protected by the Great Spirit, she suffered no harm.

It was Deerslayer's idea to ransom the prisoners with some rich brocades and carved ivory that he and Judith found in Tom Hutter's chest. Its contents had been known only to Hutter and the simpleminded Hetty, but in this emergency, Judith did not hesitate to open the coffer. Meanwhile, a young Iroquois had rowed Hetty back to the cabin on a raft. Deerslayer told him that the party in the cabin would give two ivory chessmen for the release of the captives. He was unable to drive quite the bargain he had planned. In the end, four chessmen were exchanged for the men, who were returned that night.

Hetty brought a message from Wah-ta!-Wah. Chingachgook was to meet the Indian girl at a particular place on the shore when the evening star rose above the hemlocks that night. Hurry Harry and Tom Hutter were still determined to obtain scalps. When night closed in, Hurry Harry, Hutter, and Chingachgook reconnoitered the camp. To their disappointment, they found it deserted and the Indians camped on the beach, at the spot where Wah-ta!Wah was to wait for Chingachgook.

While Hutter and Harry slept, the Delaware and Deerslayer attempted to keep the rendez-vous, but the girl was under such close watch that it was impossible for her to leave the camp. The two men entered the camp and boldly rescued her from her captors. Deerslayer, who remained to cover their escape, was taken prisoner.

When Judith heard from Chingachgook of Deerslayer's capture, she rowed Hetty ashore to learn what had become of the woodsman. Once more, Hetty walked unharmed among the superstitious savages. Deerslayer assured her there was nothing she could do to help and that he must await the Iroquois' pleasure. She returned to Judith.

As the girls paddled about, trying to find the ark in the darkness, they heard the report of a gun. Torches on shore showed them that an Indian girl had been mortally wounded by a shot from the ark. Soon the lights went out. Paddling to the center of the lake, they tried to get what rest they could before morning came.

When daylight returned, Hutter headed the ark toward the cabin once more. Missing his daughters, he had concluded that the cabin would be the most likely meeting place. Hutter and Harry were the first to leave the ark to go into the cabin. There the Iroquois, who had come aboard in rafts under cover of darkness, were waiting in ambush. Harry managed to escape into the water, where he was saved by Chingachgook. Judith and Hetty came to the ark in their canoe. After the Indians had gone ashore, those on the ark went to the cabin. They found Hutter lying dead. That evening, he was buried in the lake. Hurry Harry took advantage of the occasion to propose to Judith, but she refused him.

Shortly afterward, they were surprised to see Deerslayer paddling toward the ark. He had been given temporary liberty in order to bargain with the fugitives. The Iroquois sent word that Chingachgook would be allowed to return to his own people if Wah-ta!-Wah and Judith became brides of Iroquois warriors. Hetty, they promised, would go unharmed because of her mental condition. Although Deerslayer's life was to be the penalty for refusal, these terms were declined.

Deerslayer did not have to return to his captors until the next day, and that evening he and Judith examined carefully the contents of her father's chest. To the girl's wonder, she found letters indicating that Hutter had not been her real father but a former buccaneer whom her mother had married when her first husband deserted her. Saddened by this knowledge, Judith no longer wished to live at the lake. She intimated to Deerslayer that she loved him, only to find that he considered her above him in education and intelligence.

When Deerslayer returned to the Iroquois the next day, he was put to torture with hatchets. Hetty, Judith, and Wah-ta!-Wah came to the camp and attempted to intercede for him, but to no avail. Suddenly, Chingachgook bounded in and cut his friend's bonds. Deerslayer's release was the signal for the regiment from the nearest fort to attack, for Hurry Harry had gone to summon help during the night.

The Iroquois were routed. Hetty was mortally wounded during the battle. The next day, she was buried in the lake beside her parents. Judith joined the soldiers returning to the fort. Deerslayer departed for the Delaware camp with Chingachgook and his bride.

Fifteen years later, Deerslayer, Chingachgook, and the latter's young son, Uncas, revisited the lake. Wah-ta!-Wah was long since dead, and, though the hunter inquired at the fort about Judith Hutter, he could find no one who knew her. There was a rumor that a former member of the garrison, then living in England on his paternal estates, was influenced by a woman of rare beauty who was not his wife. The ark and the cabin in the lake were falling into decay.

Critical Evaluation:

The fifth and final volume of James Fenimore Cooper's Leatherstocking Tales, *The Deerslayer* portrays Natty Bumppo as an idealistic youth raised among American Indians. Bumppo, in this novel nicknamed Deerslayer, is somewhere between twenty-two and twenty-four years old. Despite his daring and resourcefulness, he must rise to adulthood by meeting the challenge of human conflict when he is faced with the realities of tribal warfare and is forced to kill his first foe. Deerslayer discovers not only the ruthlessness of civilized men but also encounters a different kind of danger in the will of a woman. Cooper's novel is a *Bildungsroman*, the story of a young man's gaining the courage of his convictions and a moral certainty. In *The Deerslayer*, Cooper creates an idyllic view of the early American frontier, when the western boundary was New York's Lake Ostego (renamed Lake Glimmerglass in the novel). Cooper also includes such themes as the concept of gifts, the conflict between the Native American code of behavior and that of the Europeans, and the distinction between natural law and moral law.

In the novel, Deerslayer kills his first Indian, rejects the proposal of a beautiful young woman, fends off the missionary efforts of the woman's feebleminded sister, and worries about the appropriateness of Indian customs for a white man. He often reflects on the beauties of the wilderness.

The dominant mood of the novel is peaceful and serene. Cooper digresses to stress the peace and quiet of the forest at early morning, high noon, and evening. What breaks the peace and solitude of the forest are the sounds of gunshots and passionate, invading white men. Deerslayer talks to Hetty Hutter about his reverence and awe for the forest, God's creation. He has learned more from studying "the hand of God as it is seen in the hills and the valleys, the mountain-tops, the streams, the forests, and the springs" than the invading white people in the novel have from studying the Bible. The invaders, rather than finding the beauty in nature, seldom give it a second thought while they destroy it, especially when it serves their economic purposes.

Two alien objects invade the primal scene of Lake Glimmerglass: Hurry Harry's large boat, called the ark, and Thomas Hutter's "castle," a house built on piles over the water. Both Hutter and Hurry Harry are at the bottom of the moral scale. Hurry Harry, as his name implies, is restless. He considers members of other races animals and prides himself on his good looks, physical strength, and capability to rationalize his wants. Both he and Hutter are economically motivated, and they value and respect only money. They will do anything to get it, even killing American Indian women and children for their scalps. Hutter's values are shared by his daughter Judith, who worships the physical in both her own beauty and in the handsomeness of the British soldiers. These three characters represent the more unpleasant aspects of human nature. Their notion of gifts is one of materialistic acquisition.

In opposition to the views of Thomas and Judith Hutter and Hurry Harry, Deerslayer, his Delaware friend, and Hetty live close to nature. The Delawares and Deerslayer follow their own gifts to lead a satisfactory life. They kill only what they eat. When they scalp, it is for glory. Since they are uneducated in the ways of the white people, they know no better; when they scalp they remain blameless.

Although both Hetty and Deerslayer affirm a higher good, both are relatively unthinking, Deerslayer being uneducated and Hetty having been born simpleminded. Cooper frequently describes both in childlike terms. Both are removed from the sophisticated temptations of civilized life and try to live in accordance with Christian morality. Their notion of gifts, like that of the American Indians, is to take what is necessary from nature to survive.

Hetty affirms a Christian life that is impossible in a fallen world. Cooper makes the point that the totally un-Christian life is complete chaos when he sends Hetty to the Huron camp to plead for the lives of her father and Hurry Harry. She is confounded when the Huron chief, Rivenoak, asks her why the white people do not follow the injunctions of Christ to forgive one's enemies and turn the other cheek.

Deerslayer straddles his two worlds. He follows what he calls the law of nature: "to do, lest you should be done by." Deerslayer is first a hunter, becoming a warrior when he takes his first victim's life. He graciously offers his enemy another chance at life, but it is refused. When Deerslayer shoots quickly, the American Indian notices his quick eye and renames him Hawkeye. Even in killing his second enemy, Deerslayer is not the aggressor. His actions are less than Christlike—he does not turn the other cheek—but they are practical, invoking the universal injunction of self-defense. Deerslayer himself is a compromise between the best and worst human traits. He shows that virtue does not depend on education but may be corrupted by it. Physically unattractive, he shows that a beautiful soul may reside behind an ugly exterior.

The Deerslayer does not end on an optimistic note. Lake Glimmerglass returns to its natural state, and the selfish characters move to the fort; Deerslayer and his Indian compatriots disappear into the wilderness. The reader, however, knows that settlers will use axes to clear the forests and guns to kill animals and American Indians. As Deerslayer, Chingachgook, and Uncas slip into the wilderness, they are overcome with a sense of what might have been, but the reader knows that what might have been never comes to pass.

"Critical Evaluation" by Thomas D. Petitjean, Jr.

Bibliography:
Barnett, Louise K. "Speech in the Wilderness: The Ideal Discourse of *The Deerslayer*." In *Desert, Garden, Margin, Range: Literature of the American Frontier*, edited by Eric Heyne. New York: Twayne, 1992. A well-balanced essay that deals with the differing levels of diction in the characters' voices in *The Deerslayer* and how such speech patterns work in the evolution of the frontier mythos.

Person, Leland S., Jr. "Cooper's Queen of the Woods: Judith Hutter in *The Deerslayer.*" *Studies in the Novel* 21, no. 3 (Fall, 1989): 253-267. An intriguing study of Judith Hutter and her place in the wilderness frontier as a woman in a man's world.

Ringe, Donald A. *James Fenimore Cooper.* New York: Twayne, 1962. Excellent general overview of the works of Cooper, including *The Deerslayer.* Places the works in the construction of the myth of the American frontier.

Schachterle, Lance. "Fenimore Cooper's Literary Defenses: Twain and the Text of *The Deerslayer.*" *Studies in the American Renaissance* (1988): 401-417. Schachterle takes to task Mark Twain, who criticized Cooper's prose style and *The Deerslayer* in his essay "Fenimore Cooper's Literary Offenses."

Selley, April. " 'I Have Been, and Ever Shall Be, Your Friend': *Star Trek, The Deerslayer,* and the American Romance." *Journal of Popular Culture* 20, no. 1 (Summer, 1986): 89-104. Asserts that *The Deerslayer* is a romantic novel that constructs the mythos of the American frontier, and that this mythos is carried on in late twentieth century popular culture through television's *Star Trek* series.

THE DEFENCE OF GUENEVERE AND OTHER POEMS

Type of work: Poetry
Author: William Morris (1834-1896)
First published: 1858

The Defence of Guenevere and Other Poems, the first collection of poems published by William Morris, is one of the three or four principal expressions of Pre-Raphaelitism in poetry. Although Morris had only just turned twenty-four when the volume appeared, it epitomizes his poetic qualities and foreshadows his artistic attainment. Algernon Charles Swinburne, his contemporary, wrote concerning it: "Such things as are in this book are taught and learned in no school but that of instinct." It was Swinburne's opinion that no other literary work had ever shown more distinctly the mark of native character and that the poetry was entirely original. He saw Morris as "not yet a master," but "assuredly no longer a pupil." Not unmindful of certain technical faults and an occasional hint of confusion in the work, Swinburne nevertheless went on to say that Morris' volume was incomparable in its time for "perception and experience of tragic truth" and that no other contemporary poet had a "touch of passion at once so broad and so sure."

Swinburne may have overstated the case for the originality of the poems; Morris shows strong influences of Sir Thomas Malory and Jean Froissart, though more in regard to selection of subject matter than in its presentation. His Arthurian poems reveal a genuine passion and exceptional beauty, especially in passages such as the vibrant, breathtaking narrative description that opens the title poem. Yet despite their freshness and strong feeling, these poems are in what may be designated the tapestry tradition—there is a hint of the decorative about them. Those poems derived more clearly from Froissart than from Malory, however (among them "Sir Peter Harpdon's End," "Concerning Geoffrey Teste Noir," and the grim "Haystack in the Floods"), attest Morris' realization that, even in the Middle Ages, the tourney was not the only aspect of war.

Although Morris had a lifelong passion for beauty, he also had a need for certain harsh or stark elements, and these are present in these poems. The touches of this power are evident in this first volume of his poems. An example of such stark description may be found in these lines from "Concerning Geoffrey Teste Noire":

> I think 'twas Geoffrey smote him on the brow
> With some spiked axe; and while he totter'd, dim
> About the eyes, the spear of Alleyne Roux
> Slipped through his camaille and his throat; well, well!

When Sir Peter Harpdon's wife Alice, upon hearing of her husband's death, cries: "I am much too young to live,/ Fair God, so let me die," readers recognize in the cry a kind of Shakespearean poignancy. Among the many other qualities of this first book of poems is the apparent simplicity of a lyric such as "Golden Wings," which attains deep sincerity as it smoothly reflects early memories in a manner distinctly Morris' own. There is also the plain perfection of the little poem, "Summer Dawn," in which, departing momentarily from the dreams and histories of long-past lives and battles, Morris speaks simply in his own voice of his desire for communion.

Morris, while studying medieval romances and admiring them for their curious intrinsic beauty, became convinced that if people could move backward through time to the age of the sea kings, they should find the essential characteristics of the race to be exactly like those of today. Admittedly, he found the Middle Ages much more ignorant, cruel, and savage than the ages preceding or following; nevertheless, he concluded that people of those times must have had feelings, desires, and thoughts quite like those of people of his time. His society had much in common, then, with that of the Middle Ages; one should, therefore, study the terrible times of the Middle Ages in order to understand them and to understand better one's own time.

Morris gives readers some brief, sudden, and flashing pictures of that far-off time. The title poem presents a queen about to be burned at the stake; then, at the sound of a horse's hooves, she knows that her lover is coming to her rescue. One of the most powerful of these pictures is presented in "The Haystack in the Floods." Not revealing either how the tragedy began or how it ended, the poem opens with the haunting questions:

> Had she come all the way for this
> To part at last without a kiss?
> Yea, had she borne the dirt and rain
> That her own eyes might see him slain
> Beside the haystack in the floods?

Readers are at first told only enough about the woman Jehane to make them wonder about her character and to know that as she rides along she is miserable. Her lover Robert, who rides some distance ahead of her with a few armed men, is confronted by his adversary Godmar and numerous armed men. At first she fears for her own safety rather than Robert's:

> My God! my God! I have to tread
> The long way back without you; then
> The court at Paris; those six men;
> The gratings of the Chatelet;
> The swift Seine on some rainy day
> Like this, and people standing by,
> And laughing, while my weak hands try
> To recollect how strong men swim.

In her despair she contemplates accepting Godmar, the man whom she hates. Robert, whose men refuse to fight against the heavy odds, charges the enemy and is captured, disarmed, and bound. When after long hesitation Jehane refuses to come willingly to his castle, Godmar and his men murder Robert before her eyes. The poem ends with an uncertainty about her fate. Does she go mad? Will she be taken back and burned at the castle from which she has escaped? The reader may even suspect that she is feigning madness and that before the castle is reached she will yield to Godmar, who may then retain her until he tires of her. Having given us this glimpse of medieval passion, selfishness, suffering, and cruelty, Morris ends the poem, after Godmar's men have beaten Robert's brains out, on this note:

> Then Godmar turned again and said:
> So, Jehane, the first fitte is read!
> Take note, my lady, that your way
> Lies backward to the Chatelet!
> She shook her head and gazed awhile
> At her cold hands with a rueful smile,
> As though this thing had made her mad.
> This was the parting that they had
> Beside the haystack in the floods.

Another grim, moving poem, a Browningesque monologue called "The Judgement of God," supplies a second example of the same device.

Other noteworthy poems in the book are "The Little Tower," "The Wind," "The Eve of Crecy," "In Prison," and "The Blue Closet." All extremely original, they display a wide range in idea and theme. In their ability to make readers understand the feelings of pain, terror, or heroic effort at particular moments in the lives of people, they all have great psychological insight. For example, Guenevere's horrible soliloquy, revealing that she has wondered how the fire would quiver yards above her head, in its startlingly true psychology, improves upon the narrative of the original story. Especially in his use of monologue and dialogue, Morris successfully demonstrates that the poet can best revive the past not by detailed description of things but by faithful expression of the feelings of persons who lived long ago.

Without exaggeration, William Morris' *The Defence of Guenevere and Other Poems* may be called an outstanding first volume of poetry. However, like the early volumes of most poets, it did not make any particular impact upon the reading public when it appeared in 1858. This lack of acclaim for the volume may have been a factor in Morris' withdrawing for some time from the writing of poetry. Another factor was his feeling that writing poetry was neither particularly notable nor difficult and that it had no precedence over the new and exciting experiments in tapestry weaving and dyeing in which he was already engaged. Morris was content with the appreciation accorded the volume by a few of his friends, among them Dante Gabriel Rossetti, to whom it was dedicated.

Bibliography:
Kirchhoff, Frederick. *William Morris*. Boston: Twayne, 1979. Literary biography of William Morris. Places *The Defence of Guenevere and Other Poems* within the larger context of Morris' life and creative accomplishments, especially his writings.

Morris, William. *The Defence of Guenevere and Other Poems*. Edited by Margaret A. Lourie. New York: Garland, 1981. A scholarly edition of the poems with extensive notes that explain passages in the poetry. A critical introduction with a full bibliography places this work in its setting of Victorian poetry.

Oberg, Charlotte. *A Pagan Prophet, William Morris*. Charlottesville: University Press of Virginia, 1978. A study of Morris' writings as the sum of a "living unity" of his creative vision. The poems in *The Defence of Guenevere and Other Poems* are discussed last, out of chronological order, to demonstrate their relationship to the themes of Morris' other work.

Silver, Carole. *The Romance of William Morris*. Athens: Ohio University Press, 1982. Examines the idea of romance, in its broadest literary and artistic sense, as revealed in the works of William Morris. A chapter is devoted to the way *The Defence of Guenevere and Other Poems* exemplifies Morris' concept of the genre of romance.

Tompkins, J. M. S. *William Morris: An Approach to the Poetry*. London: Cecil Woolf, 1988. A study of Morris' poetry, which is defined not only as verse but also as prose romances. The opening chapter analyzes the poems in *The Defence of Guenevere and Other Poems* with particular emphasis on explaining the sources in medieval literature that inspired Morris to compose these works.

DEFENCE OF POESIE

Type of work: Literary criticism
Author: Sir Philip Sidney (1554-1586)
First published: 1595

Sir Philip Sidney's *Defence of Poesie* is an attempt to raise poetry above the criticism that had been directed at it by contemporary critics and to establish it as the highest of the arts, best fitted both to please and to instruct, the two aims stated by Horace in his *Ars poetica* (c. 17 B.C.E.). The first part of *Defence of Poesie* is primarily theoretical; Sidney weighs the respective merits of philosophy, history, and poetry as teachers of virtue. In the final section, he surveys the state of English literature soon after 1580.

The importance of Sidney's *Defence of Poesie* can best be appreciated by understanding the political climate of the late sixteenth century. A growing number of religious leaders were condemning the production of imaginative literature; lyric and dramatic works were viewed as little more than tools for corruption. Furthermore, much of the writing being produced in England was hackneyed and trite. Nevertheless, Sidney, a student of the classics and a poet himself, believed there was both aesthetic and moral value in poetry, which he defined broadly to include all imaginative literature. Well versed in Greek and Roman literature, familiar with both classical and Renaissance defenses of the arts, the courtier-artist took it upon himself to champion the practice of writing. The task proved formidable, since no earlier justification seemed to be able to counter the charges that imaginative literature was simply a vile distraction that promoted idleness at best, immorality at worst. Sidney found that the only way to defend the practice of poetry was to redefine its function and assign it a more significant aesthetic role. Modeling his work on both classical and Renaissance predecessors, Sidney constructs in the *Defence of Poesie* a formal argument, in a style reminiscent of the Roman orator Cicero and his followers in the practice of rhetoric, to explain the value of poetry and to delineate those qualities that make the poet a valuable teacher.

Sidney's first argument for the supremacy of poetry is that it was the "first light-giver to ignorance"; the first great works of science, philosophy, history, and even law were poems. Both the Italian and English languages were polished and perfected by their poets, Dante Alighieri, Giovanni Boccaccio, and Petrarch on the one hand, Geoffrey Chaucer and John Gower on the other. Even Plato illuminated his philosophy with myths and dramatic scenes.

Both the Hebrews and the Romans gave high distinction to poets, considering them prophets, messengers of God or the gods. The Greeks called their writers "makers," creators, who alone could rise above this world to make a golden one. Sidney writes of the poet: "So as he goeth hand in hand with Nature, not enclosed within the narrow warrant of her gifts, but freely ranging only within the zodiac of his own wit."

The aim of poetry, of all earthly knowledge, is "to lead and draw us to as high a perfection as our degenerate souls, made worse by their clayey lodgings, can be capable of." The moral philosopher feels himself the best teacher, for he can define and discuss virtue and vice and their causes; the historian argues that his examples from the past are far more effective instructors than the abstractions of the philosopher. Sidney finds the virtues of both combined in the poet, who can give both precept and example. He cites Homer's demonstration of wisdom personified in Ulysses; of valor, in Achilles; of anger, in Ajax. The poet is free to portray the ideal, while the historian must be faithful to his subjects, and they, being human, mingle faults with their virtues. The poet may show evil punished and good rewarded; the historian must record the vagaries of fortune, which allows the innocent to suffer and the vicious to prosper.

The poet has other advantages over the philosopher; however true the philosopher's statements may be, they are hard to follow. The poet "doth not only show the way, but giveth so sweet prospect into the way as will entice any man to enter into it." People will willingly listen to stories of Aeneas or Achilles, unaware of the lessons they are learning. Having established the superiority of poetry to his own satisfaction, Sidney analyzes both the pleasing and the instructive aspects of the various literary genres, trying to determine what faults can have brought poetry into disrepute. The pastoral can arouse sympathy for the wretchedness of the poor or illustrate civil wrongs in fables about sheep and wolves; satire makes one laugh at folly and thus reform. Comedy, which has been disgraced by "naughty play-makers and stage-keepers," is valuable for the ridicule it casts upon our faults, making us scorn them as we laugh. Tragedy, stirring up feelings of wonder and pity, "teacheth the uncertainty of this world, and upon how weak foundations gilden roofs are builded."

Sidney finds nothing to criticize in the work of the lyric poet, who lauds virtuous acts, gives moral precepts, and sometimes praises God, and he defends epic poetry as the greatest of all the genres: "For, as the image of each action stirreth and instructeth the mind, so the lofty image of such worthies most inflameth the mind with desire to be worthy, and informs with counsel how to be worthy."

Concluding his defense, Sidney takes up the most frequently repeated criticisms of poetry: that it is merely rhyming and versifying; that there are other kinds of knowledge that are worthier of one's time; that poetry is "the mother of lies"; that it inspires evil lusts; and that Plato banished it from his commonwealth. Against the first objection Sidney reiterates his statement that poetry is not exclusively that which is written in verse, although he defends the use of verse on the grounds that it is a great aid to the memory and that it is "the only fit speech for music."

The second argument has already been answered; if poetry be the greatest of teachers and inspirations to virtue, it must be worthy of the greatest share of people's attention. To the contention that poets are liars, Sidney replies that since they never affirm their subjects to be literally true or real, they cannot lie. Although they do not reproduce details of life from specific incidents, neither do they attempt to prove the false true. They call upon the imagination for the "willing suspension of disbelief" and tell, not "what is or is not, but what should or should not be."

Sidney confesses that there is some justice in the condemnation of poetry for its scurrility, but he imputes the fault to bad poets who abuse their art, rather than to poetry itself. He suggests that Plato, in banishing poets from his Republic, was barring those bad writers who corrupted youth with false pictures of the gods, not the art of poetry itself.

Satisfied with these answers, Sidney then turns to the specific problems of literature in England in his own day. He sees no reason for poetry to flourish in Italy, France, and Scotland, and not in his own nation, except the laziness of the poets themselves. They will neither study to acquire ideas nor practice to perfect a style for conveying these ideas. A few English writers and works are, however, worthy of a place in world literature. Sidney praises Chaucer and the lyrics of the Earl of Surrey, and he finds that Edmund Spenser's *The Shepheardes Calender* (1579) "hath much poetry in his eclogues," although he objects to Spenser's use of rustic language, on the grounds that neither Theocritus nor Virgil, the most famous classical writers of pastoral, employed it. For the rest of English poetry, Sidney has only scorn, for it seemed to him meaningless: "One verse did but beget another, without ordering at the first what should be at the last; which becomes a confused mass of words, with a tinkling sound of rime, barely accompanied with reason."

The public criticism of drama seems to him justified, with a very few exceptions. He commends *Gorboduc* (1561), a melodramatic Seneca-type tragedy by Thomas Norton and Thomas Sackville, for its "stately speeches," "well-sounding phrases," and "notable morality," but he is disturbed by the authors' failure to observe the unities of time and place. The rest of the tragedies of the age seem absurd in their broad leaps in space and time, spanning continents and decades in two hours. A true Aristotelian in his views on drama, Sidney is convinced that stage action should be confined to one episode; other events may be reported in the dialogue to provide necessary background for the central events. He objects, too, to the presence of scurrilous comic scenes, chiefly designed to evoke loud laughter from the audience, in the tragedies.

Sidney's last target is the affected artificial diction of lyric poetry, especially of love poetry. He believes that the wildly imaginative conceits of the Euphuists are tedious, and he praises, in contrast, the sense of decorum, of fitting diction and imagery, of the great classical orators.

After a few comments on the relative merits of qualitative and quantitative verse and on types of rhyme, Sidney addresses his readers, promising fame and blessings to those who will appreciate the values of poetry and laying this curse on those who will not: "While you live you live in love, and never get favor, for lacking skill of a sonnet; and when you die, your memory die from the earth, for want of an epitaph."

Readers familiar with classical conceptions of poetry may find a disturbing dissonance in *Defence of Poesie*; at times, Sidney seems to speak in theoretical terms borrowed from Plato (who questioned the value of poetry); at other times he seems to focus, as did Aristotle, on the task of defining the elements of imaginative literature and championing poetry's moral value. In actuality, Sidney is attempting to synthesize the Platonic and Aristotelian conceptions of poetry, and to integrate them with the new neoclassical concept of criticism as a practical endeavor intended to assess the worth of individual works. Like Aristotle, Sidney stresses the importance of the poem as a made object. Significantly, however, he also emphasizes the importance of the imagination in the creation of art; poets rely not simply on what they see around them, but also on that inner quality that gives them the capacity to create people, places, situations, and emotions much like those of the everyday world, but in some ways better or worse, to serve as models for human behavior.

The *Defence of Poesie* presents principles generally accepted by the critics throughout the Renaissance: The author leans heavily upon the dicta of the most-noted classical critics, Aristotle, Plato, and Horace, and his standards are echoed by the major English critics of the seventeenth and eighteenth centuries, John Dryden, Alexander Pope, and Samuel Johnson. The notion that the poet is somehow an agent for good inspired not only the writers of Sidney's own day, but also those of succeeding generations; the great English Romantics—among them William Wordsworth, Samuel Taylor Coleridge, Percy Bysshe Shelley, and John Keats—are the inheritors of Sidney's belief that poetry has the power of moving people to do good. It is but one small step to move from Sidney's assertion in *Defence of Poesie* that the final end of poetry is "to lead and draw us to as high a perfection . . . as our degenerate soules" can reach, to Shelley's pronouncement in his own *Defence of Poetry* that "poets are the unacknowledged legislators of the world."

Sidney's essay is one of the most polished and interesting pieces of Elizabethan prose, and his comments on the writing of his own time have been borne out by the judgment of the centuries. Although this work is the first major piece of English literary criticism, it has seldom been surpassed in the centuries since Sidney's death.

Updated by Laurence W. Mazzeno

Bibliography:

Lawry, Jon S. *Sidney's Two Arcadias: Pattern and Proceeding.* Ithaca, N.Y.: Cornell University Press, 1972. The introduction examines *Defence of Poesie* as an expression of Sidney's ideas regarding the heroic poem and the classical idea of the poet. It is seen as a commentary on and preface to Sidney's *Arcadia* (1590).

Myrick, Kenneth. *Sir Philip Sidney as a Literary Craftsman.* 2d ed. Lincoln: University of Nebraska Press, 1965. Surveys Sidney's literary career as humanist, courtier, and poet; studies *Defence of Poesie* as a classical oration. Useful notes connect the work to other studies of the text.

Sidney, Sir Philip. *"An Apology for Poetry" or "The Defence of Poesy."* Edited by Geoffrey Shepherd. London: Thomas Nelson and Sons, 1967. Introduction analyzes the classical form of *Defence of Poesie* and its intellectual context and background. Almost a hundred pages of notes add further interpretation and contextual connections.

_____. *Defence of Poesy.* Edited by Lewis Soens. Lincoln: University of Nebraska Press, 1970. A substantial introduction analyzes and interprets Sidney's text. Further explanation is provided by extensive notes and a bibliography that lists pertinent texts in modern scholarship.

Spingarn, J. E. *A History of Literary Criticism in the Renaissance.* 2d ed. New York: Columbia University Press, 1949. This major study of the history of literary criticism argues that modern criticism began in the sixteenth century. Assigns Sidney a major role in that history and credits him with introducing the principles of classical criticism into England through *Defence of Poesie.*

A DEFENCE OF POETRY

Type of work: Essay
Author: Percy Bysshe Shelley (1792-1822)
First published: 1840

Readers familiar with other great "defenses" of poetry may find Percy Bysshe Shelley's *A Defence of Poetry* unusual, even confusing. There is little practical analysis of the elements of good literary work. There is no methodical history of poetry, as one reads in Sir Philip Sidney's *Defence of Poesie* (1595). There are no pronouncements about rules of composition. Instead, Shelley offers a philosophical analysis of the role of the poet as a special kind of person, one who can see the essential harmonies of the world beneath the discordant images people find in their everyday lives. Whereas Aristotle, Sidney, or John Dryden see the poet as a superb craftsman capable of delighting readers through the masterful blending of form and content, Shelley assigns the poet a higher calling: the revelation of truth about life, and the promotion of universal betterment.

These high claims are justified by Shelley's insistence that the production of poetry is not simply a craft. Rather, the true poet is a visionary who is inspired to create art as a means of revealing something about the nature of the world. The poem itself is merely an attempt to reproduce that vision. Such claims have been misinterpreted, and Shelley has been accused of promoting automatic writing or of devaluing the importance of craftsmanship. On the contrary: Shelley saw the imagination as a shaping power that gives form to the poet's vision, and only those who master form can hope to convey their vision to readers. Similarly, claims that Shelley is a promoter of emotional poetry are wrongheaded; he is insistent that the practice of poetry involves the intellect as well as the heart. He believes that great poets have a special gift that allows them to use the materials of their own time (the forms and subjects that might appeal to their contemporary readers), but transcend the limits of time and place to speak to people of all ages.

In this essay Shelley is defending poetry—"my mistress, Urania"—against the attack by Thomas Love Peacock in "The Four Ages Of Poetry," published in the first and only issue of the *Literary Miscellany* in 1820. The polemical exchange came to nothing, for *A Defence of Poetry* remained unpublished until 1840. In his essay, Peacock had elaborated the familiar figure of the Golden and Silver Ages of classical poetry into four (Iron, Gold, Silver, and Brass), skipped over "the dark ages," and repeated the succession in English poetry. Peacock's point was that poetry never amounts to much in civilized society; Shelley's defense is that poetry is essential. Their views were antithetical and neither made contact with the other: Peacock's attack is a boisterous satire, Shelley's defense is an elevated prose poem.

Nevertheless, Peacock's article is still a necessary preface to Shelley's arguments, not because one prompted the other or because Shelley adopted Peacock's historical method in the middle section of his essay, but because, as a pair, they show the opposing preferences of the older public for eighteenth century wit and of the younger for enthusiasm. Peacock's "The Four Ages of Poetry" has also the merit of being amusing; Shelley is never amusing. Peacock's argument is that poetry belongs properly to primitive societies, that as they become civilized they become rational and nonpoetical; hence it was not until the late seventeenth century that England equaled, in the work of William Shakespeare and John Milton, the Golden Age of Homeric Greece. Early nineteenth century England seemed, to him, to have reached the Age of Brass in poetry but a kind of Golden Age in science; therefore, poetry should be left to the primitive societies where it belongs. Peacock is most amusing in his picture of the first Age of Iron, in which the bard of the tribal chief "is always ready to celebrate the strength of his arm, being first duly inspired by that of his liquor." Apart from Homer, Peacock respects no poet, not even Shakespeare, who mixed his unities and thought nothing of "deposing a Roman Emperor by an Italian Count, and sending him off in the disguise of a French pilgrim to be shot with a blunderbuss by an English archer." Peacock's jest turns sour as he tires of his figure, and his strictures on contemporary poetry become a diatribe of which the gist is that "a poet of our times is a semibarbarian in a civilized community." Shelley, to whom Peacock sent a copy of his essay, was stirred to write his only prose statement on his craft. In it he came to the memorable conclusion that "Poets are the unacknowledged legislators of the world."

A *Defence of Poetry* falls into three parts. First, Shelley presents an argument that all people are poets in some degree, for poetry is an innate human faculty; hence, it is seen in all societies at all times and to eternity. In the second part, he attempts the historical proof, which he abandons in the third to make a subjective and poetic affirmation of the perpetual presence and ennobling virtue of poetry. In presenting his beliefs, Shelley uses the ideas that inspire his poems and attempts to codify them from the base Peacock had given him. Peacock could begin at once with his first age, however; Shelley found it necessary to begin by defining his notion of poetry. Two major ideas run through this first section and are reflected in the rest of the essay: the Platonic idea of mimesis, in which the imagination responds to the eternal verities it glimpses behind the material form, and the eighteenth century idea of the "sympathetic imagination" that, of its own initiative, extends itself and assumes an empathy with external objects and beings. The first idea leads Shelley to assert the superiority of the poet as the most active in using the glimpses of truth and conveying them to lesser beings for their uplifting; for this reason, the poet is the most powerful influence on humankind, a "legislator." The second idea gives the poet an insight into the ills of humankind which, once understood, can be corrected; here is the second meaning of "legislator."

The first part presented is in two sections, dealing first with the mimetic, then with the expressive powers of poetry, which powers are part of the definition of poetry; the other two parts of the definition are contained in four paragraphs on the form of poetry, especially on its use of language, the medium that makes it superior to other art media and which is called "measured" in contradistinction to "unmeasured" language or prose. The whole essay is prefaced by four paragraphs that define poetry in the largest or organic sense, not by its mechanics. These paragraphs go to the heart of the difference between Peacock and Shelley.

Shelley begins with a distinction between reason and imagination, leaving to the former the work of numbering, analyzing, and relating objects; the imagination perceives the similitude of objects in their innate values, not in their appearance, and synthesizes these values, presumably, into a valid and Platonic One or Truth. The synthetic principle of the imagination is poetry; the individual is compared to "an Aeolian lyre," subject to impressions external and internal but possessing an inner principle (poetry) that produces not simply melody but harmony. Poetry is thus both the name of a form of language (measured) and of the power of producing it and benefiting from the poem. Shelley asserts that poets are "the institutors of laws, and the founders of civil society" because they discover the laws of harmony and become "legislators" by giving these laws the form of a poem. The poetic product or poem may be an act of mimesis, but the act proceeds from the poetic faculty highly developed in the poet and contained in all people: "A poem is the very image of life expressed in its eternal truth."

The argument in the second section of the first part, devoted to the effects of poetry on society, has been anticipated in the foregoing analysis. A *Defence of Poetry*, as an "apologia," could well end at that point, but Shelley wanted to convince Peacock that his theory has external evidence. This he offers in the second part of the essay.

The historical method had already been touched on in Shelley's example of the propensity of the savage or child to imitate the impressions it receives, as a lyre produces melody only. Shelley's reading of history is as willful as Peacock's in his assertion that the morality of an age corresponds to the goodness or badness of its poetry; he adduces Greek classical drama as an evidence of a healthy society and Hellenic bucolic poetry as a sign of decay when the poets ceased to be the acknowledged legislators of the Alexandrian Hellenes. In order to cope with the same progression of health and decay in the literature of Rome, which would seem to prove Peacock's scheme, Shelley shifts the whole cycle into "episodes of that cyclic poem written by time upon the memories of men." He encounters further difficulty in coping with Christianity, for, by Shelley's theory, Jesus must be a great poet: "The scattered fragments preserved to us by the biographers of this extraordinary person, are all instinct with the most vivid poetry." Something went wrong in the Dark Ages, which brought "the extinction of the poetic principle . . . from causes too intricate to be here discussed." Shelley feels safer with Dante Alighieri and John Milton: "But let us not be betrayed from a defence into a critical history of poetry."

After abandoning the historical method which, had he followed Peacock step by step, would have brought him up to his contemporaries, Shelley returns to his defence by attacking "the promoters of utility" and, by implication, Peacock. To the utilitarian objection that poetry simply produces pleasure and that pleasure is profitless, Shelley asserts that the pleasure of poetry lies not in its superficial melody but in its innate harmony, alone capable of checking "the calculating faculty" that has already produced "more scientific and economical knowledge than can be accommodated to the just distribution of the produce which it multiplies." Shelley follows this with a paragraph that summarizes the duality of the "poetic faculty"; by synthesis it "creates new materials of knowledge and power and pleasure," and by its expressive powers it reproduces those materials "according to a certain rhythm and order which may be called the beautiful and the good."

Shelley's peroration, his personal and poetic justification for poetry, opens with three paragraphs beginning: "Poetry is indeed something divine"; "Poetry is the record of the best and happiest moments of the happiest and best minds"; "Poetry turns all things to loveliness." This is the moving genius of *Adonais*. Searching for the best proof to defend poetry from the rationalizations of Peacock, Shelley followed the prompting of his own "poetic principle" in concluding *A Defence of Poetry* with a sustained lyric in prose that Peacock could never match. The power of this essay is still inspiring. It constitutes Shelley's best claim outside his verse to be a "legislator" to the world.

Bibliography:
Clark, David Lee, ed. *Shelley's Prose: Or, The Trumpet of a Prophecy*. Albuquerque: University of New Mexico Press, 1954. Introduction examines Shelley's theory of poetry in relation to the larger context of his religious and other ideas. Notes accompany the text of *A Defence of Poetry*; annotated bibliography is also provided.
Daiches, David. *Critical Approaches to Literature*. 2d ed. New York: Longman, 1981. Discusses the Platonic idealism of *A Defence of Poetry* in terms of its subjects, poetry and social morality, language and imagination, and so on, and relates its ideas to those of Sir Philip Sidney, William Wordsworth, and Samuel Taylor Coleridge.
Dunbar, Clement. *A Bibliography of Shelley Studies: 1823-1950*. New York: Garland, 1976. Offers more than thirty-two hundred items that deal with Shelley and his writing; unannotated.

Fry, Paul H. *The Reach of Criticism: Method and Perception in Literary Theory*. New Haven, Conn.: Yale University Press, 1983. A chapter discusses the relation of *A Defence of Poetry* to the tenets of Longinus, John Dryden, and others. Closely analyzes the language, ideas, and theoretical basis; considers the essay one of the best works on the debate between poetry and science.

Jordan, John E., ed. *A Defence of Poetry*, by Percy Bysshe Shelley, and *The Four Ages of Poetry*, by Thomas Love Peacock. Indianapolis: Bobbs-Merrill, 1965. Introduction interprets the significance of Shelley's essay. Copious notes explain the text and connect it to the works of previous writers.

DEIRDRE

Type of work: Novel
Author: James Stephens (1882-1950)
Type of plot: Folklore
Time of plot: Heroic Age
Locale: Ireland
First published: 1923

> *Principal characters:*
> CONACHÚR MAC NESSA, king of Ulster
> CLOTHRU, his first wife
> MAEVE, his second wife
> CATHFA, his father and a magician
> LAVARCHAM, his conversation-woman
> FERGUS MAC ROY, his stepfather
> NESSA, his mother
> FELIMID MAC DALL, his storyteller
> DEIRDRE, Felimid's daughter and the ward of Conachúr
> UISNEAC, Conachúr's brother-in-law
> NAOISE,
> AINNLE, and
> ARDAN, Uisneac's sons

The Story:

The king of Ulster had a daughter who was called Assa, the Gentle. She loved knowledge and had many tutors. One day, returning from a visit to her father and finding her tutors killed, she buckled on her armor and set out to find the murderer. Henceforth her name was Nessa, the Ungentle. While she was bathing in the forest, Cathfa, the magician, saw and loved her. He offered to spare her life only if she would marry him. Their son was Conachúr mac Nessa. After a while, Nessa left Cathfa, taking her son with her.

When Conachúr was sixteen years old, Nessa was still the most beautiful woman in the land. Fergus mac Roy, the new king of Ulster, was only eighteen years old, but he fell in love with Nessa as soon as he saw her. She promised to marry him only if Conachúr could be king for a year while she and Fergus lived away from court. Fergus agreed, but after the year was up, Conachúr kept the throne, and Fergus became one of his most trusted followers.

Nessa arranged a marriage between Conachúr and Clothru, daughter of the high king of Connacht. On a visit to her father, Clothru was killed by her sister Maeve. Conachúr's first son was born just before she died. Bent on vengeance, Conachúr went to Connacht. There he saw Maeve and, changing his mind, he married her against her wishes. When she went to Ulster with him, she took along great riches and also a guard of one thousand men.

During one of his journeys at a time when Maeve had refused to accompany him, he stopped at the house of Felimid mac Dall, his storyteller. That night, Conachúr sent a servant to say that Felimid's wife should sleep with him. The servant returned to say that Felimid's wife could not accommodate him as she was then expecting a child. Soon the men heard the wail of the newborn infant. Conachúr asked his father to interpret the wail and other evil omens that the men had seen recently. Cathfa prophesied that the child then born, a girl, would be called The Troubler and that she would bring evil and destruction in Ulster. When one of his followers suggested that Conachúr have the child killed immediately, he sent for the infant; but he decided it was not becoming for a prince to evade fate, and he let the child live. Deirdre was her name.

Conachúr had Deirdre brought up at Emania by Lavarcham, his conversation-woman, who let the girl see no one but women servants and a guard of the oldest and ugliest swordsmen in Ulster. Lavarcham could adapt herself to any situation or group of people; while acting as a spy for Conachúr, she also learned everything that had to be taught to Deirdre to prepare her for the place Lavarcham had decided she should have in the kingdom.

Lavarcham reported regularly to Conachúr so that, while he never saw Deirdre, the king knew how she progressed month by month. He refused to believe Lavarcham's glowing reports; besides, at that time, he was well satisfied with Maeve. On the other hand, Lavarcham reported at length to Deirdre about Conachúr until the child knew all his whims, his boldness, and his majesty.

Maeve, who had never forgiven Conachúr for marrying her against her will, finally decided to leave him. She was so unforgiving that she refused to leave behind one thread of her clothes or one bit of her riches. Since some of the riches included great herds of cattle, flocks of sheep, heaps of silver and jewelry, and pieces of furniture, she had to make careful plans to get everything away when Conachúr was not looking. She trusted no one entirely, but she had a spy, mac Roth, who was even more diligent than Conachúr's Lavarcham. He discovered that Conachúr was to take a trip to Leinster; he even followed Conachúr's company for two full days until he felt the group was far enough away to be unable to get back in time; then he returned to help Maeve in her flight. Only Lavarcham guessed that something might happen, but her messengers did not reach Conachúr before Maeve had fled.

Conachúr grieved for Maeve, but he was unable to bring her back to Ulster. In the meantime, Lavarcham began to brood about the matter. The whole kingdom wanted the king to remarry, and Deirdre was sixteen years old. Lavarcham persuaded the king to come to see Deirdre.

Although Lavarcham had taught Deirdre all that she needed to know about Conachúr, she did not realize that the child thought of the king as ancient and feared him a little. Nor did Lavarcham know that Deirdre, longing for people of her own age, had learned how to escape the guards around Emania.

Deirdre was first tempted to go beyond the walls by a campfire that she wanted to investigate. Around it she saw three boys: Naoise, who was nineteen, Ainnle, who was seventeen, and Ardan, who was fourteen. They were the sons of Uisneac, who had married Conachúr's sister. Deirdre startled them when she first appeared in the light of the fire, but they all laughed and told so many good stories that she knew she would have to go back again. The younger boys insisted that Naoise would soon be the champion of Ulster, and Deirdre did not doubt it.

When Conachúr went to see Deirdre, he found her the most beautiful girl in Ulster, and he intended to marry her immediately. Lavarcham, however, made him wait a week, after which he would have a three-month feast. In love with Naoise, Deirdre was horrified at the idea of marrying a man who was so old and huge, but several nights passed before she could make her way to the campfire again. At her pleading, the brothers took her out of the country.

Six years later, Conachúr decided that Deirdre and the sons of Uisneac should be brought back from Scotland, their place of refuge, but the boys would not return except under the protection of one of Conachúr's trusted men. Fergus and his sons were sent to Scotland with assurances of safety. Deirdre had a dream and begged Naoise not to leave, but he declared that Fergus was honorable.

When the travelers reached the coast of Ulster, Fergus was detained by one of Conachúr's men, and Fergus' sons took Deirdre and the sons of Uisneac under their protection. Arriving at Conachúr's court at night, they were lodged in the fortress called the Red Branch. Then Deirdre knew there would be trouble, because Conachúr had not received them under his own roof.

Conachúr sent his men to batter down the doors and to bring Deirdre to him. The sons of Uisneac and Fergus made quick sallies, dashing out one door and in another, and killed so many of Conachúr's warriors that at last the king ordered the fortress to be set on fire. As Deirdre and the boys fled, Conachúr asked Cathfa to stop them. Cathfa cast a spell that made the boys drop their arms, and they were captured. Conachúr had the sons of Fergus and Uisneac killed. When Deirdre knelt over Naoise's dead body, she sipped his blood and fell lifeless.

Critical Evaluation:

One of the primary features of the Irish literary renaissance was the discovery, regeneration, and translation of ancient Irish myths into modern forms. Among the great Celtic legends, perhaps the most popular was the tragic love story of Deirdre, The Troubler, and her lover, Naoise. Probably the greatest artistic representations of this fable of fate, love, betrayal, and death are the dramatic versions by William Butler Yeats (*Deirdre*, 1907) and John Millington Synge (*Deirdre of the Sorrows*, 1910). However, although James Stephens' prose interpretation of the myth may lack the austere poetic grandeur of Yeats's play or the tragic intensity of Synge's, it has a psychological penetration and lively narrative thrust that makes it not unworthy of mention alongside those great predecessors.

In many ways, Stephens' version is the most modern one of the Deirdre legend. Although very different from each other, both Yeats and Synge sought to capture the atmosphere of the romantic Irish past of legend and folklore in their plays. Stephens, however, is more interested in a modern psychological analysis of the characters and their actions. At the same time, he did not ignore the flavor of archaic Celtic myth; in developing his story, he took great pains to present the medieval culture and background as authentically and thoroughly as he could. *Deirdre*, therefore, contains that mixture of the lyrical and the realistic, the ancient and the modern, and the solemn and the irreverent that characterizes Stephens' best work in all genres.

Stephens was a brilliant Irish writer of poetry and prose whose best work was grounded in the early literature of his own country. Just as he attempted to bring Irish folklore to life in *The Crock of Gold* (1912), so he tried to revitalize ancient Gaelic legend in *Deirdre*. In this novel, he wrote of the beautiful and mystical Deirdre, of brave and handsome Naoise, and of strong and willful Conachúr, who was loved by all his people and who was almost great. It is not only the people in the story that are remembered afterward; there are also many memorable scenes. *Deirdre* is a novel of legend and fantasy with a core of realism.

It has been claimed—with some justice—that Stephens' emphasis on detailed psychological analysis and explanation slows down the action in the first book and that he fails in the crucial scene—the flight of the lovers—by having it reported secondhand. If the first book is uneven, however, the second is delightful and occasionally powerful. Their personalities and motivations having been carefully delineated in the first book, the characters, and their decisions and actions, are thoroughly believable in the second one. All of the second book is excellent, and several moments—such as the suppressed tragedy evident in the gaiety of Naoise's younger brothers, Deirdre's realization of Conachúr's treachery, and especially Deirdre's death on the body of her dead lover—approach greatness.

It was not Stephens' purpose to idolize the old Irish myths but to make them alive and familiar for his own times. In spite of a setting eight centuries in the past, readers of *Deirdre* have little difficulty in believing in and relating to a gallery of vivid, passionate characters: the gentle, aristocratic King Fergus, too casual and perhaps lazy to avert tragedy; Conachúr, brave yet insecure, whose sense of honor and duty cannot overcome his passionate nature; the sons of Uisneac, united yet individualized, apparently carefree yet serious and heroic; and finally, Deirdre herself, intense, intuitive, innocent yet wise, who passionately and courageously strives for a happiness that she knows from the beginning will never be granted to her.

Bibliography:
Fackler, Herbert V. *That Tragic Queen: The Deirdre Legend in Anglo-Irish Literature.* Salzburg: Institut für Englische Sprache und Literatur, Universität Salzburg, 1978. Various nineteenth century versions of the Deirdre story are explored, and their bearing on early modern treatments of the legend is suggested. Stephens' work is firmly located in its various contexts. The analysis stresses the distinctive character of Stephens' imaginative reinvention of the bardic material.
Foster, John Wilson. *Fictions of the Irish Literary Revival.* Syracuse, N.Y.: Syracuse University Press, 1987. A critically sophisticated overview of the context in which Stephens' work was created. The relationship between *Deirdre* and works of other contemporary fabulists is evaluated, providing a significant sense of the novel's genre. The originality of Stephens' rhetorical strategies and modernizing emphases in *Deirdre* are also incisively assessed.
McFate, Patricia. *The Writings of James Stephens.* London: Macmillan Press, 1979. A thematic survey of Stephens' prose, plays, and poems. Discussion of Deirdre focuses on the story's origins in Irish myth, and Stephens' update of the original are highlighted. The study contains a chronology and a comprehensive bibliography.
Martin, Augustine. *James Stephens: A Critical Study.* Dublin: Gill and Macmillan, 1977. A comprehensive account on the whole of Stephens' writings. Discussion of *Deirdre* is included in the account of Stephens' artistic involvement with Irish myth, folktale, and saga. Analysis concentrates on Stephens' focus on the significance of jealousy in the plot.
Pyle, Hilary. *James Stephens: His Work and an Account of His Life.* London: Routledge & Kegan Paul, 1965. This study remains the most accessible source of biographical information about Stephens. Influences on his work, such as the poetry of William Blake and Eastern philosophy, are also discussed in detail. The full range of Stephens' writings are also considered in the light of an intimate knowledge of the contexts in which they were produced.

DEIRDRE

Type of work: Drama
Author: William Butler Yeats (1865-1939)
Type of plot: Tragedy
Time of plot: Antiquity
Locale: Ireland
First performed: 1906; first published, 1907

> *Principal characters:*
> FIRST MUSICIAN
> FERGUS, an old man
> NAOISE, a young king
> DEIRDRE, his queen
> CONCHUBAR, the old king of Uladh

The Story:

Two musicians were conversing in a woodland house. The First Musician rehearsed the background of the play: King Conchubar had found Deirdre as a young child in the wood, hired a nurse to care for her, and, as she attained womanhood, fallen in love with her. Just before Conchubar was to wed Deirdre, Naoise, a young man, climbed the hill to the woodland house where Deirdre was sequestered and abducted her.

Fergus, an old man, entered the house and informed the musicians that Deirdre and Naoise were to arrive momentarily. They had been in self-exile, hiding from Conchubar's jealous wrath. Having softened, the old king had invited them to return. Fergus insisted that King Conchubar had overcome his jealousy and forgiven the young lovers. When the musicians expressed skepticism, Fergus grew angry. Although he insisted that he would dance for pure joy at the change in King Conchubar, the First Musician noticed forbidding-looking men moving around outside.

Upon entering the house, Deirdre and Fergus expressed apprehension that King Conchubar had not arranged to welcome them. Fergus conjectured that Conchubar would appear to welcome his guests himself, and he observed to Naoise that Deirdre's uneasiness was understandable: Having been reared outside polite society, she would not understand the inviolability of the king's vow. Surrendering his own uneasiness to Fergus's assurance of safety, Naoise told Deirdre that it was ungrateful of them to doubt their host. Fergus remarked that he believed the best of everyone, and that such belief is capable of influencing people to behave well.

Deirdre spoke quickly to the First Musician, and from his veiled remarks she divined that Conchubar intended to kill Naoise and force her to become his unwilling queen. Deirdre's sudden anguished cry attracted Naoise, who admonished her not to criticize the king. Reminding her of Conchubar's oath, he instructed Deirdre that, "when we give a word and take a word/ Sorrow is put away, past wrong forgotten." Fergus pragmatically reminded the lovers that the house stood in the stronghold of King Conchubar's power and flight was impossible. Realizing that she and Naoise were trapped, Deirdre exclaimed that she would buy their freedom by mutilating herself, to "spoil this beauty that brought misery/ And houseless wandering on the man I love."

Naoise urged her to do nothing, for, indeed, their fate was unalterable. As if to punctuate Naoise's fatalism, a messenger arrived and announced that Conchubar had prepared supper and awaited the company of his guests. The faithful Fergus gushingly confessed that he, too, had begun to suspect Conchubar's intentions, but that all was well again. Naoise gently chided himself for doubting Conchubar. Deirdre, who knew better, calmly noted that the messenger had not finished delivering his message.

Only Deirdre and Fergus were being invited to supper, the messenger concluded; Naoise, "the traitor that bore off the queen," was unwelcome. The trap was sprung and Conchubar's treachery revealed. Naoise quickly discovered that the woods around the house swarmed with Conchubar's soldiers: Flight and fight were equally futile. In a defiant gesture of self-control, he and Deirdre joined in a game of chess.

Conchubar appeared at the window, then slipped back into the night. Naoise chased him, presuming that Conchubar fled from fear, but Deirdre snatched a knife from the First Musician, pretending that she would help Naoise in his flight. When Conchubar made his appearance in the room, he was gloating over Naoise who had been entangled in the net set to trap him. Conchubar first sternly warned Deirdre that he would kill Naoise unless she consented to walk into his house, in full public view, and as of her own free will. Deirdre beseeched Conchubar to allow her and Naoise to go free, emphasizing, naïvely, that his subjects would praise and extol him for his forgiveness. Realizing that Conchubar was adamant in his refusal to let her go, Deirdre then poignantly instructed Naoise to depart. "I will not live long, Naoise," she said, urging him to leave and forget her. Deirdre begged Conchubar to accept that she was to blame for the wrong he had suffered. Naoise's strength and fighting skill could prove useful to the kingdom. Even while Deirdre was begging for Naoise's life, he was taken outside to be slaughtered by the impassive and vindictive king.

When Deirdre was confronted with the bloody evidence of Naoise's death, she staggered, trembling, over to the musicians. Conchubar brutishly commanded her to come to his room: "The traitor who has carried off my wife/ No longer lives./ For he that called himself your husband is dead." At the peak of her grief, Deirdre feigned consent to Conchubar's command, ambiguously asserting, "It is but wisdom to do willingly/ What has to be done." Conchubar, for all his craftiness, imagined that Deirdre had wearied of opposing him and surrendered to his will. Deirdre then appealed to the king's vanity, asking to be allowed to gaze one last time upon Naoise's body in private. As she slipped behind the curtain, where she took her life, Conchubar boasted to Fergus, "Deirdre is mine." Conchubar's delight turned to outrage, however, when he saw that she had killed herself. Bitterly, he declared that he had chosen wisely in choosing Deirdre for his queen and that he acted correctly in preventing a boy lover from taking her from him.

Critical Evaluation:

W. B. Yeats, who is remembered primarily as one of the most celebrated and influential lyric poets of the twentieth century, produced eleven short plays based upon the heroic literature of Ireland and concerned chiefly with the exploits of the Ulster hero Cuchulain. Yeats based *Deirdre*, his second play, on a section of the translation of the Gaelic tale of *Cuchulain of Muirthemne* (1902), done by his friend, Lady Gregory, changing it slightly to suit his artistic needs. Although Padraic Colum found that the language of the play "has high excellence," he complained that the characterizations were exasperating, the result, according to A. S. Knowland of a "mixture of naturalism and lyricism," a mixture he agreed was uneasy. Lennox Robinson, however, called it "the most supremely satisfactory of Yeats's one-act verse-plays."

Yeats's dramatic method was to pit strong characterizations in opposition, juxtaposing poetic diction and rhythms with what he called "speech close to that of daily life." In his dialogue of 1915, *The Poet and the Actress*, he wrote "In every great play . . . you will find a group of characters . . . who express the dream, and another group who express its antagonist." The aim of drama was to pit these forces against one another in battle. "Those who try to create beautiful things without this battle in the soul, are merely imitators," he believed.

In *Deirdre*, Yeats presents the conflict of the otherworldly Deirdre with the powerful and crafty King Conchubar. The play proceeds in a series of oppositions. At first, Conchubar remains a foreboding presence, the dark shadow of Deirdre's hope. Deirdre's act of faith in returning to Conchubar's kingdom anticipates the faithlessness of Conchubar's vow to welcome and protect her and her lover, Naoise. Yeats emphasizes the vow, both to highlight its social significance and to contrast it with the stronger vow of love that Deirdre has pledged to Naoise. Later, Conchubar deceitfully offers to spare Naoise's life if Deirdre will pretend to the kingdom that she has returned of her own volition. Deirdre matches this double deceit with double fidelity, at first appealing as a loyal subject to Conchubar's honor as a king, then sacrificing herself to keep her pledge of love to Naoise.

A. Norman Jeffares has noted that Yeats's concern with drama was with the heroic, and the final contrast in *Deirdre* evokes the most distinctive trait of heroic literature, full belief in the unrivalled importance of enduring renown. Whereas Conchubar shrinks from the sacrifice that would ensure the regeneration of his honor, Deirdre unhesitatingly embraces it, directing the musicians to celebrate the felicity of her marriage, "knowing that all is happy, and that you know/ Within what bride-bed I shall lie this night,/ And by what man, and lie close up to him,/ For the bed's narrow, and there outsleep the cockcrow." Deirdre's last few thoughts include how she should rightfully be remembered, but Conchubar sinks into self-justification and paranoia.

Deirdre's act of heroism is an example of Yeats's notion of the dream, what Richard Ellman terms "the highest, most vigorous imaginative exercise." Whereas she has surrendered herself to a transcendent value, Conchubar, the dream's antagonist, has not. Yeats implies that Deirdre's ill-starred passion and the implacable demands of kingship are both extraordinary and irresistible and that both exact a total sacrifice of the self, a gift of one's individuality and character. Conchubar reneges on the obligations of kingship, recognizing only its prerogatives and powers. His selfishness, or his position within what Ellman categorizes as "the chaos of circumstances," overcomes him. Deirdre rises above it.

Yeats has written that in tragic art "one distinguishes devices to exclude or lessen character." By contrast, individuality belongs only to comedy. Conchubar makes a comical king only. It is a final flourish of *Deirdre*'s artfulness that in King Conchubar's acid insistence upon the appropriateness of his behavior, the audience can comprehend the scope of Deirdre's achievement in transcending hers by an act of selflessness and imagination.

Michael Scott Joseph

Bibliography:
Bushrui, S. B. *Yeats's Verse-Plays: The Revisions, 1900-1910.* Oxford, England: Clarendon Press, 1965. The most exhaustive treatment of *Deirdre*, covering all aspects of its composition and production. Bushrui's examination of Yeats's revisions strongly underscores the influence *Deirdre* continued to exert upon Yeats's imagination.

Jeffares, A. Norman, and A. S. Knowland. *A Commentary on the Collected Plays of W. B. Yeats.* New York: Macmillan, 1975. Provides detailed production information, including names of various casts of actors, performance dates, and a bibliography of printings of the play. Also includes useful literary background to the *dramatis personae* taken from analyses of traditional texts.

Knowland, A. S. *W. B. Yeats, Dramatist of Vision.* New York: Barnes & Noble Books, 1983. An inclusive study of Yeats's plays, in which one chapter offers an extended textual analysis. Readers might disagree with some of Knowland's dogmatic judgments, but his steady analysis is generally illuminating.

Taylor, Richard. *A Reader's Guide to the Plays of W. B. Yeats.* New York: Macmillan, 1984. Introductory essay that glosses the plot, characterization, construction, language, and stage imagery of *Deirdre.* Analyses of Yeats's other plays add to a broader knowledge of Yeats's aesthetic.

Ure, Peter. *Yeats, the Playwright: A Commentary on Character and Design in the Major Plays.* London: Routledge & Kegan Paul, 1963. A long, dense chapter on *Deirdre* engages the play on an intellectual level. Goes considerably beyond a concentration on character and design.

DEIRDRE OF THE SORROWS

Type of work: Drama
Author: John Millington Synge (1871-1909)
Type of plot: Tragedy
Time of plot: The past
Locale: Ireland
First performed: 1910; first published, 1910

Principal characters:
DEIRDRE, a heroine of Gaelic legend
NAISI, Deirdre's lover
CONCHUBOR, High King of Ulster
FERGUS, Conchubor's friend
LAVARCHAM, Deirdre's nurse
AINNLE and
ARDAN, Naisi's brothers
OWEN, Conchubor's attendant and spy

The Story:

King Conchubor had been keeping Deirdre, the beautiful young woman whom he had resolved to make his bride, at the home of Lavarcham, the old nurse, on Slieve Fuadh. One rainy evening, Conchubor and his friend Fergus arrived to find that Deirdre, to the king's displeasure, was still out gathering nuts and sticks in the woods. Lavarcham warned the king that Deirdre would not be anxious to see him, and she repeated the old prophecy that Deirdre had been born to bring destruction into the world. When Deirdre came in, the king presented her with rings and jewels and remonstrated with her for staying out in the woods. Deirdre defended her behavior and said that she had no desire to go to Emain to become queen.

Conchubor pleaded with her, talking of his loneliness, his love for her, and the rooms he had prepared for her in his castle at Emain. Deirdre insisted that in spite of the fact that she was pledged to Conchubor she would prefer to remain in the simple cottage with Lavarcham as long as possible. Conchubor, growing impatient, insisted that she be ready to go to Emain and become his queen within a few days.

After he left, Lavarcham urged Deirdre to be sensible and bend to Conchubor's wishes, but Deirdre kept talking about other defiant legendary heroines and about Naisi, and his brothers, the bravest men in the woods. Deirdre went to dress elegantly for one of the last nights of her freedom.

In the meantime Naisi and his brothers arrived at the cottage to take refuge from the storm. Lavarcham was not eager to let them in, but they claimed that a beautiful lady whom they had met in the woods had promised them refuge from the storm. They entered, but Lavarcham, sensing trouble, tried unsuccessfully to get rid of them. They were still in the room when Deirdre returned. Deirdre provided food for Ainnle and Ardan. When they left the cottage she asked Lavarcham to leave also. Alone with Naisi, she told him of Conchubor's imminent suit. Deeply in love by this time, they decided to marry and run away in spite of their knowledge of the troubles foretold. They asked Ainnle, who had returned to the cottage, to marry them before they fled into the night.

Seven years passed during which Deirdre and Naisi, with Ainnle and Ardan, lived happily beside the sea in Alban. One day Lavarcham arrived to announce that Fergus was on his way with peace offerings from King Conchubor and to plead with Deirdre to accept the king's offer. Deirdre insisted on her loyalty to Naisi. Owen, Conchubor's trusted man, arrived with word that Naisi and Fergus were already talking on the path below; he rudely advised Deirdre to leave Naisi and return to the king. Owen thought that seven years of love were more than enough and that Deirdre would one day be old and yearn for the comfort of the royal palace. Owen also revealed that he was jealous of Naisi and hated him because he had killed Owen's father some time before.

Fergus, on his arrival, said that Conchubor in his peace offering had invited Naisi and Deirdre back to Emain in peace. Naisi and Deirdre wondered if they should accept the offer. They talked of age, the possible death of love, and the happiness of their seven years, despite some difficult times, at Alban. They had experienced such perfect years, they decided to accept Conchubor's offer and return to Emain; they felt they would never know such complete happiness at Alban again. Owen returned, screaming that it was all a plot, and then ran out and split his head against a stone. Believing Owen mad, Naisi and Deirdre accepted Fergus' promise that no trick was involved, and they set out for Emain to meet Conchubor again.

Lavarcham, arriving first to speak with Conchubor, found him a lonely old man. After assuring the king that he could never gain Deirdre's love, she reported that Owen, despairing of ever gaining Deirdre, had run mad and destroyed himself. Conchubor's warriors arrived and reported that they had separated Naisi and Deirdre from Naisi's brothers. When Naisi and Deirdre arrived, they found themselves in a tent. A freshly-dug grave was concealed by curtains next to the tent. They spoke mournfully, for they strongly suspected a plot against them. Conchubor returned, welcomed them, and seemed, in spite of the evidence of the tent, the grave, and warriors lurking nearby, to mean his offer of peace seriously. Then, as he and Naisi were about to clasp hands of friendship, Naisi heard his brothers cry for help. Naisi started to leave, although Deirdre pleaded with him to stay. Naisi cursed the softness of women and ran out. The king's warriors killed Naisi as they had killed his brothers.

Conchubor urged Deirdre to end her mourning for Naisi and become his queen. Deirdre continued to lament and would have nothing to do with Conchubor. Fergus appeared and announced that he had burned Emain because the king had gone back on his pledge not to harm Naisi. Fergus, who had acted in good faith, tried to protect Deirdre, but Deirdre used Naisi's knife to commit suicide and join him in another world without defiling their love. After Deirdre's death, all mourned. Conchubor, old and broken, was led away by Lavarcham.

Critical Evaluation:

Deirdre of the Sorrows, John Millington Synge's last play, was not performed until after his death. The play deals with Irish legend, dramatizing an account of the beautiful Irish heroine who preferred death along with her lover to life as the wife of the king. The play is full of this romantic dedication, fully developed in Synge's rich Irish idiom. The language of the Irish peasant is given power and dignity as it is shaped into the tragic movement of the play. The play is also not without touches of humane characterization. The king is not simply a cruel ruler; he is also a sad and lonely man who deeply regrets the deaths he has caused. Naisi is not simply a martyred hero but also the husband who rants that his wife has caused him to be a softer man and allowed him to desert the ways of his brothers and his companions in arms. The play contains the rich warmth of Synge's local and distinctively Irish characterizations and the romantic quality of the legendary.

In spite of his relatively small output—four full-length plays and two one-acts—Synge is justly considered one of the finest dramatists of the modern stage and the Abbey Theatre's most important playwright prior to Sean O'Casey. Completed shortly before his death, but never revised to the author's complete satisfaction, *Deirdre of the Sorrows* can be seen as Synge's final statement on the joys of life, the possibilities, both good and bad, of love, and the inscrutability of human destiny.

The real strength of the play, and the thing that probably sets it apart from the many other dramatic versions of this famous Irish myth, comes from the way Synge combines an austere mood of classic, almost Grecian tragedy with characterizations that are immediate, human, and sympathetic. Deirdre first impresses the audience as a flighty young woman who chases in the woods gathering twigs and nuts with little concern for her future queenly role. Her initial reaction to King Conchubor's demand for immediate marriage is to beg, like a petulant child, for more time. Almost immediately, however, her mature, defiant, inner strength asserts itself. Faced with Conchubor's implacability, she grows into maturity almost instantly: "From this day," she tells her old nurse Lavarcham, "I will turn the men of Ireland like a wind blowing on the heath." She then dons her royal regalia, assuming the status of a queen, and, by giving herself without hesitation to Naisi, unflinchingly accepts the doom foretold for her. Yet, for all of her tragic grandeur, the girlish element in her character remains evident throughout.

Likewise, the other principal characters contain aspects of both the tragic and the mundane. Naisi is heroic and passionate, willing to risk exile and death for the love of Deirdre. He is also irritable, impulsive, and occasionally inconsistent. Toward the end of the play he admits to Fergus: "I've had dreams of getting old and weary, and losing my delight in Deirdre."

Conchubor is also pictured as a mixture of the grand and the petty. On the one hand he establishes himself as a ferocious king, given to extremes of heroism and violence. His desire for Deirdre is intense, and his plans for her are grandiose. The strength of his feelings are evidenced by the lengths to which he is willing to go to secure her, including the destruction of his own kingdom, and by the vengeful rage that is aroused against those who stand in his way, especially Naisi and his brothers. At the same time he is a pitiful old man desperately denying the effects of time and clinging to an image of himself as virile by taking a young and beautiful wife. "There's one sorrow has no end surely," he tells Deirdre, "that's being old and lonesome."

This powerful merging of the heroic and the human reaches its dramatic peak in the scene in which the lovers separate forever. Deirdre believes that the only way they can escape inevitable disillusionment and acrimony in their passion is to give themselves up to Conchubor's vengeance, thereby avoiding the slower, but more painful ravages of time. Naisi agrees because he, too, sees that their passion has spent itself, their youth is fading, and the price of their destiny must be paid. "It should be a poor thing to see great lovers and they sleepy and old." At the moment of parting, however, they have a bitter, petty squabble. Thus, their deaths represent not a victory of passion over fate, but a concession to human imperfection, even in the most noble of characters.

Deirdre of the Sorrows represented a change in direction for Synge. He had previously avoided Irish myth on purpose, feeling it to be unrealistic and irrelevant. What further directions he would have taken had he lived can only be left to conjecture.

Bibliography:
Kopper, Edward A., Jr., ed. *A J. M. Synge Literary Companion.* Westport, Conn.: Greenwood Press, 1988. A valuable collection of sixteen chapters by leading scholars, covering all aspects of Synge's life and work. Excellent introduction to the critical literature. Good bibliographies.

Price, Alan. *Synge and Anglo-Irish Drama*. London: Methuen, 1961. Extensive discussion of this play as a transformation of Irish legend and as the embodiment of Synge's persistent themes. Contrasts the play favorably with those of Synge's contemporaries, calling it "perhaps the finest thing Synge ever wrote."

Saddlemyer, Ann. "Deirdre of the Sorrows: Literature First. . . . Drama Afterwards." In *J. M. Synge: Centenary Papers 1971*. Edited by Maurice Harmon. Dublin: Dolmen, 1972. Focuses on Synge's blend of myth and characterization within his theory of art and drama. Traces the roots of this play to Synge's interest in music, Jean Racine, and life on the Aran Islands.

Synge, J. M. *J. M. Synge: Collected Works*. Vol. 2, edited by Alan Price. New York: Oxford University Press, 1968. Scholarly edition, providing the biographical context of Synge's last two years, when this play was being written. Contains a transcription of his worksheets, draft manuscripts, and related notebook entries.

Thornton, Weldon. *J. M. Synge and the Western Mind*. New York: Barnes & Noble Books, 1979. Argues that the play is resistant to heroic stereotypes of Celtic myth and presents Deirdre and Naisi as motivated by common needs and fears. Thus, the play is more psychologically complex than the mythic plays of his contemporaries.

DELIA

Type of work: Poetry
Author: Samuel Daniel (1562?-1619)
First published: 1592

    The evidently unauthorized publication of a portion of Samuel Daniel's sonnet sequence *Delia* in 1591, as part of Sir Philip Sidney's *Astrophil and Stella*, marked the introduction of the perfected version of a major poetic form that, within a few years, had become one of the dominant methods of expression in English poetry. While Daniel may be relatively unknown in comparison to Sidney, Edmund Spenser, or William Shakespeare, with *Delia*, first published in complete form in 1592, he became one of the important contributors to the development and growth of English poetry, and he remains a central figure in Elizabethan intellectual life.

    One of the most notable features about the English Renaissance is the extremely rapid intellectual, cultural, and artistic development of the period. Two of the major cultural and artistic accomplishments of the English Renaissance, the blank verse play and the sonnet sequence, were innovations that were introduced relatively suddenly and perfected rapidly. The forms, once available, were utilized by artists ranging across the full intellectual spectrum, and, within a single generation, often within a period of a few years, English authors produced enduring masterpieces in both forms.

    For example, *Gorboduc* (1561), by Thomas Sackville and Thomas Norton, is credited with being the first English play written in blank verse; it also served as the prototype for the five-act, multiple-scene play. *Gorboduc* spurred other writers to present a variety of plays ranging from tragedy to comedy to history. English literature reached a peak in its development by being exposed to a new and powerful method of presenting dramatic action.

    Fairly soon after its initial production, *Gorboduc* was accorded mainly historical interest and its style and stagecraft considered rudimentary and crude; still, it was an important step forward, and within thirty years the genre had developed to the point that Christopher Marlowe and Shakespeare could write their masterpieces. The relatively crude beginning present in *Gorboduc* was rapidly explored and exploited.

    A similarly rapid development and fruition took place with the sonnet sequence. The sonnet originally developed on the continent of Europe, with writers such as Petrarch and his followers fixing the major themes, forms, and poetic devices. Spreading throughout Europe, the sonnet convention gained additional refinements from French poets such as Joachim Du Bellay before gaining English attention in the early part of the sixteenth century, when Sir Thomas Wyatt introduced the form into English literature. Achieving limited circulation in manuscript form during Wyatt's life (although Wyatt seems to have planned to publish), his sonnets first saw wide distribution when they were printed in 1557 in a volume known as Tottel's *Miscellany*. Tottel's *Miscellany*, a collection of over 250 poems by various writers, was to become one of the most significant contributions to English literature; its value was not so much in its own excellence, but in the development that it inspired in other writers.

    Between 1580 and 1583, the Elizabethan courtier and soldier Sir Philip Sidney turned to the sonnet form and produced *Astrophil and Stella*, the first of the great Elizabethan sonnet sequences. Purposefully unpublished during Sidney's brief lifetime, *Astrophil and Stella* was first printed in 1591 in an unauthorized edition by the printer and publisher Thomas Newman. In addition to Sidney's sonnet sequence, the volume Newman published included twenty-eight additional sonnets by Samuel Daniel; these sonnets were the core of Daniel's own sonnet cycle,

Delia. In this fashion, two of the most influential works of this particular genre were made public. This was appropriate, for Daniel was an admirer of Sidney's poetic style, and was associated with Sidney's sister, Mary, Countess of Pembroke.

Unlike Sidney, who had adhered to the older custom of being reluctant to publish his work, once Newman had issued the pirated edition, Daniel was ready to provide the reading public with the authentic version of *Delia.* In 1592, Daniel published *Delia* as an independent volume, adding four additional poems and revising others. He continued to revise and republish the work throughout the 1590's, adding new sonnets, removing older poems, and revising others. The 1594 edition of *Delia* had fifty-five sonnets, twenty-three of them from Newman's earlier edition. In 1601, Daniel produced his most thoroughgoing revision, which left the work in substantially the form in which it is best known. Significantly, as proof of the enduring relationship between Daniel and the Sidney circle, the book was dedicated to the Countess of Pembroke.

While *Astrophil and Stella* is undoubtedly the greater of the two sonnet cycles, *Delia* is itself an outstanding example of the genre, and one of the finest and most influential produced during the Elizabethan period. In its story, themes, imagery, structure, and language it follows the particular and often quite rigorous conventions that governed how the Elizabethans believed sonnet sequences should be written.

The story of *Delia*, as with so many other sonnet sequences dating back to Petrarch, is that of unrequited love. The author of the sonnets, who need not be closely or literally identified with Daniel himself, is in despair; his beloved scorns him, preferring another suitor. The lover has tried every means he can conceive of to win the beloved's heart, but she remains as adamant as she is indifferent. In the end, there is little hope except that his poems will endure as testimony to her cruelty and his faithful love.

Some critics and scholars have sought to read into this generic setting a real situation in which Daniel himself loved and was rejected. There is a reason, or perhaps rather an excuse, for such an interpretation because Sidney's sequence in *Astrophil and Stella* alludes to his love for Penelope, Lady Rich. In Daniel's case, there is little evidence to support a real-life counterpart to his poetic misery; it would seem, instead, to be a case of the poet's following the conceits of the genre, nothing more.

In *Delia*, Daniel helps to establish the themes and imagery that rapidly came to dominate the majority of Elizabethan and sonnet sequences. His sonnets contain numerous references to classical mythology; insistent appeals to natural history as a source of moral lessons; and frequent reminders of the transitory quality of beauty, in particular the beauty of Delia, which, along with all mortal things, however lovely, is doomed to decay. This last theme was to become a central motif in later sonnet sequences, including Shakespeare's.

Daniel was a talented and conscientious craftsman, and *Delia* is structured in such a way that the individual sonnets flow from one to the other, giving a sense of organic unity and progress; the story, such as it is, is made to have sense and coherence and seems to be moving forward, even if that motion is toward an unhappy ending. Daniel frequently uses the device of sharing themes, images, and words between sonnets, thereby linking them together.

An example of this is found in sonnets 32 through 35, in which Daniel concentrates on the transitory nature of beauty, using the imagery of flowers, spring, and summer, all of which fade and give way to weeds and winter. The words "winter" and "flowers" are found throughout this particular section of the sequence.

In some cases, Daniel repeats words and phrases from one sonnet to the next. Sonnet 24, for example, ends with the line, "Reign in my thoughts, my love and life are thine," and sonnet 25 opens: "Reign in my thoughts, fair hand, sweet eye, rare voice." Sonnet 42 finishes with the thought that "women grieve to think they must be old," while the next poem opens with the poet reminding himself, "I must not grieve my Love."

Daniel's use of language is fluent and dignified, avoiding the feigned antique language of Edmund Spenser and the vigorously colloquial style of Thomas Nashe. Perhaps because of his association with the Sidney circle, Daniel was highly conscious of the ideal of poetic decorum, especially in language, which was greatly esteemed in the earlier years of the Elizabethan Renaissance. His word choice is restrained, and his images are carefully chosen. His images are often based on mythological sources. The opening lines of his most famous sonnet from the sequence displays both qualities:

> Care-charmer sleep, son of the sable night,
> Brother to death, in silent darkness borne:
> Relieve my languish, and restore the light,
> With dark forgetting of my care's return.

This verse, fluent and flowing, shows Daniel's work in *Delia* at its best, and helps explain how and why this sequence played such an important role in the development of English literature. The ability to use the sonnet form to comment on complex emotional feelings and intellectual concepts became a recognized possibility with the publication of Sidney's *Astrophil and Stella* and Daniel's *Delia*. Daniel's sonnets helped to establish the Elizabethan sonnet as a versatile and powerful instrument of English poetry.

Daniel's impact on the literature of his time was important and undeniable. The numerous editions of *Delia* that came in rapid succession clearly indicate a considerable popularity for the sequence; this popularity helps to explain the vogue for the sonnet sequence, which rapidly exerted great power over the English literary scene. Daniel was one of the first to produce, in perfect form, a genre in which English writers could write in a new and sophisticated fashion. The emotional, rhetorical, and intellectual versatility of the sonnet form provided English literature with a vehicle that it subsequently used to express some of its most profound and moving thoughts.

Michael Witkoski

Bibliography:
Lewis, C. S. *English Literature in the Sixteenth Century, Excluding Drama*. New York: Oxford University Press, 1954. Still one of the best surveys of the literature of this period of the English Renaissance and an excellent starting place. The comments on Daniel are informative and enlightening.
Rees, Joan. *Samuel Daniel: A Critical and Biographical Study*. Liverpool, England: Liverpool University Press, 1964. The standard modern biography of Daniel. Provides insight into Daniel's sonnets, especially those in *Delia*.
Seronsy, Cecil. *Samuel Daniel*. New York: Twayne, 1967. A fine introductory volume on Daniel, providing an overview of his life and works. Excellent background discussions on the period, including the political and intellectual currents of the time.
Sprague, Arthur Colby. Introduction to *Poems and A Defence of Ryme*, by Samuel Daniel. Chicago: University of Chicago Press, 1965. A brief but useful review of *Delia*, placing it within the context of Daniel's career.

Ure, Peter. "Two Elizabethan Poets: Daniel and Ralegh." In *The Age of Shakespeare*, edited by Boris Ford. Rev. ed. New York: Penguin Books, 1982. An excellent comparison of two highly accomplished poets of the period, which introduces the reader to a sense of the social, intellectual, and artistic standards of the period.

A DELICATE BALANCE

Type of work: Drama
Author: Edward Albee (1928-   )
Type of plot: Absurdist
Time of plot: October, in the mid-1960's
Locale: The living room of a large and well-appointed suburban house
First performed: 1966; first published, 1967

Principal characters:
AGNES, a handsome woman in her late fifties
TOBIAS, her husband, a few years older
CLAIRE, Agnes' sister, several years younger
JULIA, Agnes and Tobias' daughter, thirty-six years old
EDNA and
HARRY, friends of Agnes and Tobias, very much like them

The Story:

Agnes and Tobias, an affluent elderly couple married for about forty years, sipped after-dinner drinks in their living room one autumnal Friday evening. They chatted pleasantly about Agnes' persistent belief that she might one day easily go mad. Agnes' younger sister Claire came down from her room to apologize for an embarrassing incident she had caused during dinner and was severely rebuked by Agnes for her drunkenness. Agnes then went to telephone her daughter Julia, who lived some distance away. Left alone with Claire, Tobias inquired about her previous experiences with Alcoholics Anonymous. She explained that she felt alienated at those meetings and, after relating a bitter anecdote about herself, insisted that she was not an alcoholic because she drank willfully. Agnes returned, informing them that Julia was leaving her husband and would come home immediately. She reproached Tobias for having failed to admonish his daughter appropriately following her three previous divorces, and he responded by telling a story about a cat he had once owned that had stopped liking him for no apparent reason; when his efforts to regain his pet's affection failed, he had had it euthanized.

While Agnes and Claire comforted him, unexpected guests arrived. Harry and Edna, close friends for forty years, had felt uneasy and distressed at home alone. Pressed to explain, they related that after dinner they had suddenly become strangely frightened, for no particular reason. They could no longer endure remaining alone in their house. Agnes offered them Julia's room for the night, and they retired. Claire suggested that she knew exactly what had happened.

Saturday evening before dinner, Agnes tried to calm Julia, who was angry about the intruders who had remained locked in her former bedroom all day. Agnes casually described a psycho-analytical study she was reading about the reversal of sex roles in American society. Feigning the attitude of a father when Tobias entered, Agnes left Julia to be counseled by Tobias. Father and daughter merely quibbled and argued about her three previous marriages until Claire interrupted them to tell about her unsuccessful attempt to buy a topless bathing suit at a local department store. An antagonistic conversation ensued between the three. It continued until Agnes joined them for cocktails and reported that Harry and Edna had earlier requested sandwiches to be brought to their room. Julia explained that she had left her husband because of his insupportable negative attitudes. Harry and Edna came down, announcing that they were going home to get their things and would return after dinner.

Julia upbraided her mother for prohibiting any discussion of serious matters during dinner. Agnes claimed merely to have been keeping the family "in shape" on uneven ground by maintaining a reasonable balance among all the elements. Claire came in with an accordion but was persuaded not to play it. After the sisters exchanged sarcastic remarks concerning their sexual histories, they all discussed whether to permit the unwelcome guests to remain any longer. While Agnes and Tobias greeted their returning friends, Claire and Julia discussed this awkward situation. When Edna entered the room, Julia expressed her hostility quite openly, but Edna insisted that she had some rights. Julia then blocked access to the sideboard, preventing Harry from mixing drinks. Growing hysterical at the persistence of their demands, she ran screaming from the room. Tobias returned and was giving an account of Julia's continuing fit of hysteria upstairs when Julia entered with a pistol and ordered her father to expel the unwanted guests immediately. Tobias disarmed her, and while Edna was explaining that long-term friendship had given them the right to live there, Agnes led her daughter up to bed. Harry and Edna retired, along with Claire, leaving Tobias alone in the living room.

Early Sunday morning, as Tobias sat awake, Agnes came down. They discussed the changes their marriage had undergone over the years. Tobias explained that he had thought through their present dilemma during the night but, when pressed by his wife for his decision, he begged her advice. She refused, insisting that he, firmly supported by his family, should assert his authority. She reminded him of past occasions when he had failed to do so. Claire and Julia served coffee and orange juice, and Claire openly spiked her juice with vodka. They discussed their situation, Agnes pointing out that their guests had brought a disease, a plague of sorts, with them. She left it to Tobias to decide whether to permit the guests to remain.

Harry and Edna came down. Left alone by the women, Tobias and Harry had drinks. Harry explained that, were their positions reversed, he would not let unwanted guests stay in his house. Tobias, becoming emotional and eventually hysterical, insisted that Harry and Edna remain, though he confessed that he did not honestly want them to.

The women returned. Overhearing Tobias imploring Harry to stay, Edna requested that their bags be brought down so that they might leave. Julia joined Claire in a drink as the couples said good-bye. After Harry and Edna's departure, the three women praised Tobias for handling the situation effectively. Agnes pleasantly noted the possible danger of having three early-morning drinkers in the house.

Critical Evaluation:

The success of Edward Albee's first play, *The Zoo Story* (1959), was followed by that of *The American Dream* (1961) and the controversial *Who's Afraid of Virginia Woolf?* (1962). *A Delicate Balance*, a more restrained work, was awarded a Pulitzer Prize in drama in 1967, a distinction also bestowed upon *Seascape* in 1976 and *Three Tall Women* in 1994. Disliking literary labels, Albee has reluctantly identified himself as an eclectic, with dramatic roots extending as deeply into the plays of Anton Chekhov and Eugene O'Neill as into those of Samuel Beckett and Tennessee Williams. His plays generally deal with people's attempts to make sense for themselves of their senseless position in a senseless world. The plays work effectively largely through their rich verbal texture. Albee possesses an extraordinary ear for the inflections and rhythms of speech and writes lines that are essentially musical in their flow: Voices echo and answer themselves and one another like instruments of different timbres engaged in playing a chamber composition. This highly complex counterpoint of convoluted sentences set against robust American colloquialisms is filled with black humor, comic irony, and tragic sarcasm.

A Delicate Balance concerns the failure of relationships among family members and their closest friends. Albee's theme is that people often thoughtlessly espouse superficial values that later trap them into maintaining insincere relationships. Adjusting to appearances rather than to reality, they suffer through serious failures in communication and eventually lose any possibility of finding any gratifying emotional fulfillment. Evasions in the guise of "making do" and "making it work" enable the four principal characters in the play to pretend to themselves and to one another that their family is a happy one, or at least quite average, because their relationships appear similar to those prevailing in many other families around them. When forced eventually to examine their fantasy worlds honestly, they discover them to be empty and meaningless, and they are left alone, deprived of their illusions, with some new and difficult truths to face and ponder—or reject.

Agnes has established and controls a smooth surface of routine and habit in order to cover the web of interlocking illusions and self-deceptions that prevail in the minds of the other family members. This routine excludes honest self-awareness in the characters as well as sincere emotional responses in their interactions with others. Agnes tolerates the presence of her alcoholic sister in her home but never tries to understand her; Tobias gently chides his daughter for her failed marriages but ignores her unhappiness; and Agnes and Tobias live amicably together but lack deep emotional bonds. Julia tells her father that her indifference to him appeared during her adolescence, when she first perceived his withdrawal of affection from her. Claire, who alone sees reality clearly, drowns her perceptive insights in alcohol because she finds them too distressing to endure, but she sometimes blurts them out in lightning-quick flashes of sarcastic or sardonic wit. These humorous remarks provide comic relief while at the same time supplying an outsider's view of the activities of the other characters.

Harry and Edna, a couple "very much like Agnes and Tobias," have similarly devised a workable routine to fill the spiritual void hidden at the heart of their existence. When, becoming old, they perceive the imminent approach of death, they are struck with terror by the emptiness of lives based on appearances alone, without any deeply rooted values or sincere feelings to sustain them. This is the "plague" they bring with them to their friends' home—an awareness of their failure to become the persons they might have been, to have loved as they might have loved had they dared to commit themselves to the arduous quest for reality, accepting the pain and sorrow that truth brings with it as the price to be paid for spiritual progress.

The sudden awareness of emptiness that shattered the habitual, comfortable complacency prevailing in the lives of Harry and Edna could well have proved contagious to the mirror couple with whom they sought refuge, because the same void fills the house of Agnes and Tobias, although they have not yet acknowledged its presence. When Tobias must decide whether to allow these friends to reside in his house, he confronts the dilemma of illusion versus reality in his own life: To reject them would be to admit that they had wasted forty years in maintaining a pseudo-friendship based primarily on proximity rather than on affection. Because he cannot bring himself to face this terrible reality, he implores them to stay. Harry, who has already looked deeply into the void, now knows better and rejects Tobias' insincere plea.

The play ends with no definitive resolution, though alternative possible endings are suggested. The pain of failure in a relationship is hard for Tobias to bear. It is something he has always avoided; having failed years before, for example, to regain the affection of his cat, he had her killed. He has now endured an ordeal by fire and could emerge from it purified. He might yet advance to become a truly loving husband and father. Julia joins Claire for a drink, which suggests that she may adopt her aunt's solution of seeking oblivion to escape her problems. Agnes greets the morning sun ambiguously: A new era may now begin for them all, or the sunlight may illuminate merely a continued repetition of the routine that governed them in the past. The outcome appears unfavorable. Agnes observes pessimistically near the end of the last act, "[Y]ou wait; and time happens. When you *do* go, sword . . . shield . . . finally . . . there's nothing there . . . save rust; bones; and the wind."

Raymond M. Archer

Bibliography:
Amacher, Richard E. *Edward Albee.* Rev. ed. Boston: Twayne, 1982. A fine overview of Albee's plays and career. Considers the influence of the Theater of the Absurd on Albee's work.

Bigsby, C. W. E. *Albee.* Edinburgh, Scotland: Oliver & Boyd, 1969. Identifies Albee's liberal humanistic and existential concerns. An excellent analysis of Albee's thought, with a perceptive discussion of *A Delicate Balance.*

Paolucci, Anne. *From Tension to Tonic: The Plays of Edward Albee.* Carbondale: Southern Illinois University Press, 1972. One of the most insightful studies available. Focuses on Albee's use of language, especially metaphor and irony. Contains a chapter on *A Delicate Balance.*

Roudané, Matthew. *Understanding Edward Albee.* Columbia: University of South Carolina Press, 1987. An excellent starting point for the study of Albee's work. Traces the development of his affirmative existential vision.

Rutenberg, Michael E. *Edward Albee: Playwright in Protest.* New York: DBS, 1969. Written with Albee's cooperation. Concentrates on political and social dimensions of Albee's work. Contains two interviews and an interesting analysis of *A Delicate Balance* from a sociological point of view.

DELIVERANCE

Type of work: Novel
Author: James Dickey (1923-   )
Type of plot: Bildungsroman
Time of plot: Late twentieth century
Locale: Georgia
First published: 1970

Principal characters:
ED, a bored suburbanite
LEWIS, Ed's best friend, a survivalist
DREW, an executive for a soft-drink company
BOBBY, an insurance salesman
TWO MOUNTAIN MEN, who attack Ed and Bobby in the woods

The Story:

Lewis Medlock, Ed Gentry, Drew Ballinger, and Bobby Trippe were four men who decided to canoe a river in north Georgia before it was dammed. Lewis promised them an enjoyable time away from the pressures and routine of the city. The four men spent September 14 on the river and had the type of day that Lewis had promised. The next morning Ed agreed to take Bobby in his canoe since Lewis was frustrated with Bobby's ineptness and weakness.

Ed and Bobby stopped to rest on the bank since they were tired and, ironically, were well ahead of Lewis and Drew. Two men stepped out of the woods, one of them trailing a shotgun by the barrel. One man was taller and seemed to be toothless, and the shorter man had white stubble on his face and a stomach that fell through his overalls. In an attempt to pacify these mountain men, Ed told them that he and Bobby were not government agents looking for a still and would even be interested in buying some moonshine from them if they had it. This comment seemed to set something in motion for the mountain men, and they took Ed and Bobby at gunpoint deeper into the woods. The tall, lean man tied Ed to a tree with Ed's own belt and then turned to Bobby. While the tall man held the gun, the white-bearded man sodomized Bobby. They turned then to Ed and decided that he would perform oral sex on the tall man. As they exchanged the gun an arrow appeared in the middle of the tall man's chest. Lewis and Drew had come upon the scene quietly, having heard Bobby's screams, and Lewis had drawn his bow on the tall man and waited for an opportunity to let the arrow fly. The tall man died, and the white-bearded man ran off into the woods and disappeared. Drew wanted to take the body to the sheriff, but Lewis wanted to bury it in the woods because the area would be covered with water soon. The men voted with Ed because they thought his way was the least complicated for their present and future lives. They buried the man and the shotgun deep in the woods and got back on the river to go home.

Drew and Ed were paddling together in the first canoe when Drew fell out. This spill caused the other canoe to turn over in the rapids, and everyone swam for his life. The wooden canoe was broken in half, leaving only the aluminum canoe. Lewis' leg was broken as well, and Drew could not be found. Lewis told Ed and Bobby that Drew had been shot from the top of the cliff. Ed understood then that the white-bearded man was on top of the cliff waiting for them to head out in the canoe so that he could kill them. Ed realized that, in order for them to survive, he had to climb the cliff and kill the mountain man. He spent a good part of the night of September 15 climbing the cliff with his bow and arrow. He hid in a tree at the top, and, when the white-bearded man appeared at the top of the cliff, Ed shot him with an arrow. He fell out of the tree after the shot and his other arrow pierced his side. He lowered the mountain man's body down the cliff and buried it in the river.

That morning, September 16, Ed, Bobby, and Lewis started back down the river in the aluminum canoe. Before long, they saw Drew's body backed up against the rocks. He apparently had been shot. They buried his body in the river, also as a way of avoiding legal complications, and continued toward Aintry.

Once they returned, they had the problem of explaining to the authorities what had happened. They told the police that they had spilled from their canoes farther down the river than they actually did so that the police would not look for the bodies where they were. They also said that Drew had drowned in that spill. One deputy did not believe them and thought that they had come upon his brother-in-law, who had been missing. The police dragged the river where Ed had told them to and came up with nothing. Ed and Bobby drove home while Lewis stayed in the hospital because of his leg.

Ed lied to Drew's wife, telling her the same story he told the police. He never told his wife anything and lived in fear, for a while, of headlights in the night. Lewis and Ed eventually bought cabins on another lake and practiced their archery there, keeping secret the fact that they had buried three men in two days.

Critical Evaluation:

After the publication of *Deliverance* in 1970 and the release of the film in 1972, public response and critical response took opposite turns. If best-seller status and box-office records are any indication of how a public appreciates a work of literary or cinematic art, then *Deliverance* was a huge success. The initial critical response, however, was less than kind. Most critics compared James Dickey's novel with his earlier poetry and found the novel severely lacking. The film suffered a similar fate at the hands of reviewers who, predictably enough, often compared it to the novel and found the film superficial and lacking in psychological depth. Time has shown, however, that the critics might have been premature in shelving this novel under "popular fiction" or some other rubric that denotes literature offered to the masses and not worth taking seriously. In fact, this novel is one of the most profound examples of bridging popular fiction with a literary tradition, which in this case is Romanticism and mythology.

Most of the readings of *Deliverance* see traditional mythological elements at work, whether it be romantic appropriations of nature or Jungian archetypes and images of rebirth. Dickey has stated that the literary and mythological precedent for the novel comes from a review of books on mythology that he read in college. He remarks that he was especially interested in the concepts of rites of passage, in which initiates undergo a separation from their everyday world. Initiates enter a special source of power in another world, and then a life-enhancing return to that everyday world. One book that Dickey knew of was Joseph Campbell's *The Hero with a Thousand Faces*, and Campbell understands the three stages of normal world, the special world, and return as elements of all hero myths.

Ed is the main character and the hero who undergoes trials and tests, ultimately facing his own death, in order to bring meaning back to his world. Ed's everyday world is meaningless, full of the bad art that he produces for money as a graphic artist and empty of anything worthy of painting. Ed is bored, and this boredom pervades every part of his life, from his work to his archery to his home life. The world that Ed inhabits is filled with artificiality, like the paper deer he shoots at the archery range. Lewis' call to run the river offers Ed the opportunity to get out of his routine, if only for a weekend, and to experience something different, something that would soon be lost.

The nature of Ed's transformation is heroic, and thus sexual, psychological, and mythological. He encounters the earth goddess in the form of sheer cliff that he climbs in the middle of the night. This particular example of the earth presents two contradictory attributes to him. At times she seems to want to throw him off the cliff; at other times she offers him handholds from what seems to be a flat surface. As he climbs the wall, Ed's feeling of intimacy toward it grows. He describes his movements as more sensual than any sexual experience he has had.

Following an Oedipal theme, the meeting with the figure of mother earth is followed by confrontation with the father, who is represented by the man on top of the cliff. The father figure is a particularly violent one. In fact, the father is the archetypal enemy, symbolizing to the unconscious all of life's enemies. The hero must engage the father in battle, which will result in the shattering of the hero's ego and perhaps the loss of his life. Ed reflects on his unity with the mountain man, thinking so long and hard about the man on the cliff that he believes that their minds fuse in the moonlight. When Ed's arrow finds its mark and the man on the cliff dies, the mythological process is at its climactic point. The two men are one, and the world is one. All dualities are transcended; therefore, as Ed's arrow of death hits its target, his other arrow pierces Ed's flesh, "the flesh that age and inactivity were beginning to load on me." This is Ed's symbolic death. He has killed the part of him that civilization has created. Pierced by his own arrow, Ed is now complete. His limited ego-vision has been replaced by a mystical realization and experience of the one.

What Ed brings back to the everyday world from this journey is personal; what he brings back brings no boon to the world at large. Rather, his experience exists as a trace, a meaning that is never fully present but exists as a line where the unconscious once made its mark. All that is left in Ed's world are such traces of the mythical. He maintains this trace, for example, in his art, which after his return has rivers running through it. Overall, Ed's experience of return is that his life returns to something like normal. Once the river is dammed (the pun is clearly intended) he can "sleep as deeply as Drew was sleeping." Ed's experience has indeed been life-changing, but the change continues to be buried further and further under the pressure of the artificiality of everyday life. This pressure continually forces Ed's experience deeper and threatens to eliminate it altogether. Rather than resolve this tension between the influence of the mythical journey and the pressure of the everyday world to force it out of existence, Dickey leaves it unresolved. We are left doubting not only that Ed will be experiencing any more adventures, but also whether or not there will be space left for the taking of such adventures. Sacred space is disappearing, and, as Lewis might say, one ought to get up there and see it before it is gone.

Gregory Salyer

Bibliography:
Doughtie, Edward. "Art and Nature in *Deliverance.*" *Southwest Review* 64 (Spring, 1979): 167-180. An exploration of how the arts serve a mediating function in the novel. Argues that art helps negotiate the important boundaries between nature, human nature, and civilization.
Endel, Peggy Goodman. "Dickey, Dante, and the Demonic: Reassessing *Deliverance.*" *American Literature* 60 (December, 1988): 611-624. Endel offers a sophisticated and cogent reading of the novel in the light of Dante Alighieri's *Inferno* and demonstrates how Dickey

has created a presentation of unsublimated evil after the fashion of Dante and against the romantic sublime.

Foust, R. E. *"Tactus Eruditus*: Phenomenology as Method and Meaning of James Dickey's *Deliverance.*" *Studies in American Fiction* 9 (Autumn, 1981): 199-216. One of the most original interpretations of *Deliverance*. It focuses on the creative tensions in the novel and presents a "postmodern" reading, which in this case means a phenomenological and structural interpretation that centers on the characters' sense of touch. Foust also points out the problems of romantic readings of *Deliverance*.

Jolly, John. "Drew Ballinger as 'Sacrificial God' in James Dickey's *Deliverance.*" *South Carolina Review* 17 (Spring, 1985): 102-108. A mythical reading that centers not on Ed or Lewis but on Drew's affinity to the Orpheus figure in Greek mythology.

Strong, Paul. "James Dickey's Arrow of Deliverance." *South Carolina Review* 11 (1978): 108-116. Focusing on Ed's self-wounding, Strong offers an interpretation of that event and others in the light of the observations of Swiss psychologist Carl Jung.

DELPHINE

Type of work: Novel
Author: Madame de Staël (1766-1817)
Type of plot: Epistolary
Time of plot: Late eighteenth century
Locale: France
First published: 1802 (English translation, 1803)

Principal characters:

DELPHINE D'ALBEMAR, a rich, talented young widow
MATILDA DE VERNON, her kinswoman and daughter of Madame de Vernon
MADAME DE VERNON, Delphine's close friend and confidante
LÉONCE MONDEVILLE, Matilda de Vernon's fiancé
MADAME D'ERVIN, a friend of Delphine
MONSIEUR DE SERBELLANE, Madame d'Ervin's lover
MONSIEUR DE VALORBE, Delphine's beloved

The Story:

Delphine d'Albemar was a rich young widow who had been married to her guardian after her father's death. Her husband, who had been her tutor in childhood, had instilled in her the best of sentiments and virtues. As a result of her education, however, she did not wish to submit to the dogmas of society or church. Although she was a member of the French nobility, she was a believer in revolutionary doctrine, a dangerous way of thinking in France during the years immediately preceding the French Revolution. In addition, she, unlike most women of her time and position, refused to let men do her thinking for her. After her husband's death, which occurred when she was twenty years old, Delphine was emotionally, intellectually, and financially independent.

Shortly after her husband's death, Delphine proposed giving away a large part of her fortune to Matilda, a relative of her husband and the daughter of Delphine's close friend, Madame de Vernon. Despite the warnings of Mademoiselle d'Albemar, Delphine's sister-in-law, that Madame de Vernon was a very treacherous person, the gift was made so that Matilda could marry Léonce Mondeville, a Spanish nobleman. No one had met Léonce Mondeville, for the marriage had been arranged by Matilda's mother, a longtime friend of the proposed bridegroom's mother.

When Mondeville arrived in Paris, he met his future wife and Delphine. Much to Delphine's dismay, she fell in love with him and he with her. To Delphine, who had bestowed on Matilda the fortune which was making the marriage possible, it seemed that fate had played its worst trick of irony. For a time, it seemed as if the two lovers might find a way out of the difficulty. As her confidante in the problem, Delphine took Matilda's own mother, Madame de Vernon. Matilda's mother had no intention of allowing so advantageous a match to slip through her and her daughter's fingers, and she plotted to turn Mondeville against Delphine.

Meanwhile, Delphine had been aiding Madame d'Ervin in a love affair with Monsieur de Serbellane. Because de Serbellane was seen going into Delphine's house late at night, scandal linked her name with his, although he had actually gone there to see Madame d'Ervin. A short time later, Madame d'Ervin's husband surprised the two lovers in Delphine's home. When de Serbellane killed the husband in a duel, scandal named Delphine as the woman in the case.

Delphine, desiring to keep her friend's honor, did not relate the true cause of the quarrel that had precipitated the duel. Anxious to clear herself with Mondeville, however, Delphine asked Madame de Vernon to act as her friend. Instead of telling what had really happened, the older woman told him that Delphine and de Serbellane were lovers and that Delphine was about to leave France to join de Serbellane in Italy.

Mondeville prepared to marry Matilda, although he did not love her. Although Delphine realized that someone had misrepresented her to her lover, she could find no way to prevent the marriage. Only after the marriage had taken place did Delphine learn that Madame de Vernon's duplicity had caused the rift between herself and Mondeville. At that time, anxious not to hurt Matilda, Delphine promised herself not to see Mondeville and to try to forget her passion for him. Unfortunately, they continued to love each other greatly. A few months later, Madame de Vernon, on her deathbed, confessed her guilt.

Feeling themselves cheated, the lovers decided to continue seeing each other, although their course was dangerous to their honor and unfair to Matilda. Society was soon whispering that Delphine and Mondeville were lovers. Actually, there was nothing immoral in their affair, but society assumed the worst. De Valorbe, a friend of Delphine's late husband, learned of the state of affairs and resolved to marry her in order to remove her from a compromising situation. His intention aroused Mondeville's jealousy, although Delphine protested that she did not love de Valorbe and would never marry him. One night, de Valorbe went to Delphine's house in the hope that she would hide him from the police. Mondeville saw him there and challenged him to a duel. De Valorbe, hoping to escape from the country before he was imprisoned on political charges, refused to fight. A witness stirred up the scandal once again. Soon everyone believed that the two men had accidentally met while both going to assignations with Delphine, and her name was publicly dishonored. In addition, de Valorbe's refusal to meet Mondeville placed him in disgrace.

Learning at last that her husband and Delphine were in love, Matilda went to Delphine and revealed that she was to have a child. Moved by Matilda's pleas, Delphine decided to leave France. She went to Switzerland and became a pensionary at a convent which was under the direction of Mondeville's aunt. De Valorbe followed her there and caused her name to become common gossip. When he offered to clear her name by marriage, Delphine refused his proposal and decided to remain in the convent. De Valorbe, moved to distraction, committed suicide, but before he died he cleared Delphine's reputation with Mondeville.

Word came to Mondeville's aunt that Matilda was dying. She was in league with Mondeville's mother and persuaded Delphine to become a nun. They were able to have the pope waive the required year's novitiate. By the time Mondeville went to the convent to claim Delphine, she had already taken her vows.

Meanwhile the republican government had taken over in France and had disallowed the vows of religious orders. Friends persuaded Delphine that she should renounce the vows and return to France to marry her lover. She left the convent, only to discover that public opinion condemned her action. Rather than make her lover live a life of misery, she refused to marry him.

Mondeville went to join the royalist forces fighting against the republican French government, but before he could join them he was captured and sentenced to death as a traitor. Delphine tried unsuccessfully to secure his pardon. When she failed, she took poison and then joined him when he went to the execution ground. She died on the spot where he was to be executed. At first, the soldiers refused to shoot Mondeville. Having no desire to live, he taunted them until they picked up their muskets and killed him. Friends took the bodies of Delphine and her lover and buried them side by side, so that they, kept apart in life, might be close in death.

Critical Evaluation:

Delphine appears in the form of letters, the epistolary form, which was almost outmoded by the time of Madame de Staël. In addition, the tone of the novel is in the sentimental vein of many French and British novels of the first rank in the first half of the eighteenth century. The origin of the sentiment was undoubtedly Jean-Jacques Rousseau, for whom Madame de Staël had a very high regard. In *Delphine*, there is constant reflection of the ideas of Rousseau and other advanced political thinkers and philosophers of the late eighteenth century, for such doctrines as the education of women, political equality, freedom of religious conscience, anticlericalism, and devotion to reason appear constantly in the letters written by Delphine to the other characters in the novel. The novel is, therefore, an index to the temper of Madame de Staël's circle at the time.

Delphine is in many ways a *roman à clef.* It describes a strong, independent woman who is brilliant and desirable, and who lives her life in many different contexts: In the space of one novel, Delphine is a respected and financially independent widow who then becomes a destitute pensionary (almost a nun), but only after becoming a notorious figure in the eyes of her society. Madame de Staël was a woman much like Delphine. She never became a nun, but de Staël had such a forceful character and brilliant literary and social career that it was difficult for some to regard her as a woman because she resisted common definitions and paradigms for a female of that time. In fact, Prince Talleyrand, French statesman and Napoleon's most trusted adviser, once said of *Delphine*, "I understand that Madame de Staël, in her novel, has disguised both herself and me as women." This not only shows that her novel has strong autobiographical elements but also shows that she resisted, in life and in her fiction, many social norms and barriers, including those of gender. Such was the power of her charisma that it became a standard joke among polite company that after Napoleon's fall, only three major powers remained: England, Russia, and de Staël.

There are many similarities between Delphine and her creator. Both lived amid the French Revolution, and both were involved in sexual and political intrigues of the day. Delphine's journey to Switzerland and back to France echoes de Staël's life due to the fact that her father, the brilliant financier and politician Jacques Necker, had residences in both countries. De Staël had affairs with many notables, including Friedreich Schlegel and Talleyrand. Finally, note how the changing political times radically affect Delphine's fortunes: At first, she is considered a dangerous woman for resisting the mores and traditions of the time. Then, after the Revolution, things have changed so much that she is now in a convent, and it takes the state to free her because it has made such vows illegal.

De Staël had similar reversals and changes of fortune, for she and her father had to worry about the latest political change in France: With the slightest change of a minister or bureaucrat, one's head could be lost, and it is to Necker and de Staël's credit that such a thing never happened to them. *Delphine* contains some of the most penetrating examples of how individual life is altered, hemmed in, and contained by the state. Yet it also shows how the mind and spirit can overcome such limitations; Delphine always remains outside the norm, and the tension between what is expected of Delphine by state and society, and what Delphine actually does, makes the novel a classic.

Delphine is not the only character who confronts state and societal tyranny. Mondeville dies at the hands of the state. He becomes somewhat heroic at the end when he invites the guards to kill him. Through this act, he wrests power away from his executors and shows that in the face of death he is able to form a self outside the limits of the tyranny that is killing him. Both lovers take their own lives and in death are united outside the hypocritical moral strictures of their day.

Delphine is an epistolary novel, meaning that it is written in the form of letters to and from various characters. Though much has been made about the fragmented and incomplete nature of epistolary novels, it is important to understand that in an epistolary novel the author intends to represent the whole story, and that writing in epistolary form enables an author to relate a story without the confinement and sentiment of an omniscient narrator. *Delphine* ranks as one of the great Romantic novels. One of the many favorable contemporary reviews of the book commented that there were so many Parisians staying home to read *Delphine* that the streets were empty at night, and that no one was attending the theaters. De Staël, with books like *Delphine* and her masterly essay "On Literature," helped to establish Romanticism as a great movement.

Delphine agitates against the submission of women, and strives to represent how liberty is always ruined by society and its structures. However, the novel shows that is one case a social convention can be tyrannical, and in another that same convention can bring a measure of freedom. This is what makes *Delphine* so interesting as a novel. Delphine is able, at times, to change her subordinate position into one of authority and power. Normally, being a widow in her society would be a great handicap, but Delphine is able to forge an independence at least partly of her own making. She understands that she can break through the frame of the normal petit-bourgeois existence. Her time in the convent, then, can be seen as an attempt at a form of liberty, though the meddling of her relations foils this attempt. Yet at other times, what would normally be a gesture that brings power actually mires Delphine into a social web of deceit and heartbreak: When she gives money to Matilda, all her troubles begin. Hence, de Staël certainly understood the changeableness of one's fortunes in social and political contexts.

The ironic situations that ensue from the intrigues and loves in *Delphine* are frightening as well as eminently entertaining. *Delphine*'s use of irony, in fact, helps to mark the novel as a great Romantic text. Her ironic treatment of death as a bringer of life makes this novel break away from the sentiment of many novels of its time. Although it has great similarities to other lesser novels, it refrains from open moralizing and allows the characters and situations to speak in relation to themselves, rather than in a slavish relation to existing cultural constructs.

"Critical Evaluation" by James Aaron Stanger

Bibliography:
Gutwirth, Madelyn. *Madame de Staël, Novelist: The Emergence of the Artist as Woman.* Champaign: University of Illinois Press, 1978. Gutwirth, one of the most respected authorities on de Staël, represents her as a woman able to redefine the relation between art and gender. De Staël was able to deploy her art in order to emerge as a strong subject. Groundbreaking work for discussing gender issues in de Staël.
Gutwirth, Madelyn, Avriel Goldberger, and Karyna Szmurlo, eds. *Germaine de Staël: Crossing the Borders.* New Brunswick, N.J.: Rutgers University Press, 1991. Illuminating reading for those interested in reading Delphine as a transgressor of the social fabric as mapped out in late eighteenth century Europe.
Herold, J. Christopher. *Mistress to an Age: A Life of Madame de Staël.* Indianapolis: Bobbs-Merrill, 1958. Available in many libraries and by far the most informative and entertaining biography of de Staël. Relates stories and facts about her liaisons, contacts, and famous meetings with legendary cultural and literary figures. Gives complexion to de Staël, and therefore to *Delphine*.
Hogsett, Charlotte. *The Literary Existence of Germaine de Staël.* Carbondale: Southern Illinois

University Press, 1987. Examines the complex relationships between de Staël's life and her female characters. Includes an informative foreword by Madelyn Gutwirth.

Staël, Madame de. *An Extraordinary Woman: Selected Writings of Germaine de Staël*. Translated and with an introduction by Vivian Folkenflik. New York: Columbia University Press, 1987. A collection of de Staël's most memorable statements, quips, and pieces of fiction.

DELTA WEDDING

Type of work: Novel
Author: Eudora Welty (1909-   )
Type of plot: Regional
Time of plot: Early 1920's
Locale: Mississippi
First published: 1946

Principal characters:
    LAURA MCRAVEN, a cousin to the Fairchilds
    DABNEY FAIRCHILD, a bride-to-be
    ELLEN, her mother
    BATTLE, her father
    SHELLEY, her sister
    GEORGE FAIRCHILD, her uncle
    ROBBIE, George's wife
    TROY FLAVIN, a plantation manager

The Story:

Nine-year-old Laura McRaven made her first journey alone from Jackson to the Delta to visit her dead mother's people, the Fairchilds. One of her cousins, Dabney Fairchild, was to be married, and Laura's chief regret was that she could not be in the wedding party because of her mother's recent death. She remembered Shellmound, the Fairchild plantation, and knew that she would have a wonderful time with her exciting cousins and aunts. The Fairchilds were people to whom things happened, exciting, unforgettable things.

At Shellmound, Laura found most of the family assembled for the wedding. Although children her age were her companions, she was also aware of the doings of the grownups. It was obvious that the family was not happy about Dabney's marriage. Her husband-to-be was Troy Flavin, the manager of the plantation, whose inferior social position was the main mark against him. Uncle Battle, Dabney's father, was most of all reluctant to let one of his family go from him, but he could not bring himself to say anything to Dabney, not even that he would miss her. Laura found this behavior to be very strange. They seldom talked as a united family, but they always acted as one. There were so many members of the family that it was hard for Laura to keep them straight. Uncle Battle's wife was Aunt Ellen, and their oldest daughter was Shelley, who was going to be a nun. Again the whole family disapproved of her plan, but there was seldom any attempt to get her to change her mind. The obvious favorite was Uncle George, Battle's brother. Uncle George had also married beneath him. He and his wife, Robbie, lived in Memphis, where everyone knew poor Uncle George could never be happy.

When George arrived for the wedding festivities, he was alone and miserable. Robbie had left him, and he had come down alone to see his family. Not wanting to make Dabney unhappy, they did not tell her of Robbie's desertion. The children and the aunts and grandaunts were not told either, although one by one they began to suspect that something was wrong. Ellen could have killed Robbie for making George unhappy, but she kept her feelings to herself except when she was alone with Battle, her husband.

Robbie's anger at her husband began on the afternoon of a family outing. George had risked his life to save one of the cousins, a feebleminded child caught in the path of a train as they crossed a railroad trestle. After that incident, Robbie was never the same with George. She seemed to want him to prove that he loved her more than he loved his family. Probably Shelley understood the family best. She knew that they had built a wall against the outside world, but she suspected that they were more lonely than self-sufficient. Most people took the family as a group, loving or hating them all together. Only Uncle George seemed to take them one by one, loving and understanding each as an individual. Shelley thought that this was why they all loved Uncle George so much.

Dabney seemed to wish for more than she had in her love for Troy. Sometimes she felt left out, as if she were trying to find a lighted window but found only darkness. She loved Troy, but she wanted to feel even more a part of him. She also wished that her family would try to keep her with them; she wanted to make certain of their love.

Preparations for the wedding created a flurry. The dresses had been ordered from Memphis, and when some of the gowns failed to arrive, there was the usual hubbub among the women, a concern that the men could not appreciate. One of the children fell sick at the last minute, so that Laura was made one of the wedding party after all. Troy's mother sent some beautiful handmade quilts from her mountain shack. Troy felt proud, but the Fairchilds were even more self-consciously and unwillingly ashamed of his background.

After their wedding, Dabney and Troy would live at Marmion, an estate owned by the family. Dabney rode over to see the house. Looking at the stately buildings and the beautiful old trees, she knew that best of all she would love being inside it, looking out on the rest of the world. That was what she wanted the most, to be inside where she was a part of the light and warmth. That was what marriage must give her.

All the time, unknown to any of the family but Shelley, Robbie was not far away. She had come after George in hopes that he was looking for her. What had almost defeated Robbie was the fear that she had not married George but the whole Fairchild family. It was that fear which had made her angry at the affair on the railroad trestle. Wanting desperately to come first with George, she knew instinctively that he could never set her apart or above the family. Contrite and humble, she went to Shellmound. The fact that George was not even there at the moment hurt her even more, for she wanted very much for him to be miserable without her. He was, but it was not the Fairchild way to let anyone see his true feelings.

Robbie probably understood the secret of the family when she said that the Fairchilds loved each other because, in so doing, they were really loving themselves. That fact was not quite true in George's case. He was the different one. Because of his gentleness and his ability to love people as individuals, he let Robbie see his love for her without ever saying the words she had longed to hear.

The wedding was almost an anticlimax, a calm scene following gusty storms of feeling. Troy and Dabney took only a short trip, for Troy was needed to superintend the plantation. While they were gone, Battle worked the field hands hard to get Marmion ready for them. Dabney was anxious to move in, but the move was not so necessary after her marriage as it had seemed before; she no longer felt left out of Troy's life. She thought her life before had been like seeing a beautiful river between high banks, with no way to get down. Now she had found the way, and she was at peace. Indeed, the whole family seemed to have righted itself.

When Aunt Ellen asked Laura to live with them at Shellmound, her being wanted by the Fairchilds seemed too wonderful to believe. Laura knew that she would go back to her father, but still feeling that she really belonged to the Fairchilds seemed like a beautiful dream. She clung briefly to Aunt Ellen, as if to hold close that wonderful moment of belonging.

Critical Evaluation:

Eudora Welty has created in Shellmound, the home of the Fairchild family in *Delta Wedding*, a world set apart from the rest of Southern plantation society of the 1920's. Shellmound is a haven, isolated from the mainstream of Southern life and unaffected by extremes of grief and suffering: There is no racial tension, no poverty, no war or natural catastrophe, no sense of alienation and instability generated by contact with modern urban society, and no severe moral deficiencies in the characters that would preclude natural human happiness. The Fairchild estate is thus the perfect stage upon which to play out a drama about the growth of every type of love, from romantic to filial to platonic.

The main focus of the book, therefore, is on the nature of the numerous members of the Fairchild clan and on their relationships. Welty shows how the men are different from the women, how the "insiders" are different from those who have married into the family, how each person relates to the others, and how each person grows individually and privately. In order to explore these various aspects, the author utilizes different narrative voices, thus enabling the reader to view the characters from different perspectives. Aunt Tempe, for example, provides the older generation's point of view; she believes that Delta women have inherited traits that cannot be learned by outsiders, traits that enable them subtly to control their men and the plantations. At the young end of the spectrum is nine-year-old Laura, who comes to live at Shellmound temporarily after her mother's death; she provides the child's viewpoint of events during the hectic wedding preparations. The most objective, wise, and clearsighted outlook, however, is provided by Aunt Ellen. As an "outsider" (she married Battle Fairchild), she not only sees the situation more accurately than her more involved and subjective relatives but also brings to her judgment insights from the world beyond the plantation.

What distinguishes the Fairchilds most is their simultaneous independence from and reliance upon one another; each person is at once intensely caught up in family concerns and fiercely private and separate. The only member who transcends the insular closeness of the circle to achieve a more universal outlook on life is Uncle George; able to feel and see beyond the limitations of life at Shellmound, he is nevertheless tied to the Fairchilds in his heart. Through the family's constant attempts to study and understand George, and through George's emotional involvement in events at the estate, Welty reveals a group of people at once selfishly exclusive and warmly affectionate, tender, loving, and devoted.

Bibliography:

Devlin, Albert J. *Eudora Welty's Chronicle: A Story of Mississippi Life.* Jackson: University Press of Mississippi, 1983. Examines the significance of place and history in Welty's fiction. Argues that the unity of Welty's fiction results from a historical aesthetic. An excellent starting point for serious study.

Kreyling, Michael. *Eudora Welty's Achievement of Order.* Baton Rouge: Louisiana State University Press, 1980. One of the best book-length studies of Welty. Focuses on the development of Welty's fictional technique and growth of her esthetic sensibility and unique voice.

Turner, Craig W., and Lee Emling Harding, eds. *Critical Essays on Eudora Welty.* Boston: G. K. Hall, 1989. Includes three landmark essays on *Delta Wedding.* "Delta Fiction" places Welty's novel in the tradition of the old South. "*Delta Wedding* as Region and Symbol" analyzes the novel's formal structure. "Meeting the World in *Delta Wedding*" explores its mature artistry and lyricism.

Vande Kieft, Ruth M. *Eudora Welty.* Rev. ed. Boston: Twayne, 1987. A classic guide to reading

Welty. The best starting source despite more recent scholarship. Analyzes the structures, the message, and characters, focusing on the mystery and duality at the heart of Welty's fiction.

Westling, Louise. *Sacred Groves and Ravaged Gardens: The Fiction of Eudora Welty, Carson McCullers, and Flannery O'Connor*. Athens: University of Georgia Press, 1985. Explores the impact of the Southern conception of womanhood on *Delta Wedding* and two other Welty novels. Discusses Welty's fiction in relation to McCullers and O'Connor.

DEMOCRACY

Type of work: Novel
Author: Joan Didion (1934-   )
Type of plot: Political
Time of plot: Mid-1970's
Locale: Hawaii and Southeast Asia
First published: 1984

Principal characters:

INEZ CHRISTIAN VICTOR, the protagonist, a native of Hawaii and
    the wife of a liberal Democratic senator from California
HARRY VICTOR, Inez's husband
JESSICA VICTOR, the daughter of Harry and Inez, a heroin addict
ADLAI VICTOR, Jessica's dull-witted twin brother
JACK LOVETT, the love of Inez's life
PAUL CHRISTIAN, Inez's father
JANET CHRISTIAN ZEIGLER, Inez's sister
DWIGHT CHRISTIAN, Inez's uncle
BILLY DILLON, Harry's press secretary
JOAN DIDION, the author, who tells the story and appears as a
    character in it

The Story:

Inez Victor, the daughter of a once-prominent Hawaiian family and the wife of a senator, was disillusioned with her life in the political limelight. Alienated from her husband, she once again met with Jack Lovett, a man with whom she had had a brief affair as a teen. Inez and Jack, a mysterious "information specialist" working unofficially for the U.S. government, had been meeting by chance in political circles for more than twenty years.

The year had been difficult for Inez. Her husband, Harry, took the family to Jakarta on a mission to ascertain if human rights violations were occurring. However, it soon became apparent that Harry was chosen for this mission because of his willingness to overlook real political problems rather than daring to speak out and alienate the government or the voting public. Jack was finally able to rescue the Victor family by finding a place for them to stay until they were taken out of the country.

This was also the year that Inez's sister, Janet, was murdered by their father in a fit of insanity. After dealing with this situation, Inez left her marriage and went with Jack to Southeast Asia to save her heroin-addicted daughter, Jessica. Jessica had gone to Vietnam to find a job just as the U.S. armed forces were being evacuated. They were able to rescue Jessica, but Jack was killed; Inez brought his body back to Hawaii for burial. Tired of her role as a senator's wife, a role which allowed her no private life or personal freedom, Inez fled to Kuala Lumpur finally to pursue an interest of her own by working with a program to aid refugees.

Critical Evaluation:

Joan Didion's fourth novel, *Democracy*, is about American politics and the Vietnam War, public and private life, the media, and image management. However, it is mostly the story of

Inez Victor, daughter of a powerful Hawaiian family and congressman Harry Victor's wife. Didion explores the toll that living in the public eye, combined with the pressure to do "the correct thing," has taken on Inez's life.

Democracy begins in 1975 with an introduction to Jack Lovett, Inez's potential lover, and his description of the islands during the Pacific nuclear bomb tests of the 1950's. Through this scene, Jack Lovett is presented as a behind-the-scenes player in an unofficial government capacity. What Jack Lovett actually does is never clear. He arranges transport and sets up "AID funding" and "export credit programs." Even his former wives have trouble describing his occupation. His first calls him an army officer, the next an "aircraft executive." Jack Lovett operates in the shadows. He makes policy decisions and deals, he networks worldwide on behalf of the war, and he refers to himself as a "businessman" or "a consultant in international development." All of these titles are euphemisms. Jack Lovett is a troubleshooter on the business end of the war, and his approach to the problems that arise is not always legal or ethical.

Didion refers back to this opening scene, in which Jack and Inez dance in a bar as he describes the nuclear tests to her, several times throughout the novel. Didion uses the scene in the bar, along with the whole year, as the center around which all other events turn. While Inez and Jack's ongoing, generally unacknowledged feelings for each other are not primary to Inez's character, her relationship with Jack is significant. Most obviously, Jack operates as a foil for Inez's husband, Harry Victor. While Jack Lovett is a loner who feels most comfortable "in the presence of strangers," Harry Victor is always surrounded by a coterie of advisers such as his campaign manager Billy Dillon, his family, or, on at least one trip, a girlfriend. Jack Lovett assesses situations and acts accordingly, while Harry Victor spews political rhetoric designed to have the best impact on the most people and, as a result, never seems to accomplish anything. Harry Victor represents democracy in its most ironic form. So intent is he on giving the people their say that he is practically immobilized, made impotent by a fear of alienating too many people to achieve reelection. In contrast, Jack Lovett represents a more cynical brand of democracy. He is a necessary agent in a government composed of Harry Victors. Jack Lovett can be counted on to take action, to make rational decisions regardless of public sentiment.

In two instances in the novel, Jack Lovett puts Harry Victor's family members out of harm's way while Harry Victor stands by and does nothing. In the episode in which Harry takes his family into the line of fire in Jakarta, his true lack of understanding becomes apparent. Harry is a sort of government shill, prized for his willingness to overlook or not to see. As Jack Lovett says, he has blinders on, and when Harry Victor refuses to acknowledge the danger to his family in a place where there is rifle fire in the streets and a grenade has exploded in the U.S. embassy, Jack cannot keep silent. "I believe some human rights are being violated on the verandah," he says when Harry refuses to cut short a speech. It is Jack Lovett who secures safe lodging for them in the mountains until they can be transported out of the country. Later, when Jessica Victor has gone to Vietnam during the evacuation, it is Jack Lovett who flies there, locates her, and finds her a place to stay until he can get her on a flight back to the United States. Harry Victor, meanwhile, is reluctant to do anything to ensure Jessica's safety.

The implication of these two scenes is clear. The form of democracy that Harry Victor thinks he represents—with his Neighborhood Legal Coalition operating out of a Harlem storefront and his book *The View from the Street: Root Causes, Radical Solutions and a Modest Proposal* co-authored, like all of his other writing, with Billy Dillon—is a sham. His interest in the people, perhaps once rooted in a sincere concern, is hollow now. He listens and reflects what he hears, but only as long as doing so guarantees his position. Harry Victor is unable to make a move until he can gauge a potential public response to his actions. The power he thinks he has gained through his political position is illusory. What he really has is a portion of carefully managed fame.

Didion is most intent on charting the effects that this fame and living constantly in the public eye have had on Inez. In order to bring the reader closer to Inez, Didion puts herself in the novel in the character of the narrator and sometime confidante to Inez. Didion relays the events of the novel through the various accounts told to her by the actual characters and through her own personal observations of the characters in action. The effect of this metafictional device is to make the events and characters more real, more immediate.

This sense of the story as true is enhanced by the fact that Didion has included many real elements from her own life in the character of the narrator Joan Didion. Like Didion, the narrator is a reporter who has at one time worked for *Vogue* magazine and, at another, lectured at Berkeley. She even quotes a composition textbook that includes a writing assignment based on one of her essays. The fact that Didion also discusses the writing of the novel as the work progresses—careful never to let down the mask of reporting—increases the sense of immediacy the novel conveys. She presents the genesis of the novel as having been Carol Christian, Inez and Janet's mother, and mentions the various props she uses to support her writing, particularly newspaper clippings and photographs of Inez and her family members. Didion tells the reader that she has filtered out the most important elements of Inez's story. She lists the scenes, details, and story lines she has decided to leave out, the excess trimmed to leave her with an image of Jack Lovett waiting for Inez Victor. "I have been keeping notes for some time now about the way Jack Lovett waited for Inez Victor," Didion says, lending their story a sense of importance and urgency which is enhanced by the terseness of her prose. As a narrator, Didion is smart and compelling largely because she has taken the time to establish herself as a reliable observer. When she questions the account of an event she has received from one of the characters, she includes that account's probable biases. That she is a reporter and has occasion to travel on story assignments also makes her tale appear more authentic. Ironically, it is reporters and the media who have accounted for some of the major losses in Inez's life.

In a particularly revealing scene, Didion looks on as Inez gives an interview in a Miami hotel room during Harry Victor's campaign for presidential candidacy. Billy Dillon has insisted that Inez go through with the interview, explaining that it is just a game, a finite number of minutes during which she simply has to "place the ball . . . inside the lines." Inez is struggling, though, to communicate with the reporter. When asked what the major cost of public life has been, Inez replies that it is memory. She explains that the various events of her life get repeated—sometimes incorrectly—so often in print that she loses track of what really happened or of her own take on those events. In this scene, Inez is frustrated with the reporter, who seems not to follow her line of thought and becomes easily sidetracked into the status of Inez's mental health when Inez says this memory loss is "something like shock treatment." It is clear that these interviews are not just a game for Inez. They are restrictive, they necessitate self-abridgment, and Inez is never afforded the opportunity to set the record straight, to be herself.

Janet's murder is the catalyst for Inez. After looking on as her father's institutionalization, Janet's "technical death" (she has been sustained by life support and must have three flat electroencephalogram readings before her death will be official), and Harry Victor's official response to the tragedy have been negotiated, Inez leaves with Jack Lovett, the only one who has ever told her "get it while you can." Immediately Inez is afforded the freedom of relative anonymity. While Jack Lovett is searching for Jessie in Vietnam, Inez stays in Hong Kong and reads in the papers not about her presence there, but about the absence of Harry Victor's wife from his sister-in-law's funeral. She realizes how slight her connection to her husband and children feels and, less overtly, that submission to her designated role has amounted to nothing. Finally, when Inez goes to Kuala Lumpur to work with refugees, a "special interest" deemed too controversial by her husband's political advisers, it is not only significant to her assertion of her independence but also important because it calls attention to the fact that Inez is herself a sort of refugee from the public scrutiny and the familial obligations that have taken so much of her life.

Michelle Fredette

Bibliography:

Ching, Stuart. " 'A Hard Story to Tell': The Vietnam War in Joan Didion's *Democracy*." In *Fourteen Landing Zones: Approaches to Vietnam War Literature*, edited by Philip K. Jason. Iowa City: University of Iowa Press, 1992. Ching's chapter discusses Didion's portrayal of the Vietnam War in *Democracy*.

Felton, Sharon. *The Critical Response to Joan Didion*. Westport, Conn.: Greenwood Press, 1994. This text presents a sampling of the critical response to each of Didion's books. One of these criticizes Didion for "borrowing" from her former novels.

Henderson, Katherine Usher. "Joan Didion: The Bond Between Narrator and Heroine in *Democracy*." In *American Women Writing Fiction: Memory, Identity, Family, Space*, edited by Mickey Pearlman. Lexington: University Press of Kentucky, 1989. Henderson explores the effects that Didion's first-person narrator, named Didion, has on the story, particularly in terms of her relationship with Inez Victor.

Stout, Janis P. *Strategies of Reticence: Silence and Meaning in the Works of Jane Austen, Willa Cather, Katherine Anne Porter, and Joan Didion*. Charlottesville: University of Virginia Press, 1990. Stout points out that while Didion's use of white space and short "stand-alone" sentences may at first appear to be a gimmick, it lends the novel's events an appropriate urgency.

Tager, Michael. "The Political Vision of Joan Didion's *Democracy*." *Critique: Studies in Contemporary Fiction* 31, no. 3 (1990): 173-184. Tager discusses the irony in Didion's title, *Democracy*, and points out similarities between the events in the novel and the thinking behind the Iran-Contra scandal. Tager pays particular attention to the characters Harry Victor and Jack Lovett.

DEMOCRACY IN AMERICA

Type of work: Politics
Author: Alexis de Tocqueville (1805-1859)
First published: De la démocratie en Amérique: volume 1, 1835; volume 2, 1840 (English translation, 1835/1840)

Alexis de Tocqueville lived in a time of enormous political change, when every conceivable variety of political theory flourished. He was born shortly after the French Revolution had turned France into the Empire; in his lifetime occurred those further changes that transformed France, at least nominally, into a republic. His object in writing *Democracy in America* was twofold: to write about the new nation that he so much admired and to establish a new way of examining ideas of politics. Instead of proceeding from ideas of right and responsibility, Tocqueville preferred to begin by analyzing social institutions as they functioned in reality. Instead of working, as Jean-Jacques Rousseau had worked, from an arbitrary picture of the beginnings of humanity in a natural condition, Tocqueville preferred to work from what was statistically observable. Thus, *Democracy in America* begins with a picture of the geography of the new continent, its weather, its indigenous tribes, its economy, and its natural resources. In this respect, *Democracy in America* is the forerunner of the scientific spirit in the investigation of social structures.

Much of *Democracy in America* is concerned with institutions, and the first institution described by Tocqueville is that of the partition of property. He points out that it is customary in the nations of Europe to divide property by the laws of primogeniture. The result is that property remains fixed in extent and in possession; the family, no matter how changed in each generation, is linked to the wealth and political power of landed property. The family represents the estate, the estate the family, and naturally a strong inequality is carried from one generation to another. The foundations of American culture are to be found, Tocqueville points out, in the equal partition of land and fortune. Land is continually broken up into parcels, sold, developed, and transformed. The accompanying wealth and power is much more fluid than in societies in which descent really dominates fortune. The subsidiary effect of equal partition is that people have access to careers from which they might be blocked in another system.

Tocqueville was fascinated by the practice of equality, a phenomenon rarely encountered in France during his lifetime. Several chapters concern political equality; he is one of the first great commentators on the democracy of U.S. townships and corporations in the early nineteenth century. He emphasizes that it is fundamental to understand the nature of the township, particularly in its New England tradition. The key to the nature of the United States, he asserts, is the wide and responsible nature of freedom at the level of municipal government. This gives the citizen a direct voice in the government and trains the citizen for the representative democracy of the federal government. Tocqueville points out that, under this form of government, power is concentrated in the hands of the voter; the legislative and executive branches have no power of their own, but merely represent those who appoint them. To us, this fact is commonplace, but it was a new idea for the citizens of Europe in the nineteenth century.

Although much of this work is in praise of democracy in the United States, Tocqueville makes some important qualifications. His first principle is that abuse in government occurs when one special interest is served to the exclusion of all others. This kind of abuse, he remarks, formerly occurred when the upper classes imposed their will on the lower, or when military, feudal, financial, or even religious values operated to the exclusion of all others. His great qualification of democracy is that it makes possible a tyranny of the majority. He states that it is conceivable that the free institutions of the United States may be destroyed by forcing all minorities to give up their freedoms for what is supposedly the good of the majority. In that case, he concludes, democracy will give way first to despotism and then to anarchy. Above all things, Tocqueville is taken with equality, and that principle, regardless of the greatest good for the greatest number, is what animates his opinion.

Democracy in America is principally about its great subject, but there are in it many reminders of a larger view that its author has. One constant theme of the book is that the Old World must learn from the New World; in fact, the book functions not so much as an independent study of a unique phenomenon as a study of comparative political science. The French will not succeed, the author remarks, if they do not introduce democratic institutions. There will be independence for none, he adds, unless, like the republic of the United States, the French grant independence for all. With uncommon prescience, he predicts the totalitarian potentialities of the twentieth century, in which unlimited power restricted itself not to a class, but first to a party, and then to a single man. The famous ending of the first volume carries this insight to a more elaborate and specific culmination. There are two nations, Tocqueville asserts, that probably will dominate the next century, Russia and the United States. One, he says, is driven by the desire for power and war, the other by the desire to increase domestic prosperity. He predicts that there will be no peace until the aggressiveness of Russia is checked by the peacefulness of the United States: He looks to a future in which the principle of servitude will encounter that of freedom.

The second volume of *Democracy in America* was published five years after the first. The first volume had established its author as one of the best political thinkers in Europe. It won for him not only the esteem of the best minds of the Continent, but also financial and political rewards, so that from the time of its publication Tocqueville was to take an active part as a member of the French government. The second volume is concerned not with the basic economic and social characteristics of the United States, but with subsidiary questions about the nature of American culture. Tocqueville asks, for example, how Americans cultivate the arts and whether or not eloquence is to be encountered in the rhetoric of Congress. He covers the progress of science as well as that of poetry, the position of religious minorities, even the meaning of public monuments in a democracy. His general conclusion on the arts in the United States is that they do not flourish as they do in other political climates, for the arts require an atmosphere of privilege and an amount of money that a tax-conscious public is quite unlikely to spend. The useful, he says, is much preferred in a democracy to the beautiful. The artist becomes an artisan and, the author remarks with some delicacy, tends to produce imperfect commodities rather than lasting works of art.

If these qualifications are admitted they are also weighted; Tocqueville believes that a lowering of some standards is amply compensated by a heightening of others. Particularly in the matter of foreign policy, he admires the republican sense as well as form of government. Toward the end of *Democracy in America*, he ruminates on the inclinations toward war and peace of different forms of government. The democratic form, he judges, is predisposed to peace because of various influences: the rapid growth of personal wealth; the stake in property; the less material but equally important gentleness of heart that allows the citizens of a democracy a more humane view of life. Yet, when the democratic government is involved in war, the same application of ambition and energy that is so marked in commercial life results often in military success as well. Tocqueville's last thoughts about the democracy and its army deal with the danger to any society from its own standing army, and he covers substantially the same ground on this matter as do the authors of the Federalist Papers.

Democracy in America ends with the restatement that despotism may be encountered even in republics. The author admits that democracies can, on occasion, be violent and unjust, but he believes these occasions are exceptional. They will be more and more frequent, however, in the proportion that equality is allowed to lapse. Among the last of Tocqueville's animated descriptions is that of the "flock of timid and industrious animals" who have given up their individuality to a strong central government. He urges a balance between central and decentralized power, the constant consciousness of equality for all members of the polity.

Bibliography:

Commager, Henry Steele. *Commager on Tocqueville*. Columbia: University of Missouri Press, 1993. Lucid essays, written by a distinguished American historian, on Tocqueville's democratic visions. The conclusion discusses the contemporary relevance of Tocqueville's ideas for politics in the United States.

Mancini, Matthew. *Alexis de Tocqueville*. New York: Twayne, 1994. Accessible, comprehensive survey concentrates on *Democracy in America* and introduces the major themes in Tocqueville's works. A worthwhile bibliography for students new to Tocqueville's writings.

Martineau, Harriet. *How to Observe Morals and Manners*. New Brunswick, N.J.: Transaction, 1989. Published originally in 1838, this book was the first methods text in the social sciences. Clearly explicates patriarchal, classist, racist, and other biases that plague undisciplined observations such as Tocqueville employed as the empirical foundation for *Democracy in America*.

Pope, Whitney, in collaboration with Lucetta Pope. *Alexis de Tocqueville: His Social and Political Theory*. Beverly Hills, Calif.: Sage Publications, 1986. Critiques Tocqueville's pertinence for modern social theory and compares his ideas with those of Karl Marx, Emile Durkheim, and other social theorists. Useful bibliography.

Schleifer, James T. *The Making of Tocqueville's "Democracy in America."* Chapel Hill: University of North Carolina Press, 1980. A detailed, archivally based appreciation of Tocqueville's authorship of *Democracy in America*. Rewarding analysis of Tocqueville's definitions of democracy.

DEMOCRATIC VISTAS

Type of work: Social criticism
Author: Walt Whitman (1819-1892)
First published: 1871

Written when Walt Whitman was in his early fifties, *Democratic Vistas* demonstrates the author's discouragement at what he saw in America. The sobering effects of the Civil War, the death of Abraham Lincoln, and the overwhelming change resulting from the industrial revolution are quite evident as Whitman attempts to introduce a plan for the development of a golden age in the New World.

Like Whitman's poetry, the work has no substantial organization; it tends to ramble and to be repetitious. Nevertheless, in its portrait of Whitman's philosophy, and in its analysis of the potentiality of the American society, *Democratic Vistas* is extremely significant. Its criticism of American politics, culture, and values in general was partly the result of the disillusionment that existed after the Civil War, but the considerations are still quite applicable to American society.

Simply stated, the thesis of *Democratic Vistas* is that, while America is surpassing all other nations industrially and has the material facilities to continue its advancement, it lacks a distinct culture or spiritual identity. According to Whitman, such an identity could only come about through works of literature written in new literary styles by new artists. In effect, he is stating that America has the human resources, the material resources, and the sound political structure to make itself the most ideal society that has ever existed. As Whitman views the American scene, however, he sees no unique values, no real expression of these new concepts, but only a materialistic society relying on old ideas and traditional expressions. Thus, the overall result of the work is a plea for great literary works which would serve as a foundation for a new society.

Though the work has no organization other than the repetition of this same theme, Whitman's approach follows four general divisions: a portrait of the American society and its values, a statement of the basic principles and ideals which represent the goals of the "mass, or lump character" of America, the principle of the individual as the focal point for the ideal society, and great literature as the force which will bring about this society.

Whitman begins by stating his central theme—that America will never be great unless it is able to separate itself from the Old World tradition:

> I say that democracy can never prove itself beyond cavil, until it founds and luxuriantly grows its own forms of art, poems, schools, theology, displacing all that exists, or that has been produced anywhere in the past, under opposite influences.

Whitman further states that America is a new experiment founded on new principles and cannot rely on old ideas. While some might argue that the "republic is, in performance, really enacting today the grandest arts, poems, etc., by beating up the wilderness into fertile farms, and in her railroads, ships, machinery, etc.," Whitman responds that "society, in these States, is canker'd, crude, superstitious and rotten":

> The official services of America, national, state, and municipal, in all their branches and departments, except the judiciary, are saturated in corruption, bribery, falsehood, maladministration; and the judiciary is tainted.

After dwelling on the "lamentable conditions" which exist in America, Whitman states that the answer to such a problem is a "new-founded literature" which would be "consistent with science, handling the elements and forces with competent power, teaching and training men."

Having thus established the tone of his essay, Whitman proceeds to the first main consideration, an analysis of the present American society. His portrait of the "lump character" shows that the artist has, in the past, had to struggle against the masses. He also shows that the reverse has been true, for literature "has never recognized the People." It is Whitman's belief that America is experiencing the birth of a new sort of mass personality which is courageous, all-inclusive, and potentially great. To deny cultural identity to this mass would be to destroy this potentiality.

> We believe the ulterior object of political and all other government (having, of course, provided for the police, the safety of life, property, and for the basic statute and common law, and their administration, always first in order), to be among the rest, not merely to rule, to repress disorder, etc., but to develop, to open up to cultivation, to encourage the possibilities of all beneficent and manly outcroppage, and of that aspiration for independence, and the pride and self-respect latent in all characters.

In other words, Whitman believed that physical freedom is only part of America's goal. The society as a whole can progress only when it possesses a cultural freedom and a set of ideals which will enable the people to attain a transcendent spirituality. Still, the law and the political form are important to Whitman, for it is only in this governmental structure that people of all races and backgrounds can be brought together. Whitman even sees in the future a greater prosperity of the masses and a tremendous growth of society: "The true gravitation-hold of liberalism in the United States will be a more universal ownership of property, general homesteads, general comfort—a vast, intertwining reticulation of wealth."

According to Whitman, this wealth, plus a genuine solidarity of mass spirit and integrity, will make this system survive. Two examples which he gives to prove this point are that "the land which could raise such as the late rebellion, could also put it down," and that the fervor of the Americans is also evident in the interest which they show in the election of their leaders: "I know nothing grander, better exercise, better digestion, more positive proof of the past, the triumphant result of faith in human kind, than a well-contested American national election."

Having discussed the quality of America's political system and the character of the mass of its people, Whitman then turns to the individual, for "rich, luxuriant, varied personalism," argues Whitman, is the key to civilization. All else, such as literature or government, is important only insofar as it assists in the "production of perfect characters among the people." It was Whitman's belief that this principle is the basis for America's future.

Whitman defines individuality as creativity, that independent thought by which each person is able to transcend the mass, and he states that it is precisely this quality that Americans lack. He attributes this failure to an attachment to "Culture," or traditional learning. The scholar, for example, is taught what to believe, and consequently believes in nothing. Rather than serving to motivate creativity, this type of culture only systematizes and stagnates individuality.

It is not that Whitman objected to culture; he argued earlier for the necessity of a unique culture if America was to rise above materialism. He simply believed that, instead of being limited to the "parlors or lecture rooms," culture should be distributed among all people of all classes. In short, the masses should be given the opportunity to achieve identity. The nation has indeed developed people who are physically strong and educated, says Whitman, but the "gloomiest consequences" will result if people are left with an "unsophisticated Conscience."

The third and final section of the essay is devoted to the concept of a great American literature, the power that Whitman believed would enable the development of the "primary moral element" necessary for an enhanced American culture:

A boundless field to fill! A new creation, with needed orbic works launch'd forth, to revolve in free and lawful circuits—to move, self-poised, through the ether, and shine like heaven's own suns! With such, and nothing less, we suggest that New World Literature, fit to rise upon, cohere, and finalize in time, these States.

By "New World Literature" Whitman does not mean quantity; this nation has, he states, more publications than any other country. Rather, he is referring to literary forms which would represent America as the Bible, the works of Homer, Plato, and Aeschylus represent their respective civilizations. Nor should we resort to the achievements of the past, for these works were written for remote times and problems: "Ye powerful and resplendent ones! ye were, in your atmospheres, grown not for America, but rather for her foes, the feudal and the old—while our genius is democratic and modern." Whitman summarizes what has thus far been accomplished by describing the stages of development in American writing. He states that America has gone through two stages in preparation for a third and final stage, without which the first two become useless: "The First stage was the planning and putting on record the political foundation rights of immense masses of people. . . . The Second stage relates to material prosperity, wealth, produce. . . ." The third and final stage will be "a native expression-spirit," "a sublime and serious Religious Democracy sternly taking command." This spirit of impetus can come from no other land, because the foundations for this literature exist only in America.

The artist who will produce this literature will be a student of nature. "Part of the test of a great literatus," says Whitman, "shall be the absence in him of the idea of the covert, the lurid, the maleficent, the devil, . . . hell, natural depravity, and the like." More important, however, will be his faith, his simplicity of statement, and his "adherence to natural standards."

Whitman is no less explicit in his description of the themes of these great works. He says that "Nature, true Nature, and the true idea of Nature, long absent, must, above all, become fully restored, enlarged, and must furnish the pervading atmosphere to poems, and the test of all high literary and aesthetic compositions."

Here Whitman is not referring to the "posyes and nightingales of the English poets," but to the spiritual significance, symbolic and implicit, in the unity of all created matter. By means of this expression all men will be able to understand the essential harmony in the universe and thus regain their faith which has been "scared away by science."

Exactly how the artist will go about this process is not really made clear; but Whitman does say that a whole new idea of composition must be the means. In any case, he assures the reader that the nation cannot rest on what has already been accomplished; the hope of the nation is in the future.

The final tone of Whitman's essay is one which pervades the whole work; he is desperate and is trying to convince the reader that he or she should also be concerned. Earlier in his career, Whitman had thought that great American literature was on the verge of being created. At the writing of *Democratic Vistas*, he saw that that of which he had dreamed had not occurred, and he attempted to motivate the potential philosopher-artists through this essay. The result is that, when he has not obscured his message with too many words, he has given an excellent critique of American society which is as significant now as it was in Whitman's day.

Bibliography:

Aspiz, Harold. *Walt Whitman and the Body Beautiful*. Urbana: University of Illinois Press, 1980. Considers *Democratic Vistas* a mature reflection of Whitman's feminism: his belief in woman's potential, her maternal and physical capabilities, and the need for female influence on society.

Chase, Richard. *Walt Whitman Reconsidered*. New York: William Sloane, 1955. Shows the complexity of *Democratic Vistas*. In its distrust of national government and its argument for American unity, it is both radical and conservative.

Erkkila, Betsy. *Whitman the Political Poet*. New York: Oxford University Press, 1989. Examines Whitman's politics. Argues that *Democratic Vistas* moves toward socialism and affirms a more feminized, cooperative society.

Holloway, Emory. *Whitman: An Interpretation in Narrative*. New York: Biblo and Tannen, 1969. Considers *Democratic Vistas* a transitional work moving the poet from despair to hope, from physicality to spirituality, and from individuality to nationality in his writing.

Scholnick, Robert J. "The American Context of *Democratic Vistas*." In *Walt Whitman: Here and Now*, edited by Joann P. Krieg. Westport, Conn.: Greenwood Press, 1985. Considers the response found in *Democratic Vistas* to the publication of Thomas Carlyle's *Shooting Niagra: And After* (1867), other period reactions to Carlyle, and the pessimistic essays on similar themes by painter Eugene Benson.

Snyder, John. *The Dear Love of Man: Tragic and Lyric Communion in Walt Whitman*. Paris: Mouton, 1975. Argues that *Democratic Vistas* offers literature as a means of giving spiritual meaning to America's corrupt and materialistic society. Whitman's vision is both tragic concerning the present and idealistic about the future.

THE DEMON
An Eastern Tale

Type of work: Poetry
Author: Mikhail Lermontov (1814-1841)
First published: Demon, 1841 (English translation, 1875)

> *Principal characters:*
> THE DEMON
> PRINCE GOUDAL, heir to a Caucasian robber chief
> TAMARA, his daughter, a beautiful Caucasian princess
> THE YOUNG BRIDEGROOM, Tamara's betrothed
> THE GUARDIAN ANGEL
> THE AGED GUARDIAN

The Story:

The Demon, banished from heaven, flew over the earth despondent over the memories of his once glorious past. No force appeared to challenge him as he spread evil and strife throughout the world, but it had all been too easy and he had become bored and indifferent, even to the great scenic beauty of the Caucasus. The created universe left him cold and disdainful. Even the lush valleys of Georgia left him bitter and contemptuous.

The aged Prince Goudal made plans for the marriage of his only daughter, the beautiful Tamara. Outwardly at least she appeared pleased, and she danced and smiled, but within her heart she had misgivings over leaving her home and becoming subservient to her new relatives. When the Demon flew past and saw her dancing, even though the beauties of nature usually had no impact on him, he immediately fell in love with Tamara. His empty and lonely soul was aroused by her beauty and innocence, and he felt confused.

The Demon saw the bridegroom excitedly riding toward the wedding, and he saw to it that the young man became distracted by Ossetian robbers. After a brief chase, the bridegroom was shot, and a riderless horse showed up at Goudal's castle in the mountains. Tamara was anguished, but a strange voice, that of the Demon, called out to comfort her and to advise her to wait. The words inflamed her passions, but when he walked into her bedroom looking "unearthly handsome" and forlorn in his love, she saw no radiance from his head.

The twilight surrounding the Demon caused Tamara to fear him as an evil spirit, but she felt so tempted by him that she begged her father to turn the other suitors away and allow her to enter a convent as a nun. Even in a remote convent, however, secluded among the mountains and forests, she continued to feel the Demon's presence and to feel attracted by his unearthly beauty.

Because she was unable to stop thinking about the Demon, Tamara could not meditate or pray properly, and she became indifferent to the beauties of nature. When she attempted to pray to icons of the Virgin Mary, she ended up thinking about the Demon, fantasizing passionate embraces with him.

At first, the Demon did not dare enter the convent, but finally he entered the garden and serenaded Tamara with such heavenly music that he was himself overwhelmed to the point of dropping a single tear, perhaps the first since his exile from heaven. The Demon entered her room with love and joy. There, however, he was confronted by Tamara's Guardian Angel. Their standoff was brief, for the Demon turned aside the Angel with a malicious grin and claimed

Tamara as his prize because she had already sinned in her heart.

When Tamara asked the Demon what he wanted from her, he told her that it was her beauty, and he confessed all of his malice and evil, telling her, "I only kill and never save." He promised to repent if she would yield to him. When she asked him why he pursued her, the Demon was only able to tell her that he felt as if he had desired her since the beginning of Creation. He professed to regret his loneliness and he expressed some sense of hope, perhaps even for reconciliation with God. His great freedom and power over puny mortals had never meant anything to him.

Tamara attempted to resist his seduction, but she thought that if she could persuade him to renounce his evil ways and to take a solemn oath, she could accept his love. The Demon swore an elaborate and apparently sincere oath rejecting his demoniac life and insisting he desired only her love and a reconciliation with God. Holding out the promise of a life of pleasure and power beyond the transitory joys of earth, the Demon appealed to her for her love, but when Tamara succumbed and allowed him to kiss her, she gave out a single shriek and died instantly.

The Aged Guardian, the cloister's old watchman, felt a premonition after midnight. He may have been unconsciously aware both of the kiss of love's attainment and of the dying cry and moan, but when he listened he could not actually hear anything but the wind. He crossed himself, prayed silently, and continued with his dark rounds.

Tamara's beauty remained even in death. She was more richly attired at her elaborate funeral than she had ever been in life, and her lips retained a strange smile. Her grieving father built a church high in the mountains as a memorial to her. An Angel began to fly away with Tamara's sinful human soul, but the Demon attempted to claim her for himself. Only then did Tamara's soul see the anger and hatred in the Demon, and she prayed for protection. The Angel informed the Demon that Tamara's soul had been severely tried and would be granted salvation. The arrogant but defeated Demon was left cursing love, humankind, and the world itself.

Thereafter, Prince Goudal's castle was haunted by a tragic ghost, but in the village nearby life went on as usual. Nothing was left to tell succeeding generations of the old tragedy. High on a nearby mountain the church remained, often beset by snowstorms, but few people came that way.

"The Story" by Ron McFarland

Critical Evaluation:

The biographical approach to literature, which relates the art and style of a writer's work to the events of his or her life, can be problematic. Because such an approach assumes a principle of determinism, it may obscure less superficial and more significant aspects of the work. The work of Mikhail Lermontov, however, demonstrates at once unusual and very solid connections to the writer's life.

Lermontov is considered to be the outstanding representative of Russian Romanticism. Between 1826 and 1834 he imitated Lord Byron, but this imitation was more than merely a pose. In one poem, he wrote: "No I am not like Byron, like him I am a persecuted wanderer, but mine is a Russian soul. . . . I began earlier, and earlier I shall end. . . . Who will communicate my thoughts to the world? Either I, or God, or nobody." Lermontov was egoistic, but he himself saw his narcissism as a misfortune and as a self-destructive element in his personality. He believed that the poet is made for suffering in a world where angelic and demoniac principles are at constant war with each other. Lermontov's long verse narrative *The Demon* illustrates his belief in the always-present contradiction of good and evil. Unlike Byron, he often described glimpses of perfection or a state of bliss, and in *The Demon* he gave full rein to his ambivalent feelings, to his preoccupation with evil, and to his sincere though ineffectual craving for what can be defined as good.

Lermontov wrote the first draft of *The Demon* at the age of fifteen. He first reworked the theme in 1830 and 1833, and then again in 1838 after having been exiled to the Caucasus for his eulogistic poem to Alexander Pushkin. *The Demon* was finally completed, after work on several more drafts, shortly before his death in 1841. The poem was extensively reworked at least eight times, but the final variant still retained some of the original lines of 1829. The many revisions show Lermontov's intense preoccupation with the ideas of the poem.

While Lermontov was working on the first draft, he also wrote a short lyric called "My Demon." It has been said that he wrote this poem in imitation of a verse by Pushkin with the same title. Whether this is true or not, the contents of Lermontov's work express an attitude entirely his own. Instead of denouncing the spirit of negation as Pushkin had done, Lermontov was attracted to what he called the sinister collection of evils. His demon, as he first describes him, is a fierce being: "He scorns pure love; he rejects all prayers; he beholds blood indifferently." Two years later, he is less forbidding and violent. He has become more intimately bound to life, and in a sense he is a more direct representation of Lermontov himself. "The proud demon will not depart, as long as I live, from me." The dark side of the poet's personality taunts him with images of bliss and purity, but they are represented as being wholly unattainable.

In the 1838 variant of *The Demon*, Lermontov first replaces the previous indefinite locale with an exotic Caucasian setting. In his childhood, the writer had twice been to the Caucasus, where the mountains and the strange customs and folklore of the region made a strong impression on him.

The heroine of the early versions had been an anonymous nun, but in the 1838 version she has become a passionate Georgian princess named Tamara. It is believed that Lermontov used as the basis for this element an Ossetian folktale about a mountain demon in love with a beautiful mortal maiden. Perhaps he was also influenced by Byron's *Cain* (1821) and *Heaven and Earth* (1822), Thomas Moore's *Loves of the Angels* (1823), or Alfred de Vigny's *Eloa* (1824). Certainly, Lermontov took a theme that other writers had used and bent it to his own beliefs. In the dedication to the second draft, he wrote, "Like my cold and cruel Demon, I enjoyed doing evil in this world; deceit was not new to me, and my heart was full of poison. But now, like that gloomy Genius, I have been reborn through your presence for innocent delights, for hope and freedom."

Lermontov's Demon is, characteristically enough, a former angel who has rebelled against God. Despite his pride in being independent, he remembers his former bliss, and for a time he thinks that the beautiful Tamara might reconcile him to life and to God, "In Paradise again I'd shine, like a new angel in new splendor." Tamara cannot resist his impassioned words, but as soon as they kiss, she dies and her soul is taken by God. The Demon, again alone, is doomed to dwell in the same void until the end of time. Tamara redeemed her sin by death, but the Demon is incapable of sacrifice. Lermontov's Demon, who is ruled by appetite, passion, and cold self-absorption, is more human than John Milton's Satan or Johann Wolfgang von Goethe's Mephistopheles.

The Demon was censored during the reign of Nicholas I for being antireligious. It was, however, circulated privately, and by the second half of the nineteenth century it was one of the most popular poems in Russia. The lyrical, musical quality of the poem made it especially popular, and many poets, among them Aleksandr Blok, Maxim Gorky, and Boris Pasternak, have acknowledged it as a source of inspiration.

The Demon remains a powerful psychological document of an exile who, after rejecting human society, still longs to be a part of it. In using the device of confession simply and directly, Lermontov reveals a true image of himself and his life, mirrors his guilt and shame, and thereby becomes a source of repentance as well as hope. The poet attempts in this work to reconcile the angelic and demoniac elements that were aspects of his view of himself. Undeniably, *The Demon* is a personal work, yet it speaks of emotion and attitude on an unrealistic level. It was not until Lermontov wrote his most outstanding work, the novel *A Hero of Our Time* (1839), that he was able to transfer his personal complexity and contradiction to a romantic but realistically conceived tale. The protagonist of that work is no longer a demon but a very earthy soldier who is bitter and cynical and, like Pushkin's Eugene Onegin, an example of the superfluous man. The position of Lermontov's Demon as a forerunner of this idea is obvious.

Bibliography:
Eikhenbaum, B. M. *Lermontov*. Ann Arbor, Mich.: Ardis, 1981. Translated by Ray Parrott and Harry Weber. Considers *The Demon* to be the last example of the "Russian lyrico-epic narrative poem." A concise stylistic commentary on the poem's emotional-phonic qualities.
Garrard, John. *Mikhail Lermontov*. Boston: Twayne, 1982. Argues that in *The Demon* Lermontov handles an important and complex topic "in an intellectually impoverished context." Sees the characters, including the Demon, as insufficiently motivated and underrealized.
Kelly, Laurence. *Lermontov: Tragedy in the Caucasus*. New York: George Braziller, 1978. Inclines toward an autobiographical reading of the poem, seeing *The Demon* as embodying Lermontov's unhappy experiences with romantic love. Salvation through love is impossible for the Demon, as for other fictional Lermontov characters and for the author himself.
Lermontov, Mikhail. *Major Poetical Works*. Translated by Anatoly Liberman. Minneapolis: University of Minnesota Press, 1983. Useful translation of the poem and valuable textual commentary on the eight versions; includes three pages of notes. Reflects on the poem's artistic problems, notably with the character of the protagonist and the conciliatory end, which some critics believe was prompted by Lermontov's efforts to deflect objections of ecclesiastical censors.
Reid, Robert. "Lermontov's *Demon:* A Question of Identity." *The Slavonic and East European Review* 60, no. 2 (1982): 189-210. The most complete and useful commentary on the poem. Considers the polarization between humanistic and metaphysical readings. Notes that Tamara's beauty attracts the Demon because he confuses it with moral goodness; argues that natural beauty can persuade but not save or redeem.

THE DEPTFORD TRILOGY

Type of work: Novel
Author: Robertson Davies (1913-1995)
Type of plot: Moral
Time of plot: 1908-1971
Locale: Canada, England, and Switzerland
First published: 1983: *Fifth Business,* 1970; *The Manticore,* 1972; *World of Wonders,* 1975

> *Principal characters:*
> LEOLA CRUICKSHANK, a small-town beauty
> MARY DEMPSTER, a minister's wife
> PAUL DEMPSTER, her son, a magician with the stage name Magnus
>   Eisengrim
> LIESL NAEGELI, Eisengrim's lover and assistant
> DUNSTAN RAMSAY, a schoolmaster
> PERCY BOYD (BOY) STAUNTON, a wealthy lawyer
> DAVID STAUNTON, Boy's son, a criminal lawyer
> DR. JOHANNA VON HALLER, a Jungian analyst
> WILLARD, a circus magician

The Story:

Fifth Business. Even as a child, Boy Staunton played dirty. He put a stone in the snowball he lobbed at Dunstan Ramsay's back. His friend ducked, and the snowball hit Mary Dempster's head, throwing the minister's wife into premature labor. Paul Dempster weighed only three pounds at birth. He lived, but his mother was "soft in the head" ever after. The ten-year-old Dunstan knew that his fate was inextricably linked to that of Boy and the Dempsters. The snowball had been aimed at him, and he felt guilty for having ducked it. He saved the stone as a reminder.

As he reached puberty, Dunstan Ramsay was tormented by desire for the town beauty, Leola. Ridden by guilt, he sought escape in books on magic and fancied himself a magician. He performed tricks for young Paul, but he lacked dexterity. Ramsay's parents forbade him to visit the Dempsters after the young wife was caught in the arms of a tramp, on whom she said she had taken pity. On another occasion, Ramsay was severely reprimanded for bringing her home in a moment of panic when he should instead have called the doctor. He was, however, convinced that she had worked a miracle when his brother came back to life.

Ramsay came to think of Mrs. Dempster as a saint when he fought in France during World War I. He was hit by shrapnel and crawled to a ruined chapel, certain that he was dying. A bomb exploded nearby, lighting up the statue of a saint. It was Mrs. Dempster's face. The vision stayed with him while he convalesced in England and returned to Canada. Back in Deptford, he learned that Mrs. Dempster had left town; her husband had died in the swine flu epidemic, and her son had run away with a circus. Ramsay's parents were dead; his brother had died in the war; and Boy Staunton, back from private school and a desk job in the army, had won Leola.

Ramsay left Deptford, took a degree in history, and began teaching at the private school Boy had attended. One day, he met the tramp who had gotten Mrs. Dempster in trouble; the tramp, who had become a minister to the homeless, credited Mrs. Dempster with having saved him. Ramsay took summer vacations in Europe, where he studied saints' lives and wrote books on saints and myths. At a circus one evening, he saw Paul, who had become a great stage magician.

Boy and Leola raised two children, Caroline and David. Boy was egotistical and Leola, unhappy, attempted suicide. When she lost her will to live and died, Boy remarried. Ramsay made a small fortune on investments, thanks to Boy's advice, so he was able to maintain the aging and demented Mrs. Dempster in a nursing home and to continue his studies and travels. He met Paul again in Mexico, now performing under the name Magnus Eisengrim. Ramsay wrote Eisengrim's "autobiography," a total fiction. Together with Eisengrim's lover, Liesl, he devised a fortune-telling act to be performed by the "brazen head of Friar Bacon" as the finale of Eisengrim's show on his first Canadian tour.

During the Toronto engagement, Ramsay arranged a dinner with Boy and Eisengrim. He revealed the fateful connection between the three of them and produced the stone that Boy had thrown sixty years before. Boy and Eisengrim left together. Later that night, Boy's car was fished out of Lake Ontario, with Boy at the steering wheel and the stone in his mouth. "Who killed Boy Staunton?" someone cried out during the "brazen head" act on the closing night. Everyone, the riddling answer seemed to say.

The Manticore. It was David Staunton, Boy's son, who had shouted the question. The occasion made him realize that he was uncontrollably angry and needed psychological counseling. He flew to Zurich the next day and began therapy with a Jungian analyst. He recounted the events that followed his father's death: his quarreling with his stepmother; his drinking too much; his fuming about the will. He cried for the first time in years. Despite an initial resistance to self-revelation, he launched an exploration of his personal history over the past forty years and recounted his childhood in Deptford and Toronto. He remembered his parents' estrangement; his first night of drinking after his mother's death; his one true love, which was broken off by his overly protective parents; his one sexual encounter, which his father arranged for him behind his back. He told of his legal studies in Oxford, his practice of criminal law, his father's remarriage, their growing separation. The analysis continued three times a week for the next year, and Dr. von Haller played many roles as David projected one archetypal image after another onto her. She became the Shadow, the Friend, the Anima, and he began to understand his inner cast of characters. Before the Christmas holiday, she said he was ready for the second stage of analysis, which would move into the transpersonal realm.

When David shouted the question, Ramsay had had a heart attack. Liesl had taken him to a hospital, then disappeared. When Ramsay heard from her next, she was at her castle in Switzerland, where she invited him to join her and Eisengrim. He quit his teaching job, and sorted out his thoughts in a long letter to his former headmaster. He became a permanent guest at the castle. When David joined them for Christmas, they were able to cast light on the words that the "brazen head" had spoken in answer to his question. Liesl took David to an ancient cave where bears had once been worshiped. David knew he would continue his quest, whether in analysis or on his own.

World of Wonders. Liesl's castle became the scene for a television documentary on a nineteenth century magician, whose show Eisengrim was to re-create. During the filming, Eisengrim agreed to tell his real life story as the subtext for the documentary. He told of Ramsay's first lessons in magic, of his abduction by a magician named Willard, and of his work in a traveling circus called the World of Wonders. He revealed the backstage life of a circus troupe, and told of Willard's sad decline into drug addiction and total dependence. He told of his first magic shows, his work in the theater in England and Canada, and his liaison with Liesl.

The film crew moved to London for final shots, and the three friends gathered in Eisengrim's bed at the Savoy for a final discussion. Ramsay still wanted to understand the answer that Liesl had spoken through the "brazen head" after David shouted his question. Eisengrim explained to Ramsay, more fully than he had to David, exactly what happened on the last night of Boy's life. Boy had confessed that he dreaded the political office that he had long sought and finally won. Eisengrim remarked that he could always resign, not realizing that Boy's great hero had been the prince who became Edward VIII and was forced to abdicate in 1936. He recognized the suicidal thoughts that crossed Boy's mind, and did not try to stop them.

Critical Evaluation:

With *The Deptford Trilogy*, Robertson Davies went from being a respected essayist and playwright in his native Canada to an internationally acclaimed writer of moral fiction. In an earlier trilogy of novels, *The Salterton Trilogy* (1951-1958), Davies had demonstrated a talent for social satire. After *The Deptford Trilogy*, which is generally considered his masterpiece, he went on to write *The Cornish Trilogy* (1981-1988).

The first novel in *The Deptford Trilogy*, *Fifth Business*, is Ramsay's long letter to his former headmaster, in which he explains how he came to understand his role in life. *The Manticore* is David's story of how he came into analysis, followed by his journal during analysis and his diary entries during the holiday at Liesl's castle. *World of Wonders* is Eisengrim's life story as told to the film director and recorded in Ramsay's notes. Each novel stands on its own. Indeed, Davies has remarked that he did not plan the second novel until the first was in print, or the third novel until the second was finished. Yet each adds to the others and, taken together, the novels show three sides of a story begun with the spiteful throw of a snowball.

Each narrator has a story he needs to tell. Ramsay needs to establish that he is a serious scholar and not an old duffer; David, that he is a skilled lawyer and a family leader, not just an alcoholic; and Eisengrim, that he is a consummate artist as well as a dexterous deceiver. Each man is an egotist, and each has a grievance against that great egotist Boy Staunton: He was a village bully who caused a woman to go into labor and robbed her son of eighty paradisiacal days in the womb; a faithless friend; and an overbearing father. Boy also had a story to tell, but he told his to only one person in the hour before his abdication from life.

"Fifth business" is a theater term for the character who is neither hero nor heroine, confidant nor villain, but nevertheless essential to the resolution of the dramatic plot. Late in life, Ramsay discovers that the term describes him, and he comes to realize that his accusations propelled Boy toward suicide. However, his professional studies of history and myth have prepared him to recognize his own myth.

The manticore is a mythological beast with the head of a man, the body of a lion, and the tail of a scorpion. David dreams of a manticore held on leash by a sibyl. The manticore has his face and realizes that he needs a female guide. He first thinks that Dr. von Haller will be the guide, but it is with Liesl as his guide that he descends to the depths of human consciousness. David learned to cross-examine witnesses before he met the archetypal figures within himself, but depth psychology balances his legal reasoning with a better understanding of himself.

The World of Wonders is not only the circus that Paul ran off with but the phantasmagoria that he created. His stage name, which Liesl suggested, means "Great Iron Hard One"; it shows his psychological affinity with the wolf in the Grimm Brothers' fairy tales, who is often called *Eisengrim*. When he takes on the name, he ceases to be the circus performer or theatrical stuntman and becomes his real self.

Like David, Ramsay and Liesl are interested in Jungian psychology. Jung's typology of personality functions helps to explain the dynamics of character interactions in the trilogy. David learns that he is primarily a thinking type, whereas Ramsay, the scholar, discovers that he is driven by feeling, including a lifelong feeling of resentment toward Boy. Eisengrim is a sensing type, very aware of the external world, and Liesl is deeply intuitive. These are their dominant functions, but all of them become more balanced as they come to understand their life stories. It is Boy who is always a boy in some sense, always attached to a romantic dream and never quite able to accept what he has become. He abdicates; the others find new life.

Ramsay says he is "reborn" when he survives his war wounds under the watchful eye of his saint. Similarly, David is reborn when he emerges from the cave in the Alps, and Paul is reborn when he becomes Eisengrim. Those who are reborn have a sense of time outside time, which is one way of defining the mythic time of depth psychology. The "brazen head" begins by evoking time present and time past, and suggesting that its pronouncements are timeless and belong to a world when "Time is past." This is another way of defining mythic time.

The three novels have a total of twelve chapters. Such classical epics as Vergil's *Aeneid* (c. 29-19 B.C.E.) were also written in twelve books or in multiples of twelve. This may not be a complete coincidence, for Liesl and the other characters insist that a life of epic heroism is still possible. The classical epic has a mythic pattern that Ramsay finds in the saints' lives he studies and in the history he teaches. The sixth book of the *Aeneid* is a descent into the underworld in search of oracular knowledge. Similarly, the sixth chapter in Davies' trilogy concerns Boy's death, David's desperate question, and Liesl's sibylline answer through the "brazen head." The great work of the epic hero is to return from the underworld and to act on the oracular knowledge. Ramsay does this when he returns from war, Eisengrim when he emerges from hard work inside an automaton, and David when he breaks out of his long neurosis.

Davies' first readers in Canada recognized thinly disguised places and thought they recognized people, too. Readers who know of the author's colorful life story may be tempted to see autobiographical touches in the trilogy, for each of the three narrators bears a resemblance to some aspect of Davies. Dunstan Ramsay has the same initials as Robertson Davies, though in reverse, and shares Davies' teaching profession and his connection to a wealthy family. David Staunton, who is known to his friends as Davey, comes to shares Davies' interest in Jungian psychology. Magnus Eisengrim, whose initials spell "me," share Davies' interest in theater and illusion. *Fifth Business* appeared after the death of the author's father, and all the novels are concerned with fathers and sons. Readers would, however, do well to remember what Eisengrim says to David about his autobiography: It does not give the facts of his life, but it comes close to the spiritual reality. Always the master of illusion, Davies would point out that his true story is in his fiction.

Thomas Willard

Bibliography:
Cameron, Elspeth, ed. *Robertson Davies: An Appreciation*. Peterborough, Ontario: Broadview Press, 1991. Provides an interview with Davies and seventeen essays, some by such Canadian authors as John Kenneth Galbraith and Joyce Carol Oates.

Davis, J. Madison, ed. *Conversations with Robertson Davies*. Jackson: University Press of Mississippi, 1989. More than two dozen interviews with Davies, originally published in newspapers or magazines or presented over radio and television. Includes some reference to all the Deptford novels. Also provides a general introduction, a list of Davies' books, a chronology of his life, and a helpful index.

Lawrence, Robert G., and Samuel L. Macey, eds. *Studies in Robertson Davies' "Deptford Trilogy."* Victoria, British Columbia: English Literary Studies, University of Victoria, 1980. Eight essays on Davies' craft that discuss the author's interest in folklore, psychology, and theater. Davies' introductory essay, *"The Deptford Trilogy* in Retrospect," gives a valuable account of the trilogy's genesis.

Monk, Patricia. *The Smaller Infinity: The Jungian Self in the Novels of Robertson Davies.* Toronto: University of Toronto Press, 1982. Discusses Davies' knowledge of psychology, specifically that of Carl Jung. Has a separate chapter on each novel in the trilogy, as well as a bibliography and an index.
Peterman, Michael. *Robertson Davies.* Boston: Twayne, 1986. The first book-length study of Davies' life and work. Includes a long chapter on the trilogy.

DESCENT INTO HELL

Type of work: Novel
Author: Charles Williams (1886-1945)
Type of plot: Moral
Time of plot: June and July in the 1930's
Locale: Battle Hill, a residential area near London
First published: 1937

> *Principal characters:*
> PAULINE ANSTRUTHER, an orphaned woman in her twenties
> MARGARET ANSTRUTHER, her grandmother
> PETER STANHOPE, an eminent poet
> LAWRENCE WENTWORTH, a military historian
> ADELA HUNT, an aspiring actress
> HUGH PRESCOTT, her suitor
> MRS. LILY SAMMILE, a neighbor
> MRS. PARRY, a civic leader engaged in directing a play

The Story:

In the suburb of Battle Hill, Peter Stanhope was involved in the production of his verse drama. He was an eminent poet and inhabitant of the Manor House, which had belonged to his family before the housing estate was built. Under the leadership of the capable Mrs. Parry, a group of his neighbors had the privilege of performing his new play in his garden, but only one of them, Pauline Anstruther, even remotely grasped the spiritual significance of his pastoral fantasy. Pauline's sensibility was so quickened by the nuances of his verse that she confided to him the terror that had haunted her for years: the recurrent appearance of her *Doppelgänger*.

Peter Stanhope explained to her the principle of substitution: One person, through love, can assume the burden of another so that the sufferer is relieved. When Pauline became willing to accept his offer to bear her burden, she discovered that she was no longer tortured by her own problem. Instead, she was given the opportunity to bear someone else's burden of fear. Her growth in grace influenced everything around her.

As the rehearsals for the play proceeded, Pauline's role as leader of the chorus was paralleled by her role in the supernatural drama that was taking place concurrently in Battle Hill. The spiritual energy released through the play set in motion a series of events that transcended ordinary time, affecting a number of other inhabitants of the suburb. The housing estate, built in the 1920's, had taken its name from the hill, which had been a site for battles from the time of the ancient Britons to the period of the Tudors. While the estate was being built, the timeless "magnetism of death," still powerful on the Hill (as the suburb was usually called), had touched a despairing unskilled laborer, who had hanged himself on the scaffolding of an unfinished house. His restless spirit still inhabited the area, unrecognized by the occupant of the finished house, Lawrence Wentworth, a noted military historian and adviser to the producer of the play. A middle-aged bachelor, Wentworth developed a secret passion for pretty, conceited Adela Hunt, who was the heroine in the play and the girlfriend of the leading man, Hugh Prescott. Wentworth's jealousy was so consuming that he was destroying himself as surely as the suicide had. Also dying was Pauline's grandmother, Margaret Anstruther, but her death was the natural fulfillment of a well-spent life. Shortly before she died, she was visited by an unpleasantly ingratiating and vaguely sinister neighbor, Mrs. Lily Sammile, who appeared unexpectedly at several crises in the novel.

Pauline's love for her grandmother had been dutiful but detached during the years since her parents' death. She lived in Mrs. Anstruther's house as dependent and companion. It was not until Stanhope relieved her of her fear that Pauline could talk to her grandmother about it and appreciate the depth of the old woman's love. Mrs. Anstruther initiated Pauline further into the doctrine of substituted love by explaining that she could be called upon to bear the pain of their ancestor, John Struther, whose martyrdom by fire was well-known family history.

As Mrs. Anstruther approached the limits of mortality, she could see the face of the suicide as he looked into her window during his ceaseless wandering. Soon she told Pauline that Pauline had to go out in the middle of the night because someone needed her near Mr. Wentworth's. Pauline thought that Mrs. Anstruther's mind was wandering, but somehow Pauline also knew that she had to go. She discovered she no longer feared the dark, and she saw the dead man in ordinary mortal form. He asked the way to London, gently refused her offer to pay his fare, and set off to walk to the city. As she watched him, his form was transmuted into the agonized body of her ancestor, and she was given the opportunity of bearing his burden by enduring the fire in a mystical experience of real pain. This happened during the night between the dress rehearsal and the first performance of the play. Mrs. Anstruther died five minutes after Pauline got home, but the death did not keep Pauline from acting in the play, as the producer had feared. Love had given Pauline a new perspective on time and mortality.

As a counterpoint to Pauline's experience throughout the novel, Lawrence Wentworth's love operated negatively because it was focused on himself. His passion was for his idea of Adela Hunt rather than for the real person, and his jealousy of Hugh Prescott was so powerful that it created a tangible image of the woman who, he imagined, visited him with increasing frequency and became his mistress. In the bedroom where the suicide hanged himself, Wentworth's reason was destroyed by his fantasies of false love. The crisis of his descent into hell was reached on the day of the dress rehearsal, when Mrs. Parry consulted him, as a military historian, on a detail in the costumes of the guards. Wentworth knew that they were wrong and that he could arrange for them to be altered. He was so preoccupied with his erotic experience, however, that he could not be bothered and told an expedient lie instead of the truth. This sacrifice of the historian's integrity confirmed the loss of his soul. The next day his seat at the play was empty. On the afternoon of the performance, there was an unnatural stillness in the atmosphere, like the calm before a storm. Some of the cast complained of the heat, but the play proceeded successfully, and the only disturbance was Mrs. Sammile's fainting at the end. After that, a number of residents of the Hill felt unwell, but life proceeded normally. Margaret Anstruther was buried. Pauline made plans to move into London and take a job.

A few days after the funeral, Adela and Hugh were walking and carrying on a mild argument that revealed the difference between them. Hugh's love for Adela was consistent with his habit of seeing life clearly, while Adela's love for him was an aspect of her desire to manipulate others. As their walk took them near the cemetery, they met Mrs. Sammile. While they were talking to her, they become transfixed by the sight of the graves opening. Mrs. Sammile shrieked and disappeared into a small shed at the edge of the cemetery. Adela screamed and started running, pursued by Hugh shouting that the illusion was caused by the wind blowing up loose earth on the graves. His mind cleared rapidly, and as it did his love faded, so that he gave up the pursuit.

Adela's wild flight led her to the house of the man who she knew idolized her. When she looked through the window, she saw the image of herself that his diseased imagination had created, and she collapsed in terror. Found by a policeman and taken home, she awakened delirious with the impression that she had forgotten her part in the play, a key passage about perception and love. When Pauline called to see her, Adela insisted that Pauline had to find Mrs. Sammile in the shed by the cemetery, to give her Adela's part and thus make her well. Pauline, sensing that Lily Sammile was in fact Lilith, the image of false love, tried to offer Adela her own help in recovering her part, but she found that only by promising to look for the old woman could she ease Adela's tortured spirit.

The climax of love's triumph over death in the novel came when Pauline went, as she had previously gone out into the night at the request of her dying grandmother, to confront Lily Sammile in the cemetery shed. Recognizing her as the illusion rather than the reality of love, Pauline rejected her promises of rewards with a laugh of pure contented joy. Lilith dissolved into the dust and rubble of the old unused shed, which had collapsed from Pauline's push on the door. In attempting to bear Adela's burden, Pauline had thus found the completion of her own part in the drama of Battle Hill and was ready to leave for London. Seen off on the train by Stanhope, who said his own role was to comfort the many people in the community who were ill, she looked forward with joy to her new life in the city. Lawrence Wentworth traveled on the same train but refused her company and went in a daze to a historian's dinner at which his lifelong rival was honored. Wentworth sank into complete insensibility.

Critical Evaluation:

The surrealistic effect of supernatural events taking place in a natural setting is the keynote of Charles Williams' narrative treatment of spiritual experience. Ordinary life is revealed as an image of a deeper reality. The play in which all the characters are involved becomes an image of life itself in which each person must perfect his or her own role in harmony with others. The setting of Battle Hill suggests the hill of Golgotha, and Lily Sammile's lair is revealed to Pauline as an aspect of Gomorrah. For Wentworth, the journey into the city becomes the way to Gomorrah; but Pauline's destination is the Eternal City. She tells Stanhope that it seems funny to be discussing the times of trains to the new Jerusalem, but for the poet the interdependence of the temporal and the eternal is fully assimilated fact.

The characterization, like the plot, is determined by the theme. Only Pauline Anstruther and Lawrence Wentworth, who experience salvation and damnation respectively, are fully delineated. The other characters are sketched with only enough detail to give them substance as examples of different aspects of love. Stanhope and Mrs. Anstruther are seen only in relation to Pauline, Adela Hunt primarily in contrast to Pauline, and Hugh Prescott in contrast to Wentworth. Williams never falls into the error often attributed to John Milton and other authors of making his diabolical characters more attractive than the good ones. Mrs. Sammile is described with a few telling details that make her seem real, slightly pathetic, and obscurely repulsive. Peter Stanhope, in contrast, expresses his sanctity through an easy kindliness and sense of humor. The essence of goodness is seen as a quality of joy that permeates the lives of those who accept it in love. This joy is reflected not only in the characters but in the style, taking the form of wry humor in the descriptions of the play rehearsals and almost poetic rhapsody in the passages of mystical experience. The great variety in style and mood emphasizes Williams' conviction, exemplified in the plot, that reality in human life exists in multiple planes of time and space.

Of Charles Williams' eight novels, his *Descent into Hell* contains his most humane dramatization of his vision of life and the best artistic integration of fictional elements. His indebtedness to visionary poets such as Dante Alighieri, William Wordsworth, Coventry Patmore, and his

Christian colleagues (including C. S. Lewis and J. R. R. Tolkien) among the literary group called the Inklings cannot be overstated. As Williams explained it, his novels are sequels, each building upon themes established early in his writing career. The purpose of his fiction is to communicate his uniquely personal Christian vision of the good life. One may investigate, then, the extent to which *Descent into Hell* achieves Williams' purpose, and the extent to which the novel achieves his purpose without the reader's having to refer to Williams' influences.

The difficulty of such an assessment is reflected in the frustration sometimes expressed about the genre of Williams' novels. His vision is so personal that his novels may be considered a genre unto themselves, without relatives within the literary tradition. A hybrid genre—supernatural horror/thriller—has been suggested for Williams' work and has gained some acceptance. Williams is generally classified as a fantasy fiction writer, but no doubt he considered his supernatural characters and settings the least fictional aspect of his work. The suburban ordinariness of the characters of *Descent into Hell* seems to exclude this work from the horror/thriller category into which Williams' other novels may be placed. A solution to the problem of how to categorize *Descent into Hell* may lie in Williams' devotion to Arthurian legend and to medieval literary forms, among which the exemplum, or story illustrative of a point in a sermon, acts as a model for *Descent into Hell*. Williams wrote in order to convey his main theme of "co-inherence"—mutual Christian charity. His primary symbol for this theme is the City.

In his earlier novels, fictional elements of plot and character are subordinate, sacrificed to theological and thematic considerations and a sometimes undisciplined plethora of supportive images. Over time and with practice, Williams improved his control over the complex narrative form of the novel. The artistic flaws of his early novels (melodramatic and oversimplified plots and flat, stereotypical characterizations), all the result of his eagerness to present his vision, are less apparent. In *Descent into Hell* and subsequent works, plot and theme merge and complement each other, and the characters, still recognizable as Williams' types, are more fully realized and empathetic—including even the diabolical ones such as Lily Sammile.

What is central in all of Williams' work, and comes to a convincing narrative unity in *Descent into Hell*, is his fundamental theme, Christian co-inherence. Co-inherence is the interdependent relation of believers who care for and willingly help one another; these constitute the Body of Christ, the major image of which is the City—the natural city, London, and the supernatural City of God. Pauline's choice of city life is that of Christian life, present in *Descent into Hell* as "the doctrine of substituted love," based on the Gospel command, "Bear ye one another's burdens." The puzzlement that readers may experience when confronted by such terms is further complicated by Williams' repeated theme, the theology of romantic love. For Williams, this means that marriage is the primary mode of co-inherence. To Williams, sexual love stands for divine love, a doctrine that appears, from the point of view of Augustinian Christianity, eccentric at best. Christian life is traditionally a matter not of sexual joy, which is short-lived even in marriage, but of restraint over bodily claims. In *Descent into Hell*, Pauline is not concerned with eros but with *caritas*, or affection between teacher and student—Peter Stanhope and herself. Ironically, Williams' treatment of marriage is a reason for the success and credibility of *Descent into Hell*—Williams succeeds when he departs from his typical plot.

The poet T. S. Eliot considered Williams' novels entertaining reading even if a person did not want to explore deep significance in them. The characters of *Descent into Hell* are believable enough so that Eliot's observation holds true. It is informative to consult Williams' nonfiction work, such as *The Figure of Beatrice* (1943), for definition of the visionary experience of love, or *The Descent of the Dove* (1939), a history of the Holy Spirit in the church, for clarification of Williams' doctrine of co-inherence. Pauline's journey of enlightenment and her involvement with the other characters in Stanhope's play-within-the-novel, the spectators and actors, and the author Stanhope himself, are, however, interesting and enjoyable by themselves, without investigation of the ideas behind them. The lessons about true and false goals are thought-provoking, but Williams is never preachy in presenting his Christian vision. He allows it to speak for itself, as it can through the characters, who are involved in ordinary activities that are nevertheless suspenseful and engaging.

Not all Christians agree that Williams' main themes are correct or orthodox. Some traditionalists say that eros and agape are irreconcilable, but if present investigations into the role of the body in redemption proceed as it now seems they shall for some decades to come, Williams' identification of physical and divine love in the setting of Christian marriage, or perhaps even in friendship, may be prophetic. In any case, Williams' reputation in the future will hinge on the relevance of his themes, which in turn depend on the progress and direction of Christianity more than on the greatness of his fiction. Williams' greatest strengths are the force of his imagination and the clarity of his vision. His fiction meets the needs of his themes, and that is all it needs to do.

"Critical Evaluation" by Diane Brotemarkle

Bibliography:
Bleiler, Everett F. *The Guide to Supernatural Fiction.* Kent, Ohio: Kent State University Press, 1983. The treatment of Williams' novels is brief (pages 532 to 534) but places them in context of the fantasy genre.
Cavaliero, Glen. *Charles Williams: Poet of Theology.* New York: Macmillan, 1983. Explains influences on Williams and contains excellent descriptions of Williams' originality. Pages 78 to 90 give interpretative commentary on *Descent into Hell.*
Glenn, Lois. *Charles W. S. Williams: A Checklist.* Kent, Ohio: Kent State University Press, 1975. A comprehensive listing of writings about Williams up to 1975.
Hadfield, Alice Mary. *Charles Williams: An Exploration of His Life and Work.* New York: Oxford University Press, 1983. A critical biography by Williams' colleague at Oxford University Press. Hadfield understood Williams' creative intentions and was a trusted confidant in Williams' circle of family and friends.
Shideler, Mary McDermott. *The Theology of Romantic Love: A Study in the Writings of Charles Williams.* Grand Rapids, Mich.: Wm. B. Eerdmans, 1966. An indispensable study of Williams' central theological ideas and recurring symbolism.

THE DESCENT OF MAN, AND SELECTION
IN RELATION TO SEX

Type of work: Science
Author: Charles Darwin (1809-1882)
First published: 1871

The firestorm of controversy that had followed the publication of *On the Origin of Species by Means of Natural Selection* (1859) had died down considerably by the time Darwin decided to publish his book about the origin of the human species. Consistent with his meticulously detailed analysis of the origin of species within the animal kingdom, Darwin explains in *The Descent of Man* how the human animal too has evolved from lower forms. The impact of his pronouncement was somewhat blunted on his contemporaries because many had assumed these conclusions after reading the *On the Origin of the Species*; the famous argument between Thomas Huxley and Bishop Wilberforce in which the latter vehemently denied that his family tree included any apes or monkeys took place a decade before Darwin dared to publish his findings about human genealogy. Nevertheless, until Darwin spoke, lesser luminaries could be dismissed; once the great biologist made it clear that he held no privileged place for humankind in the evolutionary process, the rift between scientific and religious explanations for the creation was complete.

The chief scientific significance of Darwin's work lies in his insistence on the prominence of sexual selection in determining human evolution. Also important for the history of ideas, however, is Darwin's insistence that no special privilege should be accorded to humanity's "moral sense." He insists that the development of moral qualities in human beings is simply a part of the normal process of evolution. In his system, there is no need for a God who creates the human soul or speaks directly to humankind to explain how to live. In the twentieth century, the implications of *The Descent of Man* have proven to be more troubling for theologians than they have for scientists.

Problems beset Darwin when he turned from his brilliant biological study of 1859 to the more particular analysis of the relation of humanity to the natural world. These problems are immediately seen in the organization of Darwin's argument: More than two-thirds of the book is an exhaustive discussion of sexual selection. The book may lack the inspiration of *On the Origin of Species*, but in its summary and evaluation of the anthropological thought after the publication of that earlier masterpiece, *The Descent of Man* is one of the most important books of the nineteenth century.

In his introduction Darwin says that he plans to consider three things: whether people descended from some preexisting form, how they developed if indeed they did so descend, and what value the differences between races have to such a development. He draws evidence of the descent of the human species from his vast knowledge of medicine and biology. That people share bodily structure, embryonic development, and rudimentary organs with other mammals seems to him to be evidence enough for asserting a common ancestry. Since anthropologists and paleontologists had not at that time discovered significant relics of prehistoric human life, Darwin's affirmation of the descent of humanity is based on logic; thus he amasses an almost overwhelming number of analogies to strengthen his case. These analogies enable him to trace the development of humanity from lower animals, but in order to do so he must assume a definition of humanity. Darwin maintains that humanity's uniqueness is not due to any one characteristic but to a combination of many: upright position, acquisition of language and tools, a delicate and free hand, and superior mental powers. In the possession of these traits humanity is different only in degree. In fact, Darwin musters evidence to show that animals have curiosity, imagination, attention, and reason, attributes that earlier philosophers thought set people apart from the rest of the animal world.

Writing as a biologist, not a moral philosopher or a theologian, Darwin does not try to consider the implications that his theory has for the various religious and philosophical explanations for the origin of the human race—be they that man was made from clay and woman from a rib, or that the human form sprang from God's forehead. The single attribute that separates humanity from the rest of the animal world, Darwin thinks, is moral sense. Moral sense, the offspring of conscience, was the result of an evolutionary process; conscience came to the human race from a struggle between duty (sympathy and the social instincts) and desire (the urge for complete freedom). The belief in God also evolved, originating in dreams and developing through "spiritual agencies" into gods. It was this application, a logical outcome of Darwin's theories, that horrified both conservative Christians and idealistic philosophers, for the theory completely eliminated the validity of revelation or of supramundane enlightenment.

Darwin, well aware of the implications of his theory, concentrates on the rise of civilization from savagery. Natural selection and the struggle for survival advanced the intellectual powers so that the history of human institutions is the history of the evolution of the intelligence. As tribes grew stronger, the members learned to perceive the consequences of their actions, thereby developing moral sense. Then, as people became more and more aware of their moral sense, advanced civilizations with sophisticated religions and technologies were able to develop.

This discussion of the rise of civilization brings Darwin to the differences between races. Because individual members of different races can be mated so as to form fertile offspring and because the similarities between races far outnumber the differences, Darwin assumes that races are subsets of the one species. Furthermore, Darwin discards the hypotheses that each race descended from a primal pair, that the racial differences were caused by the conditions of life, and that the races evolved independently. The only theory that can explain the differences between races is sexual selection. The question of sexual selection, necessary to prove his assumption about race, leads Darwin into the argument that fills two-thirds of his book.

In *On the Origin of Species*, Darwin bases his theory of evolution primarily on natural selection or the struggle for survival. In other words, a slight modification in an animal's structure might allow it to survive whereas another animal that lacked this modification would die. Existence, then, is a continual warfare in which the animal with the slight advantage wins. In *The Descent of Man* Darwin considerably modifies his view of nature by analyzing sexual selection, a different kind of biological warfare. When animals have their sexes separated, the male and female organs of reproduction differ; these are primary sexual characteristics. There are other differences, however, not directly connected with the act of reproduction, and these are secondary sexual characteristics. Usually the males have the most pronounced secondary sexual characteristics (for example, the brilliant plumage of many male birds); the males acquired these characteristics not from being better fitted for existence (natural selection) but from having gained advantage over other males and having transmitted their advantages to male offspring. There are usually more males than females, so that there is a struggle among males for the possession of the female; hence the female has the opportunity of selecting one out of several males. The strongest females would have first choice among the males; therefore, the secondary sexual characteristics that pass through the strongest male and female would have the most chance of outnumbering those characteristics that pass through weaker partners. In this way, the dominant characteristics are also the strongest. The more active the rivalry among the males, the more pronounced will be the variations between male and female.

Basing his analysis of the animal world upon these principles, Darwin begins with the lower classes of the animal kingdom. In the lowest classes these characteristics are absent because most often the sexes are joined in the same individual, but in the subkingdom of the Arthropoda undoubtable examples of secondary sexual characteristics appear. Darwin presents his most convincing case, however, in his long discussions on insects and birds. In both of these subkingdoms the characteristics are so clearly noticeable that Darwin can accumulate material until he overwhelms his readers. Readers are presented with so much detailed information that they are willing to accept the evidence submitted, and the conclusions the evidence indicates, before Darwin applies his conclusions to humanity.

The secondary sexual characteristics of humanity are more complex than those of birds or insects because humanity is more complex, but this is a difference only in degree. The adult male, for example, has a beard and hairiness of the body (although there is wide variation between tribes or races); he loves to fight and has greater endurance and strength than the female. As a result of his love of battle, the male has a delight in competition and develops his intellect more than woman, who is less selfish. Having noted a few of these characteristics, Darwin asks how they came to be. Because men vied with one another for the woman, the choice of the woman led to certain secondary sexual characteristics. For example, racial differences, he theorizes, are the result of ancient concepts of beauty; the remote ancestors of the African race preferred women who were dark-skinned and flat-nosed. Thus, Darwin is able to describe the differences between races without violating his basic theory of the descent of humanity from lower forms of life.

Darwin anxiously awaited the reaction to the publication of *The Descent of Man* and was surprised when he discovered that people were interested but not shocked. In fact, the book was anticlimactic. The disturbance caused by *On the Origin of Species* had calmed and was not again stirred up, and *The Descent of Man* became a book primarily for biologists.

Bibliography:

Clark, Ronald W. *The Survival of Charles Darwin: A Biography of a Man and an Idea.* New York: Random House, 1984. Comprehensive (more than 400-page) but very readable biography that gives background on the conception, composition, and publication of *The Descent of Man*. Notes, bibliography, and index.

Desmond, Adrian, and James Moore. *Darwin.* New York: Warner Books, 1991. Chronicles Darwin's controversial life; focuses on the critical reception of *The Descent of Man* within his circle of friends and colleagues and on the business concerns of publishing the book.

Ghiselin, Michael T. *The Triumph of the Darwinian Method.* Berkeley: University of California Press, 1969. Explores the centrality of *The Descent of Man* to Darwin's thought, and in turn, the centrality of the book's chief theory, sexual selection, to the theory of evolution. Also examines Darwin's methodology.

Gruber, Howard E. *Darwin on Man: A Psychological Study of Scientific Creativity.* 2d ed. Chicago: University of Chicago Press, 1981. Gruber traces the development of Darwin's thinking and his intentionally delayed application of his theories to humanity. Analyzes the central ideas of *The Descent of Man*.

Hull, David L. *Darwin and His Critics: The Reception of Darwin's Theory of Evolution by the Scientific Community.* Cambridge, Mass.: Harvard University Press, 1973. Introductory discussion of Darwin's inductive methods and such arcane topics as teleology and the empiricist/ rationalist dichotomy. Hull includes letters and reviews from Darwin's contemporaries.

DESIRE UNDER THE ELMS

Type of work: Drama
Author: Eugene O'Neill (1888-1953)
Type of plot: Tragedy
Time of plot: 1850
Locale: A farmhouse in New England
First performed: 1924; first published, 1925

> *Principal characters:*
> EPHRAIM CABOT, a farmer
> SIMEON,
> PETER, and
> EBEN, his sons
> ABBIE, his third wife

The Story:

When the news of gold discoveries in California reached New England, Simeon and Peter Cabot, who had spent their lives piling up stones to fence their father's farm, became restless. In the summer of 1850 they were ready to tear down the fences that seemed to hem them in, to rebel against their close-fisted old father, and for once in their lives to be free. One day, Ephraim Cabot hitched up his rig and drove off, leaving the farm in charge of his three sons, Sim, Peter, and their younger half brother, Eben, all three of whom hated their father and saw him for what he was, a greedy, self-righteous hypocrite. The older brothers hated Ephraim for what he had done to them, but Eben hated his father because he had stolen the land that had belonged to his mother and had then worked her to death on the farm. Eben felt that the farm belonged to him, and he meant to have it. He had inherited some of old Ephraim's stony implacability as well as his sensuality, and he gave expression to the latter on his trips down the road to visit Minnie, the local prostitute, who had earlier belonged to his father.

Realizing that Sim and Peter wanted to go to California yet had no money to take them there, Eben thought up a plan to get rid of them once and for all. While Ephraim was away, he offered them three hundred dollars each in gold if they would sign a paper renouncing all claims to the farm. Eben had found the money, which had belonged to his mother, buried beneath the floorboards of the kitchen. The brothers accepted Eben's offer and set off for California.

Shortly afterward, old Ephraim arrived home with his third wife, Abbie Putnam. He was seventy-six, she thirty-five, but she had decided that she wanted a home of her own. When old Ephraim offered to marry her, she accepted him at once, and by the time she moved into the Cabot homestead she was determined that whatever happened the farm would be hers someday. She tried unsuccessfully to make friends with Eben, who at first hated her as he would have hated any other woman's coming to take his mother's place and the farm that rightfully belonged to him. After a time, though, Eben began to notice that life on the farm was easier since his stepmother had arrived. Yet the realization that Abbie could influence his father as she desired only strengthened Eben's determination to resist her attempts to conciliate him. Some of his taunts became so pointed that Abbie complained to Ephraim, falsely hinting that Eben had made advances toward her. When the old man thereupon threatened to kill his son, she realized that she had gone too far and must take a different approach. After that Abbie subtly instilled in Ephraim's mind the idea that a son and heir who would inherit the farm after his death would be a better way of getting back at Eben than to kill him outright. The old man, flattered at the thought that at the age of seventy-six he might have a son, agreed to leave Eben alone.

One night, after Ephraim had gone out to sleep in the barn, Abbie saw her opportunity to secure her hold on the farm. She lured Eben into his mother's parlor, a room that had not been opened since her death, and seduced him, breaking down his scruples with the suggestion that by cuckolding his father he could get revenge for Ephraim's treatment of his mother.

The result was the son Abbie had hoped for. To celebrate the child's birth, Ephraim invited all the neighbors to a dance in the kitchen of the farmhouse. Many of the guests suspected the true circumstances and said so as openly as they dared. Ephraim paid no attention to the insinuations and outdanced them all, until even the fiddler dropped from sheer exhaustion.

While the revelry still was going on the old man stepped outside to cool off. There he and Eben, who had been sulking outside, quarreled over the possession of the farm. Spitefully, Ephraim taunted his son with his knowledge of how Abbie had tricked him out of his inheritance. Furious, Eben turned on Abbie, threatening to kill her and telling her he hated her and the child he had fathered when she tricked him. By this time, however, Abbie was genuinely in love with Eben, and, thinking the child was the obstacle keeping them apart, she smothered it in an effort to prove to her lover that it was him and not the child whom she wanted. When he discovered what had happened, Eben was enraged and shocked, and he set off to get the sheriff for Abbie's arrest.

When Ephraim discovered that Abbie had killed the child that was not his, he too was shocked, but his heart filled with contempt at his son's cowardice in giving Abbie over to the law. On his return to the farm, Eben began to realize how much he loved Abbie and how great her love for him must have been to induce her to take the child's life. When the sheriff came to take Abbie away, he confessed that he was an accomplice in the crime. The two were taken off together, both destined for punishment, but happy in their love. Ephraim Cabot was left alone with his farm, the best farm in the county. It was, the sheriff told him, a place anybody would want to own.

Critical Evaluation:

Desire Under the Elms was the last of Eugene O'Neill's naturalistic plays and one of his most effective. The structural set, showing the entire farmhouse with one wall removed, was an innovation in its day. In this play, O'Neill's daring reduction of human motives to the simple impulses of love, hate, lust, and greed gives an impression of human nature as convincing and complete as the more complex studies of his later plays.

One of O'Neill's most admired and frequently performed plays, *Desire Under the Elms* provoked enormous controversy during its first stagings. Some audiences were scandalized by what one critic called "distresses" that "range from unholy lust to infanticide, and include drinking, cursing, vengeance, and something approaching incest." In Los Angeles, the cast was arrested for having presented a lewd, obscene, and immoral play. A bizarre trial followed, in which at one point the entire court witnessed a special private performance. The jury was finally dismissed when they could not resolve their deadlock, eight members voting for conviction and four for acquittal.

It gradually became apparent that O'Neill was aiming at something more than a shocking revelation of unconscious drives and primordial fears, elements that were clearly subordinate to his larger purpose of reintroducing authentic tragic vision to American theater. O'Neill's supporters could point out that the Greek and biblical sources that had inspired the play were replete with the very "immoralities" he depicted.

Euripides' *Hippolytus* (428 B.C.E.) and Jean Racine's *Phèdre* (1677) served as O'Neill's principal models. These works both draw on the archetypal plot in which a father returns from a journey with a wife who falls in love with her new stepson. This attachment, at first resisted or concealed, results in a struggle between father and son, in which the father achieves a Pyrrhic victory that costs him both son and spouse. The situation is tragic in that all participants are forced to make conscious choices of evil for the sake of a higher good. It is fate that so structures events as to necessitate the downfall of essentially noble characters. O'Neill complicates the classic plot by introducing Old Testament motifs: the hardness and vengeance of God; the superiority of justice over mercy; and the battle among sons for birthrights and fatherly favor. He also relies on Freudian psychology in his treatment of sexual relationships.

It is questionable whether O'Neill does finally succeed in giving true tragic stature to his characters. There can be no doubt that his drama possesses genuinely tragic aspects, but that the whole deserves the term "tragedy" is doubtful. Three considerations sustain this judgment. First, Eben's basic motivation remains unclear throughout the play, as does the central question whether he is the rightful heir to the farm. Second, in being as preoccupied as they are with struggles for possession and revenge, Abbie and Eben lack that nobility of purpose that we associate with truly tragic characters. Third, Eben is made to seem totally a victim of psychological drives and he does not arrive at his choices freely. This element in particular makes pathos, not tragedy, the dominant quality in *Desire Under the Elms*.

At least one critic has persuasively argued that O'Neill designed his play around a single moral fact: Ephraim Cabot ruined the life of Eben's mother—"murdered her with his hardness," as Eben says—and this sin now cries out for retribution. O'Neill's opening stage directions call for two enormous, expressionistically rendered elms that bend over the farmhouse; they should suggest suffering women and dominate the entire scene with "a sinister maternity." From the beginning, Eben proclaims his monomaniacal desire to take "her vengeance on him—so's she kin rest quiet in her grave." When Abbie enters the parlor, her scheming and erotic tendencies are momentarily subdued by the felt presence of the dead woman's spirit. Eben does not allow himself to be seduced until he is assured that he is doing his mother's will.

The structure of the action reinforces this central theme. In part 1, Eben solidifies his claim to the farm by inducing his half brothers to leave. He uses his mother's money to do this, thus depriving Ephraim of both the fortune and the assistance of his older sons. In part 2, Eben takes Ephraim's wife from him, begets a son, and sets in motion the process whereby Ephraim is humiliated in the eyes of the community. In part 3, Abbie's killing of the child prevents Ephraim from naming a new heir, and Abbie's and Eben's departure dooms Ephraim to that condition of isolation that he has always feared most. He becomes in effect an exile, living on a farm that has become a curse to him. With that, the pattern of crime and justified punishment has been completed.

Tragic in outline, *Desire Under the Elms* is less than tragic in substance. O'Neill lets the issue of Ephraim's persecution of Eben's mother become clouded. This information comes only from Eben, who is a somewhat unreliable source, given his overwhelming Oedipus complex and his deep desire to inherit the farm. That Eben stands to benefit economically by his revenge tends to tarnish his motivation and undermine his credibility. O'Neill intensifies the economic theme by showing how deeply Peter and Simeon covet the farm, and by casting doubt on Eben's claim that he has a clear legal right of ownership. Ephraim, who has worked the farm for years, discounts the claim completely.

Ironically, the fact that *Desire Under the Elms* is not fully realized tragedy probably accounts partially for its appeal, as does O'Neill's choice of a pastoral, precivilized setting that helps convey the workings of unconscious forces with astonishing power. Although outraged protests such as the sensational Los Angeles court case came from irate middle-class theatergoers, it was actually the literate American middle class that formed O'Neill's most avid audience. O'Neill was an iconoclast whose attacks, likened in one of his early poems to torpedoes fired from the submarine of his soul, were directed against middle-class complacency. Much to its credit, however, the audience whose values were under fire responded to plays such as *Desire Under the Elms* with that respect and enthusiasm that springs from recognition of the truth, however disconcerting or uncomfortable that truth may be.

"Critical Evaluation" by Leslie E. Gerber

Bibliography:
Alexander, Doris. *Eugene O'Neill's Creative Struggle: The Decisive Decade, 1924-1933.* University Park: Pennsylvania State University Press, 1992. Attempts to trace the plays to probable sources. Sees O'Neill's writing of plays as opportunities "to confront and solve" problems in his own life. Analyzes the composition and final text of *Desire Under the Elms* in relationship to O'Neill's death wish after his mother died.

Bogard, Travis. *Contour in Time: The Plays of Eugene O'Neill.* Rev. ed. New York: Oxford University Press, 1988. Recognizes O'Neill's plays as efforts at self-understanding. Attempts to analyze the plays in relationship to events in O'Neill's life. Especially effective at developing the psychological and mythic elements in *Desire Under the Elms.*

Carpenter, Frederic I. *Eugene O'Neill.* Rev. ed. Boston: Twayne, 1979. An effective, short introduction to O'Neill's life and plays, emphasizing the tragic dimensions of the dramas. Sees "the spirit of nature" as the "final hero" of *Desire Under the Elms,* since the play emphasizes that human attempts at ownership and possession result in pain and inevitable loss.

Gannon, Paul W. *Eugene O'Neill's "Desire Under the Elms."* New York: Monarch Press, 1965. Provides a clear, if oversimplified, summary of the plot and commentary on the characterization, staging, and major themes and problems in the drama.

Sheaffer, Louis. *O'Neill: Son and Artist.* Boston: Little, Brown, 1973. The most authoritative biography of O'Neill. Includes helpful details about the incidents in O'Neill's life related to *Desire Under the Elms,* as well as about the play's composition and immediate reception.

THE DEVIL UPON TWO STICKS

Type of work: Novel
Author: Alain-René Lesage (1668-1747)
Type of plot: Picaresque
Time of plot: Early eighteenth century
Locale: Madrid
First published: Le Diable boiteux, 1707; revised 1720, 1726 (English translation, 1708)

Principal characters:
 DON CLEOPHAS LEANDRO PEREZ ZAMBULLO, a student
 ASMODEUS, the demon in the bottle
 DON PEDRO DE ESCOLANO, a Spanish nobleman
 DONNA SERAPHINA, his daughter

The Story:

On a dark October night in Madrid, Don Cleophas Leandro Perez Zambullo, a student of Alcala, was in dreadful trouble. While visiting Donna Thomasa, his beloved, three or four hired bravos set upon him in her apartment, and when he lost his sword in the struggle, he was forced to take flight over the rooftops of the neighboring houses. Spying a light in a garret, he entered through a window and discovered an empty room furnished with the strange gear of a magician. As he was taking stock of the place, he heard a sigh and soon realized that he was being addressed by a demon in a bottle. To the student's questionings, the spirit replied that he was neither Lucifer, Uriel, Beelzebub, Leviathan, Belphegor, nor Ashtaroth, but Asmodeus, the Devil on Two Sticks, who always befriended hapless lovers. Cleophas thereupon broke the vial, and out tumbled a monstrous dwarf, with the legs of a goat, a stature of less than three feet, and a grotesque and grimacing face. Half concealed by extraordinary clothing and a curiously embroidered white satin cloak were the two crutches on which the dwarf hobbled about.

Because Cleophas was eager to escape his pursuers and Asmodeus wished to avoid his captor, the magician, the two did not linger in the attic. Cleophas grasped the edge of the demon's cloak, and off they flew into the sky over Madrid. For the remainder of their association together, Asmodeus entertained his companion with views of all that was happening in the city, explaining the circumstances and characteristics of those into whose houses they looked.

At first, they peered into the houses immediately beneath them. Asmodeus showed Cleophas some ridiculous views of a coquette, a nobleman, a poet, and an alchemist. At last, they came to a mansion where cavaliers and their ladies were celebrating a wedding. The demon proceeded to tell the story of the count de Belflor and Leonora de Cespedes.

The count de Belflor, a gallant young man of the court, fell in love with Leonora de Cespedes and wished to make her his mistress. By guile, the gift of a well-filled purse, and the promise of another thousand pistoles when he had accomplished his scheme, he secured the aid of her duenna, Marcella, who prevailed on the young woman to admit the nobleman to her chamber at night. One morning, as the count was making a hasty departure, for dawn was breaking, he slipped and fell while descending the silken ladder lowered from Leonora's bedchamber. The noise awakened Don Luis de Cespedes, her father, who slept in the room above. Uncovering the truth and enraged by this stain on the family honor, the old don confronted his daughter's lover. The count offered to provide for Don Pedro, Leonora's brother, who was a student, but he refused to marry the daughter, giving as his false excuse a marriage that the king had supposedly already arranged for the young courtier.

Later, after reading a reproachful letter written by Leonora, the count was moved to repentance. About the same time, Leonora's brother, Don Pedro, played truant from his studies at Alcala to pay court to an unknown young beauty whom he was secretly meeting. In a street brawl, his life was saved by the count, who happened to be passing by. The count asked the young man to go with him to act as guard while he had an interview with Leonora. The truth was revealed when Don Luis confronted his son, and the count asked for the hand of Leonora and bestowed that of his sister, Donna Eugenia, on his new friend and brother. Don Pedro was overjoyed when he discovered that his secret love was the sister of the count de Belflor. The two couples were married, and Cleophas, guided by the demon, witnessed the festivities of their double wedding. Only Marcella, the treacherous duenna, had no part in the mirth; Don Luis sent her to a nunnery where she could spend her ill-gotten pistoles and prayers to win pardon for her wickedness.

Directing Cleophas' attention to other homes in the city, Asmodeus showed him the plight of an impoverished marquis, a plagiarizing author, a procurer of young men for rich widows, and a printer of antireligious books. At Cleophas' request, the dwarf secured revenge for his mortal companion on the faithless Donna Thomasa. While she was entertaining the assassins she had hired to attack Cleophas, Asmodeus put the men into a jealous rage over her and set them to fighting. So great was the disturbance they caused that neighbors summoned the police, who on their arrival found two of the men slain. The assassins were thrown into the city dungeon, and Donna Thomasa was eventually sentenced to be transported to the colonies. Thus proud Cleophas had his revenge.

Next, Asmodeus revealed the circumstances of the wretches in the nearby prison and madhouse. Poisoners, assassins, servants falsely accused and servants deserving imprisonment, a dishonest surgeon, and others were all displayed in their cells. At the madhouse, Cleophas saw political and religious fanatics, as well as those maddened by jealousy, grief, and the ingratitude of their relatives. Asmodeus also took the opportunity of showing Cleophas other people who should have been confined in an insane asylum, for their brains were addled by avarice, egotism, and the uncontrollable pangs of love.

Suddenly, from their vantage point above the city, the two glimpsed a raging fire in a house beneath them. To everyone's horror, the beautiful Donna Seraphina, daughter of Don Pedro de Escolano, was trapped in an upstairs room. Asmodeus, at the entreaties of Cleophas, assumed the shape and appearance of the young student and brought the girl out of the burning building safely. After the rescue, Asmodeus told Cleophas that he had suddenly decided on a grand design: The young man would ultimately marry the lovely Donna Seraphina, for her noble father already believed himself deeply indebted to the handsome young cavalier.

Asmodeus continued the strange tour of Madrid with portrayals of the unrevealed secrets of those buried in the tombs of a churchyard and with glimpses of bedside death scenes of true grief, avarice, jealousy, and self-seeking. By way of contrast, he then told Cleophas a long and circumstantial tale of true friendship and love.

Don Juan de Zarata, a gallant of Toledo, had slain his false wife's lover and fled to Valencia. Near the outskirts of that city, he stopped a duel between Don Alvaro Ponzo and Don Fabricio de Mendoza, rivals for the hand of the beautiful young widow, Donna Theodora de Cifuentes. On the advice of Don Juan, the lady was allowed to choose between her suitors; her choice was Don Fabricio. Through that meeting, the young Toledan and Don Fabricio became inseparable companions. Don Fabricio, however, could not understand his friend's seeming indifference to the charms of Donna Theodora. What he did not suspect was that the Toledan had been greatly attracted to the lady and she to him, but that out of regard for friendship Don Juan made every effort to repress his passion. Unhappy in her own unrealized love for Don Juan, the lady finally decided to return to her estate at Villareal. When the Toledan confessed the truth to Don Fabricio, that gentleman was so moved by Don Juan's delicacy of feeling that he vowed no rivalry in love could ever part them.

Meanwhile, Donna Theodora had been kidnapped by Don Alvaro's ruffians and put on a vessel bound for Sardinia. Don Fabricio and Don Juan set out in pursuit, but the ship on which they sailed was overtaken by Tunisian pirates, and the two were made prisoners. Separated in their captivity, they were in despair. Don Juan, sold to the dey of Algiers, was made a gardener. At length the dey, impressed by the bearing and courtesy of his Christian slave, made him his confidant. The dey had in his harem a Spanish lady whose grief appeared inconsolable; he asked Don Juan to speak to her as a countryman and assure her of her master's tender regard. To Don Juan's surprise, the lady proved to be Donna Theodora, also taken captive when her abductors were killed by Algerian pirates.

From that time on, Don Juan planned to deliver Donna Theodora from her captivity; at last, aided by an unknown accomplice, they made their escape. Their unknown benefactor turned out to be Don Fabricio, who had been rescued aboard a French privateer. Mistaking Don Juan for the false Don Alvaro, Don Fabricio stabbed his friend and then, discovering his error, plunged his sword into his own breast. The condition of Don Fabricio grew worse, and he died soon after the arrival of the fugitives in Spain. Torn between their mutual love and grief for their friend, Donna Theodora and Don Juan were at last free to marry. A short time later, Don Juan was mortally injured in a fall from his horse. Half mad with grief, Donna Theodora soon followed him to the grave.

At length, the sleeping city awoke. Protesting that he was not weary, Cleophas urged the little demon to let him see more. Asmodeus directed his glance to the activities in the streets of beggars, artisans, a miser, and a philosopher. Then they came upon the throngs of people gathering for the king's levee: Faithless and forgetful noblemen, those seeking their own good fortune, gamblers, an honest magistrate, and others awaited their turn to appear before the king. Cleophas, however, could not be shown into the king's presence, since the royal cabinet, as Asmodeus explained, was under the exclusive control of other devils.

For diversion, Asmodeus took Cleophas to see the arrival of ransomed slaves at the Monastery of Mercy. Each captive had his own fears and hopes, and Asmodeus recounted the past and future of scores of these wretches. A few slaves met with happy circumstances upon gaining their freedom, but most of them met with grief, loneliness, and disappointment.

At that point, Asmodeus became aware that his master, the magician, had missed him, and he departed swiftly after making the student promise that he would never reveal to mortal ears all that he had seen and overheard that night. Cleophas returned to his own apartment and sank into a deep slumber that lasted a day and a night. When he awoke, he went to call on Donna Seraphina, where he was welcomed by the grateful Don Pedro, her father. During a later visit in the house where he was now an honored guest, Cleophas confessed that it was not he who had rescued the girl from the flames. Although overcome by astonishment, Don Pedro waved the explanation aside. After all, it was at Cleophas' insistence that Donna Seraphina had been brought from the blazing house unharmed. A few weeks later, the wedding of Donna Seraphina and Cleophas was celebrated with much magnificence, and the happy bridegroom never had occasion to regret the night of freedom he had provided for the Devil on Two Sticks.

Critical Evaluation:

Alain-René Lesage is chiefly remembered for his long picaresque novel, *Gil Blas* (1715-1735), but his early publication of *The Devil upon Two Sticks*, with its extensive revision and enlargement in 1726, created far more excitement in his own day and is still an interesting example of the early realistic novel of manners. As he did in most of his prose fiction, Lesage worked from a Spanish original, borrowing his title and some of the early incidents from *El Diablo Cojuelo* (1641), by Luis Vélez de Guevara. Once started, however, the novel drew further and further away from its Spanish model and entertained Lesage's contemporaries by introducing a wealth of anecdotes and reminiscences, portraits and sketches of some of the most prominent of Parisian personages, under the guise of Spanish names. Lesage's satire is trenchant and ironical, though never gross or vulgar. Lesage saw humanity with a sharp and critical eye, and he was particularly successful in his witty portrayals of authors, actors, lawyers, the social world, and "persons of quality." Like most picaresque fiction, the novel is loosely plotted; within a central narrative concerning the fortunes of Don Cleophas, a young Spanish cavalier, Lesage introduced scores of other tales, ranging from brief summaries of a few sentences to short stories running for several pages or chapters. The major plot remains in evidence throughout the book, however, and the author concludes his tale with a suitably romantic ending.

Although a satire on human nature, *The Devil upon Two Sticks* is an amiable, almost lighthearted work; the author attacks his victims with wit and grace, his high spirits and good humor balancing the grotesqueness inherent in the story. Asmodeus, the lame devil, helps Cleophas to see through the false fronts, both physical and moral, assumed by most people. The devil and his young rescuer thereby provide a framework for the stories that compose most of the narrative; Asmodeus shows Cleophas a man or woman and then exposes the person, telling his or her story with merciless truth. If there is any consistent message in *The Devil upon Two Sticks*, it is always to doubt first impressions and to seek to penetrate beneath the façades that individuals show the world.

Asmodeus is a unique character, a grotesque vision comparable to Caliban or John Milton's fallen angels. Without possessing the dark powers of the greater demons, he presides over the vices and follies of humankind rather than over the crimes. He is malicious, but not cruel, and prefers teasing and ridiculing humanity to torturing it. He possesses so much wit and playful malice and is so vividly portrayed that he almost walks away with the book, making the reader forget that he is not intended to be anything more than a momentarily friendly fiend.

Cleophas, the fiery young Spaniard, is the perfect foil for Asmodeus. He is lacking enough in discretion to be glad of the opportunity to peek behind closed doors and barred windows and discover the shocking truths about apparently respectable people. The other characters, who come and go in the secondary tales, are described with precision and amazing dexterity; few authors can summarize human nature, in its many shades and phases, in so few words. Lesage's satire is never heavy-handed, and his humor is never blunted by anticipation. In many respects, *The Devil upon Two Sticks* is surer of touch and wittier than the author's more famous *Gil Blas*; certainly, the skill he shows in drawing the scenes and completing the characterizations is reason enough for the book to be at least as well known. At times, the author reaches heights in this book that he never does in *Gil Blas*, such as in his personification of death. Even here, his humor breaks through to add still another dimension to his vision, when, having described one of the terrific phantom's wings painted with war, pestilence, famine, and shipwreck, he adorns the other with the picture of young physicians taking their degrees. The narratives that make up the book are of differing lengths and of varying interest, but all of them are entertaining and executed with wit and style.

Bibliography:

Bjornson, Richard. "The Picaresque Hero Arrives." *The Picaresque Hero in European Fiction.* Madison: University of Wisconsin Press, 1977. Comments on Lesage's adaptation of Vélez de Guevara's story and notes the dramatic significance of changes, including the transformation of the devil into a spirit presiding over the foolish as well as the evil.

Green, Frederick C. *French Novelists, Manners, and Ideas from the Renaissance to the Revolution.* New York: Frederick Ungar, 1964. Describes *The Devil upon Two Sticks* as a preparatory work for Lesage's greater novel, *Gil Blas.* Explains why the novel was popular with Lesage's contemporaries.

Mylne, Vivienne. *The Eighteenth Century French Novel: Techniques of Illusion.* Manchester, England: Manchester University Press, 1965. A chapter on Lesage provides insight into the novelist's creative process and principal themes. Notes his use of stock situations and local color to vivify the narrative of *The Devil upon Two Sticks.*

Showalter, English. *The Evolution of the French Novel 1641-1782.* Princeton, N.J.: Princeton University Press, 1972. Comments on characterization, the role of the narrator, and influences that shaped Lesage's novel; notes the author's success in using this improbable story as a means of illuminating a "moral truth."

Symons, Arthur. Introduction to *The Devil on Two Sticks.* London: Navarre Society, 1927. Discusses the literary background upon which Lesage draws for his story. Highlights the novelist's use of his tale as a satire on the supposed progress of civilization.

THE DEVIL'S ELIXIRS
From the Posthumous Papers of Brother Medardus,
a Capuchin Friar

Type of work: Novel
Author: E. T. A. Hoffmann (1776-1822)
Type of plot: Fantasy
Time of plot: Eighteenth century
Locale: Germany and Italy
First published: Die Elixiere des Teufels: Nachgelassene Papiere des Bruders Medardus, eines Kapuziners, 1815-1816 (English translation, 1824)

> *Principal characters:*
> MEDARDUS, a monk
> AURELIA, a young noblewoman
> FRANCESCO, a painter
> PRINCE VON ROSENTHURM
> COUNT VICTORIN, Medardus' brother
> LEONARDUS, a prior
> AN ABBESS
> PIETRO BELCAMPO, a hairdresser

The Story:

Francis was born at the Convent of the Holy Lime-Tree in Prussia, at the moment that his father lay dying. At Kreuzberg, the abbess of the Cistercian convent made him her pupil. When he was sixteen years old, he became a monk at the Capuchin convent in Konigswald and took the name of Medardus. Medardus was put in charge of the relics of the convent. Among them was a strange elixir. Legend said that all who drank of the potion would belong to the devil, and that if two persons drank of it, they would share the same thoughts and desires but secretly wish to destroy each other.

On St. Anthony's Day, Medardus preached a sermon about the elixir. While he was talking, he saw in the audience a painter whom he had once seen at the Convent of the Holy Lime-Tree. The sight disturbed him so much that he began to rave like a madman. Later, in an attempt to regain his full senses, he drank some of the elixir.

One day during the confessional, a beautiful woman, in appearance exactly like a painting of St. Rosalia, told Medardus that she loved him and then left. Medardus determined to run away to find her. Before he could escape from the convent, however, Prior Leonardus sent him on an errand to Rome. On the way to Rome Medardus saw an officer leaning over a precipice. When Medardus tried to save him, the officer fell over the ledge. At that moment a page appeared and told Medardus that his disguise was very good. Medardus, hardly knowing what he did, went to the nearby castle, where he met an old man, Reinhold, who seemed to be expecting him. Reinhold told him that Baron von F——, the owner of the castle, had a son, Hermogen, and a daughter, Aurelia, by an Italian wife who later died. The baron had then married Euphemia, a sinister woman who was carrying on an affair with Count Victorin, a former suitor. The count was in the habit of disguising himself in order to gain entrance to the castle.

Medardus became convinced that he was Victorin. When he saw that Aurelia was the mysterious lady who looked like St. Rosalia, he felt that fate was guiding him. He tried to approach Aurelia, but she ran away. Hermogen had witnessed the incident, so Medardus killed him. As Medardus fled from the castle, he heard that Euphemia was dying of a poison she had intended for him. Taking refuge in the woods, Medardus cut off his beard and changed into clothes that Victorin's page had brought him.

When Medardus arrived in Frankenburg, he recognized the painter who had disturbed his sermon on St. Anthony's Day. After he tried to kill the man with a stiletto, Medardus was rescued from an angry mob by Pietro Belcampo, an odd hairdresser. At the forest house of the Prince von Rosenthurm, Medardus met a monk who looked like him and who drank some of his elixir. Medardus later went to the castle, where the court physician showed him a picture of a person who again looked just like him. The man was Francesco, who, together with a strange painter, had been brought to the court by the prince's brother, the duke of Neuenburg. The duke had become engaged to an Italian countess and married her, but on their wedding night, the duke had been found murdered by a stiletto wound. The bride claimed, however, that the groom had come to the bridal chamber without a light, consummated the marriage, and left. The painter, accused of the murder, escaped, and the countess went to live in a distant castle.

Francesco was engaged to the sister of a princess. During the marriage ceremony, the painter reappeared. Francesco fainted while trying to kill the painter with a stiletto. The next day he left, still unwed. It was later learned that the Italian countess had given birth to a son named Victorin. Francesco's intended bride left to become the abbess at Kreuzberg. Hearing these tales, Medardus realized that Francesco must be his father. At a party that night, Medardus was astonished to see that the princess was accompanied by Aurelia. When Aurelia recognized him, he was charged with the murder of Hermogen and was imprisoned. Later, he was released because his double, a mad monk who greatly resembled him, had confessed to the crime. Medardus also learned that he and Victorin were stepbrothers.

Medardus became engaged to Aurelia. On the day that he was to marry her, he saw the mad monk being taken to the scaffold. Suddenly Medardus began to rave. In his frenzy he stabbed Aurelia, rescued the monk from the cart, and escaped into the woods. When he regained consciousness, he found himself dressed as a monk in an Italian madhouse. He had been taken there by Belcampo, the hairdresser, who said that he had found Medardus in the woods, naked, with a monk's robe lying beside him.

Medardus went next to a Capuchin convent near Rome. While there, he learned that Aurelia was alive. He also saw a strange book that a mysterious painter left at the convent. It contained sketches of paintings Medardus had seen at the Convent of the Holy Lime-Tree and the history of the artist. He was Francesco, a painter who had drunk of St. Anthony's elixir.

Among his works, according to the account, was a painting of the martyrdom of St. Rosalia. One day he had met a woman who looked just like the painting. They married, but his wife died soon after their son was born. Then Francesco, accused of sorcery, fled with his child, whom he nourished on the elixir. From Francesco's son the family branched out and included the Princess von Rosenthurm, the abbess, the first Baroness von F——, Euphemia, and Victorin.

Medardus, now repenting his past, punished himself so much that he became known to the Pope, who spoke of making the monk his confessor. Having incurred the antagonism of the papal confessor in this manner, Medardus, realizing that his life was in danger, left Rome.

He returned to the Cistercian monastery and saw Prior Leonardus, who said that Victorin had come there, claimed to be Medardus, and then disappeared. By piecing together the strange sequences of events, Medardus and Leonardus realized that Medardus and Victorin, two brothers who had drunk of the elixir, had tried to destroy each other. Leonardus also told Medardus that Aurelia was to become a nun that day, taking the name of Rosalia. This news so disturbed Medardus that while Aurelia was taking her vows he had an impulse to stab her, but after an inward struggle, he conquered his demon and had peace in his soul. Suddenly there was a disturbance in the church. Medardus' double, dressed in rags, ran to the altar, shouted that Aurelia was his intended bride, stabbed her in the heart, and escaped. Medardus rushed to Aurelia's side. Close by he saw the mysterious painter, who said that Medardus' trials would soon end. Aurelia regained consciousness, told Medardus that he and she were destined to expiate the guilt of their family, and then died. The people in the church, having seen the painter emerge from a picture over the altar, believed that a miracle had occurred; they regarded Aurelia, now called Rosalia, as a saint.

Medardus, having fully recovered, could clearly tell truth from falsehood, and from Leonardus and the abbess he received forgiveness for his past deeds. Leonardus then asked him to commit his life story to writing. Having completed this task, he was awaiting the time when he would join Aurelia in heaven.

Father Spiridion, the librarian of the Capuchin monastery at Konigswald, appended a note to Medardus' manuscript. He wrote that one night, hearing strange sounds from Medardus' cell, he investigated and saw a tall man who said that the hour of fulfillment would come soon. Then Medardus died, one year to the minute from the time of Aurelia's death. Father Spiridion added that the painting of St. Rosalia, which the monastery had acquired, bore, on the day of Medardus' funeral, a wreath of roses. The wreath had been put there by Pietro Belcampo, who later joined the order and became Brother Peter.

Critical Evaluation:

The Devil's Elixirs is modeled on Matthew Gregory Lewis' classic gothic novel *The Monk* (1796), which Aurelia reads. Like Lewis, E. T. A. Hoffmann employs a monk as a central character in order to emphasize the sharp difference that might exist between the image that one presents to the world, in speech and public behavior, and the inner self of one's fantasies, desires, and impulses. Lewis' Ambrosio is, however, a monster of calculated hypocrisy whose embarkation upon a career of sin, although doubtless unwise, is the result of a conscious decision; the situation of Hoffmann's Medardus is more confused.

Medardus' confusion is communicated to the text that tells his story, which becomes inordinately convoluted. Attempts to say what happens in the story are bound to fail. The linear plot of *The Monk* is much easier to follow—Ambrosio is drawn inexorably to his damnation. The plot might be deemed unsatisfactory on precisely that account. When one becomes aware of the conflicts that exist between one's social self and one's inner self, those conflicts are often confused, and it really is not clear exactly how much control one's powers of conscious reason have over the anarchic thrust of one's appetites and emotions. It never is clear, even to those who commit horrible crimes, to what extent they were driven by forces outside their control. In admitting that the business of submitting to temptation is dreadfully confused, Hoffmann offers the reader an account of an inner life that, however luridly it may be supernaturalized, is psychologically accurate. It is possible to pity Medardus.

The double is a central motif in gothic fiction, particularly that of Germany. The German word frequently applied to the motif, *Doppelgänger*, figures in a popular saying whose literal translation is: "He who sees his going double must go himself," that is, die. The double of gothic fiction carries an implicit threat of impending death. In most stories involving doubles—of which the most famous American example is Edgar Allan Poe's "William Wilson"—the double becomes an externalized projection of the inner self, and takes into the social arena all the impulses and designs that must be eliminated from the social self in order to preserve the harmony of social relationships. Such "escapes" of the inner self inevitably cause embarrassment to the social self, whose falsity stands revealed.

Medardus' double is the libertine aristocrat Victorin, the man Medardus might have become had he not been led by the ridicule of a gaggle of teasing girls to suppress his sexuality and take holy orders. Medardus thinks that Victorin has been destroyed, but he has not; he is merely submerged within Medardus' personality, ready to resurface when the conditions are right. What Medardus tries to construe as an altogether proper regard for an image of St. Rosalia eventually reveals itself as sexual attraction. St. Anthony might have been able to rise above such temptations—as symbolized by the Satanic elixir—but Medardus is not. He tries to find a way back from his commitment to celibacy, following St. Paul's advice that it is "better to marry than to burn." Alas, his secret desires are no more tolerant of the prospect of monogamy than they are of the prospect of celibacy; instead of being the instrument of his salvation, Aurelia becomes one more aspect of his confusion.

In the end, Aurelia's removal by the angry double permits Medardus a brief interval of peace. He is reassured by her dead body that he—that is, his social self—will be able to enjoy an untroubled union with her in Heaven (a place from which unruly inner selves are banned). His own account of his tribulations, given in a written confession that is of necessity the product of his conscious, rational self, ends on a very hopeful note. The appendix added by Father Spiridion seems to tell a different tale, although Spiridion does not realize it: The reader will almost certainly conclude that the "horrible voice" that summons Medardus to his fate is that of the devil.

In concluding the story thus, Hoffmann perhaps sides with those who think that if a Last Judgment occurs, then people must answer for their secret thoughts and desires as well as their public speeches and actions. On the other hand, Hoffmann has piled layers of confusion so thickly upon his plot by making Spiridion as unreliable a narrator as Medardus that one hesitates to accept this idea as final. Perhaps the ending is to be read as a calculated ambiguity, signifying a genuine uncertainty as to where the limits of personal responsibility lie—or ought to lie.

"Critical Evaluation" by Brian Stableford

Bibliography:

Cobb, Palmer. *The Influence of E. T. A. Hoffmann on the Tales of Edgar Allan Poe*. Chapel Hill: University of North Carolina Press, 1908. Includes discussion of the two authors' use of the double.

Daemmrich, Horst S. *The Shattered Self: E. T. A. Hoffmann's Tragic Vision*. Detroit: Wayne State University Press, 1973. Explores the divisions of the self in *The Devil's Elixirs* and Hoffmann's shorter works.

Herdman, John. *The Double in Nineteenth-Century Fiction*. New York: St. Martin's Press, 1991. Chapter 4, subsection 2, is a detailed analysis of *The Devil's Elixirs*.

Negus, Kenneth. *E. T. A. Hoffmann's Other World*. Philadelphia: University of Pennsylvania Press, 1965. A study of Hoffmann's use of the supernatural.

Passage, Charles E. "E. T. A. Hoffmann's *The Devil's Elixirs*: A Flawed Masterpiece." In *Journal of English and Germanic Philology* 75, no. 4 (October, 1976): 531-545. A detailed account of the novel.

THE DEVOTION OF THE CROSS

Type of work: Drama
Author: Pedro Calderón de la Barca (1600-1681)
Type of plot: Tragedy
Time of plot: Seventeenth century
Locale: Siena, Italy
First published: La devoción de la cruz, 1634 (English translation, 1832); first performed, 1643

Principal characters:
EUSEBIO, a foundling
JULIA, his sister
LISARDO, his brother
CURCIO, their father
GIL, a peasant
MENGA, a peasant woman
ALBERTO, a priest

The Story:
Two rustics, Gil and Menga, were looking for a lost donkey when they spied two men preparing to fight a duel. Lisardo, one of the men, was angry that anyone as low-born as Eusebio, the other, should aspire to marry Julia, Lisardo's sister.

Eusebio explained by telling a miraculous story. He had been one of two infants abandoned beneath a wayside cross. Taken home by a shepherd, the famished baby bit the breast of his foster mother, who threw the child into a well, where his rescuers found him floating safely with arms crossed. Later the house in which he was living burned, but the fire broke out on the Day of the Cross, and once more he survived unharmed. More recently, in a shipwreck, he had floated to safety on a raft of two crossed planks. He explained that since he had obviously acquired nobility by devotion to the cross, he deserved Julia. Lisardo denied the claim and they fought. As had happened before in Eusebio's life, no harm came to him in a dangerous situation. As Lisardo lay dying of his wound, he begged in the name of the cross for Eusebio to save him. The amazed peasants reported that they had seen Eusebio pick up his dying enemy and carry him to a convent.

Back in Siena, Julia was fearful of her father's discovery of letters she had received from Eusebio. When her lover appeared, wanting to take her away with him before she learned about her brother's death, her father's arrival forced him to hide and listen to Curcio as he voiced his long-held suspicions of his wife's infidelity. Curcio was interrupted by the arrival of four peasants carrying the body of Lisardo. Julia, grieving, ordered the killer out of her life forever.

Eusebio, broken-hearted, turned bandit and through his cruelty rose to command a troop of outlaws. Only captives mentioning the cross escaped death at his hands. One day a bullet-creased prisoner was brought in carrying a volume titled *Miracles of the Cross.* He was Father Alberto, and in gratitude for having his life spared the priest promised Eusebio that he would be on hand to hear the bandit's last confession.

News arrived that Lisardo's father, having put Julia into a convent, was pursuing Eusebio with soldiers. Scorning danger, Eusebio let his passion for Julia take him to the convent, where he found her in bed. Before he could take her, he saw on her breast the same sign of the cross that was on his own skin. The mark told him that she had been the other child left beside the cross, his sister, and so he ran away. Julia, who had tried to fight him off in her cell, began to pursue him in masculine attire. She did not know why he had refused to love her.

When the soldiers overtook him, Curcio wounded Eusebio fatally. Then the cross on the young man's body revealed to Curcio that he had slain his own son, abandoned with his twin sister because of the father's baseless suspicions of his wife's unfaithfulness.

With his dying breath, Eusebio called for Father Alberto. Four shepherds arrived to bury his body. The priest also appeared as he had promised. He explained that because of God's pleasure in Eusebio's devotion to the cross, his soul had been left in his body long enough for him to make his confession and be redeemed.

Critical Evaluation:

To understand a religious play such as *The Devotion of the Cross*, one must keep in mind that Spain was a deeply religious nation, and that Pedro Calderón de la Barca truly expressed its feelings and ideas in the seventeenth century. The most popular of Spanish playwrights after the death of Lope de Vega in 1635, he wrote secular and religious dramas until he took holy orders in 1651. From that time until his death he wrote only religious plays. *The Devotion of the Cross* is one of his early works. Since the characters and the setting are Italian, some critics assign it to the period when he was a soldier in Italy. The plot is less complicated than is usual in Calderón's work.

The Devotion of the Cross was one of the most controversial of the Baroque dramatist's works. First there was the problem of authorship; only in the latter part of the twentieth century was the play universally accepted as Calderón's. Then there were the critics whose analyses, at times oriented more toward the political and the religious than toward the literary, had more to do with Catholic Spain and Protestant England than the subject matter of the text itself.

Eighteenth and nineteenth century critics were outraged at the extravagance of the plot and the fetishism of what they claimed was the play's underlying philosophy, namely that salvation was possible through the obsessive veneration of an inanimate object. Even some of Calderón's admirers admitted that the mature Calderón himself probably was scandalized by this early work. Most chronologies give the date of composition as 1633, one that would place it close to that of Calderón's masterpiece *Life Is a Dream* (1635).

Criticism of *The Devotion of the Cross*, however, has now come full circle. Far from the derision of Protestant critics, or a mere mention in a footnote by Hispanic scholars, the play is now praised for its allegorical nature and is viewed as representative of Calderón's thematic and dramatic craftsmanship.

Curcio is the character in whom the Calderonian imprint is most evident. A tyrannical father, one of a long line of the dramatist's dysfunctional male parents, he is also afflicted by the fatal Calderonian disease, a blind self-aggrandizement which is outwardly manifested in violent spasms of honor. One such outbreak led him to commit the deed, the murder of his wife, that has poisoned his life and that eventually causes the destruction of his entire family. Rosmira died but not before giving birth to twins. Julia, one of the twins, was saved however, the other twin, Eusebio, was lost. Even though Curcio had secretly believed in his wife's innocence, and no one else had even doubted her, his pride forced him to kill her. Exterior appearances, even admitted self-delusions, are what matter to him. They are his identity. This concept of self has robbed his son of his identity, a confusion which is given dramatic irony in the scene in which Eusebio and Julia, unknown brother and sister, but also lovers, confront each other over the dead body of their brother Lisardo, who was killed because he ridiculed Eusebio's lack of family and position. (Some students of seventeenth century staging have asserted that in the performance, Lisardo would have been lying crosswise between Eusebio and Julia with the corpse's hands also placed in a position similar to a cross.

Far from being just an effective stage device or a dramatic motif, the symbol of the cross represents true identity. On an individual level, it is Eusebio's only link with his past. Found at the foot of a cross and possessed of a mysterious birthmark in the shape of a cross, Eusebio's life history has been marked by this sign. Nevertheless, his veneration of the cross is not a blind devotion to the object, the superstitious fetishism seen by early critics, but, instead, it is an authentic perception, although dimly glimpsed at times, of what the symbol can reveal to him about his life. It is a hope that Eusebio does not lose, even after he descends into a life of violence and crime. In fact, fetishism is explicitly derided in the scene in which the comic figure Gil cynically covers himself with imitation crosses and is captured, anyway.

The cross is not just the personal symbol of identity for Eusebio, but in the larger Christian worldview of this drama, it is the symbol of truth for all humanity. Some readings of *The Devotion of the Cross* have focused on the heavy allegorical content of the work. Eusebio, therefore, is marked with the sign of the cross, as are all Christians. Eusebio's fall from grace is representative of Adam's fall from paradise, and his salvation, even after death, symbolizes the powerful redemptive gift of Christ's mercy. Eusebio's life, also like that of all Christians, is colored by the original sin of the father—in a religious context again, that of Adam's fall, but in Eusebio's life, first by the decision of his father to murder his mother and, second, by his father's vengeance after Lisardo's death; his father's vengeance deprives him of his lands and possessions and forces him into a life of flight and crime.

Curcio, therefore, has twice stripped his son of his identity, and Curcio's vindictive pursuit leads to Eusebio's death. Curcio is, after all, the one who had committed murder at the foot of a cross, and every evil consequence in the play can be traced to the consequences of his actions. He is the puppet master pulling the strings, and this sense of a malevolent presence controlling their lives makes the protagonists desperate. They seem driven to lash out at anyone or anything. They lack self-control, and their lives seem predestined.

This repudiation of free will on the one hand, and the emphasis on an uncritical, all-forgiving grace—no matter what the crimes of the sinner—on the other hand, have bothered some students of Calderonian drama and have possibly contributed to the initial hesitation in attributing the play to Calderón, who has been seen as the foremost champion of free will and has repeatedly been cited as one of the precursors of Existentialism. Calderón did write several works with strong fatalistic undertones, most of which were set in pre-Christian—therefore, unredeemed—times. The mood of these works is similar to that of *The Devotion of the Cross*. In *The Great Cenobia* (1625), for example, characters such as Cenobia either accept their fate with stoic fortitude, or they rage against it. In either case, there is no thought of changing destiny. In *The Devotion of the Cross*, Eusebio and Julia are portrayed as innocent victims of their father's crime and pride, and they are branded by his follies, just as surely as by their cross birthmark. A miracle is necessary to save them and only Christ's grace triumphs over blindness and egotism and the oppression of society's rigid codes. Interpreted in this light, the dual theme of the play is Calderonian, a search for self-identity filtered through a protest at a tyrannical honor code and a vindication of free will, with the difference that here the free will belongs to God.

"Critical Evaluation" by Charlene E. Suscavage

Bibliography:
Enwhistle, W. J. "Calderón's *La devoción de la cruz.*" *Bulletin Hispanique* 50 (1948): 472-482. An important study of *The Devotion of the Cross* that should be read together with A. A. Parker's work.

Honig, Edwin. *Calderón and the Seizures of Honor.* Cambridge, Mass.: Harvard University Press, 1972. Detailed analysis of the often debated theme of honor in Calderon's plays. Selected quotes from the plays are in English, but the Spanish is given in an appendix.

McKendrick, Melveena. "The *bandolera* of Golden Age Drama: A Symbol of Feminist Revolt." *Bulletin of Hispanic Studies* 46 (1969): 1-20. Discusses the *bandolera*, a popular figure of the age. Also discusses Calderón's portrayal of Julia.

Parker, A. A. "The Father and Son Conflict in the Drama of Calderón." *Forum for Modern Language Studies* 2 (1966): 99-133. Critically acclaimed study of one of the pivotal themes in Calderonian drama. An excellent starting point for further study.

_____. "Towards a Definition of Calderonian Tragedy." *Bulletin of Hispanic Studies* 39 (1962): 223-237. One of the seminal essays of modern Calderonian criticism. Discusses Parker's famous theory of shared responsibility. His analysis of *The Devotion of the Cross* is the most widely accepted.

THE DIALOGUES OF PLATO

Type of work: Philosophy
Author: Plato (c. 427-347 B.C.E.)
First transcribed: 399-347 B.C.E. (English translation, 1804)

> *Principal personages:*
> SOCRATES, the Athenian philosopher
> GORGIAS, a Sophist
> PROTAGORAS, a Sophist
> CRITO, Socrates' contemporary, an aged friend
> PHAEDRUS, a defender of rhetoric
> ARISTOPHANES, a poet and playwright
> THEAETETUS, a hero of the battle of Corinth
> PARMENIDES, the philosopher from Elea
> PHILEBUS, a hedonist
> TIMAEUS, a philosopher and statesman
> PLATO, Socrates' pupil

The Platonic *Dialogues* rank with the extant works of Aristotle as among the most important philosophical works of Western culture. The extent of Plato's influence is partly due to the fact that his works have survived, unlike those of earlier Greek philosophers, as well as to the fact that at various times in the history of the Christian church his ideas have been used in the process of constructing a Christian theology (though in this respect Aristotle's influence was greater). The principal cause of his past and continuing effect on human thought, however, is the quality of his work.

The distinctive character of Platonic thought finds adequate expression in the dialogue form. Although Plato, like all philosophers, had his favored perspectives from which he interpreted and, consequently, saw the world, he realized better than most philosophers that philosophy is more an activity of the mind than the product of an investigation. This is not to say that philosophy does not, in some legitimate sense, illuminate the world. In the process of making sense out of experience the philosopher is restless: No one way of clarifying an idea or a view is entirely satisfactory, and there is always much to be said for an alternative mode of explanation. When distinctive Platonic conceptions finally become clear, they do so against a background of penetrating discussion by means of which alternative ideas had been explored for their own values and made to complement the conception that Plato finally endorses. As an instrument for presenting the critical point-counterpoint of ideas, the dialogue is ideal, and as a character in control of the general course and quality of the discussion, Socrates is unsurpassed.

Socrates was Plato's teacher, and it was probably out of respect for Socrates the man and the philosopher that Plato first considered using him as the central disputant in his dialogues. Reflection must have reenforced his decision, for Socrates was important more for his method than for his fixed ideas, more for his value as a philosophical irritant than as a source of enduring wisdom. The Socratic method is often described as having been designed to bring out the contradictions and omissions in the philosophical views of others; better yet, it can be understood as a clever technique for so playing on the ambiguities of claims as to lead others into changing their use of terms and, hence, into apparent inconsistency.

The extent to which Plato uses the dialogues to record Socrates' ideas and that to which he uses Socrates as a proponent of his own ideas will probably never be conclusively answered. The question is historical, but in the philosophical sense it makes no difference whose ideas found their way into the dialogues. A fairly safe assumption is that it was Socrates who emphasized the importance of philosophical problems of value, knowledge, and philosophy itself. He probably argued that it is important to know oneself, that the admission of one's own ignorance is a kind of wisdom possessed by few individuals, and that virtue is knowledge.

Certainly Socrates must have had a devotion to his calling as philosopher and critic: No one who regarded philosophy as a game would have remained in Athens to face the charge that by philosophy he had corrupted the youth of Athens, nor would he have refused a chance to escape after having been condemned to death. Socrates' courage and integrity are recorded with poignant power in the *Apology*, the dialogue in which Socrates defends himself and philosophy against the charges brought against him; the *Crito*, in which Socrates refuses to escape from prison; and the *Phaedo*, in which Socrates discusses the immortality of the soul before he drinks the hemlock poison and dies.

Of the ideas presented in the dialogues, perhaps none is more important than Plato's theory of Ideas or Forms. This theory is most clearly expressed in the *Republic*, the dialogue in which the problem of discovering the nature of human justice is resolved by considering the nature of justice in the state. Plato distinguished between particular things, the objects experienced in daily living, and the characters that things have, or could have. Goodness, truth, beauty, and other universal characters—properties that can affect a number of individual objects—are eternal, changeless, beautiful, and the source of all knowledge. Although some critics have claimed that Plato was speaking metaphorically when he talked, through Socrates, about the reality of the Forms, the dialogues leave the impression that Plato considered the Forms to be actually existing, in some sense peculiar to themselves, as universals or prototypes that things may or may not exemplify.

A survey, however brief, of the range of questions and tentative answers to be found in the dialogues, provides no more than a bare inkling of Plato's power as a philosopher. Only a careful reading leads to a true appreciation of the depth of Plato's speculative mind and the skill of his dialectic. Only a reading, moreover, can convey Plato's charm, wit, and range of sympathy. Whether the final result may be in good part attributed to Socrates as Plato's inspiring teacher is unimportant. Socrates as the subject and Plato as the writer (and philosopher—in all probability more creative than Socrates) combine to create an unforgettable image of the Hellenistic mind.

Although many of the dialogues concern themselves with more than one question, and although definitive answers are infrequent so that discussions centering on a certain subject may crop up in a number of different dialogues, certain central problems and conclusions can be isolated in the *Dialogues*.

Charmides centers on the question, "What is temperance?" After criticizing a number of answers, and without finally answering the question, Socrates emphasizes the point that temperance involves knowledge. *Lysis* and *Laches* consider, respectively, the questions, "What is friendship?" and "What is courage?" The first discussion brings out the difficulty of the question and of resolving conflicts of values; the second one distinguishes courage from a mere facing of danger and makes the point that courage, as one of the virtues, is a kind of knowledge involving willingness to act for the good. The *Ion* exhibits Socratic irony at work on a rhapsodist who is proud of his skill in the recitation of poetry. Socrates argues that poetry is the result of inspiration, a kind of divine madness. In the *Protagoras*, Socrates identifies virtue and knowledge, insisting that no one chooses evil except through ignorance. One of a number of attacks of the Sophistical art of fighting with words is contained in the *Euthydemus*.

In the *Meno*, the philosopher Socrates and his companions wonder whether virtue can be taught. The doctrine that ideas are implanted in the soul before birth is demonstrated by leading a slave boy into making the correct answers to some problems in geometry. At first it seems that since virtue is a good and goodness is knowledge, virtue can be taught. Because, however, there are no teachers of virtue, it cannot be taught; in any case, because virtue involves right opinion, it is not teachable. In the *Euthyphro*, the idea that piety is whatever is pleasing to the gods is shown to be inadequate.

The *Apology* is the most effective portrait of Socrates in a practical situation. No moment in his life had graver consequences than the trial resulting from the charge that he had corrupted the youth of Athens by his teachings, yet Socrates continued to be himself, to argue dialectically, and to reaffirm his love of wisdom and virtue. He pictured himself as a gadfly, stinging the Athenians out of their intellectual arrogance. He argued that he would not corrupt anyone voluntarily, for to corrupt those about him would be to create evil that might harm him.

Socrates is shown as a respecter of the law in the *Crito*; he refuses to escape after having been pronounced guilty. In the *Phaedo* he argues that the philosopher seeks death because his whole aim in life is to separate the soul from the body. He argues for the immortality of the soul by saying that opposites are generated from opposites; therefore, life is generated from death. The soul is by its very nature the principle of life; hence, it cannot itself die.

The dialogue *Greater hippias* does not settle the question, "What is beauty?" but it does show, as Socrates points out, that "All that is beautiful is difficult." The subject of love is considered from various philosophic perspectives in the *Symposium*, culminating in the conception of the highest love as the love of the good, the beautiful, and the true. *Gorgias* begins with a discussion of the art of rhetoric, and proceeds to the development of the familiar Socratic ideas that it is better to suffer evil than to do it, and that it is better to be punished for evil-doing than to escape punishment.

The *Parmenides* is a fascinating technical argument concerning various logical puzzles about the one and the many. It contains some criticism of Plato's theory of Ideas. Plato's increasing interest in problems of philosophic method is shown by the *Cratylus*, which contains a discussion of language beginning with the question whether there are true and false names. Socrates is not dogmatic about the implications of using names, but he does insist that any theory of language allow people to continue to speak of their knowledge of realities.

The *Phaedrus* is another discourse on love. It contains the famous myth of the soul conceived as a charioteer and winged steeds. In the *Theaetetus*, Socrates examines the proposal by Theaetetus that knowledge is sense perception. He rejects this idea as well as the notion that knowledge is true opinion.

The *Sophist* is a careful study of sophistical method with emphasis on the problem of being and non-being. In the *Statesman*, Plato continues the study of the state he initiated in the *Republic*, introducing the idea—later stressed by Aristotle—that virtue is a mean.

Socrates argues in the *Philebus* that neither pleasure nor wisdom is in itself the highest good, since pleasure that is not known is worthless and wisdom that is not pleasant is not worth having; only a combination is wholly satisfactory. A rare excursion into physics and a philosophical consideration of the nature of the universe are found in the *Timaeus*. Here Plato writes of God, Creation, the elements, the soul, gravitation, and many other matters.

The *Critias*, an unfinished dialogue, presents the story of an ancient and mythical war between Athens and Atlantis; and with the *Laws*, the longest of the dialogues, Plato ranges over most of the areas touched on in his other dialogues, but with an added religious content: Soul is the source of life, motion, and moral action; and there is an evil soul in the universe with which God must deal.

Bibliography:
Grube, G. M. A. *Plato's Thought*. Indianapolis: Hackett, 1980. A good exposition of Plato's thought designed for both specialists and nonspecialists. Focuses on broad themes (such as the Ideas, Eros, the soul, the gods, and education) rather than on individual dialogues. Includes a valuable bibliographic essay.

Guthrie, W. K. C. *Plato. The Man and His Dialogues: Earlier Period* and *The Later Plato and the Academy*. Vols. 4 and 5 in *A History of Greek Philosophy*. Cambridge, England: Cambridge University Press, 1975, 1978. Contains a lucid summary and substantial discussions of each dialogue. Scholarly and authoritative, yet fully accessible to the general reader.

Jaeger, Werner. *In Search of the Divine Centre* and *The Conflict of Cultural Ideals in the Age of Plato*. Vols. 2 and 3 in *Paideia: The Ideals of Greek Culture*. Translated by Gilbert Highet. New York: Oxford University Press, 1943. Presents an analysis of Plato's dialogues within the context of a cultural history of Greece; emphasizes the *Protagoras, Gorgias, Meno, Symposium, Republic, Phaedrus*, and *Laws*. Provocative reading for novice or specialist.

Raven, J. E. *Plato's Thought in the Making: A Study of the Development of His Metaphysics*. Cambridge, England: Cambridge University Press, 1965. Investigates the relative contributions of Socrates and Plato. Treats primarily the *Protagoras, Gorgias, Meno, Phaedo, Symposium, Republic, Phaedrus, Parmenides, Sophist*, and *Timaeus*. Appropriate for the general reader.

Shorey, Paul. *What Plato Said*. Chicago: University of Chicago Press, 1933. Chapters on Plato's life and writings precede concise summaries of all the dialogues; running references to the Platonic text being summarized are printed in the margins. A good introduction to Plato's works.

DIANA OF THE CROSSWAYS

Type of work: Novel
Author: George Meredith (1828-1909)
Type of plot: Psychological realism
Time of plot: Nineteenth century
Locale: England
First published: 1885

Principal characters:
DIANA MERION WARWICK, a young woman of beauty and charm
AUGUSTUS WARWICK, her husband
LADY EMMA DUNSTANE, Diana's friend
THOMAS REDWORTH, Diana's friend and admirer
LORD DANNISBURGH, another friend
SIR PERCY DACIER, a young politician in love with Diana

The Story:

All fashionable London was amazed and shocked when the beautiful and charming Diana Warwick suddenly left her husband's house. The marriage had been ill-fated from the start, for Augustus Warwick, a calculating, ambitious politician, had considered the marriage to Diana as largely one of convenience. Diana, for her part, had accepted his proposal as a refuge from the unwelcome attentions to which her position as an orphan had exposed her.

Diana Merion had first appeared in society at a state ball in Dublin, where her unspoiled charm and beauty attracted many admirers. Lady Emma Dunstane introduced Diana to Thomas Redworth, a friend of her husband, Sir Lukin Dunstane. Redworth's attentions so enraged Mr. Sullivan Smith, a hot-tempered Irishman, that he attempted to provoke the Englishman to a duel. Redworth pacified the Irishman, however, to avoid compromising Diana by a duel fought on her account.

Later, while visiting Lady Emma at Copsley, the Dunstane country home in England, Diana was forced to rebuff Sir Lukin when he attempted to make love to her. Leaving Copsley, she went to visit the Warwicks. Thomas Redworth told Lady Emma that he loved Diana, but by then it was too late. Diana had already agreed to marry Augustus Warwick.

In London, the Warwicks lived in a large house and entertained lavishly. Among their intimates was Lord Dannisburgh, an elderly peer who became Diana's friend and adviser. While Warwick was away on a government mission, the two were often seen together, and Diana was so indiscreet as to let Lord Dannisburgh accompany her when she went to visit Lady Emma, which gave rise to unkind gossip. On his return, Warwick, who was incapable of understanding that his wife was innocent, served Diana with a divorce suit in which he accused her of infidelity and named Lord Dannisburgh as corespondent. Diana disappeared from Warwick's house and from London. In a letter, she told Lady Emma that she intended to leave England. Her friend, realizing that flight would be tantamount to confession, felt sure that before she left the country, Diana would go to Crossways, her father's old home. Determined that Diana should remain and boldly defend herself, Lady Emma sent Redworth to Crossways with instructions to detain Diana and persuade her to stay with the Dunstanes at Copsley.

Lady Emma had guessed correctly; Diana was at Crossways with her maid. At first, she was unwilling to see Lady Emma's point of view, for she thought of her flight as a disdainful stepping aside from Warwick's sordid accusations; finally, however, she gave in to Redworth's arguments and returned with him to Copsley.

Although the court returned a verdict of not guilty to the charge Warwick had brought against her, Diana felt that her honor was ruined and that in the eyes of the world she was guilty. For a time, she was able to forget her own distress by nursing her friend, Lady Emma, who was seriously ill. Later, she left England to go on a Mediterranean cruise. Before her departure, she wrote a book entitled *The Princess Egeria.*

In Egypt, she met Redworth, now a brilliant member of Parliament. He was accompanied by Sir Percy Dacier, Lord Dannisburgh's nephew and a rising young politician, who fell in love with her and followed her to the Continent. He was recalled to London by the illness of his uncle. Diana followed a short time later and learned on her arrival in London that Redworth had been active in making her book a literary triumph. He had aroused interest among the critics because he knew that Diana was in need of money.

Lord Dannisburgh died, with Diana at his bedside during his last illness. He had been her friend, and she paid him that last tribute of friendship and respect regardless of the storm of criticism it elicited. When Lord Dannisburgh's will was read, it was learned that he had left a sum of money to Diana.

In the meantime, Diana had inadvertently made an enemy of the socially ambitious Mrs. Wathin, who thought it her social duty to tear Diana's reputation to shreds. In part, her dislike was motivated by jealousy that Diana should be accepted by people who would not tolerate her. Her actions were also inspired by Warwick, Mrs. Wathin's friend, who, once he lost his suit against Diana, tried to force his wife to return to him.

Sir Percy's attentions were distressing to Diana. She was half in love with him, but was still legally bound to Warwick. She faced a crisis when Mrs. Wathin called to announce that Warwick, now ill, wanted Diana to return and act as his nurse. Diana refused, whereupon Warwick threatened to exercise his legal rights as her husband. Sir Percy, who informed her of Warwick's intention, asked her to elope with him to Paris. She agreed but was saved from that folly by Redworth, who arrived to tell her that Lady Emma was ill and about to undergo a serious operation at Copsley. Diana went with him to be at her friend's side.

Lady Emma nearly died, and the gravity of her condition restored Diana's own sense of responsibility. She ordered Sir Percy to forget her. He continued to pursue her, however. One day, he confided the tremendous political secret that the prime minister was about to call on Parliament to pass some revolutionary reform measures. Then he attempted to resume his former courtship, but Diana refused to listen to him; she felt that if she could not have Sir Percy as a lover, she could not keep him as a friend.

Because Diana was in desperate need of money—she had been forced to sell Crossways to pay her debts, and her later novels had not brought her any money—she went to the editor of a paper that opposed the government party and sold him the information Sir Percy had given to her.

When the paper appeared with a full disclosure of the prime minister's plan, Sir Percy accused her of having betrayed him and discontinued his friendship with her. A short time later, he proposed to a young lady of fortune. About the same time, Warwick was struck down by a cab in the street and killed. Diana had her freedom at last, but she was not happy, knowing she was in public disgrace. Although she had burned the check in payment for the information she had disclosed, it was common knowledge that she had betrayed Sir Percy and that he had retaliated by marrying Constance Asper, an heiress. When Sullivan Smith proposed marriage, Diana refused him and sought refuge in the company of her old friend, Lady Emma. Her stay at Copsley freed her of her memories of Sir Percy, so much so that on her return to London she was able to greet him and his bride with dignity and charm. Her wit was as sharp as ever, and she took pleasure in revenging herself upon those who had attempted to destroy her reputation with their gossip and slander.

On another visit to Copsley, she met Redworth again, who was now a railroad promoter and still a distinguished member of Parliament. When he invited her and Lady Emma to visit Crossways, Diana learned that it was Redworth who had bought her old home and furnished it with the London possessions she had been forced to sell. He bluntly told Diana that he had bought the house and furnished it for her because he expected her to become his wife. Not wishing to involve him in the scandals that had circulated about her for so long, she at first pretended indifference to his abrupt wooing. Lady Emma urged her to marry Redworth, however, since he had loved her for many years. At last, aware that she brought no real disgrace to Redworth's name, she consented to become his wife.

Critical Evaluation:

Any novel by George Meredith requires attention not only to the actual work but also to the wider aspects of the technique of fiction. Meredith was an original writer of deep concentration and mature force. His Diana is a character who is head and shoulders above most nineteenth century fictional English heroines, offering the charm of femininity as well as the portrait of one perplexed by convention and yet aware of its force. Her predicament involves errors in judgment but becomes a glory to her, and her career compels the reader's belief that a life that will not let go its harvest of errors until they are thoroughly winnowed is a human drama of deepest interest. Diana, beautiful, witty, and skeptical of social convention and moral expediency, is the embodiment of Meredith's philosophy and art, and she shows that an individual can extract wisdom from life's experiences.

Diana of the Crossways is the most emphatically feminist of George Meredith's novels, but a woman too intelligent and spirited to accept willingly her "place," as defined by Victorian society, figures prominently in virtually all of his fiction. Some, such as Diana's friend Emma Dunstane or Lady Blandish of *The Ordeal of Richard Feverel* (1859), manage to confine their protest to witty commentary while playing their assigned roles; others, like Diana, are forced by circumstances into active rebellion.

It is generally agreed that Meredith's chief model for his beautiful, brilliant, hard-beset heroines was his own first wife. In the fine poem sequence *Modern Love* (1862), he traces, thinly disguised, the course of their marriage from its happy and passionate beginnings through the conflicts that led to his wife's running off with an artist friend of Meredith. Although bitter at first, Meredith learned much from the experience of his first marriage and came to accept major responsibility for its failure. His novels repeatedly depict a loving and loyal woman virtually driven into the arms of another man by the blind egoism of her husband or lover. Asked by Robert Louis Stevenson on whom the protagonist of *The Egoist* (1879) was modeled, Meredith replied that his fatuous hero was drawn "from all of us but principally from myself."

Meredith believed that his society was dominated by egotism, chiefly that of men, and was both fearful and suspicious of anything bright and beautiful because of the threat that it posed to complacency. He shared the Victorian belief in progress, but he defined progress in terms of intelligence and sensibility. Choosing the comedy of wit as his preferred mode, he attacked the dull and smug and called for "brain, more brain." He recognized the tragedy of life but ascribed it to human failure. As he wrote in *Modern Love*, "no villain need be. We are betrayed by what is false within." The falseness may spring from self-deception or from unquestioning acceptance of what "the world" proclaims. What can save people is the ability to be honest with themselves and to see the world as it is, as well as the courage to act on their perceptions even in defiance of social norms.

Many of Meredith's contemporaries shared his belief in a continuing evolution of human beings' spiritual and intellectual capacities, but few besides Robert Browning were as ardent in affirming also "the value and significance of flesh." For Meredith, the goal of life was to realize one's full potentialities in a vital balance: "The spirit must brand the flesh that it may live."

Meredith's Diana fully exemplifies his philosophy of life. The central metaphor of the novel is the "dog-world" in hot pursuit of its quarry, a beautiful woman too intelligent and sensitive to play the role society demands of her, that either of "parasite" or of "chalice." Diana is, however, no spotless, perfect victim of malign persecutors. In precept and practice, Meredith scorned sentimental melodrama. Young and inexperienced, Diana brings much of her trouble on herself. She marries for protection and position, a prudent move by worldly standards but disastrous in its consequences. Achieving a measure of independence, she endangers it by her extravagance, and she is finally almost destroyed by an impulsive, desperate act. Although elements of the "dog-world" are moved by envy and malice, most of Diana's adversaries act "honorably" in their own eyes; it is the conventions of honor, of respectability, and—most important—of the place of women in Victorian society that nearly overpower her.

The resolution of the plot would seem to be a compromise if the novel were the feminist tract it has been called: Diana does not finally triumph as a fully independent person, accepted by society on her own terms and admired for her wit and nerve. Only rescued from despair by her friend Emma, she proves herself capable of standing alone but chooses instead to marry again. As Meredith presents her choice, however, it is not compromise but fulfillment. Her marriage to Redworth, who truly understands and values her, represents the ideal wedding of flesh and spirit, achieved not by good luck but after a process of striving, blundering, learning from mistakes, and finally seeing and accepting life as it is.

Diana of the Crossways was an immediate success upon publication, probably because its theme had been taken from a recent scandal involving a brilliant and beautiful Irishwoman, Mrs. Caroline Norton, who had been accused (as it proved, falsely) of selling an important government secret. Critics have generally tended to rate the work high among Meredith's works, often second only to his masterpiece *The Egoist*, and its themes are of perhaps even broader interest in the late twentieth century than they were in 1885. Yet later readers have experienced some difficulty with Meredith's famous style, the joy and the despair of his admirers.

From his first work of fiction, *The Shaving of Shagpat* (1855), to his last, the prose of this admirable writer became progressively more poetic in its richness, precision, compactness, and indirection. In the earlier novels, it is a beautiful addition to plot and characterization; in the later, it sometimes detracts from or even obscures them. Oscar Wilde may not have been entirely fair in claiming that as a novelist Meredith could do everything but tell a story, yet in *Diana of the Crossways* and other later novels he often seems fastidiously averse to saying anything directly. The texture of his prose makes demands that not all readers are willing to meet, but the attentive reader is richly rewarded in beauty, wit, and subtlety of thought and expression. The very dazzle and density of Meredith's style, embodying as it does his vigorous and invigorating vision of life, continues to delight new generations of readers.

"Critical Evaluation" by Katharine Bail Hoskins

Bibliography:
Conrow, Margaret. "Meredith's Ideal of Purity." *Essays in Literature* 10, no. 2 (Fall, 1983): 199-207. Explores Meredith's definition of the ideal of sexual purity and his double standard. Examines the Lugano scene in *Diana of the Crossways*.
Daniels, Elizabeth A. "A Meredithian Glance at Gwendolen Harleth." In *George Eliot: A Centenary Tribute*, edited by Gordon S. Haight. Totowa, N.J.: Barnes and Noble Books, 1982. Like George Eliot, Meredith did not wish to overturn Victorian marriage, but he was sharply critical of the callous nature of the male ego and believed that society needed women with fuller psychic development.
Deis, Elizabeth J. "Marriage as Crossways: George Meredith's Victorian-Modern Compromise." In *Portraits of Marriage in Literature*, edited by Anne C. Hargrove and Maurine Magliocco. Macomb: Western Illinois University, 1984. Discusses Meredith's position on marriage as a transitional one.
Elam, Diane. "'We pray to be defended from her cleverness': Conjugating Romance in George Meredith's *Diana of the Crossways*." *Genre* 21, no. 2 (Summer, 1988): 179-201. Meredith's text self-consciously thematizes romance, employing it not only as a process of structuring the novel but also as a subject of the narrative. Shows that reality outside the novel is also a narrative construction.
McGlamery, Gayla. "In His Beginning, His Ends: The 'Preface' to Meredith's *Diana of the Crossways*." *Studies in the Novel* 23, no. 4 (Winter, 1991): 470-489. A close reading of the difficult opening chapters, with their contorted stylistics and philosophical pronouncements, as a demonstration of all that Meredith hopes to achieve in the rest of the novel. Notes the new direction in his handling of identity and in his relationship to the reader.

DIARY

Type of work: Diary
Author: Samuel Pepys (1633-1703)
First published: 1825; enlarged edition, 1848-1849; enlarged to 6 volumes, 1875-1879;
enlarged to 10 volumes, 1893-1899; enlarged to 11 volumes, 1970-1983

The *Diary* of Samuel Pepys is a unique document in the annals of English literature, perhaps of all literature. There are other fascinating day-to-day accounts of interesting and momentous times, and some of these were written by people of genius, but there is only one other autobiographical collection—the recently discovered journals of James Boswell—that combines fascinating subject matter and genius of composition with the intriguing story that is associated with the *Diary* of Pepys.

There is an important difference between Boswell and Pepys. Boswell, as his editors admit, was writing for posterity; Pepys was not. Pepys' *Diary* was written for himself only, apparently for the sole purpose of allowing its author to savor once more, at the end of each day, the experiences of the preceding twenty-four hours. There is no evidence of revision of any kind, and the book was written in a shorthand that protected it from posterity for more than a hundred years after its author's failing eyesight had forced him to give up keeping his diary.

Pepys' method of composition gives the *Diary* an immediacy that makes Boswell's *Journals* appear sedulously organized. The coded shorthand allows for admissions of personal animosities and revelations of scandalous behavior that otherwise would not be found in the writings of a responsible public official. That Pepys was a responsible, high-ranking public official is the last factor that contributes to the importance of his work. Boswell was the scion of an important Scottish family and a member of the Scottish bar, but (aside from his Corsican experience) the only history in which he was involved was literary history. Pepys was involved with the history of a nation at a very important time.

The *Diary* is important in a number of ways. First, it is of great value as a document of the Restoration period. No writer of a historical novel based on the history of the time could possibly create a character familiar with as many important events as was the opportunistic busybody, Samuel Pepys. One of the most influential figures in bringing about the return of the Stuarts in 1660 was the former Cromwellian, Sir Edward Montague, who was assisted by his able cousin and protégé, Samuel Pepys. It was Sir Edward who commanded the fleet that sailed from Holland and returned triumphantly with the king. On board the flagship, kissing the king's hand, firing a cannon to salute the new monarch (and burning an eye in the process), commenting on the plainness of the queen, taking charge of the king's dog in the landing at Dover was, again, Samuel Pepys.

Later, made Clerk of the Acts of the Navy Board because of his assistance to the Stuarts (Sir Edward Montague was made Earl of Sandwich), he remained at his post in London and wrote down his observations of the terrible plague from which most members of his class fled in panic. It was Pepys, again, who did his best to keep the English Navy afloat during the Dutch Wars, and Pepys who defended the Navy in a brilliant speech before Parliament in the investigation that followed (1668). Earlier (September 2, 1666), when the great fire of London broke out, it was Pepys who rushed to the king to inform him of the catastrophe and to suggest the blowing up of houses to prevent the spread of the fire. Pepys, who had a part in all these events, tells of them in a straightforward, unself-conscious account unvarnished by fear of what his contemporaries would have thought or of what posterity would think.

Along with vivid pictures of the major events of Restoration history are day-to-day accounts of the less earthshaking but equally revealing activities in the life of the London that Pepys shared, accounts that make the *Diary* a document of social, cultural, and artistic history as well. Here Pepys' concern with—his actual delight in—detail brings a particular world of the past to life. Readers see the crowded, unsanitary, and often impassable London streets. At times, during trips to Pepys' father's house in Brampton or during excursions to the country, we catch glimpses of rural existence in the days of Charles II. Readers see life in the houses of the well-to-do and the noble and, occasionally, at court. On a more mundane scale, there is Pepys' concern with clothes (his father was a tailor and he reflects a professional knowledge) and his greater concern with managing his own household. Unfortunately for revelations on this score, Pepys had no children, but his problems in household management included his handling of the affairs of his rather shiftless parents, brothers, and sister, the maintenance of a staff of servants that grew as his own wealth increased, and domestic supervision of his beautiful but erratic—sometimes docile, sometimes temperamental—young wife. In regard to the arts, there is a wealth of material on the theater and on music. Pepys was an inveterate playgoer. Though his frequent attendance bothered his basically Puritan conscience and though he made intermittent vows to refrain, it is seldom that many entries go by in which some play that he has seen is not commented on. So frequent are these comments, in fact, that the *Diary* is an invaluable source of information to the student of Restoration drama. It is equally valuable to the specialist in the history of music: Pepys was not only an accomplished musician but also a composer, and the delight in music which he expresses gives an insight into a particularly musical age.

Nor was artistic beauty the only kind that captivated the practical and mercenary Pepys. Since he was equally attracted to beauty in its carnal manifestations, his pursuit of beauty in feminine form and his diligent (but finally unsuccessful) attempts to hide these pursuits from his wife provide an insight into the mores of the Restoration period. These accounts of the diarist's philanderings—honest, but hidden by the elaborate code—are a part of the personal revelation that the work provides.

In spite of its importance as historical and social document, the *Diary* is, on its most intriguing level, the portrait of a man, a self-portrait drawn in strong and certain lines with no detail, however uncomplimentary, however compromising, omitted. That it is the portrait of a man active in the affairs of his day adds to its interest; but the main value comes from its unstinting wealth of circumstantial detail. Yet the detail and the man cannot be separated: The love of detail and the love of life that inspired the keeper of the *Diary* make up the essence of the man himself. The *Diary* is a celebration of the things of this world and a portrait of the man who praised them.

Bibliography:
Morshead, O. F. Introduction to *The Diary of Samuel Pepys: Selections*, edited by O. F. Morshead. New York: Harper & Row, 1960. Offers a brief biography of Pepys and his family, a publishing history of the diaries, and commentary on the diaries' content. Notes Pepys' energy, his artless style, and his surprising frankness.
Ollard, Richard. *Pepys: A Biography.* New York: Holt, Rinehart and Winston, 1974. Offers clarification to readers who need additional information about topics to which the diaries allude. Focuses particularly on Pepys' politics and his position in the admiralty.
Sutherland, James. *English Literature of the Late Seventeenth Century.* New York: Oxford University Press, 1969. Examines the subjects of Pepys' diary and notes his self-analysis and his remarkable honesty.

Taylor, Ivan E. *Samuel Pepys*. New York: Twayne, 1967. This general introduction to Pepys and his diaries organizes its chapters around the themes of Pepys' work, including his politics, family life, theatergoing, and womanizing.

Willy, Margaret. *English Diarists: Evelyn and Pepys*. London: Published for the British Council and the National Book League by Longmans, Green, 1963. Includes a brief sketch of Pepys' life and a discussion of the scope of his diaries with reference both to what they reveal about his personality and to the historical events they record.

THE DIARY OF A COUNTRY PRIEST

Type of work: Novel
Author: Georges Bernanos (1888-1948)
Type of plot: Psychological realism
Time of plot: 1920's
Locale: France
First published: Journal d'un curé de campagne, 1936 (English translation, 1937)

Principal characters:
A PARISH PRIEST, the diarist
THE CURÉ DE TORCY, a superior of the narrator
DOCTOR MAXENCE DELBENDE, the narrator's friend
SERAPHITA DUMOUCHEL, a young parishioner
MONSIEUR DUFRETY, a former classmate of the narrator
THE COUNT, a wealthy resident of the parish
THE COUNTESS, his wife
MADEMOISELLE CHANTAL, their daughter
MADEMOISELLE LOUISE, the governess at the chateau

The Story:

A thirty-year-old priest who was in charge of the Ambricourt Parish in France recorded in his diary his impressions and activities over a period of one year. His purpose in keeping the diary was to maintain frankness with himself in his relationships with his parishioners and in his service to God.

The priest was a man of marked humility, sympathy, simplicity, and great loneliness. Son of a poor family in which there had been much suffering and hardship, he planned to raise the scale of living in his parish. His plans for a village savings bank and for cooperative farming were discussed at his first monthly meeting with the curates, but his plans were disapproved because of their pretentious scope and his lack of personal influence in the parish. This blow, which caused him to question whether God was prepared to use his services as he did the services of others, was intensified by the words of his superior and ideal, the Curé de Torcy, and of his friend, Dr. Maxence Delbende, who soon afterward committed suicide because of his disappointment at not receiving a legacy he expected.

These two men thwarted the young priest's ambition with their belief that the poor could not be raised for religious and social reasons. God gave the poor a dignity, the Curé de Torcy said, which they do not wish to lose in His sight. According to the doctor, poverty served as a social bond and a mark of prestige among the poor. In the eyes of the church, the curate believed, the rich are on the earth to protect the poor.

Undaunted, the priest accepted an invitation to the chateau, where he hoped to get financial help for his parish projects from the count. He was unsuccessful in this, but he devoted himself with all his physical energy, which was limited because of insomnia and a chronic stomach disorder, to the spiritual advancement of his parish. Even here, however, his efforts were ill-spent. He questioned his success in teaching a catechism class when the children did not respond as he had hoped, and he was tormented by the attentions of Seraphita Dumouchel, a young student in the class, who discomfited him by her suggestive questions and remarks to the

1705

other children and by the scribbled notes she left about for the young priest to find.

Seraphita later befriended him, when on a parish visit he suffered a seizure and fell unconscious in the mud. A few days later, however, bribed by sweets, she told Mademoiselle Chantal, the count's strong-willed, jealous daughter, that the priest had fallen in drunkenness. The story was believed because it was known among the parishioners that the priest drank cheap wine and because his physical condition was growing progressively worse.

The priest's spiritual strength showed itself in his theological dealings with the count's family. In conversation and in confession, Mademoiselle Chantal had told him that her father was having an affair with Mademoiselle Louise. The daughter, believing that she was to be sent to England to live with her mother's cousin, declared that she hated everyone in her household—her father and the governess for their conduct, and her mother for her blindness to the situation. After asserting that she would kill Mademoiselle Louise or herself and that the priest would have to explain her conduct to God, she got his promise that he would discuss the girl's problems with her mother.

The priest went to the chateau to confer with the countess regarding her daughter's spiritual state. There he found the mother in an even more atheistic frame of mind than that of her daughter. Her spiritual depression resulted from the death of her baby son, twelve years earlier. During a prolonged philosophical discussion, in which she ridiculed the priest for his theological idealism and his lack of vanity and ambition, the countess described with bitterness the hateful selfishness of her daughter and related with indifference the count's many infidelities.

Before he left the chateau, the priest sensed a spiritual change in his wealthy parishioner when she threw into the fire a medallion containing a lock of her son's hair. The priest, always humble, tried to retrieve the locket. In a letter delivered to him at the presbytery later in the day, the countess told him that he had given her peace and escape from a horrible solitude with the memory of her dead child. The countess died that night.

The priest's success in helping to redeem her soul left him with an uncertain feeling. He did not know whether he was happy or not. If his reaction was happiness, it was short-lived. When the details of his session with the countess became known as a result of Mademoiselle Chantal's having eavesdropped, criticism and derision were heaped on him. The canon reprimanded him because he had assumed the role of her confessor, and the Curé de Torcy ridiculed his approach in dealing with the countess. Members of the family, unstable as they were in their relationships, accused him of subversive tactics.

His lack of social grace, his personal inadequacies, and his professional inaptitude seemed to increase as his physical condition grew worse. Because his hemorrhages continued, he therefore decided to consult Dr. Lavigne in Lille. His last major bungle was in connection with this medical aid. He had forgotten the name of the doctor recommended to him in Lille, so he turned to the directory and mistakenly chose the name of Dr. Laville. The physician, a drug addict, bluntly diagnosed the priest's ailment as cancer of the stomach. From the doctor's office, the priest went to the address of his old schoolmate at the seminary, Monsieur Dufrety, who had long been urging his friend to visit him. There he died that night.

In a letter from Monsieur Dufrety to the Curé de Torcy, details of the priest's death were described. In great suffering and anguish following a violent hemorrhage, the priest had held his rosary to his breast. When he had asked his old friend for absolution, his request was granted and the ritual performed in a manner, Monsieur Dufrety wrote, that could leave no one with any possible misgivings. The priest's last words affirmed his great faith in the whole scheme of things because of God's existence.

Critical Evaluation:

A Catholic novelist in the manner of Julien Green and François Mauriac, Georges Bernanos was a visionary for whom the forces of good and evil were genuine presences. He shows a fierce integrity in his writing, although his views are sometimes oversimplified or inconsistent. His characters, while representing extremes of human behavior ranging from saintliness to depravity, are battlegrounds for good and evil, and their souls are the prize. These priests and other individuals who devote their lives to God are powerfully imagined and realistically drawn.

The Diary of a Country Priest has a meager plot because Bernanos is more interested in showing a man's thoughts and basic principles than in describing general human behavior; this novel is a fictional presentation of priestly attitudes, functions, and tribulations. Through this philosophical and realistic treatment of life in a small French parish, readers recognize Bernanos' high regard for Joan of Arc as the symbol of France. In the simplicity of her peasantry and saintliness, the maid is not unlike the diarist. Compassion and tenderness characterize the writing, which in translation sustains the poetic charm and fluency of the original. Humankind's holiness is Bernanos' keynote.

One of the themes of *The Diary of a Country Priest* is that of the conflict between individual religious ecstasy and the day-to-day "housekeeping" of the church. The young priest's aspirations, at once naïve and noble, are touching, but his failure to live up to them causes him increasing unhappiness. He wants more than anything else to be of use to God and to his parishioners, but he feels thwarted at every step and is not sure why. The picture of the hard, narrow villagers, with their materialistic and shallow ways, their stubbornness and malice, is vivid and complete; the reader soon understands the pain of the youthful priest's frustration when he is unable to elevate them spiritually.

Boredom, Bernanos suggests, is the beginning of evil, or at least the ground in which it grows. The young priest sees that life for his parishioners is nothing but boredom. The nature of injustice worries him as does the nature of true poverty. Everyone constantly gives him advice, warning him of intolerance, excessive dedication, or pride, but none of them can see into his heart and mind and understand what really troubles him. The naïve and unworldly qualities of the young priest give him an innocent charm.

Despite his inexperience, the priest knows that "each creature is alone in his distress." His growing wisdom is a growing realization of the loneliness of the individual. From the beginning, he is beset by ailments and becomes obsessed by them; soon, illness dominates his physical existence, but his spiritual life grows richer and more intense.

At the end, the priest has learned that true humility does not lie in self-hatred, but rather that the supreme grace is to "love oneself in all simplicity." His death, revealed in a moving letter from his friend to his superior, expresses his ultimate sense of peace.

Bibliography:
Blumenthal, Gerda. *The Poetic Imagination of Georges Bernanos: An Essay in Interpretation.* Baltimore, Md.: Johns Hopkins University Press, 1965. An analysis of the poetic imagination at work in the novel. Associates this poetic vision with Bernanos' mystical explication of human behavior.
Brée, Germaine, and Margaret Guiton. "Private Worlds." In *An Age of Fiction: The French Novel from Gide to Camus.* Rutgers, N.J.: Rutgers University Press, 1957. Interprets the country priest as a figure tormented by private and public incompatibilities. His diary is therefore a reflection of what the priest cannot, perhaps dares not, communicate to his parish or to church authorities.

Bush, William. *Georges Bernanos*. Boston: Twayne, 1969. Bush discusses Bernanos' contention that evil in modern society is connected with conservative social forces and that humans secretly covet totalitarian order. Examines *The Diary of a Country Priest* as a vehicle of private thoughts that sustain the dying priest. Chief among these thoughts is the possibility that self-realization comes only with death.

Field, Frank. "Georges Bernanos and the Kingdom of God." In *Three French Writers and the Great War: Studies in the Rise of Fascism*. New York: Columbia University Press, 1975. Overestimates the effect of World War I on Bernanos' pessimism but offers insights into the political and social underpinning of *The Diary of a Country Priest*. Although impressionistic, this study links Bernanos to larger trends in 1920's ideology.

Hebblethwaite, Peter. *Bernanos: An Introduction*. New York: Hillary House, 1965. This work emphasizes the importance of childhood events as the psychological determinant of adult behavior. Offers a close reading of *The Diary of a Country Priest* with a detailed analysis of Bernanos' innovative techniques. The priest is presented as an exemplar of spiritual tenacity.

THE DINING ROOM

Type of work: Drama
Author: A. R. Gurney, Jr. (1930-   )
Type of plot: Comedy
Time of plot: Approximately 1930 to 1980
Locale: A dining room, somewhere in the Northeastern United States
First performed: 1982; first published, 1982

Principal characters:
  FATHER, a conservative autocrat
  MOTHER, his wife
  GIRL, his daughter
  BOY, his son
  GRACE, a conservative matron
  CAROLYN, her daughter
  ARCHITECT, a practical designer
  PEGGY, a philandering wife
  GRANDFATHER, a wealthy patriarch
  NICK, his grandson
  OLD LADY, an anile matriarch
  AUNT HARRIET, a grande dame
  TONY, her nephew, a student
  JIM, a beleaguered father
  MEG, his married daughter
  STANDISH, a guardian of family honor
  HARVEY, an orderly man of affairs
  RUTH, a hostess
  ANNIE, a servant
  A DINING ROOM TABLE, a venerable family heirloom

The Story:

An unnamed real estate agent and her client discussed the possible uses of the dining room in an old house available for sale. Although the client expressed some sentimental interest in the room, he declined to make an offer on the home, and the two planned to look elsewhere.

At a different time and place, the siblings Arthur and Sally argued over which of them would get the dining room table left behind by their widowed mother, who had moved to Florida. The issue remained unresolved, and the Father, a precise, finicky man, started complaining to Annie, the servant, that on the previous day he had found a seed in his orange juice. He began instructing his son and daughter in breakfast-table deportment and criticized the deficiencies of his son's teacher, Miss Kelly. The Father was joined by his wife, the Mother, while another husband, Howard, expressed irritation with his wife, Ellie, because she had started to do schoolwork on the dining room table. He complained that the table and its place mats, his family's heirlooms, were very valuable, and he tried to persuade her to work elsewhere. When she resisted, he stormed out and Ellie, unfazed, returned to her work on the table.

Carolyn, a young teenager, next explained to her unreceptive mother, Grace, why she wanted to go to the theater with her aunt Martha. Grace, who believed that the eccentric, mildly bohemian Martha would be a bad influence on Carolyn, tried to make Carolyn stay home to fulfill other obligations while insisting that Carolyn was free to make up her own mind. To Grace's chagrin, Carolyn decided to go with her aunt.

A young boy, Michael, who was sick and at home from school, tried to talk a servant, Aggie, into staying on in the family service. At the same time, an Architect and Psychiatrist began to discuss plans for remodeling the house so that it could be used both as a home and as an office. The Architect recalled his past in such a room and his unwilling participation in agonizing family-dinner rituals. To the hesitant Psychiatrist, he proposed that the dining room, a relic, be sacrificed for office and reception space.

A children's birthday party for a boy named Brewster followed, hosted by Peggy, Brewster's mother. Ted, the father of one of the children, arrived to pick him up, and as the party progressed, Ted and Peggy, sotto voce, discussed their deteriorating adulterous liaison. When the children went off to play party games, the Grandfather, an elderly man of about eighty, entered and sat at the head of the dining table. He was approached by Nick, his grandson, who had been sent to ask him for financial support for his education at a private, exclusive preparatory school. After remarking wistfully that things had been different when he was young and that times were not so easy, the Grandfather agreed to help. Toward the end of the Grandfather's litany, Paul began examining the table, checking to see why it had developed a wobble, which worried its owner, Margery. After crawling under the table with Paul, Margery discovered, to her dismay, that the table, made in 1898, was an American replica of an earlier English piece. The two planned to repair the table together and left for the kitchen to seal their partnership with a drink.

In the wake of their departure, celebrants gathered in the dining room for a Thanksgiving dinner. Two of them, Stuart and Nancy, tried to explain the situation to the Old Lady, Stuart's mother, but she was completely disoriented and failed to understand what was happening. The men at the dinner sang for her, and for a moment it appeared that she might come around, but when they finished, the Old Lady, lost in her youth, asked them to call for her carriage, noting that her mother would expect her home for tea. Stuart and his brothers escorted her out, leaving the women behind to commiserate about the situation over stiff drinks.

Two girls, Helen and Sarah, released from school, entered next and discussed raiding the pantry liquor supply. In the absence of Sarah's mother, they planned to invite some boys for a party. Kate and Gordon, illicit lovers, appeared, fresh from a guilty tryst. They attempted to regain their composure over tea, but were taken aback by the unexpected arrival of Kate's son, Chris, whose coldness toward Gordon revealed his suspicions about the relationship between Gordon and his mother. Aunt Harriet, an aristocratic hostess, lectured her nephew, Tony, a student at Amherst, on good manners and the proper use of the elegant table pieces she showed him. After taking notes and pictures, he explained that he was going to use the material in an anthropology class presentation on the WASP culture of the northeastern states. Irate over the disclosure, Aunt Harriet ordered him to leave.

Jim and his mature, married daughter, Meg, filed into the room. As Jim fortified himself with Scotch, Meg subjected him to a recital of her problems, which involved the breakdown of her marriage and her affairs with a married man and another woman. She hoped to renew herself with a visit at home, but Jim would only agree to letting her stay for a brief, temporary visit.

Standish, defending family honor, explained to his wife and children why he had to go to his club to try to force an apology from Binky Byers, who while in the steam bath had publicly alluded to the homosexuality of Standish's brother, Uncle Henry. An old man, Harvey, then began to explain to his son, Dick, that he wanted him to comply with the funeral arrangements he had made for himself. He confided that he had already written his own obituary and planned his funeral service, including very specific written directions. He also explained that he was leaving his best legacy, the dining room, to Dick.

At the end, Annie, the servant, explained to Ruth, her employer, that she was retiring and would no longer be available for service to the family. After Annie left, Ruth spoke wistfully of a recurrent dream she had, a dream of a perfect party, to which all her family and friends were invited. The Host then came in, and as the guests gathered, raised a glass of wine and proposed a toast to everyone.

Critical Evaluation:

The Dining Room resembles some of A. R. Gurney's other plays, like the earlier *Scenes from American Life* (1970), in that it develops as a series of interlocking vignettes or minidramas that only loosely relate to one another. The individual scenes are all built around the play's central stage property, the large dining room table that dominates the set and plays a role in the lives of the characters who use it.

There are fifty-seven distinct characters in the two-act comedy, none of them central. All appear only once, except Annie, a servant, who appears near the beginning of the play and at the end. The characters are not related to anyone outside their own vignette, but most share a common heritage and culture: They are upper-middle-class WASPs living someplace in the northeastern United States sometime between the Great Depression of the 1930's and the early 1980's.

The play clearly shows that their way of life is changing. In fact, a major theme of *The Dining Room*, developed through generational contrasts, is that the WASP version of American culture has become outmoded and, to the younger generation, increasingly irrelevant. The central, archetypal symbol of that culture is the dining room and the large dining table, reminders of a day when families sat down together for long formal dinners, during which children, seen but not heard, learned about their heritage, against which, to some degree, they all finally rebel.

In some of the vignettes, the generational gulf seems deep and permanent, as in the second-act episode with Tony and Aunt Harriet. To Tony, the WASPs of the northeastern United States are "a vanishing culture," like the Cree Indians of Saskatchewan and the Kikuyus of Northern Kenya, and he, one of its scions, is determined to learn about it from studying the eating habits of the culture, as if it were a long-extinct society with only fossilized artifacts remaining to bear witness to its identity. That suggestion outrages Aunt Harriet, who threatens to drive to Amherst and castrate Tony's anthropology professor with one of her pistol-handled butter knives.

Although Gurney's intent is to evoke laughter, his humor is gentle and sympathetic. His characters are mostly decent people, even when they cling to reactionary beliefs and biases or commit immoral acts. Standish's sense of honor seems a bit ludicrous, for example, but it is honor nevertheless. Nick's grandfather, in another vignette, airs his grumpy intolerances, but in the end he proves kind and generous, almost despite himself. Clearly, in Gurney's world, most of the characters at least try to do the right thing.

Gurney's comic collage is not constructed in a chronological order. Events are only occasionally given hints as to the intended time frame through references to related events, issues, and public figures. Nor is there any logical relationship between juxtaposed vignettes. They only interlock, like cinematic lap dissolves, with one minidrama beginning while another is still ending. At the openings and endings of vignettes, characters from two distinct vignettes are briefly on stage together but totally unaware of one another. The episodes are like distinct pearls strung on a delicate thread of a common ethos.

As notes to the play explain, *The Dining Room* was designed for an ensemble cast of six performers, with each actor playing several parts. The play therefore has greater continuity in performance than when read, for while characters do not reappear, the actors do. Furthermore, much of the play's comic appeal is bolstered by the fact that performers must play parts ranging from exuberant, excited children at a birthday party to octogenarians who are losing touch with reality. Because the players are transparently actors mimicking characters, the whole is given an improvisational quality that helps keep the tone light even when such serious issues as marital infidelity and dying are broached. Yet the wistful recollection of what many of the older characters consider to have been a better time and place also elicits real nostalgia in the audience. In chronicling the passing of old ways, Gurney evokes a sense of bittersweet respect that infuses his humor with warmth and wisdom.

John W. Fiero

Bibliography:
Gilman, Richard. "A Review of *The Dining Room* and *The Middle Ages*." *The Nation* 236 (April 30, 1983): 552-553. Identifies Gurney as "the poet laureate of middle-consciousness" and discusses *The Dining Room* as a typical work.
Gurney, A. R., Jr. "Pushing the Walls of Dramatic Form." *The New York Times*, July 27, 1986, pp. B1, B6. Gurney provides analysis of his own work, his methods of coping with restrictions on artistic freedom, and his new themes and experimentation in structure.
Levett, Karl. "A. R. Gurney, Jr., American Original." *Drama* 147 (Autumn, 1983): 6-7. A good survey of Gurney's work up to and including *The Dining Room*, which is identified as the play that "consolidated Gurney's reputation." Also identifies influences on Gurney using some of the playwright's own observations.
Simon, John. "Malle de Guare." *New York* 15 (March 8, 1982): 81-82. Argues that the play is derived from Thornton Wilder's *The Long Christmas Dinner* (1931) and discusses its "trickiness," its use of ingenious structural devices.
Weales, Gerald. "American Theatre Watch, 1981-1982." *Georgia Review* 36 (Fall, 1982): 517-526. Places *The Dining Room* in a group of ethnic-conscious plays successfully produced in commercial theater over two Broadway seasons.

THE DINNER PARTY

Type of work: Novel
Author: Claude Mauriac (1914-   )
Type of plot: Experimental
Time of plot: 1950's
Locale: Paris
First published: Le Dîner en ville, 1959 (English translation, 1960)

Principal characters:
BERTRAND CARNÉJOUX, the host and an editor and novelist
MARTINE (PILOU) CARNÉJOUX, his wife
EUGÉNIE PRIEUR, an aging belle of Parisian society
GILLES BELLECROIX, a scenarist and aspiring novelist
LUCIENNE OSBORN, the egocentric wife of an American film producer
ROLAND SOULAIRES, a rich but frustrated bachelor
MARIE-ANGE (MARIETTA) VASGNE, an actress and Bertrand's mistress
JÉRÔME AYGULF, a childhood friend of Martine and a substitute guest

The Dinner Party is an experimental novel. There is no narrator, and speakers are not identified except by subject matter, leitmotif, or an occasional self-apostrophe. The text is a fusion
of conversation and soliloquy. There are crosscurrents of two or three different subjects—
stichomythic or protracted, and Claude Mauriac creates the illusion of simultaneity in the varied
mental associations evoked by some passing remark. The difficulties of following such a
presentation of multiple experience are only initial; they are resolved in the development of
character patterns that emerge despite the loss in translation of the uniqueness of language
assigned to individual characters.

In the mid-twentieth century, the experimental novel became a subspecies of the traditional
novel. Examples of experimental novels such as The Dinner Party must nevertheless be
assessed as is any work of art in an established medium. What Mauriac accomplished in The
Dinner Party is impressive. To treat at book length the incidental chatter and random musing
of eight people during a dining period of perhaps two hours is an undertaking vulnerable to
arousing boredom in the reader. Not a single character in the book emerges as a great or
memorable one; their relations to one another are rather trivial and in fact represent clichés of
the beau monde. Yet without telling a significant story or symbolizing any extensive meaning,
Mauriac sustains his kaleidoscope of sophisticated sensibilities with remarkable intensity.

There is no perceptibly dominant theme, all is dinner party experience observed and recorded
by means of the dramatic method and the interior monologue. The characters, nevertheless, are
thoroughly interesting people. Their talk—about history, aristocratic genealogy, literature
(Marcel Proust, Maurice Barrès, Anatole France, Graham Greene, and Gerard Manley Hopkins), astrology, travel, God, and even intellectual parlor games—is generally absorbing,
occasionally informative, and often amusing. Their thoughts about one another, about themselves, and about the matters that happen to arise are compounded of vanity, lust, boredom,
jealousy, creative perceptivity, intelligence, insight, and hopeful intentions, all projected with a
psychological subtlety and effectiveness that impart true unity to the book. Other characters, in
the persons of the seductive servant Armande or members of fashionable society who are talked
about or recalled in memory, add to the dimensions of the emanating reality. Details of the

courses served, descriptions of spots on the tablecloth or crumbs on a chair, and appraisals of the quality of the champagne being consumed are brilliantly integrated into the vibrant texture of the writing.

The situation that Mauriac creates out of his assemblage of characters is reminiscent of Marcel Proust. The atmosphere Mauriac's characters breathe is rarefied. His people are elegant, aristocratic (or socially pretentious), artistic, and sensual. They are aware of social stratification, youth fading into age, their desire for one another, the interplay of their sensibilities, and the projection of their personae. Henri Bergson hovers over the table: The diners indulge in flights of memory stimulated by simple words or sensations; they consider their future, but everything is focused on the present moment of consciousness.

There is no head of the table as such, but the host sits as nearly opposite his wife as a round table seating four men and four women will allow. He is Bertrand Carnéjoux, the forty-six-year-old editor of the magazine *Ring* and author of a successful novel entitled *Sober Pleasures* (the original manuscript bore the more revealing title *Metaphysics of Physical Passion*). Preeminent in Carnéjoux's mind is the desire to write another novel of even greater artistic integrity, formulated in a new way that will bring the words and thoughts of his characters into immediate juxtaposition. More than once, as he notes his conversation at the table, he regrets that he does not find it possible to achieve the same brilliance, the same eloquence when he is at work over a manuscript in his study. Meanwhile, he presides over the party, secure in his knowledge of amorous success with every woman present except one. His conversation is mainly about literature, his thoughts divided between love affairs and plans for writing.

His wife, Martine, is twenty-six years old, intimately known as Pilou, and the wealthy and innocent daughter of Irene, one of Bertrand's former mistresses. Throughout the party, her thoughts are mainly radiant expressions of love for her two children, Rachel and Jean-Paul, but she is also tempted to respond to the attentions of Bellecroix.

Gilles Bellecroix is a forty-nine-year-old screenwriter who has attained greater fame than Bertrand but who is not satisfied inwardly with his achievement. He is obsessed with the idea that he must produce a good novel to realize himself. Meanwhile, he observes the dinner guests with a cinematic eye, visualizing meaningful scenes in flickers of pose or behavior. Between him and Bertrand there is a latent rivalry that carries over into Gilles's flirtation with Martine, whose dancing on an earlier occasion is unforgettable to him. Gilles finds his real center of being, however, in his wife Bénédicte; he knows that for him true happiness lies in love, fidelity, monogamy.

Eugénie Prieur, still, at sixty-seven, called "Gigi" by young blades of Paris, is the oldest guest (too old to have been one of Bertrand's conquests), full of rich nostalgic memories, the wisdom of long experience, and an intimate knowledge of social machinations. The perspective with which she endows her world is further documented by her conversations about historic family connections.

Roland Soulaires, forty-five, is temperamentally a Prufrock who hides his fears and insecurity behind his idle dreams and his clever talk with Eugénie about social identification. Extremely wealthy, but fat and bald, he fails to interest the beautiful guest at his left, the twenty-four-year-old Marie-Ange Vasgne. Formerly a Canadian farm girl named Marietta but now a sultry blonde model and aspiring actress, Marie-Ange is Bertrand's current mistress who dares near the end of the party to tease him by inquiring after Marie-Plum, another mistress whom Bertrand has never been able to forget. Everyone's knowledge of these affairs, admitted or not, is the measure of civilization for these people. Marie-Ange toys with the numbers one through six, as though seeking a pattern of sense in the world.

Lucienne Osborn, forty-two, is married to an American film producer, not present at the dinner. Her mind vapid, her body faded, she is preoccupied with thoughts of television sets, suntans, her dog Zig, and her lover, Léon-Pierre.

Jérôme Aygulf, who is twenty, finds himself out of his element. A childhood friend of Martine, he was invited only at the last moment after another guest had sent regrets. Jérôme, aspiring but naïve, is at the opposite end of the scale from Eugénie. He finds himself longing for the attention and patronage of Bertrand more than for anything else. Insecure and a little awkward in this society, he nonetheless attracts the attention of Marie-Ange.

The Dinner Party belongs in that class of novels, including also Henry James's *The Sacred Fount* (1901) and André Gide's *The Counterfeiters* (1925), in which a novelist as a character thinks interchangeably about experience and the novel. The center of interest in Mauriac's book really lies in the thoughts and comments expressed by Bertrand and Gilles about the novel form. Referring to his novel, Bertrand speaks of a new kind of fiction, one in which on some common occasion, such as the present dinner party, time and space would be suspended. Contemplating his next work, which will fuse thought and speech, Bertrand responds to Paul Claudel's definition of the simplicity of truth along the line of Denis Diderot's Proustian statement that "Everything we have ever known . . . exists within us without our knowing it." The book is studded with criticism of novelists and theories of the novel, ideas that reveal character but also illuminate the practice of Mauriac in this particular novel. In one way or another, *The Dinner Party* raises a host of interesting questions about twentieth century fiction.

Bibliography:
Mauriac, Claude. *The New Literature.* Translated by Samuel I. Stone. New York: George Braziller, 1959. Critical study of twentieth century French literature by the author of *The Dinner Party.* Especially useful for gaining appreciation of Mauriac's theory of fiction; explains his concept of *aliterature,* which he used in creating *The Dinner Party* and other novels.

Mayhew, Alice. "All Things at Once." *Commonweal* 81 (September 25, 1964): 20. Assesses the "suite of four novels" in which Mauriac explores problems of communication in the twentieth century. Discusses the role of Bertrand Carnéjoux in *The Dinner Party* and other works in Mauriac's sequence.

Mercier, Vivian. *The New Novel from Queneau to Pinget.* New York: Farrar, Straus, & Giroux, 1971. Lengthy chapter on Mauriac. Contains an extensive analysis of *The Dinner Party*; attempts to aid readers in understanding Mauriac's complex method of narration. Claims that his presentation of characters borders on stereotype and caricature.

Moore, Harry T. *Twentieth Century French Literature Since World War II.* Carbondale: Southern Illinois University Press, 1966. Brief review of Mauriac's work as a novelist. Classifies him with others writing "antinovels" after World War II. Sketches his aims in *The Dinner Party* and notes his use of readers' aids to assist in interpreting the work.

Roudiez, Leon. *French Fictions Today.* New Brunswick, N.J.: Rutgers University Press, 1972. A chapter on Mauriac includes commentary on *The Dinner Party* that focuses on the author's techniques of narration and highlights his preoccupation in the book with sex and death.

THE DISCIPLE

Type of work: Novel
Author: Paul Bourget (1852-1935)
Type of plot: Psychological realism
Time of plot: Late nineteenth century
Locale: Paris and Riom
First published: Le Disciple, 1889 (English translation, 1898)

> *Principal characters:*
> ADRIEN SIXTE, a philosopher
> ROBERT GRESLOU, his disciple
> MONSIEUR DE JUSSAT, a hypochondriac nobleman
> CHARLOTTE, his daughter
> LUCIEN, her younger brother
> ANDRÉ, her older brother

The Story:

Adrien Sixte grew up in a peculiar way. His hardworking father wanted him to study for one of the professions, but, despite the boy's early promise in school, he never studied at a university. His indulgent parents allowed him to spend ten lonely years in study. In 1868, at the age of twenty-nine, Adrien Sixte published a five-hundred-page work called *The Psychology of God.* By the outbreak of the Franco-Prussian War, Adrien had become the most discussed philosopher in the country. He followed his first study with two even more provocative books, *The Anatomy of the Will* and *The Theory of the Passions.*

Soon after the death of his parents, Adrien settled into a regular routine in Paris. So faithful was he to his schedule that the inhabitants of the quarter could set their watches by his movements. He spent eight hours of every twenty-four in work, took two walks each day, received callers (chiefly students) on one afternoon in the week, and on another afternoon made calls on other scholars. By patient labor and brilliant insight, he developed to his complete satisfaction his deterministic theory that each effect comes from a cause, and that if all causes are known, results can be predicted accurately. He applied his theory to all forms of human activity, to vices as well as to virtues.

One day, the neighbors were startled to see Adrien leave his apartment hurriedly at an unusual hour. To his great consternation, he had received a notice to appear before a magistrate in the affair of Robert Greslou, one of his students, and he also had a letter from Robert's mother saying that she would visit him that very day at four o'clock on an urgent matter.

The sophisticated judge was incredulous when he learned that Adrien never read the newspapers. The celebrated savant had not heard of Greslou's imprisonment after being charged with the murder of Charlotte de Jussat. Adrien soon learned that the suspect had been arrested on purely circumstantial evidence, that the proof of his guilt or innocence might well be only psychological. Hence Adrien, the master, must testify as to his disciple's ideas on psychological experience. Adrien explained that if a chemist can analyze water into hydrogen and oxygen, he can synthesize hydrogen and oxygen into water. Similarly, if a psychological result can be analyzed into its causes, the result can be reproduced by those same causes; that is, by the scientific method, one can predict human behavior. The judge was interested and inquired if his theory applied to vices. Adrien said that it did, for, psychologically, vices are forms of behavior that are as interesting and valid as social virtues.

When he returned home, Adrien found Robert's mother waiting for him. She protested her son's innocence and begged Adrien to save her boy. Adrien remembered Robert as a precocious student of philosophy, but he really knew little of him as a person. The mother begged Adrien to help and gave him a manuscript written by Robert while in jail. On the outside of the manuscript was a note. If Adrien read the document, he must agree not to try to save Robert; if the condition were unacceptable, he must burn the manuscript immediately. With many misgivings, Adrien took the document and read it. It was a minute and detailed account of Robert's upbringing, his studies, and his experiences in the de Jussat home.

Robert had always been brilliant. He did outstanding work in school, and early in his studies he showed a pronounced talent in psychology. Most of his time was devoted to study, but a developing sensuality showed itself sporadically. Since he had grown up at Clermont, he lacked some of the polish imparted at Paris; in consequence, he failed an examination. While awaiting another opportunity to enter the university, Robert accepted a year's appointment as tutor to Lucien de Jussat. At the de Jussat country home, Robert found an interesting household. Lucien, his pupil, was a fat, simple thirteen-year-old boy. André, the older brother, was an army officer fond of hunting and riding. The father was a hypochondriac and a boor. Charlotte, the daughter of the family, was a beautiful nineteen-year-old girl.

Robert soon began the studied seduction of Charlotte. He had three reasons for such a step. First, he wanted to have some sort of revenge against the wealthy family. Second, his developed sexuality made the project attractive. Finally, and probably most important, he wanted to test his theory that if he could determine the causes leading to love and sexual desire, he could produce desire by providing the causes. Robert kept careful notes on procedures and results.

He knew that pity is close to love. Consequently, he aroused the pity of Charlotte by mysterious allusions to his painful past. Then, by carefully selecting a list of novels for her to read, he set about inflaming her desire for passionate, romantic love. Robert, however, was too hasty. He made an impassioned avowal to Charlotte and frightened her into leaving for Paris. Just as Robert began to despair of accomplishing his purpose, the illness of Lucien recalled Charlotte. Robert wrote her a note telling her he would commit suicide if she did not come to his room by midnight. He prepared two vials of strychnine and waited. When Charlotte came, he showed her the poison and proposed a suicide pact. Charlotte accepted, provided she could be the first to die. They spent the night together. Robert had triumphed.

Robert repudiated the pact, prompted in part by a real love for Charlotte. The next day, she threatened to call her brother if Robert attempted to stop her own attempt at suicide, for she had read Robert's notes and knew she was simply the object of an experiment. After writing a letter to her brother André, telling him of her intended suicide, she drank the strychnine. Robert was arrested soon afterward on suspicion of murder.

When Adrien Sixte came to the end of the manuscript, he began to feel a moral responsibility for his disciple's act. Disregarding the pledge implicit in his reading, he sent a note to André asking him if he intended to let Robert be convicted of murder by concealing Charlotte's letter. André resolved to tell the truth, and, in a painful courtroom scene, Robert was acquitted.

Immediately after the trial, André went to look for Robert. Scarcely able to resist, since he had been ready to die with Charlotte's secret safe, Robert went with André willingly. On the street, André pulled out a gun and shot Robert in the head. Robert's mother mourned beside the coffin; Adrien also mourned because he accepted moral responsibility for the teachings that had prompted his disciple's deed.

Critical Evaluation:

Paul Bourget's most famous novel had a profound effect on the world of French letters. Its author had begun publishing as a poet in 1872; he had turned out other perceptive novels beginning in 1885. His *Essais de psychologie contemporaine* (1883) proved most influential. He has scarcely an obscure writer. Until *The Disciple*, however, he was known mostly for his social criticism (the *Essais*, describing the literary environment in which he matured, were considered a landmark) and for his highly passionate novels. Indeed, conservatives thought his work almost pornographic. With *The Disciple*, he broke unexpected ground, exploring the responsibility of those whose teachings and writings influence our actions. Adrien Sixte, in his story, is the most moral of scholars, but, however unintentionally, his doctrines lead young Robert Greslou to commit a heinous crime. Bourget blames Greslou's teacher, Adrien. In so accusing, Bourget is also peering into the mirror of his own soul, because Adrien is a thinly disguised portrait of the great French nineteenth century historian, philosopher, and literary critic Hippolyte Taine. He was Bourget's own mentor and role model, who argued that if one knows all the causes for a given action, one can inevitably predict it. The literary doctrines then in vogue, as practiced by such French novelists as Émile Zola, followed deterministic criteria, depicting characters as lacking free will and thus not responsible for their actions; heredity and environment held them in thrall. Bourget was not so much repudiating determinism as demanding religious responsibility for what he viewed as human, not inanimate, causes.

Taine was sorely wounded by his old disciple Bourget's stand, even writing the author to deny any resemblance between Adrien Sixte and himself, adding that he never would have counseled Greslou to act as Sixte did. Interestingly enough, Bourget had based his plot on two real cases, the latter, involving a writer Bourget actually knew, occurring only a few months before *The Disciple* was published. His book owed some of its popularity to its unusual mixture of psychological analysis and sensational murder mystery, not to speak of the formerly objective psychologist's new role as antipositivist, antiskeptic, Christian moralist.

For the rest of his long life, Bourget continued to compose essays and novels deploring anti-Christian, especially anti-Catholic, behavior, rigging his plots to show the tragedies that befall his heedless characters. Like so many Victorian writers (compare the plots of his good friend, the novelist Henry James), his heroes and heroines are faced with heroic dilemmas. How they deal with them reflects their character strengths and weaknesses. Such thesis literature rapidly becomes obsolete, once the social problems besetting any given age are solved. At worst, it is scarcely readable, the plots transparently contrived, the puppet characters confected of cloth. Bourget, however, wrote well and, more to the point, always remained a keen psychologist. From time to time, he even reverted to his former, determinist point of view.

To understand the excitement generated by *The Disciple*, it may help to state that the French take literary and social doctrines very seriously indeed. Since Honoré de Balzac, French literature, especially by novelists, had been moving away from its roots, emphasizing exact depictions of milieu—businesses, shops, factories, farms, the salons of the rich, the hovels of the poor, city and country, entrepreneur and peasant. As Balzac could announce, the surroundings explain the individual, even as individuals explain their milieu. The writer aims for accuracy of description, psychology being of secondary importance. The job of art, then, is to reveal truth, without concern for its effect on its audience. Bourget, in challenging this concept, was reverting to the older notion that the duty of art is to instruct while pleasing.

As well, he was returning to the French tradition of psychological realism with which the French have always felt comfortable. Arguably, the first novel, though in verse, is the *Chastelaine de Vergy*, a thirteenth century French psychological masterpiece. Madame de La Fayette's

Princesse de Clèves (1678) is universally recognized as an almost perfect gem of psychological realism. The works of Denis Diderot and Choderlos de Laclos' *Les Liaisons dangereuses* (1782) carry the tradition into the next century, followed by the works of Alfred de Musset and *Adolphe* (1816), by Benjamin Constant de Rebecque, a few generations later. The tradition persists into the present. Psychologically probing the love life of the French adolescent, mature beyond his or her years, remains a staple of the French novel. It is seen in Raymond Radiguet's *Le Diable au corps* (1923) and in any of the novels of Françoise Sagan. Bourget was quite simply acknowledging the roots of French literature. His *Essais* had revealed a perspicacious observer, his novels confirmed the diagnosis, and *The Disciple* justified his reputation.

The Disciple is also notable for the beauty of its depictions of the gentle Auvergne landscapes, which Bourget knew and loved from the days of his youth, which he spent hiking in the countryside. He always possessed a strong sense of place and subscribed to the doctrines of his friend Auguste-Maurice Barrès, whose novel *Les Déracinés* (1897) depicted the dangers of forcing people to abandon the land of their birth.

If some disliked Bourget's moralizing, Christian slant, few could deny his persuasive intensity. Many of the French youth of his day (to whom the novel is dedicated) agreed with him. He continued to exert a strong influence on France's social conscience well into the twentieth century, though after World War I his hold was destined to weaken. *The Disciple*, in any case, may still be read for its superb depiction of the need for moral responsibility.

"Critical Evaluation" by Armand E. Singer

Bibliography:
Auchincloss, Louis. "James and Bourget: The Artist and the Crank." In *Reflections of a Jacobite*. Boston: Houghton Mifflin, 1961. In this chapter, Auchincloss chides Bourget for assuming the role of France's social and moral guide.
Feuillerat, Albert. *Paul Bourget*. Paris: Plon, 1937. Fullest and most penetrating of studies in French on Bourget's work, though it omits most of the details about his life. Feuillerat was Bourget's brother-in-law and intimate friend, but he maintains critical distance.
Goetz, T. H. "Paul Bourget's *Le Disciple* and the Text-Reader Relationship." *French Review* 52 (October, 1978): 56-61. Discusses the author's concerns over the influence of the authority figure (that is, the writer) upon his or her audience, especially the nation's youth.
Secor, Walter Todd. *Paul Bourget and the Nouvelle*. New York: King's Crown Press, 1948. The short novel (*nouvelle*) is the field in which many critics believe Bourget was the most outstanding.
Singer, Armand E. *Paul Bourget*. Boston: Twayne, 1976. The only full account in English of Bourget's life and works. *The Disciple* is treated on pages 65-67 and 120-121.
Suleiman, Susan Rubin. *Authoritarian Fictions: The Ideological Novel as a Literary Genre*. New York: Columbia University Press, 1983. In this brilliant study, the author treats the thesis novel, using Bourget's *L'Étape* (1902), a later version of the type of work that includes *The Disciple*, as her model.

DISCOURSE ON METHOD

Type of work: Philosophy
Author: René Descartes (1596-1650)
First published: Discours de la méthode, 1637 (English translation, 1649)

To the French philosopher René Descartes, the act of doubting seemed clearly to mark the proper starting point for all philosophical inquiries. The methodology that flows from this approach, many of Descartes' successors have insisted, laid the foundations of modern philosophy. The beginning of *Discourse on Method* is a systematic tearing down of learning and education; understanding does not rest, Descartes implies, on received information.

Although usually identified simply as the *Discourse on Method*, the full title Descartes gave to his brief, five-part essay more accurately reveals the nature of his subject. The full title is *Discours de la méthode pour bien conduire sa raison & chercher la vérité dans les sciences* (*Discourse on the Method of Rightly Conducting the Reason and Seeking for Truth in the Sciences*). The *Discourse on Method* appeared along with three other essays that augment Descartes' fundamental propositions with details. They were all incorporated in his *Philosophical Essays*. Descartes believed that all people possess good sense and the unique ability to reason, so the *Discourse on Method* was written in French in an era when Latin was the language of Europe's academic, intellectual, and religious elites. It was Descartes' intention to reach a relatively large audience.

Descartes completed this essay well before 1637. When he was twenty-three, in fact, he recorded a series of dreams that inspired him to establish a new philosophical and scientific system. Moreover, his basic ideas and methodology were shared among his friends and correspondents for years before the book was published. Several things had dissuaded him from publishing. He was aware, first of all, of Galileo Galilei's condemnation by the Catholic church for having defended the theory of Nicolaus Copernicus (published in 1512) that Earth and the other planets revolved about the Sun. Rigorously trained by Jesuits La Flèche College and a sincere Catholic, Descartes accordingly suppressed his own cosmological ideas until he had gotten them to conform to those of his church. He also deeply valued time for meditation, thought, and reflection: time, that is, for leisure. Consequently, to publish his views was to invite the time-consuming bothers caused by approving adherents and by angry critics alike. Furthermore, since to his own satisfaction he had largely resolved many of the intellectual problems he examined, he lacked incentive to publish. The urgings of friends, a sense of social obligation, and some vanity persuaded him, at the then-advanced age of forty-one, finally to publish.

In the *Discourse on Method* Descartes approached the ancient philosophical question of What is true? or What is certain? He employed a novel method. He styled his exposition modestly. He was not interested, he wrote, in pedantically laying down precepts for others to follow. They, after all, would respond to the dictates of their own reason. He was concerned also about the possibility of being in error, so much so that he offered his "Tract . . . merely as a history, or . . . as a tale" that might yield examples worthy of emulation. Read in this light, the *Discourse on Method* recounts the steps of his intellectual adventure, the progress made en route, and the conclusions drawn when he reached his destination.

To launch himself anew Descartes describes how, figuratively, he divested himself of intellectual baggage and of prejudices acquired from his worldly experience. As one born of a seminoble class, for instance, he had engaged in the diversions of aristocrats, had served with the armies of Maurice of Nassau and Johann Tzerclaes, Count Tilly, during his early twenties, and had spent several years in Paris studying science, prior to embarking upon two decades of solitude and immersion in his work in Holland, later in Sweden. The experiences and the conventional authorities that once had nourished his mind had ceased to sustain him. The insights and methods of languages, history, theology, morals, ethics, eloquence, poetry, jurisprudence, medicine, and scholastic philosophy—in each of which he was well versed—he discarded as too obscure and too imprecise to afford him a pathway to truth and certainty.

What Descartes sought to discover was a body of self-evident truth. He sought certainties that, with the common endowments of good sense, humanity could accept. Descartes also wrote the *Discourse on Method* with another purpose in mind. What he sought to effect, in addition, was the reconciliation of the mechanical explanation of everything in nature (the assumptions of the new science of his day) with the cherished spiritual doctrines and values of Christianity.

Descartes chose mathematics as the exemplar of the precise and logical reasoning that could be applied to the resolution of philosophical problems. The rigorous rules and axioms of mathematics, it seemed evident to him, showed the way to certainties. Certain it was and always would be, for example, that three and three were six. A young child and a mathematical genius eternally arrive at the same result. Descartes had a profound interest in mathematics, and he made an indelible impact on its advancement. He has been recognized universally for his seminal contributions to algebra and, among other achievements, he is generally credited with founding analytical geometry. Important mathematical concepts continue to bear his name.

It was as a mathematician, then, that Descartes turned to rectifying philosophy, doubting everything, and reducing everything to what he alone, not authority, could establish as certain. Such reductionism established a single fact: Doubt itself could not be doubted. For, logically, to doubt was to think, and to think was to exist. From this reasoning comes the famous affirmation: *Cogito, ergo sum* (I think, therefore I am). This Descartes described as "the first and most certain knowledge that occurs to one who philosophizes in an orderly manner." Acknowledging his famous phrase to be a clear and self-evident axiom, a test of truth that provides a distinctly perceived certainty, Descartes proposed as a general rule that everything clearly perceived as its corollary is true.

Having found a starting point of self-evident truth, the next step for Descartes was to resolve another problem: What if there were no God, or if there were, what if God were a deceiver who surrounds people with illusions? To unravel these questions, he began by positing his idea that God, the Creator of all things, a perfect, infinite being, preexisted within him. The idea of God had to be innate. Nothing comes from nothing, and since there is something, God exists. Descartes had not created himself and thereby was imperfect and mortal. The conception of God had to have been received from a perfect, omnipotent, omniscient, and infinite being, therefore making it manifest that God exists. Descartes' knowledge of God implied the existence of a being greater than Descartes himself.

With God established as a certainty, Descartes then deals with the ancient philosophical problem of body and mind. It was essential for Descartes to reconcile the new science, to which he was devoted, to his religion, which claimed an equal measure of his devotion. Mounting evidence from science, most of it based upon mathematical inquiries and solutions, demonstrated that the entire physical world could be explained in mechanical terms (with God as the prime mover of the universe). God designed these mechanics, setting the physical bodies of the universe in motion in unalterable conformity with unchanging laws. For Descartes, natural laws were laws of motion, and differences between physical bodies were explicable as differences between their various parts. Having created the world as chaos, God, according to Descartes, thereafter enabled it "to act as it is wont to do": evolve in obedience to those laws.

Using medical analogies, Descartes assigned human functions to the realm of nature; they operate in accordance with its mechanical laws. He declared, however, that humanity's rational and spiritual qualities were entirely separate from bodily functions and could not be "educed from the power of nature." Humanity's "Reasonable Soul," that is, its rational and spiritual attributes, had been created by God. Occasionally, mind and body interact, which accounts for human comprehension of sensations and appetites. Descartes' notion of such "occasionalism" still left mind and body substantially separate. The mechanical and passive body that operates in accord with the laws of nature eventually dies, but the soul continues on as immortal.

The *Discourse on Method* is a master sketch. Descartes deploys the details of his theory of mathematical methodology and ways to discover scientific truth in the three essays printed along with the *Discourse on Method* as well as in his *Meditationes de prima philosophia* (1640; meditations) and his *Principia philosophiae* (1644; principles of philosophy). Collectively, neither these nor other of Descartes' writings represent a systematic theory of knowledge. His interests were never pointed in that direction. Rather, the *Discourse on Method* and his other essays expound a method of identifying truth or self-evident certainties. Alone, one's sensory experiences, he believed, can never yield either self-evident truths or certainties. Certainties result from individuals' reasoning deductively from basic principles that were inherent in the mind. Such principles are innate, fixing in the mind the standards that guide it to truth.

The *Discourse on Method*, however, leaves unexplained how innate ideas enter the mind in the first place, though the implication is that God placed them there. Descartes also remains vague about how one's faculty of reason comes to possess natural canons for assessing truth. The meaning imparted to innate ideas is likewise confused. Sometimes Descartes implies that innate ideas impress themselves on the mind. Sometimes, he calls innate ideas principles discovered in the soul. Elsewhere he suggests the soul has the power to generate the knowledge from experience. He is unclear too about how, if God is pure spirit, He could lay down the rules governing a mechanical universe or could impart motion to matter.

Critics swiftly pointed to the deficiencies of Descartes' rationalism and use of a priori reasoning. They readily comprehended that his errors stem from his attempts at reconciling a mechanistic science with Catholic theology. Before long, philosophers Gottfried Leibniz, Immanuel Kant, Nicolas Malebranche, Pierre Bayle, Baruch Spinoza, and Thomas Hobbes, among others, tried rectifying, or avoiding, Descartes' difficulties. Other philosophers such as John Locke simply rejected Descartes' entire concept of innate ideas, or the way he separated the material and the spiritual. For their part, Jesuits denounced the message of the *Discourse on Method* and officially banned it in 1663. Dutch Calvinists likewise opposed it, and many French and German universities prohibited students from reading it.

The *Discourse on Method* nevertheless won Descartes an international reputation. Cartesian philosophy soon garnered a host of disciples, drew attention to vital questions, and expounded the philosophical values of an orderly, logical mathematical method.

Clifton K. Yearley

Bibliography:
Beck, L. J. *The Method of Descartes*. New York: Garland, 1987. Provides a clear exposition of the *Discourse on Method* which, though scholarly, is easily understandable.
Descartes, René. *Discourse on Method*. 2d rev. ed. Edited and translated by Laurence J. Lafleur. New York: Liberal Arts Press, 1956. Provides informed commentary along with the text.
Grene, Marjorie. *Descartes*. Minneapolis: University of Minnesota Press, 1985. The author's

purpose is to place Descartes' work in the broader context of his life. The *Discourse on Method* is a central feature of the beginning and middle chapters.

Maritain, Jacques. *Three Reformers: Luther, Descartes, Rousseau.* Westport, Conn.: Greenwood Press, 1970. A noted French Catholic author places Descartes' major work in context with the writings of two other seminal thinkers.

Smith, Norman K. *New Studies in the Philosophy of Descartes.* New York: Garland, 1987. The author focuses his analysis on the pioneering qualities of the *Discourse on Method* as well as upon its revelations about Descartes' influences.

THE DIVAN

Type of work: Poetry
Author: Hafiz (Shams al-Din Muhammed, c. 1320-1389 or 1390)
First transcribed: Dīvān, c. 1368 (English translation, 1891)

The Divan of Hafiz is one of the glories of Persian literature in its Golden Age and a classic of Eastern literature. Hafiz was the pen name of Shams al-Din Muhammed, a Persian who, early in his life, turned to the serious study of philosophy, poetry, and theology. The pen name he adopted means "a man who remembers," a title normally bestowed upon persons who have committed the Koran to memory. In Hafiz's case, the title was not unwarranted, for he was a dervish who taught the Koran in an academy founded by his patron.

The Divan is the best known of Hafiz's works. He also wrote in various other patterns common to Persian poetry. The *Divan* itself is a collection of short poems, lyric in quality, in the form known as *ghazals.* In the original Persian, these poems consist of from five to sixteen couplets (called *baits*). The particular poetic form has been compared to the ode and the sonnet in English-language poetry because of the lyric qualities, the length, and the subject matter. One curious feature of Hafiz's *ghazals* is that the last two lines normally contain the poet's name. The first line of each *ghazal* introduces the rhyme, which is repeated in every other succeeding line within the poem.

Although relatively little known in the Western world, Hafiz's *Divan* has remained the most popular poetry ever written in his native land. It has even been considered oracular, and Persians sometimes consult it by opening the book and placing a finger on a chance passage, hoping to have an answer thereby to whatever question has arisen. Such a procedure, or a variation of it, was supposedly done at the death of the poet. Because of exception taken to some of his poems, his corpse was at first denied the usual burial rites. To settle the question, some of his *ghazals* were written on slips of paper and placed in an urn, one to be drawn out by a child. According to legend, the verse drawn by chance from the urn said that Hafiz should be given appropriate funeral rites, as he would enter Paradise; thus the question was settled.

Through the centuries there has been debate over whether his poetry should be taken literally or symbolically, with those who see in *The Divan* a serious work by a great Persian philosopher and student of the Koran taking one side of the question, and those who see it as a fine expression of a warmly alive human being taking the other. Western readers who cannot see anything religious in these superficially hedonistic poems should call to mind the religious expression, veiled in sensual imagery though it is, of poetry such as that of John Donne and Richard Crashaw in England, Saint John of the Cross in Spain, and Edward Taylor in the United States.

Whether one may wish to take it literally or on a symbolic level, the imagery of Hafiz's poetry is warm, human, even passionate. There is no escaping, even in translation, the sincerity of the poet. Like most Eastern poetry, the imagery may even seem lush to Western readers, as in the following example:

> The east wind at the dawn of day brought a perfume from the tresses of my beloved, which immediately cast my foolish heart into fresh agitation.
> I imagined that I had uprooted that flower from the garden of my heart, for every blossom which sprang up from its suffering bore only the fruits of pain.
> From fear of the attacks of her love, I set my heart free with bloody strife; my heart dropped gouts of blood which marked my footsteps.

I beheld from her terrace how the glory of the moon veiled itself in confusion, before the face of
that dazzling sun.

In his poems, Hafiz praises love between man and woman, and he praises the beauty of women,
their eyes, their lips, their hair, their features, their forms. He also sings of wine and men, as in
these lines:

O Cupbearer! bring the joy of youth; bring cup after cup of red wine.
Bring medicine for the disease of love; bring wine, which is the balm of old and young.
Do not grieve for the revolution of time, that it wheeled thus and not thus. Touch the lute in peace.
Wisdom is very wearisome; bring for its neck the noose of wine. When the rose goes, say, "Go
gladly," and drink wine, red like the rose.
If the moan of the turtle does not remain, what matter? Bring music in the jug of wine.

Whether one can interpret this praise of wine as symbolic of spiritual substance is open to
question. That there is passion, grace, and charm in the lines is, however, undeniable. The same
is true of the following, also typical of Hafiz:

O interpreter of dreams! give good tidings because last night the sun seemed to be my ally in the
joy of the morning sleep.
At the hour when Hafiz was writing this troubled verse, the bird of his heart had fallen into the snare
of love.

An interesting legend about one of Hafiz's poems in *The Divan* has come down through the
ages. In the poem, he offered willingly to exchange both the rich cities of Bokhara and
Samarkand for the mole on the cheek of his beloved. When the great conqueror Tamerlane
learned of the poem and had an opportunity, he sent for the poet and rebuked him, saying that
Hafiz should not have offered to give away what did not lay in his power to bestow. Not entirely
subdued, even in the presence of the great Tamerlane, Hafiz is supposed to have replied that it
was through such generosity that he came to the attention of the mighty conqueror. Over and
over again in *The Divan*, another city is mentioned, his own native city of Shiraz, which he
loved greatly. ("Hail, Shiraz! incomparable site! O Lord, preserve it from every disaster!")
From the fame of Hafiz and his poems, Shiraz came to be a symbol of poetic inspiration among
poets who followed him.

The reader of *The Divan* may make comparisons between Hafiz's lyrics and those of Omar
Khayyám, an earlier Persian poet and one whose work is more widely known among English-
speaking readers through the adaptation by Edward FitzGerald (published 1859). The works of
the two poets have much in common. The apparent hedonism, the similar imagery, and the same
flowing mellifluousness are found in the work of both men. The obvious difference is the
superficial one of form, Omar Khayyám having written in quatrains, as the word "Rubáiyat"
indicates, Hafiz in the form of the *ghazal*. A more important difference lies in the attitudes
expressed in the poems. Hafiz is the more serious of the two, despite an apparent hedonism.
There is a greater inclination on the part of Hafiz to be religious, to place his faith in Allah and
his wisdom, inscrutable as the poet may find it.

Bibliography:
Arberry, Arthur J. *Classical Persian Literature*. London: George Allen & Unwin, 1958. An
account by the most accessible translator of Hafiz, with a discussion of Hafiz in translation.
Hillmann, Michael C. *Iranian Culture: A Persianist View*. Lanham, Md.: University Press of

America, 1990. A younger scholar's assessment of Hafiz and his place in the Persian literary tradition.

_____. *Unity in the Ghazals of Hafez*. Minneapolis, Minn.: Bibliotheca Islamica, 1976. A survey of Hafiz scholarship from 1947 to 1976. Discusses the problems of translation.

Meisami, Julie Scott. *Medieval Persian Court Poetry*. Princeton, N.J.: Princeton University Press, 1987. Discusses Hafiz within the tradition of Persian court poetry and patronage.

Rypka, Jan. *History of Iranian Literature*. Dordrecht, The Netherlands: D. Reidel, 1968. Incorporates scholarship to 1968, especially by Iranian scholars. Emphasizes the social setting.

Schimmel, Annemarie. "The Genius of Shiraz: Sa'di and Hāfez." In *Persian Literature*, edited by Ehsan Yarshater. Albany, N.Y.: Bibliotheca Persica, 1988. The perspective of a distinguished scholar of Persian mysticism.

THE DIVINE COMEDY

Type of work: Poetry
Author: Dante Alighieri (1265-1321)
Type of plot: Allegory
Time of plot: The Friday before Easter, 1300
Locale: Hell, Purgatory, Paradise
First transcribed: La divina commedia, c. 1320 (English translation, 1802)

> Principal characters:
> DANTE
> VIRGIL, his guide
> BEATRICE, the soul of Dante's beloved

The Story:

Dante found himself lost in a dark and frightening wood. Trying to regain his path, he decided to climb a mountain to get his bearings. Strange beasts blocked his way, however, and he was forced back to the plain. As he was bemoaning his fate, the poet Virgil approached him and offered to conduct him through Hell, Purgatory, and blissful Paradise.

When they arrived at the gates of Hell, Virgil explained that here were confined those who had lived their lives without regard for good or evil. At the River Acheron, where they found Charon, the ferryman, Dante was seized with terror and fell into a trance. Aroused by a loud clap of thunder, he followed his guide through Limbo, the first circle of Hell. The spirits confined there, he learned, were those who, although they had lived a virtuous life, had not been baptized.

At the entrance to the second circle of Hell, Dante met Minos, the Infernal Judge, who warned him to be careful how he entered the lower regions. Dante was overcome by pity as he witnessed the terrible punishment these spirits were undergoing, who had been guilty of carnal sin and were for punishment being whirled around in the air without cessation. The third circle housed those who had been guilty of the sin of gluttony. They were forced to lie deep in the mud, under a constant fall of snow and hail and stagnant water. Above them stood Cerberus, a cruel monster, barking at the helpless creatures and tearing at their flesh. In the next circle, Dante witnessed the punishment of the prodigal and the avaricious, and here he realized the vanity of fortune.

He and Virgil continued on their journey until they reached the Stygian Lake, in which the wrathful and gloomy suffered. At Virgil's signal, a ferryman transported them across the lake to the city of Dis. They were denied admittance, however, and the gates were closed against them by the fallen angels who guard the city. Dante and Virgil gained admittance into the city only after an angel had interceded for them. There Dante discovered that tombs burning with a blistering heat housed the souls of heretics. Dante spoke to two of these tormented spirits and learned that all the souls in Hell knew nothing of the present, were able to remember the past, and could dimly foresee the future.

The entrance to the seventh circle was guarded by the Minotaur, and only after Virgil had pacified him could the two travelers pass down the steep crags to the base of the mountain. There they discerned a river of blood, in which those who had committed violence in their lifetimes were confined. On the other side of the river they learned that those who had committed suicide were doomed to inhabit the trunks of trees. Beyond the river they came to a desert in which were confined those who had sinned against God, Art, or Nature. A stream flowed near the desert and the two poets followed it until the water plunged into an abyss. In order that they might descend to the eighth circle, Virgil summoned Geryon, a frightful monster, who conducted them below. There they saw the tortured souls of seducers, flatterers, diviners, and barterers. Continuing along their way, they witnessed the punishment accorded hypocrites and robbers. In the ninth gulf were confined scandalmongers and spreaders of false doctrine. Among the writhing figures they saw Mahomet. Still farther along, the two discovered the horrible disease-ridden bodies of forgers, counterfeiters, alchemists, and all those who deceived under false pretenses.

A trumpet summoned them to the next circle, in which were confined all traitors. A ring of giants surrounded the circle, one of whom lifted both Dante and Virgil and deposited them in the bottom of the circle. There Dante conversed with many of the spirits and learned the nature of their particular crimes.

After this visit to the lowest depths of Hell, Dante and Virgil emerged from the foul air to the pure atmosphere surrounding the island of Purgatory. In a little while, they saw a boat conducted by an angel, in which souls were being brought to Purgatory. Dante recognized that of a friend among them. The two poets reached the foot of a mountain, where passing spirits showed them the easiest path to climb its slope. On their way up the path, they encountered many spirits who explained that they were kept in Ante-Purgatory because they had delayed their repentance too long. They pleaded with Dante to ask their families to pray for their souls when he once again returned to earth. Soon Dante and Virgil came to the gate of Purgatory, which was guarded by an angel. The two poets ascended a winding path and saw men, bent under the weight of heavy stones, who were expiating the sin of pride. They examined the heavily carved cornices they passed, and found them covered with inscriptions urging humility and righteousness. At the second cornice were the souls of those who had been guilty of envy. They wore sackcloth and their eyelids were sewed with iron thread. Around them were the voices of angels singing of great examples of humility and the futility of envy. An angel invited the poets to visit the third cornice, where those who had been guilty of anger underwent repentance. Dante was astonished at the examples of patience that he witnessed there. At the fourth cornice, he witnessed the purging of the sin of indifference or gloominess. He discussed with Virgil the nature of love. The Latin poet stated that there were two kinds of love, natural love, which was always right, and love of the soul, which might be misdirected. At the fifth cornice, avarice was purged. On their way to the next cornice, the two were overtaken by Statius, whose spirit had been cleansed and who was on his way to Paradise. He accompanied them to the next place of purging, where the sin of gluttony was repented, while voices sang of the glory of temperance. The last cornice was the place for purging by fire of the sin of incontinence. Here the sinners were heard to recite innumerable examples of praiseworthy chastity.

An angel now directed the two poets and Statius to a path that would lead them to Paradise. Virgil told Dante that he might wander through Paradise at his will until he found his love, Beatrice. As he was strolling through a forest, Dante came to a stream, on the other side of which stood a beautiful woman. She explained to him that the stream was called Lethe, and helped him to cross it. Then Beatrice descended from heaven. She reproached him for his unfaithfulness to her during her life, but the virgins in the heavenly fields interceded with her on his behalf. Convinced of his sincere repentance and remorse, she agreed to accompany him through the heavens.

On the moon, Dante found those who had made vows of chastity and determined to follow the religious life, but who were forced to break their vows. Beatrice led him to the planet

Mercury, the second heaven, and from there to Venus, the third heaven, where Dante conversed with many spirits and learned of their virtues. On the sun, the fourth heaven, they were surrounded by a group of spirits, among them Thomas Aquinas. He named each of the spirits in turn and discussed their individual virtues. A second circle of blessed spirits surrounded the first, and Dante learned from all how they had achieved blessedness.

Then Beatrice and Dante came to Mars, the fifth heaven, where the souls of those who had been martyred were cherished. Dante recognized many renowned warriors and crusaders among them.

On Jupiter, the sixth heaven, Dante saw the souls of those who had administered justice faithfully in the world. The seventh heaven was on Saturn, where Dante found the souls of those who had spent their lives in meditation and religious retirement. From there Beatrice and her lover passed to the eighth heaven, the region of the fixed stars. Dante looked back over the distance that extended between the earth and this apex of Paradise and was dazzled and awed by what he saw. As they stood there, they saw the triumphal hosts approaching, with Christ leading, followed by Mary.

Dante was questioned by the saints. Saint Peter examined his opinions about faith, Saint James those about hope, and Saint John those about charity. Adam then approached and told the poet of the first man's creation, of his life in Paradise, and of his fall and what had caused it. Saint Peter bitterly lamented the avarice displayed by his apostolic successors, and all the sainted host agreed with him.

Beatrice then conducted Dante to the ninth heaven, where he was permitted to view the divine essence and to listen to the chorus of angels. She led him to the Empyrean, from the heights of which, and with the aid of her vision, he was able to witness the triumphs of the angels and of the souls of the blessed. So dazzled and overcome was he by this vision that it was some time before he realized that Beatrice had left him. At his side stood an old man whom he recognized as Saint Bernard, who told him that Beatrice had returned to her throne. He told Dante that if he wished to discover still more of the heavenly vision, he must join with him in a prayer to Mary. Dante received the grace to contemplate the glory of God, and to glimpse, for a moment, the greatest of mysteries, the Trinity and humanity's union with the divine.

Critical Evaluation:

Dante Alighieri was born into an aristocratic Florentine family. Unusually well educated even for his time and social class, he was knowledgeable in science and philosophy and was an active man of letters as well as an artist. He lived in politically tumultuous times and was active in politics and government. All of his knowledge, his experience, and his skill were brought to bear in his writings. During an absence from Florence in 1302, he was sentenced to exile for opposing the government then in power. For a time, he engaged in revolutionary activities, but even later he was never allowed to return to his beloved Florence upon pain of being burned. Dante wrote *The Divine Comedy* in exile, and he died in Ravenna.

Dante chose to write the masterpiece *The Divine Comedy* in Italian, although the language of scholarship at that time was Latin. Dante's major writings in Latin were the political essay *De monarchia* (*About Monarchy*, c. 1313) and the treatise *De vulgari eloquentia* (*On the Vulgar Tongue*, c. 1306), a compelling defense of the use of the written vernacular, instead of Latin. Here he argued in conventional Latin the superiority of unconventional written Italian as a medium of expression. Dante used Latin for a number of very important letters and for a few poems, but his language of choice was his native Italian. His earliest major work—*La vita nuova* (*The New Life*, c. 1292), a mystical-spiritual autobiography combining prose and poetry—was written in Italian. So, too, were *Il convivio* (*The Banquet*, c. 1307), a scholarly and philosophical treatise, and a number of lyric poems. The greatest tribute to the eloquence of written Italian is, however, *The Divine Comedy*.

The work, which was first titled *La commedia* (the adjective was an afterthought), is a great and complex work. It is divided into three sections, or canticles, *Inferno* (Hell), *Purgatorio* (Purgatory), and *Paradiso* (Heaven). The entire work is composed of one hundred cantos, apportioned into thirty-four segments in *Inferno* and thirty-three each in *Purgatorio* and *Paradiso*. The rhyme scheme, called terza rima, results in each rhyme occurring three times and thus creating an interlocking scheme that produces a very closely knit poem. This structure is not arbitrary, nor is it a mere intellectual exercise.

Number symbolism plays an important part in *The Divine Comedy*. As an essentially Christian poem, it relies heavily on mystical associations with numbers. It is not difficult to discern, for example, the relationship between one poem in three canticles and one God in Three Persons. Terza rima too is significant in this regard. A higher level of complexity comes into play with the reflection of the unity or oneness of God, which is diffused on a metric basis when, for example, one is divided into one hundred cantos. Two becomes the duality of nature as seen in the opposition between corporeal and spiritual, active and contemplative, Church and State, and Old Testament and New. Three signifies Father, Son, Holy Ghost; Power, Wisdom, Love; Faith, Hope, Charity; and other combinations. Four—as in seasons, elements, humors, directions, cardinal virtues—combines with three to make a mystical seven: days of creation, days of the week (length of Dante's journey), seven virtues and seven vices (as in the seven levels of Purgatory), planets, and many more. Multiples of three—three times three equals nine—create further permutations: choirs of angels, circles of Hell, and the like. Adding the mystical unity of one to the product nine makes ten, the metric permutation of one discussed above.

Dante and other medieval writers deliberately contrived these complex relationships of number symbolism. In *Il convivio*, Dante explained his view of the four levels of interpretation of a literary work and by doing so legitimized explanations of number symbolism. He proposed that a text be read literally, following the actual story; allegorically, which uncovers hidden meanings; morally, which relates the work to human behavior; and anagogically, a reading accessible only to the most sophisticated, which pertains to the absolute and universal truths contained in a work.

The Divine Comedy offers something at each of these four levels of interpretation. As a literal story, it has the fascination of autobiographical elements as well as the features of high adventure. The protagonist, Dante, led by Virgil, undertakes a journey to learn about himself, the world, and the relations between the two. In the course of his journey, he explores other worlds in order to place his own world in proper perspective. As his journey progresses, he learns.

As an allegorical story, *The Divine Comedy* traces the spiritual enlightenment of Dante's soul. It also delineates social, political, cultural, and scientific parables. By integrating all of these aspects into an intricately interwoven pattern, the poem becomes an allegory for the real and spiritual world order.

As a moral story, the work has perhaps its greatest impact as a cautionary tale to warn the reader about the consequences of various categories of behavior. In the process, it helps the reader to understand sin (Hell), penance (Purgatory), and salvation (Heaven). On this level, *The Divine Comedy* becomes a vehicle for teaching moral behavior.

As an anagogical story, the poem offers a mystical vision of God's grand design for the entire universe. The complex interdependency of all things—including the web of interrelationships stemming from number symbolism—is, in this view, all part of the Divine Plan, which humankind can grasp only partially and dimly. God remains ineffable to the finite capacities of human beings, and His will can never be fully apprehended by humans, whose vision has been impaired by sin. The anagogical aspects of *The Divine Comedy* are but aids for the most spiritually enlightened to approach Eternal Truth.

No brief explanation can do justice to the majesty of this monumental achievement in the history of Western poetry. Its very scope and encyclopedic nature make *The Divine Comedy* a key to the study of medieval civilization. It cannot be easily or properly fragmented into neat categories for discussion, and background in history and theology is useful. Above all, the reader must recognize that no sweeping generalization can adequately account for the complexity of ideas or the intricacy of structure in *The Divine Comedy*.

"Critical Evaluation" by Joanne G. Kashdan

Bibliography:
Dronke, Peter. *Dante and Medieval Latin Traditions*. Cambridge, England: Cambridge University Press, 1986. Succinctly demonstrates in *The Divine Comedy* Dante's debt to medieval Latin conventions. Marshals impressive evidence to argue that Dante did not write the expository part of the "Epistle to Cangrande," which constitutes the cornerstone of Charles Singleton's allegorical interpretation of Dante's masterpiece.
Freccero, John. *Dante: The Poetics of Conversion*. Edited by Rachel Jacoff. Cambridge, Mass.: Harvard University Press, 1986. A collection of seventeen essays by a leading critic of Dante. Demonstrating the centrality of Augustine's thought for Dante, Freccero builds on the writings of Charles Singleton while refining many Singletonian ideas.
Jacoff, Rachel, ed. *The Cambridge Companion to Dante*. Cambridge, England: Cambridge University Press, 1993. Fifteen essays by distinguished scholars that provide essential background to and critical evaluations of Dante's life and work. Includes key studies by historians and literary scholars.
Singleton, Charles Southward. *Dante Studies*. Cambridge, Mass.: Harvard University Press, 1954 and 1958. 2 vols. Often regarded as the most influential studies published by an American Dante scholar, these classic writings interpret Dante's poem using a fourfold allegorical model. Though dated, Singleton's approach remains a point of departure for much American Dante scholarship.
Sowell, Madison U., ed. *Dante and Ovid: Essays in Intertextuality*. Binghamton, N.Y.: Medieval & Renaissance Texts & Studies, 1991. Addresses the crucial question of how the Christian poet Dante made use of the classical poet's texts. The essays highlight and offer perspicacious commentary on the Ovidian presence throughout Dante's masterpiece.

THE DIVINE FIRE

Type of work: Novel
Author: May Sinclair (1863-1946)
Type of plot: Psychological
Time of plot: 1890's
Locale: England
First published: 1904

Principal characters:
SAVAGE KEITH RICKMAN, a young writer
HORACE JEWDWINE, a literary editor
LUCIA HARDEN, Rickman's inspiration
FLOSSIE WALKER, Rickman's fiancée
MR. PILKINGTON, a financier

The Story:

Horace Jewdwine, a literary editor, thought he had discovered a genius in Savage Keith Rickman, a young and unknown poet who earned his living by making catalogs for his father, a bookseller. Jewdwine hesitated, however, to declare openly that Rickman was a genius, for his reputation could suffer if the young man then proved otherwise. He encouraged Rickman privately but failed to give him the public recognition that would have meant so much to the young writer.

Rickman himself cared little for fame or money. He knew that he was a genius, that is, that part of him was a genius. He was also a student, a young man about town, a journalist, a seeker after simple pleasures, and sometimes a drunk. He found it difficult to have so many facets to his nature. One part warred constantly with the others; but no matter in what form he found himself, honor never left him. Even when drunk, he continued to be honorable.

Rickman's intelligence and his ability to judge books were the foundations upon which the elder Rickman had built his financial success as a book dealer, yet the father and son could never understand each other. Money was the father's god; the muse was Rickman's. The father was backed by and supported by Mr. Pilkington, a financier of questionable ethics but great success. When Pilkington informed him that the Harden library might soon be on the market, the old man sent his son to evaluate it. At the same time, Miss Lucia Harden, daughter of the owner of the library, asked for someone to catalog it for her. Rickman was chosen because his knowledge of old books was infallible.

Rickman was awed by Lucia. She was the daughter of a baronet and far above him in station, but from the first, he knew that she was destined to be his inspiration. Lucia was Jewdwine's cousin, and he was unhappy when he learned of her association with Rickman. He knew Rickman was beneath her, but he also knew that his cousin was moved by poetry. Jewdwine thought that he himself would one day marry Lucia and inherit the library and the country estate, but he could not bring himself to ask for her hand; decisions were almost impossible for Jewdwine.

While working for Lucia, Rickman learned that his father and Pilkington were planning to pay a ridiculously low price for the Harden library. In order to help the girl, he wrote to Jewdwine and asked him to buy the library at a fair figure. Jewdwine failed to answer the letter. When Lucia's father died suddenly, leaving her indebted to Pilkington, Rickman went to his father and tried to persuade him to change the offer. The old man refused, and Rickman left the bookshop forever, refusing to compromise his honor in return for the partnership his father offered him if he would stay. Not wanting to hurt Lucia, he told her little of what had happened. He even tried to excuse Jewdwine's failure to buy the library and so salvage some of her father's estate.

Pilkington took the Harden house and furniture and Rickman's father the library. After Rickman left him, the old man's business began to fail, and he was forced to mortgage the library to Pilkington. The books were stored, pending redemption. Rickman did not see Lucia again for five years.

Back in London, Rickman continued to write for various journals. Jewdwine gave him a junior editorship on the journal he edited, and the job allowed Rickman to live fairly comfortably. He had put his serious writing away in a drawer. Although the product of his genius, it would bring no money. Eventually, he was trapped into a proposal of marriage by Flossie Walker, a fellow boarder. Flossie would never understand the ways of genius; her world was a house in the suburbs decorated with hideous furniture. Rickman found himself with the house bought and the wedding date set.

Chance saved him. After five years, Lucia visited a friend in Rickman's boardinghouse, and the two met again. No word of love was spoken, for Lucia, even without her fortune, was still above him, and Rickman had no desire to hurt Flossie, who had waited two years for him to accumulate enough money for their marriage. He and Lucia, however, found inspiration and comfort in their renewed acquaintance. The real blow to Flossie's dreams came when Rickman's father died, leaving him a small inheritance. With it, Rickman would be able to redeem the mortgaged Harden library from Pilkington and return it to Lucia. If he did so, he would not be able to marry for at least two more years. Flossie could not understand Rickman's belief that a debt of honor could be just as binding as a legal debt. Rickman was greatly relieved to learn that Flossie refused to wait. She quickly married another boarder and found her house in the suburbs, complete with nursery.

Rickman lived through years of grinding labor. He worked all night, starved himself, and lived in an unheated attic to redeem the complete library. He got extensions from Pilkington, who enjoyed the sight of genius chasing an impossible goal. His friends lost track of him. He lost his job with Jewdwine because he would not compromise his honor even in his desperate need to help Lucia. At last, he seemed doomed to fail, for his lack of food and his feverish work had made him desperately ill. Friends found him and took him, unconscious, to a hospital. Later, they found the work of his genius while going through his belongings. When it was published, Rickman's fame was assured. Poor Jewdwine! How he wished now that he had had the courage to claim Rickman in time. By that time, however, Jewdwine had sacrificed his own principles, and success was beyond hope for him.

When he had recovered, Rickman went to Lucia. He found her ill and unable to walk. When she learned that his illness had been caused by his having worked for her, the gift was almost more than she could bear. With his aid, she arose from her bed. Cured of the malady that she knew now was only heartbreak, she saw Rickman whole, the genius and the man fused at last.

Critical Evaluation:

May Sinclair's *The Divine Fire* deals with the frustrations of a young poet of exceptional talent whose valuable energies are wasted in the struggle to make a living and to fulfill an enormous, self-imposed financial obligation. Sinclair shows a wide variety in her work, but there are techniques in *The Divine Fire* that are characteristic of her general style; the novel also contains many of the same attitudes and psychological concerns frequently found in her fiction.

Stylistically, Sinclair is somewhat of a naturalist. In comparison with her other works, *The Divine Fire* is relatively long and leisurely paced, but it shares with them an acute attention to detail and an objectivity of observation. Through her skillful and unobtrusive selection of details to present, Sinclair creates a powerful impression of realism that carries its own meaning without need of comment by the author. Sinclair was influenced by H. G. Wells and thus interested in exposing the mediocrity of middle-class values and their deadening effect on the spirit. Her intent was to dramatize the way an individual life—whether an unusual one like Keith Rickman's or a quite ordinary one such as Flossie Walker's—is molded by external forces. Keith Rickman's career, therefore, illustrates to some extent the dictum found in Sinclair's earlier novel *Audrey Craven* (1897): "In our modern mythology, Custom, Circumstance, and Heredity are the three Fates that weave the web of human life." Sinclair, nevertheless, does not approach the pessimism of Thomas Hardy or Theodore Dreiser, and she is often unwilling to accept the naturalist solution. In *The Divine Fire*, Rickman, after all of his suffering, is finally recognized as a genius and united with Lucia.

Although Sinclair was not a Freudian, she was certainly aware of the important psychological assumptions beginning to be made in her generation and of their implications. The reader discovers in all of her work that same sensitivity and insight into emotions and motivations that inspire *The Divine Fire*. She is particularly aware of the various kinds of oppression that produce frustration; one type that appears frequently—and reminds readers of Sinclair's similarities to Henry James—is the oppressiveness parents exert over their children. Also reminiscent of James are her portraits of seemingly nice people who are in reality self-serving and unscrupulous—portraits that reflect not only her interest in the discrepancy between appearance and reality but also her desire to expose hypocrisy and false values.

Bibliography:
Bloom, Harold, ed. *May Sinclair.* Twentieth-Century British Literature 14. New York: Chelsea House, 1986. Excerpts from several sources summarizing Sinclair's accomplishments as a novelist. Includes excellent reviews of *The Divine Fire* from the time of the novel's first publication.
Boll, Theophilus. *Miss May Sinclair, Novelist: A Biographical and Critical Introduction.* Rutherford, N.J.: Fairleigh Dickinson University Press, 1973. Detailed though somewhat favorably biased study of Sinclair's life and career. Comments on the significance of *The Divine Fire* to her reputation, and offers brief analyses of plot and narrative techniques.
Brown, Penny. "May Sinclair: The Conquered Will." In *Poison at the Source: The Female Novel of Self-Development in the Early Twentieth Century.* New York: St. Martin's Press, 1992. Discusses Sinclair's work as an example of the way twentieth century female novelists portray difficulties faced by women trying to develop a sense of identity. Links *The Divine Fire* with other early Sinclair works that share affinities with Victorian fiction.
Kaplan, Sydney J. *Feminine Consciousness in the Modern British Novel.* Urbana: University of Illinois Press, 1975. A chapter on Sinclair included in a study of five female British novelists who focus on the tensions between the ideal of sexual equality and the realities of female subordination. Comments on the use of psychological techniques in her fiction.
Zegger, Hrisey. *May Sinclair.* Boston: Twayne, 1976. Good general introduction to the novelist's career. Classifies *The Divine Fire* as an idealistic novel, calling it an allegory of the individual's journey through life. Considers it one of Sinclair's least successful artistic productions, despite its popularity.

DIVINE LOVE AND WISDOM

Type of work: Religious
Author: Emanuel Swedenborg (1688-1772)
First published: Sapientia angelica de divino amore et de divina sapientia, 1763 (English translation, 1788)

Early in his life, Emanuel Swedenborg established for himself a lasting reputation as a scientist in many scientific fields, including physics, astronomy, mathematics, engineering, and human anatomy. His research in several of these fields culminated in important publications that showed him well in advance of his time. His work in anatomy, for example, anticipated some of the later theories of physiology, including those involving the functions of the ductless glands.

With respect to his later writings in religion and theosophy, Swedenborg's reputation is a mixed one. Between 1743 and 1745 he suffered a mental and religious crisis that changed his life and his work. During the crisis, according to his own report, he underwent mystical experiences in which he believed he was given access to the spiritual world. He saw visions of that world, heard and took part in celestial conversations, and received divine instruction. In 1745, during a third great spiritual experience, Swedenborg reported having witnessed the second advent of Christ and having been instructed to establish a "New Church." From his visions and the instructions he purportedly received grew Swedenborg's theosophical writings, for which he used Latin. Although he wrote voluminously on his doctrines, Swedenborg did not himself found a sect, for he believed that members of any church could follow his doctrines. Later his followers did constitute the Church of the New Jerusalem, or New Church.

Like all theosophical writings, those of Swedenborg depend for their importance on how seriously readers are willing to take the author's reports of divine inspiration and revelation. If this is accepted, the writings assume tremendous, even cosmic, significance, for Swedenborg did not attempt to disguise or conceal the supernatural source of his doctrines. He stated as actual fact that his doctrines were the results of visions granted to him by God, and he calmly and routinely noted certain facts and points either overheard in conversations among the angels or witnessed during the times he was transported spiritually to heaven. He regarded his mission seriously, sincerely believing that he had been commanded to interpret the spiritual world and explicate the Bible's true spiritual intent to humankind.

Swedenborg's most important theosophical work is *Divine Love and Wisdom,* in which he stated his system most comprehensively and succinctly. The premises of his doctrine are that God is Man (or God-Man) and that God is Love. He reported that the conception of God as Man is held in all the heavens, the reason he vouchsafed being that heaven as a whole and in every part resembles the human form, and the divine itself, together with the angels (who are also human in form), constitutes heaven. Swedenborg added that all angels and other heavenly spirits are human beings in perfect form. The essence or being of God, according to Swedenborgian doctrine, is love, an infinite love that humankind knows only as existing and not through an acquaintance with its nature, inasmuch as humankind is, without God, held to the natural world.

For Swedenborg, the manifestation of God and his infinite love is a living sun. That spiritual sun corresponds in heaven to the "dead" sun of the natural world, and is the source of spiritual life. The sun of the natural world, according to Swedenborg, is the source of life in nature, which is but a receptacle of life, not a source. Just as the spiritual sun and the natural sun are distinct but analogous in part and whole, so are heaven and earth distinct but analogous. Swedenborg warned, however, that space and time are concepts only of the natural world and are not to be found in the structure of the infinite and perfect realm of heaven. In heaven, according to the cosmology expounded in *Divine Love and Wisdom*, are three uncreated, distinct, and eternal degrees, corresponding to which in the natural world there are three finite degrees. Swedenborg did not describe in *Divine Love and Wisdom* how these degrees exist, but only stated that they are love, wisdom, and use, or to put it another way, end, cause, and effect. The three degrees exist, declared Swedenborg, in every human being at birth, although as a creature of the natural world the human being is unaware of them. As the degrees are opened successively to the individual, so is God in people and people in God, according to the doctrine. Light from the spiritual sun flows into human beings as they shun evil, meaning that they can gain in wisdom; but the "heat" of the spiritual sun, or love, cannot be received. The natural mind of the lowest degree, said Swedenborg, is a hell in itself, while the mind that is spiritualized becomes a heaven. In other words, by love and the opening of each of the successive degrees human beings can rise toward God. According to *Divine Love and Wisdom*, the end of creation, both spiritual and natural, is to become perfectly the image of God-Man.

Swedenborg undertook to answer the question of creation that has bothered countless numbers of theologically minded persons in every generation: Did God create the universe out of nothing, or did he form a cosmos from the stuff of chaos? According to Swedenborg:

> Every one of enlightened judgment sees that the universe was not created out of nothing, because it is impossible to make anything out of nothing; for nothing is nothing, and to suppose anything to be made out of nothing is absurd and therefore contrary to the light of truth, which comes from the divine Wisdom. . . . Everyone of enlightened judgment also sees that all beings were created out of self-existent substance, the very BEING out of which all things that exist come forth: and as God is the only self-existent Substance, and thus is essential BEING, it is plain that this is the source of all things that exist.

Swedenborg suggests that there are pairs in all parts of the body in order that everyone may achieve the love and wisdom of divinity. He notes that the eyes, ears, nostrils, hands, loins, and feet exist in pairs, and that the heart, brain, and lungs are divided into two parts. The right-hand parts, according to his views, have a relation to love and the left-hand parts a relation to wisdom.

The doctrine propounded in *Divine Love and Wisdom* grants to all human beings the means of achieving the spiritual heaven, for in the Swedenborgian view it is a false doctrine that the Lord arbitrarily excludes any members of the human race from salvation.

Bibliography:
Dole, George F., ed. *A View from Within: A Compendium of Swedenborg's Theological Thought.* New York: Swedenborg Foundation, 1985. A discursive and thorough survey of Swedenborg theology by a respected scholar. Well-organized and helpful to any serious student. For a more concise rendition of his biography and key concepts see *A Scientist Explores Spirit: A Compact Biography of Emanuel Swedenborg, with Key Concepts of Swedenborg's Theology.* West Chester, Pa.: Swedenborg Foundation, 1992.
James, Henry. *The Secret of Swedenborg: Being an Elucidation of His Doctrine of the Divine Natural Humanity.* 1869. Reprint. New York: AMS Press, 1983. Still an essential guide to Swedenborg's understanding of the multifold symbolic and allegorical relations between God's love and human nature.
Morris, Herbert Newall. *Flaxman, Blake, Coleridge and Other Men of Genius Influenced by*

Swedenborg. Norwood, Pa.: Norwood Editions, 1975. Aids in understanding various literary and cultural figures who were influenced by Swedenborg's philosophy.

Swedenborg, Emanuel. *Angelic Wisdom Concerning the Divine Love and Wisdom*. London: Swedenborg Society, 1969. Like many of the editions published by the Swedenborg Society and the Swedenborg Foundation, this one is authoritative.

Trobridge, George. *Swedenborg: Life and Teaching*. 5th ed. Revised by Richard Tafel, Sr., and Richard Tafel, Jr. New York: Swedenborg Foundation, 1992. Important biography of Swedenborg, with a lucid discussion of Swedenborg's belief system.

DIVING INTO THE WRECK

Type of work: Poetry
Author: Adrienne Rich (1929-   )
First published: 1973

In 1974, Adrienne Rich received the National Book Award for *Diving into the Wreck*. In a statement written with Audre Lord and Alice Walker, fellow nominees, she rejected the award as an individual but accepted it on behalf of all women, dedicating the occasion "to the struggle for self-determination of all women." This vision of herself as writing for and in the presence of women has guided her work. Feminism provides Rich with the framework for her vision of transformation for herself and for other women.

Her seventh book of poetry, the collection is, in part, a clarification of her identity as a member of the women's movement of the past decade. Receiving critical acclaim from the onset of her career, including being chosen by W. H. Auden for the Yale Younger Poets Award for her first collection, *A Change of World* (1951), the poet has sought a position in the male-dominated literary world. In the late 1960's and early 1970's she became politically active in antiwar protests and the feminist movement. Rich saw her poetic power and political ideology merge, creating a powerful poetic vision that informs *Diving into the Wreck*. Rich, one of America's foremost poets, has explored, analyzed, and depicted her own physical, psychic, and intellectual rebirth in her prose and poetry. Although her later works, including her prose text *Of Woman Born: Motherhood as Experience and Institution* (1976) and her poetry collection *The Dream of a Common Language* (1978), dramatize the theme of rebirth in detail, the initial exploration of this theme takes place in the collection *Diving into the Wreck*. In this work, the poet embraces an individual and a collective consciousness that provides for her transformation.

Rich identifies the world of the fathers as an oppressive patriarchal one that restricts a woman's existence in every way, psychologically and physically, individually and collectively. In *Of Woman Born: Motherhood as Experience and Institution*, she asserts that "the kingdom of the fathers" denies women their power, permeating every institution and experience, determining and defining women and their roles politically and socially. Further, she concedes that patriarchal assumptions have shaped both women's moral and intellectual history. For women to move from being powerless to powerful, they must confront their past and redefine themselves in the present and for the future. The central theme of a woman's coming to consciousness synthesizes the collection. Divided into four sections, the work follows the process of awakening. First, there is the discovery, then the anger, then the courage to survive, and then to seek change. Rich finds her poetic voice in this book, and with that voice the power to define a collective consciousness for all women. As Rich explains in *On Lies, Secrets, and Silences: Selected Prose 1966-1978* (1979), the poet must speak for those who "are less conscious of what they are living through." The poetry depicts the struggle of awakening. Poems such as "When We Dead Awaken" (1971) and "Waking in the Dark" (1971) indicate this theme. In each poem, the speaker describes the effort of trying to make sense of a world that, upon waking, appears so different:

> working like me to pick apart
> working with me to remake
> this trailing knitted thing, this cloth of darkness
> this woman's garment, trying to save the skein.

The poet describes the struggle to survive in a world in which she is the stranger. Her existence is questioned because the "dead language" does not describe the altered state that she has upon waking. Although the speaker knows she is awake, "yet never have we been closer to the truth," the doubt and disbelief still linger and only "the words," such as those written in "your diaries," are what keep her sane. In the poem "Waking in the Dark," the speaker characterizes the waking as almost unnatural. She sees herself as being the only one who is awake in an "unconscious forest."

The process of awakening brings anger, as illustrated in the poems "From the Prison House" (1971) and "The Phenomenology of Anger" (1972). In the first poem, the speaker paints "the world of pain" as being imminent even when she sleeps. For her, the vision "must be unblurred" and clear for her to describe in detail a better place. The poet is the one who must remember every detail, to forget nothing about the world of violence and pain that has held her prisoner. In her essay "When We Dead Awaken: Writing as Revision" (1971), Rich describes women as "sleepwalkers" who in coming awake find that they are not alone. Essentially, she envisions that in the awakening, each woman forms a "collective reality" that is critical for her survival. This concept is emphasized in both poems. Further, the persona in "The Phenomenology of Anger" reiterates Rich's view that victimization and anger are real experiences for women. In one stanza the speaker muses that the world is no longer viable as she rejects the "fantasies of murder" and resolves to hate so as to rid herself of the lies of a world that she has decided to reject. Her hate turns into fire as she ritualistically burns up the old life, cleansing herself for the new one in which she is powerful.

The process of awakening is painful and lonely. The speaker of "Merced" (1972) describes herself as crying "without knowing which thought/ forced water to my eyes." In "Song" (1971) the loneliness is defined as being the first one awake "in a house wrapped in sleep." The loneliness is necessary, however, to find one's personal strength and truth. The speaker relates that if she is lonely it is like the loneliness of one taking the first breath of a new dawn. The tone of hope, not despair, however, characterizes the process, for it is one that will produce a clearer vision of the self.

"Diving into the Wreck" (1972) is the centerpiece of the collection. "The wreck" is the history of women. Rich begins to comprehend the damage that has been done to all women by the "book of myths." In the first stanza, she readies herself by loading the camera, checking her knife, putting on her rubber suit and "the awkward mask." All of these symbolize that she must be prepared for what she may find and must remain in control. In this stage of reawakening, she has gone beyond her individual consciousness into the "hold" where other women sleep "with drowned face" and "open eyes." She clarifies her reason for the exploration:

> I came to explore the wreck.
> The words are purposes
> The words are maps.
> I came to see the damage that was done
> and the treasures that prevail.

Her tone is somber and decisive. She knows that without words, she is without meaning, yet she must go underwater, where words cannot be spoken, to gain understanding. As she circles the wreck, she becomes an androgyne, "I am she; I am he." She dives into the hold of the wreck. There she discovers the half-destroyed instruments; they represent the state of the history of women. Although they have been left to rot, there is hope because they are only half destroyed. The hope lies not in the book of myths "in which our names do not appear" but in the instrument of the poet who, "by cowardice or courage," finds her and women's way back to the surface. In the final stanza, she enacts the final step: moving from the individual's awakening to the collective state of consciousness: "We are, I am, you are."

To classify *Diving into the Wreck* as merely a collection of political poetry would be a mistake. It is poetry because of its feminism. Rich's feminism is a natural extension of her poetry; for Rich, feminism is about empathy. Rich describes conflicts on the individual and the collective levels; she discovers the living connection between the political and the personal. Her poetry chronicles an individual's transformation into a strong, artistic, powerful voice, one that attempts to articulate her own change as it mirrors the collective reality of her time.

The poet creates a powerful language capable of describing this new vision. Rich accomplishes this in *Diving into the Wreck*. The poetry in this collection heralds that of her later collections, including *The Dream of a Common Language* (1978), in which she gives birth to "a whole new poetry." To have arrived at such a point in the artist's journey, Rich had to be the explorer of the past, as she is in the poem "Diving into the Wreck." To acquire this expertise, this vital knowledge, it is necessary to "re-vision," a process she defines in an essay as that of looking back and reperceiving an old text from a new perspective. The poet revises the past history of women, the one written by men, and then guides the reader back to the present with a clearer view of both the past and the present. Adrienne Rich has a transformative power and exhibits it in *Diving into the Wreck*.

Cynthia S. Becerra

Bibliography:
Flynn, Gale. "The Radicalization of Adrienne Rich." *Hollins Critic* 11 (1974): 1-15. Describes the complex evolution of a poet through her poetry, including *Diving into the Wreck*. Examines her political ideology and its impact on her works.
Jong, Erica. "Visionary Anger." *Ms.* 2, no. 1 (July, 1973): 30-34. Thoughtfully examines *Diving into the Wreck* in the context of Rich's philosophy and past work. Assesses her impact on feminist thought.
Rich, Adrienne. *Adrienne Rich's Poetry: Texts of the Poems: The Poet on Her Work: Reviews and Criticism.* Edited by Barbara Charesworth Gelphi and Albert Gelphi. New York: W. W. Norton, 1975. A thoughtful study of the author's work.
_____. *Of Woman Born: Motherhood as Experience and Institution.* New York: W. W. Norton, 1976. Analyzes motherhood as an institution and as a personal experience, using sociological theory and history to examine the significance of motherhood.
_____. *On Lies, Secrets, and Silences: Selected Prose, 1966-1978.* New York: W. W. Norton, 1979. Presents a detailed account of her intellectual rebirth through her prose. Identifies the literary works and figures who have influenced her.

DOCTOR FAUSTUS
The Life of the German Composer Adrian Leverkühn
as Told by a Friend

Type of work: Novel
Author: Thomas Mann (1875-1955)
Type of plot: Philosophical
Time of plot: 1885-1945
Locale: Germany
*First published: Doktor Faustus: Das Leben des deutschen Tonsetzers Adrian Leverkühn,
  erzählt von einem Freunde,* 1947 (English translation, 1948)

> *Principal characters:*
> ADRIAN LEVERKÜHN, an arrogant, sickly musical genius
> SERENUS ZEITBLOM, his lifelong friend and the narrator
> WENDELL KRETSCHMAR, Adrian's music teacher
> EHRENFRIED KUMPF and
> EBERHARD SCHLEPPFUSS, teachers of theology
> RÜDIGER SCHILDKNAPP, a poet and Adrian's friend
> RUDOLF SCHWERDTFEGER, a violinist befriended by Adrian
> INEZ INSTITORIS, a woman in love with Schwerdtfeger
> CLARISSA RODDE, her sister
> MARIE GODEAU, a woman whom Adrian loves
> NEPOMUK SCHNEIDEWEIN, Adrian's young nephew

The Story:

At the outset, Serenus Zeitblom doubted his ability to narrate understandably the life story of his friend Adrian Leverkühn. His friend was a musical genius whose strange, doomed career showed many parallels with the course of German history in the twentieth century. A former professor of philology, living in retirement and out of sympathy with the Hitler regime and greatly concerned for the future of his country, Zeitblom hesitantly began his task in May, 1943.

Adrian Leverkühn was born in 1885 on a farm near Kaiseraschern, in Thuringia. His family was of superior yeoman stock, and his father, a man interested in curious natural phenomena, did everything in his power to stimulate his son's intellectual curiosity. Adrian's boyhood friend, Serenus Zeitblom, was a frequent visitor in the Leverkühn household. Years later Zeitblom could remember his friend's absorbed interest in a book filled with pictures of exotic lepidoptera. One in particular, *Heroera Esmeralda,* fascinated the boy because of its unusual beauty and protective coloring. Adrian was introduced to music by a hired girl who taught him old folk songs.

Because the farm was to go to an older brother, the family intended that Adrian, a boy of brilliant mind and arrogant disposition, would become a scholar. When he was ten years old, he entered the school in Kaiseraschern. Living in the house of his uncle, a dealer in musical instruments, he had the run of the shop and began to play chords on an old harmonium. When his uncle overheard his efforts, he decided that the boy ought to have piano lessons. Adrian began to study under Wendell Kretschmar, the organist at the cathedral. His chief interest at that time, however, was theology, and he entered the University of Halle with the intention of preparing himself for the clergy. Zeitblom, certain that his friend's choice was dictated by the arrogance of purity, went with Adrian to his theological lectures. One of the teachers was Ehrenfried Kumpf, a forthright theologian who enlivened his classes by insulting the devil with epithets that Martin Luther might have used. Another instructor was Eberhard Schleppfuss, whose lectures were filled with anecdotes and sly undertones of demonism and witchcraft.

Given the range of his talents, Adrian could have chosen a career in scholarship, theology, or music. At last, unable to reconcile his interest in philosophy and science with theological precepts, he turned to music and began, still under Kretschmar's training, experiments in theory and technique that were to determine the highly original nature of his art. Before long, the pupil had surpassed the instructor. When Zeitblom was drafted for a year of compulsory military duty, Adrian was exempted because of his frail constitution, and went to Leipzig for further study. With Kretschmar's encouragement, he began to compose. A new friend of his, Rüdiger Schildknapp, was an Anglophile poet whose enthusiasm for William Shakespeare led to Adrian's decision to plan an opera based on *Love's Labour's Lost* (1594-1595). A sinister guide, somewhat like Schleppfuss in appearance, lured Adrian to a brothel one night. When a girl in the house—an Esmeralda, he called her—approached him, he ran from the place. Later he tried to see the girl again, but she had gone to Pressburg. Adrian followed her and there voluntarily contracted the venereal infection that led to the strange flowering of his genius and the eventual wreckage of his life. Several years afterward, during a holiday in Italy, he imagined a medieval-istic encounter with the devil, who in return for his soul promised him twenty-four years in which to fulfill his powers as an artist.

Before his Italian journey, Adrian had lived for a time in Munich. There his friends were artists and young intellectuals, among them Rüdiger Schildknapp, a novelist named Jeanette Scheurl, the young violinist Rudolf Schwerdtfeger, several actors, and the daughters of his landlady, Inez and Clarissa Rodde. Zeitblom met these people through Adrian and became interested in them. In 1912, Zeitblom married. A short time later, on his return from Italy, Adrian retired to a Bavarian farm presided over by motherly Frau Else Schweigestill. In this retreat, during the next twenty years, he composed the music that established his fame, and Zeitblom taught in Freising, not far away. During that entire time, the friends saw each other frequently. Zeitblom wrote the libretto for Adrian's opera on *Love's Labour's Lost*.

When war broke out in 1914, Zeitblom went into the army and served until he was invalided home with typhus. Adrian wrote *Marvels of the Universe* and a composition based on the *Gesta Romanorum*. During the war, Inez Rodde married Dr. Helmut Institoris, but she was secretly in love with Rudolf Schwerdtfeger and maintained an adulterous relationship with the violinist for years. Adrian's health began to improve after the war. His great work of that period was an oratorio entitled *Apocalypse*. As his fame grew, he acquired a patroness, Madame de Tolna, a wealthy Hungarian widow whom Zeitblom never met. In the meantime, Schwerdtfeger had broken off his love affair with Inez. Their first meeting after their separation was at the funeral of Inez's sister, Clarissa, an actress who was driven to suicide by a blackmailing lover.

Adrian yielded at last to Schwerdtfeger's urging and composed a violin concerto for the musician. About that time Adrian met the attractive Marie Godeau. Hoping to marry her, he sent Schwerdtfeger to act as his emissary in his courtship, but the violinist fell in love with the young woman and wooed her for himself. Shortly after the engagement was announced, Inez Institoris boarded a streetcar in which her former lover was riding and shot him. Adrian blamed himself for his friend's death.

Fate had one more blow in store for the composer. Adrian's nephew, Nepomuk Schneide-wein, of whom he was paternally fond, came to stay with Adrian at the Schweigestill farm while convalescing from an illness. There little Echo, as his uncle called him, suddenly contracted cerebrospinal meningitis and died. It seemed to Adrian that he had lost the child he himself might have had. He never completely recovered from his grief.

He continued to work on his masterpiece, a symphonic cantata called *The Lamentation of Doctor Faustus*. In the early summer of 1930, he invited a number of his friends and some critics to hear excerpts from the work, but his explanation of his composition was so disordered and blasphemous that many of the guests left before he had sat down to begin playing the score. As he struck the first chords, he fell senseless to the floor.

Adrian Leverkühn lived in madness for the next ten years, and he died, tenderly cared for by his aged mother, at his Thuringian birthplace in 1940. Serenus Zeitblom was among the few old friends present at the funeral. It seemed to him then, and the certainty grew upon him while he was writing the story of Adrian's life, that his friend somehow reflected the progress of the German nation, a land that had been arrogant, isolated, and dehumanized and was now—as the old philologist penned his final pages in April, 1945—reeling toward its final destruction.

Critical Evaluation:

Doctor Faustus, like other novels by Thomas Mann, particularly his monumental *The Magic Mountain* (1927), is enormously complex and built up of layer upon layer of interlocking references not only to the present but to the entire history of European civilization. Yet it is constructed on a very simple premise, that of inversion. Throughout the book, things are turned upside-down, and the readers again and again encounter, as in a magic mirror, their expectations being stood on their heads. Where hell is expected to be hot, it is instead described as freezing cold. The devil is no burning presence; instead, a chill emanates from him. Music, far from being the result of passionate inspiration, turns out to be the result of a highly cerebral, invented system of composition. Adrian Leverkühn's art is the result not of a special blessing but of a common curse, syphilis. Finally, the narrator of this novel, which attempts to encapsulate the history of the German people while telling the tale of a heroic (or antiheroic) figure, turns out to be an insignificant professor in a provincial town.

No doubt the paradoxical nature of the plot of *Doctor Faustus* owes something to Thomas Mann's own situation. For he wrote this most German of books in Los Angeles, where he lived in exile, having been forced to leave his homeland after Adolf Hitler came to power. His home and possessions had been impounded, his honorary doctorate canceled, and his citizenship revoked. While his character Serenus Zeitblom (a name that roughly translated means "serene flower-of-the-time") is tracing the progress of World War II from within Germany, Mann was following it from eight thousand miles away.

Certainly Mann composed his novel's inversions quite deliberately and down to the smallest detail. Leverkühn's final work, *The Lamentation of Doctor Faustus*, is modeled in part on Ludwig van Beethoven's Ninth Symphony (it even takes an hour and a quarter to perform, as does Beethoven's symphony), but where the choral passages in Beethoven's symphony are based on Friedrich Schiller's "Ode to Joy," Leverkühn's last work is referred to as an "Ode to Sorrow." Mann even has Leverkühn say that his *Lamentation* is a retraction of Beethoven's Ninth Symphony.

Through Leverkühn, Mann challenges a number of ideas stemming back to the nineteenth century when Beethoven wrote his symphony. What Mann wants to question, he has Leverkühn deny: That a nation state is good, that music is a force for good, that great artists are agents of good, that history teaches that humanity is moving upward into the light and that this progression in inevitable and must succeed. Long before the end of this novel, all such assumptions have become extremely dubious.

Yet Romanticism always had within itself this darker, despairing strain, the essential doubt that existence is worthwhile. *Doctor Faustus*, to be truly anti- or un-Romantic, would have had to dispense with its tragic hero, its vast battlefields, its deal with the devil, and its focus on individual suffering and joy, which confers value and meaning on life even though Leverkühn might wish to deny that life offers these. A truer opposite to the Romantic spirit in literature would be writing that de-emphasized the role of the individual in shaping history and ignored the significance of nations and of liberty, equality, and fraternity as human rights.

It is precisely because Mann's beliefs are those Romantic ideals that he was impelled to write this novel, for he saw these ideals endangered on every side during the 1930's and 1940's. The enemy of human beings is everywhere present in Mann's world, not least in the movement in art known as modernism. Mann's description of Leverkühn's system of composition was based on information Mann received from a mutual acquaintance about Arnold Schoenberg's so-called method of composing with twelve tones related only to one another. Mann considered this method to be highly constructivist and to a considerable extent anti-inspirational and repressive of certain elements in art that he believed essentially human. Upon this basis, Mann drew connections from fascism to modernism and from both of these to disease and to the devil.

The strength of the novel derives from the interest Mann gives to these questions. Ultimately, evil may be simply more interesting than good, because it raises more forcefully the questions of free will and determinism, choice and fate. Faustian pacts with the devil, a child dying in agony from meningitis, a great composer deliberately contracting a venereal disease from a prostitute—these can make compelling literature. Mann has scruples, moral misgivings, and a very real terror of the world gone mad, but he satirizes these in the hypocritical mealy-mouthed figure of the narrator. The readers' sympathies go rather with the man who has lost his soul to accomplish something indestructible, no matter what that something, than to the ordinary narrator. Leverkühn is a highly cultured, civilized man committed to the symbolic rather than the actual acting-out of his destructive impulses. Compared to Zeitblom, however, he is a monster, a vehicle for forces both natural and supernatural, and as such, a riveting subject for a book.

"Critical Evaluation" by David Bromige

Bibliography:
Bergsten, Gunilla. *Thomas Mann's "Doctor Faustus": The Sources and Structure of the Novel.* Translated by Krishna Winston. Chicago, Ill.: University of Chicago Press, 1969. Still the best detailed treatment of the novel's background and construction. Includes a useful appendix of Mann's source materials and a thorough, though now dated, bibliography.
Heller, Erich. "Parody, Tragic and Comic." In *Thomas Mann: The Ironic German.* 1958. Reprint. South Bend, Ind.: Regnery/Gateway, 1979. A careful and approachable reading of *Doctor Faustus* as tragic parody of art and artists, history, religion, and humankind's ability to create meaning.
Kahler, Erich. "The Devil Secularized: Thomas Mann's Faust." In *Thomas Mann: A Collection of Critical Essays,* edited by Henry Hatfield. Englewood Cliffs, N.J.: Prentice-Hall, 1964. Written for *Commentary* in 1949, Kahler's essay sees *Doctor Faustus* as a radical novel and Mann's "terminal book," in which he documented all he had to say about art and life. Excellent introduction to the issues involved in the novel.
Lehnert, Herbert, and Peter C. Pfeiffer, eds. *Thomas Mann's "Doctor Faustus": A Novel at the Margin of Modernism.* Columbia, S.C.: Camden House, 1991. Originally presented at a

symposium on the novel, the essays in this volume concentrate on several central aspects of the novel: women, Jews, questions of modernism in history, music, philosophy, narcissism, love, and death. A general introductory essay situates the novel historically.

Mann, Thomas. *The Story of a Novel: The Genesis of "Doctor Faustus."* Translated by Richard and Clara Winston. New York: Alfred A. Knopf, 1961. A fascinating and enlightening account of how Mann came to write the novel. A delightful counterpart to more traditional scholarly criticism. Provides biographical connections and interesting information on the problems of writing in exile.

DOCTOR FAUSTUS

Type of work: Drama
Author: Christopher Marlowe (1564-1593)
Type of plot: Tragedy
Time of plot: Sixteenth century
Locale: Germany
First performed: c. 1588; first published, 1604

> *Principal characters:*
> FAUSTUS, master of all knowledge
> WAGNER, his servant
> LUCIFER, the fallen angel
> MEPHOSTOPILIS, a devil
> GOOD ANGEL
> EVIL ANGEL

The Story:

Faustus had been born to a common family in Rhodes, Germany. In his maturity, while living with some relatives in Wittenberg, he studied theology and was called a doctor. However, Faustus was so swollen with conceit that, Daedalus-like, he strove too far, became glutted with learning, conspired with the devil, and finally fell, accursed.

At the outset of his downward path Doctor Faustus found himself complete master of the fields of knowledge that men at that time studied. As a medical doctor he had already achieved huge success and great renown. After obtaining good health for his patients no challenge remained in medicine except immortality. Law, Faustus concluded, was nothing but an elaborate moneymaking scheme. Only divinity remained, but theology led to a blind alley. Since the reward of sin was death and since no one could say he or she was without sin, then all must sin and consequently die.

Necromancy greatly attracted Faustus. Universal power would be within his reach, the whole world at his command, and emperors at his feet, were he to become a magician. Summoning his servant Wagner, Faustus ordered him to summon Valdes and Cornelius, who could teach him their arts.

The Good Angel and the Evil Angel each tried to persuade Faustus. Faustus was in no mood to listen to the Good Angel. He exulted over the prospects of his forthcoming adventures. He would get gold from India, pearls from the oceans, tasty delicacies from faraway places; he would read strange philosophies, cull from foreign kings their secrets, control Germany with his power, reform the public schools, and perform many other fabulous deeds. Eager to acquire knowledge of the black arts, he went away to study with Valdes and Cornelius.

Before long the scholars of Wittenberg began to notice the doctor's prolonged absence. Learning from Wagner of his master's unhallowed pursuits, the scholars lamented the fate of the famous doctor.

Faustus' first act of magic was to summon Mephostopilis. At sight of the ugly devil, he ordered Mephostopilis to assume the shape of a Franciscan friar. The docile obedience of Mephostopilis elated the magician, but Mephostopilis explained that magic had limits in the devil's kingdom. Mephostopilis claimed that he had not actually appeared at Faustus' behest but had come, as he would have to any other person, because Faustus had cursed Christ and abjured the Scriptures. Whenever someone is on the verge of being doomed, the devil will appear.

Interested in the nature of Lucifer, Faustus questioned Mephostopilis about his master, the fallen angel, and about hell, Lucifer's domain. Mephostopilis was cagey. He claimed that the fallen spirits, having been deprived of the glories of heaven, found the whole world hell. Even Mephostopilis urged Faustus to give up his scheme, but Faustus scorned the warning, saying that he would surrender his soul to Lucifer if the fallen angel would give to Faustus twenty-four years of voluptuous ease, with Mephostopilis to attend him.

While Faustus indulged in a mental argument concerning the relative merits of God and the devil, the Good Angel and the Evil Angel, symbolic of his inner conflict, appeared once again, each attempting to persuade him. The result was that Faustus was more determined than ever to continue his course.

Mephostopilis returned to assure Faustus that Lucifer was agreeable to the bargain, which must be sealed in Faustus' blood. When Faustus tried to write, however, his blood congealed and Mephostopilis had to warm the liquid with fire. Significantly the words, "Fly, man," appeared in Latin on Faustus' arm. When Faustus questioned Mephostopilis about the nature of hell, the devil claimed that hell had no limits for the damned. Intoxicated by his new estate, Faustus disclaimed any belief in an afterlife. Thus he assured himself that his contract with Lucifer would never be fulfilled, in spite of the devil's warning that he, Mephostopilis, was living proof of hell's existence.

Faustus, eager to consume the fruits of the devil's offering, demanded books that would contain varied information about the devil's regime. When the Good Angel and the Evil Angel came to him again, he realized that he was beyond repentance. Again the opposing Angels insinuated themselves into his mind, until he called on Christ to save him. As he spoke, wrathful Lucifer descended upon his prospective victim to admonish him never to call to God. As an appeasing gesture Lucifer conjured up a vision of the Seven Deadly Sins.

Faustus traveled extensively throughout the world, and Wagner marveled at his master's rapid progress. In Rome, at the palace of the Pope, Faustus, made invisible by his magic arts, astounded the Pope by snatching things from the holy man's hands. Like a gleeful child Faustus asked Mephostopilis to create more mischief. When Faustus returned home the scholars questioned him eagerly about many things unknown to them. As his fame spread, the emperor invited him to the palace and asked him to conjure up the spirit of Alexander the Great. A doubtful knight scoffed at such a preposterous idea, so Faustus, after fulfilling the emperor's request, spitefully placed horns on the head of the skeptical nobleman.

Foreseeing that his time of merriment was drawing to a close, Faustus returned to Wittenberg. Wagner sensed that his master was about to die when Faustus gave his faithful servant all his worldly goods.

As death drew near, Faustus spoke with his conscience, which, assuming the form of an Old Man, begged him to repent before he died. When Faustus declared that he would repent, Mephostopilis cautioned him not to offend Lucifer. Faustus asked Mephostopilis to bring him Helen of Troy as a lover to amuse him during the final days of his life.

In his declining hours Faustus conversed with scholars who had loved him, and the fallen theologian revealed to them his bargain with Lucifer. Alone, he uttered a final despairing plea that he be saved from impending misery, but in the end he was borne off by a company of devils.

Critical Evaluation:

Doctor Faustus is probably Christopher Marlowe's most famous play. Although Marlowe, who was a contemporary of William Shakespeare and a poet as well, wrote only seven plays, if Shakespeare had died at an equally young age (twenty-nine rather than fifty-two), Marlowe would today be the more famous of the pair. Marlowe was one of the first English writers to perfect blank verse (unrhymed iambic pentameter) and to use it with flexibility and poetic effect in drama. He was killed in a tavern brawl, perhaps as a result of serving as a spy in the service of Queen Elizabeth I.

The surviving manuscripts of *Doctor Faustus* cannot be entirely attributed to Marlowe alone. The comic scenes were probably added by a collaborator. Some criticism views the comic scenes charitably, seeing them as commentary on, rather than as a distraction from, the main plot. The actions of the servants and clowns as they try to conjure devils and the bargain made with the horse-courser, who returns to pull off Faustus' leg when the horse sold him proves to be a creation of black magic, are easily seen as parodies of Faustus' more serious deviltry. In the episode with the pulled-off leg, his body disintegrates as do his chances for spiritual salvation.

Doctor Faustus is framed in a convention from the medieval drama. It presents itself, through the prologue, as a morality play, a dramatized treatise from which a serious lesson should be garnered. Faustus is a kind of Everyman; he sins and needs to repent. This moralizing is carried through in the epilogue as well, where again the audience is directly addressed and admonished. Moreover, one of the dramatic devices used by Marlowe is that of the Good and Evil Angels, as manifestations of Faustus' conscience and instinct. Although these angels are typical devices, they assume in Marlowe's play a deeper psychological and religious significance.

Medieval morality, however, is only the play's frame. The play's thematic heart is with the humanistic Renaissance. Faustus is a self-made man. He has risen above his lowly birth and exalted himself by pursuing knowledge. He is ambitious, but he is ambitious for the most that can be known and the best that can be accomplished. What entices him to black magic is in part the mystery of its books and rituals, which he longs to learn. He seeks knowledge: This good motive is what leads him to damnation. Faustus is disappointed immediately, when all he learns after the pact is that God made the universe, that hell is wherever God is not, and that Faustus has ensured that he will be in hell for eternity. All that is left him, then, is trifles: fooling the Pope, conjuring up grapes in winter, pursuing the likenesses of beautiful women who were devils or illusions. The silliness of his pact is made clear by events in the comic subplot, in which the least-educated clown can also summon forth a demon. Faustus gives up true power, the power of choice, of spirit, and of intellect, for the equivalent of parlor tricks.

The poignancy of this irony is made clear in the final scene, in which the clock counts down the minutes left in Faustus' life and he begs for a single drop of Christ's blood to save him. Faustus has committed the sin of despair, however; ultimately he thinks his sins too great for Christ's mercy. He screams with ironic futility that he would burn his books as the devils tear his flesh and take him into the fiery pit of hell.

"Critical Evaluation" by Sandra K. Fischer

Bibliography:
Brooke, Nicholas. "The Moral Tragedy of *Dr. Faustus.*" *Cambridge Journal* 5 (1952): 663-687. Focuses on the moral choices presented to Faustus. Attempts to incorporate the comic subplots in a unified reading of Renaissance dualism, which would render the play an aesthetic whole and a dramatic success.

Kirschbaum, Leo. "Marlowe's Faustus: A Reconsideration." *Review of English Studies* 19 (1943): 225-241. Examines the language of the most memorable poetry of the play, the praise of Helen of Troy, to discover when the audience ought to be seduced by the language and when it must judge and resist beautiful verse.

Kocher, Paul H. "Marlowe's Atheist Lecture." *Journal of English and Germanic Philology* 39 (1940): 98-106. Reprints the blasphemous comments allegedly made by Christopher Marlowe, attested by one Richard Baines before the Privy Council in 1593. Judging the veracity of these comments and, if they are truly Marlowe's, how typical they are of his beliefs helps readers decide their sympathies in *Doctor Faustus*.

Levin, Harry. *The Overreacher: A Study of Christopher Marlowe*. 1952. Boston: Beacon Press, 1964. Examines the sources of the Faust legend and places them in the context of the fall of Lucifer from heaven. Examines the comic scenes to find in them a burlesque of the main plot.

Mizener, Arthur. "The Tragedy of Marlowe's *Dr. Faustus*." *College English* 5 (1943): 70-75. Treats the ambivalence toward knowledge in the Renaissance evidenced in Faustus' tragic progress in the play. Examines reason versus faith and allies necromancy with the dark side of the latter.

DOCTOR PASCAL

Type of work: Novel
Author: Émile Zola (1840-1902)
Type of plot: Naturalism
Time of plot: Late nineteenth century
Locale: The south of France
First published: Le Docteur Pascal, 1893 (English translation, 1893)

Principal characters:
　　DR. PASCAL, a doctor interested in heredity
　　CLOTILDE, his niece
　　MARTINE, their devoted old servant
　　MADAME FÉLICITÉ ROUGON, Dr. Pascal's mother
　　DR. RAMOND, a friend of Dr. Pascal and Clotilde
　　MAXIME, Clotilde's brother

The Story:

The July afternoon was extremely hot, but the room was well protected from the heat by heavy wooden shutters. In front of a huge carved oak armoire, Dr. Pascal was patiently looking for a particular sheet of paper. The search was not easy. For about thirty years, the doctor had been amassing manuscripts for his work on heredity. A smile came over his face when he found the paper, and he handed it to his niece and asked her to copy it for their friend, Dr. Ramond. Clotilde took it without interrupting her work on a pastel drawing of flowers that was intended for an illustration plate in the doctor's book.

Martine, the housekeeper, came in to repair the tapestry on an armchair. She had been with the doctor for thirty years, ever since he had come to Plassans as a young doctor. Thirteen years later, following the death of his wife, Dr. Pascal's brother had sent Clotilde, then seven years old, to live with him. Martine had cared for the child according to her own zealous religious convictions.

Dr. Pascal completed Clotilde's instruction by trying to give her clear and healthy ideas on everything. The three had lived in peaceful happiness, although a certain uneasiness was now beginning to grow out of their religious conflicts. Martine considered it a pity that such a kind man as her master refused to go to church; the two women had agreed that they would force him to attend services.

Later that afternoon, old Madame Rougon came by, ostensibly for a visit, but actually to inspect everything. Hearing her son in the next room, she expressed displeasure that he was again doing what she called his "devilish cooking." She told Clotilde of the unpleasant rumors about the doctor's new drug. If only he could try spectacular cures on the famous people of the town, she declared, instead of always treating the poor. She had wanted him to be a success, like his two brothers, but Dr. Pascal was most unlike the rest of his family. He had practiced medicine for only twelve years; after that, he had invested his money with a private broker and was now living on its returns. Martine received the money every three months and used it to the best advantage. When his patients paid him, Dr. Pascal threw the money in a drawer. When he visited a poor patient, he often left money there instead of receiving payment. He was completely absorbed in his research and his fight against suffering.

Madame Rougon was upset most by the fact that the big oak armoire contained detailed information on each member of the family. Afraid that the doctor's papers might fall into the hands of a stranger, she asked Clotilde to give her the key. She opened the cupboard, but as she was reaching for the files, Dr. Pascal entered; she left demurely as if nothing had happened. It was Clotilde who received the brunt of the doctor's anger. From that time on, Dr. Pascal felt that he was being betrayed by the two human beings who were dearest to him, and to whom he was dearest. He kept all the drawers of his desk tightly locked.

One day, Maxime came for a visit. Still young, he was already worn out by his dissolute way of life. Having ascertained that his sister was not planning to get married, he asked her to come to Paris with him. Clotilde was frightened at the idea of leaving Dr. Pascal's home, but she promised to go to her brother if some day he really needed her.

After Maxime's visit, the house returned to its state of subdued tension until a Capuchin came to Plassans to preach. Clotilde, deeply shaken by his preaching, asked Dr. Pascal to burn all of his papers. He refused. He also had another fruitless discussion with his mother, who was constantly begging the young girl to destroy the files.

One night, Dr. Pascal found Clotilde trying to steal his papers. While she helped to replace them, he made a last attempt to convince her of the value of his work. He showed her the files and explained the use he was making of them. Clotilde was almost convinced but asked for time to think about the matter.

One day, the doctor returned to the house in great agitation. A patient had died of a heart attack while he was giving him an injection. Dr. Pascal refused Clotilde's attempted comfort, and when his mother hinted that he might be going insane, he nearly believed the suggestion. He felt he might be suffering from the same condition as his grandmother, who had never been well-balanced and was now, at the age of one hundred and four, living in a sanatorium. Anxious and helpless, Clotilde and Martine watched over him.

Dr. Ramond came and asked Clotilde to marry him, but she said that she needed time to consider his proposal and that she would answer him soon. In the meantime, she asked him what he thought of her uncle's condition. Dr. Pascal overheard the conversation, and from that time on, his health became worse. Although he allowed Clotilde to take care of him, he would not let her come into his room when he was in bed. She finally persuaded him to try some of his own injections, as Dr. Ramond had suggested. As he began to show improvement, she tried to restore his faith in his research. He was overjoyed when she found the key to the armoire and brought it to him.

At last, Dr. Pascal declared that he felt greatly improved, and he told Clotilde that she should begin to think about a date for her marriage. Clotilde did not seem concerned. One day, as they were coming back from a walk, she asked him to help untie her hat. Suddenly, as he bent close to her, he realized how greatly he desired her. Disturbed by the strength of his feelings, he insisted that she give Dr. Ramond a definite date for the wedding. A short time later, he bought her an extravagant present of lace, which he put on her bed. That night, Clotilde came running to his door and told him that if her marriage was the occasion for the gift, she was not going to marry Dr. Ramond. He, Pascal, was the man she loved. That night she became his.

A period of extreme happiness followed for both Clotilde and Dr. Pascal. Martine, after disappearing for a full day to show her disapproval, continued her faithful service. One day, Martine returned with the news that the broker had embezzled the doctor's funds and fled. She performed miracles in preparing meals, using the money accumulated in the drawer, but at last their situation became really desperate. Dr. Pascal and Clotilde seemed quite unconcerned and waited patiently for the matter to be settled in court.

Madame Rougon kept busy. She produced a letter from Maxime, now disabled, in which he asked for his sister, and she heaped contempt on Dr. Pascal for keeping the young woman without marrying her and for not being able to feed her properly. Dr. Pascal was happy when Clotilde refused to go to her brother, but, feeling guilty, he pretended that he needed time to devote himself to his research and insisted that she should go. Deeply hurt, Clotilde nevertheless obeyed.

Dr. Pascal went on working, waiting, meanwhile, for the painful joy of Clotilde's letters. His health suffered, and he had two heart attacks. Dr. Ramond brought him the news that some of his money had been recovered. About the same time, he received a letter from Clotilde, telling him that she was pregnant. He immediately wired her to return. She left at once, but he died two hours before she arrived. He had however mustered enough strength to complete his files concerning himself, Clotilde, and their unborn child.

While Clotilde was in Dr. Pascal's room, Madame Rougon, with the help of Martine, burned all his papers. Clotilde later used the shelves to store her baby's clothes.

Critical Evaluation:

Doctor Pascal, the twentieth and final novel in Émile Zola's Rougon-Macquart series, is significant both as a reflection of Zola's personal life and as the culmination of his vast, ambitious history of the second Empire. If *Doctor Pascal* does not possess the literary energy of some of the other novels in the Rougon-Macquart series, it nevertheless reveals many of Zola's characteristic interests and obsessions.

Doctor Pascal centers on the love between an older doctor and a young woman, his niece. This relationship mirrors Zola's love for Jeanne Rozerot, a beautiful, modest twenty-year-old seamstress whom Zola's wife had employed. Rozerot became his mistress in 1888 (he was near fifty at the time) and for her sake went on two extreme diets to lose weight. He seems to have loved her very much, and he eventually had two children by her (although he had none by his wife, Alexandrine). He was not, however, willing to divorce his wife, despite the fact that he disapproved of extramarital affairs. Alexandrine had been his loyal companion through very hard times, and he could not bring himself to desert her now. Alexandrine was unhappy about the affair, but after Zola died, she behaved most humanely; she agreed to meet his children, treated them kindly, and even made it possible for them to bear their father's name legally.

Doctor Pascal is thus a very personal novel and reflects much about the life of the novelist. It is also personal in the sense that Dr. Pascal, as much as any other character in Zola's fiction, embodies the author's own intellectual interest and commitments. Dr. Pascal the scientist is devoted to curing nervous disorders and to keeping a record of his family. Zola too often viewed himself and his work as "scientific." In opposition to what he considered to be the unreality of the Romantics, Zola was determined to place his work on a firm scientific basis; in fact, he often saw his own fiction as a form of "experimentation." Dr. Pascal's record of the Rougon-Macquart family permits Zola to review the chronicle of the figures and incidents in this "history" and, at the same time, to express his views on the significance of heredity in the affairs of men and families. Dr. Pascal—and, by inference, Zola—takes the genetic material of the Rougon-Macquarts extremely seriously. Although the laws of heredity may not be completely understood, and although Dr. Pascal's injections are not medically successful, Dr. Pascal's belief in the power and explanatory force of science remains unshaken.

In fact, Dr. Pascal's belief in science—and the opposition to that belief from those closest to him—forms the chief intellectual concern of the novel. The objections to the doctor's scientific approach are religious and social, whereby the former, although virulent, is ultimately less threatening to Zola than the latter. Dr. Pascal's treasured servant, Martine, objects to Pascal's tampering with God's plan, but she takes action to help destroy the doctor's valued historical files only after being incited by Madame Rougon, Dr. Pascal's mother.

Madame Rougon's motives are entirely selfish. She does not want the honor of the family stained by an exposure of defects. Her only pride is her family, and she cannot tolerate the prospect of family shame. Taking advantage of Martine's simplicity, Madame Rougon finally succeeds in destroying all of Dr. Pascal's meticulously recorded chronicle. In a sense, this destruction of the family records is a logical conclusion of the degeneration of the Rougon-Macquarts, a family that, despite a few branches still growing, has degenerated and become self-destructive.

If the parallel between Dr. Pascal and Zola holds, the question arises whether Zola's literary work is also metaphorically destroyed as the Rougon-Macquart series comes to an end. Perhaps Zola believed that life would take its revenge on literature, that the truth he sought to express could not be borne. The forces of reaction, both social and religious, would stifle and burn his work.

That fate was not in store for Zola's literary work, although it was, in a sense, in store for Zola himself. Shortly after the publication of *Doctor Pascal*, Zola intervened in the notorious Dreyfus affair. Alfred Dreyfus, a Jewish officer, was convicted of treason by the French authorities, and the conviction was upheld despite another officer's having confessed to the crime and fled the country. When Zola thereupon attacked the authorities for anti-Semitism, hypocrisy, and lies, he was forced into temporary exile in England.

Zola's courageous action in behalf of Dreyfus and his opposition to anti-Semitism are particularly important in evaluating Zola's naturalist theory, which occupies a central role in *Doctor Pascal*. Because of Zola's emphasis on genetic determinism, his work might be open to accusations of racialism. Because of the stress he places on forces that mold men's lives, over which they have no control, he also could be accused of fatalism. The critic Georg Lukács, for example, refuses even to include Zola in the literary tradition of progressive realism. Yet in his literary output as in his life, Zola affirmed his confidence in the forces of science, progress, and, above all, life. Despite the destruction of the doctor's files, the reader is left with the impression at the end of the novel that Dr. Pascal's work will continue after him.

The emotional interest of the narrative, the center of gravity of the fiction, lies in the love of an older man for a young woman. Zola explores their feelings with extreme delicacy and insight, and the child resulting from their love is meant to signify the rebirth of hope and humanity. The child more than compensates for the destruction of the files. If that destruction is seen as revenge against scholarship, science, and art, then the birth of the child signals the victory of the positive forces of life over the forces of despair and negativism.

Although the novel holds significant intellectual content as well as relevance to Zola's life and career, there is a certain weariness in Zola's telling that may be the result of Zola's already having written an enormous number of pages in his vast chronicle. Like his character Dr. Pascal, Zola was no longer a young man. The narrative may be judged to lack the intensity of his earlier works, but it nevertheless glows with compassion and loving faith.

"Critical Evaluation" by Howard Lee Hertz

Bibliography:
Grant, Elliott M. *Émile Zola*. New York: Twayne, 1966. Detailed analyses of Zola's works, as well as of his theories, plans, and methods. Includes a discussion of *Doctor Pascal*, the final volume of the Rougon-Macquart cycle and a pivotal work in Zola's oeuvre.

Hemmings, F. W. J. *Émile Zola*. Oxford, England: Clarendon Press, 1966. Discusses *Doctor Pascal* as the summation of the Rougon-Macquart cycle. The birth of a male child at the end illustrates the theme of rebirth and rejuvenation. The character of Dr. Pascal is interpreted as incorporating Zola's own ideas and philosophy of life.

Lanoux, Armand. *Zola*. Translated by Mary Glasgow. London: Staples Press, 1955. Lively biography that includes discussion of Zola's works. Characterizes *Doctor Pascal* as a portrait of Zola in middle life. Like Zola, the hero's chief concern is his fear of old age.

Nelson, Brian. *Zola and the Bourgeoisie: A Study of Themes and Techniques in Les Rougon-Macquart*. Totowa, N.J.: Barnes & Noble Books, 1983. *Doctor Pascal* is included in a discussion of utopia and sex in the bourgeois world. Nelson concludes that the novel illustrates themes of decadence and renewal, and he links Zola's utopian vision of progress to the value of work.

Wilson, Angus. *Émile Zola: An Introductory Study of His Novels*. New York: William Morrow, 1952. Informative theoretical background of Zola's naturalism and materialism. Wilson characterizes *Doctor Pascal* as one of Zola's novels of Aix, the scene of his provincial youth.

DOCTOR THORNE

Type of work: Novel
Author: Anthony Trollope (1815-1882)
Type of plot: Domestic realism
Time of plot: Mid-nineteenth century
Locale: Barsetshire, England
First published: 1858

Principal characters:
DOCTOR THORNE, a country doctor
MARY THORNE, his niece
SQUIRE GRESHAM, the owner of Greshamsbury Park
LADY ARABELLA, his wife
FRANK GRESHAM, their son
ROGER SCATCHERD, a stonemason and later a baronet
LOUIS PHILIPPE, his son
MISS DUNSTABLE, an heiress

The Story:

Greshamsbury Park, in the county of Barsetshire, dominated the life of the surrounding countryside. Unfortunately, Greshamsbury's lord, Squire Gresham, was rapidly spending himself into poverty. Most of his financial troubles resulted from the desire of his wife, Lady Arabella De Courcy Gresham, to get him into politics. The squire had inherited his father's seat in Parliament but had lost it because of his Whig leanings. Barsetshire was overwhelmingly Tory and did not approve of Gresham's Whig friends or the fact that his wife's aristocratic family, the De Courcys, were aggressively Whig in sentiment. Gresham twice tried to regain his seat in the Parliamentary elections because his wife fancied being the wife of a member of Parliament, but he was unsuccessful and lost a great deal of money in financing his campaigns.

When therefore his son Frank came of age, Squire Gresham had not much to offer him in the way of financial security. Lady Arabella saw as their only hope the possibility of Frank's marriage to a wealthy heiress. That he might do such a thing, however, seemed rather doubtful, for, much to the distress of his mother and her family, Frank was in love with Mary Thorne, niece of the local doctor. Frank and Mary had known each other all their lives, and Mary had been educated along with the young Greshams at Greshamsbury Park.

Mary Thorne had been brought to live with her uncle, Doctor Thorne, when she was a mere infant. The real circumstances of her birth—that she was the illegitimate child of Doctor Thorne's brother and Mary Scatcherd, a village girl—were known only to the doctor. Even Mary Scatcherd's brother Roger, who had killed his sister's betrayer, did not know that Doctor Thorne had adopted the child. Roger Scatcherd, a poor stonemason, had been sentenced to six months in prison for his crime. When his term was up, he was told that the child had died. Since the doctor stood in high favor with Squire Gresham and regularly cared for Lady Arabella, his niece, an attractive child and near the age of the Gresham children, had taken her lessons with them. By the time Frank was of age, Mary Thorne seemed part of the family. Lady Arabella, however, was determined that this was not to be the literal state of affairs, for Mary had no money.

One of Squire Gresham's greatest misfortunes was the forced sale of a particularly choice part of his estate to pay off his most pressing debts. Doctor Thorne, acting as agent for the squire, had found a buyer in Sir Roger Scatcherd, the former stonemason, who now possessed a title, a seat in Parliament, and a large fortune. Although he knew nothing of the existence of his sister's illegitimate child, Sir Roger was in close contact with Doctor Thorne because he was a chronic alcoholic, and Doctor Thorne was often called on to attend to him after his drinking bouts.

The loss of the property greatly diminished the value and extent of the estate Frank would someday inherit. Fortunately, one of the Gresham daughters was engaged to marry money, a politician who wanted the Gresham and De Courcy family connections. A second daughter was to marry the local vicar and was thus assured of a respectable position, although one without much money. Frank was his mother's real hope, and to save him from his unfortunate entanglement with Mary, Lady Arabella's family invited Frank to De Courcy Castle for a visit.

The Countess De Courcy hoped to make a match between Frank and Miss Dunstable, a family friend and a woman considered the wealthiest heiress in England. Miss Dunstable, ten years older than Frank and much more worldly-wise, was clever and sharp-tongued. When, mostly to humor his aunt, Frank pretended to woo her, he found her good company. She saw through his pretended amorous interest immediately, and they became the best of friends, after which she became Frank's confidante and adviser.

Sir Roger Scatcherd was in such poor health from excessive drinking that he decided to make his will, leaving everything to Louis Philippe, his equally alcoholic son. When Doctor Thorne learned the terms of the will, he told Sir Roger that Mary Scatcherd's child was still living, whereupon Sir Roger made her his heir in the event of his son's death.

Lady Arabella, finding Frank's attachment for Mary unchanged, would not allow the girl to visit Greshamsbury. When Frank arrived home and was made aware of this, he was furious. The family insisted, however, that he had to marry wealth, particularly because the sister who was to have made an advantageous marriage had been jilted.

Sir Roger was also in difficulties. Having discovered a fraud in his election, the committee unseated him, and the shock was too great for the old man. He went on another drinking bout and died from the effects. Louis Philippe, who inherited the estate, had meanwhile also formed an attachment for Mary, but she remained true to Frank. The only hope for the happiness of Mary and Frank seemed to lie in the death of Louis Philippe, who was well on his way to following his father to the grave. Having paid a visit to the squire for the purpose of foreclosing on some debts, Louis Philippe went on a drinking spree that left him weak and very ill.

In a stormy interview soon afterward, Lady Arabella demanded that Mary end her engagement to Frank. Mary refused to be the one to break her promise, but she did ask the young man to release her because of the hopelessness of the situation in which they found themselves. Frank refused, insisting that they loved each other. Then Louis Philippe died. When Doctor Thorne jubilantly told Mary the news of her inheritance, her marriage to Frank became possible. With Mary now an heiress, not even the proud De Courcys could object to so excellent a match. For the first time in years, an atmosphere of rejoicing hung over Greshamsbury Park.

Critical Evaluation:

Doctor Thorne is the third novel in Anthony Trollope's Barsetshire series, succeeding *The Warden* (1855) and *Barchester Towers* (1857). As in the first two novels, Trollope describes the social realities of his mythical county, providing extraordinary insight into the English class structure and the social realities of the nineteenth century. Unlike the first two works, which were concerned with the insular ecclesiastical world of a cathedral town, Trollope turns his attention in this novel to the landed wealth of Barsetshire. The gentry, represented by the Greshams, are in decline because of the political imprudence of the squire, who aligned himself with his wife's family, the De Courcys, notoriously aristocratic and notoriously Whig. Having lost his Tory constituency and his money, Squire Gresham attempts to save the estate for his son.

It is at this point that Doctor Thorne, one of Trollope's ideal gentlemen, enters the story. The squire's only confidant, he serves not only as the family physician but also as its moral and spiritual counselor. Rigorous in his ethics, proud of his social station, and in no way awed by the upper classes, Doctor Thorne supports the squire in his attempt to restore the estate to its former vigor. Despising snobbish and pretentious aristocrats such as the De Courcys, who have no loyalty to the life of the land, he seeks to help his friend by advising various economies and suggesting judicious loans.

If the moral strength that saves Greshamsbury Park comes from the doctor, it is the money of Sir Roger Scatcherd which enables Gresham to recoup and permits Frank and Mary to wed. Scatcherd, who represents the new industrial wealth, unwittingly saves the agriculture of the area from the moneylenders of London. It is in this alignment that Trollope reveals his political sympathies with the English upper middle class and his antagonism to the aristocracy and their morality.

Doctor Thorne surpasses both of its predecessors in its range of characters and situations. It relies very heavily on melodrama, and the ending is distinctly reminiscent of a fairy tale, yet the scene setting and dialogue are as good as anything Trollope ever wrote. "Frank must marry money" is the refrain that integrates the novel. Lady Arabella is quite willing to sacrifice everything—her son's happiness, Mary Thorne's reputation, Doctor Thorne's medical care of her—if only her son will attach himself to a rich woman. Lady Arabella's husband, Squire Gresham, supports her, even though in his heart he approves of Mary and wants to honor his son's love for her. Roger Scatcherd thinks the power of his money will secure Mary Thorne for his dissolute son, Louis Philippe, who thinks the same. Doctor Thorne, who is neither intimidated nor awed by the aristocratic Gresham and De Courcy families, realizes the difficulty of Mary's situation. If she does not inherit her uncle's money, the prospects for her and Frank are bleak. Even Mary, although she never disavows her love for Frank, is willing (at Lady Arabella's urging) to write him a letter releasing him from his promise to marry her.

The only character besides Frank who steadfastly refuses to concede to the power of money is Miss Dunstable. An heiress in her thirties who is tired of the many men who have courted her for her money, she tells Frank that if he sticks by his first love, his determination to marry for love will eventually provide him with a living as well. Her advice would seem sentimental if she were not presented as such a worldly character. She is one of Trollope's finest creations, a shrewd and sophisticated woman who insists that Frank act on his own feelings and principles. To marry money, Miss Dunstable implies, would be not his salvation but his ruin, for he would have lost his real self.

Through the sensible Miss Dunstable Trollope sounds his theme that it is not blood or money that makes the man or woman but rather strength of character. Miss Dunstable seems a happy and well-adjusted person precisely because she knows herself and her society so well. Unlike so many of the other characters, she is neither hypocritical, self-deceiving, nor self-serving.

Trollope's other admirable characters have similar traits. Doctor Thorne, though less polished than Miss Dunstable and considerably more abrupt in his social intercourse, exhibits the same trueness of spirit. He is quite willing to offend Lady Arabella in the defense of his niece, Mary, whose excellent character, he realizes, is her only possession. For a similar reason, Doctor Thorne admires Roger Scatcherd, a violent man and a drunkard, for his plain speaking and hard-working life.

Of course, Doctor Thorne and the other honest characters suffer for their plain speaking and their refusal to submit to money interests or the aristocracy. Trollope allows them to survive, however, and even thrive because their fierce defense of self is combined with sensitivity to the power of social norms and authorities. Thus Doctor Thorne continues to treat Lady Arabella professionally as a doctor even while he takes exception to her treatment of his niece; for one thing, he needs the income from ministering to the Gresham family. Frank Gresham, too, shows respect for his family's values by agreeing to go away for a year to test their view that his separation from Mary will destroy his love for her. Trollope's most mature characters, in other words, assert themselves without repudiating societal standards. They have firm but flexible personalities, and in due course they are rewarded with success.

Trollope's management of plot and dialogue is enthralling. He delays the announcement of Mary's inheritance of Roger Scatcherd's fortune until the end of the novel. He ingeniously takes Lady Arabella and Doctor Thorne through several confrontation scenes that gradually intensify the differences between them. Through his description of Louis Philippe's bathetic decline and death from too much drink and self-indulgence he shows someone without any inner resources dying in a surfeit of wealth.

Trollope mitigates the melodramatic and fairy-tale aspects of his story with his narrative voice. The narrator often acknowledges that he is telling a story and even apologizes for faults such as the excessive length of the novel's first two chapters; he considered them necessary to explain the social and historical background of Frank and Mary's story, but he regrets that he has to introduce so much material so early in his novel. These confessions are disarming. The reader seems to be taken into the novelist's confidence. Indeed, Trollope invites the reader to feel superior to the narrator and at the same time indulgent toward his loquacious asides and digressions.

Because Trollope's theme is the nature of society and the power of money, because he draws characters with such precision and allows them to speak for themselves, his narrator is free to embark on many asides and subplots, for each digression from the main story enriches the background. As historian and novelist, Trollope resembles in tone the Henry Fielding of *The History of Tom Jones, a Foundling* (1749). Both novelists fully immerse readers in their characters' lives and yet retain a vivid consciousness of themselves as writing literature. Trollope does not go as far as the earlier Fielding in discoursing on the conventions of storytelling; on the contrary, his voluble narrator assumes an awareness of the tradition of novel writing and confines his comments only to the shape of his own story. The relaxed, casual tone and leisurely narrative are an extension of Trollope's supple moral insights.

"Critical Evaluation" by Carl Rollyson

Bibliography:
Booth, Bradford. *Anthony Trollope: Aspects of His Life and Art.* Bloomington: Indiana University Press, 1958. Considers the novel inferior to the two earlier Barsetshire novels because of Trollope's reliance on melodrama, which detracts from the novel's realism, but concedes the enormous appeal of Trollope's storytelling. Also analyzes what he calls Trollope's conservative-liberalism.

Hall, N. John. *Trollope: A Biography.* Oxford, England: Oxford University Press, 1991. Comments on the origins of the novel's plot, its popularity in spite of the critics' reservations, the engaging narrative mode, and Doctor Thorne as a typical Trollope hero.

MacDonald, Susan Peck. *Anthony Trollope.* Boston: Twayne, 1987. Concise discussion of the narrator, showing how his interventions intensify the story's thematic and ethical complexity and enhance the novel's realism.

Overton, Bill. *The Unofficial Trollope.* Totowa, N.J.: Barnes & Noble, 1982. Extensive analysis of the novel, emphasizing Trollope's vision of contemporary history and his handling of the complex plot.

Super, R. H. *The Chronicler of Barsetshire: A Life of Anthony Trollope.* Ann Arbor: University of Michigan Press, 1988. Explains the biographical origins of the novel, its relationship with the Barsetshire series, and its critical reception. Also discusses the way in which Trollope handles the theme of marriage in this novel and others.

DOCTOR ZHIVAGO

Type of work: Novel
Author: Boris Leonidovich Pasternak (1890-1960)
Type of plot: Social realism
Time of plot: 1903-1943
Locale: Moscow, the Eastern Front, and Siberia
First published: 1957 (English translation, 1958)

Principal characters:

YURII ANDREIEVICH ZHIVAGO, a physician, poet, and man of goodwill
EVGRAF ANDREIEVICH ZHIVAGO, his half brother
NIKOLAI NIKOLAIEVICH VEDENIAPIN (UNCLE KOLIA), his maternal uncle
ANTONINA ALEXANDROVNA GROMEKA (TONIA), his wife
LARISA FEODOROVNA GUISHAR (LARA), the wife of Pavel Antipov
PAVEL PAVLOVICH ANTIPOV (PASHA), a Red commissar
INNOKENTII DUDOROV (NIKA), the son of a revolutionary terrorist
MISHA GORDON, the son of a Jewish lawyer and a friend of Yurii Zhivago
VICTOR IPPOLITOVICH KOMAROVSKY, a shady lawyer and the seducer of
    Lara
LIBERIUS AVERKIEVICH MIKULITSYN, a Red partisan leader
TANIA, the daughter of Yurii Zhivago and Lara

The Story:

Ten-year-old Yurii Zhivago, the son of a wealthy profligate who had deserted his family, attended his mother's funeral in the company of his Uncle Kolia. They stayed that night at a nearby monastery. To the boy, waking in the darkness, the snow-covered landscape beyond his window suggested an empty, alien world. Young Misha Gordon, traveling with his father, saw the older Zhivago kill himself in a leap from a moving train. Nika Dudorov, whose parents were a nihilistic terrorist and a Georgian princess, was being brought up in the household of Kilogrigov, a philanthropic industrialist. After his father, a revolutionary and a railway worker, had been exiled to Siberia, Pasha Antipov was taken in by the Tiverzin family, also revolutionaries. Amalia Guishar, the French widow of a Russian engineer, arrived in Moscow and opened a dressmaking establishment; her protector was Victor Komarovsky, an unscrupulous lawyer who eventually succeeded in seducing her daughter Lara.

Before long, these lives began to crisscross. During their school days, Yurii Zhivago and Misha Gordon lived in the home of Alexander Gromeko, a professor of chemistry; their companion was Tonia, daughter of Gromeko and his ailing wife, Anna Ivanovna. Pasha and Nika took part in student riots. One night, by chance, after Madame Guishar had attempted suicide, Yurii saw Lara looking at her betrayer and guessed their secret. Lara, following an unsuccessful attempt to shoot Komarovsky, became a governess in the Kilogrigov household; later, she married Pasha and went to live with him in a hamlet beyond the Urals. Yurii discovered his vocation as a poet but instead chose a career in medicine because he believed that art was not a vocation, any more than melancholy or cheerfulness was a profession. For him, most choices were as simple as that. During his student years, he revealed an almost Dostoevskian gift of innocence which he never lost and which made him vulnerable, in the end, to forces beyond his power to order or control. This trait was part of the greater, enveloping mystique, which in the novel threw over much that was brutal and sordid a radiance of goodness and truth, symbolized by the light seen briefly in a strange house as Yurii and Tonia drove by to a Christmas party. He married Tonia, and their first child was born shortly before World War I.

With the outbreak of the war, the tempo of events quickened abruptly. Yurii Zhivago served in a hospital unit on the front lines of battle. Wounded, he was nursed by Lara Antipov, who was to become the great love of his life. He found himself married to a wife whom he sincerely respected and loved, but at the same time, he was pulled toward Lara by a tide of passion which swept him along into the unsettled years ahead. The Moscow to which he returned after the October Revolution was a city ravaged by riots and disease, from which he fled with his family to an estate, the property of Tonia's grandfather, in the Urals. All Russia was on the move—restless, threatening, violent. In the village where the Zhivagos settled, Yurii met Lara again and was once more drawn to her until he was seized by a band of Red partisans and forced into service as their doctor during a campaign of guerrilla warfare against the White partisans in Siberia. After his escape, he returned to find that his family had gone back to Moscow. He and Lara lived together in an abandoned farmhouse for a brief period of perfect happiness. Then, about to be arrested because they had become politically suspect, he sent her to safety with Komarovsky, who had become an official of the new regime. Another great scene of the novel is that in which Zhivago encountered Pasha for the last time. Pasha, now called Strelnikov— "The Shooter"—had been a feared and hated commissar of the civil war, but he himself was in flight from Red authorities who had denounced him as he had denounced others. His suicide after a night of wild accusation and abject confession pointed eloquently to the revolutionary madness of the period.

Back in Moscow, Zhivago found his life empty and meaningless. His family had found refuge in Paris. He married a younger woman, the daughter of a former porter in the Gromeko house, practiced medicine, and wrote a few scientific papers. In the end, he was befriended by his strange half-brother, Evgraf, an ambiguous figure whose relationship with Yurii remained shadowy and symbolic. After Yurii died of a heart attack, Evgraf arranged for the publication of a collection of Yurii's poems. During World War II, he also discovered Tania, the daughter of Yurii and Lara, and provided for her future.

Critical Evaluation:

Doctor Zhivago is the final statement of a writer who lived a full and complex artistic life. His father was an accomplished painter, his mother a concert pianist. Leo Tolstoy and the composer Aleksandr Scriabin were family friends. Boris Pasternak pursued music in youth but then turned to poetry, for which he prepared by studying philosophy at Marburg University. Born of Jewish parents, Pasternak was influenced both by the theology of his ancestors and by Christianity. Though he was relatively free of religious dogma, he was strongly persuaded of the reality of spiritual life, to which he felt the artistic impulse was closely related. It is not surprising that *Doctor Zhivago* is a vivid yet complicated and somewhat uneven work.

To observe that it is a poet's novel is quite common but nevertheless instructive. Even in an English translation there are remarkably lyric passages which reflect Pasternak's deep love for his native land. The sketches of many people as they live Russian life early in the twentieth century are especially notable in Part 1 of the work. Through both parts there are expressions of opinion, wisely made to come from several of the novel's characters, which reflect a subtle intelligence in its author. The poems of Yurii Zhivago, which conclude the novel and are intended to be an integral part of the whole, exhibit qualities one might expect of a ranking Russian poet of his century.

On the other hand, there are certain evidences that *Doctor Zhivago* is the work of a writer who was not thoroughly sure of the novelist's craft. Characters are sometimes drawn with enough care to be memorable and then more or less forgotten. Various incidents in the book are connected to others in ways that are somewhat clumsy. In a writer without Pasternak's ability to make the reader suspend disbelief, the coincidences whereby important characters are not only linked, but linked repeatedly and improbably, would seem absurd. The love story of Zhivago and Lara, surrounded by the circumstances of ordinary life in a more familiar world, would seem too sentimental.

Early in *Doctor Zhivago*, Nikolai Vedeniapin, Yurii Zhivago's maternal uncle, observes that "gregariousness is always the refuge of mediocrities, whether they swear by Soloviev or Kant or Marx. Only individuals seek the truth. . . ." Yurii Zhivago is not very gregarious, even if in becoming a doctor he devotes himself to the service of other people. Like his creator, Pasternak, he feels sympathy with the plight of an oppressed people and favors the revolution, but he is an individual, as both a scientist and an artist, who keeps what distance he can between himself and the brutalities, even atrocities, committed in the name of a new and better world. The dislocations which separate him from his wife, family, and the life he expected to have are somewhat mitigated by his extended affair with Lara. His poetry, which he sees not as a vocation but as an essential part of his being, provides him with the spiritual experience that the circumstances of his time would otherwise obliterate.

A title word of the novel, also the surname of the main character, "Zhivago" is related to "zhit'," the Russian verb meaning "to live." Yurii Zhivago's engagement with life is as much a matter of the spirit as of the flesh. In some ways, he seems a passive man, not especially convincing in his role as doctor. The first of the poems with which the novel concludes is called "Hamlet," Named for William Shakespeare's irresolute hero with whom Zhivago may be identified. The concluding poem, "Garden of Gethsemane," seems to affirm the resurrection, if not of body then of spirit, toward which future centuries will "drift, trailing like a caravan. . . ."

Life, spirit, art—these are the essentials that Yurii Zhivago struggles to preserve in an epoch with which he feels sympathy but not harmony. Not a particularly strong man himself, he is supported by strong women, of whom the most important is Lara. When he is separated from her at the urging of Victor Komarovsky, an unscrupulous but capable man, Zhivago drifts back to Moscow, where he has a new marriage of sorts and something of a career in medicine. The events of his time have broken his health, and he dies in early middle age. His fictional legacy is the body of poems which complete *Doctor Zhivago* and which are unmistakably influenced by an element of Christian idealism.

The circumstances surrounding the publication of *Doctor Zhivago*, its critical reception, and the political acrimony that followed have tended to obfuscate thoughtful criticism of the novel, but they cannot be ignored and should probably be reviewed. To begin with, Pasternak, who had earned a reputation as a poet as early as the 1920's, was not unwilling to serve the revolution if he was allowed intellectual and artistic freedom. These were not allowed, however, and, from about 1933 until 1943 he could not publish original poems in the Soviet Union. He supported himself by translating, particularly the English poets. He began work on *Doctor Zhivago* shortly after World War II and had it largely completed by the mid-1950's. Joseph Stalin had died in 1953, and, with the easing of possibility for internal repercussions, it seemed possible that the Soviet Union might allow the publication of Pasternak's book if he agreed to change some things. The Hungarian Uprising of 1956, however, led to new repressions, and seeing *Doctor Zhivago* printed at home was out of the question.

Pasternak then allowed his novel to be translated and published in Italy, which led to further translation and dissemination of the book throughout the Western world. If this did not sufficiently anger the Soviet authorities, the awarding of the Nobel Prize for Literature in 1958 did. Pasternak was forced to decline the prize. To coerce him further, the Soviets jailed Olga Ivinskaya, his companion since 1946 and the model for the character of Lara. Pasternak was expelled from the Writers' Union and threatened with deportation from Russia. Not surprisingly, Western nations used these events as a weapon in the Cold War, which troubled Pasternak deeply. He had not written his novel to make a political statement, nor did he wish to be separated from his people and his homeland.

Ironically, it is the Marxists themselves who have insisted that the artifacts of any human culture include a political dimension. The events of *Doctor Zhivago*, though they might be found politically inconvenient, are the substance of the story. The novel does not reject revolution, nor political reform, nor social justice. It simply records the brutality with which these ideals may be pursued and the difficulty of preserving other ideals, spiritual or personal or artistic, in a time of violent upheaval.

"Critical Evaluation" by John Higby

Bibliography:
Erlich, Victor, ed. *Pasternak: A Collection of Critical Essays.* Englewood Cliffs, N.J.: Prentice-Hall, 1978. This collection of essays covers all important facets of Pasternak's opus, including short fiction, although the emphasis is on his poetry and *Doctor Zhivago.*
Gifford, Henry. *Boris Pasternak: A Critical Study.* New York: Cambridge University Press, 1977. Gifford follows the stages in Pasternak's life and discusses works written in those stages in order to establish his achievements as a poet, writer of prose fiction, and translator. Chapters 12 and 13 deal with *Doctor Zhivago.*
Ivinskaya, Olga. *A Captive of Time.* Garden City, N.Y.: Doubleday, 1978. Ivinskaya, Pasternak's love in the last years of his life and the model for the character Lara in *Doctor Zhivago,* provides a wealth of information about Pasternak and *Doctor Zhivago.*
Mallac, Guy de. *Boris Pasternak: His Life and Art.* Norman: University of Oklahoma Press, 1981. An extensive biography of Pasternak. The second part is devoted to Mallac's interpretation of the most important features of Pasternak's works. *Doctor Zhivago* is discussed in "Toward Doctor Zhivago."
Muchnic, Helen. "Boris Pasternak and the Poems of Yuri Zhivago." In *From Gorky to Pasternak.* New York: Random House, 1961. Muchnic discusses the poems appended to the novel as an integral and important part of the novel.
Rowland, Mary F., and Paul Rowland. *Pasternak's "Doctor Zhivago."* Carbondale: Southern Illinois University Press, 1967. This book-length interpretation of *Doctor Zhivago* attempts to clarify allegorical, symbolic, and religious meanings in the novel. Although some interpretations are not proven, most of them are plausible, making for fascinating reading.

DODSWORTH

Type of work: Novel
Author: Sinclair Lewis (1885-1951)
Type of plot: Social realism
Time of plot: 1920's
Locale: United States and Europe
First published: 1929

Principal characters:
SAM DODSWORTH, an American manufacturer
FRAN DODSWORTH, his wife
EMILY, their daughter
BRENT, their son
KURT OBERSDORF, Fran's lover
CLYDE LOCKERT, Fran's admirer
EDITH CORTRIGHT, Sam's friend

The Story:

In 1903, Sam Dodsworth married Fran Voelker, whom he had met at the Canoe Club while he was assistant superintendent at the Zenith Locomotive works. Five years later, Sam became vice-president and general manager of production for the Revelation Automobile Company. By 1925, the Dodsworths had two children, Emily, who was about to be married, and Brent, who was studying at Yale. When Sam sold his factory to the Unit Automotive Company, he and Fran decided to go to Europe for a leisurely vacation, a second honeymoon.

The first night out on the S.S. *Ultima*, Sam met Major Clyde Lockert in the smoking room. Lockert, who said he was growing cocoa in British Guiana, quickly became friends with Fran and, while Sam looked on like an indulgent parent, squired her about. He continued to see the Dodsworths after they arrived in London. Fran was snobbishly pleased when he took them to visit his cousins, Lord and Lady Herndon. Between them, Fran and Lockert made Sam feel almost like an outsider. He was a failure at the dinner party the Herndons gave, for he was unable to discuss cricket or polo, and he had no opinions about the Russian situation.

One evening, Hurd, manager of the London branch of the Revelation Motor Company, invited Sam to a gathering, along with about thirty representatives of American firms. Sam was surprised to learn that few of them wanted to go back to the United States except, perhaps, for a visit. They all preferred the leisure and freedom from moral restraint that their adopted land afforded. These arguments made Sam see Europe in a different light.

When he returned to the hotel, he found Fran in tears. Lockert had taken her out that evening and, on their return, tried to make love to her. Fran, ashamed of the situation and sure that Lockert would be laughing at her, asked that they leave for France as soon as possible. They started four days later.

France was a new experience for Sam Dodsworth. When Fran was willing to go sightseeing, he was able to see Paris and observe its people. He was less satisfied when she chose to be fashionable and take tea at the Crillon with other American tourists. The more he saw of the country, however, the more convinced Sam became that he could not understand the French. In the back of his mind, he was afraid that his inability to accept foreign ways, and Fran's willingness to adopt them, would drive them apart. He felt lonely for his old friend Tubby Pearson, president of the Zenith Bank.

Before long, Fran had many friends among expatriate Americans of the international set. Given her constant visits to dressmakers and a portrait painter, as well as outings with the leisured young men who escorted her and her friends, she and Sam saw less and less of each other. When he went home for his college class reunion that summer, he left Fran to take a villa with one of her new friends. He was to join her again in the fall, so that they might go on to the Orient together.

Back in New York, Sam felt, at first, as if he had become a stranger to the life of noise and hurry he had previously taken for granted. Nor was he interested in the newest model Revelation that had been, quite competently, developed without his aid. He discovered also that he and his son no longer shared common ground. Brent was planning to sell bonds. The newly married Emily, her father observed, was the very capable manager of her own home and needed no assistance. Even Sam's best friend, Tubby Pearson, had gone on without him to new poker-playing and golfing companions.

At first, his letters from Fran were lively and happy. Then she quarreled with the friend who shared her villa over one of their escorts, Arnold Israel, a Jew. Sam grew increasingly anxious as he realized that the man was trailing Fran from one resort to another and that their relationship was becoming increasingly more intimate. He made sailing reservations and cabled his wife to meet him in Paris.

Sam had no difficulty discovering that his wife had been unfaithful to him; she admitted as much during their stormy reunion in Paris. With the threat that he would divorce her for adultery if she did not agree to drop Israel, he forced her to leave for Spain with him the following day.

The Dodsworths wandered across Spain into Italy and, finally, on to Germany and Berlin, and Sam had ample time to observe his wife. Increasingly he noted her self-centeredness, her pretentiousness, but his pity for her restlessness made him fonder of her. At the home of the Biedners, Fran's cousins in Berlin, the Dodsworths met Kurt Obersdorf, a ruined Austrian nobleman. Kurt took them to places of interest in Berlin and became Fran's dancing companion.

When the news came that the Dodsworths were grandparents, for Emily now had a boy, they did not sail for home. In fact, they did not tell their friends of the baby's birth because Fran feared that, as a grandmother, she would seem old and faded to them. When Sam went to Paris to welcome Tubby Pearson and his wife, abroad for the first time, Fran remained in Berlin.

Sam and Tubby enjoyed themselves in Paris. Then Sam, driven by a longing to see his wife, flew back to Berlin. That night, Fran announced that she and Kurt had decided to marry and that she wanted a divorce. Sam agreed, on the condition that she wait a month before starting proceedings. Sadly, Dodsworth left for Paris and from there went on to Italy. While he was sitting on the piazza in Venice and reading one of Fran's letters, he saw Edith Cortright, a widow whom the Dodsworths had met during their earlier trip to Italy. Mrs. Cortright invited Sam home to tea with her, and on his second visit, he told her about his separation from Fran.

Sam spent most of the summer with Edith and her Italian friends. He began to gain a new self-confidence when he found that he was liked and respected by these new acquaintances, who admired him and were satisfied with him as he was. He grew to love Edith, and they decided to return to America together. Then Sam received a letter from Fran telling him that she had dropped divorce proceedings because Kurt's mother objected to his marriage with a divorced American.

Without saying good-bye to Edith, Sam rejoined Fran, homeward bound. He tried patiently to share her unhappiness and loneliness, but before long, Fran was her old self, implying that

Sam had been at fault for the failure of their marriage, and flirting with a young polo player aboard ship. After breakfast one morning, Sam sent a wireless to Edith, making arrangements to meet her in Venice. When the boat docked in New York, Sam left his wife forever. Three days later, he sailed again to Italy and to Edith Cortright.

Critical Evaluation:
Sinclair Lewis was born into the American middle class, and his novels suggest that he both loved and detested his own kind, a crucial fact in understanding the unevenness of his satirical portraits. The critic Alfred Kazin views Lewis, together with Sherwood Anderson, as new realists—post-World War I reporters freed by the war into a struggle for "freedom of conduct" in middle America. Both writers, liberating forces in American literature of the 1920's, made "transcriptions of average experience," sometimes reproducing it and sometimes parodying it, but always participating in the native culture in the course of revealing its shortcomings. A typical Lewis novel reflects a mixture of scorn and compassion for its characters.

Although Lewis published more than twenty novels, a play, short stories, and sketches between 1914 and his death in 1951, his reputation as an artist eventually came to rest on four novels of the 1920's: *Main Street* (1920), *Babbitt* (1922), *Arrowsmith* (1925), and *Dodsworth* (1929). The protagonists of these works continue to generate interest and empathy because Lewis' feeling for the characters as human beings overrode his abiding skepticism. As a result, these characters are memorable, living individuals whose natures and problems transcend caricature and the topical.

Dodsworth, whose working title was *Exile*, was written in Europe, where Lewis had journeyed in the aftermath of his ruined marriage. While there he found or imagined that he found a culture superior to that of America's half-educated, anti-intellectual boosters. Lewis' strong if troubled vision of middle America appears to have come from a deep sense of his own inferiority. Although he was the first American to receive the Nobel Prize in Literature, he later remarked that it ruined him; he could not "live up to it." This sense of native inferiority and resulting attempts to ensure self-respect and love are duplicated in Sam Dodsworth's experiences in Europe. Lewis blends autobiography with fiction in a well-controlled third-person narrative technique in *Dodsworth*, focusing primarily on the protagonist and creating a fully realistic account of Sam's travels that simultaneously documents the journeys and reasserts Dodsworth's value as a human being.

Lewis sees Dodsworth idealistically, for the most part, but so skillfully that the romantic and nostalgic are veiled by the realistic surface of events. Sam is the post-Victorian embodiment of American virtue. He is essentially honest, doggedly willing to remain open to new experience, boyish in his sincere if awed appreciation of femininity and womanliness, but reluctant to be henpecked forever. His restrained physical courtship of Edith Cortright entails only kissing her hands. He is reserved, well-mannered, and admirably dignified for an American, even while clutching his Baedeker. By contrast, most other American male characters are presented as inferior if not nefarious. Arnold Israel engages in questionable financial pursuits and is sensual and more European than the Europeans. Tub Pearson is the perennial adolescent whose idea of humor is to address French waiters as "Goosepeppy" and to ask for fricassée of birds' nests. Brent, the Dodsworths' son, decides to live by selling bonds, hoping to reach the "hundred and fifty thousand a year class."

Most significant in the characterization of Dodsworth, however, is his devotion to a work ethic of substance, which proves to be his salvation. Sam slowly but persistently weighs his values against those of older cultures: England, France, Italy, Spain, and Germany. Europeans know wine, history, women, politics, and are not afraid of things theoretical, even socialism. Therefore, they can just "be," that is, rest in the self-confidence of their familial and cultural heritage. Americans, however, Sam dimly realizes, are born apostles and practitioners of technology. They must "do." Forces beyond their knowledge and control harness their dreams and energies. Their destiny is to build more and better autos, plumbing, and electrical appliances. Sam and Edith decide to return to Zenith to work but not on what Sam calls "kitchy banalities."

Lewis uses architecture as the symbol of Dodsworth's new life and work. In Europe, Sam, becoming absorbed in architecture, observes and sketches bridges, towers, and doorways. He is impressed by their lines, their strength, their beauty, but he recognizes that they are European. Rather than return to Zenith to build a phony pastiche of villas and chalets in the San Souci development, Sam and Edith talk of building homes for Americans, native to the soil and spirit. Optimistically, Edith cries that the American skyscraper is the only new thing in architecture since the Gothic cathedral. Working together, their future promises to be a sharp contrast to that of the pitiful Fran, to whom all culture was interesting as "social adornment."

Occasionally, Lewis abandons the detached third-person narrative technique to speak directly to the reader, indulge in satirical comments about travelers, and provide a series of descriptions of American tourists complete with names in the comedy of humors tradition. Evident also are some forced metaphors, a few poorly integrated references to "morality hounds" in America or to the absurdities of Prohibition. Yet Lewis endows the novel with its power basically by making Sam Dodsworth a sympathetic, authentic American whose life matters to him and to the reader.

"Critical Evaluation" by Mary H. Hayden

Bibliography:
Bloom, Harold, ed. *Sinclair Lewis.* New York: Chelsea House, 1987. A collection of critical essays on Sinclair Lewis, including an important study of *Dodsworth* by Martin Light, who sees the novel as one of Lewis' strongest achievements and one that resolved the tension in his work between romance and realism. Bloom's introductory essay praises *Dodsworth* as an underrated masterpiece. Selected bibliography.

Bucco, Martin, ed. *Critical Essays on Sinclair Lewis.* Boston: G. K. Hall, 1986. A collection of criticism on Sinclair Lewis that begins with early reviews and goes on to later critics. A useful essay by Robert L. Coard analyzes *Dodsworth* as a generic popular novel of the early twentieth century.

Grebstein, Sheldon Norman. *Sinclair Lewis.* New York: Twayne, 1962. Standard introductory study of Lewis, with selected bibliography. Praises *Dodsworth* and *Arrowsmith* as being Lewis' best works for having the best realized and most credible characters.

Lundquist, James. *Sinclair Lewis.* New York: Frederick Ungar, 1973. A general study, which places Lewis' novels in their social context and views the writer as someone who contributed to American culture's growing self-awareness. Examines *Dodsworth* as a powerful social document in which Lewis responded to social changes in the United States. Selected bibliography.

Schorer, Mark. *Sinclair Lewis: An American Life.* New York: McGraw-Hill, 1961. Thoroughly researched study of Lewis's life and work, an indispensable reference. Explores the autobiographical aspects of *Dodsworth*, which Schorer places in the context of Lewis' role in the transformation of American manners, morals, and intellectual assumptions.

A DOLL'S HOUSE

Type of work: Drama
Author: Henrik Ibsen (1828-1906)
Type of plot: Social realism
Time of plot: Nineteenth century
Locale: Norway
First published: Et dukkehjem, 1879 (English translation, 1880); first performed, 1879

> *Principal characters:*
> TORVALD HELMER, a bank manager
> NORA HELMER, his wife
> MRS. LINDE, Nora's old school friend
> KROGSTAD, a bank clerk
> DR. RANK, a friend of the Helmers

The Story:

On the day before Christmas, Nora Helmer had busied herself with last-minute shopping, for this was the first Christmas since her marriage that she had not had to economize. Her husband, Torvald, had just been made manager of a bank and after the New Year their money troubles would be over. She had bought a tree and plenty of toys for the children and had even indulged herself in some macaroons, her favorite confection, but of which Torvald did not entirely approve. He loved his wife dearly, but he regarded her very much as her own father had, as an amusing doll—a plaything.

It was true that she did behave like a child sometimes in her relations with her husband. She pouted, wheedled, and chattered because Torvald expected these things; he would not have loved his wife without them. Actually, seven years earlier Nora had shown that she had the courage of a mature, loving woman. Just after her first child was born, when Torvald had been ill and the doctor had said that he would die unless he went abroad immediately, she had borrowed the requisite two hundred and fifty pounds from Krogstad, a moneylender. She had forged her father's name to the note, who was dying at the time, and convinced Torvald that the money for his trip had come from her father. Yet Krogstad was exacting, and since then she had had to devise various ways to meet the regular payments. When Torvald gave her money for new dresses and such things, she never spent more than half of it, and she had found other ways to earn money. One winter she did copying, which she kept a secret from Torvald.

Krogstad, who was in the employ of the bank of which Torvald was now manager, was determined to use Torvald to advance his own fortunes. Torvald disliked Krogstad, however, and was just as determined to be rid of him. The opportunity came when Christina Linde, Nora's old school friend, applied to Torvald for a position in the bank. Torvald resolved to dismiss Krogstad and hire Mrs. Linde in his place.

When Krogstad discovered that he was to be fired, he called on Nora and told her that if he were dismissed he would ruin her and her husband. He reminded her that the note supposedly signed by her father was dated three days after his death. Frightened at the turn matters had taken, Nora pleaded unsuccessfully with Torvald to reinstate Krogstad in the bank. Krogstad, receiving from Torvald an official notice of his dismissal, wrote a letter in which he revealed the full details of Nora's forgery. He dropped the letter in the mailbox outside the Helmer home.

Torvald was in a holiday mood. The following evening they were to attend a fancy dress ball, and Nora was to go as a Neapolitan fisher girl and dance the tarantella. To divert her husband's attention from the mailbox outside, Nora practiced her dance before Torvald and Dr. Rank, an old friend. Nora was desperate, not knowing quite which way to turn. She had thought of Mrs. Linde, with whom Krogstad had at one time been in love. Mrs. Linde promised to do what she could to turn Krogstad from his avowed purpose. Nora thought also of Dr. Rank, but when she began to confide in him he made it so obvious that he was in love with her that she could not tell her secret. However, Torvald had promised her not to go near the mailbox until after the ball.

What bothered Nora was not her own fate, but Torvald's. She imagined herself already dead, drowned in icy black water, and pictured the grief-stricken Torvald taking upon himself all the blame for what she had done and being disgraced for her sake. In fact, Mrs. Linde, by promising to marry Krogstad and look after his children, had succeeded in persuading him to withdraw all accusations against the Helmers. She realized, however, that sooner or later Nora and Torvald would have to come to an understanding.

The crisis came when Torvald read Krogstad's letter after their return from the ball. He accused Nora of being a hypocrite, a liar, and a criminal and of having no religion, morality, or sense of duty. He declared that she was unfit to bring up her children and that she might remain in his household but would no longer be a part of it. When Krogstad's second letter arrived, declaring that he intended to take no action against the Helmers, Torvald's attitude changed, and with a sigh of relief he declared that he was saved.

For the first time, Nora saw her husband for what he was—a selfish, pretentious hypocrite with no regard for her position in the matter. She reminded him that no marriage could be built on inequality and announced her intention of leaving his house forever. Torvald could not believe his ears and pleaded with her to remain, but she declared she was going to try to become a reasonable human being, to understand the world—in short, to become a woman, not a doll to flatter Torvald's selfish vanity. She went out and with irrevocable finality, slammed the door of her doll house behind her.

Critical Evaluation:

Although Henrik Ibsen was already a respected playwright in Scandinavia before the premiere of *A Doll's House*, it was that work that catapulted him to international fame. The earliest of Ibsen's social-problem plays, this drama must be read in its historical context to understand its impact not only on twentieth century dramaturgy but also on society at large.

Most contemporary theater up to the time, including Ibsen's earlier work, fell into two general categories, one the historical romance; the other, the so-called well-made (or "thesis") play. The well-made play was a contrived comedy of manners revolving around an intricate plot and subplots but ultimately suffocated by the trivia of its theme and dialogue as well as by its shallow characterization. There was also the occasional poetic drama—such as Ibsen's *Brand* (1866) and *Peer Gynt* (1867)—but poetic form was often the only distinction between these plays and historical romances, as the content tended to be similar.

Into this dramaturgical milieu, *A Doll's House* injected natural dialogue and situations; abstained from such artificial conventions as the soliloquy or "aside" and observance of the "unities" of time and place; and insisted on the strict logical necessity of the outcome without attempting to wrench events into a happy ending. These theatrical innovations constitute Ibsen's fundamental contribution to the form of realistic drama. This kind of drama emphasizes believability, yet there is no attempt to achieve the comprehensiveness of photographic reality;

rather, realism is selective and strives for representative examples in recognizable human experience. Through selectivity, realism implicitly assumes a critical stance. Thus the Helmers' domestic crisis had, and still has, an immediate impact on theater audiences for being potentially true of the audience as well. Drama changed radically after *A Doll's House*, for which reason Ibsen is called the father of modern drama.

Ibsen's influence on twentieth century drama was twofold, for he combined both technique and content in the realism of *A Doll's House*. Specifically, Ibsen elevated playmaking to a level above mere entertainment by validating the respectability of plays about serious social issues. One of the most volatile issues of his day was the position of women, who throughout virtually all of Western society were at that time considered by law and by custom chattel of fathers and husbands. Women were denied participation in public life; their access to education was limited; their social lives were narrowly circumscribed; and they could not legally transact business, own property, or inherit. In the mid-nineteenth century, chafing under such restrictions, some women began to demand autonomy. They pushed for the right to vote and the opportunity for higher education and entry into the professions. By the last two decades of the nineteenth century, this had turned into open defiance, which in turn evoked outrage from many.

Against this turbulent background, Ibsen presented *A Doll's House*. The response was electric. On the strength of the play, suffragists construed Ibsen as a partisan supporter, and their opposition accused the playwright of propagandizing and being an agent provocateur. Yet Ibsen was neither a feminist nor a social reformer. Indeed, Ibsen personally deplored the kind of emancipation and self-development that brought women out of the domestic sphere into the larger world; he saw women's proper role exclusively as motherhood. His feminist sympathies were but a facet of his realism. He did no more than try to describe the problems as he saw them; he did not attempt to solve them. Nevertheless, he had a sharp eye and many sharp words for injustice, and it was the injustice of Torvald's demeaning treatment of Nora—a deplorably common occurrence in real life, Ibsen conceded—that provided the impetus for the play.

In the raging debate over the morality of Nora's behavior, however, it is altogether too easy to neglect Torvald's dramatic function in the play. This smug lawyer/bank manager is meant to represent the social structure that decreed an inferior position for women. Torvald is, in effect, a symbol for male-dominated and authoritarian society. Thus he establishes "rules" for Nora—the petty prohibition against macaroons, for one, the requirement that she act like a child and believe in the rightness, empirical as well as ethical, of his view in all matters. (In fact, Ibsen remarks in his "Notes" for the play that men make the laws and judge a woman's conduct from a man's point of view, "as though she were not a woman but a man.") His contemptuous attitude toward Nora's intelligence and sense of responsibility—he calls her his "little lark," his "little squirrel," his "little featherbrain," his "little spendthrift," and so on—actually reflects the prevailing view that many men had of women: that they are owned property, playthings, dolls to be housed in toy mansions and be indulged, but only sparingly.

In this Neanderthal context, it is difficult not to view Torvald as a thoroughgoing villain. Like society, however, Torvald is not completely devoid of redeeming grace, for otherwise Nora would not have married him, or committed forgery at great personal risk and used her utmost ingenuity to protect him from shame. Nora is both sensible and sensitive, despite Torvald's disparaging insinuations, and her awareness of her own worth is gradually awakened as the play unfolds—and with it her sense of individual responsibility. When at last she insists on her right to individual self-development, the spoiled girl-doll becomes a full-fledged woman. She slams the door of the doll house in a gesture symbolic of a biblical putting away of childish things and takes her rightful place in the adult world. Needless to say, that slam shakes the very rafters of the social-domestic establishment, and the reverberations continue in the present. So powerful an echo makes a powerful drama.

"Critical Evaluation" by Joanne G. Kashdan

Bibliography:

Downs, Brian W. *Ibsen: The Intellectual Background.* New York: Octagon, 1969. Contains preface, chronology, and index, and makes multiple references to *A Doll's House.* Downs argues that the "disagreement" upon which the drama turns is not between a wife and husband as much as it is between woman and society.

Hornby, Richard. *Patterns in Ibsen's Middle Plays.* Lewisburg: Bucknell University Press, 1981. A readable, helpful, and interesting discussion of *A Doll's House* in one chapter. Indicates that the play's underlying idea is the "ethical leap" that informs the technical and aesthetic development of the play.

Mencken, H. L. Introduction to *Eleven Plays of Henrik Ibsen.* New York: Random House, 1950. Mencken's prose is worth reading for itself and especially so in this case for anyone interested in Ibsen. Mencken lauds *A Doll's House* and declares that it represents the full measure of Ibsen's contribution to the art of drama.

Meyer, Michael. *Ibsen: A Biography.* Garden City, N.Y.: Doubleday, 1971. A well-organized, readable, illustrated source with an annotated index. Includes frequent references to *A Doll's House,* especially in chapter 19. Meyer also discusses the continued focus on Ibsen's view of women's situation in a man's world, on the outcry against *A Doll's House,* and on the monetary return it brought the author.

Shafer, Yvonne, ed. *Approaches to Teaching Ibsen's "A Doll [sic] House."* New York: Modern Language Association of America, 1985. Useful for both nonspecialists and specialists. Provides section about materials available for a study of *A Doll's House* and a section on approaches to teaching it. Provides insight for understanding and interpreting the play.

DOMBEY AND SON

Type of work: Novel
Author: Charles Dickens (1812-1870)
Type of plot: Social realism
Time of plot: Early nineteenth century
Locale: England
First published: 1846-1848

> *Principal characters:*
> MR. DOMBEY, a wealthy London merchant
> PAUL, his son
> FLORENCE, his daughter
> EDITH GRANGER, his second wife
> MR. CARKER, his trusted agent
> WALTER GAY, the young man whom Florence loves

The Story:

Mr. Dombey was a stiff, dignified man who rarely showed emotion, but the birth of an infant son, who was named Paul, was cause for rejoicing. Mr. Dombey had longed many years for a child who would become the Son of his mercantile firm of Dombey and Son. The fact that Mrs. Dombey died shortly after the boy's birth did not particularly concern him; his attention centered entirely on the little infant. Mr. Dombey also had a daughter, Florence, but she meant nothing to him, for she could not take a place in the firm.

Little Paul was first given over to a wet nurse, but the woman was considered unreliable and was dismissed. After her dismissal, little Paul was cared for by Mr. Dombey's sister and one of her friends. Despite their vigilant care, however, the boy suffered from poor health. He was listless and never cared to play. At last, Mr. Dombey arranged to have him sent to a home at Brighton, together with his sister, to benefit from the sea air.

Paul loved his sister very much, and they were constant companions, but Paul's love for Florence only made Mr. Dombey dislike the girl. He resented the fact that she was healthy when his son was not, and he felt that his daughter was coming between him and his son.

One weekend while Mr. Dombey was visiting at Brighton, Walter Gay, a young clerk in his firm, came to the inn where Mr. Dombey and his children were dining. Some time before, the clerk had rescued Florence from an old thief. Now his uncle was about to become a bankrupt, and Walter had come to ask for a loan to save his uncle's shop. Mr. Dombey let little Paul, who was then six years old, make the decision. Paul asked Florence what he should do; she told him to lend the money, and he did.

Shortly afterward, little Paul was placed in a private school at Brighton, where he was to be educated as quickly as possible. The pace of his studies proved too much for him, and before the year was out his health broke down. Even after his father took him home to London, he did not seem to grow any better. He died a few months later, deeply mourned by his father and his sister, although for different reasons.

Mr. Dombey took his son's death as a personal blow of fate to his plans. His sister and her friend became so concerned about him that they persuaded him to take a trip to Leamington with Major Bagstock, a retired officer. While in Leamington, they met Edith Granger, a young widow whose mother the major had known. Mr. Dombey began to court Mrs. Granger, seeing in her a beautiful, well-bred young woman who would grace his household and provide him with an heir. Mrs. Granger, coaxed by an aged mother who was concerned for her own and her daughter's welfare, finally accepted Mr. Dombey, although she was not in love with him.

Florence Dombey had seen young Walter Gay several times since their meeting at Brighton. After her brother's death, she came to look upon young Walter as a substitute brother, despite his lowly station. Their friendship was broken temporarily when Mr. Dombey sent Walter on a mission to the West Indies. Weeks passed, and no word was heard of the ship on which he had sailed. Everyone believed that it had sunk and that Walter had been drowned.

After Mrs. Granger had accepted Mr. Dombey's suit, they began to make plans for the wedding and for reopening the Dombey house in London. Edith Granger first met Florence at the house. The two immediately became fast friends, even though Mr. Dombey disliked his daughter and made it plain that he did not want his wife to become too fond of the girl.

Mr. Dombey's second marriage was unsuccessful from the start. Edith Granger was too proud to give in to Mr. Dombey's attempts to dictate to her and to his claim upon her as a piece of merchandise, and she resisted him in every way. Dombey, who was too dignified to argue with her, began to send his business manager, Mr. Carker, to tell his wife that he was dissatisfied with her conduct. Carker warned Mrs. Dombey that, unless she obeyed Mr. Dombey, Florence would be the one to suffer. Edith Dombey thereupon became outwardly cool toward her stepdaughter, but she continued to resist her husband. Mr. Carker was dispatched to tell her that Mr. Dombey meant to be obeyed in everything.

Edith revolted by ostensibly running off with Carker, her husband's most trusted employee, who was so far below Mr. Dombey socially that the blow hurt Mr. Dombey even more. When Florence tried to comfort her father, he rebuffed her cruelly, going so far as to strike her. She ran out of the house, knowing she no longer had a home or a father, and found refuge in the shop owned by Sol Gills, Walter Gay's uncle. Gills had disappeared in search of his nephew, and his friend, an old ship's captain, was in charge. Captain Cuttle recognized Florence and took her in.

Mr. Dombey learned the whereabouts of his wife and Carker from a young woman whom Carker had seduced and deserted. Mr. Dombey followed the pair to France but failed to locate them. Carker returned to England after Edith refused to have anything to do with him. She had her revenge, she said, in having ruined him and her husband. Carker tried to escape into the English countryside, but when he met Mr. Dombey at a railway station, an accident occurred and Carker was killed by a train.

Florence continued to stay with Captain Cuttle, hoping that Walter would return, even though everyone had given him up for dead. Her faith was at last rewarded. Walter had been picked up by a vessel bound for China. Shortly after his return, he confessed to Florence that he no longer felt toward her like a brother, for she had become a woman during his absence. Realizing that she, too, had fallen in love with him, she accepted his proposal. Walter had found work as a clerk on a ship, and after their marriage, they sailed on a ship bound for the Orient.

The failure of his marriage had broken Mr. Dombey's spirit, and he took little interest in his firm from that time on. The firm had been placed in a difficult position by some of the transactions Carker had handled while he was Dombey's trusted agent. As a result of Carker's mismanagement and Dombey's lack of interest, the firm went bankrupt. After the bankruptcy, Mr. Dombey stayed alone in his house, saw no one, and gradually drifted into despair.

On the very day that Mr. Dombey had decided to commit suicide, Florence returned to London from the Orient with her one-year-old son, who was named Paul, after his dead uncle. Florence and the baby cheered up Mr. Dombey, and he began to take a new interest in life.

Reconciled to his daughter, he realized that she had always loved him even when he was cruel to her. Walter Gay succeeded in business, and all of them lived together happily; his misfortunes had made a changed man of Mr. Dombey.

Critical Evaluation:

Dombey and Son, which appeared after *Martin Chuzzlewit* (1843-1844), was Charles Dickens' effort to regain the popularity he had lost with the publication of his previous novel. *Martin Chuzzlewit*, which had heavily satirized America and Americans, had caused Dickens to lose a great deal of favor, much to Dickens' chagrin, who was by that time in something of a competition for the public's attention with another great Victorian novelist, William Makepeace Thackeray. *Dombey and Son* is unusual in Dickens' work for being set among a higher social level than his previous novels. For the first time, he indicated an interest and a sympathy in the upper-middle classes and the aristocracy. The story is a very serious one, involving the downfall of a dignified merchant and the painful process by which he learns that love is more powerful than money. As is typical of Dickens, however, there is a large cast of characters providing a rich, sometimes humorous background to the central story.

In *Dombey and Son*, Dickens for the first time attempted to portray the full panorama of English society, from beggar to magnate, from baronet to housemaid. Although less successful than *Bleak House* (1852-1853) in expressing the connections between all levels of society, the novel has a prodigious scope.

The principal theme of the work is the relationship between parents and children, chiefly Mr. Dombey's relationship with Paul and Florence and subordinately those of various parents and their offspring, ranging in social station from Mrs. Skewton and Edith down to Mrs. Brown and her Alice. Each family situation is thrown into relief by contrast with another that is similar in social class yet utterly different in kind. Edith Granger, schooled almost from infancy to be "artful, designing, mercenary, laying snares for men," is shown in contrast with the son of Sir Barnet Skettles, whose parents willingly interrupt his studies at Dr. Blimber's academy in order to enjoy his company during their trip abroad. Mr. Dombey's crude attempt to mold his fragile son to a shape that does his father honor in the world's eyes contrasts with the honest and unpretentious course that Solomon Gills recommends to his nephew Walter: "Be diligent, try to like it, my dear boy, work for a steady independence, and be happy!" The miserable devices of greed that Mrs. Brown urges on her daughter as the only recourse of the poor is proven a lie by the love and warmth shown by Polly Toodle toward her erring son Rob.

The sad ends of Edith, little Paul, and Alice Marwood all result from the corruption of childhood by adult concerns and from the disregard of individuality in children, a view of them as things, counters in a game, or a hedge against destitution or mortality. Mr. Dombey views Paul as a little mirror of his own greatness. He expects his son to reflect himself—that is, to love him as he loves himself. In his stubborn individuality, Paul perceives the merits of Florence and turns to her; Mr. Dombey is amazed and outraged, because he sees Paul as an extension of himself and cannot conceive that the little boy could have a different opinion. In Mr. Dombey's own mind, no blame accrues to himself; he decides that Florence must be the cause of the "distortion" of Paul's feelings. In this way, she falls victim to her father's self-love and becomes the object of his hatred, almost a scapegoat for his repressed feelings of guilt about Paul's death; in his view, she had destroyed Paul as a tool capable of advancing his father's self-approbation, the function for which his elaborate education was supposed to have prepared him.

Edith Granger, too, was formed in her youth to fulfill her mother's nasty ambitions. The shining ideal that both Mrs. Skewton and Mr. Dombey urge on their children is a certain standing in the eyes of the world, essentially an adult concern. In contrast, Walter's mentor in his own invincible childishness (he rebukes himself for being "old-fashioned") guides his charge in the path of honesty, which is the natural behavior of childhood. Young Paul is the chief exemplar of this virtue in the novel, and his resistance to corruption is likewise referable to that curious quality of being "old-fashioned." Paul was "born old"; he possesses that wisdom of extreme age that constitutes a return to the innocence of childhood. He is fey and resists classification. His obdurate honesty shows itself in his concern for first principles. When he inquires of his father what money can do and his father proudly replies that money can do anything, little Paul suggests two things it cannot do: bring back his mother or give him health. Then he asks the question again, still more pointedly: "What's money, after all?" as if to direct his father's attention to the extreme paltriness of those things which money can do, to that vain show that nurtures his father's pride. His father takes no notice of it then; it is not for him to learn from a child. Despised, neglected, and thought unfit to prepare for any great purpose, Florence has her brother's memory for a master and educates herself to his truth rather than to her father's ambition.

Dombey and Son is unique among Dickens' novels in its profusion of strongly drawn female characters. Indeed, the author seems intent on ringing the changes on female nature from best to worst. For the most part, these figures though vivid have but one dimension, but two characters evidence a greater depth of understanding than the author had previously achieved in his representation of women. One is the character of Florence, whose states of mind illustrate a classic psychological progression. Rejected by a loved parent, she reasons thus: "I am unloved, therefore unlovable." Her early conviction of unworthiness not only dictates her subsequent actions but indeed shapes the main plot of the novel. Florence eventually becomes the figure of ideal womanhood; she even displays talents of a housewife in Solomon Gills's parlor. Yet she is truly good without being saccharine, a major advance in Dickens' treatment of women characters. Miss Tox is even more an unusual creation; Dickens had not previously produced a female character who was at once such an object of satire and so generally sympathetic. She comes in for her share of ridicule for her delusions about Mr. Dombey's intentions and for her genteel pretensions in general, but the author allows her the virtue of her consistency: "poor excommunicated Miss Tox, who, if she were a fawner and a toad-eater, was at least an honest and a constant one. . . ." She is as unlikely a vessel of kindness and simple wisdom as the dandy Toots, or the exhausted aristocrat, Cousin Feenix; yet Dickens puts wisdom into their mouths as if to show that although corruption might seem to reign supreme everywhere, truth, though hidden, can flourish and even prevail.

"Critical Evaluation" by Jan Kennedy Foster

Bibliography:
Andrews, Malcolm. *Dickens and the Grown-up Child.* Houndmills, Basingstoke, Hampshire: Macmillan, 1994. Sees *Dombey and Son* as a reflection of the world through a child's eyes, as well as making "familiar use of the child as an agent of redemption"; Paul Dombey is radically different from earlier male children in Dickens' work.

Armstrong, Frances. *Dickens and the Concept of Home.* Ann Arbor, Mich.: UMI Research, 1990. Contains good sections on *Dombey and Son.* Concludes that Florence must make her own home "in the face of mental and physical abuse from the man that should be the center of that home." Focuses on the creative process of homemaking that increasingly leads Florence outside of herself as the novel progresses.

Auerbach, Nina. "Dickens and Dombey: A Daughter After All." *Dickens Studies Annual* 5 (1976): 95-104. Good treatment of the novel's feminist theme, which Auerbach defines as "Dickens's most thorough exploration of his own and his contemporaries' doctrine of the 'two spheres,' with each sex moving in a solitary orbit inaccessible to the other."

Donovan, Frank. *The Children of Charles Dickens*. London: Leslie Frewin, 1969. Good exploration of the themes of childhood and parenting in *Dombey and Son*. Sees Mr. Dombey as a classic "rejective parent," whose rejection of Florence is done consciously whereas his rejection of Paul is unconscious.

Shelston, Alan, ed. *"Dombey and Son" and "Little Dorrit."* Houndmills, Basingstoke, Hampshire: Macmillan, 1985. Provides a very good introduction to the novel, with information on the origins of *Dombey and Son*, an overview of contemporary critical appraisals, and several important critical studies since 1941.

DOMINIQUE

Type of work: Novel
Author: Eugène Fromentin (1820-1876)
Type of plot: Psychological
Time of plot: Nineteenth century
Locale: France
First published: 1862 (English translation, 1932)

> *Principal characters:*
> DOMINIQUE DE BRAY, a gentleman
> MADELEINE DE NIÈVRES, his beloved
> AUGUSTIN, his tutor
> OLIVIER D'ORSEL, his friend
> JULIE, Madeleine's younger sister, in love with Olivier

The Story:

The narrator of the book first met Dominique de Bray at Villeneuve. Dominique lived at the large Château des Trembles with his wife and two children. The mayor of the commune, he was shy, unpretentious, and a friend to all in the community. On St. Hubert's Day, Dominique was visited by Olivier d'Orsel, a wealthy, solitary man with captivating manners and a passion for luxury, who had retired from social life. A few days after his visit, Olivier tried to commit suicide. This event led Dominique to tell the narrator about himself.

Orphaned at an early age, Dominique grew up at Villeneuve. In his youth, he became a lover of the outdoors. He was cared for by Madame Ceyssac, his aunt, who provided him with a tutor named Augustin. The two differed greatly in temperament. Dominique was emotional and wild and loved nature; Augustin was well-read, exact, practical, and apparently oblivious to nature. When he was not tutoring Dominique, he would remain in his room, writing plays and letters. After four years the time came for Dominique to go away to school. Augustin went to Paris with high hopes of his own success.

Dominique went to live with Madame Ceyssac in her mansion at Ormesson. At school he befriended young Olivier d'Orsel, who also had an estate near Les Trembles. Dominique, who was a good student, helped Olivier with his schoolwork. Too shy to admit it, Dominique fell in love with Madeleine, Olivier's cousin. At night he would spend his time writing poetry. He also kept up a correspondence with Augustin, who warned him against confusing Olivier's love of pleasure with the true goals in life.

Dominique was surprised when Madeleine married Monsieur de Nièvres, a well-established gentleman. After the ceremony Dominique was in despair because he realized that he loved a married woman. After graduation, Dominique and Olivier went to Paris. There they saw Augustin, who grew to like Olivier but had no esteem for him. Olivier, in turn, esteemed Augustin without liking him.

Dominique, trying to forget his love for Madeleine, buried himself in his literary work. He went to libraries and lectures, and he read through the small hours of the night in the belief that the austere routine was good for him. After a few months, however, he burned his writings because he thought them stale and mediocre. Olivier, who saw what Dominique had done, told him to find other amusements and affections. Augustin, on the other hand, simply said that he

1777

would have to begin again. Augustin, who had experienced setbacks of his own, never complained. Having guessed Dominique's love problem, he told him to solve it by plunging into continuous work.

In spite of Augustin's advice and example, Dominique found it impossible to settle to his work. Through Olivier, he met a woman whom he saw steadily for two months. Then he learned that Nièvres and Madeleine were going to Ormesson, and he invited them to Les Trembles for the holidays. Although he never told Madeleine about his love for her, those were happy months for Dominique. That winter Nièvres and Madeleine decided to go to Paris.

Eventually Dominique wanted to make Madeleine admit that they loved each other, but the harder he tried to draw an admission from her the more she pretended to be quite unaware of his intention. One day, when he was determined to tell her of his love, he saw tears in her eyes; he understood then that there was nothing more to be said.

After that day their relationship became relaxed and natural, and Madeleine, wanting to encourage Dominique in his work, began to meet him at the risk of compromising her reputation. After a time, Dominique realized that Madeleine was about to surrender herself to him. He then stopped seeing her, and she became gloomy and irritable. Her reactions made Dominique realize that he had deeply troubled her conscience.

Meanwhile, Augustin had married. Visiting Augustin in his home, Dominique saw the near-poverty but great happiness in which his former tutor lived. At the same time Olivier, deeply involved with the woman he had been seeing, began to hate the world and himself. It became evident that Julie, Madeleine's younger sister, loved Olivier. Olivier, however, claimed that happiness was a myth and refused to think of marrying her; his attitude led to a loss of confidence between Dominique and Olivier.

One night, while Dominique and Madeleine were attending the opera, Dominique caught the glance of his former mistress. Madeleine saw the exchange and later told Dominique that he was torturing her and breaking her heart. That night Dominique, determined to deal honestly with Madeleine, decided to claim her. For the next three weeks, however, she was not at home to him. Frustrated, Dominique moved to new quarters and, as a final effort, tried to escape the life of emotions and concentrate on the logical disciplines of the mind. He read much, saved his money, and published anonymously two volumes of his youthful poetry. He also wrote some political books which were immediately successful. When he evaluated his talents, however, he concluded that he was a distinguished mediocrity.

Several months later, Olivier told Dominique that there was unhappiness at Nièvres, where Madeleine was staying. Julie was ill, and Madeleine herself was not well. Dominique went to Nièvres at once and there found Julie recovering. No longer needed as her sister's nurse, Madeleine, with disregard for propriety, shared three days of supreme happiness with Dominique.

On impulse, after Madeleine had led him in a dangerous ride on horseback, Dominique decided to leave as he had come, without premeditation or calculation. When he was helping her to fold a large shawl that evening, Madeleine half-fainted into his arms, and they kissed. Dominique felt very sorry for her and let her go. After dinner, Madeleine told him that, although she would always love him, she wanted him to go away, to get married, to take up a new life. That was the last Dominique saw of Madeleine. He returned to Les Trembles and settled down to a quiet country life.

Dominique told the narrator that the years had brought forgiveness and understanding. Augustin, he said, had become a respected figure in Paris. Dominique himself had never repented his early retirement; he felt, in fact, that his life was merely beginning.

Critical Evaluation:

Written after Romanticism had flowered and faded in France, *Dominique* is quite similar to the personal memoirs and novels that appeared in early nineteenth century France. François René de Chateaubriand's *René* (1802) and Benjamin Constant's *Adolphe* (1816) are examples of novels of this period. Eugène Fromentin's novel is similar to the Abbé Prévost's *Manon Lescaut* (1731) as well, because *Dominique*, like *Manon Lescaut*, has to do with irresistible and destructive passion.

Yet *Dominique*'s roots in French literary history go deeper than the Romantic and pre-Romantic eras. In some sense, the novel's hero moves in the tradition of courtly love, worshiping as he does, for at least half the novel, a beautiful woman from afar. Early in his story, Dominique places Madeleine on a pedestal; he admires her, yet he fears approaching her. His status as adoring pseudo-knightly lover is indicated ironically by his name, which derives from the Latin *dominus*, which suggests that Dominique is a lord of sorts, a man reigning over his own domain. The irony is that Dominique has deep feelings of inferiority and insecurity; he is hardly a lordly or dominating type until he reaches maturity.

The novel opens with a depiction of the mature Dominique, lord of an estate, Les Trembles, married and the father of two children. The novel's first two chapters state the theme of passion versus self-control, and, consequently, service to others. The Dominique whom readers and the first-person narrator of the first two chapters meet is a man of about forty years, known in the environs as a man dedicated to his family and to doing good for others. The lesson he has learned about self-preservation and the importance of dedicating oneself to others is what Dominique talks about in the rest of the novel.

The young Dominique was raised by his aunt in Normandy; he is a young man who loves his native countryside. Without great enthusiasm, he later goes to Paris to pursue his studies and a career as a writer. His friend and counselor in these early years is Augustin, who bears the name of a famous saint and philosopher—which emphasizes his role as the choice of traditional reason, faith, and restraint. Throughout the novel, Augustin serves as Dominique's mentor, offering an example of what one can achieve in life, not through impulse and feeling but by means of discipline. In Dominique's youth, Olivier d'Orsel also opposes Dominque's propensity to self-pity, passivity, passion, and despair. When Dominique, in despair after Madeleine marries the Count of Nièvres, becomes mired in a sense of futility and even destroys his written work, Olivier tries to convince him that love is merely a question of chance—that Madeleine is a unique woman, fated in some way to be the love of his life. Later, however, Olivier is seen to be a less than admirable character, when he spurns the love of Madeleine's sister, Julie. At that point, as Olivier explains to Dominique, he has become very much a selfish, pleasure-seeking man of the world, believing in nothing but his own satisfaction. Much later, ironically, it is Dominique's wife who, believing that doing good and committing oneself to others is one's very reason for living, unknowingly precipitates Olivier's attempted suicide. In contrast, Augustin marries, but with neither the passion Dominique feels for Madeleine, nor the cruel self-interest that motivates Olivier. Dominique despises what he calls the "movement" of life in Paris, the social frenzy that he likens to a whirlpool that threatens those in the Parisian sea with shipwreck. In his frustration with this life and with Madeleine's determination to keep him at an emotional distance, he begins to think of confessing his love for her. He conceives of an attack, a direct approach to her, thinking in terms of swordplay, a military expedition, a seduction.

Madeleine's vulnerability dissuades Dominique from this brutal attack, although she does, with chagrin, recognize the love Dominique has for her. Oddly enough, Madeleine devotes time and energy to exorcising Dominique's passion for her from his heart—destructive as it is to their well-being. This attempt at "cure," as Madeleine calls it, fails.

Madeleine's discouragement with Olivier's treatment of Julie and her frustration with her attachment to Dominique comes to a head when Madeleine leads Dominique on a horseback ride through the forest on her estate, excitedly spurs on her mount, and expresses in a brutal fashion the depth and nature of what she feels for Dominique. Her excitement, flushed cheeks, convulsive laughter, and breathless animality when she faces Dominique with her riding crop in her teeth, leads them to a revelation of the dangers unrestrained physical passion holds.

Here is the crisis, and here is where Dominique understands his need for metaphysical and for spiritual rest. At this point in his life and in his relationship with Madeleine, he decides to put his life in order. He decides, first of all, to never see Madeleine again. He then withdraws from the animation of the world, and he returns to his beloved Les Trembles. His marriage ensues.

It is only to be expected that the final image in the novel is that of the sage Augustin, at last a successful public figure and a happy one, who arrives at Les Trembles for a visit.

"Critical Evaluation" by Gordon Walters

Bibliography:
Charvet, P. E. "The Romantic Novel." In *The Nineteenth Century, 1789-1870.* Vol. 4 in *A Literary History of France.* New York: Barnes & Noble Books, 1967. A brief treatment of Fromentin's novel that places it in the context of French Romanticism.
Cruickshank, John. "The Novel of Self-Disclosure." In *The Early Nineteenth Century.* Vol. 4 in *French Literature and Its Background,* edited by John Cruickshank. New York: Barnes & Noble Books, 1969. Develops the points that the novel is autobiographical and pertinent to Fromentin's stature as a painter. Like other critics too, Cruickshank considers the ways in which the novel is both Romantic and post-Romantic.
Howard, Richard. "From Exoticism to Homosexuality." In *A New History of French Literature,* edited by Dennis Hollier with R. Howard Bloch, et al. Cambridge, Mass.: Harvard University Press, 1994. An interesting placement of *Dominique* in the tradition of exoticism and eroticism in French literature.
Levin, Harry. *The Gates of Horn.* New York: Oxford University Press, 1963. Includes a chapter on Gustave Flaubert, in which Levin draws analogies between painting and fiction.
Martin, Graham Dunstan. *"Dominique"* and *"Fromentin."* In *The New Oxford Companion to Literature in French,* edited by Peter France. New York: Oxford University Press, 1955. Notes the way in which *Dominique* endorses passion, insofar as the resolution of the conflict between reason and morality is unsatisfactory and Augustin a cold figure.

DON CARLOS
Infante of Spain

Type of work: Drama
Author: Friedrich Schiller (1759-1805)
Type of plot: Historical
Time of plot: Sixteenth century
Locale: Spain
First performed: 1787; first published, 1787 as *Don Carlos, Infant von Spanien* (English translation, 1798)

Principal characters:
DON CARLOS, the heir to the Spanish throne
PHILIP II, the king of Spain and Don Carlos' father
ELIZABETH DE VALOIS, the queen of Spain and Don Carlos' stepmother
MARQUIS DE POSA, Don Carlos' friend
DOMINGO, the king's confessor
DUKE OF ALVA, Philip II's trusted general and minister
PRINCESS DE EBOLI, an attendant to the queen

The Story:
King Philip II of Spain did not wish to trust his son, Don Carlos, with any of the crown's affairs, ostensibly because, even though Don Carlos was twenty-three years old, he was too hot-blooded. Probably the real reason was that Philip, who had forced his father, Charles V, from the throne, now feared his own son. The differences and coldness between the king and his son were aggravated by the fact that Philip was married to Elizabeth de Valois, with whom Don Carlos had been in love. Indeed, the courtship between the two had been sanctioned by France and Spain, until Philip had decided to take Elizabeth for himself.

Don Carlos hid his continuing love for Elizabeth, now his stepmother, until his friend, the Marquis de Posa, returned from Flanders, at which time Don Carlos confided in him. The marquis was horrified, but swore upon their boyhood friendship to help the prince, if the prince in turn would try to help the people of Flanders escape from the heavy and tyrannic policies forced upon them by Philip through his emissary, the Duke of Alva.

Don Carlos went to his father and pleaded that he be made the king's agent in Flanders, declaring that he would act humanely toward the people. Philip refused to listen and sent the duke over Don Carlos' protests. He did, however, request that the duke be better disposed toward his son. When the duke went to speak to the prince, he found Don Carlos in the queen's antechamber. They had words and fought, until the queen intervened.

From one of the queen's pages Don Carlos received a mysterious note and a key to a room in the queen's apartments. Hoping against hope that the queen had sent it to him, he went to the room, an act for which his jealous father would have punished him severely. Instead of the queen, he found the Princess de Eboli, who had sent him the note because she had fallen in love with him. She asked his help in evading the importunities of the king, who sought her for his mistress, but Don Carlos repelled her advances and thus incurred her anger. When he left, he took with him a letter that the king had sent her. Hoping to use the letter as proof that the king was a tyrant and an evil man, he showed it to the Marquis de Posa. The marquis tore up the letter, however, saying that it was too dangerous a weapon and might hurt Don Carlos and the queen more than the king.

In the meantime, the Princess de Eboli, infuriated at Don Carlos' refusal of her love, went to Domingo, the king's confessor and pander, and told him of her decision to become Philip's mistress. She also told about having met the prince and that he had obviously been hoping to meet the queen. That information pleased Domingo and the Duke of Alva, who wanted to rid the kingdom of both Don Carlos and the queen.

With the help of the princess, the duke and the confessor laid a trap for Don Carlos and the queen. Becoming suspicious of the conspirators' motives, Philip called in a man he thought would be completely honest in solving the problem. Ironically, that man was Don Carlos' friend, the Marquis de Posa. He quickly gained the king's confidence, even though some of his religious ideas were heretical, and he did his best to help Don Carlos. Because the marquis had to work in secret, Don Carlos considered him disloyal to himself. Other courtiers reported to Don Carlos that a file of letters he had given to the marquis had been seen in the king's chamber. What Don Carlos heard was true, for the marquis had found it necessary to tell the truth about the letters to clear Don Carlos of the charge of illicit relations with the queen.

Don Carlos, not knowing the truth concerning the marquis' activities, went to Princess de Eboli to seek her help. The Marquis de Posa, learning of Don Carlos' visit to the princess, entered immediately after the prince. Using the authority given him by the king to arrest Don Carlos, the marquis had him put incommunicado in prison, lest he talk to others who could do him harm. The easiest way to keep Don Carlos safe would have been to murder Princess de Eboli, but the marquis did not have the heart to kill her, even when his dagger was at her breast.

Instead of assuming the guilt of murder, the marquis resolved to make himself the victim. The king was convinced that Don Carlos and the queen had been involved in a treasonable plot against the crown in Flanders. To clear them, the marquis sent a letter he knew would be put into the king's hands. In it he stated that he, the marquis, was the real conspirator. Afterward the marquis had only enough time to go to the prison and reveal his true actions to Don Carlos before a shot was fired through the gratings by an assassin sent by Philip.

Popular wrath and the indignation of the grandees forced Philip to release his son, but Don Carlos refused to leave the prison until his father came in person to give him back his sword and his freedom. When Philip arrived, in the company of the grandees of the council, Don Carlos confronted him with the marquis' corpse and told him that he had caused the murder of an innocent man. Philip, seeing the truth of the accusation and filled with remorse, became ill in the prison and was carried away by the grandees.

A friend reported to Don Carlos that the king and the Duke of Alva had been enraged by public reaction in favor of the imprisoned prince. Hoping to lift the yoke of tyranny that his father and the Duke of Alva had imposed on that country and its people, Don Carlos decided to leave Spain immediately and go to Flanders. Before he left, he planned to see the queen once more and tell her of his plans. Donning a mask and the garb of a monk, he went through a secret passage to the queen's wing of the castle. Once there he walked openly through the corridors to her rooms, able to do so because of a superstition that Charles V, garbed in like manner, haunted the castle. The superstitious soldiers let him pass.

The king, meanwhile, had sent for the Cardinal Inquisitor. Asked for his advice, the churchman rebuked Philip for his waywardness in letting the heretic marquis escape proper punishment for so long and then having him killed for political reasons. They discussed also the heresy of the young prince, and Philip resolved to turn his son over to the Inquisition for punishment. Philip led the cardinal to the queen's apartments, for, having heard reports of the ghost, he guessed who was beneath the disguise. Don Carlos was found with the queen and handed over to the authorities of the Inquisition.

Critical Evaluation:

Friedrich Schiller's dramatic works are often divided into three periods: early, middle, and classical. *Don Carlos*, which took Schiller four years to write and was completed in 1787, is the single play representing the middle period. It is a melodramatic high tragedy written in blank verse, which combines complicated political ideas with a story of doomed love.

In the course of writing *Don Carlos*, Schiller's ideas about the characters changed. Because the first three acts were published in *Die Thalia* between 1785 and 1787 as they were completed, the playwright felt he had to resolve this story line, despite his preference. He would have reworked the play quite differently and created characters more suited to his new ideas had the first acts not already been in the hands of the public. Schiller said of *Don Carlos*, "The parts that first attracted me began to produce this effect in a weaker degree . . . Carlos himself lost my favor, perhaps for no other reason than because I had become his senior, and Posa replaced him. I commenced the fourth and fifth acts with quite an altered heart." The inconsistencies in *Don Carlos* are the result of this change of course. Later in his life, Schiller was extremely critical of *Don Carlos*. In his *Letters upon Don Carlos*, he wrote, "in the first (three) acts I aroused expectations that the last do not fulfill." In the final two acts, Posa does not act in accordance with his earlier course. Initially, he had proclaimed his loyalty to Carlos; then he seemed to ally himself with the king. Probably he could have used that friendship to support his goals of social justice, but when he ruined that possibility the plans for rebellion were destroyed, and all the while Carlos remained in the dark about the greater duties that drove Posa. In the first three acts, Posa is a heroic idealist; in the next acts, he is an unjustified maniac. Even his death, which he feels is purely sacrificial, does not help Carlos, his own greater cause, or anyone else.

Don Carlos was a public success, but critics pointed out some flaws. Schiller's research into the Spanish monarchy of the sixteenth century had shown him several different ways to interpret the same historical moment. He had used Louis Sebastian Mercier's factual account *Portrait of Phillipe II* (1785), which he translated into German, and for some details he drew on Robert Watson's *History of the Reign of Phillipe II* (1778). Much of the story line for *Don Carlos*, however, comes from César Vichard Saint-Réal's eighty-page *Dom Carlos, Nouvelle Historique* (1672), the least factual of his sources, and as a result Schiller's play may actually contain very little, if any, factual or historical matter.

The most important theme in the play is that of realism versus idealism. Philip represents a harsh and conservative realist who is interested in people only to the extent that they are useful to him; he is not at all interested in improving his subjects' well-being. Posa represents an idealist who strives to improve conditions for all people and to liberate them to a higher plane of existence. One of the most famous lines of this play, in the midst of the most powerful of its compelling scenes, is Posa's statement to the king, "O Give us freedom of thought." In this scene, incidentally, Schiller the philosopher overruns Schiller the poet. In presenting what amounts to a treatise on government, the action and the love story are suspended. The conclusion of the third act reflects the change that Schiller's conception of his characters has undergone, and the attempt in the following acts to justify the importance of his political views as well as to resolve the prince's love for the queen is somewhat disjointed.

The king, a realist, has developed his ideas strictly from experience and observation, as well as from the command of the Church; from these he has determined his rules of judgment and philosophy and mode of action. Posa is attractive to the king because Philip has probably never before met anyone who would not immediately come under his service. Posa claims that his sole motive is to serve others, and this too, is something the king has not experienced.

Whatever impact Posa might have had on the king is, however, annulled by the entrance of the Grand Inquisitor, who adds another ingredient to the mix of the play when he tells the king that Posa was scheduled to die long ago and the king had in effect taken property away from the Church. The Grant Inquisitor's presence is amazingly strong. He delineates the proper mentality for a monarch and sets the standard for the realist view that is the king's. The Inquisitor has no tolerance for human beings; he considers people to be a wretched lot of weaklings and fools who should be punished for their inherent flaws by servitude to the Church and the monarchy. The Inquisitor is utterly convinced of his beliefs, and he serves to set the king straight after his interview with Posa that had loosened the king's thoughts and let in a glimmer of light. The Inquisitor serves to nullify that shimmer with his own strong authority, which no one in the play can refute.

"Critical Evaluation" by Beaird Glover

Bibliography:
Crawford, Ronald L. "Masks of Deception in Schiller's *Don Carlos*." *Germanic Notes* 17, no. 3 (1986): 34-35. Crawford explores mask imagery in *Don Carlos* and considers the play's importance in eighteenth century German drama.
Harrison, R. B. "*Gott ist über mir*: Ruler and Reformer in the Twofold Symmetry of Schiller's *Don Carlos*." *The Modern Language Review* 76, no. 3 (July, 1981): 598-611. A discussion of structure, symmetry, and characterization in Schiller's *Don Carlos*. Presents an analysis of Schiller's understanding and use of structure and form.
Miller, Ronald Duncan. *Interpreting Schiller: A Study of Four Plays*. Harrogate: Duchy Press, 1986. Provides a rigorous criticism and analysis of *Don Carlos*, as well as of *Wilhelm Tell* (1804), *Jungfrau von Orleans* (1801), and *Wallensteins Tod* (1799). Analyzes the plays individually but also compares and contrasts them with one another. Gives some consideration as well to Schiller's life and times.
Sharpe, Lesley. *Schiller and the Historical Character: Presentation and Interpretation in the Historiographical Works and in the Historical Dramas*. New York: Oxford University Press, 1982. Approaches Schiller's works both as histories and as dramas and focuses on defining his historical and philosophical thought. Considers the genre of historical drama and the appropriate approach to analyzing such presentations.
Vazsonyi, Nicholas. "Schiller's *Don Carlos*: Historical Drama or Dramatized History?" *New German Review: A Journal of Germanic Studies* 7 (1991): 26-41. Discusses Johann Schiller's Don Carlos as both drama and historical drama within the context of Germanic literature.

THE DON FLOWS HOME TO THE SEA

Type of work: Novel
Author: Mikhail Sholokhov (1905-1984)
Type of plot: Historical
Time of plot: 1918-1920
Locale: Russia
First published: Tikhii Don, 1928-1940 (partial English translations, 1934 as *And Quiet Flows the Don*; 1940 as *The Don Flows Home to the Sea*; complete English translations, 1942 as *The Silent Don*; 1967 as *And Quiet Flows the Don*)

> *Principal characters:*
> GREGOR MELEKHOV, a soldier
> PANTALEIMON PROKOFFIVICH, his father
> ILINICHNA, Gregor's mother
> PIOTRA, his brother
> AKSINIA, his mistress
> NATALIA, his wife
> KOSHEVOI, a Communist

The Story:

The Germans were still carrying off flour, butter, and cattle. Every day their trucks rolled from the Don through the Ukraine. Various sections of Russia, however, were fighting one another. To the north of the Don Basin, the White Army was driving back the Bolsheviks. Most of the Cossacks were in the White forces, although some were with the Reds.

Gregor and Piotra Melekhov were leaders in the White Army. Piotra, the elder brother, was decidedly anti-Red and waged battle viciously. Gregor was of two minds; perhaps the Reds would bring stable government. Gregor was opposed to pillaging civilians and killing prisoners. As best he could, he kept his men in hand. When his father and his sister-in-law Daria visited him at the front, he was furious when they took home a wagon load of loot.

In Tatarsk, the Whites were trying to win over the Cossacks to full support of the insurgent cause. In the spring of 1918 there had been a great defection of northern Cossacks to the Reds, and the southern Cossacks were only halfhearted in throwing back the Red tide. Koshevoi, a Red sympathizer, was caught when he returned to his home in Tatarsk. His companions were killed, but he was released to join the drovers in the steppes.

Eugene Listnitsky, a rich Cossack from the district, spent a furlough with a brother officer. Eugene was attracted to Olga, the man's wife. After the officer was killed, Listnitsky married the widow. When he got home, invalided out with a missing arm, Aksinia, his former mistress, was still there, waiting for him. Eugene wanted nothing more to do with her after his marriage. He made love to her briefly under a currant bush and offered her money to go away. Aksinia was pained but stayed. Her husband Stepan, miraculously alive after years in prison, tried in vain to get her to come home.

Gradually the Cossacks returned home; as farmers, they had to till the land. The advancing Red Army passed through the village of Tatarsk. After them came the political men, and the Red government took charge. Gregor was glad to be home but had little longing now for Aksinia, who had been his mistress before she became Eugene's. After years of fighting Germans and Reds, he was content to be a little reconciled to Natalia, his wife.

Koshevoi was put in charge of the government of Tatarsk, and soon Stockman, a professional

Red, came to help him. In order to consolidate their power, they began, gradually, seizing a man here and there and spiriting him off to death or imprisonment. They wanted to arrest Piotra and Gregor. A little afraid to take Piotra, who was friendly with Fomin, a Red commander, they decided to take Gregor. Learning of their intentions in time, Gregor left Tatarsk and escaped.

As the political imprisonments and executions increased, the Cossacks revolted. The wrongs they had suffered at the hands of the Reds were so great and so many that in a comparatively short time the rebellion was succeeding. Piotra was made a commander immediately. He was a ferocious fighter and ruthless with the Reds. In a skirmish, however, he was captured by the enemy. Koshevoi, now a Communist, stepped out from a patrol and killed Piotra without compunction.

After serving under Piotra, Gregor rose to command a division. He was cold with fury toward the Communists and had the reputation of never keeping prisoners alive for long. When the Cossacks began to imprison Red sympathizers from among civilians, however, he dissented strongly. On one occasion, he even forced open a prison and released old men and women who were suspected of helping the Reds.

Stockman and the others who had been the political rulers of Tatarsk were captured when a Red regiment deserted. Stockman was killed outright, and the others were returned to run a terrible gauntlet at Tatarsk. Daria herself killed the man she thought responsible for the death of Piotra, her husband. Koshevoi was not suspected at the time.

Daria recovered from Piotra's death rather speedily and soon was carrying on various affairs. When Gregor came home on furlough, she even made tentative love to him. Gregor, however, was tired from fighting and carousing, and he still had bitter memories of Aksinia. Natalia, who had heard of Gregor's conduct on his sprees, was cold to him. The day before he was to return to the army, Gregor met Aksinia at the Don. He thought of their former love and of her affair with Listnitsky; but the old love was not dead, and he took Aksinia again.

The Soviet government realized by May of 1919 that they had a formidable task on their hands and thus increased their forces, slowly pushing back the insurgent Cossacks. The rebels retreated toward the Don, taking with them crowds of refugees. At last the Cossacks crossed the river and held their positions.

The Reds came through Tatarsk as Natalia was recovering from typhus. Koshevoi was with them; he was indignant that Dunia, Gregor's young sister, was across the Don, for he had long been in love with her. Koshevoi's own family was missing, and his father's house had been destroyed. He took pride in firing the houses of all the rich landowners in and near Tatarsk.

Gregor, busy as a division commander, took time to send for Aksinia, and she came to live near him. Stepan returned, to her embarrassment, and although she did not take him back as her husband, they preserved appearances among the refugee families.

With the arrival of the White Army, the Reds were driven back. Now that the insurgents were incorporated into a regular army, Gregor was demoted to the rank of squadron commander, for he was an uneducated man. The Whites sent punitive patrols to punish those who had aided the Reds. To the horror of the Melekhovs, all of Koshevoi's relatives were executed. Daria caught syphilis and drowned herself. When Natalia learned of Gregor's return to Aksinia, she refused to bear him another child. She had an unskillful abortion performed and bled to death.

With increasing Red pressure and desertion from the Cossack ranks, the White Army was going down in defeat. Gregor and Aksinia fled south to try to board a ship. On the way, Aksinia fell ill with typhus and had to be left behind. She later made her way back to Tatarsk. Gregor could not leave the country. With nothing better to do, he joined the Reds and fought valiantly against the Poles.

In spite of family protests, Dunia married Koshevoi, now commissar of the village. When Gregor returned home, Koshevoi at once set in motion plans to arrest him. Gregor, however, escaped again, joining up with Fomin, a deserter from the Red Army. Fomin tried to rally the Cossacks to revolt against the Communists for levying heavy taxes and collecting grain. The revolt, however, was short-lived. The rebels were killed, and only Gregor went back to Tatarsk. This time, when Gregor fled, he took Aksinia with him, but she was killed by a pursuing Red patrol. Gregor threw his weapons into the Don and went back to his house. Only his son was left to him now, and he would fight no more.

Critical Evaluation:

The Don Flows Home to the Sea is the last half of an immense historical novel, *Tikhii Don*. The novel follows a Don Cossack, Gregor Melekhov, from peacetime czarist Russia through the German-Russian War to the Russian Revolution and the Civil War. Although the focal point of the novel is war, the cultural life of Cossack Russia—its love for the land and the roles of men and women in the agrarian family—is equally well portrayed. The length of the work enables a magnificent panorama of history to unfold.

Mikhail Sholokhov intensely loved the Don, the steppe, and the cycles of the seasons, and his poetic language beautifully captures the bond of the Cossacks with their land. Theirs is a peasant's life. They are in tune with the wind, the coming of rain, the swelling and cracking of the frozen Don. Numerous scenes begin with painterly descriptions of landscape, subtle but insistent reminders that it is from the land that life comes. Death, undisguised, is omnipresent. Gory and detailed descriptions of the dying and of the dead become commonplace, but the Don and the steppe survive all tragedies. Sholokhov evokes the sights, sounds, and smells of that earthy existence so vividly that the pain of Cossack uprootedness is totally convincing. Young soldiers who fight valiantly near the Don are ineffectual, lifeless, on foreign soil; refugees wander aimlessly when forced to flee their Don home.

The Melekhov family and the other townspeople of Tatarsk are typical of agrarian society and culture. Roles within family units are assumed unquestioningly, although not always obediently. The head of the Melekhov household, old Pantaleimon Prokoffivich, Gregor's father, is responsible for all who live under his roof: his wife, his sons, their wives and children, and his daughter until she marries. He is the patriarchal authority. Pantaleimon orders the marriage of Gregor and Natalia when he learns of Gregor's affair with Aksinia; Gregor complies. Old Pantaleimon becomes confused about his authority over his sons, however, when their military ranks surpass his.

Pantaleimon expects and demands to be served and respected by women, who are, he assumes, his subordinates. In Cossack society, females are less valued than males and are treated as possessions by husbands. When Stepan Astakhov first learns of the affair between his wife, Aksinia, and Gregor, he returns home to beat, then stomp on Aksinia as if he were doing a Cossack dance. He is within his rights to thus punish her transgression.

The matriarch of the Melekhov family is Ilinichna, Pantaleimon's wife, who is not only the female head of the household (wife, mother, and grandmother) but also the mother to her sons' wives. The relationship between the mother-in-law and the daughters-in-law is an interesting one. Ilinichna gives orders to Daria, Pyotr's wife, and Natalia as a mistress would to servants. The young married women have no rights except as granted by their husbands and mother-in-law.

Children are reared in an extended family, and parental authority is often less than that of the grandparent. The middle generation, sons and daughters-in-law, are treated as overgrown children by the older generation. A major role for the young men is to serve in the military. Service is seen as an honor, a duty that is fulfilled unquestioningly. The process of maturation for young men seems to occur in the military. When Gregor and his friends return home from war, the townspeople comment on how broad-shouldered they have become.

A strain of violence permeates Cossack life. Even during peacetime there is an air of exaggerated rivalry in which anger is expressed overtly. When old Pantaleimon proudly races through the village with his hero son, Gregor, he becomes infuriated with an old woman who scolds him for nearly running over her livestock. His anger could easily lead him to using his whip on her. Wartime violence is seen both on the battlefront and within the civilian population. There is an irony in the reverence a soldier holds for his own mother when he mistreats another's mother; an irony when he who has shared another soldier's wife returns home enraged to find that his wife has been similarly unfaithful.

The length of the novel gives the feeling of the flow of history, not in generalized sweeping trends or wartime strategies, but in a long series of specific circumstances that enables the reader to become involved with numerous major characters and to care about their lives and deaths as much as about the life of the one central figure, Gregor Melekhov. A dead soldier by the side of the road becomes a vital loss, as the reader learns in retrospect from a small diary of the soldier's life and love. The relationship that grows between Podtielkov and Anna Pogodko is another mini-novel that is given life and death within the confines of Sholokhov's world. The deaths that affect Gregor most deeply are those of his and Aksinia's daughter, of Piotra on the battlefield, of Piotra's wife by suicide, of Natalia by an unsuccessful abortion, of Pantaleimon of typhus as a refugee, and, finally, of Aksinia. The reader participates in Gregor's suffering because Sholokhov has fully developed all of these characters.

This long-range focus on history through specific tragedies gives the indelible impression of the war weariness, resignation, and readiness for death that Gregor feels when he finally returns home for the last time. This work and the first part of the narrative, *And Quiet Flows the Don*, have also been published as one book.

"Critical Evaluation" by Mary Peace Finley

Bibliography:
Ermolaev, Herman. *Mikhail Sholokhov and His Art*. Princeton, N.J.: Princeton University Press, 1982. One of the best studies of Sholokhov and his works by a native scholar trained in the West. *The Quiet Don* is discussed extensively, especially regarding historical sources and Sholokhov's use of them.
Hallett, R. W. "Soviet Criticism of *Tikhiy Don*, 1928-1940." *The Slavonic and East European Review* 46, no. 106 (1968): 60-74. A brief but substantive treatment of Sholokhov's difficulties with the authorities in publishing the novel because of his objective presentation of the revolution.
Klimenko, Michael. *The World of Young Sholokhov: Vision of Violence*. North Quincy, Mass.: Christopher, 1972. A useful study of Sholokhov's early works, with the emphasis on *The Quiet Don* as the seminal work of the Russian literature about the revolution.
Medvedev, Roy. *Problems in the Literary Biography of Mikhail Sholokhov*. Translated by A. D. P. Briggs. Cambridge, England: Cambridge University Press, 1977. An informative book by a leading former Russian dissident concerning the famous controversy about the accusations of plagiarism against Sholokhov.
Ruhle, Jurgen. "The Epic of the Cossacks." *Literature and Revolution*. Translated and edited

by Jean Steinberg. New York: Praeger, 1969. Studies of the relationship between literature and revolution, viewing the historical and political background of Sholokhov's *The Don Flows Home to the Sea.*

Simmons, Ernest J. "Sholokhov: Literary Artist and Socialist Realism." In *Introduction to Russian Realism.* Bloomington: Indiana University Press, 1965. Discusses at length the basic dilemma in Sholokhov's creative life—a conflict between art and politics.

DON JUAN

Type of work: Poetry
Author: George Gordon, Lord Byron (1788-1824)
Type of plot: Satire
Time of plot: Late eighteenth century
Locale: Spain, Turkey, Russia, and England
First published: 1819-1826

Principal characters:
DON JUAN, a young Spaniard
DONNA INEZ, his mother
DONNA JULIA, his first mistress
HAIDÉE, his second love
THE SULTANA, who coveted Juan
CATHERINE, Empress of Russia
LADY ADELINE AMUNDEVILLE, Juan's adviser
DUCHESS OF FITZ-FULKE, who pursued Juan
AURORA RABY, pursued by Juan

The Story:

When Don Juan was a small boy, his father died, leaving the boy in the care of his mother, Donna Inez. Donna Inez was a righteous woman who had made her husband's life miserable. She had her son tutored in the arts of fencing, riding, and shooting, and she herself attempted to rear him in a moral manner. The young Don Juan read widely in the sermons and lives of the saints, but he did not seem to absorb from his studies the qualities his mother thought essential.

At sixteen, he was a handsome lad much admired by his mother's friends. Donna Julia, in particular, often looked pensively at the youth. Donna Julia was just twenty-three and married to a man of fifty. Although she loved her husband, or so she told herself, she thought often of young Don Juan. One day, finding herself alone with him, she gave herself to the young man. The young lovers spent long hours together during the summer, and it was not until November that Don Alfonso, her husband, discovered their intrigue. When Don Alfonso found Don Juan in his wife's bedroom, he tried to throttle him. Don Juan overcame Don Alfonso and fled, first to his mother's home for clothes and money. Then Donna Inez sent him to Cadiz, there to begin a tour of Europe. The good lady prayed that the trip would mend his morals.

Before his ship reached Leghorn, a storm broke it apart. Don Juan spent many days in a lifeboat without food or water. At last the boat was washed ashore, and Don Juan fell exhausted on the beach and slept. When he awoke, he saw bending over him a beautiful girl, who told him that she was called Haidée and that she was the daughter of the ruler of the island, one of the Cyclades. Her father, Lambro, was a pirate, dealing in jewels and slaves. She knew her father would sell Don Juan to the first trader who came by, so Haidée hid Don Juan in a cave and sent her maids to wait on him.

When Lambro left on another expedition, Haidée took Don Juan from the cave and they roamed together over the island. Haidée gave jewels, fine foods, and wines to Don Juan, for he was the first man she had ever known except her father and her servants. Although Don Juan still tried to think of Donna Julia, he could not resist Haidée. A child of nature and passion, she gave herself to him with complete freedom. Don Juan and Haidée lived an idyllic existence until Haidée's father returned unexpectedly. Don Juan again fought gallantly, but at last he was overcome by the old man's servants and put aboard a slave ship bound for a distant market. He never saw Haidée again, and he never knew that she died without giving birth to his child.

The slave ship took Don Juan to a Turkish market, where he and another prisoner were purchased by a black eunuch and taken to the palace of a sultan. There Don Juan was made to dress as a dancing maiden and present himself to the sultana, the fourth and favorite wife of the sultan. She had passed by the slave market and had seen Don Juan and wanted him for a lover. In order to conceal his sex from the sultan, she forced the disguise on Don Juan. Even at the threat of death, however, Don Juan would not become her lover, for he still yearned for Haidée. Perhaps his constancy might have wavered if the sultana had not been an infidel, for she was young and beautiful.

Eventually Don Juan escaped from the palace and joined the army of Catherine of Russia. The Russians were at war with the sultan from whose palace Don Juan had fled. Don Juan was such a valiant soldier that he was sent to St. Petersburg to carry the news of a Russian victory to Empress Catherine. Catherine also cast longing eyes on the handsome stranger, and her approval soon made Don Juan the toast of her capital. In the midst of his luxury and good fortune, Don Juan grew ill. Hoping that a change of climate would help her favorite, Catherine resolved to send him on a mission to England. When he reached London he was well received, for he was a polished young man, well versed in fashionable etiquette. His mornings were spent in business, but his afternoons and evenings were devoted to lavish entertainment. He conducted himself with such decorum, however, that he was much sought after by proper young ladies and much advised by older ones. Lady Adeline Amundeville made him her protégé and advised him freely on affairs of the heart. Another, the Duchess of Fitz-Fulke, advised him too, but her suggestions were of a more personal nature and seemed to demand a secluded spot where there was no danger from intruders. As a result of the Duchess of Fitz-Fulke's attentions to Don Juan, Lady Adeline began to talk to him about selecting a bride from the chaste and suitable young ladies attentive to him.

Don Juan thought of marriage, but his interest was stirred by a girl not on Lady Adeline's list. Aurora Raby was a plain young lady, prim, dull, and seemingly unaware of Don Juan's presence. Her lack of interest served to spur him on to greater efforts, but a smile was his only reward from the cold maiden.

His attention was diverted from Aurora Raby by the appearance of the ghost of the Black Friar, who had once lived in the house of Lady Adeline, where Don Juan was a guest. The ghost was a legendary figure reported to appear before births, deaths, or marriages. To Don Juan, the ghost was an evil omen, and he could not laugh off the tightness about his heart. Lady Adeline and her husband seemed to consider the ghost a great joke. Aurora Raby appeared to be a little sympathetic with Don Juan, but the Duchess of Fitz-Fulke merely laughed at his discomfiture.

The second time the ghost appeared, Don Juan followed it out of the house and into the garden. It seemed to float before him, always just out of his reach. Once he thought he had grasped it, but his fingers touched only a cold wall. Then he seized it firmly and found that the ghost had a sweet breath and full, red lips. When the monk's cowl fell back, the Duchess of Fitz-Fulke was revealed. On the morning after, Don Juan appeared at breakfast wan and tired. Whether he had overcome more than the ghost, no one will ever know. The duchess, too, came down, seeming to have the air of one who had been rebuked.

Critical Evaluation:

Although Byron said that *Don Juan* was to be an epic, his story does not follow epic tradition. It is a vehicle for digression on any and every subject and person that entered Byron's mind as he wrote. The plot itself is almost a minor part of the poem, for much more interesting are Byron's bitter tirades on England, wealth, power, society, chastity, poets, and diplomats. The poem holds a high place among literary satires, even though it was unfinished at Byron's death.

George Gordon Byron, who became the sixth Lord Byron by inheriting the title from his uncle, William, was born on January 22, 1788. His father, the notorious "Mad Jack" Byron, deserted the family, and young Byron was brought up in his mother's native Scotland, where he was exposed to Presbyterian concepts of predestination, which distorted his religious views throughout his life. In 1801 he entered Harrow, a public school near London; in 1808 he received the master of arts degree from Cambridge; in 1809 he took his seat in the House of Lords. From June 1809 to July 1811, Byron traveled in Europe. In 1812, he met Lady Caroline Lamb, who later became his mistress; in 1813 he spent several months with his half-sister, Augusta Leigh, who later bore a daughter who may have been Byron's. Byron married Annabella Milbanke in 1815; she bore him a daughter, Ada, a year later and left him shortly thereafter. In 1816, Byron left England, never to return. That year found him in Switzerland with the Shelleys, where in 1817 Clare Clairmont bore his illegitimate daughter Allegra. After 1819, Countess Teresa Guicciola, who sacrificed her marriage and social position for Byron, became his lover and comforter. Byron died on April 19, 1824, in Missolonghi, where he had hoped to help Greece gain independence from Turkey. His most famous works are *Childe Harold's Pilgrimage* (1812-1818, 1819), *Manfred* (1817), *Cain: A Mystery* (1821), *The Vision of Judgment* (1822), and *Don Juan*, his masterpiece.

Don Juan, a mock-epic poem written in ottava rima, is permeated with Byronic philosophy. Its episodic plot, narrated in first person by its author, tells the story of young Juan, who, victimized by a narrow-minded and hypocritical mother, an illogical educational system, and his own fallible humanity, loses his innocence and faith and becomes disillusioned. The poem's rambling style allows for Byron's numerous digressions, in which he satirizes many aspects of English life: English government and its officials, religion and its confusions and hypocrisies, society and its foibles, war and its irrationality, woman and her treachery, man and his inhumanity. Even English poets feel the fire of Byron's wrath. Thus Byron has been accused of a completely negative view in *Don Juan*—anti-everything and pro-nothing. The philosophy of *Don Juan* is not wholly pessimistic, however, and its tone is consistently, especially in the digressions, sardonic and tongue-in-cheek. Furthermore, Byron's flippant refusal to take Juan's story (or life) too seriously and his extensive use of exaggerated rhyme (such as "intellectual" and "hen-peck'd you all") are essentially comic. Thus the zest and the laughter in *Don Juan* belie the statements of despair and lend an affirmation of life despite its ironies; the lapses into lyricism reveal a heart that sings despite the poet's attempts to stifle emotion with sophistication.

In *Don Juan*, Byron's philosophical confusion seems to be caused by his natural affinity for a Platonic, idealistic view, which has been crushed under the weight of a realism he is too honest and too perceptive to ignore. He denies that he discusses metaphysics, but he comments that nothing is stable or permanent; all is mutable and subject to violent destruction. Yet Byron, in calling the world a "glorious blunder," is not totally blind to its temporary beauties. During the Juan-Haidée romance, the lovers live in an Edenic world of beautiful sunsets and warm, protective caves. Still, Juan's foreboding and Haidée's dream are reminders that nature's dangers always lurk behind its façade of beauty. Even Haidée, "Nature's bride," pursued pleasure and passion only to be reminded that "the wages of sin is death."

Byron's view of the nature of humanity is closely akin to his complex view of natural objects. People have their moments of glory, integrity, and unselfishness. For example, Juan, the novice, does not flee from the horror of battle; he shuns cannibalism even though he is starving; he refuses to be forced to love the sultana; he risks his life to save young Leila. Often Byron emphasizes humanity's freedom of mind and spirit. Yet Byron believes that human self-deceit is the chief factor in decadence; false ideas of glory lead to bloodshed. Ironically, Surrow lectures his soldiers on "the noble art of killing"; humanity kills because "it brings self-approbation." In fact, Byron suggests that men are more destructive than nature or God. Still, Byron does not condemn humanity. This is in spite of Byron's opinion that humanity is basically flawed. Lord Henry, the elder sophisticate, is perhaps the best example of the human inability to retain innocence; caught in the trap of his own greed and hypocrisy and of society's political game, Lord Henry finds that he cannot turn back, even though "the fatigue was greater than the profit." Byron also strikes out against political corruption. He had strong hopes for England's budding liberalism: a "king in constitutional procession" had offered great promise in leading the world to political freedom and morality. Yet Byron boldly declares England's failure to fulfill this promise.

Byron does, however, offer positive values in *Don Juan*. He believes that momentary happiness and glory and love are worth living for. Although "A day of gold from out an age of iron/ Is all that life allows the luckiest sinner," it is better than nothing. Humanity must fight, though it knows that it can never redeem the world and that defeat and death are certain. Since hypocrisy is one of the worst sins, people should be sincere. To Byron, the creative act is especially important, for it is humanity's only chance to transcend mortality.

Throughout *Don Juan*, then, one follows humanity through its hapless struggle with life. Born in a fallen state, educated to hypocrisy and impracticality, cast out into a world of false values and boredom, a person follows the downward path to total disillusionment. One learns, however, to protect oneself from pain by insulating oneself with the charred shell of burned-out passion and crushed ideals. Blindly, one stumbles toward that unknown and unknowable end—death. Yet one goes not humbly but defiantly, not grimly but with gusto.

Therefore, Byron's philosophy, despite its harshness, is one that embraces life, seeking to intensify and electrify each fleeting, irrevocable moment. It is a philosophy of tangibles, though they are inadequate; of action, although it will not cure humanity's ills; of honesty, although it must recognize humanity's fallen state. Although death is inevitable and no afterlife is promised, Byron maintains his comic perspective: "Carpe diem, Juan . . . play out the play."

"Critical Evaluation" by Janet Wester

Bibliography:
Bloom, Harold. "Don Juan." In *The Visionary Company: A Reading of English Romantic Poetry*. Rev. ed. Ithaca, N.Y.: Cornell University Press, 1990. Explores how Byron's attempt to straddle the worlds of fallen and reborn humanity places his epic in the same visionary landscape as that of other Romantic poets.
Byron, George Gordon, Lord. *Don Juan*. Edited by T. G. Steffan. New York: Penguin Books, 1986. Excellent edition of Byron's epic, derived from Steffan's four-volume variorum edition. Complete with extensive notes, variants, commentary, and bibliography.
McGann, J. J. *Don Juan in Context*. Chicago: University of Chicago Press, 1976. An analysis of the personal, literary, and historical influences of Byron's epic. Individual chapters discuss the problems of form, development of language, chronology of composition, and the importance of imagination as a creative and analytical faculty.
Ridenour, G. M. *The Style of Don Juan*. New Haven, Conn.: Yale University Press, 1960.

Examines the classical theory of styles and its impact on Byron's paradoxical vision and his involvement in the narrative as speaker. Particular attention is paid to the Fall as a metaphor for the creation of art, nature, sexual identity, and a persona.

Wolfson, Susan. "'Their She Condition': Cross-Dressing and the Politics of Gender in *Don Juan.*" *English Literary History* 54 (Fall, 1987): 585-617. Argues that categories that historically define "masculine" and "feminine" are often inverted in *Don Juan.* Dressing young Juan as a slave girl and the Duchess of Fitz-Fulke as the Black Friar are two examples of playful attempts at exposing and challenging the inadequacies of socially constructed gender roles.

DON JUAN TENORIO

Type of work: Drama
Author: José Zorrilla (1817-1893)
Type of plot: Comedy
Time of plot: c. 1545
Locale: Seville, Spain
First performed: 1844; first published, 1844 (English translation, 1944)

Principal characters:

DON JUAN TENORIO, a nobleman of Seville
DON DIEGO TENORIO, his father
DON LUIS MEJÍA, an Andalusian gentleman
DON GONZALO DE ULLOA, the comendador of Calatrava
INES DE ULLOA, his daughter
ANA DE PANTOJA, a young woman betrothed to Mejía
MARCOS CIUTTI, Don Juan's servant

The Story:

It was the carnival season in Seville, and the Laurel Tavern was a strange place in which to find gallant young Don Juan Tenorio, when the streets outside were filled with masked merrymakers. He was there with his servant, Marcos Ciutti, to keep a rendezvous with Don Luis Mejía, another gallant, with whom he had struck a wager as to which of them could do the most harm in the next twelve months. That night the bet was to be decided.

Don Gonzalo de Ulloa, the father of the girl whom Don Juan hoped to marry, went masked to the inn, for he wanted to hear with his own ears an account of the wild and villainous deeds attributed to his prospective son-in-law. Don Diego, Juan's father, joined him, masked as well. Several officers, friends of Don Juan and Mejía, were also loitering in the tavern to learn the outcome of the wager, which had been discussed in the city for months. Mejía appeared promptly, just as the cathedral clock was striking eight.

Good-humoredly, the rivals compared lists of the men they had slain in duels and the women they had cruelly deceived during the year. Don Juan was easily the victor. Because his roster lacked only two types of women, however, a nun and the bride of a friend, he wagered that he could add both to his list within a week. Fearing that his rival had an eye on Ana de Pantoja, whom he was planning to marry, Mejía sent his servant to call the police. Angered by the evil deeds of which Don Juan had boasted, the comendador announced that he would never consent to the young scoundrel's marriage with his daughter Ines. Instead, the girl would be kept safe in a convent. Don Diego disowned his son.

A patrol appeared to arrest Don Juan on Mejía's accusations. Other guards summoned by Ciutti took Mejía into custody at the same time.

Through the influence of powerful friends, Mejía was soon freed. He hurried at once to the house of Ana de Pantoja, where he persuaded a servant to let him into the house at ten o'clock that night. He intended to keep Don Juan from attempting an entrance. When Ana appeared at the balcony, he told her his plan, and she acquiesced to it.

Don Juan, also released from custody, overheard their conversation, which gave him the idea of impersonating his rival in order to get into Ana's room. Ciutti had already bribed Ana's duenna to secure the key to the outer door. To make sure that Mejía was out of the way, Ciutti also hired several men to impersonate the police patrol. These bravos seized Mejía and bound him.

Don Juan next interviewed Brigida, the duenna of Ines, and bribed her to deliver a note to the girl in the convent. When the old woman reported that her charge was in love with Don Juan, although she had never seen him, the gallant decided that he had time to go to the convent and abduct her before the hour for him to appear at Ana's house.

At the convent, Ines listened abashed as the abbess praised her godliness. Perhaps she had once been like that; now she no longer looked forward to taking holy orders. Half-frightened, half-eager, she kept thinking of Don Juan. The appearance of Brigida with the note upset her still more, so that when Don Juan himself appeared suddenly at the door of her cell she collapsed in a faint. It was easy for him to carry her off in her unconscious state. Don Gonzalo, worried by the young man's boasting and reports of conversations between him and Brigida, arrived at the convent too late to save his daughter. Ines remained unconscious while Don Juan took her to his house beside the Guadalquiver River. When she came to, Brigida lied to her, telling her that Don Juan had saved her life when the convent caught on fire.

Don Juan returned after he had successfully entered Ana's room. Mejía, seeking revenge, came in pursuit. Don Gonzalo, hoping to rescue his daughter, also appeared at the house. Enraged by their insults, Don Juan shot Don Gonzalo and stabbed Mejía. Then he jumped into the river to escape from police who were hammering at his front door. Abandoned by Don Juan, Ines returned to the convent and died of grief.

Five years later, a sculptor was putting the finishing touches to the Tenorio pantheon. On Don Diego's orders, the family mansion had been torn down and the grounds turned into a cemetery for his son's victims. Lifelike statues of the three chief ones, Mejía, Don Gonzalo, and Ines, gleamed in the moonlight. Patiently, the sculptor explained his labors to a stranger, who eventually terrified the craftsman by revealing himself as Don Juan.

Repentant, Don Juan knelt before Ines' monument and begged her to intercede with God for mercy. When he looked up, her statue had disappeared from its pedestal and Ines herself stood beside him, sent reincarnate from heaven either to bring him back with her to salvation or to be damned with him throughout eternity; he had until dawn to choose their fate. Don Juan, unable to believe that what was happening was real, thought it a trick of crafty priests.

When two officers who five years before had witnessed the outcome of his bet with Mejía came into the graveyard, he laughed at their fear of ghosts; fear had no entry to his heart. After inviting his old acquaintances to have supper with him and hear the story of his adventures, with rash bravado he also extended his invitation to the statue of Don Gonzalo. Only the comendador's presence at the table, Don Juan said, would convince him of a life beyond the grave. The statue kept its stony silence.

While the trio sat drinking at the table, they heard the sound of knocking, each time nearer, though all the doors were bolted. Then into the room stalked the statue of Don Gonzalo, to tell the skeptic about the life eternal that could be realized through God's mercy. The officers fainted, but Don Juan was so courteous a host that before the statue disappeared through the wall it invited him to a similar banquet in the cemetery.

Still unconvinced that one moment of repentance could wipe out thirty years of sin, Don Juan refused to be moved when Ines appeared to persuade him to make the right choice. Half believing that the whole affair was a joke concocted by the sleeping officers, he shook them back to consciousness and accused them of using him for their sport. They in turn charged him with drugging them. The argument ended in challenges to a duel.

In the half light of early morning, the statues of Ines and Don Gonzalo were still missing from the pantheon of the Tenorio family when Don Juan, melancholy because he had killed his old friends in the duel, appeared to keep his appointment. His knock at the comendador's tomb transformed it into a banquet table that parodied his own bountiful spread of the night before. Snakes and ashes were the foods, illuminated by the purging fire of God, and ghostly guests crowded around the board. Although Death was on his way, Don Juan still refused to repent as Don Gonzalo's statue once more told him about the redeeming power of heaven.

As Don Juan's funeral procession approached, Don Gonzalo seized the sinner's arm and prepared to drag him off to hell. At that moment Don Juan raised his free arm toward heaven. Ines appeared and she and Don Juan, both saved, sank together into a bed of flowers scattered by angels. Flames, symbolizing their souls, mounted to heaven.

Critical Evaluation:

Don Juan Tenorio, the boastful libertine who defies God in his search for earthly pleasures, is one of Spain's mythical figures. In the legend and in Tirso de Molina's seventeenth century masterpiece *The Trickster of Seville* (1640), time runs out and Don Juan is dragged down into hell. Heaven's justice has been appeased and the fabric of society restored.

In the nineteenth century *Don Juan Tenorio* by José Zorrilla y Moral, on the other hand, Don Juan is given time and is saved, even after death. The difference between the two works lies in the varying perspective of the hero. Although in both works the personality of Don Juan dominates the play, sweeping all other characters aside, Tirso had chosen to accentuate in the title the salient trait of his Don Juan's nature, that of gamester, the man who views life as a game and uses people, especially women, as pawns. Tirso's Don Juan is incapable of change or true affection; handsome, magnificently proud, and brave though he may be, he is not complete, not a hero. The Don Juan Tenorio of Zorrilla's play, by contrast, is a hero, the quintessential romantic hero. In one of those rare moments of inspiration, Zorrilla seems to have found the right combination of medieval lore, literary tradition, and the Romantic ideal. *Don Juan Tenorio*, appearing at the very end of the Spanish Romantic movement, resonated with the Spanish people, and every November 1, All Saints Day, the play is still performed throughout the Hispanic world.

Spanish Romantic drama extravagantly rebelled against rigid neoclassicism, and *Don Juan Tenorio*'s only concessions to unity are in the dominance of its protagonist and in its principal theme of salvation through love. It is a long operatic work of seven acts in mixed verse which, although uneven at times, reaches intense melodic heights. The action starts during carnival week in a torch-lit Seville where masked revelers await the participants in a cruel wager, and it ends in a cemetery complete with antithetical vengeful ghosts and cherubs, hellfire and flowers, funeral chants and joyous song. Its acts are titled, each stressing the dominant mood or theme. Act IV, for example, in which Don Juan carries off Ines and has his first chance at redemption, is entitled "The Devil at Heaven's Door," representing the antithesis of the devil and the angel, Don Juan and Ines.

Don Juan, in true romantic rebel fashion, had scoffed at tradition and society's mores until he meets Ines, whom he stole from her convent out of spite. Something in Ines, perhaps her innocence or her obvious adoration of him, mysteriously moves him, or perhaps he sees his only hope of salvation through her. If Don Juan is the archetypal Romantic hero, Ines is the archetypal Romantic heroine. Dreamy, delicate, unaccustomed to the world, shut up in her convent, and almost hypnotized by the force of Don Juan's personality, she forms an ideal image of him that time and death cannot break. She dies from grief after Don Juan's abandonment of her, following her father's death, and then literally sacrifices her own salvation for that of her lover. She may be weak in life, but in death she is forceful enough to make a pact with God.

Theology is not the strong point of *Don Juan Tenorio*. Don Juan is saved after death, even though God generally does not equate a sinner with a saint; an entire life of crime and scandal is rarely blotted away forever by one second of repentance. The moral linchpin of the play, however, is the fact that Don Juan had tried to repent; a moment of Gonzalo's scorn and taunting had destroyed that moment of salvation.

The play, at its most excessive, is melodrama, but it is effective. At times it is as hypnotic as its title character in the kaleidoscopic use of light and sound and changing scenes and in the seductive music of its verse. The extreme contrast between the action, mood, and scene of Acts IV and V is a good example of Zorrilla's technique of change and reversal. Act IV is all passion, light, fire, and motion, but when we meet with the characters again in Act V, the start of the second half of the play, they have been transformed into lifelike statues in a cemetery dedicated to the victims of Don Juan; their vital force has been converted into frigid marble. The light now is cold; a silver moon shines on a stillness of white and black. There is no movement; even the rhythm of the verse slows down.

The contrasting nature of the scenery and action is the medium for the expression of the work's antithetical themes. All the great dramatic dualities are present—betrayal and faith, damnation and salvation, corruption and innocence, hope and despair, hate and, above all, love. All the excess, all the music, all the disparate images coalesce around this overriding central tenet, that love is dominant, even after death, and can break down even the gates of heaven. This message is certainly one of the principal reasons for the play's continuing popularity.

In contrast to the stern retribution of God's justice in Tirso's *The Trickster of Seville*, here the audience is consoled with the prospect of divine mercy. Another reason for the play's success could be that secretly the audience has always wanted Don Juan to be saved. Even in Tirso's work, in which Don Juan deserves to be punished, it is his fire and passion that are remembered.

"Critical Evaluation" by Charlene E. Suscavage

Bibliography:

Arias, Judith. "The Devil at Heaven's Door: Metaphysical Desire in *Don Juan Tenorio*." In *Hispanic Review* 61 (Winter, 1993): 15-34. Analyzes the Romantic drama as a game and deals with the wager underlying the plot. Applies psychological theories of René Girard that show how the character's behavior is an example of mimetic desire, a desire that in Don Juan is "ultimately metaphysical in nature."

Feal, Carlos. "Conflicting Names, Conflicting Laws: Zorrilla's *Don Juan Tenorio*." In *PMLA* 96 (May, 1981): 375-387. Concludes that the work shows evidence of being an improvisation and enjoys an "exaggerated theatricality" because the figure was "a man in need of an audience." Addresses the myth and compares Zorrilla's with Tirso's version.

Firmat, Gustavo Perez. "Carnival in *Don Juan Tenorio*." In *Hispanic Review* 51 (Summer, 1983): 269-281. A structural study that disagrees with the author's self-criticism of the play. Sees flaws and inconsistencies as "harmonious elements in a coherent, if unusual, design." Concentrates on the letter motif (delivered in a prayerbook as a form of masking and unmasking) and the play's reversal of cause-and-effect patterns (metalepsis).

Howe, Elizabeth Teresa. "Hell or Heaven? Providence and Don Juan." In *Renascence* 37 (Summer, 1985): 212-219. Discusses the fact that Zorrilla's Don Juan expects damnation but gets salvation, the reverse of the situation in Tirso. Concludes that Don Juan is the "devil incarnate [and] Satan is a logical extension of the Romantic hero, pursuing self-gratification in defiance of social restraint."

Mandel, Oscar, ed. *The Theatre of Don Juan: A Collection of Plays and Views, 1630-1963.* Lincoln: University of Nebraska Press, 1963. A full study of the figure of Don Juan, which introduces Zorrilla's version with a thorough overview of his special treatment. Good for understanding the subsequent parodies, burlesques, and other travesties of the play in Spanish-speaking countries. The introductory essay on the legend is particularly insightful.

DON QUIXOTE DE LA MANCHA

Type of work: Novel
Author: Miguel de Cervantes (1547-1616)
Type of plot: Mock-heroic
Time of plot: Late sixteenth century
Locale: Spain
First published: El ingenioso hidalgo don Quixote de la Mancha, part 1, 1605; part 2, 1615
(English translation, 1612-1620)

Principal characters:
DON QUIXOTE DE LA MANCHA, a knight-errant
SANCHO PANZA, his squire
ALDONZA LORENZO, a farm girl Quixote calls Dulcinea, his "illusionary lady"
PEDRO PEREZ, a village curate
MASTER NICHOLAS, a barber
SAMSON CARRASCO, a young bachelor of arts

The Story:

A retired and impoverished gentleman named Alonzo Quixano lived in the Spanish province of La Mancha. He had read so many romances of chivalry that his mind became overwhelmed with fantastic accounts of tournaments, knightly quests, damsels in distress, and strange enchantments, and he decided one day to imitate the heroes of the books he read and to revive the ancient custom of knight-errantry. Changing his name to Don Quixote de la Mancha, he had himself dubbed a knight by a publican whose miserable inn he mistook for a turreted castle.

For armor he donned an old suit of mail that had belonged to his great-grandfather. Then, upon a bony old nag he called Rosinante, he set out upon his first adventure. Not far from his village he fell into the company of some traveling merchants who thought the old man mad and beat him severely when he challenged them to a passage at arms.

Back home recovering from his cuts and bruises, he was closely watched by his good neighbor, Pedro Perez, the village priest, and Master Nicholas, the barber. Hoping to cure him of his fancies, the curate and the barber burned his library of chivalric romances. Don Quixote, however, believed that his books had been carried off by a wizard. Undaunted by his misfortunes, he determined to set out on the road again with an uncouth rustic named Sancho Panza as his squire. As the mistress to whom he would dedicate his deeds of valor, he chose a buxom peasant wench famous for her skill in salting pork. He called her Dulcinea del Toboso.

The knight and his squire had to sneak out of the village under cover of darkness, but in their own minds they presented a brave appearance: the lean old man on his bony horse and his squat, black-browed servant on a small ass, Dapple. The don carried his sword and lance, Sancho Panza a canvas wallet and a leather bottle. Sancho went with the don because, in his shallow-brained way, he hoped to become governor of an island.

The don's first encounter was with a score of windmills on the plains of Montiel. Mistaking them for monstrous giants, he couched his lance, set spurs to Rosinante's thin flanks, and charged full tilt against them. One of the whirling vanes lifted him from his saddle and threw him into the air. When Sancho Panza ran to pick him up, Quixote explained that sorcerers had changed the giants into windmills.

Shortly afterward he encountered two monks riding in company with a lady in a coach escorted by men on horseback. Don Quixote imagined that the lady was a captive princess. Haughtily demanding her release, he unhorsed one of the friars in an attempted rescue. Sancho was beaten by the lady's lackeys. Don Quixote bested her Biscayan squire in a sword fight, sparing the man's life on the condition that he go to Toboso and yield himself to the peerless Dulcinea. Sancho, having little taste for violence, wanted to get on to his island as quickly as possible.

At an inn, Quixote became involved in an assignation between a carrier and a servant girl. He was trounced by the carrier. The don, insulted by the innkeeper's demand for payment, rode away without paying. To his terror, Sancho was tossed in a blanket as payment for his master's debt. The pair came upon dust clouds stirred up by two large flocks of sheep. Don Quixote, sure that they were two medieval armies closing in combat, intervened, only to be pummeled with rocks by the indignant shepherds whose sheep he had scattered.

At night the don thought a funeral procession was a parade of monsters. He attacked and routed the mourners and was called Knight of the Sorry Aspect by Sancho. The two came upon a roaring noise in the night. Quixote, believing it to be made by giants, wanted to attack immediately, but Sancho judiciously hobbled Rosinante so he could not move. The next day, they discovered that the noise came from the pounding of a mill.

Quixote attacked an itinerant barber and seized the poor barber's bowl, which he declared to be the famous golden helmet of Mambrino, and his packsaddle, which he believed to be a richly jeweled caparison. Next, the pair came upon a chain gang being taken to the galleys. The don interviewed various prisoners and decided to succor the afflicted. He freed them, only to be insulted by their remarks concerning his lady, the fair Dulcinea. Sancho, afraid of what would ensue from their releasing of the galley slaves, led Quixote into the mountains for safety. There they came upon a hermit, a nobleman, who told them a long story of unrequited love. Quixote and the hermit fought over the virtues of their respective loves. Deciding to do penance and to fast for the love of Dulcinea, Quixote gave a letter to Sancho to deliver to the maiden. When Sancho returned to the village, Don Quixote's friends learned from Sancho the old man's whereabouts. They returned with Sancho to the mountains, hoping they could trick Don Quixote into returning with them. The priest devised a scheme whereby a young peasant woman would pose as a princess in distress. Don Quixote, all but dead from hunger and exposure, was easily deceived, and the party started homeward.

They came to the inn where Sancho had been tossed in the blanket. The priest explained the don's vagaries to the alarmed innkeeper, who admitted that he too was addicted to the reading of romances of chivalry. At the inn, Don Quixote fought in his sleep with ogres and ran his sword through two of the innkeeper's precious wineskins. The itinerant barber stopped by and demanded the return of his basin and packsaddle. After the party had sport at the expense of the befuddled barber, restitution was made. An officer appeared with a warrant for the arrest of the don and Sancho for releasing the galley slaves. The priest explained his friend's mental condition, and the officer departed.

Seeing no other means of getting Don Quixote quietly home, his friends disguised themselves and placed the don in a cage mounted on an oxcart. He was later released under oath not to attempt to escape. A churchman joined the party and sought to bring Quixote to his senses by logical argument against books of knight-errantry. The don refuted the man with a charming and brilliant argument and went on to narrate a typical romance of derring-do. Before the group reached home, they came upon a goatherd who told them a story and by whom Quixote was beaten through a misunderstanding.

Sometime later the priest and the barber visited the convalescing Don Quixote to give him news of Spain and of the world. When they told him there was danger of an attack on Spain by the Turks, the don suggested that the king assemble all of Spain's knights-errant to repulse the enemy. At this time Sancho entered, despite efforts to bar him. He brought word that a book telling of their adventures had appeared. The sight of Sancho inspired the don to sally forth again. His excuse was a great tournament to be held at Saragossa.

Failing to dissuade Don Quixote from going forth again, his friends were reassured when a village student promised he would waylay the flighty old gentleman.

Don Quixote's first destination was the home of Dulcinea in nearby El Toboso. While the don waited in a forest, Sancho saw three peasant girls riding out of the village. He rode to his master and told him that Dulcinea with two handmaidens approached. Frightened by the don's fantastic speech, the girls fled. Don Quixote swore that Dulcinea had been enchanted.

Benighted in a forest, the knight and his squire were awakened by the arrival of another knight and squire. The other knight boasted that he had defeated in combat all Spanish knights. The don, believing the knight to be mistaken, challenged him. They fought by daylight and, miraculously, Don Quixote unhorsed the Knight of the Wood, who was Samson Carrasco, the village student, in disguise. His squire was an old acquaintance of Sancho. The don declared the resemblances were the work of magicians and continued on his way. Upset by his failure, Carrasco swore vengeance on Don Quixote.

Sancho filled Quixote's helmet with curds which he procured from shepherds. When the don suddenly clapped on his helmet at the approach of another adventure, he thought his brains were melting. This new adventure took the form of a wagon bearing two caged lions. Quixote, ever intrepid, commanded the keeper to open one cage—he would engage a lion in combat. Unhappily, the keeper obeyed. Quixote stood ready, but the lion yawned and refused to come out.

The don and Sancho joined a wedding party and subsequently attended a wedding festival at which the rejected lover tricked the bride into marrying him instead of the rich man she had chosen.

Next, the pair were taken to the Caves of Montesinos, where Quixote was lowered underground. He was brought up an hour later asleep, and, upon awakening, he told a story of having spent three days in a land of palaces and magic forests where he had seen his enchanted Dulcinea.

At an inn, Quixote met a puppeteer who had a divining ape. By trickery, the puppeteer identified the don and Sancho with the help of the ape. He presented a melodramatic puppet show which Don Quixote, carried away by the make-believe story, demolished with his sword. The don paid for the damage done and struck out for the nearby River Ebro. He and Sancho took a boat and were carried by the current toward some churning mill wheels, which the don thought were a beleaguered city awaiting deliverance. They were rescued by millers after the boat had been wrecked and the pair thoroughly soaked.

Later, in a forest, the pair met a huntress who claimed knowledge of the famous knight and his squire. They went with the lady to her castle and were welcomed by a duke and his duchess who had read of their previous adventures and who were ready to have great fun at the pair's expense. The hosts arranged an elaborate night ceremony to disenchant Dulcinea, who was represented by a disguised page. To his great discomfort, Sancho was told that he would receive five hundred lashes as his part of the disenchantment. Part of the jest was a ride through space on a magic wooden horse. Blindfolded, the pair mounted their steed, and servants blew air in their faces from bellows and thrust torches near their faces.

Sancho departed to govern his isle, a village in the domains of the duke and duchess, while the female part of the household turned to the project of compromising Quixote in his worship of Dulcinea. Sancho governed for a week. He made good laws and delivered wise judgments, but at the end of a week, he yearned for the freedom of the road. Together he and his master proceeded toward Saragossa. Don Quixote changed their destination to Barcelona, however, when he heard that a citizen of that city had written a spurious account of his adventures.

In Barcelona, they marveled at the city, the ships, and the sea. Don Quixote and Sancho were the guests of Moreno, who took them to inspect the royal galleys. The galley which they visited suddenly put out to sea in pursuit of pirates, and a fight followed. Sancho was terrified.

There came to Barcelona a Knight of the White Moon, who challenged Don Quixote to combat. After the old man had been overcome, the strange knight, in reality the student Carrasco, sentenced him to return home. Don Quixote went back, determined next to follow a pastoral shepherd life. At home, the tired old man quickly declined. Before he died, he renounced as nonsense all to do with knight-errantry, not realizing that in his high-minded, noble-hearted nature he himself had been a great, chivalrous gentleman.

Critical Evaluation:

It has been said that *Don Quixote de la Mancha* is "the best novel in the world, beyond comparison." This belief was, is, and certainly will be shared by lovers of literary excellence everywhere. Miguel de Cervantes' avowed purpose was to ridicule the books of chivalry that enjoyed popularity even in his day, but he soared beyond this satirical purpose in his wealth of fancy and in his irrepressible high spirits as he pokes fun at social and literary conventions of many kinds. The novel provides a cross-section of Spanish life, thought, and feeling at the end of the chivalric age.

"For my absolute faith in the details of their histories and my knowledge of their deeds and their characters enable me by sound philosophy to deduce their features, their complexions and their statures," says Don Quixote, declaring his expertise in knight-errantry. This declaration affords a key to understanding Cervantes' *Don Quixote de la Mancha*, for it demonstrates both the literal and the symbolic levels of the novel—and the distinction between those levels is crucial to grasping the full import of the story. The literal level is superficial; it is about the misadventures of a nut and a fool. The symbolic level, however, probes much deeper; it reveals the significance of these adventures. In fact, the symbolic level deals, as all good literature does, with values. Thus, Don Quixote's declaration is ironic on the superficial level and, in context, on the level of its true thematic message.

On the literal level, Don Quixote is eminently qualified by his extensive reading to assert familiarity with the history, the deeds, and the character of virtually every knight whose existence was recorded. Indeed, his penchant for reading books of chivalry is established on the first page of the first chapter of the book. Even his niece and his housekeeper refer frequently to his reading habits. Moreover, the inventory of the don's library, made just before the books were burned, reveals the extent of his collection, and earlier mention of his omnivorous reading leads to the assumption that he had read all of them. Further evidence of Don Quixote's erudition is his ready knowledge of the rules of knight-errantry and his recalling the legend of Mambrino's helmet in connection with his oath of knighthood. Later, after an encounter with Yanguesan herdsmen, there is evidence, in a very lucid and pragmatic statement for a presumably insane old man, of Don Quixote's having read Machiavelli, followed by the don's citation of the misfortunes that befell his hero, Amadis of Gaul.

Other adventures provide internal evidence of Quixote's knowledge about the history of chivalry. A thrashing by muleteers jogs the don's memory to analogies between his plight and similar outrages visited upon the Marquis of Mantua, Baldwin, Abindarraez, and Don Roderigo de Narvaez. After his lance is broken by a windmill, Don Quixote remembers the makeshift tree-limb weapon used by Diego Perez de Vargas when the latter's primary weapon was broken in battle. At another time, he explains and defends the code of knight-errantry to fellow travelers, citing Arthurian legend, the ever-present Amadis of Gaul, the stricter-than-monastic rules of knight-errantry, and the noble families of Italy and Spain who contributed to the tradition. In fact, incredible as it may seem, just before the don attacks the herd of sheep, he attributes to each sheep a title and an estate culled from his reservoir of reading—or from his overactive imagination. In addition, to rationalize his own designation as the Knight of the Sorry Aspect, he recalls the sobriquets of other knights-errant. In an attempt to inculcate Sancho Panza with the proper respect for his master, Don Quixote even relates biographical incidents from the lives of the squires of Amadis of Gaul and Sir Galaor. Significantly, almost craftily, he mentions that Gandalin, Amadis' squire, was also Count of the Firm Isle—a blatant inducement for Sancho to remain in the don's service. Yet, all in all, on the literal level, Don Quixote's mastery of chivalric lore seems to serve only as a rationalization for his ill luck.

On the symbolic level, more questions are raised than are answered. Quixote claims to have reached a "sound philosophy." Is, however, reliance on reading alone—as he has done—a valid basis for "sound philosophy," or has the don become so absorbed in his books that he is unable to formulate or express the applicability of his reading? Can, for example, literature serve as a basis for understanding reality as Don Quixote avers? In lieu of a clear-cut answer, Cervantes offers a paradox. Early in the text, Don Quixote learns from Sancho that the squire has never read any histories because he is illiterate; but later, trying to divert the don's attention with a story, Sancho, under questioning, admits that although he had not seen the person in question, "the man who told me this story said it was so true and authentic. . . . I could swear on my oath that I had seen it all." The issues of verisimilitude and credibility are not really resolved in this novel. Consequently, these issues generate further questions about distinctions between reality and fantasy. Sancho represents empirical, commonsensical reality; the don stands for whimsy and unfettered imagination. Whose view of the world is more accurate? Cervantes is ambiguous, at best, about the answer. The question endures. Readers are left to ponder this paradox that Emily Dickinson has so succinctly described: "Much madness is divinest sense."

Another issue raised on the symbolic level involves the possible immorality of reading "too many" books. Books, in this sense, are a symbol of education, and this facet of *Don Quixote de la Mancha* may be a veiled protest against censorship in general and the *Index Librorum Prohibitorum* in particular. The literal lesson emphasizes the corruptive power of books (and, therefore, education); however, the symbolic implication—given Cervantes' sympathetic treatment of Don Quixote—is that books and education are liberating influences on the human psyche. Thus, the symbolic purport of *Don Quixote de la Mancha* may be a parody of the Church's monopoly of literacy in the Middle Ages, with the uninhibited don a foil to the insensitive, book-burning priest.

To be sure, Don Quixote became a tragic figure toward the end of the novel, but not for the failure of his philosophy; rather, it is society's failure to accommodate a deviation from the norm. Herein lies another symbolic level of the novel: society's intolerance of deviance. For Cervantes certainly did not make the don contemptible nor did he treat him with contempt. Such treatment would have been repellent after the tolerance of the first part of the story. Despite the satirical thrust of the novel on the symbolic level, the don himself is a sympathetic character throughout the story. Although he strives to push time back, his efforts are depicted as noble, although futile. The sympathy he evokes is that popular sympathy for the underdog who defies all odds and is broken in the attempt, in contrast to the protagonist, who has everything in his favor and succumbs to a surfeit of success.

Cervantes' novel is a complex web of tangled skeins, subject to many more interpretations than those suggested here. Suffice it to say that *Don Quixote de la Mancha* is unequivocally judged the finest Spanish novel ever written and one of the greatest works in world literature.

"Critical Evaluation" by Joanne G. Kashdan

Bibliography:

Allen, John J. *Don Quixote, Hero or Fool? A Study in Narrative Technique.* Gainesville: University Presses of Florida, 1969. A sound starting place for students of postmodern criticism as it relates to the novel.

Coover, Robert. "The Last Quixote: Marginal Notes on the Gospel According to Samuel Beckett." In *In Praise of What Persists*, edited by Stephen Berg. New York: Harper & Row, 1983. Coover, a postmodern writer who admires Beckett and *Don Quixote*, connects postmodernism to Cervantes' work.

Entwistle, William J. *Cervantes.* Oxford, England: Clarendon Press, 1969. Essays on Cervantes' life and writing. The essay "The Hero as Pedant" addresses the reception of Cervantes' masterpiece and its rise to the "rank of a work of art." Indexed, with a brief biography and a chronological listing of his works.

Nelson, Lowry, Jr., ed. *Cervantes: A Collection of Critical Essays.* Englewood Cliffs, N.J.: Prentice-Hall, 1969. Gathers the best available critical opinions on Cervantes' work. Ten essays, one by Thomas Mann and another by W. H. Auden.

Predmore, Richard L. *The World of Don Quixote.* Cambridge, Mass.: Harvard University Press, 1967. Provides a brief, clear exploration of the complex world of Cervantes' great novel.

DON SEGUNDO SOMBRA
Shadows on the Pampas

Type of work: Novel
Author: Ricardo Güiraldes (1886-1927)
Type of plot: Regional
Time of plot: Late nineteenth century
Locale: Argentina
First published: 1926 (English translation, 1935)

Principal characters:
DON SEGUNDO SOMBRA, a gaucho
FABIO, a young waif
DON LEANDRO GALVÁN, a rancher
PEDRO BARRALES, a gaucho
PAULA, a pretty young woman and the beloved of Fabio

The Story:

Fabio was a young lad who lived with his two maiden aunts in a small Argentine village. He disliked his aunts, who felt, in their turn, that he was simply a bother. He was not sure that the two women were truly his relatives, for they paid him little attention as long as he gave them no trouble. Don Fabio Caceres, a rancher, occasionally came to see the boy and took him into the country for a day, but the man ceased coming when Fabio was about eleven years old.

Fabio grew up to be a mischievous youngster who showed off for the worst element of the town. He knew all the gossip and spent most of his time hanging around the saloons; no one seemed to care that he never went to school. The village loafers hinted that he was an illegitimate, unwanted child. At best, he seemed destined to be a ne'er-do-well who carried a chip on his shoulder in defiance of the rest of the world.

One night, a gaucho rode into the town as Fabio was going home from fishing. The man impressed the boy instantly, and, a little later, Fabio earned the gaucho's interest by warning him of an ambush laid by a knife-wielding bully. The kind words spoken by the gaucho, Don Segundo, went to the boy's heart, and Fabio immediately decided to follow the man when he left town. Gathering together his meager possessions, which fortunately included a saddle and two ponies, Fabio went quietly away without telling anyone where he was going in order to escape his hated aunts. He rode to the ranch belonging to Don Leandro Galván, where he knew Don Segundo was going to spend a few days breaking wild horses.

When he arrived, the boy applied for work and was accepted. By the time Don Segundo was ready to leave the ranch on a cattle drive, Fabio had convinced Don Leandro and Don Segundo that he was a willing worker, and they let Fabio go with the other gauchos on half pay. At the end of the drive, Fabio was doing well in his apprenticeship as a gaucho.

For five years, Fabio continued under the tutelage of Don Segundo. Traveling from ranch to ranch, they worked for a number of landowners. From the older man, Fabio learned to care for himself and his horses, to work cattle under various conditions, to live courageously, to get along with all kinds of people, and to have a good time singing songs, dancing, and telling stories. It was more than a way of making a living that the man passed on to the boy; it was an entire culture, a culture as old as the cattle industry and in some respects even older, going back as it did to the culture of Spain.

There were many incidents in their wanderings, including a time when Fabio won a large amount of money by picking the winning bird in a cockfight when everyone else bet against the bird. That happened in the town of Navarro, a town which remained a lucky place in young Fabio's mind. A long cattle drive to a ranch on the seashore was also an important experience for Fabio. There he found that he detested the countryside, and he experienced much bad luck; but he fell in love with a young woman there. He had picked up quite a respectable string of horses, the tools of the gaucho's trade, and he was very proud of them. In working the cattle at the seashore ranch, however, two of the horses were injured, much to the young gaucho's dismay. One of them was badly gored by a bull, and when Fabio came across the bull one evening while exploring with another young man, he vowed to break its neck. He lassoed the beast and broke its neck with the shock, but in doing so, he injured himself severely, breaking several bones.

While Fabio remained at the ranch convalescing from his injuries, he fell in love, he thought, with Paula, a pretty young woman who lived on the place. Unfortunately, she led him on while she also led on the rather stupid son of the rancher. The other lad took advantage of Fabio's crippled arm and attacked him with a knife. Fabio, not wanting to injure the owner's son, to fight over a woman, or to violate the father's hospitality, avoided the other fellow's thrusts until they became deadly. Then with a quick thrust, Fabio slashed the boy's forehead slightly, quickly taking the will to fight out of him. Paula, over whom the fight began, rebuked the crippled Fabio. Disgusted at her and at himself, Fabio, crippled as he was, mounted his horse and rode away to rejoin Don Segundo, who was working at a nearby ranch until Fabio could be ready to travel.

Don Segundo and Fabio happened into a small village on a day when people had gathered from miles around to race horses. Fabio bet and lost a hundred pesos, then another hundred, and finally the third and last hundred he possessed. Still not believing that the situation was hopeless, he gambled five of his horses and lost them as well. He came out of the afternoon's activity a sad young man.

He and Don Segundo were hired to trail a herd of cattle from a ranch near the village to the city to be butchered. It was a long, hard drive, even for experienced gauchos. It was made even more difficult for Fabio by the fact that he had only three horses, for the animals soon became fatigued from the work of carrying him and working the cattle onthe road. When the herd stopped to rest one afternoon, Fabio decided to see if he could somehow get another horse or two.

While looking about, he found Pedro Barrales, a gaucho who had traveled with him and Don Segundo several times. Pedro Barrales had a letter addressed to Señor Fabio Caceres, a letter which he gave to Fabio. The lad looked blankly at the letter, not believing it was addressed to him, for he thought he had no surname. Don Segundo opened the letter to find that the maiden aunts had been truly Fabio's relatives and that Don Fabio Caceres, who had visited him at his aunt's home, was really his father, from whom he had inherited a fortune and a large, well-stocked ranch. The news saddened Fabio because he saw that it would take him away from the life he loved. He was angered, too, because he had been left so long under the impression that he should be ashamed of his parentage.

Acting upon the good advice of Don Segundo, Fabio returned to his native town, however, and from there to the ranch where he had begun work under Don Leandro Galván, who had now become his guardian. When Don Segundo agreed to remain with him for three years on his own ranch, Fabio was willing to settle down. Yet, the three years passed all too swiftly, and at the end of that time, Fabio was exceedingly sad when Don Segundo left, answering the gaucho's call to wander.

Critical Evaluation:

The Argentine poet, short-story writer, and novelist Ricardo Güiraldes was born in Buenos Aires in 1886 to a landowning family. He lived his first years in France, returned there often, and died in Paris in 1927. Although he traveled abroad frequently, Güiraldes loved his country, especially the *pampa*, the fertile plains in the province of Buenos Aires, where his family owned a ranch called La Porteña. As a young boy, he spent summers at the ranch among the gauchos, the Argentine cowboys. He learned about gaucho life and folklore from Don Segundo Ramirez, the man immortalized in *Don Segundo Sombra*, the novel for which Güiraldes received the National Prize for Literature in 1926.

The novel is based on the author's recollections of his early life on the *pampa*. Influenced by works such as Mark Twain's *Huckleberry Finn* (1884), the regional and poetic narrative illustrates the experience of growing up in the countryside, having the ideal gaucho as a mentor and role model. *Don Segundo Sombra* symbolizes the *pampa* and its inhabitants and represents the gaucho culture as it once existed, before the invasion of economic and industrial progress in early twentieth century. Often compared to *Don Quixote de la Mancha* (1605-1615), the novel's gaucho of mythical presence is the last representative of a special kind of life that was disappearing like a shadow but leaving its essence and spirit, becoming more a legend than a way of life.

The coming-of-age story, with the typical structure of a *Bildungsroman*, is told by Fabio through recollections and memories. The twenty-seven chapters may be divided into three parts of nine chapters each. As the reader follows the narrator and protagonist Fabio in his journey toward adulthood, he or she stops with him several times so that he may retrace his steps mentally, in flashbacks. At first, when Fabio is about fourteen years old, one discovers that he considers himself an illegitimate orphan whose unhappy and purposeless life is changed drastically by the arrival of Don Segundo Sombra. Fabio sees his destiny in a nomadic free life, hoping to become a real gaucho. In the second part, Fabio reviews the five years spent learning gaucho skills and overcoming physical and spiritual tests. In the third part, the reader sees him returning to his town of origin, ready to take over his new position as a ranch owner upon the news of his legitimate right to the possessions of his father, who recognized him as his heir before dying. In the last three chapters, he recalls the departure of Don Segundo, after reviewing his life as a landowner.

The image of Don Segundo is seen through Fabio's eyes. He admires legendary gauchos and transfers his images of them to his mentor, who becomes a hero and father figure for him. Fabio is the protagonist, but Don Segundo is the main character of his recollections. He embodies the virtues of the gaucho Fabio wants to become: laconic, serene, proud, stoic, and respectful of others, prizing freedom above all else. In the journey through the *pampa*, a delinquent, lazy orphan grows up to be an honest, hardworking member of society. His love of unconditional freedom must be given up in order to fulfill his true destiny. At the end of the novel, Fabio learns to accept his fate having finally found his destiny after travelling physically and mentally in search of his true identity. Don Segundo has taught him to be tough and stoic, fearless and brave, ready to face challenges. With him, Fabio has explored moral and physical attributes that are desirable in a man, and has learned the benefits of loyalty, courtesy, understanding, and friendship. Fabio's moments of recollection take place by a stream, a river, and a pond, indicating with the imagery of water the three different stages in the life of Fabio as he moves through this journey of learning. Each kind of water symbolizes life as a current, small at first, gaining strength later, and finally reaching stability as Fabio returns to his origins.

The three moments of recollection—at departure time, during the journey, and at the return—

seem to coincide with three figures: Don Segundo, Fabio, and Raucho. Don Segundo represents the past, Fabio is the present, and Raucho, Don Leandro Galván's son, is the ideal future into which the present is changing. Fabio must learn from the past and accept the future for survival. The novel offers a lesson for the young people of Argentina. Güiraldes uses Don Segundo, the essence and spirit of an authentic Argentina, as a symbol to guide the country into the future. He wants to rescue and keep alive the soul of the nation. Don Segundo becomes the personification of tradition as a guiding light.

The *pampa* provides a stage and a space for Fabio's adventures as a gaucho. The interaction of nature and man provokes emotions which Fabio, the artist as a young man, observes and interprets poetically. The plot is subordinated to the description of nature and rural activities. Lights and colors are captured with impressionistic techniques. The inclusion of songs, traditional stories, proverbs, and colloquial expressions provides realistic authenticity. Even the most realistic scenes, however, are recreated with poetic imagery, characterizing Güiraldes' work as a lyrical novel with striking images.

Don Segundo Sombra, the allegorical farewell to a disappearing national figure and to the literary genre of the gaucho novel, is a classic example of the *novela de la tierra*, or regional novel, also called *criollista*, written in the 1920's in Latin America. The incorporation of the *pampa*, a regional landscape, into fiction expresses the search for authenticity, breaking with traditional models and establishing the foundation of the contemporary Latin American narrative.

"Critical Evaluation" by Ludmila Kapschutschenko-Schmitt

Bibliography:
Alonso, Carlos J. *The Spanish American Regional Novel: Modernity and Autochthony.* Cambridge, England: Cambridge University Press, 1990. Discusses representative novels, illustrating the search for an autochthonous artistic expression. Focuses on the complexity of *Don Segundo Sombra*'s discourse, noting the text's reference to its own process of production.
Beardsell, Peter R. "Güiraldes' Role in the Avant-Garde of Buenos Aires." *Hispanic Review* 42, no. 3 (Summer, 1974): 293-309. Explores Güiraldes' participation in the avant-garde movement of the 1920's, and shows how this is reflected in his poetry and narrative. Concludes that *Don Segundo Sombra* would not have been possible without the influence of avant-garde literature.
Fitz, Earl E. *Rediscovering the New World.* Iowa City: University of Iowa Press, 1991. Approaches the writings of the Americas as a cohesive literary type. Compares Güiraldes to writers such as Mark Twain and William Faulkner, exploring how their works transcend the local to attain the universal, representing "deep regionalism."
Franco, Jean. *Spanish American Literature Since Independence.* New York: Barnes & Noble, 1973. Compares Fabio's training to a spiritual exercise and emphasizes Don Segundo's spirituality. The regional setting of the novel is seen as conducive to attaining spiritual goals away from the industrialized world.
Vazquez Amaral, José. *The Contemporary Latin American Narrative.* New York: Las Americas, 1970. Includes the chapter "Ricardo Güiraldes and the Metaphysical Gaucho: *Don Segundo Sombra*," in which Vazquez discusses Güiraldes' "Argentinity" and the importance of *Don Segundo Sombra* as the summation of the entire literature of the gaucho.

DOÑA BÁRBARA

Type of work: Novel
Author: Rómulo Gallegos (1884-1969)
Type of plot: Regional
Time of plot: Early twentieth century
Locale: Arauca Valley, Venezuela
First published: 1929 (English translation, 1931)

Principal characters:
DOÑA BÁRBARA, a beautiful, unscrupulous mestiza
SANTOS LUZARDO, the owner of the Altamira ranch
MARISELA, the illegitimate daughter of Doña Bárbara and
Lorenzo Barquero
ANTONIO, a cowboy at the Altamira ranch
THE WIZARD, a rascally henchman of Doña Bárbara
SEÑOR DANGER, an American squatter on the Altamira ranch
DON BALBINO, the treacherous overseer at the Altamira ranch

The Story:

The Altamira ranch was a vast estate in the wildest section of the Arauca River basin of Venezuela, a ranch that had been established early in the history of the country's cattle business. Late in the nineteenth century, it had been divided into two parts by one of the owners' joint heirs. One part of the ranch kept the old name and went to the male heir of the Luzardo family. The other part went to a daughter who had married a Barquero, and it took on the name from the new owner. As the years went by, the two families carried on a feud that killed most of the men on both sides. During the Spanish-American War, the owner of Altamira quarreled with his elder son and killed him; he then starved himself to death. His wife, Doña Luzardo, took her only remaining son to Caracas to rear him in a more civilized atmosphere.

Years went by. Finally the son, Santos Luzardo, decided to sell the ranch, which had been allowed to deteriorate under irresponsible overseers. The young man went into the back country to see the place for himself and to determine what it might be worth. On his arrival, he found that the neighboring ranch of the Barqueros had fallen into the hands of Doña Bárbara, a mestiza who had been the mistress of the real owner before she ran him off his property. Doña Bárbara was in the process of taking over the Altamira ranch as well, with the help of several henchmen, including Don Balbino, the ranch's overseer. Santos decided to keep the ranch and try to make it prosperous again.

Santos was able to rely on the help of a handful of loyal cowboys who had known him as a child. These included Antonio, a cowboy who had been his playmate years before. Santos Luzardo's first move was to end the feud between himself and the Barqueros. He found Lorenzo Barquero living in a cabin in a swamp, the only land his mistress had not taken from him. After making his peace with Lorenzo and his illegitimate daughter, Marisela, Santos took them to live at Altamira ranch. Marisela was as beautiful as her mother, Doña Bárbara, and Santos wished to retrieve her from barbarity.

Most of the cattle had been stolen from the Altamira ranch, and only about one hundred head were left. Nevertheless, Antonio had seen to it that many hundreds more had been allowed to stray into wild country, thus saving them from Doña Bárbara and Señor Danger, an American squatter who was in the process of carving his own ranch out of Altamira land. One of Santos' first acts was to discharge Don Balbino, Altamira's treacherous overseer, who, since he had been working for Doña Bárbara and was her lover, thereupon sought the mestiza's protection.

Santos, who had been trained as a lawyer, decided first to try legal means of repossessing the lost parts of his ranch. He went to the local magistrate and, through his knowledge of the law, forced that official to call in Doña Bárbara and Señor Danger. They were told to permit a roundup of his cattle and to help him, since their herds were intermingled with those from Altamira. They were also told to build fences, since according to the law, they had too few cattle to let them run wild. Doña Bárbara was to help build a boundary fence between her ranch and Altamira. She accepted the decisions with surprisingly good grace. Her henchmen were amazed, for previously she had ridden roughshod over all opposition. The answer lay in the fact that she was secretly in love with Santos Luzardo and hoped eventually to inspire his love (and acquire his property) by her beauty.

As the weeks of ranch routine passed, Santos was glad that he had brought Marisela to his house, for his efforts to teach her culture kept him from losing touch with civilization. Although his interest in her was only that of a friend and tutor, Marisela had fallen in love with him.

Along the Arauca River, there were thousands of herons. When the birds molted, the people of Altamira went out to collect the valuable plumes; fifty pounds of the feathers were sent to market with two of the cowboys, and Santos intended to use the money from the sale to fence his boundaries. On their way to market, the cowboys were murdered and the feathers stolen. Their loss and the failure of the authorities to track down the culprit caused a great change in Santos. He determined to take the law into his own hands and when necessary to match violence with violence.

His first act was to have three of Doña Bárbara's henchmen captured and sent to prison, for they had long been wanted for a number of crimes. A short time later, he received word from Doña Bárbara, who was torn between her love for him and her wish for power. She told him that in a certain canyon he would find the thief who had taken the feathers. Santos went there in the night and killed the Wizard, Doña Bárbara's most trusted and bloodthirsty henchman.

By this time, Don Balbino, Doña Bárbara's lover, had become distasteful to her. She had him killed after discovering that it was he who had stolen the feathers, and, to aid Santos, she threw the blame of the Wizard's murder on Don Balbino. Having recovered the feathers, Doña Bárbara went to town to sell them for Santos. At the same time, she had documents made out to transfer the disputed lands to their rightful owner. When she returned to her ranch, she found that her people had deserted her; they could not understand why she had turned on her trusted killers. Doña Bárbara rode immediately to Altamira, where she found Santos talking to Marisela, whose father had recently died. Because the girl's love for Santos showed plainly on her face, Doña Bárbara, unseen, drew her revolver to kill her daughter. Her own love for Santos prevented the deed, however, and she rode away without revealing her presence.

Doña Bárbara was not heard from again. The next day, a large envelope was delivered to Santos. In it, he found a sheaf of documents returning the property she had stolen from him, and others transferring the Barquero ranch to Doña Bárbara's daughter, Marisela. Shortly afterward, Santos and Marisela were married, and the two ranches that had been separated for many years were once again joined under one owner.

Critical Evaluation:

Doña Bárbara is the novel of the *llanos*, the tropical grassland bordering the Orinoco River in the center of Venezuela, a republic almost as large as America's Southwest. The llanos had once supplied the cavalry that filled General Simon Bolívar's revolutionary army's ranks, giving it victory over Spain's Royalist armies during Venezuela's War of Independence from Spain. Next to the geography itself, the ranchwoman Doña Bárbara, who symbolizes barbarism, is the most clearly etched character, for she is a wild, dreadful, beautiful half-breed from beyond the remotest tributaries of the Orinoco. Her very name reeks of barbarism. Opposite her is Santos Luzardo, who symbolizes the civilizing energy that is trying to penetrate the llanos' savagery and tame it.

Rómulo Gallegos uses symbols for barbarism, such as the great *tolvaneras*, or whirlwinds, that periodically flay the llanos. There are also rampaging herds of horses and steers; a midnight-black stallion as savage as Satan before Santos Luzardo tames him; the power of flowing rivers and currents; a fire that scorches the plains and leaves a swath of blackened embers behind; and, evoking the violent spirit of the llanos, the llanero horsemen who threaten to destroy any tendrils of civilization that come within reach. Gallegos describes the area's beauties—the flowers, sunset tints, breezes, white clouds, rains, and pink herons—but ever lurking in the background is the malaria that earlier had nearly depopulated the llanos and had caused the region's inexorable decline.

To some extent, Gallegos uses standard characterizations, but he gives sensitive depictions of the llanero, or cowboy; the boatmen of the Arauca River; the typical military officials and ranch owners; and the itinerant and sometimes rascally Syrian peddlers. Some of Gallegos' sociological types are presented as clearly as if they inhabited an animated museum. Possibly his only near caricature is Señor Danger, a one-dimensional villain intended to represent the Yankee rascal of so many Spanish American novels.

Gallegos develops his plot logically. The book combines interesting subject matter and the author's knowledge of Venezuela to produce a near masterpiece. Gallegos does not exaggerate the human cruelty, his realism is convincing, and there are few distortions. The author did not, however, provide an in-depth study of the range of the llanos' society, and the novel is thus limited at times by an unconscious social prejudice and a certain superficiality. Yet most of the characters do come alive in the book and are not likely to be forgotten by the reader, for they develop and change subtly but gradually.

The basic themes of *Doña Bárbara* are universal ones. Civilization against barbarism is as dominant a theme here as in Domingo Faustino Sarmiento's *Facundo* (1845), the masterpiece of Argentine literature. Also present are such opposing forces as humans against nature, female against male, cruelty against kindness, justice against oppression, and freedom against bureaucracy.

Doña Bárbara is rich in Venezuelan expressions, idioms, and flavor of speech. Gallegos' style moves effortlessly, without excess words or structural disorganization. *Doña Bárbara*, like other Venezuelan novels, exposed and spotlighted national ills. Reform was aided by such writings but was still slow, even after Gallegos himself became president. The author was apparently not strong enough or perhaps lacked enough political acumen to accomplish what was accomplished in the nineteenth century by Argentina's two literary presidents, Bartolome Mitre and Domingo Sarmiento, who were men of action as well as of the pen.

Gallegos' *Doña Bárbara* nevertheless, represents a fine example of that important feature of Venezuelan and Latin American progress—the novel. The broadest and least restricted literary form, mirroring as it does society's ills, the novel is a supple tool in the hands of reformers such as Rómulo Gallegos, who are brave enough to risk political persecution for their writings.

"Critical Evaluation" by William Freitas

Bibliography:
Alonso, Carlos J. "'Otra sería mi historia': Allegorical Exhaustion in *Doña Bárbara*." *Modern Language Notes* 104 (March, 1989): 418-438. Examines symbolic figures and the presence of allegorical constructions in Gallegos' novel.
Amaral, José Vázquez. "Rómulo Gallegos and the Drama of Civilization on the South American Plains: *Doña Bárbara*." In *The Contemporary Latin American Narrative*. New York: Las Américas Publishing, 1970. Discusses the social background of the characters and provides information about the locale and how Gallegos used it in the development of his plot.
Brushwood, John S. "The Year of Doña Bárbara (1929)." In *The Spanish American Novel: A Twentieth Century Survey*. Austin: University of Texas Press, 1975. Analyzes the novel's characterization and narrative techniques, and situates *Doña Bárbara* in the development of the Spanish American novel.
Englekirk, John E. "*Doña Bárbara*, Legend of the Llano." *Hispania* 31, no. 3 (August, 1948): 259-270. Explains the actual terrain of the novel and compares the real characters with their fictitious counterparts.
Spell, Jefferson Rea. "Rómulo Gallegos, Interpreter of the Llanos of Venezuela." In *Contemporary Spanish-American Fiction*. New York: Biblo and Tannen, 1968. An excellent starting point for a study of *Doña Bárbara*. Discusses the novel's depiction of the struggle between civilization and barbarism.

DOÑA PERFECTA

Type of work: Novel
Author: Benito Pérez Galdós (1843-1920)
Type of plot: Tragedy
Time of plot: Late nineteenth century
Locale: Orbajosa, Spain
First published: 1876 (English translation, 1880)

> *Principal characters:*
> JOSÉ (PEPE) REY
> DOÑA PERFECTA REY, his aunt
> ROSARIO, her daughter
> DON INOCENCIO, the canon of the cathedral
> MARIA REMEDIOS, his sister
> JACINTO, María's son

The Story:

The city of Orbajosa, with its 7,324 inhabitants, was proud of its religious atmosphere. It boasted a cathedral and a seminary but possessed nothing else to make it known to the rest of Spain, having no manufacturing. Its only agricultural activity was the raising of garlic. The leading citizen of Orbajosa was Doña Perfecta Rey, a widow whose wealth was the result of legal victories her brother, an Andalusian lawyer, had won over her husband's family. Since her brother had a son, Pepe Rey, and she had a daughter, Rosario, the idea of marriage between the two young people seemed a natural arrangement to their elders. It was for this purpose that Pepe was first sent to Orbajosa.

In his busy life as a road construction engineer, Pepe had thought little about matrimony, but he began to do so after seeing the lovely Rosario. The girl, for her part, was attracted to her cousin, and in the beginning Doña Perfecta too was much taken with Pepe.

Doña Perfecta, like the other inhabitants of Orbajosa, was dominated by the Church, and as the town's most exemplary citizen she felt it necessary to be especially devout. Don Inocencio, the canon of the cathedral, had other plans for Rosario. Urged on by his sister, María Remedios, who wanted the Rey fortune for her son, Jacinto, Don Inocencio, who was far less innocent than his name implied, began conniving to end all talk of marriage between the cousins.

Pepe, through his wide travels and training, was unorthodox, though not without regard for religion. Before long, Don Inocencio made him appear a heretic, and Doña Perfecta, forgetting her indebtedness to his father and ignoring the feelings of her daughter, refused to let him see Rosario. The girl, made meek by strict education and dominated by her mother, lacked the courage to assert herself in declaring her love for her cousin. Soon everyone in Orbajosa—from the bishop to the working man in the fields—became convinced that it was a matter of religious and civic necessity to rid their city of the heretic. The unsuspecting Pepe tried to explain that he had no intention of attacking religion, but his attempts to make his position clear only made matters worse.

Finally, after several stolen interviews with Rosario in the family chapel, Pepe and Rosario decided to run away together. At the very time, however, that the conscience-stricken Rosario was revealing the plan to her mother, María Remedios arrived to warn Doña Perfecta that Pepe was entering the garden. Knowing that Pepe was coming to take Rosario away, Doña Perfecta ordered one of her acquaintances to shoot. Pepe fell, mortally wounded. His death drove Rosario insane. Don Inocencio felt himself cut off from the world, and Doña Perfecta died of cancer. Nobody gained anything, but Orbajosa was convinced it had won a victory for the faith.

Critical Evaluation:

Benito Pérez Galdós went to Madrid as a student of law in 1863, but literature and the theater proved more interesting to him than the bar. Early in his literary career, he wrote several novels about politics and social customs. Then, between 1875 and 1878, Pérez Galdós became interested in religion and published three novels dealing with its different aspects: *Doña Perfecta*, the story of a town dominated by the clergy; *Gloria* (1876-1877), a novel about a clash between the Jewish and Christian religions; and *La Familia de Leon Roch* (1878), a story of religious fanaticism that ruined a happy household. All three novels are classified as belonging to the novelist's early period, although they represent a great technical advance over his first attempts.

In *Doña Perfecta*, Pérez Galdós portrays religious intolerance and hypocrisy in a small Andalusian cathedral town removed from the main current of life. The novel graphically presents what Gerald Brennan labeled "the stagnant, stupid, fanatical Spain of the country districts." Pérez Galdós also describes the clash of modern ideas against the walls of bigotry and prejudice. Representative of the new order is the scientifically trained, clear-thinking, outspoken bridge builder Pepe. The old is represented by a wealthy woman so fanatically religious that to save her daughter's immortal soul she would even condone murder.

The shadow of intolerant Doña Perfecta hovers darkly over Orbajosa, just as the cathedral looms over plaza and town. The human beings in the cathedral make it a somber place rather than the mellow, beautiful, hope-inspiring temple of God it could be. Far from attacking religion itself, Pérez Galdós' purpose in writing *Doña Perfecta* is to reform religion. He criticizes Catholicism for its faults but acknowledges that it had once given robust, rural Spain its strength. Pérez Galdós champions the cause of progress while condemning the abuses of traditionalism, although he is aware that traditionalism could be a life-giving flame.

The novel's characterization is thinner than it is in the author's later works. Father Inocencio clearly symbolizes one of the many types of rural priests of his time, but other characters are not depicted with finesse. Character motivations are also vague at times, and gorgonlike Doña Perfecta herself is one of Pérez Galdós' weaker female characterizations. The characters are not strongly etched because Pérez Galdós viewed them not as individuals but as representatives of their class or profession. Atmosphere and setting are stressed for the same reason. An important element in *Doña Perfecta* is Pepe's hope that human beings can be led upward by education. Pepe Rey thus reflects the views of nineteenth century Spanish intellectual thought that had influenced the author, and as such he is more realistically drawn than many of the other characters in the novel.

Bibliography:

Cardwell, Richard A. "Galdós' *Doña Perfecta*: Art or Argument?" *Anales Galdosianos* 7 (1972): 29-47. Discusses and questions the idea of the work as a "thesis novel." Focuses on whether Pepe Rey is a liberal martyr to a progressive ideal in a backward rural society.

Eoff, Sherman. *The Novels of Pérez Galdós. The Concept of Life as Dynamic Process.* St. Louis, Mo.: Washington University, 1954. A study of the structure of Pérez Galdós' novels. Includes one small chapter devoted to *Doña Perfecta*.

Shoemaker, William H. *The Novelistic Art of Galdós.* 2 vols. Valencia, Spain: Albatros Hispanofila, 1980-1987. Volume 1 provides a broad literary critique of Pérez Galdós' novels in their entirety. Volume 2 discusses each of the novels in turn, giving an overall critique of the specific works, including structure, style, symbolism, and critical consensus.

Varey, J. E. *Doña Perfecta.* London: Grant & Cutler, 1971. A good critical introduction to the novel. Includes a discussion of the novel's situation and character as well as its social, moral, and political aspects. One chapter is devoted to the stylistic features of the novel.

Zahareas, Anthony N. "Galdós' *Doña Perfecta*: Fiction, History, and Ideology." *Anales Galdosianos* 11 (1976): 29-58. Focuses on the identification of certain moments in the history of Spain during the nineteenth century that might be related to Pérez Galdós' fictional events. An interesting and enlightening study.

THE DOUBLE-DEALER

Type of work: Drama
Author: William Congreve (1670-1729)
Type of plot: Comedy
Time of plot: Seventeenth century
Locale: London
First performed: 1693; first published, 1694

Principal characters:
MELLEFONT, an earnest young man
LORD and LADY TOUCHWOOD, his uncle and aunt
CYNTHIA, his sweetheart
MASKWELL, his false friend

The Story:

Lady Touchwood was infatuated with her husband's nephew, Mellefont, and confessed her ardor to him. Mellefont, who had pledged himself to Cynthia, daughter of Sir Paul Plyant, rebuked Lady Touchwood, whereupon she attempted to end her life with his sword. When he prevented her in the attempt, she vowed revenge. Fearing the designs of Lady Touchwood, Mellefont engaged his friend Careless to keep Lady Plyant, Cynthia's stepmother, away from Lady Touchwood. Careless revealed his distrust of Maskwell, Mellefont's friend, who was under obligations to Lord Touchwood. Out of sheer spite, Lady Touchwood gave herself to Maskwell. In return, Maskwell promised to help Lady Touchwood by insinuating to Lady Plyant that Mellefont really loved her, not her stepdaughter Cynthia.

Lady Touchwood's plan began to work. Old Sir Paul Plyant and Lady Plyant expressed indignation when they were told that Mellefont desired Lady Plyant. Actually, Lady Plyant was flattered and merely pretended anger, but she was nevertheless shocked that Mellefont intended to marry Cynthia for the ultimate purpose of cuckolding Sir Paul. She rebuked him but at the same time told the puzzled young man not to despair. Maskwell revealed to Mellefont that he was Lady Touchwood's agent in provoking trouble, but he did not reveal his real purpose, which was to create general confusion and to win Cynthia's hand.

Lord Touchwood, refusing to believe that his nephew played a double game, was scandalized when Lady Touchwood recommended canceling the marriage on the grounds that Mellefont had made improper advances to her. Maskwell, instructed by Lady Touchwood, ingratiated himself with Lord Touchwood by saying that he had defended Lady Touchwood's honor and had prevailed on Mellefont to cease his unwelcome attentions.

Maskwell, to further his plans, told Mellefont that his reward for assisting in the breakup of Mellefont's marriage to Cynthia was the privilege of bedding with Lady Touchwood. The fake friend pretended that he wished to be saved from the shame of collecting this reward, and he asked the credulous Mellefont to go to Lady Touchwood's chamber and there surprise him with Lady Touchwood. When Lord Plyant, frustrated by Lady Plyant's vow to remain a virgin, complained to Careless that he did not have an heir, Careless waggishly promised to see what he could do in the matter.

Mellefont, to escape the evil that was brewing, impatiently urged Cynthia to elope with him. Although she refused, she promised to marry no one but him. When she challenged Mellefont to thwart his aunt and to get her approval of their marriage, he promised to get Lady Touchwood's consent that night.

Lady Plyant, meanwhile, had consented to an assignation with Careless. When Lord Plyant appeared, Careless had to give her, secretly, a note containing directions for their meeting. Lady Plyant, anxious to read Careless' letter, asked her husband for a letter that he had received earlier. Pretending to read her husband's letter, she read the one given her by Careless. By mistake she returned her lover's letter to her husband.

When she discovered her mistake, she reported it in alarm to Careless, but Lord Plyant had already read the letter. Lady Plyant insisted that it was part of an insidious plot against her reputation, and after accusing her husband of having arranged to have it written in order to test her fidelity, she threatened divorce. Careless pretended that he had written it in Lord Plyant's behalf to test his wife's virtue. Foolish as he was, Lord Plyant was not without suspicion of his wife and Careless.

That night, Mellefont concealed himself in Lady Touchwood's chamber. When she entered, expecting to find Maskwell, Mellefont revealed himself. Lord Touchwood, informed by Maskwell, then appeared. When he threatened his nephew, Lady Touchwood pretended that the young man was out of his wits. Not suspecting Maskwell's treachery, Lady Touchwood later told him of her lucky escape. Maskwell, in a purposeful soliloquy, revealed to Lord Touchwood his love for Cynthia. Duped, the old man named Maskwell his heir and promised to arrange a marriage between Cynthia and the schemer.

Lady Touchwood learned of Maskwell's treachery when Lord Touchwood told her that he intended to make Maskwell his heir. Chagrined by her betrayal, Lady Touchwood urged her husband never to consent to Cynthia's marriage with anyone but Mellefont.

Maskwell, still pretending to be Mellefont's friend, made his final move by plotting with the unwary Mellefont to get Cynthia away from her house. His intention being to marry her himself, he privately told Cynthia that Mellefont would be waiting for her in the chaplain's chamber. Careless checked Maskwell's carefully laid plans, however, when he disclosed Maskwell's villainy to the young lovers. Cynthia and Lord Touchwood, in concealment, overheard Lady Touchwood rebuke Maskwell for his betrayal of her, and eventually she tried to stab her lover but was overcome with emotion. Maskwell then revealed the meeting place where Mellefont, in the disguise of a parson, would be waiting for Cynthia. Lady Touchwood, planning to disguise herself as Cynthia, hurried away to meet Mellefont there.

Lord Touchwood, knowing of her plan, put on a chaplain's habit and confronted his wife when she came to make overtures to the man she supposed was Mellefont. The whole plot was uncovered and Maskwell, the double-dealer, unmasked; Mellefont, cleared of all suspicion, took Cynthia for his own.

Critical Evaluation:

After the great success of his first comedy, *The Old Bachelor* (1693), William Congreve was disappointed at the poor reception of *The Double-Dealer*, which he considered a better play on a more serious theme. Serious it was; like other contemporary comedies, it satirizes the follies and vices of the time, but here the emphasis is on the vices rather than the follies. An unusual combination of Restoration comedy and Jacobean melodrama, the play's action is largely devoted to the intrigues of the villain Maskwell. Audiences were apparently uncomfortable at being forced to take such a long hard look at Machiavellian treachery and romantic knavery at work. As John Dryden pointed out, "The women think he has exposed their bitchery too much and the gentlemen are offended with him, for the discovery of their follies, and the way of their intrigues, under the notion of friendship to their ladies' husbands." Maskwell, in the depth of his resourceful villainy, is reminiscent of William Shakespeare's Iago, and Lady Touchwood compares him to a devil.

Lady Touchwood, of course, is herself a villain, but, as one of the victims of Maskwell's double-dealing, a lesser one. As she reminds Maskwell, her excuse is "fire in my temper, passion in my soul, apt to every provocation, oppressed at once with love, and with despair. But a sedate, a thinking villain, whose black blood runs temperately bad, what excuse can clear?" Unquestionably, the depiction of burning love turning into burning hatred has seldom been as powerful in a work professing to be a comedy as it is in Congreve's play. Lady Touchwood, indeed, has struck some critics as an almost tragic figure. Other indications of the playwright's striving for tragic effect are the unusual number of soliloquys and the play's ending with a piece of moralizing, rather than (as was customary for Restoration comedy) a dance.

Because Congreve's focus of attention is on Maskwell, his hero and heroine are given relatively short shrift. Mellefont and Cynthia are an agreeable pair of lovers, but no more than that. Cynthia is shown to be sensible and sincere, but she has none of the sparkling wit that was to make Congreve's Millamant so admirable. Nor are there any of the almost obligatory battles of wit between hero and heroine. Indeed, Mellefont appears much of the time to be a passive dupe and a fool, so much so, that Congreve felt obliged to defend his hero from such charges in the play's dedication.

The plot is original; Congreve was proud that "the mechanical part of [the play] is perfect." Consciously trying to incorporate the three unities into a classical form, he succeeded at least in molding a work that has unity of time (the action is continuous, over a three-hour period) and place (it all takes place in one gallery). As for unity of action, the plot is unusually tight, but there are subplots in the form of the cuckolding of Sir Paul Plyant by Careless, and of Lord Froth by Brisk. Indeed, what levity and wit the play has to offer are largely contained in these subplots. The various affectations of the minor characters, the romantic intrigues between the ladies and their gallants, and such brilliantly actable passages as the dialogue between Brisk, Lord Froth, and Careless on whether or not one should laugh at comedies, are ample evidence that Congreve had not forgotten that his prime task as a comic playwright was not to moralize— at least, not overtly—but to entertain.

Bibliography:
Birdsall, Virginia Ogden. *Wild Civility: The English Comic Spirit on the Restoration Stage.* Bloomington: Indiana University Press, 1970. Good introduction to *The Double Dealer* in chapter 7, "Congreve's Apprenticeship." Interprets the play as an exploration of the fate of the gullible in a treacherous world where appearances conceal realities.

Gosse, Anthony. "Plot and Character in Congreve's *Double Dealer*." *Modern Language Quarterly* 29 (1968): 274-288. Useful overview of the play's history, characters, and structure. Claims it was unpopular because it targeted early audiences instead of "some safe outside target, such as the cuckolded cit or booby country squire."

Hoffman, Arthur W. *Congreve's Comedies*. Victoria, B.C.: University of Victoria, 1993. Stimulating discussion in chapter 2, "The Pessimism of Comedy: *The Double Dealer*," includes the play's historical background, Dryden's protection, and verbal and structural connections with Shakespeare's *Othello* (1604).

Holland, Norman N. *The First Modern Comedies. The Significance of Etherege, Wycherley and Congreve.* Cambridge, Mass.: Harvard University Press, 1959. Chapter 13 discusses the combination in *The Double Dealer* of a serious plot with comic action. Claims that the play is a failure because the hero (the good but naïve Mellefont) is passive while the villain (the worldly-wise Maskwell) is an active and successful intriguer.

Van Voris, W. H. *The Cultivated Stance. The Designs of Congreve's Plays*. Dublin: Dolmen Press, 1965. Chapter 3 provides a good account of Congreve's imposition of a "mechanically perfect neoclassical order" on the play and a valuable discussion of its characters and political ramifications.

DOWN THERE

Type of work: Novel
Author: Joris-Karl Huysmans (1848-1907)
Type of plot: Fantasy
Time of plot: Late nineteenth century
Locale: Paris
First published: Là-bas, 1891 (English translation, 1924)

Principal characters:
DURTAL, a man of letters
DES HERMIES, a doctor
HYACINTHE CHANTELOUVE, Durtal's mistress
LOUIS CARHAIX, a bellringer
MADAME CARHAIX, his wife
GÉVINGEY, an astrologer

The Story:
Durtal had decided to write a biography of Gilles de Rais, the French marshal briefly associated with Joan of Arc, who had been the subject of a famous sorcery trial in 1430. His friend des Hermies expressed his delight that Durtal was abandoning the realistic novel, but Durtal wanted to apply the methods of modern realism to his task, in spite of the difficulties involved.

Des Hermies took Durtal to the bell tower of a church and introduced him to the bell ringer Louis Carhaix, who had asked to meet him. Carhaix thought he might be useful to Durtal's researches. Durtal described the early part of Gilles de Rais' life to des Hermies, observing that his excessively luxurious lifestyle had alarmed his expectant heirs to petition the king to prevent his selling off parts of the estate. The debts that de Rais subsequently ran up, Durtal opined, caused him to take an interest in the magical arts, by which means he hoped to learn the secret of making gold. After his alchemical experiments had failed, Durtal claimed, de Rais turned to active Satanism and the mass murder of children.

Having heard Durtal's account, des Hermies raised the subject of modern Satanism, and brushed aside Durtal's opinion that there was no such thing, with an assurance that it was rife in contemporary Paris. Durtal thought that it would help his work enormously to be able to study Satanist rites firsthand. Later, at Carhaix's house, des Hermies offered an account of the uninterrupted descent of a Satanist tradition from the time of de Rais to modern times. He then began supplying Durtal with research materials supporting this contention.

Durtal received an admiring letter from a woman who had read his last work of fiction. He replied to it, thus beginning an extensive correspondence that inflamed his curiosity considerably. She used a pseudonym, but he eventually guessed that she might be Hyacinthe Chantelouve, the wife of the historian at whose house he had first met des Hermies. This guess was confirmed when she confronted him in Gilles de Rais' castle, where he had gone to soak up the atmosphere. The two became lovers.

At Carhaix's house des Hermies introduced Durtal to an astrologer named Gévingey, with whom they discussed spiritualism and various other aspects of modern occultism, including the kinds of demon called incubi and succubi. Gévingey named a fallen priest called Canon Docre as an accomplished black magician and suggested that he was an intimate of the Chantelouves. Durtal could not believe at first that his new mistress was a Satanist, but evidence to that effect began to accumulate.

After reviewing the record of Gilles de Rais' supposed atrocities, Durtal went to visit the Chantelouves, where the conversation quickly turned to Satanism and Canon Docre. Durtal's infatuation with Madame Chantelouve was still increasing in intensity, and so was his desire to meet Canon Docre, but he found some distraction in his continuing discussions with des Hermies and Carhaix on various aspects of magic and demonology, including the exploits of a certain Dr. Johannès, who had supposedly freed Gévingey from the evil influence of Docre. He also carried his private account of Gilles de Rais' career forward to the beginning of his trial.

Madame Chantelouve eventually promised to take Durtal to a black mass conducted by Docre. She confessed to having been infatuated with the man at one time. While waiting for the appointed time, Durtal completed his account of the trial of Gilles de Rais, including his lurid confession and extravagant repentance. Madame Chantelouve took him to the place where the black mass was to be held. He watched with interest but found the experience rather disappointing; eventually he had to take Madame Chantelouve away when she seemed to be overcome by the incense that was used. They parted on bad terms.

Durtal described the black mass to des Hermies, Carhaix, and Gévingey, and they discussed its relationship to orthodox religion at some length. Carhaix argued that the prevalence of Satanism was evidence of the decadence and corruption of their society, possibly marking the nearing of its end and the second coming of Christ. Durtal agreed that the world was indeed sick and resolved not to have any further contact with Madame Chantelouve—a decision that she eventually accepted in a bitter letter.

Des Hermies told Durtal more about the virtuous magic of Dr. Johannès and his miraculous cures, but Durtal was as reluctant to credit the power of white magic as he had been to credit the power of black. Des Hermies confessed that he remained skeptical, causing Durtal to express a reluctant envy of Carhaix's faith. At Carhaix's house, Durtal added a brief appendix to his account of Gilles de Rais' career, describing the marshal's execution. The three friends delivered their final verdict on the century that seemed to them all to be moving to a sadly ignominious end as "storm-clouds of foul abomination" gathered on its horizon. Carhaix alone conserved hope for the future in his vision of a magnificent return of the Holy Spirit.

Critical Evaluation:

Down There is more a debate than a novel. In his most famous work, *Against the Grain* (1884), Joris-Karl Huysmans took a flirtatious delight in overturning all conventional evaluations of morality and art in his description of the reclusive Jean Des Esseintes' attempts to live a perfectly decadent life. Durtal is by no means as ambitious a protagonist, and his flirtation with Satanism and Madame Chantelouve is distinctly half-hearted. If Madame Chantelouve is a vampiric succubus—as Durtal briefly suspects—she is not a very effective one.

That is, in the end, the worst charge Durtal brings against Satanism: not that it is evil, but merely that it is inefficient. Its inefficiency is revealed not so much by the fact that Dr. Johannès triumphs over Canon Docre in the war for Gévingey's soul, but by the fact that the visions of grandeur and exoticism that Satanism offers prove in the end to be tawdry. When Durtal finally gets to see the black mass, he finds it sadly lacking in esthetic excitement as well as demonic power; it is not sufficiently impressive to impose itself upon him, and its failure dispels the illusion that briefly binds him to Madame Chantelouve.

Down There was researched as conscientiously by Huysmans as its imaginary biography of

Gilles de Rais was by Durtal, and many commentators have regarded the novel as a *roman à clef*. Paris was full of occultists in Huysmans' time; many of them are cited in the text. Most took their inspiration from the career of Eliphas Lévi (Alphonse Louis Constant), who had successfully posed as a practitioner of the occult arts a generation before. The most famous of these would-be magi was Joséphin Péladan, whose Rosicrucian lodge was loudly advertised in his prolific writings. His writings included a long series of novels railing against the decadence of the age and calling for its renewal by a syncretic faith whose architect he desired to be. That Huysmans ever saw an actual black mass is, however, doubtful; Satanism was then, as it is now and always has been, much more a product of lurid fantasies than the active practices of the unholy.

In all probability, the dull truth of the matter was that Gilles de Rais was innocent of all the charges brought against him. Like other victims of famous sorcery trials, he was framed by his enemies, who used the same vicious slanders to discredit and destroy him as the English had earlier used to discredit and destroy his companion-in-arms, Joan of Arc. Gilles de Rais' trial as a domestic affair, however, and later generations of the French were content to let his conviction stand so that the Church might use it as a terrible example to those who faltered in the faith. The success of *Down There* as a scary story is an ironic testament to the power of the terrorism of the imagination that killed Gilles de Rais.

It is significant that the flights of fancy on which Durtal and his two friends continually embark are forever being brought down to earth by the kindly attentions of Madame Carhaix, who is always bustling around with supplies of good hot food. She, rather than the devout bell ringer, is the novel's paragon of common sense and virtue. Her unobtrusive presence is testimony to the fact that Huysmans never lost touch with reality while he was in pursuit of his obsession of the moment.

The methodology of Durtal's historical research is explicitly modeled on that of Jules Michelet, a historian who attempted to place himself imaginatively in the shoes of the people of past ages. Michelet wrote a book, *La Sorcière* (1862), about the witch hunts and sorcery trials of the Middle Ages in which he put himself into the shoes of accused witches so as to make them into heroic rebels against the tyranny of an autocratic and misogynist Church. These witches elevated their folk medicine into a kind of Satanism in an expression of ideological resistance. Michelet's book thus became the parent of all the modern scholarly fantasies that insist (falsely) that there was a witch cult, although it was misunderstood and misrepresented by the Church. Durtal's conclusion that Gilles de Rais was eventually driven to madness and remorse by the knowledge that there were no further depths of evil to be plumbed is a fantasy similar to Michelet's, arising from the error of putting a thoroughly modern decadent consciousness into a situation in which it does not belong.

As history, therefore, *Down There* is worthless. It was not written as history, however, and ought not to be condemned on that account. As a philosophical novel debating the status and worth of religious faith in the decadent Paris of the 1890's, it is fascinating. It explores extremes of hypothetical faith and possible feeling that no one else had ever treated with such scrupulousness. As a record of Satanism it is completely unreliable, but it remains a remarkably intense examination of the possible utility of Satanism as creed and ritual. Its conclusion—that Satanism can never be anything but a hollow sham, incapable of delivering any kind of aesthetic or material gratification—is surely secure, no matter how convoluted the argument was that led Durtal to its achievement.

Brian Stableford

Bibliography:
Baldick, Robert. *The Life of J.-K. Huysmans*. Oxford, England: Clarendon Press, 1955. A useful biography, which sets *Down There* in the context of Huysmans' own explorations of the occult.

Birkett, Jennifer. *The Sins of the Fathers: Decadence in France 1870-1914*. London: Quartet Books, 1986. A useful study of the Decadent movement. Part 2, chapter 1 discusses Huysmans' work.

Brandreth, Henry R. T. *Huysmans*. London: Bowes & Bowes, 1963. A biographical and critical study. *Down There* is discussed in chapter 4, "The Devil with His Hooked Claw."

Carter, A. E. *The Idea of Decadence in French Literature 1830-1900*. Toronto: University of Toronto Press, 1958. One chapter, "*Fin-de-Siècle*," includes a discussion of *Down There* and its relationship to other works of the period.

Lloyd, Christopher. *J.-K. Huysmans and the Fin-de-Siècle Novel*. Edinburgh: Edinburgh University Press, 1990. *Down There* is discussed in terms of its relevance to all four of the book's thematic headings: "Words," "Women," "Monsters," and "Magic."

DRACULA

Type of work: Novel
Author: Bram Stoker (1847-1912)
Type of plot: Horror
Time of plot: Late nineteenth century
Locale: Transylvania and England
First published: 1897

Principal characters:
JONATHAN HARKER, an English solicitor
MINA MURRAY, his fiancée
COUNT DRACULA, a mysterious nobleman
DR. JOHN SEWARD, the director of a sanatorium for the mentally ill
DR. ABRAHAM VAN HELSING, a Dutch medical specialist
LUCY WESTENRA, Mina's friend
ARTHUR HOLMWOOD, Lucy's fiancé

The Story:

On his way to Castle Dracula in the province of Transylvania (in what is now Romania), Jonathan Harker, an English solicitor, was apprehensive. His nervousness grew when he observed the curious, fearful attitude of the peasants and the coachman after they learned of his destination. He was on his way to transact business with Count Dracula, and his mission would necessitate remaining at the castle for several days.

Upon his arrival at the castle, Harker found comfortable accommodations awaiting him. Count Dracula was a charming host, although his peculiarly bloodless physical appearance was somewhat disagreeable to Harker's English eyes. Almost immediately, Harker was impressed with the strange life of the castle. He and the Count discussed their business at night, as the Count was never available during the daytime. Although the food was excellent, Harker never saw a servant about the place. While exploring the castle, he found that it was situated high at the top of a mountain with no accessible exit other than the main doorway, which was kept locked. He realized with a shock that he was a prisoner of Count Dracula.

Various harrowing experiences ensued. When Harker secretly explored one of the rooms in the castle, three phantom women materialized and attacked him, attempting to bite his throat. Then the Count appeared and drove them off, whispering fiercely that Harker belonged to him. Later, Harker thought he saw a huge bat descending the castle walls, but the creature turned out to be Count Dracula. In the morning, trying frantically to escape, Harker stumbled into an old chapel where a number of coffinlike boxes of earth were stored. He opened one and saw the Count lying there, apparently dead. In the evening, when the Count appeared as usual, Harker demanded that he be released. The Count obligingly opened the castle door. A pack of wolves surrounded the entrance. The Count laughed maliciously. The next day Harker, weak and sick from a strange wound in his throat, saw a pack cart loaded with the mysterious boxes drive from the castle. Dracula had departed and Harker was alone, a prisoner with no visible means of escape.

Meanwhile, in England, Harker's fiancée, Mina Murray, had gone to visit her beautiful and charming friend, Lucy Westenra. Lucy was planning to marry Arthur Holmwood, a young nobleman. One evening, early in Mina's visit, a storm blew up and a strange ship was driven aground. The only living creature aboard was a gray wolflike dog, which escaped into the countryside. Soon afterward, Lucy's happiness began to fade because of a growing tendency to sleepwalk. One night, Mina followed her friend during one of these spells and discovered Lucy in a churchyard. A tall, thin man who was bending over Lucy disappeared at Mina's approach. Lucy could remember nothing of the experience when she awoke, but her physical condition seemed much weakened. Finally, she grew so ill that Mina was forced to call upon Dr. Seward, Lucy's former suitor. Lucy began to improve under his care, and when Mina received a report from Budapest that her missing fiancé had been found and needed care, she felt free to end her visit.

When Lucy's condition suddenly grew worse, Dr. Seward asked his old friend Dr. Van Helsing, a specialist from Amsterdam, for his professional opinion. Examining Lucy thoroughly, Van Helsing paused over two tiny throat wounds that she was unable to explain. Van Helsing was concerned over Lucy's condition, which pointed to unusual loss of blood without signs of anemia or hemorrhage. She was given blood transfusions at intervals, and someone sat up with her at night. She improved but expressed fear of going to sleep because her dreams had grown so horrible.

One morning, Dr. Seward fell asleep outside her door. When he and Van Helsing entered her room, they found Lucy ashen white and weaker than ever. Van Helsing quickly performed another transfusion and she rallied, but not as satisfactorily as before. Van Helsing then secured some garlic flowers and told Lucy to keep them around her neck at night. When the two doctors called the next morning, they discovered that Lucy's mother had removed the flowers because she feared their odor might bother her daughter. Frantically, Van Helsing rushed to Lucy's room and found her in a coma. Again he administered a transfusion, and again her condition improved. She said that with the garlic flowers close by she was not afraid of nightly flapping noises at her window. Van Helsing sat with her every night until he thought her well enough to leave. After cautioning her to sleep with the garlic flowers about her neck at all times, he returned to Amsterdam.

Lucy's mother continued to sleep with her daughter. One night, the two ladies were awakened by a huge wolf that had crashed through the window. Mrs. Westenra fell dead of a heart attack, and Lucy fainted, the wreath of garlic flowers slipping from her neck. Seward and Van Helsing, who had returned to England, discovered her half dead in the morning. They knew she was dying and called Arthur. As Arthur attempted to kiss her, Lucy's teeth seemed about to fasten onto his throat. Van Helsing drew him away. When Lucy died, Van Helsing put a tiny gold crucifix over her mouth, but an attendant stole it from her body.

Soon after Lucy's death, several children of the neighborhood were discovered far from their homes, their throats marked by small wounds. Their only explanation was that they had followed a pretty lady. When Jonathan Harker returned to England, Van Helsing went to see him and Mina. After talking with Harker, Van Helsing revealed to Dr. Seward his belief that Lucy had fallen victim to a vampire, one of those strange creatures who can live for centuries on the blood of their victims and breed their kind by attacking the innocent and making them vampires in turn. According to Van Helsing, the only way to save Lucy's soul was to drive a stake through the heart of her corpse, cut off her head, and stuff her mouth with garlic flowers. Dr. Seward protested violently. The next midnight Arthur, Dr. Seward, and Van Helsing visited Lucy's tomb and found it empty, but after Lucy returned the next morning, they did as Van Helsing had suggested with Lucy's corpse.

With Mina's help, Seward and Van Helsing thereupon tried to track down Dracula in London, hoping to find him before he victimized anyone else. They decided their best chance lay in removing the boxes of sterilized earth he had brought with him from Transylvania, in which he hid during the daytime. They finally trapped Dracula, but he escaped them. Before fleeing England, however, Dracula attacked Mina and promised that he would exact his revenge through her. Van Helsing put Mina into a trance and learned that Dracula was at sea and that it would be necessary to follow him to his castle. Wolves gathered about them in that desolate country. Van Helsing drew a circle in the snow with a crucifix, and the travelers rested safely within the magic enclosure. The next morning, they overtook a cart carrying a black box. Van Helsing and the others overcame the drivers of the cart and pried open the lid of Dracula's coffin. As the sun began to set, they drove a stake through the heart of the corpse. The vampire was no more and Mina was free.

Critical Evaluation:

With his horror novel *Dracula*, Bram Stoker created a work that became something of a symbol for twentieth century society and that, perhaps unlike any other, spawned a range of publications, plays, and motion pictures. The image of the vampire of course dates back several thousand years, but Stoker recast the legend in a conventionally Western tradition and provided it with an aura of dark Romanticism reminiscent of John Polidori's *The Vampyre* (1819) and of the voluptuous whisperings of Sheridan Le Fanu's *Carmilla* (1871). Stoker's novel combined the basic ingredients of the classical horror story with the author's personal experiences and inspiration.

The main character in *Dracula* is based on the historical figure of Vlad Tepes the Impaler, a fifteenth century Walachian prince who ruled Transylvania and Walachia (now Romania) and earned a bloody reputation by spearing domestic criminals and foreign invaders on wooden sticks. He assumed the name Dracula, variously interpreted as "son of the dragon" and "son of the devil," as a further reminder of his powers.

Stoker's book deals with a number of more universal themes as well, including the loneliness of death, the endless allure of erotic love, and an unnerving invocation of insanity. The author, a dreamy visionary with seemingly two sides to his nature, transfers aspects of the hate-love relationship of the vampire state to personal relationships between his characters. That lends a sexually charged underpinning to much of the narrative and creates some of the most gruesome and powerful scenes in the history of the horror novel. Stoker not only employed a series of firsthand accounts (such as diaries, journals, newspaper clippings, and other documents) to tell the story—thus returning to the epistolary technique introduced some years earlier by Wilkie Collins—he also fused several different viewpoints in the narrative. In part because he had little time at his disposal and had to write rapidly, and in part because of the Victorian cultural milieu, he lent a somewhat trite sentimentality to many sections of the book. Fortunately, however, the first few chapters of *Dracula* create a charged atmosphere of suspense that sustains the reader's interest throughout. Stoker also took great care to interlace the narrative elements of the plot; every detail counts and hardly anything is superfluous. Although he relies heavily on direct testimonials, this device also possesses the virtue of imparting an immediate and believable effect. At the time the book was published, reviewers could well still have classified *Dracula* as a traditional gothic horror story because of ingredients such as ships lost at sea, mysterious castles, and vaults resounding with the patter of rats' feet. What is unusual about this novel is the way Stoker treats his themes, the ambiguities in which he cloaks his vampire, and his use of forceful symbolism. *Dracula* has a mysterious and sinister atmosphere heightened by the narrative momentum of the vampire's actions. Stoker offers his readers neither unnameable horrors nor the kind of a rationalistic approach that might keep them from succumbing to the supernatural; rather, he concocts a suave combination of the two laced with subtle undertones of cold fear. Yet he clearly knows how to resort to nightmare horror when the occasion calls for it. Like a true horror writer, he paints with bold and deliberate strokes and as a result creates remarkable and brilliant images. For most of his life, he was deeply involved in theatrical management, and very likely his intimacy with the stage was at least partially responsible for his style. The "big" scenes are elaborate and there is a dramatic flair to almost every incident. Although Stoker had not originally thought of converting his book into a drama—the only play version given during his lifetime was done for copyright purposes—the blatant melodrama of many of the scenes cries out for stage realization. Most of Dracula's speeches to Harker, for example, are brilliantly dynamic (and have actually been put to good effect by many a film-maker). Just as effective are the tableaux framed in time, for example the moment when a small band awaits the coming of the Count in Piccadilly or watches Dracula's coffin being driven to his castle. The suspense created by these moments in slow motion is quickly relieved by the almost lightning sequence of events that tends to follow.

Stoker was never taken quite seriously as a novelist, at least not during his lifetime. Perhaps the main accusation against him was that of being a second-rate writer who churned out books and did not seem interested in refining his style. It is nevertheless his achievement that his readers are able to visualize every one of his terrifying details clearly. His blood allegory gathers to itself a host of meanings and a chilling atmosphere in which the most ordinary circumstances begin slipping into the realm of nightmare. It is precisely this ever-mounting anticipation, reeking with primordial awakenings, that creates the special style of *Dracula*. Here we are no longer dealing with a receptacle for ingenious devices of terror but with a battleground for searing issues of the body and the soul.

"Critical Evaluation" by Kathryn Dorothy Marocchino

Bibliography:

Carter, Margaret L., ed. *Dracula: The Vampire and the Critics*. Ann Arbor, Mich.: UMI Research Press, 1988. Part of the Studies in Speculative Fiction series, this work examines some of the major critical interpretations of *Dracula*.

Leatherdale, Clive. *Dracula, the Novel and the Legend: A Study of Bram Stoker's Gothic Masterpiece*. Wellingborough, England: Aquarian Press, 1985. An excellent critical study, which offers interpretation of perspectives in *Dracula* including sexual symbolism, religious themes, occult and literary myth, and political and social allegory.

Roth, Phyllis A. *Bram Stoker*. Boston: Twayne, 1982. One of the volumes in Twayne's English Authors Series, this book deals with both Stoker's life and his works. Contains an extensive chapter on *Dracula*.

Senf, Carol A., ed. *The Critical Response to Bram Stoker*. Westport, Conn.: Greenwood Press, 1994. An anthology of some of the more interesting critiques of *Dracula* from a scholarly point of view.

Stoker, Bram. *The Essential "Dracula."* Edited by Leonard Woolf and revised in collaboration with Roxana Stuart. Rev. ed. New York: Plume, 1993. Includes the original complete text of *Dracula* with notes, an introductory essay, a selected filmography of major vampire films, commentary by leading horror writers, and new illustrations by Christopher Bing. Also features an extensive bibliography.

DRAGON SEED

Type of work: Novel
Author: Pearl S. Buck (1892-1973)
Type of plot: Social realism
Time of plot: 1937-1945
Locale: China
First published: 1942

Principal characters:
LING TAN, a farmer
LING SAO, his wife
LAO TA, the eldest son
LAO ER, the second son
LAO SAN, the youngest son
PANSIAO, the daughter
ORCHID, Lao Ta's wife
JADE, Lao Er's wife
WU LIEN, The Lings' son-in-law, a city shopkeeper
MAYLI, a repatriated mission teacher

The Story:
Ling Tan and his family all lived together on their ancestral farm. In addition to Ling Tan and his wife, Ling Sao, there were three sons and a daughter. Lao Ta, one of the sons, and his wife, Orchid, had two children. Lao Er, another son, and his wife, Jade, had not been married long.

While Orchid was the conventional wife and daughter-in-law, Lao Er's wife, Jade, was different. She revealed to her husband that she wanted more than what was given and wanted to be more than what was expected of a woman. Lao Er was wise enough to realize that his strong-willed, intelligent, thoughtful wife was more blessing than encumbrance and promised that on his next visit to the city he would buy her a book, something no one else in his household had held.

In the city, Lao Er visited his older sister and her husband Wu Lien. Wu Lien was a shopkeeper, and while Lao Er was visiting, students came to the shop and destroyed all the foreign merchandise. They called Wu Lien a traitor. This was one of the earliest indications to the Ling family of the impending Japanese invasion and occupation.

One day Ling Tan was working in his fields when the first Japanese warplanes arrived. They flew over the Lings' village on the way to the city. The Lings were naïve enough not to know what had happened until that night, when We Lien brought his entire household with him, seeking refuge. His shop had been gutted by a bomb and much of the city had also been wrecked.

Ling Tan and Lao San went into the city to see the devastation for themselves, and they were caught in an air raid. When Ling Tan gathered his family and asked them what they should all do to resist the enemy, Jade and Lao Er announced their wish to flee inland to join the resistance movement. Jade was now also carrying their first child. It was decided that while Jade and Lao Er were away the rest of the family would stay and hold on to their land as best as they could.

Streams of refugees passed through the village on their way west, and firsthand accounts of

Japanese atrocities prepared Ling Tan and his fellow villagers for what they would have to do when the Japanese came. With the city in ruins and with the last of the Chinese army fled to the hills, the Japanese marched into the area. A marauding group came to the Lings' village looking for wine and women. Ling Tan sent his family to the fields. Wu Lien's mother, however, was not able to escape in time. She was raped and killed. The house was ransacked.

Ling Tan brought all the women and children in his family to the relative safety of the white missionary woman's compound. He and his sons remained on the farm. The Japanese returned, and finding no women in the Ling home, gang-raped the sixteen-year-old Lao San. Filled with hatred, Lao San left to join the resistance fighters in the hills.

Meanwhile, Wu Lien did not stay on the farm. He went back to the city to see what he could salvage of his shop and to see if he could do business with the enemy. Ingratiating himself with the conquerors, Wu Lien was appointed to a post in the new city government. He and his wife and children were then installed in generous quarters provided by the Japanese.

Tired of the monotony in the mission and curious about the new order in the city, Orchid ventured into the city. She was set upon by soldiers, raped, and killed. Ling Sao did not want to stay in the mission any more. Ling Tan came for her and the two children of Lao Ta and Orchid. Pansiao, however, they left in the care of the missionary woman, who promised to send her westward to safety and schooling.

The Lings received news of the birth of Lao Er and Jade's son. Not long after typhoid hit the village, and Lao Ta's two children were killed. Devastated, Lao Ta went to the hills too. Ling Tan and Ling Sao sent word to Lao Er and Jade to ask them to return. Ling Tan and Ling Sao started digging a secret cellar. Ling Tan had continued to work his land. The Japanese now controlled the lands and demanded most of the harvests. As the Lings' cellar grew, they could hide more of their harvests. Digging and expanding the cellar became a daily mission. When Lao Er and Jade and their baby arrived, they could be hidden underground.

With Lao Er and Jade's return, the cellar became large enough for the Ling home to become the village base for the hills resistance movement. Arms were smuggled in from the hills and stored in the cellar. All three Ling sons were now actively involved in resistance activities. Ling Tan and the other villagers also did their share. They now had the means with which to fight. Whenever they thought they could get away with it, they killed the Japanese soldiers who came to the village, carefully hiding the bodies.

With the war, Lao San had come into his own. Previously frail and innocent, he had now become a fighter and a ruthless killer. Ling Tan felt that his son needed a wife to tame him. Through Jade, he wrote to Pansiao to ask her to find her brother a wife from among the women at the mission. Pansiao set her sights on the beautiful and spirited MayLi, who had returned from abroad and was teaching in her native country. MayLi was intrigued by what Pansiao had told her of Lao San. MayLi left the mission and found her way to the Ling village. She and Lao San were attracted to each other.

After all the devastation through the years, Ling Tan's family was on the rebound. Lao Ta came home with a new wife. Lao Er and Jade had twin boys. Pansiao, although not at home, was safe and receiving an education. There was hope that Lao San would regain the humanity he had lost. He had gone inland in pursuit of MayLi.

The occupation continued and the hardships continued for Ling Tan and his family. Steadfastly holding on to his land over the years, Ling Tan had also held on to hope, but he seemed to be losing the latter. Lao Er brought him into the city to listen to the illegal radio broadcast. They heard that China was not alone anymore in fighting the Japanese. They heard that England and the United States were now fighting on their side. Ling Tan wept for joy.

Critical Evaluation:

Dragon Seed is set in the early years of World War II. More specifically, however, though the Japanese invasion of and occupation of China roughly paralleled the war years in Europe and the Pacific, the war specific to China is called the Second Sino-Japanese War. *Dragon Seed* is a chronicle of the war as experienced by the Chinese, in particular the peasants. Their country was conquered and overrun by the Japanese.

Pearl S. Buck, the first American woman to win, in 1938, the Nobel Prize in Literature, is best known for *The Good Earth* (1931). Like *The Good Earth* and many of her other novels, *Dragon Seed* is set in China, where Buck spent much of her early years with her missionary parents. Buck may perhaps be credited with introducing to the American reading public Chinese characters who were more than the figures of ridicule or contempt that had been evident in American fiction. There were a few writers who had written about Chinese or Chinese Americans prior to Buck, but Buck was the first to reach a wide audience.

It is important to note the time in which *Dragon Seed* was published. The United States had recently entered World War II, and on the Pacific front it was, with China, allied against the Japanese. It is debatable whether *Dragon Seed* was intended as propaganda, because Buck had already written extensively about China and the Chinese people. It would seem, however, that in China's war against the Japanese, Buck served to help the Chinese cause. The war novel label that is often attached to *Dragon Seed*, however, must be considered in at least two other contexts. One is the United States' own propaganda war against the Japanese of which Buck had little choice but to become part. The other is the war against Americans of Chinese ancestry that had lasted sixty years—the Chinese Exclusion Act of 1882, for example, which among other things prohibited the naturalization of Chinese as Americans, was not to be repealed until December, 1943. By default if not by design, the novel is part of these historical contexts.

The novel chronicles one family's struggles against the oppression of a foreign invader. The village and the city in which most of the action takes place are not named; the Ling family can be seen as the symbolic representative of a society built upon the unfailing unity of the family unit. In a time when all the major cities had fallen to the enemy, when the Chinese army was defeated in battle after battle, the rural family, in a country peopled primarily by rural families, seemed to be the last bastion of Chinese resistance.

The main characters are not one-dimensional, but Buck seems so intent on their struggle that the minutest everyday action is always for the cause. The characters do their part in resisting the enemy in whatever way they can, because it is demanded of the times. The "save China" message of the novel is particularly romanticized in the rhapsodic passages about Ling Tan contemplating his land. He and the farmers like him, the people who work the land, seem most deserving of the land. In contrast, the Japanese occupiers are portrayed as having little concept of the land beyond the idea of possession.

In Buck's China, everyone has his or her place. Buck examines the woman's place in the scheme of land, family, and tradition. The novel's women are not all the manipulated creatures they are supposed to be. Ling Sao and Jade are two characters who can be seen to be the progenitors of the woman warriors to come in later fiction about women of Chinese ancestry. Both are at least the equal of their husbands. Jade and Pansiao are the only two of the Ling family who are literate.

Unlike *The Good Earth*, *Dragon Seed* has not withstood the test of time. When it appeared in 1942, its topicality made it a best-seller. Today it appears simplistic, dated, and romanticized. It seems doomed to be relegated to that category of writing thought of as historical artifact rather than as literature.

Dragon Seed is an excellent example to use in the debate over what constitutes American literature. It is a seldom-read novel in the large canon of an American Nobel Prize winner. With regard to its subject matter, does one call it an American novel because it was written by an American? Does one not call it an American novel because it is not about Americans? It is noteworthy that while Buck won the Nobel Prize largely on the strength of *The Good Earth*, the novel is not always seriously thought of as qualifying for the American literary canon.

Reading *Dragon Seed* and trying to gauge its place in literature, it is also important to realize that a novel written by an American about China in the context of today's critical assessments is inherently problematic. One may ask the question: Does Buck think she can speak for the Chinese better than they can for themselves? Another critical question is: Will Chinese be confused with Chinese American? When the novel first appeared, there was little differentiation between the two. There was no expression of Chinese American consciousness in an America where even American-born Chinese were, by law, not American. Although *Dragon Seed* is clearly about China and Chinese, it is also one of the earliest instances of a novel whose characters are Chinese that was widely read by the American public. As such it is relevant in any study of how American literature has portrayed characters of Chinese ancestry and how the perception of Americans of Chinese ancestry has evolved.

"Critical Evaluation" by Pat M. Wong

Bibliography:
"Bloody Ballet." Review of *Dragon Seed*, by Pearl S. Buck. *Time*, January 26, 1942, 80, 82. Calls the novel the "strongest . . . most instructive story" about China during World War II, but criticizes the latter pages as artistically weak.

Buck, Pearl S. *My Several Worlds*. New York: John Day, 1954. Buck's autobiography describes vividly her years in China and the impact these experiences had upon her life and work. Discusses her progressive ideas on social issues.

_____. *The Story of "Dragon Seed."* New York: John Day, 1944. This monograph explains how the author came to write the novel. Describes her personal contact with Chinese farming families living near Nanking and her learning of "the horrors of the Japanese invasion."

Cavasco, G. A. "Pearl Buck and the Chinese Novel." *Asian Studies* 5 (1967): 437-450. Praises Buck's Chinese fiction, dividing her work into three categories. Argues that her novels about China are her best work and that they will always be popular because they adhere to the structure of Chinese fiction.

Doyle, Paul A. *Pearl S. Buck*. Rev. ed. Boston: Twayne, 1980. Analyzes the plot of *Dragon Seed* to show why the novel is not considered "an artistic success." Compares the work to *The Good Earth*.

DRAMATIS PERSONAE

Type of work: Poetry
Author: Robert Browning (1812-1889)
First published: 1864

When Robert Browning published *Dramatis Personae* he was beginning to gain a measure of general esteem in the eyes of the public and of the critics. The year before its publication a three-volume collection of his earlier works had sold moderately well. *Dramatis Personae* added considerably to his popularity, and a second edition was called for before the end of 1864. It is ironic that this volume, the first that can be said to have achieved popular success, contained the first clear signs of the decline of his poetic powers.

It was his first volume of new poems since *Men and Women*, published in 1855. In the interval the pattern of Browning's life had undergone complete transformation. On June 29, 1861, his wife, the poet Elizabeth Barrett Browning, had died. They had made their home in Italy; after her death, Browning returned to England. For years he had been virtually out of touch with the currents of English thought. He plunged into a society that was perplexed by what it had learned and troubled by what it had come to doubt. Browning was soon personally involved in the intellectual and religious controversies of the day.

The changes in his life produced changes in his poetry. His love poems, understandably, became more melancholy. Many of the poems in *Men and Women* have historical settings; all but a few of those in *Dramatis Personae* have contemporary settings. Even when he gives his version of an old tale, as in "Gold Hair," he manages to work in discussion of nineteenth century problems. In general, he was becoming more argumentative, more of a preacher. He still preferred the dramatic mode of utterance but the voice of the poet is often heard behind the dramatic mask.

Two of the important themes in the volume are love and death, frequently juxtaposed. The death of Mrs. Browning may have been an influence on his choice of subjects, but it should not be overestimated; a number of the poems antedate her death. "Prospice," however, written in the fall of 1861, is clearly Browning speaking in his own voice. It is an open affirmation of belief in immortality. When death ends his life, he says, as it has ended hers, "O thou soul of my soul! I shall clasp thee again,/ And with God be the rest!"

In "Too Late" another man grieves over a dead woman, but with a difference. He had never expressed his love for her and now suffers not grief alone but regret at having missed his opportunity. It is a familiar theme in Browning, love unfulfilled through negligence, expressed earlier in "The Statue and the Bust," and, elsewhere in *Dramatis Personae*, in "Youth and Art," and in "Dis Aliter Visum; or Le Byron de Nos Jours." If "Too Late" has an autobiographical element it is of an inverse order: Browning, unlike the speaker, had not missed his opportunity for love. The speaker of "Too Late" says it would have been better to

> . . . have burst like a thief
> And borne you away to a rock for us two
> In a moment's horror, bright, bloody, and brief,
> Then changed to myself again. . . .

Browning, a sedentary man, had stepped out of character once in his life, when he had spirited a middle-aged poet off to Italy.

Two of the finest poems in *Dramatis Personae*, also love poems, are "Confessions" and "James Lee's Wife" (originally called, misleadingly, "James Lee"). One reason why they are perennially satisfying is that, unlike many poems in the volume, they are free from topical controversy. In "Confessions," one of Browning's shortest dramatic monologues, a dying man recalls, with satisfaction, a love affair of long ago: "How sad and bad and mad it was—/ But then, how it was sweet!" In "James Lee's Wife," the story is that of the death of love. It is a restrained, dignified cry of heartbreak, a skillfully wrought dramatic lyric, the desolate scene and the dying year serving as mute echoes of the speaker's mood.

Of the eighteen poems originally grouped in *Dramatis Personae* (two occasional pieces were later added: "Deaf and Dumb" and "Eurydice to Orpheus"), few are not cluttered with argument. Of these, "James Lee's Wife" and "Confessions" are particularly memorable. "The Worst of It" is mawkish; "May and Death" is pleasant, but slight; "A Face" and "A Likeness" are insignificant. It should not be assumed, however, that the remaining poems, those which serve as vehicles for Browning's beliefs, can all be dismissed as inferior poems.

"Caliban upon Setebos," for example, is not only a statement of Victorian religious belief; it is as well one of Browning's successful poems of the grotesque. The element of controversy is certainly there, as indicated by the subtitle: "Natural Theology in the Island." Browning is satirizing those who, relying too closely on their own resources, posit God in their own image. Caliban is not merely a figure taken from Shakespeare's *The Tempest*; he is also a post-Darwinian figure, a poet's version of the evolutionary missing link. The topical references in the poem do not, however, prevent it from being rated one of Browning's best dramatic monologues.

"A Death in the Desert," another dramatic monologue, is perhaps more seriously marred by its attempts to promote certain religious ideas. Proponents of what was called higher criticism of the Bible—for example, David Friedrich Strauss in *The Life of Jesus, Critically Examined* (1835-1836) and Ernest Renan in *Life of Jesus* (1863)—had attempted, among other things, to prove that the Gospel of St. John had not been written, as had been assumed, by the beloved disciple. Browning's poem, an imaginative re-creation of John's death, is an argument for the authenticity of the Gospel. It contains a number of Browning's religious positions (for example, a theory about miracles). The fact that it is the dying Apostle who gives expression to these ideas is anachronistic: many of them are clearly indigenous to the middle of the nineteenth century. As a result, the dramatic effect of the poem is appreciably undercut.

The longest poem in *Dramatis Personae*, "Mr. Sludge, 'The Medium,'" is 1525 lines, or three-eighths of the entire volume. This poem is more successful. It is one of Browning's liveliest character studies, not unworthy of comparison with the great dramatic monologues in *Men and Women*. It too is tinged by Browning's growing fondness for argument. Browning satirizes spiritualism, quite a fad in the mid-nineteenth century England, by portraying a fraudulent medium whose character is based on an American, Daniel Dunglass Home, whom Browning had met. Moreover, Mr. Sludge, the speaker, gives voice, although inconsistently, to some of Browning's characteristic religious ideas. The propagandizing is done rather subtly, however, and does not strike the reader as being obtrusive.

"Rabbi Ben Ezra" and "Abt Vogler" are similar to "Mr. Sludge" in being good poems as well as statements of opinion with regard to contemporary questions. The first eight sections of "Abt Vogler" are a brilliant tour de force, a lyrical evocation of the exalted spirit of a musician improvising at the keyboard of an organ. The last four sections are not quite so successful, being too flat an exposition of one of Browning's pet theories, the "philosophy of the imperfect":

On the earth the broken arcs; in the heaven, a perfect round.
And what is our failure here but a triumph's evidence
For the fullness of the days?

The argumentative element does not predominate; sound and sense are not at odds but in harmony with each other. It was one of Browning's favorites, among his own poems, and it has since been one of the favorites of his readers.

"Rabbi Ben Ezra," another of Browning's most popular poems, is perhaps somewhat less successful than "Abt Vogler." It is unsurpassed, however, as an expression of Browning's own belief in God. The ideas contained in it are typical of Browning. He says, for example: "What I aspired to be,/ And was not, comforts me."

We are reminded of Andrea del Sarto's dictum in *Men and Women*: "A man's reach should exceed his grasp." Above all, "Rabbi Ben Ezra" is a cogent presentation of Browning's famous and frequently, if too facilely, maligned optimism.

"Gold Hair" is a curious and troubling poem. It relates an old story about the death of a young woman. She had been regarded virtually as a saint; years after her death, however, it is learned that she had been interested in earthly treasure far more than in a heavenly one. Some have objected to the story itself but that, though macabre and a bit cynical, is really unobjectionable. In the last three stanzas Browning simply lectures his readers.

The poet makes no bones about his intention to preach, and the value of his stories begins to decline as they become more and more pointedly the texts for sermons. "Apparent Failure," a lesser poem, finds Browning speaking in his own voice. The story is merely the occasion for moral instruction; it is in Browning's own words, "the sermon's text."

The final poem in *Dramatis Personae*, "Epilogue," gives brief expression to three religious positions current when Browning wrote. The "First Speaker, as David" sums up the High Church, ritualistic position; the "Second Speaker, as Renan" expresses the skepticism of one familiar with higher criticism. The "Third Speaker," Browning himself, answers the first two, calling ceremony unnecessary and belief tenable. Browning's belief, like Alfred, Lord Tennyson's, is sustained by personal feeling rather than by a process of the reason. What is really significant about the poem is that it makes no pretense of being dramatic. It sets the pattern for the bulk of his later poems, for Browning's values have changed; controversy now means more to him than writing poems, for poetry has become the vehicle for argument. As a result, the poetry suffers, as some of the poems in this volume and virtually all of the later poems, save "The Ring and the Book," clearly testify.

Bibliography:
Crowell, Norton B. *A Reader's Guide to Robert Browning*. Albuquerque: University of New Mexico Press, 1972. Criticisms of "Abt Vogler," "A Death in the Desert," "Caliban," and "Epilogue," with annotated bibliographies following each poem. Includes critical bibliography.

Erickson, Lee. *Robert Browning: His Poetry and His Audiences*. Ithaca, N.Y.: Cornell University Press, 1984. The chapter on *Dramatis Personae* interprets the poet's later work as a departure from the dramatic monologue to works such as "Epilogue to *Dramatis Personae*," in which characters express views on religion. Bibliography includes nineteenth- and twentieth-century reviews and essays.

Hudson, Gertrude Reese. *Robert Browning's Literary Life: From First Work to Masterpiece*. Austin, Tex.: Eakin Press, 1992. Two chapters on *Dramatis Personae* describe the circumstances of publication, identify sources of the poems, and ascribe the themes to contemporary religious controversies, especially higher criticism and spiritualism.

Tracy, Clarence, ed. *Browning's Mind and Art*. Edinburgh, Scotland: Oliver & Boyd, 1968. Essays written by well-known Browning critics. The Index locates references to some of the poems contained in *Dramatis Personae*.

Ward, Maisie. *Robert Browning and His World: Two Robert Brownings?* Vol. 2. New York: Holt, Rinehart, and Winston, 1969. The chapter on *Dramatis Personae* discusses Browning's friendship with Benjamin Jowett. Notes religious contrasts in the speakers of the poems.

DREAM OF THE RED CHAMBER

Type of work: Novel
Author: Ts'ao Hsüeh-ch'in (Ts'ao Chan, 1716-1763), with a continuation by Kao Ê
Type of plot: Domestic realism
Time of plot: c. 1729-1737
Locale: Peking
First published: Hung-lou Meng, 1792 (English translation, 1929)

Principal characters:

MADAME SHIH or the MATRIARCH, the matriarch of the Chia family
CHIA SHEH, her older son, master of the Yungkuofu, or western compound
MADAME HSING, his wife
CHIA LIEN, their son
HSI-FENG "PHOENIX," Chia Lien's wife
YING-CHUN "WELCOME SPRING," Chia Sheh's daughter by a concubine
CHIA CHENG, the Matriarch's younger son
MADAME WANG, his wife
CHIA PAO-YU, their son
CARDINAL SPRING, their daughter and an Imperial concubine
CHIA HUAN, Chia Cheng's son by his concubine
TAN-CHUN "QUEST SPRING," Chia Cheng's daughter by his concubine
TAI-YU "BLACK JADE," the Matriarch's granddaughter and an orphan
HSIANG-YUN "RIVER MIST," the Matriarch's grandniece
PAO-CHAI "PRECIOUS VIRTUE," Madame Wang's niece
HSUEH PAN, Precious Virtue's brother and a libertine
CHIA GEN, the master of the Ningkuofu, or eastern compound
YU-SHIH, his wife
CHIA JUNG, their son
CHIN-SHIH, Chia Jung's wife
HSI-CHUN "COMPASSION SPRING," Chia Gen's sister
HSI-JEN "PERVADING FRAGRANCE,"
CHING-WEN "BRIGHT DESIGN," and
SHEH-YUEH "MUSK MOON," Pao-yu's serving maids

The Story:

Ages ago, in the realm of the Great Void, the Goddess Nugua, whose task it was to repair the Dome of Heaven, rejected a stone which she found unsuited to her purpose. She had touched it, however, so the stone became endowed with life. Thereafter it could move as it pleased. In time, it chanced on a crimson flower in the region of the Ethereal, where each day it watered the tender blossoms with drops of dew. At last the plant was incarnated as a beautiful young woman. Remembering the stone that had showered the frail plant with refreshing dew, she prayed that in her human form she might repay it with the gift of her tears. Her prayers were to be granted, for the stone, too, had been given life in the Red Dust of earthly existence. At his birth, the piece of jade was miraculously found in the mouth of Pao-yu, a younger son of the rich and powerful house of Chia, which by imperial favor had been raised to princely eminence several generations before.

At the time of Pao-yu's birth, the two branches of the Chia family lived in great adjoining compounds of palaces, pavilions, and parks on the outskirts of Peking. The Matriarch, an old woman of great honor and virtue, ruled as the living ancestress over both establishments. Chia Ging, the prince of the Ningkuofu, had retired to a Taoist temple some time before, and his son Chia Gen was master in his place. The master of the Yungkuofu was Chia Sheh, the older son of the Matriarch. Chia Cheng, her younger son and Pao-yu's father, also lived with his family and attendants in the Yungkuofu. A man of upright conduct and strict Confucian morals, he was a contrast to the other members of his family, who had grown lax and corrupt through enervating luxury and the abuse of power.

Pao-yu, the possessor of the miraculous jade stone and a boy of great beauty and quick wit, was his grandmother's favorite. Following her example, the other women of the family—his mother, aunts, sisters, cousins, and waiting maids—doted on the boy and pampered him at every opportunity, with the result that he grew up girlish and weak, a lover of feminine society. His traits of effeminacy infuriated and disgusted his austere father, who treated the boy with undue severity. As a result, Pao-yu kept as much as possible to the women's quarters.

His favorite playmates were his two cousins, Black Jade and Precious Virtue. Black Jade, a granddaughter of the Matriarch, had come to live in the Yungkuofu after her mother's death. She was a lovely, delicate girl of great poetic sensitivity, and she and Pao-yu were drawn to each other by bonds of sympathy and understanding that seemed to stretch back into some unremembered past. Precious Virtue, warmhearted and practical, was the niece of Pao-yu's mother. She was a woman as good as her brother Hsueh Pan was vicious. He was always involving the family in scandal because of his pursuit of maidens and young boys. Pao-yu's favorite waiting maid was Pervading Fragrance. She slept in his chamber at night, and it was with her that he followed a dream vision and practiced the play of cloud and rain.

When word came that Black Jade's father was ill and wished to see her before his death, the Matriarch sent the girl home under the escort of her cousin Chia Lien. During their absence, Chin-shih, the daughter-in-law of Chia Gen, died after a long illness. By judicious bribery, the dead woman's husband, Chia Jung, was made a chevalier of the Imperial Dragon Guards in order that she might be given a more elaborate funeral. During the period of mourning, Chia Gen asked Phoenix, Chia Lien's wife, to take charge of the Ningkuofu household. This honor gave Phoenix a position of responsibility and power in both palaces. From that time on, although she continued to appear kind and generous, she secretly became greedy for money and power. She began to accept bribes, tamper with the household accounts, and lend money at exorbitant rates of interest.

One day a great honor was conferred on the Chias. Cardinal Spring, Pao-yu's sister and one of the emperor's concubines, was advanced to the rank of an Imperial consort of the second degree. Later, when it was announced that she would pay a visit of filial respect to her parents, the parks of the two compounds were transformed at great expense into magnificent pleasure grounds, called the Takuanyuan, in honor of the consort's visit. Later, at Cardinal Spring's request, the pavilions in the Takuanyuan were converted into living quarters for the young women of the family. Pao-yu also went there to live, passing his days in idle occupations and writing verses. His pavilion was close to that of Black Jade, who had returned to the Yungkuofu after her father's death.

Pao-yu had a half brother, Chia Huan. His mother, jealous of the true-born son, paid a sorceress to bewitch the boy and Phoenix, whom she also hated. Both were seized with fits of violence and wild delirium. Pao-yu's coffin had already been made when a Buddhist monk and a lame Taoist priest suddenly appeared and restored the power of the spirit stone. Pao-yu and Phoenix recovered.

A short time later a maid was accused of trying to seduce Pao-yu. When she was dismissed, she drowned herself. About the same time, Chia Cheng was informed that his son had turned the love of a young actor away from a powerful patron. Calling his son a degenerate, Chia Cheng almost caused Pao-yu's death by the severity of the beating which the angry father administered.

As Phoenix became more shrewish at home, Chia Lien dreamed of taking another wife. Having been almost caught in one infidelity, he was compelled to exercise great caution in taking a concubine. Phoenix learned about the secret marriage, however, and by instigating claims advanced by the girl's former suitor she drove the wretched concubine to suicide.

Black Jade, always delicate, became more sickly. Sometimes she and Pao-yu quarreled, only to be brought together again by old ties of affection and understanding. The gossip of the servants was that the Matriarch would marry Pao-yu to either Black Jade or Precious Virtue. While possible marriage plans were being discussed, a maid found in the Takuanyuan a purse embroidered with an indecent picture. This discovery led to a search of all the pavilions, and it was revealed that one of the maids was involved in a secret love affair. Suspicion also fell on Bright Design, one of Pao-yu's maids, and she was dismissed. Proud and easily hurt, she died not long afterward. Pao-yu became even moodier and more depressed after Bright Design's death. Outraged by the search, Precious Virtue left the park and went to live with her mother.

A begonia tree near Pao-yu's pavilion bloomed out of season. This event was interpreted as a bad omen, for Pao-yu lost his spirit stone and sank into a state of complete lethargy. In an effort to revive his spirits, the Matriarch and his parents decided to marry him at once to Precious Virtue rather than to Black Jade, who continued to grow frailer each day. Pao-yu was allowed to believe, however, that Black Jade was to be his wife. Black Jade, deeply grieved, died shortly after the ceremony. Knowing nothing of the deception that had been practiced, she felt that she had failed Pao-yu and that he had been unfaithful to her. So the flower returned to the Great Void.

Suddenly a series of misfortunes overwhelmed the Chias as their deeds of graft and corruption came to light. When bailiffs took possession of the two compounds, the usury Phoenix had practiced was disclosed. Chia Gen and Chia Sheh were arrested and sentenced to banishment. The Matriarch, who took upon herself the burden of her family's guilt and surrendered her personal treasures for expenses and fines, became ill and died. During her funeral services, robbers looted the compound and later returned to carry off Exquisite Jade, a pious nun. Phoenix also died, neglected by those she had dominated in her days of power. Through the efforts of powerful friends, however, the complete ruin of the family was averted, and Chia Cheng was restored to his official post.

In the end, however, the despised son became the true redeemer of his family's honor and fortunes. After a Buddhist monk had returned his lost stone, Pao-yu devoted himself earnestly to his studies and passed the Imperial Examinations with such brilliance that he stood in seventh place on the list of successful candidates. The emperor was so impressed that he wished to have the young scholar serve at court; but Pao-yu was nowhere to be found. The tale was that he became a bodhisattva and disappeared in the company of a Buddhist monk and a Taoist priest.

Critical Evaluation:

Dream of the Red Chamber is a long and extremely complicated domestic chronicle—the novel contains more than four hundred characters—that is at once a lively comedy of manners, a realistic fable of moral seriousness, and a metaphysical allegory. The title is capable of expressing several meanings. For example, it may be translated as "Dreams of Young Maidens," since the younger women of the Chia clan lived in the traditional "red chamber" of a palace compound. The term may also be interpreted as a reference to the metaphor "Red Dust," which in Buddhist usage is a designation for the material world with all of its pleasures, follies, and vices.

On the metaphysical level of the novel, the stone and the flower, originally located in the Ethereal, suffer a fall when they enter earthly reality in the Red Dust. Here the novel may be read as an allegory endorsing a Taoist-Buddhist system of otherworldly values (represented by the mysteriously recurring priest and monk) and rejecting the this-world view of Confucianism (represented by Chia Cheng). Interestingly enough, this novel's critique of feudalist and Confucian China has won praise from Marxist readers.

The Ethereal stone's fortunes translate into a novel of manners when the stone falls into earthly existence as the protagonist, Chia Pao-yu. In this mode, the novel becomes, through its portrayal of the Chia family, a brilliantly realistic document of upper-class life during the Ching Dynasty. It encompasses financial affairs and sexual aberrations, fraternal jealousies, and tragic suicides. The Chia fortunes reach their apogee when Cardinal Spring becomes the Emperor's concubine. The Takuanyuan Garden, built to honor Cardinal Spring, symbolizes these halcyon days; it becomes the domain of the younger Chia generation led by Pao-yu. In the garden, their way of life is carefree, innocent, almost Edenic; but, just as Pao-yu must grow into adulthood, so evil must invade this Eden. The fall begins when an indecently embroidered purse is found. A general search ensues, scandals surface, a tragic death results. Analogous disasters overtake the family. Their financial dealings incur the Emperor's displeasure; Imperial Guards ransack the Chia compound. Then bandits raid the garden itself. Finally, Pao-yu chooses to deny the folly of this world and to join the Buddhist priest and the Taoist monk journeying presumably to the Ethereal.

The eighteenth century *Hung-lou Meng*, or *Dream of the Red Chamber*, considered by scholars as the greatest of Chinese novels, comes closer to Western aesthetics than does any Chinese novel written before or after its publication. The book, perhaps first published in 1716, is generally considered to have been written by Ts'ao Hsüeh-ch'in, with the exception of the last forty chapters, which may have been written by Kao Ê, the editor of the original printed novel. Some critics believe those last forty chapters are less effective rhetorically and were the sole inspiration of Kao Ê and others; other critics believe that Kao Ê simply redacted Ts'ao Hsüeh-ch'in's original wording of the last forty chapters. Most scholars agree that, and internal evidence points to, the idea that Ts'ao Hsüeh-ch'in may have drawn upon his own experiences as the son of a once wealthy, powerful family.

The scope and depth of *Dream of the Red Chamber* has been declared by both Western and Chinese critics as a supreme study of psychological realism. The novel is not merely a story reflective of autobiographical significance. The long, complex forward motion of the plot tests ideals existent in Chinese culture: Confucian teachings, with their tenets directed toward married love, family, overindulgence, sexual obsession, and patriotism; and Buddhist and Taoist philosophy, which condemned personal obsessive desire. Although the author's inclusion of the diverse Chinese thought may create confusion at times, this phenomenon does not detract from the story's powerful, rhetorical texture, or its readability.

Dream of the Red Chamber uses allegory and symbolism to reflect Ts'ao Hsüeh-ch'in's interest in and study of tradition. Pao-yu, for example, is part of a creation myth. In further allegorical terms, the hero is put into a dream sequence. The author's response to Taoist-Buddhist thought is reflected by the symbolic technique, as well as his response to the Confucian view of the material world.

Pervading the allegory, the author also creates settings and actions suggestive of a novel of manners. Thus the highly praised realism of the novel, which has more than four hundred characters, softens the didacticism of allegory, although sometimes falling into formulaic method. The realism alone, however, provides a brilliant document of upper-class life during the Ching Dynasty. The fact that the story line does not conclude happily, that Pao-yu is acted upon in a series of climactic events toward the end of the book, introduces crucial philosophical levels with its accompanying reflection upon compassion and salvation. Thus it fulfills the criteria for serious tragedy, with its inclusion of the noble hero.

The novel's important power lies in its age-old contemporaneity: It reflects not just decadent Chinese manners, nor merely crushed nobility, nor is it solely an allegorical and symbolic argument with tradition; essentially it is a treatment of human nature's complexity—thus it speaks to all people of all ages.

"Critical Evaluation" by Dorie LaRue

Bibliography:
Knoerle, Jeanne. *"The Dream of the Red Chamber": A Critical Study.* Foreword by Lui Wu Chi. Bloomington: Indiana University Press, 1972. Evaluates *Dream of the Red Chamber* in aesthetic terms and applies Western literary tenets. Places the novel in perspective within the history of Chinese literature, and examines the novel's ethical considerations and its religious and cultural influences. Shows how the tenets of Confucianism, Taoism, and Buddhism are woven together for a unified whole. Especially helpful are the illumination of structure and technique.

Ts'ao Hsüeh-ch'in. *Dream of the Red Chamber.* New York: Twayne, 1958. Translated by Chi-Chen Wang, 1958. Most recent translation, by a well-known Chinese American scholar. Leans toward colloquial English style, and thus loses the style of the original. The symbolism, allegory, and structural significance, however, are highly accessible.

Wang, Jing. *The Story of Stone: Intertextuality, Ancient Chinese Stone Lore, and the Stone Symbolism in "Dream of the Red Chamber," "Water Margin," and "The Journey to the West."* Durham, N.C.: Duke University Press, 1992. Thorough discussion of the stone symbolism and its relationship to intertextuality, myth, and religion. An excellent section devoted to folk belief systems in the 1600-1899 Ching Dynasty period.

Wu Shih-Ch'ang. *On the Red Chamber Dream.* Oxford, England: Clarendon Press, 1961. Thorough, accessible discussion restricted mainly to textural problems that were involved when scholars attempted to identify the original/authentic version of the novel. Excellent discussion of the varying and conflicting views concerning authorship.

THE DREAM SONGS

Type of work: Poetry
Author: John Berryman (1914-1972)
First published: 1969

Begun in 1955, *The Dream Songs* combines two volumes, *77 Dream Songs* (1964) and *His Toy, His Dream, His Rest* (1968). The series of 385 songs is an ongoing, evolving account that mixes historical facts with autobiographical material, current events with philosophy, and archetypal myths with vaudeville humor. John Berryman is often associated with the confessional school of poetry, a style popular in America during the 1950's and 1960's and connected with the careers of Berryman's contemporaries Robert Lowell, Randall Jarrell, and Sylvia Plath. The design of *The Dream Songs* (that of a series of lyrics organized around a central motif) has roots in literary tradition, including *Don Juan* (1819-1824, 1826) by the British Romantic writer George Gordon, Lord Byron, and *Cantos* (1930-1970) by the American poet of the twentieth century, Ezra Pound. Berryman cited Walt Whitman, the nineteenth century American poet, as his model, claiming that he designed the poem after Whitman's "Song of Myself" (1855). In 1965, *77 Dream Songs* won a Pulitzer Prize; *His Toy, His Dream, His Rest* won the National Book Award in 1969.

At first glance, the collection seems loose, spontaneous, and improvised, but actually the individual poems are tightly structured, and they adhere technically and thematically to a complex poetic strategy. Each of Berryman's songs consists of 18 lines broken into three stanzas of six lines each. The meter is well regulated, utilizing speech patterns ranging from a parody of beatnik black dialect to baby talk to academic jargon. It takes the attitude of a hip literary insider during the late 1950's and early 1960's. In his 1979 essay "How to Read Berryman's *Dream Songs*," Professor Edward Mendelson points out an even more severe, "arithmetical precision" as a further unifying scheme built around the number seven. He demonstrates "seventy-seven Songs in the first volume . . . 77 × 5 in the completed 385 Songs . . . seven epigraphs; seven Books in all." The songs also suggest a plot, not in a linear episodic sequence of events, but as a quest of the poet's search for himself, seeking a fixed, centered ego.

Books 1 through 3 detail the metaphysical angst of Henry, the main character, recounting events and meditations. Henry is self-obsessed, petty, brilliant, dysfunctional, and damned by his need for meaning, for transcendence. The characters—including friends, enemies and acquaintances—are "zoned!" and "screwed up" or they are intellectual hustlers with their own lives to waste. Mixing slang with formal diction, discordant meter with perfect lyrical rhythms, Berryman combines pedantry with a street-smart style to portray a tragicomical blend of voices, personas, embodied in the polymorphous figure of Henry. In the preface to the one-volume edition of *The Dream Songs* (1969), Berryman writes, "The poem, then, whatever its wide cast of characters, is essentially about an imaginary character (not the poet, not me) named Henry, a white American in his early middle age, sometimes in blackface, who has suffered an irreversible loss and talks about himself sometimes in the first person, sometimes in the third, sometimes even in the second; he has a friend, never named, who addresses him as Mr Bones and variants thereof."

This "irreversible loss" may be traced, despite the disclaimer, to Berryman's own loss of innocence. When Berryman was twelve, his father shot himself to death outside the boy's window. His life after his father's suicide was punctuated by transience and dissolution, although he managed to garner prestigious poetry awards and various teaching positions, notably at Harvard, Princeton, and the University of Minnesota. Married three times, Berryman spent years fighting alcoholism, infidelity, and madness, and finally began to lose faith in his craft as a poet. The incessant strife and psychological turmoil that began so early in his life, and which is so evident in *The Dream Songs*, culminated in his own suicide in 1972.

As the title *The Dream Songs* suggests, the poems are extremely private, subjective, and personal, but as songs they are also by design public, objective, and communal. Many are introspective, confessional, self-incriminating reports from the edge of madness. Others are elegies for Berryman's contemporaries; others read like barstool editorials on political events of the day; still others come off as bitter lectures on the ironies of history. What unites the poems is the strength of the poet's personality. Berryman's genius for detail, his precise phrasing, his unrelenting insight into the heart of human experience keeps *The Dream Songs* from sinking into maudlin self-pity. The work is laced with passionate pessimism, and too often the ironic aside devolves into sour invective; nevertheless, the cynical recitals of spiritual vacuity are tempered by Berryman's stoic resignation, hope bred from despair.

The first song established Henry's disillusionment and withdrawal, contrasting his expectations with the reality he finds himself living in. The opening stanza suggests an existential conspiracy, in which "unappeasable Henry" senses that he has been fooled into believing in the possibility of happiness and fulfillment, and is suspicious of "a trying to put things over." The second stanza implies that there was a time when Henry had faith in life, when "All the world like a woolen lover/ once did seem on Henry's side." Some event, a "departure," presumably Berryman's father's death, qualifies Henry's sense of a benevolent world ripe with opportunity and promise. He feels exposed, "pried/ open," and in the third stanza seems astounded at the suffering that "the world can bear & be" (playing on the meanings of "bear") amazed that the world can produce and accept his suffering—and "be." Henry is astounded that the world exists at all and that to exist is to suffer. Once in Henry's youth he was "glad/ all at the top, and I sang." He sees life as a constant erosion, in which all endeavors lead to the same conclusion: "empty grows every bed."

The Dream Songs is, at heart, a romantic poem. In the need to discover the root of his failure in an impossible dream of transcendence, Henry becomes a tragic rebel, resenting his freedom as much as he craves it. He is a victim of his own limitations and is haunted by the infinite possibilities of his life. His muse is "Filling her compact & delicious body/ with chicken páprika." After all the strategies and evasions, "life, friends, is boring" and offers as much spiritual nourishment as "a handkerchief sandwich," the only question for Henry is: "Where did it all go wrong?" The punishment of living does not seem to fit the crime of existence. Even though "There sat down, once, a thing on Henry's heart/ so heavy," he is confused by the severity of the penitence he extracts from himself. His crime is against himself, and he complains that he would never "end anyone and hacks her body up/ and hide the pieces, where they may be found."

Book 4, the Op. posth. (opus posthumous section, songs 78-91) describes Henry's symbolic death, as he is "flared out in history." Snuffing out his will, "nourished he less & less/ his subject body." His message from the grave is filled with as much remorse as acrimony. He is both satisfied and bewildered by his condition. In his desire to selflessness, he feels "something bizarre about Henry, slowly sheered off." As he begins the process of ego extinction, he is left with only "his eyeteeth and one block of memories" which prove "enough for him." After all, he claims, it is "a *nice* pit" and "the knowledge they will take off your hands" keeps him free from the mundane habits—typewriters and deadlines—that infuriate and deaden his life. While he admits that "It would not be easy, accustomed to these things,/ to give up the old world,"

Henry gives it his best shot. Bound by guilt to experience, he hopes "Henry's brow of stainless steel/ rests free," but unable to absolve himself from the crimes of his conscience, "returning to our life/ adult & difficult," he is "collected and dug up." His return to the world is measured by "accumulated taxes" and wives "glued/ to disencumbered Henry's many ills." Seduced by the opportunity death affords him "to fold/ him over himself quietly," he "muttered for a double rum" and began "with a shovel/ digging like mad, Lazarus with a plan/ to get his own back."

Book 5 continues to catalog his psychic convalescence during a lengthy hospital stay. Caught in a cycle of recovery and relapse, his only recourse is to transform his world, or lose it. Berryman relies on his craft for salvation, in the transforming process of the imagination, rebounding with stoic persistence from one defeat after another. This attempt to impose poetic form on the contingencies of existence culminates for Berryman in book 6, beginning with a sequence of elegies for Berryman's contemporary, American poet Delmore Schwartz, "the new ghost/ haunting Henry most," before continuing through a hodgepodge of meditations, migrations, literary gossip, as "wanderers on coasts lookt for the man/ actual, having encountered all his ghost." The existential travelogue ends in book 7 with the poet in exile—literally—in Ireland, "Leaving behind the country of the dead." In Dublin, surrounded by ghosts, Berryman seems to have discovered a unified voice. The songs become more conversational, less daring. The device of the minstrel from the early songs is abandoned. The delivery becomes almost occasional, resembling letters from the poet to himself. The enervation evident in the later songs of book 7 may, however, be an inevitable result of the theme of the collection. *The Dream Songs* is about the poet's search for the form to contain experience, and therefore to control the world of the self. The shifts in syntax and perspective that mark the early songs are resolved in book 7, and the poet's project—the synthesis of experience and form in the completion of the self—is finished. In fact, the last two songs return to the poet's original source of disillusionment: Berryman as co-victim of his father's suicide. The poet makes "this awful pilgrimage" only to "spit upon this dreadful banker's grave/ who shot his heart out." Murderous with grief and anger, he will "ax the casket open ha to see/ just how he's taking it." Berryman's self-destruction, his "final card," may have been merely the poet's last futile attempt to find "a middle ground between things and the soul."

Jeff Johnson

Bibliography:
Kelly, Richard, and Alan K. Lathrop, eds. *Recovering Berryman: Essays on a Poet.* Ann Arbor: University of Michigan Press, 1993. A broad approach to Berryman's art and life. Includes Lewis Hyde's controversial essay "Alcohol and Poetry: John Berryman and the Booze Talking."
Mariani, Paul. *Dream Song: The Life of John Berryman.* New York: William Morrow, 1990. An exhaustive biography drawing on interviews and anecdotes from Berryman's colleagues and acquaintances. Attempts to connect Berryman's life with his work, stressing autobiographical elements in *The Dream Songs.*
Matterson, Stephen. *Berryman and Lowell: The Art of Losing.* New York: Barnes & Noble Books, 1987. Explores Berryman's career in the context of his contemporary, Robert Lowell. Discusses the "theme of disintegration" prevalent in Berryman's work.
Mendelson, Edward. "How to Read Berryman's *Dream Songs.*" In *American Poetry Since 1960,* edited by Robert B. Shaw. Cheadle Hulme: Carcanet Press, 1973. A brief but detailed analysis of *The Dream Songs,* providing an overview of the complete series as well as

detailed explications of selected poems; relies less on biographical material than on the more formal poetic structures and strategies.

Thomas, Harry, ed. *Berryman's Understanding: Reflections on the Poetry of John Berryman.* Boston: Northeastern University Press, 1988. Provides a broad cultural context for his work and close critical analysis of his poetry.

DRINK

Type of work: Novel
Author: Émile Zola (1840-1902)
Type of plot: Naturalism
Time of plot: Second half of the nineteenth century
Locale: Paris
First published: L'Assommoir, 1877 (English translation, 1879)

> *Principal characters:*
> GERVAISE, a laundress
> COUPEAU, a roofer and her husband
> LANTIER, her lover and the father of her first two children
> ADÈLE, Lantier's mistress
> GOUJET, a neighbor secretly in love with Gervaise
> NANA, the daughter of Gervaise and Coupeau
> VIRGINIE, Adèle's sister

The Story:

All night Gervaise had been waiting for her lover, Lantier, to come back to their quarters in Paris. When he finally came home, he treated her brutally and did not display the least affection toward Claude and Étienne, their two children. He stretched out on the bed and sent Gervaise off to the laundry where she worked.

When she was thirteen years old, Gervaise had left her country town and her family to follow Lantier; she was only fourteen years old when Étienne was born. Her family had been cruel to her, but until recently Lantier had treated her kindly. Gervaise knew that Lantier had come under the influence of both the dram shop and of Adèle, a pretty prostitute.

Gervaise herself was rather pretty, but she had a slight limp which, when she was tired, became worse; the hard life she had lived also had put its mark on her face, although she was only twenty-two. She would have been perfectly happy working hard for her own home and a decent life for her children, but all she had ever known was endless hardship and insecurity.

At the laundry she found some relief in confiding her story to Madame Boche, an older woman who had become her friend. Suddenly the children came running in with word that Lantier had deserted the three of them to go away with Adèle and that he had taken with him everything they owned.

Gervaise's first thought was for her children, and she wondered what would become of them. Soon, however, she was roused in anger by the insults of Virginie, Adèle's sister; Virginie had come to the laundry for the sadistic pleasure of watching how Gervaise would take the triumph of her rival. Gervaise was quite frail and much smaller than Virginie; nevertheless, she jumped toward her, full of rage. A struggle followed, in which the two women used pieces of laundry equipment and wet clothes to beat each other. Surprisingly, Gervaise, who had given all of her strength, came out victorious. Virginie was never to forgive her.

Madame Fauconnier, proprietress of a laundry, gave Gervaise work in her establishment. There she earned just enough money to provide for herself and her children. Another person interested in Gervaise was Coupeau, a roofer who knew all the circumstances of her unhappy life. He would have liked to have her live with him. Gervaise preferred to devote herself entirely to her two small boys; but one day, when Coupeau proposed marriage to her, she was overcome by emotion and accepted him.

The situation was not very promising at first because the couple had no money. Coupeau's sister and brother-in-law, who were as miserly as they were prosperous, openly disapproved of his marriage. Slowly, perseverance in hard work made it possible for the Coupeaus to lead a decent life and even to put a little money aside. Gervaise had quite a reputation as a laundress, and she often dreamed of owning her own shop. A little girl, Nana, was born to the couple four years later. Gervaise resumed working soon afterward.

This good fortune, however, could not last. While Coupeau was working on a roof, Nana diverted his attention for a split second and he fell. Gervaise, refusing to let him be taken to the hospital, insisted on caring for him at home. Coupeau somehow survived, but his recovery was very slow. What was worse, inactivity had a bad effect on him. He had no more ambition, not even that of supporting his family. He also went more and more often to the dram shop.

Meanwhile, Gervaise was preparing to give up her dream of a little shop of her own when Goujet, a neighbor secretly in love with her, insisted that she borrow the five hundred francs he offered her as a gesture of friendship. She opened her shop and soon had it running successfully.

Goujet's money was never returned. Instead, the family's debts kept progressively increasing, for Coupeau remained idle and continued drinking. Gervaise had become accustomed to a few small luxuries, and she was not as thrifty as she had once been. Actually, she still felt quite confident that she would be able soon to meet her obligations; she had a very good reputation in the whole neighborhood.

At this point, Virginie returned, pretending that she had forgotten the fight in the laundry. At first, Gervaise was a little startled to discover that her old enemy was going to be her neighbor once more. Unprejudiced, however, she had no objection to being on friendly terms with Virginie.

Then Lantier came back. When Gervaise heard from Virginie that he had deserted Adèle and had been seen again in the neighborhood, she had been badly frightened. So far, however, her former lover had made no attempt to see her and she had forgotten her fears.

Lantier had waited to make a spectacular entrance. He chose to appear in the middle of a birthday party hosted by Gervaise. Most unexpectedly, Coupeau, who by that time was continuously drunk, invited him in. During the weeks that followed, the two men became drinking companions. Later on, Lantier suggested that he might live and board with the Coupeaus. Gervaise's husband had reached such a state of degeneration that he welcomed the idea.

Although the agreement was that Lantier was to pay his share of the expenses, he never kept his promise, and Gervaise found herself with two men to support instead of one. Furthermore, Lantier had completely taken over the household and was running it as he pleased. Still a charming seducer, he was extremely popular with the women of the neighborhood.

Gervaise herself began to degenerate. Disgusted by her husband, she could not find the strength to refuse the embraces of her former lover. Before long her work suffered from such a state of affairs, and she eventually lost the shop. Virginie bought it and, at the same time, won the favors of Lantier.

Meanwhile, Nana had almost grown up, and she was placed as an apprentice in a flower shop. When she decided to leave home for the streets, Gervaise gave up all interest in life and joined Coupeau in the dram shop. After he finally died of delirium tremens, she tried walking the streets, but nobody would have her, wretched as she was. Goujet's timid efforts to help her were useless. Completely worn out by all the demands that had been made on her, she died alone.

Critical Evaluation:

Drink, more commonly known by its French title, *L'Assommoir*, is the seventh in a series of twenty novels written by Émile Zola about several generations of the Rougon-Macquart family. It is one of the first such generational series, and is carefully shaped by the author according to his controversial ideas for a novel that would parallel, he hoped, the objective observation he admired in the natural sciences. His notion was to treat his characters something like guinea pigs in a world that he would create for them. Narrative impartiality and objectivity were paramount.

Not surprisingly, a public that had loved the romantic version of the poor offered them in Victor Hugo's *Les Miserables* (1862) was outraged by the squalor that Zola describes in *Drink*. The raw language and the clear parallels that the author draws between his characters and barnyard animals disgusted many readers, who found such a depiction threatening to their belief that the human soul raises men and women above the frailties of their bodies. *Drink* also indicts readers who imagine the poor are ennobled by horrible living conditions.

Zola defended the book as the first novel about working-class people that does not lie about their daily lives. He claimed that the characters in *Drink* are not evil, but ignorant and victimized by the crushing work that fills their days. Pointing to the collapse of Gervaise and the others, he described the novel as morality in action, implicitly teaching his readers a lesson in the consequences of alcohol, lethargy, jealousy, and irresponsibility.

Many find the novel quite painful to read, since the downfall of several of its well-meaning characters is relentless and even cruel. The narration and characterization are also truly compelling, more like a classic Greek tragedy than a soap opera, and many readers find the experience one they never forget. Gervaise, with her limp, her youthfulness, her determination, her hard work, and her resilience in the face of great odds, wins over most readers, who cheer her success against Virginie and her initial financial good sense. Zola does all that could be expected of an author to offer readers a sympathetic character. This makes her destruction all the more painful. At the same time, he shows the less admirable side of her character—her self-destructive desire to please—and plots its effect in her disastrous decisions. She and Coupeau do not have enough character or self-definition to resist their environment; instead, they allow themselves to be shaped by it.

Except for the wedding party's interesting trip to the Louvre museum, the novel takes place exclusively within a very cramped space around Montmartre cathedral in Paris. Part of Zola's purpose in the novel is to demonstrate that the imperial grandeur that Louis Napoleon brought to Paris, the result of tearing down old tenements and replacing them with more expensive housing and broad boulevards, displaced the poorer elements of society and crowded them too closely together. The result, he shows in this novel and others of the series, is a kind of reverse evolution—a resurgence of the animal nature in his characters. The devolution accelerates under the influence of peer pressure, drunkenness, and physical abuse (the book's title can also be translated "bludgeon").

Zola was greatly influenced by Charles Darwin's notion of evolution and genetic inheritance, and by the social Darwinism that applied biological principles to social theory. Zola's experiment in this novel is a demonstration of the depressing consequences of the survival of the fittest, since in the inhuman world of the nineteenth-century Parisian poor, immoral characters such as Lantier and Virginie seem better suited to fight their way to victory. In later novels in the series Zola charts the history of Gervaise's daughter, Nana, whose prostitution brings her more raw success than her mother's hard work and affability ever achieved. As weak as Gervaise may ultimately appear to be, however, her final decision to refuse Goujet's love raises the melodrama to the level of tragedy. She has come to know her own limitations, and, loving Goujet as he loves her, she decides to go to her death alone rather than drag him down as well. The reader is left to decide whether the fittest deserve to survive.

Many critics consider *Drink* and *Germinal* (1885) the best of the novels in the Rougon-Macquart series because they most successfully wed Zola's experimental techniques to his naturalism. These were the elements that Henry James so admired in Zola's work, and that influenced the American naturalists (such as Frank Norris, Theodore Dreiser, Steven Crane, and Upton Sinclair). This is saying a lot, since the Rougon-Macquart series is considered the finest of his productions.

Zola was not as interested in portraying psychological states as in presenting the physical world in which his characters lived and in which their personalities took shape. In *Drink*, as in his other novels, the buildings, the gutters, the machines, take on an importance and prominence that had been missing in much earlier fiction. Rather than have his characters discuss the philosophy behind their existence, he "embodied" the ideas in the environment in which he placed his creations. It is of utmost importance to Zola that Gervaise and Coupeau were born in a particular place, to parents with a particular history, and that they ended up echoing each other's characteristics in the way that—inevitably—would drag them down. Their heredity, their historical moment, and their environment determine the choices that are presented to them and determine the decisions they make in response.

"Critical Evaluation" by John C. Hawley

Bibliography:
Baguley, D., ed. *Critical Essays on Émile Zola*. Boston: G. K. Hall, 1986. A collection of historical responses to Zola, including the poet Algernon Charles Swinburne's famous condemnation of *Drink*.

King, Graham. *Garden of Zola: Émile Zola and his Novels for English Readers*. New York: Barnes & Noble Books, 1978. Describes the book's compulsive readability, a result of its rise-and-fall structure. Discusses the reception of the novel, its imagery, and much else.

Lethbridge, Robert. "Reading the Songs of *L'Assommoir*." *French Studies: A Quarterly Review* 45, no. 4 (October, 1991): 435-445. Describing the twenty songs in the novel and their context in the plot, the author shows the upsetting hybridity of the narration. Zola invites the reader ironically to observe the peasants, yet at the same time excludes the reader with the songs.

_____. "A Visit to the Louvre: *L'Assommoir* Revisited." *The Modern Language Review* 87, no. 1 (January, 1992): 41-55. Demonstrates in detail what the characters notice and avoid in their visit to the Louvre, and shows the mutually self-defining distinction between verbal and pictorial cultures.

Viti, Robert M. "Étienne Lantier and Family: Two-timing in *L'Assommoir* and *Germinal*." *Neophilologus* 75, no. 2 (April, 1991): 200-206. Étienne is conflicted by his dual inheritance: his father's revolutionary and temporally disruptive existence and his mother's bourgeois ideal of order.

DRUMS ALONG THE MOHAWK

Type of work: Novel
Author: Walter D. Edmonds (1903-   )
Type of plot: Historical
Time of plot: 1775-1783
Locale: Mohawk Valley
First published: 1936

Principal characters:
GILBERT MARTIN, a young pioneer
MAGDELANA "LANA" BORST MARTIN, his wife
MARK DEMOOTH, a captain of the militia
JOHN WOLFF, a Tory
BLUE BACK, a friendly Oneida Indian
MRS. MCKLENNAR, Captain Barnabas McKlennar's widow
JOSEPH BRANT, an Indian chief
GENERAL HERKIMER and
GENERAL BENEDICT ARNOLD, military leaders against the British
NANCY SCHUYLER, Mrs. Demooth's maid
JURRY McLONIS, a Tory
HON YOST, Nancy's brother

The Story:

Magdelana Borst, the oldest of five daughters, married Gilbert Martin and together they started off from her home at Fox's Mill to settle farther west in their home at Deerfield. The time was July, 1776, and the spirit of the revolution had reached into the Mohawk Valley, where settlers who sided with the rebels had already formed a company of militia commanded by Mark Demooth. Soon after he came to his new home, Gil had to report for muster day. Some Indians had been seen in the vicinity. Also, the militia had decided to investigate the home of John Wolff, suspected of being a king's man. Finding evidence that a spy had been hidden on the Wolff farm, they arrested John Wolff, convicted him of aiding the British, and sent him to the Newgate Prison at Simsbury Mines.

A few months after their arrival at Deerfield, Gil decided to organize a logrolling to clear his land for farming. The Weavers, the Realls, and Clem Coppernol all came to help with the work. When they were about half finished, Blue Back, a friendly Oneida Indian, came to warn them that a raiding party of Seneca Indians and whites was in the valley. The settlers immediately scattered for home to collect the few movable belongings, which they might save, and then drove to Fort Schuyler. Lana, who was pregnant, lost her baby as a result of the wild ride to the fort. The enemy destroyed the Deerfield settlement. All the houses and fields were burned; Gil's cow was killed; and Mrs. Wolff, who had refused to take refuge with the people who had sent her husband to prison, was reported missing. Gil and Lana rented a one-room cabin in which to live through the winter. With spring coming and needing a job to support himself and Lana, Gil became the hired man of Mrs. McKlennar, a widow. The pay was forty-five dollars a year plus the use of a two-room house and their food.

General Herkimer tried to obtain a pledge of neutrality from the Indian chief, Joseph Brant, but was unsuccessful. At the end of the summer, word came that the combined forces of the British and Indians, commanded by General St. Leger, were moving down from Canada to attack the valley. The militia was called up, and they set out westward to encounter this army. The attack by the militia, however, was badly timed, and the party was ambushed. Of nearly six hundred and fifty men, only two hundred and fifty survived. The survivors returned in scattered groups. Gil received a bullet wound in the arm. General Herkimer, seriously injured in the leg, died from his wounds.

After the death of General Herkimer, General Benedict Arnold was sent out to reorganize the army and lead it in another attack—this time against General St. Leger's camp. When Nancy Schuyler, Mrs. Demooth's maid, heard that her brother, Hon Yost, was in the neighborhood with a group of Tories, she decided to sneak out to see him. On the way, she met another Tory, Jurry McLonis, who seduced her. Before she was able to see Hon, the American militia broke up the band. Hon was arrested but was later released when he agreed to go back to the British camp and spread false reports of American strength. As a result of her meeting with Jurry McLonis, Nancy became pregnant. About the same time, John Wolff escaped from the prison at Simsbury Mines and made his way to Canada to look for his wife.

The following spring brought with it General Butler's raiding parties, which would swoop down to burn and pillage small settlements or farms. Mrs. Demooth tormented Nancy constantly because of her condition and one night frightened Nancy so completely that she, in terror, packed a few of her belongings in a shawl and ran away. Her only idea was to try to get to Niagara and find her brother Hon, but she had not gone far before labor pains overtook her, and she bore her child beside a stream. An Indian found her there and took her with him as his wife. Lana had her child in May. The destruction by the raiding parties continued all through that summer, and the harvest was small. Mrs. McKlennar's stone house was not burned, but there was barely enough food for her household that winter. In the spring, Colonel Van Schaick came to the settlement with an army, and the militia headed west once again, this time to strike against the Onondaga towns.

Lana had her second child the following August. As a result of the lack of food during the winter, she was still weak from nursing her first boy, Gilly, and after the birth of her second boy, it took her a long time to recover. The next winter they all had enough to eat, but the cold was severe. During that winter, Mrs. McKlennar aged greatly and kept mostly to her bed. The raids continued through the next spring and summer. The men never went out to their fields alone; they worked in groups with armed guards. One day, after all the men had gone to the fort, Lana took the two boys for a walk and then sat down at the edge of a clearing and fell asleep. When she awoke, Gilly was gone. Two Indians were near the house. She put the baby, Joey, into a hiding place and then searched for Gilly. She found him at last, and the two of them also crawled into the hiding place. Meanwhile, the two Indians had entered the house and set it on fire. Overwhelmed by Mrs. McKlennar's righteous indignation, they carried out her bed for her. They fled when men, seeing the smoke, came hurrying from the fort. Gil and the two scouts, Adam Helmer and Joe Boleo, built a cabin to house them all during the coming winter.

With the spring thaws, a flood inundated the valley. As the waters receded, Marinus Willett came into the Mohawk Valley with his army, with orders to track down and destroy the British forces under General Butler. Butler's army was already having a difficult time, for British food supplies were running out and wolves killed all stragglers. The militia finally caught up with Butler, harassed his army for several miles, killed Butler, and scattered the routed army in the wilderness. The Mohawk Valley was saved.

Three years later, the war over, Gil and Lana went back to their farm at Deerfield. They now had a baby girl, and Lana and Gil felt content with their hard-won security, their home, their children, and each other.

Critical Evaluation:

During the 1930's, the historical novel became extremely popular. Most of them followed the same pattern: they were long, had many characters, were full of action and realistic detail, and usually ended happily. *Drums Along the Mohawk* has all of these qualities, and it is one of the best of the genre. In 1936, it was on the best-seller list. In his author's note, Walter Edmonds defends the genre, noting that the life presented is not a bygone picture, for the parallel is too close to the reader's own. The valley people faced repercussions of poverty and starvation and were plagued by unfulfilled promises and a central government that could not understand local problems. Thus, the valley farmers, in the typically American tradition, learned to fight for themselves and for the land they had worked so hard to wrench from the wilderness.

Contrary to the patriotic myth, the war was not a glorious fight for freedom for all American soldiers. Many fought only because it was necessary to protect their families. They never thought of the American troops in the South and East; that was too remote, while the ever-present threat of immediate disaster was too near. When Captain Demooth says to Gil, "Who gives a damn for the Stamp Tax?" Gil admits that it had not bothered him and asks the key question of most of the farmers: "Why do we have to go and fight the British at all?" The attitude of many of the men conscripted for the militia is "Damn the militia! I need to roof my barn." Yet, as the attacks upon the small settlements begin, they realize that they must band together and fight.

At times, the Western settlers wonder which side is the enemy. Denied food, munitions, and the protection of regular troops by the government at Albany, their seed grain commandeered and their fences burned for firewood, the settlers of German Flats become extremely bitter at the indifferent treatment they receive. When the widowed Mrs. Reall, with her many children, tries to collect her husband's back pay, she is denied because he is not marked dead on the paymaster's list. Even though Colonel Bellinger swears that he saw Reall killed and scalped, the money is withheld. The only alternative she is given is to file a claim before the auditor-general, which must then be passed by an act of Congress. In the meantime, the family must either starve or rely on the charity of others who cannot really afford to help. They find that the Continental currency is practically worthless, but the climax of the colonists' disillusionment with the Congress comes when the residents receive huge tax bills for land that has been abandoned, buildings that have burned, and stock that has been killed. The incredulous settlers realize that the tax list is the one formerly used by the king.

The bestiality of what war does to people dominates the book. As the Indian raids become more ghastly, the Continentals grow more brutal. Scalps are taken by both Indian and white, and the atrocities and mutilations committed by both sides become increasingly barbarous. Yet, in spite of the ever-present atmosphere of horror, fear, and death, Edmonds also presents the forces of life. There is fierce energy in the characters in spite of their hardships. This is seen most clearly in the character of Lana, who, though weakened by starvation, work, and fear, manages to bear and care for her two boys. There is a mystery about her as she nurses and cares for her babies. Although she deeply loves Gil, with the birth of the first child, her role as a mother becomes the most important. Even the rough scout Joe Boleo senses the maternal mystery she exudes. There is also beauty in life itself as seen in the human body and in reproduction. The pregnant Nancy becomes more beautiful as she carries her illegitimate child, and the marriage of young John Weaver to Mary Reall begins another generation when Mary becomes pregnant.

Edmonds' style is free flowing, and he has an excellent ear for natural speech. As omniscient narrator, he goes deeply into the minds of the main characters and captures their reactions to the many events going on about them. All of the main characters have individuality and the gift of life.

The praise that is often given the novel is for the realism that Edmonds achieves by minute detail; however, this is also a weakness. His accounts of the many battles and raids become repetitious, for in the interest of historical truth, he does not want to eliminate anything. Thus, the action becomes blurred because there are so many similar accounts.

Structurally, the book is well handled with the exception of the last chapter, "Lana," which occurs three years after the preceding one. It appears to have been tacked on simply to tie up a few loose ends and to give the story a happy ending. In a book that has proceeded slowly season by season for five years, the three-year interval startles the reader.

The theme of the novel is the strength of those who will endure anything to achieve the American Dream. Through their own efforts, they hope to earn their land, houses, animals, and the material things necessary to make life easier and more beautiful for themselves and particularly for their children. Lana and Gil begin their marriage with a cow, a few pieces of furniture, and Lana's most valued possession—a peacock feather that, with its mysterious beauty, symbolizes the beauty of the dream. All of this is lost in the war; but in the last chapter, Gil realizes his ambitions. He is farming his own land, he has built a new house, and he owns a yoke of oxen. Lana has her two boys, a baby daughter, security, and even the now battered but still gorgeous peacock feather which the Indian Blue Back returns to her. She is supremely content and secure as she tells herself, "We've got this place. . . . We've got the children. We've got each other. Nobody can take those things away. Not any more."

"Critical Evaluation" by Vina Nickels Oldach

Bibliography:
Clarke, Edward J. "Book Review: Two Historical Novels." *North American Review* 242, no. 2 (Winter, 1937): 433-438. Praises Edmonds' novel as significant American nationalist literature. Notes universal struggle for land and freedom set against natural disaster and political conflict.

Gay, Robert M. "The Historical Novel: Walter D. Edmonds." *The Atlantic Monthly* 165, no. 5 (May, 1940): 656-658. Analyzes the structure of the historical novel. Claims Edmonds avoided the common pitfalls of this genre by concentrating on simple characters and powerful narrative, achieving unity and purpose within a complex string of events.

Kohler, Dayton. "Walter D. Edmonds: Regional Historian." *English Journal* 27, no. 1 (January, 1938): 1-11. Comparative analysis of Edmonds' short stories and novels to 1938. Explains the new regionalism movement Edmonds inspired as an exploration of the New York State canal region in colonial times, not as a world separate from the contemporary reader, but as a collection of similar struggles and hopes separated from the present only by time.

Nevins, Allan. "War in the Mohawk Valley." *Saturday Review of Literature* 14, no. 14 (August 1, 1936): 5. Praises the author's ability to represent a realistic view of a region in conflict with Tories and Indians, but laments the novel's absence of any rich characterizations.

Wyld, Lionel D. *Walter D. Edmonds, Storyteller.* Syracuse, N.Y.: Syracuse University Press, 1982. Discusses Edmonds' creation of a new genre, the canal novel, and its impact on subsequent works by others using New York State themes and settings.

DUBLINERS

Type of work: Short fiction
Author: James Joyce (1882-1941)
First published: 1914

James Joyce, the preeminent experimental modernist, began *Dubliners* with a version of "The Sisters." A first-person narrative, it appeared in a 1904 issue of *Irish Homestead* under the pseudonym Stephen Daedalus. Thus the narrator was part of the story, its now mature protagonist. A character of the same name was already the protagonist of an autobiographical novel-in-progress, *Stephen Hero*, that ultimately became *A Portrait of the Artist as a Young Man* (1916). Stephen Dedalus (why Joyce changed the spelling of the last name is uncertain) would also be a major character in Joyce's masterpiece *Ulysses* (1922).

Stephen's namesake, Daedalus, first artist of Greek mythology, is most famous for inventing human flight by combining mundane things—feathers, frames, wax, and knowledge about birds. Like the father of flight, "Stephen Daedalus" uses everyday life in his art, creating soaring insights. Joyce called such insights epiphanies, analogs of the epiphanic belief of New Testament Magi that the manger-housed infant of a Jewish newlywed was their God. Joyce no longer believed in religious Epiphany but thought art should yield epiphanic insights using mundane facts and events.

Initially, he planned a dozen stories, arranged into four categories. Including a revision of "The Sisters," there would be three stories each, devoted to childhood, adolescence, mature life, and public life. By 1907, he had created a fifth category, married life. Stories on married life were inserted between the stories of adolescence and mature life. "The Sisters," first of the childhood stories, is about a boy's relationship with his teacher, Father Flynn, who has just died. The boy's uncle and aunt, who are raising him, and their friend Cotter wonder what happened between the two. The uncle defends Flynn, suggesting that he had a "great wish" for the boy—presumably the priesthood—and the speculation seems to be corroborated by what the boy studied: Latin and priestly duties to the Eucharist and the confessional, in which sinners are absolved in absolute confidentiality. The boy is awed by those duties and, it is suggested, thinks Father Flynn wanted him in the order until he learns through the denials of Flynn's sisters that Flynn spilled sanctified wine, failing in his duty to the Eucharist, and was found paralyzed, helplessly laughing to himself in the confessional. These facts, which Flynn could not share because of a "too scrupulous" duty to the confessional, enable the boy to realize epiphanically that Father Flynn did not intend to awe and attract but rather to awe and dissuade him from becoming a priest.

"An Encounter" leads to its protagonist's realization that his attitude toward his fellows has been wanting. Searching for adventure, he and his classmate Mahoney ditch school. The Dillon boys do not join them, and the protagonist takes pleasure in imagining a disciplinarian caning one of them. When a perverse, scholarly old man who disdains common children confesses to the protagonist a delight in administering whippings, the protagonist recognizes a destructive parallel in himself. "Penitent," he acknowledges the loyal Mahoney as a friend who does not deserve the disdain he felt for him.

"Araby" concludes the childhood group with an epiphanic story about love. The shy protagonist, infatuated with "Mangan's sister," is approached by her one day. She wonders whether he will be going to Araby, a bazaar. She would love to go, she says. When he asks why she cannot, she blames a retreat at her convent. Determined to buy her something, the protagonist goes to the bazaar alone and finds a saleswoman flirting with two men: She claims that she did not say something; they claim that she did. In that context, the love-smitten boy realizes that Mangan's sister had discretely offered to accompany him to the bazaar. Her covert offer would have allowed her to deny doing so if he had teased her about it; too naïve to realize what she was doing, and too shy to say, "Let's go together," he lost the opportunity by assuming she could not go. Crushed, the boy leaves without buying anything.

For the boy, experience yields insight. Protagonists of the remaining narratives, with the possible exception of "The Dead," end benighted. In the subsequent stories of *Dubliners*, epiphanies are reserved for readers.

The adolescents are all failures. Eveline, in the story that bears her name, wants her beau Frank to resemble her dead brother Ernest, who protected her from their violent father. However, doubting Frank's intentions, she fails to determine whether Frank's offer to spirit her to Buenos Aires is earnest or useful. Instead, a frightened animal, she freezes at the boarding ramp of the boat on which Frank leaves.

Jimmy Doyle of "After the Race" thinks he is a companion to the automobile racers he follows. Instead, they bilk the do-nothing butcher's son of his cash. They get him drunk, fleece him at cards, and leave him in a stupor to await "daybreak."

Lenehan and Corley, aging protagonists of "Two Gallants," the final story of adolescence, are even worse off. Lenehan, a leech in a yachting cap, follows in John Corley's wake. Both perpetually need cash, and Corley uses a stratagem to obtain some. While Lenehan eats peas, contemplates marriage to a rich woman, and worries, Corley persuades the homely servant he is servicing to steal from her employer. Thus J. C. (who aspirates the first letter of his name, rendering it Whorely) sells love, and Lenehan is his disciple.

The stories of marriage are no more idyllic. In "The Boarding House," Bob Doran only thinks he sowed wild oats. Meek, he is coerced into marrying Polly Mooney, daughter of "the Madam" who runs the house. Polly, under her mother's eye, allures him, and at the proper moment the Madam demands that Doran save her daughter's honor or face exposure. Fearful, he acquiesces in a marriage that bodes ill from before the start.

Timid Little Chandler of "A Little Cloud" is already married. Father of an infant whom his wife prefers to him, he dreams of becoming a poet. He imagines reviews of his Celtic poems, but no verse issues from him. He would like to emulate his friend Gallaher, who escaped provincial life by becoming a reporter, and when Gallaher visits, Chandler meets him at Corless', a risqué nightclub that Chandler used to hurry past in trembling excitement. Alas, Gallaher now disdains Ireland. He affects an English accent, dresses like an Englishman, and is touchy about his failure to marry. Chandler sees through Gallaher's bravado briefly but on returning home falls back into blind admiration. His wife upbraids Gallaher for upsetting her "little mannie," and Chandler weeps.

Bulky Farrington of "Counterparts" lashes out instead. A cog in the machine of modern commerce, his physical strength is useless in his job as scrivener. At work, pink, hairless Mr. Alleyne dominates him. Farrington's small wage keeps him subject, and when he wastes the six shillings he gets pawning his watch by standing a round of drinks, an aggravated awareness of his constraints grips him. His attempt to arm-wrestle a circus performer compromises his physical power, and, utterly defeated, he asserts dominance at home by beating his son, blindly striking a blow at himself through his one hope for the future.

The stories of mature life concern people with dismal pasts and no future. Maria of "Clay," a nanny once, reared children who were not hers. A woman who offered motherly attention without the office of mother, she lives now at the Dublin by Lamplight laundry, where women who once sold sex without the office of wife seek shelter. On her way to a visit with her former charge Joe, she is confused by kind words from a tipsy gentleman and disembarks without the plumcake she was bringing. Joe is gracious about it, but his children resent her suggestion that they took the cake. In a game designed to predict the future, they and the girls next door trick Maria into choosing a saucer of clay, suggesting the grave. Joe's wife substitutes a prayer-book, anticipating life in a convent, but the first choice stands. When Maria sings "I Dreamt That I Dwelt," she repeats the nostalgic first verse, leaving out the verse that refers to future love.

James Duffy of "A Painful Case" likewise lacks prospects, but he embraces bleakness. He lives at a distance even from himself, writes about himself in the third person, and, when an opportunity arises to strike up friendships with Mrs. Sinico and her daughter, becomes friendly only with the mother, possibly thinking married women physically unavailable. When she seeks intimate relations, he breaks off the friendship, noting that love between men is impossible because sex must be avoided and friendship with women is impossible because sex cannot be avoided. Disapproving his own impulses, Duffy condemns himself to an isolation that is finalized four years later by Mrs. Sinico's perhaps accidental death.

Not only isolation but absence is the highest presence in "Ivy Day in the Committee Room." At a gathering of political canvassers on the anniversary of Charles Stewart Parnell's death, when all who honor him wear sprigs of ivy, drinking outweighs politics. When Parnell's loyal follower, Joe Hynes, reads his poorly crafted but heartfelt tribute to "Ireland's uncrowned king" (Parnell), the unsympathetic Mr. Croften robs it of value by praising the writing.

Public life, whether artistic, religious, or celebratory, is equally frustrating. Mrs. Kearney of "A Mother" wants to manage her pianist daughter's career but loses sight of her goal. Her dispute with Mr. Holohan over remuneration leads him to deny future employment to the girl.

Father Purdon of "Grace" offers businessmen salvation at a price. Tom Kernan, a drunken salesman, needs to reform, and his friends, led by Mssrs. Power and Cunningham, take him to church, where Purdon's sermon twists the parable of the unjust steward (Luke 16: 8-9) into a "spiritual accountant['s]" call for compromise.

"The Dead," last in the series, combines all categories. Gabriel Conroy, attending a Feast of Epiphany party at the home of his aunts one snowy evening, likes to think of himself as liberated, but he is trapped on many fronts. He imagines that he is genteel, but, when he finds himself alone with Lily, the maid, he is attracted. A college teacher, he married Gretta, a Connacht girl disdained by his now dead mother as "country cute"; he still smarts at the characterization. Imagining himself above politics, he is wounded when his colleague, the political activist Molly Ivors, playfully accuses him of abandoning Ireland. He thinks he disdains his aunts and cousin, but he delivers a speech at the party and carves the goose. He creates a life for Gretta, but she does not play the roles he assigns; when they rent a hotel room her thoughts never approach his erotic imaginings. Gretta is thinking of sickly Michael Furey, who in her teen years exposed himself to the cold for her, worsened, and died. Gabriel, preoccupied with thoughts of being alone with his wife at evening's end, fails to see that for her the evening has been a pining regret over lost youthful love and guilt over Michael's death. Forced to confront his failures, Gabriel, in his own epiphany, sees his living relationship with his wife as less significant than the love of the long-dead Michael, and, in a snowy vision of the living and dead united, resolves to travel westward into Ireland, where he can meet demise. His understanding, however, is still partial; incomplete recognition can lead to a paralysis as damaging as ignorance.

Joyce was anticipated by the late nineteenth century Russian Anton Chekhov in the writing of apparently plotless stories of everyday life that nevertheless yielded insights into entrapment, frustration, and psychological paralysis. Joyce was first to see such stories as epiphanic and in *Dubliners* produced one of the first collections of stories geographically and thematically linked into a single work of transcendent art.

Albert Wachtel

Bibliography:

Ellmann, Richard. *James Joyce*. Rev. ed. New York: Oxford University Press, 1982. A brilliantly researched biography that traces the stories to their biographical roots.

Hart, Clive, ed. *James Joyce's "Dubliners."* New York: Viking Press, 1969. A collection of essays by outstanding scholars, full of useful facts and insights.

Kenner, Hugh. *Dublin's Joyce*. Bloomington: Indiana University Press, 1956. Wide-ranging and inventive readings of Joyce's works and sources.

Peake, C. H. *James Joyce: The Citizen and the Artist*. Stanford, Calif.: Stanford University Press, 1977. Comprehensive readings of Joyce as a writer who elucidates his time.

Wachtel, Albert. *The Cracked Lookingglass: James Joyce and the Nightmare of History*. London: Associated University Presses, 1992. Analyses of the texts as "fictional histories" in which cause and chance prove equally illuminating.

THE DUCHESS OF MALFI

Type of work: Drama
Author: John Webster (c. 1577-1580—before 1634)
Type of plot: Tragedy
Time of plot: Sixteenth century
Locale: Amalfi and Milan, Italy
First performed: 1614; first published, 1623

> *Principal characters:*
> GIOVANNA, the Duchess of Amalfi
> ANTONIO, her second husband
> FERDINAND, the duke of Calabria, the duchess' jealous brother
> THE CARDINAL, another brother of the duchess
> BOSOLA, the brothers' spy and executioner

The Story:

The Duchess of Malfi was a young widow whose two brothers, a cardinal and Ferdinand, the duke of Calabria, were desperately anxious lest she marry again, for they wanted to inherit her title and estates. Their spy in her household was Bosola, her master of horse.

The duchess fell in love with her steward, Antonio, and married him secretly. Later, she secretly bore a son. When the happy father wrote out the child's horoscope according to the rules of astrology and then lost the paper, Bosola found the document and learned about the child. He dispatched a letter immediately to Rome to inform the brothers. The duke swore that only her blood could quench his anger, and he threatened that once he knew the identity of the duchess' lover, he would ruin her completely.

The years passed and the duchess bore Antonio two more children, a second son and a daughter. Antonio told his friend Delio that he was worried because Duke Ferdinand was too quiet about the matter and because the people of Malfi, not aware of their duchess' marriage, were calling her a common strumpet.

Duke Ferdinand had come to the court to propose Count Malateste as a second husband for the duchess. She refused. Bosola had not been able to discover the father of the duchess' children. Impatient with his informer, the duke decided on a bolder course of action. He determined to gain entrance to the duchess' private chamber and there to wring a confession from her. That night, using a key Bosola had given him, the duke went to her bedroom. Under his threats, she confessed to her second marriage, but she refused to reveal Antonio's name. After the duke left, she called Antonio and her loyal servant Cariola to her chamber. They planned Antonio's escape from Malfi before his identity could become known to the duchess' brothers.

The duchess called Bosola and told him that Antonio had falsified some accounts. As soon as Bosola left, she recalled Antonio and told him of the feigned crime of which she had accused him to shield both their honors, and then bade him flee to the town of Ancona, where they would meet later. In the presence of Bosola and the officers of her guard she accused Antonio of stealing money and banished him from Malfi. With feigned indignation, Antonio replied that such was the treatment of thankless masters, and he left for Ancona. When the duped Bosola upheld Antonio in an argument with the duchess, she felt she could trust him with the secret of her marriage and asked him to take jewels and money to her husband at Ancona. Bosola, in return, advised her to make her own departure from the court more seemly by going to Ancona by way of the shrine of Loretto, so that the flight might look like a religious pilgrimage.

Bosola immediately traveled to Rome, where he betrayed the plans of Antonio and the duchess to Duke Ferdinand and the cardinal. They thereupon promptly had the lovers banished from Ancona. Bosola met the duchess and Antonio near Loretto with a letter from Duke Ferdinand that ordered Antonio to report to him, since he now knew Antonio to be his sister's husband. Antonio refused and fled with his oldest son toward Milan. Bosola took the duchess back to her palace at Malfi as Duke Ferdinand's prisoner. At Malfi, the duke again visited her in her chamber. He presented her with a dead man's hand, implying that it was from Antonio's corpse. Finally Bosola came and strangled the duchess. Cariola, and the children were also strangled, though not with the quiet dignity with which the duchess had accepted her fate. When Bosola asked Duke Ferdinand for his reward, the hypocritical duke laughed and replied that the only reward for such a crime was its pardon.

In Milan, meanwhile, Antonio planned to visit the cardinal's chamber during the night to seek a reconciliation with the duchess' brothers. He intended to approach the cardinal because Duke Ferdinand had lost his mind after causing his sister's murder. The cardinal ordered Bosola that same evening to seek out Antonio, who was known to be in Milan, and murder him, but Bosola turned on him and accused him of having plotted the duchess' murder. He demanded his reward. When a reward was again refused, Bosola decided to join forces with Antonio to avenge the duchess' death.

That night, all plans miscarried. In the dark, Bosola accidentally murdered Antonio, the man he had hoped to make an ally in his revenge on Duke Ferdinand and the cardinal. A few minutes later, Bosola stabbed the cardinal and was in turn stabbed by the mad Duke Ferdinand, who had rushed into the room. Bosola, with his last strength, stabbed the duke and they both died. Alarmed, the guards broke into the apartments to discover the bodies. Into the welter of blood, a courtier led the young son of the Duchess of Malfi and Antonio, whom Antonio had taken to Milan. He was proclaimed ruler of the lands held by his mother and uncles.

Critical Evaluation:

Little is known of John Webster's life, although the title page of his pageant, *Monuments of Honor* (1624), calls him a merchant-tailor. In the custom of Jacobean playwrights, he often collaborated, probably with Thomas Dekker, a practice supported by Philip Henslowe, whose *Diary* (published in 1961) gives much information about the theater of the period. Webster's reputation rests almost entirely upon *The White Devil* (c. 1612), and *The Duchess of Malfi* (c. 1613). Both are studies of illicit love, revenge, murder, and intrigues worthy of the Machiavellians that so appealed to Elizabethan and Jacobean audiences.

The Duchess of Malfi is a finer play than *The White Devil*, in part because of the noble character of the duchess herself. Her story has the reputation of being the best poetic tragedy written after William Shakespeare's, and the work reveals Webster's powers to present themes of great moral seriousness in magnificent language while also creating flesh-and-blood characters. Webster and Shakespeare mastered thinking in images so well that the images develop themes and meaning as fully as does the plot.

Some critics have noted that the violence of Webster's revenge-and-blood tragedies may obscure their finer qualities. George Bernard Shaw referred to Webster as "a Tussaud-laureate." Despite the melodramatic or surrealistic qualities of his work, however, few critics underestimate Webster's brilliance as a psychologist. His work shows its descent from Thomas Kyd's *The Spanish Tragedy* (1592), Senecan tragedy, and the medieval morality play, and the dramas reflect a preoccupation with death and the tempestuous history of the Renaissance period. Many of the dramas are set in Italy, the epitome of evil locales to Renaissance English.

The Duchess of Malfi was an actual Italian figure, but Webster's immediate source was William Painter's *Palace of Pleasure* (1567), a collection of tediously moral stories, which was in turn based on twenty-five novellas of Matteo Bandello that also provided themes for several plays by Shakespeare and his contemporaries. Painter concentrates on two major sins, or weaknesses: the duchess' sensuality and Antonio's excessive ambition. Bosola is referred to only once in Painter's story. Webster does not alter Painter's version so much as he enlarges it by surrounding the limited world of the lovers with other worlds: the corrupt court of Amalfi and the religious state of Rome. He thereby exposes a universal corruption that expands concentrically beyond the lovers' chambered world. He enlarges and magnifies the role of the villain Bosola and uses him to bind the various worlds together. The resulting revenge tragedy treats the question of personal honor (still tied to feudal values), the political and moral problems of lawlessness, and the supreme question—human vengeance and divine or Providential vengeance.

Webster creates this fallen world through the actions of the duchess, Ferdinand, the cardinal, Antonio, and Bosola, particularizing the questions as to what true love should do in the presence of family pride and social taboos; how an individual can rise in an evil, power-dominated world without undergoing corruption; and finally, whether people create their own heaven or hell. The topic of free will is both implicit and explicit throughout the play: People are responsible for the choices they make. Webster forces the smaller worlds into collision in the working out of these themes, and tragic destruction ensues. Providence finally asserts its influence through the hope vested in the duchess' and Antonio's innocent son.

The duchess of the play is a headstrong but noble woman who says to her executioners: "Pull, and pull strongly, for your able strength/ Must pull down heaven upon me." Nobility notwithstanding, her "passion is out of place," for Antonio is but head steward of her household. She denies the chain of being on its social level in wooing Antonio. Even at the moment when she and Antonio confess their love, they are therefore threatened. In Act I, scene iii (lines 176-181), she tries to ease his fears:

> ANT.: But for your brothers?
> DUCH.: Do not think of them:
> All discord without this circumference
> Is only to be pitied, not fear'd:
> Yet, should they know it, time will easily
> Scatter the tempest.

Her optimism is that of the pure soul, but she misjudges the power of those outside "this circumference." Her willfulness and passion are lust in the eyes of her brothers, the Church, and society at large. Webster communicates the sweetness of the romance, however, so thoroughly that the lovers are totally sympathetic throughout.

Second to the duchess in importance is Bosola, a symbol of Webster's disgust with an era that admired ambition but provided little opportunity for its honest realization. This melancholy scholar perverts his intelligence to "serve" Ferdinand and the cardinal, representatives of political and ecclesiastical corruption. Bosola's evil actions continue after the duchess' murder so that Webster can complete the theme of corruption. This accounts for the extended action of Acts IV and V, which some critics have found objectionable. Ultimately, Bosola recognizes his misplaced devotion and his responsibility for the horrors, a recognition too sudden for some readers. Outside of Shakespeare's works, however, dramatic characters of the period seldom changed gradually, a vestige of the parent morality plays.

Even Ferdinand (who may hide incestuous feelings for his sister) accepts his guilt when he says, "Whether we fall by ambition, blood, or lust,/ Like diamonds, we are cut with our own dust." Ferdinand's marvelous image, which refers to all the characters, is characteristic of the powerful figurative language throughout the play. The image identifies the characters as the most precious of jewels, yet paradoxically made of dust. The place of human beings a little below the angels is secure, Webster declares, only so long as they act in accordance with the moral laws established by Providence. People rise or fall by their own acts. Delio's words that close the play are Webster's imagistic final comment upon the fallen of Amalfi:

> These wretched eminent things
> Leave no more fame behind 'em, than should one
> Fall in a frost, and leave his print in snow.

"Critical Evaluation" by Mary H. Hayden

Bibliography:
Bloom, Harold, ed. *John Webster's "The Duchess of Malfi."* New York: Chelsea House, 1987. An anthology of eight important articles on the play, including Lisa Jardine's provocative feminist reading. In his introduction, Bloom provides a useful history of the villain-as-protagonist tradition.

Boklund, Gunnar. *"The Duchess of Malfi": Sources, Themes, Characters.* Cambridge, Mass.: Harvard University Press, 1962. A thorough overview of *The Duchess of Malfi*, including a helpful discussion of the narrative sources on which Webster relied. Boklund finds the play unified in its design and provides a highly detailed analysis of the major characters.

Ornstein, Robert. *The Moral Vision of Jacobean Tragedy.* Madison: University of Wisconsin Press, 1960. A substantial chapter on Webster treats the moral vision of *The Duchess of Malfi* and finds spiritual victory, rather than defeat, in the duchess's resolute stand against her brothers.

Peterson, Joyce E. *Curs'd Example: "The Duchess of Malfi" and Commonweal Tragedy.* Columbia: University of Missouri Press, 1978. Peterson argues the controversial thesis that it is the duchess' prideful defiance of order and class that leads to the catastrophe.

Rabkin, Norman, ed. *Twentieth Century Interpretations of "The Duchess of Malfi."* Englewood Cliffs, N.J.: Prentice-Hall, 1968. Presents nine interpretive articles and a number of responding "View Points" on Webster and his play. The editor's introductory essay places Webster's work in the context of the decline of tragedy seen in the distinctly unheroic Jacobean society.

DUINO ELEGIES

Type of work: Poetry
Author: Rainer Maria Rilke (1875-1926)
First published: Duineser Elegien, 1923 (English translation, 1930)

For the reader who must rely on a translation of Rainer Maria Rilke's culminating work, the story and the man behind its appearance may overshadow the poem itself. No translation of the elegiac German original can do justice to the philosophy of the man who wrote it or be as deeply affecting as the inspiration that produced the work.

Rilke is often ranked with William Butler Yeats as one of the preeminent poets of the twentieth century. His poetic innovations might, however, be better compared with those of Gerard Manley Hopkins, though in the case of Rilke experimentation with rhythm and rhyme never took precedence over content. Like Yeats, he often let the content find the form. Of the three, Rilke was the most intuitive, rhapsodic, and mystical, and he was perhaps the most consummate craftsman.

In October, 1911, the poet visited his friend Princess Marie von Thurn und Taxis-Hohenlohe at Duino Castle, near Trieste. He remained at the castle alone throughout the winter until April, and there he composed the first and second elegies and parts of several others. The opening stanza, which begins, "Who, if I cried, would hear me among the angelic orders?" came to him while he was walking in a storm along a cliff two hundred feet above the raging sea—a romantic interlude worthy of an atmospheric passage in a gothic novel. Rilke conceived the plan of all ten elegies as a whole, though ten years elapsed before the poem found its final form.

The first elegy, like the first movement of a musical work, presents the central theme and suggests the variations that follow. From the opening line to the last, Rilke invokes the angels, not those of Christianity but of a special order immersed in time and space, a concept of being of perfect consciousness, of transcendent reality. As a symbol appearing earlier in Rilke's poetry, the angel represents to him the perfection of life in all the forms to which he aspired, as high above humankind as God is above this transcending one. Nearest to this angelic order are the heroes—later he praises Samson—and a woman in love, especially one who dies young, as did Gaspara Stampa (1523-1544), whom Rilke celebrates as a near-perfect example. Like the lover, human beings must realize each moment to the fullest rather than be distracted by things and longings. With this contrast of people and angels, of lovers and heroes, and with the admission of life's transitoriness, the poet suggests the meaning of life and death as well as words can identify such profound things.

If the introduction or invocation is a praise of life, the second elegy is a lament for life's limitations. Mortals must, at best, content themselves with an occasional moment of self-awareness, of a glimpse at eternity. Unlike the Greeks, people in later times have no external symbols for the life within. In love, were humans not finally satiated, they might establish communication with the angels; finally, though, human intuitions vanish, leaving only a fleeting glimpse of reality.

Rilke began the third elegy at Duino and completed it in Paris the following year; during an intervening visit to Spain, he composed parts of the sixth, ninth, and tenth elegies. In the third section, he confronts the physical bases of life, especially love. He suggests that woman is always superior in the love act, man a mere beginner led by blind animal passion, the libido a vicious drive. Sublime love is an end in itself, but human love is often a means to escape life. Even children have a sort of terror infused into their blood from this heritage of doubt and fear.

From this view of mortality, Rilke would lead the child away, as he says in a powerful though enigmatic conclusion:

> . . . Oh gently, gently
> show him daily a loving, confident task done,—guide him
> close to the garden, give him those counter-
> balancing nights. . . .
> Withhold him. . . .

Perhaps the advent of war made the fourth elegy the most bitter of all, written as it was from Rilke's retreat in Munich in 1915. The theme of distraction, of humankind's preoccupation with fleeting time and time-serving, makes of this part a deep lament over the human condition. People are worse than puppets who might be manipulated by those unseen forces, angels. Attempts to force destiny, to toy with fate, cause mortals to break with heaven's firm hold. People must be as little children, delighted within themselves by the world without, and with their attention and energies undivided, alone. Here, they will find the answer to death as the other side of life, a part of life and not the negation or end of it.

The fifth elegy, the last from the standpoint of time, written at the Château de Muzot in 1922, was inspired by Pablo Picasso's famous picture of a group of acrobats. Here again the circumstances of the writing overshadow the very real worth of the poem. Picasso's *Les Saltimbanques* was owned by Frau Hertha Koenig, who allowed Rilke the privilege of living in her home in 1915 so that he could be near his favorite painting. Either the poet imperfectly remembered the details of the painting when the poem was finally written or he included the recollections of acrobats who had delighted him during his Paris years. Regardless of influences, however, the poem is remarkable in its merging of theme and movement with a painting, emphasizing Rilke's conviction that a poem must celebrate all the senses rather than appeal to eye or ear alone.

The acrobats, symbolizing the human condition, travel about, rootless and transitory, giving pleasure to neither themselves nor the spectators. Reality to the acrobat, as to humankind, is best discovered in the arduousness of the task; routine, though, often makes the task a mockery, especially if death is the end. If death, however, is the other side of life and makes up the whole, then life forces are real and skillfully performed to the inner delight of performers and spectators, living and dead alike.

The hero, Rilke asserts in the sixth elegy, is that fortunate being whose memory, unlike that of long-forgotten lovers, is firmly established by his deeds. Being single-minded and single-hearted, the hero has the same destiny as the early departed, those who die young without losing their view of eternity. The great thing, then, is to live in the flower of life with the calm awareness that the fruit, death, is the unilluminated side of life. For the hero, life is always beginning.

In the seventh elegy, the poet no longer worries about transitory decaying or dying. Now he sings the unpremeditated song of existence:

> Don't think that I'm wooing!
> Angel, even if I were, you'd never come.
> For my call
> is always full of 'Away!' Against such a
> powerful
> current you cannot advance. Like an
> outstretched
> arm is my call. And its clutching,

> upwardly
> open hand is always before you
> as open for warding and warning,
> aloft there, Inapprehensible.

From this viewpoint, Rilke attempts in the eighth elegy, dedicated to his friend Rudolph Kassner, to support his belief in the "nowhere without no," the "open" world, timeless, limitless, inseparable "whole." "We," contrasted to animals, are always looking away rather than toward this openness.

Rilke continues the theme of creative existence in the ninth elegy, possibly begun at Duino but certainly finished at Muzot. He suggests that the life of the tree is superior in felicity to human destiny. People should, perhaps, rejoice in the limiting conditions of mortality by overcoming the negation of the flesh with a reaffirmation of the spirit. Death then holds no fears; it is not opposite to life, not an enemy but a friend. This work possibly represents the author's own recovery from the negating, inhibiting conditions of World War I to a renewed faith in life.

The tenth elegy, the first ten lines of which came to Rilke in that burst of creativity at Duino, contains a satiric portrait of the City of Pain, where man simply excludes suffering, pain, and death from his thoughts; where distractions, especially the pursuit of money, are the principal activities. This semiexistence of the poet contrasts with that in the Land of Pain, Life-Death, where there is continuous progress through insights of a deeper reality to the primal source of joy.

> And we, who have always thought
> of happiness climbing, would feel
> the emotion that almost startles
> when happiness falls.

Perhaps Rilke means that by complete submission or attunement to universal forces individuals are suspended or even fall into the "open." This deeply realized philosophy he developed in *Sonnets to Orpheus* (1923), a work that complements *Duino Elegies*, though it does not surpass it in deep emotional undertones and sheer power of expression.

Taken together, the elegies offer a mural of Rilke's inner landscape. Internalization of travel experiences, the lonely scenery of Duino Castle, the flight of birds, mythological constructs, and other phenomena create a background of timeless "inner space" against which the author projects his coming to grips with the existential polarities of life and death. Progressing from lament to profound affirmation of mortality, the poems glorify the fulfillment of humanity's promise to maintain all things of value through a process of transformation that rescues external nature by placing it in the protected realm of the spirit. The power by which this is accomplished is love. By bringing together earth and space, life and death, all dimensions of reality and time into a single inward hierarchical unity, Rilke sought to ensure the continuation of humanity's outward existence.

The definitive English translation of the *Duino Elegies* remains the 1939 version produced by J. B. Leishman and the renowned poet Stephen Spender, who established a standard of literary accuracy and fluency that few later translators have been able to match. Other useful editions include C. F. MacIntyre's 1961 dual-language version and Elaine Boney's literal 1975 rendering.

Bibliography:
Brodsky, Patricia Pollock. *Rainer Maria Rilke*. Boston: Twayne, 1988. A straightforward life-and-works volume; an excellent starting point for beginning students of Rilke. Chapter 7 explores the *Duino Elegies* and Rilke's other poems of the period. Useful primary and secondary bibliographies, notes, index.

Heller, Erich. "Rilke in Paris." In *The Poet's Self and the Poem: Essays on Goethe, Nietzsche, Rilke, and Thomas Mann*. London: The Athlone Press, 1976. The text of a series of lectures originally delivered at the University of London. A brief but perceptive attempt to place Rilke in the context of the major German literary and intellectual figures of his day; pays particular attention to the early elegies.

Komar, Kathleen L. *Transcending Angels: Rainer Maria Rilke's Duino Elegies*. Lincoln: University of Nebraska Press, 1987. The major English-language study of the *Duino Elegies*. Komar devotes a chapter to each of the ten elegies and includes a short biographical sketch of Rilke. Excellent bibliography and index.

Mandel, Siegfried. *Rainer Maria Rilke: The Poetic Instinct*. Carbondale: Southern Illinois University Press, 1965. A landmark study of Rilke's poetic evolution. Of special interest is chapter 1, which provides a fascinating account of the tragedies that shaped the poet's character.

Prater, Donald. *A Ringing Glass: The Life of Rainer Maria Rilke*. Oxford, England: Clarendon Press, 1986. A well-documented, scholarly biography derived largely from Rilke's extensive private correspondence. Focuses on the details of the poet's life, with only occasional attention to his work; chapters 4 to 6 cover the period of the *Duino Elegies'* composition. Notes, bibliography, index.

DULCE ET DECORUM EST

Type of work: Poetry
Author: Wilfred Owen (1893-1918)
First published: 1920

Wilfred Owen set his poem "Dulce et Decorum Est" during World War I on the Western Front in France. His purpose—to protest against the mentality that perpetuates war—is unmistakable, but what sets the work apart from much other antiwar literature is the effectiveness of his tightly controlled depiction of war.

The first fourteen of the poem's twenty-eight lines comprise a sonnet that vividly describes a single terrible moment. The last twelve address the reader directly, explaining the significance or moral of the incident. The speaker is among a company of exhausted men who after a stint at the front are marching unsteadily toward the rear when they are suddenly overtaken by poison gas. After they hastily pull on their gas masks, the speaker sees through the misty lenses that one of them, somehow maskless, is staggering helplessly toward him. He watches the man succumb to the gas, desperately groping the air between them as he drops to the ground, like someone drowning. The third stanza shifts the context to the speaker's dreams. In a single couplet, the speaker declares that in all his dreams he sees that soldier plunging toward him. In the final stanza, he turns to the readers, telling them that if they too could have experienced such dreams and watched the soldier dying on the wagon into which the soldiers flung him, they would never repeat to their children "The old Lie: Dulce et decorum est/ Pro patria mori."

Throughout the war, this Latin phrase—a quotation from the Roman poet Horace (*Odes* III. 2.13, 23 and 13 B.C.E.)—was frequently used in inspirational poems and essays. In a letter to his mother, Owen provides the translation, "It is sweet and meet to die for one's country," and he expostulates sarcastically, "*Sweet!* And *decorous!*"

Wilfred Owen is often judged to be the most remarkable of the group of "war poets" who emerged during World War I. Although "Dulce et Decorum Est" is seldom considered to be technically Owen's finest poem, it is nevertheless among his most famous because it captures so compellingly not only the tribulations of the soldiers who fought in the war but also their belief that the patriotic rhetoric on the home front and the government's refusal to negotiate a peace were more to blame for their suffering than the opposing soldiers. Owen, who was an officer with the Manchester Regiment, planned to publish "Dulce et Decorum Est" in a volume that was to present the truth about the war, which he knew to be utterly at odds with the belligerent cant that appeared daily in newspapers and magazines in England.

Two drafts of the poem carry the dedication "To Jessie Pope etc" (two other drafts simply say "To a certain Poetess"), suggesting that Owen had originally specifically targeted such individuals as Jessie Pope, whose collection of children's verses, *Simple Rhymes for Stirring Times,* was intended to kindle enthusiasm for the war.

In the end, Owen removed the sarcastic dedication, perhaps so as to make clear that he wished to address a much broader readership. Most English men and women had greeted the outbreak of war in August, 1914, with enthusiasm. Wars of recent memory had been limited, distant affairs; the people expected adventure and heroism from a contained conflict that would be over by Christmas. Instead, after the second month of the war, when Germany's march on Paris was halted at the Marne, the opposing armies dug themselves into trenches facing each other across a narrow strip known as "No Man's Land" along a line that stretched across Belgium and France. In part because of the efficiency of machine guns and because tanks were not deployed until near the end of the war, neither side was able to dislodge the other. Millions of men lost their lives in costly and fruitless attempts to break the stalemate; in just one day, July 1, 1916, the great offensive at the River Somme took the lives of 60,000 men. Rats, lice, and the sight of exposed corpses were inescapable conditions of trench warfare. By the time the war ended, all those who had experienced the horrors of trench warfare had been forced to abandon their belief in the superiority of European civilization and the idea of European progress.

In the opening lines of "Dulce et Decorum Est," Owen vividly portrays the price of trench warfare, the exhaustion of soldiers who have become like old women, "hags," coughing, lame, blind, and deaf. The poet speaks for these individuals who, though they no longer function in tidy military unison, are joined by their shared experience of a nightmare that seems just at the point of being over when the new assault arrives. The deadly gases (at first chlorine, later phosgene and mustard gas) that remain a hallmark of World War I, were first used on a large scale on the Western Front. Although soldiers were equipped with respirator masks, more than one million men died from such attacks. The gas whose effects Owen describes in the second stanza is the odorless and colorless mustard gas that was frequently used after July, 1917. Detectable only by its sting, it gave its victims only seconds to protect themselves and caused severe, often fatal, burns to exposed skin and lungs. Owen also mentions other miseries of the "Great War" such as the unusually heavy rainfalls that turned the fighting zone into a bog in which the men suffered crippling foot ailments and sometimes even drowned.

The poem also expresses "the pity of war," the theme Owen also articulated in the short preface he drafted for the intended collection. English poetry, he explains, is "not yet fit to speak" of heroes, but speaking the truth of war may act as a warning to the next generation. Owen uses the word "pity" in a special sense, one that encompasses a profound fellow feeling for all those who suffer; and, ultimately, that includes everyone. Hence, his protest against war transcends itself and becomes a protest against all inhumanity. The ability of Owen's poems to transcend the particular circumstances of their creation was a quality some of his early critics, including the poet W. B. Yeats, failed to see. "Dulce et Decorum Est" accomplishes this as effectively as anything Owen wrote, for the focus of its protest is not the pain suffered by a few men but rather the transhistorical "Lie." The horrible death of the gassed soldier exposes the fallacy behind the oft-repeated, high-sounding Latin epigram: The poem's protest is against an abuse of language.

Owen drafted the poem in August, 1917, at the age of twenty-four, while he was convalescing at Craiglockhart War Hospital in Edinburgh. He finished it about one year later, perhaps shortly before his death. The event described in the poem is almost certainly based on actual experience, as Owen reported such "smothering" dreams to his doctor. Recovering from concussion, trench fever, and "shell shock" or "neurasthenia" (terms that were often used as euphemisms for exhaustion), Owen's stay at Craiglockhart was crucial in his poetic development, in part because he became acquainted with the more experienced soldier-poet Siegfried Sassoon but, even more important, because it gave him a chance to work steadily during a period when his sense of poetic purpose was most urgent.

Owen was deeply concerned about the technical problems involved in the expression of his passionate convictions. Some of his later poems use striking methods such as half-rhyme, but in this poem too, Owen's technical mastery is impressive. The first stanza employs heavy, single-syllable rhymes throughout; to convey exhaustion, Owen breaks up the rhythm, which only composes itself in the third line. After several comparatively regular lines, a dramatic shift occurs with the fragmentary syntax of the first lines of the stanza about the gas. The four repeating "um" sounds of those line in the words "fumbling," "clumsy," "someone," "stumbling" produce interior rhymes that create a sudden, panicked sense of double-time. After the ellipsis, an eerie, dreamlike calm sets in as the poet coolly, objectively describes the man drowning "as in a green sea." The couplet literally rehearses the moment as do the dreams, and in place of a rhyme it repeats the falling cadence of "drowning" with extraordinary effect, as though poetry itself must stumble and fall at this juncture. The final stanza exploits the steady, relentless rhythm of iambic pentameter for the purpose of "accumulatio," heaping up declarations in couplets that each describe more of what could be seen. "My friend" announces a last turn: a direct accusation against the time-honored, respectable, capitalized "Lie." The extra foot in line 25 shatters the iambic pentameter and produces particularly heavy stresses on the two long syllables of "old Lie," enhancing the resonance of the foreshortened half-line that ends the poem.

In a late revision, Owen substituted lines 23 and 24 ("Obscene as cancer, bitter as the cud/ Of vile, incurable sores on innocent tongues,—") for two lines that had introduced a note of eroticism that might have distracted attention from Owen's main purpose ("And think how, once, his head was like a bud,/ Fresh as a country rose, and keen, and young,—") The new lines recall images from Dante's *Inferno* (c. 1320), and their guttural sounds enhance the impression of outrage.

After a year of convalescence, Owen returned to the front in August, 1918. In October, he received the Military Cross, and on November 4, 1918, just one week before the Armistice, he was gunned down on the Sambre Canal. Owen published only five poems during his lifetime, and "Dulce et Decorum Est" was first published posthumously in *Poems* (1920), the eleventh poem in a volume of only twenty-three. His reputation grew rapidly after the publication of Edmund Blunden's 1931 edition of his poems, which included a lengthy memoir. Although the C. Day Lewis edition of Owen's poems is now considered standard, "Dulce et Decorum Est" is often reprinted in versions that differ significantly. In particular, some editors follow Blunden in preferring a manuscript variant of line 8, "Of gas shells dropping softly behind."

Matthew Parfitt

Bibliography:

Griffith, George V. "Owen's 'Dulce et Decorum Est.'" *Explicator* 41, no. 3 (1983): 37-39. Provides a detailed reading of the poem, with an emphasis on images of voice. Griffith argues that "Dulce et Decorum Est" is as much a poem about poetry as it is about "the pity of war."

Hibberd, Dominic. *Owen the Poet.* Basingstoke, England: Macmillan, 1986. An illuminating study of Owen's "poethood" based primarily on careful readings of the poems, including "Dulce et Decorum Est."

Owen, Wilfred. *The Collected Poems of Wilfred Owen.* Edited with an introduction and notes by C. Day Lewis. New York: New Directions, 1964. The definitive edition of Owen's poetry includes juvenilia, notes concerning manuscript variants, and two essential essays by accomplished poets. Also includes a memoir by Edmund Blunden.

Stallworthy, Jon. *Wilfred Owen.* London: Oxford University Press, 1974. This definitive biography sheds valuable light on the context and occasion of "Dulce et Decorum Est."

Welland, Dennis. *Wilfred Owen: A Critical Study.* Rev. ed. London: Chatto and Windus, 1978. In this first and perhaps most influential study of Owen's poetry, Welland argues that "Dulce et Decorum Est," though masterly, is inferior to later, less strident poems such as "The Sentry."